Tables

Colonial Colleges   122
Navigation Acts   72

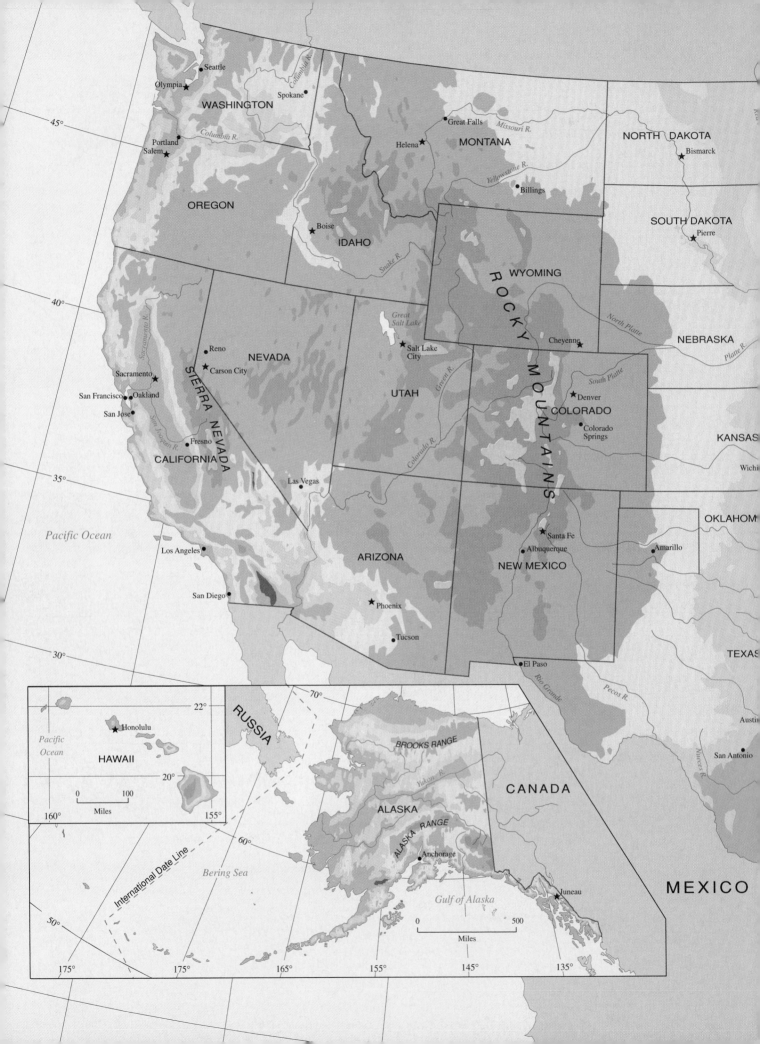

Seattle
Olympia★
WASHINGTON
Spokane

Portland
Salem★
OREGON

Columbia R.
Columbia R.

Great Falls
Helena★
MONTANA
Missouri R.

NORTH DAKOTA
Bismarck★

Boise★
IDAHO
Snake R.
Yellowstone R.
Billings

SOUTH DAKOTA
Pierre★

R O C K Y   M O U N T A I N S
WYOMING

Cheyenne★
North Platte

NEBRASKA
Platte R.

Great
Salt Lake
Salt Lake
City★

Reno
Carson City★
NEVADA
UTAH
Green R.
South Platte
Denver★
COLORADO
Colorado
Springs

KANSAS
Wichit

Sacramento★
San Francisco
Oakland
San Jose
SIERRA NEVADA
Sacramento R.
San Joaquin R.
Fresno
CALIFORNIA

Las Vegas
Colorado R.

Los Angeles

San Diego

ARIZONA
Phoenix★
Tucson

Santa Fe★
Albuquerque
NEW MEXICO

El Paso
Rio Grande
Pecos R.

Amarillo
OKLAHOM

TEXAS
Austin

San Antonio
Nueces R.

Pacific Ocean

Pacific
Ocean
22°
Honolulu★
HAWAII
20°
0   100
Miles
160°   155°

70°
RUSSIA

BROOKS RANGE
Yukon R.
ALASKA
ALASKA RANGE
Anchorage

CANADA

Juneau★

MEXICO

International Date Line
60°
Bering Sea

Gulf of Alaska

50°
175°   175°   165°   155°   145°   135°

0   500
Miles

45°
40°
35°
30°

CANADA

MINNESOTA

Duluth

St. Paul

Minneapolis

ux Falls

IOWA

Omaha

Lincoln

L. Superior

WISCONSIN

Wisconsin R.

Milwaukee

Madison

Mississippi R.

MICHIGAN

L. Huron

L. Michigan

Lansing

Detroit

Chicago

Gary

Des Moines

peka

Kansas City

Jefferson City

St. Louis

MISSOURI

ILLINOIS

Springfield

Illinois R.

Wabash R.

INDIANA

Indianapolis

Ohio R.

Louisville

KENTUCKY

Frankfort

Cincinnati

Cleveland

L. Erie

OHIO

Columbus

Wheeling

Pittsburgh

L. Ontario

Buffalo

Allegheny R.

St. Lawrence R.

MAINE

Augusta

Burlington

Montpelier

N.H.

VT.

Concord

Portland

Manchester

Albany

NEW YORK

MASS.

Boston

Hartford

Providence

CONN.

R.I.

Newark

New York

PENNSYLVANIA

Harrisburg

Trenton

NEW JERSEY

Philadelphia

Hudson R.

Baltimore

MD.

Dover

DELAWARE

Annapolis

Potomac R.

WASHINGTON D.C.

WEST
VIRGINIA

Charleston

VIRGINIA

Richmond

Norfolk

Missouri R.

Lincoln

oklahoma City

Canadian R.

Arkansas R.

ARKANSAS

Little Rock

Memphis

Nashville

TENNESSEE

Cumberland R.

Knoxville

Tennessee R.

APPALACHIAN MOUNTAINS

Roanoke R.

Raleigh

NORTH CAROLINA

Charlotte

Cape Fear R.

SOUTH
CAROLINA

Columbia

Santee R.

Charleston

Atlantic Ocean

Dallas

rth

s R.

Sabine R.

Trinity R.

Red R.

LOUISIANA

MISSISSIPPI

Jackson

Birmingham

ALABAMA

Montgomery

Alabama R.

Chattahoochee R.

GEORGIA

Atlanta

Altamaha R.

Tallahassee

Jacksonville

Houston

Baton Rouge

New Orleans

rado R.

Gulf of Mexico

FLORIDA

Miami

BAHAMAS

Atlantic
Ocean

67°

66°

San Juan

PUERTO RICO

18°

Ponce

Caribbean Sea

0   50

Miles

CUBA

Elevation

Feet		Meters
9,843		3,000
6,562		2,000
3,281		1,000
1,640		500
656		200
0		0
Below sea level		Below sea level

0   200   400

Miles

95°   90°   85°   80°   75°

160° 140° 120° 100° 80° 60° 40° 20°

80°

GREENLAND
(KALAALIT-NUNAAT)
(DEN.)

Arctic Circle

ALASKA
(U.S.)

ICELAND

60°

CANADA

UNIT
KINGI

IRELAND

40°

UNITED STATES

*Atlantic
Ocean*

PORTUGAL

SP

AZORES
(PORT.)

MADEIRA IS.
(PORT.)

MOROCCO

MEXICO

BAHAMAS

Tropic of Cancer

CANARY IS. (SP.)

WESTERN
SAHARA
(MOR.)

HAWAII (U.S.)

CUBA

DOMINICAN
REPUBLIC

PUERTO RICO (U.S.)

20°

MAURITANIA

HAITI

ANTIGUA AND BARBUDA

BELIZE
HONDURAS

JAMAICA
ST. KITTS-NEVIS

DOMINICA
ST. VINCENT AND
THE GRENADINES

CAPE
VERDE

SENEGAL

GUATEMALA
EL SALVADOR

NICARAGUA

GRENADA

GAMBIA

BUI

GUINEA-
BISSAU

GUINEA

COSTA RICA

BARBADOS
TRINIDAD AND TOBAGO
GUYANA

SIERRA
LEONE

PANAMA

VENEZUELA

SURINAME

LIBERIA

CÔTE
D'IVOIRE

COLOMBIA

FRENCH GUIANA (FR.)

Pacific   Ocean

Equator

0°

GALAPAGOS IS.
(ECU.)

ECUADOR

KIRIBATI

PERU

WESTERN
SAMOA

AMERICAN
SAMOA (U.S.)

FRENCH POLYNESIA

BRAZIL

TONGA

BOLIVIA

20°

Tropic of Capricorn

CHILE

PARAGUAY

Atlantic

ARGENTINA

URUGUAY

Ocean

40°

FALKLAND IS. (U.K.)

60°

Antarctic Circle

80°

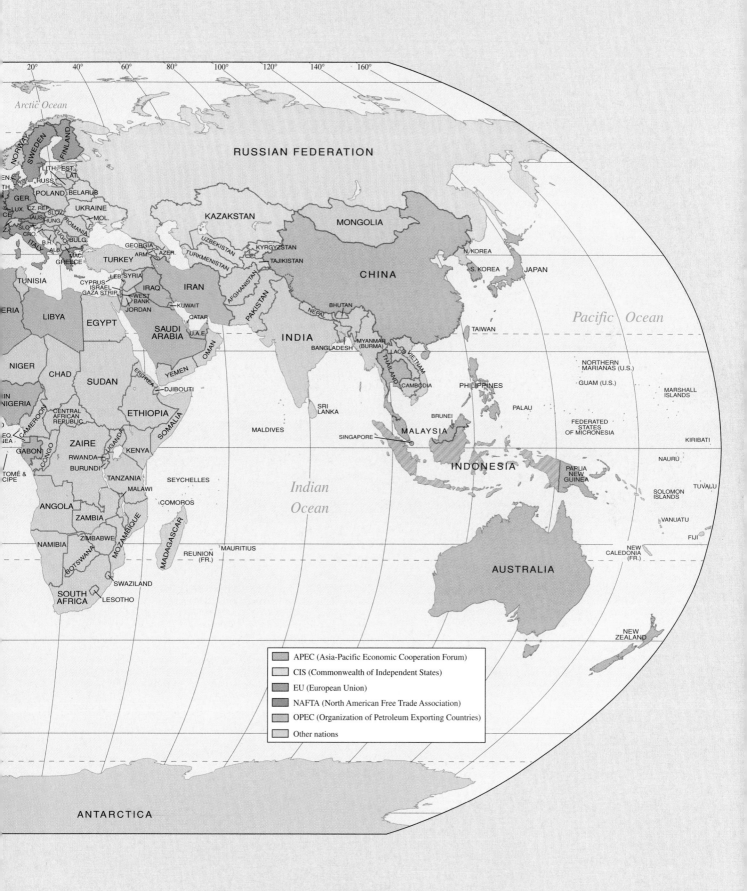

Arctic Ocean

RUSSIAN FEDERATION

NORWAY SWEDEN FINLAND
EN.S
TH. LITH. EST.
GER. RUSS. LAT.
POLAND BELARUS
LUX. CZ. REP.
CE AUS. SLOV. UKRAINE
SLO. HUNG. ROMANIA MOL.
CRO. YUGO. BULG.
ITALY B.H. MAC.
ALB.
GREECE TURKEY
CYPRUS LEB. SYRIA
ISRAEL IRAQ
GAZA STRIP WEST BANK IRAN
JORDAN KUWAIT
QATAR

KAZAKSTAN

MONGOLIA

GEORGIA
ARM. AZER.
UZBEKISTAN KYRGYZSTAN
TURKMENISTAN TAJIKISTAN
AFGHANISTAN
PAKISTAN

N. KOREA
S. KOREA JAPAN

CHINA

TUNISIA

LIBYA EGYPT

SAUDI
ARABIA U.A.E.
OMAN

NIGER CHAD SUDAN

ERIA

NIGERIA

YEMEN
DJIBOUTI

NEPAL BHUTAN

INDIA

TAIWAN

Pacific Ocean

BANGLADESH MYANMAR
(BURMA)
LAOS VIETNAM
THAILAND
CAMBODIA

NORTHERN
MARIANAS (U.S.)

GUAM (U.S.)

MARSHALL
ISLANDS

CAMEROON
CENTRAL
AFRICAN
REPUBLIC ETHIOPIA
EQ.
UEA
GABON CONGO UGANDA KENYA
RWANDA
TOMÉ & BURUNDI
CIPE TANZANIA

SOMALIA

SRI
LANKA

MALDIVES

SINGAPORE

PHILIPPINES
PALAU

BRUNEI

MALAYSIA

FEDERATED
STATES
OF MICRONESIA

KIRIBATI

NAURU

MALAWI

SEYCHELLES

Indian
Ocean

INDONESIA

PAPUA
NEW
GUINEA

SOLOMON
ISLANDS

TUVALU

ANGOLA ZAMBIA
COMOROS

NAMIBIA ZIMBABWE
BOTSWANA
MOZAMBIQUE MADAGASCAR

REUNION
(FR.)

MAURITIUS

VANUATU

FIJI

NEW
CALEDONIA
(FR.)

AUSTRALIA

SOUTH SWAZILAND
AFRICA LESOTHO

NEW
ZEALAND

APEC (Asia-Pacific Economic Cooperation Forum)
CIS (Commonwealth of Independent States)
EU (European Union)
NAFTA (North American Free Trade Association)
OPEC (Organization of Petroleum Exporting Countries)
Other nations

ANTARCTICA

Michael P. Conzen
University of Chicago

Advisory Editor for Cartography

America's History

Volume 1 TO 1877

The Britton family settled in Germantown, Pennsylvania, before the American Revolution, but little is known of William Britton, who painted this and several other scenes of the town in the 1820s.

Germantown was founded in 1683 by German Mennonites, and it soon became a hub for trade between nearby Philadelphia and outlying communities. In this view of the market square, Britton depicts several residences, the markethouse (shed at center), the prison (white building behind the markethouse, partly obscured by trees), and the firehouse (building with steeple).

William Britton *Market Square, Germantown,* c. 1820
Oil on canvas, 12 1/4 x 19 7/8". Philadelphia Museum of Art:
Collection of Edgar William and Bernice Chrysler Garbisch

THIRD EDITION

America's History

Volume 1 TO 1877

James A. Henretta
University of Maryland

W. Elliot Brownlee
University of California, Santa Barbara

David Brody
University of California, Davis

Susan Ware

Marilynn S. Johnson
Boston College

Worth Publishers

America's History, Volume 1: To 1877, *Third Edition*

For our families

Library of Congress Catalog Card Number: 96-060600

ISBN: 1–57259–213–3

Printing: 1 2 3 4 5 — 01 00 99 98 97

Executive editor: Paul Shensa

Development editor: Jennifer E. Sutherland

Design: Malcolm Grear Designers

Art director: George Touloumes

Production editor: Laura Rubin

Production supervisor: Stacey B. Alexander

Layout: Fernando Quinones

Picture editor: Deborah Bull/Photosearch

Picture researcher: Joanne Polster/Photosearch

Line art: Demetrios Zangos

Cartography: Mapping Specialists, Ltd.

Composition and separations: TSI Graphics

Printing and binding: Von Hoffmann Press, Inc.

Cover: William Britton, *Market Square, Germantown*, c. 1820
Oil on canvas, 12 1/4 × 19 7/8″. Philadelphia Museum of Art:
Collection of Edgar William and Bernice Chrysler Garbisch, (detail)

Worth Publishers
33 Irving Place
New York, NY 10003

Contents in Brief

Contents

Chapter Features

★   ★   ★

Preface

★   ★   ★

We live in troubled intellectual times. Political turmoil in the academic world and in the wider culture has forced close scrutiny of established beliefs and methods. These "culture wars," as they have been called, have had a direct impact on the interpretation and teaching of history. The debate over the *National Standards for History* provided a forceful reminder that historians assume a great social responsibility when they define the content, structure, and meaning of the nation's past.

We welcome this challenge. From the very inception of *America's History*, we set out to write a *democratic* history, one that would convey the experiences of ordinary people even as it recorded the accomplishments of the great and powerful. We focused not only on the rich diversity of peoples who have become Americans but also on the institutions—political, economic, and social—that forged a common national identity. And we presented political and social history in an integrated way, using each perspective to make better sense of the other. The recent debates over the purposes and meaning of history have confirmed our belief that this is the right approach, and we have therefore continued and improved upon it.

The Third Edition of *America's History* remains committed to presenting a balanced and comprehensive narrative of our nation's past. In our discussion of government and politics, diplomacy and war, we show how they affected—and were affected by—ethnic groups and economic conditions, intellectual beliefs and social changes, and the religious and moral values of the times. Just as important, we place the American experience in a global context. We trace aspects of American society to their origins in European and African cultures, consider the American Industrial Revolution from the perspective of the world economy, and plot the foreign relations of the United States as part of an ever-shifting international system of imperial expansion, financial exchange, and diplomatic alliances.

Organization

As historians explore ever more diverse aspects of the American experience, the need to organize this disparate material for the student becomes more and more imperative. We have therefore given *America's History* a clear chronology and a strong conceptual framework. Volume 1 is divided into three Parts, with each Part corresponding to a distinct phase of development. Each Part begins at a crucial turning point, such as the American Revolution, and emphasizes the dynamic forces that it unleashed and that symbolized the era. To aid student comprehension, each Part begins with a two-page overview: first, a **Thematic Timeline** highlights the key developments in government, the economy, society, culture, and foreign affairs; then these themes are summarized in a brief **Part essay**. Each Part essay focuses on the crucial engines of historical change—in some eras primarily economic, in others political or diplomatic—that created new conditions of life and transformed social relations. The essays and the Part organization help students understand the major themes and periods of American history, to see that bits and pieces of historical data acquire significance as part of a larger pattern of development.

In telling this complex story, we give equal attention to historical actors and to historical institutions, customs, and forces—writing what the historian Lawrence Stone has called "the new narrative history." At the center of our narrative are the actions of individual Americans: we show how people of all classes and groups make their own history. But we also make clear how people's choices are influenced and constrained by circumstances: the customs and institutions inherited from the past and the distribution of power in the present. Such a presentation not only conveys the diversity of the American experience but also helps students understand their own potential for purposeful action as responsible citizens.

Changes in the Third Edition

Those acquainted with the Second Edition will find much that is familiar and many changes as well. The most important change is the addition of a new author, Professor Marilynn S. Johnson of Boston College. The author of the prize-winning monograph, *The Second Gold Rush: Oakland and the East Bay in World War II*, Dr. Johnson now shares with Susan Ware the major responsibility for twentieth-century America and has used her specialized knowledge to augment our treatment of California and the western United States.

Other changes have resulted from the extraordinarily helpful suggestions of instructors who have used *America's History*. Responding to their concerns, we have made major changes in many chapters. Chapters 1, 2, and 8 now provide a much more detailed picture of native American cultures west of the Mississippi and Spanish–native American interactions in the Southeast and Southwest. Chapters 13 and 14, on antebellum society and politics, have been significantly reorganized to provide a much stronger chronological emphasis.

In addition, we have revised many sections of the text to reflect newly published scholarship. We have expanded our treatment of African peoples in the seventeenth and eighteenth centuries and free African-Americans in the nineteenth century. Reflecting recent work on gender, we have sharpened our analysis of men's as well as women's lives. We have drawn on the new western history to enrich the coverage of Spanish- and English-speaking settlers in Texas and the Southwest in the nineteenth century. We tell the story of cultural interaction in the West from the perspective of all participants—the resident native Americans as well as incoming groups: Mormons, miners, ranchers, and farm families. Drawing on yet another emergent field of scholarship, the Third Edition of *America's History* incorporates more material on the role of the state throughout American history.

Features

The Third Edition of *America's History* contains a wealth of special features, all closely tied to the main text. We have expanded our much-hailed **American Lives** feature so that every chapter now includes an incisive biography of an important individual or group. Among the new Lives are studies of the seventeenth-century Powhatan chief Opechancanough, Federalist politician Gouverneur Morris, social reformer Dorothea Dix, and Civil War general William T. Sherman.

We have also expanded our coverage of the lives of ordinary Americans and, to enhance their presence in the historical record, we have refined our **American Voices** feature. Each chapter contains two or three contemporary first-person accounts from the letters, diaries, autobiographies, and public testimony of ordinary Americans that paint a vivid portrait of the social or political life of the time. Finally, recognizing the challenge of technological change in the present, we have deepened our discussion of **New Technology** in the past; major essays focus on the technical aspects of innovations and how they affected everyday life. Taken together, these documents and essays provide instructors with a range of teaching materials and assist students to enter the life of the past and see it from within.

At the beginning of each chapter, we have added a brief **outline** to provide students with an overview of the main themes. Then, at the end of the chapter, we reiterate the themes in an analytic **Summary** and remind students of important events in an expanded **Timeline**. The annotated **Bibliography** that follows every chapter now begins with a general section containing two or three books of general interest or particular importance.

We have improved and expanded our illustration program. Professor Michael R. Conzen, our advisory editor for cartography, has prepared seven entirely new maps, including detailed treatments of Africa during the era of the Atlantic slave trade and New Spain's northern borderland empire in the late eighteenth century. In addition, each chapter includes around fifteen photographs, carefully selected to enhance a particular aspect of the text. Finally, in response to numerous requests, we have added the Articles of Confederation to the documents at the end of the book.

Supplements

Student Guide

by Stephen J. Kneeshaw (College of the Ozarks), Timothy R. Mahoney (University of Nebraska, Lincoln), Linda Moore (Eastern New Mexico University), and Barbara M. Posadas (Northern Illinois University)

The *Student Guide* is designed to help students improve their performance in the course. Not only will their comprehension of the textbook and their confidence in their abilities be advanced through its conscientious use, but they will develop better learning skills and study habits. The guide begins with an introduction by Gerald J. Goodwin (University of Houston) on how to study history. Each chapter includes a summary of the essential facts and ideas of the text chapter, with fill-in questions; the timeline from the textbook with short explanations of the significance of each event; a glossary; skill-building exercises based on a map, table, or figure from the textbook; exercises for the American Voices documents and the American Lives and New Technology essays; and a self-test.

Instructor's Resource Manual

by Timothy R. Mahoney (University of Nebraska, Lincoln) and Linda Moore (Eastern New Mexico University)

The *Instructor's Resource Manual* contains an abundance of materials to aid instructors in planning the course and enhancing student involvement. For each chapter of the textbook the resources include chapter themes, a brief summary, the timeline from the textbook with additional details, lecture suggestions, class discussions starters, topics for writing assignments, and topics for research. In addition, the manual includes seven historiographic essays on a variety of topics by outstanding scholars in these fields. For courses with a topical focus, special documents sets (modules) are provided for constitutional, southern, and diplomatic history, as well as the history of African-Americans, Latinos, native Americans, and women. The *Instructors Resource Manual* also includes a guide to writing about history by Gerald J. Goodwin, a guide to the use of computers and the Internet in teaching history by James B. M. Schick (Pittsburg State University), and a film and video guide by Stephen J. Kneeshaw.

Test Bank

by Thomas L. Altherr and Adolph Grundman (Metropolitan State College of Denver), and James Miller

The test bank provides 120 to 150 questions for each chapter, including multiple-choice questions, fill-ins, map questions, and short and long essay questions. Computerized test-generation systems are also available for IBM-compatible and Macintosh platforms.

Documents Collection

by Cathy Matson (University of Delaware), John K. Alexander (University of Cincinnati), and Louis S. Gerteis (University of Missouri, St. Louis)

The *Documents Collection*, containing approximately 160 key documents, is packaged with the textbook (if required) or available separately. Each document is preceded by a brief introduction and followed by questions to help students understand its context and significance.

Transparencies

A set of 56 full-color acetate transparencies reproduces maps, figures, and fine art from the textbook, along with teaching suggestions.

Lecture Presentation CD-ROM Archive

New for the Third Edition, the presentation CD-ROM software will make it easy for instructors to include multimedia in classroom lectures. The disk, available in Mac and Windows formats, includes electronic lecture outlines and digital images of maps, figures, and fine art from the textbook.

Acknowledgments

We are extremely grateful to the many scholars and teachers who reported on their experiences with the Second Edition or reviewed manuscript chapters of the Third Edition. Their comments often challenged us to rethink or justify our interpretations and always provided a check on accuracy down to the smallest detail.

John K. Alexander, University of Cincinnati

Richard Baquera, El Paso Community College

Frederick Blue, Youngstown State University

Nancy H. Bowen, Del Mar College

Dickson D. Bruce, Jr., University of California, Irvine

Jane Turner Censer, George Mason University

Doug Clark, Linn-Benton Community College

Cheryl Ann Cody, Houston Community College

Richard S. Cramer, San Jose State University

Thomas Dublin, Binghamton University

Aaron S. Fogelman, University of South Alabama

Dr. Patrick Foley, Editor, *Catholic Southwest: A Journal of History and Culture*

Louis S. Gerteis, University of Missouri–St. Louis

Paul A. Gilje, University of Oklahoma

Thavolia Glymph, Pennsylvania State University

Linda Dudik Guerrero, Palomar College

Stephen Haar, Texas Technical University

Leslie Harris, Emory University

Herman M. Hattaway, University of Missouri–Kansas City

Colette A. Hyman, Winona State University

Joy E. Ingram, Pellissippi State Technial Community College

Frederic Cople Jaher, University of Illinois, Champaign–Urbana

William J. Gilmore-Lehne, Richard Stockton College

Cathy Matson, University of Delaware

George S. McCowen, Williamette University

Samuel T. McSeveney, Vanderbilt University

John S. Nader, State University of New York at Delhi

Benjamin H. Newcomb, Texas Technical University

Rich Newman, State University of New York at Buffalo

Margaret E. Newell, Ohio State University

Gregory H. Nobles, Georgia Institute of Technology

Leonard Riforgiato, Pennsylvania State University, Shenango Campus

Nancy Shoemaker, University of Wisconsin–Eau Claire

Barbara Warnick Silberman, Germantown Historical Society

Marshall F. Stevenson, Jr., Ohio State University

Melvin I. Urofsky, Virginia Commonwealth University

Laga Van Beek, Brigham Young University

Robert M. Weir, University of South Carolina

As the authors of *America's History*, we know better than anyone else just how much of this book is the work of other hands and minds. We are grateful to R. Jackson Wilson, who conceived the intellectual scaffolding of the project, and to David Follmer, who in various guises as our editor, publisher, and agent, has helped us to create it. We are equally appreciative of the assistance provided by three very special people at Worth Publishers: Bob Worth gave us the resources and the incentive to develop the full potential of *America's History*. Paul Shensa provided us with constant stimulation and extraordinarily helpful advice. And Jennifer Sutherland held us to the highest scholarly standards as she masterfully edited our text.

Special thanks are also due to many other individuals: Deborah Bull and the staff of Photosearch; the fine assistant editors who worked closely with us on the Third Edition—Jeannine Ciliotta, Phyllis Fisher, Barbara Gerr, and Debra Osnowitz; our project editor, Laura Rubin; and the Worth production and editorial staff: Stacey Alexander, George Touloumes, Demetrios Zangos, Brad A. Fox, and Yuna Lee.

We also want to express our thanks for the valuable research assistance provided by Andrew Laas, University of Maryland, Amy Richter of New York University, and Beverly Bastian and Michael Adamson of the University of California, Santa Barbara.

From the very beginning we have considered this book as a joint intellectual venture and with each edition our collaborative effort has grown. We are proud to acknowledge our collective authorship of *America's History*.

James A. Henretta
W. Elliot Brownlee
David Brody
Susan Ware
Marilynn S. Johnson

About the Authors

★   ★   ★

James A. Henretta is Priscilla Alden Burke Professor of American History at the University of Maryland, College Park. He received his undergraduate education at Swarthmore College and his Ph.D. from Harvard University. He has taught at the University of Sussex, England; Princeton University; UCLA; Boston University; as a Fulbright lecturer in Australia at the University of New England; and in 1991–92 at Oxford University as the Harmsworth Professor of American History. His publications include *The Evolution of American Society, 1700– 1815: An Interdisciplinary Analysis*; *"Salutary Neglect": Colonial Administration under the Duke of Newcastle*; *Evolution and Revolution: American Society, 1600–1820*; *The Origins of American Capitalism*; and important articles in early American and social history. He recently completed a fellowship at the Woodrow Wilson Center working on a study of *The Transformation of the Liberal State in America, 1800–1970*.

W. Elliot Brownlee is Professor of History at the University of California, Santa Barbara. He is a graduate of Harvard University, received his Ph.D. from the University of Wisconsin, Madison, and specializes in U.S. economic history. He has been awarded fellowships by the Charles Warren Center, Harvard University, and the Woodrow Wilson International Center for Scholars. He has been a visiting professor at Princeton and was Bicentennial Lecturer at the U.S. Department of the Treasury. His published works include *Dynamics of Ascent: A History of the American Economy*; *Progressivism and Economic Growth: The Wisconsin Income Tax, 1911–1929*; *Women in the American Economy: A Documentary History, 1675–1929* (with Mary M. Brownlee); *The Essentials of American History* (with Richard N. Current, T. Harry Williams, and Frank Freidel); *Funding the Modern American State: The Rise and Fall of the Era of Easy Finance, 1945–1995*; and *Federal Taxation in America: A Short History*.

David Brody is Professor Emeritus of History at the University of California, Davis. He received his B.A., M.A., and Ph.D. from Harvard University. He has taught at the University of Warwick in England, at Moscow State Univer-

sity in the former Soviet Union, and at Sydney University in Australia. He is the author of *Steelworkers in America*; *Workers in Industrial America: Essays on the 20th Century Struggle*; and *In Labor's Cause: Main Themes on the History of the American Worker*. He has been awarded fellowships from the Social Science Research Council, the Guggenheim Foundation, and the National Endowment for the Humanities. He is past president (1991–92) of the Pacific Coast Branch of the American Historical Association. His current research is on industrial labor during the Great Depression.

Susan Ware specializes in twentieth-century U.S. history and the history of American women. From 1986 to 1995 she taught at New York University and is now an independent scholar based in Cambridge, Massachusetts. She received her undergraduate degree from Wellesley College and her Ph.D. from Harvard University. Ware is the author of *Beyond Suffrage: Women in the New Deal*; *Holding Their Own: American Women in the 1930s*; *Partner and I: Molly Dewson, Feminism, and New Deal Politics*; *Modern American Women: A Documentary History*; and *Still Missing: Amelia Earhart and the Search for Modern Feminism*. She serves on the national advisory boards of the Franklin and Eleanor Roosevelt Institute and the Schlesinger Library of Radcliffe College and has been a historical consultant to numerous documentary film projects.

Marilynn S. Johnson is Assistant Professor of History at Boston College, where she teaches American urban and social history. She received her B.A. degree from Stanford University and her M.A. and Ph.D. from New York University. She is the author of *The Second Gold Rush: Oakland and the East Bay in World War II* and is currently working on a study of urban police violence in the late nineteenth and twentieth centuries. Her articles and reviews have appeared in *Pacific Historical Review*, *Journal of American History*, *Journal of Urban History*, and *Labor History*. She recently served on the editorial board of *Pacific Historical Review*.

America's History

Volume 1 TO 1877

1

The Creation of American Society

1450–1775

	Economy	Society	Government	Religion	Culture
	From Staple Crops to Internal Growth	**Ethnic, Racial, and Class Divisions**	**From Monarchy to Republic**	**From Hierarchy to Pluralism**	**The Creation of American Identity**
1450	Native American subsistence economy Europeans fish off North American coast	Sporadic warfare among Indian peoples Spanish conquest of Mexico, 1519–21	Rise of monarchical nation-states in Europe	Protestant Reformation, 1517	
1600	First staple crops: furs and tobacco	English-Indian warfare African servitude begins in Virginia, 1619	James I rules by "divine right" Virginia House of Burgesses, 1619	Persecuted English Puritans and Catholics migrate to America	Puritans implant Calvinism, education, and freehold ideal
1640	New England trade with sugar islands Mercantilist regulations: first Navigation Act, 1651	White indentured servitude in Chesapeake Indians retreat inland	Puritan Revolution Stuart restoration, 1660 Bacon's rebellion, 1675	Religious liberty in Rhode Island	Aristocratic aspirations in Chesapeake
1680	Tobacco trade stagnates Rice cultivation expands	Indian slavery in Carolinas Ethnic rebellion in New York, 1689	Dominion of New England, 1686–89 Glorious Revolution	Rise of toleration	Emergence of African-American language and culture
1720	Mature subsistence economy in North Imports from Britain increase	Scots-Irish and German migration Growing rural inequality	Rise of the assembly Challenge to "deferential" policies	German and Scots-Irish Pietists in mid-Atlantic region Great Awakening	Expansion of colleges, newspapers, and magazines Franklin and the American Enlightenment
1760	Trade boycotts encourage domestic manufacturing	Uprisings by tenants and backcountry farmers Artisan protests	Ideas of popular sovereignty Battles of Lexington and Concord, 1775	Evangelical Baptists Quebec Act allows Catholicism, 1774	Sense of "American" identity Innovations in political theory

Societies are made, not born. They are the creation of decades, even centuries, of human endeavor and experience. America is no exception to this rule. The first Americans were hunting and gathering peoples who migrated to the Western Hemisphere from Asia many centuries ago. Over many generations these migrants—the native Americans—came to live in a wide variety of societies. In much of North America they developed kin-based cultures that relied on farming and hunting. But in the lower Mississippi region a hierarchical society that was influenced by the great Indian civilizations of Mesoamerica emerged and then slowly declined. The coming of Europeans tore the fabric of native American life into shreds. Native Americans increasingly confronted a *new* American society, one dominated by men and women of European origin.

The Europeans who settled America sought to transplant their traditional societies to the New World—their farming practices, their social hierarchies, their culture, and their religious ideas. But in learning to live in the new land, the Europeans who came to England's North American colonies created distinctly new societies.

First, many settlers compiled an impressive record of economic achievement. Traditional Europe was made up of poor and unequal societies racked by periodic famine. But in the bountiful natural environment of North America, plenty replaced poverty, and the settlers created a bustling economy and prosperous communities of independent farm families. Indeed, the northern mainland colonies became the "best poor man's country" for migrants from the British Isles and Germany.

Second, the new society became a place of oppressive captivity for Africans. Tens of thousands of Africans, from many peoples, were transported to America in chains to labor as slaves on tobacco and rice plantations. Slowly and with great effort, they and their descendants created an African-American culture within a social order dominated by Europeans.

Third, whites in the emerging American societies created an increasingly free and competitive political system. The first English settlers transplanted authoritarian institutions, and the English government sought to manage their lives. But after 1689 traditional controls gradually gave way to governments based in part on representative assemblies. Eventually, the growth of self-rule led to demands for political independence and government based on the sovereignty of the people.

Fourth, the American experience profoundly changed religious institutions and values. Many migrants came to America in search of the right to practice their religion, and the society they created became increasingly religious, especially after 1740. But many Americans rejected the harshest Calvinist beliefs, while others embraced the rationalist view of the European Enlightenment. As a result, American Protestant Christianity became increasingly tolerant, democratic, and optimistic.

Fifth, the new American society was marked by change in the family and the local community. The first English settlers lived in patriarchal families in which the father exercised supreme authority. Their close-knit communities were strictly ruled by religious leaders or men of high status. By 1750, however, many American fathers no longer tightly controlled their children's lives and lived in more diverse and open communities. Many men—and some women—began to enjoy greater personal independence.

Sixth, the new American society was increasingly pluralistic, composed of migrants from varied backgrounds: English, Scots, Scots-Irish, Dutch, Germans, and West Africans as well as many native American peoples. Regional cultures developed in New England, the mid-Atlantic colonies, and the Chesapeake and Carolina areas. An American identity—based on the English language, British legal and political institutions, and shared experiences—emerged only slowly.

The story of the colonial experience is thus both tragic and exciting. The settlers created a new American world but one that warred with native Americans and condemned most African-Americans to bondage even as it offered Europeans rich opportunities for economic security, political freedom, and spiritual fulfillment.

An Indian View of the Spanish Conquest

Spear-throwing Aztec warriors confront armored Spanish
soldiers during the battle for Tenochtitlán.

Worlds Collide: Europe and America

1450–1630

★   ★   ★

The United States had its origins in two great historical events—first, the settlement of the Western Hemisphere over thousands of years by various native American peoples and, second, the emergence of a dynamic commercial sector in the traditional agricultural society of Western Europe. Beginning in 1492, these stories fused into a single historical drama that changed the course of world history. The subsequent arrival in the Western Hemisphere of enslaved Africans—in Brazil and the West Indies after 1550 and in North America after 1600—added another dimension to the unfolding drama (see Chapter 3).

Originally migrants from northern Asia, the native Americans were isolated from the rest of the human race for over 12,000 years. Over the course of 400 generations their numbers grew from tens of thousands to tens of millions, and they divided into scores of language groups and hundreds of distinct societies, each with its own culture. By A.D. 1450 some native American peoples were living under vast empires, but many more resided in smaller agricultural societies in which kinship and community formed the primary bonds of government.

Across the Atlantic Ocean, most people in Europe lived in agricultural communities. A small class of armed aristocrats, the feudal nobility, ruled over a mass of illiterate peasants. Except for the city-states of Italy, which had established themselves as centers of trade, European society had little potential for sustained economic growth or expansion into foreign lands. During this period it was the Muslim peoples of the Mediterranean region who controlled the trade among Europe, Asia, and Africa and who led the world in scholarship.

By 1630 all this had changed, in no small measure because of the penetration of Portuguese and Dutch merchants into the trade of Asia and that of Spanish adventurers into the lands of the Western Hemisphere.

The Age of Exploration fueled economic activity in Europe and created prosperity for the upper and middling classes.

For native Americans, European expansion proved to be a tragedy. At first they had to confront military adventurers who came to plunder their wealth and exploit their natural resources. Later, as the pace of change quickened in Europe, as peasants were forced off their land and religious dissenters were persecuted, Indian peoples had to face thousands of Europeans migrating to the Western Hemisphere. The contest was never an equal one, primarily because of the devastating impact of European diseases, so many native American peoples found that their very existence was at risk.

How did Europeans come to replace Arabs as the leaders in world trade and extend their influence across the Atlantic? What made native Americans vulnerable to conquest by Spanish adventurers? How did England, a small and insignificant nation in 1492, acquire the political will and economic resources to establish colonies in the Western Hemisphere? And what led to the transatlantic trade in enslaved Africans? In the answers to these questions lie the origins of the United States.

Native American Worlds

When the Europeans arrived, at least 40 million native Americans were living in the Western Hemisphere in environments as cold as the Arctic and as lush as the tropics. Many North American Indians lived in decentralized hunter-gatherer or kinship-based agricultural societies, but some lived in richer and more complex communities. And in Mesoamerica (present-day Mexico and Guatemala) and Peru some of them had created brilliant civilizations whose art, religion, social structure, and economic practices were as complex as those of Europe and the Mediterranean.

The First Americans

The first people to live in the Western Hemisphere were large family-based groups of hunter-gatherers who migrated from northeastern Asia during the last great Ice Age, which began about 30,000 B.C. and ended about 12,000 B.C. They traveled from Siberia to Alaska, both of which consisted of ice-free tundra, across a land bridge formed when glaciation lowered the sea level and exposed dry land at the Bering Strait. These first "migrants" were not consciously migrating at all but were following herds of caribou and other wild game. Archeological evidence suggests that this haphazard peopling of the American continents continued in successive waves for thousands of years, until the glaciers melted

and the rising ocean waters submerged the land bridge. The people of the Western Hemisphere were then cut off from the rest of the world and would remain so for 400 generations.

Following wild herds and looking for edible plants and fresh water, some of the earliest Americans moved eastward. Crossing the northern Rocky Mountains, they probably traversed an ice-free corridor along the eastern side of the mountains from present-day Alaska to Montana, a land where game animals, nuts, berries, and nutritious grasses were abundant. Over the generations in which the corridor remained free of glaciers, they moved south and then spread out in all directions. By 8000 B.C., when the glaciers finally retreated, groups of hunter-gatherers were already established throughout the hemisphere, from the tip of South America to the Atlantic coast of North America. For another 3,000 years these first Americans subsisted as foragers, living off the wildlife and vegetation they found.

About 5000 B.C. some native American peoples began to develop horticulture—most notably in present-day Mexico. They planted avocado, chili peppers, and cotton; most important, they discovered how to breed maize, or Indian corn, either from a wild grass (teocentli) or from a now-extinct wild maize, creating an ear of grain about the size of an acorn. Over the next 3,000 years they bred this grain into Indian corn, a much larger, extremely nutritious plant that was a good deal hardier than wheat or barley, the staple cereals of Europe and Asia, and had more varieties and a higher

Gold Piece from Peru
Skilled Inca artisans created gold jewelry of striking beauty. Note the intricate detail on the headdress and the stylized treatment of the face.

yield per acre. They also learned to cultivate beans and squash and to plant them together with corn. Since the beans preserved the fertility of the soil by restoring its nitrogen, this trio of vegetables allowed intensive farming and high yields; equally important, it provided a balanced diet rich in calories and essential amino acids. Cultivation of these crops thus provided an agricultural surplus, laying the economic foundation for a settled society and a complex civilization with a population of many millions.

The Maya and the Aztecs

By 100 B.C. the people of Teotihuacán in the central highland valley of present-day Mexico and the Maya in the Yucatan Peninsula and the rain forests of Guatemala had begun to develop sophisticated cultures that would remain vital for a thousand years. Both of these civilizations drew on the culture of the earlier Olmec peoples, who beginning about 1200 B.C. created substantial ceremonial centers in the lowland tropical forests along the Gulf of Mexico. These centers contained colossal stone heads, probably portraits of Olmec rulers, and intricate jade carvings, probably representing their deities, especially the *were-jaguar,* which merged the features of a snarling jaguar and those of a crying human infant.

Around A.D. 300, the Maya began building large religious centers in the rain forests where the flat Yucatan Peninsula rises gradually to the highlands of present-day Guatemala. These were urban communities with elaborate systems of water storage and irrigation. Tikal, one of the largest, had at least 20,000 inhabitants, mostly farmers who worked nearby fields and whose labor was used to build huge stone temples. An elite class that claimed descent from the gods ruled Mayan society, living in splendor on goods and taxes extracted from peasant families. Skilled artisans decorated temples and palaces with magnificent friezes and paintings that often depicted warrior gods and complex rituals. Mayan astronomers developed a complex and precise calendar that recorded historical events and predicted eclipses of the sun and the moon with remarkable accuracy centuries in advance of their occurrence. Most fascinating of all, perhaps, was Mayan hieroglyphic writing, which recorded the royal lineage of the various city-states and noteworthy events, including warfare conducted primarily for taking captives of high status.

Beginning around A.D. 800, Mayan civilization fell into decline for reasons that are still debated. Recent research suggests that a two-century-long dry period caused a significant decline in the population. Faced with ever-increasing burdens imposed on them by the ruling elite, the remaining farmers probably deserted the temple cities and set up small agricultural communi-

Chacmool Statue
Striking statues of a reclining man, called Chacmools, were prominent features of many Mayan temples. Priests placed sacrifices and gifts to the gods on the Chacmools' flat stomachs.

ties in the countryside. Whatever the cause, by A.D. 900 many cities had been abandoned and ritually desecrated, with their monuments mutilated, and had begun to revert to tropical forest.

Teotihuacán and Tula. The other major native American civilization developed in the highlands, centered on the city of Teotihuacán in the central Valley of Mexico. The city, a center of trade between the highland and lowland regions, spread over 8 square miles. At its zenith about A.D. 500, it had more than 100 temples, at least 4,000 apartment buildings, and a population of at least 100,000. It also boasted the Pyramid of the Sun, a huge religious monument that was as large at its base as the great pyramid of Cheops in Egypt.

The Teotihuacán people were headed by an elite of religious leaders, bureaucrats, and military officials who ruled over a vast assemblage of farmers and a variety of artisans. The farmers were agricultural innovators, developing a cultivation system known as *chinampas*—small, intensively cultivated islands that were constructed on a network of natural and artificial lakes. Teotihuacán artisans were no less inventive, working in stone, pottery, cloth, leather, and especially obsidian (hard volcanic glass used for sharp-edged weapons and tools). Teotihuacán had declined by A.D. 700, probably because of a long-term drop in rainfall and persistent invasions by seminomadic peoples, who burned and destroyed many parts of the city. Eventually the militant Toltecs from the deserts of northern Mexico took control of the region, absorbed its culture, and created a great empire. The Toltecs built their capital at the ancient religious site of Tula, northwest of Teotihuacán, and adopted Quetzalcoatl, the feathered serpent, as their major deity. Tula in its turn was captured in A.D. 1168 by other warrior tribes.

The Aztecs. The last great expression of the Teotihuacán civilization was the Aztec empire. The Aztecs entered the Valley of Mexico from the north toward the end of the twelfth century and attempted to settle among the surviving Toltecs. After being rebuffed, they finally found an unoccupied island in the middle of Lake Texcoco. There, about A.D. 1325, they built a new capital, Tenochtitlán (present-day Mexico City), just 30 miles south of Teotihuacán. Like the Toltecs before them, they learned the settled ways of the resident peoples and mastered their complex irrigation systems. However, they remained an aggressive tribe. Inspired by the sun god, Huitzilopochtli, who was also their god of war, they eventually subjugated the entire central Valley of Mexico.

The Aztecs established a hierarchical society dominated by a celibate priesthood and a warrior noble caste whose members married exclusively among themselves. The priests incorporated the were-jaguar god of the earlier Olmec culture into their religion, along with Quetzalcoatl from the Toltecs. Nobles and priests ruled over twenty clans of free commoners, who farmed communally owned land, as well as huge numbers of slaves and serfs, who worked the private estates of the nobility. Aztec merchants, organized in a hereditary guild (*pochteca*), created trading routes throughout the highland regions and imported furs, gold, textiles, food, and obsidian, while Aztec warriors used brute military force to extend the bounds of the empire. Aztec rulers demanded both economic and human tribute from scores of subject tribes, gruesomely sacrificing untold thousands of men and women to Huitzilopochtli; they feared that without these human sacrifices the sun would cease its daily journey across the sky. By A.D. 1500 Tenochtitlán had grown into a great metropolis with splendid palaces and temples and over 200,000 inhabitants, a monument to centuries of agricultural ingenuity and to the skills of its Aztec rulers.

The Indians of North America

In A.D. 1500, as many as 10 million native Americans were living north of the Rio Grande, in habitats as diverse as the dry lands of the Southwest and the heavily forested lands east of the Mississippi River (see Map 1.1). Like the Mesoamericans, these peoples were descendants of the hunter-gatherers who had crossed the land bridge from Asia—an epic journey that was kept alive from one generation to the next in stories and leg-

ends. A tale of the Tuscarora Indians, who occupied the area of present-day North Carolina, tells of a famine in the old world and a journey over ice toward where "the sun rises," a long trek that finally brought their ancestors to a lush forest with abundant food and game, where they settled.

The Hopewell Culture. Over the centuries, some peoples who lived in the eastern woodlands of North America developed more complex cultures as they domesticated various wild plants, increasing the food supply and promoting the growth of a larger, more sedentary population (see New Technology, page 8). Cultivating small gourds, sunflowers, and small grains and constructing numerous burial mounds, the Adena peoples flourished in southern Ohio and the neighboring regions by 700 B.C. Around A.D. 100 an even more vigorous Hopewell culture spread its influence through trade over the entire Mississippi Valley from Wisconsin to Louisiana. The Hopewell people built large burial mounds that were 30 feet high and 90 feet across at the base, often surrounding them with extensive circular, rectangular, or octagonal earthworks up to 1,500 feet in diameter. They buried their dead with elaborate artifacts: copper beaten into elaborate designs, crystals of quartz, mica cut into the shape of serpents and human hands, and stone pipes carved in the images of frogs, hawks, bears, and other animals. For unknown reasons, the elaborate Hopewell trading network, which stretched from Wyoming to Ontario to the Gulf coast, gradually collapsed around A.D. 400.

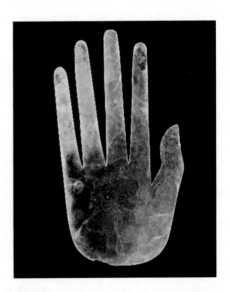

Hopewell Art
The Hopewell people had a rich artistic tradition. Carved objects, such as this elegant (and strikingly modern) mica hand, were commonly placed in burial mounds as gifts to the spirits of the dead.

MAP 1.1

Native American Peoples, 1492
Native Americans populated the entire Western Hemisphere at the time of Columbus's
arrival, having learned how to live in many environments. They created diverse cultures
that ranged from the centralized agriculture-based empires of the Maya and the Aztecs
to seminomadic tribes of hunter-gatherers. The sheer diversity among Indians—of culture, language, tribal identity—inhibited united resistance to the European invaders.

New Mexico and California. As the Hopewell culture
declined in the East, three important native American
cultures developed along the river valleys of the Southwest. By A.D. 600 farmers of the Hohokam culture in
present-day Arizona were using irrigation to grow two
crops a year, fashioning pottery with red-on-buff designs and, under Mesoamerican influence, building ball
courts and low platform mounds. To the east, in the
Mimbres Valley of New Mexico, the Mogollon peoples
developed a distinctive black-on-white pottery and,
after A.D. 1000, large multiroom stone structures. The

Anasazi of northern Arizona and New Mexico fully developed this architecture, building elaborate residential-
ceremonial villages in steep cliffs as well as devising an
elaborate ceremonial road system and various astronomical devices. All three peoples, however, fell into decline after A.D. 1250 as long periods of drought and
invasions by the Navajo and the Apache disrupted their
precarious system of food production. But the descendants of these Pueblo peoples—including the Zuni and
the Hopi—were able to sustain their vigorous village
societies.

8

Indian Women and Agriculture

Corn was the dietary staple of most native Americans, and its cultivation shaped their vision of the natural world. The Agawam Indians of Massachusetts began their year with the month of Squannikesas, a word that meant "when they set Indian corn," and subsequent months had names that referred to the weeding, hilling, and ripening of corn. To appease the spirit forces in nature and ensure a bountiful harvest, the Seneca Indians of New York held a corn-planting ceremony. They asked the Thunderers, "our grandfathers," to water their crops and beseeched the sun, "our older brother," not to burn them.

Among the eastern woodland tribes, growing corn was women's work. Indian women prepared the ground with wooden hoes tipped with bone, flint, or clamshells. According to a Dutch traveler, they made "heaps like molehills, each about two and a half feet from the others" and planted "in each heap five or six grains." As the tall slender plants appeared, the women piled on more dirt to support the roots. They also "put in each hill three or four Brazilian [kidney] beans. When they grow up, they interlace with the corn, which reaches to a height of from five to six feet; and they keep the ground free of weeds."

The planting of corn and beans together represented a major technological advance, for it dramatically increased total yields. The beans fixed nitrogen in the soil, preserving fertility, and conserved moisture, preventing erosion. Beans and corn provided a diet rich in vegetable proteins. By cultivating 2 acres, an Indian woman typically harvested 60 bushels of shelled corn—half the calories required by five persons for a year.

This economic contribution enhanced the political influence of women in some tribes, especially those in which names and inheritance rights passed through women (matrilinealism). Thus, among the matrilineal Seneca and the other Iroquois nations, women chose the clan leaders. To preserve their status, women jealously guarded their productive role. A Quaker missionary reported as late as 1809 that "if a man took hold of a hoe to use it, the Women would get down his gun by way of derision & laugh and say such a Warrior is a timid woman."

In seventeenth-century America, English farmers appropriated Indian corn technology and made it part of their own culture. Protestant ministers as well as Indian spiritual leaders prayed for a bountiful harvest of corn. But among European settlers men planted, tended, and harvested the crop—and they worked with horses and plows, not hoes. After clearing their fields of tree stumps, English farmers plowed furrows at 3-foot intervals from north to south. Then they cut east-west furrows, heaping up the soil into Indian-style cornhills at the intersecting points. English planting methods were less labor-intensive than Indian techniques and far less productive, averaging from 10 to 15 bushels per acre, not 30. And, in combination with patrilineal naming and inheritance practices, that meant that women played a subordinate role in the productive life of the society.

Nevertheless, corn became the premier American food crop, and with good reason. As a Welsh migrant to Pennsylvania noted, corn "produced more increase than any other Graine whatsoever." Pigs and chickens ate its kernels, and cows munched its stalks and leaves. Ground into flour and made into bread, cakes, or porridge, corn became the dietary staple of poor people in the northern English colonies and of white tenant farmers and enslaved blacks in the South and the West Indies.

The horticultural work of native American women underlay the political and artistic achievements of the Hopewell and Mississippian cultures and the military strength of the Iroquois and other Indian peoples. Moreover, their presence in the fields constantly reminded English settlers that their own division of labor between the sexes was neither universal nor necessarily the most efficient method of production.

Timucuan women in Florida plant beans and maize while men break up the soil.

Casas Grandes Pot
The artistically and architecturally talented Mogollon and Anasazi peoples of Arizona and New Mexico took utilitarian objects—such as this ordinary pot—and decorated them with black-on-white designs. Their cultures flourished from 1000 to 1250, after which they slowly declined.

In California, distinct environmental zones helped produce a complex pattern of native American life as more than 500 small tribes with diverse forms of speech, religion, and economic life appeared by A.D. 500. The various peoples traded surplus foodstuffs and artifacts—finely woven baskets, carved stone bowls, and sturdy canoes—with one another, allowing a relatively dense population. Political authority was vested in the hands of local big men who presided over kin-based societies.

Mississippian Society. A new burst of creative energy transformed the culture of the Mississippi Valley beginning about A.D. 800. One stimulus was the spread of technology from Mesoamerica. For example, new strains of maize and beans were cultivated that, when eaten together, provided all the amino acids required for a protein-rich diet and, when planted on productive river bottomland, could support a population of ten persons per square mile—about ten times the population density of hunter-gatherers. The resulting agricultural surpluses laid the foundation for a culture based on small fortified temple cities and a ranked social system. The largest city, at Cahokia (present-day East St. Louis, Missouri), probably had a population of 10,000 at its peak around A.D. 1150 and boasted more than

100 temple mounds, including the immense Monks Mound, which was 90 feet high and 900 feet at the base. These fortified temple cities were governed, as in Mesoamerica, by chiefs and in some cases by a privileged class of nobles and priests. This elite was supported in comfort by the handiwork of skilled artisans and the agricultural surplus paid in tribute by a caste of peasant cultivators in the surrounding countryside.

By A.D. 1350 the largest centers of Mississippian civilization were in rapid decline, most likely because of the combined impact of high mortality—from malnourishment stemming from iron deficiency and from urban diseases such as tuberculosis—and warfare prompted by competition for fertile bottomlands. Still, the values and institutions of this civilization lingered for centuries and accounted for the fierce resistance by the Indians of this region to Spanish and French invaders beginning in the 1540s.

The Natchez people of Mississippi maintained elements of the old temple mound culture into modern times. French traders and priests who encountered the Natchez around A.D. 1700 found a rigidly stratified four-class society (see American Voices, page 10). There was the highest caste of Suns, the hereditary leaders of the chiefdom; two intermediate groups of Nobles and Honored People; and a bottom class of peasants, called Stinkards, who cultivated the land. Descent was matrilineal, so that a Great Sun was succeeded not by his own son but by the son of his sister. Undoubtedly influenced by Mesoamerican rituals, the Natchez practiced human sacrifice; the death of a Great Sun called for the sacrifice of his wives and an enlargement of a ceremonial mound to bury their remains. Other Mesoamerican practices persisted among some tribes in Florida and also among the Choctaw, who regarded a mound in present-day Winston County, Mississippi, as *ishki chito*, the "great mother." There, according to a Choctaw legend, "the Great Spirit created the first Choctaws, and through a hole or cave, they crawled forth into the light of day." Class divisions also marked some Muskhogean peoples: the Creek, the Chickasaw, and the Iroquoian-speaking Cherokee. Because of their hierarchical social order and cultural achievements, eighteenth-century British settlers called them the Civilized Tribes.

For the rest of North America, the most important legacy of the Mississippian civilization was its agricultural practices, including the use of flint hoes and superior strains of corn, beans, and squash. This new horticultural technology produced a more reliable and abundant food supply, permitting the tribes of the eastern region to enjoy a more fixed and stable way of life after A.D. 1000. As better nutrition improved health and lengthened the life span, communities grew in size and developed more complex cultures.

Father le Petite

The Customs of the Natchez

Traditional beliefs and institutions from the earlier Mississippian culture (A.D. 1000–1450) served to fortify the Natchez in their resistance to French Jesuit missionaries. In this letter, written about 1730, a missionary accurately describes many Indian customs but misinteprets the rules governing the succession of the chief, which simply followed the normal practice of descent and inheritance in a matrilineal society.

My Reverend Father, The peace of Our Lord.

This Nation of Savages inhabits one of the most beautiful and fertile countries in the World, and is the only one on this continent which appears to have any regular worship. Their Religion in certain points is very similar to that of the ancient Romans. They have a Temple filled with Idols, which are different figures of men and of animals, and for which they have the most profound veneration. Their Temple in shape resembles an earthen oven, a hundred feet in circumference. They enter it by a little door about four feet high, and not more than three in breadth. Above on the outside are three figures of eagles made of wood, and painted red, yellow, and white. Before the door is a kind of shed with folding-doors, where the Guardian of the Temple is lodged; all around it runs a circle of palisades, on which are seen exposed the skulls of all the heads which their Warriors had brought back from the battles in which they had been engaged with the enemies of their Nation. . . .

The Sun is the principal object of veneration to these people; as they cannot conceive of anything which can be above this heavenly body, nothing else appears to them more worthy of their homage. It is for the same reason that the great Chief of this Nation, who knows nothing on the earth more dignified than himself, takes the title of brother of the Sun, and the credulity of the people maintains him in the despotic authority which he claims. To enable them better to converse together, they raise a mound of artificial soil, on which they build his cabin, which is of the same construction as the Temple.

The old men prescribe the Laws for the rest of the people, and one of their principles is . . . the immortality of the soul, and when they leave this world they go, they say, to live in another, there to be recompensed or punished.

This Government is hereditary; it is not, however, the son of the reigning Chief who succeeds his father, but the son of his sister, or the first Princess of the blood. This policy is founded on the knowledge they have of the licentiousness of their women. They are not sure, they say, that the children of the chief's wife may be of the blood Royal, whereas the son of the sister of the great Chief must be, at least on the side of the mother.

In former times the Nation of the *Natchez* was very large. It counted sixty Villages and eight hundred Suns or Princes; now it is reduced to six little Villages and eleven Suns.

Source: The Jesuit Relations and Allied Documents, ed. by Reuben Gold Thwaites (Cleveland: The Murrow Brothers, 1900), vol. 68, pp. 121–135.

The Woodland Indians. On the eve of European contact, most Indian peoples in the eastern woodlands of North America lived in self-governing tribes composed of clans. A *clan* was a group of related families that had a common identity and a real or legendary common ancestor. Clan elders' power came from their ties to this ancestor, and they led ceremonies and regulated personal life in the interests of the tribe as a whole. For example, elders prevented marriage between members of the same clan, a rule that helped prevent genetic inbreeding; they also granted families use rights over certain planting grounds or hunting areas, since the concept of private ownership of land was virtually unknown in Indian culture. Clan leaders also resolved personal feuds, disciplined individuals who violated customs, and decided whether to go to war against their neighbors. However, their power was far less than that of Mayan or Aztec rulers, because their kinship-based system of government worked by consensus, not by coercion.

The peoples of eastern North America spoke at least sixty-eight mutually unintelligible languages that fell into five separate families. Most of the Indians who lived between the St. Lawrence River and Chesapeake Bay, such as the Pequot and the Delaware, spoke Algonquin dialects. The Five Nations of the Iroquois, who dominated the region between the Hudson River and the Great Lakes—the Mohawk, Oneida, Onondaga, Cayuga, and Seneca—spoke Iroquoian languages. The tribes in the territory between the southern Atlantic coast and the Mississippi River, such as the Creek and the Choctaw, were primarily Muskhogean and Sioux speakers, whereas most of the tribes living in Florida used varieties of the Timucuan and Calusan tongues.

Each people claimed its own territory, but most Indians did not live in permanent settlements. Instead, bands of people moved about, using different parts of their domain on a seasonal basis. Throughout much of eastern North America women and children gathered berries and seeds year-round, while men hunted and fished. In the summer, villages were established near arable lands, where women, using hoes, planted native grasses or, increasingly after A.D. 1000, corn, squashes, and beans that had been carried northward from Mesoamerica. Prospering tribes built semipermanent villages of domed wigwams (or, among the Iroquois, longhouses) near their cornfields and lived there from April to October, celebrating the yearly agricultural cycle with religious ceremonies such as the Iroquois green corn and strawberry festivals. Among the Iroquois, who had made slash-and-burn maize-based agriculture their dominant means of support, women's central role in food production probably enhanced their authority, which was already considerable because of the Iroquois' matrilineal-based clan and inheritance system. Use rights to land and other property passed from mother to daughter, and the senior women of each clan chose the (male) clan chief.

After the harvest, clans often broke into groups consisting of three or four families, with the men hunting together for large game. Given this subsistence economy—a combination of hunting, gathering, and simple hoe agriculture—the woodland peoples lived harsh and rather limited material lives; they did not make intensive use of the environment, and their populations did not grow rapidly. Consequently, these peoples, unlike the native Americans in Mesoamerica, did not live in densely populated communities with elaborate religious sites or trade extensively with other peoples. Instead, each group's economic life depended primarily on the climate and natural resources of its territory. For example, the short growing season along the St. Lawrence River diminished the importance of horticulture for northern Algonquians, such as the Abenaki and Passamaquoddy of present-day Maine, who lived by hunting wild animals, fishing, and gathering wild grasses, nuts, and berries. By contrast, the more southerly Algonquins, such as the Delaware and the Powhatan, depended on farming by women for most of their food. In many cases, foraging peoples traded furs for the foodstuffs grown by the farming groups. Even before the arrival of the Europeans, a long-distance trade in corn, *wampum* (shell money), and furs linked the distant communities of Long Island and Maine. Whatever their economic base, by A.D. 1500 most of the Indian peoples had been living a relatively settled existence on their lands for generations.

Traditional European Society in 1450

Europeans came to America from a predominantly agricultural society. Before 1450 most Europeans were peasants who farmed the soil and were at the mercy of forces beyond their control—from kings and aristocrats who imposed high taxes and rents to bandits, predatory armies, droughts, and plagues that threatened the safety of their families and the livelihood of their communities. Amid these dangers, the main comfort was the Christian religion, which offered the hope of eternal salvation.

The Peasantry

There were only a few large cities in Western Europe before 1450—Rome, Paris, Amsterdam, London, Madrid, the city-states of northern Italy—home to merchants and artisans. More than 90 percent of the population lived in small, relatively isolated rural communities separated from each other by rolling hills or dense forests. A settlement typically consisted of a compact village surrounded by extensive fields. Each peasant family owned or leased a small dwelling in the village and had the right to farm several strips of land in the fields. These fields were "open"—that is, not divided by fences or hedges—making cooperative farming a necessity. Each year the male householders decided which crops to plant and how many cows and sheep each family could graze on the commonly owned meadows.

The open-field system of land tenure produced a strong sense of community that was reinforced by the confiningly primitive state of transportation. Villages were linked only by rough dirt roads and ox-drawn carts. Travel was slow and cumbersome at best and nearly impossible in heavy rain or deep snow. Since there were few merchants, most peasant families exchanged surplus grain or meat with their relatives and neighbors and bartered their produce for the services of local artisans: millers, weavers, blacksmiths, roof thatchers.

Village life was tightly restrictive. Although by 1450 peasants in Western Europe were no longer serfs legally bound to the land, their mobility was limited by geographical isolation and a lack of work outside agriculture. A man might seek a job (or a wife) in a nearby village or be forced to fight as a foot soldier in a distant war. A woman might leave her village to marry, work as a domestic servant, or sell homespun textiles at a regional fair. If she was really lucky, she would make a pilgrimage to a famous shrine or cathedral, such as Canterbury or Chartres. But these events were extraordinary. Most men and women lived hard, unvarying lives in the towns or regions of their birth.

An Idealized Medieval World
In this illustration from a medieval manuscript, well-dressed
peasants labor effortlessly in front of a beautiful palace.
Only the fortifications hint at the warfare of the era and the
nobility's power over the lives of ordinary men and women.

The Seasonal Cycle. As among native Americans,
nearly all aspects of European peasant life followed a
seasonal pattern. The agricultural year began in March,
when the ground thawed and dried, allowing villagers
to plow and plant. In England the farming season formally began on Lady Day, March 25, the day in the
Christian calendar on which the church celebrated the
Annunciation to the Virgin Mary of the impending
birth of Jesus Christ. Accordingly, in ceremonies that
probably derived from pagan fertility rites, pious peasants prayed to the Virgin for a bountiful crop. With less
enthusiasm, they paid the first quarterly installment of
rent to their landlords.

Once the agricultural year was under way, the pace
of life quickened. Peasants sowed their fields in April
and May and cut the first crop of hay in June, storing it
as winter fodder for their livestock. During these busy
spring months, men sheared the thick winter wool of
their sheep, which the women then washed and spun
into yarn. After the exhausting work of spring planting
and haymaking, life became more relaxed. Families
took to mending their fences or repairing their barns
and houses. Then, following the strenuous fall harvest,
they celebrated with riotous bouts of merrymaking. As
winter approached, peasants slaughtered excess live-

stock and salted or smoked the meat. During the cold
months, they completed the time-consuming tasks of
threshing grain and weaving textiles and had more
leisure time to visit friends or relatives in nearby villages. Just before the cycle began again in the spring,
rural folk held carnivals to celebrate with drink and
dance the end of the long winter night.

Death also followed a seasonal pattern (see Figure
1.1). Many rural folk died in January and February, victims of the cold and viral diseases. August and September were even worse, as infants and old people
succumbed to epidemics of fly-borne dysentery. More
mysteriously, births also followed a seasonal rhythm. In
European villages (and later in rural British America),
the greatest numbers of babies were born in February
and March, with a smaller peak in September and October. The precise causes of this pattern are unknown.
Religious practices—for example, abstention from sexual intercourse by devout Christians during Lent—
might have affected the number of conceptions. Even
more likely, fluctuations in the food supply or in female
work patterns from month to month might have altered
a woman's ability to carry a child to full term. One
thing is certain. This seasonal pattern of births does not
exist in modern urban societies, so it must have been a
reflection of traditional rural life.

Over the generations, this pattern of exhausting effort during the spring and summer alternating with exuberant play during the fall and winter became a custom,
one that European migrants would bring with them to
America. A German who settled in Pennsylvania refused to move farther south because, a traveler reported, he loved his winter leisure. Without cold and
snow, "people must work year in, year out, and that
was not his fancy; winter, with a warm stove and slug-
gish days being indispensable to his happiness."

The Peasant's Lot. Most peasants wanted to be
yeomen, owning enough land to support a family in
comfort, but relatively few achieved this goal. For most
peasants, a difficult, unpredictable life and an early, arbitrary death were the natural conditions of existence.
Mere survival required heavy labor. Other than water-
or wind-powered mills for grinding grain, raw muscle
was the major source of energy. While horses and oxen
strained to break the soil with primitive wooden plows,
men staggered as they guided them from behind. At
harvesttime, workers cut hay, wheat, rye, and barley
with hand sickles, but even when fine weather brought
a good harvest, output was at most 10 bushels of grain
per acre—one-tenth of a modern yield.

The margin of existence was thin, and it corroded
family relations. Before 1650 about half of those born
in Europe died before the age of twenty-one. Malnourished mothers fed their babies sparingly, calling them
"greedy and gluttonous" little beasts, and many new-

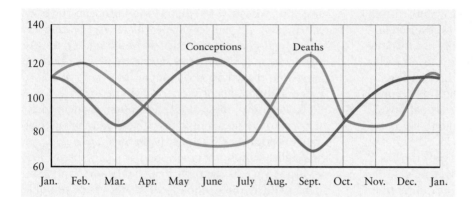

FIGURE 1.1

The Yearly Rhythm of Rural Life
The annual cycle of nature profoundly
affected life in the traditional world.
Deaths were about 20 percent above
normal in February and September.
Summer was the healthiest season, with
the fewest deaths and the greatest number of successful conceptions (as measured by births nine months later).

An Artisan Family
Work was slow and difficult in a world dependent on simple
tools and hand labor, and survival required the efforts of
all family members. Here a fifteenth-century French wood-
worker planes a panel of wood as his wife twists flax fibers
into linen yarn for the family's clothes and their son fashions
a basket out of reeds.

born girls were "helped to die" so that their older
brothers would have enough to eat. To relieve over-
crowding at home and instill discipline, English parents
commonly sent eight-year-old children to live as servants in other households, where they were often mis-
treated. Those who survived the rigors of infancy and
childhood found hunger, disease, and violence to be
constant companions. "I have seen the latest epoch of
misery," a French doctor reported as famine and plague
struck. "The inhabitants . . . lie down in a meadow to
eat grass, and share the food of wild beasts."

Often destitute, usually exploited and dominated
by landlords and aristocrats, many peasants simply accepted their condition. Others did not. It would be the
deprived rural classes of England and Western Europe,
hoping for a better life for themselves and their children, who would supply the majority of white migrants
to the Western Hemisphere.

Hierarchy and Authority

In the traditional European social order, as in the Aztec
and Mayan empires, authority came from above. Aristocrats, priests, and government officials intruded into
the affairs of peasants, and the peasants organized their
families and communities in a hierarchical manner.
Nearly everywhere the individual submitted to the discipline of superiors or to the consensus of the village community. In such a society dependent relationships were
the accepted social norm; few men—and even fewer
women—had much personal freedom or developed a
strong sense of individual identity. Most people's behavior was shaped by powerful social institutions—family,
community, and nobility.

The Family. Social discipline began at home. The man
was the head of the house, a patriarch who made all the
important decisions. His power was justified by the
teachings of the Christian Church. As one English pastor
put it, "The woman is a weak creature not embued with

like strength and constancy of mind"; law and custom consequently "subjected her to the power of man." Upon marriage, an English woman not only assumed the family name of her husband and usually moved to his village but also was required under the threat of legally sanctioned physical "correction" to submit to her husband's orders—be they for service or for sexual favors. Moreover, she surrendered to her husband all her property, including her clothes. In her new legal state of *coverture*, a married woman was allowed only the "use" of her personal possessions; upon her husband's death, she received only a dower—usually the use during her lifetime of one-third of the family's land and goods.

Fathers controlled the lives of children in an equally encompassing and authoritarian way. Landowning peasants in Western Europe normally retained legal control of farms until their physical strength ebbed. Only then, after age fifty, did they provide land to sons and dowries (usually livestock or furnishings) to daughters, permitting their children to marry. Consequently, most young men and women worked for their fathers until their middle or late twenties, enduring years of emotional domination and sexual deprivation. When they finally did marry, it was often to someone not of their liking, since most marriages were arranged, with parents choosing partners of comparable wealth and status to protect the family's economic position.

Within the family, children were not born equal: their social position depended on their sex and birth order. In many regions cultural rules dictated that a father bestow most of his land on his oldest son (primogeniture). That son became the new patriarch, responsible for the welfare of his siblings. Custom called for landless brothers and sisters to work on their brother's farm in return for food and shelter, but the small size of most peasant holdings forced many younger children to join the ranks of the roaming poor, condemned to desperate lives on the edge of respectable society.

The Community. In a world of scarcity, the price of survival was unremitting social discipline. Village authorities strictly regulated individual behavior for the common good; for example, in Germany they granted marriage licenses only to couples with sufficient property to support a family. Officials also imposed limits on what could be charged for the staff of life: a loaf of bread, a sack of flour or grain. Fearful of change, they made tradition the measure of all existence. "After a thing had been practiced for so long that it becomes a Custom," an English clergyman proclaimed, "that Custom is Law."

Monarchs and Manorial Lords. The monarchs of Western Europe owned vast tracts of land and, like Aztec and Mayan rulers, lived in splendor off the labor of the masses of peasants. Gradually, the European rulers extended their power, levying royal taxes, creating law courts, and conscripting men for military service. Yet they were far from supreme, given the power of the nobility, who played a major role in the affairs of the villages and kingdoms of Western Europe.

Collectively, these noblemen often challenged the authority of princes and kings. They had their own legislative institutions, such as the French *parlements* and the English House of Lords, and enjoyed special legal privileges, such as the right to a trial before a jury composed of their own (noble) peers. And because nobles had direct control over the peasantry, monarchs had little choice but to appoint them as local judges and militia officers.

Such legacies of the medieval feudal order, when most kings were dependent on the nobility, worked against the formation of strong centralized states. Other privileged groups whose wealth and status limited the rulers' power were the clergy and the merchants. In the Beauvais region of France the Catholic Church and the aristocracy controlled nearly half the land, leaving individual peasants and village communities, who made up more than 95 percent of the population, to divide the rest.

Hierarchy and authority reigned supreme in the traditional European social order both because of the power of established institutions and because, in a harsh and unpredictable world, they offered ordinary people a measure of security and certainty. These values, which migrants carried with them to America, would shape the character of family life and the social order there well into the eighteenth century.

The Power of Religion

The Catholic Church served as one of the great unifying forces in Western European society. By A.D. 1000 Christianity had converted virtually all of pagan Europe, extending its spiritual jurisdiction over Latins, Germans, Celts, Anglo-Saxons, and western Slavs. The pope, as head of the Catholic Church, directed a vast hierarchy of cardinals, bishops, and priests. Latin, the language of scholarship, was preserved by Catholic priests and monks, and Catholic dogma provided a common understanding of God, the world, and human history. Equally important, the church provided another bulwark of authority and discipline in society.

Religion in Daily Life. Christian doctrine penetrated deeply into the everyday lives of peasants. Over the centuries, the church adopted a calendar that accommodated the agricultural cycle and incorporated various pagan festivals, such as the winter solstice, which

Christ's Crucifixion
This graphic portrayal of Christ's death on the cross, by the
German painter Grünewald, sought to remind believers of
the reality of death and the need for repentance. (Central panel
of closed Isenheim Altarpiece, Colmar, Musée Unterlinden)

marked the return of the sun and the victory of light
over darkness. The Christian celebration of the birth of
Jesus Christ on December 25, a few days later, grafted a
new religious meaning onto the solstice, encouraging
pagan conversions.

In the spring, when the warmth of the sun revived
the earth, the church celebrated Christ's resurrection
from the dead on Easter Sunday. This holy day absorbed pagan spring fertility festivals and gave them a
distinctively Christian meaning. Christian and pagan
traditions blended again in the autumn months as ancient harvest festivals gradually evolved into holy days
of thanksgiving.

This merging of the sacred and the agricultural cy-
cles endowed all worldly events with meaning. Few
Christians believed that events occurred by chance; they
must be the result of God's will. If crops rotted in the
ground or withered under a hot sun, the Lord must be
displeased with his people. According to the Bible, "The
earth is defiled under its inhabitants' feet, for they have
transgressed the law" (Isaiah 24:5). To avert calamities,
peasants turned to priests for spiritual guidance and to
confess their transgressions of God's commands and the
church's laws. Every village had a church, and holy
shrines dotted the map of Europe, tangible points of
contact between the material and spiritual worlds. By

offering prayers to Christ and the saints, whose statues
stood in the shrines and churches, Christians hoped to
stave off worldly disasters.

God's presence in the world was continually renewed through the Mass and the sacrament of Holy
Communion. According to Catholic doctrine, priests
had the power to change sacramental bread and wine
into the body and blood of Christ. In this way, peasants—along with priests and aristocrats—could partake
in the divine.

There was another supernatural force at large in the
world: Satan. Satan challenged the majesty of God by
tempting people into evil. If prophets spread unusual
doctrines, they were surely the tools of Satan. If a devout Christian fell mysteriously ill, the sickness might
be the result of an evil spell cast by a witch in league
with Satan. Fear of Satan's wiles justified periodic
purges of heretics—men and women who questioned
the church's doctrine and practices.

The Crusades. As the Catholic Church consolidated its
power in Europe, popes and priests urged their followers to crush all those who held other religious beliefs.
Muslims became a prime target. After the death of the
prophet Muhammad in A.D. 632, the newly united peoples of Arabia set out to convert and conquer the world.
They spread the Muslim faith and Arab civilization far
beyond its homeland—into sub-Saharan Africa, India,
and Indonesia and deep into southern Europe. Between
A.D. 1095 and 1272 successive armies of Christians, led
by the flower of the nobility, embarked on a series of
great Crusades against Muslim "infidels." They halted
Arab advances into southern Europe and invaded Palestine, seeking to expel Muslims from the Holy Land
where Christ had lived.

The Crusades had some success in their military
mission, gaining control of much of Palestine for nearly
200 years, but their spiritual impact on Europe was
more profound, strengthening the Christian identity of
its population. The resulting religious fervor also contributed to the renewed persecution of Jews in many
European countries. England expelled most of its Jewish population in 1290, and France did the same in
1306. Jewish refugees went mostly to Germany, the
great center of European Jewry, only to be driven farther east, to Poland, over the next century. At the same
time, the Crusades broadened the intellectual and economic horizons of the privileged classes of Western Europe, bringing them into contact with the advanced
civilizations of the Middle East and Asia. A fresh wind
blew through Europe, resulting in marked changes in
that continent's commercial interests and military
power—changes that in turn would cause slower but
equally significant alterations in its traditional agricultural society.

The Spice Trade
This French manuscript illustration (circa 1380) shows workers in Malabar (near Calicut on the western coast of India) harvesting pepper for the spice trade. The white-skinned man is meant to be Marco Polo, one of the few Europeans to visit India or China before the Portuguese voyages.

Europe and the World, 1450–1550

Europe changed dramatically after 1450. First, a major revival of learning, the Renaissance, expanded the horizons of the commercial and political classes. Second, Portuguese merchants found new trade routes to India and China and became leaders in world commerce. Finally, Spanish adventurers found and invaded the Western Hemisphere, conquering the wealthiest native American empires and, through the spread of European diseases, devastating their peoples. For the first time since the Roman Empire, Europeans became major actors in world history.

Renaissance Beginnings

Beginning about A.D. 1300, first Italy and then the countries of northern Europe experienced a rebirth of learning and cultural life. The main stimulus came from the Crusaders' exposure to the highly developed civilization of the Arab world. Arab traders had access to the fabulous treasures of the East: luxurious Chinese silks, brilliant Indian cottons, precious stones, and exotic spices, including pepper, nutmeg, ginger, and cloves. Arab inventors had developed magnetic compasses, water-powered mills, and mechanical clocks, and from their trading contacts in China, they had learned the properties and uses of gunpowder. In great cultural centers such as Alexandria and Cairo in Egypt, Arab scholars carried on the legacy of Christian Byzantine civilization, which had preserved the great achievements of the Greeks and Romans in religion, medicine, philosophy, mathematics, astronomy, and geography.

At the same time, from Toledo and other cities in Moorish Spain, Arab learning gradually filtered into Europe. The Moors were Arabs who had invaded the Iberian Peninsula centuries before and still controlled its southern region. Moorish scholars had translated Aristotle, Ptolemy, and other ancient writers into Latin, reacquainting the peoples of Europe with their classical heritage.

Astronomers at Istanbul, 1581
Arab and Turkish scholars transmitted ancient texts and learning to Europeans in the Middle Ages and, during the age of discovery, contributed to the expansion of geographical and astronomical knowledge.

The Italian Renaissance. During the Crusades, merchants from the Italian city-states of Venice, Genoa, and Pisa had wrested away a share of the Arab trade with the East. Dispatching ships to Alexandria, Beirut, and other eastern Mediterranean ports, these merchants purchased goods that originally had come from China, India, Persia, and Arabia and sold them throughout Europe. The enormous profits from this commerce created a new class of merchants, bankers, and textile manufacturers who conducted trade, lent vast sums of money, and spurred technological innovation in silk and woolen production. This moneyed elite ruled the republican city-states of Italy, and in *The Discourses*, Niccolò Machiavelli articulated its political culture of *civic humanism*—an ideology that celebrated public virtue and service to the state and that would profoundly influence European and American conceptions of government.

In what was to become the fashion of the age, wealthy Italian families became patrons of the arts and sciences, subsidizing a remarkable array of artistic and intellectual projects. Perhaps no other age in European history has produced such a flowering of artistic genius. Michelangelo, Andrea Palladio, and Filippo Brunelleschi designed and built great architectural masterpieces, while Leonardo da Vinci and Raphael produced magnificent religious paintings, creating styles and setting standards that have endured into the modern era.

Humanism. The Renaissance did not directly affect the average European peasant, but it had a profound impact on the upper classes. The artists and intellectuals of the Renaissance were optimistic in their view of human nature—they were humanists who celebrated individual potential. Whereas traditional paintings had depicted, often grimly, religious themes and symbols, Renaissance works of art and literature showed real men (and a few women) with complex personalities and creative talents. Those who embraced the psychology of the Renaissance saw themselves not as prisoners of blind fate or victims of the forces of nature but as many-sided individuals with the capacity to change the world.

Renaissance Architecture
The columned buildings of the Renaissance recalled the classical world of Greece and Rome, and the symmetrical design reflected the impulse to create a world of ordered beauty.

Renaissance Princes. The idea that the world could be shaped by human ingenuity was particularly appealing to Renaissance rulers, who were eager to shape it to their own benefit. In *The Prince* (1513), Machiavelli provided unsentimental advice on how monarchs could increase their political power. Machiavelli's hero in this treatise was the Italian ruler Cesare Borgia, but he was inspired by the state-building activities of the ambitious monarchs of France and Western Europe.

These monarchs—among them France's Louis XI (1461–1483), England's Henry VII (1485–1509), and Spain's Ferdinand (1479–1516) and Isabella (1474–1504)—created royal law courts and bureaucracies to reduce the power of the landed classes and formed alliances with commercial interests to build strong and prosperous national states. They allowed merchants to trade throughout their realms and granted privileges to artisan guilds, thus encouraging both foreign trade and domestic manufacturing. In return, they extracted taxes from towns and loans from merchants to support their armies and officials. The alliance of monarchs, merchants, and royal bureaucrats challenged the primacy of the agrarian nobility. Indeed, the increasing wealth and power of the monarchical nation-state propelled Europe into its first age of expansion.

Portugal Penetrates Africa and Asia

In 1450 Western Europe was a collection of poor agricultural societies lying isolated and unimportant at the far edge of the Eurasian land mass. Strangely, it was Portugal, a small Atlantic country of only 1.5 million people, that led the way in the great surge of exploration. Portugal boasted political stability, a tradition of seafaring, and a fleet of merchant ships. It also had a prince, Henry the Navigator, who was determined to contest the dominant position of Muslim and Italian merchants by finding a new ocean route to the wealth of Asia.

Henry the Navigator. Prince Henry (1394–1460) was the younger brother of King Edward I of Portugal. Henry was a complex, many-sided individual, at once a Christian warrior and a Renaissance humanist. As a knight of the Order of Christ, Henry had fought against the Arabs in North Africa, an experience that reinforced his desire to extend Portuguese power and the bounds of Christendom. As a humanist, Henry patronized Renaissance thinkers who drew inspiration from classical Greek and Roman (rather than Christian) sources, and he relied on Arab and Italian geographers for the latest knowledge about the shape and size of the continents. In the activist spirit of the Renaissance, Henry sought to fulfill the predictions of his horoscope: "to engage in great and noble conquests and to attempt the discovery of things hidden from other men."

African Slavery. In the 1420s, Prince Henry established a center for exploration and ocean mapping and from there sent out ships to sail the African coast and probe the Atlantic. His seamen soon discovered and settled Madeira and the Azores. By 1435 Portuguese sea captains were regularly roaming the coast of West Africa, seeking ivory and gold in exchange for salt, wine, and fish. By the 1440s they were trading in humans as well, the first Europeans to engage in African slavery. For centuries Arab merchants had conducted a brisk overland trade in slaves, buying sub-Saharan Africans captured during local ethnic conflicts and selling them throughout the Mediterranean region. The Portuguese extended this commerce, at first transporting West Africans from Senegambia to sugar estates in Madeira and the Azores. Eventually they would bring hundreds of thousands of slaves across the Atlantic to toil on the sugar plantations of Brazil and the West Indies (see Chapter 3).

The Portuguese Maritime Empire. After Henry's death in 1460, Portuguese navigators and adventurers continued their explorations, looking for a direct ocean route to Asia. In 1488 Bartholomew Diaz rounded the Cape of Good Hope, the southern tip of Africa. Ten years later Vasco da Gama sailed all the way to India. The Arab, Indian, and Jewish merchants and traders on India's Malabar Coast shunned da Gama as a dangerous commercial rival, but he returned to Portugal with a valuable cargo of cinnamon and pepper, the latter being in such great demand for flavoring and preserving meat that the voyage realized a profit of 6,000 percent. Da Gama returned to India in 1502 with twenty-one fighting vessels and immediately attacked his rivals in a naked challenge for commercial dominance. Square-rigged Portuguese caravels outmaneuvered and outgunned Arab fleets, while on land plunder-hungry Portuguese adventurers burned cities and seized the property of rival traders.

The Portuguese government set up fortified trading posts for its merchants at key points around the Indian Ocean—at Goa in India, Hormuz in Arabia, and Malacca in Malaysia—and soon opened trade routes from Africa to Indonesia and up the coast of Asia to China and Japan. Portuguese merchants easily undersold Arab traders, for their ships held more and traveled faster than overland caravans. In a momentous transition, Portuguese Christians replaced Arab Muslims as the leaders in world commerce and in the trade in African slaves (see Map 1.2).

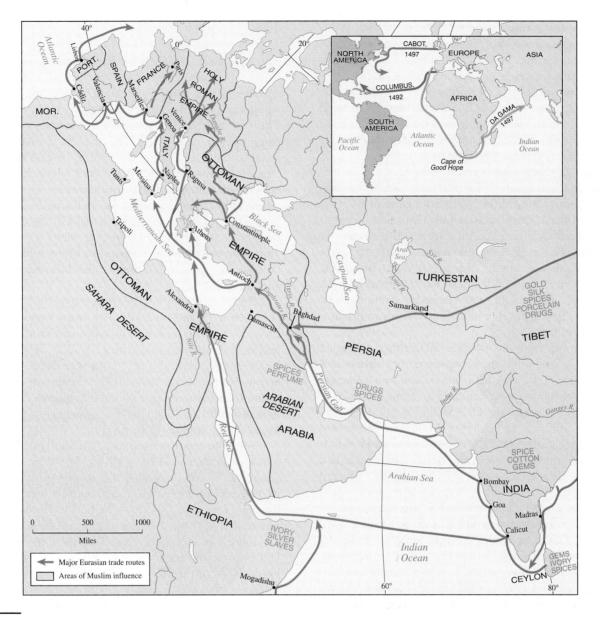

MAP 1.2

Europeans Seek Control of World Trade
For centuries the Mediterranean Sea was the meeting point for the commerce of
Europe, northern Africa, and southern Asia. Beginning in the 1490s, Portuguese, Spanish, and Dutch adventurers and merchants opened up new trade routes, challenging
the primacy of the Muslim-dominated Mediterranean.

Spain and America

Spain quickly followed Portugal's example. As Renaissance rulers, King Ferdinand of Aragon and Queen Isabella of Castile saw national unity and commerce as
the keys to prosperity and power. Married in their teens
in an arranged match, the young rulers had combined

their kingdoms. They devoted their energies and resources to the *reconquista*, the centuries-long campaign
to oust the Moors from Spanish soil. In 1492 their
armies finally reconquered Granada, the last outpost of
Islam in Western Europe. Continuing their effort to use
religion to build a sense of "Spanishness," Ferdinand
and Isabella launched a brutal Inquisition against sus-

pected Christian heretics and expelled (or forcibly converted) thousands of Jews. Then they turned their attention to expansion, looking across the seas for new opportunities for trade and empire.

Because Portugal controlled the southern, or African, approach to Asia, Isabella and Ferdinand sought a western route and soon were giving a hearing to a Genoese sea captain, Christopher Columbus. Columbus was familiar with the findings of Italian geographers who had rediscovered the maps of the ancient Greeks and had reached the mistaken conclusion that Europe, Africa, and Asia covered more than half the earth's surface. Accepting these miscalculations, Columbus believed that the Atlantic Ocean, long feared by Arab sailors as an endless "green sea of darkness," was little more than a narrow channel of water separating Europe from Asia. With financial backing from Spanish merchants, Ferdinand and Isabella commissioned Columbus "to discover and acquire islands and mainland in the Ocean Sea."

Columbus set sail with three small ships on August 3, 1492. An ambitious man, he wanted not only to discover a new route to China but to find and rule new lands, receiving from his monarch-patrons the titles of viceroy and governor as well as that of admiral. On October 12, 1492, after a voyage of 3,000 miles, he landed at one of the islands of the present-day Bahamas. Whatever his original intentions, the Italian adventurer had "discovered" for Europeans the lands of the Western Hemisphere.

Columbus set about exploring the Caribbean islands, claiming them for Spain and demanding gold from the local Carib and Arawak peoples. Believing that he had reached Asia, or "the Indies" in fifteenth-century parlance, he called these native inhabitants "Indians," and the Caribbean islands thus became known as the West Indies. Buoyed by the natives' stories of rivers of gold lying "to the west," Columbus left forty men on the island of Hispaniola and returned triumphantly with several Caribs to display to Queen Isabella and King Ferdinand.

Those monarchs were sufficiently impressed by Columbus's discovery that over the next twelve years they supported three more voyages. During those expeditions Columbus began the transatlantic trade in slaves, carrying a few hundred Indians to slavery in Europe and importing black slaves from Africa to work as artisans and farmers in the Spanish settlements, but he failed to find great kingdoms or valuable goods; his death in 1506 went virtually unrecognized. In one of the more curious ironies of history, the two continents that Columbus revealed to Europe were named by a German geographer after the Florentine merchant Amerigo Vespucci, who had traveled in South America around 1500 and had called it a *nuevo mundo*, a New World.

The Conquest

The Spaniards who followed Columbus, settling on Cuba, Hispaniola, and other Caribbean islands, were hardened men. Many were soldiers, veterans of the *reconquista* and of subsequent wars in North Africa. They were eager to spread the Christian faith and equally eager to get rich. The Spanish Crown licensed some of them as *adelantados* (entrepreneurs or proprietors), and this entitled them to land, plunder, the management of conquered territory, and titles of nobility; in return they pushed forward the boundaries of the empire. After subduing the Arawak and Caribs and wiping out, through disease and war, as many as a million Tainos on the island of Hispaniola, these military chieftains quickly penetrated the mainland in search of gold and other booty.

Disappointment and death greeted some adventurers, such as Juan Ponce de León, who went searching for gold and slaves along the coast of Florida in 1513 and gave the peninsula its name; in 1521 his attempt to conquer and settle the new land was cut short by an arrow from a Calusa Indian. Other Spaniards won fame rather than fortune: Vasco Núñez de Balboa crossed the Isthmus of Darien (Panama) in 1513, becoming the first European to see the Pacific Ocean.

Some Spanish adventurers fulfilled their fondest dreams. Between 1519 and 1535 a few thousand Spaniards seized control of the powerful Aztec empire in the Mexican highlands, the Mayan settlements in the Yucatan Peninsula, and the rich Inca civilization in the mountains of Peru. Within a generation these adventurers and their monarch, King Charles I (1516–1556), had become masters of the wealthiest and most populous regions of the Western Hemisphere.

The Fall of the Aztecs. In 1519, Hernando Cortés, the first of the great Spanish *conquistadors* (conquerors), landed on the Mexican coast near Veracruz, leading a Spanish force of 600 men. Drawn by rumors of the golden splendor of the Aztec empire, Cortés and his men marched inland. Within two years they had conquered the entire Aztec empire (see Map 1.3). This impressive feat was partly the result of a startling coincidence. Cortés arrived in the very year in which Aztec mythology had predicted the return of the god Quetzalcoatl to his earthly kingdom. Believing that Cortés was indeed that god, Moctezuma, the Aztec ruler, received him with great ceremony and initially allowed him free rein.

European technology was also an important factor in Cortés's triumph, both as a sign of Cortés's divinity and as an instrument of warfare. The sight of the Spaniards in full armor, with cannon that shook the heavens, made a deep impression on the Aztecs. The Aztecs had learned how to purify gold and fashion it

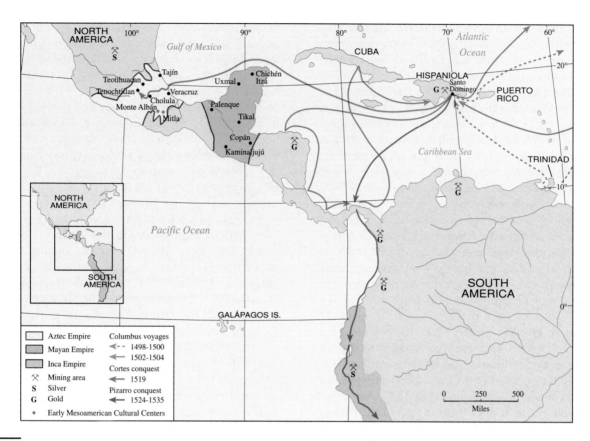

MAP 1.3

The Spanish Conquest

The Spanish first invaded the islands of the Caribbean. Rumors of a magnificent golden civilization led to Cortés's invasion of the Aztec empire in 1519. By 1535 other Spanish conquistadors had conquered the Mayan temple cities and the Inca empire in Peru, completing one of the great conquests in world history.

into ornate religious objects, but they did not produce iron for tools or weapons. Moreover, they had no wheeled carts or cavalry, for horses, once abundant in the Western Hemisphere, had died out thousands of years before. Consequently, Aztec warriors, fighting on foot with flint- or obsidian-tipped spears and arrows, were no match in small-group combat for Spanish conquistadors seated high on their horses, protected by heavy armor, and wielding steel swords.

Still, the peoples of the Aztec empire, who numbered in the millions, could have crushed the European invaders if they had presented a united front. But Cortés deftly exploited existing conflicts within Indian society. The various tribes and nations dominated by the Aztecs had long resented their cruel and oppressive rulers, who had seized their finest goods and sacrificed vast numbers of their people to the Aztec gods. To rid themselves of their overlords, many of these subject peoples rebelled, providing Cortés with supplies, information, and thousands of soldiers. Moctezuma had been killed early in the struggle (probably by followers upset by his weak military policies), and after a three-month siege the

main city of Tenochtitlán fell and the Aztec empire collapsed, the victim not only of superior Spanish military technology but of the rebellion by its subject Indian peoples.

Events then took an unexpected turn, thwarting the hopes of the subject Indian peoples and allowing the conquistadors to take over the centralized Aztec political system. The Western Hemisphere had been isolated from the viral illnesses of Europe and Asia for thousands of years, so native Americans lacked resistance to ordinary European diseases such as smallpox, influenza, and measles. A savage smallpox epidemic devastated the Aztec capital of Tenochtitlán even as the Spanish attacked, and new epidemics were swiftly spread throughout the region by Indian traders and Spanish explorers. Diseases struck down tens of thousands of native Americans, depriving the Indian peoples of leaders and warriors and sapping the morale of the survivors. Cortés quickly extended Spanish rule over the entire Valley of Mexico, and his lieutenants subdued the rest of the highland peoples and then moved against the Maya in the Yucatan, quickly conquering them as well.

The Incas. In the 1520s Francisco Pizarro, another conquistador, embarked on an expedition to the mountains of Peru, home of the rich and powerful Inca empire. Starting around A.D. 1440 as a small chiefdom centered on the Andean valley of Cuzco, some 9,000 feet above sea level, the Inca state quickly extended its control over lands stretching 2,000 miles along the Pacific coast of South America. Some 24,000 miles of roads and carefully placed administrative centers linked the far-flung empire, which boasted cities constructed of finely crafted stone. A semidivine Inca king ruled the empire, assisted by a hierarchical bureaucracy staffed by noblemen, many of whom were his relatives. By the time Pizarro reached Peru, half the population had already died from European diseases. Weakened militarily and emotionally by this abrupt loss of people and fighting among themselves over succession to the throne, the Inca nobility was easy prey for Pizarro and his army.

The Northern Frontier. Even as Pizarro conquered the Incas, other Spanish adventurers sought wealth in North America, establishing a short-lived settlement in present-day Georgia in 1526. Cortés himself dispatched expeditions along the Pacific coast; in 1533, one of his pilots, Fortún Jiménez, discovered the peninsula of Baja California and, drawing on a popular tale of chivalry that described a mythical island of California, named the region after it. A decade later Juan Rodríguez Cabrillo, a veteran of the conquest of Tenochtitlán, became the first European to reach the Pacific coast of the present-day United States. His expedition explored the California coast as far north as Oregon.

Meanwhile, the Viceroy of New Spain, Antonio de Mendoza, commissioned Francisco Vázquez de Coronado to penetrate into the heart of North America in search of the fabled seven cities of Cíbola, said by previous Spanish explorers to lie north of present-day Albuquerque and to be capped with golden towers. Coronado's expedition of 1540–1542 included 300 Spanish adventurers (including at least 3 women), 6 Franciscan missionaries, 1,000 Indian allies, and 1,500 pack horses. Traveling over well-worn Indian trails, Coronado reached and captured the alleged Cíbola, which turned out to be a poor Zuni pueblo of 100 families. Refusing to abandon his quest, Coronado dispatched expeditions that discovered the Grand Canyon in Arizona and explored much of the Rio Grande Valley in New Mexico, where they encountered the Pueblo people for the first time. Coronado himself drove eastward, pursuing more empty rumors, eventually reaching the grasslands of central Kansas (see Map 2.1, page 39).

Simultaneously, Hernando de Soto, driven by visions of gold and glory and subsidized by Genoese merchants based in Seville, embarked from Florida on a *adelantado* mission of conquest and plunder. De Soto's force of 600 adventurers cut a bloody swath across the densely populated Southeast, enslaving native peoples and doing battle with the chiefdoms of the once-powerful Mississippian culture: the Apalachee of northern Florida, the Cofitachequi of South Carolina, and the Coosa of northern Alabama. In 1541 he crossed the Mississippi, going into Arkansas and parts of Texas, but to no avail. De Soto found caches of freshwater pearls but, like Coronado in the west, no gold, with the result that until the activities of Pedro Menéndez de Avilés in the 1560s (see American Lives, pages 24–25), Spain largely ignored North America.

The Legacy of the Conquest. The Spanish invasion forever changed life throughout the Western Hemisphere, first and foremost through its devastation of the native population. Although estimates vary, it seems likely that as many as 25 million Indians were living in present-day Mexico and Guatemala at the time of the Spanish invasion of 1519. Disastrous epidemics in 1521, 1545, and 1575 took millions of lives; by 1650, only 3 million native Americans were left. In Peru, the population plummeted from 9 million in 1533 to fewer than one-half million a century later. The Pueblo peoples of the Southwest and the Mississippian chiefdoms of Florida and the Southeast may have suffered declines of an equal magnitude as a result of European diseases.

Warfare and economic exploitation hastened the decline of the population. As Bartolomé de Las Casas argued, the Indians derived few material benefits from Spanish rule (see American Voices, page 23). Spanish overlords expelled native Americans from their agricultural lands, which had provided corn, squash, and beans for human consumption, and used their labor on vast new plantations, raising wheat and livestock for export to Europe. Spanish priests suppressed their traditional gods and converted them to Catholicism; Spanish bureaucrats imposed taxes and supervised their lives; and 500,000 Spanish migrants eventually settled on their lands.

The change was profound on both sides of the Atlantic. The coming of the Spanish altered the character of the American environment as imported grains and grasses supplanted native flora. Horses, which were first brought over by Cortés, began to spread throughout the Western Hemisphere and in the following centuries would change the way of life of hundreds of Indian communities, especially on the Great Plains of the United States. The food products of the Western Hemisphere—maize, tomatoes, manioc—had an equally great impact on Europe and Africa, increasing agricultural yields and stimulating the growth of populations. Nor was that all. The gold and silver that had honored Aztec gods now flowed into the counting houses of Spanish mine owners and merchants and the treasury of the Spanish kings, making that nation the most powerful in Europe until 1650.

Bartolomé de Las Casas

The Spanish Conquest Condemned

In 1542 Bartolomé de Las Casas, Dominican friar and Bishop of Chiapas (in present-day Mexico), wrote to the Spanish king to condemn the brutal treatment of native Americans by the conquistadors. Las Casas's books were widely read throughout Europe, creating the Black Legend, a picture of Spain as a vicious and cruel nation, determined at all costs to impose Catholicism on Indians—and on Protestant Europeans.

Now to come to the continent, we dare affirm of our own knowledge that there were ten kingdoms as large as the kingdom of Spain. . . . Of all this the inhumane and abominable villainies of the Spanish have made a wilderness, for though it was formerly occupied by vast and infinite numbers of men, it has been stripped of all people . . . over twelve million souls innocently perished, women and children being included in the sad and fatal list. . . .

As for those that came out of Spain, boasting themselves to be Christians, they had two ways of extirpating the Indian nation from the face of the earth: the first was by making bloody, unjust, and cruel wars against them; the second was by killing all those that so much as sought to recover their liberty, as some of the

braver sort did. And as for the women and children that were left alive, the Spaniards let so heavy and grievous a yoke of servitude upon them that the condition of beasts was much more tolerable. . . .

What led the Spanish to these unsanctified impieties was the desire for gold to make themselves suddenly rich, in order to obtain dignities and honors that were in no way fit for them. . . . The Spanish so despised the Indians (I now speak what I have seen without the least untruth) that they used them not like beasts, for that would have been tolerable, but looked upon them as if they had been the dung and filth of the earth, and so little did they regard the health of their souls that they permitted the great multitude to die without the least light of religion. . . .

From which time forward the Indians began to think of ways that they might take to expel the Spaniards from their country. And when the Spanish saw this they came with their horsemen well armed with swords and lances, making a cruel havoc and slaughter among them, overrunning cities and towns and sparing neither sex nor age. Nor did their cruelty take pity on women with children, whose bellies they ripped up, taking out the infants to hew them to pieces. They

Bartolomé de Las Casas

would often lay wagers as to who could cleave or cut a man through the middle with the most dexterity, or who could cut off his head at one blow. The children they would take by the feet and dash their innocent heads against the rocks. . . . They erected a kind of gallows broad and low enough so that the tormented creatures might touch the ground with their feet, and upon each one of these they strung thirteen persons, blasphemously affirming that they did it in honor of our Redeemer and his apostles.

Source: Bartolomé de Las Casas, *The Tears of the Indians, Being an Historical and True Account of the Cruel Massacres and Slaughters of above Twenty Millions of Innocent People,* trans. John Phillips (London, 1656), 4–9.

By that time, the once magnificent civilizations of Mexico and Peru lay in ruins, and the surviving native Americans had lost much of their identity as separate peoples. Most Spanish settlers were men and many married Indian women, so their descendants eventually formed a predominant *mestizo* population with a mixed cultural heritage. As early as 1531 an Indian convert to Christianity began this process of cultural blending, reporting a vision of a dark-skinned Virgin Mary. Known as the Virgin of Guadalupe, this new Christian symbol became the object of great devotion and eventually of Mexican cultural nationalism. Resisting such assimi-

lation, small groups of Maya and other peoples left their lands and retreated into the mountains and preserved their traditional agricultural practices and values. In the centuries to come, their descendants, unlike the inhabitants of Africa and India, would never have the numbers or the power to oust the Europeans and so remained dependent peoples. Today only a single Indian tongue, Guarani in Paraguay, is a recognized national language, and no native American state sits in the United Nations. For the original Americans, the consequences of the Spanish intrusion in 1492 were tragic and irreversible.

Luis de Velasco/Opechancanough/ Massatamohtnock: Multiple Identities

Long before the Chesapeake Bay took its present name, it was known as the Bahía de Santa María (the Bay of Saint Mary), claimed by Spain and part of the giant colony of Florida that stretched from present-day Texas to Newfoundland. And long before the first English adventurers set foot in the colony they called Virginia, Spanish Jesuits established a mission there (in 1571) at Ajacán, the name they imposed on the land near the bay; they came to convert the local Algonquian inhabitants, the Powhatan people, to the Catholic faith.

For eighty years, from the 1560s to the 1640s, this land would be contested ground, as Spanish conquistadors and English adventurers and native chiefs vied with each other for control of the land and its people. The life of one man spanned this eighty-year struggle for power. The Spanish knew him as Don Luis de Velasco, a young Indian *cacique* (or chief) who had lived in Spain and become a pious convert to the Catholic faith. A generation later the English encountered him as Opechancanough, a local chief, "the King of the Pamaunches" (Pamunkey), who was also the elder brother of the Powhatan of the region and an astute negotiator who seemed to be a force for interracial peace. Finally, when he succeeded his brother as the main chief in 1621, at the age of seventy-seven, this man assumed a new name, Massatamohtnock, and a new role: a diplomat-warrior who led two Indian uprisings.

Spanish Catholic convert, pacific leader and diplomat, zealous native American patriot: Was this a case of multiple identities? A confused response to contradictory cultural pressures? Or simple deception?

This puzzle has its origins in 1561, when two vessels commanded by the famous Spanish mariner and adventurer Pedro Menéndez des Avilés sailed into the Bahía de Santa María. Like other conquistadors, Menéndez came looking for gold and plunder, but he also sought good harbors for naval garrisons that would protect Spanish treasure ships from pirates. Menéndez went away without riches but with a plan to return as an *adelantado*, the conqueror-proprietor of the entire east coast of North America. He also took with him the seventeen-year-old son of a local chief, an Indian youth "of fine presence and bearing," whom he

promised to take to Europe "that the King of Spain, his lord, might see him." King Philip II was equally impressed by the imposing stature of the young *cacique*, who must have stood more than six feet tall, and by his intelligence, for he granted him an allowance and had Dominican friars teach him the Spanish language and the principles of the Catholic faith.

Three years later, the young man was in Mexico, where he acquired a new patron, Don Luis de Velasco, the Viceroy of New Spain, who became his godfather and gave the Indian his own name. Anxious to return to his people, in 1566 the Indian Don Luis accompanied a expedition to the Bahía de Santa María that was blown off course, and he found himself once again in Spain. Now taught by Jesuits, a contemporary chronicler noted, "he was made ready and they gave him the holy sacraments of the altar and Confirmation." For his part, Don Luis convinced the Jesuit Father Juan Baptista de Segura of his "plan and determination . . . of converting his parents, relatives, and countrymen to the faith of Jesus Christ, and baptizing them and making them Christians as he was."

Thus it was that the young Christian convert and eight Jesuit missionaries landed in 1570 in Ajacán, 5 miles from the later site of Jamestown. Once restored to the land of his childhood, Don Luis readopted its customs, taking a number of wives. When he was publicly chastised for adultery by Father Segura, he returned to his native village. When three missionaries came to fetch him, Don Luis had them killed with a "shower of arrows"; then, according to one account, he murdered Father Segura and the rest of the Jesuits with his own hand. This massacre brought quick retribution. In 1572 Menéndez personally led a punitive expedition that killed dozens of Indians, but his onetime protégé escaped his wrath. Renouncing his Spanish identity, the young *cacique* took a new name, Opechancanough, "He whose soul is white," and joined his younger brother, the Powhatan, in building the strongest chiefdom in the region.

As Spanish dreams of an eastern North American empire faded in the face of fierce native American resistance, England dispatched its own adventurers to search for gold and propagate "the Christian religion to such People as yet live in Darkness." Opechancanough first confronted the new invaders in December 1607, when he captured Captain John Smith but spared his life. Two years later, when Smith grabbed the chief "by the long lock of his head; and with my pistol at his breast . . . made him fill our bark with twenty tuns of corn," Opechancanough did not seek revenge. Instead, for the next decade, the Pamunkey chief pursued a complicated diplomatic strategy: he "stood aloof" from the English and "would not be drawn to any Treaty," strongly resisting proposals to take Indian children from their parents so that they might be "brought upp in Christianytie." At the same time, he served the cause of interracial peace by acquiescing in the marriage of his niece Pocahontas to John Rolfe and by arranging a treaty between the Chickahominy and the English. Opechancanough stood between the two peoples, an Algonquin in culture and purpose but one whose was soul was still "white."

Then, once again, the chief assumed a new identity, taking the name Massatamohtnock in 1621 when he succeeded his younger brother as the Powhatan. The number of English migrants had increased significantly, leading many Algonquins to believe that the English would take up "all their lands and would drive them out the country." To prevent this, the aging Massatamohtnock played a double game. While assuring Governor Wyatt that "the Skye should sooner falle than Peace be broken, on his parte," he secretly mobilized the Pamunkey and more than two dozen other Indian peoples for a surprise attack that took the lives of 347 English men, women, and children (see Chapter 2). Urging the chief of the Potomacks to continue the onslaught, Massatamohtnock declared his goal: "before the end of two Moons there should not be an Englishman in all their Countries."

Finally defeated in the late 1620s by English scorched-earth warfare, the old chief reappeared in 1644, orchestrating a surprise assault that took the lives of "near five hundred Christians." Now a hundred years old, "so decrepit that he was not able to walk alone but was carried about by his men," Massatamohtnock was captured by the English and taken to Jamestown, where an ordinary soldier "basely shot him through the back . . . of which wound he died."

The absence of Algonquin sources makes it unlikely that we will ever know the complete history or the real motives of this remarkable man called Opechancanough for most of his life. But the violent treatment Don Luis meted out to Father Segura and the resistance Massatamohtnock unleashed in 1622 and 1644 suggest that ultimately he defined himself as an Indian patriot, a resolute enemy of the European invaders and their Christian religion.

The murder of Father Segura by the Indian Don Luis de Velasco at Ajacán in 1571, as depicted in a European engraving.

The Protestant Reformation and the Rise of England, 1500–1630

While Spain was conquering the indigenous societies of the New World, traditional European society was under siege from within. In 1517 a major schism divided the Catholic Church, plunging Europe into religious wars that lasted for decades. Simultaneously, gold and silver from America set off a great inflation, which altered traditional European society. England in particular was reshaped by these forces. Inflation, along with the enclosure of open fields, disrupted the lives of the peasantry, laying the foundation for a vast transatlantic migration. At the same time, English monarchs, seeking greater wealth, assisted the expansion of shipping and trade, creating the maritime resources required to establish overseas colonies. Finally, these rulers, trying to impose a single national Protestant church, persecuted Calvinist Protestants and Roman Catholics, prompting thousands to seek refuge in America.

The Protestant Movement

For more than a millennium the peoples of Western and Central Europe had been united in a common faith and their allegiance to the pope in Rome. The Protestant Reformation, which began in 1517, ushered in an era of war and social turmoil that lasted more than a century, forever shattering that unity.

At first, reformers wanted only to cleanse the church of corruption and abuses. Over the centuries the Catholic Church, through gifts, fees, and taxes, had become a large and wealthy institution, owning vast estates throughout Europe. Some bishops and cardinals, the princes of the church, used the income from church lands to live well, often luxuriously. Corruption became all too common. Pope Leo X (1513–1521), a member of the powerful Italian Medici family, received half a million ducats a year from the sale of religious offices, a practice known as *simony*. In England, Cardinal Thomas Wolsey set an equally poor example by giving church positions to his relatives. Ordinary priests and monks extracted their share of the spoils, using their authority to obtain economic or sexual favors. These abuses ignited a smoldering anticlericalism. One reformer proclaimed that the clergy were a "gang of scoundrels" who should be "rid of their vices or stripped of their authority." But until 1517 those raising their voices in protest had been either ignored or condemned as heretics and executed.

Martin Luther. In 1517, Martin Luther, a German monk and a professor at the university in Wittenberg, publicly challenged church leaders by nailing his famous Ninety-five Theses to the door of the town cathedral. This document, which was widely reprinted, condemned the church's pervasive and highly lucrative practice of selling *indulgences*—official dispensations that promised the purchasing sinner release from punishments in the afterlife. Luther argued that indulgences were worthless; redemption could come only from God through grace, not from the church, for a fee. When Luther refused to recant his views, he was excommunicated by Pope Leo X and threatened with punishment by King Charles I of Spain, who was also head of the Holy Roman Empire (see Table 1.1). The sentiment for reform was particularly strong in the German states, and northern German princes embraced Luther's doctrines and protected him from arrest. Soon Europe was at war as Charles dispatched armies to restore his authority, and Catholicism, throughout the Holy Roman Empire.

Luther broadened his attack, lashing out at church dogma and ritual not explicitly based on Scripture. His beliefs differed from Roman Catholic doctrine in four major respects. First, Luther rejected the doctrine of St.

TABLE 1.1

Spanish Monarchs, 1474–1598

Monarch	Dates of Reign	Achievements
Ferdinand and Isabella	1474–1516	Expelled Moors
Charles I	1516–1566	Dispatched Columbus; also Holy Roman Emperor, 1519–1566
Philip II	1566–1598	Attacked Protestantism; mounted Spanish Armada

Thomas Aquinas, the great medieval philosopher, that Christians could win salvation by their faith and good deeds (what Luther called "justification by works"). Stressing God's power and human weakness, Luther argued that people could be saved only by faith ("justification by faith") and that faith—and salvation—came as a gift of grace from God, not as a result of human action.

Second, Lutherans—and all Protestants—rejected the spiritual authority of the pope, partly because of corruption in the Italian-controlled papacy and partly because of political developments. As the Reformation gathered force, the rulers in many Protestant states declared themselves to be the official head of the churches within their realms, gaining the power to appoint bishops and control the church's property. Third, Luther downplayed the role of priests as mediators between God and the people, denying, for example, that priests had the power to grant absolution for sins. Instead he proclaimed the priesthood of all believers: "Our baptism consecrates us all without exception and makes us all priests." Fourth, Protestants considered the Bible the sole authority in matters of faith, raising the prospect of a multitude of individual interpretations. So that everyone could read the Bible, it was translated from Latin into the languages of the common people: German, French, and English. Luther himself did the German translation.

Social Revolution. Luther's attacks on existing authority encouraged the proliferation of radical religious doctrines and, in 1524, popular revolt against manorial landlords by the oppressed peasantry in Germany. The revolt was ruthlessly suppressed (a response that was applauded by Luther), but dissenting ideas continued to simmer below the surface. Ten years later a group of Anabaptists, religious radicals who rejected the doctrine of infant baptism, seized control of the city of Münster. They placed political power in the hands of "Saints"—those who felt God had saved them through grace—and their new government promptly abolished most rights to private property.

Fearing such social revolutions, most rulers in southern Europe did not contest the authority of the pope. Luther also affirmed the need for social discipline, arguing that whereas spiritual liberty was a private matter, Christians owed complete obedience to established political authorities. In the Peace of Augsburg in 1555, which ended a generation of religious wars, princes in the old Holy Roman Empire won the right to decide whether their subjects were to be Catholic or Protestant. Northern German princes made Lutheranism the official state religion, to which all members of the realm had to conform.

The Teachings of John Calvin. A more rigorous version of Protestantism appeared in Geneva, Switzerland, under the leadership of the great French theologian John Calvin. Even more than Luther, Calvin stressed the omnipotence of God and the corruption of human nature caused by Adam's sin. His masterly *Institutes of the Christian Religion* (1536) depicted God as an awesome and absolute sovereign, governing the "wills of men so as to move precisely to that end directed by him." Relentlessly pursuing this train of thought to its ultimate conclusion, Calvin enunciated the doctrine of *predestination*, the idea that God had "predestined" certain women and men for salvation even before they were born, condemning the rest to the eternal misery and torture of hell.

In Geneva, Calvin set up a model Christian community. He eliminated bishops altogether and placed spiritual power in the hands of ministers chosen by the members of each congregation. In the eyes of Calvinists, the state was an instrument of the church; its duty was to remake society into a disciplined religious community. Accordingly, ministers and pious laymen ruled the city, prohibiting all frivolity and luxury and banishing those who resisted.

Calvinism won converts all over Europe despite persecution by princes determined to suppress religious minorities in the name of national unity. Calvinism was the creed proclaimed by French Huguenots, by Protestants in Belgium and Holland, by Presbyterians in Scotland, and by Puritans in England and, eventually, America (see Map 1.4, page 28).

Spain's Rise and Decline

Luther's challenge to Catholicism in 1517 came just two years before Cortés conquered the Aztec empire, and the two sets of events remained linked. Gold and silver from rich mines in Mexico and Peru poured into Spain at the rate of 3 million ducats per year between 1550 and 1575 and averaged about 9 million ducats annually for the rest of the century, making Spain the wealthiest nation in Europe. Twenty percent of this immense treasure—the Royal Fifth—went directly to the Spanish monarch, helping Philip II (1556–1598), the great-grandson of Ferdinand and Isabella, become the most powerful ruler in Europe. From the Escorial, a massive monastery-palace that he built outside Madrid, Philip presided over a vast empire that included the wealthiest states of Italy, the commercial and manufacturing provinces of the Spanish Netherlands (Holland and Belgium), and, after 1580, Portugal and all its possessions in America, Africa, and the East Indies.

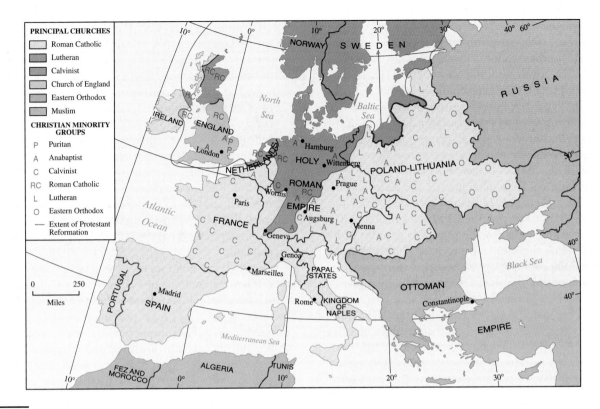

MAP 1.4

Religious Diversity in Europe

By 1600 Europe was permanently divided. Catholicism remained dominant in the south, but Lutheran princes and monarchs ruled northern Europe, and Calvinism had strongholds in Switzerland, Holland, and Scotland. Radical sects were persecuted by legally established Protestant churches as well as by Catholic clergy and monarchs. These religious conflicts encouraged the migration of minority sects to America.

The Dutch Revolt. Philip was an ardent Catholic and used his American wealth in a decades-long struggle against Protestantism in the Netherlands. Calvinism had taken strong root in these Dutch- and Flemish-speaking provinces, which had become wealthy from deep-sea fishing, commercial ties with the Portuguese empire, and the manufacture of woolen and linen fabrics. Their inhabitants feared that Philip would extend the Spanish Inquisition to wipe out their faith and take away their traditional political liberties. A popular anti-Catholic and anti-Spanish uprising in 1566 brought fierce repression by Philip's armies, but the revolt continued nonetheless.

Led by William of Orange in the province of Holland, the seven northern provinces declared their independence from Spain in 1581, becoming the Dutch Republic (or the Netherlands). To support the new Protestant state, Queen Elizabeth of England dispatched 6,000 troops to the Continent in 1585. In response, Philip assembled the Spanish Armada, and in 1588 he sent this impressive fleet of 130 ships (with 30,000 men and 2,400 pieces of artillery) to attack England. To Philip, this was the start of a holy crusade, for

he intended to conquer England, reimpose Catholicism there, and then wipe out Calvinism in Holland. But the Armada failed utterly, as English ships and a fierce storm destroyed the Spanish fleet and Philip's dream of a Catholic Europe along with it.

The Dutch were the big gainers. In 1609 Philip's successor tacitly accepted Dutch independence, and Amsterdam quickly emerged as the financial and commercial capital of northern Europe. After the formation of the Dutch East India Company, the Netherlands replaced Portugal as the dominant European power in Asia and coastal Africa. The Dutch also looked across the Atlantic, investing in sugar plantations in Brazil and the Caribbean and establishing fur-trading posts in North America (see Chapter 2).

As the Netherlands prospered, Spain faltered. Philip had spent much of his American bullion outside Spain, contributing to a long-term decline of the Spanish economy. Seeking greater opportunities, hundreds of thousands of Spaniards migrated to the new empire in America. Philip's massive expenditure of bullion also doubled the money supply of Europe, contributing to a runaway inflation that historians now refer to as the

A Dutch Merchant Family
This painting captures the serious Calvinist ethos—and the prosperity—of Holland in the sixteenth century and also the character of the patriarchal family, with its rigid hierarchy of gender and age.

price revolution of the sixteenth century. The price of a bushel of wheat, for example, rose by 300 percent between 1530 and 1600 because more money was "chasing" the limited supply of food and handmade goods and because a sharp rise in Europe's population was increasing the demand for them (see Figure 1.2). The chief beneficiaries of the price revolution were the Netherlands, France, and England. Stimulated by the influx of Spanish gold and silver, their economies boomed, enabling them to seize the initiative in commerce, manufacturing, and diplomacy. At Philip's death in 1598, Spain was in serious decline, exhausted financially and psychologically by war and inflation.

Social Change and Migration from England

England's rise came slowly. As early as 1497, John Cabot had explored the coasts of Newfoundland and Nova Scotia, establishing an English claim to the region, but for the next half century England was too weak in numbers, wealth, and military power to do more than send fishing fleets across the Atlantic. Then a decline in the death rate (because of fewer plagues and epidemics) prompted a sustained rise in the population from 3 million to 5 million between 1500 and 1630. A larger population created more wealth but also caused shortages of food, clothes, and housing. With goods in

FIGURE 1.2

Inflation and Living Standards
The influx of Spanish bullion was the main cause of the great inflation in grain prices, but increased demand (from a constantly growing population) also played a role. Higher prices cut real wages, resulting in lower living standards.

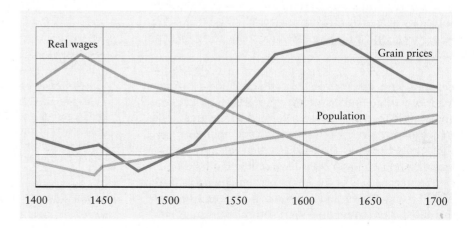

short supply and bullion plentiful, prices spiraled upward, bringing economic changes that profoundly altered the traditional class structure and, beginning in the 1550s, encouraged commercial expansion and overseas settlement.

Aristocracy, Gentry, Yeomanry. Most profoundly affected by the price revolution were the nobility, who had customarily rented out their estates on long leases for fixed rents. In the past, such arrangements had provided them with a secure income and plenty of leisure. As one English nobleman put it, "We eat and drink and rise up to play and this is to live like a gentleman." Then inflation struck. In the space of two generations, prices tripled on virtually everything, but the nobility's income from the rents on its farmlands remained virtually the same. Consequently, the wealth and status of the aristocracy declined both in local communities and in the nation as a whole.

Two other social groups benefited from the price revolution: the yeomen and the gentry. The *gentry* were substantial landholders who lacked the titles and legal privileges of the aristocracy. The gentry's estates were usually smaller than those of the nobility but they managed them more efficiently. For instance, the gentry rented their lands on short leases so they could raise rents to keep pace with inflation. Some yeomen also benefited from rising prices. Described by a European traveler as "middle people of a condition between gentlemen and peasants," *yeomen* owned some land, which they worked with family help. Since their labor costs remained constant, the yeomen's sale of grain brought increasing profits, which the more affluent among them used to build substantial houses and provide land for their children.

As aristocrats lost wealth, their branch of Parliament, the House of Lords, declined in influence. At the same time, members of the rising gentry, supported by the votes of other rural property owners, entered the House of Commons, the political voice of the propertied classes. The gentry demanded new rights and powers for the Commons, such as control of taxation. Thus the price revolution encouraged the rise of governing institutions in which property owners had a voice, a development with profound consequences for American political history.

Peasants and Enclosures. Peasants and farm laborers made up three-fourths of the population of England, and their lives, too, were transformed by the great inflation. As in the rest of Western Europe, many of these rural folk lived in open-field settlements, owning or leasing a house plot in the village center and holding the right to farm strips of the large surrounding fields. After 1500, rising prices and a growing demand for wool disrupted this communal agricultural system. Profit-

minded landlords and wool merchants used their influence in Parliament to pass *Enclosure* acts, which allowed owners to fence in the open fields and put sheep to graze on them, pushing villagers off their lands.

Thus dispossessed, families moved to small cottages in the countryside, creating a new class of landless laborers known as *cotters.* Constantly on the brink of poverty, cotters spun and wove the wool of the sheep that had taken their place on the land or worked as wage laborers on large estates owned by merchants or the gentry. Wealthy men had "taken farms into their hands," a critical observer noted in 1600, "and rent them to those that will give most, whereby the peasantry of England is decayed and become servants to gentlemen." English agriculture thus became increasingly capitalistic, with a few families owning the land and many other families working for them (see Figure 1.3).

These changes in English rural life precipitated a substantial migration to North America after 1600. As the population grew and land prices rose, thousands of yeoman farm families migrated to the English colonies to maintain their status as landowners. The enclosure

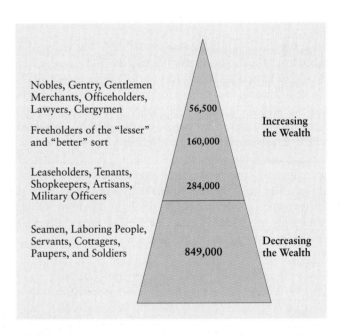

FIGURE 1.3

The Structure of English Society: 1688
This famous table of the structure of English society, devised by Gregory King in the 1680s, shows the result of centuries of aristocratic rule and of the enclosure movement. The majority of English families (some 849,000, according to King) lacked land or other productive resources and therefore, he thought, were "Decreasing the Wealth of the Kingdom." In fact, the labor of the propertyless produced a good deal of the wealth owned by those 500,500 families at the middle and top of the social scale.

movement created even greater numbers of dispossessed and impoverished peasants, many of whom crossed the Atlantic as humble indentured servants in hopes of a better life in the New World.

Mercantilist Expansion

The migration of so many English men and women would not have been possible without a vigorous and expanding merchant community. Beginning about 1350, English merchants began to sell high-quality English wool to manufacturers in France and the Netherlands. After 1500, English merchants themselves became textile manufacturers, creating a new *outwork* system of rural household production that was an early form of capitalist industry. In this system the merchants bought wool from landowners and provided it to landless cotters, who spun and wove the wool into cloth. The merchants then sold the finished product in English and foreign markets.

The Crown helped merchant capitalists expand the putting-out system and export goods to foreign markets. In 1563, the Statute of Artificers (artisan workers) gave justices of the peace the authority to fix wages, preventing cotters from demanding higher pay for their work. A new Poor Law in 1601 further ensured manufacturers a pool of cheap labor by making it more difficult for poor people to receive public assistance or private charity. Under the Tudor monarchs, especially Elizabeth I (1558–1603), special monetary bonuses were awarded to manufacturers who exported goods. Moreover, the government negotiated commercial treaties with foreign states and gave special privileges to merchant groups. In 1555, the Crown gave a royal charter to the Muscovy Company, providing it with a monopoly on the export of English cloth to Russia. Similar charters were granted to the Levant Company (Turkey) in 1581, the Guinea Company (Africa) in 1588, and the East India Company in 1600.

Mercantilism. The sixteenth-century system of state-supported manufacturing and trade became known in later centuries as *mercantilism*. English monarchs, like the rulers of many European states, pursued mercantilist policies to increase national power and wealth. By encouraging merchants to invest in domestic manufacturing, the Crown reduced the importation of foreign-made goods and boosted exports, a strategy designed to give England a favorable balance of trade. Gold and silver flowed into the country in payment for English manufactures, stimulating further economic expansion and enriching the merchant community. Increased trade meant higher revenues from import duties, which swelled the royal treasury and enhanced the power of the national government.

The success of these mercantilist policies made overseas colonization possible. The first attempts to establish a permanent English presence in America were small-scale efforts backed by individual aristocrats. All of them failed. In the 1580s, Sir Humphrey Gilbert's settlement in Newfoundland collapsed for lack of sufficient financial backing. Sir Ferdinando Gorges's colony along the coast of Maine also failed because of inadequate supplies and the harsh climate. Sir Walter Raleigh's three expeditions to North Carolina ended in failure, with one, the famous "lost" colony of Roanoke, completely vanishing, its 100 men, women, and children gone without a trace or any apparent cause.

What finally made English colonization possible was the banding together of successful merchants in *joint-stock companies*, which sold shares of stock to many investors, thus raising substantial amounts of money for commercial enterprises. It was a royally chartered joint-stock venture, the Virginia Company of London, that founded the first permanent English settle-

Sir Walter Raleigh and His Son
Raleigh was one of the great figures of his age. A distinguished courtier (as this portrait suggests), he was also a man of action—as a conquering soldier in Ireland, an explorer in South America, and the organizer of England's first colonial ventures.

ment in America at Jamestown (Virginia) in 1607. The investors hoped, like the Spanish, to grow rich by finding gold and by trading with the natives or exploiting their labor.

The English Reformation and the Puritan Exodus

While English merchants sought wealth in Virginia, thousands of other English men and women migrated to Massachusetts and Maryland to escape religious conflict and persecution. King Henry VIII (1509–1547) had initially opposed the spread of Protestantism in his kingdom. Then he petitioned the papacy for a divorce from Catherine of Aragon, an aunt of Charles V, the Holy Roman Emperor. When his request was denied, Henry broke with Rome, established a national Church of England (which granted his divorce), and declared himself supreme head of that church with complete control over ecclesiastical appointments. This break from Rome set in motion a series of religious conflicts that ended in a massive migration to America and civil war in England.

The Church of England. Henry VIII made few changes in traditional religious dogma, organization, or ritual. Priests, sacraments, and elaborate ceremonies remained important, and spiritual authority still flowed downward in a hierarchical and authoritarian fashion—from king to bishops to priests. Indeed, except for its emphasis on the authority of the Bible and its recognition of justification by faith, the Church of England under Henry was barely Protestant. But Henry's severance of the link with Rome was crucial. When his elder daughter, Queen Mary (1553–1558), briefly restored Catholicism as the state religion, her action was deeply resented, and her execution of 300 Protestant clergymen further inflamed anti-Catholic sentiment.

By the time Henry's younger daughter, Elizabeth I (1558–1603), ascended the throne, pressure for Protestant reform was irresistible, and the new queen was quick to respond by approving a Protestant confession of faith. The Thirty-nine Articles were carefully crafted to appeal to as many English Christians as possible. They incorporated both the Lutheran doctrine of justification by faith and the Calvinist belief in predestination but retained the clerical hierarchy of bishops and archbishops as well as traditional religious services—now conducted in English rather than Latin.

Elizabeth I (1558–1603)
Attired in richly decorated clothes, Queen Elizabeth I celebrates the destruction of the Spanish Armada (pictured in background) and proclaims her nation's imperial ambitions. The Queen's hand rests on a globe, asserting England's claims in the Western Hemisphere.

Presbyterianism. In an age of passionate religious controversy, Elizabeth's compromise was bound to be challenged. Many English Protestants condemned the power of bishops as "anti-Christian and devilish and contrary to the Scriptures" and called for a more radical change in church organization. Some reformers took inspiration from Calvin's Geneva, where the laity of each church controlled all of its affairs. Others preferred the presbyterian system devised by John Knox for the Calvinist Church of Scotland; there, local congregations elected lay elders (presbyters), who assisted ministers in running the church. By 1600, 500 ministers in the Church of England wanted to eliminate bishops and install a presbyterian form of church government.

The Puritans. Other reform-minded English Protestants focused their attention on religious practice. Calling themselves "unspotted lambs of the Lord" or (embracing a term used to insult them) "Puritans," they sought to purify the church of "false" teachings and practices. Although Puritans differed among themselves, they were generally united on three basic principles of ritual and doctrine. First, they wanted the authority over spiritual and financial matters to rest primarily with the lay members in each local congregation, not with bishops or even Presbyterian synods. Second, Puritans asserted the priesthood of each individual, maintaining that all Christians, not only ministers, could understand and interpret the Bible. Third, they condemned most traditional religious rites as magical or idolatrous. Puritans were offended by elaborately robed priests and by gaudy churches filled with statues and fragrant with incense; they denied that the sacraments of Baptism and Communion had miraculous powers.

As part of their attack on what they saw as magical religion, Puritans denied that God spoke to people through the *senses*. True spirituality and genuine religious knowledge, they argued, came through the *mind*. Consequently, they taught their children the importance of reading the Bible (which produced a highly literate population). The centerpiece of their religious service was the sermon—a finely wrought argument on dogma and ethics.

Religious Persecution. King James I (1603–1625), a Scot who was the first Stuart to rule England, continued Elizabeth's policy of resisting radical religious reform. He remarked bitterly that presbyterians favoring representative institutions of church government "agreeth as well with a monarchy as God with the Devil." James endorsed the absolute power of kings, not shared power with Parliament. In *The True Laws of Free Monarchy*, he maintained that kings drew their authority directly from God and thus had a *divine right* to rule. As for the congregationalist-minded Puritans, James threatened to "harry them out of the land, or else do worse."

Radical Protestants took the king at his word and fled England to avoid persecution. To preserve their "pure" Christian faith, some sects separated completely from the Church of England (and hence were called "Separatists"). One such group was the Pilgrims, who left England and settled among like-minded Dutch Calvinists at Leiden in Holland. Fearing the loss of their English way of life, some Pilgrims decided to migrate to America to preserve both their religious freedom and their sense of national identity. Led by William Bradford, thirty-five Pilgrims, joined by sixty migrants from England, founded the Plymouth colony in 1620.

During the next two decades, the repressive policies of James I and Charles I (1625–1649) drove thousands of Puritans across the Atlantic to establish settlements in the West Indies and at Massachusetts Bay. Like the Pilgrims, the Puritans envisioned a reformed Christian society, a genuinely "new" England. However, rather than break with the Church of England, they hoped to reform it; hence, they were "non-Separatist" congregationalists. They were strict Calvinists nonetheless, and the colonies they founded embodied some of the most radical thought of the Protestant Reformation.

Religious intolerance drove English Catholics to America as well. Persecuted by the dominant Church of England for their religious beliefs and their allegiance to the pope, they began settling in America in 1634, establishing the colony of Maryland. Thousands of other settlers accompanied the Catholics and Puritans, fleeing poverty or hoping for greater prosperity in the new settlements.

The English Legacy to America. The economic and religious transformation of England during the sixteenth century greatly influenced the character of its North American settlements. Since the aristocracy was on the decline and played a small role in colonization, the American settlements were not dominated by a legally privileged nobility. Conversely, the rise of English merchants enhanced their role in overseas expansion and resulted in the rapid creation of a transatlantic trading economy. Moreover, the social upheaval produced by enclosure and agricultural capitalism in England prompted the migration of thousands of yeomen and peasant families seeking land to farm. Finally, as a result of the influence of Calvinism on English Protestantism, many of these migrants carried radical forms of Christianity to North America.

The legacy was rich and complex. As products of traditional Europe, the settlers brought with them age-old principles of authority and a hierarchical social organization. Yet the old European order had already been partially overturned: the English colonies in America were founded by a nation in the midst of violent economic, political, and religious transformation. Their character and their fate were unpredictable.

Summary

The first inhabitants of the Western Hemisphere were hunter-gatherers from Asia who migrated across a land bridge during the last Ice Age. Their descendants settled throughout North and South America, establishing a great variety of cultures. In Mesoamerica, the Mayan and Aztec peoples developed densely populated agricultural societies with highly sophisticated systems of art, religion, and politics. In North America, the peoples of the Hopewell and Mississippian cultures created elaborate ceremonial and urban sites, as did the Pueblo peoples of the Southwest. Most North American Indians, however, lived in small-scale, self-governing communities of foragers, hunters, and horticulturalists.

The Europeans who invaded America came from an agricultural society in which an elite ruled a mass of peasants. The Christian religion gave emotional richness and meaning to life. Church and state endorsed values of hierarchy and authority, demanding strict discipline as the price of survival in a world of scarcity.

Europeans gradually acquired the skills and power required to colonize the Western Hemisphere. The Crusades opened their eyes to the learning of the Arab Muslim world, while the Italian Renaissance and the emergence of strong monarchical nation-states began to transform Europe from a static to a dynamic society. Portugal broke the Arab monopoly of trade with Asia by dispatching merchants around the African continent. After completing the *reconquista*, Spain sent the Italian sea captain Christopher Columbus to find a westerly route across the Atlantic. Instead of Asia, Columbus found a "new world." Within a generation, Spanish conquistadors had pillaged the wealthy civilizations of Peru and Mexico, but they failed to find gold and empire north of the Rio Grande. The coming of Europeans—and their diseases, government, and religion—brought death to millions of native Americans and changed forever the lives of those who survived.

Gold and silver from America changed European society as well, triggering a price revolution that disrupted traditional society, which was already reeling from the Protestant Reformation. These twin forces—inflation and religious dissent—undermined Spain's dominant position in Europe while encouraging the maritime expansion of Holland, France, and England. In England, monarchs used mercantilist policies to promote manufacturing, foreign trade, and colonization. The enclosure movement and religious conflicts likewise prompted a mass migration to America. Coming from a society in flux, the migrants carried both traditional and modern ideas and institutions across the Atlantic.

TIMELINE

30,000–10,000 B.C.	Settlement of eastern North America
3000–2000 B.C.	Cultivation of crops begins in Mesoamerica
1200 B.C.	Olmec culture appears
A.D. 100–400	Hopewell culture in Mississippi Valley
300	Rise of Mayan civilization
500	Zenith of Teotihuacán civilization
600	Emergence of Pueblo cultures
700–1100	Spread of Arab Muslim civilization
800–1350	Mississippian culture
1096–1291	Crusades bring Europeans into contact with Islamic civilization
1212–1492	Spanish *reconquista*
1300–1450	Italian Renaissance
1325	Aztecs establish their capital at Tenochtitlán
1415–1500	Portuguese establish maritime empire
1440s	Portugal enters trade in African slaves
1492	Christopher Columbus's first voyage to America
1513	Juan Ponce de Leon explores Florida
1517	Martin Luther starts Protestant Reformation
1521	Hernando Cortés leads Spanish conquest of Mexico
1534	Henry VIII establishes Church of England
1536	John Calvin's *Institutes of Christian Religion*
1539–1543	Hernando de Soto invades southeastern region of America
1540–1542	Francisco Vázquez de Coronado searches for Cíbola
1550–1630	Price revolution English mercantilism Enclosure movement
1556	Philip II becomes king of Spain
1558–1603	Elizabeth I, queen of England
1560s	English Puritan movement begins
1560s	Pedro Menéndez de Avilés plans North American empire
1603–1625	James I, first Stuart king of England

BIBLIOGRAPHY

One of the few works that covers the history of the various European and native American peoples is Eric Wolf, *Europe and the People without History*. See also Alfred W. Crosby, Jr., *Ecological Imperialism: The Biological Expansion of Europe, 900–1900* (1986); Robert R. Reynolds, *Europe Emerges: Transition toward an Industrial World-Wide Society, 600–1750* (1961); and G. V. Scammell, *The World Encompassed: The First European Maritime Empires* (1981).

Native American Worlds

Brian M. Fagan, *The Great Journey; The People of Ancient America* (1987), synthesizes recent scholarship on prehistoric American Indians, while his *Kingdoms of Gold, Kingdoms of Jade: The Americas before Columbus* (1991) does the same for the Mesoamerican peoples. See also Stuart J. Fiedel, *Prehistory of the Americas* (1992); Inga Clendinnen, *Aztecs: An Interpretation* (1991); John S. Henderson, *The World of the Maya* (1981); David Carrasco, *Quetzalcoatl and the Irony of Empire* (1982); R. C. Padden, *The Hummingbird and the Hawk* (1962); and R. Tom Zuidema, *Inca Civilization in Cuzco* (1992). Two fine supplements are Michael Coe et al., *Atlas of Ancient America* (1986), and Manuel Lucena Salmoral, *America in 1492* (1991), a photographic survey of dress, artifacts, and architecture.

Alfred W. Crosby, Jr., *The Columbian Exchange: Biological and Cultural Consequences of 1492* (1972), traces the impact of European diseases. See also Henry F. Dobyns, *Their Numbers Became Thinned: Native American Population Dynamics in Eastern North America* (1983), and William M. Denevan, *The Native Population of the Americas in 1492* (1992).

On North America, consult Alvin M. Josephy, Jr., ed., *America in 1492* (1993); Linda S. Cordell, *Ancient Pueblo Peoples* (1994); Bruce D. Smith, ed., *The Mississippian Emergence* (1990); Carl Waldman and Molly Braun, *Atlas of the North American Indian* (1985); and Robert Silverberg, *Mound Builders of Ancient America: The Archaeology of a Myth* (1968). Roger Kennedy, *Hidden Cities* (1994), surveys the early Indian civilizations of the Mississippi Valley.

Traditional European Society

Barbara W. Tuchman, *A Distant Mirror: The Calamitous Fourteenth Century* (1978), and Johan Huizinga, *The Waning of the Middle Ages*, present vivid portraits of the late medieval world. Two wide-ranging studies of subsequent developments are George Huppert, *After the Black Death: A Social History of Modern Europe* (1986), and Henry Kamen, *European Society, 1500–1700* (1984). Illuminating specialized studies include Peter Burke, *Popular Culture in Early Modern Europe* (1978); Pierre Goubert, *The French Peasantry in the Seventeenth Century* (1986); Philippe Ariès, *Centuries of Childhood* (1962); B. H. Slicher Van Bath, *The Agrarian History of Western Europe, A.D. 500–1850* (1963); and Emanuel Le Roy Ladurie, *The Peasants of Languedoc* (1974). See also Joel Mokyr, *The Lever of Riches: Technological Creativity and Economic Progress* (1990), and E. P. Thompson, *Customs in Common: Studies in Traditional Popular Culture* (1991).

Europe and the World

The preconditions for European expansion are treated in James D. Tracy, ed., *Rise of Merchant Empires: Long Distance Trade in the Early Modern World, 1350–1750* (1990). For the southern European background, read selectively in Fernand Braudel's massive and stimulating *The Mediterranean and the Mediterranean World in the Age of Philip II* (1949).

Paul H. Chapman, *The Norse Discovery of America* (1981), and Boies Penrose, *Travel and Discovery in the Renaissance, 1420–1620* (1952), illuminate the growth of geographical knowledge. For the expansion of the Iberian peoples see Bailey W. Diffie and George Winius, *Foundations of the Portuguese Empire, 1415–1580* (1977), and Henry Kamen, *Crisis and Change in Early Modern Spain* (1993). A good short biography of Columbus and his times is Felipe Fernández-Armesto, *Columbus* (1991).

For the Spanish and Portuguese colonial empires, see Charles R. Boxer, *The Portuguese Seaborne Empire* (1969), and James Lockhard and Stuart B. Schwartz, *Early Latin America: Colonial Spanish America and Brazil* (1984). Fine accounts of the Spanish conquest include the memorable first-hand report by Bernal Diaz del Castillo, *The Discovery and Conquest of Mexico* (ed. by I. A. Leonard, 1956); Leon Portilla, *Broken Spears: The Aztec Account of the Conquest of Mexico* (1962); and Hugh Thomas, *Conquest: Montezuma, Cortés and the Fall of Old Mexico* (1994). The impact on native society in New Spain is portrayed in Daniel T. Reff, *Disease, Depopulation, and Culture Change in Northwestern New Spain, 1518–1764* (1991); for the story north of the Rio Grande, see David J. Weber, *The Spanish Frontier in North America* (1992), and Ramon Gutiérrez, *When Jesus Came, the Corn Mothers Went Away: Marriage, Sexuality, and Power in New Mexico, 1500–1846* (1991).

The Protestant Reformation and the Rise of England

On the European Reformation, consult William J. Bouwsma, *John Calvin* (1987), and De Lamar Jensen, *Reformation Europe: Age of Reform and Revolution* (1981). For England, see Patrick Collinson, *The Religion of the Protestants: The Church in English Society, 1559–1625* (1982), and Susan Doran and Christopher Durston, *Princes, Pastors, and People: The Church and Religion in England, 1529–1689* (1991).

On the decline of Spain, consult Henry Kamen, *Spain: A Society in Conflict, 1479–1714*, 2d ed. (1991), and John Lynch, *The Hispanic World in Crisis and Change, 1598–1700* (1992), which also traces the growing economic independence of New Spain. For a general analysis of economic change in Europe, see T. S. Ashton, ed., *The Brenner Debate* (1987).

A brilliant and forceful portrait of English preindustrial society is offered by Peter Laslett, *The World We Have Lost*, 3d ed. (1984). Other important works are Keith Wrightson, *English Society, 1580–1680* (1982), and two books by Lawrence Stone, *The Crisis of the Aristocracy* (1965), and *Family, Sex, and Marriage in England, 1500–1800* (1977). On the movement of people, see Ida Altman and James Horn, eds., *"To Make America": European Emigration in the Early Modern Period* (1991).

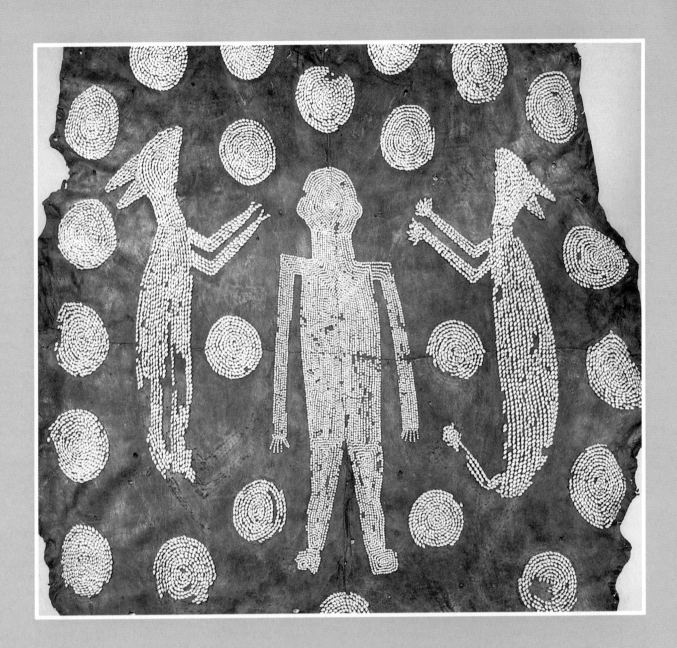

Cloak Worn by Powhatan

This deerskin, decorated with shells, is believed to be one of
the ceremonial cloaks worn by Powhatan, the leading chief
of the Indians of eastern Virginia. It was taken to England in
1614, a few years after the English first settled at Jamestown.

CHAPTER 2

Invasion and Settlement
1565–1675

★   ★   ★

By 1565 Spain had established a permanent settlement in North America, and France, Holland, and England would soon claim shares of the continent. For the next century those four nations battled for control of North America. In the process, they established very distinct colonial systems, focused either on religious conversion, the fur trade, or the settlement of European colonists. Spanish priests and a few Spanish colonists spread their religion and culture into Florida and New Mexico; French peasants farmed the St. Lawrence valley while French and Dutch merchants negotiated with Indian peoples over the fur trade; and English settlers along the Atlantic seaboard slowly moved westward.

English expansion began slowly. By 1625 England had established only two tiny colonies on the mainland: Jamestown and Plymouth, both in eastern North America. Then, between 1625 and 1675, tens of thousands of English men and women migrated to America, buying or seizing land from the Indian peoples, first in the Chesapeake Bay region and then in New England. These colonists came from markedly different backgrounds, and life in America pushed them in fresh directions. The Chesapeake was invaded primarily by adventurers seeking wealth and power, and it developed as an export-oriented plantation society in which life for most people was short, hard, and so oppressive that it sparked a violent civil war.

By contrast, New England evolved in an orderly fashion. Its settlement was directed by a purposeful group of leaders who had strong religious and communal values. Many settlers arrived in families, bolstering social cohesion, and joined Puritan churches, which enforced strict moral standards. Consequently, New England developed as a tightly governed society with a relatively egalitarian and self-sufficient yeoman economy.

This first century of European settlement prefigured the course of North American history. The triumphs of the invaders—as missionaries, fur traders, or settlers—came largely at the expense of the various Indian peoples, who gradually—through European diseases, sporadic wars, and religious conversions—lost their lives, lands, and cultural values.

Spanish, French, and Dutch Goals

Largely ignored before 1600, North America became the object of European diplomatic and religious rivalries. Spanish and French missionaries encouraged native Americans to renounce their ancestral religions and become Catholics. French and Dutch merchants sought to control the fur trade, often by setting one Indian people against another. To the Indians, these strangers had to be treated with great care, for they might be either benefactors or dangerous enemies. Wherever Europeans went as missionaries or fur traders rather than as settlers, the white population remained small, and the Indians had a much better chance of retaining their traditional lands and identities. But nearly everywhere the native peoples eventually rose in revolt.

Imperial Rivalries and American Settlements

By the 1560s few Spaniards still dreamed of finding rich Indian empires in North America. However, officials in New Spain wanted to reinforce their claims to the continent and protect the treasure fleets that skirted its eastern coast on their way to Spain. The danger was real, for Spanish gold was a powerful lure to English adventurers. In the 1560s Sir John Hawkins and other "sea dogs" plundered Spanish possessions in the Caribbean.

The Contest for Florida. France was also on the move. As far back as the 1530s Jacques Cartier had sailed into the Gulf of St. Lawrence in search of a northwestern passage to Asia and had laid France's claim to all the adjacent lands. Then, in the late 1550s, French corsairs systematically attacked Spanish treasure ships, cutting the Spanish Crown's revenue in half. French Protestants settled in Brazil in 1555, and in 1564 they moved into the Florida peninsula, land long claimed by Spain, constructing a fort on the St. John River.

King Philip II acted quickly, appointing Pedro Menéndez de Avilés as *adelantado* of the province of Florida, directing him to find the encroaching Frenchmen and "cast them out by the best means." Menéndez carried out his orders with a vengeance, massacring about 300 members of the "evil Lutheran sect." In 1565 Menéndez established a Spanish fort at St. Augustine, the first permanent European settlement in the future United States, and six other bases, the most important at Saint Elena on Port Royal Sound in present-day South Carolina. From there he sent expeditions into the interior and to the Bahía de Santa María (Chesapeake Bay), where in 1571 Spanish Jesuits founded a short-lived mission (see American Lives, Chapter 1). However, attacks by the Calusa and Timucuan peoples soon destroyed most of the Spanish settlements, causing Menéndez to condemn them as an "infamous people, Sodomites, sacrificers to the devil . . . [who should be] given as slaves."

New Mexico and California. The Spanish Crown adopted a more pacific policy toward native Americans. The Comprehensive Orders for New Discoveries, issued in 1573, placed the "pacification" of new lands primarily in the hands of missionaries, excluding adventurers such as Menéndez. In the 1580s Franciscan friars rediscovered the Pueblo world visited by Coronado two generations before, naming the area San Felipe del Nuevo México and establishing missions among the Indian settlements (see Map 2.1). But in 1598, the *adelantado* Juan de Oñate led an expedition of 500 soldiers and settlers into New Mexico to establish a military *presidio* (fort) and a trading villa. As their supplies dwindled, Oñate's men seized corn and clothing from the Pueblo peoples and murdered and raped those who resisted. Indians of the pueblo of Acoma struck back, killing 11 Spanish soldiers and prompting the remaining Spanish troops to destroy the pueblo, killing 500 men and 300 women and children. Faced by now-hostile Indian peoples, most of the settlers withdrew to New Spain.

English Ventures. Meanwhile, English adventurers stepped up their attacks on the Spanish empire. In 1577 Sir Francis Drake sailed around the tip of South America and attacked a Spanish bullion fleet in the Pacific. After landing in California, which he claimed for England, Drake sailed west to Asia. Circumnavigating the globe, he returned home with £600,000 in bullion (equal to about $30 million in 1995), twenty times the annual income of the wealthiest aristocrat. A decade later, in 1586, Drake sacked the treasure port of Cartagena (in present-day Colombia) and then razed St. Augustine, nearly wiping out the fledgling garrison-colony.

These attacks, along with Raleigh's expeditions to North Carolina, alarmed Spanish officials. They grew more concerned as the Virginia Company's settlement at Jamestown in 1607 and the founding of French Quebec in 1608 challenged Spain's monopoly over North America. This rivalry with France and England prompted Spain to maintain a token presence north of the Rio Grande, as did the continuing desire to convert the Indian peoples. In 1608 the Spanish Crown decided to maintain the garrison in St. Augustine and authorized Franciscans to remain in New Mexico. However, Spanish officials decided that an outpost in California

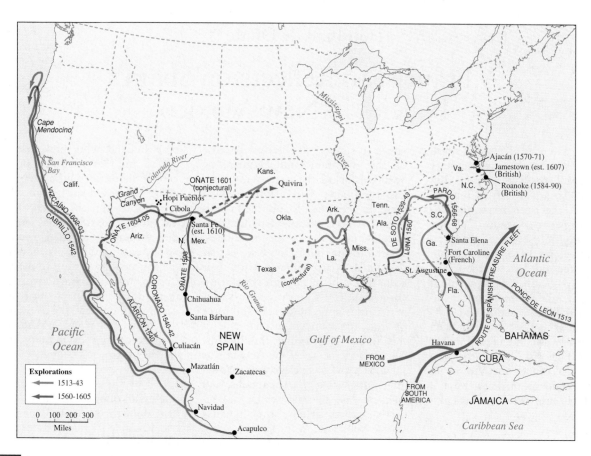

MAP 2.1

New Spain Looks North, 1513–1610

The quest for gold drew Spanish adventurers deep into North America. Hernando de Soto and Francisco Vázquez de Coronado led wide-ranging expeditions in the 1540s, but the first permanent settlement to the north of New Spain came only in 1565, at St. Augustine in present-day Florida. A generation later, following the explorations of Juan de Oñate, the Spanish founded Santa Fe in New Mexico.

would not be worth the cost, delaying permanent European occupation of that area until 1769.

New Spain: Territory and Missions

The Catholic Church was the primary force in colonizing New Spain north of the Rio Grande. Throughout the seventeenth century, Franciscan friars established missions among the Pueblo peoples of New Mexico and the Muskhogean-speaking villagers of Georgia and the north Florida peninsula, baptizing tens of thousands. Personal zeal accounted in part for the Franciscans' success; disdaining personal comfort, the friars built their missions and churches near existing pueblos and villages and often learned Indian languages. But government support in the form of supplies and soldiers also played a role in their success. Protected by soldiers, friars smashed the religious idols of the native Americans and, to win their allegiance to Christ and the concepts

of sin and heaven and hell—all new ideas for the Indians—dazzled them with rich vestments, gold crosses, and silver chalices (see American Voices, page 40).

For the Franciscans, religious conversion and cultural assimilation went hand in hand. The missionaries introduced European agricultural practices, with men instead of women growing most of the crops, and imposed Spanish language and customs, encouraging the Indians to farm, cook, eat, dress and walk like Spaniards. Those who committed sexual sins or worshiped traditional spirits were punished, usually by whipping.

For most native Americans, the missions were coercive institutions. They tolerated the Franciscans out of fear of military reprisals or in hopes of gaining access to their spiritual secrets. When prayers to Jesus and the Christian saints failed to prevent European diseases and rapacious soldiers and settlers from devastating their communities, many Indians turned back to their traditional deities.

Don Juan de Oñate

A Franciscan Reflects on Spain's Policies in New Mexico

New Spain extended its empire north of the Rio Grande through military force and religious conversion. But Spanish *adelantados* such as Juan de Oñate and Franciscan friars had differing interests and goals and frequently came into conflict. However, these two agents of Spanish expansionism often needed to cooperate. The friars frequently called on troops stationed in military *presidios* to induce local Indians to settle (and stay) at the missions and protect them from attacks by nomadic Indian peoples. As a close reading will suggest, this plea from a Franciscan to the Viceroy of New Spain endorses the limited use of military force even as it condemns past excesses.

The first and foremost difficulty, from which have sprung all the evils and the ruin of this land, is the fact that this conquest was entrusted to a man of such limited resources as Don Juan de Oñate. The result was that soon after he entered the land, his people began to perpetrate many offenses against the natives and to plunder their pueblos of the corn they had gathered for their own sustenance; here corn is God, for they have nothing else with which to support themselves. Because of this situation and because the Spaniards asked the natives for blankets as tribute, even before teaching them the meaning of God, the Indians began to get restless, abandon their pueblos, and take to the mountains. Your lordship must not believe that the Indians part willingly with their corn, or the blankets with which they cover themselves; on the contrary, this extortion is done by threats and force of arms, the soldiers burning some of the houses and killing the Indians. This was the cause of the Acoma war [of 1598], as I have clearly established after questioning friars, captains, and soldiers. And the war which was recently waged against the Jumanas started the same way. In these conflicts, more than eight hundred men, women, and children were killed, and three pueblos burned.

I do not hesitate to say that his majesty could have discovered this land with fifty well-armed Christian men, giving them the necessary things for this purpose, and that what these fifty men might discover could be placed under the royal crown and the conquest effected in a Christian manner without outraging or killing these poor Indians, who think that we are all evil and that the king who sent us here is ineffective and a tyrant. By so doing we would satisfy the wishes of our mother church, which, not without long consideration and forethought and illuminated by the Holy Spirit, entrusted these conquests and the conversions of souls to the kings of Castile, our lords, acknowledging in them the means, Christianity, and holiness for an undertaking as heroic as is that of winning souls for God.

Because of these matters (and others that I am not telling), we cannot preach the gospel now, for it is despised by these people on account of our great offenses and the harm we have done them. At the same time it is not desirable to abandon this land, either for the service of God or the conscience of his majesty since many souls have already been baptized. Besides, this place where we are now established is a good stepping stone and site from which to explore this whole land.

Source: G. P. Hammond and Agapito Rey, *Don Juan de Oñate, Colonizer of New Mexico, 1595–1628* (Albuquerque: University of New Mexico Press, 1953), Part II, pp. 692-695.

And well they might, for the resident Spaniards systematically exploited their labor. Franciscans ran their missions with Indian workers, who grew their crops and carried them to market, often on their backs. Spanish settlers, some of them privileged citizens, or *encomenderos*, collected tribute from the natives, usually in goods but often through a system of forced labor known as *repartimiento*. Still other native Americans, often women and children captured by nomadic Indian peoples, were ransomed by Spanish settlers and forced to work as slaves. Elaborate codes of Spanish law meant to regulate or prohibit the exploitation of Indian labor were rarely enforced in frontier regions.

Native peoples tried to save themselves, sometimes rising in disorganized revolts. By 1680 years of forced tribute, drought, and raids by nomadic Navajos and Apaches combined to threaten many Pueblos with extinction. Led by Popé, an Indian shaman (priest) accused of sorcery by the Spanish, the peoples of two dozen pueblos mounted a carefully coordinated rebellion. They killed over 400 Spaniards and forced the remaining 2,000 colonists to flee 300 miles down the Rio Grande to El Paso. Overtly rejecting Christianity, the Pueblo peoples desecrated churches and tortured and killed twenty-one missionaries. Reconquered a decade later by Diego de Vargas, the Indians rebelled again in 1696,

Conversion in New Mexico
Franciscan friars introduced Catholicism to the Indian peoples north of the Rio Grande, assisted by nuns of various religious orders. This 1631 engraving shows La V. M. María de Jesús de Agreda preaching to a nomadic people (*los chichimecos*) in New Mexico.

only to be subdued. Exhausted by war but now able to practice their own religion and avoid forced labor, for the next century the Pueblo peoples accepted their dependent position, joining with the Spanish to defend their lands against attacks by nomadic Indian peoples.

New France: Furs and Souls

The French came late to North America, and even after the founding of Quebec in 1608, they came only in small numbers. Therefore, in 1627 the French Crown chartered the Company of New France to encourage migration to the settlement. The company recruited few women (only about 12 percent of the total), and the men were mostly young peasants who had fled rural poverty and ended up in the cities of western France. And most of them, probably 70 percent of the 67,000 migrants to Quebec between 1608 and 1763, eventually returned to France, their hopes for prosperity dashed by the realities of life in the northern colony with its long, bitter winters.

Nor did conditions in France encourage migration. Many French peasants held strong legal rights to their village lands, and few had been displaced by the enclosure of common fields. Moreover, the French government discouraged migration in order to ensure an ample supply of farm laborers and military recruits—and thus preserve French power in Western Europe. Finally, the Catholic monarchs of France barred Huguenots (French Protestants) from seeking refuge in the colony, where the Crown feared they might undermine state interests. Consequently, New France proved a failure as a settler colony: in 1698 its European population was only 15,200, a much lower number than the 100,000 settlers then residing in the English colonies.

Instead, French Canada became a vast fur-trading enterprise as explorers traveled deep into the continent seeking new suppliers and claiming new lands for France (see Map 2.2). In 1673 Jacques Marquette, a priest of the Society of Jesus (Jesuits), journeyed west from Quebec with the fur trader Louis Joliet, eventually reaching the Mississippi River and traveling down it from present-day Wisconsin to Arkansas. René Robert Cavelier, Sieur de La Salle, completed the exploration of the majestic river in 1681, asserting French sovereignty over the entire Mississippi Valley while seeking a personal fortune. As a French priest noted with disgust, La Salle's party hoped "to buy all the Furs and Skins of the remotest Savages, who, as they thought, did not know their Value; and so enrich themselves in one single voyage." La Salle named the region Louisiana in honor of Louis XIV, the Sun King. By the early eighteenth century, despite Spain's renewed claims to Texas and the lower Mississippi Valley, New France included a thriving port at New Orleans, on the Gulf of Mexico.

The intrusion of French traders and explorers had a catastrophic impact on native Americans living near the Great Lakes. The *coureurs de bois* (runners of the woods) introduced deadly European diseases that killed anywhere from 25 to 90 percent of the native population. Moreover, as they exchanged European manufactures such as blankets and steel knives for partially tanned deerskins and beaver pelts, they set in motion a devastating series of Indian wars.

The Iroquois of New York had been organized since 1550 in large towns of 500 to 2,000 persons and were united in a great "longhouse" confederation, the Five Nations. In the 1640s they embarked on a decades-long war to seize control of the lucrative trade in furs from their neighbors. Becoming what one historian has called an "engine of destruction," the Five Nations virtually destroyed two western Iroquois tribes, the Eries and the Neutrals; forced the Iroquois-speaking Huron

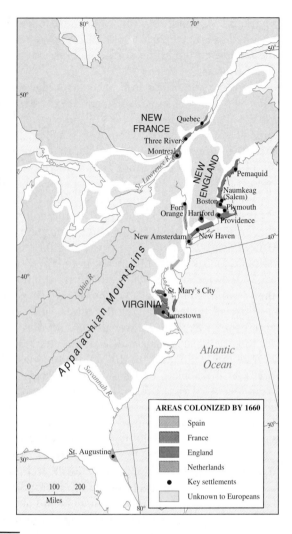

MAP 2.2

Eastern North America in 1660
Four European nations had permanent settlements
in eastern North America by 1660 but only England
had substantial numbers of settlers—some 25,000 in
New England and another 15,000 in the Chesapeake. Even so, the English settlements hugged the
coastline, leaving most of the land in the hands of
native American peoples.

to move north of the Great Lakes; and pushed a dozen
Algonquian-speaking peoples—Ottawas, Fox, Sauks,
Kickapoos, Miamis, Illinois—out of their traditional
lands north of the Ohio River. The Algonquian refugees
crowded into a newly formed multitribal region west of
Lake Michigan (present-day Wisconsin) and, to protect
themselves against the powerful Iroquois, allied themselves in the 1670s with the French, who also feared the
Five Nations. By 1701 Algonquin-French attacks had so
weakened the Iroquois that they agreed to the Grand
Settlement, promising neutrality in French-British warfare and abandoning efforts to dominate the western Indian nations.

French priests sought to expand the fur trade
among the Huron and pacify the Iroquois by converting
the native peoples to Catholicism. Between 1625 and
1763 hundreds of Jesuit priests lived among the Indians,
sharing their hardships and, to a greater extent than the
Spanish friars, coming to understand their values. One
Jesuit reported a belief among the Huron that "our
souls have desires which are inborn and concealed, yet
are made known by means of dreams" and used it to
explain the Christian doctrines of immortality and salvation. Indians responded in an equally pragmatic way,
at first welcoming the Black Robes as *manitou*, powerful spiritual beings who held magical secrets, such as the
way to forge iron. Gradually they demoted the missionaries to the status of ordinary men when prayers to the
Christian God (the "Great Manitou") did not protect
them from disease, famine, or enemy attack. "His fables
are good only in his own country," charged a leading
Peoria chief; "we have our own, which do not make us
die as his do."

However, unlike the Spanish Franciscans, the
French missionaries did not use Indians for forced labor,
and they protected the native Americans by preventing
brandy from becoming a bargaining item in the French
fur trade (even as rum fueled the English trade in pelts).
Moreover, the Jesuits won converts by advancing Christian doctrines that addressed the needs of some Indians.
In the 1690s young women among the Illinois embraced
the cult of the Virgin Mary in part because they could
use its emphasis on chastity to assert the common Algonquin belief that unmarried women were "masters of
their own body." Yet most native Americans who had
the choice found it more satisfying to hold on to their
traditional religion and culture. It was primarily Indians
who had been subdued by force and confined to praying
towns or reservations who adopted European religious
beliefs.

New Netherland: Commerce

Unlike the French and Spanish, the first Dutch settlers
in North America had little interest in religious conversion. Instead, commerce was their overriding concern.
Like France and England's New World colonies, New
Netherland was sponsored by private companies. The
Dutch Republic had become the commercial hub of Europe after it had wrested independence from Spain (see
Chapter 1), and its American settlements were part of
its worldwide empire. Henry Hudson, an Englishman in
the service of the Dutch East India Company, found and
named the Hudson River in 1609, and a few years later
the Dutch established fur-trading posts on Manhattan
Island and at Fort Nassau (present-day Albany). In
1621 the Dutch government chartered the West India
Company, giving it a trade monopoly in West Africa

and the exclusive authority to establish settlements in America. The new company took over the trading post at Fort Nassau (which it renamed Fort Orange) and set up new posts in Connecticut, New Jersey, Delaware, and Pennsylvania. In 1624 the director of the company, Peter Minuit, "purchased" all of Manhattan Island from the Indians and founded the town of New Amsterdam as the capital of the New Netherland colony (see Map 2.1).

These wilderness outposts attracted few settlers because New Netherland did not have a surplus agricultural population, and their small size made them vulnerable to invasion from New England or New France. To encourage migration, the West India Company granted huge estates along the Hudson River to wealthy Dutchmen, stipulating that each proprietor, or *patroon*, settle fifty tenants on his land within four years or the estate would revert to the company. Among all the patroons, only Kiliaen Van Rensselaer, a diamond merchant, brought over enough peasant-tenants to retain his vast American holding, the manor of Rensselaerswyck. By 1646 the population in Dutch North America had reached only 1,500.

Although New Netherland failed as a settler colony, it flourished briefly as a fur-trading enterprise, albeit a bloody one. In the 1640s Governor William Kieft embarked on an expansionist policy, dispatching armed Dutch bands to seize prime farming land from the neighboring Algonquian peoples and take over their trading network, in which corn and wampum from Long Island were exchanged for furs from Maine. Threatened by the Dutch guns supplied to their traditional Iroquois enemies, the Algonquians responded with force. By the end of "Kieft's War" (1643–1646), more than two hundred Dutch residents and a thousand Indians had been killed, many in brutal massacres of women, children, and elderly men. In the wake of this disaster, the Dutch West India Company largely ignored its crippled North American settlement, concentrating instead on the profitable importation of African slaves to its sugar plantations in Brazil.

Local Dutch officials ruled as they thought best. Continuing Kieft's expansionist policies, Governor Peter Stuyvesant ordered the conquest in 1655 of New Sweden, a small fur-trading rival on the Delaware River. Stuyvesant also rejected the demands of English settlers on Long Island for a representative system of government, alienating the colony's increasingly diverse population of Dutch, English, and Swedes. Consequently, in 1664, during one of a series of Anglo-Dutch wars, the population of New Amsterdam offered little resistance to English invaders and generally accepted English rule. For the rest of the century the renamed towns of New York and Albany remained small fur-trading centers, Dutch-English outposts in a region still dominated by native Americans.

Social Conflict in the Chesapeake

The English came to the Chesapeake Bay region of present-day Virginia and Maryland seeking gold, furs, and trading opportunities. Quite unexpectedly, they developed a settler society with a booming tobacco economy based on the exploitation of native American lands and the labor of white indentured servants. The Chesapeake settlements were an economic success but a social and moral failure. Settlers fought with Indians to acquire land, and prominent families used wealth, deceit, and force of arms to rule the society.

The English Invasion

Like New Netherland, the first English settlement in North America was a corporate colony, an enterprise of ambitious merchants. In 1606 the merchant stockholders of the Virginia Company of London received a charter from James I that granted them the right to exploit the riches of North America from present-day North Carolina to southern New York. The company's directors had chosen the name Virginia both to honor Elizabeth I, the "Virgin Queen" who had died in 1603, and to enhance their chances of obtaining a charter. As an additional inducement, they promised to "propagate the *Christian* religion" among "infidels and Savages." Charter in hand, the company's directors were able to raise funds from no fewer than 56 London commercial firms and 659 individual investors. Their goal was to find and exploit rich and populous Indian peoples.

In 1607 the company dispatched an expedition to Virginia to found a trading outpost, not a settler colony. Only men and boys—not families—were aboard the three small ships—*Sarah Constant, Goodspeed*, and *Discovery*—that set sail from London. The company retained ownership of all the land in Virginia and appointed a governor and a small council to direct the migrants, who were its employees or "servants." The company expected them to procure their own food and ship anything of value—gold, exotic crops, or Indian merchandise—back to England.

The migrants were unprepared for the challenges they faced. Some were young gentlemen with financial or personal ties to the shareholders of the Virginia Company but no experience in living off the land—a bunch of "unruly Sparks, packed off by their Friends to escape worse Destinies at home," as one observer put it. The rest were cynical adventurers, men bent on conquering the Indians for their gold or turning a quick profit from trade. Like the company's directors, they expected to find established towns with ample supplies of food and labor and Indians with gold to trade for English cloth and tinware.

The "Starving Time." They were soon disappointed. Arriving in the spring, after a hazardous voyage of four months, the newcomers laid out the settlement of Jamestown on a swampy peninsula on the James River (both named after the new king) and explored the region. They found forty Algonquian-speaking Indian peoples, among them the Monacan and the Chickahominy, who willingly exchanged corn for English goods but had little else to offer and no interest in working for the traders. And the traders were not much interested in working for themselves, at least not in planting crops and raising food. All they wanted, one of them noted, was to "dig gold, refine gold, load gold." But there was no gold.

Of the 120 Englishmen who embarked on the expedition, only 38 were still alive after nine months in America, the rest having fallen victim to malnutrition and disease. Only the determination of Governor John Smith, a soldier of fortune who ran the infant colony like a dictator, saved the enterprise from total collapse, and when Smith left, starvation loomed. As of 1611, the Virginia Company had sent 1,200 settlers to Jamestown, but fewer than half had survived. "Our men were destroyed with cruell diseases, as Swellings, Fluxes, Burning Fevers, and by warres," one of the leaders reported, "but for the most part they died of meere famine." Desperate for food, survivors raided Indian villages, provoking hostility. The new governor, Thomas West, imposed military discipline on the migrants and demanded that the native Americans acknowledge the sovereignty of James I.

The Powhatan, the leading chief of a loose confederation of some two dozen tribes, was prepared to extend privileges to the English traders if they would support him against his Indian rivals. But faced with food seizures and West's haughty demands, the chief accused the English of coming "not to trade but to invade my people and possess my country." Nevertheless, Powhatan, whom Smith described as a "grave majestical man," accepted the presence of the English, giving his daughter Pocahontas in marriage to the adventurer John Rolfe in 1614.

Rolfe had come to Virginia in 1610, and he would play a leading role in the colony until his death in 1622. Soon after his arrival Rolfe imported tobacco seeds from the West Indies and began to cultivate the crop. Tobacco was already popular in England as a result of imports from Spanish America. Within a few years Virginia was exporting tobacco to London; and the colony's leading men wanted more workers to grow it, so they imported hundreds of poor white men from England. And, Rolfe noted in 1619, "a Dutch man of warre . . . sold us twenty Negars." These black laborers, who probably worked as servants rather than slaves,

Carolina Indians, 1585
John White was one of the first English settlers in Sir Walter Raleigh's colony on Roanoke Island, and his watercolors provide a rich visual record of native American life. The shallow waters inside the Outer Banks (Albemarle Sound in present-day North Carolina) provided Indian peoples with a protein-rich diet of fish. (© British Museum)

were the first Africans in British North America and, in a sense, the first African-Americans.

As hopes for the Indian trade declined and the prospect of exporting tobacco rose, the Virginia Company instituted a new and far-reaching set of policies. In 1617 it allowed individual settlers to own land, granting 100 acres of land to every freeman in Virginia, and it established a *headright* system, by which every incoming head of a household had a right to 50 acres of land and 50 additional acres for every adult family member or servant. The company also approved a new "charter of privileges, orders, and Lawes" that provided for a system of representative government. The House of Burgesses (so called because its election procedures followed those of the English boroughs, or "burgs") was first convened by Governor George Yeardley in Jamestown in 1619. This body had the authority to make laws and levy taxes, although its legislative acts could be vetoed by the governor or nullified by the company. Together, these two incentives—land ownership and local self-government—achieved the desired result: between 1617 and 1622, about 4,500 new recruits set sail from England. Virginia was about to become a settler colony.

The Indian Uprising of 1622. The sudden influx of settlers sparked all-out war with the resident Indians. The new migrants were farmers who wanted land that the Indians had long since cleared and were using for their own crops. The Englishmen's demands alarmed Opechancanough, Powhatan's brother and his successor as the leading chief of the region (see American Lives, Chapter 1). Forming an alliance with other Chesapeake tribes, the chief launched a surprise attack, killing nearly a third of the white population and vowing to drive the rest back across the ocean. The English retaliated by burning the Indians' cornfields, depriving them of food, a strategy that secured the safety of the colony by the late 1620s.

The cost of the war was high. The Indians killed many settlers and burned a lot of property, but their own losses were even worse. Moreover, the time of coexistence was past; as one English militiaman put it, "[we now felt we could] by right of Warre, and law of Nations, invade the Country, and destroy them who sought to destroy us; whereby wee shall enjoy their cultivated places, turning the labourious Mattock [hoe] into the victorious Sword (wherein there is more ease, benefit, and glory) and possessing the fruits of others' labour."

Royal Government. Two years after the Indian uprising of 1622, James I dissolved the Virginia Company, accusing its directors of mismanaging the increasingly valuable tobacco colony. Thereafter, Virginia became a *royal colony*, the first in English history. A governor and the members of a small advisory council were appointed by the king. The House of Burgesses was retained, but any legislation it enacted required ratification by the king's Privy Council. James also legally established the Church of England in Virginia; this meant that all property owners had to pay taxes to support the clergy. These institutions—a royal governor, an elected assembly, and an established Anglican church—became the model for royal colonies throughout America.

The Founding of Maryland. The neighboring settlement of Maryland also became a tobacco-growing colony, but it was founded on a completely different political and religious basis. Maryland was a *proprietary colony*, meaning that it was owned by a "proprietor." In 1632 Charles I (1625–1649), James's successor, gave Cecilius Calvert, Lord Baltimore, a charter that made him the proprietor of the territory between the Potomac River and the Delaware Bay. Lord Baltimore owned all the land in his colony and could sell it, lease it, or give it away as he wished. He also had the authority to appoint the governor and all public officials and could found churches and appoint ministers.

A Catholic, Baltimore wanted Maryland to become a refuge for his coreligionists, such as the Brent family (see American Lives, pages 46–47), who were being persecuted in England. He therefore devised a policy of religious toleration to minimize confrontations between Catholics and Protestants. He instructed the governor (his brother, Leonard Calvert) to allow "no scandall nor offence to be given to any of the Protestants" and to "cause All Acts of Romane Catholicque Religion to be done as privately as may be."

The settlement of Maryland began in 1634. Twenty gentlemen (mostly Catholics) and 200 artisans and laborers (mostly Protestants) established St. Mary's City high on a bluff overlooking the mouth of the Potomac River. The population grew quickly, for the Calvert family carefully planned and supervised the colony's development, hiring skilled artisans and offering ample grants of land to wealthy migrants. Since Maryland's soil proved almost as suitable for the cultivation of tobacco as Virginia's, the booming European market for the new crop helped ensure the success of the colony.

The main problems were political. Baltimore's charter specified that the proprietor had to govern with the "Advice, Assent, and Approbation" of the freemen of the colony. However, Governor Leonard Calvert tried to ignore that stipulation. Beginning in 1638, a representative assembly elected by the freemen insisted on the right to initiate legislation, which Baltimore grudgingly granted. After an armed uprising by Protestants, in 1649 the assembly enacted a Toleration Act that granted religious freedom to all Christians, thus protecting the Catholic settlers, who remained a minority of the population. By 1650 Baltimore had accepted the separation of the legislature into an upper house consisting of an appointed council and a lower house filled with leading men elected by propertied freeholders. As in Virginia, local self-government was balanced by limits on the settlers' autonomy; all laws passed by the assembly and the council and approved by the proprietor had to be consistent with those of England. But the fluid conditions of life in America—notably the absence of traditional authoritarian institutions—enhanced the political power of ordinary people and their ambitious leaders.

Margaret Brent: A Woman of Property

In 1647 the new Maryland colony was in crisis. Protestants had revolted against the Catholic government and seized control of the colony. To preserve Maryland as a refuge for Catholics and safeguard his family's interests, Governor Leonard Calvert hired mercenary soldiers from Virginia. Lacking hard currency to pay them, he pledged his estate and that of his brother, Cecilius Calvert (Lord Baltimore, the proprietor of Maryland), as security for their wages. But just as his soldiers put down the revolt, Governor Calvert died, plunging the government into disarray, without authority or funds to pay the restless mercenaries. On his deathbed Leonard

Calvert named Thomas Green to succeed him as governor but entrusted his personal estate to a prominent landowner, Margaret Brent. Telling her "I make you my sole Exequtrix. Take all, pay all," he left the resolution of the crisis in her hands.

The woman who accepted this challenge was born around 1601 in Gloucestershire, England, into a substantial gentry family. But as Catholics, the Brents' religious freedom and fortune were increasingly precarious. Since the death of Queen Mary in 1557, English Catholics had endured almost continuous religious persecution, and the growing power of militant Puritans

A nineteenth-century painting depicts Margaret Brent asking for voting rights in the Maryland assembly.

during the 1630s promised new hardships for the Brents and other Catholics. The family faced a troubled financial future as well. With thirteen children, Margaret Brent's parents had done their utmost to propagate their Catholic faith, but their fruitfulness threatened the next generation with economic decline. In migrating to Maryland, the Brent children hoped to use the modest funds provided by their parents and their ties with the Calverts to maintain their gentry status.

Margaret Brent, her sister Mary, and their brothers Giles and Fulke arrived in Maryland in 1638. They carried a letter from their coreligionist Lord Baltimore recommending that they be granted land on favorable terms, and the grant was made. Margaret and Mary took up the "Sisters Freehold" of 70 acres in St. Mary's City, the capital of the colony. Four years later Margaret acquired another 1,000 acres on Kent Island from her brother Giles. Margaret soon won the trust and favor of Governor Calvert, sharing with him the guardianship of Mary Kitomaquund, the daughter of a Piscataway chief, who was being educated among the English.

The governor's death during the 1647 crisis threatened the Brents' ambitions, which depended on Catholic rule and access to the governing family and its allies in the assembly. To preserve her family's religious freedom—and its wealth and influence—Margaret Brent would have to save the colony from the mutinous soldiers. Now a mature woman of forty-six, Brent was unusually well qualified for this task. Like many women of gentle birth, she had received some preparation for public affairs; she had enjoyed a basic education in England and had watched her father conduct the business of his estate. But, almost unheard of for a woman, she also had considerable experience in the public arena. As a single woman of property in Maryland, she had appeared frequently before the Provincial Court to file suits against her debtors. In addition, she had occasionally acted as an attorney, pleading the cases of her brother Giles and various women before the court.

Brent did not hesitate to use the power and authority Calvert had assigned to her. First, since food was in short supply and the soldiers camped in St. Mary's City were demanding bread, she arranged for corn to be imported from Virginia. Then, to pay the soldiers, she spent all of Leonard Calvert's personal estate. When that proved inadequate, she adroitly exploited her position as the governor's legal executor to draw on the resources of the Lord Proprietor. Using the power of attorney Governor Calvert had held as Baltimore's representative, Brent sold the proprietor's cattle to pay the troops. Once paid, the soldiers promptly dispersed—some becoming settlers—allowing Governor Green to

restore order to the increasingly Protestant colony. To preserve Maryland as a refuge for Catholics, Lord Baltimore had the assembly pass a Toleration Act (1649), which allowed the free exercise of religion by all Christians.

Margaret Brent's vigorous advocacy of the interests of her family and the Calverts did not go unchallenged. In January 1648 she demanded two votes in the assembly, one for herself as a freeholder and one in her role as the proprietor's attorney. For reasons that do not appear on the record, the Provincial Court opposed her claim: it "denyed that the said Mrs. Brent should have any vote in the house." From England, Lord Baltimore launched a "bitter invective" against Brent, protesting against the sale of his cattle and accusing her of wasting his estate. Baltimore's attack was partly designed to convince the Puritan Parliament, which had just defeated the king in the English Civil War, that he did not favor Catholics. He also hoped to recover some of his property, which he suspected had fallen into the hands of the Brent family. Although the Maryland assembly declined to grant Margaret Brent a vote, it did defend her stewardship of Baltimore's estate, advising him that it "was better for the Collonys safety at that time in her hands than in any mans . . . for the Soldiers would never have treated any others with that Civility and respect. . . ."

No longer assured of the proprietor's favor, the Brents turned to new strategies to advance their interests. Giles Brent married Mary Kitomaquund, the Piscataway Indian, perhaps hoping to gain land or power from her influential father, and moved with her to Virginia in 1650. The next year Margaret and Mary Brent also took up lands in Virginia, on the Northern Neck, gradually settling their estate with migrants from England. Margaret Brent never married, making her one of the very few English women in the early Chesapeake not to do so. She died on her Virginia plantation, named "Peace," in 1671, bequeathing extensive property in Virginia and Maryland, mostly to her brother Giles and his children.

Margaret Brent is often hailed as an early feminist and woman lawyer, but viewed in the context of the time, her actions and achievements were essentially those of an "adventurer" and an assertive woman of property. Born into privileged circumstances and determined to maintain that status, she had struck out on her own—settling in the wilderness of Maryland, defending her interests before the Provincial Court, asserting her rights as a property owner in the assembly, and helping to save the colony—and her family's fragile stake in America—in a time of crisis.

Tobacco and Disease

Tobacco and disease shaped the early history of Maryland and Virginia. Indians in North America and the West Indies had long cultivated the tobacco plant, using its leaves as a medicine and a stimulant. By the 1620s tobacco was popular in England as well, as men and women of the upper and middling classes developed a craving for it and the nicotine it contained. They found many ways to use tobacco: smoking, chewing, or snorting it in its powdered form, snuff. Initially King James I was not impressed. He condemned the use of this "vile Weed" and warned that its "black stinking fumes" were "baleful to the nose, harmful to the brain, and dangerous to the lungs." But his attitude changed as the "vile weed" proved to be a valuable crop. In 1619 he imposed a duty (an import tax) on tobacco, and the revenues filled the royal coffers.

The demand for tobacco in Europe set off a forty-year economic boom in the Chesapeake. The exotic crop commanded such high prices that thousands of profit-hungry migrants flocked to the region, where tobacco thrived in the warm, humid climate. "All our riches for the present do consist in tobacco," a happy planter remarked in 1630. The Chesapeake colonies exported about 3 million pounds of the plant in 1640 and 10 million pounds in 1660. The tobacco leaf became the symbol of the new colonies of Virginia and Maryland, and the tobacco plantation became a characteristic form of settlement. Planters moved up the river valleys, establishing large farms at a considerable distance from one another but easy to reach by water (see Map 2.3). Few towns grew up in the Chesapeake colonies, and there

was a much weaker sense of community there than in the open-field villages of rural England.

Unfortunately, tobacco was not the only thing that flourished in the mild Chesapeake climate. Mosquitoes bred quickly and spread malaria through their bites. Malaria made people weak to the point where they were unable to resist other diseases. It struck pregnant women especially hard; many died after bearing their first or second child, and so settler families were small. Malaria and other sicknesses—smallpox, fevers, dysentery—took such a high toll that although more than 15,000 settlers arrived in Virginia between 1622 and 1640, the population rose only from 2,000 to 8,000.

For most of the seventeenth century life in the Chesapeake colonies remained harsh and short (see Figure 2.1). Most men never married because there were few women settlers. The marriages that did take place often ended abruptly with an early death, destroying the normal bonds of family, friendship, and community. Rarely did both parents survive to see their children grow to adulthood. Unmarried young men and orphaned children accounted for a substantial portion of the population.

The precarious state of family life altered the traditional male system of authority in the household. Because men could expect their male relatives to die young, many Chesapeake husbands deviated from custom and named their wives as the executors of their wills. Those wills enhanced the position of widows (in relation to child-heirs) by giving them the use of more of the family property than was strictly required by law. Frequently a man's will permitted his widow to retain an ample legacy even if she remarried, as most women

---

MAP 2.3

River Plantations in Virginia
The first migrants settled in widely dispersed plantations along the James River. The growth of the tobacco economy continued this pattern as wealthy planter-merchants traded with English ship captains from their riverfront plantations. Consequently, few substantial towns or trading centers developed in the Chesapeake region.

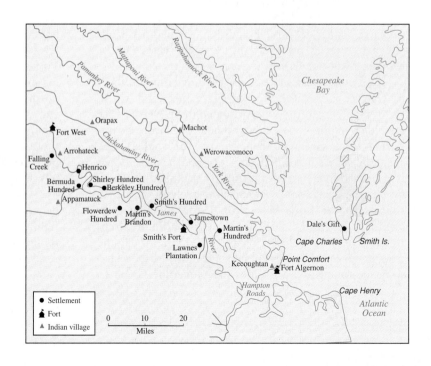

FIGURE 2.1

Average Life Expectancy at Age Twenty in Virginia and New England, 1640–1700

Malaria and other diseases brought early death to English migrants in the Chesapeake region, producing a society filled with orphaned children. Settlers in New England lived into their sixties, often transmitting their customs and values to their grandchildren.

Married women in Middlesex County, Virginia	39
Married men in Middlesex	48
Women in Andover, Massachusetts Bay Colony	62
Men in Andover	64
Women in Plymouth Colony	62
Men in Plymouth Colony	69

The Tobacco Economy

Most poor farmers raised tobacco, for it grew well in small fields and was easy to process. But larger plantations, such as the one pictured above, used the labor of indentured servants and slaves. The workers cured the tobacco stalks by hanging them for several months in a well-ventilated shed; then they stripped the leaves and packed them tightly into large barrels, or "hogsheads," for shipment to Europe.

did. In fact, women who survived the rigors of life in the Chesapeake often improved their social position and legal privileges through inheritance and remarriage.

Indentured Servitude

Despite the dangers, the lure of land ownership and tobacco wealth was so strong that between 1640 and 1700 over 80,000 English settlers moved to Virginia and at least 20,000 more sought their fortunes in Maryland. Shipping registers from the port of Bristol provide a glimpse of the lives of 5,000 people among these English emigrants. As was the case among migrants to New France, three-quarters of them were men, and most were under twenty-five years old; many had traveled hundreds of miles to Bristol, some intent on embarking for Virginia and others simply looking for work. Taking full advantage of their plight, merchants and sea captains concluded labor contracts called *indentures* with these youths. Indentures bound them to work in return for room and board for a period of four or five years (or, in the case of younger servants, until the age of twenty-one). Upon reaching Virginia or Maryland, the merchants assigned the contracts to local planters in return for cash or tobacco.

Indentured servitude was very profitable for those who owned the contracts. For merchants servants were valuable cargo, because they fetched high prices in the labor-starved Chesapeake. For plantation owners, they were an incredible bargain. In return for providing food, clothing, and shelter for their indentured workers, the planters received all the profits of their servants' labor for four or five years. With the price of tobacco at six pence a pound, a male indentured servant could produce five times his purchase price in a single year. Furthermore, indentured servants were counted as household members, so planters in Virginia received 50 acres of land for every servant they acquired.

Masters had the legal right to regulate nearly every aspect of their servants' lives. They could beat them for disobeying or slacking off; they could withhold permission to marry. If servants ran away or became pregnant, a master could go to court to increase their term of service. Planters often abused their female servants. As a Virginia law of 1692 put it, "dissolute masters have gotten their maids with child; and yet claim the benefit of their service." Planters could get rid of uncooperative servants by selling their contracts to new masters. As an Englishman in Virginia remarked in disgust, "servants were sold up and down like horses."

And so, for most of these migrants, indentured servitude did not provide the escape from poverty they had sought. Half the men died before receiving their freedom, and another quarter remained poor. The remaining quarter got some benefit from their ordeal, acquiring property and respectability. If they survived, women servants generally fared better, prospering because men in the Chesapeake had grown "very sensible of the Misfortune of Wanting Wives." Some married their masters or other men with substantial incomes. By migrating to America, these few—and very fortunate—men and women escaped a life of landless poverty in England.

The Seeds of Revolt

During the boom years of the 1620s tobacco sold for twenty-four pence or more a pound; forty years later it was fetching only a few pence per pound—barely one-tenth as much. Overproduction in the Chesapeake was the prime cause of the bust in the tobacco market, but political decisions made in England also played a role.

The Navigation Acts. In 1651, in an effort to exclude Dutch ships and merchants from England's overseas possessions, Parliament passed an *Act of Trade and Navigation*. As revised and extended in 1660 and 1663, the Navigation Acts permitted only English or colonial-owned ships to enter American ports. They also required the colonists to ship certain "enumerated articles," including tobacco, only to England. Chesapeake planters could thus no longer legally trade with Dutch merchants, who traditionally paid the highest prices for tobacco.

Moreover, the English monarchs continually raised the duty on tobacco in order to increase royal revenues. Those duties, by keeping the price of imported tobacco high, stifled the growth of the market, and planters received only one penny a pound for their crop by the 1670s. Yet as living conditions improved and more children were born and survived to adulthood, the number of planters in Virginia and Maryland grew each year, as did tobacco exports—from about 20 million pounds

annually in the 1670s to 41 million pounds between 1690 and 1720, more than the slowly expanding market could absorb. Profit margins were very thin, and few planters prospered.

Poor Tenants, Rich Planters. Economic stagnation after 1660 meant that the Chesapeake ceased to be a land of upward social mobility. Yeomen families earned just enough to scrape by. Each year a typical small freeholder family grew about 1,800 pounds of marketable tobacco. Taxes (often paid in tobacco) amounted to 200 pounds of the crop and clothes accounted for another 800, leaving only about 800 pounds to be sold or bartered for supplies and equipment. Many freeholders fell into debt and had to sell their land.

Even harder hit were newly freed indentured servants, who found it nearly impossible to save the money required to become property owners. Under the head-right system, freed servants could *patent* (be granted) 50 acres of uncleared land, provided that they could afford to pay the fees for surveying the land and recording the deed. Then, to become planters, they had to buy tools, seed, and livestock. Few succeeded, and most had to sell their labor once again—as wage laborers, tenant farmers, or even servants.

Established planters weathered the decline in tobacco prices with greater success. Many had accumulated large landholdings; now they leased small plots to the growing army of tenant farmers. They also lent money at high rates of interest to hard-pressed yeomen families. Some well-to-do planters became commercial middlemen, setting up small retail stores or charging a commission for storing the tobacco of their poorer neighbors or selling it to English merchants.

Gradually the economic life of the Chesapeake colonies came to be dominated by an elite of planter-merchants. In Virginia those men were able to accumulate nearly half the patented land by using their political power to extract huge land grants from the royal governor and in some cases by claiming headright shares for fictitious migrants. In Maryland wealthy planters controlled labor with equal success; in Charles County they owned about 40 percent of the work force through the indenture system. As aggressive entrepreneurs confronted a growing number of young, landless laborers, social divisions intensified.

Governor William Berkeley. Tensions in Chesapeake society reached a breaking point during the corrupt regime of Governor William Berkeley. Berkeley, who served as governor of Virginia between 1642 and 1652, had won fame in 1644 by repulsing a second Indian uprising led by Opechancanough and concluding a peace treaty that, by guaranteeing certain lands to the Indians, preserved peace for a generation. When he became governor again in 1660, he made large land grants to him-

Green Spring
Governor Berkeley ran Virginia from his country estate at Green Spring, with its large but architecturally undistinguished residence. The wooden outbuildings housed equipment and the indentured servants who worked as farm laborers.

self and members of his council. Berkeley's Green Spring faction, named after his country estate, soon became a corrupt oligarchy. Council members exempted their own lands from taxation and appointed friends as county judges and local magistrates. Berkeley suppressed dissent in the House of Burgesses through the lavish use of patronage, assigning land grants to friendly legislators and appointing their relatives to the profitable posts of sheriff, tax collector, and justice of the peace.

Berkeley staved off every challenge to his rule for fifteen years. Once his favorites were in the House of Burgesses, he refused to call new elections. When the demand for elections could no longer be ignored, the corrupt Burgesses changed the voting system to exclude landless freemen, who constituted half the population of the adult white men. Property-holding yeomen retained the vote, but they were unhappy about falling tobacco prices, rising taxes, and political corruption. The Virginia elite—unlike the English aristocracy and gentry—was too newly formed and too crudely ambitious to command the respect of the lower orders. Social and political unrest began to reach the boiling point.

Bacon's Rebellion

Conflict with the Indians. In 1675 there were 40,000 whites in Virginia, and their views of frontier issues were based largely on class and geography. Most of the wealthy planters lived in the coastal districts and opposed a policy of armed expansion into Indian territory, as did the planter-merchants who traded with the native Americans for furs. However, poor freeholders and aspiring tenant farmers who had settled farther inland, seeking cheap land, insisted that the Indians be expelled or exterminated.

The Indians in Virginia were few and weak, their numbers having dwindled from about 30,000 in 1607 to 2,000 in 1675. Most lived on lands guaranteed by treaty—lands now coveted by the frontier settlers. But the Susquehannock people had migrated into the region

from the north, settling on the upper reaches of the Potomac River, and actively encouraged the other Indians to resist white expansion.

War broke out in the summer of 1675, when Virginia militiamen crossed the Potomac River into Maryland and without provocation murdered thirty Indians. Defying orders from Governor Berkeley, a larger force of 1,000 militiamen then surrounded a fortified Susquehannock village. Under a flag of truce, they lured four chiefs out of the stockade and killed them on the spot. The outraged Susquehannock retaliated by killing eighty whites in raids on outlying plantations.

Berkeley did not want war, which would disrupt the fur trade, and proposed a defensive military policy, asking the House of Burgesses in March 1676 to raise money to build a series of forts to protect the frontier plantations. Western settlers dismissed this strategy as useless against roving Indian bands and an excuse to levy high taxes. Berkeley's plan, one freeholder argued, was a plot by the coastal planters and the political elite—the "grandees," as he called them—to break the freeholders financially and take "all our tobacco into their own hands."

Nathaniel Bacon. Nathaniel Bacon emerged as the leader of the western settlers. A wealthy young man, he had recently arrived from England and settled on a frontier estate. Although he was only twenty-eight, Bacon commanded the respect of his neighbors in part because of his high status, for Berkeley had made him a member of the governor's council, but more because of his personality. Bacon was forceful and bold, confident of his goals and purposeful in pursuing them. When Berkeley refused to grant Bacon a military commission, the young man marched his frontiersmen against the Indians anyway, slaughtering members of the peaceful Doeg people.

The massacre triggered a political upheaval that completely overshadowed the Indian question. Condemning Bacon's men as "rebels and mutineers," Berkeley expelled Bacon from the council and placed him under arrest. Then, realizing that the rebel leader commanded a large military force, the governor reinstated Bacon, gave in to the demand for legislative elections, and accepted the far-reaching political reforms enacted by the new House. The Burgesses, who now included influential supporters of Bacon, curbed the powers of the governor and the council to grant lands and allow tax exemptions. And to cut the patronage powers of the Green Spring faction, the Burgesses converted many local offices into elected posts, giving yeomen freeholders more control over the government. The legislature also restored voting rights to landless freemen.

These much-needed reforms did not end the rebellion, however. Bacon, who was well connected in England, was bitter at having been treated by the governor as a young upstart; the men in his army, resentful of exploitation by the "grandees," were eager to flaunt their newly won power. Backed by 400 armed men, Bacon forced the governor and the Burgesses to commission him "General of Virginia." Then he toppled Berkeley and seized control of the colony.

Popular Rebellion. In August 1676 Bacon announced his goals in an uncompromising "Manifesto and Declaration of the People." It demanded the death or removal of all native Americans and an end to the rule of wealthy "parasites." "The poverty of the country," Bacon proclaimed, "is such that all the power and sway is got into the hands of the rich, who by extorious advantages, having the common people in their debt, have always curbed and oppressed them in all manner of ways."

Bacon's coup brought civil war to Virginia. Berkeley led 500 armed supporters in a successful attack on Jamestown, after which Bacon's army promptly recaptured the capital, burned it to the ground, and plundered the plantations of Berkeley's allies. Only Bacon's sudden death from dysentery in October gave Berkeley the upper hand. The governor dispersed Bacon's army of frontiersmen and servants and then took his revenge, seizing the estates of well-to-do rebels and hanging twenty-three men.

Bacon's rebellion was a pivotal event in the history of the Chesapeake region. Planter-merchants continued to dominate the colony, but they realized that it was dangerous to let a governor and a corrupt oligarchy rule unchecked. In the future they would limit the governor's authority and find public positions for substantial property owners who, like Bacon, had political ambitions. The planter-merchant elite also learned how to contain the fury of the lower social orders, supporting an expansionist military policy that won the votes of tenants and poor yeomen by promising them access to Indian lands.

The uprising also contributed to the emergence of a new labor system: African slavery. Slavery in the Chesapeake had already grown for economic reasons, such as the scarcity of English indentured servants and a surge in the transatlantic trade in African captives (see Chapter 3). Now its expansion was fueled by the Chesapeake elite's desire to forestall another rebellion by freed white servants. In All Hallows Parish in Maryland, permanently enslaved Africans made up 10 percent of the population in 1675; by 1700 they accounted for 35 percent. Thus, to maintain their privileged class position, the leaders of Virginia and Maryland committed themselves and their descendants to a social system based on the exploitation of enslaved blacks.

Puritan New England

Adopting the Puritans' view of themselves, many historians depict the Puritan exodus to America as a heroic effort to preserve the "pure" Christian faith. Yet many Puritans migrated for economic reasons, and their desire for land to provide food and farmsteads for their growing families was only slightly less intense than that of the openly profit-minded adventurers in Virginia. Puritan magistrates found biblical justification for seizing lands from the native Americans, imposed strict religious orthodoxy on their own followers, and condemned dozens of women to death for the crime of "witchcraft." However, the Puritan story does have impressive qualities. These religious migrants created a stable society of independent farm families in New England and gave a moral dimension to American history.

The Puritan Migration

The Pilgrims at Plymouth. The histories of New England and Virginia differed from the beginning. Jamestown was settled by unruly male adventurers; Plymouth, the first permanent community in New England, was filled with pious Protestant families—English Pilgrims who had settled in Holland and other religious dissenters who wished, as they put it, to advance the true "gospell of the Kingdome of Christ in those remote parts of the world."

Before sailing to America aboard the *Mayflower* in September 1620, the Pilgrims had organized themselves into a joint-stock corporation to secure financial backing from sympathetic Puritan merchants. Their stated intention was to settle in the territory granted to the Virginia Company, but either by accident or, more likely, by design they landed far to the north, on the rocky coast of New England. There, outside the jurisdiction of Virginia and lacking a charter from King James I, they created their own covenant of government, the Mayflower Compact, to "combine ourselves together into a civill body politick." This document, which was signed by forty-one adult men, was the first "constitution" adopted in North America. It translated into political terms the Pilgrims' long-standing belief in the autonomy of the religious congregation and, while recognizing the sovereignty of the king, produced a system of self-government based on the rule of law.

That first winter in America tested the Pilgrims' spiritual mettle. In Plymouth, as in Jamestown, hunger and disease took a heavy toll: of the 100 migrants who arrived in November, only half survived until the spring. Thereafter the Plymouth colony—unlike Virginia—became a healthy and thriving community because of the cold climate, which inhibited the spread of mosquito-borne diseases, and the religious discipline of the determined settlers. Unlike the gold-hungry adventurers in Virginia, the Pilgrims set about building small, solid houses and planting ample crops of grain and vegetables. The settlement grew quickly through natural increase and migration and had a population of 3,000 by 1640. Aided by epidemics that killed off the Indians, the settlers spread across the landscape and established ten new towns with extensive powers of self-government.

New England Domestic Architecture
Well-to-do Puritans affirmed their commitment to America by building well-constructed dwellings. Most late-seventeenth-century houses were built of wood and had plain symmetrical facades and substantial central chimneys—to preserve heat during the cold New England winters.

In 1636 they adopted a legal code that provided for a colonywide system of representative government and contained a rudimentary bill of rights.

The Pilgrims were devout Christians and tried to live according to the laws and ethics of the Bible, which in their view required limiting the power of the state over religion. As "Separatists," they had cut themselves off from the Church of England and believed that each congregation should be self-governing, free from control by either a religious or a political hierarchy. In that limited sense, they anticipated the "separation of church and state."

Religious Conflict in England. Meanwhile, England was plunging deeper into religious turmoil. King Charles I, James I's successor, reaffirmed his father's support for the Church of England and its traditional liturgy and ecclesiastical hierarchy. But Charles personally repudiated some of the Calvinist doctrines of the Anglican creed, such as justification by faith. The Puritans, who had gained many seats in Parliament, directly challenged the king, accusing him of "popery."

Charles's response was to dissolve Parliament in 1629. For the next decade he ruled by "divine right," raising money on his own authority through royal edicts, higher customs duties, and the sale of monopolies. The king's arbitrary rule struck at the dignity of the landed gentry, who expected to exercise authority through the House of Commons. The merchant community, another stronghold of Puritanism, was also displeased as higher tariffs ate away at their profits.

Religious strife intensified when the king chose William Laud to be bishop of London in 1628. Laud loathed Puritans and, when he became archbishop of Canterbury in 1633, banished hundreds of Puritan ministers from their pulpits, forcing Anglican rituals on their congregations. Tens of thousands of ordinary men and women felt the impact of arbitrary rule. However, their faith in the Puritan creed remained unshaken: they conducted services in secret, and some of them went further, planning to seek refuge in America.

The Massachusetts Bay Colony. In 1630, 900 Puritans boarded eleven ships and sailed across the Atlantic under the leadership of John Winthrop, a well-educated, highly regarded country squire. Having obtained a charter from Charles I, the Puritans established a new settlement, the Massachusetts Bay colony, in the area around Boston. Even more than the Pilgrims, the Puritans saw themselves as central actors in a great historical drama. They were a "saving remnant" chosen by God to preserve the true faith in America. The Lord "has sifted a whole nation," a Puritan minister declared, "that he might send choice grain over into this Wilderness."

Governor John Winthrop
This portrait captures the gravity and intensity of Winthrop, whose policies of religious orthodoxy and elite rule shaped the early history of the Massachusetts Bay colony.

Winthrop decided to go to America for economic as well as religious reasons. Believing England to be corrupt in morals and "overburdened with people," he sought land and opportunity for his children. But he also saw a chance to preserve the true Christian church and set an example for all Europe to follow. "We must consider that we shall be as a City upon a Hill," Winthrop told his fellow passengers aboard the ship *Arbella* in 1630. "The eyes of all people are upon us." Though the Puritan experiment has long since vanished, Winthrop's words still evoke in Americans a vision of their destiny as a people and a nation.

Once they arrived in America, Winthrop and his associates transformed their joint-stock business corporation, the General Court of shareholders, into a legislature that was empowered to enact laws for the new colony. Over the next decade about 10,000 Puritans migrated to the Massachusetts Bay colony, along with 10,000 others—yeomen and artisan families, along with their servants—fleeing from hard times in England (see Map 2.4). To ensure rule by the godly, the Puritans enacted a law limiting the right to vote and hold office to men who were members of an approved Puritan church.

By the mid-1630s the General Court had become a representative assembly elected by the members of Puritan congregations in the various towns. With John Winthrop as governor (he served for fifteen years), the General Court sought to create a religious common-wealth, establishing Puritanism as the official state-supported religion and barring members of other faiths from conducting services. The Bible was the basis for some of the laws enacted by the Massachusetts Bay government. For example, the Puritans followed a biblical rule by dividing inheritances among all heirs, with a double portion going to the oldest son, thus rejecting the custom of many English families of giving all the land to the eldest son (primogeniture). "Where there is no Law," the court advised local magistrates, they should rule "as near the law of God as they can."

Puritans and Pequots

The Puritans' conception of themselves as God's chosen people shaped their relations with native Americans. Initially they felt obliged to justify their intrusion into the Indians' domain. "By what right or warrant can we enter into the land of the Savages," they asked themselves while still in England, "and take away their rightfull inheritance from them and plant ourselves in their places?" An answer to this question was provided by John Winthrop, who suggested that a disastrous small-pox epidemic that killed hundreds of Indians in 1633 was in fact a mark of divine favor. "If God were not pleased with our inheriting these parts," he asked, "Why doth he still make roome for us by diminishing them as we increase?"

For a second justification the Puritans turned to the Book of Genesis, which instructed them to "be fruitful, and multiply, and replenish the earth, and subdue it." From this, the magistrates of Massachusetts Bay argued that because the Indians had not "subdued" most of their land by plowing or fencing it, they had no "just right" to it.

Bolstered by these religious beliefs, the Puritans often treated native Americans with a brutality equal to that of Spanish conquistadors and Nathaniel Bacon's frontiersmen. A vivid instance of this occurred in 1637, when Pequot warriors attacked Puritan farmers who had begun to intrude onto their fertile lands in the Connecticut River Valley. As sporadic violence escalated into war, Puritan militiamen and their Indian allies led a surprise attack on a Pequot village and massacred about 500 men, women, and children. "God laughed at the Enemies of his People," one soldier boasted, "filling the Place with Dead Bodies." Puritan forces ruthlessly tracked down the survivors, selling many into slavery in the Caribbean. In the end, the Pequot people were virtually exterminated.

Like most Europeans, the English invaders viewed the Indians as "savages," culturally inferior people who did not deserve civilized treatment. Indeed, to some Puritans the Indians were latter-day "Philistines," a biblical people that had been justly slain by the Jews, God's

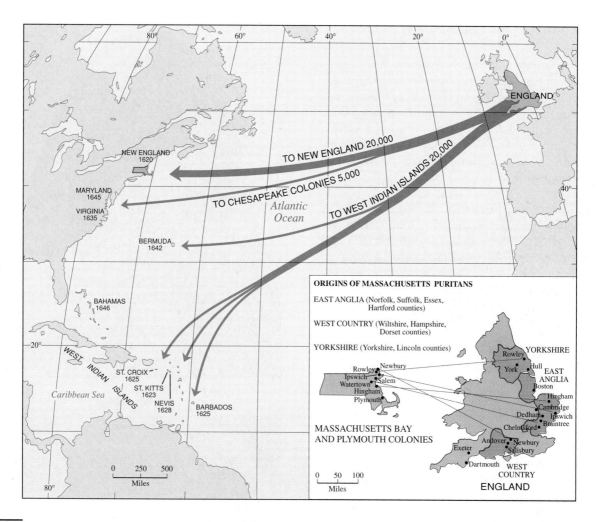

MAP 2.4

The Puritan Migration to America
Nearly 50,000 Puritans left England between 1620 and 1640. In New England, migrants from the three major areas of English Puritanism—Yorkshire, East Anglia, and the West Country—commonly settled among those from their own region. They named American communities after their English towns of origin and transplanted regional customs, such as the open-field agriculture practiced in Rowley in Yorkshire and Rowley in Massachusetts Bay.

original chosen people. Yet the Puritans were not racist as the term is understood today. To them, native Americans were not genetically inferior and indeed were not even members of a different race—they were white people with sun-darkened skins. Not race but sin accounted for the Indians' "degenerate" condition. "Probably the devil" delivered these "miserable savages" to America, wrote the Puritan minister Cotton Mather, "in hopes that the gospel of the Lord Jesus Christ would never come here to destroy or disturb his absolute empire over them."

This interpretation of Indian history inspired attempts at conversion. John Eliot, a Puritan minister, translated the Bible into Algonquian and undertook missions to Indians outside Boston and on Cape Cod. Because Puritans demanded that the Indians conform to

English customs and master Puritan theology, only a few native Americans became full members of Puritan congregations. However, the Puritans achieved what the Spanish Franciscans had only hoped for in New Mexico: a controlled Indian population. Within a generation there were more than a thousand "praying Indians" living under Puritan supervision in fourteen special mission towns. Their numbers severely diminished by European diseases and English arms, their traditional kinship and communal institutions in shreds, these "survivors" placed themselves under Puritan political and religious control. Thus, a combination of European diseases, military force, and Christianization pacified most of the seaboard Algonquian peoples, guaranteeing, at least temporarily, the safety of new white inhabitants of New England.

Religion and Society, 1630–1670

Unlike the Separatist Pilgrims, the Puritans' wish was to reform the Church of England from within. Disposing of ostentatious "Catholic" features such as bishops and elaborate rituals, they followed what they believed to be the practice of the first Christians, devising a simple church structure controlled by the laity, or the ordinary members of the congregation. Hence their name, *Congregationalists*.

The Elect. According to Puritan theology, which was derived mainly from the teachings of John Calvin (see Chapter 1), God had chosen a few "elect" men and women for salvation—they were predestined for heaven even before they were born. The doctrine of predestination was a harsh one, for it seemed to deny people any control over their salvation. Moreover, it led to a sharp division between church members, the Elect or Saints, as they were called, and the rest of the population, who constituted a majority of the adult population of New England. The Saints set extraordinarily high standards for church membership. Many people did not even bother to apply; those who did were subjected to a rigorous oral examination of their morals and beliefs. Even the Saints lived in great anxiety, for they could never be sure that they were really among the elect. Consequently, Puritan deathbeds were scenes of agony and doubt. "I have seen Persons Quaking on their Death Beds, and their very beds therewith Shaking under them," Cotton Mather reported, with their deathbed utterances testifying to their terror: "O! The wrath of a Dreadful God, Makes me Tremble; I Tremble, I Tremble, at that wrath."

Puritans dealt with the uncertainties of divine election in three ways. Some congregations pointed to the transforming effect of the conversion experience: as God infused the sinner's soul with grace, he or she was "born again" and *knew* that salvation was at hand

Changing Images of Death
Death—sudden and arbitrary—was a constant presence in the preindustrial world. Pre-1700 New England gravestones often depicted death as a frightening skull, warning sinners to repent of their sins. After 1700 a smiling cherub adorned many gravestones, suggesting a more optimistic view of the afterlife.

A Puritan Meetinghouse
Puritan churches were plain but handsome buildings. Inside, the most prominent feature was the pulpit, symbolizing the importance of the sermon and the Word of God. Outside, most meetinghouses were painted in bright colors (not white, as they are today).

John Dane

The Life Story of a Puritan Tailor

The conscience of a Puritan was always active, always seeing God's hand in ordinary events and prompting self-examination and self-control in an unending battle against the temptations of the world. John Dane migrated to Massachusetts Bay in the 1630s and, after surviving a near suicide, lived in Ipswich until his death in 1684.

I first settled in Berkhampstead [England]. . . . On a night when most folks was abed, a maid came into the shop and sat with me, and we jested together, but at the last she carried it so, and put herself in such a posture, as that I made as if I had some special occasion abroad and went out, for I feared if I had not [left] I should have committed folly with her. But I often thought that it was the prayers of my parents that prevailed with God to keep me.

[Subsequently, at Hereford:] There was, whether fly, wasp, or hornet I cannot tell, but it struck my finger, and water and blood came out of it and pained me much. I went up to a house and showed it [to the people there], but they knew not what a sting I had

at my heart. Now I thought of my mother's words, that God would find me out. . . . The pain and swelling increased and swelled up to my shoulder. I prayed earnestly to God that He would pardon my sin and heal my arm. I went to a surgeon and asked him what it was. He said it was "take." I asked him what he meant. He said it was taken by the providence of God. This knocked home on my heart what my mother said, "God will find you out." Now I made great promise that if God would hear me this time I would reform.

I then bent myself to come to New England, thinking that I should be more free here than there from temptations, but I find here a devil to tempt, and a corrupt heart to deceive. . . . Many troubles I passed through, and I found in my heart that I could not serve God as I should. . . . [At that time] with my gun on my shoulder charged, in the mile brook path beyond Deacon Goodhewe's, I had several thoughts [which] came blocking into my mind that I had better make away [with] myself than to live longer. I walked discoursing with such thoughts

[for] the best part of an hour, as I judged it. At length I thought [that] I ought of two evils to choose the least, and that it was a greater evil to live and to sin against God than to kill myself—with many other satanical thoughts. I cocked my gun, and set it on the ground, and put the muzzle under my throat, and took up my foot to let it off. And then there came many things into my head, one [was] that I should not do evil that good might come of it. . . . I was then much lost in my spirit, and, as I remember, the next day Mr. Rogers preached, expressing himself that those were blessed that feared God and hoped in His mercy. Then I thought that blessedness might belong to me, and it much supported my spirit. . . . Thus God hath all along preserved and kept me all my days. Although I have many times lost His special presence, yet He hath returned to me in mercy again.

Source: John Dane, "A Declaration of Remarkable Providences in the Course of My Life." *New England Historical and Genealogical Register*, VIII (1854), 149–156.

(see American Voices, above). Other Puritans stressed "preparation," the confidence that came from years of spiritual guidance and church discipline. Many of these "preparationists" followed the Dutch Protestant theologian Jacob Arminius in conceiving of God as a more reasonable and merciful deity than the one portrayed by Calvin. If a person expressed "the merest desire to be saved," declared one Arminian-influenced Puritan, God would bestow His saving grace. Still other New England Puritans reassured themselves by embracing a collective interpretation of their destiny. They believed that God had entered into a *covenant*, or contract, with the Puritans, promising to treat them as a divinely "chosen people" as long as they ordered their lives in accordance with His laws.

Roger Williams and Rhode Island. To remain in God's favor, Puritan magistrates purged their society of religious dissidents. One target was Roger Williams, who had become the minister of the Puritan church in Salem in 1634. Williams applauded the Pilgrims' separation of church and state and condemned the legal establishment of Congregationalism in Massachusetts Bay. He taught that political magistrates should have authority only over the "bodies, goods, and outward estates of men," not over their spiritual lives. Moreover, the outspoken Salem preacher questioned the moral and legal justification for seizing (rather than buying) Indian lands. When Williams refused to end his criticism, the Puritan magistrates banished him from Massachusetts Bay in 1635.

Williams and his followers resettled in Rhode Island in 1636, founding the town of Providence on land acquired from the Narragansett Indians. Other religious dissidents joined him in nearby Portsmouth and Newport. In 1644 these towns obtained a corporate charter from the English Parliament, which was controlled by Puritans, granting them full authority "to rule themselves." Rhode Islanders used their new political freedom to ensure religious liberty. In Rhode Island there was no legally established church; every congregation was autonomous, and individual men and women could worship God as they pleased.

The Heresy of Anne Hutchinson. Puritan magistrates detected another threat to their holy commonwealth in the person of Anne Hutchinson, a middle-aged woman, the wife of a merchant and the mother of seven, who worked as a midwife. Hutchinson held weekly prayer meetings in her house—often attended by as many as sixty women—in which she questioned the teachings of certain Boston clergymen, saying that they placed undue emphasis on church laws and good behavior. In words that recalled Martin Luther's rejection of indulgences (see Chapter 1), Hutchinson argued that salvation was not something that people could earn; there was no "covenant of works." Rather, salvation was bestowed by God through the "covenant of grace." Hutchinson stressed the importance of revelation: the direct communication of truth by God to the individual believer. Since this doctrine diminished the role of ministers and, indeed, of all established authority, Puritan magistrates found it threatening.

The magistrates also resented Hutchinson because of her sex. Like other Christians, Puritans believed in the equality of souls—both men and women could be saved; they also believed that the soul had a feminine nature. When it came to practical matters regarding the governance of church and state, however, women were seen as being clearly inferior to men. As the Pilgrim minister John Robinson put it, women "are debarred by their sex from ordinary prophesying, and from any other dealing in the church wherein they take authority over the man." Puritan women could never be ministers, lay preachers, or even voting members of the church.

In 1637 the Massachusetts Bay magistrates put Hutchinson on trial for heresy as an *antinomian*, a person who looks inward for grace or truth and asserts freedom from the rules of the church. Hutchinson defended her beliefs with great skill and tenacity, and even Winthrop admitted that she was "a woman of fierce and haughty courage." But the odds were against her. The judges not only found her guilty of heresy for claiming a direct relationship with God but also condemned her for exceeding her proper station in life. In Winthrop's words, she should have "attended her household affairs, and such things as belong to women."

The General Court banished Hutchinson from the Massachusetts Bay colony. Her merchant allies, affluent men who also resented the power of the clergy, were unable to protect her. Defeated, she followed Roger Williams into exile in Rhode Island, where she and a small group of supporters founded Portsmouth. Later Hutchinson moved to Westchester County, New York, where she was killed in an Indian raid. Puritan magistrates noted Hutchinson's death with grim satisfaction, interpreting it as a sign of God's approval of their enforcement of religious orthodoxy.

The Connecticut Colony. The banishing of dissidents prompted some devout Puritans, among them the Reverend Thomas Hooker of Newtown (Cambridge), to flee from the authority of the Massachusetts Bay magistrates. In 1636 Hooker led a hundred settlers to the Connecticut River Valley, where they established the town of Hartford. Other Bay colony residents followed, settling along the river at Wethersfield and Windsor. In 1639 the Connecticut Puritans adopted the Fundamental Orders, a plan of government that included a representative assembly and a popularly elected governor. A royal charter from King Charles II in 1662 bestowed self-government on these Connecticut towns, whose population had grown to almost 5,000, and joined them to another Puritan settlement at New Haven. Connecticut was patterned after Massachusetts Bay, with a firm union of church and state and a congregational system of church government, but voting rights were extended to most property-owning men—not just church members (see Table 2.1).

The Cambridge Platform. In Massachusetts Bay leading magistrates and ministers gave up their efforts to impose a single definition of orthodoxy. In the Cambridge Platform of 1648, the laity won a written guarantee that each church would be independent and equal. Although the platform specified that "consociations" of clergy might meet to discuss church dogma and discipline, most Puritan congregations could act as they pleased, deciding matters of doctrine, choosing and dismissing ministers, and admitting new members. In religion as in politics, hierarchy gave way to local self-rule.

The Puritan Revolution. Many migrants had expected that the settlement of New England would be the beginning of the *millennium*, the thousand-year rule of Christ on earth predicted in the Book of Revelation. At first, events in England appeared to bear them out. In 1637 Archbishop Laud imposed a new prayer book on Presbyterian Scotland and threatened to send bishops to impose religious discipline. Popular riots against Laud's edicts led to armed resistance. In 1639 a Scottish Presbyterian army invaded England, forcing Charles to call Parliament into session to vote funds for the war. The

TABLE 2.1

European Colonies in North America before 1660

	Date	First Settlement	Type	Religion	Chief Export or Economic Activity
New France	1608	Quebec	Royal	Catholic	Furs
New Netherland	1613	New Amsterdam	Corporate	Dutch Reformed	Furs
New Sweden	1628	Fort Christina	Corporate	Lutheran	Furs; farming
English Colonies					
Virginia	1607	Jamestown	Corporate (Merchant)	Anglican	Tobacco
Plymouth	1602	Plymouth	Corporate (Religious)	Separatist Puritan	Mixed farming; livestock
Massachusetts Bay	1629	Boston	Corporate (Religious)	Puritan	Mixed farming
Maryland	1634	St. Mary's	Proprietary	Catholic	Tobacco; grain
Connecticut	1635	Hartford	Corporate (Religious)	Puritan	Mixed farming; livestock
Rhode Island	1636	Providence	Corporate (Religious)	Separatist Puritan	Mixed farming; livestock

Puritan-dominated House of Commons seized the chance to demand an end to arbitrary measures. When Charles resisted, the nation divided into Royalist and Parliamentary factions. In 1642 thousands of English Puritans—and scores of Puritans who had returned from America—took up arms against the king. After four years of civil war, the Parliamentary forces led by Oliver Cromwell were victorious. In 1649 Parliament executed Charles, proclaimed a republican commonwealth, and imposed Presbyterianism on the Church of England. God's rule on earth seemed imminent.

But the Puritan experiment in England lasted just a decade. Popular support for saintly rule quickly declined, especially when Cromwell took dictatorial control of the government in 1653. After Cromwell's death a repentant Parliament summoned Charles I's son, Charles II, back to the throne. In 1660 the monarchy was restored, and bishops reclaimed their authority in the Church of England. For many steadfast Puritans the Restoration represented the victory of the Antichrist—a false church preaching false Christian doctrines.

The Halfway Covenant. The outlook in New England seemed equally grim. Puritans in America were experiencing grave doubts about their religious "errand into the wilderness," for the second generation had not sustained the intense religious spirit of the original migrants. Many younger Puritans had been baptized as infants but, perhaps intimidated by the religious zeal of their parents, had not experienced conversion and become full church members. Their "deadness of soul" threatened to end the Puritan experiment, since the un-

Richard Mather (1596–1669)
Mather migrated to New England in 1635 after Archbishop Laud stripped him of his pulpit. His son Increase Mather was a leading Boston clergyman, as was his grandson Cotton Mather, the author of *Magnalia Christi Americana*, an epic of the Puritan adventure in New England.

converted could not present their own children for baptism. Never more than a bare majority, the Saints had imposed their religious vision out of determination, not numbers. If Puritans became a small minority, they might well lose control of the colony.

To keep the churches vigorous, Puritan ministers devised the Halfway Covenant in 1662. This covenant altered Calvinist theology by making salvation more predictable, indeed almost hereditary. Under its terms, the children of all baptized Puritans could be presented for baptism and thus become "halfway" members. Not conversion but birth became the key to Puritan identity. For example, the First Church of Milford, Connecticut, had 962 members in the period 1639–1770. No fewer than 693 of these Puritan Saints (72 percent) were members of the thirty-six families who had established the original congregation.

The Halfway Covenant began a new phase of the Puritan experiment. Puritans had come to America to preserve the "pure" Christian church; many of them half expected to return in triumph to a Europe ready to receive the true Gospel. In the course of events, that sacred mission had been dashed, and so Puritan ministers instead exhorted their congregations to create in the American wilderness a new society based on high moral and intellectual principles.

The Puritan Imagination and Witchcraft

Like the native Americans they encountered in New England, the Puritans (and other seventeenth-century Europeans) thought that the physical world was full of supernatural forces. This belief in "spirits" was not completely inconsistent with their Christian heritage, since Catholics believed in supernatural miracles and Protestants hoped that "grace" would infuse their hearts. However, it stemmed primarily from the system of pagan beliefs that were still current in Christian Europe, among both ordinary people and highly educated individuals.

The diary of Samuel Sewall provides a glimpse into the Puritan imagination. Sewall was born in England in 1652 and educated at Harvard College, which had been founded by Massachusetts Bay Puritans in 1635. He enjoyed a long and distinguished life as a Boston merchant, politician, and judge. Sewall was a devout Puritan: the Bible shaped his consciousness and provided him with clues to the meaning of events. Thus, he applauded a proposal to establish a French Protestant colony in territory claimed by Catholic Spain, interpreting it as part of God's plan to pull down "the throne of Antichrist, as is so designed in the [Book of] Revelation."

Sewell constantly sought a supernatural design in natural events. For example, he spent an evening with Cotton Mather, an influential minister, discussing why "more Ministers' Houses than others proportionably had been smitten with Lightning; inquiring what the meaning of God should be in it." At times this belief in supernatural forces led Sewall into pagan practices. For example, before occupying a new addition to his house, he drove a metal pin into the floor to fend off evil spirits.

Devout Protestants such as Sewall thought they received many celestial signs or warnings from God in the form of blazing stars, deformed births, and rainstorms of blood. They also followed pagan astrological charts printed in farmers' almanacs. Those charts, along with diagrams and pictures, correlated the movements of the planets and stars with the signs of the zodiac. By deciphering the charts, farmers determined the best times to plant crops, marry off their children, and make other important decisions.

Zealous Protestant ministers attacked such beliefs and practices and condemned "cunning" individuals who claimed to have special powers as healers or prophets. Many ordinary Christians looked on folk doctors or conjurers as "wizards" or "witches" who acted at the command of Satan. Between 1647 and 1662, civil authorities in Massachusetts and Connecticut hanged fourteen people for witchcraft. Most of the victims were older women, who, their accusers claimed, were "double-tongued," "had an unruly spirit," or in some way challenged prevailing customs.

The most dramatic episode of witch-hunting took place in Salem, Massachusetts, in 1692. The causes are complex and not easily discovered, but they seem to have involved group rivalries and blatant deception. Poor and resentful Puritan farmers in rural Salem village apparently sought revenge against certain wealthier church members, who lived near the seaport of Salem town, by bringing charges of witchcraft against their families and friends. This community conflict got out of hand, in part because judges allowed the introduction of dubious evidence; Massachusetts authorities arrested 175 people and executed 22 of them—again mostly women. Fear and suspicion spread into the neighboring village of Andover. Its people "were much addicted to sorcery," claimed one observer, and "there were forty men in it that could raise the Devil as well as any astrologer."

The Salem episode, in concert with the imposition of royal government in Massachusetts (see Chapter 3), marked a major turning point in the history of New England. The intense government-supported religiousness of the first two generations of Puritans was dealt one blow by popular revulsion against the hysteria—and the mass executions—at Salem; there would be no more legal prosecutions for witchcraft. The European Enlightenment (see Chapter 4), which began around 1675, delivered a second blow by propagating a more rational understanding of the natural world. Increasingly people explained events such as an unforeseen accident or a sudden death as being caused by natural forces, not by God or Satan or the movements of the stars or a witch's spell. Unlike Sewall and Cotton Mather, well-read men of the next generation, such as Benjamin Franklin, would conceive of lightning not as a supernatural sign but as a natural phenomenon.

A Freeholding Society

Essential to the Puritans' God-fearing "just society" was the freeholder ideal. In creating New England communities, they consciously avoided the worst features of the traditional agricultural regime of Europe. They did not wish to live in a society where a few wealthy landowners dominated a large population of poor landless families or in a state where a strong central government levied oppressive taxes. The Puritans wanted a world of independent communities and churches made up of landowning, socially responsible families.

Local Government. New England governments used land-grant policies to fashion a new social order. The General Courts of Massachusetts Bay and Connecticut did not adopt the Chesapeake headright system, which enabled wealthy planters to accumulate land patents. Nor did they normally give thousands of acres of land to favored individuals. Instead, they bestowed the title to a township—usually measuring about 6 miles by 10 miles—on a group of settlers. These settlers, or *proprietors*, then distributed the land among themselves, giving the largest amounts to men of high social status, who often became the political leaders of the town. However, all male heads of families had a voice in the town meeting, the main institution of local government. Each year the town meeting chose *selectmen* to manage town affairs. It also levied taxes; enacted ordinances regarding fencing, lot sizes, and road building; and regulated the common fields used for grazing livestock and cutting firewood. These communities had much more power over taxes and local affairs than was the case in most peasant villages in Europe.

The political power of the towns determined the structure of colonywide government. Beginning in 1634, each town in the Massachusetts Bay colony elected its own representatives to the General Court. As the number of towns increased, the Court gained authority at the expense of the governor and magistrates in Boston.

Town autonomy encouraged diversity in social and cultural practices. For instance, most of the settlers of Rowley, Massachusetts, came from the East Riding region of Yorkshire in northern England and brought with them many Yorkshire manorial customs, such as communally regulated open-field agriculture. In contrast, the proprietors of Watertown, who came primarily from the East Anglia region northeast of London,

quickly duplicated that area's system of enclosed fields and separate family farmsteads.

Land and Social Authority. Whatever their county of origin, Puritans were careful not to transplant feudal land customs. New England governments granted land to town proprietors or to individuals in *fee simple*. This form of title meant that the holders owned the land outright, free from manorial obligations or feudal dues; they could sell, lease, or rent it as they pleased. Moreover, fee simple owners did not have to pay the government (or an aristocrat) an annual *quitrent*, a token sum of money that symbolized the authority of the state or the lord. Puritan leaders wanted a society of independent freeholders (see Map 2.5).

Widespread ownership of land did not imply equality of wealth or status. Like most Europeans of the time, Puritans accepted—indeed, embraced—a social and economic hierarchy that provided order and security in an uncertain world. "God had Ordained different degrees and orders of men," proclaimed the wealthy Boston merchant John Saffin, "some to be Masters and Commanders, others to be Subjects, and to be commanded." Otherwise, Saffin noted with disdain, "there would be a meer parity among men."

An Affluent Puritan Woman
This well-known painting of Elizabeth Freake and her daughter, Mary, is perhaps the finest portrait of a seventeenth-century American and suggests the growing prosperity of the Boston merchant community. (*Mrs. Elizabeth Freake and Baby*, circa 1671–1674)

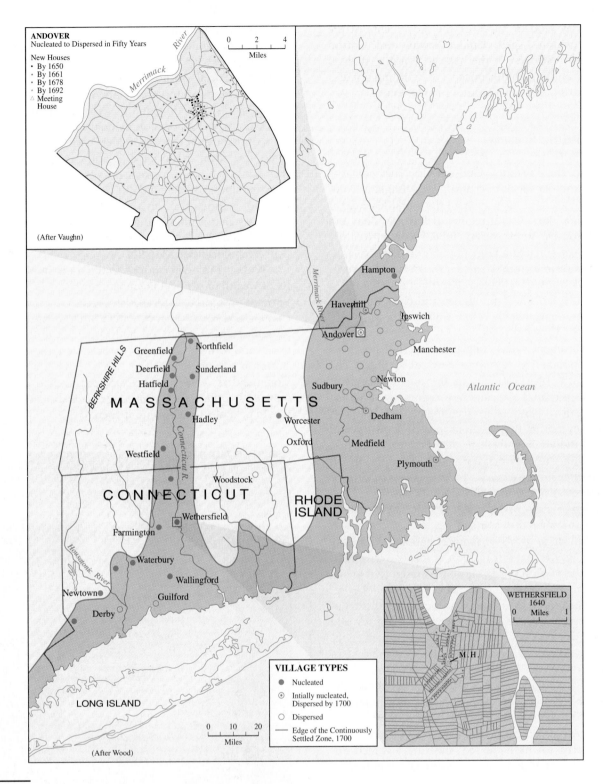

MAP 2.5

Settlement Patterns in New England
Initially, most Puritan towns were compact; families lived close to one another in the "nucleated" village center and traveled daily to the surrounding fields. In 1640 this pattern was apparent in Wethersfield, which was situated on the broad plains of the Connecticut River Valley. The rugged geography of eastern Massachusetts encouraged a more dispersed form of settlement. By 1692 many residents of Andover lived outside the village center—on their own farms.

Migrants from privileged backgrounds in England used their high social status to reap immediate material benefits in America. For example, Edward Johnson came to New England from Kent, where he had been a man of "rank and quality." Johnson became well known on both sides of the Atlantic as the author of the *Wonder-Working Providence of Zion's Saviour*, a prophetic tract published in 1650, but he prospered in Massachusetts Bay primarily because, as a gentleman, he was able to claim a large land grant in Woburn. The most influential proprietors received the lion's share of land in many other towns. In Windsor, Connecticut, for example, the upper tenth received 40 percent of the land, and the lowest fifth of the settlers only 4 percent.

Occasionally the General Court did make large grants to individuals. John Pynchon was given thousands of acres along the Connecticut River at Springfield, Massachusetts, as a reward for his exploits as an Indian fighter. More than most important migrants, Pynchon was able to live like a landed English gentleman, presiding over dozens of tenants. In 1685 Pynchon rented land or housing to 49 of the 120 male adults in Springfield. Thanks to his wealth and status, he dominated the political life of the town.

The rough economic equality among New England farm families would soon be challenged. Initially, the larger proprietors owned sizable farms, ranging in area from 200 to 600 acres—enough land to divide among all their sons, usually three or four. Smallholders were less fortunate and usually could provide land for only some of their sons. Nonproprietors were the least well off, for they had to buy land or work as tenants or laborers. By 1702, in Windsor, Connecticut, about 30 percent of adult male taxpayers were landless. It would take years of saving, or migration to a new town, for these men and their families to become freeholders.

Despite these inequalities, nearly all New England settlers had a real opportunity to acquire property, and even those at the bottom of the social scale enjoyed some economic security. When he died in the 1690s, Nathaniel Fish was one of the poorest men in Barnstable, Massachusetts, yet he owned a two-room cottage, 8 acres of land, an ox, and a cow. For him and thousands of other settlers, New England had proved to be the promised land, a new world of opportunity.

The Indians' New World

Native Americans, whose ancestors had lived on the American continents for millennia, found that they too were living in a new world, but for them it was a bleak, dangerous, and conflict-ridden place, rendered deadly by European diseases and thousands of armed settlers.

They responded in a variety of ways: banding together in new tribes, retreating to mountainous areas to preserve their culture, and on occasion doing battle with the invading Europeans.

Metacom's War

By the 1670s the white population of New England had grown to 55,000. The Indian population of southern New England continued to decline: from 120,000 in 1570, to 70,000 in 1620, to barely 16,000 in 1670. Like Opechancanough in Virginia and Popé in New Mexico, Metacom, leader of the Wampanoag tribe, concluded that only united resistance could stop the relentless advance of the Puritans, whose towns now stretched along the Massachusetts coast and deep into the Connecticut River Valley (see Map 2.2).

Metacom (King Philip), Chief of the Wampanoag
The Indian uprising of 1675 left an indelible mark on the historical memory of New England. This painting of 1850 was used by traveling performers to tell the story of King Philip's War and was done on semitransparent cloth so that it could be lit from behind for dramatic effect. (Shelburne Museum)

Mary Rowlandson

A Captivity Narrative

Mary Rowlandson, a minister's wife in Lancaster, Massachusetts, was one of many settlers taken captive by the Indians during Metacom's War. Some young captives remained with the Indians for their entire lives, gradually becoming Indians in manner and outlook, but most captives were ransomed. Mrs. Rowlandson spent eleven weeks and five days in captivity, traveling constantly, until her family ransomed her for £20. Her account of this adventure, published in 1682, became one of the most popular prose works of its time.

On the tenth of February 1675, came the Indians with great numbers upon Lancaster: their first coming was about sunrising; hearing the noise of some guns, we looked out; several houses were burning, and the smoke ascending to heaven. . . . [T]he Indians laid hold of us, pulling me one way, and the children another, and said, "Come go along with us"; I told them they would kill me: they answered, if I were willing to go along with them, they would not hurt me. . . .

The first week of my being among them I hardly ate any thing; the second week I found my stomach grow very faint for want of something; and yet it was very hard to get down their filthy trash; but the third week . . . they were sweet and savory to my taste. I was at this time knitting a pair of white cotton stockings for my [Indian] mistress; and had not yet wrought upon a sabbath day. When the sabbath came they bade me go to work. I told them it was the sabbath-day, and desired them to let me rest, and told them I would do as much more tomorrow; to which they answered me they would break my face. . . .

Then I went to see King Philip. He bade me come in and sit down, and asked me whether I would smoke . . . but this no way suited me. For though I had formerly used tobacco, yet I had left it ever since I was first taken. It seems to be a bait the devil lays to make men lose their precious time. . . .

. . . During my abode in this place, Philip spake to me to make a shirt for his boy, which I did, for which he gave me a shilling. I offered the money to my master, but he bade me keep it; and with it I bought a piece of horse flesh. Afterwards he asked me to make a cap for his boy, for which he invited me to dinner. I went, and he gave me a pancake, about as big as two fingers. It was made of parched wheat, beaten, and fried in bear's grease, but I thought I never tasted pleasanter meat in my life. . . .

Hearing that my son was come to this place, I went to see him. . . . He told me also, that awhile before, his master (together with other Indians) were going to the French for powder; but by the way the Mohawks met with them, and killed four of their company, which made the rest turn back again, for which I desire that myself and he may bless the Lord; for it might have been worse with him, had he been sold to the French, than it proved to be in his remaining with the Indians. . . .

My master had three squaws, living sometimes with one, and sometimes with another one. . . . [It] was Weetamoo with whom I had lived and served all this while. A severe and proud dame she was, bestowing every day in dressing herself near as much time as any of the gentry of the land: powdering her hair, and painting her face, going with necklaces, with jewels in her ears, and bracelets upon her hands. When she had dressed herself, her work was to make girdles of wampom and beads. . . .

About that time there came an Indian to me and bid me come to his wigwam at night, and he would give me some pork and ground-nuts. Which I did, and as I was eating, another Indian said to me, he seems to be your friend, but he killed two Englishmen at Sudbury, and there lie their cloaths behind you. I looked behind me, and there I saw bloody cloaths, with bullet-holes in them. Yet the lord suffered not this wretch to do me any hurt. . . .

On Tuesday morning they called their general court (as they call it) to consult and determine, whether I should go home or no. And they all as one man did seemingly consent to it, that I should go home. . . .

Source: C.H.Lincoln, ed., *Original Narratives of Early American History, Narratives of Indian Wars, 1675–1699*, vol. 14 (New York: Barnes and Noble, 1952).

Forging a military alliance with the Narragansett and Nipmuck peoples in 1675, Metacom, whom the Puritans called King Philip, attacked white settlements throughout New England. Bitter fighting continued into 1676, ending only when Metacom was killed. By the end of the war the Indians had burned 20 percent of the English towns in Massachusetts and Rhode Island and had killed 5 percent of the adult white population (see American Voices, above). But the Indians' losses—from war, famine, and disease—were even higher: 4,000 native Americans, or 25 percent of an already severely diminished population. Many of the survivors were sold into slavery, including Metacom's wife and nine-year-old son.

The outcome of Metacom's revolt was typical. By 1700 the English invaders had conquered many of the native peoples along the Atlantic coast. Small remnants of those groups, stripped of their lands and traditions, survived on the margins of white society and live on into the present. But they had suffered a double tragedy, failing both to repel the English and to maintain the integrity of their traditional cultures.

The Fur Trade and the Inland Peoples

For the time being the Indian peoples in the interior of North America were able to maintain their identity, independence, and, with more difficulty, traditional way of life. Traders brought European diseases as well as brandy and rum, so that epidemics and drunkenness sapped the vitality of some peoples. Moreover, as native Americans exchanged furs for iron utensils and cloth blankets, they made fewer flint hoes, clay pots, and skin garments. After two or three generations, some eastern Indians had come to rely on European manufacturers for many basic goods. Among Indian peoples to the west of the Appalachians and the Great Lakes, however, imported goods were in short supply, in part because canoes carried small cargoes, and traditional subsistence activities remained strong.

Everywhere competition for beaver and deer pelts led to conflict among native Americans. Families or villages within a tribe would claim exclusive hunting and trapping rights over an area, undermining clan unity. Conflict between Indian peoples also increased as the population of fur-bearing animals dwindled and rival bands of hunter-warriors competed for new trapping areas. After subduing the Huron and Erie peoples, the Iroquois extended their dominion southward to include the Delaware and the Susquehannock. As in all societies, a commitment to warfare increased the influence of those who made war, so the balance of power shifted from elders to headstrong young warriors.

The fur trade also transformed the Indians' relationship with the natural world. Native Americans were animists in religion, believing that everything in nature—animals, trees, rocks—had a living spirit that demanded respect. The members of each clan in a tribe venerated an animal as its *totem*, or symbol, often considering themselves actual descendants of that animal. Tribesmen could hunt those totem animals—fox, deer, beavers—only if they followed certain customs. As they skinned beavers or butchered deer for their food and clothing, they thanked the spirits of the animals and a principal guardian spirit, a "master of the animals," by offering prayers or burning tobacco. They also respectfully buried the carcasses and the entrails. To throw the bones into a fire or a river was taboo, an act that might bring misfortune.

In bringing about the deaths of millions of beaver, the European fur trade altered the ecology of eastern North America, for their dams no longer controlled the flow of creeks and streams. It brought spiritual upheaval to the Indians as well. Warriors now hunted ceaselessly in order to trade with the French in Quebec and the English in New York. As they killed more and more deer and beaver, the Indians sensed the displeasure of the spirits in nature. The epidemics that swept their communities confirmed their fears: the spirits of the animals were taking their revenge. The warriors of the Micmac of Nova Scotia confessed that they no longer knew "whether the beavers are among our friends or our enemies." No less than military conquest and religious conversion, the fur trade drastically altered the character of Indian society.

America had become a new world for Indians as well as for Europeans. All the invaders—Dutch and French fur traders no less than Spanish conquistadors and English settlers—destroyed traditional native American societies, forcing their members to fashion new ways of life.

Ætatis suæ 21. Aᵒ. 1616.

An English View of Pocahontas
By depicting the Indian princess Pocahontas as a well-dressed European woman, the artist implicitly casts her as a symbol of peaceful assimilation to English culture. In actuality, marriages between white men (often fur traders) and Indian women usually created a bilingual hybrid culture that existed uneasily between the two societies.

Summary

Beginning in 1575, first Spain and then England, France, and Holland established permanent settlements in North America. Spain claimed most of the continent, but its empire consisted primarily of a few military garrisons and Franciscan missions in Florida and New Mexico. Both soldiers and friars exploited the labor of the native peoples and threatened their culture, prompting Indian revolts that expelled most Spaniards by 1700. Far to the northeast, the fur trade became the lifeblood of New France and New Netherland. French fur traders and Jesuit priests extended France's influence among the native peoples of the Mississippi Valley. The English came primarily as settlers, and their relentless quest for land brought war with the Indian peoples.

The English created two very different types of colonies in North America. Settlers in the Chesapeake region overcame a disease-ridden environment to create a plantation society that raised tobacco for export to Europe. Wealthy planters controlled Chesapeake society, dominating a population of freeholding farm families, propertyless freemen, and white indentured servants. The pursuit of self-interest by Governor Berkeley and his faction in Virginia and the end of the tobacco boom prompted Nathaniel Bacon's unsuccessful rebellion of 1675–1676. Subsequently, planters made some concessions to white freeholders and turned increasingly to slave labor from Africa.

The English migrants who settled amid the rocky soil and harsh climate of New England grew rapidly in numbers and raised crops mostly for their own consumption. Reacting against the religious hierarchy and economic hardships they had experienced in England, Puritan settlers consciously created a society based on widespread ownership of land and self-governing churches and towns. At first Puritan magistrates enforced religious orthodoxy, banishing Roger Williams, Anne Hutchinson, and other religious dissidents, but eventually they conceded extensive power to local Congregational churches, ensuring political stability.

Wherever Europeans intruded, the native peoples died from new epidemic diseases and went to war to defend their lands. The Pueblo peoples rose in major revolts in 1598 and 1680, the Chesapeake Indians nearly wiped out the Virginia colony in 1622, and Metacom's forces dealt New England a devastating blow in 1675–1676. By 1700, however, many native American peoples along the Atlantic seaboard had been nearly annihilated by disease and warfare, and the lives of most Indians east of the Mississippi River had been transformed by the fur trade.

TIMELINE

1560s	English and French attack Spanish treasure ships
1565	Spain establishes St. Augustine, Florida
1573	Spanish Comprehensive Orders for New Discoveries
1580s	Failure of Roanoke and other English colonies
1598	Acoma War in New Mexico
1600	Franciscans in Florida and New Mexico
1603–1625	King James I of England
1607	English adventurers settle Jamestown, Virginia
1608	Samuel de Champlain founds Quebec
1613	Dutch fur traders on Manhattan Island
1619	First Africans arrive in Chesapeake Virginia House of Burgesses convened
1620	Pilgrims found Plymouth colony
1620–1660	Tobacco boom in Chesapeake colonies
1621	Dutch West India Company chartered
1622	Opechancanough's uprising
1624	Virginia becomes a royal colony
1625	Jesuits undertake missionary work in Canada
1625–1649	King Charles I of England
1627	Company of New France urges migration to Quebec
1630	Puritans found Massachusetts Bay colony
1634	Maryland settled
1635–1637	Pequot War Roger Williams, banished, settles in Rhode Island Anne Hutchinson expelled from Massachusetts Bay
1640s	Five Iroquois Nations go to war over fur trade
1649–1660	Puritan Commonwealth in England
1651	First Navigation Act passed
1660	William Berkeley Governor of Virginia until 1678
1660–1720	Poor tobacco market
1662	Connecticut receives royal charter Halfway Covenant revises Puritan theology
1664	English conquer New Netherland
1670s	Indentured servitude declines
1673	Marquette and Joliet explore Mississippi
1675–1676	Bacon's rebellion Metacom's uprising Expansion of African slavery in the Chesapeake
1680	Popé's rebellion in New Mexico
1681	La Salle claims Louisiana for France
1692	Salem witchcraft trials

BIBLIOGRAPHY

David Weber, *The Spanish Frontier in North America* (1992), and Richard White, *The Middle Ground: Indians, Empires, and Republics in the Great Lakes Region, 1650–1815* (1991), are magisterial studies, while Bernard Bailyn, *The Peopling of British North America* (1986), offers a useful overview of the early English colonies.

Spanish, French, and Dutch Goals

For Spain's northern empire see, in addition to Weber, Ramón Gutiérrez, *When Jesus Came, the Corn Mothers Went Away: Marriage, Sexuality, and Power in New Mexico, 1500–1846* (1991). The French threat to its domain is traced by Robert S. Weddle, *The French Thorn: Rival Explorers in the Spanish Sea, 1682–1762* (1991), and Daniel H. Usner, Jr., *Indians, Settlers, and Slaves in a Frontier Exchange Economy: The Lower Mississippi Valley Before 1783* (1991).

The best general studies of French Canada are by W. J. Eccles, *The Canadian Frontier, 1534–1760* (1983) and *France in America*, rev. ed. (1990). French interaction with native Americans is covered by Bruce G. Trigger, *The Children of Aataentsic: A History of the Huron People to 1660* (1976); Daniel K. Richter, *The Ordeal of the Long House: The Peoples of the Iroquois League in the Era of European Colonization* (1992); and Patricia O. Dickason, *Canada's First Nations: A History of the Founding Peoples from Earliest Times* (1992).

For English expansion, see Kenneth Andrews, *Trade, Plunder, and Settlement: Maritime Enterprise and the Genesis of the British Empire, 1480–1630* (1984); Nicholas Canny, *Kingdom and Colony: Ireland in the Atlantic World, 1560–1800* (1988); A. L. Rowse, *Sir Walter Raleigh* (1962); David B. Quinn, *England and the Discovery of America, 1481–1620* (1974); and Karen O. Kupperman, *Roanoke* (1984). The interaction of the English and Dutch with native Americans can be followed in Gary B. Nash, *Red, White, and Black: The Peoples of Early America* (1982); Francis Jennings, *The Invasion of America* (1975); and two works by James Axtell, *The European and the Indian* (1981) and *The Invasion Within: The Contest of Cultures in Colonial North America* (1985).

Social Conflict in the Chesapeake

Alden Vaughan, *American Genesis: Captain John Smith and the Founding of Virginia* (1975), covers the earliest years, while Edmund S. Morgan, *American Slavery, American Freedom: The Ordeal of Colonial Virginia* (1975), provides a brilliant analysis of the rest of the colonial period. Important essays appear in Thad W. Tate and David L. Ammerman, eds., *The Chesapeake in the Seventeenth Century* (1979), and Lois Green Carr, Philip D. Morgan, and Jean B. Russo, *Colonial Chesapeake Society* (1989). Significant community studies include Carville Earle, *The Evolution of a Tidewater Settlement Pattern: All Hallows Parish, Maryland, 1650–1783* (1975), and Lois Green Carr et al., *Robert Cole's World: Agriculture and Society in Early Maryland* (1991).

For a discussion of political institutions, see W. F. Craven, *The Southern Colonies in the Seventeenth Century, 1607–1689* (1949), and David W. Jordan, *Foundations of Representative Government in Maryland, 1632–1715* (1988).

Contrasting accounts of Bacon's rebellion can be found in T. J. Wertenbaker, *Torchbearer of the Revolution* (1940), and Wilcomb B. Washburn, *The Governor and the Rebel* (1958).

Puritan New England

For the Puritan migration, see Edmund Morgan, *The Puritan Dilemma: The Story of John Winthrop* (1955); Sumner Chilton Powell, *Puritan Village: The Formation of a New England Town* (1963); David Grayson Allen, *In English Ways: The Movement of Societies and the Transferral of English Local Law and Custom to Massachusetts Bay in the Seventeenth Century* (1981); and David Cressy, *Coming Over: Migration and Communication between England and New England in the Seventeenth Century* (1987).

Puritanism as an intellectual movement is best explored in the works of Perry Miller; see especially *The New England Mind: The Seventeenth Century* (1939). Charles Hambrick-Stowe, *The Practice of Piety: Puritan Devotional Disciplines* (1982), discusses the emotional dimension of Puritanism, while David D. Hall, *World of Wonder, Days of Judgment: Popular Religious Belief in Early New England* (1989), explores its nonrational aspects. See also Andrew Delbanco, *The Puritan Ordeal* (1989).

For a discussion of dissent in early New England, consult Philip Gura, *A Glimpse of Sion's Glory: Puritan Radicalism in New England, 1620–1660* (1984); Edwin S. Gaustad, *Liberty of Conscience: Roger Williams in America* (1991); Amy Schrager Lang, *Prophetic Woman: Anne Hutchinson and the Problem of Dissent in the Literature of New England* (1987); Paul Boyer and Steven Nissenbaum, *Salem Possessed: The Social Origins of Witchcraft* (1974); Carol F. Karlsen, *The Devil in the Shape of a Woman: Witchcraft in New England* (1987); and David D. Hall, ed., *Witch Hunting in Seventeenth-Century New England: A Documentary History, 1632–1691* (1991).

Community studies that reveal the lives of ordinary New England men and women include John Demos, *The Little Commonwealth: Family Life in Plymouth Colony* (1971), and Kenneth A. Lockridge, *A New England Town . . . Dedham, Massachusetts, 1636–1736* (1970). See also John Demos, *The Unredeemed Captive: A Family Story from Early America* (1994).

The Indians' New World

James H. Merrell, *The Indians' New World: Catawbas and Their Neighbors from European Contact through the Era of Removal* (1989), is a pathbreaking study. Douglas Leach, *Flinthawk and Tomahawk: New England in King Philip's War* (1958), is the standard treatment of the conflict. See also Karen Ordahl Kupperman, *Settling with the Indians: The Meeting of English and Indian Cultures in America, 1580–1640* (1981); Bernard Sheehan, *Savagism and Civility: Indians and Englishmen in Colonial Virginia* (1980); and Daniel K. Richter and James H. Merrell, *Beyond the Covenant Chain: The Iroquois and Their Neighbors in Indian North America* (1987). Two illuminating ecological studies are Calvin Martin, *Keepers of the Game: Indian-Animal Relations and the Fur Trade* (1978), and William Cronon, *Changes in the Land: Indians, Colonists, and the Ecology of New England* (1983).

Bristol Docks and Quay (detail)

The bustle and prosperity of the English port of Bristol is well conveyed in this eighteenth-century painting. Thousands of migrants embarked for America from Bristol, which became a hub of the triangular trade with Africa, the West Indies, and the mainland colonies.

CHAPTER 3

The British Empire in America
1660–1750

★   ★   ★

By 1660 English traders and settlers had pushed aside native American peoples and founded two clusters of colonies along the eastern coast of North America. The English government used mercantilist policies to profit from the products and commerce of those colonies, creating an empire based on trade. To protect their increasingly valuable colonies from European rivals in the West Indies and on the Continent—the Dutch in New Netherland, the French in Quebec, and the Spanish in Florida—English officials expanded the navy and repeatedly went to war.

The West Indian sugar islands were England's most prized overseas possessions. Sugar produced with enslaved labor from Africa brought wealth to English planters and merchants and would soon make England a world power. Settler colonies from New England to the Carolinas bolstered this economic empire by providing crucial supplies to the sugar islands and shipping tobacco and rice to European markets.

England's dominion in America rested on a combination of force and consent. English planters used brute force to control the tens of thousands of African slaves who labored on the plantations, while English governors and bureaucrats won the voluntary support of white settlers by granting power to their representative assemblies. The result, as defined by a British imperialist in 1745, "was a magnificent superstructure of American commerce and British naval power on an African foundation."

The Politics of Empire, 1660–1713

By 1660 England had thriving colonies in America but lacked a firm, uniform policy for governing them. Over

69

the next twenty-five years England tightened its control, first by imposing strict trade regulations and then by centralizing colonial government. Accustomed to running their own affairs, the colonists resisted those efforts, sometimes through open rebellion. Then upheaval in England brought to power new political leaders who consented to a measure of American self-government.

The Restoration Colonies

In 1660 Charles II (1660–1685) returned from exile and restored the Stuart monarchy. Like the earlier Stuarts, Charles supported the Anglican Church and believed in the divine right of kings. A robust and vigorous man, Charles offended many of his subjects by marrying a Portuguese Catholic princess and presiding over a sexually permissive royal entourage. His generosity and extravagance kept him in debt—a fact of considerable importance for American affairs.

On ascending the throne, Charles rewarded the aristocrats who supported the Restoration by giving them millions of acres of land in America. In 1663 he gave the Carolinas, which included much of Spanish Florida, to eight aristocrats, including Sir George Carteret, Lord John Berkeley, and his brother Sir William Berkeley, the governor of Virginia. In 1664 the

king granted the territory between the Delaware and Connecticut rivers to his brother James, the duke of York. Later that year James also took possession of the newly captured Dutch colony of New Netherland, renaming it New York after his title. Because he wished to concentrate on governing New York, James gave ownership of New Jersey to two of the Carolina proprietors, Sir George Carteret and Lord John Berkeley. And so, in just two years, vast tracts of land fell into the hands of a few English noblemen.

The new colonies were proprietorships in which all the land belonged to the proprietors to do with as they pleased. As in Maryland, their charters required only that their laws conform broadly to those of England. These generous provisions allowed the proprietors to shape the character of their possessions. Most proprietors sought to create a traditional social order, presided over by a gentry class and a legally established Church of England (see Table 3.1).

The Carolinas. The Carolina proprietors were especially determined to build a traditional rural society. They instructed John Locke, who would later become the political theorist of propertied individualism and popular government, to devise a scheme of government for the new colony. The result, the Fundamental Constitutions of Carolina (1669), prescribed a manorial sys-

A King in Waiting, circa 1655
While Oliver Cromwell imposed stern Puritan rule on England, the future Charles II (1660–1685) danced his way across Europe. As king, Charles presided over a court known for its extravagance and debauchery.

TABLE 3.1

English Colonies in North America, 1660–1750

	Date	Type	Religion	Status in 1775	Chief Export or Economic Activity
Carolina	1663	Proprietary	Church of England	Royal	Mixed farming; naval stores
North	1691				
South	1691				Rice; indigo
New Jersey	1664	Proprietary	Church of England	Royal	Wheat
New York	1664	Proprietary	Church of England	Royal	Wheat
Pennsylvania	1681	Proprietary	No established church	Proprietary	Wheat
Georgia	1732	Trustees	Church of England	Royal	Rice
New Hampshire (separated from Massachusetts)	1739	Royal	Congregationalist	Royal	Mixed farming; lumber; naval stores
Nova Scotia	1749	Royal	Church of England	Royal	Fishing; mixed farming; naval stores

---

tem in which land was equated with political power and social rank: noble "landgraves" were to preside over baronies populated both by free families and by "leet men"—serfs bound to the land.

This aristocratic fantasy bore no relation to reality. The first settlers in North Carolina, poor families from Virginia, refused to work on large manors and lived instead on modest farms, raising grain and tobacco. Ignoring this repudiation of their manorial plans, the proprietors continued to grant deeds that required the payment of an annual quitrent. Farmers in Albemarle County, angered by the cost of this claim of lordship and by taxes on tobacco exports, rebelled in 1677. Led by John Culpepper, they deposed the governor and forced the proprietors to abandon most of their legal claims.

The settlement of South Carolina was equally unsuccessful for the landed proprietors. The colonists, many of whom had come from Barbados, by then an overcrowded sugar island, refused to accept the Fundamental Constitutions or the proprietors' demands for quitrents. The Barbadians introduced racial slavery, using a small number of African slaves to raise cattle and food crops for export to the West Indies. They also opened a lucrative trade with native Americans, exchanging English manufactured goods for furs and Indian slaves. This commerce encouraged slave-raiding attacks on Franciscan missions in Florida, which could have led to war with Spain, and in 1715 prompted a violent war with the resident Yamasee people. These struggles made South Carolina an ill-governed, violence-ridden frontier settlement until the 1720s.

William Penn and Pennsylvania. In stark contrast to the Carolinas, the proprietary colony of Pennsylvania devel-oped into a peaceful and prosperous settlement. In 1681 Charles II bestowed this land on William Penn, primarily in payment of a large debt the king owed to Penn's father, the admiral Sir William Penn. The younger Penn was an enigmatic man. Born to wealth, he seemed destined for renown as a friend and servant of kings but in his early twenties he converted to the Society of Friends (Quakers), a radical Protestant sect, and became one of its ardent supporters. His pamphlet *No Cross, No Crown* offered an articulate defense of the Quakers' belief in religious liberty, and he used his prestige to spread their influence. Pennsylvania, his greatest achievement, was designed as a refuge for Quakers, who were persecuted in England because they refused to serve in the army or pay taxes to support the Church of England.

Like the Puritan migrants to New England, Quakers wanted to restore to religion the simplicity and spirituality of early Christianity. But Quakers were not Calvinists, who restricted salvation to a small elect. Rather, Quakers followed the teachings of their founders, the English visionary George Fox and his associate Margaret Fell, who argued that all women and men could be saved because God had imbued each person with an inner "light" of grace or understanding. The principal Quaker religious institution—the weekly meeting for worship—was designed to help members to discover this inner light. The meetings were not led by a minister and did not center on a sermon. Instead, Friends encouraged anyone, man or woman, who felt the promptings of the inner light to speak. "Nearest the front by the wall are two benches," a traveler reported after a visit to a Philadelphia meetinghouse. "In these pews sit those of both sexes who either are already accustomed to preach or expect to be inspired by the Holy Ghost."

Penn's Frame of Government, which he drew up in 1681, guaranteed political liberty and religious freedom: it prohibited an established church and religious taxes and allowed Christians of all faiths to vote and hold office. During the 1680s thousands of Quakers, primarily from the middling classes of northwestern England, came to Pennsylvania. Most settled along the Delaware River, in or near the city of Philadelphia, which Penn himself planned. To attract more settlers, the proprietor sold land at low prices—and in fee simple, without quitrents or other obligations—and had his *Brief Account of the Province of Pennsylvania* translated into Dutch and German. In 1683 migrants from Krefeld in Saxony founded Germantown just outside Philadelphia, and thousands of other Germans soon joined them.

In 1682 James, duke of York, gave Penn another colony, Delaware, originally a Swedish settlement that had been conquered first by the Dutch and then, in 1664, by the English. The Quaker leader incorporated the Delaware settlements into Pennsylvania as the Lower Counties, and after 1703 he allowed the inhabitants to select their own representative assembly. Religious liberty and ethnic diversity made Pennsylvania and the Lower Counties the most open and democratic of all the Restoration colonies.

The New Mercantilism

Although Charles II was generous with land, giving away vast domains to pay his political and financial debts, he kept a tight grip on colonial trade by enacting new mercantilist legislation. His policies were meant to channel the trade of the empire through England and raise royal revenues from custom duties.

Before 1650 the English government followed traditional mercantilist thinking, encouraging exports while restricting imports. These policies were designed to give England a favorable balance of trade with European countries, forcing those countries to pay the difference in gold or silver. After 1650, as the economic potential of the colonies became apparent, the government devised new mercantilist policies to regulate their trade. The initial phase of this policy, expressed in the Navigation Act of 1651, was aimed expressly at Dutch merchants who were supplying the English colonies with European manufactures and carrying their sugar and tobacco directly to European markets. To help English traders and secure shipping fees for English merchants, the act required that all goods imported into England or the colonies be carried on ships registered in England, Ireland, or the colonies.

Upon ascending the throne in 1660, Charles II endorsed the Navigation Act. He also created a new committee of the Privy Council, the Lords of Trade and Plantations, to formulate colonial policy. The king had Parliament pass a new Navigation Act (1660) that strengthened the ban on foreign shipping and stipulated that sugar, tobacco, and indigo could be shipped only to other English possessions. In 1663 the Staple Act required that these crops be sent directly to England, from which they could be reexported to other countries at a great profit. The Staple Act also stipulated that European exports to America be shipped through England, inflating the prices of those goods and thus increasing the sale of English manufactures.

To enforce these laws and raise money, Parliament passed the Revenue Act of 1673; it imposed a special "plantation duty" on certain American exports and created, for the first time, a staff of customs officials to col-

TABLE 3.2

Navigation Acts, 1651–1751

	Date	Purpose	Result
Act of 1651	1651	Cut Dutch trade	Mostly ignored
Act of 1660	1660	Ban foreign shipping; enumerated goods only to England	Partially obeyed
Act of 1663	1663	European imports only through England	Partially obeyed
Staple Act	1663	Enumerated goods and European imports pass through England	Mostly obeyed
Revenue Act	1673	Impose "plantation duty"; create customs system	Mostly obeyed
Act of 1696	1696	Prevent frauds; create Vice-Admiralty Courts	Mostly obeyed
Woolen Act	1699	Prevent export or intercolonial sale of textiles	Partially obeyed
Hat Act	1732	Prevent export or intercolonial sale of hats	Partially obeyed
Molasses Act	1733	Cut American imports of molasses from French West Indies	Extensively violated
Iron Act	1750	Prevent manufacture of finished iron products	Extensively violated
Currency Act	1751	End use of paper currency as legal tender in New England	Mostly obeyed

lect the levy in American ports. In 1696 another Navigation Act required American governors to enforce trade regulations and increased the legal powers of customs agents. This act replaced the Lords of Trade with a new administrative body, the Board of Trade, composed of politicians and officials with knowledge of colonial affairs. During the following decades the board proposed new laws to regulate specific American industries (see Table 3.2).

The English government backed its mercantilist policy with force. "What we want," declared the duke of Albemarle, "is more of the trade the Dutch now have." In three commercial wars between 1652 and 1674 the English navy broke Dutch supremacy in world trade, driving the Dutch from New Netherland, their only base in North America, and ending their dominance of the West African slave trade. Meanwhile, English merchants expanded their fleets and established a dominant position in Atlantic commerce.

The Dominion of New England

For England, the new mercantilism was a spectacular success. In America, however, Charles II's policies were resented as an economic burden and an intrusion into the colonies' internal affairs, so most of the colonies initially resisted the new measures. In Massachusetts, a customs official named Edward Randolph reported that the Puritan government took "no notice of the laws of trade," welcoming Dutch merchants as usual and importing goods directly from the French sugar islands. Indeed, Puritan leaders claimed that their original royal charter exempted them from most of the regulations. Outraged, Randolph called on his superiors to use English troops to "reduce Massachusetts to obedience."

At Randolph's urging, the Lords of Trade and Plantations decided to assert their authority over the Puritan colonies. In 1679 they denied the claim the Massachusetts Bay colony had laid to the adjoining frontier province of New Hampshire and created a separate colony with a royal governor. Then, in 1684, the Lords of Trade persuaded the English Court of Chancery to annul the charter of Massachusetts Bay on the grounds that the Puritan government had virtually outlawed the Church of England and violated the Navigation Acts.

The accession of James, duke of York, to the throne as James II (1685–1688) gave the Lords of Trade an opportunity to increase royal authority. James was an admirer of Louis XIV, the despotic king of France, and was bent on curbing the power of Parliament at home and that of representative institutions in America. With James's support, in 1686 the Lords revoked the corporate charters of Connecticut and Rhode Island and merged them with the Massachusetts Bay and Plymouth colonies to form a new royal province, the Dominion of New England (see Map 3.1). Two years later the Lords added New York and New Jersey to the dominion, creating a single colony stretching from the Delaware River to Maine.

The Dominion of New England represented a new authoritarian model of colonial administration. As the name implied, New England was to be the king's own "dominion." James named Sir Edmund Andros, a military officer and former governor of New York, to rule the new entity. Dispatched to Boston with orders to abolish the existing legislative assemblies, Andros ruled Massachusetts Bay by administrative fiat, attacking all the major institutions of Puritan society. He advocated public worship in the Church of England, offending Puritan Congregationalists. He banned town meetings and so undermined the local autonomy of settlers in scores of rural villages. And he levied arbitrary taxes and challenged the validity of all land titles granted under the original Massachusetts charter. While Andros offered to provide new deeds, they were not in fee simple; title holders were required to pay an annual quitrent. The Puritans protested vigorously against the new regime, but James refused to restore the old charter.

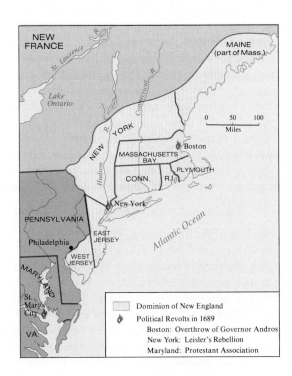

MAP 3.1

The Dominion of New England 1688–1689
The Dominion created a vast new royal colony stretching nearly 500 miles along the Atlantic coast. After the Glorious Revolution in England, revolts in Boston and New York City ousted royal officials, effectively ending the Dominion. In Maryland a Protestant Association mounted a third revolt, deposing the Catholic proprietary governor.

The Glorious Revolution of 1688

Fortunately for the colonists, James made as many enemies at home as Andros made in the colonies. The new monarch angered political leaders by revoking the charters of many English towns and corporate bodies and rejecting the advice of Parliament. He also offended many English people by openly practicing Roman Catholicism and prosecuting Anglican bishops when they questioned his authority over church appointments.

Dissent reached a crisis in 1688, when James's second wife, a Spanish Catholic princess, gave birth to a son. The prospect of a Catholic heir to the throne ignited a quick and bloodless coup known as the Glorious Revolution. Backed by popular protests and the army, Protestant parliamentary leaders forced James into exile and enthroned Mary, his Protestant daughter (by his first wife), and her Dutch husband, William of Orange. Queen Mary II (1689–1694) and King William III (1689–1701) agreed to rule as constitutional monarchs, forgoing the Stuarts' claim to a "divine right," and accepted a Declaration of Rights. This document limited the powers of the monarch and enhanced both the liberties of subjects and the powers of Parliament.

The political philosopher John Locke tried to justify the Glorious Revolution. In his *Two Treatises on Government* of 1690, Locke argued that individuals are endowed with inalienable natural rights to life, liberty, and property and that the legitimacy of government rests on the consent of the governed. Locke's views on liberty and popular sovereignty—and his advocacy of representative government—had a lasting influence on many Americans, especially those who sat in the colonial assemblies and wanted to increase their powers. More immediately, the Glorious Revolution sparked popular rebellions in Massachusetts, Maryland, and New York.

The Fall of the Dominion. When news of the accession of William and Mary reached Boston in April 1689, Congregational ministers immediately circulated a printed manifesto calling on the townspeople to "seize the vile persons who oppressed us." The town militia took Governor Andros prisoner, and a hastily formed Committee of Safety forced him to return to England. In London the eminent American Puritan minister Increase Mather petitioned the new monarchs for restoration of the old charter of 1629.

William and Mary agreed to break up the Dominion of New England, which many English Parliamentary leaders viewed as a symbol of Stuart despotism. They insisted, however, on retaining close supervision of the dominant northern colony of Massachusetts Bay. In 1691 a new charter combined Massachusetts Bay, Plymouth, and Maine into the new royal colony of Massachusetts. The Crown would appoint the governor

The Target of the Glorious Revolution
The stance and facial expression of James II (1685–1688) suggest his forceful, arrogant personality. His arbitrary measures and Catholic sympathies prompted rebellions in England and America and cost him the throne.

(and naval officers to supervise the ports), while the townspeople would elect delegates to the assembly, the House of Representatives. The charter broadened the franchise to include property owners who were not members of Puritan congregations and guaranteed religious freedom to members of the Church of England. This new charter, which gave Massachusetts considerable political autonomy while increasing royal control over trade and military defense, worked well for the next seventy years.

Uprising in Maryland. In Maryland the result of James II's overthrow was bitter religious conflict. A Protestant Association led by John Coode quickly removed the officials appointed by the Catholic proprietor, Lord Baltimore, accusing them of "Popish Idolatry and Superstition." Coode's rebellion reflected the longstanding conflict between Protestants, who constituted the majority of the residents, and Catholics, who held most of the wealth and political offices. But economic problems were also important in Maryland. The stagnant tobacco market had struck hard at the finances of smallholders, tenant farmers, and former indentured servants. Like Nathaniel Bacon's followers in Virginia, they were suffering not only from falling prices but also from rising taxes and the high fees imposed by proprietary officials.

To quiet the Protestant rebels, the Lords of Trade suspended Lord Baltimore's proprietorship, imposed royal government, and established the Church of England as the colony's official church. This settlement lasted until 1715, when Benedict Calvert, the fourth Lord Baltimore, converted to the Anglican faith and the Crown restored the proprietorship to the Calvert family (which held it until the American Revolution). With the government firmly in Protestant hands and with Catholics forced to practice their faith in private, political conflict diminished, and a united governing class emerged. As in Virginia, the main lines of social division in Maryland now involved class and race, with a planter elite controlling a population of servants, slaves, and tenants. In Maryland, the uprisings of 1689 had eliminated Catholicism as a major political force.

Ethnic Rebellion in New York. In New York the Glorious Revolution produced even more ethnic and religious strife, class tension, and political instability. After England conquered New Netherland in 1664, James II (as duke of York) imposed strict authoritarian rule, prohibiting representative institutions. However, he did not expel or persecute the Dutch residents; indeed, he allowed the Rensselaers and other Dutch manorial lords to retain their large land holdings, and most of the Dutch inhabitants remained in the colony. Thirty years later nearly 60 percent of the taxpayers in New York City were Dutch artisans and shopkeepers. As proud Protestants from Holland, they welcomed the accession of Mary and her Dutch husband to the English throne.

In 1689, a month after the uprising in Boston, the New York militia ousted Colonel Francis Nicholson, who, under Sir Edmund Andros, was lieutenant governor of New York and New Jersey. Dutch artisans in New York City joined with Puritan farmers on Long Island in this attack on Nicholson, an alleged Catholic sympathizer, and other "Popish Doggs & Divells" appointed by James II. They replaced Nicholson with Jacob Leisler, a migrant German soldier who had married into a prominent Dutch merchant family. At first Leisler had the support of all classes and ethnic groups, but when he freed debtors from prison and urged the creation of a more democratic, town-meeting form of government, this solidarity disintegrated.

In the political struggle that followed, Dutch artisans in New York City sided with Leisler, taking control of the ten-member Board of Aldermen, while wealthy merchants, who had traditionally controlled the city government, attacked the legitimacy of Leisler's seizure of power. Class animosity suffused a pamphlet written by a merchant, Nicholas Bayard, who accused Leisler of being like a "Masaniello," the peasant fishmonger who in 1647 had led a popular revolt in Naples, Italy. Leisler held on to power until 1691, when he was forced to surrender to Henry Sloughter, the new royal governor. Influenced by Bayard and his wealthy merchant friends, Sloughter had Leisler and seven of his associates indicted for treason. An English jury convicted Leisler and Jacob Milburne, his son-in-law, and the two men were hanged and then decapitated—treatment reserved for those found guilty of the most heinous crimes. A new Board of Aldermen, dominated again by merchants, passed ordinances reducing artisans' wages. These measures broke the power of the Dutch artisans, but political conflict between the Leislerian and anti-Leislerian factions continued until the 1710s.

The Glorious Revolution of 1688–1689 began a new phase in English imperial history. In America, the uprisings in Boston and New York toppled the authoritarian institutions of the Dominion of New England and restored internal self-government. In England, a new constitutional monarchy gave effective control of the affairs of state to representatives of the propertied classes. These men promoted an empire based on commerce by curbing royal monopolies (such as the East India and Royal African companies), giving free rein to enterprising merchants and financiers, and developing the American colonies as a source of trade.

A Prosperous Dutch Farmstead
Many Dutch farmers in the Hudson River Valley prospered, because of easy access to markets and their exploitation of black slaves. To record his success, Martin Van Bergen of Leeds, New York, had this mural painted over his mantelpiece.

The Empire in 1713

To preserve its growing power in Europe, England fought two great wars at the end of the seventeenth century, the first against France—the War of the League of Augsburg (1689–1697)—and the second against France and Spain—the War of the Spanish Succession (1702–1713). In both conflicts England's prime goal was to prevent Louis XIV (the "Sun King") from extending France's boundaries and gaining dominance in Europe, but the fighting spilled over into the three nations' empires in North America. There Britain fought to save its foothold along the eastern coast, while France extended its dominion over the lower Mississippi Valley. Spain assumed a defensive posture, viewing its North American colonies as marginal and dispensable (see Table 3.3).

War in America. During the War of the League of Augsburg (known in America as King William's War), New England troops and their Iroquois allies fought against French troops and their Algonquin allies, mostly in Indian territory. French and Indian forces destroyed the frontier town of Schenectady, New York, in 1690, while Massachusetts troops captured Port Royal, the capital of Acadia. The Treaty of Ryswick, which ended the war in 1697, returned all captured territory in North America but confirmed French control of the western half of the rich sugar island of Santo Domingo, present-day Haiti.

Two years later France broke Spain's exclusive control of the Gulf coast of North America, establishing a fort at the mouth of the Mississippi River. In 1702, however, France and Spain became allies during the War of the Spanish Succession when the grandson of Louis XIV of France ascended to the Spanish throne. In that conflict, called Queen Anne's War in America, English forces from South Carolina burned the Spanish town of St. Augustine but failed to capture the fort.

Then, in 1704, the Carolinians mobilized a force of thousands of Creek warriors (won over by the promise of rum, guns, plunder, and trade goods) and rebel mission Indians (who resented the forced-labor system). This army destroyed the remaining Franciscan missions in northern Florida, attacked the Spanish settlement at Pensacola, and massacred those Apalachee who remained loyal to the Spaniards. A joint Spanish-French force twice assaulted Charleston but failed to capture it.

Far to the northeast, Abenaki warriors joined with the French to destroy English settlements in Maine, and in 1704 a force of Abenaki and Mohawk attacked the western Massachusetts town of Deerfield, killing 48 residents and making captives of 112 more. The New York frontier remained quiet because the Iroquois had been forced by a French-Algonquin alliance to accept a general settlement in 1701 and because no one wanted to disrupt the lucrative fur trade. In 1710 British troops, augmented by New England volunteers who feared French Catholicism, again seized Port Royal, but a major expedition against the French stronghold at Quebec in 1711 failed miserably despite the presence of twelve British men-of-war and more than 5,000 troops.

Although there were few major battles, the stakes in these American confrontations were high: for Britain and France, nothing less than the future control of the continent was at issue; for Spain, the defense of its empire in Mesoamerica and the Caribbean. To preserve control of Florida and protect Havana in nearby Cuba, the Spanish reinforced St. Augustine. And to safeguard the rich silver mines in northern New Spain from attack by the new French colony of Louisiana, the Spanish established permanent settlements in Texas, beginning at San Antonio in 1718. Four years later there were 250 Spanish soldiers and 10 Franciscan missions in the infant frontier colony.

Native Americans, caught in the middle of these European-bred conflicts, maneuvered to protect their interests. The prosperous town-dwelling Caddo peo-

TABLE 3.3

English Wars, 1650–1750

	Date	Purpose	Result
Anglo-Dutch	1652–1654	Commercial markets	Stalemate
Anglo-Dutch	1664	Markets—conquest	England takes New Amsterdam
Anglo-Dutch	1673	Commercial markets	England makes maritime gains
King William's	1689–1697	Maintain European balance of power	Stalemate in North America
Queen Anne's	1702–1713	Maintain European balance of power	British get Hudson Bay and Nova Scotia
Jenkins' Ear	1739	Expand markets in Spanish America	Stalemate
King George's	1740–1748	Maintain European balance of power	Capture and return of Louisbourg

ples, one of whose confederacies, the "Kingdom of Tejas," would give Texas its name, expelled the first Spanish Franciscan missionaries in 1693, blaming them for a fatal smallpox epidemic. A generation later the Tejas refused baptism (believing "that the [holy] water kills them") and successfully resisted Spanish control by turning to the French for firearms and trade goods.

In New York, the Five Iroquois peoples—the Mohawk, Oneida, Onondaga, Cayuga, and Seneca—had long lived in a strong political confederation. Now, by means of astute diplomacy, the Iroquois created a "covenant chain" of treaties with tribes in Pennsylvania and the Ohio River Valley and adopted a policy of "aggressive neutrality," exploiting their central geographical location by trading with the English and the French but refusing to fight for either. The Delaware leader Teedyuscung explained this strategy by showing his people a pictorial message from the Iroquois: "You see a Square in the Middle, meaning the Lands of the Indians; and at one End, the Figure of a Man, indicating the English; and at the other End, another, meaning the French. Let us join together to defend our land against both."

In 1713 the Treaty of Utrecht ended this series of wars and provided Britain with major territorial and commercial gains (see Map 3.2). From France, Britain obtained Newfoundland, Acadia (Nova Scotia), the Hudson Bay region of northern Canada, and, most important, suzerainty over the Iroquois and access to the western Indian trade. As a result, Albany and Oswego in New York soon rivaled Montreal as commercial centers of the fur trade. From Spain, Britain acquired commercial privileges in Spanish America and the strategic fortress of Gibraltar at the entrance to the Mediterranean. These gains solidified Britain's commercial supremacy and brought peace to North America for the next generation.

Limited Administrative Reform. The wars focused attention on the English empire in America, which had developed in a haphazard fashion. Some colonies produced crops for export and were commercially tied to England; others were settlements of religious dissidents who wanted to be left alone. Some colonies had corporate charters, others were proprietary ventures, and still others had royal governors.

In 1696 Parliament sought to establish a uniform system by creating a new Board of Trade and filling it with rising politicians and experienced bureaucrats, who drew upon the thinking of leading economist theorists—such as John Locke. The Board sought to install royal governors in all the American settlements but lacked the political influence to do so. Colonists and proprietors resisted reforms, as did English political leaders: Parliament had just overthrown a power-hungry monarch at home and was unwilling to increase royal power in America.

MAP 3.2

Britain's American Empire, 1713

Britain's West Indian possessions were small—mere dots on the Caribbean Sea. However, in 1713 they were by far the most valuable parts of the empire. Their sugar crops brought wealth to English merchants, trade to the northern colonies, and a brutal life (and early death) to African workers.

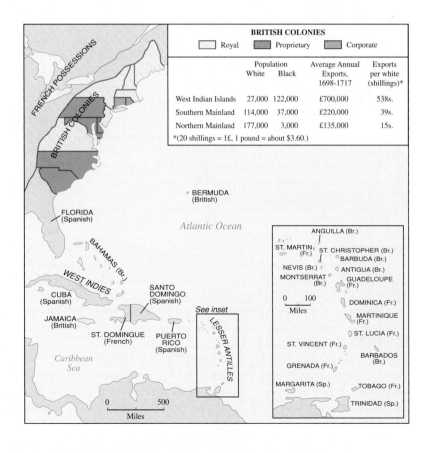

BRITISH COLONIES				
☐ Royal	▨ Proprietary	▨ Corporate		
	Population		Average Annual	Exports
	White	Black	Exports, 1698-1717	per white (shillings)*
West Indian Islands	27,000	122,000	£700,000	538s.
Southern Mainland	114,000	37,000	£220,000	39s.
Northern Mainland	177,000	3,000	£135,000	15s.

*(20 shillings = 1£, 1 pound = about $3.60.)

Consequently, the empire retained a diverse set of governing institutions. New York continued as a royal province; the separate settlements of East and West New Jersey came under royal control in 1702. As in other royal colonies, a governor was appointed by the Crown and an assembly was elected by the people. Connecticut and Rhode Island, as corporate colonies, had greater political autonomy. Like all colonies, they were bound by the Navigation Acts and their laws were subject to review by the Privy Council in London, but they elected their governors and all other local officials. The proprietors retained uneasy control of Carolina, which was formally divided into two colonies in 1713. In Maryland and Pennsylvania, the Calvert and Penn families retained their land rights and political authority. In 1713, as in 1660, the English settlements in North America resembled a patchwork quilt, its colors and textures representing corporate, proprietary, and royal colonies. Those colonies, however, were no longer mere religious outposts or baronial fantasies. They were parts of a thriving commercial empire.

The Imperial Slave Economy

Between 1550 and 1700 European merchants and migrants created a new type of agricultural system. Using land seized from native Americans and the labor of enslaved Africans, the migrants created plantations in Brazil and the West Indies that raised sugar, tobacco, and other valuable crops, which the merchants then brought to markets in Europe. This transoceanic trade in American products, known as the South Atlantic system, changed the history of four continents. It sapped the human resources of West Africa, set off a commercial revolution in Europe, and populated North America and South America with a score of racially mixed societies (see Table 3.4). This slave-based economy also provided markets for farmers in England's northern mainland colonies and stimulated the growth of seaports and merchant communities.

The African Background

West Africa is a vast and diverse region that stretches along 2,000 miles of coastline from present-day Senegal to Cameroon and includes the modern states of Liberia, the Ivory Coast, Ghana, and Nigeria. To the south along another 1,200 miles of that coast lie Gabon, the Congo, Zaire, and Angola, also important sources of the transatlantic trade in slaves. In 1500 a thick expanse of tropical rain forest covered much of the coast, but a series of great rivers—the Senegal, Gambia, Volta,

TABLE 3.4

Slave Destinations, 1520–1810

Destination	Number of Africans Exported
South America	
Brazil	3,650,000
Dutch America	500,000
West Indies	
British	1,660,000
French	1,660,000
Central America	
Spanish	1,500,000
North America	
British colonies	500,000
Europe	175,000
Total	9,645,000

Niger, and Congo—provided relatively easy access to the woodlands, plains, and savanna of the interior.

Most residents were farmers who lived in extended families in small villages and cultivated plots of 6 to 8 acres. Normally, men cleared the land and women planted and harvested the crops. On the plains of the savanna, millet, cotton, and livestock were the prime products, while the forest peoples grew yams, which they ate in the form of porridge or dough, and harvested palm nuts for oil. Forest dwellers exchanged kola nuts, a mild stimulant, for the textiles and leather goods produced by savanna dwellers. Salt produced along the seacoast was also traded, often for iron or gold mined in the hills of the interior.

Political and Social Organization. Most West Africans spoke related Congo-Kordofanian languages, but they were divided into hundreds of distinct cultural and political groups. A majority of the people in both the savanna and the forest lived in hierarchical, socially stratified societies ruled by princes. For example, the Akan peoples organized themselves into complex states ruled by kings whose powers were limited by a council of ministers. The Wolof kings of Senegambia were much more powerful. Warrior-rulers with an army of soldier-slaves, they appointed local chiefs and grew rich from tax revenues and from levies on merchants and conquered peoples. Women of the royal Wolof clans exercised considerable power as well, collecting tribute from various villages and judging cases of adultery.

Many other West Africans resided in stateless societies organized by family and lineage, much as the Woodland Indians of North America did (see Chapter 1). The Tiv people along the Niger River, for example, created a relatively egalitarian society in which land was available to all; chiefs and elders administered justice but could neither impose taxes and rents nor control individual laborers. Other West Africans lived in communities managed by a village council.

Both women and men had secret societies, corporate bodies that unified society by cutting across lineage and clan loyalties in stateless cultures and by checking the powers of rulers in princely states. The most important societies were the *Poro* for men and the *Sande* for women; they provided sexual education for the young, conducted adult initiation ceremonies, and, by shaming individuals or officials, enforced a code of public conduct and private morality.

Supernatural beliefs underlay the power of the *Poro* and the *Sande*. Although some West Africans had been converted to the Muslim faith and believed in a single god, most recognized a variety of deities ranging from a remote creator-god who seldom interfered in human affairs to numerous spirits that lived in the earth, animals, and plants. Male blacksmiths (who had mastered the secrets of iron making) and female potters (who had transformed the basic elements of earth, water, and fire) captured these spiritual powers in amulets, "power generators" that protected those who wore them. Africans also paid homage to their ancestors, the "living dead," who were believed to inhabit a spiritual world from which they could intercede on behalf of their descendants. Royal families paid elaborate homage to their ancestors, endowing themselves with an aura of divinity.

European Traders and African Society. At first European traders had a positive impact on life in West Africa by introducing new plants and animals. Portuguese merchants carried coconuts from East Africa, oranges and lemons from the Mediterranean, and pigs from Western Europe. From the New World traders brought sweet potatoes, peanuts, papaya, pineapples, and tobacco. The most important plants were American maize and cassava (manioc), which gradually displaced millet and yams as the staple foods in the West African diet; indeed, their higher yields per acre prompted growth of the population in many areas.

Early Portuguese merchants also expanded existing trade networks, stimulating the domestic economy. European iron bars and metal products joined kola nuts and salt moving inland, whereas grain, gold, ivory, and cotton textiles flowed to the coast to provision and stock European ships heading for Asia and other regions of West Africa. This inland trade remained in the hands of Africans, in part because of disease: Europeans were quickly stricken by yellow fever, malaria, and dysentery, and their death rate was more than 50 percent a year.

Europeans also joined in the trade in human laborers. Unfree status had existed for many centuries in West Africa. Some people were held in bondage as security for debts; others were sold into servitude by their kin, often in return for food in times of famine; still others were enslaved war captives. Although treated as property and exploited as agricultural laborers, these slaves usually were considered members of the society that had enslaved them and often were treated as kin. Most retained the right to marry, and their children were often free.

A small proportion of unfree West Africans were "trade slaves," sold from one kingdom to another or carried overland to the Mediterranean region, mostly by Arab Muslim traders. The first Portuguese in Senegambia found that the Wolof king, the Buurba Jolof,

> supports himself by raids which result in many slaves from his own as well as neighboring countries. He employs these slaves in cultivating the land allotted to him: but he also sells many to the Azanaghi merchants in return for horses and other goods, and also to the Christians, since they have begun to trade with these blacks.

An African King
This striking bronze plaque, circa 1550–1680, from Benin, an important kingdom in West Central Africa, depicts a mounted king, his attendants, and (probably) his children.

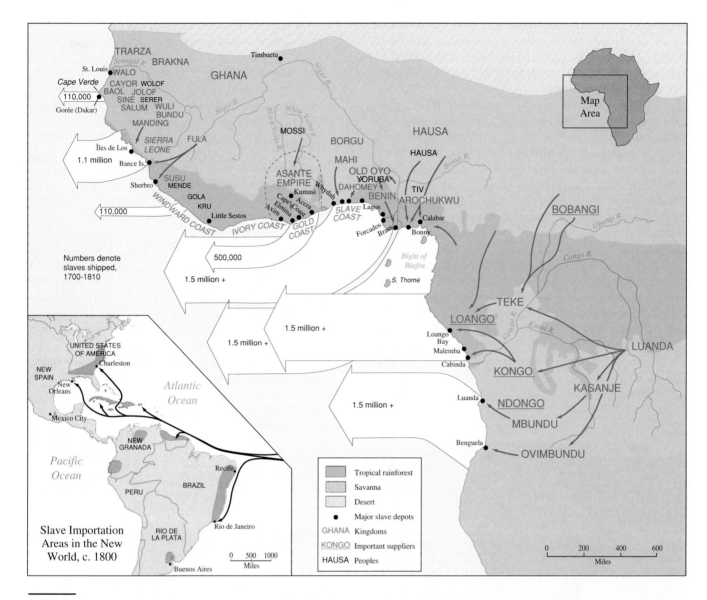

MAP 3.3

Africa in the Eighteenth Century

The tropical rain forest region of West Africa was home to scores of peoples and dozens of kingdoms. Some, such as Dahomey, became aggressive slavers, taking tens of thousands of war captives and funneling them to the seacoast, where they were purchased by European traders. About 15 percent of enslaved Africans died on the transatlantic voyage, the feared "middle passage"; most of the survivors labored on sugar plantations in Brazil and the British and French West Indies (see Table 3.4).

tuguese and then Dutch merchants annually transported about 10,000 Africans across the Atlantic to Brazil and the Caribbean. After England's triumph in the Anglo-Dutch wars, English and French merchants took over this trade in humans, developing African-run slave-catching systems that extended far into the interior. Between 1700 and 1810 they carried over 6 million Africans—800,000 in the 1780s alone—to toil and die in the Americas, primarily on sugar estates in the West Indies.

The South Atlantic System

The demand for labor in Europe's New World plantations gradually transformed the scale and nature of African slavery (see Map 3.3). Between 1440 and 1550 Portuguese traders carried a few thousand Africans each year to labor on sugar plantations in Madeira and the Canary Islands. Then, between 1550 and 1700, Por-

Sugar from Brazil and the West Indies was the cornerstone of the South Atlantic system. Before 1500 Europeans had few sources of sweetness—primarily honey and fruit juices. The cultivation of sugarcane and later the sugar beet changed the diet of Europe and the world. Once people had tasted sweetness, they craved it. They added sugar to tea and coffee, pies and cakes, and ate it straight in the form of candy. (By 1900 sugar accounted for 20 percent of the calories consumed by people throughout the world.)

Like other European nations, England met the demand for sugar by expanding its plantations. Beginning about 1650, English merchants developed Barbados as a sugar colony. Around 1700 they invested heavily in the Leeward Islands and then turned to Jamaica; by 1750 Jamaica had 700 large sugar plantations worked by more than 105,000 African slaves.

Sugar and the English Economy. Sugar production was complex and expensive. It required fertile land on which to grow the cane, labor to plant and cut it, and heavy equipment to process it into raw sugar and molasses. Because only wealthy merchants or landowners had the capital to outfit a plantation, a planter-merchant elite developed in the sugar industry. Successful planters earned 8 to 10 percent annually on their investment, double the rate of return on government bonds. Their enrichment led the Scottish economist Adam Smith to declare in *The Wealth of Nations* (1776) that sugar was the most profitable crop in either Europe or America.

The South Atlantic system made England a wealthy nation, stimulating its economy in four ways. First, it absorbed the direct profits of sugar production because most West Indian planters lived in England as "absentees." Second, the Navigation Acts, by requiring that American staple crops be exported through England, raised the level of English trade; by 1750 reexports of sugar and tobacco accounted for half of all British exports. Third, English merchants enjoyed a bonanza; for example, in the 1680s the Royal African Company sold male slaves in the West Indies for five times what it had paid for them. Such profits made England the leading maritime power in Europe. Its shipyards built hundreds of vessels to transport slaves, machinery, and settlers to the Western Hemisphere. Commercial expansion also provided England with a supply of experienced sailors, helping to make the Royal Navy the most powerful fleet in Europe. Fourth, transatlantic commerce expanded the domestic economy of England (and Scotland), creating thousands of jobs as men built the port facilities, warehouses, and dwellings of Liverpool, London, and Glasgow—the cities that became the centers of the trade in slaves, sugar, and tobacco. More men and women worked as sugar or tobacco refiners, rum distillers, and manufacturers of textiles and iron products for the growing markets in Africa and America.

Thanks to the South Atlantic system, England was no longer dependent for its prosperity on the raw wool trade. Transatlantic commerce and the mercantilist policies of the Navigation Acts advanced the development of capitalist institutions, making England a wealthy and powerful nation.

The Impact on Africa. Whatever the benefits for Europeans, the South Atlantic system was a tragedy for West Africa and certain parts of East Africa, such as Madagascar. Between 1550 and 1870, the Atlantic slave trade uprooted about 15 million Africans, draining the resources of the continent and provoking untold human misery. Overall, the iron, tinware, rum, and cloth that entered the African economy in exchange for slaves was worth from one-tenth (in the 1680s) to one-third (by the 1780s) as much as the goods those slaves produced. Thus Atlantic slavery enhanced the prosperity of Europe even as it diminished the wealth and population of Africa.

The spiritual and political cost of the slave trade cannot be calculated. The European demand for slaves made kidnapping common in much of West Africa, disrupting the lives of millions of African families (see American Voices, page 82). More significantly, it encouraged violence among peoples; an observer noted in 1739 that "whenever the King of Barsally wants Goods or Brandy . . . , the King goes and ransacks some of his enemies' towns, seizing the people and selling them." Indeed, slaving became a way of life in Dahomey, where the royal house made the sale of slaves a state monopoly between 1730 and 1800 and used the resulting access to European guns to create a centralized military despotism. Dahomey's army, which included a contingent of 5,000 women, became a war-making machine that systematically raided the interior for captives, exporting thousands of slaves each year. The Asante kings also used the firearms and wealth acquired through the Atlantic trade to create a bureaucratic empire of 3 million to 5 million people. Yet active slaving remained a choice, not a necessity. The old and still powerful Kingdom of Benin, famous for its output of superb cast bronzes and carved ivory, resolutely opposed the slave trade, prohibiting the export of men for over a century.

Nonetheless, the South Atlantic slave trade transformed West African life by encouraging powerful centralized states to conquer egalitarian stateless societies. Class divisions also hardened as people of noble birth sold those of lesser status. Law courts became vindictive, selling into slavery even those people who had committed minor crimes. Women's lives changed as well, for more men (about 65 percent of the total) than women were consigned to the transatlantic slave trade, both because European planters preferred male laborers and because African traders withheld female captives for the domestic slave trade market. Thus more African men took several wives, from whom they extracted agricultural labor as well as marital pleasures. Most important, harsh forms of slavery that denied marriage rights or were hereditary gradually became a characteristic institution in Africa, eroding the dignity of human life there as well as on the plantations of the Western Hemisphere.

AMERICAN VOICES

Olaudah Equiano

The Brutal "Middle Passage"

Olaudah Equiano, also known as Gustavus Vasa, experienced domestic slavery in Africa and plantation slavery in Barbados and Virginia. After buying his freedom in 1766, he fled to London, where twenty years later he published a memoir of his life.

My father, besides many slaves, had a numerous family of which seven lived to grow up, including myself and a sister who was the only daughter. . . . I was trained up from my earliest years in the art of war, my daily exercise was shooting and throwing javelins, and my mother adorned me with emblems after the manner of our greatest warriors. One day, when all our people were gone out to their works as usual and only I and my dear sister were left to mind the house, two men and a woman got over our walls, and in a moment seized us both, and without giving us time to cry out or make resistance they stopped our mouths and ran off with us into the nearest wood. I was left in a state of distraction not to be described. I cried and grieved continually, and for several days I did not eat anything but what they forced into my mouth. At length, after many days' travelling, during which I had often changed masters, I got into the hands of a chieftain in a very pleasant country. This man had two wives and some children, and they . . . could to comfort me, particularly the first wife, who was something like my mother. Although I was a great many days' journey from my father's house, yet these people spoke exactly the same language with us. This first master of

Olaudah Equiano

mine, as I may call him, was a smith, and my principal employment was working his bellows.

I was again sold and carried through a number of places till . . . at the end of six or seven months after I had been kidnapped I arrived at the sea coast.

The first object which saluted my eyes when I arrived on the coast was the sea, and a slave ship which was then riding at anchor and waiting for its cargo. I now saw myself deprived of all chance of returning to my native country . . . ; and I even wished for my former slavery in preference to my present situation, which was filled with horrors of every kind. . . . I was soon

put down under the decks, and there I received such a salutation in my nostrils as I had never experienced in my life; so that with the loathsomeness of the stench and crying together, I became so sick and low that I was not able to eat, nor had I the least desire to taste any thing. I now wished for the last friend, death, to relieve me; but soon, to my grief, two of the white men offered me eatables, and on my refusing to eat, one of them held me fast by the hands and laid me across I think the windlass, and tied my feet while the other flogged me severely. I had never experienced anything of this kind before, and although, not being used to the water, I naturally feared that element the first time I saw it, yet nevertheless could I have got over the nettings, I would have jumped over the side, but I could not. . . .

At last we came in sight of the island of Barbados; the white people got some old slaves from the land to pacify us. They told us we were not to be eaten but to work, and were soon to go on land where we should see many of our country people. This report eased us much; and sure enough soon after we were landed there came to us Africans of all languages.

Source: The Interesting Narrative of the Life of Olaudah Equiano, or Gustavus Vasa, the African, Written By Himself (London, 1789).

Slavery and Society in the Chesapeake

Africans first arrived in Virginia in 1619, but for the next forty years their numbers remained small, and they were not legally enslaved. English common law acknowledged varying degrees of bondage, such as indentured servitude, but not the concept of *chattel*

slavery—the ownership of one human being by another. If legalized slavery was to exist in the English colonies, the settlers would have to create it.

Virginia's Decision for Slavery. The decision in favor of slavery was easy for some migrants. The English in the West Indies and those who migrated from there to

South Carolina simply imitated the labor system used by the Spanish, Portuguese, and Dutch sugar planters and soon gave it legal form. In the tobacco colonies of Maryland and Virginia slavery developed more slowly. Three or four hundred Africans lived in the Chesapeake colonies in 1649, making up about 2 percent of the population; by 1670 the proportion of blacks was still only 5 percent. These Africans were forced to work hard and were ill fed and ill clothed, but so too were most English indentured servants in this exploitative tobacco economy. And a significant number of black workers (one-third in one Maryland community) received their freedom by completing the term of service or converting to Christianity. Some African Christian freemen even purchased slaves or bought the labor contracts of English servants. In this raw and unformed society there were few set rules.

The success of these Africans suggests that religion and personal initiative were initially as important as race in determining social status. The English in the Chesapeake had always seen Africans as "different," sometimes referring in personal letters and official documents to skin color or language but focusing primarily on religion. To the colonists, Africans were first and foremost pagans or Muslims. Thus, by becoming a Christian and a planter, an enterprising African could aspire to near equality with the English settlers.

Beginning in the 1660s, however, new laws gradually lowered the status of all Africans. The reason for this change is not clear. Perhaps the English elite grew more conscious of race as the number of Africans increased, or perhaps the end of the tobacco boom prompted greater social control over blacks as well as over white servants and poor farmers. In any event, new legislation in Virginia forbade Africans to own guns or join the militia. Between 1667 and 1671 the House of Burgesses abridged the property rights of Africans, barring them—"tho baptized and enjoying their own Freedom"—from buying the labor contracts of white servants and specifying that conversion to Christianity did not qualify Africans for eventual freedom. Being black was becoming a mark of inferior legal and social status.

After Bacon's rebellion of 1675–1676, planters imported thousands of Africans, primarily because it had become cheaper to buy blacks than to import white servants and also because slaves had few legal rights and could be disciplined more strictly. A law of 1692 prohibiting sexual intercourse between English and Africans was intended to separate the two laboring groups and create a racially divided society. Blacks found that their servitude was permanent and hereditary, binding their children as well as themselves. Finally, in 1705, a Virginia statute explicitly defined virtually all resident Africans as slaves: "All servants imported or brought into this country by sea or land who were not Christians in their native country shall be accounted and be slaves." The English elite in the Chesapeake colonies had chosen to create a society based on slave labor.

The New Chesapeake Social Order. The social order in the Chesapeake changed significantly after 1700. As settlement moved inland, away from swampy lowlands, disease took fewer lives, and English migrants lived long enough to form stable families and communities. Men reassumed control of family property, no longer naming their wives as executors of their estates and legal guardians of their children (as they did when death rates were high) but bestowing those powers on their male kin. Reaffirming the primacy of male heirs, they also restricted widows' estates to the customary one-third share.

The reappearance of strict patriarchy within the family mirrored larger social developments. As the planter elite consolidated its authority, it created a rural social hierarchy that reflected European traditions, with a few gentry families on the top, a small yeoman class, a much larger group of white tenant farmers, and an army of dependent black laborers. Thousands of African slaves grew their masters' food as well as their export tobacco; built houses, wagons, and tobacco casks; and made shoes, clothes, and other necessities. Their increased self-sufficiency helped wealthy Chesapeake planters weather the depressed tobacco market between 1680 and 1720. Small-scale planters fared less well, falling deeper into debt to their creditors among the elite.

To prevent another rebellion like Bacon's, the Virginia gentry reduced taxes on these middling and poor whites. The annual poll tax paid by every free man fell from 45 pounds of tobacco in 1675 to only 5 pounds a year by 1750. When Royal Governor Alexander Spotswood tried to raise the property requirement for voting, the gentry strongly opposed him. Their strategy was to curry the favor of voters at election time, bribing them with rum, food, and money; once in office, they enacted laws that favored small-scale farmers. In return, yeomen planters elected their wealthy neighbors to political office and deferred to their authority. By creating solidarity among whites, this political compromise prevented a black uprising; by enhancing the power of the planter elite, it limited the authority of the royal governor.

This political compromise worked because most Chesapeake white men shared a common culture. The gentry was still a boisterous, aggressive class, and poor and wealthy planters enjoyed many of the same amusements, from hunting, hard drinking, and gambling on horse races and cockfights to sharing tales of their manly prowess in seducing female servants and slaves. As time passed, however, affluent Chesapeake planters took on the trappings of wealth, modeling themselves after the English aristocracy (see American Lives, pages 86–87). Between 1720 and 1750 they replaced their modest wooden houses with mansions of brick and mortar. Increasingly, planters—and their wives—sought elegance and refinement, avidly reading English newspapers and pamphlets, importing English clothes, and dining in the English fashion, with an elaborate afternoon tea. They hired English tutors to teach etiquette to their daughters and sent their sons to London to pass a few years at the Inns of Court (the training ground for English lawyers) and to be educated as gentlemen. Most of these young men returned to America, married young ladies (preferably charming and rich ones), and took up the life of slave owning planters, managing plantations and participating in politics. Gentry women now lived in less raucous and more genteel households, their identities increasingly shaped by the conventions of domesticity: deferring to their husbands' authority, rearing pious children, and maintaining elaborate social networks. Committed to life in America, the planter-merchants of the Chesapeake used the profits from the South Atlantic system to form a stable ruling class that was increasingly well educated and refined.

The Expansion of Slavery

The wealth of the white elite came from the labor of black slaves. By 1770 slaves numbered about 500,000 and made up about a third of the southern population. Yet black slavery became an institution not because it was "necessary"—whites grew most of the tobacco and could have cultivated rice and sugar—but because it meant less work and greater profits for those who owned slaves. African labor not only supported a wealthy elite of planter-merchants—such as the Carters, Lees, Burwells, and Randolphs in the Chesapeake and the Bulls, Pinckneys, and Gadsdens in South Carolina—but also raised the living standards of many other white southerners: 60 percent of farm families owned at least one slave by the 1770s.

In contrast to the comfortable lives it provided for planters, eighteenth-century slavery was a brutal experience for Africans. Torn from their villages, they were marched in chains to coastal ports. From there they made the infamous "middle passage"—the perilous voyage to the New World in disease-ridden ships so overcrowded that there was barely room to move. Some Africans jumped overboard, choosing to drown rather

Two Views of the Middle Passage
As the slave trade boomed, ship designers packed in more and more human cargo (below), treating enslaved Africans with no more respect than hogsheads of sugar or tobacco. By contrast, the watercolor, painted by a naval officer, captures their humanity and dignity.

than endure more suffering. Others—about 15 percent of the total and no fewer than 750,000 during the eighteenth century—died aboard ship from sickness or disease, mostly dysentery, smallpox, or scurvy. The survivors, headed mostly for Brazil or the West Indies, faced a degrading life of backbreaking labor.

The Sugar Islands. The waste of human life in the West Indies was staggering. Disease was rampant; thousands of Africans died in epidemics of yellow fever, smallpox, and measles. Thousands more were killed by inadequate food, oppressive work, and inhuman living conditions. Planting and harvesting the sugarcane required intense labor under a subtropical sun, with a pace often set by the overseer's whip. Some planters were little more than killers; with sugar prices high and the cost of slaves low, they worked slaves to death and then imported more. In fact, the mortality rate was so high that although British sugar planters on Barbados imported about 85,000 Africans between 1708 and 1735, the black population of the island increased by only 4,000 (from 42,000 to 46,000).

Initially, because West Indian planters purchased four men for every woman, most slaves could not marry. But women survived at a much higher rate, possibly because they were whipped less often, and gradually female slaves formed half the work force. These women bore few children, because planters forced pregnant women to work in the fields up to the time of birth and miscarriages were frequent. In the sugar colonies, the African population did not increase through reproduction until after slavery was abolished.

The Chesapeake. In Maryland and Virginia living conditions for slaves were less severe, and many lived relatively long lives. Producing tobacco was less physically demanding than growing sugar, and because plantations in the Chesapeake were small and dispersed, epidemic diseases did not spread easily. Moreover, since tobacco planting was only modestly profitable, planters could not constantly buy new slaves and therefore treated those they had less harshly.

Tobacco planters sought to increase their work force through reproduction, purchasing higher numbers of female slaves and encouraging Africans to have large families. In 1720 women made up about a third of the African population of Maryland, and the black population had begun to increase through reproduction. One absentee owner instructed his plantation agent "to be kind and indulgent to the breeding wenches, and not to force them when with child upon any service or hardship that will be injurious to them." And, he added, "the children are to be well looked after." Planters imported Africans again when tobacco prices rose after 1720, but by midcentury American-born slaves formed a majority among Chesapeake blacks. The tobacco

economy, with its relatively healthful plantations and modest profit margin, permitted the emergence of a large African-American population.

South Carolina. In South Carolina, which was settled by land-hungry whites from Barbados in the 1680s, slaves lived under a more demanding regime. The colony grew slowly until Africans from rice-growing cultures, who knew how to plant, harvest, and process that nutritious grain, turned rice into a profitable export crop (see New Technology, page 88). By 1730 Charleston merchants were shipping about 17 million pounds of rice a year to southern Europe, where it was in demand; by 1775 annual rice exports had reached 75 million pounds.

To expand production of their lucrative crop, white planters and merchants imported tens of thousands of Africans (see Figure 3.1). As early as the 1710s Africans made up a majority of the population of South Carolina and about 80 percent of those living in the rice-growing lowlands, but most met an early death. Mosquito-borne epidemic diseases flourished in the hot swampy lowlands of coastal Carolina and took the lives of thousands of slaves. Overwork killed many other Africans, for moving tons of dirt to construct irrigation works was brutally hard work. As in the West Indies, there were many deaths and few births.

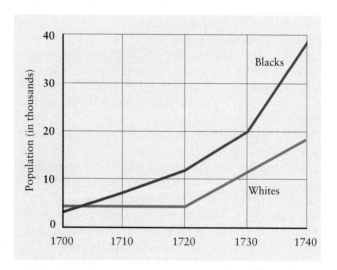

FIGURE 3.1

The Growth of Slavery in South Carolina
To grow more rice, white planters imported thousands of African slaves, giving South Carolina a black majority and prompting the development of a strong Afro-centric language and culture.

William Byrd II and the Maturation of the Virginia Gentry

William Byrd aimed high. In 1692, a mere stripling of eighteen, he sought a post with the Lords of Trade, the body charged with administering England's colonial empire. Nearly two decades later, like his father before him a member of the Virginia Council, Byrd again sought preferment from imperial authorities, trying to become governor of Virginia. He renewed this unsuccessful quest in 1714 and again in 1722.

His father's ambition explained much. The son of a goldsmith and a London tradesman turned Virginia Indian trader and planter-merchant, the older William Byrd had high hopes for his son, shipping him across the Atlantic at age seven to be educated as an English gentleman at the Felsted School. The goal was elusive. Apparently ostracized as a "colonial" by his status-conscious classmates, the young Byrd nonetheless embraced his father's vision: Living in England for the next twenty-four years, he consciously practiced the precepts of self-control and courtesy laid down in a well-known manual of etiquette, Richard Brathwait's *The Perfect Gentleman*. He became a learned man who read Hebrew, Greek, Latin, French, and Italian, and he wrote witty (and minor) poetry and prose.

All to little avail. While living in London from 1692 to 1705, Byrd practiced the arts of a young gentleman and man-about-town, but he never mastered them. As he confessed in a revealing self-portrait, "Inamorato L'Oiseaux" (the Enamored Bird, a word play on his family name), "He wou'd look like a fool, and talk like a Philosopher, when both his eyes and his Tongue shou'd have sparked with wit and waggery." The failure might have been personal, for despite his attempt at gallantry, Byrd was essentially a shy man. Or perhaps it was cultural, for the stigma of birth to a colonial family with few aristocratic connections was difficult to overcome. Whatever the cause, Byrd failed utterly in his almost desperate attempts to secure a rich post or a rich wife.

The death of his father brought him back to reality—in Virginia, a "lonely . . . silent country" that sometimes seemed like "being buried alive." Indeed, Virginia was not only culturally isolated but also medically dangerous, still beset by epidemic disease and early death. But Byrd survived his provincial exile and

there, between 1705 and 1714, gradually assumed a coherent identity. As a merchant, slaveowning planter, and receiver of royal revenues, the young Virginian commanded a handsome annual income of some 1,500 English pounds sterling. And after taking as a wife Lucy Parke, the daughter of the colonial-born governor of the Leeward Islands, he succeeded his father as the proprietor of Westover, a tobacco estate on the James River, and as a local and provincial magnate. The parish vestry awarded him "the best pew in the church"; he was appointed commander in chief of the militia in Henrico and Charles City counties; and, the biggest prize of all, the king's ministers named him a member of the Council, the advisory body to the governor and the highest court in the colony. By 1710, at age thirty-six, Byrd had risen about as high as a Virginia-born gentleman could go.

It was not enough. Driven—perhaps by his father's ambition or by his own compulsions, perhaps by the allure of imperial prestige or English high society—Byrd embarked on a decade-long quest for power and wealth. The result was nearly calamitous for Byrd, even as it reveals the inner dynamics of the politics and culture of his time.

Byrd's first goal was political power: the governorship of Virginia, the most prestigious imperial post on the mainland. From his long stay in England he had aristocratic friends, including Sir John Perceval, the earl of Egmont, and Sir John Campbell, the duke of Argyll, who had influence in high places, such as the Board of Trade. But these patronage connections were frail. The great duke of Marlborough, whose army would best that of France's King Louis XIV, curtly dismissed Byrd's petition, stating that "no one but soldiers should have the government of a plantation." Marlborough needed lucrative offices for his retired generals, and he wanted governors with military expertise in the event of an attack from New France or New Spain. Rather than Byrd, he named Sir Alexander Spotswood to govern Virginia.

Rebuffed politically, the ambitious young man sought greater wealth. To inherit the Virginia estate of his wife's deceased father, Byrd agreed in 1712 to "pay all Colonel Parke's debts," a financial miscalculation

William Byrd in the pose of an English aristocrat, London, circa 1702. (Colonial Williamsburg Foundation)

that cost him dearly. Unknown to his son-in-law, Parke had incurred debts in England of £3,000, a burden that would weigh down Byrd for the next thirty years. Like most wealthy eighteenth-century Virginia planters (who fell into debt because of extravagant life-styles), he found himself in a position of humiliating dependence on the credit of London merchant houses.

In 1714 Byrd returned to England to deal with Parke's debts and to undermine Governor Spotswood, whose policies threatened the power of the Council and Byrd's business in the Indian trade. Two years later Lucy Parke Byrd joined him, only to succumb to smallpox: "Gracious God what pains did she take to make a voyage hither to seek a grave," Byrd lamented. In premodern England as in early Virginia, death struck quickly and arbitrarily, without regard to age or social status.

The next years were unhappy ones for Byrd, who was unable to dislodge Spotswood from the governorship, pay off Parke's debts, or marry a rich woman. As he avidly (and awkwardly) pursued an heiress twenty years younger than himself with flowery letters addressed to "Sabina" from "Veramour" (True Lover), Byrd satisfied his sexual desires with a string of prostitutes, recording the encounters and his daily routine in the "Secret Diaries," which he wrote in code during most of his adult life:

> [January 26, 1719] I rose about 8 o'clock, having taken my asses' milk, and read a chapter in Hebrew and some Greek in Lucian. I said my prayers and had milk porridge for breakfast. About 10 o'clock came Annie Wilkinson and I rogered her. . . .

Once again Byrd's colonial origins defeated him: his Virginia estate of 43,000 acres and 200 black slaves failed to impress Sabina's father: "an Estate out of this Island appears to him little better than an Estate in the moon." Rejected as a suitor, Byrd vented his hostility against Sabina in verse:

> *Let Age with double speed oretake her;*
> *Let Love the room of Pride supply;*
> *And when the Fellows all forsake her*
> *Let her gnaw the sheets & dy.*

Byrd once again faced the prospect of a living death in Virginia. In 1719 the Board of Trade ordered him to return to the colony (and threatened to remove him as a councillor if he did not comply), but Byrd stayed in Virginia for only eighteen months before returning to London, where he lived for another five years.

Only in 1726, at age fifty-two and driven by financial necessity, did Byrd finally renounce his quest to be an English gentleman or imperial governor. He returned to Virginia with a young wife (who brought only a small dowry and bore him four children), at last prepared emotionally to accept a lesser destiny as a member of the Virginia gentry. Finally giving up his "rooms" in London in 1728, he built an elegant two-story brick mansion on the family's estate at Westover. From there, he led the Virginia gentry in an unsuccessful effort to prevent Parliamentary approval of the Colonial Debts Act (1732), which allowed English creditors to seize American lands and slaves to pay off debts. And there, during the 1730s, he wrote an unpublished "History of the Dividing Line" between Virginia and North Carolina, an ironic yet celebratory portrait of America and its people.

The personal odyssey of William Byrd II mirrored that of the Virginia gentry as a whole. They had come to America to get rich and return to England in triumph, only to discover that they were bound to Virginia by the curse of their inferior colonial birth. It was a hard and bitter lesson but far from a tragic one, for they remained members of a privileged slaveowning provincial gentry. As Byrd put it after his return to America: "Like one of the patriarchs, I have my flocks and my herds, my bond-men and bond-women, and every soart of trade amongst my servants, so that I live in a kind of independance on every one, but Providence."

Rice: Riches and Wretchedness

Technology always has cultural significance, for its use reveals the systems of value and power in a society. Occasionally, as in the case of the introduction of rice to America, the relation between culture and technology is particularly dramatic. Rice was not grown in England, and the first white settlers in South Carolina failed to plant it successfully during the 1670s and 1680s. As a planter later recalled, "The people being unacquainted with the manner of cultivating rice, many difficulties attended to the first planting and preparing it, as a vendable commodity."

Unlike Europeans, many West Africans had a thorough knowledge of rice. Along the Windward Coast of Africa, an English traveler noted, rice "forms the chief part of the African's sustenance." As he explained, "The rice fields or *lugars* are prepared during the dry season, and the seed sown in the tornado season, requiring about four or five months to bring it to perfection." Enslaved blacks brought these skills to South Carolina. As early as 1690 an Englishman named John Steward was actively promoting rice production both as a potential export and as a cheap food for his slaves. For their part, Africans welcomed the cultivation of a familiar food, and their knowledge was crucial to its success.

English settlers had been unable to master not only the planting and harvesting of rice but also its hulling. At first they tried to come up with a machine—a "rice mill"—to separate the tough husk of the rice seed from the nutritious grain inside. Thus, in 1691 the government awarded Peter Jacob Guerard a two-year patent on a "Pendulum Engine, which doeth much better, and in lesser time and labour, huske rice." Machines did not prove equal to the task, however, and English planters turned to African technology. In 1700 a royal official informed the English Board of Trade that the settlers had "found out the true way of raising and husking rice" by having slave women use traditional mortar and pestle methods to process it. The women placed the grain in large wooden mortars hollowed from the trunks of pine or cypress trees and then pounded it with long wooden pestles, quickly removing the husks and whitening the grains. Their labor was prodigious. By the 1770s slaves were annually processing 75 million tons of rice for export and millions more for their own consumption.

African labor and technology brought both wealth and wretchedness to South Carolina. The planter-

In this early twentieth-century photograph, the descendants of enslaved women use African technology to hull rice in South Carolina.

merchant aristocracy that controlled the rice industry became immensely wealthy; for example, nine of the ten richest Americans who died around 1770 came from South Carolina and had grown rich from rice. The tens of thousands of enslaved Africans who labored in the rice swamps and plantations lived hard and short lives; many died of disease, and until the late eighteenth century, those slaves who survived had little to show—in material comforts or a stable family life—for their years of labor. Although the technology of rice production was not inherently elitist, in America it became part of a slave-based plantation society with immense racial and economic divisions.

The Creation of an African-American Community

Chesapeake planters imported slaves from many regions of West Africa, but about 60 percent of the Africans landing along the York River in Virginia in the 1720s came from Calabar and other lands near the Bight of Biafra. South Carolina slave owners preferred laborers from the Gold Coast and Gambia, but because the slave trade shifted to the south after 1730, they got more than 30 percent of their work force from Angola. In no colony, however, did any African people or language group become dominant, primarily because white planters consciously attempted to ensure security through cultural diversity. "The safety of the Plantations," declared a widely read English pamphlet, "depends upon having Negroes from all parts of Guiny, who do not understand each other's languages and Customs and cannot agree to Rebel."

The slaves regarded each other not as "Africans" but as members of specific peoples or language groups. Gradually, however, enslaved Africans found it in their interest to transcend their diverse identities. In the low-lands of South Carolina, which were populated largely by African-born blacks, they created a new language, the Gullah dialect, which incorporated English and African words in an African grammatical structure and so was widely understood. In the Chesapeake, with more American-born blacks and a less concentrated slave population, many Africans gave up their native tongues for English. "All the blacks spoke very good English," a European visitor to Virginia in the mid-eighteenth century noted with surprise.

The acquisition of a common language, whether Gullah or English, was a prerequisite for the creation of an African-American community. The growth of stable family and kin networks was another requirement. In South Carolina a high death rate prevented long-term family formation, but after 1725 Chesapeake blacks created strong nuclear families and extended kin relationships. These "African-Americans" gradually developed a culture of their own, passing on family names, traditions, and knowledge to the next generation.

In this newly formed ethnic community, aspects of the slaves' African heritage could be seen in wood carvings, the giant wooden mortars and pestles used for hulling rice, and the design of shacks, which often had

African Culture in South Carolina
The dance and the musical instruments are of Yoruba origin, the contribution of Africans from the Niger River–Gold Coast region (the homeland of the Yoruba), an area that accounted for one-sixth of the slaves imported into South Carolina.

rooms arranged from front to back in a distinctive "I" pattern (not side by side, as was common in English houses). Many African-Americans retained their traditional religious beliefs, observing Muslim religious practices or relying on the spiritual powers of conjurers. But others adopted Protestant Christianity, reshaping its doctrines, ethics, and rituals to fit their needs. For their part, whites were influenced by African musical rhythms. Virginians have "what I call everlasting jigs," reported Nicholas Creswell, an Englishman. "A Couple gets up and begins to dance a jig (to some Negro tune)."

Yet slavery drastically limited African-American creativity. Slaves had few opportunities for education and self-expression because most blacks worked as farm laborers and accumulated few material goods. "We entered the huts of the Blacks," commented a well-traveled European who visited Virginia in the late eighteenth century:

> They are more miserable than the most miserable of the cottages of our peasants. The husband and wife sleep on a mean pallet, the children on the ground; a

very bad fireplace, some utensils for cooking. . . . They work all week, not having a single day for themselves except for holidays.

He concluded that without question, "the condition of our peasants is infinitely happier." The comparison between slaves and peasants was apt. Both African-American slaves and European peasants were peoples who, because of their poverty and dependence, had only limited ways to express their identity. Consequently, they bequeathed to posterity not great works of art or literature but distinctive cultures based on language, family, community, and religion.

Moreover, African-American society was still in the process of formation. The parents or grandparents of eighteenth-century slaves had come to the American mainland in chains and as strangers to one another. Yet unlike their fellow Africans in the West Indies, they not only had survived but also had developed family networks, a common language, and a culture of their own. The power of that culture is conveyed by a story told by a traveler in the southern backcountry. He came upon

Slave Dwellings at Mulberry Plantation
Most plantation scenes depict the imposing mansions of the slave owners. This view of Mulberry plantation in South Carolina, however, steals a look behind the big house to the meager dwellings of the slaves, whose labor produced the wealth of the plantation.

an African-American who had been taken prisoner and adopted by Indians, who had given him "a wife, a mother, and plenty of land to cultivate if he chose it, and the liberty of doing everything but making his escape." But the black man rejected this freedom, rendering "himself up a voluntary slave to his former master, that he might there once more embrace those friends and relatives from whom he had been so long separated." To this African-American, family and cultural identity were worth more than greater freedom in an alien society.

Oppression and Resistance

Returning to slavery was an act of great courage: slave owners were not a forgiving group. They came from a culture in which the poor were systematically oppressed, religious heresy ended in bloodshed, and minor crimes were punishable by death. Masters did not hesitate to impose harsh discipline on white indentured servants, whipping them without mercy or doubling their time of service for running away, and because African slaves were an alien people, all moral restraints vanished. In the West Indies English planters routinely branded troublesome slaves with hot irons. To keep their slaves in submission, Chesapeake planters resorted to castration, nose slitting, and the amputation of fingers, toes, and ears. Declaring the chronic runaway Ballazore an "incorrigeble rogue," Robert "King" Carter of Virginia ordered his toes cut off: "nothing less than dismembering will reclaim him." The worst aspects of human nature and of the harsh traditions of early modern Europe found expression in a slave-based society.

Terror and Control. White violence was related to the size and density of the slave population. On the malaria-ridden lowland plantations of South Carolina a few whites generally had charge of twenty-five to a hundred slaves and they could maintain authority only by inspiring fear. Black workers were forbidden to leave the plantation without special passes, and rural patrols enforced those regulations. Slaves who disobeyed, refused to work, or ran away were punished brutally. Even in the Chesapeake, where slaves constituted a minority of the population, planters often resorted to the whip.

Whites who grew up in this society learned to use terror to maintain their superior position. No one knew this better than Thomas Jefferson, who witnessed brutality on his father's plantation in the mid-eighteenth century. Each generation of whites, he noted, was "nursed, educated, and daily exercised in tyranny," for the relationship "between master and slave is a perpetual exercise of the most unremitting despotism on the one part, and degrading submission on the other. Our children see this and learn to imitate it."

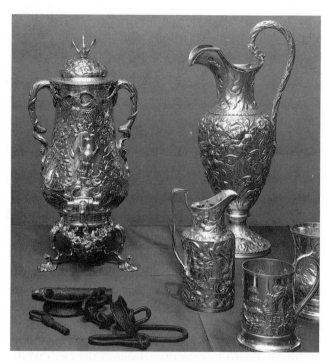

Iron Shackles and a Silver Service
Colonial metalworkers fashioned shackles for enslaved Africans as well as elaborate silver urns and cups for wealthy slave owners. The juxtaposition of these objects of beauty and oppression confronts the vast disparity of life in a slave society.

Slaves dealt with their plight in a variety of ways. Some cooperated with their owners, agreeing to do extra work in return for better food or clothes. Others resisted by working slowly or carelessly or by stealing from their masters. Still others attacked their owners or overseers, taking a small measure of revenge, though it was punishable by mutilation or death.

A successful rebellion was nearly impossible on the mainland, because whites were both numerous and armed. Full-fledged slave revolts occurred mostly on densely settled sugar plantations, and then only in areas where nearby mountains offered a secure refuge, such as Jamaica. But some newly arrived slaves without ties to African-American culture escaped to the frontier, where they tried to establish African villages (for example, near Lexington, Virginia, in 1728) or, more often, married into Indian tribes. Others, especially those who were fluent in English, fled to towns, where they tried to pass as free blacks.

The Stono Rebellion. Imperial rivalries sparked a major slave revolt in British North America. In the late 1730s the governor of Spanish Florida promised freedom and land to slaves who fled from South Carolina.

By February 1739 at least sixty-nine slaves had reportedly escaped to St. Augustine, and rumors circulated "that a Conspiracy was formed by Negroes in Carolina to rise and make their way out of the province." When war between England and Spain broke out later that year, the conspirators acted. Banding together near the Stono River, seventy-five Africans, some of them Portuguese-speaking Christians from the African Kingdom of Kongo, killed a number of whites, stole guns and ammunition, and marched south toward Florida "with Colours displayed and two Drums beating." Unrest swept the countryside, but the white militia killed many of the Stono rebels and dispersed the rest, preventing a general uprising.

The Stono rebellion frightened whites throughout the mainland. South Carolina planters tightened plantation discipline and bought fewer new Africans. Elsewhere slaveholders acted vigorously to quell discontent. After several unexplained fires and burglaries in New York City in 1741, the authorities alleged a plot among slaves, who formed almost 20 percent of the population and were owned by over 40 percent of the city's white households. After a judicial inquisition, they hanged or burned to death twenty blacks and four whites—alleged accomplices in the conspiracy—and transported eighty slaves to the West Indies. For Africans, the price of active resistance was high.

The Northern Economy

The West Indies Trade. Not only New York City but the entire northern mainland economy participated in the South Atlantic system. The sugar islands provided a ready market for American bread, lumber, fish, and meat. As a West Indian explained as early as 1647, planters in the islands "had rather buy food at very dear rates than produce it by labour, so infinite is the profit of sugar works." By 1700 the economic systems of the West Indies and New England were tightly interwoven. After 1720 farmers and merchants in New York, New Jersey, and Pennsylvania entered this trade, shipping wheat, corn, and bread to the West Indies.

This commerce tied the empire together economically. In return for sugar exports to England, West Indian planters received bills of exchange—basically credit slips—from London merchant houses. The planters then used those bills to pay slave traders for newly arrived Africans and to reimburse mainland merchants for the agricultural goods produced by northern farmers. The merchants in turn exchanged their bills for British manufactures, thus completing the cycle.

The West Indian trade created the first American merchant fortunes and major urban industries. New England merchants built factories in Boston, Newport, and Providence to process raw sugar, imported from the islands, into refined sugar, which previously had been imported from England. They also invested in distilleries to turn West Indian molasses into rum for domestic and foreign consumption. By the 1740s Boston distillers were exporting more than half a million gallons of rum annually.

Seaport Cities. As a result of this mercantile activity, American port cities grew rapidly. By 1750 Newport, Rhode Island, and Charleston, South Carolina, had nearly 10,000 residents apiece; Boston had 15,000, and New York had almost 18,000. The largest port, Philadelphia, whose population would reach 30,000 by 1776, was the size of most European provincial cities and formed the center of a sprawling regional economy.

Trade was the lifeblood of these cities. Merchants in Boston and Philadelphia, along with those in New York, handled most of the mainland's imports from Britain and managed exports to the West Indies. A bustling export trade in wheat transformed Baltimore from a sleepy village to a major port in the two decades after 1740. Charleston, the only major southern seaport, shipped deerskins, indigo, and rice to European markets. In addition, New England merchants, operating out of Boston, Salem, Marblehead, and smaller ports, built a major fishing industry, providing mackerel and cod to feed the slaves of the sugar islands and to export to southern Europe. By 1750 the New England fishing fleet numbered more than 600 ships and provided employment for over 4,000 men.

Coastal towns were centers of the shipbuilding and lumber industries. By the 1740s seventy sawmills dotted the Piscataqua River in New Hampshire, providing low-cost wood for homes, warehouses, and especially shipbuilding. Scores of shipwrights turned out oceangoing vessels, while hundreds of other artisans made ropes, sails, and metal fittings for the new fleet. Shipyards in Boston and Philadelphia launched about 15,000 tons of oceangoing vessels annually, augmenting English shipbuilding so successfully that colonial-built ships eventually made up about a third of the British merchant fleet.

Interior Towns. The impact of the South Atlantic system extended far into the interior of North America, because of an intricate transportation network. For instance, a small fleet of trading vessels sailed back and forth between Philadelphia and the villages along the Delaware Bay, exchanging cargoes of European goods for barrels of flour and wheat. Land-based transport in Maryland, meanwhile, was handled by hundreds of professional teamsters who by the 1750s annually moved to market 370,000 bushels of wheat and corn and 16,000 barrels of flour, representing 10,000 wagon trips. To accommodate this traffic, entrepreneurs and artisans set up taverns, livery stables, and barrel-making shops in small towns along the wagon roads, providing additional jobs.

Prosperous towns attracted a wide variety of artisans; for example, Lancaster, Pennsylvania, had more than 200 German and English artisans. The South Atlantic system thus provided not only markets for farmers, by far the largest group of northern residents, but also opportunities for merchants, artisans, and workers in country towns and seaport cities.

Seaport Society

American Merchants. A small group of wealthy merchants stood at the top of urban society. The Apthorp, Bowdoin, Faneuil, and Oliver families in Boston; the Beekmans, Crugers, Waltons, and Roosevelts in New York; and the Norris and Pemberton clans in Philadelphia were among the first great American entrepreneurs, and their ventures in West Indian and European trade reaped handsome profits (see Map 3.4). By 1750 about 150 merchants controlled 70 percent of Philadelphia's trade. Their taxable assets averaged £3,000, a huge sum at the time.

Like the Chesapeake gentry, wealthy northern merchants imitated the British upper classes in their cultural tastes. Guided by imported design books from England, merchants built mansions in the new Georgian architectural style—grand houses that, with their large windows symmetrically flanking elaborate columned porticoes, conveyed the wealth of their owners. Their wives created a genteel culture, decorating their houses with the best furniture and entertaining guests at elegant dinners.

Artisans. Artisans and shopkeepers, along with their families, constituted nearly half the seaport population and provided the residents with food, housing, and clothing. Their ranks included innkeepers, butchers, seamstresses, shoemakers, weavers, bakers, carpenters,

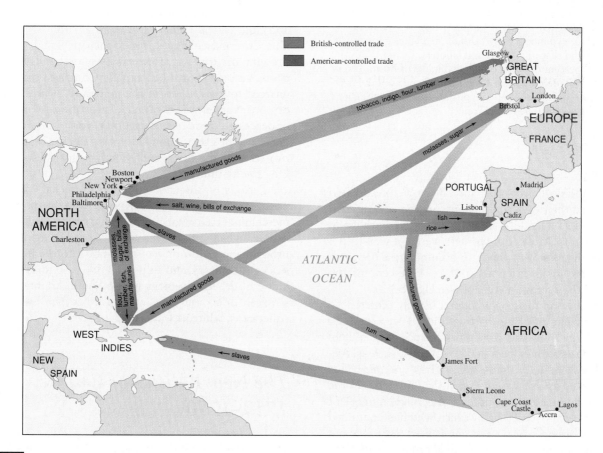

MAP 3.4

The Rise of the American Merchant, circa 1750
In accordance with mercantilist doctrine, British merchants controlled most of the transatlantic trade in manufactures, sugar, tobacco, and slaves. However, merchants in Boston, New York, and Philadelphia seized control of the West Indian trade, while Newport traders imported slaves from Africa, and Boston and Charleston merchants carried fish and rice to southern Europe.

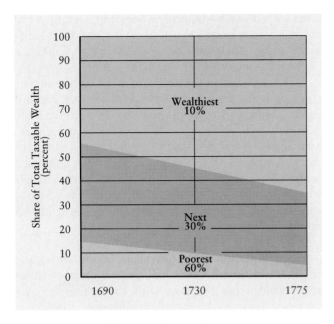

FIGURE 3.2

Wealth Inequality in the Northern Cities
As commerce expanded, the wealth of merchants grew much faster than did that of artisans and laborers. By the 1770s the poorest 60 percent of the taxable inhabitants of Boston, New York, and Philadelphia owned less than 5 percent of the taxable wealth, whereas the top 10 percent—the merchant elite and its allies—controlled 65 percent.

masons, and dozens of other specialists. Well-to-do artisans owned their own tools, shops, and houses and had taxable assets averaging about £300, a tenth those of the merchants. Most craft workers were not well-to-do, however. A tailor was lucky to accumulate £30 worth of property in his lifetime, a mere 1 percent of the wealth of the average merchant (see Figure 3.2).

Artisans had their own culture, usually centered on their particular craft and its traditions. They socialized among themselves and sometimes formed mutual-help societies to assist members in times of need, such as a serious illness or a business loss. Wives and husbands often worked as a team and taught the "mysteries of the craft" to their children. Indeed, a discernible number of shops were run by widowed women who had continued the family business. Some artisans aspired to wealth and status, an entrepreneurial ethic that prompted them to hire apprentices and expand production. But the goal of most artisans was a "competency"—an income sufficient to maintain the family in modest comfort and dignity.

Laborers and Slaves. Laboring men and women formed the lower ranks of the urban social order. Hundreds of

well-muscled men worked as stevedores on the docks of Boston, Philadelphia, and New York, transferring tons of manufactured goods and molasses from inbound ships to warehouses and then loading the ships with barrels of wheat, fish, and rice for export. Hundreds of other men worked for wages in a variety of semiskilled jobs, while poor women—whether single, married, or widowed—eked out a living washing clothes, spinning wool, or working as servants. Black slaves and white indentured servants performed many of the most menial and demanding jobs. In Philadelphia, African-American slaves and indentured German migrants made up about 20 percent of the city's residents but held nearly half the laboring jobs.

Whether enslaved, indentured, or merely poor, wage workers and merchant seamen were indispensable to the economy of every port city. Yet they owned little property. Most lived in small rented houses or tenements in the back alleys of the crowded waterfront districts, scraping by on household budgets that left no margin for sickness, accidents, or unemployment. To make ends meet, women took in washing and sewing and children were sent out to work as soon as they were able. In good economic times such personal sacrifices brought security or, for many sailors and laborers, enough money to drink cheap New England rum in waterfront taverns, often in the company of adventurous or poor women who worked as prostitutes. But periods of depressed trade meant irregular work, hunger, dependence on the charity handed out by the town-appointed overseers of the poor, and—for the most desperate—a life of petty thievery.

Periods of stagnant commerce affected all townspeople, the rich as well as the poor. Even the most astute merchants faced financial hardship and possible bankruptcy when prices plunged. Commerce not only brought jobs and opportunities but also the uncertainties of a complex and unpredictable system of transatlantic trade. Involvement in the South Atlantic system between 1660 and 1750 transformed the lives of all Americans, white as well as black.

The New Politics of Empire, 1713–1750

The triumph of trade changed the politics of empire. The British government, pleased with the prosperous commerce in staple crops, ruled its colonies with a gentle hand. This policy of "salutary neglect" gave the colonists a significant degree of self-government and economic autonomy and ultimately allowed Americans to challenge the rules of the British mercantilist system.

The Rise of the Assembly

Before 1689 political affairs in most colonies were dominated by royal governors or authoritarian elites. The duke of York ran New York by fiat, Puritan magistrates suppressed dissent in New England, and Governor Berkeley and his Green Spring faction ruled Virginia with an iron hand. These oligarchs denounced critics of their policies as traitors and condemned opposition groups as illegitimate "factions." Such arrogance reflected a widespread belief that power came from above, not from below. In the words of Robert Filmer, a royalist political philosopher in England, "Authority should Descend from *Kings* and *Fathers* to *Sons* and *Servants*."

As the American settlements became mature provinces after 1700, they developed a more representative system of politics. The seeds of this change were planted during the Glorious Revolution in England, when the political faction known as the Whigs led the fight for a constitutional monarchy that limited the authority of the Crown. The English Whig ideal was a "mixed government," one that divided power among the three social orders: the monarchy, the aristocracy, and the commons. Whigs did not advocate democracy, but they did believe that property owners (the "commons") should have some political power, especially with regard to the levying of taxes. When Whig politicians forced William and Mary to accept a Declaration of Rights in 1689, they strengthened the powers of the House of Commons at the expense of the Crown.

Emulating the English Whigs, the leaders of the American representative assemblies established the same committees that existed in the House of Commons, such as those on rights and privileges. They insisted on the assemblies' authority to levy taxes and demanded a position of constitutional equality with the royal or proprietary governor. Gradually, colonial leaders won partial control of patronage and the budget, angering imperial bureaucrats and absentee proprietors. "The people in power in America," complained the proprietor William Penn during a struggle with the Pennsylvania Assembly, "think nothing taller than themselves but the Trees."

The American political system remained more elitist than democratic. Although most property-owning white adult men had the right to vote after 1700, in some colonies—Virginia and South Carolina, for example—only men of considerable wealth and status stood for election. By the 1750s seven members of the Lee family, representing five counties, sat in the Virginia House of Burgesses and—along with members of other powerful Virginia families, such as the Byrds, Randolphs, and Carters—dominated its major committees.

Similar family dynasties and alliances appeared in the northern colonies (see Figure 3.3). In New England,

the children and grandchildren of the original Puritans had intermarried and formed a core of political leaders. "Go into every village in New England," John Adams said in 1765, "and you will find that the office of justice of the peace, and even the place of representative, have generally descended from generation to generation, in three or four families at most." Marriage ties created powerful political networks. A European traveler noted that the political leaders in New Brunswick, New Jersey, were "General White, Colonel Bayard, and Judge Patterson—all these families are related and live in close contact."

Although the royal governors remained powerful, dispensing patronage and land grants, political authority came increasingly to reside in local leaders and the assemblies in which they sat. Most assemblymen had first been elected to office as town selectmen, county justices of the peace, or officers in the militia and could count on local support to resist governors or royal bureaucrats. These self-confident American politicians used the "power of the purse"—their control of taxation and revenue—to prevent the implementation of unpopular imperial policies. In Massachusetts during the 1720s, for example, the assembly refused repeatedly to obey the king's instructions to provide a permanent salary for the royal governor and, adding insult to injury, refused to pay even a yearly stipend to Governor Shute as long as he continued to press the issue.

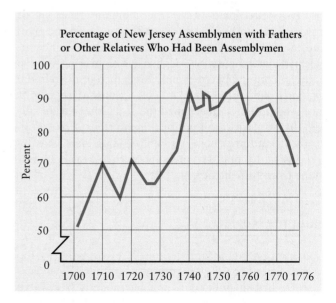

FIGURE 3.3

Family Connections and Political Power
By the 1750s nearly every member of the New Jersey assembly came from a family with a history of political leadership, clear testimony to the emergence of an experienced governing elite in the colonies.

Like Shute, most royal governors lacked the political clout to impose controversial policies on the powerful assemblies. And neither governors nor assemblies had the power to impose unpopular edicts on the people. The crowd actions that overthrew the Dominion of New England in 1689 were a regular part of political life in both England and America and were used to achieve social and economic aims. To uphold community values, for example, a mob in New York closed houses of prostitution, and one in Salem, Massachusetts, ran people with infectious diseases out of town. In Boston during Queen Anne's War (1702–1713), hungry artisans and laborers rioted to prevent merchants from exporting much-needed grain. A generation later in New Jersey, farmers closed down the law courts to prevent proprietary claimants from seizing disputed lands. In New England, lumbermen attacked the king's Surveyors of the Woods when they sought to reserve certain tall pine trees as masts for the British navy.

Crowds were often outmaneuvered by astute officials who waited for their passion to subside, or they were outlasted by entrepreneurs or land speculators who had money and often law on their side. But mobs were forces to be reckoned with. When officials in Boston sought to restrict the sale of farm produce to a designated public marketplace, a crowd destroyed the building and defied the authorities to arrest them. "If you touch One you shall touch All," an anonymous letter warned Sheriff Edward Winslow, "and we will show you a Hundred Men where you can show one."

This letter made clear the changing relations of power. The expression of popular opinion—in the give-and-take of New England town meetings, in the rum-warmed conviviality of Virginia electioneering, in the political contests between ambitious men in the Middle Colonies, and ultimately in the actions of rebellious mobs—gradually undermined the old authoritarian system. In its place stood political institutions—local governments and provincial assemblies—that were broadly responsive to popular pressure and increasingly immune from British control.

Salutary Neglect

Contributing significantly, though unwittingly, to the rise of American self-government were the policies pursued by British politicians and bureaucrats (see Table 3.5). During the reigns of George I (1714–1727) and George II (1727–1760), royal bureaucrats relaxed their supervision of internal colonial affairs, focusing instead on defense and trade. Two generations later the eminent British political philosopher Edmund Burke would praise this strategy of mild rule as one of "salutary neglect," a mercantilist strategy that Burke believed had

contributed to the colonies' wealth and population growth.

Sir Robert Walpole. Salutary neglect was a by-product of the political system developed by Sir Robert Walpole, leader of the Whigs in the House of Commons, who served as the king's chief minister between 1720 and 1742. By strategically dispensing appointments, pensions, and gifts, Walpole won parliamentary support for his policies, transforming the formerly antagonistic relationship between king and Parliament into one of harmonious cooperation. In effect, he governed in the monarch's name but with Parliament's consent.

Walpole's tactics offended some members of Parliament. His chief opponents, who called themselves Real Whigs, argued that by using patronage and bribery to create a strong *Court* (or *Crown*) *party*, he had betrayed the constitutional monarchy established by the Glorious Revolution of 1688. Other critics, organized in a loose *Country party* of landed gentlemen, celebrated the independence of the individual members of Parliament. They condemned Walpole's close ties with merchants and financial institutions such as the Bank of England and his creation of a large national debt, warning that high taxes, a bloated royal bureaucracy, and a standing army threatened the liberties of the people.

American Real Whigs. The arguments of the Real Whigs and the Country party appealed to Americans who wanted to preserve the hard-won powers of the provincial assemblies. In their eyes, the royal governors in America still had too much arbitrary power: they could veto legislation and use land grants and political appointments to influence voting in the assemblies. "By increasing the number of officers dependent on the Crown," a writer in the Boston *Weekly Newsletter*

TABLE 3.5

English Monarchs, 1660–1760

	Dates of Reign	Family/Dynasty of Origin
Charles II	1660–1685	Stuart
James II	1685–1688	Stuart
Mary II and William III	1689–1694 / 1689–1702	Stuart / House of Orange
Anne	1702–1714	Stuart
George I	1714–1727	House of Hanover
George II	1727–1760	House of Hanover

Sir Robert Walpole, the King's Minister
Walpole (left) offers advice to the Speaker of the House of Commons. A brilliant tactical politician, Walpole used patronage to command a majority in the Commons. By looking out for the financial interests of George I and George II—the German-speaking monarchs from the duchy of Hanover—he won their support as well. Walpole's personal motto, "let sleeping dogs lie," helps to explain his colonial policy of salutary neglect. (© National Trust Photographic Library/John Hammond)

charged, the royal governor sought to destroy "the liberties of the people." Such rhetoric was excessive. Few governors could actually wield despotic power, but the accusation nevertheless stirred public anxiety.

Even as Walpole's political tactics were alarming Americans, his patronage policies were undermining the royal bureaucracy in America. His ministers filled colonial posts with mediocre officials who had good political connections and whose main goal was not to advance imperial policies but to enrich themselves. In New York, for example, William Cosby became governor during the 1730s primarily because his wife was related to Lord Halifax, an influential aristocrat. Cosby was hungry for money, and his salary demands and selling of offices threw the province into political chaos for a decade. His successor, George Clinton, appointed

through a family connection with the duke of Newcastle (Walpole's chief political manager), lacked the will or political acumen to uphold imperial interests. In 1744, for example, he cautioned his superiors against imposing a stamp tax, warning that "the people in North America are quite strangers to any Duty but such as they raise themselves." Rather than challenging this outlook, Clinton simply accepted it as a fact of political life (see American Voices, page 98).

Patronage also weakened the Board of Trade as Walpole and Newcastle packed it with their supporters in Parliament. These mediocre *placemen* (so called because they did little work but merely occupied a "place") weakened the morale of capable imperial officials. Governor Gabriel Johnson went to North Carolina in the 1730s as a potential reformer determined to "make a mighty change in the face of affairs" by curbing the power of the assembly, but he soon became discouraged by the lack of support at home. Like other imperial officials during the era of salutary neglect, he became a cautious governor, deciding "to do nothing which can be reasonably blamed, and leave the rest to time, and a new set of inhabitants."

Thus Walpole's political strategy weakened imperial rule in America in three different ways. First, his support for a merchant-run empire based on trade inhibited forceful imperial rule, allowing the "rise of the assembly" in America. Second, his corrupt domestic policies persuaded American Real Whigs that British rule posed a threat to their political liberties, weakening respect for royal governors. Third—and most directly—his patronage system weakened the royal bureaucracy in America. Salutary neglect did not "cause" Americans to seek independence; in fact, in the short run mild rule actually strengthened the colonists' allegiance to Britain (as did the increasing popularity of British goods and culture). But the legislative autonomy allowed by salutary neglect did encourage Americans to expect a position of political equality within the empire and eventually to claim it.

Consolidating the Mercantile System

Beginning in the 1730s Walpole's ministry did act decisively in protecting British commercial interests in America, both from foreign military threats and American economic competition. One major initiative was to provide a subsidy for the new colony of Georgia.

The Founding of Georgia. In the early 1730s General James Oglethorpe and a group of social reformers influenced by the Enlightenment (see Chapter 4) successfully petitioned King George II for land south of the Carolinas. They named the new colony Georgia (in honor of the king) and planned it as a refuge for Britain's poor.

Governor George Clinton

The Waning of British Authority

Authority has to be exercised firmly to command respect. Lax administration in London and weak officials in America opened the way for colonial assemblies to defy imperial policy. In a letter to the Lords of Trade written in 1742, Governor Clinton confesses his inability to control the provincial New York Assembly.

My Lords,

I have in my former letters inform'd Your Lordships what Incroachments the Assemblys of this province have from time to time made on His Majesty's Prerogative & Authority in this Province in drawing an absolute dependence of all the Officers upon them for their Saleries & Reward of their services, & by their taking in effect the Nomination to all Officers. . . .

1stly, That the Assembly refuse to admit of any amendment to any money bill, in any part of the Bill; so that the Bill must pass as it comes from the Assembly, or all the Supplies granted for the support of Government, & the most urgent services must be lost.

2ndly, It appears that they take the Payment of the [military] Forces, passing of Muster Rolls into their own hands by naming the Commissaries for those purposes in the Act.

3rdly, They by granting the Saleries to the Officers personally by name & not to the Officer for the time being, intimate that if any person be appointed to any Office his Salery must depend upon their approbation of the Appointment . . . .

I must now refer it to Your Lordships' consideration whether it be not high time to put a stop to these usurpations of the Assembly on His Majesty's Authority in this Province and for that purpose may it not be proper that His Majesty signify his Disallowance of the Act at least for the payment of Saleries.

Source: E. B. O'Callaghan, ed., *Documents Relative to the Colonial History of the State of New York* (Albany, 1860–).

Envisioning a society of small farms worked by independent landowners and white indentured servants, the trustees of Georgia limited most land grants to 500 acres and, unlike all other British colonies, outlawed slavery.

Walpole provided Georgia with a subsidy from Parliament, not because he shared the founders' vision, but because he wished to protect the increasingly valuable rice colony of South Carolina from attack from Spanish Florida. Spain had long resented the British presence in Carolina and was outraged by the expansion into Georgia, where Spanish Jesuits and Franciscans had established Indian missions. Responding to Spanish threats, Walpole dispatched a regiment of troops to Georgia in 1737 and appointed Oglethorpe commander in chief of all military forces in Georgia and South Carolina. Simultaneously, merchant interests in Parliament formed an alliance with the Georgia trustees to push for an aggressive anti-Spanish policy. After the Treaty of Utrecht in 1713 British merchants had steadily increased their trade in slaves and manufactured goods to Spain's American colonies, eventually controlling two-thirds of their overseas trade. Spanish officials began to resist this commercial imperialism, much of it illegal, so the merchants wanted their government to go to war.

War with Spain. In 1739 Spanish naval forces sparked the so-called War of Jenkins' Ear by physically mutilating Robert Jenkins, an English sea captain who was trading illegally with the Spanish West Indies. Britain used this provocation to begin the first significant military conflict in America in a generation. In 1740 British regulars commanded by Governor Oglethorpe, together with provincial troops from South Carolina and Georgia and some Indian allies, launched an unsuccessful expedition against St. Augustine, which was defended by Spanish soldiers and escaped African slaves. Later that year the governors of the other mainland colonies raised 2,500 volunteers, who joined a British naval force in an assault on the Spanish seaport of Cartagena in present-day Colombia. The attack failed, and instead of enriching themselves with Spanish booty, hundreds of colonial troops died of tropical diseases.

The War of Jenkins' Ear became part of a general European conflict, the War of the Austrian Succession (1740–1748). This struggle pitted Britain and its traditional ally, Austria, against Spain, France, and Prussia. Although the British and French navies clashed in the West Indies, the long frontier between the British colonies and French Canada remained calm. Then, in 1745, more than 3,000 New England militiamen, supported by a British naval squadron, captured the powerful French naval fortress of Louisbourg on Cape Breton Island near the mouth of the St. Lawrence River; the fort surrendered without a fight.

The Treaty of Aix-la-Chapelle, which ended the war in 1748, mandated the return of all captured territory in

North America, and this bitterly disappointed the New England provinces. Yet the war secured the territorial integrity of Georgia by reaffirming British military superiority in the region. British merchants continued to expand their commerce within the Spanish empire.

The Politics of Mercantilism. The expansion of British commerce that had opened the way to the era of salutary neglect ultimately brought it to a close. As American economic growth threatened various British interests, pressure mounted in England to assert greater administrative control over the colonies. In general, mercantilist policy called for colonies to produce only agricultural goods and raw materials, reserving the more profitable provision of manufactured goods and commercial services for artisans and merchants in the home country. Parliament implemented this policy by enacting the Woolens Act of 1699 and the Hat Act of 1732, which prohibited the intercolonial sale of American-produced textiles and hats, and the Iron Act of 1750, which allowed the export of pig iron to England but banned new iron-working forges and mills in the colonies.

The Navigation Acts, however, had a major loophole. By allowing Americans to own ships and transport goods, they enabled colonial merchants to gain control of 95 percent of the commerce between the mainland and the West Indies. American merchant houses also carried three-quarters of the manufactures shipped across the Atlantic from London and Bristol. Quite unexpectedly, British mercantilism had created a dynamic and wealthy community of colonial merchants.

The Molasses Act. American enterprise eventually clashed with the powerful British interests. By the 1720s the rapidly growing mainland settlements were producing more flour, fish, and barrels than the British sugar islands had use for, and so colonial merchants began to sell them in the French West Indies. These inexpensive foodstuffs and supplies helped French planters produce low-cost sugar and control the competitive European market. American rum distillers imported cheap French molasses, cutting off another market for British sugar products. By the 1730s the British sugar industry was on the verge of collapse.

British sugar producers petitioned Parliament for help and won passage of the Molasses Act of 1733. This act permitted the mainland colonies to export fish and farm products to the French islands but placed a high tariff (6 pennies per gallon) on molasses imported from non-British colonies. Parliament expected the act to benefit British planters by making their prices competitive.

American merchants and public officials strongly protested the Molasses Act, arguing not only that it would cut farm exports and cripple their distilling industry but also that the resulting loss of revenues would make it more difficult for colonists to purchase British goods. When Parliament ignored their protests, American merchants simply refused to obey the act, importing French molasses and bribing customs officials to ignore the new tax. Fortunately for the Americans, sugar prices rose in the mid-1730s, quieting the concerns of the British planters, so that the act was never enforced and the Royal Customs Service collected only a pittance. But the act foreshadowed a new era of imperial control.

Currency and Trade. The financial policies of the provincial assemblies also troubled imperial officials. Because American merchants sent most of the bullion and bills of exchange from the West Indian trade to Britain to pay for manufactures, the colonists lacked an adequate amount of currency. To create a domestic money supply, the assemblies of ten colonies established land banks, which lent money. Farmers gave the banks a mortgage on their land (hence the term *land bank*) and received loans in the form of paper currency. This creative system of finance stimulated both trade and investment by providing ordinary people with a medium of exchange and landowners with money to invest in equipment.

In some colonies the misuse of paper currency created conflicts with merchants, both British and American. The Rhode Island assembly paid its expenses not by levying taxes but by printing paper money (not backed by land mortgages), producing a severely depreciated currency. Eventually a Rhode Island bill with a face value of £10 would buy only £5 worth of goods. Creditors, many of them British merchants, rightly complained that they were being financially harmed because Rhode Islanders could pay off old debts with new, depreciated currency.

Because Rhode Island was a small colony and did not have a royal governor, British officials tolerated this fiscal abuse. But when Massachusetts tried to issue paper currency in 1740, the British government intervened, strongly supporting Governor Belcher's veto, even though the currency would be backed by a land bank. Then, in 1751, Parliament passed a broad Currency Act that prevented all the New England colonies from establishing new land banks and, with Rhode Island in mind, prohibited the use of public bills of credit to pay private debts. Many British merchants thought such decisive action was long overdue.

Imperial officials were equally distressed by the growing power of the provincial assemblies and seized on the currency issue as a case in point. Charles Townshend of the Board of Trade charged that American assemblies had assumed many of the "ancient and established prerogatives wisely preserved in the Crown." By 1750 many British political and financial leaders were determined to replace salutary neglect with a more rigorous system of imperial control.

Summary

When Charles II was restored to the English throne in 1660, he paid his political and personal debts by bestowing land in America as proprietary colonies. The Carolina colony was given to a group of aristocrats. New York, conquered from the Dutch in 1664, fell to Charles's brother James, duke of York. Pennsylvania was awarded to William Penn. However, Charles adopted new mercantilist policies, securing the enactment of Navigation Acts, which tightly regulated colonial exports and imports. In 1685, the new king, James II, tried to impose tighter political controls as well, abolishing the existing charters of the northern mainland colonies and creating the Dominion of New England. The Glorious Revolution of 1688 cost James his throne, and revolts in Boston, New York, and Maryland helped secure the restoration of the colonists' traditional rights and institutions.

The South Atlantic system, based on the West Indian sugar trade, laid the foundation for England's wealth and power. To work the sugar plantations of the West Indies and Brazil, millions of Africans were forced into slavery and premature death. In Virginia, where Africans mainly raised tobacco and the conditions of servitude were less severe, the number of black laborers grew dramatically through importation and natural increase. In North America, the South Atlantic system brought great profits to white planters, the creation of African-American communities, and prosperity for northern seaports, merchants, and farmers.

The Treaty of Utrecht (1713) ushered in a generation of peace among the European powers in North America, leaving the British colonies free to develop their social and political institutions. Aided by the unofficial British policy of salutary neglect, American political leaders strengthened the power of the provincial assemblies, which were controlled by the elite but responsive to the views of ordinary people. After 1730 pressure from British interests prompted greater imperial control of American affairs.

In 1733, alarmed by the decline of the British sugar industry because of colonial trade with the French West Indies, the British passed the Molasses Act, again tightening mercantilist controls on colonial trade. Additional legislation restricting manufacturing in the colonies and regulating their financial policies signaled that by 1750 the era of salutary neglect was rapidly coming to an end.

TIMELINE

1651	First Navigation Act Barbados becomes sugar island
1660	Restoration of Charles II
1660s	Virginia moves toward slave system New Navigation Acts
1663	Carolina proprietorship granted
1664	New Netherland captured; becomes New York
1669	Fundamental Constitution of Carolina
1681	William Penn founds Pennsylvania
1685	James II becomes king of England
1685–1689	Dominion of New England
1688	Glorious Revolution
1689	Rebellions in Massachusetts, Maryland, and New York
1689–1702	Mary II and William III govern England
1689–1713	Intermittent war in Europe and America
1696	Board of Trade created
1699	Woolens Act
1705	Virginia statute defines slavery
1713	Treaty of Utrecht
1714–1750	British policy of "salutary neglect" Rise of American assemblies British "reexport" trade in sugar and tobacco Dahomey becomes "slaving" state
1718	Spanish missions and garrison in Texas
1720–1742	Sir Robert Walpole chief minister
1720–1750	Black natural increase in Chesapeake African-American society created Rice exports from Carolina soar Africans in Carolina create Gullah language Planter aristocracy in southern colonies Expansion of seaport cities on mainland
1732–1733	Georgia colony chartered; Spain protests Hat Act and Molasses Act
1739	Florida governor encourages slave desertions Stono rebellion War of Jenkins' Ear
1740	Veto of Massachusetts land bank
1740–1748	War of the Austrian Succession
1750	Iron Act
1751	Currency Act

★   ★   ★

BIBLIOGRAPHY

The best short overview of England's empire is Michael Kammen, *Empire and Interest: The American Colonies and the Politics of Mercantilism* (1970), but see also Alison Olson, *Making the Empire Work: London and American Interest Groups, 1690–1790*. On Africa, see Paul Bohannan and Philip Curtin, *Africa and the Africans*, 3d ed. (1988). For the mingling of cultures in Virginia, read Mechel Sobel, *The World They Made Together* (1987).

The Politics of Empire

Robert Bliss, *Revolution and Empire: English Politics and the American Colonies in the Seventeenth Century* (1990), explores the impact of the Puritan Revolution, whereas Jack M. Sosin, *English America and the Restoration Monarchy of Charles II: Transatlantic Politics, Commerce, and Kinship* (1980), does the same for the restored king. See also Stephen S. Webb, *1676: The End of American Independence* (1984). For the events of 1688–1689 see David S. Lovejoy, *The Glorious Revolution in America* (1972). More specific studies include Jack M. Sosin, *English America and the Revolution of 1688: Royal Administration and the Structure of Provincial Government* (1982), and Lois Green Carr and David W. Jordan, *Maryland's Revolution of Government, 1689–1692* (1974). Ethnic tension in New York can be traced in Robert C. Ritchie, *The Duke's Province: Politics and Society in New York, 1660–1691* (1977); Thomas J. Archdeacon, *New York City, 1664–1710: Conquest and Change* (1976); Donna Merwick, *Possessing Albany, 1630–1710: The Dutch and English Experiences* (1990); and Joyce Goodfriend, *Before the Melting Pot: Society and Culture in Colonial New York City, 1664–1730* (1992). Jack M. Sosin, *English America and Imperial Inconstancy: The Rise of Provincial Autonomy, 1696–1715* (1985), outlines the new imperial system.

The Imperial Slave Economy

For the African background, see John Thornton, *Africa and Africans in the Making of the Atlantic World, 1400–1680* (1992), and Richard Olaniyan, *African History and Culture* (1982). Specialized studies of forced African migration include Philip Curtin, *The Atlantic Slave Trade: A Census* (1969); Paul Lovejoy, ed., *Africans in Bondage: Studies in Slavery and the Slave Trade* (1986); James A. Rawley, *The Transatlantic Slave Trade* (1981); Joseph E. Inikori and Stanley L. Engerman, eds., *The Atlantic Slave Trade* (1992), and Barbara L. Solow, ed., *Slavery and the Rise of the Atlantic System* (1991).

Richard S. Dunn, *Sugar and Slaves: The Rise of the Planter Class in the English West Indies, 1624–1713* (1972), provides a graphic portrait of the brutal slave-based economy, whereas Sidney W. Mintz, *Sweetness and Power: The Place of Sugar in Modern History* (1985), explores the impact of its major crop. Winthrop D. Jordan, *White over Black, 1550–1812* (1968), remains the best account of Virginia's decision for slavery. T. H. Breen and Stephen Innes, *"Myne Owne Ground": Race and Freedom on Virginia's Eastern Shore, 1640–1676* (1980), closely examines the lives of the first slaves and free blacks. For the creation of African-American society see Allan Kulikoff, *Tobacco and Slaves: Southern Cultures in the Chesapeake, 1680–1800* (1986); Daniel C. Littlefield, *Rice and Slaves: Ethnicity and the Slave Trade in Colonial South Carolina* (1981); and Peter H. Wood, *Black Majority: Negroes in Colonial South Carolina through the Stono Rebellion* (1974). See also Orlando Patterson, *Slavery and Social Death: A Comparative Study* (1982); Richard Price, ed., *Maroon Societies: Rebel Slave Communities in the Americas* (1973); and Ira Berlin and Philip D. Morgan, eds., *Cultivation and Culture: Labor and the Shaping of Slave Life in the Americas* (1992).

On white society in the South, see Daniel Blake Smith, *Inside the Great House: Planter Family Life in Eighteenth-Century Chesapeake Society* (1980); Rhys Isaac, *The Transformation of Virginia, 1740–1790* (1982); Timothy H. Breen, *Tobacco Culture* (1985); and the fine older study by Charles Sydnor, *American Revolutionaries in the Making: Political Practices in Washington's Virginia* (1952). Urban society and trade are explored in Gary B. Nash, *The Urban Crucible* (1979); Gary M. Walton and James F. Shephard, *The Economic Rise of Early America* (1979); and Christine L. Heyrman, *Commerce and Culture: The Maritime Communities of Colonial Massachusetts, 1690–1750* (1984). See also Marcus Rediker, *Between the Devil and the Deep Blue Sea: Merchant Seamen, Pirates, and the Anglo-American Maritime World, 1700–1750* (1987).

The New Politics of Empire

The appearance of a distinctive American polity is traced in Jack P. Greene, *The Quest for Power: The Lower Houses of Assembly in the Southern Royal Colonies, 1689–1776* (1963); Bernard Bailyn, *The Origins of American Politics* (1968); Patricia U. Bonomi, *A Factious People: Politics and Society in Colonial New York* (1971); A. Roger Ekirch, *"Poor Carolina": Politics and Society in Colonial North Carolina, 1729–1776* (1981); and Richard Bushman, *King and People in Provincial Massachusetts* (1985). John Schutz, *William Shirley* (1961), shows how a competent colonial governor wielded power, whereas Thomas C. Barrow, *Trade and Empire: The British Customs Service in Colonial America, 1660–1775* (1967), and Alison G. Olson, *Anglo-American Politics, 1660–1775* (1973), explore various aspects of British mercantilism.

Douglas E. Leach, *Roots of Conflict: British Armed Forces and Colonial Americans, 1677–1763* (1986), and Howard H. Peckham, *The Colonial Wars, 1689–1762* (1964), cover the diplomatic and military conflicts of the period, but these Anglo-American perspectives should be balanced by David J. Weber, *The Spanish Frontier in North America* (1992).

An English Country House

Imported English books and art, such as this painting of the English gentry at play, defined cultural standards for many upper-class Americans. (Colonial Williamsburg Foundation)

CHAPTER 4

Growth and Crisis in American Society

1720–1765

★　　　★　　　★

Britain's North American settlements grew spectacularly, from about 400,000 residents in 1720 to nearly 2 million by 1765. Widespread ownership of land made American farming communities very different from peasant villages in Europe, but throughout British North America old family values remained intact: men owned most of the property, and women were accorded an inferior legal and social position.

Regional differences among the northern colonies grew more pronounced. New England continued to be dominated by Puritans and freeholding farm families. A population explosion and economic hardship in Europe prompted a massive migration of Germans and Scots-Irish to the mid-Atlantic colonies, giving them greater ethnic and religious diversity than was the case in New England and, indeed, any society in Western Europe. The resulting cultural and religious tensions were offset, at least to a degree, by economic prosperity, resulting from a growing international trade in wheat.

Before 1720 most Americans lived much simpler lives than Europeans, because they were unable to re-create the cultural sophistication of their homelands. After 1720 mainland settlers began participating in the intellectual and religious movements of the larger world. Many educated Americans embraced the ideas of the European Enlightenment, or Age of Reason. Far more residents, of African as well as European ancestry, were swept up in a new wave of religious enthusiasm that derived from European Pietism.

Americans also were swept up in the Great War for Empire, known in the colonies as the French and Indian War, which gave Britain control of all of eastern North America, and in the great expansion of trade sparked by the early stages of the British Industrial Revolution. The colonists sent huge quantities of tobacco, rice, and wheat to European markets and, after 1750, consumed 15 to 20 percent of all British exports. Now larger, with

Freehold Society in New England

Even though their religious vision faltered after a century in America, the Puritans achieved many of their social goals. In 1720 New England remained a predominantly rural society in which most men owned their own land, farming it with the aid of their dependent wives and children. By 1750, however, the population threatened to outstrip the supply of arable land and pastureland, posing a severe challenge to the freehold ideal.

Farm Families: Women's Place

In America as in Europe, law and custom elevated men over women. Men claimed not only political power in the state but also, particularly in New England, domestic authority within the family. As the Reverend Benjamin Wadsworth of Boston advised women in his pamphlet *The Well-Ordered Family* (1712), it made no difference if they were richer, more intelligent, or of higher social status than their husbands: "Since he is thy Husband, God has made him the head and set him above thee." Therefore, Wadsworth concluded, it is "thy duty to love and reverence him."

All through their lives women had it impressed on them that theirs was a subordinate role. Small girls watched their mothers defer to their fathers. As they grew to adulthood, they learned that their marriage portions would be different from and smaller than those of their brothers: they would receive not land but money, livestock, or household goods. In a typical will, Ebenezer Chittendon of Guilford, Connecticut, left all his land to his sons, decreeing that "Each Daughter have half so much as Each Son, one half in money and the other half in Cattle."

In rural New England—indeed, throughout the colonies—a woman's place was as a dutiful daughter to her father and a helpmeet (helpmate) to her husband,

The Character of Family Life: The Cheneys
Life in a large early American family was very different from that in a small modern one. Mrs. Cheney's face shows the rigors of having borne ten children, a task that occupied her entire adult life. Her children grew up with many older (or younger) siblings, which blurred differences between the generations.

who tilled the land and represented the family in the community. Some farmwives fulfilled these roles in an exemplary fashion. They spun thread and yarn from flax or wool and wove it into shirts and gowns; knitted sweaters and stockings; made candles and soap; learned the difficult arts of turning milk into butter and cheese, brewing malt into beer, and preserving meats; and mastered dozens of other productive household tasks.

The community lavished praise on these "notable" women, setting them up as models. "I have a great longing desire to be very notable," one woman wrote upon her marriage. Women who lacked skills felt their shortcomings keenly, although their labor was no less crucial to the rural household economy. As Abigail Hyde, a New England farmwife, confessed in a letter, "The conviction of my deficiencies as a mother is overwhelming."

Bearing and raising children was not an easy task. Most women in the northern colonies married in their early twenties and bore five to seven children before the onset of menopause in their early forties. There were no drugs to ease the pain of labor and no antibacterial medications to prevent infections. Yet most women survived numerous childbirths, helped by midwives—women who prepared them emotionally for the experience of giving birth, stayed with them during labor, and attended to the needs of the newborn and the mother. A large family sapped a woman's emotional strength and kept her energies focused on domestic activities. For about twenty of her most active years a woman was either pregnant or breast-feeding. Sarah Ripley Stearns, a Massachusetts farmwife, explained that she had no time for religious activities because "the care of my Babes takes up so large a portion of my time and attention."

Over time, the shrinking size of farms prompted many couples to choose to have fewer children. After 1750 families in long-settled communities such as Andover, Massachusetts, had an average of only four children. Smaller families meant that women had fewer mouths to feed, fewer clothes to wash and mend, and more time to pursue other tasks. Susan Huntington of Boston, who had the good fortune to be rich, spent more time in "the care & culture of children, and the perusal of necessary books, including the scriptures." With fewer children, ordinary farm women could make extra yarn, cloth, or cheese to exchange with their neighbors or sell to shopkeepers, thus enhancing the family's standard of living. (After 1770 some would become wage workers in a new merchant-run putting-out system, stitching the soft upper parts of women's shoes.)

But women's participation in the daily affairs of life was limited by cultural rules. For example, Puritan men were reluctant to have their wives work in the fields. "Women in New England," Timothy Dwight reported approvingly, "are employed only in and about the house and in the proper business of the sex." Yet strong-

Tavern Culture
By the eighteenth century, many taverns were run by women, such as this "Charming Patroness," who needed all her charm to deal with her raucous clientele. It was in taverns, declared puritanical John Adams, that "diseases, vicious habits, bastards, and legislators are frequently begotten."

minded wives often defied their husbands and assumed authority in the household or over their own lives.

One such woman was Hannah Heaton of North Haven, Connecticut, a devout Puritan wife who reproved her husband's family for "wicked practices" and left his church. Like other Puritan women, Heaton had taken advantage of the Protestant emphasis on reading the Bible and had learned to read and write. She chafed under the restrictions in most Congregational churches that denied women the opportunity of voting or even speaking. Like Anne Hutchinson (see Chapter 2), Heaton questioned the authority of her minister, thinking him unconverted and a "blind guide." Eventually she joined an evangelical congregation that, like more radical Protestant churches, gave women an active role in religious matters. For example, Quakers believed "that women can be called to the ministry as well as men," as a French visitor noted, and Baptists in Rhode Island permitted women to vote on church affairs. Yet these differences among churches were only variations on the general theme of female subordination. Despite their increasing freedom from child-rearing most women—not only in New England but also in other regions of British America—remained in an inferior position, their lives tightly bound by a web of laws, cultural expectations, and religious restrictions.

Farm Property: Inheritance

By contrast white American men had escaped many traditional constraints. Whereas in England the nobility and the gentry owned 75 percent of the arable land and had it farmed by servants, tenants, and wage laborers, in the northern mainland colonies 70 percent of the settled land was owned by yeomen freeholders. "The hope of having land of their own & becoming independent of Landlords is what chiefly induces people into America," an official reported in the 1730s.

Not that it was easy to get hold of even a small farm in the colonies. Children from poor families often began their working lives as indentured servants. Their parents, unable to provide them with work or food, bound them out to farmers who could. Young men ended their indentures at age eighteen or twenty-one with many farming skills but without land. For ten or

twenty years they struggled as wage-earning farm laborers or tenants to save enough to buy a few acres of their own. And if they failed to acquire enough property to leave a landed estate, their children would have to repeat the slow climb up the agricultural ladder: from servant, to laborer, to tenant, to freeholder.

Having learned the importance of a landed inheritance from bitter experience in Europe, most yeomen farmers assumed responsibility for the economic fate of their children. As their sons and daughters reached marriageable age—usually twenty-three to twenty-five—these farmers provided them with a *marriage portion* consisting of land, livestock, and sometimes farm equipment. The marriage portion repaid children for their labor on the parents' farm and ensured their future loyalty. Parents knew they would need help in their old age (there were no pension or social security systems). To guarantee that they would not be left helpless, some farmers kept legal title to the land until they died.

Because parents began to transfer their hard-earned land and goods to their children upon marriage, a family's future prosperity depended on a wise choice of marriage partners. Yeomen parents usually decided whom their children would marry. Normally, children had the right to refuse an unacceptable match, but they did not have the luxury of "falling in love" with whomever they pleased.

Once married, a woman had fewer property rights than did her husband and children. A new bride gave legal ownership of all her personal property to her husband. Any land a woman might possess fell under the

Lady Undressing for a Bath, circa 1730–1740
This delightful painting attributed to Gerardus Duyckinck captures a moment of intimacy between an unknown but obviously well-to-do American couple. Many marriages were "arranged" but grew into love matches. Others began with strong emotional bonds that withered over time. One affluent Philadelphia woman found herself in a perfect romantic match, writing to her husband: "Our Hearts have been united from the first, in so firm, so strong, so sweet an affection, that words are incapable of setting it forth."

control of her husband. English and colonial law compensated married women for this loss of property by giving them *dower rights*. When a woman's husband died, she had the right to use a third of the family's estate during her lifetime. If she remarried, however, she forfeited this right. And she could not sell her one-third interest, for it legally belonged to her children; her rights were restricted to use. The wife's property rights were subordinated to those of the family "line," which stretched, through the children, across the generations.

To preserve the ideal of a freehold society based on family property, American farmers followed a number of strategies. Some fathers used the traditional English legal device of *entail* by willing the farm to a male child and specifying that it remain undivided and in the family forever. For example, Ebenezer Perry of Barnstable, Massachusetts, willed his land to his son, Ebenezer, Jr., stipulating that it devolve in turn on the younger Ebenezer's "eldest son surviving and so on to the male heirs of his body lawfully begotten forever."

Other farm parents in New England used a *stem family* system to preserve a freehold estate. They chose a married son or son-in-law to work the farm with them and he became the "stem," or center, of the entire family, inheriting the farm after the father's death. Still other parents wrote wills that gave the family farm to the oldest son but required that he pay money or goods to the younger children. All these devices—entail, the stem system, and legally binding wills—favored one son to keep the family farm intact across the generations. Most parents, however, provided their other children with money, apprenticeship contracts, or frontier tracts to enable them to become freeholders in other communities.

Farmers in New England who wished to give land to all their male children divided their farms, a pattern common among 90 percent of the fathers in Chebacco, Massachusetts. Division could be a risky strategy, because many sons ended up with too little land to provide a comfortable living. A better solution, chosen by other equality-minded farmers, was to move their young families to frontier regions, where life was hard but land was cheap and abundant. "The Squire's House stands on the Bank of the Susquehannah," a traveler named Philip Fithian reported from the Pennsylvania backcountry in the late colonial period. "He tells me that he will be able to settle all his sons and his fair Daughter Betsy on the Fat of the Earth."

The historic accomplishment of New England farmers was the creation of communities composed of independent property owners. A French visitor remarked that the sense of personal worth and dignity in this rural world contrasted sharply with European peasant life. In America he found "men and women whose features are not marked by poverty, by lifelong deprivation of the necessities of life, or by a feeling that they are insignificant subjects and subservient members of society."

The Crisis of Freehold Society

Yet the threat of deprivation was increasing because the number of residents doubled with each generation, mostly as a result of natural increase. The Puritan colonies had about 100,000 people in 1700, 200,000 in 1725, and almost 400,000 by 1750. In long-settled areas, lands that had been ample for the original migrant families had been divided and then subdivided until many parents could no longer provide land for their children. The Reverend Samuel Chandler of Andover, Massachusetts, noted in the 1740s that he had "been much distressed for land for his children," seven of whom were boys. Dispersing the land among so many heirs usually meant a decline in living standards (see Table 4.1). In

TABLE 4.1

Diminishing Property in the Fuller Family, Kent, Connecticut

	Date of Birth	Highest Assessment on Tax List
First Generation		
Joseph Fuller	1699	203 pounds
Second Generation		
Joseph Jr.	1723	42
Zachariah	1725	103
Jeremiah	1728	147
Nathaniel	?	67
Adijah	?	46
Simeon	?	49
Abraham	1737	136
Jacob	1738	59
Isaac	1741	7
	Average:	72 pounds
Third Generation		
Abel	?	40
Abraham, Jr.	?	50
Oliver	1747	50
Daniel	1749	65
Howard	1750	28
Benejah	1757	32
Ephraim	1760	100
John	1760	?
Asahel	1770	48
James	1770	40
Revilo	1770	35
Samuel	?	14
	Average:	42 pounds

Concord, Massachusetts, by the 1750s, about 60 percent of farmers owned less land than their fathers had.

Because parents had less to give their children, they had less control over their children's lives. The system of arranged marriages broke down. Young people moved to newly settled regions or had premarital sex and used pregnancy to win permission to marry. The number of firstborn children conceived before marriage rose spectacularly throughout New England, from about 10 percent in the 1710s to 30 percent in the 1740s and, in some communities, to 40 percent by the 1760s. If these young people had it to do over, they "would do the same again," an Anglican minister observed, "because otherwise they could not obtain their parents' consent to marry."

On the eve of the American Revolution, farm communities in New England responded to the threat to their freehold ideal in three basic ways. First, many towns petitioned the provincial government for assistance. In 1740 Massachusetts farmers unsuccessfully demanded a land bank that, by issuing paper currency, would provide them with loans and stimulate trade. With greater success, they sought new land grants along the frontier. Settlers continually moved inland—into New Hampshire and the future Vermont—hacking new farms out of the virgin forest and creating new communities of freehold farmers.

Second, settlers who remained on the original farmsteads planted different crops. Even before 1750 they had replaced the traditional English crops of wheat and barley (for bread and beer) with a grazing economy based on corn, cattle, and hogs. Corn offered a hardy food for humans, and its abundant leaves furnished feed for cattle and pigs, which provided milk and meat. The physician William Douglass observed in the 1720s that poor people in New England subsisted on "salt pork and Indian beans, with bread of Indian corn meal, and pottage of this meal with milk for breakfast and supper." After 1750 New England farmers raised the output of this mixed-crop grazing economy by planting potatoes, whose high yield offset the disadvantage of smaller farms. Farmers also introduced nutritious English grasses, such as red clover and timothy, to provide forage for their livestock and nitrogen for the depleted soil (though they didn't know the chemistry). These innovative measures not only averted a food shortage but also generated a surplus for export. New England became the major supplier of salted and pickled meat to the West Indies; in 1770 preserved meat accounted for about 5 percent of the value of all exports from the mainland colonies.

Third, to compensate for the reduced size and limited resources of their properties, farm families not only had fewer children but also increased productivity by helping one another. Men lent each other tools, draft animals, and grazing land. Women and children joined other families in spinning yarn, sewing quilts, and shucking corn. Farmers plowed the fields of artisans, who in turn fixed the pots, plows, and furniture brought to them for repair. By sharing labor and goods, every farm—and the entire economy—was able to achieve maximum output at the minimum cost.

This system of economy and exchange—the "household mode of production," as one historian has called it—worked well because New England was a homogeneous, close-knit society. Typically, no money changed hands between relatives or neighbors. Instead, farmers, artisans, and shopkeepers recorded debts and credits in personal account books, and every few years the accounts were "balanced" through the transfer of small amounts of cash. Thus, New England farmers averted a social crisis and preserved their freehold society well into the nineteenth century.

The Mid-Atlantic: Toward a New Society, 1720–1765

The middle colonies—New York, New Jersey, and Pennsylvania—lacked the cultural uniformity of New England, containing instead a mixture of settlers from many European countries with diverse traditions and religions (see Map 4.1). Yet these settlements had more order and purpose than one might think. Strong ethnic ties bound German settlers to one another, as did deep religious loyalties among the members of various churches: Scots-Irish Presbyterians, English and Welsh Quakers, German Lutherans, and Dutch Reformed Protestants. These religious and ethnic ties generated conflicts among cultural groups, as did increasing economic inequality.

MAP 4.1

Ethnic and Racial Diversity, 1775
In 1700 most colonists were English, but by 1775 those of English descent constituted a minority. African-Americans accounted for one-third of the population of the South, while the presence of Germans and Scots-Irish created ethnic and religious diversity in the middle colonies and southern backcountry.

FIGURE 4.1

Population Growth, Wheat Prices, and English Imports in the Middle Colonies

Wheat prices soared in Philadelphia because of demand in the West Indies and Europe. Exports of grain and flour paid for English manufactures, which were imported in large quantities after 1750.

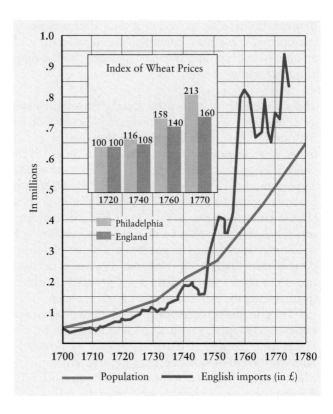

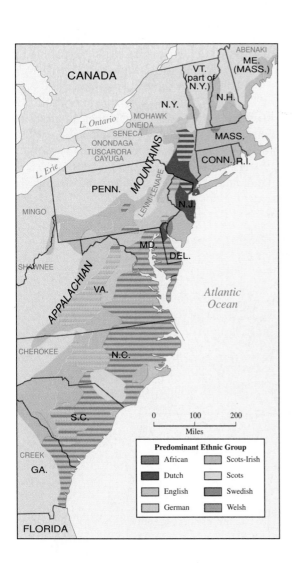

Opportunity and Equality

Pennsylvania, New York, and New Jersey attracted huge numbers of migrants in the eighteenth century, with the combined population rising from 50,000 in 1700 to 120,000 in 1720 and to 350,000 by 1765. An ample supply of fertile land and a long frost-free growing season of about 180 days attracted migrants, who prospered because the population explosion in Western Europe had created a huge demand for wheat, which they were able to supply. Wheat prices doubled in the Atlantic world between 1720 and 1770, and profits from wheat financed the settlement of the region. By 1770 the value of the wheat, corn, flour, and bread shipped from the middle colonies amounted to over 15 percent of all mainland exports (see Figure 4.1).

Many farm families prospered from growing grain, but few became large-scale producers, because preindustrial technology greatly limited output. A worker with a hand sickle could reap only half an acre a day, and if ripe grain was not cut promptly, it sprouted, rendering it useless. The *cradle*, a long-handled scythe with wooden fingers that arranged the wheat for easy collection and binding, was introduced during the 1750s and doubled or tripled the amount a worker could cut. Even so, a family with two adult workers could not easily harvest more than about 15 acres of wheat in a growing season, from which it could thresh perhaps 150 to 180 bushels of grain. After meeting its own needs, the family might sell the surplus for £15, enough to buy salt and sugar, tools, cloth, and perhaps a few acres of new land.

The Emergence of Inequality. Rural Pennsylvania was initially a land of economic equality. In Chester County, for example, the original migrants came with approximately the same resources (see Figure 4.2). In 1693, the poorest 30 percent of the taxpayers owned a substantial 17 percent of the assessed wealth and the top 10 percent controlled only 23 percent. Most families lived in small houses with one or two rooms. Their furniture consisted of a few benches or stools and a bed in a loft. Only the wealthiest families ate off pewter or ceramic plates imported from England or Holland. The great majority consumed their simple fare from wooden *trenchers* (platters) and drank from wooden *noggins* (cups).

The rise of the wheat trade—and the influx of poor settlers—introduced marked social divisions. By the 1760s some farmers had grown wealthy by hiring the poor and using their labor to raise large quantities of wheat for market sale. Others had become successful entrepreneurs, providing newly arrived settlers with land, equipment, goods, and services. These large-scale farmers, rural landlords, speculators, storekeepers, and gristmill operators gradually formed a new class of wealthy agricultural *capitalists*—the owners of productive property. The estate inventories of this economic elite include mahogany tables, four-poster beds, table linen, couches, and imported Dutch dinnerware—all of which testify to growing economic inequality. In the 1760s the richest 10 percent of the Chester County's property-owning families controlled 30 percent of their

communities' assets, while the poorest 30 percent held a mere 6 percent.

Moreover, a new landless class, one with no taxable property, had appeared at the bottom of the social order. In five agricultural towns in New Jersey in the 1760s, half the white men aged eighteen to twenty-five were without land, while in Chester County, Pennsylvania, nearly half of *all* white men were propertyless. Some landless men were the sons of property owners and would eventually inherit at least a part of the family estate. But just as many were Scots-Irish *inmates*, single men or families "such as live in small cottages and have no taxable property, except a cow," as the tax assessor in the Scots-Irish township of Londonderry explained. There was also an "abundance of Poor people" in the predominantly German settlement of Lancaster, Pennsylvania. A merchant noted that they "maintain their Families with great difficulty by day Labour."

These landless Scots-Irish and German migrants hoped to improve their lot by becoming tenants and then landowners, but such goals were either unrealistic or very hard to achieve. Land prices had risen sharply in settled areas with good transportation, and the acquisition of a farmstead was the work of a lifetime. Merchants and artisans took advantage of the ample supply of labor by organizing a putting-out system: they bought wool or flax from some farm families and paid others to spin it into yarn or weave it into cloth. An English traveler reported in the 1760s that hundreds of Pennsylvanians had turned "to manufacture, and live upon a small farm, as in many parts of England." By that time eastern areas of the middle colonies, as well as New England, had become as crowded and socially divided as many regions of rural England.

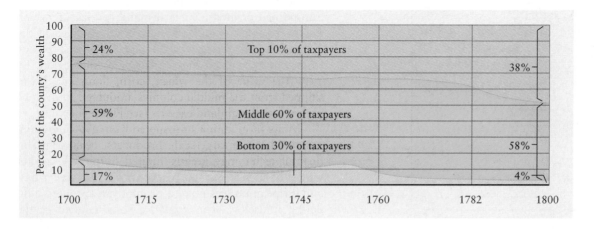

FIGURE 4.2

Increasing Social Inequality in Chester County, Pennsylvania
By renting land and selling goods to a growing population, the county's landed and commercial elite grew rich. Eventually the top tenth of the taxpayers commanded nearly 40 percent of the wealth, far above the paltry 4 percent owned by the poorest 30 percent.

Tenancy on the Hudson Manors. Migrants to New York faced an even more arduous road to land ownership. Long-established Dutch families—the Rensselaers, the Van Cortlandts, the Philipses—still presided over the patroonships created by the Dutch West India Company in the fertile Hudson River Valley (see Map 4.2). The first English governors of New York augmented the ranks of this landowning class by bestowing huge tracts of land on the Livingston, Morris, and Heathcote families. These clans had a stranglehold on the best land and refused to sell an acre of it. They wanted to live like European aristocrats, masters of scores of tenant families.

For that reason, many migrants refused to settle in the Hudson River Valley. In 1714 the manor of Rensselaerswyck had only 82 tenants on hundreds of thousands of acres. But gradually population growth caused a scarcity of freehold land in eastern New York, and more families were forced to accept tenancy leases. To attract tenants, the lords of the manors began to grant long leases and the right to sell (to the next tenant) any improvements made to the property. Thus, Rensselaerswyck had 345 tenants in 1752 and nearly 700 by 1765. With determination, luck, and wheat profits, some tenants saved enough to buy freehold property, but the Hudson River Valley remained primarily a region of tenant farmers, distinct from the predominantly freehold communities in Pennsylvania, New Jersey, and New England.

Even communities of yeomen farm families were increasingly divided by economic interests and class position. In Pennsylvania, gentlemen farmers and commercial middlemen had grown rich whereas German and Scots-Irish inmates still struggled for subsistence. In New England, which lacked a major export crop, many small-scale freeholders had fallen into debt; even the most creative farmers could generate only a limited surplus. Throughout the mainland colonies, smallholding farm families worried about finding enough land to give their children and feared—with good reason—a return to the exploited status of the European peasantry.

Ethnic Diversity

When the Swedish traveler Peter Kalm visited Philadelphia in 1748, he found no fewer than twelve religious denominations, including Anglicans, Quakers, Swedish and German Lutherans, Scots-Irish Presbyterians, and even Roman Catholics. Large communities of German sectarians, such as the Moravians in the Pennsylvania towns of Bethlehem and Nazareth, added to this religious diversity.

The Quaker Experiment. Members of the Society of Friends (Quakers) were the dominant social group in

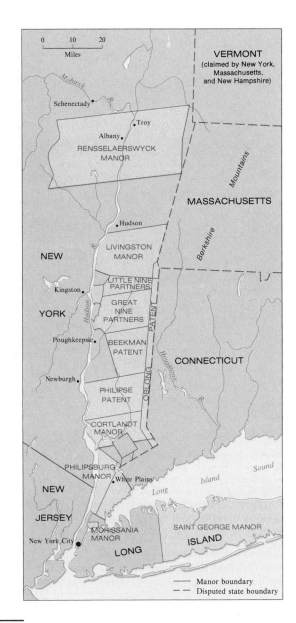

MAP 4.2

The Hudson River Manors
Dutch and English manorial lords dominated the fertile eastern shores of the Hudson River Valley—leasing small farms to German tenant families and refusing to sell land to migrants from overcrowded New England. From this powerful elite emerged Patriot leaders, such as Gouverneur Morris (see *American Lives*, pages 204–205), and influential American families, such as the Roosevelts.

A Quaker Meeting for Worship
Quakers dressed plainly and met in plain, unadorned buildings. They sat in silence, speaking only when inspired by the "inner light." Women spoke frequently and were listened to with respect, an experience that prepared Quaker women to take a leading part in the nineteenth-century women's rights movement. This British work, entitled *Quaker Meeting*, shows an elder (his hat placed temporarily on a peg above his head) exhorting the congregation.

Pennsylvania, at first because they outnumbered the others and later because, despite a huge influx of new migrants after 1720, they retained wealth and influence. Quakers controlled Pennsylvania's representative assembly (established by the proprietor William Penn's Frame of Government) until the 1750s and exercised considerable power in New Jersey.

Quakers had a distinct social ethic. They wore plain clothes without elaborate decoration and refused to defer to their "superiors" by removing their hats. In talking among themselves and with strangers, they used the familiar "thee" and "thou" rather than the more formal "you." Friends refused to use law courts to settle disputes among themselves, relying instead on arbitrators to judge what was "right," not simply what was "legal." Around 1750 some Quakers extended these egalitarian values to their relations with blacks, freeing their own slaves. Indeed, some Quaker meetings not only condemned the institution of slavery but also expelled any members who continued to keep slaves, making Quakers the first religious group to advocate the abolition of slavery.

Quakers were pacifists, and so they avoided war with native Americans. Penn negotiated the first treaty with the Delaware Indians in 1682, and the Pennsylvania government purchased Indian land rather than seizing it by force. These conciliatory policies enabled Pennsylvania to avoid a major Indian war until the 1750s, a record unmatched elsewhere in the British colonies. In diplomacy as in religious matters,

the Quakers' radical social experiment was largely successful and attracted thousands of migrants from eighteenth-century Europe.

The Pennsylvania Germans. Germans came to the middle colonies in a series of waves, fleeing their homeland because of war, religious persecution, and poverty. First to arrive, in 1683, was a group of Mennonites attracted by Penn's pamphlet promising religious freedom. Beginning in 1709, boatloads of impoverished peasants from the Palatine region of western Germany, an area devastated by religious warfare, settled as tenants on Hudson River manors. Then, in the 1720s, continuing religious upheaval and population growth in southwestern Germany and Switzerland stimulated another wave of migrants. "Wages were far better than here," Heinrich Schneebeli reported to his friends in Zurich after an exploratory trip to Pennsylvania, and "one also enjoyed there a free unhindered exercise of religion." Thirty citizens of Zurich immediately asked the authorities for permission to emigrate. Many Germans and Swiss had the resources to pay their own way; they migrated to provide better opportunities for their children. Others signed on as *redemptioners,* a kind of indentured servant, to get to Pennsylvania (see American Voices, page 113).

In 1749, after the War of the Austrian Succession, thousands of Germans and Swiss fled their overcrowded and war-torn homeland for the middle colonies. By 1754, when the outbreak of the Seven Years War (the European component of the Great War

Gottlieb Mittelberger

The Perils of Migration

The lure of ample land and a better life prompted thousands of Germans to endure the hardships of migration, which were described in a book published by Gottlieb Mittelberger in 1750. A Lutheran minister who returned to Germany, Mittelberger viewed America with a critical eye, warning his readers of the difficulties of life in a competitive, pluralistic society.

[The journey from Germany to Pennsylvania via Holland and England] lasts from the beginning of May to the end of October, fully half a year, amid such hardships as no one is able to describe adequately with their misery. Both in Rotterdam and in Amsterdam the people are packed densely, like herrings so to say, in the large sea-vessels. One person receives a place of scarcely 2 feet width and 6 feet length in the bedstead, while many a ship carries four to six hundred souls. . . .

During the journey the ship is full of pitiful signs of distress—smells, fumes, horrors, vomiting, various kinds of sea sickness, fever, dysentery, headaches, heat, constipation, boils, scurvy, cancer, mouth-rot, and similar afflictions, all of them caused by the age and the highly-salted state of the food, especially of the meat, as well as by the very bad and filthy water, which brings about the miserable destruction and death of many. . . . All this misery reaches its climax when in addition to

everything else one must also suffer through two to three days and nights of storm with everyone convinced that the ship with all aboard is bound to sink. In such misery all the people on board pray and cry pitifully together.

Children between the ages of one and seven seldom survive the sea voyage; and parents must often watch their offspring suffer miserably, die, and be thrown into the ocean, from want, hunger, thirst, and the like. I myself, alas, saw such a pitiful fate overtake thirty-two children on board our vessel, all of whom were finally thrown into the sea. Their parents grieve all the more, since their children do not find repose in the earth, but are devoured by the predatory fish of the ocean. It is also worth noting that children who have not had either measles or smallpox usually get them on board the ship and for the most part perish as a result.

When the ships finally arrive in Philadelphia after the long voyage only those are let off who can pay their sea freight or can give good security. The others, who lack the money to pay, have to remain on board until they are purchased and until their purchasers can thus pry them loose from the ship. In this whole process the sick are the worst off, for the healthy are preferred and are more readily paid for. The miserable people who are ill must often still remain at sea and in

sight of the city for another two or three weeks—which in many cases means death. Yet many of them, were they able to pay their debts and to leave the ships at once, might escape with their lives.

Thus let him who wants to earn his piece of bread honestly and in a Christian manner and who can only do this by manual labor in his native country stay *there* rather than come to America.

But the fact that so many still go to America and especially to Pennsylvania is to be blamed on the swindles and persuasions practiced by so-called Newlanders. These thieves of human beings tell their lies to people of various classes and professions, among whom may be found many soldiers, scholars, artists, and artisans. They abduct people from their Princes and Lords and ship them to Rotterdam or Amsterdam for sale. There they get three florins, or one ducat, from the merchant, for each person ten years or older. On the other hand the merchants get from sixty to seventy or eighty florins for such a person in Philadelphia, depending on the debts that said person has incurred on the voyage. . . .

Source: Gottlieb Mittelberger, *Journey to Pennsylvania* (1756), ed. and trans., Oscar Handlin and John Clive (Cambridge, Mass.: Harvard University Press, 1960).

---

for Empire) abruptly halted migration, 37,000 new settlers (of a pre-1776 total of 102,000) had landed in Philadelphia. German settlements soon dominated certain areas of the rich Lancaster plain in Pennsylvania. Other groups moved down the Shenandoah Valley into the western districts of Maryland, Virginia, and the Carolinas. Most of them managed to improve their lives. As the German minister Gottlieb Mittelberger re-

ported from Pennsylvania in the 1750s, "Even in the humblest or poorest houses, no one eats bread without butter or cheese."

These migrants did not seek to create an all-German colony but were content to live in a British-defined political community. This decision reflected their class origins and religious ideology; few came from politically active segments of German society, and many

German Artisanry
German artisans in Pennsylvania, carrying on the traditions of the old country, frequently decorated their furniture with abstract designs and simple folk motifs, such as the rectangular patterns and angels on this chest of drawers.

religious sectarians explicitly rejected political activism. They slid easily into the status of loyal subjects of the German (and German-speaking) Hanoverian king of England, engaging in politics only to protect their religious liberty and property rights. Most Germans, however, sought to guard their linguistic and cultural heritage. A minister in North Carolina admonished his congregation "not to contract any marriages with the English or Irish," explaining that "we owe it to our native country to do our part that German blood and the German language be preserved in America." In fact, most American-born Germans took marriage partners of their own ancestry, spoke to each other and read newspapers in German, and attended church services conducted in German. They also continued German agricultural practices: English visitors to the middle colonies remarked that German women were "always in the fields, meadows, stables, etc. and do not dislike any work whatsoever."

The Scots-Irish. The Scots-Irish made up the largest group of new migrants to British North America, with some 150,000 arriving between 1720 and 1776. They settled throughout the mainland but primarily in the middle colonies and the southern backcountry. These migrants were Presbyterians, the descendants of Scots who had been sent to northern Ireland to bolster English control there in the mid-seventeenth century. In Ireland the Scots had faced discrimination and economic regulation from the dominant English. For example, the Test Act of 1704 excluded both Scottish Presbyterians and Irish Catholics from holding public office in Ireland, reserving this privilege for members of the Church of England. English mercantilist regulations placed heavy import duties on the woolen goods produced by Scots-Irish farmers and weavers.

Rising taxes and poor harvests stimulated a major Scots-Irish migration to America during the 1720s. "Read this letter, Rev. Baptist Boyd," a New York settler wrote back to his minister, "and tell all the poor folk of ye place that God has opened a door for their deliverance. . . . all that a man works for is his own; there are no revenue hounds [tax collectors] to take it from us here." Lured by such reports, thousands of Scots-Irish sailed for Philadelphia and spread out across the mid-Atlantic region and southward down the Shenandoah Valley. Like the Germans, the Scots-Irish were determined to keep the culture of their homelands alive. They held to their Presbyterian faith and encouraged marriages within the church.

The middle colonies were not a "melting pot"; the diverse European cultures did not blend together to produce a homogeneous "American" outlook but kept their separate identities. Thus, defying New York law, many Dutch families maintained inheritance practices that favored wives over children. The major exception to cultural separatism was the Huguenots, French Calvinists who were expelled from France and settled in New York and various seacoast cities; they intermarried with other Protestants during the eighteenth century. More typical was the experience of Welsh Quakers; 70 percent of the children of the original migrants to Chester County, Pennsylvania, married other Welsh Quakers, as did 60 percent of the third generation. By marrying within their own groups, these and other European settlers created a pluralistic society of diverse nationalities, cultures, and religions in the middle colonies.

A Pluralistic Society

In their religious and ethnic diversity, the mid-Atlantic colonies constituted a society distinct from Europe (see Map 4.3). In Western Europe pluralism in religion was an untried experiment, and even in America most European-trained ministers remained committed to religious uniformity enforced by an established church backed by the government. "Throughout Pennsylvania the preachers do not have the power to punish anyone, or to force anyone to go to church," Gottlieb Mittelberger complained. As a result, "Sunday is very badly kept.

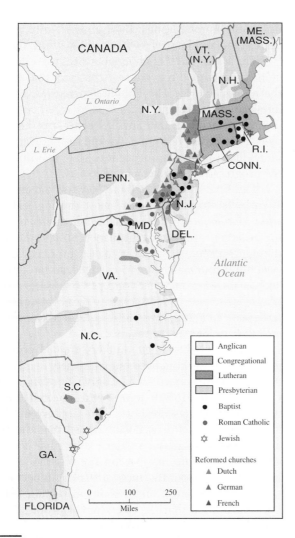

MAP 4.3

Religious Diversity in 1750

By 1750 religious diversity was on the rise. Baptists had grown in numbers in New England—long the stronghold of Congregationalism—and would later dominate Virginia. Already there were pockets of Presbyterians and Lutherans in the South, where Anglicanism was the established religion.

children received proper religious instruction. The committee also reported on the moral behavior of adults. In Chester County the men acted on such a report by disciplining one of their members "to reclaim him from drinking to excess and keeping vain company."

Communal sanctions also effectively sustained a self-contained and prosperous Quaker community. Permission to marry was granted only to couples with sufficient land, livestock, and equipment to support themselves and their future children. Marriage with non-Quakers usually was prohibited, and those who disobeyed were treated as outcasts. In Chester County about two-thirds of the young men and women who married outside the faith were barred from Quaker meetings. Over the generations this strict system shaped the character of the Quaker community. The children of well-to-do Friends had ample marriage portions and usually married within the sect. Those who lacked the resources remained unmarried or left the Society. Thus the Quakers created a prosperous religious community of urban merchants and rural freeholders. Clearly, a single established church was not necessary to avoid social chaos.

Yet Pennsylvania did not escape the tensions inherent in a society composed of distinct ethnic groups. By the 1750s Pennsylvania politics was sharply divided along cultural and religious lines. Scots-Irish Presbyterians on the frontier were challenging the pacifism of the Quaker-dominated assembly and demanding a more aggressive policy toward the Indians. Newer German migrants, many of whom belonged to Lutheran and Reformed churches, also opposed the Quakers; they wanted laws that respected their inheritance customs (which gave the community some say in the disposition of a family's property) and representation in the provincial assembly in proportion to their numbers. Other Germans, particularly the Mennonites, supported the Quakers because of their pacifism. Religious outlook increasingly determined political allegiance. As one observer noted, Scots-Irish Presbyterians, German Baptists, and German Lutherans had begun to form "a general confederacy" against the "ruling party" of Quakers in Pennsylvania, but this alliance was fragile. A foreign visitor remarked during the 1750s that these groups had "a mutual jealousy, for religious zeal is secretly burning." Latent religious and ethnic passions would break out during the following decade and again during the War for Independence, nearly destroying the new republican government of Pennsylvania.

Yet this experiment in freedom and diversity, which would survive the revolutionary era, offered a glimpse of the future. Cultural pluralism and an open religious and political order subject to passionate ethnic and social conflicts would characterize much of American society in the nineteenth and twentieth centuries.

Many people plough, reap, thresh, hew or split wood and the like." He concluded that "Liberty in Pennsylvania does more harm than good to many people, both in soul and body."

Mittelberger failed to appreciate the power of communal self-discipline. The various religious sects in Pennsylvania enforced moral behavior among their members. Each Quaker family, for example, regularly attended a weekly meeting for worship and a monthly meeting that handled discipline. A committee met with each family four times a year and made certain that its

The Enlightenment and the Great Awakening, 1740–1765

Two great European cultural movements swept across the Atlantic to America between the 1730s and the 1760s: the Enlightenment and Pietism. The *Enlightenment* emphasized the power of human reason to shape the world; it appealed especially to better-educated men and women, mostly from merchant or planter families, and to urban artisans. *Pietism* was an emotional, evangelical religious movement that stressed people's dependence on God. Although Pietism attracted all social groups, it was most successful among farmers, urban laborers, and slaves. Both the Enlightenment and Pietism promoted independent thinking, but in different ways. Together they transformed American intellectual and cultural life.

The Enlightenment in America

Americans of European ancestry came from a Christian culture, and some believed they had been sent to the New World on a religious mission. Many others found formal religion less persuasive than superstitions and folk wisdom. They saw the world in animistic terms: spirits and powers were everywhere and could be used for good or evil. Swedish settlers in Pennsylvania ascribed magical powers to the great white mullein, a common wild plant. When they had a fever, a traveler reported, they would "tie the leaves around their feet and arms." Even educated people believed that events occurred for reasons that today would be called magical. When a measles epidemic struck Boston in the 1710s, the Puritan minister Cotton Mather sought to contain its spread by "getting the Blood of the Great Passover sprinkled on our Houses." Like most Christians of the time, Mather believed that the earth stood at the center of the entire universe and that God intervened directly in human affairs.

The New Learning. The Scientific Revolution of the seventeenth century challenged these traditional world views, altering the outlook of the educated elite. The observation of the sixteenth-century astronomer Copernicus that the earth travels around the sun, not vice versa, had offered a new and more modest view of humankind's place in the universe. Other scholars conducted experiments using empirical methods—actual observed experience—to discover more about natural phenomena such as earthquakes and lightning. These intellectual innovations convinced many educated Euro-

peans that human beings could analyze—and ultimately understand and improve—the world in which they lived.

The European Enlightenment began around 1675, coinciding with discoveries of the laws that governed the natural world. The Enlightenment was a complex intellectual movement, but it was based on four fundamental principles: the lawlike order of the natural world; the power of human reason; the natural rights of individuals, including the right to self-government; and the progressive improvement of society.

The English scientist Isaac Newton did more than anyone else to advance this "new learning." His *Principia Mathematica* (1687) used mathematics to explain the orderly movement of the planets around the sun. Although Newton retained a belief in magical forces (seeking through alchemy to change lead into gold), his laws of motion and his concept of gravity described how the universe could operate without the constant intervention of a god, thus challenging traditional Christian explanations of the cosmos.

Other Enlightenment thinkers applied critical, rational modes of thought to human society in an effort to define its natural laws. In his *Essay Concerning Human Understanding* (1690), John Locke rejected the belief that human beings are born with God-given "innate" ideas. On the contrary, Locke argued that the infant's mind was a *tabula rasa*, a "blank slate" that was gradually filled with information conveyed by the senses and arranged by reason. By emphasizing the impact of environment, experience, and reason on human behavior, Locke proposed that the character of people and societies could be changed through education and purposeful action. Indeed, in his *Two Treatises on Government* (1690) justifying the Glorious Revolution of 1688, Locke advanced a revolutionary theory of government: political authority was not divinely ordained but sprang from "*social compacts*" that people made to preserve their "natural" rights to life, liberty, and property. Not princes but people conferred political legitimacy, so that governments might change through the decision of a majority.

The Enlightment in the Colonies. The Enlightenment ideas of Locke and others came to America with books and travelers and quickly affected the colonists' conceptions of religion and science. As early as the 1710s the Reverend John Wise of Ipswich, Massachusetts, combined Locke's political principles and Calvinist theology to defend the decision of Congregational churches to vest power in their lay members. Wise argued that just as the "social compact" formed the basis of political society, the religious covenant made the congregation—not bishops or monarchs, as in the Church of England—the interpreter of spiritual authority. Similarly, Enlightenment science influenced Cotton Mather when a smallpox epidemic threatened Boston in the 1720s. Mather sought a scientific remedy, joining with Zabdiel Boylston, a prominent Boston physician, in supporting the new technique of inoculation (with a less virulent strain of the smallpox virus) against the disease.

By midcentury Enlightenment ideas had become second nature to many educated Americans. Elizabeth Smith, an upper-class mother, invoked Lockean principles when, in a letter to a friend, she wrote about her newborn child: "The Infant Mind is a blank that easily receives my impression." Some upper-class colonists—Virginia planters and New York merchants—as well as urban artisans became *deists*. Influenced by Enlightenment science, deists believed that God had created the world but allowed it to operate according to the laws of nature. Their God was a rational being, a divine "watchmaker" who did not intervene directly in history or in people's lives. Rejecting the authority of the Bible and established churches, deists relied on people's "natural reason" to define a moral code, adherence to which would be punished or rewarded after death.

Franklin and the American Enlightenment. Benjamin Franklin was the epitome of an Enlightenment thinker in America. Born into the family of a devout Calvinist candlemaker in Boston in 1706, Franklin had little formal schooling. He was self-taught, having acquired a taste for knowledge as a printer's apprentice, and he mastered a wide variety of political and scientific works. Franklin's imagination was shaped by Enlightenment literature, not by the Christian Bible. In fact, as he explained in his *Autobiography*, "from the different books

I read, I began to doubt of Revelation itself." Franklin became a deist.

As a tradesman, printer, and journalist in Philadelphia, Franklin formed "a club of mutual improvement," which met every Friday evening to discuss "Morals, Politics, or Natural Philosophy." Although personally somewhat of a skeptic, Franklin propagated the outlook of the rational Enlightenment—optimistic, secular, and materialistic—in *Poor Richard's Almanac,* which was read by thousands of farmers. In 1743 he helped found the American Philosophical Society, an institution devoted to "the promotion of useful knowledge." He came up with an improved stove (the Franklin stove) and invented bifocal lenses for eyeglasses and the lightning rod. His research in the infant science of electricity won international acclaim. In fact, the English scientist Joseph Priestley praised Franklin's book on electricity, first published in England in 1751, as the greatest contribution to science since the work of Newton.

Franklin's Philadelphia became the showplace of the American Enlightenment. It boasted a circulating library filled with the latest scientific treatises from Europe. The first American medical school was founded there in 1765. Quaker and Anglican merchants built a Hospital for the Sick Poor in 1751 and then, in 1767, added a Bettering House to shelter the aged and disabled and offer employment to the poor. These philanthropists were acting as much from economic self-interest as from moral conviction, for they hoped these institutions would reduce the taxes they paid for relief of the poor. Nonetheless, the hospital and the bettering house were expressions of the Enlightenment belief that purposeful human action could improve society.

Enlightenment Philanthropy: The Philadelphia Hospital

This imposing structure, built in 1753 with public funds and private donations, embodied two Enlightenment principles—that purposeful action could improve society and that the world should express reason and order (exhibited here by the symmetrical facade). Etchings such as this one, *A Southeast Prospect of the Pennsylvania Hospital*, circa 1761 by John Streeper and Henry Dawkins, bolstered Philadelphia's reputation as the center of the American Enlightenment.

The life of the mind came of age in British North America as educated men founded clubs, schools, and publications. The first American newspapers had appeared in Boston in 1704 and Philadelphia in 1719, but their numbers increased dramatically after 1740; by 1765 nearly every colony had a regularly published newspaper. Ambitious printers produced magazines aimed at wealthy gentlemen, including the *New York*, the *Massachusetts*, and Franklin's *General*. Although most of them were failures—local newspapers and books from Europe filled the needs of the reading public—they were the first significant nonreligious publications (apart from newspapers) to appear in the colonies. The European Enlightenment had added a secular dimension to colonial intellectual life, preparing the way for the great American contributions to republican political theory during the Revolutionary Era.

Pietism in America

While American deists challenged old religious views, many other Americans embraced the new European devotional movement known as *Pietism*. Pietism paid little attention to theological dogma, emphasizing instead moral behavior, emotional church services, and a mystical union with God. Pietist preachers appealed to the hearts, not the minds, of their followers. They exhorted people to be devout—that is, "pious"—Christians; hence the name. Their teachings were particularly popular among the lower orders of European society, and peasants, artisans, and laborers joined pietistic churches by the thousands.

Pietism came to America with German migrants in the 1720s and led to a religious revival in the middle colonies. In Pennsylvania and New Jersey the Dutch minister Theodore Jacob Frelinghuysen moved from church to church, preaching to German settlers and arousing them with vigorous, emotional sermons. Frelinghuysen then harnessed their enthusiasm, organizing private prayer meetings and encouraging lay members of the congregation to preach a message of spiritual urgency to growing congregations. William Tennent and his son Gilbert were Presbyterian clergymen who copied Frelinghuysen's approach and during the 1730s led a series of revivals among Scots-Irish migrants in New Jersey and Pennsylvania.

Simultaneously, an American pietistic movement was born in Puritan New England. Puritanism had been part of an upsurge of piety in sixteenth-century England, but over the years many Puritan congregations had lost their religious zeal. During the 1730s Jonathan Edwards sought to restore spiritual commitment to the Congregational churches of the Connecticut River Valley, urging people—especially young men and women—to commit themselves to a life of piety and prayer (see American Lives, pages 120–121).

George Whitefield and the Great Awakening

Religious revival was carried to new heights in the 1740s by George Whitefield, a young English evangelist. Whitefield had experienced conversion in England after reading German pietistic tracts. He became a disciple of John Wesley, the founder of Methodism, who himself had been inspired by German Moravian Pietists during a stay in Georgia. Wesley combined enthusiastic preaching with disciplined "methods" of worship. Soon he had persuaded thousands of Anglicans and scores of ministers to become pietistic Methodists within the Church of England.

Whitefield preached with equal success in America, where, outside of New England, he found a society with few ministers and a weak churchgoing tradition. Whitefield established an orphanage in Georgia in 1738 and then returned to preach throughout the colonies from 1739 to 1741. Huge crowds of "enthusiasts" greeted the young preacher wherever he went, from Georgia to Massachusetts. "Religion is become the Subject of most Conversations," the Pennsylvania *Gazette* reported. "No books are in Request but those of Piety and Devotion." The usually skeptical and restrained Benjamin Franklin was so impressed by Whitefield's oratory that when the preacher asked for contributions, Franklin emptied his pockets "wholly into the collector's dish, gold and all." By the time the evangelist reached Boston, the Reverend Benjamin Colman reported that the people were "ready to receive him as an angel of God."

Whitefield owed his appeal partly to his compelling personal presence. "He looked almost Angelical—a young, slim, slender youth," according to one Connecticut farmer. And he spoke magnificently and with great force, impressing on his audience that they all had sinned and must seek salvation. Like most evangelical preachers, Whitefield did not read his sermons but spoke from memory, as if inspired, raising his voice for dramatic effect, gesturing eloquently, and making striking use of biblical metaphors. The young preacher evoked a deep emotional response. Hundreds of men and women suddenly felt the "new light" of God's grace within them; strengthened and self-confident, these New Lights were prepared to follow in Whitefield's footsteps. The evangelist's eloquence transformed the local revivals in the Connecticut Valley and the middle colonies into a genuine Great Awakening that spanned the mainland settlements, spreading a set of shared religious values.

Religious Upheaval in the North

Old Lights versus New Lights. Like all cultural explosions, the revival was controversial. Conservative ministers such as Charles Chauncy of Boston condemned the "cryings out, faintings and convulsions" produced by emotional preaching. These "Old Lights," as they were called by the awakeners, feared—with good reason—that revivalism would destroy the established churches. Inspired by Whitefield's example, dozens of farmers, women, and artisans roamed the countryside, preaching that the Old Lights were "unconverted" sinners.

To silence the revivalists, the Old Lights in Connecticut persuaded the legislative assembly to prohibit traveling preachers from speaking to established congregations without the ministers' permission. Thus, when Whitefield returned to Connecticut in 1744, he found many pulpits closed to him. But the New Lights stoutly resisted attempts by civil authorities to silence them. "I shall bring glory to God in my bonds," a dissident preacher wrote from a Massachusetts jail. The New Lights won repeal of the Connecticut law in 1750, but the battle was far from over.

The Awakening's Significance. The Great Awakening gradually altered American perceptions of the proper religious order. One major confrontation involved the issue of religious taxes and, beyond that, the legitimacy of an established church. As outsiders, many New Lights and Baptists questioned government involvement in religion and favored a greater separation between church and state. According to the Baptist preacher Isaac Backus, "God never allowed any civil state upon earth to impose religious taxes." In New England many New Lights simply left the established Congregational Church; by 1754 they had founded 125 "separatist" churches. Other dissidents joined growing Baptist congregations (see Figure 4.3). In New York and New Jersey, the Dutch Reformed Church split into two factions as New Lights resisted the conservative church authorities in the Netherlands. After the Great Awakening, established churches lost their aura of authority; many people reluctantly paid taxes to the established minister but joined other congregations. State-supported religion was no longer an unquestioned norm.

The Awakening also challenged the authority of the ministry. Traditionally, preachers had commanded respect because of their education in theology and knowledge of the Bible. But Gilbert Tennent questioned these criteria in his influential pamphlet *The Dangers of an Unconverted Ministry* (1740). Tennent maintained that what qualified ministers to hold office was not theological training but conversion—the experience through which a person came to know the grace of God. Thus, anyone who was saved could speak with ministerial authority. Traditional churches—formal, hierarchical, doctrine-bound—began to lose members to denominations, such as the Baptists, that emphasized piety rather than theology, emotions rather than dogma, lay preaching rather than clerical wisdom. By reasserting Luther's commitment to "the priesthood of all believers," Pietists created a more democratic religious community.

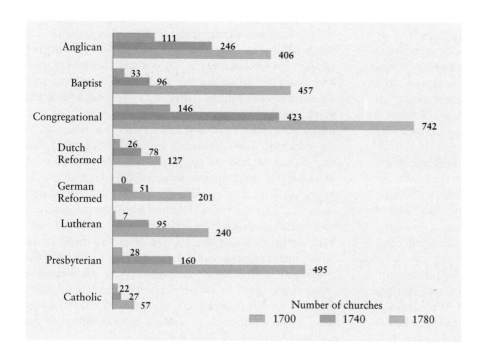

FIGURE 4.3

Church Growth by Denomination, 1700–1780

Some churches, such as the Dutch Reformed, grew only from the natural increase of their members. After 1740, the fastest-growing denominations were immigrant churches—the German Reformed and Lutheran—and those with an evangelical message, such as the Baptists.

Jonathan Edwards: Preacher, Philosopher, Pastor

Jonathan Edwards did not mince words. Echoing the harsh theology of John Calvin, Edwards preached that men and women were helpless creatures completely dependent on God: "There is Hell's wide gaping mouth open; and you have nothing to stand upon, nor any thing to take hold of: there is nothing between you and Hell but the air; 'tis only the power and mere pleasure of God that holds you up."

Edwards spoke (a listener noted) with great "inward fervor, without much noise of external emotion," and without a single gesture. His controlled demeanor underlined the torments that awaited those who fell into the eternal flames:

> How dismal will it be . . . to know assuredly that you never, never shall be delivered from them; . . . after you shall have endured these torments millions of ages . . . your bodies, which shall have been burning and roasting all this while in these glowing flames, yet shall not have been consumed, but will remain to roast through an eternity yet.

Such was the terrible—and inevitable—fate that Edwards the preacher promised to complacent Christians in his most famous sermon, *Sinners in the Hands of an Angry God* (1742). But Edwards the pastor preached a more hopeful message of personal repentance and spiritual rebirth, telling congregations that this fate awaited only those who "never passed under a great change of heart, by the mighty power of the spirit of God upon your souls; all that were never born again, and made new creatures."

With such impassioned words, Edwards inspired a religious revival in the Connecticut River Valley in the mid-1730s and helped George Whitefield stir up an even greater one in the 1740s. But this minister, one of the leading revivalists of his age, was also a profound and original philosopher, perhaps the most intellectually brilliant colonial American.

Jonathan Edwards was born in East Windsor, Connecticut, in 1703, the fifth child and only son among the eleven children of Timothy and Esther Stoddard Edwards. The parents' identities shaped their son. The father came from a wealthy family but ended up a poorly paid rural minister who fought constantly with his congregation over his salary and authority, battles that Jonathan would also fight with his church. The mother was the daughter of Solomon Stoddard, a great revivalist and the most famous churchman in Connecticut, a family legacy that would both help and haunt Jonathan Edwards throughout his life.

As a child Jonathan embraced his grandfather Stoddard's theology, rejecting the Calvinist belief in God's omnipotence over people's lives and labeling it "a horrible doctrine." But as a preacher, he became a committed Calvinist, explaining in a *Personal Narrative* written later in life that at age seventeen he experienced "a *delightful* conviction" of the Almighty's absolute sovereignty, an "inward sweetness . . . [of] sweetly conversing with Christ, and wrapt and swallowed up in God." In fact, Edwards found his Calvinist God only with great difficulty. He came to adopt a Calvinist outlook only after many years of personal torment as a young adult and a series of physical and emotional collapses.

The Enlightenment came more easily to Edwards. While studying for the ministry at Yale College, he read the works of Isaac Newton, John Locke, and other Enlightenment thinkers, starting a lifetime of philosophical inquiry into the meaning of words and things. He accepted Locke's argument in the *Essay Concerning Human Understanding* (1690) that our ideas are not innate from birth but are the product of experience and the senses—our ability to see, hear, feel, and taste the world around us. A person who has never *tasted* a pineapple, said Locke, will never have "the true idea of the relish of that celebrated and delicious fruit." But Locke's theory was less successful in explaining *abstract* ideas—God, man, angel, love, salvation—and it was here that Edwards made his contribution. Locke had suggested that such ideas resulted when the mind mixed together various sense experiences, but Edwards—who had worked out his theological doctrines through intense personal torment—argued that they involved emotional apprehension as well—since, for example, "love" (whether of God or a fellow human) was "felt" and not merely understood. It followed that abstract ideas were emotional as well as rational entities, the product of the passions as well as the senses.

Edwards used his theory of knowledge to justify his

This portrait, painted by Joseph Badger in 1720, suggests that even as a young man Edwards was grave and dignified.

style of preaching, arguing that vivid words promoted conversions by conveying abstract ideas in their full emotional intensity. As he put it in *A Treatise Concerning Religious Affections* (1746), "true religion, in great part, consists in holy affection," an emotional state created by words that evoked the terrors of eternal damnation and the necessity of repentance. It was reasonable, Edwards declared, "to endeavor to fright persons away from Hell." In the end the philosopher was at one with the preacher.

Edwards put these ideas into practice as pastor of the Congregational church in Northampton, Massachusetts, taking over that position from his grandfather, Solomon Stoddard, in 1729. He worked hard, spending thirteen hours a day composing sermons and treatises, and more than matched his grandfather's success as a revivalist, especially among young people. Beginning in 1734, Edwards reported, "the number of true saints multiplied . . . the town seemed to be full of the presence of God: it never was so full of love, nor so full of joy; and yet so full of distress as it was then." News of the Northampton revival stimulated religious fervor up

and down the Connecticut River Valley "till there was a general awakening."

Edwards interpreted his success as "a remarkable Testimony of God's Approbation of the Doctrine . . . that we are justified only by faith in Christ, and not by any manner of virtue or goodness of our own." He maintained that uncompromising Calvinist position during the widespread revivals of the 1740s. Also seeking to restore an older communal order, he took issue with New Lights who asserted "the absolute Necessity for every Person to act singly . . . as if there was not another human Creature upon earth." Repudiating that spirit of individualism, Edwards insisted that aspiring Saints should heed their pastors, who were "skilful guides," and then make a "credible Relation of their inward Experience" to the congregation, thus strengthening the covenant bonds that knit members together in a visible church. Edwards extended his critique of individualism to economic affairs, speaking out against "a narrow, private spirit" among merchants and landlords, those men who "are not ashamed to hit and bite others [and] grind the faces of the poor. . . ."

Edwards's rigorous standards and assault on religious and economic individualism deeply offended the wealthiest and most influential members of his congregation. Continuing struggles over his salary and disciplinary authority culminated in a final battle in 1750, when Edwards repudiated Stoddard's practice of admitting almost all churchgoers to Communion and thus full church membership, adhering instead to the Calvinist doctrine that God bestowed grace only on chosen Saints. By a vote of 200 to 20, the Northampton congregation dismissed the great preacher and philosopher from his pastorate. Impoverished and with a family of ten children to support, Edwards moved to Stockbridge, Massachusetts, a small frontier outpost. There he ministered, without great success, to the Housatonic Indians and wrote an impressive philosophical work, *Freedom of the Will.* Just as he was about to take up the presidency of the College of New Jersey (Princeton) in 1757, Edwards was inoculated against smallpox, took the inoculation badly, and died. He left a pair of spectacles, two wigs, three black coats, and some 300 books, including 22 written by himself—but not much else in the way of earthly goods.

As he lay dying, this turn of fate puzzled America's first great philosopher. Why had God called him to Princeton only to give him no time to undertake his duties? As a preacher and pastor Edwards had always responded to such questions by stressing God's arbitrary power and the "insufficiency of reason" to understand God's purpose. Now he himself had to accept that grim and emotionally unsatisfying answer, showing through his personal experience why Calvinism was such a hard faith by which to live . . . or die.

By reinforcing the strong community values of ordinary farmers and rural people, some pietistic revivals also questioned the morality of economic competition and growing disparities in wealth. Many rural Pietists were suspicious of merchants and land speculators, fearing that the mercenary values of the marketplace had eroded traditional moral principles. Jonathan Edwards spoke for many rural Americans when he said that a "private niggardly spirit" was more suitable "for wolves and other beasts of prey, than for human beings." By joining and participating in religious revivals, many farm families reaffirmed their commitment to the cooperative ethic of rural life. "In any truly Christian society," Gilbert Tennent explained, "mutual *Love* is the *Band and Cement*."

The Awakening also injected new vigor into education and intellectual pursuits, especially religious learning, as the various churches founded new colleges to educate the youth and train ministers (see Table 4.2). New Light Presbyterians established the College of New Jersey (Princeton) in 1746, and New York Anglicans founded King's College (Columbia) in 1754. Baptists set up the College of Rhode Island (Brown); the Dutch Reformed Church subsidized Queen's College (Rutgers) in New Jersey. The true intellectual legacy of the revival was not education for the few, however, but a new sense of spiritual power and independence among the many. The Baptist preacher Isaac Backus captured the democratic thrust of the Awakening when he noted that "the common people now claim as good a right to judge and act in matters of religion as civil rulers or the learned clergy."

Social and Religious Conflict in the South

In the southern colonies religious conflict took an intensely social form, especially in Virginia. The Church of England, the established church, was supported by public taxes, yet it had never ministered to most Virginians. About 40 percent of the population was made up of African-Americans, who generally were excluded from membership. Whites were required by law to attend services, but many landless families—another 20 percent of the population—came irregularly. Middling white freeholders, who made up 35 percent of the population, formed the core of most Anglican congregations, but it was the remaining 5 percent, the prominent planters, who held power in the church. They controlled the parish vestries, the lay organizations that helped ministers manage church affairs. Indeed, these vestrymen used their control of parish finances to keep Anglican ministers under control. One clergyman complained that vestrymen dismissed any minister who "had the courage to preach against any Vices taken into favor by the leading Men of his Parish."

New Light Presbyterians. The vestry's power could not inhibit the new religious fervor. In 1743 a bricklayer named Samuel Morris, who had been inspired by reading George Whitefield's sermons, led a group of Virginia Anglicans out of the established church to seek a more vital religious experience. Morris and his followers invited New Light Presbyterian ministers from Scots-Irish settlements along the Virginia frontier to lead prayer meetings. Soon local revivals spread across the back-

TABLE 4.2

Colonial Colleges

	Date of Founding	Colony	Religious Affiliation
Harvard	1636	Massachusetts	Puritan
William and Mary	1693	Virginia	Church of England
Yale	1701	Connecticut	Puritan
College of New Jersey (Princeton)	1746	New Jersey	Presbyterian
King's (Columbia)	1754	New York	Church of England
College of Philadelphia (University of Pennsylvania)	1755	Pennsylvania	None
College of Rhode Island (Brown)	1764	Rhode Island	Baptist
Queen's (Rutgers)	1766	New Jersey	Dutch Reformed
Dartmouth	1769	New Hampshire	Congregationalist

country and into the so-called Tidewater region along the Atlantic coast.

The political leaders of Virginia feared that a full-scale Presbyterian pietistic revival would undermine their authority. It was their custom to attend Church of England services with their families and display their fine clothes, well-bred horses, and elaborate carriages to the assembled community. Some vestrymen flaunted their power by marching in a body to their seats in the front rows. These opportunities for a show of their authority would vanish if freeholders joined the New Light Presbyterians, and religious pluralism might threaten the gentry's ability to tax the masses to support the Church of England. The fate of the established church seemed to hang in the balance.

To restrain the New Light Presbyterians, Governor William Gooch denounced their "false teachings." Anglican justices of the peace closed down Presbyterian meetinghouses and harassed Samuel Davies, a popular New Light preacher. These actions kept most white yeomen within the Church of England, as did the elitist outlook of most Presbyterians. Presbyterian ministers—even New Lights such as Davies—were highly educated and sought converts among skilled workers and propertied farmers, seldom preaching to poor whites and enslaved blacks.

Baptist Revivals and Black Protestantism. Baptists succeeded where Presbyterians failed. Like the Quakers, Baptists were a radical offshoot of the Protestant Reformation, direct descendants of the Anabaptists (see Chapter 1). Condemned or outlawed by the authorities throughout Europe, Baptists drew their congregations from among the poor, developing emotionally charged rituals—such as baptizing adults by full immersion—that offered solace and hope in a world of trouble. During the 1760s thousands of yeomen and tenant farm families in Virginia flocked to revivalist meetings, drawn by the enthusiasm and democratic ways of Baptist preachers.

Slaves were welcome at Baptist revivals. As early as 1740 George Whitefield had openly condemned the brutality of slaveholders and urged that Africans be brought into the Christian fold. A handful of New Light planters took up this challenge in South Carolina and Georgia, but with limited success. The hostility of the white population and the commitment of many Africans to their ancestral religions kept the number of converts low. The first significant conversion of slaves took place two decades later among second- or third-generation African-Americans in Virginia. Hundreds of those slaves, who knew English and English ways, joined Baptist churches run by ministers who taught that all men and women were equal in God's eyes.

The ruling gentry reacted violently to this courting

of blacks and poor whites. Anglican sheriffs and justices of the peace organized armed bands of planters who broke up Baptist services by force. In Caroline County, Virginia, an Anglican posse attacked one Brother Waller. Waller was attempting to pray when, a fellow Baptist reported, "he was violently jerked off the stage; they caught him by the back part of his neck, beat his head against the ground, and a gentleman gave him twenty lashes with his horsewhip."

The intensity of the gentry's response reflected class antagonism, loyalty to the Anglican church, and fear: the Baptists posed a threat to their traditional culture. Baptist ministers condemned as vices such customary pleasures of Chesapeake men as gambling, drinking, whoring, and cockfighting and proposed to replace those boisterous habits with puritanical, cooperative Christian living. Baptist preachers urged their followers to work hard and lead virtuous lives. They emphasized equality by calling one another "brother" and "sister."

Their central ritual, of course, was baptism. In contrast to most other Christian churches, in which people were baptized as infants, Baptists received this sacrament as adults, often by complete immersion in water. Once men and women had experienced the infusion of grace—had been "born again"—they were baptized in an emotional public ceremony that was a celebration of shared fellowship. One Sunday "about 2,000 people came together," a Baptist minister noted:

> We went to a field and making a circle in the center, there laid hands on the persons baptized. The multitude stood around weeping, but when we sang *Come we that love the lord* they lifted up their hands and faces toward heaven and discovered such cheerful countenances in the midst of flowing tears as I have never seen before.

The appeal of Baptist preaching and ritual was overwhelming. Despite fierce resistance from the gentry, by 1775 about 20 percent of Virginia's whites and hundreds of enslaved blacks belonged to Baptist churches.

Anglican slaveholders retained their economic and political power, but the revival threatened their control and privileged position. For one thing, it spread democratic principles of church organization among white yeomen and tenant farmers. Also, belief in a living God gave meaning to the lives of poor families and better prepared them to assert their social values and economic interests. Finally, as Baptist—and, later, Methodist—ministers spread Christianity among the slaves, the cultural gulf between blacks and whites shrank, undermining one justification for slavery and giving blacks a new sense of spiritual identity. Within a generation African-Americans would develop their own version of Protestant Christianity.

The Midcentury Challenge: War, Trade, and Land

Between 1740 and 1765 colonial life was transformed not only by Pietism and the Enlightenment but also by war, economic change, and frontier violence. First, Britain embarked on a major war in America, the so-called French and Indian War, which became a worldwide conflict and redefined the British empire. Second, the expansion of transatlantic trade increased colonial prosperity but put Americans into debt to British creditors. Third, Britain's ouster of the French from North America in 1763 stimulated a great westward migration that led to new battles with the Indians, armed conflicts between settlers and landowners, and frontier rebellions against eastern governments.

The French and Indian War

In the aftermath of the War of Jenkins' Ear, British officials began to appreciate the economic and military potential of their colonial empire. Governor William Shirley of Massachusetts predicted that within a century the population of the mainland colonies would equal that of France and "lay a foundation for a Superiority of British power upon the continent of Europe."

Population and Diplomacy. Before the middle of the eighteenth century few Europeans had settled in the vast Mississippi Valley. The main French settlements, including the fur-trading centers of Montreal and Quebec, were along the St. Lawrence River, with only forts and fur-trading posts dotting the interior of the North American continent. British settlers had not moved across the Appalachians because there were few natural transportation routes. Moreover, the territory was a stronghold of the Iroquois, who were still allied with western native Americans in a covenant chain. For a generation the Iroquois and the western Algonquin had extorted guns and subsidies from English and French officials and traded with merchants for blankets and metal goods, holding off white settlements with threats of war. In the late 1740s this "play-off" system broke down for three interrelated reasons: both the British and the French refused to pay the rising cost of "gifts" to native Americans; Delaware and Shawnee Indians along the Ohio River declared their autonomy, disrupting the Iroquois' covenant chain; and a land shortage in New England and the influx of European migrants into the middle colonies increased Anglo-American migration on to Indian lands. During the 1750s William Johnson, the Indian agent for the British government in New York, bestowed manufac-

tured goods on the Mohawk nation to win its permission to settle Scottish migrants west of Albany but earned only distrust.

In the South land-hungry settlers and speculators were also on the march. In 1749 Governor Robert Dinwiddie of Virginia and a group of prominent planters organized the Ohio Company, which enlisted the support of John Hanbury and other London merchants with political connections and obtained a royal land grant of 200,000 acres along the upper Ohio River and the promise of 300,000 more acres (see Map 4.4). These initiatives infuriated the Iroquois, who told the British in 1753: "We don't know what you Christians, English and French intend; we are so hemmed in by both, that we have hardly a hunting place left."

The Road to War. To secure British claims to the Ohio region, Governor Dinwiddie sent Colonel George Washington—a young planter eager to speculate in western lands—to ward off the French with a force of the Virginia militia. This initiative raised the prospect of war. French officials and merchants wanted to reestablish their influence among the newly strident Delaware and Shawnee and viewed Washington's expedition as a threat to France's claim of sovereignty over the entire Mississippi Valley. To deter Indian rebellions and British incursions, they ordered the construction of Fort Duquesne at the point where the Monongahela and Allegheny rivers join to form the Ohio (present-day Pittsburgh). In July 1754 French troops repulsed the Virginia force and captured Washington and the garrison at Fort Necessity (a hastily built military redoubt 60 miles south of Fort Duquesne). Virginia was at war with France in the American backcountry, and the Ohio Indians, like the Iroquois, regarded themselves as potential victims of a European military contest.

MAP 4.4

European Spheres of Influence, 1754

France and Spain laid claim to vast areas of North America and sought to use Indian allies to combat the numerical advantage of British settlers. For their part, native Americans played off one European power against another. As a British official observed: "To preserve the Ballance between us and the French is the great ruling Principle of Modern Indian Politics." By expelling the French from North America, the Great War for Empire disrupted this balance, leaving Indian peoples on their own to resist encroaching Anglo-American settlers.

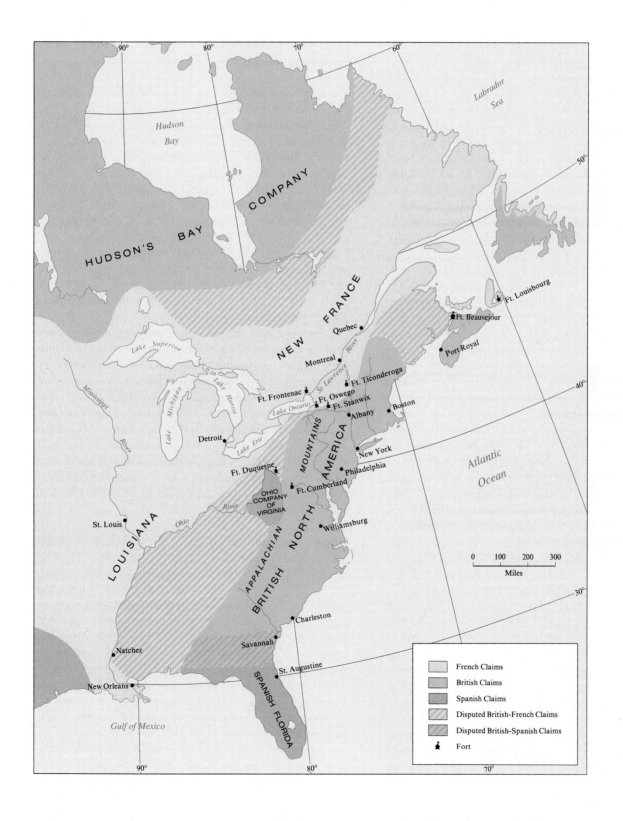

The British government had no desire to see this fighting continue. Its coffers were still empty from the long and expensive war with France that had ended in 1748. Wars required new taxes, which were strongly opposed in Parliament, as Prime Minister Henry Pelham knew: "There is such a load of debt, and such heavy taxes already laid upon the people, that nothing but an absolute necessity can justifie our engaging in a new War."

But Pelham could not control the march of events. William Pitt, a rising statesman, demanded a policy of expansionism in the colonies, as did Lord Halifax, the energetic new head of the Board of Trade. To coordinate the efforts of the American settlements, the board proposed a "union between ye Royal, Proprietary, & Charter Governments." Some American political leaders were thinking along similar lines. Delegates from most of the northern governments and the Six Iroquois Nations had met at Albany in June 1754 to discuss war policies, and the colonial representatives had adopted a Plan of Union, which was primarily the work of Benjamin Franklin. Under the Albany plan, each colony would send delegates to an American continental assembly, which would be presided over by a royal governor-general. This assembly would assume responsibility for all western affairs: trade, Indian policy, and defense. The proposed union never materialized because the provincial assemblies wanted to preserve their autonomy and the imperial government feared the consequences of convening a great American assembly.

To counter the French presence in the Ohio region, Britain dispatched Sir Edward Braddock and two regiments of troops to America. In May 1755 Braddock started marching through the wilderness with this force of 1,400 regulars and 450 Virginia militiamen. He never reached Fort Duquesne. In July a small force of French and a larger group of Delaware and Shawnee, who had now decided to side with the French, launched a surprise attack, killing Braddock and half his men. With this battle, the skirmish between France and Virginia escalated into a European war.

Initially there were few battles. The Ohio Indians adopted a defensive posture, fighting only when Europeans entered their territory. And because hundreds of miles of forest separated the populated areas of Canada and British America, military action by Britain and France was limited primarily to water-borne expeditions. In June 1755 British and New England naval and military forces captured Fort Beauséjour in Nova Scotia (Acadia). To eliminate the French from this region, the British deported 6,000 Acadians, some of whom eventually settled in Louisiana. Just before war was formally declared in 1756, the French sent the Marquis de Montcalm to command their forces in North America. Montcalm promptly captured and destroyed Fort Oswego on Lake Ontario.

The Great War for Empire

Two years of fighting in America precipitated the Seven Years' War in Europe. In 1756, France made a pact with Austria, Britain's longtime continental ally, and French and Austrian armies threatened Hanover, the homeland of King George II of England, as well as Prussia, the territory of Britain's new ally, Frederick the Great. When armed conflicts broke out in India and West Africa as well as in North America and the West Indies, the struggle became a Great War for Empire.

Pitt's Imperial Strategy. In 1757 William Pitt replaced the irresolute Henry Pelham as the leader of the government. Pitt honored Britain's commitment to its Prussian ally by sending large subsidies and a small expeditionary force, but his main interest lay overseas. The Seven Years' War would not be just another in a long string of European dynastic struggles with colonial episodes. Instead, it would be a Great War for Empire. Britain had reaped unprecedented wealth from its trading empire in the West Indies, North America, and India, and Pitt was determined to crush France, which was the main obstacle to further expansion. Pitt used the British fleet to bottle up the French navy in its home ports and began a systematic attack against overseas French possessions.

Pitt planned the critical campaign against New France with special care. He sought out vigorous military leaders, giving top commands to three impressive young officers: James Wolfe, Jeffrey Amherst, and William Howe. And he exploited a demographic advantage: Britain's 2 million mainland residents outnumbered the French settlers by 14 to 1. Pitt provided the colonies with generous subsidies, agreeing to pay half the cost of the troops raised there and supply them with arms and equipment. Finally, he committed main units of the British navy and thousands of British regulars to the American conflict.

The Capture of Quebec. In 1758 the British launched attacks on the perimeter of New France's defenses, forcing the French to abandon Fort Duquesne and capturing Louisbourg. The following year the British moved on Quebec from three directions. Colonel John Stanwix moved to the northeast from Fort Duquesne—renamed Fort Pitt—and General Amherst led an Anglo-American army northward from New York. These expeditions were designed to distract French forces and their Indian allies from the major British force—50 warships, 200 transports, and 8,500 troops—which sailed up the St. Lawrence River under the command of General Wolfe in June 1759 (see Map 4.5).

The attack on Quebec was the turning point of the war in North America. General Wolfe probed the city's strong defenses for three months. Then one day, in the

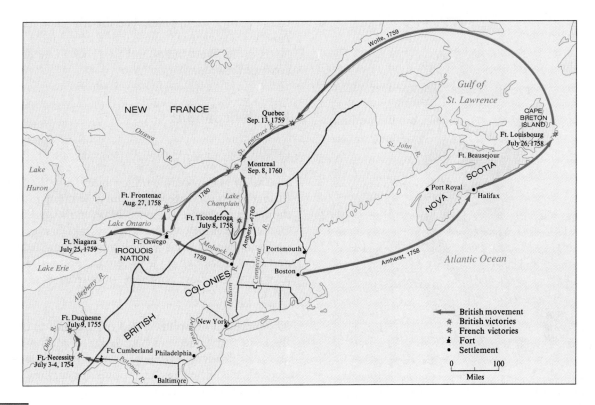

MAP. 4.5

The Anglo-American Conquest of New France
After years of preparation, British and American forces attacked the heartland of
New France, capturing Quebec in 1759. The conquest both united and divided the
allies. Colonists celebrated the great victory—"The Illuminations and Fireworks
exceeded any that had been exhibited before," reported the South Carolina *Gazette*—
but British officers viewed provincial soldiers with disdain: "the dirtiest, most con-
temptible, cowardly dogs you can conceive."

hours before dawn, 4,000 British troops scaled the 200-
foot cliffs behind the city and took up positions on the
high plains. French troops led by Montcalm advanced
against Wolfe's army but were overwhelmed by British
discipline and firepower. Quebec fell. The Royal Navy
prevented French reinforcements from crossing the Atlantic, and when British forces captured Montreal in
1760, the conquest of Canada was complete.

Pontiac's Uprising. The war in America had one more
scene to play. Early in 1763 the Ottawa chief Pontiac
led a group of loosely linked uprisings by tribes from
New York to Michigan. During the war the tribes had
been defrauded by rum-peddling British traders, and
they resented the British military occupation of the old
French forts as well as General Amherst's decision to
curtail "gifts" and supplies of gunpowder. Fearing the
influx of Anglo-American settlers, Pontiac hoped to re-

store the old French alliance, declaring, "I am French,
and I want to die French." Other Indians were inspired
by Neolin, a Delaware prophet who, blending Christian
doctrine with native American beliefs, urged the repudiation of all Europeans—along with their tools and
clothes—and a return to traditional customs.

Acknowledging this separatist pan-Indian outlook,
Pontiac astutely directed it against the British, capturing
nearly every British garrison west of Fort Niagara. The
uprising ended ultimately with the British in control:
the Indians returned British prisoners, surrendered
some of their leaders for punishment, and accepted the
British as their new political "fathers." For their part,
the British evinced somewhat greater respect for native
Americans, bargaining with them and, in the Proclamation Line of 1763, which temporarily forbade settlement west of the Appalachians, safeguarding their
territory from land-hungry settlers.

Pontiac

This portrait depicts Pontiac both as an Indian, symbolized by the necklace of bear claws, and as a European-style ruler with a regal demeanor and a flowing robe. Pontiac did indeed partake of two worlds, absorbing French culture as he asserted his Indian identity.

The Treaty of Paris. On the other battlefronts around the world, the British went from success to success. The East India Company captured French commercial outposts and took control of trade in large sections of India. British forces seized French Senegal in West Africa, the French sugar islands of Martinique and Guadeloupe, and the Spanish colonies of Cuba and the Philippine Islands. When the war ended, Pitt was no longer in office, but his maritime strategy had extended British power all over the world. The first British empire was at the height of its power.

The Treaty of Paris of 1763 confirmed the triumph of British arms. Britain gained sovereignty over half the continent of North America, including French Canada, all French territory east of the Mississippi River, and Spanish Florida. As recompense, Spain received all of Louisiana west of the Mississippi River, which it ruled for the next forty years, along with the restoration of

Cuba and the Philippines. The French empire in North America was reduced to a handful of valuable sugar islands in the West Indies and two rocky islands off the coast of Newfoundland.

British Economic Growth

Britain owed its triumph in large part to its unprecedented economic resources. Ever since it had wrested control of many oceanic trade routes from the Dutch at the end of the seventeenth century, Britain had been the dominant commercial power. Now, in the middle of the eighteenth century, it was becoming the first country to undergo the Industrial Revolution. Its new technology and work discipline made Britain the first—and for over a century the most powerful—industrial nation in the world.

The Industrial Revolution and the Expansion of Trade. By 1750 British artisans had designed and built water- and steam-driven machines that powered lathes for shaping wood, jennies and looms for making textiles, and hammers for forging iron. The new machines produced goods far faster than human labor could. Furthermore, the entrepreneurs who ran the new factories drove their employees hard, forcing them to labor long hours and keep pace with the machines. This new work discipline made it possible for the British to produce more wool and linen textiles, iron tools, paper, chinaware, and glass than ever before—and sell those goods at lower prices.

English and Scottish merchants launched aggressive campaigns to market their products in the rapidly growing mainland colonies. They extended a full year's credit, instead of the traditional six months, to American traders. Colonial shopkeepers and merchants took advantage of these liberal terms to expand their inventories and increase their sales to distant backcountry farmers. Americans increased their consumption and soon accounted for 20 percent of all British exports (see Figure 4.4). The settlers bought equipment for their farms and all kinds of household goods—cloth, blankets, china, and cooking utensils. This first "consumer revolution," as some historians have called it, raised the living standard of many Americans.

American Exports. To pay for these imports, Americans increased their agricultural exports. Tobacco from the Chesapeake remained the most important export, accounting for about 25 percent of the total. Planters sent 52 million pounds of tobacco abroad in 1740 and more than 75 million pounds in 1765. Entrepreneurs in Scotland financed this expansion by subsidizing Virginia planters and Scots-Irish migrants who moved into

A Philadelphia Merchant
James Tulley stands well-dressed and proud in his counting-house, his ships in the background preparing for the next voyage. Merchants like Tulley were the first great American entrepreneurs, organizing trade between the mainland, the West Indies, and Britain.

the Piedmont, a region of plains and rolling hills inland from the Tidewater counties. Scottish-run stores granted ample credit to these white settlers—to purchase land, slaves, and equipment—and took part of their tobacco crop in payment. By the 1760s Scottish merchants were buying nearly half the annual Chesapeake tobacco crop and reexporting most of it to expanding markets in France and central Europe.

Agricultural exports also supported the luxurious life-style of the white slaveowners of South Carolina. The British government subsidized the cultivation of indigo, and by the 1760s planters were annually sending indigo valued at £117,000 to English textile factories while carrying on an expanding export trade in rice to Holland and markets in southern Europe, selling about 65 million pounds of rice a year.

A booming export trade in wheat and flour permitted residents of the mid-Atlantic region to participate in the consumer revolution. With Europe in the throes of a population explosion, Continental merchants were buying wheat from America—at first only in poor harvest years, then regularly. Wheat prices in Philadelphia jumped almost 50 percent between 1740 and 1765, bringing high profits to farmers and merchants. New York, Pennsylvania, Maryland, and Virginia became the breadbasket of the Atlantic world.

But even this boom in exports could not defray the cost of the consumer frenzy. During the 1750s and 1760s exports paid for only 80 percent of imported British goods. The remaining 20 percent—millions of pounds—was financed by British merchants who extended credit. The first American spending binge, like most subsequent splurges, landed many consumers in debt.

FIGURE 4.4

Population, British Imports, and the American Trade Deficit
Around 1750 the rate of growth of British imports into the American colonies outpaced their rate of population growth, indicating that consumption per capita was increasing. The colonists then went into debt to pay for these goods, running an annual deficit with their British suppliers.

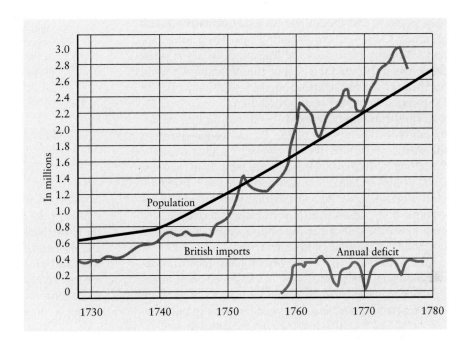

The return of peace after the Great War for Empire brought an end to boom times. Britain slashed its troop levels and military expenditures in America, and the loss of military markets, contracts, and cash subsidies made it more difficult for Americans to purchase British goods. Merchants looked anxiously at their over-stocked warehouses and feared bankruptcy. "I think we have a gloomy prospect before us," a Philadelphian noted in 1765, "as there are of late some Persons failed, who were in no way suspected." The increase in transatlantic trade had raised living standards but also had made Americans more dependent on overseas creditors and the world economy.

Land Conflicts

In times of prosperity and in times of stagnating trade, the colonial population continued to grow. By 1750 the shortage of arable land in long-settled areas had become so acute that political conflicts broke out over land rights (see Map 4.6). With each new generation the problem got worse. In 1738, for example, men and women who traced their American ancestry back four generations founded the new town of Kent in western Connecticut. Their families had been moving slowly to the north and west for a century, and Kent was at the generally accepted western boundary of the colony. The next generation would have to find somewhere else to go.

Migration out of New England. In the 1750s Connecticut farmers formed the Susquehannah Company and petitioned the Connecticut legislature to help them claim lands in the West. According to the colony's seventeenth-century charter, its boundaries stretched all the way to the Pacific Ocean, yet those claims crossed land granted by Charles II to William Penn. The Susquehannah Company persuaded the legislature to assert jurisdiction over disputed territory in the Wyoming Valley in northeastern Pennsylvania and then sold land titles to Connecticut migrants who settled there.

The Penn family resisted this intrusion into its domain. With the support of the Pennsylvania assembly, the Penns reaffirmed their proprietary rights over the Wyoming Valley and issued their own land patents. Rival groups of land claimants proceeded to burn down each other's houses. To avert further violence, the Pennsylvania and Connecticut governments referred the dispute to British authorities in London, where it remained undecided at the time of independence.

Land disputes also broke out on New York's border with Massachusetts and New Hampshire. The boundaries were not precise, and hundreds of families from New England moved into disputed territory in the Hud-

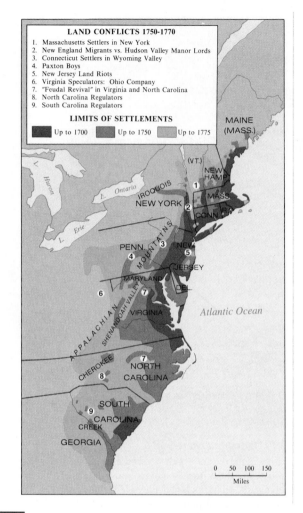

MAP 4.6

Westward Expansion and Armed Conflict
Between 1750 and 1775 the mainland population doubled—from 1.2 million to 2.5 million—sparking legal battles over land, which became increasingly valuable. Violence broke out in newly settled regions as backcountry settlers fought with Indians, rival claimants, and eastern-dominated governments.

son River Valley. New England yeomen farmers refused to accept the tenancy leaseholds that were customary on the great New York manorial estates. Instead, they purchased freehold titles from Massachusetts land speculators and roused the long-settled Dutch and German tenants to repudiate their manorial leases.

Manorial lords enforced their claims in New York courts, setting off a rebellion. In 1766 New England migrants and tenant farmers in Westchester, Dutchess, and Albany counties refused to pay rent and used the threat of mob violence to close the courts. At the behest of the royal governor, General Thomas Gage led two British regiments to assist local sheriffs and manorial bailiffs in suppressing the tenant uprising and evicting New England squatters.

Proprietary Power. Other large landowners also won legal and political battles. In New Jersey and throughout the southern colonies, resident landowners and English aristocrats revived old land grants from the time of Charles II (1660–1685), and judges supported their claims to quitrents in regions settled by yeomen farmers and to vast tracts of undeveloped land. Lord Granville, an heir of one of the original Carolina proprietors, collected quitrents in the Granville district of North Carolina, and a legal suit gave Lord Fairfax ownership of the entire northern neck of Virginia along the Potomac.

Long-established proprietary families profited anew from the increased demand for land. Many farmers in settled regions could not afford "improved" freehold properties with cultivated fields, orchards, and fenced grazing land. Reluctantly, they turned to proprietors for tenancy leases on manorial estates or for undeveloped land. By the 1760s the Maryland proprietor, Lord Baltimore, was one of the richest men in England because of his American real estate. The Penn family reaped great profits from land sales and rents in Pennsylvania.

This revival of proprietary power underscored the growing strength of the landed gentry and the increasing resemblance between rural societies in Europe and America. High-quality land east of the Appalachians was getting more expensive, and much of it was controlled by English aristocrats, manorial landlords, and wealthy speculators. Unless something changed, tenants and even yeomen farmers might soon be reduced to the status of European peasants.

Uprisings in the West

As farmers moved west in search of land, they found themselves in the middle of new political and economic conflicts over Indian policy, political representation, and bankruptcy. Events erupted in violence on the frontiers of Pennsylvania and North and South Carolina.

The Paxton Boys. In Pennsylvania the white community came to blows over Indian policy. As long as Quakers had dominated Pennsylvania politics, relations with native American tribes had remained peaceful. After 1740, however, when large numbers of Scots-Irish migrants settled along the frontier, they wanted to push the Indians off the land. When the Quakers refused to help them, the frontiersmen reacted with violence. In 1763 the Paxton Boys, a band of Scots-Irish farmers, massacred twenty members of the Conestoga tribe, which included the last remnants of the once numerous Susquehannock people. When Governor John Penn attempted to protect the tribe and bring the murderers to justice, about 250 armed Scots-Irish advanced on Philadelphia, forcing the governor to mobilize the militia to defend the city. Benjamin Franklin intercepted the angry mob at Lancaster to seek a compromise, and a battle outside Philadelphia was narrowly averted (see American Voices, page 133).

Ultimately, the prosecution of the accused men failed for lack of witnesses, and the Scots-Irish dropped their demands for the expulsion of the Indians. But the episode left a legacy of racial and ethnic hatred and political resentment. During the independence crisis the Scots-Irish would take their revenge against both Indians in the West and the Quaker and Anglican elite in the East.

The South Carolina Regulators. During the French and Indian War there had been brutal warfare between land-seeking whites and the Cherokee in the backcountry of South Carolina. After the war outlaw bands of whites continued to roam the countryside, unchallenged by government authority. To subdue the outlaw bands and restore order, slaveowning planters and yeomen farmers banded together in an armed vigilante group called the Regulators. They took it upon themselves to impose moral discipline on the "low people"—the hunters, squatters, and landless laborers who lived on the fringes of society—by whipping people suspected of poaching or stealing goods.

The Regulators also struggled for western rights, presenting a list of demands to the eastern authorities: they wanted more local courts, fairer taxes, and greater representation in the provincial assembly. The South Carolina government accepted Regulator rule in the west despite its illegal character. Both the royal governor and the members of the provincial assembly were afraid to send troops to the backcountry because they feared slave revolts on the lowland rice plantations if the militia was away. They therefore compromised with backcountry insurgents, creating locally controlled courts in the west in 1767 and reducing the fees for legal documents. Lowland planter-merchants kept a firm grip on political power, however, refusing to reapportion the legislature to give western settlers representation proportionate to their growing numbers. The assembly also continued to tax the thin soil of the upland region at the same rate as the fertile lands of the low country.

A Backcountry Road
The first settlers in interior valleys lived in small, crude log cabins that were strung
out along the road. Loneliness and desolation, suggested here by a solitary rider, were
overcome by concerted efforts to build social communities, often through church-
centered activities. (Collection of The New-York Historical Society)

Because many western residents resisted their arbitrary assumption of power, the Regulators could not continue the struggle. Vowing to end Regulator rule, men
who had previously served as justices of the peace in the
backcountry organized a Moderator movement. In
March 1769, 600 armed supporters of each faction met
near the Saluda River and exchanged angry words, then
gunshots. Only an agreement to restore authority to the
provincial government averted wholesale violence. Like
the Paxton Boys in Pennsylvania, the Regulators attracted
attention to western interests but failed to alter the balance of power. Eastern interests remained dominant.

The North Carolina Regulators. In North Carolina the
key issue dividing east and west was commercial credit.
By the 1760s the transatlantic market system extended
far into the backcountry. At small stores owned by Scottish merchants, farmers and planters exchanged tobacco, wheat, and hides for manufactured goods and
bought land and slaves on credit. The more ambitious
among them created small-scale slave plantations, so
that the number of blacks rose. In Orange County, North
Carolina, the number of enslaved African-Americans
jumped from 45 in 1754 to 729 by 1767.

But tobacco prices plummeted after the Great War
for Empire, and many farmers found themselves deeply

in debt. In one three-year period, merchants in
Granville County brought 350 debt suits to local courts.
Judges directed sheriffs to seize the property of bankrupt farmers and sell it at auction to pay creditors and
court costs. Backcountry farmers resented this recourse
to the courts both because it generated high fees for
lawyers and court officials and because it violated local
customs. As in rural communities in New England,
loans among neighbors were based on trust and often
ran for years.

To save their farms, North Carolina debtors created
their own Regulator movement. At first the Regulators
intimidated judges, closed courts by force, and broke
into jails to free their leaders. Then they sought to elect
planters and farmers to the legislature. Their leader, a
migrant from Maryland named Herman Husband, told
his followers not to vote for "any Clerk, Lawyer, or
Scotch merchant. We must make these men subject to
the laws or they will enslave the whole community."
The Regulators demanded a law allowing them to pay
their taxes in the "produce of the country" rather than
in cash; they also wanted legal fees reduced, and—like
the South Carolina Regulators—they asked for fairer
taxes and greater legislative representation.

The North Carolina Regulators developed the most
broad-based and democratic program of all the back-

Henry Melchior Muhlenberg

The Paxton Boys March on Philadelphia

Racial conflict on the frontier sparked ethnic and religious confrontation in Pennsylvania as armed Scots-Irish Presbyterians marched on Philadelphia. Lutheran Germans opposed many of the policies of the politically dominant (and usually pacifist) Quakers and their German Moravian allies. This journal entry by the leading Lutheran minister Henry Melchior Muhlenberg mocks the hypocrisy of the Quakers and, in the process, reveals the extent of ethnic antagonism in Pennsylvania.

February 5. Toward evening the rumor sprang up that a corps of backwoods settlers—Englishmen, Irishmen, and Germans—were on the march toward Philadelphia to kill the Bethlehem Indians at the barracks outside the city. Some reported that they numbered seven hundred, others said fifteen hundred, etc. The Friends, or so-called Quakers, and the Moravians ran furiously back and forth to the barracks, and there was a great to-do over constructing several small fortresses or ramparts near the barracks. Cannons were also set up. Some remarked concerning all this that it seemed strange that such preparations should be made against one's own fellow citizens and Christians, whereas no one ever took so much trouble to protect from the Indians His Majesty's subjects and citizens on the frontier.

As far as I can learn, the opinion and sentiment of various ones of our German citizens is as follows:

That the Quakers and Bethlehemites had only used some of the aforesaid Indians as spies and that they had in view only their own selfish interests . . . which explained why the Quakers, etc. in Philadelphia did not exhibit the least evidence of human sympathy, etc. when Germans and other settlers on the frontiers were massacred and destroyed in the most inhuman manner by the Indians.

After two o'clock at night the watchmen began to cry, "Fire!" I asked our watchman, who is a member of our congregation, where the fire was. He said there was no fire, but that the watchmen had orders to cry out, "Fire," because the above-mentioned backwoodsmen were approaching. Thereupon all the alarm bells began to ring at once and a drum was sounded to summon the inhabitants of the city to the town hall plaza. The ringing sounded dreadful in the night.

A whole *troup* of small boys followed a prominent Quaker down the street shouting in amazement, "Look, look! a Quaker carrying a musket on his shoulder!" Indeed, the older folks also looked upon it as a miraculous portent to see so many old and young Quakers arming themselves with flintlocks and daggers, or so-called murderous weapons! What heightened their amazement was this: that these pious sheep, who had such a tender conscience during the long Spanish, French, and Indian War, and would rather have died than lift a hand for defense against the most dangerous enemies, were now all of a sudden willing to put on horns of iron like Zedekiah, the son of Chenaanah (I Kings 22), and shoot and smite a small group of their poor, oppressed, driven, and suffering fellow inhabitants and citizens from the frontier!

Source: Theodore G. Tappert and John W. Doberstein, eds., *The Notebook of a Colonial Clergyman* (Philadelphia, 1959).

---

country movements. In Anson County, for example, they argued that each person should pay taxes "in proportion to the profits arising from his estate." But the North Carolina insurgents were no more successful than were the other western protesters. In 1771 Governor William Tryon mobilized the militia and defeated a large Regulator force at the Alamance River; seven insurgent leaders were summarily executed. Not since Leisler's 1689 revolt in New York had political conflict in America resulted in so much bloodshed.

In 1771 as in 1689, colonial conflicts became intertwined with imperial politics. In far-off Connecticut, the Reverend Ezra Stiles defended the Regulators. "What shall an injured & oppressed people do," he asked, when they are faced with "Oppression and tyranny (under the name of Government)?" Stiles saw himself as an American patriot, and his condemnation of Governor Tryon in 1771 reflected American resistance to British imperial control. But Stiles's remarks also served as a commentary on developments in the mainland colonies between 1720 and 1765. These were years of crisis—agricultural, religious, ethnic, and military—but also of transformation. In 1765 America was still a dependent society closely tied to Britain by trade, culture, and politics, but it was also an increasingly complex society with the potential for an independent existence. British policies would determine the direction the maturing colonies would take.

Summary

By 1720 a freeholding yeoman society had developed in New England. Its families were controlled by men, who assumed ownership of their wives' property and provided inheritances for the children. When rapid population growth began to threaten the freehold ideal, New England farmers averted a crisis by planting higher-yielding crops, sharing their labor and goods with each other, and moving farther to the west.

In the mid-Atlantic colonies the rising European demand for wheat, their principal crop, brought prosperity to many farmers. A great influx of German and Scots-Irish migrants created an ethnically diverse society where religious groups held to their own beliefs but tolerated the traditions of others. Ethnic conflict did break out, especially over the Quakers' pacifist Indian policy, and the emergence of stark economic inequality created new tensions. While some gentlemen farmers and entrepreneurs grew wealthy, a new landless class began to appear at the bottom of the social order.

As the American colonies became more integrated into the world economy, they also participated more fully in the intellectual life of Europe. Enlightenment rationalism influenced educated Americans such as Benjamin Franklin, and pietistic religion reinvigorated colonial churches. The preaching of George Whitefield prompted a Great Awakening in the early 1740s that brought spiritual renewal to thousands of Americans, but not without sparking conflict. In the northern colonies enthusiastic New Lights condemned traditional Old Lights, and in Virginia evangelical Baptists converted white tenant farmers and enslaved blacks, challenging the religious and social dominance of the Anglican elite.

Beginning in the 1740s, the mainland colonies experienced a series of upheavals. Manorial lords in New York suppressed tenant uprisings, and proprietors in many colonies successfully asserted their economic and legal rights. Yeomen families who had migrated into the backcountry of the Carolinas fought with native Americans and other settlers over land and challenged the authority of eastern political leaders. And British and American soldiers fought a major war against the French, conquering Quebec and driving the French out of North America. These conflicts, along with the expansion of transatlantic trade, testified to the growing involvement of the colonies in the diplomacy, commerce, and intellectual life of Europe. Britain's North American provinces were growing—in economic complexity, political vitality, and military potential.

TIMELINE

1700	Freehold ideal in rural communities Household mode of production Arranged marriages common Woman's "place" as subordinate helpmate Female literacy in New England expands
1700–1714	New Hudson River manors created
1720s	German migrants settle in middle colonies Scots-Irish migration grows Enlightenment ideas spread to America Frelinghuysen holds revivals
1730s	Tennents lead Presbyterian revivals Jonathan Edwards preaches in New England
1739	George Whitefield and the Great Awakening War of Jenkins' Ear
1740–1760s	Population pressure in New England Smaller family size; more premarital pregnancies Women active in religion and market activities Ethnic pluralism in middle colonies Rising grain and tobacco prices Increasing rural inequality
1740s	Old Lights versus New Lights Religious establishment questioned New colleges founded Newspapers increase Enlightenment ideas (Locke, Newton) spread
1743	Franklin founds American Philosophical Society
1749	Ohio Company formed Susquehannah Company in Connecticut
1750s	Proprietary resurgence Industrial Revolution begins in England Consumer "revolution" raises American debt Indian "play-off" system breaks down
1754	French and Indian War begins Albany Congress
1755	French Acadians deported
1759	Fall of Quebec
1760s	New York and New England border conflicts Regulator movements in the Carolinas Evangelical Baptists in Virginia
1762	Treaty of Fontainebleau gives Louisiana to Spain
1763	Treaty of Paris ends Great War for Empire Florida and Canada ceded to Britain Postwar colonial recession Pontiac leads Indian uprising Paxton Boys in Pennsylvania

★   ★   ★

BIBLIOGRAPHY

A fine collection of important articles can be found in Stanley Katz, John Murrin, and Douglas Greenberg, eds., *Colonial America: Essays in Politics and Social Development*, 4th ed. (1993). John J. McCusker and Russell R. Menard, *The Economy of British America, 1607–1783* (1985), survey economic change, whereas Jon Butler, *Awash in a Sea of Faith: Christianizing the American People* (1990), covers religious developments. Jack P. Greene, *Pursuits of Happiness* (1988), offers a provocative comparative analysis of regional social evolution.

Freehold Society in New England

A good local study is Daniel Vickers, *Farmers & Fishermen: Two Centuries of Work in Essex County Massachusetts, 1630–1830* (1994), whereas Bruce C. Daniels, *The Fragmentation of New England: Comparative Perspectives on Economic, Political, and Social Divisions in the Eighteenth Century* (1988), and Allan Kulikoff, *The Agrarian Origins of American Capitalism* (1992), offer a wider view. See also Robert Gross, *The Minutemen and Their World* (1976), and Richard Bushman, *From Puritan to Yankee: Character and the Social Order in Connecticut, 1690–1765* (1967). On women's lives, see Laurel Thatcher Ulrich, *Good Wives: Image and Reality in the Lives of Women of Northern New England, 1650–1750* (1982), and Marylynn Salmon, *Women and the Law of Property in Early America* (1986). For studies of material culture that reveal the character of society, see Robert B. St. George, ed., *Material Life In America, 1600–1860* (1988).

The Mid-Atlantic: Toward a New Society

On Pennsylvania, consult Michael Zuckerman, ed., *Friends and Neighbors: Group Life in America's First Plural Society* (1982); Allan Tully, *William Penn's Legacy: Pennsylvania, 1726–1755* (1978); and Barry J. Levy, *Quakers and the American Family* (1988). James T. Lemon, *The Best Poor Man's Country* (1972), pays some attention to ethnicity, as does Marilyn J. Westerkamp, *Triumph of the Laity: Scots-Irish Piety and the Great Awakening, 1625–1760* (1988). On white indentured servants and ethnic migration, see the classic study by Abbot E. Smith, *Colonists in Bondage* (1947); R. Greg Roeber, *Palatines, Liberty, and Property: German Lutherans in Colonial British America* (1993); R. J. Dickson, *Ulster Immigration to Colonial America, 1718–1775* (1966); Jon Butler, *The Huguenots in America* (1983); Ned Landsman, *Scotland and Its First American Colony, 1683–1775* (1985); and A. Roger Ekirch, *Bound for America: The Transportation of British Convicts to the Colonies, 1718–1775* (1987). Other important studies include Patricia U. Bonomi, *A Factious People: Politics and Society in Colonial New York* (1971), and Thomas L. Purvis, *Proprietors, Patronage, and Money: New Jersey, 1703–1776* (1986).

The Enlightenment and the Great Awakening

Henry F. May, *The Enlightenment in America* (1976), is still the standard treatment, but see also Paul Merrill Spurlin, *The French Enlightenment in America* (1984), and Herbert Leven-thal, *In the Shadow of the Enlightenment: Occultism and Renaissance Science in Eighteenth-Century America* (1976). For medical knowledge see Richard Shryock, *Medicine and Society in America, 1660–1860* (1960). Brooke Hindle, *The Pursuit of Science in Revolutionary America, 1735–1789* (1956), and John C. Greene, *American Science in the Age of Jefferson* (1984), are also relevant.

Good studies of the Great Awakening include David S. Lovejoy, *Religious Enthusiasm in the New World: Heresy to Revolution* (1985); Patricia U. Bonomi, *Under the Cope of Heaven: Religion, Society, and Politics in Colonial America* (1986); and Harry S. Stout, *The New England Soul: Preaching and Religious Culture in Colonial New England* (1986). Three good biographies of New England revivalists are Patricia Tracy, *Jonathan Edwards, Pastor* (1979); W. G. McLoughlin, *Isaac Backus and American Pietistic Tradition* (1957); and Christopher Jedrey, *The World of John Cleaveland* (1979). Richard Bushman, ed., *The Great Awakening* (1970), and Rhys Isaac, *The Transformation of Virginia, 1740–1790* (1982), capture the emotions of ordinary participants.

Bernard Bailyn, *Education in the Forming of American Society* (1960), is a stimulating introduction, while Lawrence A. Cremin, *American Education: The Colonial Experience, 1607–1783* (1970), offers a comprehensive treatment. William L. Joyce et al., eds., *Printing and Society in Early America* (1983), assesses the impact of books, pamphlets, and newspapers on the American mind.

The Midcentury Challenge: War, Trade, and Land

Douglas E. Leach, *Roots of Conflict: British Armed Forces and Colonial Americans, 1677–1763* (1986), sets the Great War for Empire in a larger context. See also Edward P. Hamilton, *The French and Indian Wars* (1962); Guy Fregault, *Canada: The War of the Conquest* (1969); George F. G. Stanley, *New France: The Last Phase, 1744–1760* (1968); and Fred Anderson, *A People's Army: Massachusetts Soldiers and Society in the Seven Years' War* (1984). Richard White, *The Middle Ground* (1991), and Francis Jennings, *Empire of Fortune: Crown, Colonies, and Tribes in the Seven Years' War* (1988), describe the crucial role played by Indians in the conflict. See also Richard Aquila, *The Iroquois Restoration: Iroquois Diplomacy on the Colonial Frontier, 1701–1754* (1983), and David H. Corkran, *The Cherokee Frontier: Conflict and Survival, 1740–1762* (1966).

Gary M. Walton and James F. Shepherd, *The Economic Rise of Early America* (1979), trace the growing importance of commerce. See also Paul G. E. Clemens, *The Atlantic Economy and Colonial Maryland's Eastern Shore: From Tobacco to Grain* (1980), and Jacob M. Price, *Capital and Credit in British Overseas Trade: The View from the Chesapeake, 1700–1776* (1980).

Backcountry political agitation forms the focus of Richard D. Brown, *The South Carolina Regulators* (1963), and some of the essays in Alfred Young, ed., *The American Revolution: Essays in the History of American Radicalism* (1976). See also W. Stitt Robinson, *The Southern Colonial Frontier, 1607–1763* (1979); Charles E. Clark, *The Eastern Frontier: The Settlement of Northern New England, 1610–1763* (1970); and Richard Beeman, *The Evolution of the Southern Backcountry* (1984).

Occupation of Concord by the British (detail)

The British marched to Lexington and Concord in force and searched houses in the town center for arms and munitions. Hearing of the skirmishes, the New England portraitist Ralph Earl visited the sites, creating this and other paintings of the campaign.

Toward Independence: Years of Decision

1763–1775

★   ★   ★

At the end of the Great War for Empire the American colonists were loyal subjects of Great Britain. Twelve years later the colonies stood on the brink of civil war—angry, armed, and resistant to British authority. How had it happened, asked the president of King's College in New York, that such a "happily situated" people should decide to "hazard their Fortunes, their Lives, and their Souls, in such a Rebellion"?

This rapid and unexpected change had two broad sets of causes. First, the character of the American political and social system fostered dreams of autonomy. Unlike most colonial peoples, Americans lived in a prosperous, stable society with a strong tradition of representative government. This unique historical experience created vigorous, experienced leaders and a self-confident populace capable of supporting an independence movement. Still, most Americans had been content for generations under British rule. What sparked them to rebel—the second, and immediate, cause of the independence movement—was Britain's attempt to reform the imperial system.

The story of the rebellion unfolded in four distinct phases. First, a British reform initiative began during the war and culminated in the Stamp Act of 1765. This tax legislation led to the second phase, an angry protest against new economic burdens and the constitutional principles on which they were based. A political compromise provided only a temporary respite; between 1767 and 1770 the third phase of the confrontation witnessed the imposition of new British taxes, the revival of American resistance, and a second compromise. Then a final crisis precipitated by a tax on tea unleashed the deep passions stirred up by a decade of reform and resistance, producing a civil war within the British empire.

The Reform Movement, 1763–1765

Military power made Britain the dominant nation in Europe after the Great War for Empire. France had been checked on the Continent, and Britannia ruled the waves for the next century and a half. By driving the French out of Canada, Britain had also achieved dominance over eastern North America (see Map 5.1). The way was clear for Britain to impose central control on its American colonies.

Tensions in the Imperial System

The Great War for Empire strained the imperial political system and brought to light deep-seated differences between Britain and its colonies. Before 1754 only royal governors and a few merchants and naval officers had experienced life in the American provinces. During the conflict, however, hundreds of British army officers and middle-level bureaucrats came to the mainland colonies, and they did not like what they saw. Provincial soldiers were drawn from the dregs of society, General James Wolfe told a friend. "There is no depending on them in

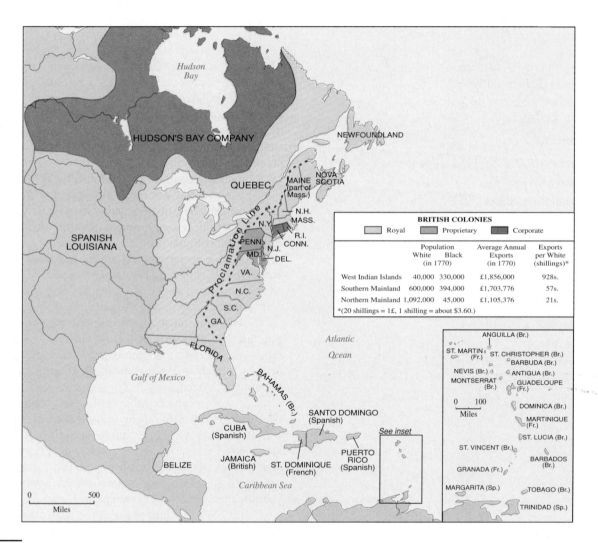

BRITISH COLONIES		
Royal	Proprietary	Corporate

	Population White (in 1770)	Black	Average Annual Exports (in 1770)	Exports per White (shillings)*
West Indian Islands	40,000	330,000	£1,856,000	928s.
Southern Mainland	600,000	394,000	£1,703,776	57s.
Northern Mainland	1,092,000	45,000	£1,105,376	21s.

*(20 shillings = 1£, 1 shilling = about $3.60.)

MAP 5.1

Britain's American Empire in 1763

In 1763 Britain was dominant in the West Indies and controlled all of eastern North America. British ministers dispatched troops to the conquered colonies of Florida and Quebec and, with the Proclamation Line of 1763, sought to prevent Anglo-American settlement west of the Appalachian Mountains.

action." For their part, Americans were shocked by the arrogance of upper-crust British officers and by the rigors of military discipline. British troops, a Massachusetts militiaman wrote in his diary, "are but little better than slaves to their officers."

Disputes over Taxes and Trade. The war also exposed the weakness of British administrative control, especially as it was wielded by the royal governors. In theory, governors had extensive political powers, including command of the provincial militia. In reality, they had to share power with the colonial assemblies, which refused to support the war effort with taxes and troops unless the governor relinquished control over military appointments and operations. Britain's Board of Trade complained that in Massachusetts "almost every act of executive and legislative power is ordered and directed by votes and resolves of the General Court."

In Virginia the assembly refused to levy additional taxes to pay for the war. The Burgesses resorted instead to deficit financing, printing paper currency in amounts sufficient to pay the province's bills. As the colony's government bought military supplies and paid troops, the purchasing power of the currency fell nearly 20 percent. Yet Virginia law required merchants and other creditors to accept the currency as legal tender, at face value. British merchants in the colony refused to accept payment in depreciated currency and applied to Parliament for relief. Parliament had helped before, passing a Currency Act in 1751 that had placed strict regulations on the issuing of government bills of credit by the New England colonies and had prohibited their use as legal tender to pay private debts. Now the British legislature passed another Currency Act (1764), banning the use of paper money as legal tender in Virginia and all the colonies. Americans would have to pay their debts to merchants with British currency, foreign coins, or bills of exchange. Equally important, Parliament had seized control of the colonial monetary system from the American assemblies.

Imperial authorities also began to enforce the Navigation Acts, regulating colonial trade more strictly. Before the war American merchants had routinely bribed colonial customs officials to circumvent the Molasses Act of 1733. To curb such corruption, in 1762 Parliament passed a Revenue Act, which prohibited officeholders in the customs department from leasing offices to deputies, who had often accepted bribes to support themselves while paying the absentee officeholders. Moreover, the Royal Navy was instructed to block all trade with the French islands. Royal officials had been shocked to find that during the war with France colonial merchants had continued to ship food and supplies to the French islands. It was absurd, declared an outraged British politician, that French armies attempting

"to Destroy one English province, are actually supported by Bread raised in another." Such commerce, the British ministry charged, allowed the French "to sustain and protract this long and expensive war."

British Troops in America. The most striking evidence of Britain's determination to protect and control its colonies was the decision in 1763 to station a large peacetime army—fifteen regiments of infantry, about 10,000 men—in North America. There were three reasons for this move. First, because most French settlers, some 60,000 in number, chose to remain in Canada, Britain needed troops to discourage rebellion in the newly captured province of Quebec. British troops also occupied Florida, which Spain wanted back but whose Spanish residents had mostly fled to Havana.

Second, officials in London feared another Indian war. The rebellion begun by the Ottawa chief Pontiac in May 1763 was still raging (see Chapter 4) and seemed to confirm the wisdom of maintaining substantial garrisons in the forts taken from the French. Pontiac's rebellion had also taught the British that what the Indians most feared was white settlement. In October, as an additional step to prevent trouble in the Ohio River Valley, King George III issued the Proclamation of 1763, which prohibited white settlement west of the crest of the Appalachians and regulated the fur trade with the Indian peoples. The Proclamation angered American land speculators, whose drive for expansion in the Ohio River Valley had started the war with France in the first place, and was ignored by thousands of land-hungry white settlers. As many as 50,000 whites—"too Lawless and Licentious ever to be restrained," according to one British official—may have lived west of the Appalachians by 1775.

The third reason for deploying the troops was the apprehension on the part of some British politicians of an American independence movement, a fear that had been growing since the late 1740s. "I have been publickly told," the Swedish traveler Peter Kalm reported from America in 1748, "that within thirty or fifty years, the English colonies may constitute a separate state, wholly independent of England." Only the danger of a French invasion from Canada, Kalm thought, deterred colonists from demanding greater autonomy. For that reason, some British officials argued during the peace negotiations of 1763 that it would be prudent to return Canada to France while keeping the West Indian sugar islands of Guadeloupe and Martinique. Given the decision to keep Canada, officials such as Henry Knox, a former treasury official in Georgia, recommended a strong British military presence in the mainland colonies. Indeed, Knox wrote in a memorandum to policy makers, "The main purpose of Stationing a large Body of Troops in America is to secure the Dependence of the Colonys on Great Britain."

Of course, the presence of British troops would not necessarily stop Americans from demanding political autonomy. In the 1740s, when land riots had broken out in New Jersey, Governor Jonathan Belcher had advised royal authorities that simply stationing British troops in the colony would not "drive Assemblies or people from their Obstinate ways of Thinking, into reasonable measures." Belcher knew that to be effective, military power had to be used to impose royal edicts or curb the power of local officeholders. In establishing a large military presence in America, the British ministry showed that it might be prepared to use force to preserve and extend imperial rule.

The Financial Legacy of the War

Britain paid a substantial price at home for its military successes abroad. During the Great War for Empire the British East India Company had routed the French in India, opening up the rich subcontinent to British commerce and eventual conquest, but the conflict had drained the company. Its well-connected officials looked to the British government for new subsidies and privileges, but the Treasury was empty. The government had borrowed heavily from British and Dutch bankers to finance the war, and the national debt had almost doubled, from £75 million in 1754 to £133 million in 1763.

This huge war debt placed a new financial burden on the British prime minister, Lord Bute, the lackluster favorite of George III who had replaced William Pitt in 1761. As the war came to a close, Bute's ministry had to find funds to pay the interest on the debt as well as the normal expenses of government. Treasury officials advised against raising the land tax, which was already at an all-time high and was paid by the propertied classes, whose support the government needed. The ministry therefore imposed higher import duties on tobacco and sugar, which manufacturers passed on to consumers in the form of higher prices. The government also increased *excise levies*—sales taxes—on goods such as salt and beer and distilled spirits, once again passing along the costs of the war to ordinary people.

To collect these taxes and duties, the British government had to expand its bureaucracy (see Figure 5.1). Between 1750 and 1775 the number of royal officials in Britain jumped from about 5,000 to more than 11,000. Parliament gave the new bureaucrats increased administrative and legal powers. Customs agents and informers patrolled the coasts of southern Britain, arresting smugglers and seizing tons of goods—such as French wines and Flemish textiles—on which import duties had not been paid. Convicted smugglers faced heavy penalties, including death or "transportation" to America as indentured servants.

The legacy of the war was therefore a paradoxical mix. Along with immense military power and increased national pride for Britain came huge debts, tighter governmental control, and rising domestic dissent. Beginning with the ascendancy of Sir Robert Walpole in the 1730s, radical Real Whigs and conservative Country party landlords had emphasized the dangers of unlimited government, and now their worst fears seemed to have come to pass. The Treasury was at the mercy of the "monied interest"—the banks and financiers who had paid for the war and were reaping millions of

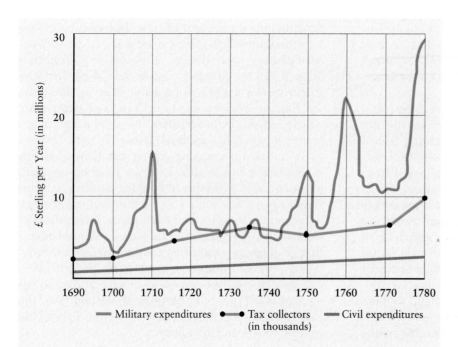

FIGURE 5.1

The Growing Power of the British State

As Britain built a great navy and subsidized the armies of its European allies, the government's military expenditures soared, as did the number of tax collectors. The tax bureaucracy doubled in size between 1700 and 1735 and doubled again between 1750 and 1780.

Britain Triumphant
This painting celebrates the Great War for Empire by praising two of its heroes, Prime Minister William Pitt and General James Wolfe, who was killed during the battle of Quebec. It also conveys a political message with Real Whig overtones, warning the king against "Evil and Corrupt Ministers."

pounds in interest from government bonds. And with the number of royal officers skyrocketing, the evils of patronage and administrative abuse became more apparent. Warning that a corrupt Parliament filled with "worthless *pensioners* and *placemen*" had embarked on a systematic plan to extinguish British liberty, reformers demanded that Parliament be made more representative. In 1763, for example, the Radical Whig John Wilkes demanded an end to *rotten boroughs*—tiny districts whose voters were controlled by wealthy aristocrats and merchants. The price of empire abroad was debt and dissent at home.

British Reform Strategy

The Great War for Empire brought a decisive end to the era of salutary neglect. During the war a new generation of British political leaders had come to power, determined not only to defeat France but also to reform the imperial system. Charles Townshend of the Board of Trade and Prime Minister William Pitt had a broad vision. They agreed with Thomas Pownall, the former governor of Massachusetts, that "the spirit of *commerce* will become the predominant power, which will rule the powers of Europe" and that the American colonies were the key to commercial success. In their eyes, the mainland settlers had systematically evaded their responsibilities, defying the Navigation Acts by smuggling, trading with the French during wartime, and refusing to pay a fair share of the cost of their military defense. The continued growth of British trade and national power depended on the reform of imperial administration and taxation.

At first political instability in Britain hampered the quest for reform. When George III came to the throne in 1760, he reasserted the power of the monarchy, disrupting Walpole's system of cooperation between the king and Parliament. In particular, George insisted in 1761 on installing Lord Bute, his favorite, as prime minister even though Bute did not control a majority in the House of Commons. Bute successfully negotiated the Treaty of Paris, ending the war, but resigned in 1763, unable to resolve the growing financial crisis. The king then turned reluctantly to George Grenville, who enjoyed strong support in Parliament.

The Sugar Act. Grenville, an astute politician, embraced the cause of imperial reform. Shortly after becoming prime minister, he introduced the Sugar Act of 1764. This new Navigation Act, a revision of the Molasses Act of 1733, resulted from a wide-ranging review of the West Indian trade system by Treasury officials Thomas Whatley and Charles Jenkinson. Whatley and Jenkinson had long been governmental contacts for colonial agents—resident Americans or English merchants who represented the interests of the colonial assemblies in London. They knew that the mainland settlers had to sell their wheat, fish, and lumber in the French islands. Without the molasses, sugar, and bills of exchange that those sales brought, the colonists would lack the funds to buy British manufactured goods. The Treasury officials therefore resisted demands from British sugar planters to cut off this trade by enforcing the Molasses Act's high duty of 6 pence per gallon on molasses imported from the French West Indies. Instead, they instituted a smaller duty of 3 pence per gallon, arguing that this levy would allow British molasses to compete with the cheaper

French product without destroying the mainland's export trade or distilling industry.

But American merchants and manufacturers refused to accept this compromise. Many New England traders, such as John Hancock of Boston, had made their fortunes by smuggling huge quantities of French molasses without paying any duty. Their profits—illegally gained in the first place—would be severely cut by the new regulations. The merchants, joined by New England distillers who feared higher costs, orchestrated a petition campaign against the Sugar Act. Publicly, they protested that the tax called for in the Sugar Act would wipe out trade with the French islands. Privately, they vowed to evade the duty by smuggling or by bribing officials.

Imperial reform had legal and political as well as economic consequences as merchants and their allies raised constitutional objections to the Sugar Act. Thomas Cushing, speaker of the Massachusetts House of Representatives, argued that the duties constituted a "tax," so that the Sugar Act was "contrary to a fundamental Principall of our Constitution: That all Taxes ought to originate with the people." A House committee went further, declaring that such parliamentary acts "have a tendency to deprive the colonies of some of their most essential Rights as British subjects." Whatley and Jenkinson's attempt to balance the interests of British sugar planters and those of mainland settlers had become a bitterly contested constitutional issue. The terms of debate had shifted, and fatefully so.

Vice-Admiralty Courts and the "Rights of Englishmen." In addition to levying duties, the Sugar Act of 1764 extended the jurisdiction of *vice-admiralty courts*—maritime tribunals that operated without the procedures and protections of English common law. There was no trial by jury in those courts. Rather, a judge—usually one with British sympathies—heard arguments and decided cases solely on the basis of Parliamentary legislation.

For half a century colonial legislatures had vigorously opposed vice-admiralty courts, which had been introduced to put teeth in the Navigation Acts. To limit the power of these courts, which had long been opposed in Britain not only by smugglers but also by principled opponents of royal power, the assemblies extended the jurisdiction of their own courts over all customs offenses occurring in American seaports or coastal waters. Thus merchants charged with violating the Navigation Acts often were acquitted by well-disposed common-law juries or American-born judges. By extending the jurisdiction of vice-admiralty courts to all customs offenses wherever they occurred, the Sugar Act closed this loophole.

The powers given to the vice-admiralty courts thus revived old American fears and raised new constitu-

tional objections. Richard Bland, an influential Virginia planter, charged that the courts illegally discriminated against British subjects living in America; the colonists "were not sent out to be the Slaves but to be the Equals of those that remained behind," Bland asserted. John Adams, a young Massachusetts lawyer who defended John Hancock on a charge of smuggling, took a similar position:

> Here is the contrast that stares us in the face. The Parliament in one Clause guarding the People of the Realm, and securing to them the benefit of a Tryal by the Law of the Land, and by the next Clause, depriving all Americans of that Privilege. What shall we say to this Distinction? Is there not in this Clause a Brand of Infamy, or Degradation, and Disgrace, fixed upon every American? Is he not degraded below the rank of an Englishman?

The logic of Adams and Bland was compelling, though they had some of the facts wrong. Vice-admiralty courts had long played a major role in Britain. Adams and Bland were unaware of this or, caught up in the debate over imperial reform and American rights, were deliberately misleading their fellow colonists. In any case, the new vice-admiralty legislation did not discriminate against Americans. Instead, it extended British legal practices—albeit unpopular ones—to America.

The real issue was not the suppression of traditional American liberties but the growing authority of the British state both at home and abroad. The expanded royal bureaucracy was determined to root out smuggling and to raise revenues in Britain and North America. The colonists' righteous anger reflected their past experience; raised under a policy of salutary neglect, they instinctively resisted the new rules and procedures.

Yet in a larger sense, knowledgeable Americans such as Bland and Adams were right when they claimed that British policy challenged the existing constitutional structure of the empire. After the war many British officials denied that the colonists had the right to claim either the privileges inscribed in their royal charters or the traditional "rights of Englishmen." For example, when Royal Governor Francis Bernard of Massachusetts heard that the Massachusetts assembly had objected to the Sugar Act, claiming no taxation without representation, he asserted that the people in America did not have that constitutional right. "The rule that a *British* subject shall not be bound by laws or liable to taxes, but what he has consented to by his representatives," Bernard argued, "must be confined to the inhabitants of Great Britain only." In Bernard's eyes and those of many British political leaders, Americans were second-class subjects of the king, their rights limited by the Navigation Acts and the national interests of the British state as determined by Parliament.

The Stamp Act

The issue of taxation brought about the first great imperial crisis. When Grenville introduced the Sugar Act in Parliament in 1764, he also announced his intention to seek a colonial stamp tax the following year. He hoped that part of the £200,000 per year needed to clothe, house, feed, and pay the 10,000 soldiers the ministry planned to station in America would be covered by this new measure, which would require tax stamps on court documents, land titles, contracts, playing cards, newspapers, and other printed items. A similar English tax levied since 1694 had yielded an annual revenue of £290,000, and Grenville hoped the American levy would raise at least £60,000 (about $5 million today). The prime minister knew that some Americans would object to the tax on constitutional grounds, so he asked explicitly if any member of the House of Commons doubted "the power and sovereignty of Parliament over every part of the British dominions, for the purpose of raising or collecting any tax." No one rose to object.

Grenville informed the American assemblies that unless they could "raise a sum adequate to their defence,"

George Grenville, Architect of the Stamp Act
As prime minister from 1764 to 1766, Grenville assumed leadership of the movement for imperial reform and taxation. But most British politicians believed that the colonies should be better regulated and share the cost of the empire.

a stamp tax would be voted in 1765. This challenge threw the London agents of the colonial legislatures into confusion. They all agreed that the assemblies could not apportion the defense budget among themselves; the colonies had met together only on a single occasion, the Albany Congress of 1756, and not a single assembly had accepted its proposals. Agent Richard Jackson, an English merchant, advised the assemblies to accept the stamp tax because he believed that their long-standing claim to the sole right of taxation lacked a firm constitutional basis and that the tax would be imposed on them whether they liked it or not.

Benjamin Franklin, representing the Pennsylvania assembly, countered with a proposal for American representation in Parliament. "If you chuse to tax us," he suggested to a British friend, "give us Members in your Legislature, and let us be one People." But with the exception of William Pitt, who prepared a draft proposal for American representation in Parliament, British politicians rejected this radical idea. They argued that the colonists were "virtually" represented by the merchants who sat in Parliament and by other members with interests in America. Even colonial leaders were skeptical of Franklin's plan; they were "situate at a great Distance from their Mother Country," the Connecticut assembly declared in a printed pamphlet dispatched to London and therefore "cannot participate in the general Legislature of the Nation." Influential Philadelphia merchants, worried that a handful of colonial delegates would be powerless in Parliament, warned Franklin "to beware of any measure that might extend to us seats in the Commons."

But American leaders had no alternative to the plan proposed by Grenville, who was determined to assert the constitutional supremacy of Parliament. The Stamp Act was "the great measure of the Sessions," Grenville's chief assistant observed, "on account of the important point it establishes, the Right of Parliament to lay an internal Tax upon the Colonies." The ministry's plan worked smoothly. The House of Commons refused to accept American petitions opposing the new legislation, which it passed by an overwhelming vote of 205 to 49. Parliament also approved Grenville's proposal that violations of the Stamp Act be tried in vice-admiralty courts so that the colonists would have no hope of acquittal by friendly juries in local common-law courts.

Finally, at the request of General Thomas Gage, commander of British military forces in America, Parliament passed a Quartering Act that directed colonial governments to provide barracks and food for the British troops stationed there. During the French and Indian War the assemblies of Massachusetts and New York had refused to accept this financial burden, and the ministry was determined to force the colonists into compliance.

Grenville's design was complete. He had firmly declared the supremacy of the British Parliament and pushed forward the movement for imperial reform. But he also provoked a constitutional confrontation with the American assemblies not only on the crucial issue of taxes but also on the right to a trial by a local jury and on the support of a standing army. The intentions of the imperial authorities had become clear.

The Dynamics of Rebellion, 1765–1766

With the Sugar and Stamp acts, Grenville had thrown down the gauntlet to the American colonists. Would they resist this curtailment of the political autonomy achieved during the decades of salutary neglect? If they did, what were their chances of success? Settlers in various colonies had opposed unpopular laws or arbitrary governors, but they had never before faced a reform-minded ministry and Parliament. Some Patriots—as the defenders of American rights came to be called—resisted the new British measures forcefully by organizing resistance committees, rioting in the streets, or delivering speeches that bordered on treason. Many other Americans, moved by anti-imperial sentiments, economic self-interest, and religious and constitutional principles, rallied to the Patriot side. Still others, perhaps a majority, remained loyal to the king even as they questioned the wisdom of his ministers' policies.

The Crowd Rebels

The American response to the Stamp Act was more drastic than Grenville had predicted. Disciplined mobs led by men who called themselves the Sons of Liberty demanded the resignation of newly appointed stamp-tax collectors, most of whom were native-born colonists. One of the first incidents took place in Boston in August 1765, when the Boston Sons of Liberty made an effigy of the collector Andrew Oliver, which they beheaded and burned before destroying a new brick building that he owned. Boston merchants who opposed the Stamp Act advised Oliver to resign; otherwise "his House would be immediately destroyed and his Life in Continual Danger." Two weeks later Bostonians attacked the house of Lieutenant Governor Thomas Hutchinson. As a defender of social privilege and imperial authority, Hutchinson had many enemies. Now, in the heat of crisis, the common people took their revenge by destroying his house and burning his library.

In nearly every colony similar crowds of angry but purposeful people—the "rabble," as their American and

A British View of American Mobs
The artist depicts the Sons of Liberty as sadists, subjecting a British excise officer to physical abuse, and as wanton destroyers of property, dumping tea into the harbor. The Liberty Tree in the background raises the question: Does Liberty mean Anarchy?

British detractors called them—intimidated royal officials. Near Wethersfield, Connecticut, 500 farmers and artisans confronted the tax collector Jared Ingersoll. Ingersoll had been born into a prominent Connecticut family and had served as the assembly's agent in London. He had worked actively against the Stamp Act, but once it passed, he sought to profit from it by becoming a tax collector. Confronted by the fruits of that decision, Ingersoll debated with the leaders of the crowd for hours, but they refused to be swayed by his previous service to the colony or his high social status. An observer heard one rioter shout that he "lookt upon this as the Cause of the People" and would not "take Directions about it from any Body." Ingersoll finally capitulated. At the behest of the mob, he gave three cheers for "Liberty and Property," tossed his hat into the air, and, humbled, resigned from his office.

Motives of the Crowds. The strength of the Liberty mobs was surprising, but such crowd actions were a fact of political life in both Britain and America. For example, Protestant mobs burned the pope in effigy every November 5 to celebrate the failure of Guy Fawkes, a Catholic, to overturn the English government in 1605. Colonial mobs regularly destroyed houses used as brothels and often expressed anti-imperial sentiments. In 1747 Boston crowds rioted for three days to protest the impressment of merchant seamen for service in the Royal Navy. The crowds protesting the Stamp Act were simply acting according to tradition—beheading an effigy of Oliver reenacted the ritual killing of the pope on Guy Fawkes Day, and destroying Hutchinson's dwelling recalled attacks on houses of prostitution (see American Voices, page 146).

The social composition of the rioters was as traditional as their behavior, for premodern mobs usually represented a cross section of the middle and lower orders of society. Most Sons of Liberty were property-owning artisans who had previously known each other in jobs, churches, or neighborhoods. For example, of the thirty-six young men who formed the Sons of Liberty of Albany, New York, in 1765, twenty belonged to the same firefighter's club and twelve sat together in the balcony of the Dutch Reformed Church. The crowds themselves—which usually numbered in the hundreds and occasionally reached a few thousand—were more diverse. Seeking adventure and excitement, young apprentices and journeymen marched with their artisan masters, as did day laborers and unemployed sailors, the "rabble" of the port cities.

What distinguished the Stamp Act rioters were the motives of many of the participants. Some urban artisans joined the Liberty mobs out of economic self-interest. Imports of low-priced British shoes and other products were threatening their livelihood, and they feared that the stamp tax would lower their standard of living further—for the benefit of a rich governing class in Britain and America. Unlike "the Common people of England," a well-traveled colonist observed, "the people of America . . . never would submitt to be taxed that a few may be loaded with palaces and Pensions and riot in Luxury and Excess, while they themselves cannot support themselves and their needy offspring with Bread."

The religious passions aroused by the Great Awakening were another source of popular resistance. Some skilled workers were evangelical Protestants who led disciplined, hardworking lives, and they resented the arrogance and immorality of many British officers and the corrupt behavior of many royal bureaucrats. The image of the greedy British official seeking only the "gratification of his private Passions" loomed large in the pages of the *Independent Reflector*, a Real Whig newspaper published in New York during the 1750s.

Still other artisans had carried over from Britain the antimonarchical sentiments of the seventeenth-century Puritan revolution. A letter sent to a Boston newspaper promising to save "all the Freeborn Sons of America" from "tyrannical ministers" was signed "Oliver Cromwell." Other letters and handbills signed "O.C." threatened British officials and sympathizers with violence. The cry of "Liberty and Property" forced on Jared Ingersoll echoed ideological resistance to the taxes imposed by the Stuart kings. Thus, traditional fears of tyrannical power merged with economic self-interest and religious passion to create a potent anti-imperial outlook among the artisans and workers of the colonial cities.

Growing Popular Resistance. When the Stamp Act went into effect on November 1, 1765, most influential Americans advocated nonviolent resistance. In New York City, 200 merchants announced a boycott, vowing not to import British goods. Traders in Boston and Philadelphia quickly followed their example, but popular resentment against British policy was not easily contained. In New York less prosperous merchants such as Isaac Sears mobilized shopkeepers, tradesmen, artisans, laborers, and seamen in a mass protest meeting. They marched through the streets, breaking streetlamps and windows and crying "Liberty!" On November 2 nearly 3,000 New Yorkers joined a mob that plundered the house of an unpopular British officer and surrounded Fort George, where the tax stamps were stored, threatening to seize and destroy them.

On Guy Fawkes Day, November 5, Lieutenant Governor Cadwallader Colden feared an open assault on the fort and called on General Gage to use his small military force against the crowd. But the British commander refused. "Fire from the Fort might disperse the Mob, but it would not quell them," he told Colden, "and the consequence would in all appearances be an Insurrection, the Commencement of Civil War." Colden had to surrender the tax stamps.

Popular resistance nullified the Stamp Act throughout the colonies. Frightened collectors distributed few stamps to angry Americans, and royal officials and judges were at a loss. Slow communications across the Atlantic meant that the ministry's response to the riots would not be known until the following spring. In the meantime officials had to accept legal documents without the stamps.

The popular revolt of 1765 not only repudiated British authority but also gave a democratic cast to the emerging sense of American political identity. "Nothing is wanting but your own Resolution," a New York Son of Liberty declared during the upheaval, "for great is the Authority and Power of the People." Royal officials could no longer count on the deferential behavior that had ensured political stability for three generations. "What can a Governor do without the assistance of the

William Almy

A Stamp Act Riot, 1765

The Sons of Liberty attacked stamp-tax collectors in many cities, including Newport, Rhode Island. This letter describes the rituals observed by the Newport mob and the political awareness of its leaders (the devil-infested "Boot" is a satiric reference to Lord Bute, the prime minister from 1761 to 1763). It also suggests the high emotional and material price paid by those who opposed the Patriots by speaking and writing in defense of the Stamp Act.

In the morning of the 27th Inst. between five and six a Mob Assembled and Erected a Gallows near the Town House and then Dispers'd, and about Ten A Clock Reassembled and took

The Effigys of the Above Men and the Stamp Master and Carted them up Thames Street, then up King Street to the said Gallows where they was hung up by the Neck and Suspended near 15 feet in the Air, And on the Breast of the Stamp Master, was this Inscription THE STAMP MAN . . . and upon the Breast of the Doct'r was write, THAT INFAMOUS, MISCRE-ATED, LEERING JACOBITE DOCT'R MURFY. . . . And about five A Clock in the Afternoon they made a Fire under the Gallows which Consum'd the Effigy's, Gallows and all, to Ashes. I forgot to tell you that a Boot hung over the Doctor's Shoulder with the Devil Peeping out of it. . . .

We thought it was all over. But last Night about Dusk they all Muster'd Again, and first they went to Martin Howard's, and Broke Every Window in his house, Frames and all, likewise Chairs Tables, Pictures and every thing they cou'd come across. . . .

This Moment I'v Rec'd a Peace of News which Effects me so Much that I Cant write any More, which is the Demolition of your worthy Daddy's house and Furniture etc. But I must just let you know that the Stamp Master has Resign'd. . . .

Source: William Almy to Dr. Elisha Story, *Proceedings of the Massachusetts Historical Society*, vol. 55 (1921-1922), pp. 235–236.

Governed?" the Philadelphia customs collector lamented. The Stamp Act crisis of 1765 eroded the emotional foundations of power and left the British government on the defensive in America.

Ideological Roots of Resistance

Merchants and Lawyers Take the Lead. The American resistance movement began in the seaport cities, and for good reason. Urban residents—artisans, merchants, and lawyers—were directly affected by British policies. The Stamp Act taxed city-based products and services, such as newspapers and legal documents. The Sugar Act and the accompanying customs reform raised the cost of molasses to urban merchants and distillers, while the Currency Act complicated their trade and financial transactions. To make matters worse, beginning in the early 1750s, British firms had begun to sell goods directly to colonial shopkeepers at special auction sales, bypassing American mercantile houses and cutting their profits. The combination of British governmental regulation and business competition undermined the merchants' loyalty to the empire. As an official in Rhode Island reported in 1765, the interests of Britain and the colonies were increasingly "deemed

by the People almost altogether incompatible in a Commercial View."

American lawyers were prominent in mobilizing public opinion against the British. In part, the lawyers reflected the views of the merchants who hired them to prevent seizure of their ships by zealous customs officials or vice-admiralty judges. But their own professional values also prompted lawyers to contest the legality of various imperial measures. When the Board of Trade changed the terms of appointment for colonial judges from "during good behavior" to "at the pleasure" of the royal governor, lawyers protested that the new procedure compromised the independence of the judiciary. American lawyers also opposed the extension of vice-admiralty courts; as men trained in English common law, they favored trial by jury. A deep respect for established institutions ultimately led many older lawyers to remain loyal to the Crown, but young lawyers embraced the revolutionary cause; of the fifty-six men who signed the Declaration of Independence in 1776, twenty-five were lawyers.

As merchants and lawyers debated political and constitutional issues in taverns and coffeehouses, on street corners, and in public meetings, they broadened the terms of debate. Initially they argued for particularistic "liberties and privileges" embodied in colonial charters or political traditions. But they also drew on the works of seventeenth-century English philosophers such as Thomas Hobbes, James Harrington, and John Locke, who had advanced the concept of natural rights; the French theorists Montesquieu and Voltaire, who argued against the arbitrary exercise of political power; and the Scottish Enlightenment thinkers David Hume and Frances Hutcheson, who advocated skeptical philosophical inquiry.

Influenced by an emerging Enlightenment tradition, the arguments of the American urban elite took on a more universal cast. Liberty became more an abstract ideal than a set of historical privileges. Pamphlets of remarkable political sophistication circulated throughout the colonies, providing the resistance movement with an intellectual rationale and a political agenda. This urban-based political agitation swayed the outlook of men from rural communities, who dominated the American assemblies numerically, and encouraged them to make a principled defense of American rights.

Intellectual Traditions. Educated colonists drew on three intellectual traditions to build their arguments. The first was English common law, the centuries-old body of legal rules and procedures that protected the king's subjects against arbitrary acts by other subjects or by the government. As early as 1761 James Otis of Boston had cited English legal precedents in the famous Writs of Assistance case, disputing the constitutionality of a general search warrant that permitted customs officials to inspect the property and possessions of any person. Similarly, when John Hancock, an influential Boston merchant, was accused of smuggling, his young lawyer, John Adams, used common-law principles to demand a jury trial. "This 29th Chap. of Magna Charta" respecting jury trials, Adams argued in a legal treatise of 1765, "has for many Centuries been esteemed by Englishmen, as one of the noblest Monuments, one of the firmest Bulwarks of their Liberties." An essential argument of Otis, Adams, and other New England lawyers was that customary or common-law rights could not be abridged by parliamentary statutes. The Georgia assembly took a similar position. Although there were only twenty-nine British soldiers in the colony, it refused on principle to comply with the Quartering Act to prevent establishing "a precedent they by no means think justifiable." Because the colonists' "essential rights as British subjects" were being violated, such resistance was imperative.

A second major intellectual resource for educated Americans was the rationalism cultivated during the Enlightenment. Unlike common-law attorneys, who valued precedent and venerated the ways of the past, Enlightenment philosophers questioned the past and appealed to reason to discover and correct the ills of so-

Sam Adams, Boston Agitator
This painting by John Singleton Copley, *Samuel Adams* (circa 1772), shows the radical Patriot pointing to the Massachusetts Charter of 1692, suggesting that "charter rights" accounted for Adams's opposition to British policies. But Adams also was influenced by the natural rights tradition.

ciety. Most Enlightenment thinkers followed John Locke in believing that all individuals possessed certain "natural rights"—such as life, liberty, and property—and that it was the responsibility of government to protect those rights. For many educated colonists this belief provided an intellectual justification for resistance to British authority. Samuel Adams, John's cousin and a radical Patriot, asked rhetorically if it was "lawful to resist the Supreme Magistrate, if the Commonwealth cannot be otherwise preserved" and used arguments based on the individual's natural rights to justify the Stamp Act uprising.

English political tradition provided a third ideological basis for the American Patriot movement. Some Americans, particularly those in Puritan New England, venerated the Commonwealth era, the brief period between 1649 and 1660 when England was a republic. These republicans joined with members of the provincial assemblies in applauding the Glorious Revolution of 1688 and the various constitutional restrictions placed on the monarchy by the English Whigs, such as the ban on royally imposed taxes. Subsequently, many educated

Americans absorbed the arguments of Real Whig spokesmen such as John Trenchard and Thomas Gordon (the authors of *Cato's Letters*), who attacked the power of government financiers and condemned the idea of standing armies. Well-informed colonists also joined in criticizing Walpole and his successors as politically corrupt. "Bribery is so common," John Dickinson of Pennsylvania noted during a visit to London in the 1750s, "that there is not a borough in England where it is not practiced." This critical Real Whig view of British politics predisposed many Americans to distrust any attempt at imperial reform. Joseph Warren, a Boston physician and Patriot, reported that many townspeople thought the Stamp Act was intended "to force the colonies into rebellion," after which the ministry would use "military power to reduce them to servitude."

The rhetoric was exaggerated, but the charges had a basis in fact. British administrative reform threatened the interests of many Americans. The Proclamation Line of 1763, for example, protected Indian peoples by curbing the activities of white land speculators, fur traders, and westward migrants. In 1764 the Sugar Act extended the jurisdiction of the vice-admiralty courts, and in 1765 the Stamp Act imposed British taxes directly on Americans. Finally, Britain's growing economic presence threatened the colonists' sense of control over their financial lives. It seemed to one pamphleteer that Americans were being compelled to give the British "our money, as oft and in what quantity they please to demand it."

Many Americans viewed these events narrow-mindedly as threats to their self-interest, but common-law attorneys, natural-rights theorists, and Real Whig critics of ministerial policy stated their objections in broad philosophical terms. Their ideological statements endowed colonial opposition to British control with high moral significance, turning a series of particularistic tax protests into a broad resistance movement.

The Informal Compromise of 1766

While mobs protested in the streets, opposition-minded politicians sharpened their arguments in the assemblies. In May 1765 the eloquent young Virginian Patrick Henry urged the House of Burgesses to condemn the Stamp Act. Conservative Burgesses silenced Henry when the young orator compared George III to Charles I and seemed to call for a new Oliver Cromwell to seize power in Britain. However, the Burgesses endorsed many of his resolutions, declaring that any attempt to tax the colonists without their consent "has a manifest Tendency to Destroy AMERICAN FREEDOM." More significantly, the Stamp Act provoked the first effort by the colonial assemblies to speak with one voice. Even before the Burgesses' resolutions reached Boston, the

Patrick Henry, A Great Orator
Henry drew on evangelical Protestantism to create a new mode of political oratory. "His figures of speech . . . were often borrowed from the Scriptures," a contemporary noted, while his style and speech conveyed "the earnestness depicted in his own features."

Massachusetts House of Representatives had called for a meeting of the colonies in New York in October to consider a "loyal and humble representation" to the king and Parliament "to implore Relief."

Nine colonial assemblies sent delegates to the Stamp Act Congress. As politicians trained in the art of compromise, the twenty-eight delegates did not threaten to rebel but devised a set of Stamp Act Resolves that contested the constitutionality of the Stamp and Sugar acts. The Resolves declared that only the colonists' elected representatives could impose taxes on them and that because of their distance from Britain and their distinct interests, Americans could not be represented in the House of Commons. The delegates protested strongly against the loss of American "rights and liberties," especially trial by jury. Then, assuring Parliament that Americans "glory in being subjects of the best of Kings having been born under the most perfect form of government," the delegates humbly petitioned for repeal of the Stamp Act.

TABLE 5.1

Ministerial Instability in Britain

Leading Minister	Dates of Ministry	American Policy
Lord Bute	1760–1763	Mildly reformist
George Grenville	1763–1765	Ardently reformist
Lord Rockingham	1765–1766	Accommodationist
William Pitt/ Charles Townshend	1766–1770	Ardently reformist
Lord North	1770–1782	Coercive

The Stamp Act Resolves were received by a Parliament in turmoil. George III had lost confidence in Grenville (because of issues unrelated to the Stamp Act) and had replaced him as prime minister with Lord Rockingham (see Table 5.1). For Americans, Rockingham was an ideal prime minister. Young, inexperienced, and open to persuasion, he led a party of Old Whigs hostile to Grenville's American policies. Indeed, the Rockingham Whigs stood for the earlier policy of salutary neglect, believing that America was important as a source of "flourishing and increasing trade" that added to the national wealth, not as a source of tax revenue. Some Old Whigs even agreed with the colonists that the new tax was unconstitutional. Lord Camden, chief justice of the Court of Common Pleas, told his Parliamentary colleagues that "taxation and representation are inseparably united" and concluded, "I can never give my assent to any bill for taxing the American colonies while they remain unrepresented."

British merchants also favored the colonists' cause. The decision by most American traders not to import British goods had caused a drastic fall in sales, and Britain had large inventories of goods on hand. "The Avenues of Trade are all shut up," a Bristol merchant complained. "We have no Remittances and are at our Witts End for want of Money to fulfill our Engagements with our Tradesmen." In January 1766 the leading commercial centers of London, Liverpool, Bristol, and Glasgow deluged Parliament with petitions, arguing that as a result of the colonial boycott, the Stamp Act threatened British prosperity.

Neither this argument nor those of the Old Whigs persuaded the members of Parliament who were outraged by the popular rebellion in America. These hard-liners demanded that substantial numbers of British soldiers be sent to the seaport cities to suppress the riots and that Americans submit to the constitutional supremacy of Parliament. "The British legislature," declared Chief Justice Sir James Mansfield, "has authority to bind every part and every subject, whether such subjects have a right to vote or not." He insisted that the ministry discipline the upstart colonists, warning that "when the supreme power abdicates, the government is dissolved."

William Pitt, pro-American in sentiment yet firmly committed to British national power, devised yet a third, more ambiguous, response to the American resistance movement. Stating that Parliament had no right to tax the colonies, Pitt demanded that "the Stamp Act be repealed absolutely, totally, and immediately," but at the same time he acknowledged that British authority over America was "sovereign and supreme, in every circumstance of government and legislation whatsoever."

Rockingham tried to reconcile these conflicting opinions and factions. First, to mollify colonial opinion and assist British merchants, he secured the repeal of the Stamp Act. He also instructed army commanders in the colonies not to use troops against the crowds, and he refused to send additional troops to the seaport cities. Next, Rockingham fashioned a compromise to change the Sugar Act: he reduced the duty on French molasses from 3 pence to 1 penny a gallon, but he risked another constitutional confrontation by applying the duty to imports of British molasses as well. Thus, the revised Sugar Act not only regulated foreign trade, which most American politicians accepted, but also raised revenue through a tax on a British product, which some colonists challenged as unconstitutional. Rockingham sharpened the constitutional debate—and pacified imperial reformers and hard-liners—with the Declaratory Act of 1766, which explicitly reaffirmed

Mixing Business and Politics, 1766
Hurt by the colonists' trade boycott, British manufacturers campaigned for repeal of the Stamp Act. To celebrate the repeal—and expand the market for its teapots in America—the Cockpit Hill factory in Derby quickly produced a commemorative design.

Eliza Lucas Pinckney

The Wedding of George III, 1762

As a young woman, Eliza Lucas (1722–1793) won acclaim for producing indigo dye in South Carolina. In 1744 she married Charles Pinckney (1699–1758), an influential Charleston lawyer and politician, and from 1753 to 1758 she lived with him in London, where she left her two sons to continue their education. A member of the Anglo-American elite, Mrs. Pinckney in 1762 expressed a natural loyalty to Britain and great curiosity about "my Sovereign and his Consort," King George III and his bride, Charlotte Sophia of Mecklenburg. And she acknowledged the great tax burdens assumed by her British friends. Beginning in the late 1760s her allegiance to the empire slowly waned. By 1775 Mrs. Pinckney supported Patriot calls for independence, and her sons became leaders of the rebellion.

How, dear Madam, could you think of this remote spott in the midsts of the splendour of Royal Weddings, Coronations, Gay Courts and the attendant cheerfulness that must follow in their train long after. . . .

You cant think how many people you have gratified by your obliging me with so particular a discription of the Queen. We had no picture of her Majesty nor discription that could be depended upon till I received your favour. . . . If, Madam, you have ever been witness to the impatience of the people of England about a hundred mile from London to be made acquainted with what passes there, you may guess a little at what our impatience is here when I inform you that the curiosity increases with the distance from the Center of affairs; and our impatience is not to be equaled with any peoples within four thousand mile.

In half an hour after I was favoured with a vizet from our new Gov., Mr. B[oone], lately arrived here from his former Government in the Jerseys, who I found (tho' he has an extensive good acquaintance in England) knew as little of the New Queen as we did here. I had the pleasure to read him also the discription. . . . On the whole I am a very Loyal Subject and had my share of Joy in the agreeable account of my Sovereign and his Consort.

When, my Dear Madam, shall we have peace? Till then I have little prospect of seeing my Children and friends in England; and a Spanish warr we are told is unavoidable. We are pretty quiet here just now, but 'tis much feared it will continue no longer than the winter. We never was so taxed in our lives, but what is our taxes to yours [?]. However, we are a young Colony and our Seas does not throw up sands of gold, as surely the British does to enable you to bear such prodigious Expences.

Source: The *Letterbook of Eliza Lucas Pinckney, 1739–1762,* edited by Elise Pinckney (University of North Carolina Press, 1972), 174–176.

the "full power and authority" of the British Parliament to "bind the colonies and people of America in all cases whatsoever."

Despite these strong words, the Stamp Act crisis ended in an informal compromise. The Americans had won an important victory. Their riots, boycott, and petitions had secured repeal of the hated tax. Yet Grenville and other advocates of imperial reform also triumphed. In a showdown with the provincial assemblies they had obtained a statement of Parliamentary supremacy. Rockingham's compromise gave each side just enough to claim victory. And because the confrontation had ended quickly, it seemed possible that it might be forgotten even more quickly. The constitutional status of the American provinces remained uncertain, but political positions had not yet hardened. Leaders of goodwill could still hope to work out an imperial relationship acceptable to both sides (see American Voices, above).

The Growing Confrontation, 1767–1770

The compromise of 1766 was short-lived. Within a year political rivalries in Britain sparked a new and more prolonged struggle with the American provinces over taxes. Economic self-interest and ideological rigidity on both sides of the Atlantic aggravated the conflict. Only after a lengthy commercial boycott and the threat of military action was a second compromise finally achieved.

The Townshend Initiatives

Often the course of history is changed by a small event—a leader's illness, a personal grudge, a chance remark. So it was in 1767, when Rockingham's Old Whig ministry collapsed and George III named William Pitt to head a new ministry. Pitt, the master strategist of the Great War for Empire, now sat in the House of Lords as the earl of Chatham, but he was chronically ill with gout. Because of Chatham's frequent absences from cabinet meetings and Parliamentary debates, Chancellor of the Exchequer Charles Townshend assumed command. Chatham was sympathetic toward America; Townshend was not. Since his service on the Board of Trade in the 1750s, Townshend had favored imperial reform; now he had the power to push it through.

What prompted Townshend to act was a chance confrontation with his longtime political rival George Grenville. As the chancellor presented the military budget to Parliament in 1767, Grenville rose from his seat to demand that the colonists pay for the British troops in America. Grenville's challenge put Townshend on the defensive, and he made an unplanned, fateful policy decision. Convinced of the necessity of imperial reform and eager to reduce the English land tax, Townshend promised that he would find a new source of revenue in America.

The new tax legislation, known as the Townshend Act of 1767, imposed duties on paper, paint, glass, and tea imported into the colonies. The tax was expected to raise between £35,000 and £40,000 a year—a small sum but one that Townshend was determined to use shrewdly. To mollify Grenville, he allocated part of the revenue for military expenses, but he reserved the major part "to defray the costs of Civil Government"—that is, to pay the salaries of governors, judges, and other imperial officials.

Townshend's initiative was intended to change the political balance of power in the colonies. He wanted to free royal officials from financial dependence on the American legislatures, enabling them to enforce Parliamentary laws and royal directives and depriving the colonial assemblies of much of their political leverage. To enhance the power of the royal bureaucracy, Townshend devised the Revenue Act of 1767, reorganizing the Customs Service. The new act created a Board of American Customs Commissioners in Boston and four vice-admiralty courts, in Halifax, Boston, Philadelphia, and Charleston. These administrative innovations were far-reaching and posed a greater threat to American autonomy than did the small sums raised by the import duties.

In fact, Townshend's overriding concern was to diminish the powers of the American representative assemblies, and events in New York gave him a chance. As in Georgia, the New York assembly had refused to comply with the Quartering Act of 1765, which required the lodging of British troops. Fearing an unlimited drain on its treasury, the New York legislature initially denied General Gage's requests for barracks and supplies and

later limited its assistance to the housing of two infantry battalions and one artillery company. The struggle intensified when the ministry instructed the New Yorkers to assume complete financial responsibility for defense against Indian attacks. If the New York assembly refused, some members of Parliament were ready to impose an extra port duty on New York imports and exports to raise the needed funds.

The secretary of state, William Petty, earl of Shelburne, came up with a stronger, more coercive set of policies. He suggested a military governor for New York, with authority to seize funds from the colony's treasury to quarter the troops and "to act with Force or Gentleness as circumstances might make necessary." Ultimately, Townshend decided on a less provocative measure, pushing through Parliament the so-called Restraining Act of 1767, which suspended the New York assembly until it submitted to the Quartering Act. Faced with the loss of self-government, the New Yorkers finally gave in. They appropriated funds to support the resident military garrison and defend themselves against Indian attacks.

The Restraining Act was an important innovation. The British Privy Council had always supervised the colonial assemblies, over the decades invalidating about 5 percent of all colonial laws—such as those establishing land banks or vesting new powers in the assemblies—as contrary to British laws or policy. The Restraining Act was a much more powerful administrative weapon because it threatened not just particular laws but the existence of the lawmaking body itself. Townshend, like his critic Grenville, was determined to tax the colonists and subordinate their representative political institutions to Parliamentary authority.

America Again Resists

The debate on the Townshend duties, which most American public officials condemned as unconstitutional, hinged superficially on a distinction between "internal" and "external" taxes. In response to the Stamp Act, Daniel Dulany, a conservative Maryland lawyer, had suggested that Americans would accept external duties on trade even as they opposed internal taxes. Benjamin Franklin had made essentially the same argument to the House of Commons in seeking repeal of the Stamp Act. Colonists would more readily accept higher prices for molasses and rum arising from duties on imported goods, he argued, than they would agree to the directly collected taxes of the Stamp Act. Townshend thought that this distinction between internal and external taxes amounted to "perfect nonsense," but he told Parliament that "since Americans were pleased to make that distinction, he was willing to indulge them [and] . . . to confine himself to regulations of Trade."

In reality, only a few colonial leaders saw any difference between internal taxes and external duties; the majority agreed with John Dickinson, author of *Letters from a Farmer in Pennsylvania* (1768), that the real issue was the intention or goal of the legislation. Because the Townshend duties were not designed to regulate trade but to bring revenue to the imperial government, they amounted to taxes imposed without consent. As Dickinson sarcastically declared, "I think it evident that we *must* use paper and glass; that what we use *must* be *British*; and that we *must* pay the duties imposed, unless those who sell these articles are so generous as to make us presents of the duties they pay."

The Massachusetts House of Representatives took the lead in opposing the new duties. In February 1768 it sent a letter to other assemblies condemning the Townshend Act for infringing on the colonists' "natural & constitutional Rights." This initiative received a lukewarm response, primarily because the American merchant community was divided. To pressure Parliament to repeal the legislation, Boston merchants began a new boycott of British imports in April 1768; New York traders followed suit in August. Philadelphia merchants, however, refused to join the boycott because they were more heavily involved in direct trade with Britain and believed that they had too much to lose. Philadelphia's sailors and dockworkers supported this decision, for they also feared that a lengthy boycott would ruin them financially. In Pennsylvania, therefore, protests were confined to words, with residents encouraging the assembly to petition the king for repeal of the Townshend duties.

Nonimportation. In 1768, unlike 1765, many Americans questioned the wisdom of a nonimportation strategy. Nonetheless, public support for the boycott gradually spread from Boston and New York to smaller port cities, such as Salem, Newport, and Baltimore, and into the countryside. In Puritan New England ministers and public officials supported nonimportation by condemning "luxury and dissipation" and decrying the use of "foreign superfluities." They discouraged reliance on imported goods and promoted the domestic manufacture of necessities such as cloth and paper.

American women, especially religious women, added their support to the nonimportation movement. Ordinarily women were excluded from prominent roles in public affairs; in times of religious and social upheaval, such as the Great Awakening or a severe shortage of food, a few women would emerge as prophets or preachers or would lead a mob, demanding that shopkeepers provide reasonably priced grain. But the boycotts prompted a more sustained involvement by women in the public world. During the crisis over the Stamp Act groups of young women with ties to Patriot leaders declared their support for the American cause.

For example, in Providence, Rhode Island, in March 1766, "eighteen daughters of liberty, young ladies of good reputation," met to spin yarn, declaring that they would not purchase British manufactures. The contest over the Townshend duties elicited support from a much broader group, religious women in New England, who organized spinning matches, bees, and demonstrations at the homes of their ministers. Some gatherings were openly patriotic, such as that at Berwick, Maine, where the spinners, "as true Daughters of Liberty," celebrated American goods, "drinking rye coffee and dining on bear venison." But many more combined support for nonimportation with the fulfillment of social obligations and charitable work by gathering to spin flax and wool, which they donated to their ministers and needy members of the community. Just as the tradition of crowd actions influenced men's response to the imperial crisis, so women's concerns with the well-being of their communities guided their efforts.

Ultimately, the efforts of patriotic young ladies and religious women prompted thousands of other women to redouble their efforts at the spinning wheel and the loom and won broad public support. Newspapers celebrated these patriotic heroines, whose production of "homespun" cloth made America less dependent on British textile imports, which totaled about 10 million yards a year. It was a newsworthy event when the women of the Freeman, Smith, and Heard families of Woodbridge, New Jersey, announced that they had attained an annual household output of 500 yards. Town-wide production was also a source of pride. One Massachusetts town claimed an annual output of 30,000 yards of cloth; East Hartford, Connecticut, reported 17,000 yards.

The men of Boston and New York had other methods of promoting nonimportation. The Sons of Liberty published the names of merchants who refused to comply with the boycott, broke their store windows, and harassed their employees. In Charleston, South Carolina, the merchant Christopher Gadsden joined the Liberty Boys and helped persuade his fellow traders to support the boycott. But in many seaports merchants deeply resented the crowd's attacks on their reputations and property. Fearing mob rule, they condemned nonimportation and stood by the royal governors.

Despite this split between radical Patriots and future Loyalists, the boycott gathered momentum, uniting thousands of Americans in a common political movement. In March 1769, responding to public pressure, most Philadelphia merchants finally stopped importing British goods. Two months later the members of the Virginia House of Burgesses agreed not to buy dutied articles, British luxuries, or slaves. "The whole continent from New England to Georgia seems firmly fixed," the Massachusetts *Gazette* proudly announced; "like a strong, well-constructed arch, the more weight there is

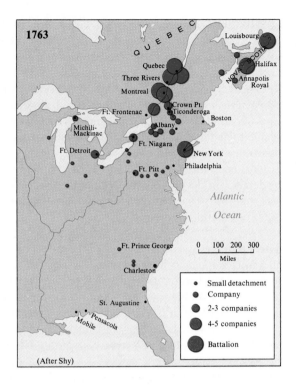

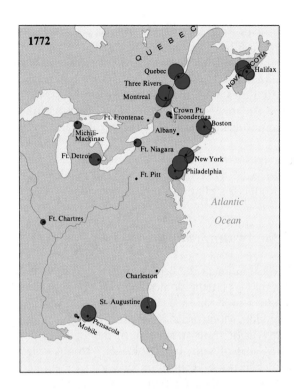

laid upon it, the firmer it stands; and thus with America, the more we are loaded, the more we are united." Reflecting colonial self-confidence, Benjamin Franklin called for a return to the pre-1763 imperial system. "It is easy to propose a plan of conciliation," Franklin declared: "*repeal* the laws, *renounce* the right, *recall* the troops, *refund* the money, and *return* to the old method of requisition."

Britain Responds. The home authorities had something very different in mind. The boycott and crowd violence had exhausted their patience. When a copy of the Massachusetts House's letter opposing the Townshend duties reached London in mid-1768, Lord Hillsborough, the secretary of state for American affairs, branded it as "unjustifiable opposition to the constitutional authority of Parliament." He told Governor Francis Bernard to dissolve the House if it refused to rescind its action. Hillsborough backed up his words by dispatching four regiments of troops to Boston to strengthen the "Hand of Government," particularly the hand of the customs commissioners, who had been forced by a mob of furious Bostonians protesting the seizure of John Hancock's ship *Liberty* on a smuggling charge to take refuge on the British warship *Romney*. Hillsborough's main goal was not to prevent smuggling along the seacoast but to prepare for an armed showdown with the radical Boston Patriots.

By the end of 1768 a thousand British regulars were encamped in Boston, and military coercion was a very real prospect (see Map 5.2). General Gage accused Massachusetts public leaders of "Treasonable and des-

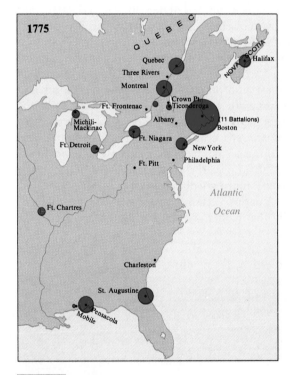

MAP 5.2

British Troop Deployments, 1763–1775

As the imperial crisis deepened, British military priorities changed. In 1763 most British battalions (the large circles represent 350 men) were stationed in Canada to deter Indian attacks and French-Canadian revolts. After the Stamp Act riots of 1765, the British established larger garrisons in New York and Philadelphia. By 1775 eleven battalions of British regulars occupied Boston, the center of the American Patriot movement.

perate Resolves" and advised the ministry to "Quash this Spirit at a Blow." Parliament threatened to appoint a special commission to hear evidence of treason. King George supported Hillsborough's plan to repeal the Townshend duties in all the colonies except Massachusetts, thus isolating the agitators, and then use the British army to bring the rebellious New Englanders to their knees.

The stakes had risen. In 1765, American resistance to taxation had provoked an argument in Parliament; in 1768, it produced a plan for military coercion.

The Second Compromise

At this critical moment the British ministry's resolve faltered. Britain was having domestic problems. Poor harvests caused a food shortage in 1768, and riots swept the countryside. Mobs protested against high prices and raided supplies of grain and bread. In the highly publicized "Massacre of Saint George Fields," troops killed seven demonstrators. Opposition politicians exploited the situation and called for a new ministry. Supported by associations composed of merchants, tradesmen, and artisans (who resented corrupt aristocratic government) the Radical Whig John Wilkes stepped up his attacks on government corruption and won election to Parliament. American Patriots identified with Wilkes, drank toasts in his honor, and purchased thousands of teapots and drinking mugs that carried his picture. They followed events apprehensively as on four occasions the ministry denied Wilkes his seat when the popular leader was elected, and reelected, to Parliament in 1768 and 1769. Riots in Ireland over the growing military budget there added to the ministry's difficulties.

The American trade boycott also began to hurt. Normally the mainland colonies had an annual deficit of £500,000 in their trade with Great Britain, but in 1768 they imported far fewer goods, cutting the deficit to £230,000. In 1769 the boycott had a major impact on the British economy (see Figure 5.2). By continuing to export tobacco, rice, fish, and other goods to Britain while refusing to buy its manufactured goods, Americans accumulated a huge trade surplus of £816,000. To revive their flagging fortunes, British merchants and industrialists petitioned Parliament for repeal of the Townshend duties. The decline in manufacturing and trade also bit deeply into government revenues, since no less than 68 percent came from excise taxes and duties on exports and imports.

The Crisis Resolved. By late 1769 the threat of military coercion seemed to have passed. Merchants' petitions had persuaded some ministers that the Townshend duties were a mistake, and the king no longer supported Hillsborough's plan to punish the Massachusetts Patriots. Early in 1770 Lord North became prime minister, and he pointed out that it was "contrary to the true principles of commerce" for Britain to tax its own exports to America, because the goal of mercantilism was to encourage the consumption of British products in the colonies. North arranged a compromise by which Parliament repealed the Townshend Act's duties on glass, paper, paint, and other manufactured items but retained the tax on tea as a symbol of Parliament's supremacy. This stratagem worked. In a spirit of goodwill (and to restore their own flagging fortunes), merchants in New York and Philadelphia rejected pleas from Patriots in Boston to continue the boycott. Most Americans did not insist on strict adherence to their constitutional principles, contesting neither the duty on British molasses required by the Sugar Act of 1766 nor the symbolic tax on tea. They simply avoided paying those taxes by smuggling and bribing customs agents.

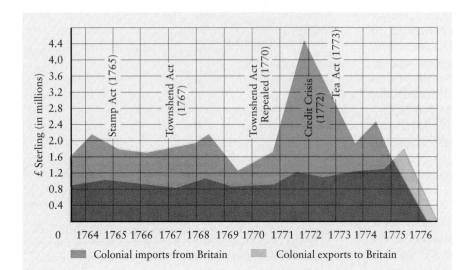

FIGURE 5.2

Trade as a Political Weapon, 1763–1776
Political upheaval did not affect the mainland colonies' exports to Britain, which rose slightly over the period, but imports fluctuated greatly. The American boycott of 1768–1769 brought a sharp fall in the importation of British manufactures, which then soared after the repeal of the Townshend duties.

John Wilkes, British Radical
Wilkes won fame as the author of *North Briton, Number 45,* a pamphlet that called for political reform in Britain. At a dinner in Boston, Radical Whigs raised their glasses to Wilkes—toasting him 45 times!

Not even a new outbreak of violence in New York City and Boston in 1770 could disrupt the spirit of compromise. During the boycott New York artisans and workers had taunted British regulars in the resident garrison, mostly with words but occasionally with stones and fists. In January 1770 the troops responded by tearing down a Liberty Pole in front of a tavern, setting off a week of sporadic street fighting—the Golden Hill riots—in which both sides suffered only minor injuries. In Boston, where a much larger group of British soldiers competed with townsmen for the favor of local women and for part-time jobs, tensions came to a head in the "Boston Massacre" of March 1770. A mob of laborers and seamen attacked a group of soldiers, who fired into the crowd, killing five men, including one of the leaders—Crispus Attucks, a mulatto who had escaped from slavery in Massachusetts in 1750 and worked as a seaman. Seeking to uphold the honor of Boston while condemning British policy, Patriot leaders played a double game. No less a Patriot than John Adams defended the soldiers in a Boston court, blaming the incident on "a motley rabble of saucy boys, negroes and mulattoes,

Irish teagues and outlandish jack tarrs," and won their acquittal. Simultaneously, another Patriot, James Bowdoin, wrote *A Short Narrative of the Horrid Massacre in Boston*, accusing the British of deliberately planning the killing. This pamphlet circulated widely in the colonies and inflamed public opinion against the imperial authorities.

Sovereignty Debated. Most Americans still remained loyal to the empire, but five years of conflict over taxes and constitutional principles had built ill will on both sides of the Atlantic. Even Lord Chatham thought the American merchants and assemblies had carried "their notions of freedom too far" and were unwilling, on a number of crucial issues, to "be subject to the laws of this country." Benjamin Franklin recognized that the colonies had repudiated the power of Parliament to impose taxes and had questioned other aspects of its authority as well. He wanted to redefine the imperial relationship, giving America political equality within the empire. Perhaps thinking of various European "composite monarchies" (in which kings ruled far-distant and semiautonomous provinces acquired by inheritance or conquest), Franklin suggested that the colonies were now "distinct and separate states" but ones that had "the same Head, or Sovereign, the King."

Thomas Hutchinson, the American-born royal governor of Massachusetts, was horrified at Franklin's proposal, rejecting the idea of "two independent legislatures in one and the same state." For Hutchinson, the British empire was a single entity, and sovereignty was indivisible—all or nothing. "I know of no line," he told the Massachusetts House of Representatives, "that can be drawn between the supreme authority of Parliament and the total independence of the colonies." But a House committee disagreed, adopting Franklin's position: if Britain and its American colonies were united by the king as their "one head and common sovereign," they could "live happily in that connection." (More than a century and a half later this idea would come to fruition in the British Commonwealth of Nations.)

The second crisis—and compromise—had significantly altered the terms of the debate. In 1765 American public leaders had accepted Parliament's authority. The Stamp Act Resolves had opposed only certain "unconstitutional" legislation. By 1770 the most outspoken Patriots—including Franklin, Patrick Henry of Virginia, and Samuel Adams and his followers in the Massachusetts House—had repudiated Parliament and claimed equality for their assemblies under the king. Nor did they flinch when reminded that George III condemned their agitation. As the Massachusetts House told Hutchinson, "There is more reason to dread the consequences of absolute uncontrolled supreme power, whether of a nation or a monarch, than those of total independence."

There the matter rested. The British had twice tried to impose taxes on the colonies, and American Patriots had twice forced them to retreat. It was now clear that if Parliament insisted on exercising its claim to sovereignty, at least some Americans would have to be subdued by force. Fearful of civil war, the ministry hesitated to take the final fateful step.

The Road to War, 1771–1775

The repeal of most of the Townshend duties in 1770 restored harmony to the British empire, and for the next three years most disputes were resolved peacefully or were confined to individual colonies. The continued existence of the empire seemed assured. Yet history moves in unpredictable ways, and below the surface lay strong fears and passions—and mutual distrust. Suddenly, in 1773, those undercurrents erupted, overwhelming any hope for compromise. In less than two years the Americans and the British stood on the brink of war.

The Tea Act

Parliament's repeal of the Townshend duties did not satisfy radical Patriots, who now wanted American independence. They kept the Boston Massacre vivid in public memory and exploited events—such as a British credit crisis in 1772, which caused economic distress in the colonies—to warn Americans about the dangers of imperial domination. In November 1772 Samuel Adams persuaded the Boston town meeting to establish a Committee of Correspondence "to state the Rights of the Colonists of this Province." Within a few months eighty Massachusetts towns had set up similar committees. This movement spread to other colonies when, in January 1773, the British government set up a royal commission to investigate an incident involving the *Gaspée*, a British customs vessel Rhode Island Patriots had burned in June 1772 to protest the diligence of its captain in enforcing the Navigation Acts. The royal commission's powers, particularly its authority to send Americans to Britain for trial, aroused Patriot sentiment. In Virginia the House of Burgesses created a Committee of Correspondence "to communicate with the other colonies" about the situation in Rhode Island. By July 1773 similar committees had sprung up in Connecticut, New Hampshire, and South Carolina.

The Compromise Overturned. However, the first link in the chain of events that led directly to war was Parliament's passage of a Tea Act in May 1773. The purpose of the act was to provide financial relief to the British East India Company, a royally chartered firm that was deeply in debt both because of mismanagement and because of the cost of military expeditions that extended British trade in India. The Tea Act provided a government loan to the company and, more important, eliminated the customs duties on the tea that it brought to Britain and then reexported to America. This provision cut costs for the East India Company, allowing it to undersell other British merchants, who had to pay the customs levies, and giving it a virtual monopoly of the provincial market.

Lord North knew that the Tea Act would be unpopular in America but failed to gauge just how unpopular it would be. Since 1768, when the Townshend Act had placed a duty of 3 pence a pound on tea, American traders had boycotted the British product, buying illegally imported tea from the Dutch instead. By the 1770s about 90 percent of the tea consumed in America was contraband. But the Tea Act would make East India Company tea cheaper than the smuggled Dutch tea, and American merchants and consumers in those circumstances might choose to buy the British tea and pay the 3-pence duty. Colonial opponents of the act charged that the ministry was bribing Americans to give up their principles; as an anonymous woman put it in the *Massachusetts Spy*, "the use of tea is considered not as a *private* but as a *public* evil . . . a handle to introduce a variety of . . . oppressions amongst us." This was exactly what North wanted. Like Grenville and Townshend before him, he was not content to declare Parliament's authority to tax the colonies—he wanted to demonstrate it.

North's insensitivity to the fragile state of the colonial relationship cost the empire dearly, for it revived American resistance. The East India Company decided to distribute the tea directly to shopkeepers in major American cities, a tactic that shocked colonial merchants. The Tea Act would not only eliminate the illegal Dutch trade but also cut American merchants out of the British tea business. "The fear of an Introduction of a Monopoly in this Country," General Haldimand reported from New York, "has induced the mercantile part of the Inhabitants to be very industrious in opposing this Step and added Strength to a Spirit of Independence already too prevalent."

The Committees of Correspondence took the lead in organizing resistance to the Tea Act. All along the seaboard the Sons of Liberty prevented East India Company ships from landing tea, forced the captains to return it to Britain or store it in public warehouses, and held public bonfires at which they persuaded their fellow citizens (sometimes gently, sometimes not) to consign their tea to the flames. By these means, Patriots effectively nullified the Tea Act.

The Boston Tea Party. In Boston events took a more ominous turn. For decades Massachusetts had steadfastly resisted British authority, and in the 1760s had assumed leadership of the anti-imperial movement. Boston lawyers James Otis and John Adams had raised the first constitutional objections to legislation enforcing imperial reform, Boston mobs were the first to oppose the Stamp Act, and Boston merchants such as John Hancock had led colonial opposition to the Townshend duties. As early as 1768 Bostonians had condemned the tax on tea as a devious plot by "the politicians who planned our ruin," and it was they who provoked the Boston Massacre two years later. Boston was destined to spark the final conflagration with Great Britain.

Chance also figured in this outcome. The governor of Massachusetts, Thomas Hutchinson, bitterly opposed the Patriots, and with good reason. Stamp Act rioters had looted his house; Benjamin Franklin and Boston Patriots had smeared his reputation by stealing and publishing his private correspondence; and the Massachusetts House had condemned his defense of Parliamentary power. A combination of personal grudges and constitutional principles made Hutchinson determined to uphold the Tea Act.

The governor had a scheme to collect the tax and land the tea. Several of the agents chosen by the East India Company to handle the tea in Boston were Hutchinson's sons. When the tea arrived on the *Dartmouth*, the governor had his sons pass the ship through customs. Once this legal entry had been achieved, the *Dartmouth* could not depart without paying the duties on its cargo. Hutchinson had time on his side. If the tea duty was not paid within twenty days, customs officials could seize the cargo, land it with the help of the British army, and sell the tea at auction.

The Massachusetts Patriots met the governor's challenge. The Boston Committee of Correspondence sent Paul Revere, William Molineaux, and Thomas Young to lead a group of Patriots, most of whom were artisans, aboard the *Dartmouth*. On a cold night in December 1773 they boarded the ship while disguised as Indians, broke open the 342 chests of tea (valued at about £10,000, or about $800,000 today), and threw them into the harbor. "This destruction of the Tea is so bold and it must have so important Consequences," John Adams wrote in his diary, "that I cannot but consider it as an Epoch in History" (see American Lives, pages 158–159).

The Coercive Acts. Adams was not exaggerating. The British Privy Council was outraged, as was the king. There would be no more compromises. "Concessions have made matters worse," George III declared. "The time has come for compulsion." Parliament decisively rejected a proposal to repeal the duty on American tea. Instead, in the spring of 1774 it enacted four Coercive Acts to force Massachusetts into submission. A Port Bill closed Boston Harbor until the East India Company received payment for the destroyed tea. A Government Act annulled the Massachusetts charter and prohibited most local town meetings. A new Quartering Act required the colony to build barracks or put soldiers into private houses. And an Administration of Justice Act allowed royal officials accused of capital crimes to be tried in other colonies or in Britain.

Hillsborough had proposed a similar "divide-and-rule" strategy in 1769 when he had suggested isolating Massachusetts from the other mainland colonies. By 1774, however, the boycott against the Townshend duties and the activities of the Committees of Correspondence had created a firm sense of unity among the colonies. In far-off Georgia, a Patriot warned the "Freemen of the Province" that "every privilege you at present claim as a birthright, may be wrested from you by the same authority that blockades the town of Boston." "The cause of Boston," George Washington declared from Virginia, "now is and ever will be considered as the cause of America."

Religion and Rebellion
Many American Protestants hated bishops and the ecclesiastical power they represented. This cartoon warns that the Quebec Bill of 1774, which allowed the practice of Catholicism in Canada, was part of a plot by the hierarchy of the Church of England to impose bishops on the American colonies.

George R. T. Hewes and the Meaning of the Revolution

George Hewes, 1835
This portrait of George Hewes was painted by Joseph Cole.

George Robert Twelves Hewes was born in Boston in 1742. He was named George after his father, Robert after a paternal uncle, and Twelves after his maternal grandmother, whose maiden name was Twelves. Apart from his long name, Hewes received little from his parents—not size, for he was unusually short at five feet, one inch; not wealth, for his father, a failed tanner, died a poor soap boiler when Hewes was seven; not even love, for Hewes spoke of his mother only as someone who whipped him for disobedience. When he was fourteen she apprenticed him to a shoemaker, one of the lower trades.

This harsh upbringing shaped Hewes's personality. As an adult he spoke out against all brutality, even the tar and feathering of a Loyalist who had almost killed him. And throughout his life he was extremely sensitive about his class status. He was "neither a rascal nor a vagabond," Hewes retorted to a Boston gentleman who pulled rank on him, "and though a poor man was in as good credit in town as he was."

The occupation of Boston by 4,000 British soldiers in 1768 drew the twenty-six-year-old Hewes into the resistance movement. At first his concerns were personal: he took offense when British sentries challenged him and when a soldier refused to pay for a pair of shoes. Then they became political: Hewes grew angry when some of the poorly paid British soldiers moonlighted, taking jobs away from Bostonians, and even angrier when a Loyalist merchant fired into a crowd of apprentices who were picketing his shop, killing one of them. And so on March 5, 1770, when British soldiers came out in force to clear the streets of rowdy civilians, Hewes joined his fellow townspeople: "They were in the king's highway, and had as good a right to be there" as the British troops, he said.

Fate—and his growing political consciousness—had placed Hewes in the middle of the Boston Massacre. Not only did he know four of the five workingmen shot down that night by British troops, but one of them, James Caldwell, was standing by his side, and Hewes caught him as he fell. Outraged, Hewes armed himself with a cane, only to be confronted by Sergeant Chambers of the 29th British Regiment and eight or nine soldiers, "all with very large clubs or cut-

lasses." Chambers seized his cane, but as Hewes stated in a legal deposition, "I told him I had as good a right to carry a cane as they had to carry clubs." This deposition, which went on to tell of the soldiers' threats to kill more civilians, was included in *A Short Narrative of the Horrid Massacre in Boston* published by a group of Boston Patriots.

Hewes had chosen sides, and his political radicalism did not go unpunished. His outspokenness roused the ire of one of his creditors, a Loyalist merchant tailor. Hewes had never really made a go of it as a shoemaker and constantly struggled on the brink of poverty. Unable to make good on a two-year-old debt of £6. 8s. 3p. (about $300 today) for "a sappled coat & breeches of fine cloth," he landed in debtor's prison in September 1770. Such extravagance of dress on Hewes's part was rare; his purchase of the suit had been the desperate ploy of a propertyless artisan to win the hand of Sally Summer, the daughter of the sexton of the First Baptist Church, whom Hewes had married in 1768. Prison did not blunt Hewes's enthusiasm for the Patriot cause. On the night of December 16, 1773, he turned up as a volunteer at the Tea Party organized by the radical Patriot leaders of Boston. He "daubed his face and hands with coal dust in the shop of a blacksmith" and then found, somewhat to his surprise, that "the commander of the division to which I belonged, as soon as we were on board the ship, appointed me boatswain, and ordered me to go to the captain and demand of him the keys to the hatches."

Hewes had been singled out and made a minor

leader, and he must have played the part well. Thompson Maxwell, a volunteer sent to the Tea Party by John Hancock, recalled that "I went accordingly, joined the band under one Captain Hewes; we mounted the ships and made tea in a trice." In the heat of conflict the small man with the large name had been elevated from a poor shoemaker to "Captain Hewes."

A man of greater ability or ambition might have seized the moment, using his reputation as a Patriot to win fame or fortune, but that was not Hewes's destiny. During the War of Independence he fought as an ordinary sailor and soldier, shipping out twice on privateering voyages and enlisting at least four times in the militia, about twenty months of military service in all. He did not win riches as a privateer (although, with four children to support, that was his hope) or find glory, or even adequate pay in battle: "we received nothing of the government but paper money, of very little value, and continually depreciating." Indeed, the war cost Hewes the small stake he had in society: "The shop which I had built in Boston, I lost"; it was pulled down and burned by British troops.

In material terms, the American Revolution did about as much for Hewes as his parents had. When a journalist found the shoemaker in New York State in the 1830s, he was still "pressed down by the iron hand of poverty." The spiritual reward was greater. As his biographer, Alfred Young, put it: "He was a nobody who briefly became a somebody in the Revolution and, for a moment near the end of his life, a hero." Because Americans had begun to celebrate the memory of the Revolution, Hewes was brought back to Boston in 1835 in triumph as one of the last surviving participants in the Tea Party—the guest of honor on Independence Day.

But a more fundamental spiritual reward had come to Hewes when he became a revolutionary, casting off the deferential status of "subject" in a monarchy and becoming a proud and equal "citizen" in a republic. What this meant to Hewes, and to thousands of other poor and obscure Patriots, appeared in his relationship—both real and fictitious—with John Hancock. As a young man Hewes had sat tongue-tied and deferential in the rich merchant's presence. But in his story of the Tea Party Hewes made Hancock his equal, placing him at the scene (which was almost certainly not the case) and claiming that he "was himself at one time engaged with him in the demolition of the same chest of tea." In this lessening of social distance—this declaration of *equality*—lay one of the profound meanings of the American Revolution.

The Boston "Tea Party"
Led by radical Patriots disguised as Mohawk Indians, Bostonians dump taxed British tea into the harbor. The rioters underlined their political motives by punishing those who sought personal gain; a man who stole some of the tea was "stripped of his booty and his clothes together, and sent home naked."

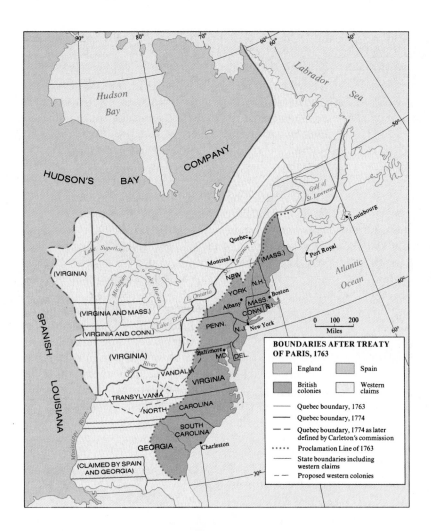

MAP 5.3

British Western Policy, 1763–1774
The Proclamation Line of 1763 restricted white settlement west of the Appalachian Mountains. Nevertheless, colonial land speculators planned the new colonies of Vandalia and Transylvania. However, the Quebec Act of 1774 designated these western lands as Indian reserves and, by vastly increasing the boundaries of Quebec, eliminated the sea-to-sea land claims of many eastern colonies. The act angered many Americans: settlers and land speculators who wanted easy access to the west, New England Protestants who had long feared Catholicism in French Canada, and colonial political leaders who condemned its failure to provide a representative assembly in Quebec.

In 1774 Parliament passed the Quebec Act, heightening the Americans' sense of common danger. This law extended the boundaries of Quebec into the Ohio River Valley, thus threatening to restrict the western land boundaries of Virginia and other seaboard colonies (see Map 5.3). It also gave legal recognition to Roman Catholicism, a concession to the French residents of Canada that aroused old religious hatred, especially in New England, where Puritans detested Catholicism and associated it with arbitrary royal government. The ministry had not intended the Quebec Act as a coercive measure, but many colonial leaders saw it as another demonstration of Parliament's power to intervene in American domestic affairs.

The Continental Congress Responds

To respond to the new British measures, American leaders called for a new all-colony assembly, the Continental Congress. The newer colonies—Florida, Quebec, Nova Scotia, and Newfoundland—did not attend, but delegates from all the other mainland provinces (except Georgia, whose assembly was effectively controlled by a royal governor) met in Philadelphia in September 1774.

New England delegates to the First Continental Congress advocated political union and immediate military preparations. Southern leaders, fearing a British plot "to overturn the constitution and introduce a system of arbitrary government," also favored resistance. Many delegates from the middle colonies held out for a political compromise. Led by Joseph Galloway of Pennsylvania, these men of "loyal principles" outlined a scheme for a new imperial system resembling the Albany Plan of Union of 1754. Under Galloway's proposal, America would have a legislative council selected by the colonial assemblies and a president-general appointed by the king, with the new government having veto power over Parliamentary legislation affecting America. Despite this feature, the delegates refused to endorse Galloway's plan; with British troops "occupying" Boston, it was thought to be too conciliatory.

Instead, the First Continental Congress passed a Declaration of Rights and Grievances that condemned the Coercive Acts and demanded their repeal. The Congress also repudiated the Declaratory Act of 1766, which had proclaimed Parliament's supremacy over the colonies, and demanded that Britain restrict its supervision of American affairs to matters of external trade. Finally, the Congress began a program of economic retaliation. It decreed that new nonimportation and nonconsumption agreements would come into effect in December 1774, and if Parliament did not repeal the "Intolerable Acts," as the Patriots called them, by September 1775, all colonial exports to Britain, Ireland, and the West Indies would be cut off. Ten years of constitutional conflict had ended in all-out commercial warfare.

Even at this late date a few British leaders continued to hope for a compromise. In January 1775 the earl of Chatham (William Pitt) proposed the removal of British troops from Boston and asked Parliament to give up its claim to tax the colonies and to recognize the Continental Congress as a lawful body. In return for these and other concessions, he proposed that the Congress acknowledge Parliamentary supremacy and grant a continuing revenue to cover part of the British national debt.

Chatham's dramatic intervention, like Galloway's in the colonies, was doomed to failure. The British ministry was unyielding. Twice it had backed down; a third retreat was impossible. The honor of the nation was at stake. The ministry rejected Chatham's plan, branding the Continental Congress an illegal assembly, and also rejected a proposal by Lord Dartmouth, the colonial secretary, to send commissioners to America to negotiate a settlement.

Instead, Lord North set stringent terms: Americans must pay for their own defense and administration and must acknowledge Parliament's authority to tax them. To give teeth to these demands, North imposed a naval blockade on American trade with foreign nations and ordered General Gage to suppress dissent in Massachusetts. Former Governor Thomas Hutchinson, now living in exile in London, reported that the British prime minister had told him, "Now the case seemed desperate. Parliament would not—could not—concede. For aught he could see it must come to violence."

The Rising of the Countryside

Although the Patriot movement began in the seaport cities, its success depended on the support of the predominantly rural population. Most farmers initially had little interest in imperial issues. Their lives were deeply rooted in the soil, and their prime allegiance was to their families and communities. Then the French and Indian War took their sons away from home and nibbled at their income. In the community of Newtown on Long Island, for example, farmers had paid an average of 10 shillings (about $20 today) in taxes before 1754;

William Pitt
Hobbled by gout and age, William Pitt (Lord Chatham) addresses the House of Lords on the American question. By 1775 Pitt's eloquence could not soothe the mutual suspicion and anger created by a decade of conflict. (Metropolitan Museum of Art)

by 1756 taxes had jumped to 30 shillings to cover New York's military expenses. Peace brought only slight relief; the Quartering Act cost each Newtown resident 20 shillings in taxes in 1771. Many rural Americans found these exactions onerous, although in fact they paid much less in taxes than did most Britons (see Table 5.2).

The Patriots. Political as well as economic issues infiltrated from the cities into the countryside. Rural Patriots rallied to support the nonimportation movements of 1765 and 1769, and the Daughters of Liberty in hundreds of small towns and villages spun and wove wool into homemade cloth to support American resistance. It was this outburst of rural patriotism that encouraged the Continental Congress to declare a new economic boycott of British goods in 1774 and to create a network of local Committees of Safety and Inspection to enforce it. The Congress identified ways of supporting the boycott. For example, it condemned Americans who wore expensive imported clothes at funerals, approving only "a black crape or ribbon on the arm or hat for gentlemen, and a black ribbon and necklace for ladies."

These symbolic affirmations of traditional rural thriftiness reflected harsh economic realities for many

TABLE 5.2

Patriot Resistance, 1762–1775

British Action	Date	Patriot Response
Revenue Act	1762	Merchants complain privately
Proclamation Line	1763	Land speculators voice discontent
Sugar Act	1764	Protests by merchants and Massachusetts House
Stamp Act	1765	Riots by Sons of Liberty Stamp Act Congress First nonimportation movement
Quartering Act	1765	New York Assembly refuses to implement until 1767
Townshend Duties	1767	Second nonimportation movement Harassment of pro-British merchants
Troops occupy Boston	1768	Boston Massacre of 1770
Gaspée affair	1772	Committees of Correspondence created
Tea Act	1773	Widespread resistance Boston Tea Party
Coercive Acts and Quebec Act	1774	First Continental Congress Third nonimportation movement
British raids on Lexington and Concord	1775	Armed resistance by Minutemen Second Continental Congress

smallholders. The yeoman tradition of agricultural independence was everywhere under attack. In long-settled regions arable land was scarce and expensive, while in many new communities merchants were seizing farmsteads for delinquent debts. In New York manorial landlords were demanding higher rents, and entrepreneurial speculators controlled large frontier tracts. The new demands of the British government would further drain "this People of the Fruits of their Toil," complained the town meeting of rural Petersham, Massachusetts. "The duty on tea," added a Patriot pamphlet, "was only a prelude to a window-tax, hearth-tax, land-tax, and poll-tax, and these were only paving the way for reducing the country to lordships." By the 1770s many northern yeomen felt personally threatened by British policies.

Chesapeake slaveowners had similar fears despite their much higher standard of living. Beginning in the 1750s, many planters had sunk into debt. A Virginia

planter observed in 1766 that a debt of £1,000 had once been considered excessive, but "ten times that sum is now spoke of with indifference and thought no great burthen on Some Estates." High living had led to economic anxiety. Slaveowners, accustomed to being masters on their plantations, resented their financial dependence on British merchants. Moreover, the Coercive Acts raised the threat of political dependence in the minds of many planters. They worried that once Parliament had subdued Massachusetts, it might seize control of Virginia's county courts and House of Burgesses. This prospect moved many planters to action. "The spark of liberty is not yet extinct among our people," one planter declared, "and if properly fanned by the Gentlemen of influence will, I make no doubt, burst out again into a flame."

The Loyalists. Support for the Patriot cause, however, was far from unanimous. As early as 1765 various groups of Americans had worried that resistance to Britain would destroy respect for all political institutions and end in mob rule. This fear was particularly strong among propertied families—large landowners, substantial slaveowners, and wealthy merchants—and their fears increased as the Sons of Liberty used violence to enforce nonimportation. One well-to-do New Yorker complained, "No man can be in a more abject state of bondage than he whose Reputation, Property and Life are exposed to the discretionary violence . . . of the community."

Thousands of ordinary colonists became Loyalists, for a variety of reasons. Class antagonism was one factor. Many Hudson Valley tenant farmers turned to Loyalism when their landlords embraced the Patriot cause. Similar social divisions prompted backcountry Regulators in North Carolina and Maryland farmers on the eastern shore of the Chesapeake Bay to oppose the policies advocated by the Patriot gentry. Ethnicity and religion also played a role, as many Quakers and Germans in Pennsylvania, Dutch and Germans in New York and New Jersey, and Scots in the Carolinas supported the king both because of conflicts with their Patriot neighbors and because they feared political change.

Beginning in 1774, these conservative Americans of "loyal principles" began joining together to denounce Patriot schemes of independence. Royal governors—such as Thomas Hutchinson of Massachusetts, Benning Wentworth of New Hampshire, and Lord Dunmore of Virginia—stood at the head of the Loyalists. They mobilized royal officials, merchants with military contracts, clergy of the Church of England, and well-established lawyers into a small but wealthy and articulate pro-British party. Clergymen such as Jonathan Boucher of Virginia denounced Patriot agitators from their pulpits, while Loyalist landlords and merchants used the threat of economic retaliation to

at which the people were advised to close the royal courts of justice and transfer their political allegiance to the popularly elected House of Representatives. Crowds of armed men prevented the Court of General Sessions from meeting, and rural Patriots harassed supporters of the royal regime.

General Thomas Gage, now governor of Massachusetts as well, tried desperately to maintain imperial power. In September 1774 he ordered British troops to march out of Boston and seize Patriot armories and storehouses at Charlestown and Cambridge. Far from subduing the Patriots, this action only created more support for their cause. Twenty thousand colonial militiamen mobilized to safeguard depots of military supplies at Concord and Worcester. The Concord town meeting voted to raise two companies of troops to "Stand at a minutes warning in Case of alarm," thus creating the famous Minutemen. Eighty percent of male heads of families and a number of single women in Concord signed a Solemn League and Covenant vowing support for nonimportation, and other rural towns also expressed allegiance to the rebellious Patriot government. Gage's authority was increasingly limited to Boston, where it rested primarily on the bayonets of his 3,500 troops.

This stalemate lasted for six months. Gage, unwilling to undertake new raids that might precipitate an armed conflict, waited for orders from Britain. In the meantime, the Massachusetts House met on its own authority. It issued regulations for the collection of taxes, assumed the responsibilities of government, and strengthened the militia. Even before the news of Massachusetts's defiance reached London, the Colonial Secretary, Lord Dartmouth, declared Massachusetts to be in a state of "open rebellion." He told Gage that "force should be repelled by force" and sent orders to the governor to march quickly against the "rude rabble."

On the night of April 18 Gage followed his orders and dispatched troops to capture colonial leaders and supplies at Concord. Paul Revere and two other Bostonians warned the Patriots, however, and at dawn on April 19 local militiamen met the British at Lexington. Shots rang out, and a British volley killed 8 Americans and wounded several others. Pressing on to Concord, the 700 British soldiers confronted 400 Patriots. This time the British took the heavier losses: 3 dead and 12 wounded. The worst was yet to come. As the British retreated along the narrow, winding roads to Boston, they were repeatedly ambushed by 1,000 militiamen from neighboring towns. By the end of the day, 73 British soldiers lay dead, 174 were wounded, and 26 were missing. British fire had killed 49 American militiamen and wounded 39.

Too much blood had been spilled to allow a peaceful compromise. Twelve years of economic conflict and constitutional debate had ended in civil war.

Political Propaganda: The Empire Strikes Back
A British cartoon attacks the women of Edenton, North Carolina, for supporting the boycott of British trade, hinting at their sexual lasciviousness and—by showing an enslaved black woman among these supposed advocates of liberty—their moral hypocrisy.

persuade indebted tenants and workers to oppose radical demands. But in most areas there were too few Loyalists, and they were too poorly organized to affect the course of events in 1774 and 1775. A Tory Association started by Governor Wentworth in New Hampshire had only fifty-nine members, fourteen of whom were Wentworth's relatives. At this crucial point Americans who favored resistance to British rule commanded the allegiance—or at least the acquiescence—of the majority of white Americans.

The Failure of Compromise

When the Continental Congress met in September 1774, New England already stood in open defiance of British authority. In August 150 delegates from neighboring towns had gathered in Concord, Massachusetts, for a Middlesex County Congress, an illegal convention

Summary

The Great War for Empire brought a decisive end to the era of salutary neglect and began an era of imperial reform. The war had exposed the weakness of Britain's control over its American colonies and had left that nation with a crushing load of debt. When George Grenville became prime minister in 1763, he embraced the cause of reform. To raise money—and reassert British authority—he enacted the Sugar Act, which extended the jurisdiction of vice-admiralty courts, and the Stamp Act, which imposed a direct tax for the first time.

The colonists resisted reform, protesting against the stamp duty through mob violence, a trade boycott, and an extralegal Stamp Act Congress. Educated colonists based their arguments for American rights on English common law, Enlightenment thought, and the writings of Real Whigs, whereas the Sons and Daughters of Liberty drew inspiration from evangelical Protestantism and the English republican tradition. To assist British merchants and manufacturers, Parliament repealed the Stamp Act in 1766, but it explicitly reaffirmed its complete authority over the colonies.

In 1767 Charles Townshend undermined this first informal compromise by imposing a new tax on trade. Americans responded with a second nonimportation movement and new constitutional arguments proclaiming the authority of their assemblies over provincial affairs. While the British ministry nearly adopted a plan to crush American resistance by force, domestic problems prompted it to repeal most of the Townshend duties by 1770.

Lord North disrupted this second compromise by passing the Tea Act in 1773. When Bostonians resisted the new law, the British used coercion in Massachusetts to try to destroy the Patriot resistance movement. In 1774 American political leaders met in the First Continental Congress, which challenged British authority and devised a new program of economic warfare. The Congress had the support of a majority of American farmers and planters, who were now prepared to resist British rule. The failure to find a new compromise resulted in bloodshed at Lexington and Concord in April 1775 and then in civil war.

TIMELINE

1754–1763	Salutary neglect ends British national debt doubles
1760	George III becomes king
1761	Lord Bute becomes prime minister
1762	Revenue Act reforms customs service Royal Navy stops trade with French islands
1763	Treaty of Paris ends Great War for Empire Spanish evacuate Florida Proclamation Line restricts western settlement Peacetime army in America Grenville becomes prime minister John Wilkes demands reform of Parliament
1764	Currency Act Sugar Act Colonists oppose vice-admiralty courts Franklin proposes American representation in Parliament
1765	Stamp Act Quartering Act Patrick Henry and Virginia Resolves Stamp Act Congress Riots by Sons of Liberty
1765–1766	First nonimportation movement
1766	First Compromise: Rockingham repeals Stamp Act and enacts Declaratory Act
1767	Townshend duties "Restraining Act" in New York Second nonimportation movement begins Daughters of Liberty make homespun cloth Increased illegal imports of Dutch tea
1768	British army occupies Boston Support for boycott grows
1770	Second Compromise: North repeals most Townshend duties Golden Hill riots in New York Boston Massacre
1772	*Gaspée* burned in Rhode Island Colonial Committees of Correspondence
1773	Tea Act Boston Tea Party
1774	Coercive Acts punish Massachusetts Quebec Act First Continental Congress Third nonimportation movement Loyalists organize
1775	British ministry orders Gage to suppress rebellion Battles of Lexington and Concord

★   ★   ★

BIBLIOGRAPHY

Jack P. Greene and J. R. Pole, eds., *The Blackwell Encyclopedia of the American Revolution* (1991), illuminates both obscure and well-known aspects of the Revolutionary Era. A good interpretive synthesis is Edward Countryman, *The American Revolution* (1985).

The Reform Movement

For the state of the empire in 1763, see Alison Gilbert Olson, *Making the Empire Work: London and the American Interest Groups, 1690–1790* (1992), and Jack P. Greene, *Peripheries and Center: Constitutional Development . . . 1607–1788* (1986). The impact of the Seven Years' War is traced in the classic study by Lawrence H. Gipson, *The Coming of the Revolution, 1763–1775* (1954), and the following works: Richard Middleton, *The Bells of Victory: The Pitt-Newcastle Ministry and the Conduct of the Seven Years' War, 1757–1762* (1985); Alan Rogers, *Empire and Liberty: American Resistance to British Authority, 1755–1763* (1974); Howard H. Peckham, *Pontiac and the Indian Uprising* (1947); and Joseph A. Ernst, *Money and Politics in America, 1755–1775* (1973). Marc Egnal, *A Mighty Empire: The Origins of the Revolution* (1988), attempts an interpretive synthesis.

British politics and imperial reform can be traced in John Brewer, *Party Ideology and Popular Politics at the Accession of George III* (1976); P. D. G. Thomas, *British Politics and the Stamp Act Crisis: The First Phase of the American Revolution, 1763–1767* (1975); Thomas C. Barrow, *Trade and Empire: The British Customs Service in Colonial America, 1660–1775* (1967); John L. Bullion, *A Great and Necessary Measure: George Grenville and the Genesis of the Stamp Act, 1763–1765* (1982); Carl Ubbelohde, *The Vice-Admiralty Courts and the American Revolution* (1960); and Philip Lawson, *George Grenville: A Political Life* (1984).

The Dynamics of Rebellion

For the American response to the British reform laws, see Edmund S. Morgan and Helen M. Morgan, *The Stamp Act Crisis: Prologue to Revolution* (1963); Pauline Maier, *From Resistance to Revolution: Colonial Radicals and the Development of American Opposition to Britain, 1765–1776* (1972); and Gary B. Nash, *The Urban Crucible: Social Change, Political Consciousness, and the Origins of the American Revolution* (1979). Merrill Jensen, *The Founding of a Nation: A History of the American Revolution, 1763–1776* (1968), and Robert Middlekauff, *The Glorious Cause: The American Revolution, 1763–1789* (1982), provide detailed narratives.

Studies of individual colonies capture the spirit of the resistance movement. See Paul A. Gilje, *The Road to Mobocracy: Popular Disorder in New York City, 1763–1834* (1986); David Lovejoy, *Rhode Island Politics and the American Revolution* (1958); and Ronald Hoffman, *A Spirit of Dissension: Economics, Politics, and the Revolution in Maryland* (1973). The motives of Patriots are best addressed through biographies. See Leo J. Lemay, ed., *Reappraising Benjamin Franklin: A Bicentennial Perspective* (1993); Pauline Maier, *The Old Revolutionaries: Political Lives in the Age of Samuel Adams* (1980); Library of Congress Symposium, *The Development of a Revolutionary Mentality* (1972); Milton E. Flower, *John Dickinson, Conservative Revolutionary* (1983); Richard R. Beeman, *Patrick Henry: A Biography* (1974); John R. Alden, *George Washington: A Biography* (1984); and Helen Hill Miller, *George Mason: Gentleman Revolutionary* (1975).

The most important single study of Patriot ideology is Bernard Bailyn, *The Ideological Origins of the American Revolution* (1967), but see Robert M. Calhoon, *Dominion and Liberty: Ideology in Anglo-American Political Thought, 1660–1801* (1994). Other works include Caroline Robbins, *The Eighteenth-Century Commonwealthman* (1959); Morton White, *The Philosophy of the American Revolution* (1978); Garry Wills, *Inventing America: Jefferson's Declaration of Independence* (1978); and H. T. Dickinson, *Liberty and Property: Political Ideology in Eighteenth-Century Britain* (1978). For a discussion of the legal tradition, see Charles H. McIlwain, *The American Revolution: A Constitutional Interpretation* (1923), and John Phillip Reid, *Constitutional History of the American Revolution: The Authority of Rights* (1986).

The Growing Confrontation

Peter D. G. Thomas, *The Townshend Duties Crisis: The Second Phase of the American Revolution, 1767–1773* (1987), is the most comprehensive treatment, but see Colin Bonwick, *English Radicals and the American Revolution* (1977), and Ian R. Christie and Benjamin W. Labaree, *Empire or Independence, 1760–1776* (1976). On American resistance, consult Richard Alan Ryerson, *The Revolution Is Now Begun: The Radical Committees of Philadelphia, 1765–1776* (1978); Peter Shaw, *American Patriots and the Rituals of Revolution* (1981); and Stanley Godbold, Jr., and Robert W. Woody, *Christopher Gadsden* (1982). The confrontation between Patriots and British authority is covered in John Shy, *Toward Lexington: The Role of the British Army in the Coming of the American Revolution* (1965), and Hiller B. Zobel, *The Boston Massacre* (1970).

The Road to War

Benjamin Labaree, *The Boston Tea Party* (1964), is comprehensive and stimulating and can be supplemented by Peter D. G. Thomas, *Tea Party to Independence: The Third Phase of the American Revolution* (1991); Bernard Donoughue, *British Politics and the American Revolution: The Path to War, 1773–75* (1972); and David Ammerman, *In the Common Cause: American Response to the Coercive Acts of 1774* (1968). A fine study of the resistance movement is Edward F. Countryman, *A People in Revolution: The American Revolution and Political Society in New York* (1983). On prewar Loyalism, see Bernard Bailyn, *The Ordeal of Thomas Hutchinson* (1974), and Janice Potter, *The Liberty We Seek: Loyalist Ideology in Colonial New York and Massachusetts* (1983). For the rising of the countryside, see David Hackett Fischer, *Paul Revere's Ride* (1994); Gregory H. Nobles, *Divisions throughout the Whole: Politics and Society in Hampshire County, Massachusetts, 1740–1775* (1983); Jere R. Daniell, *Experiment in Republicanism: New Hampshire Politics and the Revolution, 1741–1790* (1970); and Richard Bushman, *King and People in Provincial Massachusetts* (1985). The transfer of authority is described in Jerrilyn Greene Marston, *King and Congress: The Transfer of Political Legitimacy, 1774–1776* (1987).

P A R T **2**

The New Republic

1775–1820

	Government	Diplomacy	Economy	Society	Culture
	Creating Republican Institutions	**European Entanglements**	**Expansion of Commerce and Manufacturing**	**Defining Liberty and Equality**	**Pluralism and National Identity**
1775	State constitutions written	Independence declared (1776) French alliance (1778)	Wartime expansion of manufacturing	Slavery emancipation in the North Murray, "On the Equality of the Sexes" (1779)	Paine's *Common Sense* calls for a republic
1780	Articles of Confederation ratified (1781) Legislative supremacy in states Philadelphia convention drafts U.S. Constitution (1787)	Treaty of Paris (1783) British trade restrictions in West Indies	Bank of North America (1781) Commercial recession (1783–89) Western land speculation	Virginia Statute of Religious Freedom (1786) Idea of republican motherhood	Land ordinances create a national domain in the West German settlers preserve own language Webster defines American English
1790	Bill of Rights (1791) First national parties: Federalists and Republicans	Wars of the French Revolution Jay's and Pinckney's treaties (1795) Undeclared war with French (1798)	First Bank of the United States (1792–1812) States charter business corporations Outwork system expands	Sedation Act limits freedom of the press (1798)	Indians form Western Confederation Sectional divisions emerge between South and North
1800	Revolution of 1800 Activist state legislatures Chief Justice Marshall asserts judicial power	Napoleonic wars (1802–15) Louisiana Purchase (1803) Embargo of 1807	Cotton expands into Old Southwest Farm productivity improves Embargo encourages domestic manufacturing	Youth-run marriage system New Jersey ends woman suffrage (1807) Atlantic slave trade legally ended (1808)	African-Americans absorb Protestant Christianity Tecumseh develops Indian identity
1810	Triumph of Republican party State constitutions democratized	War of 1812 Treaty of Ghent (1816) Monroe Doctrine (1823)	Second Bank of the United States (1816–36) Supreme Court protects contracts and corporations Emergence of a national economy	Expansion of suffrage for white men New England abolishes established church (1820s)	War of 1812 tests national unity Second Great Awakening shapes American identity

The American war is over, the Philadelphia Patriot Benjamin Rush declared in 1787, "but this is far from being the case with the *American revolution*. On the contrary, nothing but the first act of the great drama is closed. It remains yet to establish and perfect our new forms of government." The job was even greater than Rush imagined, for the republican revolution of 1776 challenged the values and institutions of the colonial social order, forcing changes in many spheres of life—economic, religious, cultural.

The first and most fundamental task was to devise a republican system of government. In 1775 no one in America knew what powers the central and state governments should have or how they should be organized. It took time and experience to find out. The states wrote constitutions by 1780, but their legislatures pursued prodebtor policies that were controversial and socially divisive. It took another decade for Americans to reach agreement on a national government, and even longer to assimilate a new institution, the political party, into the workings of government. These years of experiment and party strife witnessed the success not only of popular sovereignty—government of the people—but also the rise of activist state legislatures—government for the people—and a slow but steady movement toward political democracy—government by the people.

Second, to create and preserve their new republic, Americans had to fight two wars against Great Britain, an undeclared war against France, and many battles with Indian peoples and confederations. The wars against Britain divided the country into bitter factions—Patriots versus Loyalists in 1776, and prowar Republicans against antiwar Federalists in 1812—and expended much blood and treasure. Tragically, the extension of American sovereignty over the trans-Appalachian West brought about the demise of many Indian peoples—their lives taken by European diseases, their lands seized by white settlers. Yet by 1820 the United States was a strong independent state, free at last from a half-century of entanglement in the wars and diplomacy of Europe.

Third, by this time the expansion of the market system had laid the foundations for a strong national economy. Merchants financed a banking system and devised extensive outwork industries. State governments used charters and legal incentives to spur improvements in transportation, finance, and manufacturing. Southern planters carried slavery west to Alabama and Mississippi and grew rich by exporting a new crop—cotton—to markets in Europe and the North. Vast numbers of farm families settled new lands in the West or undertook additional labor as handicraft workers in the Northeast. By 1820 the new American republic had begun to achieve economic as well as political independence.

Fourth, Americans tried to define the nature of their republican society, but found themselves divided along lines of gender, race, religion, and class. Then as now, Americans disagreed on fundamental issues—legal equality for women, the future status of slavery, the meaning of free speech and religious liberty, and the extent of public responsibility for social inequality. These years saw the triumph of liberty of conscience and, except in New England, the end of established churches. The northern states gradually emancipated their slaves, but social equality—not only for blacks, but for women and many white men—remained elusive. In 1820, as in 1775, authority in the family and society remained firmly in the hands of men of property.

The fifth and final task Americans set themselves—creating a distinct culture and identity—was very hard to achieve. The United States remained a land of diverse peoples and distinct regions. Native Americans still lived in their own clans and nations, while black Americans, one-fifth of the enumerated population, were developing a new, African-American culture. The white inhabitants, divided among those of English, Scots-Irish, German, and Dutch ancestry, also preserved many aspects of their traditional cultures. Nevertheless, political institutions united Americans, as did their engagement in the market economy and their increasing participation in evangelical Protestant churches. By 1820, to be an American meant, for the dominant white population, being a republican, a Protestant, and an enterprising individual in a capitalist-run market system.

***The Attack on Bunker Hill with the Burning of
Charles Town*** (detail)

The British attacked Patriot militiamen, who were dug in on
Breed's Hill and Bunker Hill, on June 17, 1775. Before
dislodging the rebel troops, the British suffered heavy losses.

CHAPTER 6

War and Revolution

1775–1783

★   ★   ★

With the battles at Lexington and Concord in April 1775, the American Patriots became rebels, willing to use military force to achieve their political ends. Only a minority of Patriots demanded independence at that point, but the outbreak of fighting gave the advantage to the most intrepid, perhaps even the most foolhardy. During the last months of 1775 these radical Patriots began to dominate local meetings, provincial assemblies, and the Continental Congress, urging a complete break from British rule.

On July 4, 1776 the Patriots formally became rebels by agreeing to a Declaration of Independence that severed their ties to Great Britain. More momentously, they became revolutionaries, for the insurgents followed the advice of the Continental Congress and created new republican state governments. Repudiating aristocratic and monarchical rule, the Patriots vested sovereignty in the people as a whole, only to argue among themselves over what that meant in practice. Thus began the age of the democratic revolutions.

To defend their state governments, Patriot men and women went to war against an invading British army. Initially, most of the battles took place in the North, devastating dozens of communities between New York and Philadelphia. Simultaneously, the cost of fighting the war devastated the fiscal resources of the Continental Congress and the state governments. Only a miraculous victory at Saratoga and an alliance with France saved the fledgling rebellion.

Thereafter the fighting shifted to the South, where British forces again initially gained the upper hand. Gradually, a bitter war of attrition sapped the strength of the British army, while political unrest at home undermined the resolve of the British ministry. In a stunning diplomatic triumph, the rebel Patriot statesmen won independence largely on their own terms.

Nonetheless, the War of Independence had lasted six years, taken thousands of lives, and required vast expenditures of scarce resources. By the time it ended, the war had sharpened social divisions among the American people, had nearly destroyed their new financial institutions, and had tested their commitment to republican ideals.

Toward Independence, 1775–1776

The Battle of Concord was fought on April 19, 1775, but another fourteen months would elapse before the rebels made a final break with Britain. In the intervening time, the most vocal Patriots decided that preserving the "rights of Englishmen" wasn't enough: they wanted independence. In one colony after another Patriot legislators threw out the royal governors and created the two essentials for independence: a government and an army. Loyalists protested in vain against the rebellious fervor sweeping the colonies.

Civil War

The Second Continental Congress. The outbreak of fighting in Massachusetts lent great urgency to the Second Continental Congress, which met in Philadelphia in May 1775. With John Adams exhorting its members to rise to "the defense of American liberty," radical Patriots pressed for a Continental army. They wanted George Washington of Virginia to take command of the New England forces that had surrounded the British in Boston, and they wanted to call for new volunteers. More cautious delegates and those with Loyalist sympathies opposed these measures, warning that they would lead to more violence and commit the colonists irretrievably to rebellion. After bitter debate, Congress approved the proposals—but, as Adams lamented, only "by bare majorities."

While Congress deliberated in Philadelphia, hostilities continued to rage in Massachusetts. On June 17 more than 3,000 British troops attacked new American fortifications on Breed's Hill and Bunker Hill, which overlooked Boston. It took three assaults, during which 1,000 British soldiers were killed or wounded, to dislodge the Patriot militiamen. Despite the bloodshed, a majority in Congress still hoped for reconciliation with Britain. Led by John Dickinson of Pennsylvania, a moderate Patriot, they passed an Olive Branch petition, expressing loyalty to George III and asking him to repeal oppressive parliamentary legislation. Zealous Patriots in the Congress, such as Samuel Adams of Massachusetts and Patrick Henry of Virginia, countered by winning passage of a somewhat contradictory Declaration

of the Causes and Necessities of Taking Up Arms, asserting that Americans dreaded the "calamities of civil war" but were "resolved to die Freemen rather than to live [as] slaves."

King George did not exploit these divisions among the Patriots. He refused even to receive the Olive Branch petition, which the Loyalist Richard Penn brought to London in August. Instead, he issued a Proclamation for Suppressing Rebellion and Sedition, expressing his determination to crush the American revolt. By that time his intemperate words were perhaps justified, for Congress had decided at the end of June to invade Canada, hoping to unleash a popular uprising and add a fourteenth colony to the rebellion. Patriot forces easily took Montreal, but in December 1775 they failed to capture Quebec.

Meanwhile, Patriot merchants resorted to financial warfare, implementing Congress's resolution to cut off all exports to Britain and its West Indian possessions. By disrupting the tobacco trade and sugar production, they hoped to undermine the British economy. Parliament retaliated in December 1775 with a Prohibitory Act outlawing all trade with its rebellious colonies.

Rebellion in the South. In the meantime, the fighting in Massachusetts had sparked skirmishes between Patriots and Loyalists in the southern colonies. In June 1775 the Patriot-dominated House of Burgesses seized authority in Virginia, forcing the royal governor, Lord Dunmore, to take refuge on a British warship in Chesapeake Bay. From there Dunmore organized two military forces: one of whites, the Queen's Own Loyal Virginians, and one of blacks, the Ethiopian Regiment. Citing the king's proclamation, Dunmore branded the Patriots "traitors" and declared martial law. Then, in November, the governor issued a controversial proclamation of his own, offering freedom to slaves and indentured servants who belonged to rebels but joined the Loyalist cause. Patriot slaveowners now faced the possibility of black uprisings as well as military attack. Alarmed by Dunmore's proclamation, many planters threatened runaway slaves with death and called for a final break with Britain.

In the Carolinas, too, demands for independence grew more insistent in response to British military threats. Early in 1776 North Carolina's royal governor, Josiah Martin, tried to reestablish his authority with a force of 1,500 Scottish Highlanders from the Carolina backcountry. The Patriot militia quickly mobilized, and in February they defeated Martin's army in the Battle of Moore's Creek Bridge, capturing more than 800 of his troops. In Charleston, South Carolina, in June 1776 a group of armed artisans joined three Continental regiments and repelled a British naval assault.

As the violence escalated, radical Patriots seized control and moved toward independence. Early in 1776 the rebels transformed the North Carolina assembly into an independent Provincial Congress; in April that body instructed its representatives "to concur with the Delegates of other Colonies in declaring Independency, and forming foreign alliances." Virginia followed suit. Led by George Mason, James Madison, Edmund Pendleton, and Patrick Henry, Patriots called a special convention in May at which they resolved unanimously "to declare the United Colonies free and independent states."

Common Sense

The break with Britain did not come easily. It was not difficult for Patriots to repudiate Parliament—the author of the hated tax laws—but most Americans retained a deep loyalty to the Crown. Joyous crowds had toasted the health of King George III after the repeal of the Stamp Act, and even as the imperial crisis worsened, Benjamin Franklin proposed that the king rule over autonomous American assemblies. Americans condemned the legislation enacted by Parliament, not the king or the institution of monarchy.

The roots of this loyalty ran deep in the structure of American society. Like most men and women in the early modern world, Americans used metaphors of age and family to describe the system of social authority and imperial rule. Colonists often pictured their society as the dependent offspring—the child—of Britain, the "mother country." They respected "elders" in town meetings and church congregations. In their minds, the family was a "little commonwealth" ruled by its male head and the king was the "father" of his people. Denial of the legiti-

macy of the monarchy threatened paternal authority and the hierarchical order of society. Yet events had prepared Americans to reject their political father. Economic and religious changes had lessened the power and authority of fathers and traditional leaders. And by 1775 zealous Patriots were accusing George III of supporting ministers who passed oppressive legislation and of ordering the use of military force against them.

Agitation against the king became especially intense in Philadelphia, the largest American city but not previously a bastion of Patriot sentiment because of the Loyalist sympathies of many of its merchants. Now artisans took the initiative. Constituting about half the city's population, artisans owned nearly 40 percent of its wealth but feared for their future prosperity. Many felt that British imports threatened their small-scale manufacturing enterprises and that Parliament was bent on eliminating their "just Rights and Privileges." After the outbreak of fighting in Massachusetts the artisans, now organized into a Mechanics Association, became a powerful force in the Patriot movement. By February 1776 forty artisans were sitting alongside forty-seven merchants on the Philadelphia Committee of Resistance, the extralegal body that enforced the latest trade boycott.

More than economic self-interest was at work here. Some artisans and more of the city's laborers were Scots-Irish Presbyterians who had migrated to Pennsylvania to escape oppressive British rule in northern Ireland, and many adhered to the doctrine of religious equality propounded by Gilbert Tennent and other New Light ministers. As pastor of Philadelphia's Second Presbyterian Church, Tennent had told his congregation

The Royal Family
George III strikes a regal pose, surrounded by his queen and numerous offspring, all brilliantly attired. Patriots repudiated not only monarchy but also the fancy dress and aristocratic manners of the *ancien régime*, championing a society of republican simplicity.

that all men and women are equal before God. Translating religious equality into political terms, New Light Presbyterians shouted in street demonstrations that they had "no king but King Jesus." In addition, republican ideas derived from the European Enlightenment circulated freely in Pennsylvania. Well-educated scientists and statesmen—such as Benjamin Franklin, David Rittenhouse, Charles Thomson, and Benjamin Rush—joined artisans in questioning not only the wisdom of George III but also the legitimacy of the monarchy.

At this pivotal moment, with popular sentiment in a state of flux, a single pamphlet tipped the balance. In January 1776 Thomas Paine published *Common Sense,* a call for independence and republicanism. Paine, a corset maker and minor bureaucrat in Britain, had been fired from the English Customs Service for agitating for higher wages. He migrated to Philadelphia in 1774, armed with a letter of introduction from Benjamin Franklin. There he met Benjamin Rush and others who shared his republican sentiments. "Monarchy and hereditary succession have laid the world in blood and ashes," Paine proclaimed in *Common Sense,* leveling a personal attack against the king, "the hard hearted sullen Pharaoh of England." Mixing insults with biblical quotations, Paine blasted the British system of "mixed government," which yielded only "monarchical tyranny in the person of the King and aristocratical tyranny in the persons of the peers."

Paine presented the case for independence in a way that the general public could understand and respond to, suggesting the absurdity of an island ruling or conquering a continent. *Common Sense* went through twenty-five editions and reached hundreds of thousands of homes. Its message was clear: reject the arbitrary powers of king and Parliament and create independent republican states. "A government of our own is our natural right," Paine concluded. "'TIS TIME TO PART."

Independence Declared

Fired by Paine's arguments and the escalating military conflict with Loyalists, the American call for a break with Britain sounded with increasing urgency in Patriot conventions throughout the colonies. In June 1776 these disparate demands were given a single voice in the Continental Congress when Richard Henry Lee presented the Virginia Convention's resolution: "That these United Colonies are, and of right ought to be, free and independent states . . . absolved from all allegiance to the British Crown." Faced with certain defeat, staunch Loyalists and anti-independence moderates withdrew from the Congress, leaving committed Patriots to take the fateful step. On July 4, 1776, the Congress approved the Declaration of Independence.

The main author of the Declaration was Thomas

Affirming the Declaration of Independence
The mood in the room is solemn as Congress formally declares independence from Great Britain. The delegates were now traitors to their country and king, their fortunes and even their lives hinging on the success of Patriot arms.

Jefferson, a young Virginia planter and legislative leader whose pamphlet *A Summary View of the Rights of British America* had mobilized resistance to the Coercive Acts. In composing the Declaration, Jefferson primarily wanted to justify Congress's action both to domestic critics and to foreign observers by putting the blame for the rupture on the king. To this end, he enumerated the acts of the imperial government that had oppressed Americans, suggesting that powerful centralized governments are inherently dangerous to liberty. Simultaneously, he provided a detailed indictment of the king's conduct, discrediting monarchical rule. Through the power of his prose, Jefferson sought to convince his fellow Americans of the perfidy of George III: "He has plundered our seas, ravaged our coasts, burned our towns, and destroyed the lives of our people. . . . A prince, whose character is thus marked by every act which may define a tyrant, is unfit to be the ruler of a free people."

In ringing phrases Jefferson proclaimed a series of "self-evident" truths: "that all men are created equal"; that they possess the "unalienable rights" of "life, liberty, and the pursuit of happiness"; that government derives its "just powers from the consent of the governed" and can rightly be overthrown if it "becomes destructive of these ends." His prose, steeped in the ideas and rhetoric of the European Enlightenment and the Glorious Revolution of 1688, celebrated the doctrines of individual liberty and popular sovereignty. All Americans are heirs of this revolutionary republican tradition.

For Jefferson, as for Paine, the pen was mightier than the sword. Almost overnight many halfhearted Americans were radicalized into republican revolutionaries. In rural hamlets and seaport cities, crowds celebrated the Declaration by burning George III in effigy; in New York City, they toppled a huge statue of the king. With these acts of destruction, Patriots broke their psychological ties to the mother country and the father monarch. Americans were now ready to create republics, state governments that derived their authority from the people.

The Perils of War and Finance, 1776–1778

The Declaration of Independence brought an end to the minor skirmishing of a civil war. For the next two years Britain mounted large-scale offensives against the Continental army commanded by George Washington, defeating the rebel forces in nearly every battle. A few inspiring American victories kept the rebellion alive, but in late 1776 and again during the winter of 1777–1778, at Valley Forge, the fate of the Patriot cause hung in the balance.

War in the North

Early in 1776 the British ministry decided to use overwhelming military force to crush the American revolt. The task looked easy. Great Britain had a population of 11 million, compared with about 2.5 million in the thirteen rebel colonies, nearly 20 percent of whom were African-American slaves. The British enjoyed a great economic advantage because of the immense profits of the South Atlantic system and the newly emerging Industrial Revolution. Militarily, Britain enjoyed clear superiority: it had a standing army of 48,000 men (and the financial resources to hire or raise thousands more) and the most powerful navy in the world. The imperial government also expected support from the tens of thousands of Loyalists in America and from various Indian tribes hostile to white expansion.

In contrast, the rebellious Americans looked weak. They had no navy, and their small Continental army consisted mostly of militiamen whose enlistments would expire at the end of 1776. True, the Patriots could field thousands of militiamen, but only for short periods and only near their own farms or towns. Assessing the two antagonists in 1776, few observers would have given the rebels a chance for victory.

Lord North, who was still the prime minister, moved quickly to put down the rebellion. Alarmed by the American invasion of Canada in 1775, he ordered an ambitious military mobilization and replaced the ineffective General Gage with a new commander, General William Howe. Howe had served in the colonies during the French and Indian War and had distinguished himself in Wolfe's siege of Quebec. North ordered him to capture New York City and seize control of the Hudson River, isolating the radical Patriots in New England from the rest of the colonies.

Howe proceeded with dispatch. In March 1776 he transferred the British forces in Boston to a new military headquarters in Halifax, Nova Scotia, where they were joined by dozens of new regiments. By the summer he was ready to move. While the Continental Congress was declaring independence in Philadelphia, Howe was landing 10,000 troops—British regulars and German mercenaries—outside New York City. By August the

The Evacuation of Boston
Surrounded by American militiamen and facing bombardment by Patriot artillery, General Howe directs the withdrawal of British troops from Boston in March 1776. Four months later he launched a major offensive against Washington's army near New York City.

British army had swollen to 32,000 soldiers, supported by a fleet of thirty warships and 10,000 sailors. This formidable force faced, on the American side, General Washington's newly formed, poorly trained army of about 18,000 troops, nearly half of whom were short-term militiamen hastily recruited by the state governments of Virginia and New England. Many American officers were capable men who had served in the French and Indian War, but even the most experienced had never commanded a large force or faced a disciplined army capable of the intricate maneuvers of European warfare. The advantage of the British forces was overwhelming; their officers had been tested in combat, and their soldiers were well armed.

British superiority was immediately apparent. On August 27, 1776, Howe attacked the Americans in the Battle of Long Island and forced them to retreat to Manhattan Island. There Howe outflanked Washington's troops, nearly trapping them on several occasions. Outgunned and outmaneuvered, the Continental army again retreated, first to Harlem Heights, then to White Plains, and finally across the Hudson River to New Jersey. Howe pursued the Americans cautiously, seeking to envelop Washington's main force in a pincer movement. By December the British army had pushed the Continental troops out of New Jersey and across the Delaware River into Pennsylvania, and Congress was forced to flee from Philadelphia to Baltimore.

From the Patriots' perspective, winter came just in time, for it was customary in the eighteenth century to halt military campaigns during cold and snowy weather. Moreover, the overconfident British let down their guard, allowing the Americans to score a few triumphs. On Christmas night in 1776 Washington crossed the Delaware River and staged a surprise attack on Trenton, New Jersey. About a thousand Hessians, German mercenaries who had long fought for the British army, were forced to surrender. Then, on January 3, 1777, the Continental army won a small engagement at nearby Princeton. These victories raised sagging Patriot morale and prompted the British to evacuate New Jersey, a withdrawal that allowed the Continental Congress to return to Philadelphia and worried potential Loyalists throughout America. Bright stars in a dark night, the American triumphs could not mask British military superiority. These are the times, wrote Tom Paine, that "try men's souls."

Armies and Strategies

British superiority did not break the will of the Continental army, and the rebellion continued. Howe himself was partly responsible for prolonging the conflict. While in Britain he had opposed the Coercive Acts, and as the British military commander he still hoped for a compro-

mise—indeed, he had authority from Lord North to negotiate with the rebels. Consequently, instead of following up his early victories with a ruthless pursuit of the retreating American army, Howe was content to show his superior power and tactics, hoping to convince the Continental Congress that resistance was futile.

Howe's cautiousness reflected the conventions of eighteenth-century warfare, in which generals sought to outmaneuver the opposing forces and win their surrender rather than destroy them. Of course, he was also aware that his troops were 3,000 miles from supplies and reinforcements; in case of a major defeat, it would take six months to replenish his forces, especially since neither the ministry nor the royal governors had encouraged Loyalists to join or supply the army. However understandable Howe's tactics were, they cost the British the opportunity to nip the rebellion in the bud. Instead, Howe allowed the American army to survive to fight another day and to claim victories at Trenton and Princeton.

Howe's failure to win a decisive victory was paralleled by Washington's success in avoiding a spectacular defeat. He, too, was cautious, challenging Howe's army on selected occasions but retreating in the face of superior strength. As Washington told Congress, "On our

Washington at the Battle of Trenton
Washington told Congress that "on our Side the War should be defensive," but his bold attack across the Delaware on Christmas night, 1776, gave Americans their first military victory.

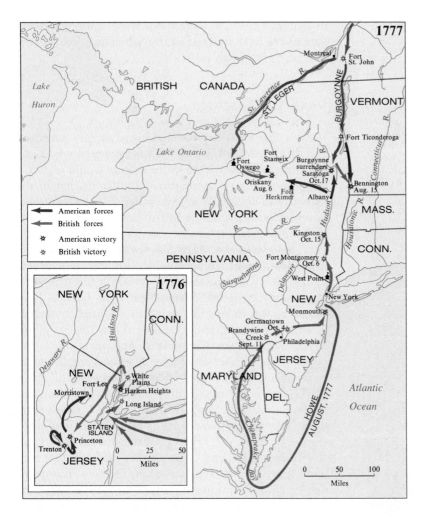

The War in the North

In 1776 the British army drove Washington's forces across New Jersey into Pennsylvania. The Americans counterattacked at Trenton and Princeton, setting up winter headquarters at Morristown. In 1777 General Howe captured Philadelphia from the south, while General Burgoyne and Colonel St. Leger launched invasions from Canada. Aided by thousands of New England militia, troops commanded by General Horatio Gates defeated Burgoyne at Bennington and then at Saratoga, the military turning point of the war.

Side the War should be defensive." The American general's strategy was to draw the British away from the seacoast to extend their lines of supply and sap their morale. His primary goal was to keep the Continental army intact as a symbol and instrument of American resistance (see Map 6.1).

In achieving this goal, Washington had more to contend with than Howe. Congress vowed to field a regular force of 75,000 men, but the Continental army never reached half that number; at its peak Washington's main force had only 18,000 men, few of whom were experienced soldiers. Yeomen farmers and trained militiamen preferred to serve in local units near their fields and families and refrained from joining the Continental forces. Consequently, the American army drew its recruits from the lower ranks of society. For example, the soldiers in the Continental units commanded by General William Smallwood of Maryland were either poor American-born youths or older foreign-born men—British ex-convicts and former indentured servants. They enlisted not to express their patriotic fervor but to make their way in the world, enlisting for three years in return for a bonus of $20 in cash (about $200 today) and the promise of 100 acres of land. Even so,

the declining purchasing power of Continental currency hurt the soldiers and their families financially, undermining their morale. Moreover, it took time to mold these men into a fighting force. In the face of a British artillery bombardment or a flank attack, many recruits panicked; hundreds of others deserted, unwilling to submit to the discipline and danger of military life. They also resented the contemptuous way Washington and other American officers treated the camp followers—the women who came along with the recruits and took care of their material and emotional needs.

Such support was crucial, for the Continental army did not receive much encouragement from the public. Radical Whig Patriots had long viewed a peacetime standing army as a threat to liberty and even in wartime hesitated to create a professional force. They placed their hopes in the militia, men organized in local units and supplied and aided by their families and communities. The Continental army went begging, without adequate goods from the populace or money from the Congress. General Philip Schuyler of New York complained that his troops were "weak in numbers, dispirited, naked, destitute of provisions, without camp equipage, with little ammunition, and not a single piece

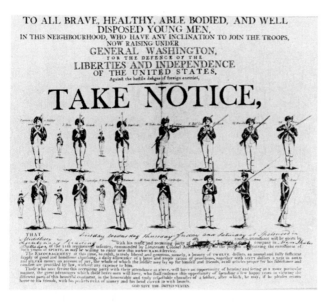

Patriots Recruit an Army
Some Americans became soldiers because of the glamour of bearing arms, but the citizens of Peacham, New Hampshire, were motivated by Real Whig fears of British tyranny: "Although we . . . had but six or eight men in the town, we sent two of them . . . for we feared if the British were not going to be stopped, we shall all be ruined."

Joseph Brant
The Mohawk chief Thayendanegea, known to the whites as Joseph Brant, secured the support of four of the Six Iroquois Nations for the British. In 1778 and 1779 he led Iroquois warriors and Tory Rangers in attacks on American settlements throughout western New York. This portrait by Charles Willson Peale was painted in 1797.

of cannon." Given this situation, Washington was fortunate not to have suffered an overwhelming defeat in the first year of the war.

Victory at Saratoga

Howe's failure to achieve a decisive victory surprised and dismayed Lord North and his ministers, who came to realize that restoration of the empire would require a long-term military commitment similar to that in the French and Indian War. Accepting the challenge, the government increased the British land tax to finance the war and prepared to mount a major campaign in 1777.

The isolation of New England remained the primary British goal. To accomplish this, the colonial secretary, Lord George Germain, devised a three-pronged attack converging on Albany, New York. General John Burgoyne was to lead the main force, a large contingent of British regulars, from Quebec down the St. John's River, across Lake Champlain, and then down the upper Hudson River to Albany. A second, smaller force under Lieutenant Colonel Barry St. Leger would attack Albany from the west, moving through the Mohawk River Valley. Leger's troops were mostly Iroquois warriors from central New York. The Iroquois had allied themselves with the British to protect their land from American settlers, and Germain was confident that they would cut down the rebels all along the New York frontier. Finally, to reinforce Burgoyne from the south, Germain ordered Howe to dispatch a contingent from his army northward from New York City.

Howe had a plan of his own. He proposed to attack Philadelphia, the home of the Continental Congress, hoping to force Washington into a fixed battle and end the rebellion with a single major victory. With Germain's apparent approval, Howe set his forces in motion—but very slowly. Rather than march overland through New Jersey, the troops sailed south from New York and then up Chesapeake Bay to approach Philadelphia from the southwest. Once on the ground, however, the British army showed its tactical skill. Howe's troops easily outflanked the American positions along Brandywine Creek, forcing Washington to withdraw. The British marched triumphantly into Philadelphia on September 26, half assuming that the capture of the rebels' capital would end the uprising. However, the Continental Congress fled into the interior, first to Lancaster and then to York, and would hear no words of surrender.

The British paid a high price for this victory. Howe's leisurely advance against Philadelphia exposed Burgoyne to defeat in the north. Initially, Burgoyne's troops had sped across Lake Champlain, overwhelming the American defenses at Fort Ticonderoga and driving onward toward the upper reaches of the Hudson River.

Moses Hall

Partisan Warfare in the South

The British campaign in the South un-leashed a bitter struggle between resident Patriots and Loyalists, many of whom had old grudges to settle. Patriots labelled British Lieutenant Colonel Banastre Tarleton "Bloodly Tarleton" because of his wanton disregard for the rules of warfare; but the Patriots responded in kind, and the war in the southern backcountry left a trail of brutality.

Our troops and this body of Tories and Colonel Tarleton['s Tories] all being in the same neighborhood, our troops on the march met said body of Tories at a place called the Race Paths, and [the Tories], mistaking our troops for Tarleton's, Colonel Lee and Officers kept up the deception and Colonel Lee and his light horse marching in one column or line, and Major or Colonel Dixon's command in another, some interval apart, the Tories passed into this interval between our lines. . . .

They frequently uttered salutations of a friendly kind, believing us to be British. Colonel Lee knew what he was about and so did Major Dixon. . . . In a few minutes or less time, and at the instant they, the Tories, were completely covered by our lines upon both flanks, or front and rear as the case may have been, the bugle sounded to attack, and the slaughter began, the Tories crying out, "Your own men, your own men, as good subjects of His Majesty as in America." It was said that upwards of two hundred of these Tories were slain on the ground.

The evening after our battle with the Tories, we having a considerable number of prisoners, I recollect a scene which made a lasting impression upon my mind. I was invited by some of my comrades to go and see some of the prisoners. We went to where six were standing together. Some discussion taking place, I heard some of our men cry out, "Remember Buford" [a slaughter of Virginian troops by Tarleton's Tories], and the prisoners were immediately hewed to pieces with broadswords. At first I bore the scene without any emotion, but upon a moment's reflection, I felt such horror as I never did before nor have since, and, returning to my quarters and throwing myself upon my blanket, I contemplated the cruelties of war until over-come and unmanned by a distressing gloom from which I was not relieved until commencing our march next morning before day by moonlight. I came to Tarleton's camp, which he had just abandoned leaving lively rail fires. Being on the left of the road as we marched along, I discovered lying upon the ground something with appearance of a man. Upon approaching him, he proved to be a youth about sixteen who, having come out to view the British through curiosity, for fear he might give information to our troops, they had run him through with a bayonet and left him for dead. Though able to speak, he was mortally wounded. The sight of this unoffending boy, butchered, . . . relieved me of my distressful feelings for the slaughter of the Tories, and I desired nothing so much as the opportunity of participating in their destruction.

Source: Hall's Pension application, Record Group 15 of the Records of the Veterans Administration, National Archives. Available in John C. Dann, ed., *The Revolution Remembered: Eyewitness Accounts of the War for Independence* (Chicago: University of Chicago Press, 1980), 201–204 *passim.*

Then they stalled, for Burgoyne—"Gentleman Johnny," as he was called—fought with style, not speed. His heavy baggage train moved slowly, weighed down with comfortable tents and ample stocks of food and wine (see American Voices, above). Its progress was further impeded by the Continental forces of General Horatio Gates, who felled trees across the crude wagon trail and raided the long, thinly stretched supply lines to Canada. By the end of the summer Burgoyne's army—6,000 regulars (half of them German mercenaries) and 600 Loyalists and Indians—was in trouble, bogged down in the wilderness near Saratoga, New York.

The Patriot militia delivered the final blow. On August 16 at a military depot at Bennington, Vermont, 2,000 militiamen left their farms to fight a bitter pitched battle that deprived British raiders of much-needed sup-plies of food, horses, and oxen. Burgoyne then received more bad news: Patriot militiamen in the Mohawk Valley had forced St. Leger's troops to retreat. And to meet Howe's request for additional troops to occupy Philadelphia, the British commander in New York City had to recall the relief force he had sent toward Albany. While Burgoyne waited in vain for help, thousands of Patriot militiamen from Massachusetts, New Hampshire, and New York joined Gates's forces. They "swarmed around the army like birds of prey," an English sergeant wrote in his journal, and on October 17, 1777, forced Burgoyne to surrender.

The battle of Saratoga proved to be the turning point of the war. The Americans captured 5,000 British troops and their equipment—a price in men and materiel that far outweighed Howe's capture of Philadelphia. More important, the victory virtually assured the success of American diplomats in Paris, who were seeking a military alliance with France. Patriots on the home front were equally delighted, though their joy was muted by an awareness of the difficulties that lay ahead.

Wartime Trials

In the twentieth century two world wars disrupted the lives of millions of ordinary women and men, conscripting them into war industries, destroying their property, turning them into refugees, taking their lives. On a much smaller scale, the American War of Independence exposed tens of thousands of civilians to deprivation, displacement, and death. "An army, even a friendly one, are a dreadful scourge to any people," a Connecticut soldier wrote home from Pennsylvania. "You cannot imagine what devastation and distress mark their steps." New Jersey was particularly hard hit by the fighting as British and American armies marched back and forth across the state. Those with reputations as Patriots or Loyalists fled from their homes to escape arrest—or worse. Soldiers and partisans looted farms, seeking food or political revenge. Drunk and disorderly troops harassed or raped women and girls. Wherever the armies went, families lived in fear.

People learned to fear their neighbors as well, for the War of Independence was in many respects a civil war. Mobs of Patriot farmers in New England beat suspected Tories or destroyed their property. "Every Body submitted to our Sovereign Lord the Mob," a Loyalist preacher lamented. "Now we are reduced to a State of Anarchy." Patriots in most communities quickly organized a new institution of local government called a Committee of Safety. Those committees collected taxes, sent food and clothing to the Continental army, and imposed fines or jail sentences on those who failed to support the Patriot cause. "There is no such thing as remaining neutral," declared the Committee of Safety of Farmington, Connecticut.

Financial Crisis. Wars are not won by guns alone. Armies have to be fed, clothed, and paid. Victory often goes to the side that has the most money or is prepared to make the greatest financial sacrifices. When the War of Independence began, the new American governments were neither wealthy nor politically secure. Since opposition to taxes had fueled the independence movement in the first place, Patriot officials were reluctant to increase taxes for fear of undermining their fragile authority. To finance the war, the state governments first borrowed money, in gold or silver or British currency, from wealthy individuals. Those funds quickly ran out, so the states created a new monetary system based on the dollar (not the English pound) and issued $260 million in

currency and transferable bonds, using the new money to pay soldiers and purchase supplies. Theoretically the new notes could be redeemed at a stated time in gold or silver. But since they were printed in huge quantities and were not backed by tax revenues or mortgages on land, many Americans questioned their worth and refused to accept them at the face value. Indeed, North Carolina's paper money came to be worth so little that the state government refused to accept it. Many state governments teetered on the brink of bankruptcy.

The monetary system created by the Continental Congress collapsed as well, despite the best efforts of the Philadelphia merchant Robert Morris, the "financier of the Revolution." Until 1781 the Congress was essentially an ad hoc coalition of independent state governments without legal authority of its own and completely dependent on funds requisitioned from the member states, which frequently paid late or not at all. To raise money, Congress depended on loans, but with no funds of its own, the government could not assure creditors that they would be repaid. Congress therefore borrowed $6 million from France and pledged it as security; wealthy Americans promptly purchased $27 million in Continental loan certificates, essentially gambling on the Patriot cause. When those funds and other French and Dutch loans were exhausted, Congress followed the lead of the states and financed the war by printing money. Between 1775 and 1779 it issued $191 million in currency. By 1780 tax revenues from the states had retired only $3 million of those bills

A Flood of Paper Currency
The Continental Congress issued this bill in 1776, declaring it to be worth "SIX Spanish Milled DOLLARS" or the equivalent in gold or silver, but by 1780 most Americans no longer had confidence in the currency and its value collapsed to virtually nothing—giving rise to the phrase "not worth a continental."

from circulation, so the value of the remaining bills continued to fall.

Indeed, the enormous increase in the volume of paper currency created the worst inflation in American history. The amount of goods available for purchase—both domestic foodstuffs and foreign manufactures—had shrunk significantly because of the fighting and the British naval blockade, even as the amount of currency had multiplied. Inevitably, consumers "bid up" the prices of goods. In Maryland, for example, a bag of salt that had cost $1 in 1776 was valued at $3,900 a few years later. This soaring inflation forced nearly every family to look out for its own interests. Unwilling to accept worthless currency, hard-pressed farmers refused to sell their crops, even to the American army. To supply their own needs, farmers resorted to barter—trading wheat for tools or clothes—or sold goods only to those who could pay in gold or silver. In towns, women led mobs that seized overpriced sugar, tea, and bread from storekeepers. With civilian morale and social cohesion crumbling despite the victory at Saratoga, some Patriot leaders began to doubt that the rebellion could succeed.

Valley Forge. Fears reached their peak during the winter of 1777–1778. After the capture of Philadelphia, Howe established winter quarters there, and he and his officers partook of the finest wines, foods, and entertainment the city could offer. Washington's army retreated into the Pennsylvania countryside, establishing its base for the winter some 20 miles to the west, in Valley Forge. About 12,000 soldiers, accompanied by hundreds of camp followers, arrived at the camp in December. Everyone suffered horribly. "The army . . . now begins to grow sickly," a surgeon confided to his diary. "Poor food—hard lodging—cold weather—fatigue—nasty clothes—nasty cookery. . . . Why are we sent here to starve and freeze?" Many soldiers deserted, unable to endure the harsh conditions; by spring over a thousand men had vanished into the countryside. Another 3,000 soldiers and scores of camp followers died from malnutrition and disease. One winter at Valley Forge took as many American lives as had two years of fighting against General Howe.

Precarious public backing for the rebellion also threatened the army, which could not depend on farmers for support. Ethnic and religious divisions among Americans who lived near Valley Forge directly affected military operations. For example, most New Light members of the Dutch Reformed Church in nearby New Jersey actively supported the American cause, joining the militia and raiding British encampments, but many Old Lights were Loyalists and fed information and supplies to the British. A number of Quakers and German sectarians in Pennsylvania were pacifists, unwilling to support either side.

Self-interest also contributed to the deprivation of Washington's army at Valley Forge. Many farmers hoarded their grain over the winter, hoping to profit from high prices in the spring. Others bullied their way through Patriot roadblocks to Philadelphia, where British quartermasters paid in gold and silver. Even farmers who supported the rebellion could not afford to supply the American army when their labors were rewarded with rapidly depreciating Continental Congress dollars. "Such a dearth of public spirit, and want of public virtue," Washington complained—but to no effect. The suffering at Valley Forge continued, graphic testimony to divided loyalties among the public and the inability of the Congress to raise sufficient revenue.

In this dark hour Baron von Steuben, a former Prussian military officer, raised the morale and self-respect of both officers and enlisted men by instituting a standardized system of drill and maneuver at Valley Forge. Von Steuben was one of a handful of foreigners who had volunteered their services to the American cause. His efforts encouraged officers to become more professional in their demeanor and behavior and instilled greater order and discipline in the ranks. Thanks to von Steuben, the smaller Continental army that emerged from Valley Forge in the spring was a much tougher and better disciplined force with a renewed sense of purpose.

The Path to Victory, 1778–1783

The Patriots' prospects improved dramatically in 1778, when the United States formed a military alliance with France, the most powerful nation on the European continent. The alliance not only brought the Americans money, troops, and supplies but also changed the conflict from a colonial rebellion to an international war.

The French Alliance

Negotiating the Treaty. In 1777 Benjamin Franklin and two other diplomats, Arthur Lee and Silas Deane, had begun negotiations for a commercial and military treaty with France. Since 1763 France had been seeking revenge for its defeat in the French and Indian War and its loss of Canada. The French foreign minister, the comte de Vergennes, was a determined opponent of Britain and an early supporter of American independence. In 1776 he persuaded King Louis XVI to extend a secret loan to the rebellious colonies and supply them with gunpowder. When news of the American victory at Saratoga reached Paris in December 1777, Vergennes urged the king to approve a formal alliance with the Continental Congress.

Franklin and his associates craftily exploited the rivalry between France and Britain. They used the threat of a negotiated settlement with Britain to win an explicit French commitment to American independence. The Treaty of Alliance of February 6, 1778 specified that after France entered the war against Great Britain, neither partner would sign a separate peace before the "liberty, sovereignty, and independence" of the United States was assured. In return, the American diplomats pledged that their government would recognize any French conquests in the West Indies.

France and America were unlikely partners. France was Catholic and a monarchy; the United States was largely Protestant and a federation of republics. The two peoples had been on opposite sides in wars from 1689 to 1763. But now they were united against a common enemy. After two years of armed resistance, the fledgling American federation had earned the respect of the nations of Europe and had come to figure in the international balance of power. The Franco-American alliance isolated Britain diplomatically and placed it militarily on the defensive: British forces not only confronted the Patriots in North America but had to defend Gibraltar against Spain, and the West Indies, India, and Britain itself against France.

The British Response. The war became increasingly unpopular in Britain. Radical agitators and republican-minded artisans supported American demands for greater rights and campaigned for political reforms at home—such as broadening the right to vote and eliminating electoral corruption. The landed gentry and urban merchants protested against rising taxes. To meet the military budget, the government had already increased the land tax and the stamp duty and imposed new levies on carriages, wine, and imported goods. "It seemed we were to be taxed and stamped ourselves instead of inflicting taxes and stamps on others," a British politician complained. Yet George III continued to demand that the rebellion be crushed at any cost. If America won independence, he warned Lord North, "the West Indies must follow them. Ireland would soon follow the same plan and be a separate state, then this island would be reduced to itself, and soon would be a poor island indeed."

Lord North took a more pragmatic position. To forestall a Franco-American alliance and keep the colonies in the British empire, North announced his intention in February 1778 to seek a negotiated constitutional settlement. At his bidding, Parliament repealed the Tea and Prohibitory acts and, in an amazing concession, renounced its right to tax the American colonies. The prime minister then appointed a commission, headed by Lord Carlisle, to negotiate with the Continental Congress and offer a return to the constitutional relationship that had existed in 1763, before the Sugar and Stamp acts. But it was too late. By early 1778, not only had the military pact with France been signed but a majority of Americans had embraced independence and republicanism.

The Impact of the Alliance. The alliance with France infused new life into the Patriots' cause. With access to military supplies and European loans, the American army soon improved and hopes soared. "There has been a great change in this state since the news from France," a Patriot soldier reported from Pennsylvania; farmers—"mercenary wretches," he called them—"were as eager for Continental Money now as they were a few weeks ago for British gold."

The Congress also showed renewed energy and purpose, finally addressing the demands of the officer corps for pensions. Most officers came from the upper ranks of society and used their own funds to equip not only themselves but sometimes their men as well; in return they demanded pensions for life at half pay. Although John Adams condemned the petitioners as "Mastiffs, scrambling for rank and pay like apes for nuts," Congress agreed to give the officers half pay after the end of the war, though only for seven years. General Washington had urged Congress to make this concession, warning the lawmakers that "the salvation of the cause depends upon it."

War in the South

The French alliance expanded the war without bringing it to a rapid conclusion. When France entered the conflict in June 1778, it had other goals besides a quick victory over the British forces in North America. Hoping to capture a rich sugar island, France concentrated its naval forces in the West Indies. Spain, which entered the war in 1779, also had its own agenda: in return for providing naval assistance to France, it hoped to win back Florida and Gibraltar in the peace settlement. The destiny of the new American republic was enmeshed in a web of European alliances and territorial quarrels.

This diplomatic morass gave Britain one more opportunity to crush the rebellion—or at least limit it. Saratoga had spelled an end to British hopes of recapturing New England and holding all the rebellious mainland colonies. But in many ways New England was the least valuable part of the empire. Far more important to the South Atlantic system were the southern colonies, with their rich crops of rice and tobacco. The British ministry, beset by a war on many fronts, settled on a more modest strategy in America. It would use its army to recapture Virginia, the Carolinas, and Georgia and then rely on Loyalists to hold and administer the reconquered territory.

Until that time the British had made little use of Americans who remained loyal to the king. They knew, however, that recent migrants with little sympathy for the rebel cause made up a sizable portion of the population of the southern backcountry. Some, such as the Scottish Highlanders in North Carolina, retained an especially strong allegiance to the Crown. The British hoped to recruit other Loyalists from the ranks of the Regulators, who had opposed the political dominance of low-country planters. They also hoped to take advantage of racial divisions in the South. Over 1,000 Virginia slaves had fought for Lord Dunmore in 1776 under the banner "Liberty to Slaves!" and thousands more might support a new British offensive. At the least, racial divisions would undermine the Patriots' military efforts. Blacks formed 30 to 50 percent of the population, yet whites were afraid to arm them. Many planters refused to allow their sons or white overseers to join the Continental forces, keeping them home to prevent slave revolts.

Implementing this southern strategy became the responsibility of Sir Henry Clinton, who had replaced the discredited Howe early in 1778. In June 1778 Clinton ordered the main British army to evacuate Philadelphia and move to more secure quarters in New York. In De-

cember he finally launched his southern campaign, landing a force of 3,500 men near Savannah, Georgia. The British army took the city, mobilized hundreds of blacks to build barricades and unload military supplies, and then moved inland, capturing Augusta early in 1779. By the end of the year the British had reconquered Georgia and had 10,000 troops poised for an assault on South Carolina. To counter this threat, the Continental Congress suggested that South Carolina raise 3,000 black troops, but the state assembly overwhelmingly rejected the proposal.

During most of 1780 British forces moved from one victory to another. In April Clinton laid siege to Charleston, South Carolina, which surrendered six weeks later. He captured General Benjamin Lincoln and his 5,000 troops in the single largest American surrender of the war. After this success Lord Cornwallis assumed control of the British forces and sent out expeditions to secure the countryside. In August Cornwallis routed an American force commanded by General Horatio Gates, the hero of Saratoga, at Camden in the heart of the Carolina pine barrens, giving the British control of South Carolina (see Map 6.2).

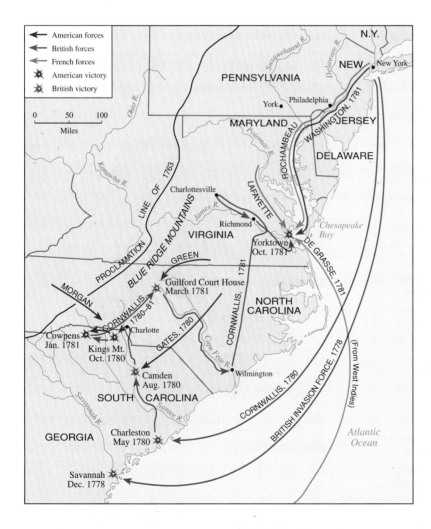

MAP 6.2

The Campaign in the South

The British ministry's southern strategy started well. British forces captured Savannah in December 1778 and Charleston in May 1779. Brutal warfare raged in the interior over the next eighteen months, fought more by small bands of irregulars than by disciplined armies. When Cornwallis carried the battle into Virginia in late 1781, a Franco-American army led by Washington and Lafayette surrounded his forces at Yorktown, aided by the French fleet under Admiral de Grasse.

This victory seemed to confirm the wisdom of the southern strategy. After the British attack, hundreds of blacks fled to Florida and hundreds more sought protection behind British lines, providing labor for the invading army. Moreover, southern Loyalists rallied to the support of the Crown, forming military units and providing supplies and information to British forces as they moved through Georgia and South Carolina. In contrast, the local Patriots were of little use to General Gates's army. Only about 1,200 militiamen joined Gates at the battle of Camden—a fifth of the number of local Patriots at Saratoga—and many of them panicked and fled without firing a shot.

Then the tide of battle turned. Far off in Europe, the Dutch declared war against Britain, making its diplomatic isolation complete; of more immediate importance, France dispatched troops to America. The French decision was partly the work of the marquis de Lafayette, a republican-minded French aristocrat who had offered his services to the American cause long before the alliance of 1778. Lafayette had returned to France early in 1780 to persuade Louis XVI to change French military priorities and prosecute the war against Britain in North America more vigorously. In July 1780 a French army of 5,500 men commanded by General comte de Rochambeau arrived in Newport, Rhode Island, where it posed a threat to the British forces in New York.

In the South, Washington replaced Gates with Nathanael Greene as the American commander, and Greene immediately devised new military tactics and strategies. To make the best use of the Patriot militiamen, many of whom were "without discipline and addicted to plundering," Greene divided them into small groups under strong leaders and used them to harass the larger but less mobile British forces. A militia force of Patriot farmers defeated a regiment of Loyalists at King's Mountain, North Carolina, in October 1780, taking about a thousand prisoners. American guerrillas led by the "Swamp Fox," General Francis Marion, won a series of small but fierce battles in South Carolina, while General Daniel Morgan led another American force to a bloody victory over a British regiment at Cowpens, North Carolina, in January 1781. On March 15 General Greene's force fought Cornwallis's seasoned army to a draw at North Carolina's Guilford Court House.

Patriot forces had broken the back of the British offensive, but Loyalist garrisons and militia remained powerful, and the well-organized Cherokee posed an additional threat to Patriot forces. Determined to protect their lands, the Cherokee attacked American settlers in the southern backcountry, preventing them from joining the battle against the British. Nonetheless, Greene's army slowly began to wear down the British and reconquer the Carolinas and Georgia. "We fight, get beaten, and fight again," General Greene declared.

In the spring of 1781 Cornwallis made the crucial decision to concede the southernmost states to Greene and seek a decisive victory in Virginia. Aided by reinforcements from Clinton in New York, Cornwallis moved through eastern North Carolina and into Virginia's Tidewater region. His forces, led by Benedict Arnold, the infamous traitor to the Patriot cause (see American Lives, pages 184–185), ranged up and down the James River, meeting only slight resistance from a small American force commanded by Lafayette. Then, in May 1781, as the armies of Lafayette and Cornwallis sparred near the York Peninsula in Virginia, the French monarch ordered the large fleet in the West Indies commanded by Admiral François de Grasse to sail to North America.

Emboldened by the ample forces at his disposal, Washington launched a well-coordinated attack. To keep Clinton's troops in the North, he feinted an assault on New York City and secretly had General Rochambeau's army march from Rhode Island to Virginia, where it joined Washington's troops. Simultaneously, Admiral de Grasse positioned his fleet off the coast of Virginia, where, in combination with a smaller French naval force from Rhode Island, it established control of Chesapeake Bay. By the time the British discovered Washington's audacious plan, it was too late. Cornwallis found himself surrounded, his army of 9,500 men outnumbered two to one on land and cut off from reinforcement or retreat by sea. Abandoned by the British navy, he surrendered at Yorktown on October 19, 1781.

James Lafayette
Born into slavery in Virginia, James Lafayette served as a spy in 1781 for the American army commanded by the marquis de Lafayette, receiving his freedom as a reward and taking Lafayette's surname as his own. The two Lafayettes met again in 1824, when the Frenchman visited the United States.

American Soldiers at Yorktown, 1781
A French observer captured the diversity of the American army: a black infantryman from Rhode Island, a French-Canadian volunteer, a buckskin-clad rifleman from Virginia, and (holding the gunnery torch) an artilleryman from the Continental army.

The Franco-American victory at Yorktown broke the resolve of the British government. "Oh God! It is all over!" Lord North exclaimed when he heard the news. His ministry lacked the will or resources to raise a new army to fight a long war of attrition in America, and Britain's European rivals posed an immediate threat. The combined fleets of France and Spain were menacing the British sugar islands, Dutch merchants were recapturing American and European markets from English and Scottish traders, and a newly formed group of European states—the League of Armed Neutrality—was threatening to use force to break Britain's commercial blockade of France. Isolated diplomatically in Europe, stymied militarily in America, and—perhaps most important—lacking public support at home, the British ministry gave up active prosecution of the war. Only isolated attacks by Loyalists and Indians reminded Americans that their country was still at war.

The Patriot Advantage

Angry members of Parliament demanded an explanation for this stinging military defeat. How could mighty Britain, victorious in the Great War for Empire, with its formidable financial and military resources, be defeated by a motley group of upstart colonists? The ministry blamed the military leadership, pointing with some justification to a series of blunders made by British generals. Why had Howe not been more ruthless in his pursuit of Washington's army in 1776? How could Germain have failed to coordinate the movements of Howe's and Burgoyne's armies in 1777? Why had Cornwallis been allowed to march deep into the powerful rebel state of Virginia in 1781?

Historians have been equally critical of the military command, but they also have pointed out the high odds against British success, given the broad-based support for the rebel cause. While only a third of the white population consisted of "true Patriots," deeply committed to the rebellion, another third was supportive enough to pay the taxes imposed by the state governments. Unlike most revolutionaries, the Patriots had assumed control of well-established institutions, and their leaders were experienced politicians who could command public support and manage governments. And while the Continental army had to be built from scratch and was never very large, it was fighting on its own territory with the assistance of thousands of militiamen. Even the substantial number of Loyalists and Indian allies—more than 55,000 Tories fought as regular soldiers or militiamen during the war, and thousands of native Americans served as auxiliary troops—could not offset these advantages.

The odds changed over time. Once the rebels had the military, diplomatic, and financial support of France, they could reasonably hope for victory. Britain now faced an expanding conflict, requiring more resources. A charismatic leader such as William Pitt or a great general might have rallied British political opinion to the cause, suppressed the American rebellion, and restored imperial authority. But ordinary politicians and mediocre generals were destined to fail.

Americans, by contrast, were extremely lucky to have George Washington as commander of the Continental army, for his leadership was inspired. The American general deferred to the civil authorities, winning respect—and political and financial support—from the Congress and the state governments alike. He exercised firm control over his subordinates yet supported their just complaints. Confident of his own abilities, he recruited outstanding men such as Baron von Steuben to instill discipline into the ranks of the fledgling Continental army and turn it into a respectable fighting force. Washington also came to understand that warfare in a lightly governed agricultural society required the deft use of rural militia units.

The Enigma of Benedict Arnold

Benedict Arnold was different: a military hero for both sides in the same war. He began his career as an American Patriot in May 1775, when he and Ethan Allen led the brigade that captured Fort Ticonderoga on Lake Champlain. Arnold's heroics continued in September, when he led an expedition of 1,150 riflemen against Quebec, the capital of British Canada. The American commander drove his men hard through the Maine wilderness, overcoming leaky boats, spoiled provisions, treacherous rivers, and near starvation to arrive at Quebec in November, his force reduced to 650 men. These losses did not deter Arnold. Joined by General Richard Montgomery, who had arrived with 300 troops after capturing Montreal, Arnold's forces attacked the strongly fortified city, only to have the assault end in disaster. A hundred Americans were killed, including

Montgomery; 400 were captured; and many were wounded, including Arnold, who fell as he stormed over a barricade, a ball through his leg.

Quebec was only the beginning. For the next five years Arnold served the Patriot side with distinction in one battle after another, including a dangerous assault against the center of the British line at Saratoga, where he was again wounded in the leg. No general was more imaginative than Arnold, no field officer more daring, no soldier more courageous.

Yet Arnold has gone down in history not as a hero but as a villain, a military traitor who, as commander of the American fort at West Point, New York, in 1780, schemed to hand it over to the British. Of his role in this conspiracy there is no doubt. His British contact, Major John André, was caught with incriminating documents in Arnold's handwriting, including routes of access to the fort. Arnold, fleeing down the Hudson River on a British ship, defended his treason in a letter to Washington, stating that "love to my country actuates my present conduct, however it may appear inconsistent to the world, who very seldom judge right of any man's actions."

But judge we must. Why did Arnold desert the cause for which he had fought so gallantly and twice been wounded? Was there any justification for his conduct?

When the fighting began at Lexington and Concord in April 1775, Arnold was thirty-four, an apothecary and minor merchant in New Haven, Connecticut—but also a militia captain and ardent Patriot. "Good God," he had exclaimed at the time of the Boston Massacre, "are the Americans all asleep and tamely giving up their Liberties?" Eager to support the rebellion, Arnold coerced the town's selectmen into supplying powder and ball to his men and promptly marched them to Boston, which was under siege by the New England militia. On the way Arnold thought up the attack on Fort Ticonderoga (realizing that the fort's cannon could be used to force the British out of Boston) and persuaded the Massachusetts Committee of Safety to approve his plan and make him a colonel. That done, he raced to New York to take command so that the glory would be his. The victory achieved, Arnold submitted an inflated

Benedict Arnold

Major John André Executed as a British Spy
Unable to catch the traitor Benedict Arnold, the American army executed his British accomplice, whose elegance, intelligence, and dignity won the hearts of his captors: "He died universally esteemed and universally regretted," noted Alexander Hamilton.

claim for expenses (£1,060 in Massachusetts currency, or about $60,000 today) and protested vehemently when legislators closely examined each item.

These events illuminated Arnold's great strengths and fatal flaws and were prophetic of his ultimate fate. He was bold and creative, a man who sized up a situation and acted quickly. He was ambitious and extravagant, an egocentric man who craved power and the financial rewards that came with it. He was intrepid and ruthless, willing to risk his life—and the lives of others—to get what he wanted.

Such men often are resented as much as they are admired, and so it was with Arnold. At Quebec some New England officers accused him of arrogance and tried to withdraw from his command, but Congress rewarded the intrepid colonel by making him a brigadier general. When Arnold again distinguished himself in battle in early 1777—having his horse shot out from under him—Congress promoted him to major general and gave him a new horse "as a token of their admiration of his gallant conduct." But then, in the middle of the struggle at Saratoga, General Horatio Gates, the American commander, relieved Arnold of his command, partly for insubordination and partly because Gates considered him a "pompous little fellow." Washington rewarded Arnold nonetheless, appointing him commandant at Philadelphia in July 1778, after the British evacuation of the city.

By then Arnold was an embittered man, disdainful of his fellow officers and resentful toward Congress for not promoting him more quickly and to even higher rank. A widower, he threw himself into the social life of the city, holding grand parties, courting and marrying Margaret Shippen—a talented young woman of good family, who, at nineteen, was half his age—and falling deeply into debt. Arnold's extravagance drew him into shady financial schemes and into disrepute with Congress, which investigated his accounts and recommended a court-martial. "Having . . . become a cripple in the service of my country, I little expected to meet [such] ungrateful returns," he complained to Washington.

Faced with financial ruin, uncertain of future promotion, and disgusted with congressional politics, Arnold made a fateful decision: he would seek fortune and fame in the service of Great Britain. With cool calculation, he initiated correspondence with Sir Henry Clinton, the British commander, promising to deliver West Point and its 3,000 defenders for £20,000 sterling (about $1 million today), a momentous act that he hoped would spark the collapse of the American cause. Persuading Washington to place the fort under his command, Arnold moved in September 1780 to execute his audacious plan, only to see it fail when André was captured. As André was executed as a spy, Arnold received £6,000 from the British government and appointment as a brigadier general.

Arnold served George III with the same skill and daring he had shown in the Patriot cause. In 1781 he led devastating strikes on Patriot supply depots: in Virginia he looted Richmond and destroyed munitions and grain intended for the American army opposing Lord Cornwallis; in Connecticut he burned ships, warehouses, and much of the town of New London, a major port for Patriot privateers.

In the end, Benedict Arnold's moral failure lay not in his disenchantment with the American cause—for many other officers returned to civilian life disgusted with the decline in republican virtue and angry over their failure to win a guaranteed pension from Congress. Nor did his infamy stem from his transfer of allegiance to the British side—for other Patriots chose to become Loyalists, sometimes out of principle but just as often for personal gain. Arnold's perfidy lay in the abuse of his position of authority and trust: he would betray West Point and its garrison—and if necessary the entire American war effort—to secure his own success. His treason was not that of a principled man but that of a selfish one, and he never lived that down. Hated in America as a consort of "Beelzebub . . . the Devil," Arnold was treated with coldness and even contempt in Britain. He died as he lived—a man without a country.

Finally, Washington had a greater margin for error than did the British generals who opposed him. He needed only to maintain an army in the field to keep the cause alive, given the fact that for every active Loyalist there were two Patriots and that the rebels usually controlled the local governments. Though they often wavered in their support, these ordinary citizens mobilized the economic resources required to fight a long war and came through at crucial moments in the military campaigns. Patriot partisans deprived the British troops of safe camps and local supplies. Thousands of militiamen besieged General Gage in Boston in 1775, surrounded Burgoyne at Saratoga in 1778, and forced Cornwallis to relinquish the Carolinas in 1781.

In the end, the allegiance of the American people decided the outcome of the conflict. Preferring Patriot rule, the majority of farmers and artisans refused to support Loyalist forces or accept imperial control in areas occupied by the British army. Consequently, though the British won many military victories, they achieved little, whereas their two major defeats—at Saratoga and Yorktown—proved catastrophic.

Diplomatic Triumph

After Yorktown it took the diplomats two years to conclude the war. Peace talks began in Paris in April 1782, but the French and Spanish stalled for time, hoping for a major naval victory or territorial conquest. Their delaying tactics infuriated the American diplomats—Benjamin Franklin, John Adams, and John Jay—who feared that drawn-out negotiations would tempt France to sacrifice American interests. Consequently, the Americans negotiated secretly with the British; if necessary, they

were prepared to cut their ties to France and sign a separate peace. The British ministry was also eager to obtain a quick settlement, because many members of Parliament no longer supported the war, and ministers feared the loss of a rich sugar island in the West Indies or the creation of a new French empire in North America.

Astutely exploiting the rivalry between Britain and France, Franklin and his colleagues won a major victory at the bargaining table. The Treaty of Paris, signed in the French capital on September 3, 1783, formally recognized the independence of the United States. Britain retained Canada, but only the part north and west of the Great Lakes. All the land between the Appalachian Mountains and the Mississippi River that Britain had wrested from France twenty years before was ceded to the new American republic. This was still the domain of undefeated native American peoples, but Britain made no attempt to secure the land rights of its Indian allies. Instead, it promised to withdraw its garrisons across the trans-Appalachian West "with all convenient speed," leaving native Americans to their fate. As an Indian of the Wea people complained, "In endeavouring to assist you it seems we have wrought our own ruin."

Other provisions granted Americans fishing rights off Newfoundland and Nova Scotia, forbade the British from "carrying away any negroes or other property of the American inhabitants," and guaranteed freedom of navigation on the Mississippi to British subjects and American citizens "forever." In its only concession, the American government promised "earnestly" to recommend to the state legislatures that they return Loyalist property seized in the war and treat Loyalists as free and equal citizens.

In the Treaty of Versailles, signed at the same time as the Treaty of Paris, Britain made peace with France

Making Peace
Benjamin West's uncompleted painting of 1783, *American Commission of the Preliminary Peace Negotiation with Great Britain* (detail), portrays the American negotiators, including Benjamin Franklin, John Jay, and John Adams. The Americans bargained hard with the British during the fall of 1782 and signed the preliminary treaty on November 30. A Patriot diplomatic triumph, the treaty acknowledged the independence of the United States and extended its boundaries to the Mississippi River.

and Spain. France had diminished the size and wealth of the British empire, but its only territorial gain was the Caribbean island of Tobago. More significant for the future, by joining the war of American independence France had quadrupled its national debt, and in six years cries for tax relief and for political liberty at home would spark the French Revolution. Spain failed in its main objective of retaking Gibraltar, but it did reacquire Florida from Britain. Americans welcomed this diplomatic outcome, for Spain was a far weaker power than Britain or France.

However, the two treaties were vague in defining the boundaries between the United States and its British and Spanish neighbors, so that territorial disputes would mar relations for another thirty years. But the peace settlement opened the interior of the continent to American expansion and made possible the development of a large and powerful nation.

Republicanism Defined and Challenged

From the moment of its creation, Americans began to define the character of their new republican society. In the Declaration of Independence Thomas Jefferson proclaimed that all individuals have the right to "life, liberty, and the pursuit of happiness." Jefferson drew his list from the writings of John Locke, but he substituted the word *happiness* for Locke's *property*. Jefferson's choice reflected the idealism of many Patriots and their commitment to *republican virtue*, an enlightened quest for the public interest. But it also suggested that many Americans considered the private ownership of property a prerequisite for happiness. The tension between self-interest and the public interest—between individual property rights and the welfare of the community—would shape the history of the new nation.

Republican Ideals and Wartime Pressures

The Republican Ideal. In the simplest terms, a republic is a state without a monarch. For many Americans, republicanism was much more—not simply a political system but a social philosophy. "The word *republic*," wrote Thomas Paine, "means the *public good*, or the good of the whole" (from the Latin *republica*: thing, *res*; of the people, *publica*). It followed that the members of a republic assumed important social responsibilities. "Every man in a republic is public property," asserted the Philadelphia Patriot Benjamin Rush (who eventually extended this notion to include women as well). "His time and talents—his youth—his manhood—his old age—nay more, life, all belong to his country."

Wartime fears allowed this collectivist vision to find ample expression, often at the cost of individual choice. When a local Patriot Committee of Safety suppressed a dissenting Loyalist or demanded that a merchant lower prices, its members saw themselves as acting in the public interest, according to the maxim of ancient Rome: "Take care that the commonwealth should receive no damage." Similarly, when General Howe occupied Philadelphia in 1777, the Pennsylvania legislature invoked republican principles to justify the extreme steps it took to safeguard the state. It required loyalty oaths of all citizens, expelled suspected Tories, and executed two Quakers on charges of treason. Ultimately the assembly, dominated by Scots-Irish Presbyterians, went further, invoking evangelical Protestant values in a controversial campaign to outlaw gambling, horse racing, theatrical shows, and all "evil practices which tend to debauch the minds and corrupt the morals of the subjects of the Commonwealth."

The Ideal Tested in the Military. Because republicanism lauded public virtue, the Continental Congress praised the self-sacrifice of the militiamen who fought and fell at Lexington and Concord, Saratoga, and Camden. In contrast, its members deprecated the Continental officer corps's demand for lifetime pensions as a "total loss of virtue," as Henry Laurens of South Carolina put it. Having been raised as gentlemen, officers were supposed to be the prime exemplars of the ideal of republican virtue—far from demanding recompense, they should give freely to the republic.

As the war continued, the zeal for self-sacrifice diminished. Continental troops stationed at Morristown, New Jersey, mutinied during the winters of 1779 and 1780, unable or unwilling to endure the harsh conditions. To restore authority, Washington ordered the execution of several leaders of the mutiny, and despite its precarious finances, Congress used monetary incentives—back pay and new clothing—to pacify the rest of the recruits. Unrest among higher-ranking military men lurked below the surface throughout the war, erupting finally at Newburgh, New York, in 1783, when Washington had to use his personal authority to thwart a potentially dangerous challenge to Congress's policies by a group of disgruntled officers.

Republican Virtue versus Self-Interest in the Marketplace. Civilians also found it difficult to sustain their virtue as economic hardship brought the war closer to home. The British naval blockade nearly eliminated the New England fishing industry along the Atlantic coast and cut off the supply of European manufactured goods to American consumers. Domestic trade and production declined as well. The British occupation of Boston, New York, and Philadelphia put thousands of people out of work. Unemployed shipwrights, dock laborers, masons, coopers, and bakers left the cities and drifted into the countryside; the population of New York City declined from 21,000 in 1774 to less than half that at the war's end. In the Chesapeake the British blockade deprived tobacco planters of markets in Europe, forcing them to turn to the cultivation of wheat, corn, and other foodstuffs. All across the land the pace of commercial activity slackened as farmers and artisans adapted to a war economy.

The scarcity of imported goods brought a sharp rise in prices and widespread appeals for government regulation. Consumers decried merchants and traders as "enemies, extortioners, and monopolizers." In 1777 a convention of New England states restricted increases in the price of domestic commodities and imported goods to 75 percent above their prewar level; to enforce this directive, the Massachusetts legislature passed an "Act to prevent Monopoly and Oppression." Many farmers and artisans refused to sell goods at the established prices. Some wanted to pass along their own rising costs, but others were determined to profit from wartime shortages. In the end consumers had to pay the market price, a government official admitted, "or submit to starving."

Personal distress prompted many Americans to re-examine the meaning of republican virtue. Philadelphia, where severe food shortages and soaring prices followed the British withdrawal in 1778, saw the most spirited debate. In May 1779 a crowd of artisans and laborers, having caught a merchant illegally exporting flour, called a town meeting and created a Committee on Prices that set wholesale and retail rates for thirty-two commodities. The artisan-led committee justified these restraints by invoking the traditional concept of the "just price," reflecting their fear of exploitation by well-to-do merchants and calculating storekeepers.

Led by the influential Patriot financier Robert Morris, Philadelphia merchants argued against price controls and articulated a "classical liberal" ideology of free trade and enlightened self-interest. They pointed out that regulation would only cause farmers to store their crops, whereas allowing prices to rise would bring goods to market and relieve scarcity. Morris's arguments found favor among farmers, who wanted to sell their goods at the highest prices, and members of the Continental Congress, including Benjamin Franklin, who condemned price controls as "contrary to the nature of commerce."

But most Philadelphians were skeptical. At a town meeting in August 1779, 2,115 voters endorsed government regulation of the market and only 281 opposed it. Most craft workers and laborers wanted fair trade (rather than free trade) and supported republican community controls—at least in *principle*. In practice, many artisan-republicans—shoemakers, tanners, and bakers—found that they could not support their families on

fixed prices and so refused to abide by them. In civilian life as in the military, self-interest tended to triumph over republican virtue.

Women and Household Production. Faced with a shortage of goods and with constantly rising prices, government officials found it nearly impossible to purchase supplies for the troops. They met this challenge by requisitioning goods directly from the people. For example, in 1776 Connecticut officials called on the citizens of Hartford to provide 1,000 coats and 1,600 shirts and assessed smaller towns on a proportionate basis. In 1777 officials again pressed the citizenry to provide shirts, stockings, and shoes for the men from their communities serving in the Continental army. Soldiers added their own pleas to these exhortations. During the Battle of Long Island, for example, Captain

War Mobilization
A few American women actually fought in the war (see American Lives, Chapter 9) and many thousands more traveled with the Continental army, providing the troops with food and support. This 1779 woodcut (which accompanied a poem by Molly Guttridge, a "Daughter of Liberty") symbolizes the contributions of the Patriot women of war-torn Marblehead, Massachusetts. (Collection of The New-York Historical Society)

Edward Rogers lost "all the shirts except the one on my back," he wrote to his wife. "The making of cloath . . . must go on. . . . I must have shirts and stockings & a jacket sent me as soon as possible & a blankit."

Patriot women seized this opportunity to contribute to the war effort, increasing their production of homespun cloth. One Massachusetts town claimed an annual output of 30,000 yards of cloth, while women in Elizabeth, New Jersey, promised "upwards of 100,000 yards of linnen and woolen cloth."

With their husbands and sons away, many women assumed the burden of farm production. Some went into the fields themselves, plowing or cutting and loading grain. Others supervised hired laborers or slaves, acquiring a taste for decision making in the process. "We have sow'd our oats as you desired," Sarah Cobb Paine wrote to her absent husband; "had I been master I should have planted it to Corn." Taught from childhood to act selflessly—to value the welfare of their fathers, brothers, and husbands above their own—most Patriot women did not experience the conflict between republican virtue and self-interest that plagued men. The production of cloth, meat, and grain boosted their self-esteem as contributors to the war effort and prompted some women to claim greater rights in the new republican society; and it began the process of increasing productivity within farm households that pushed forward the American transition to a capitalist economy (see Chapters 7 and 9).

Fiscal Crisis. Nearly all Americans—women as well as men—found that they could maintain their standard of living only by carefully calculating every economic transaction. The cost of the war was the main culprit, since it was paid for primarily by printing money, which steadily depreciated in value. By 1778 so much currency had been printed that it took $7 in Continental bills to buy goods worth $1 in gold or silver. And things only got worse, with the ratio increasing to 42 to 1 in 1779 and 100 to 1 in 1780. When the rate of exchange between Continental currency and specie reached 146 to 1 in 1781, not even the most virtuous Patriots would accept paper money.

Congress tried to halt the spiraling inflation by redeeming its currency and removing it from circulation. In 1780 it asked the states to assess taxes that could be paid in Continental currency at the rate of 40 paper dollars for every silver dollar owed by a taxpayer. This initiative resulted in the redemption of $120 million in Continental bills and yielded a substantial profit to astute speculators, who had seen a future value in the currency. They had bought Continental bills from thousands of ordinary citizens at rates of 80, 100, or 120 to 1, and they now used those bills to pay their taxes, receiving credits worth double or triple their investment. At the end of the war speculators still held $71 million in Continental notes; they hoped that the currency eventually would be redeemed at its face value, giving them an even greater profit.

In this financial game there were more losers than winners. The big losers were farmers and artisans who had received Continental bills for supplies and soldiers who had taken them as military pay. As soon as they received the currency, it lost purchasing power, literally depreciating in their pockets. Individually these losses were small, amounting to a tiny "tax" every time an ordinary citizen received a paper dollar, kept it for a week, and then spent it. But collectively these "currency taxes" paid the huge cost of the war. It was these personal sacrifices, willing or not, made by hundreds of thousands of American citizens that financed the struggle for independence.

The experience was a sobering one. "Private Interest seemed to predominate over the public weal," a leading Patriot complained as the war came to an end, and "avaricious and ambitious men" seemed to be everywhere. Was this the society for which Americans had fought and died? "Let us have patience," Benjamin Rush replied to such questions. He admitted that self-interest might be in the ascendancy, but he had faith that "our republican forms of government will in time beget republican opinions and manners. All will end well." Events would not completely bear this out, but for Rush and many other Patriots, public virtue remained the preeminent principle of the new American republics.

The Loyalist Exodus

As the war turned in favor of the Patriots, Loyalists faced disaster. Fearing for their lives, more than 100,000 Tories emigrated to Canada, the West Indies, or Britain. This exodus disrupted the established social order, for some of the Loyalists were wealthy and politically powerful merchants, lawyers, and landowners. Some of those who migrated to Canada—where they became known as the United Empire Loyalists—assumed the leadership of the English-speaking colonies of Nova Scotia, New Brunswick, and Ontario.

The land, buildings, and goods left behind by the Loyalists raised the touchy issue of the sanctity of property rights. Some Patriots wanted to confiscate the property of "traitors," and the passions of war lent urgency to their arguments. Initially, the government of North Carolina rented out Loyalists' estates, but when the British army invaded the South, the Patriot-dominated assembly confiscated the estates outright. Officials in New York also seized Loyalists' lands and goods, claiming the "sovereignty of the people of this state in respect to all property."

Many public officials opposed the seizure of Loyalist property as contrary to Patriot principles. Following the classical liberal thought of John Locke as well as the dictates of common law, the Massachusetts Constitution of 1780 declared that every citizen should be protected "in the enjoyment of his life, liberty, and property, according to the standing laws," and state officials extended these rights to Loyalists. Most Tory property in Massachusetts was handled by the court system under the Act to Provide for the Payment of Debts. The courts mandated the seizure of land and goods needed to reimburse creditors, but the remaining property reverted to the agents of departed Loyalists.

Thus, there was no government-led social revolution. Respect for property rights and the states' need to raise revenue meant that most states seized only a limited amount of property—that owned by notorious Loyalists—and they generally sold it to the highest bidder, which usually meant a wealthy Patriot rather than a poor yeoman or foot soldier. For example, Georgia seized 128,000 acres of land from 166 Tories but sold it to only 188 Patriots. In a few cases the sale of Loyalist property produced a more democratic result. In North Carolina about half the new owners of Loyalist lands were small-scale farmers. And on the former Philipsburg manor in New York, Patriot tenants successfully converted their leases into fee-simple ownership. But unlike France after 1789 or Russia after 1917, the revolutionary upheaval did not drastically alter the structure of rural society.

Social turmoil was greater in the cities as upwardly mobile Patriot merchants replaced Tories at the top of the economic ladder. In Massachusetts, the Lowell, Higginson, Jackson, and Cabot families moved their trading enterprises to Boston to fill the vacuum created by the departure of the Hutchinsons and Apthorps and their friends. Small-scale traders in Philadelphia and its environs stepped into the vacancies created by the collapse of Anglican and Quaker mercantile firms during the war. In the countinghouses as on the battlefield, Patriots emerged triumphant. The War of Independence drove out thousands of Loyalist merchants and shopkeepers, replacing a tradition-oriented economic elite—one that invested primarily in foreign trade and urban real estate—with a group of entrepreneurial-minded republican merchants.

The Problem of Slavery

The American Revolution generated intense debate over the institution of slavery, in part because of the active role played by African-Americans on both sides of the struggle. Thousands of slaves in the South sought freedom by taking refuge behind British lines. Two neighbors of Richard Henry Lee, the Virginia Patriot, lost "every slave they had in the world" during the war.

Fifty-three blacks, including eight mothers and their children, fled from another Virginia plantation, subsequently winning their freedom by working or fighting for the king. When the British army evacuated Charleston, more than 6,000 former slaves went with the troops; another 4,000 left Savannah with the British. Hundreds of black Loyalists settled permanently in Canada, but over 1,000 others, poorly treated and settled on inferior land in Nova Scotia, sought a better life in the abolitionist settlement in Sierra Leone in West Africa.

Just as many African-Americans served the Patriot cause. Free blacks from New England enrolled in Patriot units such as the First Rhode Island Company and the Massachusetts "Bucks." In Maryland, Patriots recruited a large number of slaves for military duty and later freed them in return for their service, a policy that was rejected by other southern states. In those states many slaves struck informal bargains with their Patriot masters, trading loyalty in wartime for a promise of liberty. The Virginia assembly passed an act allowing *manumission* (literally, "letting go from the hand") in 1782, and planters freed 10,000 slaves within a decade.

These events revealed a contradiction in the Patriots' republican ideology. "How is it that we hear the loudest *yelps* for liberty among the drivers of Negroes?" the British author Samuel Johnson chided, and some white Patriots took his point to heart. "I wish most sincerely there was not a Slave in the province," Abigail Adams wrote to her husband, John, as Massachusetts went to war. "It always appeared a most iniquitous Scheme to me—to fight ourselves for what we are daily robbing and plundering from those who have as good a right to freedom as we have."

Gradual Emancipation in the North. This intense questioning of slavery was fairly new. In the prerevolutionary world inequality of condition and status was accepted as the norm for all people, part of God's design for the world. Racial slavery was only the most extreme form of natural inequality. Significantly, it was the Quakers, whose belief in religious equality had made them sharp critics of many inequities in social life, who took the lead in condemning slavery. Beginning in the 1750s, the evangelist John Woolman and a few other Quakers had urged their coreligionists to free their slaves. The outbreak of the war led many North Carolina Quakers to "clear their hands" of the institution by manumitting their slaves. Other rapidly growing pietistic groups, notably the Methodists and the Baptists, advocated emancipation and admitted both enslaved and free blacks into their congregations. In 1784 a conference of Virginia Methodists declared that slavery was "contrary to the Golden Law of God on which hang all the Law and Prophets."

Enlightenment principles of knowledge also played a role in the debate over slavery. John Locke had argued that ideas were not innate but stemmed from impressions and experience. Accordingly, Enlightenment thinkers pointed out that the oppressive conditions of slavery accounted for the debased situation of Africans in the Western Hemisphere; the slaves were not an inherently inferior people. "A state of slavery has a mighty tendency to shrink and contract the minds of men," an American observer noted. Anthony Benezet, a Quaker philanthropist who funded a school for blacks in Philadelphia, contradicted popular belief by declaring that African-Americans were "as capable of improvement as White People."

These religious and secular arguments placed slavery on the defensive, especially in the North, where there were relatively few African-Americans. By 1784, Massachusetts had abolished slavery outright and three other states—Pennsylvania, Connecticut, and Rhode Island—had provided for its gradual end. Within another two decades every state north of Delaware endorsed gradual emancipation, which meant that liberty came slowly to northern blacks. For example, the New York Emancipation Edict of 1799 granted freedom only to the *children* of slaves, and only when they reached the age of twenty-five. As late as 1810, 30,000 slaves in the northern states—nearly a fourth of their African-American populations—still served masters.

Emancipation came slowly for several reasons. Many whites feared that black freedom would mean competition for jobs and housing and, even more threatening, a melding of the races. Consequently, in 1786 Massachusetts reenacted a colonial-era law that prohibited whites from marrying blacks, Indians, or mulattoes. Moreover, state lawmakers wanted to protect property rights, and gradual emancipation was a means of providing compensation to slaveowners in the form of a few more years of enforced African-American labor. Even in the North the whites' right to property had priority over the blacks' right to liberty.

Emancipation in the Chesapeake Region. The tension between the republican values of liberty and property was greatest in the South. Slaves made up 30 to 60 percent of the population and represented a huge financial investment. Most political leaders were slaveholders, and they used state power to preserve slavery. In 1776 the North Carolina legislature condemned Quaker manumissions as "highly criminal and reprehensible" and passed a number of laws ordering the enslavement of freed blacks or their expulsion from the state (see American Voices, page 192). Yet many Chesapeake slaveholders, moved by religious principles or oversupplied with workers on their declining tobacco plantations, allowed blacks to buy their freedom through paid work as artisans or laborers. By 1810 manumission and self-purchase had raised the number of freed blacks in Maryland to about a third of the African-American population. In Delaware freed blacks outnumbered slaves three to one.

But these forces were not strong enough to overthrow slavery in the Chesapeake. Most whites did not want a society filled with freed blacks. The Virginia legislature discussed emancipation but in 1792 imposed financial conditions that made it more difficult for whites to free their slaves. Following the lead of Thomas Jefferson, who owned more than a hundred slaves, many Chesapeake planters argued that slavery was a "necessary evil" required to maintain white supremacy and their luxurious life-styles.

And so, within a decade after the end of the Revolution, the tide had turned against emancipation in the Chesapeake. (It was never seriously considered by the expansionist-minded, rice-planting gentry of South Carolina and Georgia.) Its fate was sealed in 1800 when Virginia authorities discovered and prevented a slave uprising planned by Gabriel Prosser and then hanged him and about thirty of his followers. "Liberty and equality have brought the evil upon us," a letter to the *Virginia Herald* proclaimed in the aftermath of the abortive rebellion, for such doctrines are "dangerous and extremely wicked in this country, where every white man is a master, and every black man is a slave." Throughout the South, most whites reaffirmed their commitment to slavery and white property rights, whatever the cost to republican principles.

Symbols of Slavery—and Freedom
The scar on the forehead of this black woman, widely known as "Mumbet," underlined the cruelty of slavery. Winning emancipation through a legal suit, she chose a name befitting her new status: Elizabeth Freeman.

African-American Freemen from North Carolina Petition Congress

To safeguard the institution of slavery, the North Carolina legislature enacted a law in 1788 that allowed whites to reenslave African-Americans who had been manumitted by their owners. To escape this fate, these former slaves fled the state, and in 1797 they petitioned the national legislature to protect their rights as free citizens. At the insistence of southern representatives, Congress refused to accept their petition.

That, being of African descent, late inhabitants and natives of North Carolina, to you only, under God, can we apply with any hope of effect, for redress of our grievances, having been compelled to leave the State wherein we had a right of residence, as freemen liberated under the hand and seal of humane and conscientious masters, the validity of which act of justice in restoring us to our native right of freedom, was confirmed by judgment of the Superior Court of North Carolina, wherein it was brought to trial; yet, not long after this decision, a law of that State was enacted, under which men of cruel disposition, and void of just principle, received countenance and authority in violently seizing, imprisoning, and selling into slavery, such as had been so emancipated.

I, Jacob Nicholson, also of North Carolina, being set free by my master, Joseph Nicholson, but continuing to live with him till, being pursued day and night, I was obliged to leave my abode, sleep in the woods, and stacks in the fields, &c., to escape the hands of violent men who, induced by the profit afforded them by law, followed this course as a business; at length, by night, I made my escape, leaving a mother, one child, and two brothers, to see whom I dare not return.

I, Job Albert, manumitted by Benjamin Albertson, who was my careful guardian to protect me from being afterwards taken and sold, providing me with a house to accommodate me and my wife, who was liberated by William Robertson; but we were night and day hunted by men armed with guns, swords, and pistols, accompanied with mastiff dogs; . . . I was discovered and seized by Alexander Stafford, William Stafford, and Thomas Creesy, who were armed with guns and clubs. After binding me with my hands behind me, and a rope round my arms and body, they took me about four miles to Hartford prison, where I lay four weeks, suffering much for want of provision; from thence, with the assistance of a fellow-prisoner, (a white man,) I made my escape, and for three dollars was

conveyed, with my wife, by a humane person, in a covered wagon by night, to Virginia, where, in the neighborhood of Portsmouth, I continued unmolested about four years, being chiefly engaged in sawing boards and planting.

I, Thomas Pritchet, was set free by my master Thomas Pritchet, who furnished me with land to raise provisions for my use, where I built myself a house, cleared a sufficient spot of woodland to produce ten bushels of corn; the second year about fifteen, and the third, had as much planted as I suppose would have produced thirty bushels; this I was obliged to leave about one month before it was fit for gathering, being threatened by Holland Lockwood, who married my said master's widow, that if I would not come and serve him, he would apprehend me, and send me to the West Indies.

We beseech your impartial attention to our hard condition, . . . both for our relief as a people, and towards the removal of obstructions to public order and well-being. . . .

JACOB NICHOLSON,
JOB ALBERT, his mark,
THOMAS PRITCHET, his mark.

Source: Annals of Congress, Fourth Congress, Second Session (Washington, D.C., 1855), 2015–2017.

A Republican Religious Order

Before 1776 only the Quaker- and Baptist-controlled colonies of Pennsylvania and Rhode Island had repudiated the idea of an established church and celebrated religious liberty of conscience. Political revolution, however, had broadened the appeal of these libertarian principles, forcing Patriot lawmakers to devise new and distinct relationships between churches and state governments.

Separation of Church and State. The most dramatic change in the religious situation came in Virginia, where the Church of England was the established church. To preserve their legally privileged position, most Anglicans quickly renounced allegiance to the king, the head of the Church of England, and reorganized themselves as the Protestant Episcopal Church of America. Moreover, the Anglican gentry stopped harassing New Light Presbyterians and Baptists in order to win their support for the military effort. Finally, leading Virginia Patriots who embraced the Enlightenment questioned the wisdom of an established church. In 1776 James Madison and George Mason persuaded the Virginia convention to issue a Declaration of Rights that guaranteed the "free exercise of religion" to all Christians. Later that year the Virginia legislature passed an act exempting dissenters from paying taxes to support the Anglican Church.

The debate over state support for religion continued after the war. In general, Baptists in all the states opposed the use of taxes to support religion. Their political influence in Virginia prompted lawmakers to reject a bill supported by George Washington and Patrick Henry that would have imposed a general assessment tax to provide funds for all Christian churches. Instead, in 1786 the Virginia legislature enacted Thomas Jefferson's Bill for Establishing Religious Freedom, which made all churches equal before the law and granted direct financial support to none. A similar result obtained in New York and New Jersey, where the sheer number of churches—Episcopalian, Presbyterian, Dutch Reformed, Lutheran, and Quaker, among others—prevented legislative agreement on an established church or compulsory religious taxes.

Yet many Americans still clung to traditional European principles, arguing that a firm union of church and state promoted morality and respect for authority. "Pure religion and civil liberty are inseparable companions," a group of North Carolinians advised their minister. "It is your particular duty to enlighten mankind with the unerring principles of truth and justice, the main props of all civil government."

Thus the separation of church and state came slowly, especially in New England, where Congregationalist ministers had strongly supported the independence movement and would use their prestige to maintain a legally established church until the 1830s. Now, however, New England Congregationalists no longer attempted to suppress Baptist and Methodist churches and allowed them to use religious taxes to support their own ministers. After the Revolution, the primacy of a single established church was no longer the norm.

Freedom of Conscience. Nonetheless, the extent of religious freedom remained the subject of debate. In Virginia, Jefferson's Bill for Establishing Religious Freedom endorsed the principle of liberty of conscience and outlawed religious requirements for political and civil posts. Many states, however, continued to offer tax exemptions on church property, enforce religious criteria for voting and officeholding, and penalize individuals who questioned the doctrines of Protestant Christianity. For example, the North Carolina constitution of 1776 disqualified from public office any citizen "who shall deny the being of God, or the Truth of the Protestant Religion, or the Divine Authority of the Old or New Testament." New Hampshire had a similar provision in its constitution until 1868.

Such restrictive doctrines commanded widespread support both among the public at large and in courts of law. In one celebrated case Chancellor James Kent of the New York Supreme Court flouted the principle of religious liberty by upholding the conviction of Timothy Ruggles for blasphemy (publicly and disrespectfully shouting the name of Christ). Kent overruled Ruggles's contention that the charge infringed his liberty of conscience under the New York constitution of 1777, which guaranteed "the free, equal and undisturbed enjoyment of religious opinion." Kent declared that "the people of this State profess the general doctrines of Christianity," and for Ruggles to slander Christ was "to strike at the root of moral obligation and weaken the security of social ties." For Kent, religion underpinned the authority of the republic and had a higher priority than the individual's right of free speech.

Americans who were influenced by Enlightenment values condemned interference in matters of conscience whether by courts or by churches. Thomas Paine attacked religious institutions as "no other than human inventions set up to terrify and enslave mankind, and monopolize power and profit." Rationalist thinkers extended republican principles to religion, arguing that God had given human beings the power of reason so that they could determine moral truths for themselves. Ethan Allen of Vermont, whose Green Mountain Boys had captured Fort Ticonderoga in 1775, wrote a widely circulated pamphlet called *Reason: The Only Oracle of Man* (1784).

Allen was a deist, as were many of the leading American Patriots, such as Thomas Jefferson and Benjamin Franklin. They thought God had created the world the way a watchmaker builds a clock; once set in motion, it ran according to its own laws. "God Almighty is himself a Mechanic," proclaimed Thomas Cooper, president of the College of South Carolina. Philip Freneau, an ardent Patriot poet and deist, wrote that in "Nature" one could

> *see, with most exact design,*
> *The world revolve, the planets shine.*
> *The nicest order, all things meet,*
> *A structure in itself complete.*

To protect society from what they called "ecclesiastical tyranny," most deists demanded complete freedom of expression.

Many evangelical-minded American Protestants also favored freedom of conscience, but their goal was to protect themselves and their churches from state control. Isaac Backus warned New England Baptists not to incorporate their churches or accept tax funds under the general assessment laws of Massachusetts. Instead, Backus favored voluntary church support. In Connecticut a devout Congregationalist layman approved of voluntarism because it undermined the clerical hierarchy and thus furthered "the spirit of toleration" and "the principles of republicanism." In the aftermath of the Revolution, for a variety of causes, American Protestant Christianity became increasingly republican in structure and spirit.

Summary

Beginning in April 1775, civil war disrupted the British empire. Small-scale battles between Loyalist and Patriot militias brought more bloodshed and made compromise difficult, as did George III's determination to crush the rebellion. Thomas Paine's *Common Sense* attacked the monarchical system and persuaded many Americans to support republicanism and independence, which was declared by the Continental Congress on July 4, 1776.

British troops under General Howe defeated Washington's Continental army in a series of battles during 1776, but Patriot triumphs at Trenton and Princeton revived American morale. Howe captured Philadelphia, the Patriots' capital, in the summer of 1777, but because of poor British planning, the rebels won a major victory at Saratoga in October. The Patriots nearly lost their main army to cold and hunger at Valley Forge during the winter of 1777–1778. Simultaneously, a severe inflation caused by the excessive distribution of paper money by the Continental Congress and the states undermined Patriot morale and nearly destroyed public support for the new republican governments.

The tide turned in February 1778, when an alliance with France aided the Patriot cause financially, militarily, and diplomatically. Congress rejected British overtures for a negotiated settlement, and Lord North embarked on a southern military strategy. British troops won major victories in Georgia and the Carolinas during 1779 and 1780, but Patriot troops and guerrillas finally forced General Cornwallis into Virginia, where he suffered a major defeat at Yorktown in October 1781, the last great battle of the war. The Treaty of Paris in 1783 acknowledged the independence of the United States and defined its western boundary at the Mississippi River, opening the trans-Appalachian West to white settlement.

During the war idealistic Americans attempted to define the social and economic values of republicanism as pursuit of the common good and stressed the citizen's responsibility to the community. Some Americans embraced a Lockean liberal outlook that celebrated the pursuit of individual achievement and self-interest. Moreover, most Americans suffered financially during the war because of inflation—a hidden tax that paid for the Patriots' military effort—making it necessary for many soldiers and civilians to give the highest priority to the economic security of their families. Even so, independence and republicanism initiated significant changes in American society and public values, bringing about the immediate departure of thousands of Loyalists, the gradual abolition of slavery in the North, and a growing commitment to freedom of religious worship and separation of church and state.

TIMELINE

1775	Second Continental Congress Battle of Bunker Hill Olive Branch petition Lord Dunmore's proclamation to slaves American invasion of Canada British Prohibitory Act
1776	Patriots skirmish with Loyalists in South Thomas Paine's *Common Sense* Declaration of Independence (July 4) Howe defeats Washington in New York Virginia Declaration of Rights American victories at Trenton (December 26) and Princeton (January 3, 1777)
1777	Patriot women assist war economy Howe occupies Philadelphia Horatio Gates defeats Burgoyne at Saratoga Continental army suffers at Valley Forge Patriot paper currency creates inflation
1778	Franco-American alliance (February 6) Lord North seeks negotiated settlement Congress grants officers half-pay pension British begin "southern" strategy by capturing Savannah
1779	Confrontation in Philadelphia over price regulation Seizure and sale of Loyalist property begins
1780	General Clinton captures Charleston French army lands in Rhode Island Patriots prevail at King's Mountain Greene's forces harass Cornwallis's army Continental currency continues to depreciate
1780s	Debate over religious establishment: general assessment laws and freedom of conscience
1781	Cornwallis invades Virginia; surrenders at Yorktown Large-scale Loyalist emigration to Canada and Britain Partial redemption of Continental currency Escaped slaves depart with British
1782	Slave manumission act in Virginia (reversed in 1792)
1783	American officers at Newburgh, New York, plot against Congress Treaty of Paris (September 3)
1784	Ethan Allen publishes *Reason: The Only Oracle of Man*
1786	Virginia Bill for Establishing Religious Freedom
1799	New York enacts Gradual Emancipation Act
1800	Gabriel Prosser's rebellion in Virginia

BIBLIOGRAPHY

Gordon Wood, *The Radicalism of the American Revolution* (1992), offers a fine overview of the Revolutionary Era; for a contrasting interpretation, see the essays in Alfred F. Young, ed., *Beyond the American Revolution: Explorations in the History of American Radicalism* (1993).

Toward Independence

Jerrilyn Green Marston, *King and Congress: The Transfer of Political Legitimacy, 1774–1776* (1987), and Jack N. Rakove, *The Beginnings of National Politics: An Interpretative History of the Continental Congress* (1979), discuss the movement toward independence. See also Eric Foner, *Tom Paine and Revolutionary America* (1976), and Garry Wills, *Inventing America: Jefferson's Declaration of Independence* (1978). On Loyalism, read William N. Nelson, *The American Tory* (1961), and Robert M. Calhoon et al., *The Loyalist Perception* (1989).

The Perils of War and Finance

The military history of the war is covered in James L. Stokesbury, *A Short History of the American Revolution* (1991), and Piers Mackesy, *The War for America, 1775–1783* (1964). Don Higginbotham, *George Washington and the American Military Tradition* (1985), and Ronald Hoffman and Peter Albert, eds., *Arms and Independence: The Military Character of the American Revolution* (1984), offer a more analytic perspective. The war in the North can be followed in Ira D. Gruber, *The Howe Brothers and the American Revolution* (1972), and Richard J. Hargrove, Jr., *General John Burgoyne* (1983).

Studies of the soldiers who fought the war include Rodney Attwood, *The Hessians* (1980); Sylvia R. Frey, *The British Soldier in America* (1981); Robert K. Wright, Jr., *The Continental Army* (1983); and John C. Dann, ed., *The Revolution Remembered: Eyewitness Accounts of the War for Independence* (1980). For the importance of the military bureaucracy, see R. Arthur Bowler, *Logistics and the Failure of the British Army in America, 1775–1783* (1975), and E. Wayne Carp, *To Starve the Army at Pleasure: Continental Army Administration and American Political Culture, 1775–1783* (1984).

Local studies include Jean Butenhoff Lee, *The Price of Nationhood: The American Revolution in Charles County* (1994); Robert A. Gross, *The Minutemen and Their World* (1976); Richard Buel, Jr., *Dear Liberty: Connecticut's Mobilization for the Revolutionary War* (1980); and Donald Wallace White, *A Village at War: Chatham, New Jersey, and the American Revolution* (1979).

African-American participation in the war is discussed by Gary A. Puckrein, *The Black Regiment in the American Revolution* (1978), and Sidney Kaplan, *The Black Presence in the Era of the American Revolution* (rev. ed., 1989). The native American response is described in Barbara Graymont, *The Iroquois in the American Revolution* (1972); Isabel T. Kelsey, *Joseph Brant, 1743–1807* (1984); and James H. O'Donnell III, *Southern Indians in the American Revolution* (1973).

Two classic discussions of the fiscal problems created by the war are E. James Ferguson, *The Power of the Purse: A History of American Public Finance: 1776–1790* (1961), and Clarence L. Ver Steeg, *Robert Morris, Revolutionary Financier* (1954). A more recent study is William G. Anderson, *The Price of Liberty: The Public Debt of the American Revolution* (1983).

The Path to Victory

Bradford Perkins, *The Creation of a Republican Empire, 1776–1865* (1993), and Jonathan R. Dull, *A Diplomatic History of the American Revolution* (1985), provide good overviews of this topic. More specialized studies include James H. Hutson, *John Adams and the Diplomacy of the American Revolution* (1980); Richard B. Morris, *The Peacemakers: The Great Powers and American Independence* (1965); and Ronald Hoffman and Peter Albert, eds., *Peace and the Peacemakers: The Treaty of 1783* (1986).

For the southern campaign, consult W. Robert Higgins, ed., *The Revolutionary War in the South* (1979); Ronald Hoffman, Thad W. Tate, and Peter J. Albert, eds., *An Uncivil War: The Southern Backcountry during the American Revolution* (1985); and Jeffrey J. Crow and Larry E. Tise, eds., *The Southern Experience in the American Revolution* (1978). Studies of military action include Hugh F. Rankin, *Francis Marion: The Swamp Fox* (1973), and John S. Pancake, *The Destructive War, 1780–1782* (1985).

Republicanism Defined and Challenged

Milton M. Klein et al., *The Republican Synthesis Revisited* (1992), is a good historiographical introduction. Charles Royster, *A Revolutionary People at War: The Continental Army and American Character, 1775–1783* (1979), explores the fate of republican ideals. On women's lives during the war, see Ronald Hoffman and Peter J. Albert, eds., *Women in the Age of the American Revolution* (1989); Mary Beth Norton, *Liberty's Daughters: The Revolutionary Experience of American Women, 1750–1800* (1980); Lynn Withey, *Dearest Friend: A Life of Abigail Adams* (1980); and Joy Day Buel and Richard Buel, Jr., *The Way of Duty: A Woman and Her Family in Revolutionary America* (1984).

On the black experience, consult Sylvia R. Frey, *Water from the Rock: Black Resistance in a Revolutionary Age* (1991); Ira Berlin and Ronald Hoffman, eds., *Slavery and Freedom in the Age of the American Revolution* (1983); Gary B. Nash, *Forging Freedom: The Formation of Philadelphia's Black Community, 1720–1840* (1988); and David Brion Davis, *The Problem of Slavery in the Age of Revolution, 1770–1823* (1975). See also James W. St. G. Walker, *The Black Loyalists: The Search for a Promised Land in Nova Scotia and Sierra Leone, 1783–1870* (1976), and Shane White, *Somewhat More Independent: The End of Slavery in New York City, 1770-1810* (1991).

On changes in American religion, see Ronald Hoffman and Peter J. Albert, eds., *Religion in a Revolutionary Age* (1994); Rhys Isaac, *The Transformation of Virginia, 1740–1790* (1982); Fred Hood, *Reformed America 1783–1837* (1980); and Nathan O. Hatch, *The Democratization of American Christianity* (1989). The spiritual roots of a new secular religion are traced by Catharine Albanese, *Sons of the Fathers: The Civil Religion of the American Revolution* (1976), and Ruth Bloch, *Visionary Republic: Millennial Themes in American Thought* (1985).

The American Star

The portraits of kings and queens had traditionally served as icons or symbols of their monarchical nations. This idealized portrait of Washington by Frederick Kemmelmeyer celebrates his prowess and seeks a symbolic way of depicting a republic.

The New Political Order

1776–1800

★ ★ ★

Many wars for national independence end in political chaos or military rule, but the United States escaped those unhappy fates. The departure of the Loyalists, who would have formed a reactionary monarchist opposition, eliminated a potential political threat to the new republic. The attitude of General Washington, who firmly supported civilian rule and refused to consider becoming king, lessened the danger of a military coup d'état. Authority remained firmly in the hands of the leaders of the Patriot resistance movement, who wished to establish governments based on popular sovereignty and republican principles.

Beginning in 1776, state officials undertook the daunting task of devising new constitutions acceptable to the people. The Continental Congress also sought a constitutional mandate for its rule to enable it to address the vexing issues of war finance, inflation, the disposition of western lands, and social unrest—all of which were made more difficult by a postwar economic recession. These problems prompted a movement for a stronger national government, which found expression in the Philadelphia constitution of 1787. A controversial document, the new constitution was hotly debated and was ratified only by narrow majorities in key states.

Political life remained conflict-ridden during the 1790s. Alexander Hamilton's system of public finance and the ideological passions of the French Revolution divided Americans into warring camps and led to the rise of organized political parties. Before the election of President Thomas Jefferson ended the political crisis of the 1790s, the national government had curtailed the rights of citizens and had almost gone to war with France.

Despite these conflicts—and in part *because* of them—the period between 1776 and 1800 was the most creative era in American political and constitutional development. It was one of the most successful periods as well. Everywhere people with democratic views saw the United States as the exemplar of political liberty, and, as Tom Paine had put it, "the last best hope of mankind."

Creating New Institutions, 1776–1787

The Revolution of 1776 was both a struggle for home rule (independence) and, in the words of the historian Carl Becker, a conflict over "who should rule at home." The first conflict ended with a military victory over Britain. The second, a struggle over the character of state constitutions and governments, was less easily resolved and involved both a debate over centuries-old issues of political theory and practical politics. Who would control the new republican institutions, the traditional elites or ordinary citizens?

The State Constitutions: How Much Democracy?

Patriot leaders acted swiftly and decisively to establish the legitimacy of their rule. On May 10, 1776, Congress urged Patriots to suppress royal authority and establish institutions based on popular rule. Most states readily complied. By the end of 1776, Virginia, Maryland, North Carolina, New Jersey, Delaware, and Pennsylvania had written new constitutions; Connecticut and Rhode Island had transformed their colonial charters, which provided for extensive self-government, into republican charters by deleting all references to the king.

The Dilemma of Popular Sovereignty. The Declaration of Independence stated the principle of popular sovereignty—governments derive "their just powers from the consent of the governed"—but left unclear exactly what that meant in practice. In 1776 the Virginia constitutional convention adopted a comprehensive "declaration of rights" as the "foundation of government," and the Delaware constitution of that year linked popular sovereignty with political power: "the Right of the People to participate in the Legislature, is the Foundation of Liberty and of all free government."

But which people? During the colonial period, most political offices were occupied by the rich and wellborn, and ordinary Americans deferred to their "social betters." Even after the Revolution leading Patriots employed a narrow definition of the political nation: voting and office holding were the province of propertied white men; women, blacks, native Americans, and propertyless whites were excluded. Conservative Patriots went further, denying that popular sovereignty

meant political rights for those who owned only a little property. Thus Jeremy Belknap of New Hampshire insisted that "the people be taught . . . that they are not able to govern themselves."

Radical Patriots turned this argument on its head. In the heat of revolution they frankly embraced a democratic outlook: every citizen who supported the rebellion—property owner or not—had "an equal claim to all privileges, liberties and immunities," declared an article in the Maryland *Gazette*. The backcountry farmers of Mecklenburg County, North Carolina, instructed their representatives to the state's constitutional convention of 1776 to "oppose everything that leans to aristocracy or power in the hands of the rich and chief men exercised to the oppression of the poor." Voters in Virginia felt the same way, electing a new assembly that, an observer remarked, "was composed of men not quite so well dressed, nor so politely educated, nor so highly born. . . . They are the People's men."

Democratic-republicanism received its fullest expression in Pennsylvania, where a coalition of Scots-Irish farmers, Philadelphia artisans, and Enlightenment-influenced intellectuals took control of state politics and formulated a constitution that created the most democratic institutions of government in America or Europe. The Pennsylvania constitution of 1776 abolished property owning as a qualification for political participation, giving all men who paid taxes the right to vote and hold office. It also rejected the system of mixed government and created a *unicameral* (one-house) assembly that had complete legislative power. No council or upper house was reserved for the wealthy, and no governor exercised executive authority. Other clauses mandated an extensive system of elementary education, protected citizens from imprisonment for debt, and called for a society of economically independent freemen.

Pennsylvania's radical constitution alarmed leading Patriots in other states, most of whom did not believe in democracy. Conservatives feared that popular rule would lead to the tyranny of legislative majorities, with ordinary citizens using their numerical advantage to tax the rich. In Philadelphia, prosperous Anglican merchants founded a Republican Society to lobby for repeal of the constitution. In Boston, John Adams denounced Pennsylvania's unicameral legislature as "so democratical that it must produce confusion and every evil work."

To thwart the spread of democratic institutions, Adams dispatched copies of his *Thoughts on Government* to friends at constitutional conventions in other states. In this political treatise Adams adapted the theory of mixed government devised by English Whigs (a system with a monarch, a house of lords, and a house of commons) to a republican society. Instead of dividing state power along social lines, he assigned each function—lawmaking, administering, and judging—to a distinct branch of government. Adams argued that his scheme was republican because the people would elect the chief executive and the members of a two-house *(bicameral)* legislature. It would also preserve liberty because the various branches would check and balance each other: men of property in the upper house could check the excesses of popular majorities in the lower house, and an appointed—not elected—judiciary would review legislation. As a further curb on democracy, an elected governor would have the power to veto laws.

Leading Patriots in most states preferred Adams's mixed and balanced government, in part because it was less democratic than Pennsylvania's system and in part because it was more familiar. Most colonies had an elected assembly, an appointed council (upper house), and a royal governor. Adapting existing institutions seemed easier than beginning anew. Consequently, the framers of most state constitutions retained the existing bicameral legislature but made both houses elective. Reacting against royal governors, they reduced the powers of the executive; only three constitutions gave veto power to the governor. One of those states was New York, which was dominated by a conservative Patriot elite. The New York constitution of 1777, written chiefly by John Jay (with a copy of Adams's *Thoughts on Government* by his side), provided for a bicameral legislature with seats in the lower house apportioned by population, a governor with veto power, an appointed judiciary, and suffrage limited by property qualifications so that only 40 percent of white men were eligible to vote for the governor and the upper house.

The most flagrant use of property qualifications to maintain elite power occurred in South Carolina. That state's constitution of 1778 required candidates for governor to have a debt-free estate of £10,000 (about $450,000), senators to be worth £2,000, and assemblymen to have property valued at £1,000. These provisions ruled out office holding for about 90 percent of the white adult population; high property qualifications similarly restricted voting to a minority of South Carolina's white men.

Toward a Democratic Polity. Nonetheless, the character of American politics became more democratic for two reasons. First, the state constitutions apportioned seats in the lower houses of the legislatures on the basis of population, giving yeomen farmers in western areas the representation they had long demanded. Second, the Revolution had raised the political consciousness of ordinary Americans. During the war Patriot militiamen had claimed the right to elect their officers, "for annual election is so essentially necessary to the Liberty of Freemen." Subsequently, many veterans, whether or not they had property, demanded the right to vote and no longer automatically elected their social betters; rather, one observer noted, they chose men of "middling circumstances" who knew "the wants of the poor."

These democratic tendencies changed the composition of American legislatures (see Figure 7.1). Before the war, 85 percent of the assemblymen in the six colonies of New York, New Hampshire, New Jersey, Maryland, Virginia, and South Carolina were wealthy men with estates averaging in excess of £2,000. By 1784, however, middling farmers and artisans controlled the lower houses of the three northern states and formed a sizable minority in those of the three southern states. Flexing their new political muscles, these middling citizens successfully opposed the collection of back taxes and other measures that tended "toward the oppression of the people." In most states, backcountry residents were able to transfer the state capital from merchant-dominated seaports (such as New York City and Philadelphia) to inland cities (Albany and Harrisburg); even conservative South Carolina moved its seat of government inland from Charleston to Columbia.

The political legacy of the Revolution was complex. Conservative Patriots such as John Adams had blunted the edge of the democratic movement in that the structure of most political institutions remained conservative. Only in Pennsylvania—and Vermont, which copied Pennsylvania's constitution—were radical Patriots able to take power and create new democratic-republican insti-

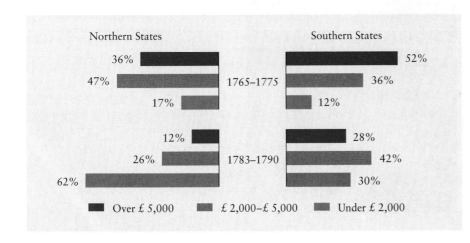

Northern States   Southern States

36%   52%
47%   1765–1775   36%
17%   12%

12%   28%
26%   1783–1790   42%
62%   30%

■ Over £ 5,000   ▦ £ 2,000–£ 5,000   ▨ Under £ 2,000

FIGURE 7.1

Change in the Wealth of Elected Officials, 1765–1790

Before the Revolution men of wealth and property predominated in the colonial assemblies. In the new republic the proportion of less prosperous men in state legislatures increased dramatically, especially in the North.

Source: Adapted from Jackson T. Main, "Government by the People: The American Revolution and the Democratization of the Legislatures," *William and Mary Quarterly,* 3d ser., vol. 23 (1966).

tutions. Yet political life—day-to-day electioneering and interest-group bargaining—had become more responsive to a broader segment of white men who owned property.

The Political Status of Women. Although debate continued over property requirements for voting, custom dictated that only men could engage in political discourse, just as the army, the militia, legislatures, juries, and other public institutions were limited to men. The extraordinary excitement of the Revolutionary Era, however, tested this division of the social order by gender. Upper-class women entered into political debate, filling their letters and diaries (and undoubtedly their conversations) with opinions on public issues. "The men say we have no business [with politics]," Eliza Wilkinson of South Carolina complained in 1783, "but I won't have it thought that because we are the weaker sex as to bodily strength we are capable of nothing more than domestic concerns. They won't even allow us liberty of thought, and that is all I want."

On the surface, Wilkinson was not asking for much. Like other wealthy, well-educated, politically aware American women, she did not demand complete equality with men by seeking voting rights or membership in public bodies such as juries. But Wilkinson's demands and those of other women were potentially revolutionary, for they challenged long-established customs and legal rules. A case in point was the proposal by Abigail Adams that Patriots create a republican *legal* order that would give women greater autonomy. Under American common law, marriage saddled a woman with the subordinate status mandated by the English feudal "law of baron and feme" ("lord and woman"); her civic and economic identity was subsumed under that of her "lord" (see Chapter 1). Thus, a married women could not own property or enter into contracts or make legal decisions by herself. If they continued to hold such power over women, "men would be tyrants," Abigail Adams chided her husband, John, in a famous exchange of letters. Even as her husband and other Patriots were busy "emancipating all nations" from monarchical despotism, she astutely pointed out, "you insist upon retaining absolute power over Wives."

Male leaders paid some attention to women's requests for greater social and legal rights. In Pennsylvania a new law in 1785 allowed women to seek either an absolute divorce or a separation with discretionary alimony, enhancing their legal position somewhat. In Massachusetts the state attorney general persuaded a jury that girls had equal rights to schooling under the state's constitution. Over time, these changes promoted gender equality. With greater access to public elementary schools as well as new female academies, many young women became literate and knowledgeable, intellectually prepared to play a larger role in the public world. By the mid-nineteenth century in the northeastern states, the percentage of women who could read and write would be nearly the same as that of men. Women authors would command a large readership among men as well as women, and literate women would again challenge their subordinate legal and political status.

But for two generations after the Revolution politics remained a male preserve. The new state constitutions either explicitly restricted suffrage to men or imposed property qualifications for voting that effectively excluded married women. An exception was New Jersey. Its constitution of 1776 granted suffrage to all free adult inhabitants worth £50, ambiguous phrasing that—apparently intentionally—permitted widows and unmarried women with property to vote. Few women exercised this option until the late 1790s, when a series

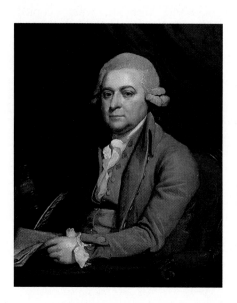

John and Abigail Adams
Both Adamses had strong personalities. In 1794 John fondly accused his wife of being a "Disciple of Wollstonecraft," but Abigail's commitment to legal equality for women long predated Wollstonecraft's *A Vindication of the Rights of Woman* (1792).

of fierce electoral battles prompted party politicians to encourage propertied women to go to the polls. To dampen competition (and preserve men's prerogatives), the New Jersey legislature redefined the franchise in 1807, bestowing voting rights on all white men who paid taxes and excluding property-owning women, African-Americans, and non-tax paying whites.

Even though the revolutionary upheaval did not seriously challenge the legal and political privileges of men, it did prompt a few American women to repudiate prevailing assumptions of women's inferiority. In 1779 Judith Sargent Murray, the daughter of a wealthy New England merchant, wrote an essay entitled "On the Equality of the Sexes," which she published in 1790. This treatise took issue with the widely accepted view of Lord Halifax, a prominent British statesman and essayist, that men had been endowed with "the larger share of reason." To refute this view, Murray systematically compared the intellectual faculties of men and women. She argued that women had a capacity for memory equal to that of men and more imagination. In judgment and reasoning, she conceded that most women were inferior to men, but she argued that this deficiency was due to lack of training. "We can only reason from what we know," she wrote, and most women had been denied "the opportunity of acquiring knowledge." Education would permit women to assume a more equal position in society, Murray concluded, invoking natural-rights arguments. Her goal was no less than "the female right to that *equality with their brethren which . . . is assigned them in the Order of Nature.*"

The most famous call for equality of the sexes—in politics as well as education—came not from America but from Britain. In 1792 Mary Wollstonecraft, a British republican influenced by the French Revolution, published the pathbreaking feminist manifesto *A Vindication of the Rights of Woman*. Reasoning from liberal ideals of natural rights and republican principles of civic equality, she demanded equal status for women in all public and political activities. Her demands received mixed reviews in elite social circles in America. Women universally condemned Wollstonecraft's sexually adventurous personal life but respected her political arguments. American men generally read the *Rights of Woman* with a disdain born of a lack of understanding. Despite their commitment to republican principles, they were unable or unwilling to question men's dominant position within the household. Some husbands remained patriarchs, and even young men who embraced the new ideal of a republican "companionate" marriage (see Chapter 9) assumed a dominant position in the partnership and refused to support a public role for their wives and daughters. Women remained second-class citizens, unable to participate directly in American political life.

Judith Sargent (Murray), Age 19
The well-educated daughter of a wealthy Massachusetts merchant, Judith Sargent was no ordinary woman. She endured a difficult seventeen-year marriage to John Stevens, a bankrupt who fled from his creditors and died in the West Indies, and in 1788 wed the Reverend John Murray, who became a leading American Universalist. Her portrait, painted around 1771 (when she was nineteen) by the renowned artist John Singleton Copley, captures Murray's skeptical view of the world, an outlook that enabled her to question customary gender roles.

The Articles of Confederation

As Patriot men moved toward independence in 1776, they confronted the troubling question of a central government. Most Patriot leaders envisioned a Continental Congress with limited powers. For example, Carter Braxton of Virginia thought Congress should have the power to "regulate the affairs of trade, war, peace, alliances, &c." but "should by no means have authority to interfere with the internal police [governance] or domestic concerns of any Colony."

The Articles of Confederation, based on a draft by John Dickinson of Pennsylvania and passed by Congress on November 15, 1777, was the first national constitution. It provided for a loose confederation in which "each state retains its sovereignty, freedom, and independence" and all powers and rights not "expressly delegated" to the United States. Most of these delegated powers pertained to diplomacy and defense. The Confederation government had the authority to declare war and peace, make treaties with foreign nations, adjudicate disputes between the states, borrow and print money, and requisition funds from the states "for the common defense or general welfare." The body charged with exercising these powers was a central legislature, the Congress, in which each state had one vote regardless of its population. There was no separate executive branch or judiciary, and important laws had to be approved by at least nine of the thirteen states. The Articles were not innovative; they simply described the way the Continental Congress had been operating since 1775.

Nonetheless, the Articles of Confederation were not ratified by all the states until 1781. The problem was western land. The Articles gave Congress authority over land disputes between states but did not provide for a national domain under Congressional control. Consequently, states with no western land claims, such as Maryland and Pennsylvania, would not ratify the Articles until states that did have such claims—based on royal charters that granted land extending in principle to the Pacific Ocean—relinquished them to Congress. But Virginia and other states bitterly resisted proposals to confine their territory. The pressure of war finally broke the deadlock. Threatened by Cornwallis's army, Virginia ceded its land claims to Congress in 1781, and Maryland, the final holdout, ratified the Articles.

The Ongoing Fiscal Crisis. Formal ratification was anticlimactic because the Confederation Congress had been exercising de facto constitutional authority for four years. The Congress raised the Continental army, negotiated the Franco-American treaty of 1778, and financed the war effort. The failures of the Congress stemmed primarily from its limited fiscal powers. Lacking the authority to impose taxes, it could only requisition funds from the state legislatures and hope they paid; it had no means of disciplining states that did not pay. Faced with the prospect of Confederation bankruptcy in 1780, General Washington called urgently for a national system of taxation, warning Patriot leaders that "unless the Congress are vested with powers competent to the great purposes of the war, our cause is lost."

In response, nationalist members of Congress sought greater powers for the Confederation. Some tried to amend the Articles; others, such as Robert Morris, who became superintendent of finance in 1781, expanded existing governmental powers. Morris won a Confederation charter for the Bank of North America, a private Philadelphia institution, hoping to use its notes to stabilize the currency throughout the country. In concert with Gouverneur Morris (see American Lives, pages 204–205), he developed a comprehensive financial plan, apportioning some war expenses among the states in proportion to their landed wealth while centralizing control of army expenditures and foreign debts in the hands of Congress. Morris hoped that a national debt would demonstrate the continuing importance of the Confederation and its need to impose taxes.

But Morris was stymied when he tried to raise revenue. Unanimous consent was required to amend the Articles, and in 1781 Rhode Island rejected Morris's proposal for a national *tariff*, an import duty of 5 percent on foreign goods. Two years later New York exercised a similar veto, blocking another proposed national tariff. State leaders pointed out that they had resisted British import duties and would not accept similar levies by another central government, even their own. In another setback to Morris's plan, each state began to assume its share of the national debt by paying interest on it directly to its own citizens rather than sending funds to Congress, which might use them to pay debt-holding citizens of other states. By 1786 Pennsylvania, Maryland, New York, and New Jersey had assumed nearly one-third of the national debt, showing that the Confederation was essentially a league of states, not a powerful government in its own right.

Western Lands and the Northwest Ordinance. Despite its limited powers, the Confederation Congress successfully implemented its plan for settling the trans-Appalachian West, which it had acquired as a result of the Treaty of Paris and the cessions of the states. The Congress had two goals. First, it needed to assert its title to this great treasure so that it could sell most of it to help pay the government's expenses. Standing in the way of this scheme were the native Americans who occupied most of those lands as well as thousands of white squatters who also asserted ownership rights. In 1783 Congress began negotiating with Indian tribes to persuade them that the Treaty of Paris had extinguished their land rights. It also rejected the claims of white squatters, allowing them to stay only if they paid the Confederation government for their lands.

Second, Congress was determined to bind western settlements to the United States by providing for their orderly settlement and eventual admission to the Union. Given the mountain barrier between the seaboard and the interior, Congress feared that westerners might try to create states on their own, establish separate republics, or even link up with Spanish Louisiana. The danger was real: in 1784 thousands of settlers—"white savages," John Jay called them—in what is now eastern Tennessee unilaterally set up a new state, Franklin, and applied for admission to the Confederation. To preserve its authority over the West, Congress refused to recognize the new state or consider its application.

To thwart similar unauthorized actions, Congress pursued a dual policy. It directed Virginia, North Carolina, and Georgia to assume temporary control of the western lands south of the Ohio River. To the north of the Ohio, Congress established a national domain, issuing three ordinances for the settlement and administration of this Northwest Territory (see Map 7.1). The Ordinance of 1784, written by Thomas Jefferson, called for the admission of the states carved out of the territory as soon as their populations equaled that of the smallest state. The Land Ordinance of 1785 established a rectangular grid system for surveying land (see Map 8.2) and a set of legal rules that spurred the creation of a full-fledged capitalist economy. These rules specified that western lands be surveyed before settlement to deter squatters, transferred in fee simple without quitrents or other dues to encourage an active land market, and sold mostly in large blocs to favor large-scale investors and land speculators.

The Northwest Ordinance of 1787 applied these general principles by providing for the creation of three to five territories in the Old Northwest—the national domain north of the Ohio River—eventually comprising the states of Ohio, Indiana, Illinois, Michigan, and Wisconsin. Reflecting the antislavery sentiments of Jefferson and many other Patriots, the ordinance prohibited slavery in those territories. It encouraged education, directing that funds from the sale of certain lands go toward the support of schools. It specified that initially each new territory would be ruled by a governor and judges appointed by Congress. Once the number of free adult men reached 5,000, the settlers could elect their own legislature. When the population grew to 60,000, the residents could write a republican constitution and apply to join the Union. Once admitted, a new state would enjoy all the rights and privileges of the existing states.

The ordinances of the 1780s were a great and enduring achievement. They provided for the orderly settlement of the West while reducing the prospect of secessionist movements and preventing the emergence of dependent "colonies." Moreover, the ordinances added a new dimension to the national identity, providing both a source of revenue for the central government and a new vision for the young nation. Whatever the continuing problems in the West—native American land claims, illegal British forts, threats from Spanish officials—the United States was no longer confined to thirteen governments on the eastern seaboard. It had the potential to become a dynamic, expanding society.

MAP 7.1

The Confederation and Western Land Claims

The Confederation Congress resolved the conflicting land claims of the states by creating a "national domain" to the west of the Appalachian Mountains. From 1781 to 1802 all the seaboard states with western land claims ceded them to the national government. The Confederation Congress established territories with democratic political institutions in this domain and declared that all of those territories were to be open to settlement by citizens from every state.

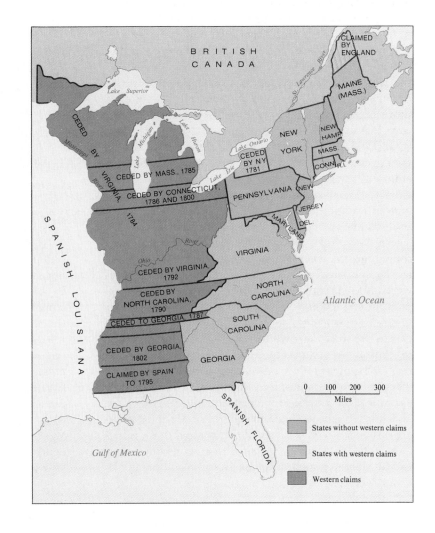

Gouverneur Morris:
An Aristocratic Liberal
in a Republican Age

The American Revolution had many meanings, and the life of Gouverneur Morris reveals one of them. Born into the New York aristocracy, Morris had an acute understanding of the dangers to his class posed by a "democratic" revolution supported by social nobodies such as Robert Twelves Hewes (see American Lives, Chapter 5). In 1774, at the tender age of twenty-two, Morris advised the New York elite "to seek for reunion with the parent state." Otherwise, "I see, and I see it with fear and trembling, that . . . we shall be under the worst of all possible dominions . . . the domination of a riotous mob." "The mob begin to think and reason," he warned again in 1775 after watching a debate between radical tradesmen and conservative Patriot merchants. "Poor reptiles! it is with them a vernal [spring] morning, . . . they bask in the sunshine, and ere noon they will bite, depend on it."

Family background had a lot to do with Morris's disdain of ordinary men and women. His grandfather, Lewis Morris, was the first lord of Morrisania, a 1900-acre manor in Westchester County, New York, and from 1738 to 1746 served as the king's governor of New Jersey. His father, Lewis Jr., was judge of the vice-admiralty court of New York and on his deathbed provided that Gouverneur, a younger son, should have "the best Education that is to be had in Europe or America": study at the Academy of Philadelphia and King's College in New York followed by an apprenticeship with the eminent lawyer William Smith, Jr. But since he lacked inherited wealth, the young Morris's choices were stark. He could either live in genteel poverty or exploit his social connections and personal talents—a fine mind, sophisticated manners, and great personal charm—to make his own fortune.

For all his aristocratic beliefs, Morris became a Patriot, refusing to follow his mother, many relatives, and his legal mentor, Smith, into Loyalism. In 1775 he won election to the Patriot Provincial Congress of New York and soon sought to shape the course of the revolutionary struggle. At the Provincial Convention that drafted New York's relatively conservative constitution of 1777, Morris argued strenuously for maintaining the

Gouverneur Morris, Federalist Statesman

old aristocratic method of voting by public declaration but more republican-minded members mandated voting by ballot. Still, the convention heeded Morris's ultra-conservative voice by imposing a property qualification for voting: ownership of a freehold worth 20 pounds.

Morris was equally active at the national level. As one of New York's delegates to the Continental Congress, he was shocked by the financial weakness of the Confederation and tried to enhance its authority. As early as 1778 Morris proposed the elimination of state currencies, the creation of a national domain in the West, and national tariffs to pay off the growing war debt. Three years later he happily enlisted as the assistant to the new superintendent of finance, the merchant

Robert Morris. Together the Morrises (who were not related) devised measures to restore the government's credit. In 1781 they won approval for the Bank of North America; the following year they issued a "Report on Public Credit," which called for the Confederation government to assume the entire national debt, issue new interest-bearing debt certificates, and impose tariffs and internal taxes to pay the interest costs. Here in outline was the fiscal program implemented a decade later by Alexander Hamilton.

Like Hamilton, Gouverneur Morris was a man of "spirit and nerve" who never doubted his own judgment and rarely respected that of others. George Washington chastised Morris for displaying his "brilliant imagination" too quickly and recklessly, whereas a French aristocrat observed that "his [air of] superiority, which he has taken no pains to conceal, will prevent his ever occupying an important place" in republican America. Never humbled, not even by an accident in 1780 that left him with a wooden leg, Morris used charm and brilliance to compensate for these flaws in his character. He played a prominent role at the Philadelphia convention in 1787, insisting that "property was the sole or primary object of Government & Society." To protect property rights, Morris argued for an aristocratic-type Senate whose members would serve without pay and for life, a national freehold property qualification for voting, and a strong president with the power of the veto.

Significantly, Morris did not defend aristocratic property. In debates in 1777 over the New York constitution, Morris had argued for "abolishing all quit rents within this State." He also called for the end of "domestic slavery . . . so that in future ages, every human being who breathes the air of the State, shall enjoy the privileges of a freeman," a proposition he reiterated with great force at the Philadelphia convention.

Morris's defense of freedom—of individuals, of the alienation of land, of commerce and legal contracts—aligned him with those Patriots who gave a "classical liberal" definition to the American Revolution. Valuing individual liberty higher than majority rule, liberal Patriots such as Morris hoped the new Constitution would protect property rights from popularly elected state legislatures and encourage economic growth. Indeed, Morris's outlook—and increasingly his life—reflected the emergent principles of laissez-faire capitalism. After serving as Robert Morris's assistant, Gouverneur became his business partner. The two men invested jointly in land in New York and Pennsylvania, in a maritime venture in Massachusetts, and in supplying tobacco to the French tobacco monopoly. Even as such speculations landed Robert Morris in debtor's prison, they made Gouverneur Morris a rich man, finally able to live in the aristocratic style to which he had been bred.

Beginning in 1788, Morris resided in Europe for ten years, first as a speculating merchant, then as the American minister to France (1792–1794), and finally as a cultured man of independent wealth. Fluent in French, polished in manners, confident of his talents, Morris fit easily into Parisian high society, taking as a mistress the young wife of an aging aristocrat, forming a lifelong friendship with the formidable Madame de Staël, and sharing the hopes and the fears of the endangered *ancien régime*. While disparaging the French nobility for "Hugging the Privileges of Centuries long elapsed," Morris refused to support the republican reforms proposed by Lafayette and others, declaring that he was "opposed to the Democracy from Regard to Liberty." Indeed, as republicans took control of France in 1792, Morris joined an unsuccessful aristocratic plot to smuggle King Louis XVI out of Paris.

In the end Gouverneur Morris stands forth as an aristocratic liberal, an American precursor of Alexis de Tocqueville (see Chapter 10). Aristocratic in manners and fearing mob rule, Morris wanted to limit the new republican polity to men of property and status even as he celebrated classical liberal principles of personal freedom, economic enterprise, and equal opportunity.

The Postwar Crisis

Success was far from assured, however, and the 1780s were a critical decade for the new nation. Peace did not bring a return to prewar prosperity. The war had destroyed many American merchant ships and disrupted trade; exports—especially of Chesapeake tobacco—declined because of the loss of long-established ties with British merchant houses. Deprived of a subsidy from the British government, South Carolina's lucrative indigo industry nearly vanished. The British Navigation Acts, which had contributed to the expansion of colonial commerce, now worked against the United States as American-owned ships were barred from trading with the sugar islands in the British West Indies.

Economic Hard Times. The postwar recession lowered the American standard of living. The population of the United States continued to grow—from 2.4 million to 3.6 million between 1775 and 1787—but exports increased only slightly, from $10.7 million to $11.6 million. As a result, individual Americans had less income to spend on imported manufactures. Nevertheless, low-priced British goods flooded urban markets, driving many artisans and war-created textile firms out of business. Responding to protests by artisans, New York, Rhode Island, Pennsylvania, and Massachusetts imposed tariffs on imported manufactures.

The financial legacy of the war compounded these problems. Most state governments emerged from the conflict with worthless currencies and big debts. North Carolina owed its creditors $1.7 million, while Virginia was liable for $2.7 million in war bonds. Speculators—wealthy merchants and landowners—had purchased many state debt certificates for far less than their face value. Now these shrewd and influential men advocated high taxes so the states could redeem the bonds quickly and at full value.

As economic recession and high taxes pressed hard on debtors, they sought political solutions to their financial problems. In South Carolina farmers won the passage of a law that prevented sheriffs from selling seized farms to repay debts; instead, creditors had to accept installment payments over a three-year period. South Carolina legislators also assisted debtors by increasing the supply of paper currency. But these prodebtor measures were controversial. David Ramsay, a physician and the future author of the well-known *History of the American Revolution* (1789), assailed the South Carolina legislature for undermining "the just rights of creditors." To avert similar prodebtor legislation and preserve elite rule in Maryland, Charles Carroll of Carrollton persuaded wealthy Maryland landowners to adopt conciliatory economic policies toward yeomen and tenant farmers. Accordingly, the Maryland legislature replaced the customary poll tax, which bore hard on the poor, with a graduated property tax. When the Maryland House of Delegates enacted profarmer and prodebtor measures in 1785 and 1786, they were rejected by the more conservative state senate.

As James Madison of Virginia pointed out, these political struggles were not primarily between "the Class with, and Class without, property." The real battle was between wealthy merchants and landowners on the one hand and a larger coalition of middling farm owners, small-scale traders, artisans, and tenant farmers on the other. Creditors might be angered by legislation favoring farmers and artisans, but prodebtor laws eased the financial strain and probably prevented a major social upheaval.

Shays's Rebellion. The absence of debtor-relief legislation in Massachusetts provoked the first armed uprising in the new nation. When the war ended, merchants and creditors in eastern Massachusetts lobbied successfully for high taxes and against paper money. These procreditor policies facilitated rapid repayment of the state's war debt but undermined the fragile finances of farmers in newly settled areas. Creditors and sheriffs hauled delinquent farmers into court, saddled them with high legal fees, and threatened to imprison them for debt or repossess their property. In 1786 residents of western counties called extralegal meetings and protested against high taxes and aggressive eastern creditors. Meanwhile, bands of angry farmers closed the courts by force and freed debtors and fellow protesters from jail. Resistance gradually grew into a full-scale revolt. Ignored by the state legislature, hundreds of farmers in western and central Massachusetts organized an army under the leadership of Daniel Shays, a former Continental army captain, and prepared to use force to resist state authority.

Shays's Rebellion, a struggle against high taxes and nonlocal political control, resembled the American resistance movements between 1763 and 1775. "The people have turned against their teachers the doctrines which were inculcated to effect the late revolution," complained the conservative Massachusetts political leader Fisher Ames. Radical Patriots were no less troubled by popular conventions and crowd actions. As Samuel Adams put it, "those Men, who . . . would lessen the Weight of Government lawfully exercised must be Enemies to our happy Revolution and Common Liberty."

To preserve its authority, the Massachusetts legislature passed a Riot Act outlawing illegal assemblies. With the financial support of nervous eastern merchants, Governor James Bowdoin equipped a strong fighting force to put down the rebellion and called on the Confederation Congress to supply an additional 1,300 soldiers. A national army was not needed. Shays's army dwindled during the winter of 1786–1787, falling victim to freezing weather and inadequate supplies.

"Gen. Daniel Shays, Col. Job Shattuck."
This woodcut was published in *Bickerstaff's Boston Almanack* for 1787 by Friends of Government who attacked the rebel leaders as upstarts and demagogues. "Liberty is still the object I have in view," a Shaysite declared in reply, but the former radical Sam Adams would have none of it: "The man who dares to rebel against the laws of a republic ought to suffer death." Shattuck was sentenced to death for treason but then pardoned; Shays fled to New York State, where he died in 1821, still a poor farmer.

Bowdoin's military force easily dispersed the rebels, and state authority was restored.

Though the rebellion collapsed, the discontent that caused it was not so easily suppressed. Massachusetts voters turned Governor Bowdoin out of office, and farmers in New York, northern Pennsylvania, Connecticut, New Hampshire, and Vermont (a separate republic until 1791, when it was admitted to the Union over the protests of New York land speculators) closed courthouses and demanded economic assistance. British officials in Canada predicted the imminent demise of the United States, and many Americans feared for the success of their republican experiment. Indeed, Shays's Rebellion was important primarily for its political impact. It prompted leaders with a national perspective to redouble their efforts to create a stronger central government.

The Constitution of 1787

From the moment of its creation, the Constitution was a complex and controversial document. Written in a time of crisis, it embodied the values and interests of men with a personal stake in its outcome. But, reflecting the intellectual talents of the framers and intense debates over political principles, the Constitution was also a principled and innovative statement of republican political theory. Beyond that, it addressed the pressing issue of the distribution of power between the states and the central government.

The Rise of a Nationalist Faction

Prominent among the Patriots who favored a stronger central government were military officers, diplomats, and officials who had served in the Continental Congress. Their experiences during the war of independence had made their political outlook national rather than state or local. General Washington, the financier Robert Morris, and the diplomats Benjamin Franklin, John Jay, and John Adams were all advocates of giving the national government the power to control foreign commerce and impose tariffs.

Americans were well acquainted with restrictions on commerce in the form of the Navigation Acts, and after independence key commercial states in the North—New York, Massachusetts, Pennsylvania—devised their own trade policies, providing subsidies to merchants and imposing protective tariffs. But the nationalists' proposals to place trade in the hands of Congress ran afoul of regional interests: southern planters wanted free trade with Europe, whereas northern merchants, artisans, and manufacturers called for protective tariffs and preferential treatment for American ships.

Tax policy was another divisive issue. Nationalist leaders were particularly troubled by the poverty of the Confederation government. The refusal by Rhode Island and New York to levy a national import duty and the decision by other states to assume and discharge some of the national debt had undermined Robert Morris's scheme to prop up the Confederation. Without tax revenue or state contributions, Congress was unable to pay even the interest on the foreign debt. To many nationalists, the American republic seemed on the verge of collapse. "I am really more distressed by the posture of our public affairs, than I ever was by the most gloomy appearances during the war," confessed William Livingston of New Jersey. The "stubborn Dignity" of the states, another nationalist complained, "will never permit a federal Government to exist."

By 1786 nationalists had yet another reason for concern: the fiscal policies of the states. Legislatures in Virginia and other southern states were granting tax relief to various groups of citizens, thus diminishing public revenue and delaying redemption of government debts. Public creditors feared that their government-issued bonds would become worthless; as Charles Lee of Virginia lamented, taxpayers were being led to believe "they will never be compelled to pay." State governments also jeopardized the sanctity of private debts by providing relief to debtors—staying the collection of private debts or exempting personal property from seizure. Four states had gone much further, forcing merchants and creditors to accept depreciated paper currency in payment for debts. "The debtor interest . . . operates in all the forms of injustice & oppression," a South Carolina creditor complained. "While men are madly accumulating enormous debts, their legislators are making provisions for their nonpayment."

Adding these concerns to their agenda, the nationalists took the initiative in 1786. Madison persuaded the Virginia legislature to call a commercial convention in Annapolis, Maryland, to discuss tariff and taxation policies. After this discussion (by twelve delegates from only five states), the nationalists called for another meeting, in Philadelphia, to undertake a broad review of the responsibilities and powers of the Confederation. Shays's Rebellion raised the prospect of social revolution and underscored the need for action. In January 1787 nationalists in Congress won the passage of a resolution supporting a revision of the Articles of Confederation to make them "adequate to the exigencies of government and the preservation of the Union." To many nationalists the Philadelphia meeting seemed the last opportunity to save the republic. "Nothing but the adoption of some efficient plan from the Convention," a fellow Virginian wrote to James Madison, "can prevent anarchy first & civil convulsions afterwards."

The Philadelphia Convention

The Philadelphia convention began in May 1787. Fifty-five delegates attended, representing every state except Rhode Island, whose legislature opposed any increase in central authority. Some members, such as Benjamin Franklin of Pennsylvania, had been leaders of the independence movement. Others, including George Washington and Robert Morris, had come to prominence during the war. Most were merchants, slaveholding planters, or "monied men"; there were no artisans, backcountry settlers, or tenants and only a solitary yeoman farmer.

Several of the most famous Patriots missed the convention. John Adams and Thomas Jefferson were in Europe, serving as the American ministers to Britain and France. Thomas Paine was also in Europe, and his fellow radical Samuel Adams was not chosen as a delegate by the Massachusetts legislature. The Virginia firebrand Patrick Henry was selected but refused to attend because he favored a limited national government. Their places were taken by capable younger men such as James Madison and Alexander Hamilton. Both were nationalists, committed to the creation of a central government that, as Hamilton put it, would protect the republic from "the imprudence of democracy" in the state legislatures.

Hamilton's views were extreme, but most of the delegates shared his procreditor and nationalist outlook. The Philadelphia convention was filled with men who supported creditor factions in their own states and wanted to protect property rights. They believed in a stronger central government that would curb what

Madison, in an important memorandum of 1787, would call the "Vices of the Political System" of the various states. They differed only on the means by which to accomplish this goal.

The Virginia Plan. The delegates began the convention by electing Washington as the presiding officer and deciding to deliberate behind closed doors to forestall popular opposition. (In fact, Americans knew little about the proceedings of the convention until the 1840s, when Madison's notebooks were published.) They agreed that each state would have one vote at the convention, as in the Confederation, and that a majority would decide an issue. Then the delegates exceeded their mandate to revise the Articles of Confederation by agreeing to consider the Virginia Plan, a scheme devised by James Madison that called for a different constitutional framework: a truly national government.

Madison arrived in Philadelphia determined to fashion a new political order. He was a graduate of Princeton,

Portrait of James Madison, 1805–1807, by Gilbert Stuart
An intellectual, Madison was also a successful politician, especially in the decade after 1785—when he helped enact the Virginia Statute of Religious Liberty, write and ratify the Constitution of 1787, win passage of the Bill of Rights, and found the Democratic-Republican party.

where he had read classical and modern political theory, and had served in both the Confederation Congress and the Virginia assembly. His experience in Virginia convinced him of the "narrow ambition" of many state political leaders and their lack of public virtue. He wanted to design a national government that would curb factional disputes and ensure the rule of men of high character.

The Virginia Plan differed from the Articles of Confederation in three crucial respects. First, it rejected state sovereignty in favor of the "supremacy of national authority." In Madison's scheme the central government had the power "to legislate in all cases to which the separate States are incompetent" and to overturn state laws. Second, it called for a *national* republic that drew its authority directly from all the people of the United States and would have direct power over them. As Madison explained, the new central government would bypass the states and operate directly "on the individuals composing them." Third, the Virginia Plan would create a three-part national government structured like many state governments. It called for a lower house elected by the voters, an upper house elected by the lower house, and an executive and judiciary chosen by the entire legislature.

From a political perspective, Madison's plan contained a fatal flaw: because it assigned great authority to the lower house and based its composition on population, the plan would dramatically increase the power of the larger states. Consequently, delegates from the less populous states rejected this plan out of hand. Their states had enjoyed equal representation in both the Continental Congress and the Confederation Congress. They feared that, as a Delaware delegate proclaimed, the populous states would "crush the small ones whenever they stand in the way of their ambitious or interested views."

To protect their interests, delegates from small states rallied behind a plan devised by William Paterson of New Jersey. The New Jersey Plan had many nationalist aspects: it would transform the Confederation by giving the central government the power to raise revenue, control commerce, and make binding requisitions on the states. But it would preserve equality among the states by limiting each state to one vote in a unicameral legislature, as in the Articles of Confederation. Of course, this provision made the New Jersey Plan unacceptable to delegates from the larger states. After a month of debate a bare majority of the states voted to accept the Virginia Plan as the basis for further discussion.

This decision changed the course of American history, for it raised the prospect of a new constitutional structure. Although two New York delegates walked out in protest, the rest redoubled their efforts. They met six days a week during the hot, humid summer of 1787, debating high principles and working through a multitude of technical details. As experienced and realistic politicians, the delegates knew that their plan had to be acceptable to existing political factions and powerful social groups. Pierce Butler of South Carolina expressed this dilemma by invoking a classical Greek precedent: "We must follow the example of Solon, who gave the Athenians not the best government he could devise but the best they would receive."

The Great Compromise. Representation remained the central problem. To satisfy all the states, large and small, the Connecticut delegates suggested changing the Virginia Plan so that the upper house, the Senate, would have two members from each state regardless of a state's size. In the lower chamber, the House of Representatives, seats would be apportioned on the basis of population, which would be determined every ten years by a national census. Delegates from the large states accepted the Great Compromise, but only after bitter debate; it seemed to them less a compromise than a victory for the smaller states.

Having resolved this major issue, the delegates quickly settled other matters that involved the interests of the existing state governments. One delegate objected to a proposal to extend the national judiciary into the states, declaring that "the states will revolt at such encroachments." The convention therefore defined the judicial power of the United States in broad terms and vested it "in one supreme Court," leaving to the new national legislature the thorny issue of establishing lower national courts in the states. The convention also decided against imposing a uniform freehold property qualification for voting in national elections. "Eight or nine states have extended the right of suffrage beyond the freeholders," George Mason of Virginia pointed out. "What will people there say if they should be disfranchised?"

Ultimately, the delegates devised ingenious ways to give the states a prominent role in the new constitutional structure. For example, they placed the selection of the president, the chief executive official, in the hands of an *electoral college* that would be chosen on a state-by-state basis. The delegates also specified that state legislatures, not the voters at large, would elect the members of the Senate. By giving state governments an important role in the new system, the delegates hoped those governments would accept the reduction of their sovereign power.

Compromise over Slavery. Although the conflict between the large and small states dominated the convention's debates, another kind of conflict—a regional division between the North and the South on the slavery issue—also began to emerge. While no one proposed the abolition of slavery, Gouverneur Morris of New York condemned it as "a nefarious institution" and George Mason of Virginia argued eloquently for national laws against the slave trade. Delegates from the Carolinas and Georgia insisted that the trade continue. As John Rutledge of South Carolina warned his colleagues, "the true question at present is whether the Southern states shall or shall not be parties to the Union."

To maintain a national union, the delegates treated slavery as a political question, not a moral issue. Compromise was the watchword. Thus, the Constitution contained a "fugitive" clause enabling masters to reclaim slaves or servants who had taken refuge in other states. This provision appealed to the white planters who controlled Georgia and the Carolinas, as did a clause that denied Congress the power to regulate the importation of slaves for twenty years after ratification. To mollify antislavery sentiment in the northern states, the delegates agreed that the slave trade could thereafter be abolished by legislative action.

Another compromise resolved the slavery-related issues of taxation and representation. Southern delegates wanted to include slaves in a state's population for the purpose of determining representation in Congress. Northerners objected, arguing that propertyless slaves, lacking the vote, were not full members of the republic and should not be counted at all. The convention finally agreed that for the purposes of representation and taxation a slave (slaves were carefully referred to in the Constitution as "all other Persons") would be counted as three-fifths of a free person.

National Power. Having allayed the concerns of small states and slave states, the delegates proceeded to fulfill their goal of creating a powerful, procreditor national government. The finished document declared that the Constitution and all national legislation and treaties made under its authority were to be the supreme law of the land. It gave the national government broad powers over taxation, military defense, and external commerce as well as the authority to make all laws "necessary and proper" to implement those and other provisions. To establish the fiscal credit of the central government, the Constitution mandated that the United States honor the existing national debt.

As the Constitution enhanced national authority, it restricted that of the states. State governments could no longer issue money to assist debtors in paying their bills. Prodebtor legislatures were also forbidden to enact any "Law impairing the Obligation of Contracts," thus prohibiting debtor-relief legislation.

The proposed Constitution was not a "perfect production," Benjamin Franklin admitted on September 17, 1787, as he urged the forty-one delegates still present to sign it. Yet the great diplomat confessed his astonishment "to find this system approaching so near to perfection as it does." His colleagues apparently agreed; all but three signed the document. Their handiwork would now be judged by their fellow Americans.

The Debate over Ratification

The procedures for ratifying the new Constitution were controversial. The convention hesitated to submit its nationalist scheme to the state legislatures for their unanimous consent, as required by the Articles of Confederation, because it undoubtedly would be rejected by Rhode Island and possibly a few other states. The delegates therefore specified a different procedure: the Constitution would go into effect upon ratification by special conventions in at least nine of the thirteen states. Because of its nationalist sympathies, the Confederation Congress winked at this extralegal procedure and sent the new Constitution to the states. Surprisingly, the state legislatures complied, calling for the election of delegates to state ratification conventions.

A great national debate began almost immediately. The nationalists seized the initiative with two bold moves. First, they called themselves "Federalists," a term that suggested a loose, decentralized system of government and thus partially obscured their goal of establishing a strong central authority. Second, they undertook a coordinated political campaign, publishing dozens of pamphlets and newspaper articles. In this literature they argued that the proposed Constitution would remedy the acknowledged defects of the Articles of Confederation and create a strong and prosperous Union.

The Antifederalists. The opponents of the Constitution became known as the Antifederalists. They came from diverse backgrounds and were less organized than the Federalists. Some, like Governor George Clinton of New York, enjoyed great power and patronage in their states and feared losing it. Others were agrarian democrats who had long opposed merchants and creditors. "These lawyers and men of learning and monied men expect to be managers of this Constitution," argued a biblically minded Massachusetts farmer, "and get all the power and all the money into their own hands and then they will swallow up all of us little folks . . . just as the whale swallowed up Jonah."

Highly educated Americans with a "traditional" republican outlook provided ideological leadership for the Antifederalist cause. Following the argument of the French political philosopher Montesquieu, they believed that republican institutions were suitable only for cities or small states. "No extensive empire can be governed on republican principles," James Winthrop of Massachusetts declared. Like most Antifederalists, Winthrop worried that a strong national administration would restore the worst features of British rule—high taxes, an oppressive bureaucracy, and a standing army controlled by a tyrant—thus ending the republican experiment in popular government. George Mason of Virginia, one of the three delegates who refused to sign the

Constitution, argued that the new charter was "totally subversive of every principle which has hitherto governed us. This power is calculated to annihilate totally the state governments." Because they were committed to keeping government "close to the people," Antifederalists maintained that keeping the old Articles was preferable to adopting a new document with such obvious defects.

Many Antifederalists stressed the danger of tyranny and elite rule. Melancton Smith of New York warned that the Constitution's provision for creating large electoral districts would inevitably lead to the concentration of power in the hands of a few wealthy upper-class men, since only such men would be prominent enough to be elected. Yet it was well known, Smith maintained, that "a representative body, composed principally of respectable yeomanry, is the best possible security to liberty." Patrick Henry of Virginia called attention to the immense taxing power of the central government. "A great and mighty President" would "be supported in extravagant munificence," he predicted; "the whole of our property may be taken by this American government, by laying what taxes they please, and suspending our laws at their pleasure." Henry and other Antifederalists envisioned the new nation as a collection of small sovereign republics tied together only for trade and defense—not the "United States" but the "States United."

The Federalist. In New York, where ratification was hotly contested, James Madison, John Jay, and Alexander Hamilton countered these arguments in a series of newspaper articles called *The Federalist.* These ardent nationalists stressed the need for a strong government to conduct foreign affairs and insisted—also invoking Montesquieu—that central authority would not foster domestic tyranny. In his *Thoughts on Government* John Adams had adapted Montesquieu's well-known analysis of British institutions, *The Spirit of the Laws* (1748), to fit American conditions, suggesting that a "separation of powers" within the government would preserve the liberty of citizens. The authors of *The Federalist* expanded this argument, pointing out that authority in the national government would be divided among a president, a bicameral legislature, and a judiciary. Each branch of government would "check and balance" the others, thus preserving liberty.

James Madison went further, denying that republicanism was suited only to small states. Indeed, in *The Federalist,* No. 10, he maintained that the sheer size of the national republic would be the greatest deterrent to tyranny. It was "sown in the nature of man," Madison wrote, that individuals would seek power and form factions to advance their own interests. Indeed, "a landed interest, a manufacturing interest, a mercantile interest, a moneyed interest, with many lesser interests, grow up of necessity in civilized nations." The task of govern-

ment in a free society, the young Virginian continued with true brilliance, was not to suppress those groups but to prevent any single faction from becoming dominant. This end could best be achieved not in a small republic, as Montesquieu and James Winthrop had maintained, but in a large one. "Extend the sphere," Madison concluded, "and you take in a greater variety of parties and interests; you make it less probable that a majority of the whole will have a common motive to invade the rights of other citizens."

Madison's hardheaded realism—his classical liberal emphasis on self-interest as the source of human conduct—was tempered by a traditional republican belief in public virtue. "I go by this great republican principle," Madison told the Virginia ratifying convention, "that the people have virtue and intelligence to select men of virtue and wisdom"—and, he undoubtedly hoped, to ratify the new Constitution.

The Ratification Conventions. Madison's hopes were tested in the ratifying conventions, which met in twelve states between December 1787 and June 1788. (Rhode Island again was the exception; it ratified only in 1790.) Unlike the men at the Philadelphia convention, the delegates to the state caucuses represented a wide spectrum of Americans: untutored farmers and middling artisans as well as educated gentlemen. In general, delegates from the backcountry were Antifederalists whereas those from the seacoast strongly supported the Federal-

Artisans Support the Constitution
Seeking tariff protection from lower-priced British tinware, New York's Society of Pewterers supported ratification of the Philadelphia constitution. Their call for "Sons Joined in One Social Band" conveyed the ideal of an artisan republican community, and in its call for brotherhood, anticipated the French Revolutionary slogan of "Liberty, Equality, and Fraternity." (Collection of The New-York Historical Society)

ists. Thus, in Pennsylvania a coalition of merchants, artisans, and commercial farmers from Philadelphia and its vicinity spearheaded an easy Federalist victory. Other early Federalist successes came in the less populous states of Delaware, New Jersey, Georgia, and Connecticut. In each case the delegates hoped that a stronger national government would offset the power of their large neighbors.

The Constitution's first real test came in January 1788 in Massachusetts, one of the most populous states and a hotbed of Antifederalist sentiment (see Map 7.2). Influential Patriots—including Samuel Adams and Gover-

nor John Hancock—publicly opposed the new charter, as did Shaysite sympathizers in the west. But astute Federalist politicians won over wavering delegates by warning of political chaos, and Boston artisans, who hoped for tariff protection from British imports, supported ratification. By a close vote of 187 to 168, the Federalists carried the day (see American Voices, page 213).

Spring brought Federalist victories in Maryland and South Carolina. When New Hampshire ratified in June (by 57 votes to 47), the required nine states had approved the Constitution. But the outcome was still in doubt, for the powerful states of Virginia and New

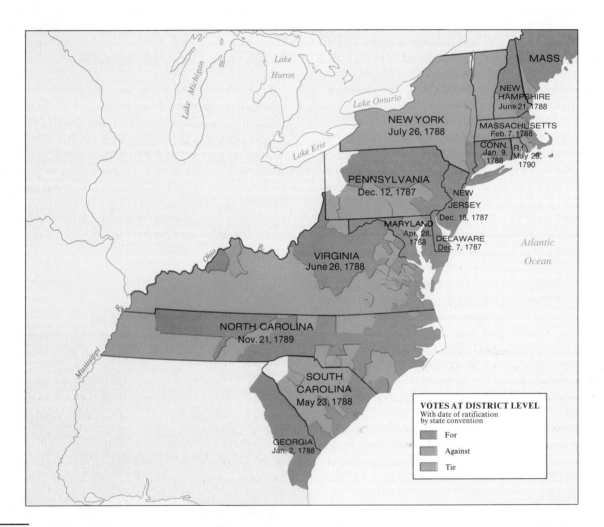

MAP 7.2

Ratifying the Constitution
In 1907 the geographer Owen Libby plotted the votes of the state ratification conventions on a map. He noted that most delegates from seaboard or commercial farming districts favored the Constitution whereas those from backcountry areas opposed it. Subsequent research has confirmed Libby's socioeconomic interpretation in North and South Carolina and Massachusetts; however, other factors influenced delegates in some states with frontier districts, such as Georgia, where the Constitution was ratified unanimously.

Jonathan Smith

A Farmer Praises the Constitution

Scores of ordinary men—middling farmers, shopkeepers, artisans—sat alongside their social betters in the state ratifying conventions; their opinions and votes were often crucial to the outcome. Here a farmer explains his support of the constitution to the Massachusetts convention in language that is plain but effective, punctuated with phrases taken from the Bible and analogies drawn from personal experience.

Mr. President, I am a plain man, and get my living by the plough. I am not used to speak in public. . . . I have lived in a part of the country where I have known the worth of good government by the want of it. There was a black cloud [Shays's Rebellion] that rose in the east last winter, and spread over the west. It brought on a state of anarchy that led to tyranny. . . . People, I say, took up arms, and then, if you went to speak to them, you had the musket of death presented to your breast. They would rob you of your property, threaten to burn your houses. . . .

When I saw this Constitution, I found that it was a cure for these disorders. I got a copy of it and read it over and over. I had been a member of the convention to form our own state constitution, and had learnt something of the checks and balances of power; and I found them all here. . . .

I don't think the worse of the Constitution because lawyers, and men of learning, and moneyed men are fond of it. [They] are all embarked in the same cause with us, and we must all swim or sink together. Suppose two or three of you had been at the pains to break up a piece of rough land, and sow it with wheat—would you let it lie waste because you could not agree what sort of fence to make? There is a time to sow and a time to reap. We sowed our seed when we sent men to the federal convention. Now is the harvest; now is the time to reap the fruit of our labor. And if we won't do it now, I am afraid we never shall have another opportunity.

Source: Jonathan Elliot, ed., *The Debates. . .on the Adoption of the Federal Constitution* (Washington, D.C.: 1830), II, pp. 101–102.

York had not yet acted. Now Madison, Jay, and Hamilton, writing in *The Federalist,* used their superb rhetorical skills to win over delegates in those key states. In addition, leading Federalists promised that the Constitution would be amended to include a Bill of Rights. This promise addressed the most powerful argument of the Antifederalists, that the new national Constitution, unlike most state constitutions, failed to protect basic individual rights, such as liberty of conscience in religious matters and the right to a jury trial. In the end, the Federalists won a narrow victory in Virginia, 89 votes to 79, and this success carried them to victory in New York by the even smaller margin of 30 votes to 27.

Few Federalists had expected a more resounding victory in light of the resistance during the 1780s to a strong central government. Working against great odds, they had created a national republic, a triumph that had profound ideological and social implications. The United States Constitution of 1787 represented the resurgence of the traditional political elite and the decline of the yeomanry. At least temporarily, creditors and merchants were in the ascendancy. The Revolutionary Era had come to an end.

The Constitution Implemented

The Constitution gave American political life a new, national dimension. Voters had long chosen local and state officials; now they elected national officeholders as well. A single political system was beginning to tie together the interests and concerns of Georgia planters, Pennsylvania artisans, Massachusetts merchants, and scores of other social groups.

Devising the New Government. The Federalists who had written the Constitution swept the election of 1788. No fewer than forty-four of the ninety-one members of the first United States Congress, which met in 1789, had helped write or ratify the Constitution. Only eight Antifederalists were elected to the House of Representatives, and they never formed a cohesive political faction. The Constitution specified that "electors" chosen by voters in the various states would select the president and vice-president. As expected, the electors chose George Washington of Virginia as president; John Adams of Massachusetts received the second highest number of electoral votes and became vice-president. The newly elected officials took up their posts in New York City, the temporary home of the national government.

Washington, the military savior of his country, now became its political father, establishing many enduring institutions and practices. At fifty-seven years of age, he was a man of great personal dignity and influence. Instinctively cautious, the new president followed many administrative practices of the Confederation government. Washington asked Congress to reestablish existing executive departments—Foreign Affairs (State), Finance (Treasury), and War—but demanded that the president have administrative control of the bureaucracy. The chief executive also had the power to appoint major officials with the consent of the Senate, and Washington insisted on his authority to remove them at will. To head the Department of State, Washington chose Thomas Jefferson, a fellow Virginian and an experienced diplomat. For secretary of the treasury he turned to Alexander Hamilton, a lawyer and a wartime military aide. Washington designated Jefferson, Hamilton, and Secretary of War Henry Knox as his *cabinet*, or body of advisers.

Congress also set about implementing the Constitution. The new national charter created a Supreme Court but left it to Congress to establish the number and jurisdiction of the lower courts. In law as in politics, Federalists wanted national institutions to supersede state institutions and act directly on individual citizens. Consequently, in the Judiciary Act of 1789 they created a comprehensive and hierarchical federal system with thirteen district courts, one for each state, and three circuit courts to hear appeals from the district tribunals. As the Constitution specified, the Supreme Court had the final say. Moreover, the Judiciary Act permitted appeals to the Supreme Court on state court decisions that involved matters specified in the Constitution, ensuring that national judges would have the final say.

The Bill of Rights. The Federalists kept their promise to amend the Constitution to protect the liberties of citizens. Drawing on lists of rights in state constitutions, James Madison, now a member of the House of Representatives, submitted nineteen amendments to the first Congress after carefully weeding out most of those that would have weakened the national government. Ten amendments received legislative approval and were ratified by the states, eventually becoming known as the Bill of Rights. Most of these amendments guaranteed legal procedures such as the right to a jury trial and freedom from arbitrary arrest; others safeguarded sacred political rights such as freedom of speech and freedom of assembly. The Second Amendment guaranteed citizens the right to bear arms so that they might protect themselves, serve in the militia, and defend their liberties. The Tenth Amendment limited the potential authority of the national government by reserving nondelegated powers to the states or the people.

As a political maneuver, the Bill of Rights yielded immediate results, quieting the fears of many Antifederalists and enhancing the legitimacy of the Constitution of 1787. As a constitutional safeguard, the amendments have had a complex history. Like all constitutional clauses and ordinary laws, they have been subject to interpretation, which has changed with time and circumstance. Moreover, in 1833 the Supreme Court (in the case of *Barron v. Baltimore*) declared that the amendments safeguarded rights only from infringement by the national government; for protection from state authorities, citizens would have to rely on the state constitutions. Nearly a century later, in the 1920s, the national courts began to use the Fourteenth Amendment (1868) to protect the rights enumerated in the first ten amendments against violation by governments at every level—national, state, and local.

The ratification of the Bill of Rights completed the implementation of the Constitution. The president and the Congress had given definite form to the executive, legislative, and judicial departments, creating the intricate mechanism of "balanced" government envisioned by the Philadelphia convention. The Bill of Rights demanded by the Antifederalists ensured broad political support for the new national government.

The Political Crisis of the 1790s

Although the new Constitution was in place by 1790, the final decade of the century brought fresh political crises. The Federalists split into two irreconcilable factions in regard to financial policy, and the French Revolution caused rifts over political ideology. The wars sparked by the revolution in France (1793–1801) expanded American trade, bringing substantial profits to farmers and spectacular fortunes to merchants, but also divided American public opinion between pro-British Federalists and pro-French Republicans. Political conflict culminated in an undeclared naval war against France in the Atlantic and the repression of free speech at home.

Hamilton's Program

One of George Washington's most important decisions was his choice of Alexander Hamilton to be secretary of the treasury. Hamilton was an ambitious self-made man, the son of a Scottish merchant in the West Indies; he was raised by his mother, Rachel Faucett, after his father abandoned the family. The precocious child learned the ways of trade from his mother, who ran a small store, and was soon apprenticed to a prominent import-export firm. Hamilton moved to the mainland in 1772

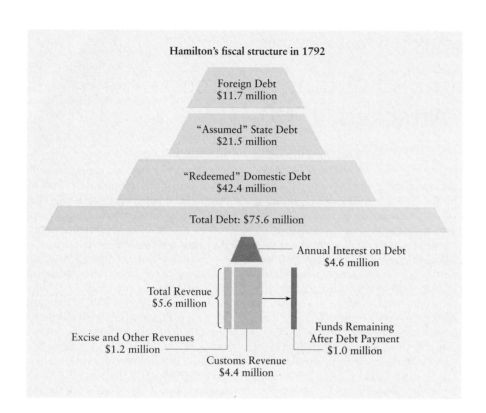

Hamilton's fiscal structure in 1792

Foreign Debt
$11.7 million

"Assumed" State Debt
$21.5 million

"Redeemed" Domestic Debt
$42.4 million

Total Debt: $75.6 million

Annual Interest on Debt
$4.6 million

Total Revenue
$5.6 million

Excise and Other Revenues
$1.2 million

Customs Revenue
$4.4 million

Funds Remaining
After Debt Payment
$1.0 million

FIGURE 7.2

Hamilton's Fiscal Structure, 1792
Hamilton used the revenue from excise taxes and customs duties to defray the annual interest on the national debt. Hamilton did not pay off the debt because he wanted to tie wealthy American bondholders to the new national government.

and enrolled at King's College in New York. His military abilities and personal charm impressed Washington, who chose him as a personal aide during the war. In the 1780s Hamilton married Elizabeth Schuyler, the daughter of a wealthy Hudson River landowner, and established close connections with the mercantile community, becoming one of the leading lawyers in New York City. At the Philadelphia convention he condemned the "amazing violence and turbulence of the democratic spirit" and called for an authoritarian government headed by a president with nearly monarchical powers. Although he left the convention early, Hamilton championed the new Constitution in *The Federalist.*

As treasury secretary, Hamilton devised innovative financial policies to overcome the fiscal problems that had bedeviled the Confederation (see Figure 7.2). Not surprisingly, his ambitious program favored men of his immediate acquaintance: financiers and seaport merchants. His recommendations took form in three major reports to Congress: on public credit (January 1790), on a national bank (December 1790), and on manufactures (December 1791).

Public Credit. The financial and social implications of Hamilton's "Report on the Public Credit" made it instantly controversial. The report asked Congress to redeem at face value the millions of dollars in securities issued by the Confederation government. Redeeming the debt in full would bolster the credit of the national

treasury but would also provide a windfall to speculators who had invested heavily in depreciated securities. For example, in one transaction the Burrell & Burrell merchant house of Boston had paid about $600 for Confederation notes with a face value of $2,500. If those notes were paid off in full, the firm would reap an enormous profit. Hamilton hoped that such windfalls, together with the strong credit of the new government, would induce financiers to continue in their role as public creditors. He proposed to redeem the old notes with new government securities, which would pay interest at about 4 percent. Creating a permanent debt would tie the interests of wealthy Americans to the new national government.

Hamilton's scheme reawakened fears of British monopolies and governmental corruption. Republican ideology warned that wealth—and the luxury that went with it—undermined public virtue, a particular concern among leaders in the southern agricultural states. "Money in a state of civilization is power," argued John Taylor of Virginia, who was wary of the rising wealth and power of the northern commercial elite. His thought might have been finished by Patrick Henry, who proclaimed on behalf of the Virginia assembly that "to erect, and concentrate, and perpetuate a large monied interest, must prove fatal to the existence of American liberty."

But Hamilton ignored those objections and advanced a second proposal that favored wealthy credi-

A Pennsylvania Farmer

Hamilton's Funding Scheme Attacked, 1790

Hamilton's plan to redeem at full value the remaining war debt of the Continental Congress roused widespread anger, for most of the money—which would be raised by import duties on goods like tea and sugar—would go to speculators, not to the soldiers and farmers who originally held the certificates.

In a former letter I took notice of the injuries which the proposed funding system will do the soldiers and other original holders of certificates, by compelling them to pay taxes in order to increase the value of certificates in the hands of quartermasters, speculators, and foreigners. The Secretary of the Treasury has declared that these people sold their certificates from choice. This I believe is true only in a few instances. A hungry creditor, a distressed family, or perhaps, in some instances, the want of a meals victuals, drove most of them to the brokers' offices, or compelled them to surrender up their certificates. . . .

This case I shall mention is of a sick soldier, who sold his certificates of £69.7.0 for £3.0.11 to a rich speculator. He went to this speculator after he recovered, and offered to redeem his certificate—but he refused to give it up. Now, can it be right that this poor soldier, every time he sips his bohea tea, or tastes a particle of sugar, should pay a tax to raise £3.0.11 to £67.7.0 in the hands of this speculator?

Thus we see public credit (that much hackneyed and prostituted phrase) must be established at the expense of national justice, gratitude, and humanity. . . .

Would it not be proper for the farmers to unite immediately, and remonstrate against all these evils? They never were in half the danger of being ruined by the British government that they now are by their own.

Had any person told them in the beginning of the war that, after paying the yearly rent of their farms for seven years to carry on this war, at the close of it their farms would only be worth one-fourth of their original cost and value, in consequence of a funding system—is there a farmer that would have embarked in the war? No, there is not. Why then should we be deceived, duped, defrauded, and ruined by our new rulers?

Source: Pennsylvania Gazette, February 3, 1790.

---

tors. He devised an *assumption* plan in which the national government would take on all the outstanding war debts of the states (see American Voices, above). This proposal unleashed a flurry of financial speculation and even an episode of governmental corruption. Before Hamilton announced the plan, Assistant Secretary of the Treasury William Duer used insider knowledge to buy up the depreciated bonds of the southern states. By the end of 1790 Duer and other northern speculators owned more than half the war bonds of Virginia and the Carolinas, selling them as their value rose.

Secretary of State Jefferson and other southern leaders condemned such shady dealings and the "corrupt squadron of paper dealers" who arranged them. Concerned members of Congress pointed out that some states, such as Virginia and Maryland, had already levied high taxes to pay off their war debts; now they would be taxed to pay the debts of other states as well, mostly for the benefit of rich northern speculators. To win support for assumption, Hamilton proposed to repay those states and struck a deal with members of Congress from Maryland and Virginia. He agreed to support their plan to locate the national capital (which the Constitution specified would consist of a special "district") along the banks of the Potomac. In return, they gave him the votes he needed to secure passage of his assumption plan in the House of Representatives.

This bargain only sharpened fears of Hamilton's plans. James Madison had questioned the morality of Hamilton's redemption and assumption proposals, since the financial rewards would go to the present holders of Confederation securities, not to the original owners—the thousands of shopkeepers, farmers, and soldiers who had accepted government certificates during the dark days of the war. Now Madison presented Congress with legislation that would give present holders only "the highest price which has prevailed in the market," with the remaining funds going to the original owners. His scheme, Madison argued, "will do more real justice . . . than any other expedient."

Madison's proposal was impractical because of the difficulty of identifying the original owners. Furthermore, nearly half the members of the House of Representatives were owners of Continental or Confederation securities and stood to profit from Hamilton's plans. Melding practicality with self-interest, the House defeated Madison's proposal by a solid margin of 36 to 13. Madison became an avowed opponent of Hamilton's economic program—and he was not alone. By way of protest, an angry citizen composed an ode, "On the Rejection of Mr. Madison's Motion":

> A soldier's pay are rags and fame,
> A wooden leg—a deathless name.
> To specs, both in and out of Cong.
> The four and six per cents belong.

The Bank of the United States. Hamilton outraged Madison again by asking Congress to charter a national financial institution, the Bank of the United States. The bank's stock would be owned by both private investors and the national government. The bank would make loans to merchants, handle government funds, and issue financial notes, thus providing a respected medium of exchange for the specie-starved American economy. These considerable benefits persuaded a majority of both houses to enact the bank bill and send it to President Washington for approval.

At this critical juncture Secretary of State Thomas Jefferson joined ranks with Madison against Hamilton. Jefferson believed that Hamilton's scheme for a national bank was unconstitutional. "The incorporation of a Bank," Jefferson told President Washington, was not "delegated to the United States by the Constitution." Adopting a *strict* interpretation of the national charter, Jefferson maintained that the central government had only the limited powers explicitly assigned to it in the document.

In response, Hamilton articulated a *loose* interpretation of the Constitution, noting that Article I, Section 8, empowered Congress to make "all Laws which shall be necessary and proper" to carry out the Constitution. In Hamilton's view, "if the *end* be clearly comprehended within any of the specified powers, and if the measure is not forbidden by any particular provision of the Constitution, it may safely be deemed to come within the compass of national authority." Washington agreed with Hamilton and signed the legislation creating the bank, which was to have its headquarters in Philadelphia.

The Report on Manufactures. As an advocate of an economically powerful nation, Hamilton had a vision of America as self-sufficient in manufactures. In 1790 he appointed Tench Coxe, the secretary of the Pennsylvania Manufacturing Society, as an assistant secretary of the treasury. With Coxe's aid, Hamilton prepared a "Report on Manufactures," which provided the first comprehensive survey of American manufacturing and, more important, presented a coherent rationale for an American mercantilist system. In the report Hamilton took issue with the view put forth by the Scottish economist Adam Smith in his influential treatise *The Wealth*

of Nations, which had been published the same year as the Declaration of Independence. Smith had condemned traditional state-directed mercantilist regulations, arguing that they subsidized inefficient producers and inhibited personal enterprise. Instead he had advocated a *laissez-faire* (leave alone) economy in which the demand for goods would determine their production and price. Following this logic, Smith suggested that the United States raise farm products—which it could do more cheaply than could European countries—and exchange them for foreign manufactures, which were less expensive than American products.

Hamilton disputed Smith's reasoning, pointing out that manufacturing costs were not fixed but could be lowered by technological innovation or public policy. If American manufacturers were given tariff protection or direct subsidies—what Hamilton called "the patronage of government"—they could compete with European producers. Yet Hamilton hesitated to impose high tariffs; instead, he joined with Coxe to create a private Society for Establishing Useful Manufactures, a venture that met with little success. Effective national support for manufacturing came only in the 1810s, with a new generation of politicians.

Factions and Taxes. As Washington began his second four-year term as president in 1793, Hamilton's financial measures split the national legislature into irreconcilable factions. Hamilton had formed political alliances in Congress to support his program; now Madison, joined by Jefferson, who resigned as secretary of state at the end of 1793, organized the opposition. "Mr. Madison, co-operating with Mr. Jefferson," Hamilton complained, "is at the head of a faction decidedly hostile to me . . . and subversive of good government." At first these groups divided along North-South lines. For example, northern congressmen had supported the Bank of the United States by a margin of 33 to 1, while southern representatives had opposed it by 19 to 6. By the elections of 1794 the factions had a more diverse makeup and had acquired names—Federalists supported Hamilton; Democratic-Republicans followed Madison and Jefferson.

Meanwhile, Hamilton pushed for the enactment of the final element of his financial system: a national revenue that would be used to pay interest charges on the permanent debt. At Hamilton's insistence, Congress imposed a variety of domestic excise taxes, including a duty on spirits, such as whiskey, distilled in the United States. It also revised the schedule of tariffs. In 1789 Congress had imposed a tax of 50 cents a ton on foreign ships entering American ports and a duty of 5 to 15 percent on the value of imported goods. Hamilton did not propose drastic increases—high "protective" tariffs that would exclude foreign goods—because that would have hurt his merchant allies and cut government revenues.

Technology and Republican Values

In 1805 the young American scientist Benjamin Silliman visited the industrial city of Manchester, England. Silliman was impressed by the great factories, "the wonder of the world and the pride of England," but disturbed by the condition of the workers—"at best an imbecile people," degraded by the conditions in which they lived and worked. "Heaps of dung, rubble from buildings, putrid, stagnant pools are found here and there among the houses, and a sort of black smoke covers the city," another visitor reported. "Under this half daylight 300,000 human beings are ceaselessly at work . . . the crunching wheels of machinery, the shriek of steam from boilers, the regular beat of the looms, the heavy rumble of the carts, these are the noises from which you can never escape."

Silliman contrasted this dismal scene of early industrialization with a peaceful image of rural America: "fields and forests, in which pure air . . . and simple manners, give vigour to the limbs, and a healthful aspect to the face." Were the wonders of British technology, he asked, worth "the physical and . . . moral evils which they produce?"

No American struggled harder with this question than Thomas Jefferson. "Those who labour in the earth are the chosen people of God," Jefferson wrote in his *Notes on the State of Virginia* (1785), and he remained committed to the moral superiority of a society of yeomen farm families. Yet Jefferson knew that "a people who are *entirely* dependent upon foreigners for food or clothes, must always be subject to them." Even before the Embargo of 1807 and the War of 1812 convinced him of the necessity of American manufacturing, Jefferson advocated the use of advanced technology. He introduced cast-iron plows and improved threshing machines on his plantation near Monticello, Virginia, and rotated crops in accordance with the latest scientific theory.

The household as factory

Jefferson championed manufacturing on the plantation as well. As early as 1796 he bought an iron-cutting machine to make nails and, by employing a dozen slave men, made 10,000 nails a day. By 1812 Jefferson had built two water-powered mills at another plantation and had equipped his Monticello slaves to manufacture textiles. He and other Americans, the former president boasted to a European friend, "have reduced the large and expensive machinery for most things to the compass of a private family. . . . I need 2,000 yards of linen, cotton and woolen yearly, to cloth my family [of slaves], which this machinery, costing $150 only, and worked by two women and two girls, will more than furnish."

Here, then, was Jefferson's way of avoiding the "dark Satanic mills" of Manchester. Each American household would become a small factory, using the labor

But he won Congressional approval for a modest increase in customs duties. As a result, customs revenue rose steadily, providing about 90 percent of the national government's income from 1790 to 1820 and ensuring the financial success of Hamilton's redemption and assumption programs.

Hamilton's design was now complete. His bold, if controversial, policies created a fiscally strong national government, protected the financial investments and commercial interests of the merchant class, and laid out a program for national economic development.

Jefferson's Vision

Few southern planters and western farmers shared Hamilton's view of the American future, and Thomas Jefferson spoke for them. A man of great learning as well as a politician and diplomat, Jefferson was well read in architecture, natural history, scientific farming, and political theory. Embracing the optimistic spirit of the Enlightenment, he declared his firm conviction in the "improvability of the human race." But progress was not inevitable, and Jefferson deplored both financial

of "women, children, and invalids" to enhance the prosperity and independence of American freehold farmers. For Jefferson, the key was democratic ownership of the means of agricultural and industrial production.

Jefferson's dream was noble and not at all unrealistic. The United States did become a nation of household producers between 1790 and 1820 (see Chapter 9). Hundreds of rural men made nails as a wintertime employment, thousands of farm women made butter and cheese for market sale, and tens of thousands of families worked in their homes manufacturing shoes, textiles, and other goods for merchant entrepreneurs. Particularly in the Northeast, the American countryside became a vast workshop.

Yet Jefferson's vision concealed important aspects of American rural life and was flawed by internal contradictions. Many families in the Northeast were driven to home manufacture by the threat of poverty; their subdivided farms yielded only a bare subsistence. The situation in the southern states was even more problematic. Was the enslaved labor that made Jefferson's nails and textiles more consonant with republican moral and economic principles than was the wage labor in Manchester factories? And over the long run, could household producers compete successfully with the water- and steam-driven factories owned by wealthy capitalists?

A candid observer must answer no to these questions. With his customary skill, Jefferson had identified the crucial issues: how the means of production should be owned and organized and who should benefit financially from the new technology. He was unable, however, to show how the technological advances and social conditions of his age could be made compatible with the republican value of liberty and the democratic ideal of equality. That question remains unresolved to this day.

An iron works, one of the "dark Satanic mills" of industrial England.

speculation and an urban industrial society. He had visited the manufacturing regions of Britain and had seen the masses of propertyless laborers there. He concluded that those workers, poor and dependent on wages, lacked the economic independence required to sustain a republican polity (see New Technology, above).

Jefferson's vision of the American future was more agrarian and more democratic. Although he had grown up as a privileged and well-educated slaveowner among the Virginia elite, he understood the values and needs of yeomen farmers and other ordinary white Americans.

In the Declaration of Independence Jefferson had proclaimed the primacy of "life, liberty, and the pursuit of happiness," and he gave form and substance to this vision in his *Notes on the State of Virginia* (1785). "Those who labor in the earth are the chosen people of God," he declared; independent yeomen farmers formed the very soul of the republic. When Jefferson drafted the Ordinance of 1784, he pictured a West settled by families who would produce bountiful harvests. Their grain and meat would feed European nations, who "would manufacture and send us in exchange our clothes and

Two Visions of America
Thomas Jefferson and Alexander Hamilton confront each other in these portraits, as they did during the 1790s. Jefferson was pro-French; Hamilton, pro-British. Jefferson favored farmers and artisans; Hamilton supported merchants and financiers. Jefferson believed in democracy and rule by legislative majorities; Hamilton argued for a strong executive and for judicial review.

other comforts." Jefferson hoped that westward expansion and foreign commerce would remedy two of the worst features of eighteenth-century agriculture—widespread tenancy in the South and subdivided farms in New England—while preserving its best features. He wanted to ban slavery from the territories (though he did not advocate abolishing it in the South) so that the American West would become a vigorous, incorruptible society of independent white yeomen farm families.

War and Politics

Events in Europe created opportunities for both Jeffersonian farmers and Hamiltonian merchants, pulling the United States out of the economic doldrums of the 1780s. The French Revolution began in 1789; four years later, the French republican government went to war against a British-led coalition of monarchical states. With the war disrupting European farming, wheat prices in Europe leapt from 5 to 8 shillings a bushel and remained at that level for twenty years. Farmers in the Chesapeake and the Middle Atlantic states capitalized on the situation, increasing their grain exports and reaping substantial profits.

Simultaneously, a boom in cotton exports revived the southern economy. Americans had expanded cotton production during the War of Independence so that they could make their own textiles. Subsequently, the mechanization of cloth production in Britain created a huge market for raw cotton. During the 1790s the invention of gins—machines that combed seeds from cotton fibers— cut costs dramatically (see Chapter 8). Soon the annual value of American cotton exports outstripped that of to-

bacco, the traditional southern export crop. As Jefferson had hoped, European markets brought high prices and prosperity to many American planters and farmers.

American merchants profited even more handsomely from the European war. President Washington issued a Proclamation of Neutrality enabling U.S. citizens to trade legally with the belligerents on both sides. As neutral carriers able to pass through the British naval blockade of the French coastline, American merchant ships took over the lucrative trade between France and its West Indian sugar islands. The American merchant fleet became one of the largest in the world, increasing from 355,000 tons in 1790 to more than 1.1 million tons in 1808. Commercial earnings rose spectacularly, averaging $20 million annually in the 1790s—twice the value of cotton and tobacco exports.

After two decades of stagnation American ports came alive. Shipowners invested part of their rising profits in new vessels, providing work for thousands of shipwrights, sail makers, laborers, and seamen. Hundreds of carpenters, masons, and cabinetmakers found work building warehouses and elegant Federal-style town houses for newly affluent merchants. New buildings went up in Philadelphia, a European visitor reported, "chiefly of red brick, and in general three stories high. A great number of private houses have marble steps to the street door, and in other respects are finished in a style of elegance." Real estate values jumped, reflecting the growth in population and wealth. During the 1790s the assessed value of property in New York City soared from $5.8 million to $20.7 million.

The French Revolution and America. Commerce with Europe engaged Americans with the differing political

Federalist Gentry
A prominent New England Federalist, Oliver Ellsworth served as Chief Justice of the United States (1796–1800); his wife, Abigail Wolcott Ellsworth, was the daughter of a Connecticut governor. In 1792 the artist Ralph Earl captured the aspirations of the Ellsworths by giving them an aristocratic demeanor and prominently displaying their mansion (in the window).

Urban Affluence
New York merchants built large town houses and furnished them with fine pieces of furniture. John Rubens Smith's painting *The Shop and Warehouse of Duncan Phyfe* illustrates the success of America's most skilled artisan entrepreneur. (Metropolitan Museum of Art)

ideologies and naval policies of the belligerents. Many Americans had welcomed the French Revolution of 1789 because it abolished the last vestiges of feudalism and established a constitutional monarchy. Yet the creation of the more democratic French republic in 1792 and the execution of King Louis XVI the next year divided public opinion in the United States.

On one side many American artisans praised the egalitarianism of the French republicans. In New York, they had King Street renamed Liberty Street; in Boston, Royal Alley became Equality Lane. More important, artisans founded Democratic-Republican clubs modeled on the radical Jacobin clubs in Paris. In Philadelphia Democratic-Republicans had a dinner to celebrate the beheading of Louis XVI; there, an observer reported, "the head of a roasted pig was severed from its body, and being recognized as an emblem of the murdered King of France, was carried round to the guests. Each one placing the cap of liberty on its head, pronounced the word 'tyrant'." Adopting French republican practice, many Americans began addressing each other as "citizen," a symbol of equality; some condemned Hamilton's economic policies as "aristocratic."

On the other side of this ideological controversy were men and women of wealth, conservative religious convictions, or Hamiltonian sympathies. They denounced the Terror—the executions of Louis XVI and his aristocratic supporters—and condemned the new French regime for abandoning Christianity in favor of a

Peter Porcupine (William Cobbett)

A Federalist Attacks French Republicanism

American Democratic-Republicans declared that "he who is an enemy to the French Revolution, cannot be a firm republican." In reply, William Cobbett, a British journalist who settled in Philadelphia and supported the Federalist party in caustic and very effective pamphlets, invokes the horrors of the Terror in France, during which hundreds of aristocrats and ordinary citizens were executed, warning Americans of the dangers of radical republicanism.

France is a *republic*, and the decrees of the Legislators were necessary to maintain it a republic. This *word* outweighs, in the estimation of some persons (I wish I could say they were few in number), all the horrors that have been and that can be committed in that country. One of these modern republicans will tell you that he does not deny that hundreds of thousands of innocent persons have been murdered in France; that the people have neither religion nor morals; that all the ties of nature are rent asunder; . . . that its riches, along with millions of the best of the people, are gone to enrich and aggrandize its enemies; that its commerce, its manufactures, its sciences,

its arts, and its honour, are no more; but at the end of all this, he will tell you that it must be happy, because it is a *republic*. I have heard more than one of these republican zealots declare, that he would sooner see the last of the French exterminated, than see them adopt any other form of government. Such a sentiment is characteristic of a mind locked up in a savage ignorance.

Shall we say that these things never can take place among us? . . . We are not what we were before the French revolution. Political projectors from every corner of Europe, troublers of society of every description, from the whining philosophical hypocrite to the daring rebel, and more daring blasphemer, have taken shelter in these States.

We have seen the *guillotine* toasted to three times three cheers. . . . And what would the reader say, were I to tell him of a Member of Congress, who wished to see one of these murderous machines employed for lopping off the heads of the French, permanent in the State-house yard of the city of Philadelphia?

If these men of blood had succeeded in plunging us into a war; if

they had once got the sword into their hands, they would have mowed us down like stubble. The word *Aristocrat* would have been employed to as good account here, as ever it had been in France. We might, ere this, have seen our places of worship turned into stables; we might have seen the banks of the Delaware, like those of the Loire, covered with human carcasses, and its waters tinged with blood: ere this we might have seen our parents butchered, and even the head of our admired and beloved President rolling on a scaffold.

I know the reader will start back with horror. His heart will tell him that it is impossible. But, once more, let him look at the example before us. The attacks on the character and conduct of the aged *Washington*, have been as bold, if not bolder, than those which led to the downfall of the unfortunate French Monarch. Can it then be imagined, that, had they possessed the power, they wanted the will to dip their hands in his blood?

Source: William Cobbett, *Peter Porcupine in America*, ed. by David A. Wilson (Ithaca: Cornell University Press, 1994), 150–154.

new religion of reason (see American Voices, above). American politics was soon dominated by the passions of the French Revolution, with admirers of the French republic toasting the diplomat Edmond Genêt and advocating war against Britain. Federalists accused Genêt of violating Washington's Proclamation of Neutrality and persuaded the president to demand his recall. In 1794 the Federalist-dominated Congress passed a Neutrality Act that prohibited American citizens from fighting in the war and barred the belligerents' naval vessels from American ports.

The Whiskey Rebellion. Meanwhile, a domestic issue sparked violence in western Pennsylvania. In 1792 farmers began protesting against Hamilton's excise tax on spirits. The tax had raised the price—and thus cut

the demand—for the corn whiskey the farmers sold locally and bartered for eastern manufactures. As resistance grew, an extralegal assembly in Pittsburgh challenged the constitutionality of the tax. Like the Patriots of 1765 and the Shaysites of 1785, the Whiskey rebels attacked tax collectors and challenged the authority of a distant government. Only now they waved banners proclaiming the French revolutionary slogan "Liberty, Equality, and Fraternity!"

The ideology of the French Revolution had sharpened the debate over Hamilton's economic policies and helped justify domestic rebellion. To uphold national authority (and deter secessionist movements along the frontier, where he owned extensive property), President Washington raised an army of 15,000 troops and suppressed the rebels.

GENERAL GEORGE WASHINGTON.
Reviewing the Western army at Fort Cumberland the 18th of October 1794

Jay's Treaty. Britain's maritime strategy widened the growing political divisions in the United States. In November 1793 the Royal Navy began seizing American ships bound for France from the West Indies. In six months the British took more than 250 vessels and confiscated their cargoes of sugar as contraband, invoking the so-called Rule of 1756. (This British legal doctrine restricted the commerce of neutral states during wartime to the amount conducted during peacetime.) Federalist merchants denied that the rule was an accepted principle of international law, but their claims usually were rejected by British admiralty courts. Yet the merchants did not demand retaliation, fearing that a war against Great Britain would throw the United States into the arms of radical French republicans, destroy the American merchant fleet, and undermine Hamilton's system of public finance.

To avert war, President Washington sent John Jay to negotiate with Britain. Jay returned with a comprehensive treaty that addressed the maritime issues as well as territorial and financial disputes dating back to the War of Independence. Jay's Treaty required the United States to make "full and complete compensation" to British merchants for all prewar debts owed by American citizens. It also acknowledged Britain's right to remove French property from neutral ships, thus relinquishing the American merchants' claim that "free ships make free goods." In return, the treaty allowed American merchants to submit claims of illegal seizures to an arbitration tribunal, ended British aid to western Indians,

and mandated the withdrawal of British military garrisons from six forts in the American Northwest.

Jefferson and his Democratic-Republican followers denounced Jay's Treaty as too conciliatory and tried to prevent its ratification. The Senate did ratify the treaty in June 1795, but only by a vote of 20 to 10, barely winning the two-thirds majority required by the Constitution. This outcome reaffirmed the government's diplomatic position. As long as Hamilton and his Federalist allies were in power, the United States would have a pro-British foreign policy.

The Rise of Parties

Political conflicts over foreign affairs, taxes and tariffs, and fiscal policy spurred the appearance of rival political parties during the presidential election of 1796. Indeed, the election marked a new stage in American politics as candidates for local, state, and national office were elected not as individuals but as representatives of parties that stood for political principles. To prepare for the election, the Federalists and Democratic-Republicans (who were now known simply as Republicans) called legislative caucuses in Congress and in the states. The members of those informal conventions discussed policies, nominated candidates, and mobilized support among the voters.

Parties were a new phenomenon. Colonial legislatures had often divided into factions based on family alliances, ethnicity, or regional concerns, but those groups were poorly organized and usually temporary. The new state and national constitutions made no provision for parties because their authors assumed that representative institutions adequately expressed the will of the people. As president, Washington had tried to stand above parties, but his continuing support for Hamilton's policies exposed him to partisan attack and influenced his decision not to seek a third term. Jefferson too believed that parties were unnecessary and dangerous. Only Madison accepted the inevitability of political parties, and even he assumed that they would be temporary coalitions that would form around a specific issue and then disappear.

Born into a world of deferential politics, these leaders underestimated the impact of the revolutionary ideology of popular sovereignty. A politically active citizenry laid the basis for a competitive party system. Once political parties appeared, they attracted the long-term allegiance of regional or occupational groups. Merchants and creditors in the northeastern states supported the Federalist party, as did wheat-exporting slaveholders in the Tidewater districts of the Chesapeake states. The Republican coalition was more diverse. By the mid-1790s it included mechanics and artisans in seaport cities, southern tobacco planters, German and Scots-Irish settlers, and subsistence farmers throughout the country. Republican policies appealed to a wider range of social groups, but the Federalists' prestige, wealth, and experience made them a potent political force.

In 1796, in an election dominated by conflict over ideology and foreign policy, Federalist candidates triumphed, winning a majority in Congress and in the electoral college. The electors chose John Adams as president. When some Federalist electors refused to vote for Adams's choice for vice-president, Thomas Pinckney of South Carolina (offended by a treaty he had negotiated with Spain), Thomas Jefferson, the Republican candidate for president, won the second highest number of electoral votes and, as stipulated in the Constitution, became vice-president. Thus the nation had a divided administration.

As chief executive, John Adams upheld the Federalists' pro-British foreign policy. He condemned French seizures of American merchant ships and accused France of meddling in the American domestic affairs. When three agents of Prince Talleyrand, the French foreign minister, solicited a loan and a bribe from American diplomats, Adams urged Congress to prepare for war. To overcome Republican objections, he charged that Talleyrand's agents, whom he dubbed X, Y, and Z, had insulted the honor of the United States. The Federalist-controlled Congress cut off trade with France and authorized American privateers to seize French ships. Between 1798 and 1800 the United States became an unofficial ally of Great Britain—a monarchy and its recent enemy—and fought an undeclared war against France, a republic and its major supporter during the War of Independence.

The Crisis of 1798–1800

The Alien and Sedition Acts. For the first—but not the last—time in American history, a controversial foreign war prompted domestic protest and governmental repression. Pro-French immigrants from Ireland viciously attacked Adams's foreign policy in newspapers and pamphlets. To silence them, in 1798 the administration enacted an Alien Act that authorized the deportation of foreigners. A few Federalist supporters favored even harsher treatment. "Were I president, I would hang them for otherwise they would murder me," declared a Philadelphia pamphleteer. To allay such exaggerated concerns, the administration passed a Naturalization Act, which increased the residence requirement for citizenship from five to fourteen years. Also in 1798, the Federalist Congress enacted a harsh Sedition Act, prohibiting the publication of ungrounded or malicious attacks against the president or Congress. "He that is not for us is against us," thundered the Federalist *Gazette of*

An Anti-French Cartoon
A five-headed monster, representing the leaders of France under the Directory, demands a bribe ("Money, Money, Money") from American diplomats. Federalists used the incident, named the XYZ affair for the three anonymous French agents who asked for the bribe, to whip up anti-French sentiment in the United States and launch an undeclared naval war.

the United States. Using the legal powers of the new act, Federalist prosecutors arrested more than twenty Republican newspaper editors and politicians, charged them with sedition, and sent some of them to prison.

Republicans assailed the Sedition Act as contrary to the Bill of Rights. Because the First Amendment to the Constitution prohibits the national government from "abridging the freedom of speech, or of the press," the Sedition Act was probably unconstitutional. But Republican leaders did not turn to the Supreme Court for redress. The Court's powers were still vague, particularly with regard to the "judicial review" of Congressional legislation. Besides, the Court was an appointed body packed with Federalists, who would probably have upheld the Sedition Act.

Madison and Jefferson instead took the fight to elected bodies—the state legislatures not dominated by Federalists. In November 1798 the legislature of Kentucky—the first western territory to become a state, in 1792—passed a resolution declaring the Alien and Sedition Acts to be "unauthoritative, void, and of no force." More important, the resolution asserted that the national government owed its existence to a compact among the states, which meant that "each party has an equal right to judge by itself." The Virginia resolution similarly claimed that the states had the right to refuse to enforce federal laws that exceeded the powers granted by the Constitution. The Kentucky and Virginia resolutions thus laid the theoretical basis for subsequent "states' rights" interpretations of the Constitution.

In 1798, as in the ratification conventions in 1788, Federalist assertions of national authority provoked a debate over the nature of the Union. Even Madison—the architect of the Constitution—had second thoughts and argued that the national government had resulted from a compact among the states. In the heat of partisan conflict Jefferson also experienced ideological conversion; once opposed in principle to political parties, he now endorsed them as valuable "to watch and relate to the people" the activities of the government.

The Election of 1800. The debate over the Sedition Act set the stage for the election of 1800. Republicans supported Jefferson's bid for the presidency by pointing to the wrongful imprisonment of newspaper editors and championing the rights of the states. President Adams responded to these attacks by reevaluating his foreign policy. Adams was a complicated man, often vain, easily offended, dogmatic, but possessed of great personal strength and determination. He showed his quality as a statesman by rejecting the advice of Hamilton and other Federalist leaders to intensify the undeclared war with France and benefit politically from nationalistic fervor. Instead, he entered into diplomatic negotiations that brought the war to an end.

Federalists attempted to win the election by depicting Jefferson as an irresponsible pro-French radical—"the archapostle of irreligion and free thought"—but they were unsuccessful. The Republicans won a resounding victory. Voters had registered their protest against a foreign war—and a special national tax on land and houses levied in 1798 to pay for it—by giving Republicans a majority in both houses of Congress and a narrow edge in the electoral college. The electors, however, gave Jefferson and Aaron Burr of New York (Jefferson's choice for vice-president) the same number of votes for the office of president. In the event of such a tie, the Constitution specified that the House of Representatives would select the president, with each state having one vote to cast. (The Twelfth Amendment, ratified in 1804, remedied this constitutional defect by requiring the electors to cast separate ballots for president and vice-president.)

Alexander Hamilton played a crucial role in the drama that followed. For thirty-five ballots Federalists in the House of Representatives blocked Jefferson's election. Then the former treasury secretary intervened. Calling Burr an "embryo Caesar" and the "most unfit man in the United States for the office of president," Hamilton persuaded key Federalists to permit the selection of Jefferson, his longtime rival. The Federalists' concern for political stability also played a role. As Senator James Bayard of Delaware explained, "It was admitted on all hands that we must risk the Constitution and a Civil War or take Mr. Jefferson."

Jefferson called the election the "Revolution of 1800," and so it was. It signaled the twilight of Federalism and its aristocratic outlook and the dawn of a more democratic era. The election also testified to the strength of the American experiment in self-government. Federalists had attacked Republicans as social radicals, traitors, and atheists for nearly a decade, with all sincerity, yet they peacefully relinquished power to their enemies. This bloodless transfer of power was genuinely revolutionary. It demonstrated that governments elected by the people could be changed by the people in an orderly, civilized way even in times of bitter partisan conflict. In his inaugural address in 1801 Jefferson referred to this achievement, declaring: "We are all Republicans, we are all Federalists." He called on Americans to temper the "will of the majority" with respect for the rights of those in the minority, "which equal laws must protect, and to violate would be oppression."

Over the course of a quarter century Jefferson had remained true to his principles. In 1801, as in the Declaration of Independence of 1776, he defined the American republic as a government based on both majority rule and minority rights, with laws that treated citizens equally and respected their liberty.

Summary

The state constitutions of 1776–1780 created new institutions of republican government. Most had property qualifications for voting and a separation of powers that inhibited popular rule. The Pennsylvania and Vermont constitutions were more democratic, with broad voting rights for men and a powerful one-house legislature. For a time New Jersey permitted women with property to vote, but most women continued to be excluded from the political sphere. A few women asserted claims of intellectual and social equality and sought greater legal rights, mostly without success. On the national level the government created by the Articles of Confederation began the orderly settlement of the trans-Appalachian West, but it lacked the authority to regulate foreign trade or raise enough revenue to pay off wartime debts. Power remained with the states, where clashes over financial policy culminated in Shays's Rebellion, an uprising of indebted farmers in western Massachusetts.

The perceived weaknesses of the Confederation led nationalists and creditors to convene a constitutional convention in Philadelphia in 1787. The delegates devised a new constitution that derived its authority not from the states but directly from the people, who were represented in the lower house of the legislature. They also created a strong national government with the power to levy taxes, issue money, and control trade. Its legislation was to be the supreme law of the land. In several important states the Constitution was ratified by only narrow margins because it diminished the sovereignty of the states and seemed to provide for a potentially oppressive central government immune from popular control.

George Washington was elected as the first president under the new government and, along with the first Congress, established the executive and judicial departments. The economic policies of Washington's secretary of the treasury, Alexander Hamilton, favored northern merchants and financiers. To oppose them, Thomas Jefferson and James Madison organized farmers, planters, and artisans into the Democratic-Republican party. The French Revolution and naval warfare led to bitter ideological struggles and, during an undeclared war with France, to political repression in the form of the Alien and Sedition Acts of 1798. The peaceful transfer of power to Jefferson and the Democratic-Republicans in 1800 ended a decade of political strife.

TIMELINE

1776	Declaration of Independence Pennsylvania's democratic constitution John Adams, *Thoughts on Government*
1777	Articles of Confederation (ratified 1781) New York's conservative constitution
1779	Judith Sargent Murray, "On the Equality of the Sexes"
1780	Postwar commercial recession Burdensome debts and creditor-debtor conflicts in states
1781	Robert Morris superintendent of finance Bank of North America Rhode Island vetoes national import duty
1784	Ordinance outlines policy for new states
1785	Land Ordinance sets up survey system Jefferson's *Notes on the State of Virginia*
1786	Annapolis commercial convention Shays's Rebellion
1787	Northwest Ordinance Philadelphia convention Madison's "nationalist" Virginia Plan
1788–1789	Ratification conventions *The Federalist* (Jay, Madison, Hamilton)
1789	George Washington becomes first president Judiciary Act establishes federal court system Outbreak of French Revolution National tariff; aid to American shipping
1790s	Boom in wheat and cotton exports Expansion of American commerce
1790	Alexander Hamilton's program: redemption and assumption
1791	Bill of Rights ratified
1792	Debate over Bank of United States Mary Wollstonecraft, *A Vindication of the Rights of Woman* First French Republic declared; Louis XVI executed (1793)
1793	Democratic-Republican party founded War between Britain and France Washington's Proclamation of Neutrality
1794	Whiskey Rebellion
1795	Jay's Treaty
1796	John Adams elected president
1797	XYZ Affair
1798	Undeclared war against France Alien, Sedition, and Naturalization acts Kentucky and Virginia resolutions
1800	Jefferson elected in "Revolution of 1800"

★   ★   ★

BIBLIOGRAPHY

Richard B. Bernstein and Kym S. Rice, *Are We to Be a Nation? The Making of the Constitution* (1987), provides a general discussion of constitution making, whereas Stanley Elkins and Eric McKitrick, *The Age of Federalism: The Early Republic, 1788–1800* (1993), offers a comprehensive assessment.

Creating New Institutions

Elisha P. Douglass, *Rebels and Democrats* (1965), documents the struggle for equal political rights. See also Jackson T. Main, *The Sovereign States, 1775–1783* (1973), and Ronald L. Hoffman and Peter Albert, eds., *Sovereign States in an Age of Uncertainty* (1981). Important studies of state constitutions include Willi Paul Adams, *The First American Constitutions* (1980); Edward Countryman, *A People in Revolution: The American Revolution and Political Society in New York, 1760–1790* (1981); and Donald Lutz, *Popular Consent and Popular Control: Whig Political Theory in the Early State Constitutions* (1980).

On women and republicanism, see Linda K. Kerber, *Women of the Republic: Intellect and Ideology in Revolutionary America* (1980), and Ronald Hoffman and Peter Albert, eds., *Women in the Age of the American Revolution* (1989). Fine in-depth studies include Rosemarie Zagarri, *A Woman's Dilemma: Mercy Otis Warren and the American Revolution* (1995); Judith Sargent Murray, *The Gleaner*, ed. by Nina Baym (1992); and Edith B. Gelles, *Portia: The World of Abigail Adams* (1992).

Gordon Wood, *The Creation of the American Republic, 1776–1790* (1965), links state and national constitutional development. It should be supplemented by Merrill Jensen's two classic studies, *The Articles of Confederation, 1774–1781* (1940) and *The New Nation, 1781–1789* (1950). Other important works on the 1780s include Peter S. Onuf, *The Origins of the Federal Republic: Jurisdictional Controversies in the United States, 1775–1787* (1983); Roger H. Brown, *Redeeming the Republic: Federalists, Taxation, and the Origins of the Constitution* (1993); Richard B. Morris, *The Forging of the Union, 1781–1789* (1987); and Robert A. Gross, ed., *In Debt to Shays: The Bicentennial of an Agrarian Rebellion* (1993).

The Constitution of 1787

In 1913 two studies initiated the modern analysis of the Constitution: Charles A. Beard, *An Economic Interpretation of the Constitution of the United States*, and Max Farrand, *The Framing of the Constitution*. For critiques of Beard's work, see Leonard Levy, ed., *Essays on the Making of the Constitution* (rev. ed., 1987); a recent narrative similar to that of Farrand is Christopher Collier and James L. Collier, *Decision in Philadelphia* (1987).

Other important works include Forrest McDonald, *Novus Ordo Seculorum: The Intellectual Origins of the Constitution* (1985); Edmund S. Morgan, *Inventing the People: The Rise of Popular Sovereignty in England and America* (1988); and Michael Kammen, *A Machine That Would Go by Itself: The Constitution in American Culture* (1986). Three fine collections of essays are Richard R. Beeman et al., eds., *Beyond Confederation: Origins of the Constitution and*

American National Identity (1987); Ellen Frankel Paul and Howard Dickman, eds., *Liberty, Property and the Foundations of the American Constitution* (1989); and Herman Belz et al., eds., *To Form a More Perfect Union: The Critical Ideas of the Constitution* (1992).

On the Antifederalists and ratification, see Patrick T. Conley and John P. Kaminski, eds., *The Constitution and the States* (1988); Stephen L. Schechter, *The Reluctant Pillar: New York and the Adoption of the Federal Constitution* (1985); and Herbert Storing, *The Antifederalists* (1985). Two recent studies of the Federalist papers are David F. Epstein, *The Political Theory of "The Federalist"* (1984), and Charles R. Kesler, ed., *Saving the Revolution: "The Federalist Papers" and the American Founding* (1987).

R. A. Rutland, *The Birth of the Bill of Rights, 1776–1791* (rev. ed., 1983), offers the basic narrative; more analytic treatments include Michael J. Lacey and Knud Haakonssen, *A Culture of Rights* (1991); David J. Bodenhemer and James W. Ely, Jr., *The Bill of Rights in Modern America* (1993); and Joyce Lee Malcolm, *To Keep and Bear Arms: The Origins of an Anglo-American Right* (1993).

The Political Crisis of the 1790s

A good synthesis is James Rogers Sharp, *American Politics in the Early Republic: The New Nation in Crisis* (1993). Studies of important statesmen include Forrest McDonald, *Alexander Hamilton: A Biography* (1979), and James T. Flexner, *George Washington and the New Nation, 1783–1793* (1970) and *George Washington: Anguish and Farewell, 1793–1799* (1972). For Jeffersonian ideology, see Joyce Appleby, *Capitalism and a New Social Order: The Republican Vision of the 1790s* (1984); Drew McCoy, *The Elusive Republic: Political Economy in Jeffersonian America* (1982); and Lance Banning, *The Jeffersonian Persuasion: The Evolution of a Party Ideology* (1978).

Richard Hofstadter, *The Idea of a Party System: The Rise of Legitimate Opposition in the United States, 1790–1840* (1969), offers an overview of the subject; also see William Nisbet Chambers, *Political Parties in the New Nation: The American Experience* (1963), and John F. Hoadley, *Origins of American Political Parties, 1789–1803* (1986). More detailed studies are Thomas P. Slaughter, *The Whiskey Rebellion* (1986), and Richard J. Twomey, *Jacobins and Jeffersonians* (1989). On diplomatic and military history, consult Henry Ammon, *The Genêt Mission* (1973); Jerald A. Combs, *The Jay Treaty* (1970); Richard H. Kohn, *Eagle and Sword: The Federalists and the Creation of the Military Establishment in America, 1783–1802* (1975); and Lawrence D. Cress, *Citizens in Arms: The Army and the Military to the War of 1812* (1982).

On Adams's administration, see Ralph Brown Adams, *The Presidency of John Adams* (1975), and Stephen G. Kurtz, *The Presidency of John Adams: The Collapse of Federalism, 1795–1800* (1957). More specialized studies are William Sinchcombe, *The XYZ Affair* (1980), and Leonard Levy, *The Emergence of a Free Press* (1985).

Good state histories include Patricia Watlington, *The Partisan Spirit: Kentucky Politics, 1779–1792* (1972); Richard R. Beeman, *The Old Dominion and the New Nation, 1788–1801* (1972); and Mary K. Bonsteel Tachau, *Federal Courts in the Early Republic: Kentucky, 1789–1816* (1978).

Settlers Move West through Pennsylvania (detail)

Thomas Birch captured the spirit of families moving to
the West to clear and farm the land in his 1816 painting
Conestoga Wagon on the Pennsylvania Turnpike.

Toward a Continental Nation

1790–1820

★ ★ ★

When they declared independence in 1776, the thirteen colonies were confined to a narrow strip of land along the Atlantic seaboard. But in 1783 Britain surrendered its claim not only to those settled areas but also to vast stretches of the North American interior, more than tripling the size of the new United States. The land beyond the Appalachians was mostly forested, dotted with French and British forts and fur-trading posts and peopled by tens of thousands of native Americans. Yet within fifty years all this would change. White Americans would drive the Indians toward the Mississippi River, found new communities in the trans-Appalachian region, and build turnpikes and canals to tie them to eastern markets.

Even before this process was well begun, President Thomas Jefferson doubled the size of the nation. The Louisiana Purchase added most of the lands between the Mississippi River and the Rocky Mountains. To assert control over the western lands and resolve maritime conflicts, the United States embarked on a new war with Britain. Before the War of 1812 was over, Indians in the trans-Appalachian region rose in revolt and eastern Federalists threatened secession from the Union. Only a surprising victory at the Battle of New Orleans preserved the honor of the United States.

Regional differences within the new nation determined the course of the war and of subsequent cultural developments. Traditional institutions shaped life in the various seaboard societies, and westward-moving migrants transplanted many customs, re-creating a yeoman farm society in the Old Northwest and a plantation economy based on slave-produced cotton in the Old Southwest. Migration to the West had a particularly disruptive impact on African-Americans, destroying well-established communities and kinship groups, and on native Americans, forcing tens of thousands of

Indians from their ancestral lands. It also ignited new diplomatic conflicts with Spain, which was trying to create a North American empire stretching from Florida to California. With the settlement of the trans-Appalachian West and the exploration of the trans-Mississippi region, a new "continental" phase of American history had begun.

Westward Expansion

Between 1776 and 1790 the combined white and black population of the United States had grown from 2.5 million to 3.9 million people, but only 200,000 Americans lived west of the Appalachian Mountains. During the next thirty years the geographical dimensions of the United States multiplied along with the population. By 1820 there were 9.6 million white and black Americans, and 2 million of them—a number almost as high as the total population in 1776—inhabited nine new states and three territories west of the Appalachians.

Native American Resistance

The American War of Independence was an unmitigated disaster for most native American peoples. Although

most Indians had fought on the Loyalist side, British negotiators failed to protect their lands or independence at the Paris peace conference. As one British statesman put it, the Indian nations were "remitted to the care of their neighbours." That care was far from benevolent. The new American republic asserted its ownership of all Indian lands west of the Appalachians both by right of conquest and by the terms of the Paris treaty of 1783. Native Americans refused to honor this claim, pointing out that they had not signed the treaty and had never been conquered.

The Confederation Congress brushed aside those arguments. In 1784 it dispatched commissioners to meet with representatives of the four pro-British Iroquois tribes—the Mohawk, Onondaga, Cayuga, and Seneca—and insist that they accept the treaty. The commissioners got their way by threatening to use military force. In the second Treaty of Fort Stanwix, signed in October 1784, the Iroquois relinquished most Seneca land in Pennsylvania and western New York and gave away territories they claimed in Ohio but hadn't controlled for a generation. That was just a taste of what was to follow. Pennsylvania officials coerced the Iroquois into surrendering more territory, as did Governor George Clinton of New York. Freely dispensing liquor, manufactured goods, and bribes, New York officials and land speculators secured new treaties that gave them title to millions of acres of Indian land in central

Treaty Negotiations at Greenville
In 1785 the Shawnee, Chippewyan, Ottawa, Miami, and other tribes formed the Western Confederacy to stop white settlement at the Ohio River. The American victory at the Battle of Fallen Timbers (1794) opened up the region, but the Treaty of Greenville (1795) recognized many Indian rights.

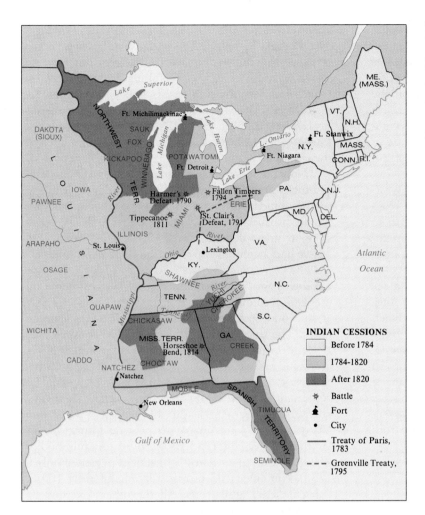

MAP 8.1

Expansion: Military and Diplomatic
The United States claimed sovereignty over the entire trans-Appalachian West by right of conquest of Britain. When the tribes of the Western Confederacy contested this claim, the American government upheld it by force, sending armies into the West during the 1790s and the War of 1812. During the 1820s and 1830s this armed diplomacy forced native American peoples to cede by treaty most of their lands east of the Mississippi River.

and western New York. By 1800 the once-powerful Iroquois peoples were confined to relatively small reservations. Even the Oneida and Tuscarora, who had supported the Patriot cause, lost most of their lands.

The American commissioners used similar tactics to extract agreements from tribes farther to the west. In 1785 the Chipewyan, Delaware, Ottawa, and Wyandot signed away most of the future state of Ohio, but they later repudiated the agreements, claiming—justifiably—that the treaties had been signed under duress. Soon those peoples, along with the Miami, Shawnee, and Potawatomi, formed a Western Confederacy to defend their lands and lives from aggressive settlers from Kentucky. Led by Little Turtle, they defeated an American expeditionary force commanded by General Josiah Hamar in 1790 and in 1791 crushed General Arthur St. Clair's army, killing 600 soldiers at the cost of only twenty-one Indian lives.

The American government's aggressive stance toward the Indians divided political opinion. Eastern critics charged that using force against native Americans

was immoral and warned that a "standing" army also could be used to suppress domestic political dissent. Westerners worried that an army would not only fight Indians but also impose national authority over settlers and squatters. Yet a majority in Congress feared an alliance between the Western Confederacy and the British in Canada and therefore supported President Washington's decision to double the army to 5,000 men. Washington chose General "Mad Anthony" Wayne to lead the western army. In August 1794 Wayne defeated the Indian allies in the Battle of Fallen Timbers (near what is present-day Toledo, Ohio).

Despite Wayne's victory, the Western Confederacy remained strong, forcing the American negotiators to compromise (see Map 8.1). In the Treaty of Greenville (Ohio) in 1795, the United States acknowledged Indian ownership of the trans-Appalachian West, renouncing a claim to the land that had been based on the right of conquest. The treaty, however, required native Americans to cede the southeastern corner of the Northwest Territory as well as certain strategic areas on the Great

Lakes, including Detroit and the future site of Chicago, and to acknowledge American sovereignty over the entire region. The Indians agreed to place themselves "under the protection of the United States, and no other Power whatever." This agreement had great diplomatic significance, for it prevented an Indian alliance with Britain and increased the likelihood that Britain would comply with its obligation (reaffirmed in Jay's Treaty of 1795) to withdraw its military garrisons from American territory in the West.

As the fighting ended, white families moved westward. Ohio entered the Union in 1803 and two years later had more than 100,000 residents, many of them clamoring for fertile Indian lands. Thousands more migrants moved into Indiana and Illinois, sparking conflicts with the native peoples over hunting rights. As the Delaware put it, "The Elks are our horses, the buffaloes are our cows, the deer are our sheep, & the whites shan't have them." To meet the Americans' land hunger, William Henry Harrison, governor of the Indiana Territory, used threats, bribes, and deceit to purchase millions of acres. State officials and land speculators in Georgia, Tennessee, and the Mississippi Territory made similar deals with other Indian nations. All along the western frontier the remorseless advance of white settlement threatened native Americans with eviction from their ancestral lands.

Settlers and Speculators

From the North and the South, migrants poured across the Appalachians. Settlers heading for Kentucky and Tennessee came from the Chesapeake region; they were primarily white tenant farmers, poor yeomen, and young couples. Fleeing the depleted soils and planter elite of the Tidewater region, these migrants—no fewer than 225,000 between 1790 and 1810—sought freedom and fertile land. Landlords tried to stop this massive loss of farm labor. A worried planter warned readers of the Maryland *Gazette* that "boundless settlements open a door for our citizens to run off and leave us, depreciating all our landed property and disabling us from paying taxes." But the exodus continued.

Land Conflict in Kentucky. Having defied their planter landlords, migrants who moved through the Cumberland Gap into the Kentucky territory had to battle Virginia authorities and land speculators. Basing their claims on "the ancient cultivation law" governing frontier tracts, an assembly of migrants asked the Virginia government, which administered the territory, to confirm their "Preoccupancy" (squatter's) titles. They invoked the argument of Hermon Husband, leader of the North Carolina Regulators (see Chapter 4), that the poor had a customary right "from time out of Mind" to occupy "back waste vacant Lands" sufficient "to pro-

vide a subsistence for themselves and their posterity." The Virginia legislature responded by allowing "actual settlers" to purchase up to 1,400 acres but then bestowed handsome grants averaging 100,000 acres on twenty-one wealthy individuals and partnerships. The result was predictable. When Kentucky became a state in 1792, a handful of speculators held title to one-fourth of the entire state, while half the adult white men owned no land and lived as squatters or tenants.

Nonetheless, thousands of new settlers flocked into Kentucky and along the Knoxville Road into Tennessee (which joined the Union in 1796), confident that they would prosper by growing cotton and hemp, which were in great demand. By 1820 Kentucky and Tennessee had a combined population of nearly a million.

Exodus from New England. A northern wave of migrants flowed out of New England into New York State and beyond, seeking to plant new yeomen farm communities. The quest for land had already propelled New England farmers north into New Hampshire and Vermont and east along the coast of Maine. Now, after two centuries of population growth, many New England communities were crowded with small subdivided farms, their rocky soils on the verge of exhaustion. Many parents were unable to provide farmsteads for the four or five children who survived to adulthood. In 1796, for example, Kent, Connecticut (founded only in 1738), contained 103 farmsteads inhabited by 100 fathers and 109 adult sons. All the other sons and the daughters who had not married local men had moved away, mostly to the West.

The lands of New York beckoned. In 1796 ten Kent families moved toward the Hudson River to Amenia, New York. By selling their small but well-established farms in Kent for $20 to $30 per acre, they were able to buy enough uncultivated land—at $2 to $3 per acre—to provide farmsteads for all their children. Hundreds and then thousands of farm families followed their example. They hitched their oxen and horses to wagons and carried tools, plows, and household goods into the plains and rolling hills of upstate New York. By 1820, 800,000 migrants were living in a string of settlements stretching from Albany to Buffalo. Thousands more New Englanders traveled on to Ohio.

This vast migration was carefully organized not by joint-stock companies or governments but by the people themselves. To lighten the economic and emotional burdens of migration, many settlers moved in large family groups. As a traveler reported from central New York: "The town of Herkimer is entirely populated by families come from Connecticut. We stayed at Mr. Snow's who came from New London with about ten male and female cousins." Members of Congregational churches often migrated together, transplanting the strong religious and cultural traditions of New England directly into western communities.

A Roadside Inn
Dozens of inns dotted the roads of the new republic, providing food and accommodation for settlers moving west and for cattle drovers and teamsters taking western produce to eastern markets.

As in Kentucky, much land fell initially into the hands of politically well-connected speculators. In the 1780s the financier Robert Morris acquired 1.3 million acres in the Genesee region of central New York for $75,000—about 6 cents an acre. Morris took a quick profit by selling the land to a group of British investors headed by Sir William Pulteney. Those investors made their profits over the long run; by 1829 Pulteney's agents in New York had received $1.2 million from sales to migrant farmers. Elsewhere in New York the Dutch-owned Holland Land Company acquired and gradually sold millions of acres of land.

Because speculators drove up the price of farms, many aspiring yeomen could not realize their dream of landed independence. In New York's Genesee region the Wadsworth family bought thousands of acres of prime land and created leasehold estates similar to the manors of the Hudson River Valley. To attract tenants, the Wadsworths leased farms rent-free for the first seven years, after which they charged rents. Seeking freehold ownership, many New England yeomen shunned these terms. They preferred to sign lease-purchase agreements with the Holland Land Company so that they would have a claim to the land while saving the money to buy it. In fact, high interest rates and the difficulty of transporting goods to market put many farmers in debt and

forced them to remain tenants indefinitely. Soon the combined debt of farmers in the counties west of the Genesee River amounted to $5 million, and tenants far outnumbered freeholders. These American farmers had fled declining prospects in the East only to find themselves at the bottom of a new economic hierarchy in the West.

Eastern Agricultural Change. The massive exodus to the West left eastern towns drained of labor and capital, and many eastern farmers compensated by planting different crops and improving their methods of cultivation. In New England more farmers turned to potatoes, a high-yielding nutritious crop. In the wheat-growing Middle Atlantic states enterprising farmers replaced metal-tipped wooden plows with cast-iron models, which dug a deeper furrow and required a single yoke of oxen instead of two or three. By reducing the cost of livestock and labor, cast-iron plows enabled small-scale farmers to keep up production even though their sons and daughters had gone west.

Wealthier eastern farmers prospered by adopting the progressive farming methods advocated by British agricultural reformers. They rotated their crops to maintain the fertility of the soil, ordering their workers or tenants to plant nitrogen-rich clover and follow it with wheat, corn, wheat, and then clover again. In

The "Onion Maidens" of Wethersfield, Connecticut
Founded in 1634 and densely settled by 1750, Wethersfield remained prosperous through agricultural innovation, turning after 1790 to market gardening. Women assumed a dominant role in this intensive horticulture and made Wethersfield the "onion capital" of the United States.

Pennsylvania and the Chesapeake region crop rotation doubled the average wheat yield from 12 to 25 bushels per acre.

Yeomen also adopted crop rotation to increase the variety of what they produced. In the fall they planted winter wheat to sell as a market crop and provide bread for their families. In the spring they sheared flocks of sheep, selling the wool to expanding textile manufacturers, and planted corn to feed milk cows during the winter. Women and girls milked the cows and developed a major new industry, making butter and cheese for market sale in the growing towns and cities.

Rural families now worked harder, laboring all twelve months of the year, but whether they were hacking fields out of western forests or carting manure to replenish eastern soils, their labor was rewarded by higher output and income. Westward migration thus boosted the entire American economy and improved the quality of rural life.

The Transportation Bottleneck

The geography of the American continent threatened to cut short this economic advance. In both Europe and America the pattern of settlement and trade had long been determined by water routes. Chesapeake planters and Hudson River manor lords relied on river transportation—which was convenient and cost only 5 or 6 cents a ton-mile—to get their crops to market. Farmers without access to rivers had to haul their crops by ox-cart over narrow dirt trails that turned into mudholes during wet seasons. Even in dry weather, ox-drawn carts moved slowly and carried only small loads. They were expensive, too, costing farmers 30 cents a ton-mile. Incredibly, Pennsylvania farmers paid as much to send their wheat and corn 30 miles overland to Philadelphia as they spent to ship it from Philadelphia to London by sea. Without improved transportation, settlers in most interior regions—especially those west of the Appalachian Mountains—could not afford to send goods to eastern markets.

The enhancement of inland travel and trade therefore became a high priority of the new state governments, which actively encouraged transportation ventures. The Pennsylvania legislature granted corporate charters to fifty-five private turnpike companies between 1793 and 1812; Massachusetts chartered over a hundred similar enterprises. The turnpike companies charged tolls for the use of the level, graveled roads they built, but the roads cut travel time significantly. State governments and private entrepreneurs also undertook the construction of inland waterways, which were even more cost-efficient. They dredged rivers to make them navigable and constructed canals, mostly to bypass waterfalls or rapids. In 1816 the United States had about 100 miles of canals, but only three canals were more than 2 miles long and none breached the great Appalachian barrier (see the physical features map at the front of the book).

The great rivers of the interior represented the hope of the West. Western settlers paid premium prices for land along navigable streams, and speculators bought up likely sites for towns along the Ohio, Tennessee, and Mississippi rivers. To take cotton and surplus grain and meat to market, western farmers and merchants built shallow barges and floated them down this interconnected river system to the port of New Orleans. By 1815 the southern port was shipping about $5 million in agricultural products yearly.

The tens of thousands of migrants in the interior of New York faced a bigger transportation problem, for no rivers connected their settlements to the East. As one pioneer recalled:

In the early years, there was none but a home market and that was mostly barter—it was so many bushels of

The River Town of Cincinnati
Thanks to its location on the Ohio River, Cincinnati became one of the great market cities of the trans-Appalachian West. By the 1820s, passenger steamboats as well as freight barges connected the city with Pittsburgh and the ocean port of New Orleans. (M. and M. Karolik Collection. Courtesy Museum of Fine Arts, Boston)

wheat for a cow; so many bushels for a yoke of oxen. The price of a common pair of cowhide boots would be $7, payable in wheat at 62 cents per bushel.

Only in 1819, when the first section of the Erie Canal connected the central counties of New York with the Hudson River, could farmers ship their crops to eastern markets (see Chapter 10).

Despite these transportation bottlenecks, white Americans continued to move westward. They knew that it would take the labor of a generation to clear land; build houses, barns, and roads; and plant orchards. Even if markets remained elusive, they were confident that their sacrifices would yield future security—a farmstead that would provide an independent livelihood for themselves and their children. The humble achievements of thousands of yeomen and tenant farm families transformed the landscape of the trans-Appalachian West, turning forests into farms and beginning the conquest of the interior of the North American continent.

Republican Policy and Diplomacy

Between 1801 and 1825 three Republicans from Virginia—Thomas Jefferson, James Madison, and James Monroe—each served two terms as president. Supported by strong majorities in Congress, this Virginia Dynasty reversed many Federalist policies, completing what Jefferson called the Revolution of 1800. The West played a prominent role in Republican policy and, together with maritime disputes with Great Britain, precipitated the War of 1812.

The Jeffersonian Presidency

Thomas Jefferson was a brilliant man, perhaps the most accomplished and versatile statesman in American history. A seasoned diplomat and an insightful political philosopher, he was also a superb politician. On becoming president in 1801, Jefferson moved quickly to win over his Federalist opponents. Reserving the crucial post of secretary of state for his Virginia ally James Madison, he appointed three men from Federalist New England to major government posts: Levi Lincoln as attorney general, Henry Dearborn as secretary of war, and Gideon Granger as postmaster general. To prepare for new electoral battles, Jefferson used patronage appointments to bolster the Republican party in New England.

Politics and Courts. Jefferson was the first chief executive to be inaugurated in the District of Columbia, the new national capital. But he did not begin with a clean slate, for after a dozen years of Federalist presidents, he inherited a government filled with his political opponents. In addition to the bureaucracy that managed the day-to-day operations of the small national government, the judiciary was packed with Federalists. Among these men the most important was John Marshall of Virginia, who had been appointed chief justice of the United States by John Adams in January 1801 (he would serve until 1835). Most frustrating of all for Jefferson, the outgoing Federalist-controlled Congress had passed a Judiciary Act in 1801, creating sixteen new judgeships, six additional circuit courts, and a variety of posts for marshals and court clerks. Adams filled those positions in a series of "midnight appointments" just before he left office. The Federalists "have retired into the judiciary as a stronghold," Jefferson complained, ". . . and from that battery all the works of Republicanism are to be beaten down and destroyed."

The Republicans fought back. The new Congress repealed the controversial Judiciary Act, dismissing the midnight judges as superfluous. It also used constitutional provisions to punish Federalist judges for their political partisanship on the bench. The Constitution empowered the House of Representatives to bring impeachment charges against officials for "high crimes and misdemeanors"; the accused was then brought to trial before the Senate. First the House impeached a mentally unstable Federalist judge, John Pickering of New Hampshire, and won his removal from office. Then House Republicans brought impeachment charges against Supreme Court Justice Samuel Chase in retaliation for his overzealous enforcement of the Sedition Act. But enough senators balked at this obviously political move to allow Chase to escape removal by a narrow vote.

Jefferson pursued a more conciliatory policy. He supported repeal of the recent Judiciary Act but judged Federalist bureaucrats on the basis of ability, not party loyalty. During eight years as chief executive he removed only 109 of 433 Federalist officeholders, 40 of whom had been midnight appointees of Adams.

The "Revolution of 1800." Jefferson was determined to change the character of the national government. The Federalists, he charged, had swollen its size and power; Republicans would shrink it back to its constitutional size and shape. When the Alien and Sedition Acts expired in 1801, Congress did not reenact them, charging that they were politically motivated and unconstitutional. The Naturalization Act was amended to permit resident aliens to become citizens after five years.

For his part, Jefferson modified many Federalist policies. During the 1790s Federalist administrations had paid tribute to the Barbary States of North Africa—that is, bribed them to spare American merchant ships from attack in the Mediterranean Sea. Jefferson stopped the payments in 1801, and when the city-states of Tunis, Morocco, Tripoli, and Algiers renewed their assaults, he ordered U.S. naval and marine units to retaliate. But Jefferson knew that an extended campaign would require a buildup of the army and navy, which would increase taxes and the national debt. He therefore accepted a diplomatic solution, reviving the Federalist tribute system but, by threatening new military action, at a much lower cost.

In domestic affairs, too, Jefferson set his own course—moderate but clearly Republican. He abolished all internal taxes, including the excise tax that had sparked the Whiskey Rebellion of 1794. Addressing his party's fears of a military takeover of the government, Jefferson reduced the size of the permanent army. He came to accept the Bank of the United States, which he

had condemned as unconstitutional in 1791, because of its importance to the nation's economy, but he was still opposed to a large public debt. One of his most important appointments was that of Albert Gallatin, a brilliant Swiss-born Republican, as secretary of the treasury. Gallatin was a fiscal conservative who believed that the national debt was "an evil of the first magnitude." By carefully controlling government expenditures and using customs revenues to redeem government bonds, he reduced the debt from $83 million in 1801 to $45 million in 1808. After the "Revolution of 1800" Jefferson and Gallatin saw to it that the nation was no longer run in the interests of northeastern creditors and merchants.

Jefferson and the West

The main objective of the Jefferson administration was to help the yeomen farm families who were settling the West. Long before his presidency Jefferson had championed western prosperity. He had celebrated the pioneer farmer in *Notes on the State of Virginia* (1785), helped compose the Confederation's land ordinances, and strongly supported Pinckney's Treaty of 1795, which allowed westerners to ship crops down the Mississippi for export through Spanish-held New Orleans. Now he had the opportunity to shape the nation's land policy.

The Northwest Territory. The settlement of the Old Northwest had been carefully planned by the Confederation Congress. The ordinances of 1785 and 1787, which had created the Northwest Territory, had divided it into uniform sections or townships. Townships were about the same size as New England communities, 6 miles square, and were divided into thirty-six sections of 1 square mile, or 640 acres, surveyed in a grid pattern (see Map 8.2).

Despite Jefferson's efforts, the ordinance of 1785 had a class bias, favoring speculators over yeomen. It specified a minimum price of $1 per acre and required that half the townships be sold in single blocks of 23,040 acres each, making direct purchase impossible for all but the wealthy. The other half of the townships were divided into parcels of 640 acres. But even this was too expensive for many migrants; only well-to-do farmers could afford the $640 cash price for an ordinary farmstead, not to mention the considerably higher amount needed to buy high-quality or well-placed land. Poorer migrants demanded better terms, but the Federalist-dominated Congresses of the 1790s turned a deaf ear. Many Federalist politicians were eastern landlords and had no desire to lose their tenants to cheap land in the West. In fact, the Federalist Land Act of 1796 doubled the minimum price to $2 per acre. Much of the best land fell into the hands of speculators, such as those in the Ohio and Scioto land companies, as the authors of the ordinances had intended.

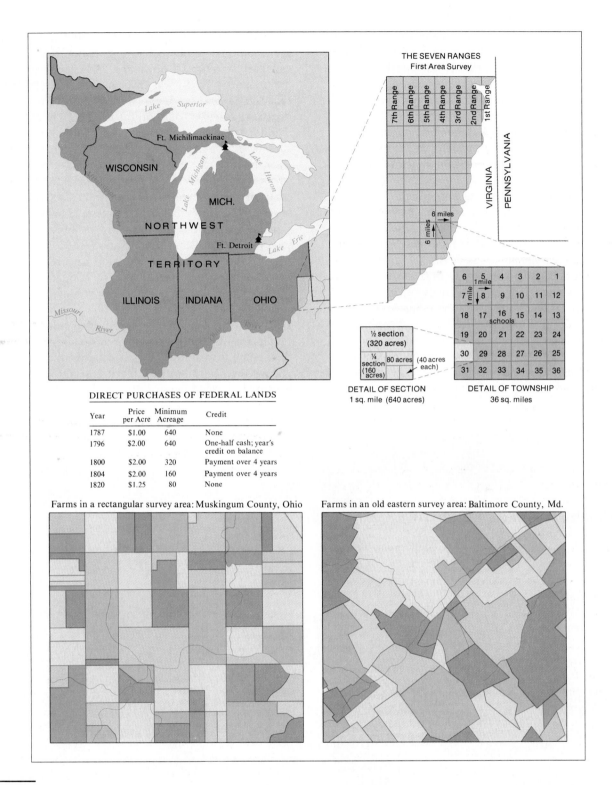

THE SEVEN RANGES
First Area Survey

7th Range | 6th Range | 5th Range | 4th Range | 3rd Range | 2nd Range | 1st Range

VIRGINIA

PENNSYLVANIA

6 miles

6 miles

DETAIL OF SECTION
1 sq. mile (640 acres)

½ section (320 acres)

¼ section (160 acres) | 80 acres | (40 acres each)

DETAIL OF TOWNSHIP
36 sq. miles

6	5	4	3	2	1
7	8	9	10	11	12
18	17	16 schools	15	14	13
19	20	21	22	23	24
30	29	28	27	26	25
31	32	33	34	35	36

1 mile

Lake Superior
Ft. Michilimackinac
WISCONSIN
Lake Michigan
Lake Huron
MICH.
NORTHWEST
Ft. Detroit
Lake Erie
TERRITORY
ILLINOIS | INDIANA | OHIO
Missouri River

DIRECT PURCHASES OF FEDERAL LANDS

Year	Price per Acre	Minimum Acreage	Credit
1787	$1.00	640	None
1796	$2.00	640	One-half cash; year's credit on balance
1800	$2.00	320	Payment over 4 years
1804	$2.00	160	Payment over 4 years
1820	$1.25	80	None

Farms in a rectangular survey area: Muskingum County, Ohio

Farms in an old eastern survey area: Baltimore County, Md.

MAP 8.2

Land Divisions in the Northwest Territory

Throughout the Northwest Territory, surveyors imposed a rectangular grid on the landscape in advance of settlement, so that farmers bought neatly defined properties. Thus the right-angled property lines in Muskingum County, Ohio (lower left), contrasted sharply with those in Baltimore County, Maryland (lower right), where—as in most eastern states—boundaries followed the contours of the land.

Because Jefferson wanted to see the West populated with yeomen farm families, his Republican colleagues in Congress passed legislation that assisted cash-poor migrants. New laws in 1800 and 1804 reduced the minimum allotment to 320 and then 160 acres, and allowed payment in installments over four years. Eventually, the Land Act of 1820 reduced the minimum purchase to 80 acres and the price to $1.25 per acre, enabling a farmer with only $100 in cash to buy a farm in the West.

The Louisiana Purchase. It was not only the Federalists who jeopardized Jefferson's dream. In 1799 Napoleon Bonaparte, a daring thirty-year-old general, seized power in revolution-torn France and immediately began an ambitious campaign to establish a French empire both in Europe and in America. In 1800 he coerced Spain into signing a secret treaty that returned Louisiana to France; two years later Spanish officials began restricting American access to New Orleans. Meanwhile, Napoleon mobilized an expeditionary force to restore French rule in Haiti, the rich sugar island then called Saint-Domingue, which was under the control of rebellious blacks led by Toussaint L'Ouverture.

Napoleon's actions prompted Jefferson to question the traditional pro-French foreign policy of the Republican party. The trade down the Mississippi guaranteed by Pinckney's Treaty was crucial to the West; any nation that denied Americans access to New Orleans, Jefferson declared, must be "our natural and habitual enemy." To avoid crossing swords with Napoleon, he instructed Robert R. Livingston, the United States minister in Paris, to purchase New Orleans. Simultaneously Jefferson sent James Monroe, a former congressman and governor of Virginia, to Britain to seek its assistance in case of war. "The day that France takes possession of New Orleans," the president warned, "we must marry ourselves to the British fleet and nation." Secretary of State James Madison took the first step toward war by encouraging American merchants to cooperate with the black government of Haiti in its resistance against the French.

Jefferson's determined diplomacy yielded a magnificent prize—the entire territory of Louisiana. By 1802 the French invasion of Haiti had faltered, the victim of yellow fever and spirited black resistance. Napoleon hesitated to send reinforcements because a new war

The American Eagle over New Orleans
Jefferson's purchase of Louisiana made New Orleans an American city, but the architecture (note the steeply pitched roofs on the right) and culture of the French settlers (Creoles) remained strong for decades. A traveler noted that "the great enmity existing between the Creoles . . . & the Americans results in fights and Challenges—there are some of both sides in jail."

with Britain threatened in Europe and he feared that American troops would invade Louisiana. Acting with characteristic decisiveness, Napoleon gave up his dream of an empire in America, and in April 1803 he offered to sell not only New Orleans but the entire territory of Louisiana as well. For about $15 million ($180 million today), Livingston and Monroe, who had joined him in Paris, concluded what became known as the Louisiana Purchase (see Map 8.3). "We have lived long," Livingston remarked to Monroe, "but this is the noblest work of our lives." The Republican statesmen had acquired the vast region between the Mississippi River and the Rocky Mountains, doubling the size of the nation.

The magnitude of the Louisiana Purchase overwhelmed the president's reservations. Jefferson had always advocated a strict construction of the Constitution, arguing that it limited action by the national government to "expressly" delegated powers. Yet the Constitution contained no provision for adding new territory. Given his dreams for the West, Jefferson was pragmatic and used the treaty-making powers in the Constitution to complete the deal with France. Federalists roundly criticized Jefferson's inconsistency but

The Continent Described

Meriwether Lewis and William Clark fulfilled Jefferson's injunction to explore the trans-Mississippi West, filling their journals with drawings and descriptions of its topography, plants, and animals, such as this detailed report on the white salmon trout.

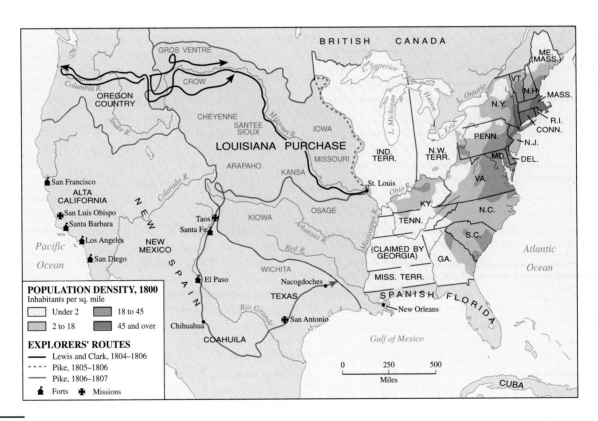

MAP 8.3

The Louisiana Purchase, 1803

The Louisiana Purchase ended France's quest for a North American empire. It doubled the size of the United States, prompting Jefferson to predict that the vast Mississippi Valley "from its fertility . . . will ere long yield half of our whole produce, and contain half of our whole population." Now only Spain stood in the way of an American continental empire.

largely approved his diplomatic triumph, with the Senate ratifying the treaty by a vote of 26 to 6.

A scientist as well as a statesman, Jefferson wanted detailed information about the physical features of the Louisiana Territory and its plant and animal life. He sent out his personal secretary, Meriwether Lewis, to explore the region. Aided by Indian guides, Lewis and William Clark, an army officer, traveled up the Missouri River, across the Rocky Mountains, and down the Columbia River to the Pacific Ocean. After two years the explorers returned with the first maps of this immense wilderness and vivid accounts of its natural resources and native American inhabitants.

Threats to Union. The Louisiana Purchase had been a magnificent acquisition, but it brought a threat to the American Union. New England Federalists had long feared that western expansion would diminish their region's political power. Now some Federalists, including the Massachusetts congressman Timothy Pickering and the geographer Jedidiah Morse, talked openly of the secession of the northeastern states. They approached Alexander Hamilton, but the great New York Federalist refused to support their plan for a separate Northern Confederacy—a scheme that they continued to advocate until the Hartford convention of 1814.

The secessionists then turned to Aaron Burr, the ambitious Republican vice-president. When Burr accepted the support of secessionist Federalists in his campaign for the governorship of New York in 1804, Hamilton accused him of plotting to dismember the Union. In reply Burr challenged his longtime enemy to a duel, the preferred aristocratic method for settling personal disputes. The illegal duel took place in New Jersey in July 1804. Hamilton died from a gunshot wound, and Burr was indicted for murder by state courts in New York and New Jersey.

This tragic event led Burr to yet another secessionist scheme. He completed his term as vice-president early in 1805 and then moved west to avoid prosecution. There he conspired with General James Wilkinson, the American military governor of the Louisiana Territory, although their plan remains a mystery. It involved capturing Spanish territory in Mexico or leading a rebellion to establish Louisiana as a separate nation headed by Burr. In any event, Wilkinson got cold feet and betrayed his ally, arresting him on a charge of treason as the former vice-president led an armed force down the Ohio River. Chief Justice Marshall presided over Burr's trial, which was both a political and a legal contest. Jefferson tried to get Burr convicted by giving a loose construction to the definition of treason in the Constitution. But Marshall repeatedly intervened from the bench, insisting, for a change, on a strict reading of the Constitution. Burr was acquitted.

The decision in Burr's trial was less important than the dangers to national unity that it revealed. The Republicans' expansionist policies had increased sectional tension and party conflict, giving new life to states' rights sentiments and secessionist schemes.

Crisis at Sea

The outbreak of the Napoleonic Wars in Europe (1802–1815) distracted attention from the West and, despite American efforts to avoid involvement, enmeshed the new nation in European political conflicts. Great Britain and France, the major belligerent powers, refused to respect American neutrality, claiming the right to board its merchant ships and confiscate their cargoes, just as they had in the wars of the 1790s.

Naval Blockades. This economic warfare intensified in 1805 when Admiral Horatio Nelson resoundingly defeated the French navy in the Battle of Trafalgar, enabling Britain to tighten its naval blockade of the Continent. The British promptly seized the American freighter *Essex* for carrying sugar and molasses from the West Indies to France and refused to classify those products as American reexports, even though the *Essex* had intentionally stopped at a U.S. port in order to make that claim. This action threatened the profits of American merchants and revived anti-British sentiment.

Napoleon replied to the British blockade with a blockade of his own. The Berlin (1806) and Milan (1807) decrees, known collectively as the Continental System, banned British ships—and neutral vessels that stopped in Britain—from European ports under French control. To counter Napoleon's strategy to destroy its export trade, Britain required neutral shippers to obtain a special license—and carry British goods—to pass through its naval blockade of Europe. American merchants were trapped. If their ships stopped at a British port to pick up a license or cargo, they faced seizure by France; but if they refused to carry British permits, their cargoes might be seized by the British as contraband. American traders were more afraid of the Royal Navy than of French customs officials, so they carried British goods to Europe, thus undermining Napoleon's Continental System.

Impressment. Both Federalists and Republicans resented British high-handedness. They railed against the British policy of stopping American merchant ships to search for sailors who had deserted from the Royal Navy and *impress* them (force them back into military service). During the wars of the 1790s British warships had seized about 2,400 sailors from American ships; but between 1802 and 1811 they had impressed nearly

8,000. Some of the men seized were British subjects carrying forged identity papers; others were Americans impressed by accident—or, more and more frequently, by design.

Long-simmering American resentment erupted in 1807 when the British warship *Leopard* attacked the U.S. frigate *Chesapeake*, killing or wounding twenty-one men and seizing four alleged deserters. "Never since the battle of Lexington have I seen this country in such a state of exasperation as at present," Jefferson declared. But instead of retaliating, Jefferson demanded monetary reparations and an end to impressment. To demonstrate his resolve, he barred British warships from entering American ports for resupply. The astute British government apologized and promised eventual compensation, but continued its blockade and impressment policies.

The Road to War

The Embargo of 1807. To protect American interests while avoiding war, Jefferson adopted a policy of *peaceful coercion.* Working closely with Secretary of State Madison, the president devised the Embargo Act of 1807. As passed by Congress, this legislation prohibited American ships from leaving their home ports until Britain and France repealed their restrictions on U.S. trade. The embargo was imaginative—an economic weapon similar to the nonimportation movements between 1765 and 1775—but naive. Jefferson and Madison overestimated the dependence of Britain and France on American shipping and underestimated the determination of both countries to continue the war despite the economic cost. The Republican leaders also underestimated the cunning of Federalist merchants, who subverted the Embargo Act by ordering their captains to steer clear of American harbors and sail between foreign ports until the embargo was lifted. Trade was the merchants' lifeblood; they were prepared to take their chances with the British navy and Napoleon's officials rather than pass up wartime profits.

However, the embargo did cripple the trade in American exports, which plunged from $108 million in 1806 to $22 million in 1808, and Federalists who represented the interests of New England merchants in Congress attacked Jefferson and Madison for jeopardizing the nation's economy. Federalists grew more alarmed when the Republican Congress passed a Force Act to prevent smuggling across the border between New England and Canada. The act gave customs officials extraordinary legal powers, reviving fears of government tyranny. "Would to God," exclaimed one Federalist, "that the Embargo had done as little evil to ourselves as it has done to foreign nations."

Madison as President. Despite public discontent with the embargo, the voters elected one of its authors, James Madison, to the presidency in 1808, giving him 122 electoral votes to 47 for the Federalist Charles C. Pinckney. As the main architect of the Constitution, an advocate of the Bill of Rights, and a congressman and party leader, Madison had served the nation well. But he was not a diplomat. He had performed poorly as secretary of state, and he lacked administrative skills. As John Beckley, a loyal Republican activist, observed in 1806, "Madison is deemed by many too timid and indecisive as a statesman." Thus, at a crucial juncture in foreign affairs, a man with little understanding of the devious, cutthroat world of international politics became president.

Madison did try to find an effective diplomatic policy. In 1809 he acknowledged the failure of the embargo, secured its repeal, and replaced it with the Nonintercourse Act. This legislation benefited merchants by permitting trade with all nations except France and Britain and offered the two belligerents the promise of normal commerce if they respected America's neutral rights. When Britain and France ignored

Poking Fun at the Federalists
A Republican cartoon of 1812 shows the Federalist Josiah Quincy—whose wealth came from the fish trade—as Grand Master of the Cod Fishes and gives him the face of a fish, mocking the Federalists' claim of social superiority.

this overture, Madison bowed to pressure from Congress and accepted a legislative act called Macon's Bill No. 2, named after Congressman Nathaniel Macon. The act reopened legal trade with Britain and France in 1810 but authorized new sanctions if either nation interfered with American commerce. The British ministry refused to alter its policies, daring the United States to cut off trade. Napoleon exploited this ill-conceived legislation more astutely. Publicly he exempted American commerce from the Berlin and Milan decrees, but privately he instructed customs officials to enforce them. "The Devil himself could not tell which government, England or France, is the most wicked," the exasperated Macon declared.

Tecumseh's Challenge. Other Republicans were pretty sure it was Britain. In 1809 eastern party leaders such as George Clinton of New York, Madison's vice-president, began to take a stand against British maritime policies. The following year Republican congressmen from the West—the future War Hawks of 1812—accused Britain of arming the Indian tribes in the trans-Appalachian region. Governor-General James Craig of Canada had in fact quietly renewed military assistance to native Americans in the Ohio River Valley, hoping that the Indians could defend their territory and continue to trade with the British. The Shawnee chief Tecumseh, assisted by his brother, the Prophet Tenskwatawa, revived the Western Confederacy of the 1790s and extended it to the southern tribes. To prevent further cessions, they revived the old doctrine of common tribal ownership of the territory north of the Ohio River and vowed to exclude white settlers.

Tecumseh and Tenskwatawa constructed a new ideology that blended ancestral religious values and various Christian teachings. Like Indian leaders before them, they called for a ban on liquor, less dependence on European goods, and an end to the cohabitation of Indian women with white men. The Shawnee leaders exploited pride in Indian ways to encourage military alliances among the western tribes, and Tenskwatawa prophesied that Indian warriors would emerge from battle unscathed. To symbolize the religious roots of Indian resistance, Tecumseh centered his confederacy at a sacred town at the junction of the Tippecanoe and Wabash rivers. He also traveled widely among southern tribes to win their allegiance, raising the prospect of war along the entire frontier.

The Decision for War. The presence of thousands of white settlers in the West began to affect American foreign policy. Expansionists in Congress condemned British support for the Western Confederacy and threatened to retaliate by seizing Florida from Spain, Britain's ally. Urged on by such talk, some Americans invaded the western (panhandle) region of Florida and sought to

Tenskwatawa, "The Prophet," 1836
Tenskwatawa added a spiritual dimension to native American resistance, urging a holy war against the invading whites. His religious message transcended differences among Indian peoples, helping to create a formidable political and military alliance.

annex it to the United States. Southern planters campaigned for the conquest of eastern Florida to prevent slaves from taking refuge among the Seminole Indians.

Meanwhile, Republican politicians claimed that it would be just as easy to conquer British Canada. Henry Clay, an avowed War Hawk from Kentucky and the new Speaker of the House of Representatives, pushed Madison toward war with Great Britain, as did John C. Calhoun, a rising young congressman from South Carolina. The outbreak of fighting with the Shawnee and their allies in the Indiana Territory might have decided the issue. In 1811 Governor William Henry Harrison defeated the Shawnee in the Battle of Tippecanoe and burned their sacred town (see American Voices, page 243).

With fighting along the frontier, influential Republicans in Congress pressing for war, and national elections quickly approaching, Madison abandoned the strategy of economic coercion. He demanded that the British respect American territorial sovereignty in the West and neutral rights in the Atlantic. When the British failed to respond quickly, Madison asked Congress to declare war. In June 1812 a sharply divided Senate voted 19 to 13 for war; the House of Representatives concurred, 79 to 49.

Chief Shabonee

The Battle of Tippecanoe

His mind sharpened by defeat, the Potawatomi chief Shabonee offers a penetrating view of reality: the unfaithfulness of allies, the confidence and impulsiveness of youth, and the false promises of war leaders.

It was fully believed among the Indians that we should defeat General Harrison, and that we should hold the line of the Wabash and dictate terms to the whites. The great cause of our failure, was the Miamies, whose principal country was south of the river, and they wanted to treat with the whites so as to retain their land, and they played false to their red brethren and yet lost all. They are now surrounded and will be crushed. The whites will shortly have all their lands and they will be driven away. . . .

Our young men said: We are ten to their one. If they stay upon the other side, we will let them alone. If they cross the Wabash, we will take their scalps or drive them into the river. They cannot swim. Their powder will be wet. The fish will eat their bodies. The bones of the white men will lie upon every sand bar. Their flesh will fatten buzzards. These white soldiers are not warriors. Their hands are soft. Their faces are white. One half of them are calico peddlers. The other half can only shoot squirrels. They cannot stand before men. They will all run when we make a noise in the night like wild cats fighting for their young. . . .

Such were the opinions and arguments of our warriors. They did not appreciate the great strength of the white men. I knew their great war chief, and some of his young men. He was a good man, very soft in his words to his red children, as he called us; and that made some of our men with hot heads mad. I listened to his soft words, but I looked into his eyes. They were full of fire. I knew that they would be among his men like coals of fire in the dry grass. The first wind would raise a great flame. I feared for the red men that might be sleeping in its way. . . .

Our women and children were in the town only a mile from the battlefield waiting for victory and its spoils. They wanted white prisoners. The Prophet had promised that every squaw of any note should have one of the white warriors to use as her slave, or to treat as she pleased. Oh how these women were disappointed! Instead of slaves and spoils of the white men coming into town with the rising sun, their town was in flames and women and children were hunted like wolves and killed by hundreds or driven into the river and swamps to hide. With the smoke of that town and the loss of that battle I lost all hope of the red men being able to stop the whites.

Source: David J. Rothman and Sheila Rothman, eds., *Sources of the American Social Tradition* (New York: Basic Books, 1975).

The causes of the War of 1812 have been much debated. Officially, the United States went to war because of violations of its neutral rights—the seizure of its ships and the impressment of its sailors. But Congressional voting and the results of the election of 1812 suggest that the War of 1812 was "a western war with eastern labels," that is, a war fought for land rather than maritime rights. The war was opposed by Federalist merchants and seamen as well as by a majority of voters in the maritime states. The Federalist candidate for president, De Witt Clinton of New York, received 89 electoral votes, primarily from New England and the Middle Atlantic states.

In contrast, Madison amassed 128 electoral votes, mostly from the South and West—regions whose congressmen had heeded the demands of their constituents and voted for war. Western farmers were angry because the British blockade had cut the price of their crops, while settlers in frontier districts demanded war against the Indians and their British allies. War Hawks in Congress not only had their eye on expansion into Florida and Canada but saw political advantage in a war. It might discredit the Federalists and drive home once and for all America's independence from Britain.

Whatever their motives, the Republicans translated them into elevated moral principles, claiming that the pride of the nation was at stake. As President Madison declared in his second inaugural address on March 1813, when the fighting was already under way, "National honor is national property of the highest value."

The War of 1812

The War of 1812 was a near disaster for the United States, both militarily and politically. Republican congressmen had predicted an easy military victory in Canada, but when General William Hull, governor of the Michigan Territory, invaded western Canada in the summer of 1812, he had to retreat almost immediately because of attacks from Indians under Tecumseh and lack of reinforcements. American forces, however, enjoyed naval superiority on the Great Lakes as Commodore Oliver Hazard Perry defeated a small British flotilla on Lake Erie, and so the United States remained on the offensive. General William Henry Harrison launched a land attack on British and Indian forces near Detroit, forcing the British to withdraw and killing Tecumseh, who had become a British general, at the Battle of the Thames in October 1813. Another American force captured and burned the Upper Canadian capital of York (now Toronto) but, short of men and supplies, immediately withdrew.

A second major invasion of Canada was impossible because of political divisions in the United States. New England governors opposed the war effort and prohibited their states' militiamen from fighting outside the nation. Boston merchants and banks declined to lend money to the national government—some actually invested in British funds instead—making it difficult to finance the war. In Congress, Daniel Webster, a dynamic young representative from New Hampshire, led Federalist opposition to higher taxes and tariffs. To force a negotiated peace, he also discouraged army enlistments and prevented the conscription of state militiamen into the American army. Having led a divided nation into war, Madison and the Republicans were unable to strike the British in Canada—their weakest point.

The American navy was no more successful in the Atlantic Ocean. The British lost scores of merchant vessels to American privateers in the first months of the war, but thereafter the powerful Royal Navy redeployed its fleet and British commerce moved in relative safety. By 1813 Britain had taken the initiative at sea. A flotilla of British warships moved up and down the American coastline, interfering with shipping and threatening seaport cities. In 1814 the fleet sailed up Chesapeake Bay, and British army units stormed ashore. They attacked the District of Columbia and set government buildings on fire in retaliation for the burning of York. The British then advanced on Baltimore but were repulsed by courageous resistance at Fort McHenry. After two years of sporadic warfare the United States was stalemated in Canada and on the defensive along the Atlantic coast, its new capital city in ruins.

Sectional political opposition to the war became even stronger in 1814. The Massachusetts legislature called for a convention "to lay the foundation for a radical reform in the National Compact," and Federalists from all the New England states gathered in Hartford, Connecticut, in December. Some delegates to the Hartford convention proposed secession from the Union, but the majority moderately called for a revision of the Constitution. Their object was to reverse the declining role of the Federalist party—and of New England—in the expanding nation. To end the Virginia Dynasty, delegates proposed a constitutional amendment limiting the presidency to one four-year term and rotating the office

among citizens from different states. Other Federalists suggested amendments restricting commercial embargoes to sixty days and requiring a two-thirds majority in Congress to declare war, prohibit trade, or admit a new state into the Union. A minority in the nation and divided among themselves, the Federalists could not hope to prevail unless the war continued to go badly.

That was a very real prospect. In the late summer of 1814 a major British invasion of the Hudson River Valley had been narrowly averted by an American naval victory at the Battle of Lake Champlain. In December British transports landed thousands of seasoned veterans at New Orleans, threatening to cut off the West's access to the sea. The United States was now under siege from both the north and the south. The only hopeful sign was that Britain had finally defeated Napoleon in Europe and was interested in securing peace with the United States to lower taxes at home and reestablish trade with America.

The British began negotiations with an American delegation at Ghent, Belgium, late in 1814. The American commissioners—John Quincy Adams, Albert Gallatin, and Henry Clay—initially demanded territory in Canada and Florida. British diplomats insisted on a buffer state between the United States and Canada to serve as a refuge for their native American allies. In the end, both sides realized that the small concessions that might be won at the bargaining table were not worth the cost of protracting the war. The Treaty of Ghent, signed on Christmas Eve, 1814, restored the prewar borders and referred unresolved disputes to future negotiations.

Andrew Jackson and the Battle of New Orleans. These results hardly justified three years of fighting and a sharply divided nation. Indeed, the outcome confirmed the view of contemporary critics (and later historians) that the War of 1812 was unnecessary and was undertaken primarily for partisan reasons. But a final victory in combat lifted American morale and, for many citizens, justified the fighting. Before news of the Treaty of Ghent reached the United States, newspaper headlines proclaimed "ALMOST INCREDIBLE VICTORY!! GLORIOUS NEWS." On January 8, 1815, troops commanded by General Andrew Jackson crushed the British forces attacking New Orleans.

The victory at New Orleans brought a very different kind of leader onto the American national scene. A son of the West, Jackson was a rugged slaveowning planter from Tennessee. He first came to public attention as an Indian-fighter after leading a troop of militia in a series of battles against the Creek in 1813 and 1814. After winning the Battle of Horseshoe Bend, he forced the Indian chiefs to sign a treaty ceding 23 million acres of land. These actions earned Jackson a reputation as a ruthless man determined to remove the Indians from the path of white settlement.

The Battle of New Orleans (detail)
As shown in Jean Hyacinthe de Laclotte's painting, British troops attacked the center and the right flank of the American defenses. Secure behind their battlements, Jackson's troops repelled the assaults and took thousands of prisoners.

Jackson's victory at New Orleans made him a national hero and a symbol of the emerging West, the land of frontier fighters. Yet Jackson won the contest at New Orleans not with Kentucky sharpshooters in coonskin caps but with a traditional deployment of regular troops, including a contingent of French-speaking black Americans, the Corps d'Afrique. The Americans fought from carefully constructed breastworks and were amply supplied with cannon, which rained "grapeshot and cannister bombs," on the massed British formations. "The slaughter must have been great," remarked one American witness. Indeed it was. The British lost thousands of their finest troops, with 700 dead and 10,000 wounded or taken prisoner. American casualties totaled only 13 dead and 58 wounded.

For Americans, the Battle of New Orleans was the most significant event of the war, testifying, as one headline put it, to the "RISING GLORY OF THE AMERI-CAN REPUBLIC!" It redeemed the nation's battered pride and, along with the coming of peace, undercut the Hartford convention's demands for a revision of the Constitution. The political institutions of the new nation had survived a war and a generation of sectional strife.

The tumultuous era of the early republic had come to an end. Peace in Europe had ended two decades of conflict over foreign policy, and the continuing success of the Republicans brought about the demise of the Federalists, whose eastern-oriented policies and elitist outlook received little support in an expanding, increasingly democratic nation. "No Federal character can run with success," Gouverneur Morris of New York lamented, and the election results of 1818 bore out his pessimism. After the voting, Republicans outnumbered Federalists in the Senate by 37 to 7 and in the House of Representatives by 156 to 27.

The decline of the Federalists prompted contemporary observers to call the two terms of President James Monroe, from 1817 to 1825, the Era of Good Feeling. Actually, national political harmony was more apparent than real, for the dominant Republican party—now home to many former Federalists—split into factions that struggled over power and patronage, and, after 1820, economic policy.

Regional Diversity and National Identity

The political divisions manifested during the War of 1812 showed that regional differences were stronger than ever. There were four American cultures—New England, Middle Atlantic, Chesapeake, and Lower South—each with distinctive values and political interests (see Map 8.4). As migrants transplanted those cultures to the Old Northwest and Old Southwest, American life became even more diverse, divided between complex seaboard societies and frontier farming regions. To unify this increasingly fragmented society, politicians and statesmen defined a new national goal: a continental American empire.

Northern Seaboard Societies

Generations of observers had contrasted the race- and class-divided societies of the Chesapeake with the freehold farming regions of the North, particularly New England. Popular speech reflected some of these differences: "Yankee," a foreign traveler learned, was "a name given derisively, or merely jestingly," to the residents of New England because of their shrewd bargaining habits. "The name of 'Buckskin' is given to the inhabitants of Virginia," he went on to observe, "because their ancestors were hunters and sold buck, or rather deer skins."

European visitors saw genuine cultural differences in the popular stereotypes. In 1800 a British observer detected religious "fanaticism" in New England as well

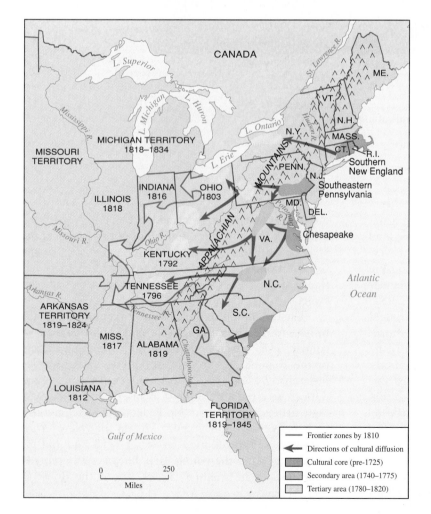

MAP 8.4

Regional Cultures Move West, 1720–1820

By 1720 four distinct "core" cultures had developed along the Atlantic seaboard. By 1775 settlers from the mid-Atlantic and Chesapeake regions had carried their customs and institutions into the southern backcountry. Then, between 1780 and 1820, settlers from New England and the Lower South transplanted their regional cultures into other parts of the trans-Appalachian West. Extensive cultural intermixture—and conflict—occurred only in certain regions, such as southern Ohio, Kentucky, and Tennessee.

as "a great strain of industry among all ranks of people." He thought that "the lower orders of citizens have a better education, are more intelligent, and better informed" than those he met in the southern states. Visitors to the Chesapeake commented on the rude manners and heavy drinking of white tenant farmers and small freeholders. They had a "passion for gaming at the billiard table, a cock-fight or cards."

New Englanders did indeed set a higher store by education than did residents of the Chesapeake. The Puritan legacy included strong traditions of primary schooling and Bible reading. As a result, most of the men and more than half the women in New England in 1790 could read and write. In Virginia, most white women and a third of adult white men could not even write their names; they signed legal documents such as wills and marriage licenses with an "X" or another mark. This disparity in the literacy rate reflected different social and fiscal priorities. The slaveholding elite that ruled southern society refused to provide services or schooling for ordinary white families. In 1800 the 4,000 free inhabitants of Essex County in Virginia spent about $1,000 for local government, including schooling. The same year the 900 residents of Acton, Massachusetts, spent $950 for public purposes—four times as much per capita as in Essex County—$550 on education alone.

Regional differences were also apparent in the observance of holidays. In Virginia, South Carolina, and other states with an Anglican heritage, Christmas was an occasion for feasting and celebration. Not so in New England, where Puritans condemned such celebrations as profane. Most New England churches did not celebrate Christmas until the 1850s; for them, Thanksgiving Day, commemorating the trials and triumphs of the first Pilgrim and Puritan settlers, was the focus of celebration. During the War of Independence New England customs had become political symbols as Congress frequently declared days of fasting and thanksgiving.

Regional identity was especially intense in New England because of ethnic and religious uniformity. By the 1820s most men and women in the region could trace their American roots back six or seven generations. No fewer than 281 members of the Newhall family resided in Lynn, Massachusetts, along with 259 Breeds, 195 Alleys, and 162 Johnsons. A list of only twelve family names encompassed 1,660 persons, or 27 percent of the town's population. In a very real sense New England was a "big family" composed of large, interrelated groups.

The culture of the Middle Atlantic region was more diverse, because the people came from different ethnic backgrounds. In Pennsylvania and New Jersey, Quakers, Germans, and Scots-Irish married largely within their own ethnic groups, and to a lesser extent so did the Dutch. Germans held on to their language as well as

Puritan Culture Persists
Like good Puritans, this prosperous New England couple wear plainly cut clothes and hold the symbols of piety and literacy—a book and a pen. The artist shows his stepmother looking directly at him (and us), suggesting that he enjoyed a better relationship with her than with his stern-faced father, a traditional New England patriarch.

their customs, especially in the small agricultural villages of Pennsylvania and the isolated backcountry districts of Maryland, Virginia, and North Carolina. A visitor to Hanover, Maryland, noted around 1820, "The inhabitants are all German. Habits, speech, newspapers, cooking—all German." In nearby Frederick Town the Lutheran church kept all its records and held Sunday-school classes in German.

This diversity among and within the various regions inhibited the establishment of an American national identity. Until the growth of interregional commerce created a national economy (see Chapter 9), only certain political events—such as the War of 1812—reminded people that they were citizens of the United States. For example, the term "Uncle Sam" came into use during the War of 1812. "This cant name for our government has got almost as common as John Bull [for the British]," a newspaper in Troy, New York, reported: "The letters U.S. on government waggons &c are supposed to have given rise to it." The immediate popular-

German Dress and Manners in America
A gentleman in traditional dress strolls among giant tulips, a familiar motif in Pennsylvania German folk art. The lace cuffs, white stockings, and walking stick suggest his high social status, as does the genteel way he holds his pipe.

ity of "The Star Spangled Banner," written by Francis Scott Key during the battle at Fort McHenry, also testified to the role of the war in promoting an American national identity.

Newspapers played an increasingly important role in fostering national identity and common cultural values. By 1820 the cities of the United States boasted thirty daily newspapers. Another thousand newspapers, mostly four-page weeklies, provided national news, market information, and advertisements to people in small towns and rural areas. Political parties subsidized some of these newspapers, creating a national debate on various legislative issues. The influential *Niles Weekly Register,* established in Baltimore in 1811, and the *North American Review,* founded in Boston in 1815, carried news from Europe and the East to every region. But only members of certain elites—merchants, politicians, lawyers—participated fully in this national culture. Most Americans lived out their lives within the regional culture into which they had been born.

The Old Northwest

When Jedidiah Morse published *American Geography* in 1793, he listed three "grand divisions of the United States": northern, middle, and southern. In the edition of 1819 he added a new section: "Western States and Territories." Some seventy years later, in an essay called "The Significance of the Frontier in American History" (1893), the historian Frederick Jackson Turner placed the West at the center of the American experience. Turner argued that an identifiable national character first developed in the West because that area was controlled by the national government. He also maintained that the western frontier experience itself—the life-or-death struggle with nature—created a character and a system of values that were distinctly American: individualistic, optimistic, pragmatic, and democratic.

Turner's theories provoked a generation of scholarly research and debate, but historians no longer accept many of his views. For instance, Turner underestimated the force of cultural tradition. Most migrants to the West, like most Europeans who came to America, sought to preserve their old values and customs. Thus, when 176 residents of Granville, Massachusetts, decided to move to Ohio, they carefully chose a site whose "peculiar blending of hill and valley" resembled the landscape of their New England community. They transplanted their Congregational church to Ohio whole, complete with ministers and elders, along with their system of freehold agriculture. So it was throughout the trans-Appalachian West: in many respects "new" communities were not new—they were old communities that had moved inland.

Yet Turner was right about the self-sufficiency of the majority of frontier communities. Cut off from most trade with outside markets, settlers made their own clothes, repaired old tools, and lived in a local barter economy, exchanging goods or labor with their neighbors. "A noble field of Indian corn stretched away into the forest on one side," an English visitor to an Ohio farm in the 1820s noted, waxing romantic,

> and immediately before the house was a small potato garden, with a few peach and apple trees. The woman told me that they spun and wove all the cotton and woollen garments of the family, and knit all the stockings; her husband, though not a shoemaker by trade, made all the shoes. She manufactured all the soap and candles they use. All she wanted with money, she said, was to buy coffee, tea, and whiskey, and she could "get enough any day by sending a batch of butter and chickens to market."

A low standard of living prevailed for this and other farm families for more than a generation. As late as 1840, per capita income in the Old Northwest was only 70 percent of the national average.

Apart from its relative poverty, the distinctiveness of the region lay in the conflict among competing cultural traditions. In Indiana, education-conscious migrants from New England set up a system of public primary schools, but only after a twenty-year battle with tax-shy yeomen from the southern states. Although the New England influence was strong, the states of the Old Northwest developed largely along the model of the Middle Atlantic states—Pennsylvania, New Jersey, and New York—with their diverse cultural traditions and ethnic political factions.

Slavery Moves into the Old Southwest

As poor whites fled from the Chesapeake states to Kentucky and Tennessee, wealthy planters and up-and-coming young men from the Chesapeake and the Lower South set up new slave plantations in the Old Southwest—the future states of Alabama, Mississippi, and Louisiana. Consequently, the southwestern frontier became a stronghold not of Turner's individualism and democracy but of slavery.

Indeed, slavery expanded in newly settled areas. As planters from the Lower South states of Georgia and South Carolina moved into the backcountry, they imported new slaves from Africa. They had used their influence at the Philadelphia convention of 1787 to protect this trade from national regulation for twenty years, and when the time limit expired in 1808, Congress responded to antislavery settlement in the North by banning American participation in the transatlantic slave trade. But by that time 250,000 new slaves had entered the United States, a number equal to that of all slaves imported during the colonial period. The black population had also grown through reproduction, increasing from half a million in 1775 to 1.8 million in 1820.

Many of these Africans and African-Americans still toiled on tobacco and rice plantations. When soil exhaustion caused tobacco production to stagnate in the Tidewater region of the Chesapeake, white planters took the crop into the Virginia Piedmont, North Carolina, Kentucky, and Tennessee. The rice industry of South Carolina and Georgia expanded until the 1820s, when many of its overseas markets were lost to cheaper rice imports from Asia. By that time white planters in Louisiana—some of them refugees from black-controlled Haiti—had established a booming economy based on sugar. Slaves in Louisiana, like those on the sugar plantations of the West Indies, were brutally exploited and died quickly from disease and overwork.

The Coming of Cotton. However, it was a new crop—cotton—that provided the impetus for the expansion of slavery. For centuries most Europeans had worn clothing made from wool or flax; cotton textiles imported from India were only for the rich. Cotton spinning and weaving had been taken up in England but had remained a minor industry. Then, after 1750, the European population explosion increased the demand for woolen and cotton cloth just as the technological breakthroughs of the Industrial Revolution were boosting production and lowering prices. Soon consumer demand and the newly invented water-powered spinning jennies and weaving mules generated a seemingly insatiable demand for raw cotton.

Beginning in the 1780s, American planters responded to this demand by importing a rot-resistant, smooth-seed, long-fiber variety of cotton from the West Indies and planting it on sea islands along the southern Atlantic coast. Then, in the 1790s, a number of inventors—including Connecticut-born Eli Whitney—developed machines to separate the seeds from the fiber of short-staple cotton, which grew well in many regions of the South.

The combination of British demand and American innovation created a new agricultural industry and a massive demand for land and labor. Thousands of white planters moved into the interior of South Carolina and Georgia to grow cotton. After the War of 1812, production spread into Alabama and Mississippi, which entered the Union in 1817 and 1819, respectively. In a single year a government land office in Huntsville, Alabama, sold $7 million of uncleared land. The expression "doing a land-office business"—a metaphor for rapid commercial expansion—dates from this time.

Cotton's Impact on African-Americans. For enslaved blacks the coming of cotton meant social upheaval. Entire black communities were uprooted from the Chesapeake and Lower South and forced to move west with their owners; even more wrenchingly, thousands of young women and men were taken away from their families through a new domestic slave trade. By 1820 whites had displaced more than 250,000 African-Americans from their birthplaces to new tobacco regions and the booming cotton states.

The history of the Tayloe family's Mount Airy plantation in Virginia illustrates the impact of cotton on the lives of blacks. In 1747 John Tayloe owned 167 slaves at Mount Airy. Over the next sixty years twice as many slaves were born as died on this plantation, creating a large, interrelated African-American community—and, from the Tayloes' point of view, a "surplus" of workers. Hence, in 1792 John Tayloe III advertised a sale of 200 slaves, at least 50 of whom were from Mount Airy. Between 1828 and 1860 Tayloe and his sons would move 180 Mount Airy slaves to their new cotton plantations in Alabama.

These sales and forced migrations brought great wealth to a few white families and untold misery to blacks. Torn from their loved ones, African-Americans

Arise! Arise! and weep no more
dry up your tears, we Shall part
no more. Come rose we go to
Tennessee,
that happy Shore. to old virginia
never — never — return. —

The Internal Slave Trade
Mounted whites escort a convoy of slaves from Virginia to Tennessee in Louis Miller's
Slave Trader, Sold to Tennessee. The trade was a lucrative one for whites, pumping
money into the declining Chesapeake economy and valuable workers into the plantations of the cotton belt. For blacks it was a traumatic journey, a second Middle Passage that broke up families and communities.

had to rebuild their lives, laboring "from day clean to
first dark" on frontier plantations in Alabama and Mississippi. "I am Sold to a man by the name of Peterson a
trader," lamented one Georgia slave. "My Dear wife for
you and my Children my pen cannot Express the griffe I
feel to be parted from you all."

Antislavery Efforts and the Missouri Compromise. The
expansion of slavery into the Old Southwest dashed the
hopes of those who thought slavery would "die a natural death" after the decline of the tobacco economy
and the end of the Atlantic slave trade. Some antislavery
advocates had worked to prevent the illegal importation
of enslaved Africans. Others had persuaded the legislatures of northern states to pass *personal liberty laws*
protecting free blacks from kidnapping or seizure under
the terms of the Fugitive Slave Act of 1793.

More important, reformers had opposed the expansion of slavery into the western territories. Despite their
efforts, Louisiana, Mississippi, and Alabama joined the
Union with state constitutions permitting slavery. When

Missouri applied for admission on a similar basis in
1819, the antislavery forces rallied. Congressman James
Tallmadge of New York proposed a ban on the importation of slaves into Missouri and the gradual emancipation of its black inhabitants. When Missouri whites
rejected those conditions, the northern majority in the
House of Representatives blocked the territory's admission to the Union. In response, southerners used their
power in the Senate, which was equally divided between
eleven free and eleven slave states, to withhold statehood from Maine, which was seeking to separate itself
from Massachusetts. Tempers flared in the heat of debate. Senator Thomas W. Cobb of Georgia accused Tallmadge of kindling "a fire which all the waters of the
ocean cannot put out and which seas of blood can only
extinguish."

Controversy raged for two years before Congress
resolved the stalemate. Representative Henry Clay of
Kentucky and other skilled politicians put together a series of agreements known collectively as the Missouri
Compromise, by which Maine entered the Union as a

MAP 8.5

The Missouri Compromise, 1820
The Missouri Compromise resolved for a generation the issue of slavery in the lands of the Louisiana Purchase. Slavery was forbidden north of the Missouri Compromise line (36° 30' north latitude), with the exception of the state of Missouri. To maintain an equal number of free and slave states in the U.S. Senate, the compromise provided for the nearly simultaneous admission of Maine and Missouri.

free state in 1820 and Missouri was admitted as a slave state the following year (see Map 8.5). This bargain preserved the existing sectional balance in the Senate and set a precedent for the future admission of states in pairs—one free and one slave. To mollify antislavery sentiment in the House of Representatives, southern congressmen accepted the restriction of slavery in the rest of the Louisiana Territory north of latitude 36° 30', the southern boundary of Missouri.

The tradition of political compromise on the issue of slavery thus continued. In 1821 as in 1787, the white leaders of the North and the South gave priority to the Union, finding complex but workable ways to reconcile the interests of their regions. But the task had become more difficult. The Philadelphia delegates had resolved their sectional differences in two months; Congress took two years to work out the Missouri Compromise, and there was no guarantee that it would work. The fates of the West, the Union, and the black race had become inextricably intertwined, raising the prospect of civil war. As Thomas Jefferson exclaimed at the time of the Missouri controversy, "This momentous question, like a fire-bell in the night, awakened and filled me with terror."

African-American Society and Culture

After 1800 a more unified African-American culture began to develop in the United States for three reasons. First, the end of the transatlantic slave trade in 1808 eliminated the need to assimilate newly arrived Africans. Even in South Carolina, only about 20 percent of the enslaved population in 1820 had been born in Africa. Second, the movement of slavery into the Old Southwest reduced differences among slaves; for example, the black Gullah dialect of the Carolinas disappeared on the cotton plantations of Alabama and Mississippi because slaves from the Chesapeake had adopted English. Third, free blacks, especially in northern cities, consciously began to foster a sense of a distinct African-American culture.

Many African elements persisted in the new African-American culture. About half the slaves who entered the United States between 1800 and 1808 came from the Congo and Angola, making those regions important sources of African influences. As the traveler Isaac Holmes reported in 1821:

> In Louisiana, and the state of Mississippi, the slaves . . . dance for several hours during Sunday afternoon. The general movement is in what they call the Congo dance; their music often consists of nothing more than an excavated piece of wood . . . one end of which is a piece of parchment.

Similar descriptions of blacks who "danced the Congo and sang a purely African song to the accompaniment of . . . a drum made by stretching a skin over a flour barrell" appeared as late as 1890.

Marriage and Family Life. African-Americans also maintained some of the social rules of their West

African-American Banjos
In 1794 an Englishman in Virginia watched slaves dancing to the music of an African-style banjo "made of a gourd something in the imitation of a Guitar, with only four strings and played with the fingers in the same manner."

tween blacks so that they could sell their slaves without breaking a marriage bond. Enslaved African-Americans therefore devised their own marriage rituals. Young men and women first asked their parents' consent to marry and then sought their owner's permission to live together in their own cabin. Following African custom, many couples signified their union in a public ceremony by jumping over a broomstick together. Christian blacks often had a religious service performed by a white or black preacher, but these rites never ended with the customary phrase "until death do you part." Everyone knew that black marriages could end with the sale of one or both of the spouses.

Many married slaves who were not separated by sale lived in stable unions. Among the slaves on the Good Hope plantation in South Carolina, about 70 percent of the women had all their children by the same man. Most other women had their first child (with an enslaved man) before marriage in what the community called an "outside" birth and bore the rest of their children within a stable union. On plantations in Louisiana black family ties were much more fragile, in part because labor in the sugar fields killed many men. Thirty percent of the slave women on one Louisiana plantation lived alone with their children, who were fathered by a succession of men.

Thus, the oppressive conditions of slavery only partially undermined blacks' efforts to create solid family bonds. To maintain their identity, many recently imported slaves in South Carolina and Georgia bestowed African names on their children; males born on Friday were often called Cuffee—the name of that day in several West African languages. Most Chesapeake slaves chose names of British origin and bound one generation to another by naming sons after fathers, uncles, or grandfathers; daughters were often named after grandmothers. Names had great social importance, for they acknowledged the biological ties of kinship (see Table 8.1). Like incest rules and marriage rituals, naming patterns created order in a harsh and arbitrary world.

As an African-American cultural community developed, the quality of slave life gradually improved. During the eighteenth century a lack of social organization among African-born slaves resulting from their diverse origins had made it easy for white men to take advantage of blacks. They had raped women and punished defiant men in horrible ways, branding them, or cutting off their fingers or ears, or even castrating them. Such abuses did not stop after 1800, but they were questioned more often. White politicians condemned rape as an aristocratic vice that was ill suited to life in a republican society. The spread of evangelical Christianity encouraged many masters to treat their slaves more humanely. African-Americans also put themselves in a position to resist the worst forms of oppression by forming stable families and strong communities. They insisted that work gangs be sold "in families" and de-

African homeland, such as rigid incest taboos. Unlike the white elite of South Carolina, which practiced cousin marriage to keep property in the family and maintain an intermarried ruling group, enslaved blacks shunned marriages between cousins even on relatively self-contained plantations. For example, on the Good Hope plantation in South Carolina about 175 slave children were born between 1800 and 1857, and no fewer than 40 percent of those children were related by blood to three slaves from Africa. Within this elaborate tangle of kinship, only one marriage between cousins took place.

Masters and slaves also had different ideas about the sanctity of marriage. Whites insisted on legally binding marriage contracts among themselves both to regulate sexual behavior and to establish the ownership of property. But slaveowners forbade legal marriage be-

TABLE 8.1

African-American Naming Patterns

Good Hope Plantation Slaves, Orangebury, South Carolina

Date of Birth	Baby's Name	Parents' Names	Source of Baby's Name
1793	Hector	Bess, Hector	Father
1806	Clarinda	Patty, Primus	Mother's mother
1811	Sambo	Affy, Jacob	Mother's father
1813	Primus	Patty, Primus	Father
1824	Sarah	Phoebe, Jack	Mother's mother
1828	Major	Clarinda, Abram	Father's father

fied their owners when they were not. Faced with transport to Mississippi and separation from his wife, one Maryland slave, his owner reported, "neither yields consent to accompany my people, or to be exchanged or sold." Masters ignored such resistance at their risk. They now faced the prospect that a slave's relatives might retaliate for violence or arbitrary sale with arson, poison, or destruction of crops or equipment.

Work and Community. Blacks in the rice-growing lowlands of South Carolina were particularly successful in gaining control over their work lives. By the Revolutionary Era those slaves had won the right to labor by the *task*. Each day a worker had to complete a precisely defined task—turn up a quarter acre of rice land, hoe a half acre, or pound seven mortars of rice. Many slaves finished their task "by one or two o'clock in the afternoon," a Methodist preacher reported. They had "the rest of the day for themselves, which they spend in working their own private fields, consisting of 5 or 6 acres of ground . . . planting rice, corn, potatoes, tobacco &c. for their own use and profit." African-Americans extended these customary rights during the War of Independence, as black drivers took over the management of many plantations, and jealously guarded them afterward. "Should any owner increase the work beyond what is customary," a South Carolina rice planter warned around 1800, "he subjects himself . . . to such discontent amongst his slaves as to make them of little use to him."

Still, white masters had virtually unlimited power—both legal and physical—over their slaves. In upland cotton-growing regions of South Carolina and Georgia and in Alabama and Mississippi, owners forced workers to labor in supervised "gangs." They sold those who were recalcitrant and punished those they viewed as lazy. Particularly on newly settled plantations, profit-conscious masters used the lash to extract labor.

Enslaved blacks found ways to resist the tyranny of slavery. Some, such as Gabriel Prosser of Virginia, plot-

ted mass uprisings and murders. Denmark Vesey, a free black married to a slave woman, planned a rebellion in Charleston, South Carolina, in 1822, but, like Prosser's, it was discovered and crushed at the last moment. Most blacks knew that a successful revolt was highly unlikely because of white strength in numbers and military superiority. Flight was also perilous. The northern and western states were hotbeds of racial prejudice, and masters could use the Fugitive Slave Law (1793) to carry them back to bondage. Yet hundreds of Chesapeake slaves fled to the free states, and thousands more threatened to do so, forcing their masters to treat them better.

Enslaved blacks in the Lower South and Old Southwest had fewer options. One avenue of escape—to Spanish Florida—was cut off in 1819 when the United States annexed Florida. Slaves had no option but to build the best possible lives for themselves where they were. As the black abolitionist Frederick Douglass would observe, these slave communities were "pegged down to a single spot" and "must take root there or nowhere." Enslaved blacks developed a culture similar to that of European peasants. They worked as dependent agricultural laborers and built close-knit communities based on family, kinship, and religion.

Meanwhile, the relatively small population of free African-Americans (about 5 percent of the total by 1820) explored the dimensions of its newfound liberty. The great majority lived on low wages from menial jobs as farm workers or city laborers and laundresses, and their lives were circumscribed by racial prejudice. But a few blacks were able to make full use of their talents and achieved great distinction. The mathematician and surveyor Benjamin Bannaker published an almanac and helped lay out the new national capital; Phyllis Wheatley won praise for her poetry, as did Joshua Johnston for his portraiture; and Robert Sheridan acquired a small fortune from his mercantile enterprises. But even more impressive and enduring were the institutions created by this first generation of free African-Americans (see American Lives, pages 254–255). Hundreds of

Richard Allen and African-American Identity

Richard Allen was a success. Born into slavery in Philadelphia in 1760, he died in 1831 not only free but influential, a founder of the African Methodist Episcopal Church and its first bishop. Allen's rise has much of the classic American success story about it, but he bears a larger significance: Allen, as one of the first African-Americans to be emancipated during the Revolutionary Era, had to forge an identity for his people as well as for himself.

Sold as a child along with his family to a farmer in Delaware, Allen began his ascent in 1777, when he was converted to Methodism by Freeborn Garretson, an itinerant preacher. Garretson also converted Allen's master and convinced him that on Judgment Day slaveholders would be "weighted in the balance, and . . . found wanting." Allowed by his repentant owner to buy his freedom, Allen earned a living sawing cordwood and driving a wagon during the Revolutionary War. After the war he furthered the Methodist cause by becoming a "licensed exhorter," preaching to blacks and whites from New York to South Carolina. His efforts attracted the attention of Methodist leaders, including Francis Asbury, the first American bishop of the Methodist Church. In 1786 Allen was appointed as an assistant minister in Philadelphia, serving the racially mixed congregation of St. George's Methodist Church. The following year he and Absalom Jones, another black preacher, joined other ex-slaves and Quaker philanthropists to form the Free African Society, a quasireligious benevolent organization that offered fellowship and mutual aid to "free Africans and their descendants."

Allen remained a staunch Methodist throughout his life. In 1789, when the Free African Society adopted various Quaker practices, such as having fifteen minutes of silence at its meetings, Allen led a withdrawal of those who preferred more enthusiastic Methodist practices. In 1794 he rejected an offer to become the pastor of the church the Free African Society had built, St. Thomas's African Episcopal Church, a position ultimately accepted by Absalom Jones. A large majority of the society had chosen to affiliate with the white Episcopal (formerly Anglican) Church because much of the city's black community had been Anglican since the 1740s. "I informed them that I could not be anything else but a Methodist, as I was born and awakened under them," Allen recalled.

To reconcile his faith and his African-American identity, Allen decided to form his own congregation. He gathered a group of ten black Methodists and took over a blacksmith's shop in the increasingly black southern section of the city, converting it to the Bethel African Methodist Episcopal Church. Although the Bethel Church opened in a ceremony led by Bishop Francis Asbury in July 1794, its tiny congregation worshiped "separate from our white brethren."

Allen's decision to found a black congregation was partly a response to white racism. Although most white Methodists in the 1790s favored emancipation, they did not treat free blacks as equals. They refused to allow African-Americans to be buried in the congregation's cemetery and, in a famous incident in 1792, segregated them into a newly built gallery of St. George's Methodist Church. But Allen's action also reflected a desire among African-Americans to control their religious lives, to have the power, for example, "to call any brother that appears to us adequate to the task to preach or exhort as a local preacher, without the interference of the Conference." By 1795 the congregation of Allen's Bethel Church numbered 121; a decade later it had grown to 457, and by 1813 it had reached 1,272.

Bethel's rapid expansion reflected the growth of Philadelphia's black population, which numbered nearly 10,000 by 1810, and the appeal of Methodist practices. Newly freed blacks welcomed "love feasts," which allowed the full expression of emotions repressed under slavery. They were attracted as well by the church's strict system of discipline—its communal sanctions against drinking, gambling, and infidelity—which helped them bring order to their lives. Allen's preaching also played a role; the excellence of his sermons was recognized in 1799, when Bishop Asbury ordained him as the first black deacon of the Methodist Church.

The Mount Bethel African Methodist Episcopal Church, Philadelphia

But over the years Allen and other blacks grew dissatisfied with Methodism, as white ministers retreated from their antislavery principles and attempted to curb the autonomy of African-American congregations. In 1807 the Bethel Church added an "African Supplement" to its articles of incorporation; in 1816 it won legal recognition as an independent church. In the same year Allen and representatives from four other black Methodist congregations (in Baltimore; Wilmington, Delaware; Salem, New Jersey; and Attleboro, Pennsylvania) met at the Bethel Church to organize a new denomination, the African Methodist Episcopal Church. Allen was chosen as the first bishop of the church, the first fully independent black denomination in America. He had succeeded in charting a separate religious identity for African-Americans.

Allen also recognized the importance of education to the future of the African-American community. In 1795 he opened a day school for sixty children and in 1804 founded the "Society of Free People of Colour for Promoting the Instruction and School Education of Children of African Descent." By 1811 there were no fewer than eleven black schools in the city.

But where did Allen think "free people of colour" should look for their future? This question had arisen in Philadelphia in 1787, when William Thornton had promoted a plan devised by antislavery groups in London to settle free American blacks (and emancipated slaves from the West Indies) in Sierra Leone, an independent state they had founded on the west coast of Africa.

Many blacks in Boston and Newport had endorsed this scheme, but the members of Philadelphia's Free African Society had rejected it. They preferred to seek advancement in America, but on their own cultural terms. The process took place on two levels: as a social group, Philadelphia blacks embraced their ancestral heritage by forming "African" churches and benevolent societies. As individuals, however, they affirmed their American identity by taking English names (although virtually never those of their former owners). This dual strategy brought pride but not significant gains in wealth and status. Nonetheless, Philadelphia's African-Americans rejected colonization; when the issue was raised again just after 1800, only four people signed up for emigration to Sierra Leone.

Instead, the city's black community petitioned the state and national governments to end slavery and the slave trade and repeal the Fugitive Slave Act of 1793, which allowed slaveowners to seize blacks without a warrant. As if to underline the importance of these political initiatives, Allen was temporarily seized in 1806 as a fugitive slave, showing that even the most prominent northern blacks could not be sure of their freedom. This experience may account for Allen's initial support for the American Colonization Society, a predominantly white organization founded in 1817 to promote the settlement of free blacks in Africa. This scheme was immediately condemned at a mass meeting of nearly 3,000 Philadelphia blacks, who set forth a different vision of the African-American future: "Whereas our ancestors (not of choice) were the first successful cultivators of the wilds of America, we their descendants feel ourselves entitled to participate in the blessings of her luxuriant soil."

Philadelphia's black community, including Allen, was more favorably inclined toward the Haitian Emigration Society, which was founded in 1824 to help African-Americans settle in that island republic. But when that venture failed, Allen forcefully urged blacks to remain in the United States. In November 1827 he made a compelling argument in *Freedom's Journal*, the nation's first black newspaper: "This land which we have watered with our *tears* and our *blood* is now our *mother country*."

Born a slave of African ancestry, Allen learned to live as a free man in white America, rejecting emigration and preserving his cultural identity by creating separate African-American institutions. But it meant that he cast his lot, and that of his descendants, with a society pervaded by racism. It was a brave decision, both characteristic of the man who made it and indicative of the limited choices available to those freed from the bonds of slavery.

them joined together to found black schools, mutual-benefit and fellowship societies, antislavery organizations, and religious denominations. Over the years these institutions helped create a sense of cultural autonomy among African-Americans and gave public expression to their lives and values.

African-American Religion. After the family, the religious community played the most important role in lives of enslaved African-Americans. Many blacks maintained African practices, invoking traditional spirits in time of need. In Louisiana, some slaves from Haiti practiced the folk religion of voodoo, a blend of African and Catholic customs. Many enslaved African-Americans in the Chesapeake became Christians, absorbing and adapting the religious views of white Baptists and Methodists. As black ministers preached or founded churches (which often met in secret to avoid repression), they advanced their own interpretation of Christian doctrines. Black theology generally ignored the issues of original sin and predestination. It also downplayed biblical passages in which the church is viewed as lawgiver and symbol of authority. Black Christians preferred to envision God as a warrior who had liberated his chosen people. "Their cause was similar to the Israelites'," Martin Prosser (Gabriel's brother) told his fellow slave conspirators during the thwarted rebellion in Virginia in 1800. "I have read in my Bible where God says, if we worship him, we should have peace in all our land and five of you shall conquer a hundred and a hundred of you a hundred thousand of our enemies."

The Christian message valued spiritual endurance as well as physical resistance. Some slaves identified with the persecuted Christ, who had suffered and died so that his followers might find peace and justice in the next world. Amid the manifest injustice of their lives, these African-Americans used Christian principles to affirm their equality with whites in the eyes of God. They took the language and religion of their masters but adapted them for their own ends. Trapped in a bicultural world, these African-Americans learned from whites but lived as blacks.

The Fate of Native Americans

"Next to the case of the black race within our bosom," James Madison remarked as he left the presidency in 1817, "that of the red race on our borders is the problem most baffling to the policy of our country." Most American political leaders had fewer misgivings than Madison did. They wanted to open lands in the trans-Appalachian West, regardless of the cost to the native American inhabitants. "Cut up every Indian Cornfield and burn every Indian town," proclaimed William Henry Drayton of South Carolina, so that their "nation be extirpated and the lands become the property of the public." For many educated whites the conquest of the interior and its aboriginal inhabitants represented the historical progress of humanity in which primitive life would be replaced by higher cultural forms. As a congressional committee put it in 1818, "Those sons of the forest should be moralized or exterminated."

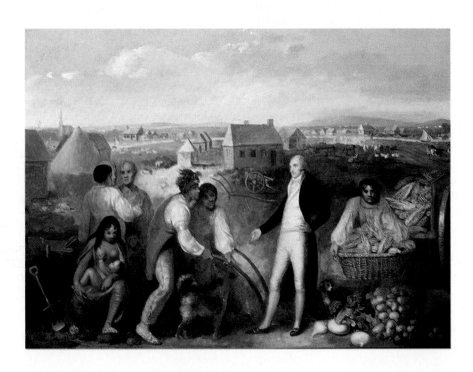

Cultural Assimilation, circa 1805
Merchant Benjamin Hawkins points to a plow, encouraging Creek Indians to adopt European farming techniques. By this time the Creeks were bartering corn and other crops (as well as furs) for manufactured goods.

Red Jacket

A Seneca Chief's Understanding of Religion

The Seneca chief Red Jacket (c. 1758–1830) acquired his name during the Revolutionary War, when he fought for the British "redcoats." Reconciling himself to American rule, he joined an Indian delegation that met George Washington. He rejected Christianity, however, and in 1805 he explained why to a group of missionaries, whom he addresses as "Brother."

Brother: Continue to listen. You say that you are sent to instruct us how to worship the Great Spirit agreeably to his mind; and, if we do not take hold of the religion which you white people teach, we shall be unhappy hereafter. You say that you are right, and we are lost. How do we know this to be true? We understand that your religion is written in a book. If it was intended for us as well as you, why has not the Great Spirit given to us, and not only to us, but why did He not give to our forefathers, the knowledge of the book, with the means of understanding it rightly?

Brother: The Great Spirit has made us all, but he has made a great difference between his white and red children. He has given us different complexions and different customs. To you He has given the arts [i.e., manufacturing]. To these He has not opened our eyes. We know these things to be true. Since He has made a great difference between us in other things, why may we not conclude that He has given us different religion according to our understanding? The Great Spirit does right. He knows what is best for his children; we are satisfied.

Source: David J. Rothman and Sheila Rothman, eds., *Sources of the American Social Tradition* (New York: Basic Books, 1975).

Attempts at Assimilation. In the name of "civilization," government officials sought to destroy the traditional cultural practices of native Americans. Henry Knox, Washington's first secretary of war, had advocated breaking up commonly owned tribal lands and distributing farming plots to individual Indian families as private property, a concept alien to the Indians, who did not own wealth as individuals but circulated goods to fulfill social obligations. Thomas Jefferson was also an assimilationist, hoping that Americans would "form one people" as Indians would "mix with us by marriage." To this end, white leaders demanded that Indians abandon tribal governments and submit to the authority of the state and the nation. Public officials also encouraged the efforts of missionaries to change the Indians' religious beliefs. The object, as one Kentucky minister put it, was to make the Indian "a farmer, a citizen of the United States, and a Christian."

Many native Americans actively resisted such attempts to redefine their identity. "Born free and independent," an observer noted, Indians were "struck with horror at whatever has the shadow of despotic power." Many tribes drove out white missionaries and forced Christian converts to participate in traditional Indian rites. To justify their ancestral values, native American leaders devised theories of cultural and religious dualism (see American Voices, above). They argued that the Great Spirit had made the two races different; as a Munsee prophet put it, "there are two ways to God, one for the whites and one for the Indians."

Nevertheless, under pressure from white missionaries, many tribes broke into hostile religious factions. Among the Seneca of New York, for example, the prophet Handsome Lake promoted traditional agricultural ceremonies—the green corn dance, the strawberry festival, and the false-face pageant—that gave ritual thanks to the earth, plants, animals, water, and sun. But Handsome Lake also adopted some Christian precepts, such as belief in heaven and hell, and used them to discourage his followers from drinking alcohol, gambling, and practicing witchcraft. More conservative people among the Seneca clung to the old ways, believed in witchcraft, and resisted the influence of white missionaries.

Strong ancestral values prompted Indians to reject European agricultural methods. Handsome Lake's political enemy, Red Jacket, led the Seneca in opposing innovations such as having men work in the fields. Traditionally, Indian women were responsible for providing much of the food supply—growing corn, squash, beans, and other basic foods—and because of matrilineal customs they often controlled the inheritance of cultivation rights on certain lands. Unlike white farm women, they enjoyed authority over property rights, and among most Eastern Woodland peoples, women's economic importance led to political responsibility. For example, the Shawnee chose female "war" and "civil" chiefs; the latter could prevent the dispatch of war parties and save captives from being tortured. Consequently, Indian women insisted on retaining their role as cultivators, and few Indian men wished to assume traditional female responsibilities, preferring the roles of hunter and warrior.

Even Christian Indians would not give up their social identity. They viewed themselves not as individuals but as members of a clan, all descendants of the same person. Most clans adopted an animal—a deer, turtle, fox, or bear—as their *totem*, or designation, often because of a vision of their original ancestor. Indians also superimposed new Christian identities onto familiar clan spirits. To accept European views of the individual or the family would be to repudiate clan identity and the essence of Indian life.

The Cherokee. Native Americans assimilated European ways only under special circumstances and for specific purposes. Beginning in the late eighteenth century, the Cherokee of Georgia and the Carolinas organized an unusually centralized political system to resist the advancing white settlers who wanted their lands for growing cotton. A Cherokee national council headed by two respected chiefs oversaw all 13,000 members of the tribe with respect to certain activities—maintaining a mounted police force, abolishing clan revenge for murder, and establishing a limited *patrilineal* inheritance system.

These innovations were implemented by a small faction of Christian Cherokee mixed-bloods. Most mixed-bloods were the offspring of white fur traders and Indian women. Growing up in a bicultural world, they learned the language and political ways of white people. A few were quite prosperous and dressed and behaved like white planters. James Vann, a Georgia Cherokee, owned more than twenty black slaves, two trading posts, and a gristmill. Forty other Cherokee mixed-blood families owned a total of more than 1,000 slaves. When whites attempted to oust the Cherokee from their ancestral land, first in 1806 and again in 1817, the mixed-bloods attempted to forge a strong national identity among their people. Sequoyah, a mixed-blood, developed a system of writing for the Cherokee language, and the tribe published a newspaper. In 1827 the Cherokee introduced a new charter of government modeled directly on the U.S. Constitution.

Mixed-blood Christians were caught between two cultures and accepted by neither. Whites treated them as Indians, to be pushed ever westward, and full-blooded Cherokee condemned their white values. During the 1820s full-bloods seized power in the Great Smoky Mountains and, because of their numbers, gradually took control of the national council, which then resisted both cultural assimilation and forced removal. Like

Divisions among the Cherokee
In 1821 Sequoyah, a mixed-blood, devised a written script for the Cherokee language, and the tribe published a newspaper printed in both English and Cherokee. Few full-blooded Cherokee could read either language; they maintained the traditional oral culture.

most native Americans, the Indians of the Old Southwest wanted to practice their traditional culture on ancestral lands. "We would not receive money for land in which our fathers and friends are buried," a Creek chief declared. "We love our land; it is our mother."

Continental Empire: Spain and the United States

As the United States challenged Indian control of the Old Southwest, Spain reasserted its claims to the lands stretching from Texas to California. Before the 1760s Spain had suffered one setback after another in North America, losing control of the Carolinas and Georgia to British settlers and Louisiana to French fur traders. A further blow came in 1763, at the end of the French and Indian War, when the Spanish monarchy was forced to cede Florida to Britain.

Yet Spain also profited from the peace settlement of 1763. When France ceded Canada to Britain, it withdrew completely from North America, ceding Louisiana to its Spanish ally. Once again Spain held title to all lands west of the Mississippi River (see Map 8.6). Title

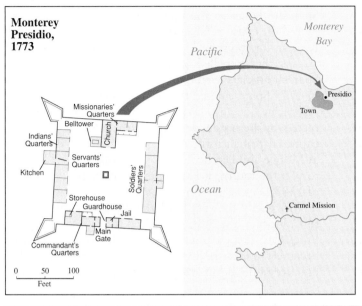

Monterey Presidio, 1773

Missionaries' Quarters
Belltower
Indians' Quarters
Church
Kitchen
Servants' Quarters
Soldiers' Quarters
Storehouse
Guardhouse
Jail
Commandant's Quarters
Main Gate

0   50   100
Feet

Pacific

Monterey Bay

Presidio

Town

Ocean

✝ Carmel Mission

Spanish Land Grants in Northern New Mexico

Rio Chama
Rio Grande
Rio Puerco
Pecos River
Santa Fe
Rio San Juan
Albuquerque
Rio Grande

▨ Land grants to 1799

0   25   50
Miles

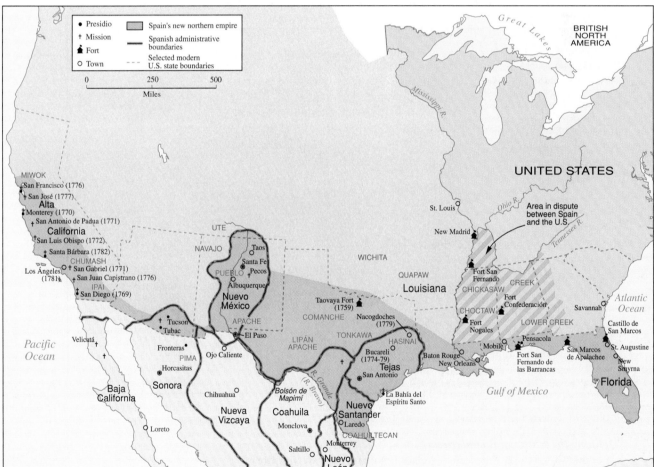

MAP 8.6

New Spain's Northern Empire in the Late Eighteenth Century

Following its acquisition of Louisiana in 1763, Spain tried to create a great northern empire. It established missions and forts in California (such as that at Monterey), expanded Spanish settlements in New Mexico, and by joining in the American War of Independence, reclaimed Florida from Britain. By 1800, this dream had been shattered by Indian uprisings in California and Texas, Napoleon's seizure of Louisiana, and American threats to Florida.

did not mean control. Louisiana remained primarily a French colony, inhabited in 1763 by 4,000 French-speaking whites and 5,000 enslaved blacks, while much of Texas, New Mexico, and southern Arizona was dominated by Apache peoples, who raided the scattered small Spanish settlements for horses and supplies.

Spain's Borderlands Empire. During the reign of Carlos III (1759–1788), a dynamic and American-oriented monarch, Spanish officials attempted to create a grand continental empire by uniting these territories on the northern border of New Spain with new settlements in California. Under the direction of José de Gálvez, Spanish troops established military presidios at San Diego, Santa Barbara, Monterey, and San Francisco while the Franciscan friar Junípero Serra set up missions there and elsewhere along the California coast. To protect

Spanish claims to the region, a naval expedition explored the coast as far north as Alaska, seeking to expel Russian fur trappers.

As they repelled Russian advances in the west, Spanish officials tried to dislodge the British in the east. In 1779 Spain entered the War of Independence on the American side and, in a series of daring campaigns directed by Bernardo de Gálvez (the nephew of José), captured British forts along the Mississippi River and at Mobile and Pensacola. Those victories enabled Spain to win the return of Florida in the Paris peace accords of 1783.

To pacify the vast borderland region from Florida to California, the Spanish devised a new Indian policy. Emulating French practice, Bernardo de Gálvez, who became the viceroy of New Spain in 1785, pursued a practice of divide and rule. His *Instructions of 1786* or-

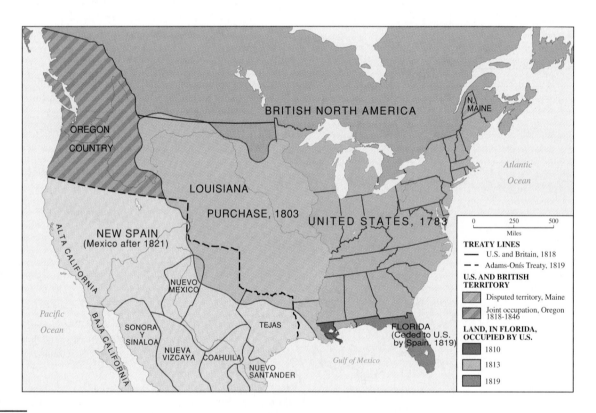

MAP 8.7

Defining the National Boundaries

After the War of 1812, American diplomats negotiated treaties with Great Britain and Spain that defined the boundaries with Canada in the north and New Spain (which in 1821 became the independent nation of Mexico) in the west. These treaties eliminated the threat of war until the 1840s, providing the United States with a much-needed period of peace and security.

dered local commanders to contain or exterminate the warlike Apache, if possible by fomenting disputes between them and other Indian peoples so that they would "destroy one another." More cooperative peoples would be offered treaties and gifts—especially arms and alcohol—to make them dependent on Spanish trade.

These treaties and trade brought peace to New Spain's northern frontier by the late eighteenth century and allowed the movement of Spanish ranchers and farmers from Mexico into Texas, New Mexico, and Arizona. In California, however, Spanish policy led to rebellion as troops raped native women and drafted labor for work at the missions. Also, as the missionaries converted the Indians to Christianity and a more settled life, European diseases cut the native population along the coast nearly in half, from 60,000 in 1769 to 35,000 in 1800.

After only a few decades of restored vigor the Spanish Borderlands Empire came under pressure from the newly independent and highly aggressive American republic. To deter American settlement west of the Appalachians, Spanish authorities restricted American trade on the Mississippi River in 1784 and entered into an alliance with the Creek peoples, who also feared American frontiersmen. But American threats and military setbacks in Europe forced Spain to accept Pinckney's Treaty of 1795, which gave Americans free access to the great river and voided Spanish land claims in the Ohio River Valley and along the Mississippi. To curry favor with Napoleon and prevent further American expansion, Spain ceded Louisiana to France in 1800 and reacted strongly when the Louisiana Purchase undermined this strategy. Spanish diplomats argued that Louisiana was limited to lands along the Mississippi River (the present-day states of Louisiana, Arkansas, and Missouri). In contrast, Thomas Jefferson claimed that the territory extended to the Rio Grande and the Rocky Mountains, which would place all of Texas and half of New Mexico under American control. This issue remained unresolved at the end of the War of 1812, as did the status of West Florida, which had been occupied by American troops during the war. American adventurers also had their eye on East Florida and mounted insurrections against Spanish authorities there (see Map 8.7).

John Quincy Adams and the West. All the disputes between Spain and the United States were resolved by John Quincy Adams. Although he was the son of John Adams, the Federalist president, John Quincy joined the Republican party before the War of 1812. As secretary of state under President Monroe, the younger Adams pursued an expansionist western policy that would have astounded his father. In 1817, when General Andrew Jackson led an expedition into East Florida, seized two Spanish forts, and executed two British subjects, accusing them of encouraging Seminole raids into the United States, Adams defended the general despite strong reservations about his conduct.

Indeed, Adams used the diplomatic crisis created by Jackson's attack to put Spain on the defensive. Threatening to invade Florida, he secured the Adams-Onís Treaty of 1819, in which East Florida was annexed to the United States. In return, the American government accepted responsibility for the financial claims of American citizens against Spain, renounced its dubious claim to Spanish Texas, and agreed on a compromise boundary between New Spain and the Louisiana Territory.

Adams also negotiated important agreements with Great Britain. The Rush-Bagot Treaty of 1817 eliminated a long-standing source of conflict by limiting British and U.S. naval forces on the Great Lakes. More important, in 1818 the two countries agreed to establish the border between the Louisiana Territory and British Canada at the 49th parallel. As a result of Adams's diplomatic efforts, the United States gained undisputed possession of nearly all of the land south of the 49th parallel and between the Great Lakes and the Rocky Mountains.

The Monroe Doctrine. Secretary Adams and President Monroe had this continental empire in mind when they outlined a new foreign policy that, thirty years later, became known as the Monroe Doctrine. In an address to Congress in 1823, Monroe, at Adams's behest, warned Spain and other European powers to stay out of the Western Hemisphere. During and after the Napoleonic Wars, patriots in Mexico and other Spanish colonies had revolted and established independent republics. The United States had extended diplomatic recognition to the new republics, and now Monroe warned Spain not to try to subdue them. The president, hoping to prevent the Russians from extending their fishing camps and fur-trading posts south of Alaska, declared that the American continents were not "subject for further colonization" by the nations of Europe. In return, Monroe reiterated that it was the policy of the United States "not to interfere in the internal concerns" of European nations. Monroe and Adams had turned their backs on Europe. They now looked purposefully westward, envisioning an American empire that would stretch from the Atlantic to the Pacific.

Summary

With the acquisition of Louisiana and white settlement of the trans-Appalachian West, the United States became a continental nation. The pace of white advance was slowed by native Americans fighting to defend their lands, the difficulties of transport and trade across the mountains, and the high price of land sold by both the U.S. government and speculators. Nonetheless, by 1820, 2 million Americans, white and black, were living west of the Appalachians.

Led by Thomas Jefferson, who favored westward expansion, the Republicans wrested political power from the Federalists. While retaining the Bank of the United States and many Federalist bureaucrats, Jefferson eliminated excise taxes, reduced the national debt, cut the size of the army, and lowered the price of national lands in the West. Faced with British and French seizures of American ships and sailors, he devised the Embargo of 1807, but it failed to change the belligerents' policies. Eventually, Indian uprisings and expansionist demands by western Republicans led President Madison into the War of 1812. The war split the nation, prompting a secessionist movement in New England, but a negotiated peace ended the war, and Jackson's victory at New Orleans preserved American honor.

The war strengthened American national identity, but regional customs remained strong. Migrants from New England carried their way of life to the Old Northwest whereas southern planters grew cotton and created a slave-based society in the Old Southwest. Enslaved blacks adopted English and some white religious practices but, along with free blacks in northern cities, also forged a distinct African-American culture. American society was increasingly divided by region and race, creating a sectional confrontation over slavery that the Missouri Compromise of 1820 did not resolve. The Cherokee and other native American peoples in the West sought to preserve their culture and territory from both Christian missionaries and land-hungry settlers from New Spain and the United States. Spanish officials tried to create a vast Borderlands Empire stretching from Florida to California but failed because of Indian resistance, European diplomatic setbacks, and pressure from the expansion-minded American government. The diplomacy of John Quincy Adams led to the annexation of Florida and the settlement of boundaries with British Canada and Spanish Texas.

TIMELINE

1784	Treaty of Fort Stanwix
1787	Northwest Ordinance
1790s	Western (Indian) Confederacy White settlers move into Northwest Territory Cotton production expands Agricultural "improvement" in East Turnpikes and short canals built
1790–1791	Little Turtle defeats American armies
1792	Kentucky joins Union; Tennessee follows (1796)
1794	General Wayne wins Battle of Fallen Timbers
1795	Treaty of Greenville Jay's Treaty Pinckney's Treaty
1800s	Chesapeake blacks adopt Protestant beliefs Handsome Lake revival among Iroquois
1800	Gabriel Prosser's rebellion in Virginia Political "Revolution of 1800"
1801	Judiciary Act passed and repealed Spain restores Louisiana to France
1801–1807	Presidency of Thomas Jefferson Gallatin reduces national debt Naval war with Barbary States Price of federal land reduced
1802–1815	Napoleonic Wars in Europe Seizures of American ships and sailors
1803	Louisiana Purchase
1804–1805	Lewis and Clark expedition Aaron Burr and western secession
1807	Embargo
1808	Tecumseh and Tenskwatawa mobilize Indians Congress bans importation of slaves
1810s	Expansion of slavery into Old Southwest Cherokee resist white advance Decline of Federalist party
1811	War Hawks call for expansion Battle of Tippecanoe
1812	War of 1812
1814	Hartford convention
1815	Andrew Jackson wins Battle of New Orleans Treaty of Ghent ratified
1817	Rush-Bagot Treaty Alabama joins Union; Mississippi follows (1819)
1817–1825	Era of Good Feeling
1819	Adams-Onís Treaty: Florida annexed, and Texas boundary defined
1820	Missouri Compromise
1823	Monroe Doctrine

BIBLIOGRAPHY

Gregory Evans Dowd, *A Spirited Resistance: The North American Indian Struggle for Unity, 1745–1815* (1992), offers a fine comparative analysis of the Indian peoples, and Donald R. Wright, *African Americans in the Early Republic, 1789–1831* (1993), provides a good overview. Donald R. Hickey, *The War of 1812: A Forgotten Conflict* (1989), puts the war in an economic and diplomatic context.

Westward Expansion

For studies of white policy toward native Americans see Bernard Sheehan, *Seeds of Extinction: Jeffersonian Philanthropy and the American Indian* (1973); Reginald Horsman, *Expansion and American Indian Policy, 1783–1812* (1967); Dorothy Jones, *License for Empire: Colonialism by Treaty in Early America* (1982); and Richard Slotkin, *Regeneration through Violence: The Mythology of the American Frontier* (1973). Works dealing with the impact of Christian missions on native American culture include Henry Warner Bowden, *American Indians and Christian Missions: Studies in Cultural Conflict* (1981); William W. Fitzhugh, ed., *Cultures in Contact* (1985); William G. McLoughlin, *Cherokees and Missionaries, 1789–1839* (1984); and Earl P. Olmstead, *Blackcoats among the Delaware* (1991). Other analyses of cultural interaction include William G. McLoughlin, *Cherokee Renascence in the New Republic* (1986), and J. Leitch Wright, Jr., *Creeks and Seminoles: The Destruction and Regeneration of the Muscogulge People* (1986).

A fine account of settlers and speculators is Alan Taylor, *Liberty Men and Great Proprietors: The Revolutionary Settlement on the Maine Frontier, 1760–1820* (1990). For developments west of the mountains, see Malcolm J. Rohrbough, *The Transappalachian Frontier: Peoples, Societies, and Institutions, 1775–1850* (1978), and John Mack Faragher, *Sugar Creek: Life on the Illinois Prairie* (1986).

Republican Policy and Diplomacy

Two good general accounts are Marshall Smelser, *The Democratic Republic, 1801–1815* (1968), and Ralph Ketcham, *Presidents above Party: The First American Presidency, 1789–1829* (1984). Detailed studies of Jefferson's presidency include Daniel Sisson, *The Revolution of 1800* (1974); Dumas Malone, *Jefferson the President* (2 vols., 1970 and 1974); Richard E. Ellis, *The Jeffersonian Crisis: Courts and Politics in the New Republic* (1971); and Noel Cunningham, *The Process of Government under Jefferson* (1978). For the Louisiana Purchase, see Alexander DeConde, *This Affair of Louisiana* (1976); Donald Jackson, *The Letters of the Lewis and Clark Expedition* (1963); and James P. Ronda, *Lewis and Clark among the Indians* (1984).

The activities of Aaron Burr are covered in Milton Lomask, *Aaron Burr* (1979), whereas the Federalists are discussed in David Hackett Fischer, *The Revolution of American Conservatism: The Federalist Party in the Age of Jeffersonian Democracy* (1965); Linda K. Kerber, *Federalists in Dissent: Imagery and Ideology in Jeffersonian America* (1970); and James Banner, *To the Hartford Convention: The Federalists and the Origins of Party Politics in the Early Republic, 1789–1815* (1970).

American attempts to avoid involvement in the Napoleonic Wars are traced in Lawrence Kaplan, *"Entangling Alliances with None": American Foreign Policy in the Age of Jefferson* (1987), and Bradford Perkins, *The First Rapprochement: England and the United States, 1795–1805* (1967) and *Prologue to War: England and the United States, 1805–1812* (1961). See also Clifford L. Egan, *Neither Peace nor War: Franco-American Relations, 1803–1812* (1983), and Doron S. Ben-Atar, *The Origins of Jeffersonian Commercial Policy and Diplomacy* (1993). On Madison, see Robert A. Rutland, *The Presidency of James Madison* (1990); J. C. A. Stagg, *Mr. Madison's War: Politics, Diplomacy, and Warfare in the Early Republic, 1783–1830* (1983); and Drew McCoy, *The Last of the Fathers: James Madison and the Republican Legacy* (1989). Native American involvement in the war is discussed in R. David Edmunds, *The Shawnee Prophet* (1983) and *Tecumseh and the Quest for Indian Leadership* (1984), as well as H. S. Halbert and T. H. Ball, *The Creek War of 1813 and 1814* (1970).

Regional Diversity and National Identity

For life in the northern seaboard states, see Benjamin W. Labaree, *The Merchants of Newburyport, 1764–1815* (1962), and Sean Wilentz, *Chants Democratic: New York City and the Rise of the American Working Class, 1788–1850* (1984). The essays in R. A. Burchell, ed., *The End of Anglo-America* (1991), document various shifts in cultural identity.

F. S. Philbrick, *The Rise of the West, 1754–1830* (1964), provides an overview of life in the Old Northwest; a more sophisticated analysis is Andrew R. L. Cayton and Peter S. Onuf, *The Midwest and the Nation* (1990). More detailed studies include Richard C. Wade, *The Urban Frontier: The Rise of Western Cities, 1790–1840* (1973), and Andrew Cayton, *The Frontier Republic: Ideology and Politics in the Ohio Country, 1789–1812* (1986).

Peter Kolchin, *American Slavery, 1619–1877* (1993), provides a fine overview. On the expansion of slavery, see Ira Berlin and Ronald Hoffman, eds., *Slavery and Freedom in the Age of the American Revolution* (1983); Donald L. Robinson, *Slavery in the Structure of American Politics, 1765–1820* (1971); and Albert Raboteau, *Slave Religion* (1968). Also see Ira Berlin and Philip D. Morgan, eds., *Cultivation and Culture: Labor and the Shaping of Slave Life* (1993), and Dena J. Epstein, *Sinful Tunes and Spirituals: Black Folk Music to the Civil War* (1977). Two good studies of the Carolina region are Joyce E. Chaplin, *Agricultural Innovation and Modernity in the Lower South, 1730–1815* (1993), and Peter A. Coclanis, *The Shadow of a Dream: Economic Life and Death in the South Carolina Low Country, 1670–1920* (1988).

For blacks in the northern states, see Gary B. Nash, *Forging Freedom: Philadelphia's Black Community, 1720–1840* (1988). Glover Moore, *The Missouri Compromise* (1953), provides a detailed analysis of that crisis. See also Merton L. Dillon, *Slavery Attacked: Southern Slaves and their Allies, 1619–1865* (1990).

Spain's quest for empire is covered in David Weber, *The Spanish Frontier in North America* (1992), whereas American initiatives are the subject of Walter LaFeber, ed., *John Quincy Adams and American Continental Empire* (1965), and Ernest May, *The Making of the Monroe Doctrine* (1976).

Launching of Fame, *Essex, Massachusetts, 1802* (detail)

The work of twenty shipwrights in Becket's yard, *Fame* was destined for the East India trade, carrying American goods and furs to China and returning with ceramics and tea.

CHAPTER 9

Toward a Capitalist Protestant Republic

1790–1820

★   ★   ★

On the fiftieth anniversary of the founding of the United States white Americans had cause for celebration. They lived free of an arbitrary government that imposed high taxes and an established church that enforced rigid dogma. They also had cause for mourning. On July 4, 1826, within a few hours of each other, John Adams and Thomas Jefferson died. The deaths of two former presidents on Independence Day seemed to many Americans to be a sign that God looked with favor on their experiment in self-government. Two of the greatest Founders had died, but the republic lived on.

Indeed, the years between 1790 and 1820 marked the maturation of the republican economic and social order begun during the American Revolution. That society had a number of distinct characteristics. First, it boasted a new system of political economy intended to enhance the welfare of the American people by increasing the "common-wealth." To that end, state legislatures embarked on ambitious programs of economic development, investing public resources in some projects and encouraging private investors to sponsor others. For the first but not the last time in American history, the state became an active force in economic life. Governmental initiatives pushed forward an already dynamic economy. In 1820 nearly 10 percent of the population resided in cities or small towns, and more people were sending crops and manufactured products into the market, expanding the commercial sector of the agricultural system.

A second prominent feature of the new society was its increasingly republican culture. Beginning in 1776, leading Americans developed a political system based on the republican principle of "ordered liberty" and gradually expanded suffrage to include most adult white men. They also applied republican ideals to reorganize traditional social institutions such as families and schools and reevaluated customary rights and duties. As a result, many individuals—women as well as men—gained more freedom to choose their marriage partners and social values.

Third, Americans reassessed women's place in the social order. Even as political and religious leaders advocated a separate sphere of domestic concerns, white women assumed a public role in American life by joining the Second Great Awakening and organizing new religious associations. Together with evangelical preachers and male laymen, they pushed forward a continuous wave of religious revivals that made Protestant Christianity one of the defining features of the national character of the United States.

This new capitalist, republican, Protestant society had its flaws, but for the white population it balanced private freedom with public responsibility. Reflecting the patriotism and self-confidence of the age, its proponents hailed the new social order as a model for all peoples. "The temperate zone of North America," a Kentucky judge declared in a Fourth of July speech, "already exhibits many signs that it is the promised land of civil liberty, and of institutions designed to liberate and exalt the human race."

Political Economy: The Capitalist Commonwealth

The nation that declared its independence in 1776 was overwhelmingly agrarian and dependent on Great Britain for markets, credit, and manufactured goods. Over the next fifty years the United States achieved a measure of economic independence, as rural Americans became manufacturers, bankers supplied credit to expand industry and trade, merchants developed regional market economies, and state governments took an active role in encouraging economic development. This emerging economy was capitalist not only because it was based on private property and market exchanges but also because capitalists—moneyed men—shaped its political and economic policies. Yet the new economy was also shaped by the ideology of the republican commonwealth and therefore was governed in part by policies that emphasized the common good.

A Capitalist Society

American Merchants. Merchants had dominated the economic life of port cities in colonial times, and with the departure of the British they began to set the social and cultural tone as well. "It is a Nation of Merchants," a British visitor reported from Philadelphia in 1798, "always alive to their interests; and keen in the pursuit of wealth in all the various modes of acquiring it."

A Cloth Merchant
Elijah Boardman and other American merchants annually imported millions of yards of cloth from Britain. When war cut off trade, some merchants financed the domestic production of textiles, first in rural households and then in factories.

After the economic contraction that followed independence, European wars from 1792 to 1815 brought rising profits to established merchant houses and fortunes to daring entrepreneurs. Among the many success stories were those of two immigrants, Robert Oliver and John Jacob Astor, who prospered phenomenally. Oliver arrived in Baltimore in 1783 as the American agent for Irish merchants who sold linens in the United States and foodstuffs in the West Indies. Two years later he began his own business—a mercantile partnership—and watched his investment of £2,000 grow slowly to £3,300 during the recession of the 1780s. Then, during the wartime shipping boom, his firm's assets soared to £110,000. Caught up in a restless pursuit of wealth, Oliver began to trade on his own, reaping enormous profits from the West Indian coffee trade and speculating in gold and silver from Spanish America. By 1807 he was a millionaire.

John Jacob Astor, who migrated from Germany to New York City in 1784, became wealthy by exploiting the fur trade in the Pacific Northwest. Soon Astor emerged as the leading New York merchant trading with China. Investing his profits in real estate, he became the largest landowner in the rapidly growing port of New York. Astor's success was unusual only in its extent; the wartime commercial boom brought prosperity to the mercantile elite in all the seacoast cities and fostered the emergence of a distinct "business class" (see Chapter 10).

Banking and Credit. To finance the expansion of mercantile enterprise, Americans had to devise an entirely new banking system. Before 1776 the colonists had found it difficult to secure loans. Farmers had relied on government-sponsored land banks, pledging their land as security, while merchants such as Oliver arranged partnerships, borrowed funds from other merchants, or relied on British suppliers to extend credit. Then, in 1781, several Philadelphia merchants, Robert Morris among them, persuaded the Confederation Congress to charter the Bank of North America to provide short-term commercial loans. Traders in Boston and New York founded similar banks in 1784. These institutions provided merchants with the credit they needed to finance their transactions. "Our monied capital has so much increased from the Introduction of Banks, & the Circulation of the Funds," the Philadelphia merchant William Bingham noted as early as 1791, "that the Necessity of Soliciting Credits from England will no longer exist, & the Means will be provided for putting in Motion every Specie of Industry."

In 1791 Congress chartered the Bank of the United States as part of Alexander Hamilton's plan to centralize the expanding American financial system. The bank had the power to issue notes and make commercial loans, and by threatening to demand payment in specie, it restrained state banks from issuing too many notes. Although the bank's managers used their lending powers cautiously, limiting loans to three times the value of the bank's holdings in gold and silver, profits still averaged a handsome 8 percent annually. By 1805, in response to the continuing demand for commercial credit, the managers had set up branches in eight major cities.

Nonetheless, for political reasons, the First Bank of the United States did not survive. Jeffersonians had long condemned a national bank, warning that it would produce "a consolidated, energetic government supported by public creditors, speculators, and other insidious men lacking in public spirit of any kind." Consequently, when the bank's twenty-year charter expired in 1811, President Madison did not seek its renewal, forcing merchants, artisans, and farmers to turn to state legislatures to support banking. New York chartered the Mechanics' and Farmers' Bank of Albany in 1811, and other states followed suit. By the time Madison chartered the Second Bank of the United States in 1816, also for twenty years, there were 246 state-chartered banks. Unfortunately, many state banks issued notes without

adequate reserves of specie, causing the notes to fall in value and inhibiting commercial growth.

Poorly managed state banks were one cause of the Panic of 1819, a credit crisis sparked by a sharp drop in world agricultural prices. Their income suddenly cut by a third, many American farmers were unable to pay their creditors, setting in motion the successive bankruptcies of local storekeepers, wholesale merchants, and scores of overextended state banks. Economic recession continued for two years as many Americans got their first taste of the "business cycle" of a capitalist market. Nonetheless, the American economy had entered a new phase. With the rapid emergence of the banking system, the United States was no longer completely dependent on British credit. The new nation had its own financial institutions that promoted foreign trade and domestic development.

Rural Manufacturing. Since colonial times American artisans had handcrafted furniture, tools, wagons, shoes, saddles, clothing, and dozens of other items. Especially in New England and the Middle Atlantic states, many artisans enjoyed a modest but comfortable life from their labor, selling or exchanging their goods mostly within the local community. For example, during the 1780s John Hoff of Lancaster, Pennsylvania, sold his fine wooden-cased clocks locally or bartered them with his neighbors for such things as a dining table, a bedstead, shoes, pine boards, and labor on his small farm.

Some artisans—especially those who worked in large, specialized groups—had their eyes on more distant markets. Shipbuilders in seacoast towns, iron smelters in Pennsylvania and Maryland, and shoemakers in Lynn, Massachusetts, all sold their products to customers outside their regions. During the Revolutionary War merchants financed the expansion of various enterprises, encouraging rural men and women to make cheese, textiles, paper, and gunpowder. After the war national pride prompted calls for the expansion of *all* domestic handicrafts. "Until we manufacture more," the Boston *Gazette* declared in 1788, "it is absurd to celebrate the Fourth of July as the birthday of our independence."

With peace restored, many merchants ignored pleas to invest in domestic manufacturing; it was more profitable to sell low-priced British goods. Still, some entrepreneurs continued to develop wider markets for American rural manufactures. For instance, merchants sold goods made on Massachusetts farms not only in Boston but also in the other seaport towns of New England. As a Polish traveler in central Massachusetts reported in 1798, "Along the whole road from Boston, we saw women engaged in making cheese."

Some inland merchants were not content with marketing farm-produced goods and handicrafts and devel-

American Country Furniture
Country artisans, such as the unknown maker of this high chest of drawers from Norwich, Vermont (circa 1780), simplified high-style English designs. Using common woods, such as birch and pine, these rural manufacturers built furniture that was both useful and elegant. (Shelburne Museum)

oped their own version of the European *outwork* or *putting-out* system (see Chapter 1, page 31). These capitalist entrepreneurs actively recruited and organized households in rural communities to manufacture specific goods. The experience of Berlin, New Hampshire, was typical. For many years Berlin artisans had made tinware—baking pans, cups, eating utensils, lanterns—and carried it to local farmers with "a horse and two baskets." After the Revolutionary War, merchants in Berlin paid artisans to increase their output and hired young men, whom they furnished "with a horse and a cart covered with a box or with a wagon," to market the tinware in the South, a market long dominated by British imports. Soon these traders blanketed areas of the South, acquiring the dubious reputation of crafty, hard-bargaining "Yankees." Their commercial success extended the size of the capitalist sector of the American domestic economy.

The greatest success of the putting-out system occurred in the shoe and boot trade, which also found markets in the South, especially on slave plantations. In the 1780s merchants and master craftsmen in Lynn, Massachusetts, began buying large quantities of leather, thread, and awls and soon put thousands of families in the New England countryside to work. Farm women and children stitched together the thin leather and canvas uppers of the shoes, and the half-finished shoes were taken by wagon to Lynn for assembly by journeymen shoemakers. When the Embargo of 1807 cut off competition from British-made shoes, merchants in Lynn and over thirty other Massachusetts towns expanded their output and produced millions of shoes. By the 1820s these entrepreneurs had mobilized an enormous work force in the New England countryside and had begun to create a *national* market.

Their success stemmed primarily from innovations in organization and marketing, not in technology. Even as their markets expanded, tinworkers, shoemakers, and other artisans continued to use their traditional *preindustrial* handcraft technology. The use of power-driven machines—the product of the Industrial Revolution in Britain—came slowly to America, beginning with the textile industry. In the 1780s merchants built hundreds of small mills along the creeks and rivers of New England and the Middle Atlantic states. They installed water-powered machines and hired workers to card and comb wool—and later cotton—into long strands. For several decades the next steps in the manufacturing process were accomplished under the outwork system. Farm women and children spun the strands into yarn, receiving wages for their work, while men, usually in other households, wove the yarn into cloth. In his *Letter on Manufactures* (1810), Secretary of the Treasury Albert Gallatin reported that there were about 2,500 outwork weavers in New England. A decade later more than 12,000 household workers in that region were weaving woolen cloth, which was then taken to water-powered fulling mills, where it was pounded flat and given a smooth finish. Thus, even before textile production was centralized in factories, the nation had a profitable and expanding outwork system of manufacturing.

From a Market Economy to a Capitalist Economy. With these advances in rural manufacturing, the United States took yet another step toward a capitalist economy. At the center of this developing system stood a dynamic group of merchant-entrepreneurs who organized production; at the periphery were hundreds of thousands of farm families who supplied the labor. When a French traveler visited central Massachusetts in 1795, he found "almost all these houses . . . inhabited by men who are both cultivators and artisans; one is a tanner, another a shoemaker, another sells goods, but all are farmers." As these families made cheese, yarn, shoes, nails, and dozens of other products for market sale, they looked for better ways of making goods and then patented their inventions. The American countryside emerged as a center not only of production but also of invention and technical change.

Indeed, the rise of rural manufacturing transformed the local agricultural economy. To supply merchants and artisans with raw materials, ambitious farm families switched from mixed-crop agriculture to raising livestock. The shoe business consumed thousands of beef hides each year, the new cheese industry required large herds of dairy cows, and textile producers purchased the wool from tens of thousands of sheep. High prices for these raw materials brought prosperity and new businesses to many farming towns. In 1792 Concord, Massachusetts, had one slaughterhouse and five small tanneries; a decade later there were eleven slaughterhouses and six large tanneries in the town. Foul odors from the stockyards and tanning pits drifted over Concord, but its people were able to purchase more goods.

The emergence of a full-fledged cash-based market economy took decades, as the experience of the book-manufacturing firm of Ebenezer and Daniel Merriam of Brookfield, Massachusetts, demonstrates. When the Merriams began selling books to publishing houses in New York City, Philadelphia, and Boston during the 1810s, they received neither cash nor credit in return but other *books*—which they had to barter with local storekeepers to get supplies for their business. The Merriams paid their own workers on a barter basis as well; a journeyman printer received the use of a small house, credits to his accounts at local stores, and no less than one-third of his "wages" in books, which he had to peddle for himself if he wanted more than a literary profit from his labors.

Yet gradually a cash economy replaced this complex barter-exchange system. As farm families joined the outwork system, they stopped producing all their own food and making their own clothing and bedding. Instead of bartering their surplus crops for household necessities, they supplied merchants with specialized goods in return for cash or store credit. "Straw hats and Bonnets are manufactured by many families," a Maine official commented in the Census of Manufacturing of 1820, while another observer noted that "probably 8,000 females" in the vicinity of Foxborough, Massachusetts, braided rye straw into hats for market sale. These women used the income from the sale of their labor to shop in local stores.

The new capitalist-run market economy had its drawbacks. Rural parents—and their children—worked longer and harder, making shoes or hats or cloth during the winter as well as planting, weeding, and harvesting crops during the warmer seasons. Perhaps more important, they lost some of their economic independence. Instead of working completely for themselves as yeomen farm families, they toiled as part-time wage laborers for merchants and manufacturers. Thus the new market system decreased the self-sufficiency of both individual families and whole communities even as it made them more productive.

Increased output boosted the income of farm families and the collective wealth of the United States. Beginning around 1800, the per capita income of Americans increased at a rate of more than 1 percent per year—more than 30 percent in each generation. By the 1820s the extraordinary increase in output, artisan skills, and merchant capital had laid the foundation for the American Industrial Revolution (see Chapter 10). After a half century of political independence, the nation was beginning to achieve economic independence from Britain.

State Mercantilism: The "Commonwealth" System

Throughout the nineteenth century state governments were the most important political institutions in the United States. State legislatures took the lead in regulating social life, for example, abolishing slavery in the North and retaining it in the South. State governments enacted laws governing criminal and civil affairs, set voting requirements, established the taxation system, and oversaw county, city, and town officials. Beginning in the late 1810s, many states rewrote their constitutions in order to make them more democratic, decreasing property requirements for voting, reapportioning legislatures, and increasing the number of elected (rather than appointed) officials. Consequently, state governments—particularly state legislatures—had a much greater impact on the day-to-day lives of Americans than did the national government.

Beginning in the 1790s, many state legislatures sought to enhance prosperity by devising a new, American system of mercantilism known as the "commonwealth" system. Just as the British Parliament had promoted the imperial economy by passing Acts of Trade, state legislatures enacted measures to stimulate commerce and economic development in America. In particular, state governments granted hundreds of *corporate charters* to private businesses that were intended to be, as the act establishing the Massachusetts Bank put it, "of great public utility." Chartered companies were not new, of course—English investors had used them to establish the first American colonies. Under English law, however, colonial governments were discouraged from creating corporations, so merchants had financed mills, shipyards, and trading ventures through private partnerships, which lacked the legal and economic advantages of government-chartered corporations.

Private partnerships also lacked the funds required to build the large-scale transportation projects—the economic infrastructure—that had become a high priority for many state governments. State legislatures therefore issued numerous charters of incorporation to promote investment in roads, bridges, and canals. For example, after receiving a monopoly charter from the

Pennsylvania assembly, the Lancaster Turnpike Company opened a graded gravel road between Lancaster and Philadelphia in 1794. Its success set off a boom in turnpike construction. Soon improved roads connected dozens of inland market centers to seaport cities, but it would take a generation to build an integrated system of all-weather roads.

By 1800 state governments had granted more than 300 corporate charters. Legal incorporation enhanced the status of private companies in two ways. First, some charters protected investors through *limited liability*: in the event of business failure, the shareholders' personal assets could not be used to pay the debts of the corporation. Second, most transportation charters included the power of *eminent domain*, a legal provision that allowed turnpike, bridge, and canal corporations to force the sale of land along their routes. This power—previously available only to the government—permitted private corporations to take lands from property owners for a reasonable price even if the owners did not want to sell. By infringing on private property rights, eminent domain promoted economic development for the good of the commonwealth.

Such uses of state power by private companies were controversial and, in the eyes of some critics, contrary to republicanism, "which does not admit of granting peculiar privileges to any body of men." Charters not only violated the "equal rights" of all citizens, opponents argued, but also infringed on the sovereignty of the state. As a Pennsylvanian put it, "whatever power is given to a corporation, is just so much power taken from the State, in derogation of the original power of the mass of the community."

Nonetheless, state courts consistently upheld the validity of corporate charters. Judges routinely approved grants of eminent domain to private corporations even when they infringed on the property rights of citizens, arguing that economic development was in the public interest. "The opening of good and easy internal communications is one of the highest duties of government," a New Jersey court declared.

State mercantilism soon encompassed much more than transportation. After the Embargo of 1807, which cut off goods and credit from Europe, the New England state governments awarded charters to 200 iron-mining, textile-manufacturing, and banking firms. Over the next few decades the Pennsylvania legislature was even more active, chartering more than 1,100 corporations and authorizing them to hold over $150 million in capital. Corporations—in the form of incorporated towns and cities, incorporated charitable institutions, and chartered private business organizations—were becoming a central institution in American society. As one contemporary put it, "the whole political system" was "made up of concatenations of various corporations, political, civil, religious, social and economical."

Thus, by 1820, the innovative policies of the state governments had created a new political economy: the commonwealth system. This system elevated the good of the public—the common-wealth—above that of private individuals, but because it used private corporations for public purposes, it also enhanced the economic and political power of capitalist entrepreneurs. This instrumental use of state legislation to improve the general welfare would continue for another generation. In 1820 Missouri lawmakers incorporated this outlook into that state's first constitution, specifying that "internal improvements shall forever be encouraged by the government of this state."

Law and the "Commonwealth": Republicans versus Federalists

Both Federalists and Republicans endorsed commonwealth ideology, but in different ways. Federalists looked to the national government for economic leadership. Most Federalists supported Hamilton's program of *national* mercantilism, in which the central government encouraged economic development through tariff and banking policies. Jeffersonian Republicans generally opposed such schemes, relying instead on the state legislatures. After the War of 1812, however, some Republicans, led by Henry Clay of Kentucky, began to support national economic initiatives. As Speaker of the House of Representatives, Clay supported the creation of the Second Bank of the United States in 1816. The following year he won passage of the Bonus Bill, sponsored by Representative John C. Calhoun of South Carolina, which would have established a national fund for roads and other internal improvements. But most Republicans still opposed national mercantilist policies; they agreed with President Madison, who vetoed the Bonus Bill because he felt it exceeded the powers delegated to the national government by the Constitution. This fundamental disagreement over the role of the national government would become a major issue of political debate for the next thirty years (see Chapter 11).

Common Law and Statute Law. Differing conceptions of law also separated Federalists and Republicans. From the earliest colonial times American jurisprudence had been shaped by English common law. In deciding cases, judges relied on *precedents*—decisions in similar earlier cases—and they assumed, as a Maryland lawyer put it, that "the Common Law takes in the Law of Nature, the Law of Reason and the Revealed Law of God." In this view, held by many Federalists, law was a venerable and unchanging entity.

The revolutionary republican doctrine of popular sovereignty undermined the intellectual foundations of this old legal order. As Americans debated constitutional principles, many of them recognized that law was a human invention—the product of politics—and not a sacred body of timeless truths. In fact, during the 1790s Thomas Jefferson and other leaders of the Republican party directly attacked the common-law system. They maintained that law made by judges following common-law precedents was inferior to the statute ("positive") law enacted by the representatives of the people. As a Republican jurist put it, a magistrate "should be governed himself by *positive* law, and executes and enforces the will of the supreme power, which is the will of THE PEOPLE."

Federalist judges and politicians warned that popular sovereignty had to be curbed. Without safeguards, Federalists feared, representative government would result in the "tyranny of the majority"—the passage of statutes that would infringe on the existing property rights of individual citizens. To keep property rights from being overridden by state legislatures, Federalist lawyers asserted that judges had the power to void laws that violated traditional common-law principles or were contrary to "natural law" or "natural rights" (see Chapter 4).

Common Law versus Economic Development. Because common-law precedents had evolved in a relatively static agricultural economy, they often discouraged new modes of enterprise, such as manufacturing. For example, capitalist entrepreneurs who erected dams to operate flour or textile mills often flooded adjacent farmlands; outraged farmers sued, arguing that the dams not only infringed on their property rights but also were a "nuisance" to the public and should be pulled down. At first the farmers won most of these cases. In 1795, for example, a New Jersey court used common-law precedents in ruling that it was illegal to interfere with the natural flow of a river for nonfarming purposes "without the consent of all who have an interest in it."

Such decisions threatened to stifle economic development. Consequently, republican-minded state legislatures enacted statutes that overrode the common law by limiting the legal recourse available to landowners. In Massachusetts, the Mill Dam Act of 1795 allowed mill proprietors to flood adjacent farmlands and prevented farmers from blocking the construction of dams or seeking damages, forcing them to accept "fair compensation" for their lost acreage. This prodevelopment legislation justified the taking of private property by asserting the superior rights of individuals who made a dynamic, rather than a static, use of their property.

State judges with Republican leanings accepted the doctrines of popular sovereignty and legislative power and therefore usually upheld mill acts, just as they supported legislative statutes that granted eminent domain to private turnpike and canal corporations. To these

judges, *social utility*—the greatest good for the greatest number—justified the government's intrusion into the property rights of individual citizens. Such rulings shocked Daniel Webster, the great Federalist lawyer and politician, who considered them no less than a "revolution against the foundations on which property rests." Both parties favored economic development, but they prescribed different political and legal paths to that goal. Federalists favored national mercantilism, common law, and a static theory of property rights; Republicans advocated state activism, statute law, and a dynamic concept of property.

Federalist Law: John Marshall

Upon becoming president in 1801, Thomas Jefferson warned that his Federalist opponents were retreating into the judiciary, and from that fortress "all the works of Republicanism are to be beaten down and erased." The legal career of John Marshall confirmed Jefferson's prediction. Appointed chief justice of the Supreme Court by John Adams in 1801, Marshall upheld Federalist principles until his death in 1835. His success stemmed not from a mastery of legal principles and doctrines—indeed, his opinions usually cited very few precedents—but from the power of his logic and the

Chief Justice John Marshall
Marshall had a commanding personal presence and made over the United States Supreme Court in his image, elevating it from a minor department into a major institution in American legal and political life.

force of his personality. Until 1821 Marshall dominated his colleagues on the Supreme Court, and they largely accepted his definition of its powers and interpretation of the law.

Three principles shaped Marshall's Federalist jurisprudence: a commitment to judicial power, the supremacy of national over state legislation, and a traditional, static view of property rights.

Judicial Power: *Marbury v. Madison*. The celebrated case of *Marbury v. Madison* (1803) demonstrated Marshall's commitment to the preeminent authority of the judiciary. The case arose from the controversial "midnight" appointments of President John Adams in 1801 (see Chapter 8). As Jefferson's secretary of state, James Madison had refused to deliver a commission appointing William Marbury as a justice of the peace. When Marbury asked the Supreme Court to intervene by issuing a legal writ directing his appointment, Marshall ruled that while Marbury had a right to his commission, that right was not enforceable by the Court. This was so, Marshall declared, because the section of the Judiciary Act of 1789 that gave the Supreme Court the power to issue writs in such cases was unconstitutional. Marshall's decision was politically astute, condemning Madison's actions while avoiding a direct confrontation with the Republican administration.

More important, this decision marked the first time the Supreme Court had overturned a national law. Five years earlier, during the dispute over the Alien and Sedition Acts, the Republican-dominated Kentucky and Virginia legislatures had asserted the authority of state legislatures to determine the constitutionality of national laws. But the Constitution implied that the Supreme Court had this power of *judicial review*, and now Marshall claimed it explicitly: "It is emphatically the province and duty of the judicial department to say what the law is." The doctrine of judicial review evolved slowly. During the first half of the nineteenth century the Supreme Court and the state courts used it to overturn *state* laws that conflicted with constitutional principles, but not until the *Dred Scott* decision of 1857 would the Supreme Court void another national law. After the Civil War, however, the Court frequently invoked judicial review to overturn Congressional as well as state legislation.

Nationalism: *McCulloch v. Maryland*. Marshall's nationalism was most eloquently expressed in the controversial case of *McCulloch v. Maryland* (1819). When Congress created the Second Bank of the United States in 1816, the bank was given the authority to handle the notes of the state banks, a power that it used to monitor their financial reserves and create a national system of credit.

Many state governments resented the dominant position of the new national bank. The Maryland legislature imposed an annual tax of $15,000 on notes issued by the Baltimore branch of the Second Bank and, to preserve the independence and competitive position of its own state-chartered banks, limited the Second Bank's powers. The national bank contested the constitutionality of Maryland's action, claiming that it infringed on the powers of the national government. In response, lawyers for the state of Maryland adopted Jefferson's argument against the First Bank of the United States, maintaining that Congress lacked the constitutional authority to charter a national bank. Even if such a bank could be created, the lawyers argued, Maryland had a right to tax its activities within the state.

Marshall firmly rejected both arguments. He declared that the Second Bank was constitutional because its existence was "necessary and proper," given the national responsibility to control currency and credit. Like Alexander Hamilton and other Federalists, Marshall preferred a loose construction of the Constitution: "Let the end be legitimate, let it be within the scope of the Constitution and all means which are appropriate, which [are consistent] . . . with the letter and the spirit of the constitution, are constitutional."

As for Maryland's right to tax all institutions within its borders, the chief justice embraced the nationalist position advanced by Daniel Webster, a fellow Federalist and legal counsel to the Second Bank. "The power to tax involves the power to destroy," Marshall observed, suggesting that Maryland's tax would render the national government "dependent on the states"—a situation that "was not intended by the American people" when their representatives ratified the Constitution. With this decision, Marshall asserted the dominance of national statutes over state legislation and, by outlining a broad interpretation of the Constitution, laid the legal foundation for the subsequent expansion of national authority.

Two years later Marshall declared the supremacy of national courts of law over state tribunals. In the case of *Cohens v. Virginia* (1821) he proclaimed that the Constitution had diminished the sovereignty of the states. State courts did not have the last say on issues that fell within the purview of the national Constitution, and their decisions could be appealed to the federal judiciary.

Property Rights: *Fletcher v. Peck*. Marshall found in the national Constitution the basis for legal guarantees that protected property rights against claims by governments and by developers. With respect to governments, Marshall noted that the *contract clause* of the Constitution (Article I, Section 10) prohibits the states from passing any law "impairing the obligation of contracts." The delegates had included this clause primarily to assist merchants and other creditors by voiding state laws that protected debtors. Marshall, however, used the contract clause to defend other property rights against legislative challenge. For example, the case of *Fletcher v. Peck* (1810) involved a large grant of land made by the Georgia legislature to the Yazoo Land Company. A newly elected state legislature later canceled the grant, alleging that it had been obtained through fraud and bribery, and speculators in other states who had purchased Yazoo lands appealed to the Supreme Court. Speaking for the Court, Marshall ruled that the purchasers had valid contracts whose obligations could not be impaired by the state of Georgia. This decision was far-reaching. It not only gave constitutional protection against subsequent state legislation to those who purchased state-owned lands but also, by upholding the rights of out-of-state speculators, encouraged the development of a national capitalist economy.

The case of *Dartmouth College v. Woodward* (1819) gave property owners even greater protection against state interference. Dartmouth was a private institution established by a charter granted by King George III in 1769. In 1816 the Republican-dominated legislature of New Hampshire tried to convert the college into a public university so that it could educate more students and enhance the common-wealth of the state. The Dartmouth trustees resisted the plan and engaged Daniel Webster to plead their case before the Supreme Court. Webster based his argument squarely on the Court's decision in *Fletcher v. Peck*. The royal charter had bestowed "corporate rights and privileges" on the college, Webster maintained; therefore, the charter constituted a contract and could not be tampered with by the New Hampshire legislature. Dartmouth College was in effect private property.

Marshall had difficulty persuading his colleagues to accept Webster's argument. Although he was still the dominant member of the Court, by 1819 five Supreme Court justices had been appointed by the Republican presidents Jefferson, Madison, and Monroe. Some of those justices favored the commonwealth system and believed that a public university would better serve the common good. Others hesitated to restrict the powers of the state legislatures or endorse the broad legal protection of property rights set forth in *Fletcher v. Peck*. Only after months of deliberation—and the preparation of a precedent-filled decision by Associate Justice Joseph Story, a New England jurist with strong Federalist leanings—did the justices follow Marshall and rule in favor of the college. *Dartmouth v. Woodward* not only endorsed a static, or "vested," conception of property rights (repudiating the dynamic, commonwealth-oriented view of the New Hampshire legislature) but extended those rights from individuals to business corporations. Thereafter, corporations would claim that their state-granted charters were "contracts" that protected them—forever—from regulation or control by the governments that had created them.

Marshall's triumph seemed complete. In the decisions handed down between 1819 and 1821—*Dartmouth*, *McCulloch*, and *Cohens*—he had incorporated Federalist principles into the law of the land, championing judicial review, nationalism, and a static conception of property rights. Many of Marshall's legal principles, such as judicial review and corporate rights, became central fixtures of the American legal order. But even before the chief justice's death in 1835, states' rights–minded jurists qualified his nationalist vision, and republican-minded state legislators used commonwealth ideology to justify the taking of private property for public purposes. Yet this legal conflict was primarily over means, not ends. Both Marshall and his Republican opponents strongly supported the private ownership of property and the expansion of a market economy. Together they laid the legal and political foundations for the American Industrial Revolution (see Chapter 10).

Visions of a Republican Social Order

After independence, Americans tried to become "republicans" in their political outlook, social behavior, and cultural values. American men applied the doctrines of legal equality and social mobility to gain the right to vote and improve their social status. Some young people sought more egalitarian marriages and more affectionate ways of raising and educating their children. Many more members of the rising generation condemned the aristocratic pretensions of old-style political leaders and the cold formality of conservative lawyers and judges. The pursuit of republican ideals was complex and conflict-ridden, but it gradually changed the character of American society.

Mobility and Democracy for Men

Between 1780 and 1820 hundreds of well-educated Europeans visited the United States to acquire firsthand knowledge of life in a republican society. These visitors came from countries characterized by political hierarchy, religious orthodoxy, patriarchal families, and profound social inequality. They wondered—as successive generations of historians have wondered—whether America represented a more just social order. The French-born essayist Crèvecoeur had no doubts. Com-

A Country Tavern
The stylishly dressed dancers command the attention of the onlookers, but the scene suggests the social cohesion and equality in rural communities and the spontaneous character of leisure-time activities.

paring the Old World and the New in his famous *Letters from an American Farmer* (1782), Crèvecoeur wrote that European society was composed "of great lords who possess everything, and of a herd of people who have nothing." In America, by contrast, there "are no aristocratical families, no courts, no kings, no bishops." Reflecting these conditions, many Americans maintained—as a letter to a newspaper put it—that people should be valued not for their "wealth, titles, or connections" but for their "talents, integrity, and virtue."

Social Mobility. To many Europeans, America was distinctive in regard to the availability of economic opportunity—it was the "best poor man's country," at least for whites. As an Englishman explained, "A consciousness of independence forms the character of the American because the means of subsistence being so easy in this country, and their dependence on each other consequently so trifling, the spirit of servility to those above them so prevalent in European manners is wholly unknown to them" (see American Voices, page 275).

Republican ideology emphasized legal equality for all free men and thus further undermined traditional hierarchical authority. "The law is the same for everyone both as it protects and as it punishes," one European noted. "In the course of daily life everyone is on the most perfect footing of equality." Foreign visitors were well aware that class divisions existed in the United States but saw them as different from those in Europe. The American colonies had never had—and the republican state and national constitutions had in fact prohibited—a legally defined, privileged nobility. The absence of an aristocracy of birth encouraged enterprising American men to seek upward social mobility and jus-

tify class divisions based on achievement. "In Europe to say of someone that he rose from nothing is a disgrace and a reproach," an aristocratic Polish visitor explained. "It is the opposite here. To be the architect of your own fortune is honorable. It is the highest recommendation."

Only a few disagreed. American men who owed their position to inherited wealth and social status questioned the moral legitimacy of a social order determined by personal effort or financial success. "The aristocracy of Kingston [New York] is more one of money than any village I have ever seen," complained Nathaniel Booth in 1825. Booth's ancestors had once ruled Kingston but had later lost predominance in the rapidly growing Hudson River town. "Man is estimated by dollars," he lamented; "what he is worth determines his character and his position at once." But Booth spoke for a minority. For most white American men republicanism meant the opportunity to advance their interests and those of their families.

Extending the Franchise. By the 1820s republicanism had also come to mean voting rights for free white men. Political democracy reflected the decline of class as the foundation of citizenship. In repudiating the hierarchical ideal of Federalists such as Samuel Stone, who called for "a *speaking* aristocracy in the face of a *silent* democracy," Americans rejected the "deferential" political practices of the eighteenth century. They refused to vote for Federalist politicians who flaunted their high social status, with their hair in "powder and queues" and their "top boots, breeches, and shoe buckles"; instead, they elected Republican politicians who dressed simply and advocated an extension of the franchise.

Charles W. Janson

Manners in the New Republic

Most European immigrants were from the poorer classes and welcomed the absence of strong class barriers in the United States, but many upper-class visitors took offense at American presumptions of social equality. This account by an English traveler also shows that the dignity felt by some whites came at the expense of blacks.

Let me suppose, like myself, you had fallen in with an American innkeeper who at the moment would condescend to take the trouble to procure you refreshment. . . . He will sit by your side, and enter in the most familiar manner into conversation; which is prefaced, of course, with a demand of your business, and so forth. He will then start a political question (for here every individual is a politician), force you to answer, contradict, deny, and, finally, be ripe for a quarrel, should you not acquiesce in all his opinions. . . .

If you arrive at the dinner hour, you are seated with "mine hostess" and her dirty children, with whom you have often to scramble for a plate. This is esteemed wit, and consequently provokes a laugh, at the expense of those who are paying for the board. . . .

The arrogance of servants in this land of republican liberty and equality is particularly calculated to excite the astonishment of strangers. To call persons of this description servants, or to speak of their master or mistress, is a grievous affront.

Having called one day at the house of a gentleman of my acquaintance, on knocking at the door, it was opened by a servant-maid, whom I had never before seen, as she had not been long in his family. The following is the dialogue, word for word, which took place on this occasion:

"Is your master at home?"
"I have no master."
"Don't you live here?"
"I stay here."
"And who are you then?"
"Why, I am Mr. ——— 's help. I'd have you to know, man, that I am no sarvant. None but negers are sarvants."

Source: C. W. Janson, *The Stranger in America, 1793–1806* (1807), 85–88.

Concurrently, legislators redefined political citizenship on the basis of gender and race, raising the status of middling and poor white men by elevating them above white women and free black men. A number of states, such as Pennsylvania and New York, denied the franchise to free African-Americans or subjected them to high property qualifications for voting. Because women traditionally had been banned from public life, they were routinely excluded from the franchise either by custom or by state constitutional fiat. The New Jer-

The Old House of Representatives, 1822

Representative government is the essence of republicanism. By highlighting the august red draperies and golden candlelight, this painting by Samuel F. B. Morse (who would later invent the telegraph) celebrates the deliberations of the popularly elected national legislature.

sey constitution of 1776, however, granted suffrage to all propertyholders, and beginning in the 1790s, propertied women became active participants in electoral battles between Federalists and Republicans. In 1807 a Republican-dominated legislature in New Jersey abolished property-holding requirements for voting and consciously defined full citizenship as an attribute of men, excluding women from suffrage. To justify this exclusion of women, legislators invoked traditional biological and social arguments. As one letter to a newspaper put it, "Women, generally, are neither by nature, nor habit, nor education, nor by their necessary condition in society fitted to perform this duty with credit to themselves or advantage to the public."

Other states also moved toward political democracy for men. Maryland extended the vote to all adult men in 1810, and the constitutions of the new states of Indiana (1816), Illinois (1818), and Alabama (1819) prescribed a broad male franchise. By the end of the 1820s only a few states—North Carolina, Virginia, Rhode Island—required the ownership of freehold property for voting.

Others, such as Ohio and Louisiana, limited suffrage to men who paid taxes or served in the militia, but a majority of the states had instituted universal white manhood suffrage (see Map 9.1).

Popular pressure brought other constitutional changes as well. Between 1818 and 1821 reform-minded politicians in Connecticut, Massachusetts, and New York pushed through important revisions in their state constitutions, reapportioning their legislatures on the basis of population and instituting more democratic forms of local government—such as the election rather than the appointment of judges and justices of the peace. If such "democratic doctrines" had been advanced ten years earlier, Chancellor James Kent of New York protested, they "should have struck the public mind with astonishment and terror."

The Legal Profession. A similar democratic revolution took place in the legal profession. During the Revolutionary Era, American attorneys had raised the standards of their profession by establishing bar

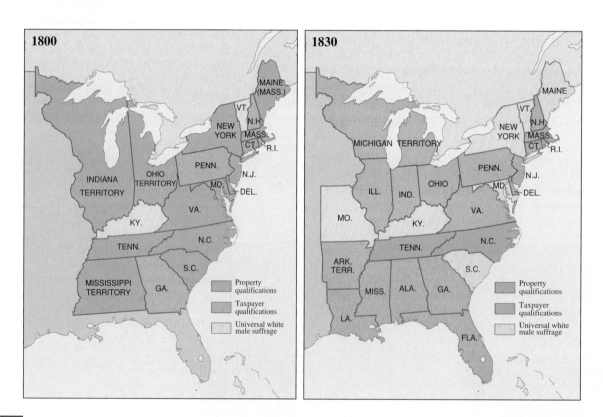

MAP 9.1

The Expansion of Voting Rights for White Men
Between 1800 and 1830 the United States moved steadily toward political democracy for white men. Many existing states revised their constitutions, replacing property ownership with taxpaying or militia service as a qualification for voting. Some new states in the West extended the franchise to all adult white men. As parties sought votes from a broader electorate, the tone of politics became more open and competitive—swayed by the interests and values of ordinary people.

TABLE 9.1

Number of Lawyers in Three Selected States, to 1820

	Number of Lawyers	Lawyers per 10,000 Population
Massachusetts (including Maine)		
1740	15	10
1775	71	24
1780	34	11
1785	92	24
1790	112	24
1800	200	35
1810	492	70
1820	710	87
Connecticut		
1790	129	54
1800	169	67
1820	248	90
South Carolina		
1771	24	19
1820	200	40

Source: George Dargo, *Law in the New Republic: Private Law and the Public Estate* (New York: Knopf, 1983), 49. Reprinted by permission of McGraw-Hill, Inc.

Judge Tapping Reeve
The founder of Litchfield Law School, Reeve sits in his study surrounded by volumes of reports of English and American cases. Published reports enhanced the authority of judges, who cited them as precedents for their rulings.

associations and winning legislation that prevented untrained lawyers—whom they called "pettifoggers"—from practicing law. By 1800 most of the sixteen states required lawyers to have three to seven years of formal schooling or apprenticeship training. Harvard, Columbia, and William and Mary colleges all offered lectures on legal issues, and in 1784 Judge Tapping Reeve founded the famous Litchfield, Connecticut, law school. By the 1820s Litchfield had graduated more than a thousand lawyers, including three future Supreme Court justices and two vice-presidents (Aaron Burr of New York and John C. Calhoun of South Carolina).

As legal rules became a more central part of American life, the legal profession grew in importance. In many states (as Table 9.1 suggests) the number of lawyers grew faster than did the population. Lawyers gained in prestige, impressing the voters with their eloquence in local courtrooms, and increasingly won election to public office. As early as 1820, 15 percent of the members of the Massachusetts assembly and 35 percent of those in the Senate were lawyers, though men of the law constituted only 1 percent of the state's adult male population. Thoroughly conversant with law as a system of power, lawyers pushed forward the activism of state legislatures, which enacted hundreds of statutes affecting many aspects of life.

The growing power of the legal profession inspired calls for its reform. Republican-minded critics attacked what they called the "professional aristocracy" of lawyers, demanding the regulation of attorneys' fees and the creation of small-claims courts in which ordinary citizens could represent themselves. Both reforms made the legal system more accessible to those without means. Reformers also succeeded in obtaining more relaxed standards for admission to the bar. By the 1820s only eleven of the twenty-six states required a fixed period of legal instruction. These reforms lowered the intellectual quality of the legal profession but made it more democratic in composition and spirit.

Republican Families

Republicanism was a potent ideology that, as John Adams lamented, "spread where it was not intended," deep into the heart of the social order. For example, the republican emphasis on equality and independence directly challenged the traditional concept of family life, which was patriarchal and constricting. In Europe and in British North America husbands had dominated their wives and maintained legal control over the family's property. Now, in the eyes of some women who wanted to control an inheritance or speak out on public matters, their subordination to men seemed arbitrary, at odds with a belief in equal natural rights. Patriarchy was no longer seen as "natural"; it could be justified only on pragmatic grounds, "for the sake of order in families," as Mercy Otis Warren put it.

Economic and cultural changes also contributed to the erosion of customary family relations. Traditionally, parents arranged marriages to ensure the economic well-being of both their children and themselves during old age. As land holdings shrank in long-settled rural communities, however, parents could no longer bequeath substantial farms to their children and so lost the economic incentives by which they had controlled their children's lives. Increasingly, sons and daughters chose their own partners.

Sentimentalism. In making these choices, many young Americans were influenced by the new cultural attitude of *sentimentalism*. Originating in Europe during the so-called Romantic movement of the late eighteenth century, sentimentalism celebrated the importance of "feeling"—that is, an emotional understanding of life's experiences. People that were influenced by sentimentalism sought a physical, sensuous appreciation of God, nature, and other human beings. By 1820 sentimentalism had touched all classes of American society. It dripped from the pages of German and English literary works read in educated circles. It fell from the lips of actors in tear-jerking melodramas, which soon became the most popular theatrical entertainments in the United States. And it infused the rhetoric of revivalist preachers, who appealed to the passions of the heart rather than the cool logic of the mind.

Sentimentalism encouraged couples to marry for love. Parents had always taken physical attraction and emotional compatibility into account in arranging marriages for their children, but romance did not have a high cultural value. Most parents were realists, influenced mostly by the character and financial resources of a prospective son- or daughter-in-law. One skeptical Virginia mother argued that young women should remain single "till they were old enough to form a proper *judgement* of mankind" and not be deceived by their emotions. Wealthy fathers were equally concerned; after the Revolution they tended to bequeath more resources to their children (often at the expense of their widowed wives) and often placed funds in legal trusts so that their daughters would not be completely dependent on their husbands. As a Virginia planter wrote to his

lawyer, "I rely on you to see the property settlement properly drawn before the *marriage*, for I by no means consent that Polly shall be left to the Vicissitudes of Life." By such means parents became paternalists, protecting the interests of those who married for love.

Republican Marriages. Republicanism made marriage, rather than parenthood, the fundamental family relationship, and the new youth-run marriage system gave young adults greater freedom. Magazines promoted marriages "contracted from motives of affection, rather than of interest," encouraging a young person to seek a spouse who was, as Eliza Southgate of Maine put it, "calculated to promote my happiness" (see American Voices, page 279). Yet many young adults lacked the maturity and experience to choose wisely. Many were disappointed when their spouses failed as financial providers or faithful companions. Divorce petitions reflected their fate. Before 1800 the few people who petitioned for divorce had charged their spouses with neglect, abandonment, or adultery—serious offenses against the moral order of society. Now emotional complaints dominated divorce petitions. One woman complained that her husband had "ceased to cherish her," and a male petitioner lamented that his wife had "almost broke his heart." Reflecting these changed cultural values, some states expanded the legal grounds for divorce to include personal cruelty and drunkenness and made divorces available through judicial decree, rather than, as in the past, only through a special act of the legislature.

Still, most unions, happy or not, lasted until death and, especially among urban Americans of middling status, were affected by the republican ideal of a "companionate" marriage. This noble ideal, in which husbands and wives had "true equality, both of rank and fortune," sharing responsibility for decisions and treating each other with respect, foundered in the face of deeply ingrained cultural habits that favored men and legal rules that placed all property in their hands. Moreover, since the new marriage system discouraged parents from playing an active role in their children's lives, young wives could no longer rely on their parents for emotional or financial support and became more dependent on their husbands.

Consequently, the net effect of republican marriage patterns was to diminish the control of parents over children but not the power of husbands over wives. The marriage contract "is so much more important in its consequences to females than to males," a young man at the Litchfield Law School noted astutely in 1820, "for besides leaving everything else to unite themselves to one man, they subject themselves to his authority. He is their all—their only relative—their only hope."

Eliza Southgate

The Dilemmas of Womanhood

Eliza Southgate was born into a wealthy Maine family in 1783. At school in Boston, she discovered both radical doctrines of sexual equality and the reality of female subordination. In this letter to a male cousin, written in 1801, she tries to resolve these contradictory messages and define her own stance toward the world of men.

But every being who has contemplated human nature on a large scale will certainly justify me when I declare that the inequality of privilege between the sexes is sensibly felt by us females, and in no instance is it greater than in the liberty of choosing a partner in marriage; true, we have the liberty of refusing those we don't like, but not of selecting those we do. This is undoubtedly as it should be....

I never was of opinion that the pursuits of the sexes ought to be the same; on the contrary, I believe it would be destructive to happiness, there would be a degree of rivalry incompatible with the harmony we wish to establish. I have ever thought it necessary that each should have a separate sphere of action—in such a case there could be no clashing unless one or the other should leap their respective bounds. Yet to cultivate the qualities with which we are endowed can never be called infringing the prerogatives of man....

The cultivation of the power we possess, I have ever thought a privilege (or I may say duty) that belonged to the human species, and not man's exclusive prerogative. Far from destroying the harmony that ought to subsist,

it would fix it on a foundation that would not totter at every jar. Women would be under the same degree of subordination that they now are; enlighten and expand their minds, and they would perceive the necessity of such a regulation to preserve the order and happiness of society....

It does not follow (O what pen!) that every female who vindicates the capacity of the sex is a disciple of Mary Wolstoncraft. Though I allow her to have said many things which I cannot approve, I confess I admire many of her sentiments.

Source: David J. Rothman and Sheila Rothman, eds., *Sources of the American Social Tradition* (New York: Basic Books, 1975).

Raising and Educating Republican Children

In all societies, marriage has many purposes: it channels sexuality, facilitates the inheritance of property, and by creating strong family and kinship ties, eases the raising of children. In the United States the triumph of republican values altered assumptions not only about marriage but also about inheritance and child-rearing. Republican-minded state legislators provided for the equal distribution of estates among child-heirs when the property owner died without a will. In conjunction with longer-term social changes, republican ideology also altered the size and values of many American families.

Fewer Children. In long-settled regions of the United States the creation of a republican society coincided with a dramatic fall in the birth rate. For example, in the farm village of Sturbridge, Massachusetts, women who had married around 1750 bore an average of 8.8 children whereas women who married around 1810 had only about 6 children. The decline was even greater

in the urban areas of Massachusetts, where by the 1820s native-born white women bore an average of 4 children. This urban birth rate barely sufficed to maintain the population, for one-third of all children in the cities died from measles, diphtheria, or smallpox.

The United States was one of the first countries in the world to experience this sharp decline in the birth rate, which is known as the *demographic transition*. The causes were several. The migration of thousands of young men to the trans-Appalachian West left many women without marriage partners and delayed the marriages of many more. Women who married later—say, at age 26 rather than age 20—had fewer children because they were married for fewer of their most fertile years. More important, thousands of white American couples deliberately limited the size of their families. After having four or five children, they used birth control or abstained from sexual intercourse to avoid conception. Farms were shrinking in size, and parents wanted to provide each of their children with an adequate inheritance.

The New Conjugal Family
Grace and Philip Schuyler pose informally with their daughters and encourage their musical and literary talents. The affectionate mood of this early nineteenth-century scene stands in sharp contrast to the hierarchy and discipline seen in the family portraits painted in earlier eras (see pages 29 and 104). (Collection of The New-York Historical Society)

Rearing the Young. At the same time, many American parents raised their children in new ways. Child-rearing practices are difficult to document, not being matters of public record, but reports from foreign visitors suggest that white Americans indulged their children and failed to discipline them. "Mr. Schuyler's second son is a spoiled little child, as are all American children, very willful, mischievous, and likeable," the Marquis de Chastelleux observed in 1780.

Visitors attributed this behavior, at least in part, to republican ideology. Because of the "general ideas of Liberty and Equality engraved on their hearts," a Polish aristocrat suggested, American children had "scant respect" for their parents. A British traveler was dumbfounded when an American father excused his son's "resolute disobedience" with a smile and the remark "A sturdy republican, sir." Foreigners guessed that parents encouraged such independence to enable young people to "go their own way" in the world.

The child-rearing literature of the period gives some support to this interpretation. Ministers, who wrote most of the pamphlets and books giving advice on raising children, were divided into two camps. Religious writers influenced by John Locke and the Enlightenment argued that children were "rational creatures" who should be encouraged to act correctly by means of praise, advice, and reasoned restraint. Those who held to Calvinist principles taught that infants were "full of the stains and pollution of sin" and needed strict discipline.

These two approaches—the authoritarian Calvinist and the affectionate rationalist—appealed to different social and religious groups in the United States. Edu-

cated or wealthy Americans, who were often members of Episcopal or Presbyterian churches, usually treated their children kindly. Since foreign commentators usually mixed with these well-to-do Americans, they reported this set of customs as the social norm. Actually, most yeomen and tenant farmers were much stricter and more authoritarian in their dealings with children, especially in families that belonged to Baptist or Calvinist-oriented Congregational churches.

Republican ideals affected this outlook. Evangelical Baptists and Methodists in the early nineteenth century still insisted on the need to instill humility in children and teach them to subordinate their desires to God's will. Fear was a "useful and necessary principle in family government," the minister John Abbott advised parents; a child "should submit to your authority, not to your arguments or persuasions." Yet even Abbott cautioned that it was wrong "exclusively to control him by this motive."

Rationalist writers placed more and more emphasis on children's capacity for education. They suggested that training should be focused on developing children's consciences so that young people would learn to police their own behavior. To that end, affectionate parents read their children stories that stressed self-discipline and neatness. They encouraged children to accept the burdens of independence: they must think and act for themselves. Foreigners observed that American children had greater freedom than did their counterparts in Europe, being allowed to participate in conversations among adults and venture into public without a chaperon. What passed unnoticed was the responsibility these young Americans had to assume for their own lives. In private life as in public, republicanism balanced rights with duties.

Education Debated. Some Americans were well aware of the fragility of their republican experiment and sought to buttress its principles through education. Before independence, formal education had played a minor role in the lives of most American youth. In New England locally funded public schools provided most children with basic instruction in reading and writing. In other regions fewer children were given an education: about a quarter of the boys and perhaps 10 percent of the girls attended privately funded schools or had personal tutors. Even in New England, only a small fraction of the men—and almost no women—went on to grammar (high) school, and only 1 percent of men graduated from college.

After independence, Caleb Bingham, an influential textbook author from Boston, called for "an equal distribution of knowledge to make us emphatically a 'republic of letters.'" Thomas Jefferson and Benjamin Rush, the Philadelphia physician, separately proposed ambitious schemes for educational reform. Both mapped out plans for a comprehensive system of primary and secondary schooling, followed by colleges to educate young men (but not women) in the liberal arts—classical literature, history, and philosophy. They also proposed the establishment of a university where distinguished scholars would lecture on law, medicine, theology, and political economy.

These ideas fell on deaf ears. To ordinary citizens such elaborate schemes smacked of elitism. Farmers, artisans, and laborers looked to schools for basic instruction in the "three R's": reading, 'riting, and 'rithmetic. They supported public funding for primary schools but not for secondary schools or colleges, which were of no use to their teenage children, who already labored as apprentices, domestic servants, or farm workers. "Let anybody show what advantage the poor man receives from colleges," an anonymous "Old Soldier" wrote to the Maryland *Gazette*. "Why should they support them, unless it is to serve those who are in affluent circumstances, whose children can be spared from labor, and receive the benefits?" New or revised state constitutions responded to the wishes of the majority by calling for the legislatures to fund a broad system of primary education.

Even plans for basic education made little headway before 1820, when a new generation of reformers campaigned successfully for the improvement of public elementary schools. Led by merchants and manufacturers, they raised standards by certifying qualified teachers and appointing state superintendents of education. Self-interest as well as public virtue motivated these gentlemen reformers, many of whom were old Federalists suspicious of the popular will. They wanted schools to instill the virtues of self-discipline and individual enterprise. Consequently, textbooks praised honesty and hard work while condemning gambling, drinking, and laziness. Gentlemen reformers also demanded that students be required to study American history, for they thought patriotic instruction would foster shared cultural ideals. The experience of Thomas Low, a New Hampshire schoolboy of the 1820s, would have satisfied their fondest hopes:

> We were taught every day and in every way that ours was the freest, the happiest, and soon to be the greatest and most powerful country of the world. This is the religious faith of every American. He learns it in his infancy and can never forget it.

The task of educators had been to transmit widely accepted knowledge and values from one generation to the next. In the new republican society they were also entrusted with instilling patriotism.

Literary Independence. Patriotism—the sense of an American identity—appeared again in the quest for a distinctive republican literature. Before the Revolution most American writers were ministers who published sermons, moral tracts, and commentaries on religious experience. Many books imported from Europe were religious in character: the Bible, commentaries on Scripture, moral advice, and the like. Most of the political treatises and literary works read in America were also by European writers. With respect to literary matters, the British mainland colonists were a dependent people.

As early as the 1780s Noah Webster had asserted that "America must be as independent in *literature* as she is in politics." Webster's contribution, in his *Dissertation on the English Language* (1789), was to standardize the American spelling of various words (such as *labor* for the British *labour*). His "blue-backed speller," first published in 1783, sold 60 million copies over the next half century and helped give Americans of all backgrounds a common vocabulary and grammar. "None of us was 'lowed to see a book," an enslaved black recalled, "but we gits hold of that Webster's old blue-back speller and we . . . studies that spelling book." Webster blended instruction in grammar and pronunciation with moral principles: "Vir-tue ex-alt-eth a na-tion, but sin is a re-proach to a-ny peo-ple" was a typical example. In other works Webster called on his fellow republican citizens to detach themselves "from the dependence on foreign opinions and manners, which is fatal to the efforts of genius in this country."

Echoing Webster's plea, Joel Barlow, a Yale graduate and an ardent Jeffersonian Republican, called for an epic literature that would celebrate America. To that end he offered his own epic poem, *The Columbiad* (1807), an ambitious but undistinguished work that

The Genius of Washington Irving
In fashioning his stories, Irving drew upon the history and folk traditions of the early Dutch settlers of New York. Ichabod Crane (shown here with the "Headless Horseman") was one of his most popular characters.

had Columbus predict the future glory of North America. Charles Brockden Brown of Philadelphia, the first American novelist, wrote six psychologically informed gothic novels between 1798 and 1801, but they all attracted few readers. Mercy Otis Warren's *History of the American Revolution* (1805) contained stirring portraits of leading American patriots, as did the best-selling *Life of George Washington* written around 1800 by "Parson" Mason Weems, an Episcopal minister. Neither work had much literary or historical merit; still, they won acclaim as contributions to popular culture and patriotism.

The most accomplished and successful writer in the new republic was Washington Irving, a Federalist in politics and outlook. His essays and histories, including *Salmagundi* (1807), *Diedrich Knickerbocker's History of New York* (1809), and *The Sketch Book* (1819), had substantial American sales and won fame abroad because Europeans were fascinated by his tales of Dutch-American life. Irving lived in Europe for seventeen years, drawn by its aristocratic manners and intense intellectual life.

Apart from Irving, no American author was well known in Europe, partly because most American writers had their primary careers as planters, merchants, or lawyers. "Literature is not yet a distinct profession with us," Thomas Jefferson told an English friend, explaining the dearth of intellectual life in the United States. "Now and then a strong mind arises, and at its intervals from business emits a flash of light. But the first object of young societies is bread and covering." Not until Emerson and the Transcendentalists would native-born authors make a real contribution to the great literature of the Western world (see Chapter 12).

Protestant Christianity and Women's Lives

Religion had always been a significant aspect of American life, but in the decades between 1790 and 1820 a series of revivals planted the values of Protestant Christianity deep in the American national character. In the process, religious revivalism created new public roles for women, initially by enlarging the dimensions of women's sphere.

The Second Great Awakening

The revivals that began around 1790 were much more complex than those of the First Great Awakening. In the 1740s most revivals occurred in existing congregations; fifty years later they also took place in camp meetings and often involved the creation of new churches and denominations. Even more strikingly, the Second Great Awakening spawned a wide variety of organizations dedicated to the cause of social and political reform.

Evangelical Churches. The churches that prospered in the new nation were typically well suited to a republican society. Because of its hierarchical structure, for example, the Roman Catholic Church attracted few converts either among Protestants, who embraced Luther's doctrine of the priesthood of all believers, or among the unchurched, who feared priestly power. Few ordinary Americans joined the Episcopal Church; not only was it dominated by the wealthy and snobbish, but power flowed downward—from bishops to ministers and then to the congregations. In contrast, the Presbyterian Church was more popular, in part because it was more "republican": ordinary members elected laymen to the synods (congresses) where doctrine and practice were formulated.

Methodism attracted even more adherents. It retained a religious hierarchy, as bishops took the lead on theological issues and enforced order in the church, but the evangelical fervor of early Methodism fostered lay preaching, emotional worship, and communal singing, creating an egalitarian religious culture. The most democratic forms of church government belonged to Quakers, Baptists, and Congregationalists. No bishops or governing bodies stood above the local congregations, and most church decisions—on matters of theology as well as administration—rested with church members. Partly because of their democratic features, Methodist and Baptist churches grew spectacularly, and by the early nineteenth century they had become the largest religious denominations in the United States (see Map 9.2).

Revivalism. Between 1790 and 1830 every decade brought another upsurge of Protestantism somewhere in the new nation. Baptists and Shakers evangelized the New England backcountry. Then a new sect of Universalists, who repudiated the Calvinist doctrine of predestination and taught that salvation was universal, attracted thousands of converts in northern New England.

After 1800 enthusiastic camp meeting revivals swept across the frontier regions of South Carolina, Kentucky, Tennessee, and Ohio. James McGready, a Scots-Irish Presbyterian preacher, "could so array hell before the wicked," an eyewitness reported, "that they would tremble and Quake, imagining a lake of fire and brimstone yawning to overwhelm them." When frontier preachers got together at a revival meeting, they were electrifying. As a young man of twenty, James Finley attended the Cane Ridge, Kentucky, revival of 1802 and was so moved that he became a Methodist minister:

> The noise was like the roar of Niagara. The vast sea of human beings seemed to be agitated as if by a storm. I counted seven ministers, all preaching at one time, some on stumps, others on wagons. . . . Some of the people were singing, others praying, some crying for mercy. A peculiarly strange sensation came over me. My heart beat tumultuously, my knees trembled, my lips quivered, and I felt as though I must fall to the ground.

Through such revivals, Baptist and Methodist preachers reshaped the spiritual landscape of the South and the Old Southwest. They won over most of the white population and, with the assistance of black ministers, began to implant evangelical Protestant Christianity among African-Americans as well.

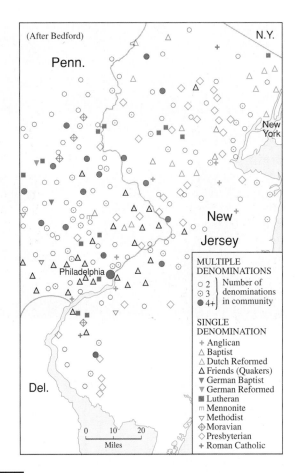

MAP 9.2

Ethnicity and Religion in Eastern Pennsylvania and New Jersey, circa 1780
Long-established churches, founded by English Quakers and Dutch Reformed Protestants, nested side by side with those established by new ethnic groups, such as German Lutherans and Scots-Irish Presbyterians. Many communities had churches from two or three different denominations, a situation that fostered religious toleration and undermined the idea of a legally established church.

Unlike the First Great Awakening, which in the 1740s had split many churches into hostile New Light and Old Light factions, the Second Awakening brought friendly competition among Protestant churches, each seeking new members among the unconverted and new methods of spreading the faith. In New England and the Middle Atlantic states pious women supplemented the work of preachers and lay elders, doubling the amount of organized spiritual energy. In the South and West, Baptist and Methodist preachers traveled constantly. Instead of settling in a congregation, a Methodist cleric followed a circuit, "riding a hardy pony or horse . . . with his Bible, hymn-book, and Discipline." Wherever they went, these "circuit riders" established new

churches by searching out devout families, bringing them together for worship, and then appointing lay elders to lead the congregation and enforce moral discipline until they returned.

Evangelical ministers copied the techniques of George Whitefield and other eighteenth-century revivalists, codifying their intuitive genius in manuals on "practical preaching." To attract converts, preachers were cautioned to emphasize piety as opposed to theology and learning and were told that extemporaneous speech was more powerful than a written sermon. "Preach without papers," advised one minister, "seem earnest & serious; & you will be listened to with Patience, & Wonder; both of your hands will be seized, & almost shook off as soon as you are out of the Church." Vigorous preaching imparted enthusiasm and a sense of purpose to hundreds of local revivals.

These missionary innovations shifted the denominational base of American religion toward the Baptists, Methodists, and other evangelical churches, which grew rapidly because they actively sought converts. The leading churches of the Revolutionary Era—the Congregationalists, Episcopalians, and Quakers—declined in relative membership. Their leaders and members were content for the most part to maintain existing congregations or grow slowly through natural increase.

New Religious Thought and Institutions. The Second Great Awakening changed the character of American thought—and social action—in dramatic ways. Before the Awakening, a Calvinist preoccupation with human depravity and weakness had shaped the thinking of many writers, teachers, and statesmen. Then, in the early nineteenth century, ministers—whether or not they were revivalists—began placing greater stress on human ability and individual free will. This view imparted a new optimism to the intellectual culture of the United States.

In New England, the primary source of the new theology, many educated and economically well-off Congregationalists became Unitarians. Rejecting the concept of the Trinity—God the Father, Son, and Holy Spirit—Unitarians believed in an indivisible and "united" God (hence the name Unitarians). Reacting against the emotionalism of Methodist and Baptist services, Unitarians stressed the power of human reason. "The ultimate reliance of a human being is, and must be, on his own mind," argued the famous Unitarian minister William Ellery Channing, "for the idea of God is the idea of our own spiritual nature, purified and enlarged to infinity." This emphasis on a believer's reason, a legacy of the Enlightenment, gave Unitarianism a humanistic and individualistic thrust.

Optimistic ideas affected mainstream Congregational churches as well. Lyman Beecher, the leading New England clergyman of the first half of the nineteenth century, accepted the anti-Calvinist idea of universal salvation. Although Beecher insisted that humans had a natural tendency to sin, he repudiated the doctrine of predestination, declaring that all men and women had the capacity to choose God. In Beecher's sermons, redemption referred to a self-induced spiritual awakening, not an arbitrary summons from a stern God. By emphasizing choice—the free will of the believer—he testified to the growing confidence in the power of human action.

Samuel Hopkins—a disciple of the great philosopher of the First Awakening, Jonathan Edwards—linked individual salvation with social reform through the concept of religious *benevolence*. Benevolence was the practice of disinterested virtue, to be undertaken by those who had received God's sanctifying grace. Those people "are thereby constituted his *Almoners*," suggested the New York Presbyterian minister John Rodgers, with a duty "to dole out his charity to their poorer brothers and sisters." Inspired by such arguments, merchants and philanthropists founded the New York Humane Society and the New York Dispensary to unite "the different classes of the community." Similar charitable organizations appeared in most cities and towns, marking the beginning of the Benevolent Empire (see Chapter 10). By the 1820s some conservative church leaders complained that through their benevolence lay men and women were devoting themselves to secular reforms—such as antislavery and the prevention of pauperism—and neglecting spiritual goals.

These new religious ideas spread quickly as a result of the founding of theological seminaries such as the Congregationalist institutions of Andover in Massachusetts and Lane in Ohio. Even more than the older divinity schools at Harvard, Yale, Princeton, and other colleges, these institutions fostered cooperation among the clergy, creating loyalty to nationwide denominations. As individual clergymen cooperated with one another, American Protestant churches became less dogmatic in their teachings. Many congregations abandoned books and pamphlets such as the orthodox *Watts Hymnal*, which took controversial stances on old theological debates over predestination and the efficacy of the sacraments, replacing them, a layman explained, with publications that would not give "offense to the serious Christians of any denomination."

Indeed, five interdenominational societies were founded between 1815 and 1826: the American Education Society (1815), the American Bible Society (1816), the American Sunday School Union (1824), the American Tract Society (1824), and the American Home Missionary Society (1826). The new organizations were based in New York, Boston, and Philadelphia but ministered to a national—and eventually an international—congregation. Each year they dispatched hundreds of missionaries to frontier regions and foreign lands—Africa, India, China—and distributed tens of thousands of religious pamphlets.

Organization on this scale gave momentum and power to the Second Great Awakening. National institutions united the individual energies of thousands of church members in a great collective undertaking, unleashing their ambitions and freeing their imaginations. "I want to see our state evangelized," declared one pious New York layman:

Suppose the great State of New York in all its physical, political, moral, commercial, and pecuniary resources should come over to the Lord's side. Why it would turn the scale and could convert the world. I shall have no rest until it is done.

For the first time in America, men and women in small villages scattered across the landscape saw themselves as part of a large religious movement, one that could change the course of history.

As a result of the Second Awakening, religion had become too important a force in American society to be kept separate from secular affairs. On July 4, 1827, the Reverend Ezra Stiles Ely called on the members of the Seventh Presbyterian Church in Philadelphia to begin a "Christian party in politics." In the sermon "The Duty of Christian Freemen to Elect Christian Rulers," Ely set out a new goal for the American republic—a religious goal that Thomas Jefferson and John Adams would have found strange, if not troubling. The two presidents, who had died the year before, believed that America's mission was to spread political republicanism. Ely urged the United States to become an evangelical Christian nation dedicated to religious conversion at home and abroad. As Ely put it, "All our rulers ought in their official capacity to serve the Lord Jesus Christ." The Second Great Awakening had added an intense religious dimension to American politics and the emerging national identity.

Women and Religion

Republican ideology raised the question of women's rights and, along with changes in social and economic life, had created new opportunities for American women. During and after the Revolutionary Era, a few women proclaimed the goal of complete equality with men, and many young women took advantage of new educational possibilities. Still other women took a more direct role in the market, producing farm goods for sale or working in expanding outwork industries. And an increasing number of women embraced the new ideal of companionate marriage, which raised the prospect of a more equal division of authority within the family. Despite these changes, deeply ingrained cultural patterns of male dominance remained intact. Indeed, the early nineteenth century brought a new ideology that limited women's sphere to domestic responsibilities. Only in American religious life did women achieve a significant public presence.

Women's Sphere. Traditionally, most American women had focused their lives on domestic duties: the bearing and raising of children and work in the home or on the

Separate Spheres
Art often reveals cultural values—here the new emphasis on child-rearing and women's domestic authority. The mother sits in the center of the room, controlling the household domain. The father enters from the outside, his prime concerns lying elsewhere, in the world of business.

farm. As the changing political order challenged longstanding relations of authority, a few upper-class women sought a public voice, but most women—and certainly most men—did not assume that the egalitarian logic of republican ideology would affect their customary gender roles. Few demanded or even supported a substantial public role for women in American society. Instead, many clergymen and political leaders promoted the notion of a separate women's sphere. Women had special domestic skills and responsibilities, they argued, and should devote themselves to the running of the home and family life.

Women's enhanced domestic role stemmed in part from changes in Christian thought. Traditionally, most religious writers had viewed women as morally inferior to men, as sexual temptresses or witches. By 1800 the clergy had revised this image, and religious teaching held men responsible for sexual misconduct. Indeed, moralists claimed that modesty and purity were inherent in the nature of women, giving them a unique ability to educate the spirit. The sustaining of virtue became part of women's sphere.

Political leaders also called on women to ensure the future of the new American republic. In his *Thoughts on Female Education* (1787), Benjamin Rush argued that a young woman should be given intellectual training so that she would be a fit republican wife, "an agreeable companion for a sensible man" who would, as another moralist put it, "excite his perseverance in the paths of rectitude." Rush and other men of affairs welcomed the emergence of loyal "republican mothers"

who would instruct "their sons in the principles of liberty and government." As a list of "Maxims for Republics" put it, "Some of the first patriots of ancient times were formed by their mothers."

Ministers embraced the idea of republican motherhood and devised new roles for women in moral and religious education. "Preserving virtue and instructing the young are not the fancied, but the real 'Rights of Women,'" the Reverend Thomas Bernard told the Female Charitable Society of Salem, Massachusetts, in 1803. He urged his audience to forget about the public roles advocated by Mary Wollstonecraft and other feminists. Instead, women should remain content to care for their children, because this gave them "an extensive power over the fortunes of man in every generation." Bernard wanted women to remain in their traditional domestic sphere while insisting that its value should be enhanced.

Many American women from the middling classes accepted this limited revision of their social identity. As a young New England woman wrote in 1803, "She is still *woman*, with duties prescribed her by the God of Nature essentially different from those of *man*." Some educated upper-class women, however, insisted on equality of the separate male and female worlds. "I will never consent to have our sex considered in an inferior point of light," Abigail Adams, the wife of President John Adams, proclaimed in 1799. And some ministers envisioned a public role for women's domestic virtues. As Thomas Grimké, a South Carolina minister, said, "Give me a host of educated pious mothers and sisters and I will revolutionize a country, in moral and religious taste."

Public Women.   Taking advantage of their enhanced moral status, women in Britain and America undertook new religious initiatives in the late eighteenth century. Mother Ann Lee founded the Shaker sect in Britain and migrated in 1774 to America, where she and a handful of followers attracted numerous recruits. The Shakers were a controversial sect; their enthusiasm, clannishness, celibacy, and commitment to female equality set them apart. By the 1820s Shaker communities dotted the countryside from New Hampshire to Kentucky and Indiana (see Chapter 12). In Rhode Island, Jemima Wilkinson, a female revivalist, won hundreds of converts to her sect (see American Lives, pages 288–289). Women in mainstream churches also became more active. In New Hampshire women managed more than fifty local "cent" societies that raised funds for the Society for Promoting Christian Knowledge; evangelical women in New York City founded a charitable institution, the Society for the Relief of Poor Widows; and young Quaker women in Philadelphia ran the Society for the Free Instruction of African Females.

Women became active in religion and charitable

work partly because they were excluded from other spheres of public life and partly because they formed a substantial majority in many denominations. For example, after 1800 about 70 percent of the members of New England Congregational churches were women. Ministers acknowledged this female presence by changing their religious practices. In many Protestant faiths men and women traditionally sat on opposite sides of the church during regular Sunday services, and ministers often conducted separate prayer meetings for each sex. Now evangelical Methodist and Baptist preachers encouraged mixed praying, which critics condemned as "promiscuous." But Presbyterian and Congregational churches in frontier areas adopted this innovation with impressive results. "Our prayer meetings have been one of the greatest means of the conversion of souls," a minister in central New York reported in the 1820s, "especially those in which brothers and sisters have prayed together."

As women's involvement in religion began to challenge traditional gender roles, their activities and organizations became controversial. Many laymen resented the emphasis on women's moral superiority and the religious and social activism that sprang from it. "Women have a different *calling*," one man argued. "They are neither required nor permitted to be exhorters or leaders in public assemblies. . . . That they *be chaste, keepers at home* is the Apostle's direction." But many ministers continued to encourage the creation of women's organizations, and women became increasingly conscious of their new social power. By the 1820s mothers throughout the United States had founded local maternal associations to encourage Christian child-rearing. Newsletters such as *Mother's Magazine* were widely read in hundreds of small towns and villages, giving women a sense of shared purpose and identity.

In their capacity as moral paragons, women had an immediate and direct impact on social behavior. Imbibing the principle of female virtue, many young women and the men who courted them postponed sexual intercourse until after marriage—a form of self-restraint that had not been common in the eighteenth century. In Hingham, Massachusetts, and many other New England towns about 30 percent of the women who married between 1750 and 1800 had borne a child within eight months of their wedding day; by the 1820s the proportion had dropped to 15 percent.

Women's Education. Female religious activism pushed forward the education of women. Churches established scores of seminaries and academies where girls—primarily from the middling classes—were given sound intellectual training as well as moral instruction. Emma Willard, the first American to advocate higher education for women, opened the Middlebury Female Seminary in Vermont in 1814 and later founded schools for girls in Waterford and Troy, New York.

Women educated in female seminaries and academies gradually displaced men from their traditional roles as teachers in locally supported public schools. By the 1820s women were teaching the summer session in many schools; in the following decade they would work the more demanding winter term as well. Women took over teaching in primary schools because they had few other job opportunities and because school authorities could pay them less than they paid men. Women earned $12 to $14 per month as schoolteachers, with room and board—less than a farm laborer. But they were also beneficiaries of the higher moral status now accorded to women and the imperatives of republican motherhood; they would instruct the young not only at home but also in school. As schoolteachers, these women had an acknowledged place in public life that had been beyond their reach in the colonial and Revolutionary periods. Through their active presence in the Second Great Awakening, thousands of American women had enhanced their personal identity and won for their sex a public role in the life of the American republic.

A Young Ladies Seminary, circa 1810–1820
Female academies equipped young women from middling and elite families with cultural skills and knowledge of the world. In this miniature panorama, two students master the intricacies of geography while another girl sharpens her musical talents.

Unruly Women: Jemima Wilkinson and Deborah Sampson Gannett

1776 was a year of new beginnings: In July the thirteen colonies repudiated 150 years of monarchical rule and declared themselves independent republics—the United States of America. In October Jemima Wilkinson of Cumberland, Rhode Island, became ill with a fever and had a vision in which she died and her body was now inhabited by the "Spirit of Light"; repudiating her birth name, Wilkinson declared herself the founder of a new religion—the Publick Universal Friend. And, beginning in 1776, Deborah Sampson, a tall and strong sixteen-year-old indentured servant in Middleborough, Massachusetts, first realized that "my mind became agitated with the enquiry—why a nation, separated from us by an ocean . . . [should] enforce on us plans of subjugation." Sampson's resolution "to become one of the severest avengers of the wrong" led her in 1782 to join the army—a cross-dressing American soldier.

George Whitefield had a hand in all these new beginnings. Since 1739 the great English evangelist had inspired Americans to turn to God and question established authority. By the 1760s New Light Presbyterians in Philadelphia and elsewhere had declared they had "no king but King Jesus" and had joined the Patriot movement. At about the same time—around 1768, when she was sixteen—Jemima Wilkinson discovered Whitefield by reading his sermons; two years later she joined the religious revival that followed his final visit to New England. By 1776 she had forsaken Quakerism, the faith of four generations of Rhode Island Wilkinsons, and joined the New Light Baptists.

In 1780 Deborah Sampson also became a Baptist, though she was expelled two years later for behaving in a "verry loose and unchristian" fashion. Accused of "dressing in men's clothes, and enlisting as a Soldier in the Army," Sampson had resisted the admonitions of her brethren to give "Christian satisfaction" for her conduct. Nor was this the end of the tale. Compressing her breasts with cotton cloth and enlisting again, Sampson served in the Light Infantry 4th Massachusetts Regiment of the Continental army for seventeen months and, while scouting the enemy in war-torn Westchester County, New York, was wounded in an engagement with the Tory militia. Like Whitefield's preaching, Sampson's adventure had "turned the world up-side down."

Sampson and Wilkinson were "disorderly women,"

Jemima Wilkinson, the "Universal Friend"

as contemporaries put it, examples of what the historian Natalie Zemon Davis has called the "woman-on-top." Both in Europe and in America, such audacious women challenged the social conventions that bound their sex, sometimes acting in "unwomanly" ways by leading food riots or political protests, sometimes donning the garb of men in symbolic protests against women's inferior status. "I burst the tyrant bands, which held my sex in awe," Sampson would proclaim in her public lectures in 1802.

Jemima Wilkinson was no less daring. A tall and graceful woman with dark hair and dark eyes, she had a magnetic personality and a powerful preaching style that created fervent disciples. Judge William Potter of Rhode Island was so moved by the Universal Friend that he gave up a promising political career, freed his slaves, and built a fourteen-room addition to his mansion for Wilkinson to use. Another wealthy farmer provided her with a home in Pennsylvania, and supporters built churches in three New England towns. Wilkinson's success—and notoriety—stemmed in part from her religious message, which blended the Calvinist warning of "a lost and guilty, gossiping, dying World" with a Quaker-inspired social gospel that advocated plain dress, pacifism, and the emancipation of slaves. But even more it reflected her revolutionary persona. Like

Mother Ann Lee, the founder of the Shakers, Wilkinson preached celibacy and never married. More controversial still, she dressed like a man, wearing a black robe similar to a clergyman's gown, and—emphasizing the ambiguity of her gender—told her followers to address her not as "she" or "her" but as "the Friend."

This radicalism—of social doctrine and personal identity—alienated more people than it attracted. Although she was touted by some of her disciples as a messiah, Wilkinson's attempts at faith healing and prophesying scandalized even the tolerant Quakers and Baptists of Rhode Island and Pennsylvania, where she was attacked by a stone-throwing mob. Forsaking evangelism, she gave up preaching to the "wicked world" and turned to utopianism, in 1790 establishing the community of Jerusalem in the wilderness of western New York; ten years later the settlement had 260 inhabitants. But few new recruits joined the sect, and its purpose and energy gradually drained away. Within two decades of Wilkinson's death in 1819 her sect had disappeared. Its only legacy is a short doctrinal pamphlet, *The Universal Friend's Advice to Those of the Same Religious Society* (1794).

Deborah Sampson left a slightly deeper imprint on American history, in part because she participated in the nation's founding war and in part because her personal radicalism was less extreme. Returning to Massachusetts after the war, she married Benjamin Gannett, a poor farmer with whom she had three children. To alleviate the family's poverty, Deborah Gannett showed the same "enterprise" that had sent her off to war. She cooperated with the author of her memoir in 1797 and, to win support for her petition for a soldier's pension, undertook a speaking tour throughout New England and New York in 1802.

In her lecture to curious audiences attracted by her military exploits and cross-dressing, Gannett conveyed a mixed message. On the one hand, she celebrated her decision in 1782 to throw off "the soft habiliment of my sex" and reaffirmed her culturally revolutionary act by performing a military drill, "Equipt in complete uniform." On the other hand, Gannett confessed her "error and presumption" in swerving "from the accustomed flowery path of female delicacy." By asking forgiveness from her "respectable" listeners for this "unnatural, unwise and indelicate" behavior, she affirmed women's traditional roles, which had been redefined as those of the proper "republican wife" and the pious "republican mother." Her performance was a study in ambiguity, at once dangerously assertive and socially reassuring.

In the broad sweep of history, the contributions of figures such as Deborah Sampson Gannett and Jemima Wilkinson are often ignored. Neither had won a major battle or devised an enduring religious doctrine. Yet their lives are important for what they reveal about the age in which they lived. Wilkinson attacked slavery, as did many others in the North, bringing about its gradual demise there. She called for a more enthusiastic religion and, along with other inspired preachers, sparked the Second Great Awakening. She showed that women could take an active part in religious affairs, and thousands of American women made the same choice, gradually changing the composition, practice, and outlook of many Protestant churches. First as a soldier and then more prominently a speaker, Deborah Sampson Gannett also claimed a public presence for women. Her long and ultimately successful public campaign for a Revolutionary War pension bridged differences of gender in asserting the sense of entitlement felt by all the veterans who had fought for their country.

But the most enduring legacy of Gannett and Wilkinson was their remarkable efforts—partly instinctive, partly conscious—to transcend the cultural limits of their time. Their lives challenged the increasingly influential ideology of "separate spheres," which divided the world into a masculine domain of public affairs and a feminine world of domestic concerns. This challenge was revolutionary even in an age of revolution and remains controversial two centuries later.

Deborah Sampson, Soldier and Speaker

Summary

By the 1820s a distinct national character had emerged in the United States, reflecting three long-term historical developments that shaped the lives of most white Americans. First, as a result of their increasing involvement in an ever shifting capitalist market economy, Americans became a competitive and "calculating" people. Between 1780 and 1820 merchant capitalists sought profits by creating a flourishing outwork system of rural manufacturing, and state governments devised a commonwealth system of political economy—awarding corporate charters and subsidies to assist transportation companies, manufacturers, and banks. Republican-minded state legislatures enacted statutes that encouraged economic development by redefining common-law property rights. Led by John Marshall, the Supreme Court protected the traditional rights of property owners and the charter privileges of business corporations. Entrepreneurs took advantage of state legislation and judicial protection to create new business enterprises, strong regional economies, and the beginnings of a national market system.

Second, republican precepts of liberty and equality created a citizenry that was suspicious—if not hostile—toward anyone with aristocratic pretensions. Taking advantage of legal and commercial equality, ambitious men sought to rise in the world. In contrast, political and religious leaders promoted the notion of a separate "women's sphere" consisting of domestic responsibilities. Republicanism—in concert with sentimentalism—influenced the private lives of many Americans, encouraging young people to marry for love as well as for economic security and prompting parents to raise their children using reason as well as authority.

Third, the Second Great Awakening made Americans a fervently Protestant people and dramatically increased the influence of evangelical Baptist and Methodist churches. Religious revivalism also enhanced the status of women, whose moral activism broadened the dimensions of their "sphere" to encompass teaching in public schools and the creation of female-run charitable groups and religious societies. Developing religious institutions thus gave women a new and growing presence in the public life of the United States.

The shared historical experiences of hundreds of thousands of white Americans between the 1770s and the 1820s—fervent Protestantism, entrepreneurial capitalism, and social republicanism—formed the core of an emerging national identity. Within this new framework of life and thought, Americans struggled to work out their individual destinies.

TIMELINE

1780s	Rural outwork system, especially shoes and textiles
1781	Philadelphia merchants found Bank of North America
1782	St. Jean de Crèvecoeur, *Letters from an American Farmer*
1783	Noah Webster's *American Spelling Book* ("the blue-backed speller")
1787	Benjamin Rush, *Thoughts on Female Education*
1790s	State mercantilism encourages economic development Parents limit family size Second Great Awakening Republican motherhood defined
1791	First Bank of the United States founded; dissolved in 1811
1794	Lancaster Turnpike Company
1795	Massachusetts Mill Dam Act
1800s	State-chartered banks proliferate Legal profession democratized Rise of sentimentalism and republican marriage system Women's religious activism Spread of evangelical Baptists and Methodists Beginnings of Benevolent Empire
1801	John Marshall becomes chief justice
1803	*Marbury v. Madison* states theory of judicial review
1805	Mercy Otis Warren, *History of the American Revolution*
1807	New Jersey excludes propertied women from suffrage
1809	Washington Irving, *Diedrich Knickerbocker's History of New York*
1810s	Expansion of suffrage for men Lawyers important in politics
1810	Albert Gallatin, *Report on Manufactures* *Fletcher v. Peck* expands contract clause
1816	Second Bank of the United States chartered
1817	Bonus Bill vetoed by Madison
1819	*McCulloch v. Maryland* enhances power of national government *Dartmouth College v. Woodward* protects corporate property rights
1818–1821	Democratic revision of state constitutions
1820s	Expansion of public primary school system Women become schoolteachers Growth of cash-based market economy
1821	*Cohens v. Virginia* declares supremacy of national courts

★   ★   ★

BIBLIOGRAPHY

Two penetrating local studies, Christopher Clark, *The Roots of Rural Capitalism* (1990), and Laurel Thatcher Ulrich, *A Midwife's Tale: The Life of Martha Ballard* (1990), capture the texture of life in the early republic. Nathan O. Hatch, *The Democratization of American Christianity* (1987), offers an interpretation of religious change.

Political Economy: The Capitalist Commonwealth

Thomas Doerflinger, *A Vigorous Spirit of Enterprise: Merchants and Economic Development in Revolutionary Philadelphia* (1986); John Denis Haeger, *John Jacob Astor* (1991); and Stuart Bruchey, *Robert Oliver: Merchant of Baltimore* (1956), are fine studies of merchant enterprise. The standard history is Curtis R. Nettels, *The Emergence of a National Economy, 1775–1815* (1965). See also Diane Lindstrom, *Economic Development in the Philadelphia Region, 1810–1860* (1983); Ronald Hoffman, John J. McCusker, and Peter Albert, eds., *The Economy of Revolutionary America* (1987); and Daniel P. Jones, *The Economic and Social Transformation of Rhode Island, 1780–1850* (1992).

On banking, see Bray Hammond, *Banks and Politics in America* (1957), and Richard H. Timberlake, *Monetary Policy in the United States* (1992). Studies of manufacturing are Thomas C. Cochran, *Frontiers of Change: Early Industrialism in America* (1981); David Jeremy, *Transatlantic Industrial Revolution: The Diffusion of Textile Technology between Britain and America, 1790–1830* (1981); and Judith A. McGaw, *Early American Technology* (1994).

The classic studies of state mercantilism are Oscar and Mary Handlin, *Commonwealth: A Study of the Role of Government in the American Economy: Massachusetts, 1774–1861* (1947), and Louis Hartz, *Economic Policy and Democratic Thought: Pennsylvania, 1776–1860* (1948). State support for transportation can be traced in Carter Goodrich, *Government Promotion of American Canals and Railroads* (1960); Erik F. Hiates et al., *Western River Transportation: The Era of Early Internal Development, 1810–1860* (1975); Philip Jordan, *The National Road* (1948); and Harry N. Scheiber, *Ohio Canal Era: A Case Study of Government and the Economy* (1969).

Two good introductions to legal issues are George Dargo, *Law in the Early Republic* (1982), and Jamil S. Zainaldin, *Law in Antebellum Society* (1983). The legal implications of commonwealth ideology are analyzed by Leonard Levy, *The Law of the Commonwealth and Chief Justice Shaw* (1955), and Morton Horwitz, *The Transformation of American Law, 1790–1860* (1976). R. Kent Newmyer, *The Supreme Court under Marshall and Taney* (1968), offers a concise treatment. See also Robert K. Faulkner, *The Jurisprudence of John Marshall* (1968); Francis N. Stites, *John Marshall: Defender of the Constitution* (1981); and Thomas C. Shevory, ed., *John Marshall's Achievement* (1989). A fine case study is C. Peter McGrath, *Yazoo: Law and Politics in the New Republic* (1966).

Visions of a Republican Social Order

Warren S. Tryon, *A Mirror for Americans: Life and Manners in the United States, 1790–1870, as Recorded by European Travelers* (3 vols., 1952), suggests the distinctive features of republican society. Michael Grossberg, *Governing the Hearth* (1985), discusses changing marriage rules. Catherine M. Scholten, *Childrearing in American Society, 1650–1850* (1985), should be supplemented by Philip Greven's pathbreaking analysis, *The Protestant Temperament: Patterns of Childrearing, Religious Experience, and the Self in Early America* (1977). Other important works include Daniel Blake Smith, *Inside the Great House: Planter Family Life in Eighteenth-Century Chesapeake Society* (1980); Bernard Wishy, *The Child and the Republic* (1970); and Jan Lewis, *The Pursuit of Happiness: Family and Values in Jefferson's Virginia* (1983).

On education, see Lawrence Cremin, *American Education: The National Experience, 1783–1861* (1981), and Carl F. Kaestle, *Pillars of the Republic: Common Schools and American Society, 1780–1860* (1983). Russell B. Nye, *The Cultural Life of the New Nation, 1776–1830* (1960), is comprehensive; a recent penetrating analysis is Richard Bushman, *The Refinement of America* (1992). Important studies of American literature include Cathy N. Davidson, *Revolution and the Word: The Rise of the Novel in America* (1986), and Jay Fliegelman, *Prodigals and Pilgrims: The American Revolution against Patriarchal Authority, 1750–1800* (1982). See also William L. Hedges, *Washington Irving: An American Study, 1802–1832* (1965).

Clement Eaton, *Henry Clay and the Art of American Politics* (1957), perceptively describes the coming of political democracy. More detailed studies are Ronald Formisano, *The Transformation of Political Culture: Massachusetts Parties, 1790s–1840s* (1983), and Chilton Williamson, *American Suffrage from Property to Democracy* (1960).

Protestant Christianity and Women's Lives

For women's lives see Harriet B. Applewhite and Darline G. Levy, eds., *Women and Politics in the Age of Democratic Revolution* (1990), and Linda Kerber, *Women of the Republic: Intellect and Ideology in Revolutionary America* (1980). Specialized studies include Joan M. Jensen, *Loosening the Bonds: Mid-Atlantic Farm Women, 1750–1850* (1986); Nancy F. Cott, *The Bonds of Womanhood: "Women's Sphere" in New England, 1780–1835* (1977); Jeanne Boydston, *Home and Work* (1990); and Susan Juster, *Disorderly Women: Sexual Politics and Evangelicalism in Revolutionary New England* (1994).

Women's religious initiatives are discussed in Mary P. Ryan, *Cradle of the Middle Class* (1981); Barbara Epstein, *The Politics of Domesticity: Women, Evangelism, and Temperance* (1978); and Keith Melder, *Beginnings of Sisterhood: The American Women's Rights Movement, 1800–1850* (1977), which also traces the growth of female academies.

Perry Miller, *The Life of the Mind in America* (1966), offers a good overview of the Second Great Awakening. For revivalism see Stephen A. Marini, *Radical Sects of Revolutionary New England* (1982); Bernard A. Weisberger, *They Gathered at the River* (1958); Jon Butler, *Awash in a Sea of Faith* (1989); and P. Jeffrey Potash, *Vermont's Burned Over District* (1991). The course of religious thought in New England is traced in D. P. Edgell, *William Ellery Channing* (1955), and Daniel Walker Howe, *The Unitarian Conscience* (1970).

Early Industrialization and the Sectional Crisis

1820–1877

THEMATIC TIMELINE

	Economy	Society	Culture	Politics and Government	Sectionalism
	The Industrial Revolution Begins	**The Emergence of a New Class Structure**	**Reform and Reaction to Reform**	**Democratization and Western Expansion**	**From Compromise to Civil War and Reconstruction**
1820	Waltham textile factory (1814) Erie Canal (1825)	Business class emerges Rural women and girls recruited as factory workers	The Benevolent Empire dominates reform Charles Finney leads revivals	Most adult white men gain the vote The rise of Jackson and the Democratic party	Missouri Compromise (1820) South becomes world's largest cotton producer
1830	American textile manufacturers achieve competitive superiority over British Panic of 1837	Mechanics form craft unions Depression shatters labor movement	Joseph Smith founds Mormon church (1830) Garrison abolitionism (1831)	Indian Removal Act (1830) Whig party formed (1834); Second Party System emerges	Nullification crisis (1832) Compromise Tariff (1833) Texas Republic
1840	Stationary steam engines used to power factories Modern factories built in East Coast cities	Working-class districts emerge in cities Irish immigration accelerates	Brook Farm (1841) Seneca Falls convention (1848)	Manifest Destiny (1845) Mexican War (1846–47) Free Soil party (1848)	South attempts to win guarantees for slavery
1850	Railroad trunk lines Panic of 1857	Settlement of Oregon and California	*Uncle Tom's Cabin* (1852)	Whig party disintegrates; Third Party System emerges *Dred Scott* (1857)	Compromise of 1850 Kansas-Nebraska Act (1854) John Brown's raid
1860	War industries thrive in the North Republicans enact economic program	Emancipation Proclamation (1863) Free blacks struggle for control of land	Thirteenth Amendment abolishes slavery (1866)	Lincoln elected (1860) Civil War (1861–65) Reconstruction	South Carolina secedes (1860) Confederate States of America (1861–65)
1870	Panic of 1873	Rise of debt peonage in the South	Fifteenth Amendment (1870) Free black communities	Compromise of 1877	Southern states readmitted to Union

In 1820 America was still a predominantly agricultural society; by 1877 it had become one of the world's most powerful industrial economies. This profound transformation began slowly in the Northeast and then, during the 1840s and 1850s, accelerated and spread throughout the northern states. During this half century the Industrial Revolution had an impact on virtually every aspect of American life.

First, technological and organizational innovations transformed the economy. High-speed machines and a new system of factory labor boosted production while canals and railroads created a vast national market. The industrial sector produced an ever increasing share of the country's wealth—from a negligible proportion in 1820 to a third in 1877.

Second, industrialization spurred the creation of a society divided by new social classes. Many Americans—middle-class people as well as the very wealthy—benefited from the new economic opportunities. An ambitious and powerful business class emerged and sought to assert its leadership, often enlisting religion to justify the new economic order and promote its reformist agenda. Many other Americans, however, lost wealth or status. Especially threatened were artisans whose skills were made redundant by technological advances. By 1840, half the nation's free workers labored for wages, and income and wealth had increasingly become more concentrated in the hands of relatively fewer families.

Third, industrialization increased pressures to democratize political life. Most important, rival social groups organized to advance their interests and at times even to challenge the power of the business class. Farmers turned to political action to address problems involving land, credit, and monopoly power. Some workers proposed the reform of industrial society through the workingmen's parties of the 1820s and 1830s. And immigrant groups arriving from Ireland, Germany, and Canada during the 1840s and 1850s espoused social and religious values that often differed from those of the business class. Under the leadership of Andrew Jackson, the Democratic party became the major vehicle for advancing the interests of those groups. To compete with the Democratic party, the parties of the business class, first the Whigs and then the Republicans, embraced tactics that encouraged wider participation in politics.

Fourth, many Americans became profoundly troubled by the changes sweeping the country. Some sought radical reform—equal rights for women and the abolition of slavery. Abolitionists at first condemned slavery as a sinful expression of arbitrary personal power, but during the 1840s many shifted their ground, attacking a "Slave Power" that seemed to threaten free labor and the economic foundations of the republic.

Fifth, industrialization sharpened sectional divisions. The North was developing an urban industrial economy whereas the South remained a predominantly rural slave-holding society. During the 1840s and 1850s each section tried to impose its distinctive labor system on the West. The defeat of the South in this competition and the fear that it could no longer protect its vital interests led to the secession movement. The secession of a large number of southern states, met by the resolve of Abraham Lincoln's Republican government to preserve the Union, produced the Civil War.

Each side believed that it was fighting to preserve its fundamental institutions and values. Each side fought to preserve a democratic republic and a labor system regarded as essential to democracy. Eventually the North declared its intention to smash slavery. The war became a total war—a war between two societies as well as two armies—and with industrial technology at their disposal, the two sides endured unprecedented casualties and costs.

The war lasted long enough for the North to build the most potent military machine in the world. The fruits of victory were substantial. During Reconstruction, the North imposed its interpretation of the Constitution on the nation, built an enduring base of power for the Republican party, eradicated slavery, and began to extend the benefits of democracy to African-Americans. But the North lacked the will to complete its work—to undertake the economic restructuring that was required to enable freed slaves to participate with full equality in American society.

Lockport on the Erie Canal (detail)

This 1852 watercolor by Mary Keys portrays Lockport, New York, a town that grew up around the locks of the Erie Canal near Buffalo.

The Industrial Revolution

1820–1840

★   ★   ★

In 1831–1832 Alexis de Tocqueville, a French aristocrat, visited the United States; in 1835 he wrote a famous treatise, *Democracy in America*, which described for a European audience the character of republican society in America. Tocqueville observed Americans at work and remarked, "What most astonishes me . . . is not so much the marvelous grandeur of some undertakings, as the innumerable magnitude of small ones." Tocqueville astutely identified a key feature of the Industrial Revolution in America: it was the product of thousands of small innovations—and thousands of small innovators.

In the late eighteenth century those innovators began the transformation of America from a predominantly agricultural society to what would become, a century later, the world's most powerful industrial economy. The 1820s and 1830s were crucial decades in this process, for they saw the most dramatic acceleration of the innovations in manufacturing that had begun so tentatively and in a piecemeal fashion during the 1790s. And even though most Americans remained farmers and most manufacturing was done by craftsmen in traditional shops until after the Civil War, the era of early industrialization was quite distinct from the preindustrial period.

For one thing, by the 1820s the very meaning of the word *manufacturing* had changed. From its original sense of making things by hand, it had come to mean production carried on in factories by workers tending power-driven machinery. More important, industrialization enabled Americans to produce far more goods and services per person. And innovations in pioneering industries such as textiles triggered additional advances—in agriculture, transportation, and other industries—which increased productivity further. Thus the new, more productive era that began in the 1820s provided the basis for a great rise in the living standards for the vast majority of Americans.

Americans sensed that they were living in a new era. Some welcomed it, but many feared the disruption of traditional social relationships. For many, religion provided the glue to keep society—and the new social classes—together.

The Rise of Northeastern Manufacturing

The Industrial Revolution had originated in Great Britain in the middle of the eighteenth century (see Chapter 4). Britain's head start gave it an early advantage that endured for many years. The first factories of the American Industrial Revolution, concentrated in the Northeast, used machines copied from British models and often were supervised by British technicians. But by 1840 Americans had reduced their reliance on British technology and were developing their own machinery and factory organization in order to exploit the nation's main advantage—an abundance of natural resources.

New Organization and New Technology

The first increases in productivity had resulted from the outwork system of rural manufacturing organized by merchants after the Revolutionary War (see Chapter 9). The new ways of organizing workers made manufacturing more efficient even without any technological improvements. As late as 1850 shoe manufacturers running complex outwork systems were the largest employers in Massachusetts but still did not use modern machinery.

Upper Falls of the Genesee River, 1835
Like many early industrial sites, these prosperous flour mills at Rochester, New York, were located to take advantage of natural resources. The Genesee River provided water to irrigate the wheat farms of the Genesee Valley and to transport the grain to mills; its falls powered the mill machinery. (Collection of The New-York Historical Society)

For tasks that were not suited to the outwork system, manufacturers developed a different approach to organizing workers: they brought them all together under one roof. They created the modern *factory*, which concentrated as many of the elements of production as possible in one place and divided the work into specialized tasks. For example, in the 1830s Cincinnati merchants built slaughterhouses that included "disassembly" lines for butchering hogs. A simple system of overhead rails moved the carcasses past workers who were assigned specific tasks: splitting the animals, removing various organs, trimming, weighing, and, finally, hosing down the cleaned carcasses before packers pickled them

and stuffed them in barrels. All these tasks could have been done on any Ohio farm, and the workers were no more skilled than was the typical Ohio farmer. But in the factory the entire butchering and packing process required less than one minute. By the 1840s Cincinnati was disassembling so many hogs that the city had become known as "Porkopolis."

Technological improvements alone could also increase productivity. As early as 1782 the prolific Delaware inventor Oliver Evans had built a highly automated, labor-saving flour mill driven by water power. His machinery lifted the grain to the top of the mill, cleaned the grain as it fell into hoppers, ground it into flour, conveyed the flour back to the top of the mill, and then cooled the flour during its descent into barrels. Evans needed only six men to mill 100,000 bushels of grain a year. His labor-saving techniques spread quickly and became permanent elements in flour milling.

What made industrial development in the United States distinctive during the 1820s and 1830s was the fact that for the first time manufacturers *combined* organizational and technological innovations. By applying technological advances to a factory setting, Americans finally achieved the dramatic productivity gains of the Industrial Revolution. In the United States the first technologically advanced factories were the New England mills that made woolen and cotton cloth.

The Textile Industry

The Industrial Revolution had begun in the textile mills of northern England in the middle of the eighteenth century. After the Revolutionary War their cheap factory-made cloth flooded the American market, threatening the livelihood of hand spinners and weavers. Desperate to recapture the domestic market, American merchants resolved to copy—or steal if necessary—the new British technology.

The earliest practitioners of industrial espionage in America were British *mechanics,* as skilled workers were then called. These workers pursued crafts or what were known as "the mechanical arts." Lured by high wages or offers of partnerships, thousands of British mechanics—who often were machine builders—pirated the detailed and up-to-date information American manufacturers coveted and set sail for the United States. Since British law prohibited the emigration of mechanics as well as the export of textile machinery, many disguised themselves as ordinary laborers or crossed the Atlantic hidden in barrels. In 1812 there were more than 300 British mechanics at work in the Philadelphia area alone.

Samuel Slater. The most important of these mechanics was Samuel Slater, who emigrated from the industrial district of Derbyshire, England, in 1789. He had served as an apprentice to Jedediah Strutt, a partner of Richard Arkwright, the inventor and operator of the most advanced machinery for spinning cotton. Having memorized the design of Arkwright's machinery, the young Slater, disguised by a beard, set sail for New York. There he contacted Moses Brown, a wealthy merchant who had been trying unsuccessfully to duplicate British spinning machinery in his cotton mill in Providence, Rhode Island. Slater took over the management of Brown's mill and replicated the entire set of Arkwright's machines. This was by far the most advanced mill in America, and for that reason the year of its opening—1790—is often considered to mark the beginning of the Industrial Revolution in the United States (see New Technology, page 298).

Pork Packing in Cincinnati
This pork-packing plant in Cincinnati used little modern technology except an overhead moving pulley system that carried hog carcasses past the workers. The plant's efficiency was primarily organizational: each worker was assigned a specific task. Such plants pioneered the design of the moving assembly lines that reached a high level of sophistication in the twentieth-century automobile factories of Henry Ford.

Cotton-Spinning Machines

The Industrial Revolution in America began in the textile factories of New England. By 1800 a wide array of machines were being used to card cotton—turning raw cotton into clean fibers—and prepare the fibers for weaving. *Carding machines*, which consisted of two or more cylinders covered with wire pins, combed the fibers into parallel strands. *Roving machines* rolled the carded cotton into a loose roll called a roving.

The real revolution in textile manufacturing came with changes in spinning technology. Rates of production had been severely limited by the slow process of spinning cotton fibers into yarn. As late as the 1760s all yarn was spun by individuals—usually young women—at hand-turned spinning machines. In 1765 the British inventor James Hargreaves invented the *spinning jenny*. (The name likened the machine to a young woman.) The key tool in spinning had always been the spindle, which first elongated and then twisted together strands of fiber to make yarn. Hargreaves's spinning jenny imitated the function of spinning wheels. The operator manually turned a wheel that spun a series of spindles, each of which simultaneously drew out the roving and twisted it into thread.

Jennies saved labor by turning from 24 to more than 100 spindles at once. However, a jenny required a skilled operator. The spinner placed bobbins (spools) with roving on the machine's frame and tied a bit of roving from each bobbin to a spindle, first passing the fibers through a carriage that moved back and forth on the frame. After elongating the roving by moving the carriage, the spinner clamped the rovings to the carriage and then turned the wheel to spin the spindles. When the thread had been given enough twist, the operator moved the carriage forward again while turning the spindles more slowly to wind the thread onto the bobbins. The jenny had to be stopped between the drawing and the twisting and slowed before winding, so it had to be driven by hand. Because of the labor costs involved, relatively few American manufacturers adopted jennies for cotton spinning.

Americans preferred the *spinning frame*, or *water frame* (a *frame* was a common name for a loom). Richard Arkwright patented this loom in Britain in 1769, and Samuel Slater brought it to the United States. Its chief innovation was to separate the functions of drawing and twisting. After two pairs of rollers had elon-

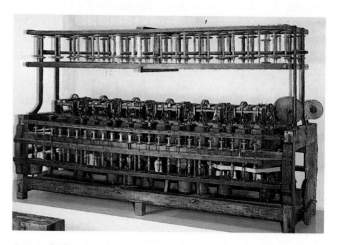

Samuel Slater's Water Frame
Samuel Slater's water frame had two rows of bobbins, twenty-four in each row, on the front and back of the lower portion of the machine.

gated the thread, it was passed down the arm of a flier, a device attached to a spindle. The flier twisted the thread and wound it onto a bobbin attached to the spindle.

The only skill needed to operate a water frame was the ability to knot a broken thread. The machine ran continuously on inexpensive water power. In addition to saving expensive labor, the frame worked much faster than did the jenny. A single water frame produced as much yarn as several hundred spinning wheels working together could. Moreover, the water frame produced yarn that was coarse enough for the rugged cloth used for most clothing in America. Even more significantly, its yarn was strong enough to be used on power looms for the warp, the vertical rows of yarn strung in tension, through which the weft yarn was woven to form the finished cloth.

American inventors quickly made significant improvements in the water frame. By 1830 virtually all the processes involved in the manufacture of cotton cloth had been mechanized in the United States, and most new mills had separate departments for carding, dressing, spinning, and power-loom weaving. The enormous gains in textile productivity and profitability inspired a host of inventors and entrepreneurs to mechanize other industries. The Industrial Revolution had seized the American imagination.

Problems of Competition. Even a mill as advanced as Slater's had difficulty competing with British mills, but Americans had one major advantage: an abundance of natural resources. America's rich agriculture produced a wealth of cotton and wool, and its rivers provided a cheap source of energy. From Maine to Delaware, all along the *fall line*, where the Appalachian foothills drop to the Atlantic coastal plain, the rivers cascade downhill in falls and rapids that can easily be harnessed to run power machinery.

Against this the British had numerous advantages. Falling shipping rates made it cheaper to ship goods across the Atlantic than to transport them within the United States, given its primitive transportation network. British interest rates were lower, so British firms could build factories and market their goods less expensively. And because British companies were better established, they could afford to engage in cutthroat competition, cutting prices briefly but sharply to drive the newer American firms out of business.

The most important British advantage was cheap labor. Britain had a larger population—about 12.6 million in 1810 compared with 7.3 million Americans—and its workers were paid less. Landless agricultural workers and underemployed urban laborers were more than willing to perform simple, repetitive factory jobs, even for low wages. Since unskilled American workers could obtain good pay for farm or construction work, American manufacturers had to offer relatively high wages to attract them to factory jobs.

To make matters worse, the federal government did little to protect the nation's high-wage workers and high-cost industries as they were learning how to meet British competition. Congress did not pass its first major protective *tariff*—a tax on imported goods—until 1824. The measure levied a fairly modest 35 percent tax on imported iron, woolens, cotton, and hemp. But in 1833, under pressure from southern planters and western farmers who wanted to keep down the price of manufactured goods, Congress began to reduce even those tariffs (see Chapter 11).

As a consequence of all these factors, American textile manufacturers often failed. Even those who survived made good profits only when the Embargo of 1807 and the War of 1812 cut off British competition. To overcome their British rivals, American textile manufacturers would have to address the central problem of low-cost British labor.

The Boston Manufacturing Company

In 1811 Francis Cabot Lowell, a wealthy Boston merchant, spent an apparently casual holiday touring British textile mills. A well-educated and charming young man, he flattered his hosts by asking a great many questions, but his easy manner hid a serious purpose. Lowell paid close attention to the answers he received, and later, in his hotel rooms, secretly made detailed drawings of the mills and power machinery he had seen. On returning to the United States, Lowell turned over his drawings to an experienced American mechanic, Paul Moody, who made additional improvements. Lowell then joined with two other merchants, Nathan Appleton and Patrick Tracy Jackson, to raise the staggering sum of $400,000 to form the Boston Manufacturing Company. In 1814 they opened a textile plant in Waltham, Massachusetts, on the Charles River. The Waltham plant was the first in America to perform all the operations of cloth making under one roof. More important, thanks to Moody's improvements, Waltham's innovative power looms operated at even higher speeds

Women Workers in a Textile Mill
This lithograph shows women working in a British cotton factory that closely resembled those in America. They tended spinning machines and looms driven by water power transmitted by a system of belts and wheels. The women here are probably knotting broken threads while the man is most likely adjusting the machinery.

than did those Lowell had seen in Great Britain, making it possible to produce cloth with fewer workers. Improved technology was one part of the answer to Britain's cheaper labor; finding less expensive American workers was the other.

The Waltham Plan. The Boston Manufacturing Company solved the other part of its problem by pioneering a manufacturing system that became known as the Waltham plan. It recruited thousands of farm girls and women as operators of textile machinery, offering them higher wages than they could earn in the outwork system of shoe and broom production or in service as maids or cooks. In addition, manufacturers provided company-run boardinghouses and cultural activities such as evening lectures. The mill owners reassured anxious parents by enforcing strict curfews, prohibiting alcoholic beverages, and requiring regular church attendance. At Lowell (1822), Chicopee (1823), and other sites in Massachusetts and New Hampshire, the Boston company built new cotton factories on the Waltham plan. During the 1820s and 1830s other Boston-owned firms, such as the Hamilton, Suffolk, and Tremont corporations, also adopted the Waltham plan (see Map 10.1).

Some of the young women working under the Waltham plan banked their wages. One worker wrote to a cousin that she wanted to attend Oberlin College (the first coeducational U.S. college, founded in 1833) "because I think it the best way of spending the money I have worked so hard to earn." Others used their wages to help support their families and parents. A girl might help her father to pay off a farm mortgage, a brother to acquire more schooling, or her family to accumulate a dowry for her own marriage. In 1835 eleven-year-old Lucy Larcom of Lowell, Massachusetts, went to work in a textile mill. In 1889 she recalled that she started work "with a light heart" because the work meant that she "was not a trouble or burden or expense" to her widowed mother (see American Voices, page 301). Regardless of what the young women did with their wages, they enjoyed the greater degree of personal independence that their incomes provided. "Don't I feel independent!" another mill worker wrote to her sister in the 1840s. "The thought that I am living on no one is a happy one indeed to me."

Throughout the 1820s and 1830s young women made up a majority of all workers in the cotton-textile industry and nearly half the workers in woolen-textile manufacturing. In the early 1830s more than 40,000 women were working in textile mills. Most of the remaining 20,000 textile workers were children under the age of fourteen, the majority of whom were girls. Men constituted only a small fraction of the textile operatives. The few men in the industry worked primarily in Rhode Island under the Fall River plan, which offered unskilled factory work to entire families. The success of

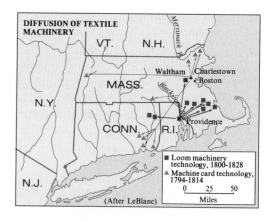

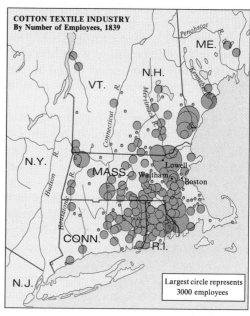

———

MAP 10.1

Early Industrial Enterprise in New England
As new and improved textile machinery spread across New England, modern textile factories sprang up and became concentrated at locations such as Waltham and Lowell in eastern Massachusetts. On the lower map each circle is placed on a town with one or more textile factories. The size of each circle indicates the relative number of spindles or employees in that town; the data are sufficiently similar for historians to be able to trace and compare the development of the industry over this period.

the Waltham and Fall River plans was due largely to the meager profitability of New England agriculture and the high birth rate among New England farm families, which led most of their young people to seek other opportunities. The region's poorer farms could not hold young people, who quickly turned to factory work even though it meant operating fast-moving machines, doing highly repetitive tasks, and disrupting traditional family life (see Chapter 11).

Lucy Larcom

Early Days at Lowell

Lucy Larcom (1824–1893) went to work in a textile mill in Lowell, Massachusetts, when she was eleven years old. She remained there until 1846, when she moved west to Illinois with her sisters and a great tide of other New Englanders. In later life she became a teacher and a writer; this selection is from her autobiography, *A New England Girlhood*.

I never cared much for machinery. The buzzing and hissing and whizzing of pulleys and rollers and spindles and flyers around me often grew tiresome. I could not see into their complications, or feel interested in them. But in a room below us we were sometimes allowed to peer in through a sort of blind door at the great waterwheel that carried the works of the whole mill. It was so huge we could only watch a few of its spokes at a time, and part of its dripping rim, moving with a slow, measured strength through the darkness that shut it in. It impressed me with something of the awe which comes to us in thinking of the great Power which keeps the mechanism of the universe in motion.

. . . We did not call ourselves ladies. We did not forget that we were working girls, wearing coarse aprons suitable to our work, and that there was some danger of our becoming drudges. I know that sometimes the confinement of the mill became very warisome to me. In the sweet June weather I would lean far out of the window, and try not to hear the unceasing clash of sound inside. Looking away to the hills, my whole stifled being would cry out

Oh, that I had wings!

Still I was there from choice, and

The prison unto which we doom ourselves,
No prison is.

I regard it as one of the privileges of my youth that I was permitted to grow up among these active, interesting girls, whose lives were not mere echoes of other lives, but had principle and purpose distinctly their own. Their vigor of character was a natural development. The New Hampshire girls who came to Lowell were descendants of the sturdy backwoodsmen who settled that State scarcely a hundred years before. Their grandmothers had suffered the hardships of frontier life. . . . Those young women did justice to their inheritance. They were earnest and capable; ready to undertake anything that was worth doing. My dreamy, indolent nature was shamed into activity among them. They gave me a larger, firmer ideal of womanhood. . . .

Country girls were naturally independent, and the feeling that at this new work the few hours they had of every-day leisure were entirely their own was a statisfaction to them. They preferred it to going out as "hired help." It was like a young man's pleasure in entering upon business for himself. Girls had never tried that experiment before, and they liked it. It brought out in them a dormant strength of character which the world did not previously see.

Source: Lucy Larcom, *A New England Girlhood* (Boston: Houghton Mifflen, 1889), 153–155, 181–183, 196–200.

New England's Success. Less than forty years after the founding of Slater's mill, New England companies finally achieved competitive superiority over the British in American markets. In 1825 Thomas Jefferson, who had earlier warned against the dehumanizing perils of industrialization, was moved to express his pride in the American achievement: "Our manufacturers are now very nearly on a footing with those of England. [England] has not a single improvement which we do not possess, and many of them adopted by ourselves to our ordinary use." The Waltham and Fall River plans also gave New England manufacturers a competitive edge over other American textile manufacturers. In New York and Pennsylvania, where agricultural employment was far better paid than in New England, textile producers were slower to adopt the technology of the Industrial Revolution. They concentrated on modifying traditional technology to produce higher-quality cloth than the British and New England mills manufactured. In the South textile entrepreneurs almost always failed because they lacked a cheap supply of labor. Poor whites disdained factory work, and the cost of buying or renting slaves was prohibitive because of the huge profits slaveowners could earn by growing cotton. The southern textile industry languished until after the Civil War.

American Mechanical Genius

Until the 1840s individuals of modest wealth provided most of the capital required to start new manufacturing firms. Only in Massachusetts did wealthy merchant capitalists such as Francis Cabot Lowell invest in modern industry. More typically, it was mechanics and small merchants who took the risks, pooling their capital and often borrowing from family members and friends to start factories. Some storekeepers, hoping to expand their business, invested in small mills. A mill could increase a storekeeper's ability to purchase supplies for his store and, by generating jobs and income, increase the local market for his goods. Storekeeper-manufacturers commonly tried to pay workers with credit at their stores in order to make certain they spent their wages on store goods.

Rockdale. The early history of industry in Rockdale, Pennsylvania, a small mill village in the Delaware Valley near Philadelphia, illustrates the entrepreneurial role of small manufacturers. In 1825 there were four cloth manufacturers in Rockdale. One was William Martin, a young, modestly wealthy Philadelphia merchant who had purchased his mills at a sheriff's sale (a sale of bankrupted property), using his savings and those of his brother-in-law. He expanded the mills by borrowing from an uncle and mortgaging the property. In 1829, however, cloth prices tumbled and he was forced into bankruptcy. The second manufacturer was John Phillips, the son of a once-prominent Philadelphia merchant who had fallen on hard times. John had married well, and he borrowed from his new brother-in-law to buy mills. Strong family support and prudent management enabled him to survive and, in 1835, to relocate his machinery to a new mill in Philadelphia. The third entrepreneur was John Crozer, a farmer and the owner of a failing sawmill. He bought a textile mill at a sheriff's sale by mortgaging his farm and borrowing from a brother-in-law. With enormous personal energy and sustained family assistance, he built the mill into a thriving business and became one of the wealthiest men in Rockdale. The fourth manufacturer, John Carter, was an immigrant and the only one of the four with experience in textiles, from his years as a mill manager in Britain. Because of his expertise, he was able to borrow extensively from local banks. Nonetheless, largely because he lacked relatives with capital, he suffered a devastating bankruptcy in 1826. The lesson was clear: success was impossible without determination, skill, and family finances.

Mechanics often crossed into the ranks of small manufacturing entrepreneurs by joining them as partners or by starting their own manufacturing firms. Literally thousands of modest mechanics developed the simple inventions that cumulatively revolutionized American manufacturing. Few of these craftsmen had formal education, but they had learned about machinery in small, traditional craft shops and, increasingly, in modern factories.

One such inventor, Richard Garsed, started working in a textile mill in New Hope, Pennsylvania, when he was only eight years old. Ten years later, in 1837,

after his father had purchased a small mill in Rockdale, Garsed experimented with improvements on his father's power looms. In three years he nearly doubled their speed. By 1842 he had invented a cam and harness device (patented in 1846) that allowed elaborately figured fabrics such as damask to be woven by machine.

The Sellars Family and the Franklin Institute. Garsed was only one of the many American mechanics who by the 1820s had replaced British immigrants at the cutting edge of technological innovation, usually basing their success on elaborate ties of family and friendship. In the Delaware Valley the remarkable Sellars family dominated an interrelated group of inventors who transmitted their mechanical knowledge from one generation to the next. Samuel Sellars, Jr., invented a machine for twisting worsted woolen yarn. His son John harnessed water power for the efficient operation of the family's sawmills and gristmills and devised a machine to weave wire sieves. John's sons and grandsons built machine shops that turned out a variety of new products: riveted leather fire hoses, papermaking equipment, and eventually locomotives.

In 1824 members of the Sellars family and other mechanics and small manufacturers founded the Franklin Institute in Philadelphia. Named after Benjamin Franklin, whom the mechanics admired for his scientific accomplishments and idealization of hard work, the institute fostered the mechanics' sense of professional identity. It also underscored the fact that mechanics had become more than traditional craftsmen. Increasingly, mechanics included engineers and inventors at the forefront of the Industrial Revolution. The institute published a journal; provided high school instruction in mechanics, chemistry, mathematics, and mechanical drawing; and organized annual fairs to exhibit the most advanced products and reward their designers. At the 1842 fair the institute's judges awarded a silver medal to Richard Garsed for cotton and worsted damask tablecloths that promised "successful competition with the imported." Craftsmen in Ohio and other states soon established their own mechanics institutes, offering the same kinds of programs that the Franklin Institute had pioneered.

Machine Tools. The most outstanding contribution of American mechanics to the Industrial Revolution was the development of machines capable of making other machines, that is, *machine tools*. In the textile industry mechanics invented devices—lathes, planers, and boring machines—that could make interchangeable textile-machine parts. These machine-tooled parts, which required only a minimum of filing and fitting, made it possible to manufacture textile machinery that was low in price and precise enough in design and construction to operate at higher speeds than British equipment.

Once American craftsmen had perfected machine tools for the textile industry, the Industrial Revolution swept through the rest of American manufacturing. If anything, the impact of machine tools was even greater in industries that produced goods made of iron or steel, such as plows, scythes, and axes. In 1832 the mechanics David Hinman and Elisha K. Root, employed by Samuel W. Collins in his Connecticut ax-making company, built a vastly improved die-forging machine—a device that pressed and hammered hot metal into *dies,* or cutting forms. Using the improved machine, a skilled worker could increase his production of ax heads from 12 to 300 a day.

Some of the most important machine-building innovators worked in the firearms industry. Beginning in the 1790s, the federal government created a demand for muskets that traditional producers, relying almost entirely on skilled workers and the slow crafting of muskets one-by-one, could not meet. Eli Whitney, an inventor and business promotor, was the first to receive a federal contract for muskets so large that it required mass-production techniques to fulfill. The machine tools he and his co-workers designed in his New Haven factory between 1798 and his death in 1825 represented the first major steps toward realizing the idea that interchangeable parts could make possible large-scale, high-speed production (see American Lives, pages 304–305).

After Whitney's death, his work was completed by his partner John H. Hall, an engineer at the federal armory at Harpers Ferry, Virginia. Hall developed all the basic machine tools required to produce modern arms: turret lathes, milling machines, and precision grinders. By 1840 Hall and other American mechanics had created the first modern machine-tool industry in the world. Thereafter, manufacturers could use machine tools to produce complicated machinery at high speed and in great quantity. The direct transmission of information and insight across just two generations of engineers connected the innovations of Whitney and Hall with Henry Ford's introduction of the first fully automated assembly line in 1913.

The Expansion of Markets

During the 1820s and the 1830s the Industrial Revolution stimulated the rapid expansion of the American marketplace. Manufacturers and merchants in the industrializing Northeast developed a national system of markets, stimulated the growth of cities and towns, and promoted the construction of a massive transportation system to link the Northeast and the Old Northwest.

Regional Trade Patterns

In the first forty years after independence Americans relied on the exportation of farm products to Europe. Between 1790 and 1810 as much as 15 percent of the national product was exported—roughly the level that had prevailed in the mid-eighteenth century. However, this changed dramatically during the 1820s. By enhancing the incomes of Americans, the Industrial Revolution enabled Americans to consume a larger share of the production of domestic farmers and manufacturers. American producers in turn sharply reduced their reliance on European markets. By 1830 they were exporting only 6 percent of the national product, a level that remained constant until the mid-twentieth century.

Eli Whitney's Factory and Village
Whitney's Mill Rock armory, which he began building in 1798 near New Haven, Connecticut, produced inexpensive, high-quality guns until his death in 1825. Whitney tried to supervise every detail of his workers' lives in the mill village of Whitneyville.

Eli Whitney:
Machine Builder and Promoter

Eli Whitney once described the world as "a Lottery in which many draw blanks." But he was often lucky during a life (1765–1825) that spanned the chaotic years between the American Revolution and the Industrial Revolution. His luck, combined with relentless social ambition and exceptional talents for self-advertisement and mechanical innovation, allowed him to exert a major influence on the course of the Industrial Revolution in the United States.

Whitney was born on a Westborough, Massachusetts, farm in economic circumstances that were typical of many farm families in New England during the late eighteenth century. His family's land was relatively poor, but the farm produced enough for the family to live comfortably, and Eli's father, who served for many years as a justice of the peace, was a respected member of the community.

As a child, Eli found routine farm chores boring and even depressing. As often as he could, he fled to the farm's workshop to fashion and repair household furniture and farm tools. Early on, Eli showed a talent for crafting wood and metal, and he preferred tinkering in the shop to the drudgery of the barns and fields. The young Whitney also found that he enjoyed talking with neighboring townspeople. His sister recalled that as a child he "possessed a great measure of affability." It was probably in those conversations that Whitney sharpened his awareness of how the marginal and overcrowded land in the settled parts of New England constrained economic opportunities for young people.

The death of his mother in 1777 and the nearly simultaneous outbreak of the American Revolution opened new doors for Eli. His father remarried in 1779, but in the interim Eli had the freedom to employ his mechanical and social skills and explore new economic horizons. When he was fourteen, Whitney persuaded his father to install a forge in the workshop so that he could produce nails and knife blades as substitutes for the British imports that were no longer available. His enterprise flourished, as did many like it in New England, and he soon hired a worker to help him meet the demand. Two years later an avalanche of cheap nails from Britain ruined Eli's market. But he demonstrated his exceptional flexibility by shifting his efforts to the

production of women's hatpins and men's walking sticks.

Despite his successes in household manufacturing, Whitney knew that the family farm could not provide a living for himself, two younger brothers, and four sisters. In any case, farm life did not appeal to him. Whitney aspired to greater wealth and status and concluded that college would provide the most reliable access to the traditional elites of New England. But he lacked the required college preparation in English grammar, classics, and mathematics. He enrolled at Leicester Academy, a private secondary school, and to finance his studies taught school for six years (1783–1789) in neighboring towns. There he made the connections that would eventually get him into Yale College.

At Yale, Whitney might have studied engineering or science if the college had offered those subjects. But like the other colleges of the day, Yale did not. In any event, Whitney was more interested in the social connections the school provided. At graduation in 1792 the president of Yale and Phineas Miller, a Yale alumnus in Georgia, found Whitney a job as tutor on a plantation.

In traveling south Whitney met Catherine Greene, the young widow of the Revolutionary War general Nathanael Greene. Whitney's tutoring position fell through, and she invited him for an extended visit to her Georgia plantation, Mulberry Grove, which Miller managed. Mrs. Greene found Whitney charming and recognized that his "affability" and Yale-bred manners would make him a social asset. Whitney, for his part, became fascinated by the exclusive world of the planters. He paid close attention to their concerns and discovered a way to employ what he learned as a youth to help them solve an economic problem, win social acceptance, and make a fortune at the same time. With the encouragement of Catherine Greene and Phineas Miller, he set up a rough workshop and applied the technique he had used to produce women's hatpins to fashion the tines for the prototype of the cotton gin, the machine that would revolutionize cotton production.

In 1793 Whitney returned to New Haven and began manufacturing gins in quantity by using special machine tools he had developed. He hoped to maintain a monopoly for his gin, which he had patented in 1794.

Eli Whitney

Eli Whitney posed for this portrait in the 1820s, when he had achieved both prosperity and social standing. His success inspired his admiring portraitist and New Haven neighbor, Samuel F. B. Morse, to shift his energy from painting to industrial technology in the 1830s and 1840s, during which he devised the first successful commercial telegraph.

He proudly reported to his father that "One of the most Respectable Gentlemen in N. Haven [said] that he would rather be the author of the Invention than the prime minister of England."

But the patent did not protect Whitney from the numerous planters who made their own gins or from manufacturers who made slight improvements on his design. A year after he took out his patent, hundreds of southern operators employed gins modeled after Whitney's but paid him no royalties. Over the years Whitney continued to market his own gins but spent much of the profit on largely futile lawsuits to protect his patent rights.

To get out of debt, Whitney turned to manufacturing a product that would have a larger—and guaranteed—market. His Yale network again served him well. In the effort to patent his gin, he had formed a friendship with another Yale alumnus, Oliver Wolcott, who became secretary of the treasury in 1795. In 1798 Whitney persuaded Wolcott that he knew how to mechanize the production of firearms and thus produce them at an unprecedented scale and pace. Whitney's information and timing were superb. The federal government had established two armories, in Springfield, Massachusetts, and Harpers Ferry, Virginia, but their production was dismal. Congress feared war with France and just before Whitney's petition to Wolcott it had authorized the Treasury to contract for arms with private parties. Almost immediately Wolcott offered Whitney a contract

to manufacture 10,000 muskets in only twenty-eight months.

Whitney knew little about the details of musket manufacture, but he did understand the potential of machine tools. He was confident that he could design tools that would enable him to produce interchangeable musket parts and thus speed the production of muskets. He assured a doubtful Wolcott that he would "form the tools so that the tools themselves shall fashion the work and give to every part its just proportion—which when once accomplished will give expeditious uniformity, and exactness to the whole." Whitney went on to devise improved forms and jigs to guide the hands of mechanics; he also crafted the first milling machine, which used sharp teeth on a gearlike wheel to cut metal; and he achieved a greater degree of interchangeability of parts than had anyone before him.

Nonetheless, Whitney was unable to develop all the tools he needed to fulfill his original contract on time. It was 1809 before he produced the 10,000 muskets, and even then he had to resort to traditional handicraft. But Wolcott remained loyal, as did the government inspector in New Haven, who was another Yale alumnus. Also helpful was a group of ten prominent citizens of New Haven, including Pierpont Edwards, the wealthy son of Jonathan Edwards. This group, most of whose members were Yale graduates, guaranteed an additional advance of federal money to Whitney. Whitney also won important supporters outside the Yale circle. The most influential was Thomas Jefferson, who had been interested in interchangeability since the 1780s. He had followed Whitney's career from the time Whitney had applied for a patent for the cotton gin, and as president-elect, had witnessed a dramatic public demonstration of interchangeability that Whitney staged in Washington. Jefferson understood what the perfection of Whitney's techniques could do for the productivity of industry.

With Jefferson's encouragement, Whitney continued to develop his techniques. During the War of 1812 and afterward, he won new federal contracts. He also had contracts to supply muskets to the militias of Connecticut and New York. The new work, along with shrewd investment advice from Oliver Wolcott, provided Whitney with the wealth and social position of which he had dreamed. He dined regularly with New Haven's elite, and Yale awarded him an honorary master's degree. In 1817 Whitney joined one of New England's most respected families by marrying Henrietta Edwards, the daughter of Pierpont Edwards.

When Whitney died in 1825, he had still not achieved his goal of complete mass production. But his self-promotion, linked with his promotion of interchangeability and mechanization, did much to ensure that the Industrial Revolution would spread throughout American manufacturing during the next seventy years.

The Yankee Peddler
Even as late as 1830, the approximate date of this painting, most Americans lived too far from town markets to shop there regularly. Farm families, such as this affluent one represented by an unknown artist, purchased most of their tinware, silverware, clocks, yard goods, pins and needles, and notions from peddlers, often New Englanders, who traveled far and wide with their vans.

While exports declined in significance, the domestic trade in agricultural and manufacturing goods flourished. Americans traded with one another in two ways. First, they exchanged goods *within* regions. Philadelphians, for example, traded locally manufactured textiles for farm products grown nearby: flour and corn; dairy products; fruits and vegetables; hay for the horses that pulled carriages, coaches, and omnibuses; and wood for heating and cooking. Second, Americans exchanged products *among* regions. Most important, merchants in the industrializing Northeast exchanged textiles, clothing, boots and shoes, muskets, and farm equipment for wheat, corn, whiskey, and hogs from farms in the Great Lakes Basin and the Ohio Valley. Manufacturers and farmers in the Northeast and the Old Northwest specialized in production for shipment to other regions. Because this interregional trade grew rapidly, they increased their scale of production, became more efficient, and enlarged their profits.

The exception to the trend of increased domestic trade was the South, which continued to produce primarily for international markets. As the Cotton Kingdom expanded across the Old Southwest, the United States became the world's largest cotton producer. Although southern farmers supplied the textile mills of the Northeast, they exported most of their cotton to Britain. And although the flow of manufactured goods from the Northeast to the South increased, southerners continued to import the majority of their manufactured goods from British suppliers. Southerners also obtained most of their financial and marketing services from British import houses. Food did not figure in this trade:

Southerners fed themselves almost entirely from nearly self-sufficient plantations and small farms on the fringe of the cotton economy.

Thus the South's economy remained tied not to other parts of the United States but to Britain. Its plantation economy more closely resembled those of Brazil and Cuba. As in those colonial economies, earnings from exports went largely to Europeans and local planters. Like the landed classes in other plantation societies, southern planters reinvested their profits by expanding their slave labor force and increasing the size of their estates.

The Growth of Cities and Towns

Industrialization and the expansion of interregional trade stimulated the growth of northern cities and towns in the 1820s. For the first time urban places—defined as localities with more than 2,500 inhabitants—began to grow more rapidly than did the population as a whole. There were also more such places: the number of towns and cities with 2,500 to 50,000 people more than doubled in twenty years, from 58 towns in 1820 to 126 in 1840. The total urban population grew fourfold, from 443,000 in 1820 to 1,844,000 in 1840.

Fall-Line Towns. The most rapidly growing urban areas were the new industrial towns. Since early mills used water power to run their machinery, factory towns sprang up all along the fall line. In 1822, for example, the Boston Manufacturing Company decided to build a new complex of mills in East Chelmsford, Massachusetts, on the Merrimack River. Within a few years the sleepy village was transformed into a bustling town, now named Lowell in honor of the company's founder. Hartford, Connecticut; Trenton, New Jersey; and Wilmington, Delaware, also surged as mill owners recruited workers from the surrounding countryside.

Western Cities. Western cities grew almost as rapidly. In 1830 New Orleans, Pittsburgh, Cincinnati, and Louisville accounted for almost three-quarters of the urban population in the West. St. Louis joined the West's largest cities by 1840, its growth stimulated by increased traffic to and from the territory west of the Mississippi. Rochester, Buffalo, Cleveland, Detroit, and Chicago also grew rapidly during the 1830s. The initial expansion of all these cities resulted from their location at points where goods had to be transferred from one mode of transport, such as canal boats or farmers' wagons, to another, such as steamboats or sailing vessels. Merchants and bankers took advantage of the special location of these cities to develop the marketing, provisioning, and financial services that were essential to farmers and small-town merchants in the hinterland.

Despite their commercial dynamism, however, manufacturing in these communities remained mostly traditional in technology and organization. At this time no western city challenged the industrial preeminence of the eastern seaport cities.

The Rise of New York. The old Atlantic seaports—Boston, New York, Philadelphia, and Baltimore—remained the largest American cities, but of the four only New York grew more rapidly than did the population as a whole. New York's growth rate was phenomenal, twice that of the nation as a whole during the 1820s and 1830s. New York overtook Philadelphia as the nation's largest city in 1810 and over the next two decades became the economic center of America (see Map 10.2).

New York boasted the best harbor in the United States. Ocean vessels could sail or steam 150 miles up the Hudson River to Albany; no other Atlantic port provided such deep penetration of the interior. Moreover, ships had unobstructed, yet protected, access to the docks on Manhattan Island. And New York merchants were unusually enterprising. They had made their city the smuggling center of British North America during the eighteenth century and had used their wits to survive British occupation during the Revolution. New York merchants, more so than merchants in Boston or Philadelphia, welcomed outsiders and their money. In 1817 New York merchants founded the New York Stock Exchange, which soon became the nation's chief market for securities.

In their most aggressive stroke, New York merchants persuaded their state government to enact a law that earmarked tax revenues for the construction of a project private investors regarded as too risky—the Erie Canal. It would stretch from Albany to Buffalo and Lake Erie. Opened in 1825, the canal connected New York City and Albany with the vast interior—the burgeoning farming communities of upstate New York and the entire Great Lakes region (see pages 310–311).

New York merchants sought to control foreign commerce as well. In 1818 four Quaker merchants founded the Black Ball Line to carry goods between New York and European ports such as Liverpool, London, and Le Havre. This was the first transatlantic *packet service*. The ships carried cargo, people, and mail on a regular schedule, and their dependability made the

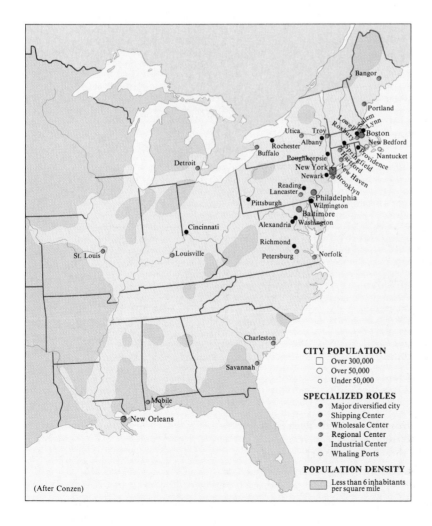

(After Conzen)

CITY POPULATION
- ☐ Over 300,000
- ◯ Over 50,000
- ○ Under 50,000

SPECIALIZED ROLES
- ● Major diversified city
- ● Shipping Center
- ● Wholesale Center
- ● Regional Center
- ● Industrial Center
- ○ Whaling Ports

POPULATION DENSITY
- Less than 6 inhabitants per square mile

MAP 10.2

The Nation's Major Cities in 1840
By 1840 American cities developed specialized roles—Cincinnati and Pittsburgh became industrial centers, Hartford and Lancaster grew as regional centers for farm communities, and Brooklyn and Buffalo developed as wholesaling centers. The oldest ports on the Atlantic seaboard remained the most diversified and played a critical role in managing and organizing the national economy.

service extremely attractive to international traders. New York merchants also gained an unassailable lead in commerce with the newly independent Latin American nations of Brazil, Peru, and Venezuela. Finally, they controlled a small but growing portion of the cotton trade. Their agents in southern ports offered finance, insurance, and shipping to cotton exporters and won for New York a dominant share of the cotton that passed through northern harbors. By 1840 New York's mercantile community controlled almost two-thirds of the nation's foreign imports and almost half of all foreign trade, both imports and exports.

The West: Farming New Land

The Industrial Revolution affected farming people in the United States in a far different way than it did in Europe. In Europe it forced a massive reduction and relocation of rural populations; in the United States it promoted the rapid occupation of new lands by farmers and a huge increase in the rural population (see Map 10.3). At the same time that the nation's industrial

towns and seaport cities were gaining in size and importance, millions of farming families were still moving west.

Migration Routes. These pioneers migrated in three great streams. In the South, cotton producers continued the migration into the Old Southwest that had begun after the War of 1812. They moved their slaves and the Cotton Kingdom into the new states of Mississippi (admitted to the Union in 1817) and Alabama (1819) and on into Louisiana (1812), Missouri (1821), Arkansas (1836), and Texas (1845). Southerners also pioneered the early settlement of the Old Northwest. Small farmers from the Upper South, especially Virginia and Kentucky, created a second stream as they followed westward routes that had been established as early as the 1790s. They ferried their wagons across the Ohio River and introduced corn and hog farming to the southern parts of Ohio (1803), Indiana (1816), and Illinois (1818).

The third stream of migrants came from the Northeast. This flow had begun during the 1790s when settlers had poured into upstate New York; it reached the

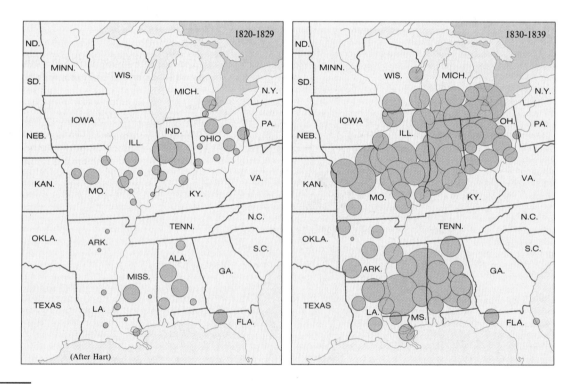

MAP 10.3

Western Land Sales, 1820–1839
Land offices opened up on the frontier to sell government land. Each circle centers on a land office, and the area of each circle represents the relative amount of land sold at that office. The maps show how settlement spread and intensified in the farmland of the Ohio Valley and the cotton plantations of the Old Southwest during the 1820s and the 1830s.

trans-Appalachian West during the 1820s. During that decade and the next, settlers from New England and the Middle Atlantic states, particularly New York, traveled along the Erie Canal to establish wheat farms in the Great Lakes Basin: northern Ohio, northern Illinois, Michigan (1837), and Wisconsin (1848).

Westward migration significantly shifted the population center of American society. In 1830 about 3 million people—more than a fourth of the nation's population—lived west of the Appalachians. By 1840 the figure was over 5 million, more than a third of all Americans. Western growth often entailed the stagnation or decline of eastern communities. Vast numbers of men and women left the seaboard states where they were born, taking with them their savings, personal property, and skills. During the 1820s and 1830s the Carolinas, Vermont, and New Hampshire lost nearly as many people through migration as they gained through the excess of births over deaths. In New England abandoned farms and homes dotted the countryside, their owners gone in search of better lands farther west.

The Incentives. Farmers moved west for complex and various reasons. Some simply wanted to increase their profits, and others wanted to acquire enough land to maintain their children in traditional rural communities. However, all farmers appreciated the economic opportunities offered by the virgin soils of the West. A cotton planter from upland Georgia, a prosperous wheat farmer from the Connecticut Valley, and a hardscrabble subsistence farmer from Vermont might have very different values, but all could recognize the economic advantage of farming on new land. Cotton planters who moved to new lands in the Southwest were glad to leave behind soil depleted by relentless cultivation. Wheat farmers migrating to the prairies of the Old Northwest were relieved of the heavy labor required to clear land of forests and rocks. The settlers soon discovered that the sweat and toil expended on a patch of fresh prairie yielded a much larger crop than could be obtained from a plot of the same size in the East.

The Tools. New and improved tools made farmers even more eager to occupy new lands. During the 1830s farmers throughout the North bought the new cast-iron plow invented in 1819 by Jethro Wood, a farmer in upstate New York. With this device, farmers could cut their plowing time in half and till much larger fields. Wood's plow, which could be repaired with replaceable cast-iron parts, spelled doom for village blacksmiths. Their handmade product could not compete with this low-cost, high-quality product of northeastern foundries. Western farmers purchased many other sturdy, inexpensive mass-produced necessities: shovels and spades, which Alan Wood began fabricating

from rolled iron at his Delaware Iron Works in 1826; axes, which the Collins Company of Connecticut began forging in the same year; and horseshoes, which Henry Burden of Troy, New York, began to make in 1835.

The Land. Cheap land prices made western settlement an even more practical choice. In 1820 Congress reduced the price of federal land from $2.00 an acre to $1.25—just enough to cover the cost of surveying and sale. For $100 a farmer could buy 80 acres, the minimum required under federal law. With the federal government offering huge quantities of public land at that price, the basic market price for all undeveloped land remained low. Purchasing land was well within the reach of most migrating people. During the 1820s and 1830s the average American family could save enough in two years to make the minimum purchase even without raising money from the sale of an old farm.

Effects on Industrialization. Although farms, not factories, dominated the economic life of the West, western settlement did promote industrial development indirectly. Efficient western farms provided eastern manufacturers with low-cost cotton, wool, leather, and other raw materials, thus helping them compete with the British. In addition, these farms supplied abundant and inexpensive grain, meat, vegetables, and fruit that helped maintain the health and strength of factory workers. The growing urban populations of the Northeast increased the demand for, and the prices of, all types of farm goods. Western markets in turn were of growing importance to eastern industry. During the 1830s the production of farm implements—horseshoes, plows, shovels, scythes, hoes, and axes—accounted for fully half the nation's consumption of pig iron. Westward expansion enabled industrializing America to take advantage of cheap land and realize the economic advantages of regional specialization.

The Transportation Revolution

The dramatic expansion of the domestic economy during the Industrial Revolution required a revolution in transportation. The road building that had begun in the 1790s achieved little by 1820. In that year the nation had no true road system, particularly in the West. Spring thaws, rainstorms, and winter conditions often made dirt roads impassable. Western settlers complained to the federal government that they lacked roads to get their goods to market. To correct that problem and integrate large chunks of territory into their buoyant economy, Americans rapidly built a transportation system of unprecedented size, complexity, and cost (see Figure 10.1).

FIGURE 10.1

Inland Freight Rates, 1784–1900
The costs of shipping goods inland on rivers, canals, and railroads fell as new technologies were developed between 1784 and 1900. If a logarithmic scale had not been used for cents per ton-mile, a much larger chart would have been necessary to show the enormous gap between wagon rates and the other rates.

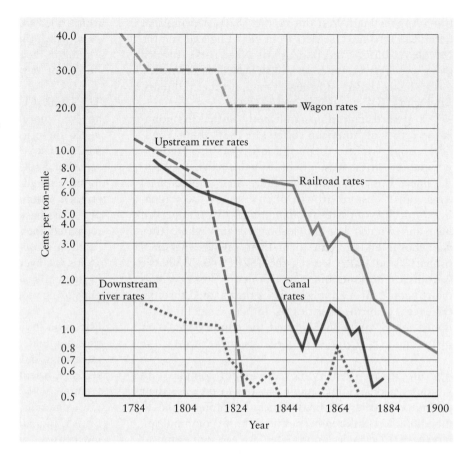

Roads. After 1820 local road building continued, especially in long-settled areas, but the quality of roads did not improve until the introduction of automobiles early in the twentieth century, and no interregional system of roads emerged until the 1830s. Then, in cooperation with state governments, the federal government built interregional roads for pedestrians, horses, herds of livestock, and heavily loaded wagons. The federal government regarded the creation of this vital infrastructure as a legitimate part of its responsibilities. The most significant feat was the National Road, which started in Cumberland, Maryland, passed Wheeling (then in Virginia) in 1818, crossed the Ohio River in 1833, and reached Vandalia, Illinois, in 1850. By that time construction of major interregional roads had ceased, their role taken over by canals and railroads.

Canals. After the War of 1812 Americans began to build canals to connect the inland areas along rivers and lakes with coastal cities and towns, but progress was slow. When the New York legislature began the Erie Canal in 1817, no canal in the United States was longer than 28 miles—a reflection of the huge capital investment required for canals and the lack of engineering expertise. A canal frenzy swept the nation, and canals became the most important part of the transportation revolution.

New Yorkers drove hard to complete the Erie Canal. Three key advantages made the project possible: the vigorous support of New York City merchants; the backing of De Witt Clinton, New York's powerful governor; and the relative gentleness of the terrain. Even amateur surveyors—such as James Geddes and Benjamin Wright, who had been trained as lawyers—were able to design and construct much of the canal.

The Erie Canal was an instant success. The first section, a stretch of 75 miles opened in 1819, immediately generated large revenues for New York State. When the canal was completed in 1825, the 40-foot-wide ribbon of water, complete with locks to raise and lower boats, reached 364 miles from Albany to Buffalo and reduced the journey for passengers traveling from New York City to Buffalo from twenty days to six. The canal also greatly accelerated the flow of goods. On a road in upstate New York, four horses would take an entire day to pull a 1-ton load 12 miles. On the canal, two horses on the towpath could pull a 100-ton load 24 miles in a day.

The Erie Canal fulfilled every promise made by its promoters. It moved settlers from the East to the Old Northwest. It gave the new western farmers of the Great Lakes Basin, as well as those of upstate New York, cheap access to the port of New York. And it placed western communities within easy reach of eastern manufacturers and the merchants of New York City.

Construction of the Erie Canal

Gangs of construction workers on the Erie Canal had to excavate deep cuts through rough land. The artist who sketched this scene, like the canal planners, was more interested in the scale of the project than in the personalities of the faceless workers. Working conditions were even worse in the marshes near Syracuse where, in 1819, a thousand workers fell ill with fever, many of whom died.

After a trip on the Erie Canal in 1830, the novelist Nathaniel Hawthorne wrote:

> Surely the water of this canal must be the most fertilizing of all fluids, for it causes towns with their masses of brick and stone, their churches and theaters, their business and hubbub, their luxury and refinement, their gay dames and polished citizens, to spring up, till in time the wondrous stream may flow between two continuous lines of buildings, through one thronged street, from Buffalo to Albany.

The spectacular benefits and profits brought by the Erie Canal prompted a national canal boom. Civic and business leaders in major cities and towns competed to build their own canals to capture trade with the West. Some promoters took advantage of New York's experience by hiring the young men who had learned canal engineering while building the Erie. Many promoters also copied New York's fiscal innovations. They persuaded their state governments to charter companies, guarantee the companies' credit, and invest directly in them or force mutual savings banks to do so—sometimes even to take over the ownership of such companies. Altogether, state governments provided—often by borrowing from British and Dutch investors—almost three-quarters of the $200 million invested in canals by 1840. By then the new canals had provided three critical transportation links: (1) from the coastal plain to the upcountry of the Atlantic seaboard states, (2) from the seaboard states to the Great Lakes Basin and the Ohio Valley, and (3) from the Great Lakes to the Ohio and Mississippi rivers (see Map 10.4).

The Romance of the Erie Canal

Apart from this artist's romanticized portrayal of life on and along the completed Erie Canal, the canal was a great commercial success. Among the economic benefits to communities along the canal was the demand for skilled carpenters to build and maintain facilities such as wharves and locks. The artist depicted those workers, but not the day laborers who labored in the thousands along the canal. (Collection of the New-York Historical Society)

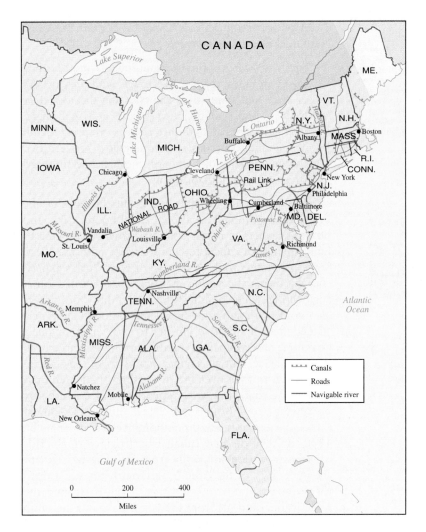

MAP 10.4

The Transportation Revolution: Roads and Canals, 1820–1860

By 1840 the United States had completed a transportation system based on roads, natural waterways, and canals. Even though this system lacked railroads until the 1840s, it was adequate for launching the Industrial Revolution.

Steamboats. The steamboat, another product of the industrial age, ensured the success of America's vast water transportation system. On canals, rivers, and lakes, steamboats traveled faster, met tighter schedules, and carried more cargo than did sailing ships.

The engineer-inventor Robert Fulton built the first American steamboat, the *Clermont*, which he navigated up the Hudson in 1807. But steamboats' large consumption of wood or coal for fuel made them very expensive to run, and they could not navigate shallow western rivers. During the 1820s engineers broadened the hulls of these boats—to increase their cargo capacity and, most important, to give them a shallower draft—and reduced their weight by using lighter wood. Able to navigate in as little as 3 feet of water, the new steamboats could maneuver around tricky snags and sandbars. Moreover, the wider, flat decks speeded the loading and unloading of cargo. During the 1820s alone, the new steamboats cut in half the cost of upstream river transport. By 1830 steamboat travel dominated the major rivers and lakes of the country.

The canals and the new boat technology increased the flow of goods dramatically. In 1835 farmers in the Old Northwest shipped 268,000 barrels of flour on canal boats to eastern markets; just five years later they shipped more than 1 million barrels. Water transport also enabled people to travel more cheaply and sped the exchange of news, technical information, and business advice (see Map 10.5). In 1830 a traveler or a letter from New York could go by water to Boston in a day and a half, to Charleston in five days, and to New Orleans or Detroit in two weeks. Thirty years earlier the same journeys, by road or sail, would have taken twice as long. Businesses and individuals communicated far more efficiently than ever before, and this in turn stimulated business.

The system of long-distance interregional water travel was essentially complete by 1840. But another transportation era was about to dawn: the Baltimore and Ohio Railroad had received a charter in 1828. But railroads were small, unconnected systems in 1840; the great era of railroad building lay in the future.

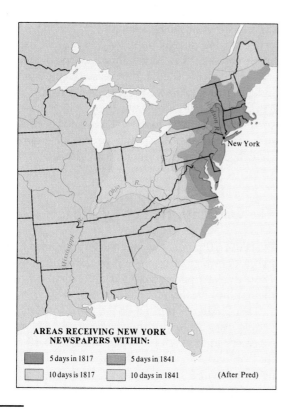

MAP 10.5

The Speed of Business News

The transportation revolution and aggressive entrepreneurs increased the speed of trade and communication between the Atlantic seaboard and the interior. The national circulation of newspapers grew along with trade, and New York's dailies became the most important sources of economic news. This map shows the dramatic improvements in communication between 1817 and 1841.

(Map legend:)

AREAS RECEIVING NEW YORK NEWSPAPERS WITHIN:

- 5 days in 1817
- 10 days is 1817
- 5 days in 1841
- 10 days in 1841

(After Pred)

Government and the Business Corporation

State governments had been granting charters to corporations since the 1790s (see Chapter 9). By extending such privileges to transportation companies in the 1820s, the states accelerated the accumulation of the huge amounts of capital needed to build transportation systems and reduced the need to tax the public for that purpose. Banks also incorporated, but few mercantile firms and almost no manufacturers did. Until after the Civil War manufacturers did not need large accumulations of capital and preferred to continue as partnerships or sole proprietorships to remain free from state regulation.

States gradually made the ability to incorporate a right rather than a privilege. During the 1820s states reduced the conditions necessary for incorporation, and in the 1830s legislatures stopped granting corporate charters one by one through the passage of special acts. Instead, they established general incorporation acts that turned over the chartering process to administrators. As more businesses received charters, however, it became difficult to protect the monopoly privileges that corporate charters often guaranteed. Younger entrepreneurs frequently challenged the monopoly privileges of established businesses for being inconsistent with the ideals of a republic. State courts responded to these challenges by weakening the legal definition of corporate privilege and thus promoting more entrepreneurial uses of property.

The Supreme Court under John Marshall also encouraged business enterprise. In the crucial case of *Gibbons v. Ogden* (1824) the Court struck down a monopoly the New York legislature had granted to Aaron Ogden for steamboat passenger service across the Hud-

An Eastern Steamboat

This watercolor by the Russian artist Pavel Petrovich Svinin (1787–1839) portrays deck life on the *Paragon*, which was owned by Robert Fulton and traveled the Hudson River. Designed primarily for passengers, eastern steamboats lacked the great paddle wheels and superstructures that became characteristic of steamboats on western rivers during the 1840s.

son River between Manhattan and Elizabethport, New Jersey. The Court's ruling, however, did not clearly favor an instrumental view of property, that is, a view hostile toward monopolies and favorable to entrepreneurial competition. The Court overturned Ogden's monopoly because the competitor, Thomas Gibbons, had a federal coasting license, and the Court believed that the federal government had paramount authority over the regulation of interstate commerce.

An instrumental view of property triumphed fully only after John Marshall died in 1835. In the landmark case of *Charles River Bridge v. Warren Bridge* (1837) the new chief justice, Roger B. Taney, ruled in favor of the Warren Bridge Company, which in 1828 had received a charter from the Massachusetts legislature to collect tolls for crossing the Charles River. He ruled against the Charles River Bridge Company, which had received an earlier charter that, the company claimed, granted an *exclusive* right to collect bridge tolls on that river. Taney did adhere to Marshall's doctrine that state governments had to respect charters, but he also argued that a legislature could not be *presumed* to have granted an exclusive, monopolistic right. His language affirmed wide access to the benefits of government: "While the rights of private property are sacredly guarded, we must not forget that the community also has rights, and the happiness and well-being of every citizen depends on their faithful preservation." In effect, he claimed that the destruction of monopoly and the consequent stimulation of competition were in the best interests of the community.

The courts thus reconciled government-granted privileges with the ideals of a republican society. State governments could follow both Marshall and Taney: Following Marshall, they could protect the privileges granted in corporate charters; following Taney, they could diffuse those privileges as widely as possible through society. State governments thus could maintain privilege but reduce its significance. Widening access to privilege increased the flow of capital to corporations and promoted the construction of the national transportation system.

Social Structure in an Industrializing Society

The Industrial Revolution transformed the material life of people in the United States. For most Americans the bonanza of factory-produced goods meant an improved standard of living. But industrialization was a socially disruptive process; the new affluence had its costs. The economic system sharpened and widened class distinctions based on the ownership and use of property and stirred animosity between classes. For a small elite—mostly merchants, factory owners, and financiers concentrated in northeastern cities and towns—industrialization meant great wealth. But for wage earners who did not own property, industrialization sometimes meant a loss of status and an uncertain future. Industrialization thus posed an unprecedented challenge to American republican ideals.

The Concentration of Wealth

By 1800, 10 percent of the nation's families owned between one-third and one-half of the nation's wealth. By 1860 that 10 percent owned more than two-thirds of the nation's wealth.

Especially in the major Atlantic seaports, wealthy people owned most of the property. In 1840 the richest 1 percent in those cities owned as much as 10 percent of the population had owned fifty years earlier. This top 1 percent owned more than 40 percent of all *tangible* property—land, ships, buildings, and household furnishings. In New York City the richest 4 percent of the population owned more than three-quarters of the tangible property. Their share of *intangible* property—stocks, bonds, and mortgages—was even greater.

The growing concentration of wealth in the cities had come about primarily as a result of the opportunities created by industrial and commercial expansion. Hence, great concentrations of wealth were less common in smaller towns or agricultural areas. Yet similar trends existed there as well. Even in modest-sized, non-industrial Massachusetts towns the richest 10 percent of families increased their holdings so that by 1840 they typically owned 50 percent or more of the tangible property.

The new manufacturers, such as Francis Cabot Lowell, increased their fortunes most rapidly. More generally, the Americans whose incomes rose most were those who exploited the innovations of the Industrial Revolution. Since technical advances were concentrated primarily in the textile, machine-tool, and firearm industries, owners and skilled workers in those industries benefited the most. Individuals who designed or adapted the most modern machinery and mobilized and disciplined the labor needed to operate it enjoyed the most rapidly growing profits, salaries, or wages.

The concentration of wealth increased more rapidly than did the pace of technological and organizational change. This occurred partly because the wealthy, often linked by business and family ties, could more easily acquire the best information about new investment opportunities. Moreover, nineteenth-century governments almost never taxed inheritances or intangible property and usually taxed real estate and personal property (furniture, tools, and machinery, for example) at extremely low rates. Although wealthy Americans paid the largest share of state and local taxes, government was small and taxes were modest. Therefore, wealthy manufacturing and mercantile families could retain their fortunes, and their economic power, into the second or third generation.

But wealthy families often failed to keep their hard-earned assets. Foolish investments, poor business sense, imprudent living, or bad luck took their toll. In fact, the Industrial Revolution increased the rate at which fortunes, large and small, were lost. Financial panics drove growing numbers of even the most cautious and calculating investors into bankruptcy. Jeremiah Thompson, New York's largest cotton trader and an organizer of the Black Ball Line, went bankrupt in 1827. Philip Hone, a wealthy merchant and mayor of New York in the 1820s, never recovered from his losses and the bankruptcy of his son during the Panic of 1837, the worst financial crisis before the Civil War.

Middle-Class Property Owners. Far more people, however, improved their economic and social standing than lost ground. The middle class grew rapidly in size and importance. Most mechanics found their skills in high demand and their wages rising. Building contractors, grocers, shopkeepers, and butchers in booming urban areas profited from an abundance of prosperous customers. The growing urban demand for meat, dairy products, and perishables, as well as for staples such as wheat, corn, and cotton, increased farmers' incomes. Most Americans saved about 15 percent of their income, often placing their surplus funds in local banks and new savings institutions. Many eventually bought property with their savings. By 1840 about half of all free American men over the age of thirty had acquired at least moderate wealth—a house, furniture, a little land, and some savings. In agricultural communities an even higher percentage owned some land. The new members of the middle class hoped to pass on to their children the advantages of skills, education, and property ownership.

The New Urban Poor

For many Americans, however, the Industrial Revolution meant a loss of opportunity and a betrayal of republican ideals. By 1840 as many as half the nation's free workers were laboring for wages rather than for their own profit. Among these workers, those who lacked skills, education, or property found that even though their real wages were rising, the gap between themselves and other Americans was widening. For ordinary laborers social mobility was extremely limited and difficult. They could look forward only to a life of work for others in factories, machine shops, and stores and on construction projects and sanitation crews. No matter how hard they worked or how thrifty they were, most could accumulate only modest savings. And an economic recession or sickness could quickly dash their hopes of rising in the world. They faced a high probability of a lifetime with little chance to buy a home or land, let alone start a business. For wage laborers who acquired no property, hope for upward social mobility rested with their children. But those workers had few resources to pass on. In fact, most could not afford to educate their offspring, apprentice them, or accumulate small dowries so that their daughters could marry men with better prospects. Instead, their children had to work to help support their families.

In Massachusetts in 1825, the daily wage of a common (unskilled) laborer—about 75 cents—was about two-thirds that of a mechanic. By the 1840s, the laborer's wage had increased to about $1 but was now less than half the typical mechanic's earnings. More-

A Chimney Sweep
The low-paid and exceedingly dirty and unhealthy work of cleaning chimneys, which were a major fire hazard in the cities of the Northeast, became largely the work of Irish immigrants and African-Americans. An Italian artist, Nicolino Calyo, painted this portrait in New York City in the early 1840s.

over, the poorest workers in the cities in the 1830s had to spend $2 of every $3 they earned just to feed their families, so they had relatively less money left to take advantage of the rapidly falling prices of manufactured goods. Middle-class families, in contrast, could feed themselves on less than a third of their earnings. Thus during the early years of the Industrial Revolution people who lacked skills or property were even worse off in relative terms than their low wages indicated.

And unskilled work offered little satisfaction. Raised in rural areas, most wage laborers were accustomed to the seasonal and task-oriented work regime of agricultural society. They resented the strict year-round labor schedule of most urban jobs. These workers often did not report to their jobs on time, and they sometimes skipped whole days of work when they were not in dire need of money.

The wage laborers who faced the worst conditions were casual workers—those hired on a short-term basis, often by the day, for the most arduous jobs. Altogether, casual workers accounted for about 10 percent of the labor force. The day laborers who dug out dirt and stones to build canals, carried lumber and bricks for construction projects, and loaded and unloaded ships and wagons were the most numerous. In 1840 nearly 25,000 day laborers serviced the traffic on the Erie Canal. Among the casual workers the poorest were free African-Americans and Irish immigrants, who began arriving in the cities of the Northeast during the 1830s (see Chapter 14).

Day laborers owned no property except the clothes they wore, and their work did not provide economic security. In depressions they bore the brunt of unemployment, and even in the best of times their jobs were unpredictable, seasonal, and dangerous. Serious injury, which was common, often meant that a worker could no longer support his family. Disease took a toll. Laborers building canals through swamps often contracted malaria or yellow fever. In 1831 the economist Mathew Carey reported that 5 percent of the workers on the Erie Canal returned to their families in the winter with their health broken "by fevers and agues."

Since nothing tied them down, casual laborers were the most geographically mobile workers, and many looked eagerly to the West. Joining casual laborers on the way west were people who had once been prosperous but had suffered economic reversals. Many household weavers, blacksmiths, and harness makers, for example, left eastern towns and cities when their customers turned to cheap goods produced in factories. Some craftsmen were fortunate enough to reestablish their trade farther to the west, where high transportation costs made goods from eastern factories more expensive. But others with traditional skills had to work for wages in the West, even as casual laborers, easing their hardship by maintaining a garden or keeping a few animals to supplement the family diet. This recourse, however, was of only slight assistance during the winter, when food was scarce and storms and frozen rivers and canals could shut down trade. Winter was often a season of appealing for charity and searching continuously, sometimes fruitlessly, for a little work chopping wood or cutting ice.

In cities, most wage laborers and their families lived in conditions that discouraged any hope for the future. By the 1830s factory workers, journeymen, and unskilled casual laborers in northeastern towns and cities lived in well-defined neighborhoods. Certain blocks became dominated by large, crowded boardinghouses where many single men and women lived together in unhealthy conditions. Landlords converted houses, including basements and attics, into apartments and then used the profits from rentals to build more workers' housing. Often the developers squeezed a number of buildings, interspersed with outhouses and connected by foul-smelling courtyards and dark alleys, onto a single lot.

The Hot Corn Seller
Free African-Americans such as this woman, painted (1840–1844) by Nicolino Calyo, persisted in the face of discrimination and harsh economic conditions. She might have been lucky enough to have a garden plot that grew more food than her family needed to survive. The extra produce offered an opportunity to supplement her meager income.

Philip Hone

A Food Riot in New York

Philip Hone (1780–1851) was a carpenter's son who made a fortune in the New York auction business. He entered civic affairs and in 1825 was elected to a one-year term as mayor. He presided over New York's reception of Lafayette and the opening of the Erie Canal. From 1828 until five days before his death he kept a secret diary, which presents a detailed picture of New York life.

Monday, Feb 13 [1837]—*Riots*. This city was disgraced this morning by a mob regularly convened by public notice in the park for the notable purpose of making bread cheaper by destroying the flour in the merchants' warehouses. The following notice was extensively published on Saturday by placards at the corners of the streets:

Bread, Meat, Rent, Fuel—Their Prices Must Come Down.

The Voices of the People Shall be Heard and Will Prevail.

The People will meet in the Park, rain or shine, at four o'clock on Monday afternoon to inquire into the cause of the present unexampled distress, and devise a suitable remedy. All friends of humanity, determined to resist Monopolists and Extortioners, are invited to attend.

Many thousands assembled on this call. The day was bitter cold and the wind blew a hurricane, but there was fire enough in the speeches of Messrs. Windt and Ming to inflame the passions of the populace. These two men . . . did not tell them in so many words to attack the stores of the flour merchants, but stigmatized them as monopolists and extortioners, who enriched themselves at the expense of the laboring poor. They said that Eli Hart & Co. had 50,000 barrles of flour in their store, which they held at an exorbitant price whilst the poor of the city were starving. This was a fire-

brand suddenly thrown into the combustible mass which surrounded the speaker, and away went the mob to Hart's store in Washington near Cortland Street, which they forced open, threw 400 or 500 barrels of flour and large quantities of wheat into the street, and committed all the extravagant acts which usually flow from the unlicensed fury of a mob. The mayor and other magistrates, with the police officers, repaired to the spot, and with the assistance of many well-disposed citizens, succeeded after a time in clearing and getting possession of the store. From thence the mob went to Herrick & Co. in Water Street, and destroyed about fifty barrels of flour. The mayor ordered out a military force, which with the other measures adopted, kept the rioters in check.

Source: Allan Nevins, ed., *The Diary of Philip Hone* (New York: Dodd, Mead, 1936) 241–242.

Under such conditions, the lives of many wage earners deteriorated. Emotional tension and insecurity took hold; they became anxious over the breakdown of the traditional order, their loss of social status, and their worsening working and living conditions (see American Voices, above). To alleviate their distress, many workers turned to the dubious solace of alcohol.

In the eighteenth century liquor had been an integral and accepted fact of American life; it had lubricated ceremonies, celebrations, work breaks, barn raisings, and games. But during the 1820s urban wage earners led Americans to new heights of alcohol consumption. Aiding them were the nation's farmers, who increasingly chose to distill gin and whiskey as a low-cost way to get their grain to market. Falling prices led drinkers to switch from rum to these "spirits." By 1830 per capita consumption of gin and whiskey had risen to more than 5 gallons a year, more than twice the present-day levels of liquor consumption.

Drinking habits changed as well. At work, those workers who were not members of craft unions committed to abstinence began to drink on the job—and not just during the traditional 11 A.M. and 4 P.M. "refreshers." Journeymen used apprentices to smuggle whiskey into shops, and then, as one baker recalled, "One man was stationed at the window to watch, while the rest drank." Grogshops and tippling houses appeared on almost every block in working-class districts, and many workers who frequented these saloons became less interested in casual camaraderie than in solitary and heavy drinking. The saloons became focal points for urban disorder and crime, including assault, burglary, and vandalism. Fueled by unrestrained drinking, a fistfight among young men one night could turn into a brawl the second night and a full-scale riot the third. The urban police forces, consisting of low-paid watchmen and amateur constables, were unable to contain the lawlessness.

The Rise of the Business Class

In 1800 most whites in rural America shared a common culture. Gentlemen farmers talked easily with yeomen about crop yields, livestock breeds, and the unpredictability of the weather. Poor southern whites and aristocratic slaveowners shared the same forms of amusement: gambling, cockfighting, and horse racing. In the North poor and rich Quakers attended the same meetinghouse, as did Presbyterians, Episcopalians, and Congregationalists of different economic groups. "Almost everyone eats, drinks, and dresses in the same way," a European visitor to Hartford, Connecticut, reported in 1798, "and one can see the most obvious inequality only in the dwellings." Social hierarchies existed in these towns and villages, but the various levels of society shared many cultural and religious values.

Origins of the Business Class. The Industrial Revolution shattered this social order. The wealthiest merchants and manufacturers—the new business elite—began the process of fragmentation by setting themselves apart as a social group. They did this first by reorganizing work in ways that separated them from wage earners. With the outwork and factory modes of organization, a new, more impersonal system of wage labor and large-scale production replaced the small, intimate shops where masters, journeymen, and apprentices had worked side by side. This separation of employers and wage earners affected residential patterns. Before the Industrial Revolution most wage earners had lived close to their employers, often in the same homes. By the 1830s, though, most employers in the largest northeastern cities had stopped providing their employees with housing and many had fled to residential communities on the urban fringe, destroying the continuity between household and workplace.

During the 1820s and 1830s another social group emerged: affluent property owners who were, in economic terms, literally a "middle class"—standing between the very wealthy factory owners, merchants, financiers, and landowners at one extreme and the non-propertied wage earners at the other. Middle-class men and women sensed growing differences between themselves and the rapidly increasing numbers of those who owned nothing and had to struggle just to survive. Their education, material well-being, and aspirations led growing numbers of middle-class Americans, especially in the North, to identify with the wealthy families of the business elite. Together, the middle class and the business elite formed a truly new social stratum—the *business class*. There might be an enormous economic gulf between a wealthy factory owner and his clerks, foremen, and mechanics, but they were beginning to share the same moral and religious ideas and, therefore, membership in the business class.

Most members of the business class were the relatives of men who had accumulated enough money to live comfortably. They were the contractors, foremen, and mechanics valued by manufacturers; they were prosperous farmers; they were professional men of modest means; and they were shopkeepers or manufacturers' clerks and agents. They owned small enterprises or worked in large banks, firms, or stores that they did not own. Typically, they had been able to buy a house and perhaps a little land.

Such people dressed well. They could afford a small carriage and a good horse or two. Their wives and daughters were literate and could play the pianos that graced the carefully decorated front parlors of their well-built houses. There were books on the shelves and usually a servant or two in the kitchen and stables. They attended church and sent their sons and daughters to good schools. They were most numerous in New England, but there were business-class families in every American town, even in the agrarian South.

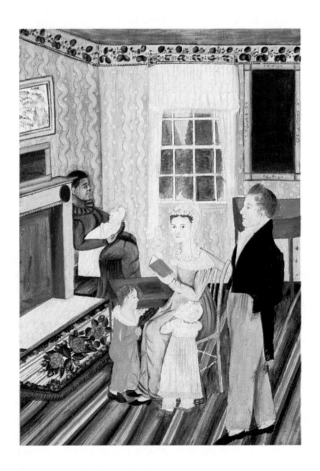

Pennsylvania Family with Servant
Women as well as men worked as day laborers, usually in domestic service. Discrimination limited employment opportunities for free African-Americans and forced them to work in disproportionate numbers as domestic servants, like the woman with this middle-class family painted by an unknown artist in York, Pennsylvania.

Ideology of the Business Class. The members of the business class defined themselves by how they thought about themselves and their relationship to society. They developed their own ideology of work, redefining traditional Christian moral injunctions. The founders of seventeenth-century New England had believed that hard work in an earthly "calling" was a duty that people owed to God. The Puritans had stopped short of believing that God would reward good Christians with worldly riches. In contrast, the business class embraced a secular ideal of work. In the late eighteenth century Benjamin Franklin had expressed this secular ideal in his *Autobiography*, in which he implied that an industrious man would become a rich one. When Franklin's *Autobiography* was finally published in full in 1818, it found a huge audience, mostly young men ready and willing to believe that if they followed Franklin's example—worked hard, saved their money, and were temperate in their habits and honest in their dealings—success would be theirs. The same lessons were taught in countless magazines, children's books, self-help manuals for young men, and novels. The business class made the ideal of the "self-made man" a central part of American popular culture.

Perceptive members of the business class sensed a contradiction between their wealth and their ideology. They urged all Americans to adopt the virtues of industry and rise in the world. At the same time, they recognized that industrialization had widened economic divisions and that many Americans would never improve their status. A yeoman society made up of independent families of farmers and artisans no longer seemed possible. "Entire independence ought not to be wished for," Ithamar A. Beard, the paymaster of the Hamilton Manufacturing Company, told a mechanics association in 1827. "In large manufacturing towns, many more must fill subordinate stations and must be under the immediate direction and control of a master or superintendent, than in the farming towns."

The message was clear. Business-class values were democratic, but the economic system that supported them was not. The clash between the democratic values of the business class and its privileged financial position became a persistent preoccupation for many Americans.

Every day this contradiction was visible in the streets of cities and towns when employers and middle-class property owners brushed up against the new urban poor. Even though neighborhoods were growing more distinct, no class dominated any single section of the city. People across the social spectrum retained a high degree of day-to-day physical proximity even in the largest cities. These were cities where most people lived within walking distance of work, schools, churches, shops, and saloons. Most middle-class housing remained within walking distance of cheap rooming houses and factories. As the horse-drawn bus—too costly for most workers—moved slowly through the late afternoon crowds, the wealthy could not avoid the sight of disorderly, sometimes drunken crowds in the muddy cobblestone streets.

When the wealthy began to ponder this disturbing reality and attempted to resolve conflicts of conscience, they did not seek to halt or reverse the Industrial Revolution. Instead, they worked to eradicate its negative aspects and control the social disorder it had created. They attempted to introduce new forms of discipline, first into their own lives and then into the lives of ordinary working people.

The Benevolent Empire

The leaders of the business class attempted to create a society marked by moral discipline. During the 1820s ministers in Congregational and Presbyterian churches, together with well-established merchants and their wives, launched programs of social regulation. One of the ministers' leading spokesmen, the Presbyterian Lyman Beecher of Boston, proclaimed their purpose: to restore "the moral government of God." Because of this aggressive quest for moral purity and firm belief in charity, historians have labeled the movement the "Benevolent Empire." It was never a formal organization, however, just a collection of reform organizations linked by overlapping membership and shared ideals.

The Benevolent Empire targeted age-old evils such as drunkenness, prostitution, and crime, but its methods were new. Instead of relying on charity, church sermons, and other traditional local initiatives, the reformers set out to institutionalize charity and combat evil systematically. They established large-scale regional and even national organizations, for example, the Prison Discipline Society and the American Society for the Promotion of Temperance. Each organization had a managing staff, a network of volunteers and chapters, and a newspaper. Together the groups set out to "rescue" prostitutes and save the abandoned children of the poor. Some reformers worked to have the insane taken from attics and cellars and put into well-ordered and disciplined asylums. Other reformers labored to change the mission of the criminal justice system from the punishment and humiliation of criminals to their rehabilitation in penitentiaries where moral self-discipline would be emphasized. By removing from their midst individuals whom they viewed as both incompetent and evil, the reformers claimed that they would ensure the vitality and independence of the citizenry and consequently strengthen the republic.

Women played an increasingly active role in reforms inspired by the Benevolent Empire. Since the 1790s upper-class women had sponsored a number of charitable organizations, such as the Society for the Relief of Poor Widows with Small Children founded in New York in 1797 by Isabella Graham, a devout Presbyterian widow. By the 1820s Graham's society was assisting hundreds of widows and their children in New York City. Her daughter, Joanna Bethune, set up other charitable institutions, including the Orphan Asylum Society and the Society for the Promotion of Industry, which gave subsidized employment to hundreds of poor women.

Keeping the Sabbath. The most deeply held conviction of the men and women who ran the Benevolent Empire was that religion provided the answers to social problems. One of the greatest threats they saw to the "moral government of God" was the decline of the traditional Sabbath. The conduction of business on Sunday became increasingly common during the 1820s, especially among merchants and shippers who did not want their goods and equipment to lie idle one day of every seven. Congress had even passed a law in 1810 that allowed mail to be transported—though not delivered—on Sunday. In 1828 Lyman Beecher and other Congregationalist and Presbyterian ministers formed the General Union for Promoting the Observance of the Christian Sabbath. To these reformers, the question of the Sunday mail law was not important in itself. It was a symbolic issue chosen to rally Christians to the task of social purification. The Union spread its chapters—usually with women's auxiliaries—from Maine to the Ohio Valley. It lobbied for local Sabbath regulations, collected funds, published tracts, organized rallies, and circulated petitions. In short, the Union behaved much like a political party.

Although the Benevolent Empire found support in every community, it also met resistance, especially with respect to keeping the Sabbath. Owners of barges on the Erie Canal and proprietors of taverns and hotels refused to close on Sundays. Men who labored twelve or fourteen hours a day six days a week scorned the notion that they ought to spend their one day of recreation in meditation and prayer. Baptist and Methodist clergymen, whose congregations tended to be poorer than those of the Congregationalists and Presbyterians, objected to the patronizing tone of the General Union. And when the Benevolent Empire proposed to teach Christianity to the slaves or send missionaries among the Indians, white southerners were outraged.

Such popular resistance or indifference limited the success of the Benevolent Empire, whose purpose was all too obviously to regulate the behavior of others—by persuasion if possible, but by law if necessary. A different kind of message was required if religious reformers were to do more than preach to the already converted and discipline the already disciplined.

Business-Class Revivalism and Reform

Charles Grandison Finney. Beginning in 1825, the Presbyterian minister Charles Grandison Finney brought a new message to people living along the Erie Canal: evil was avoidable, and *all* sinners could be saved. His ministry accelerated the pace of the Second Great Awakening—the wave of Protestant revivalism that had begun after the Revolution (see Chapter 9). Finney was not part of a traditional religious elite. Born to poor farmers in Connecticut in 1792, he was determined to make himself part of the new middle class as a lawyer. But in 1823 he underwent a highly emotional conversion experience, and he was ordained as a minister after two years of informal religious study.

In strikingly emotional revival meetings Finney preached that God waited to welcome any sinner who

Charles Finney, Evangelist
Finney (1792–1875) had a long and influential career after his New York revivals. In 1835 he established a theology department at the newly founded Oberlin College, where he helped train a generation of ministers. Finney served as president of the college from 1851 to 1866. This daguerreotype was taken in 1850, while Finney and his second wife, Elizabeth Atkinson, were on an evangelistic tour of Great Britain.

truly wanted salvation and that only God's grace, poured into the heart of the believer, made a moral life possible. He rejected an emphasis on original sin and stressed that the exercise of free will—submission to the Holy Spirit—could lead to a Christian conversion. He believed that religious instruction in official church doctrine by a trained minister did not bring—and might even hinder—salvation. What counted, Finney proclaimed, was not a person's belief in the technical doctrines of a church but the will to be saved. His was an emotional faith that rejected the intellectually based faith of many established Protestant churches.

Wherever he preached, Finney won converts among churchgoing Protestants and those who had drifted away from their churches. The conversions were dramatic and often tearful. Although most of Finney's converts were members of the middle class, he became famous for converting wealthy individuals and the poor, who seemed lost to drink, sloth, and misbehavior. Finney used religious conversion to bring everyone, rich and poor, into the same moral community. The pride of the rich (if not their wealth) and the shame of the poor (if not their poverty) would give way to an exultant celebration of a new brotherhood in Christ. Conversion changed not only people's eternal fate but also their moral standing, identifying them spiritually with earnest, pious, middle-class respectability.

The Rochester Revival. Finney's most spectacular triumph came in 1830 when he moved his revivals from small towns to Rochester, New York, a major Erie Canal city, at the invitation of local business and political leaders. For six months he preached every day. He employed a new tactic: group prayer meetings in family homes, in which women played an active role. Finney's wife, Lydia, took a visible part in his ministry. She and other pious middle-class wives visited the homes of the unconverted, often while disapproving husbands were at work. Week after week Rochester was saturated with the evangelical message. Schools and businesses stopped for prayer. Spontaneous religious meetings were held in houses and in the streets.

Finney won over members of the business elite and their wives and soon claimed that he had converted the "great mass of the most influential people" of Rochester, especially the manufacturers and merchants who shipped grain on the Erie Canal. As part of their conversion, those "influential people" often confessed that their lives had been overly governed by money and too little devoted to the moral well-being of their own souls and those of their employees. With this confession came a pledge to reform their lives and those of their workers. They would attend church, drink only water, work steady hours, and encourage their employees to follow suit. In 1831 one of Rochester's Presbyterian churches rewrote its covenant in a way that gave a new meaning to the concept of "business." Every member pledged to "renounce all the ways of sin, and to make it the business of our life to do good and promote the glory of God."

A Family's Morning Devotional
This 1842 illustration from *Godey's Lady's Book*, a leading influence on the tastes of the emerging business class, portrays the kind of family Bible reading and prayer that the Finney revivals encouraged. Here, *Godey's* idealizes an affluent young mother and father who are trying to set a good example for their child and two servants.

And so the business leaders of Rochester set out to reform their city. Their favorite target was alcohol, which seemed to be the most wasteful and damaging social habit of their workers and the most obvious sign of a collapsing social order. But they also tried to meet what they thought were the workers' spiritual needs. In 1832 wealthy businessmen founded a new Free Presbyterian Church—called "free" because members did not have to pay for pew space. This church was specifically designed to serve canal workers, transients, and the settled poor. Soon two similar evangelical churches were founded in the city. To reinforce the work of those churches, Rochester's business elite founded other institutions: a savings bank to encourage thrift, Sunday schools for poor children, and the Female Charitable Society to provide relief for the families of the unemployed.

Within limits, the attempt to create a harmonious community of morally disciplined Christians was effective. During the 1830s many workers, often led by their wives, followed their employer's example and became converts and church members. And employers who had been "saved" often confirmed the respectability of the newly converted with raises, promotions, or bonuses. However, Finney's revival seldom moved poor people. Least responsive to the Protestant evangelists were the Irish-Catholic immigrants who had recently begun arriving in American cities, including Rochester. Skilled workers who belonged to strong craft organizations—bootmakers, carpenters, stonemasons, and boat builders—also resisted the message.

Some even supported newspapers opposing the revival, arguing that workers needed organization, higher wages, and schools more than sermons and prayers (see Chapter 11). But these critics only heightened the converts' zeal for rebuilding society into an evangelically defined Christian order.

The Spread of Business-Class Revivalism. During the 1830s revivals swept through cities and towns from New England to the Ohio Valley. Dozens of younger ministers—Baptist and Methodist as well as Congregationalist and Presbyterian—energetically adopted the evangelical message and its techniques. They succeeded wherever the middle class was large and considerable numbers of workers had reaped benefits from the Industrial Revolution. In New York City, where Finney successfully established himself soon after leaving Rochester, the wealthy silk merchants Arthur and Lewis Tappan founded a magazine, *The Christian Evangelist*, to promote his ideas. With the assistance of manufacturers and merchants, evangelists soon reached sinners the way that most aggressive businessmen reached customers: They standardized and simplified their religious message, aimed it at masses of people, and measured their success in quantitative terms—by the number of converts (see Figure 10.2).

Temperance. The temperance movement proved to be the most effective arena for evangelical reform on a national scale. Evangelicals gained control of the American Temperance Society, which had been organized in

***The Ecstasy of a Camp Meeting
(detail)***
In isolated rural areas, especially those with many Baptists and Methodists, the camp meeting was a more common forum for evangelical revivals than were church and prayer meetings. Such meetings, organized while farm work was slack, attracted families who camped in wagons and tents for as long as a week to join in the intense religious excitement and social life.

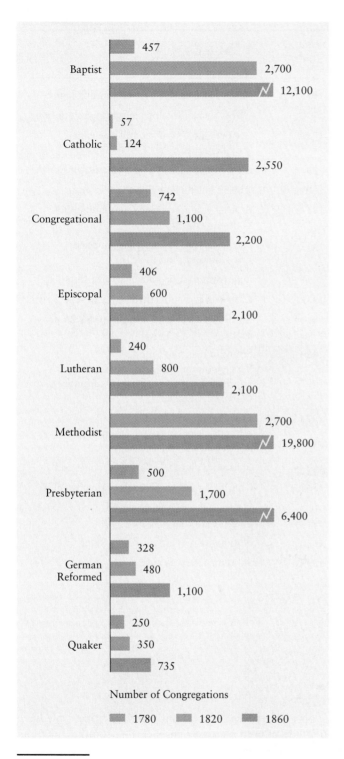

Number of Congregations

■ 1780 ■ 1820 ■ 1860

FIGURE 10.2

Church Growth by Denomination, 1780–1860

Christian congregations increased phenomenally between 1780 and 1860—nearly three times more rapidly than did the population. With the state now removed from religion, all denominations grew but revivialism played an especially important role in Protestant expansion.

1828. By the mid-1830s it had grown to 2,000 chapters with more than 200,000 members. The society adapted the methods that had worked so well in the revivals—group confession and prayer, a focus on the family and the spiritual role of women, and sudden, emotional conversion—and took them into virtually every town and city in the North. These techniques worked best among the families of the business class, for whom drink was becoming a fearful mark of social disrepute. Some business-class wives embraced temperance reform as a way to curb alcoholic husbands. On one day in New York City in 1841, 4,000 people took the temperance "pledge." The average annual consumption of spirits fell from about 5 gallons per person in 1830 to about 2 gallons in 1845.

The Work Ethic. Evangelical reformers also turned their efforts to revising and invigorating the work ethic that had been so important to the American tradition. They put a religious twist on Benjamin Franklin's formula for success. Laziness, drinking, and other wasteful habits could not, they preached, be cured simply by Franklin's patient methods of self-discipline. Instead, people had to undergo a profound change of heart, possible only through religious conversion. With God's grace would come the determination to turn away from drink, sloth, and sin. Then even the poorest family could look forward to a prosperous new life.

Only a minority of the large and diverse communities of laboring men and women joined the evangelical movement. Most of the religious converts were at least moderately prosperous and enjoyed a respectable standing in their communities. Evangelical religion reinforced the sense of common identity within the business class and that group's commitment to the concepts of individual enterprise, success, and moral discipline that constituted the ethic of the Industrial Revolution. Those Americans who joined the business class saw religion as a powerful cement for holding society together in the face of industrialization, which threatened to overwhelm the nation with social disorder and class animosity and conflict. But evangelical reform could not be contained within the Benevolent Empire, and it soon spilled over into the radical and utopian movements discussed in Chapter 12.

Summary

During the 1820s the nation's merchants, mechanics, and small manufacturers brought the Industrial Revolution to America. Through innovations in manufacturing organization and technology, Americans become more efficient producers. The combination of low-cost natural resources, the development of labor-saving innovations, and the recruitment of an industrial labor force consisting largely of women and children enabled textile manufacturers in the Northeast to become economically independent of the British.

Manufacturers and merchants in the Northeast and Northwest developed a vigorous domestic trade in agricultural and manufactured goods. Southerners participated in that trade but remained dependent on the exportation of cotton, the importation of British manufactured goods, and British commercial services. As domestic commerce grew, urbanization accelerated in the Northeast, led by New York City, which became the nation's leading trading center. Industrialization also stimulated the settlement of the West, resulting in increasing agricultural production that helped sustain the nation's economic growth. To integrate the national market, Americans built a transportation system. To encourage the flow of capital into the building of that system, state governments encouraged the use of the corporate form of organization by transportation companies. By 1840 the new national transportation system, based heavily on waterways, was unprecedented in size and complexity. In that year, however, the railroad was only in its infancy. America had launched the Industrial Revolution without the benefits of a modern railroad system.

Economic growth meant that most Americans, especially those who could take advantage of modern technological change, improved their standard of living. But industrialization widened distinctions among classes, disrupted working relations and residential patterns, and offered little opportunity for the large number of Americans who did not acquire skills, education, or property.

Economic growth fostered the development of a new social class: the business class, which consisted of middle-class property owners led by a business elite. Its members publicly acknowledged the disorder that accompanied industrialization and tried to harmonize class interests. They joined revivals led by evangelical clergymen such as Charles Finney, who believed that Christian conversions could mobilize the free will of individuals on behalf of worldly perfection. In Finney's re-

TIMELINE

1765	James Hargreaves invents spinning jenny
1782	Oliver Evans develops automated flour mill
1790	Samuel Slater's cotton mill opens in Providence, R.I.
1793	Eli Whitney manufactures cotton gins
1807	Robert Fulton launches the *Clermont*
1814	Boston Manufacturing Company builds Waltham cotton mill
1817	New York Stock Exchange founded Erie Canal begun
1818	First transatlantic packet service founded
1819	Cast-iron plow invented
1820	Price of federal land reduced to $1.25 per acre
1824	Franklin Institute founded Passage of a major protective tariff Supreme Court strikes down a monopoly in *Gibbons v. Ogden*
1825	Erie Canal completed Jefferson proclaims U.S. technological independence
1828	Baltimore and Ohio Railroad chartered
1831	Charles Grandison Finney begins Rochester revival
1832	First die-forging machine built
1833	National Road crosses Ohio River
1837	Supreme Court decides *Charles River Bridge v. Warren Bridge*

vivals business leaders and middle-class citizens pledged to attend church regularly, respect their families, abstain from alcohol, and urge others to embrace religion. A temperance pledge became an important badge of respectability. Revivalism and reform made the members of the business class even more certain that they were special—united, they believed, not only by material success but also by moral and spiritual superiority.

BIBLIOGRAPHY

The Rise of Northeastern Manufacturing

Surveys of the broad economic setting and impact of the Industrial Revolution include W. Elliot Brownlee, *Dynamics of Ascent: A History of the American Economy* (1979); Stuart Bruchey, *Enterprise: The Dynamic Economy of a Free People* (1990); Thomas C. Cochran, *Frontiers of Change: Early Industrialism in America* (1981); and Douglass C. North, *The Economic Growth of the United States, 1790–1860* (1961). Another useful survey is the pioneering work in economic geography, Donald W. Meinig, *The Shaping of America: A Geographical Perspective on 500 Years of History*, Volume 2: *Continental America, 1800–1867* (1993).

Books on the role of technological change include Gary Cross and Rick Szostak, *Technology and American Society: A History* (1995); H. J. Habakkuk, *American and British Technology in the Nineteenth Century: The Search for Labour-Saving Inventions* (1962); David Freeman Hawke, *Nuts and Bolts of the Past: A History of American Technology, 1776–1860* (1988); Brooke Hindle and Steven Lubar, *Engines of Change: The American Industrial Revolution, 1790–1860* (1986); David A. Hounshell, *From the American System to Mass Production, 1800–1932: The Development of Manufacturing Technology in the United States* (1984); Harold C. Livesay, *American Made: Men Who Shaped the American Economy* (1979); Nathan Rosenberg, *Perspectives on Technology* (1976); and Barbara M. Tucker, *Samuel Slater and the Origins of the American Textile Industry* (1984).

Stanley Lebergott, *Manpower in Economic Growth: The United States Record since 1800* (1964), provides a useful survey of the contribution of labor to the Industrial Revolution. An in-depth analysis of a critical group of women workers is Thomas Dublin, *Women at Work: The Transformation of Work and Community in Lowell, Massachusetts, 1826–1860* (1979), and *Transforming Women's Work: New England Lives in the Industrial Revolution* (1994). Regional studies of the early Industrial Revolution include Peter J. Coleman, *The Transformation of Rhode Island* (1963), and Dianne Lindstrom, *Economic Development in the Philadelphia Region, 1810–1850* (1978); and Anthony F.C. Wallace, *Rockdale: The Growth of an American Village in the Early Industrial Revolution* (1978).

The Expansion of Markets

Urban development in this period is best explored in R. G. Albion, *The Rise of New York Port, 1815–1860* (1939); Eric E. Lampard, "The Evolving System of Cities in the United States: Urbanization and Economic Development," in *Issues in Urban Economics* (ed. Harvey S. Perloff and Lowdon Wingo, Jr., 1968); Richard C. Wade, *The Urban Frontier: Pioneer Life in Early Pittsburgh, Cincinnati, Lexington, Louisville, and St. Louis* (1964); and Alan R. Pred, *Urban Growth and the Circulation of Information: The United States System of Cities, 1790–1840* (1973). The best introductions to the agricultural expansion in this period are Paul W. Gates, *The Farmer's Age: Agriculture, 1815–1860* (1960), and Lewis C. Gray, *History of Agriculture in the Southern United States to 1860* (1933). The classic history of the role of transportation is George R. Taylor,

The Transportation Revolution, 1815–1860 (1951). On the role of canals, consult Carter Goodrich et al., *Canals and American Economic Development* (1961), and Ronald E. Shaw, *Canals for a Nation: The Canal Era in the United States, 1790–1860* (1990). On the contribution of the law to early industrialization, see Oscar Handlin and Mary Flug Handlin, *Commonwealth: A Study in the Role of Government in the American Economy, Massachusetts, 1774–1861* (1947); Morton J. Horwitz, *The Transformation of American Law, 1780–1860* (1977); and James Willard Hurst, *Law and the Conditions of Freedom in the Nineteenth-Century United States* (1964).

Social Structure in an Industrializing Society

The following provide a good introduction to the study of the distribution of wealth and income in the early nineteenth century: Frederic C. Jaher, *The Urban Establishment: Upper Strata in Boston, New York, Charleston, Chicago, and Los Angeles* (1982); Edward Pessen, *Riches, Class, and Power Before the Civil War* (1973); and Jeffrey G. Williamson and Peter H. Lindert, *American Inequality: A Macroeconomic History* (1980). These studies should be supplemented with analyses of social mobility such as Robert Doherty, *Society and Power: Five New England Towns, 1800–1860* (1977); Don H. Doyle, *The Social Order of a Frontier Community: Jacksonville, Illinois, 1825–1870* (1978); Peter R. Knights, *The Plain People of Boston, 1830–1860* (1976); and Stanley Lebergott, *The American Economy: Income, Wealth, and Want* (1976). Some of the disruptive effects of mobility on urban life are addressed in Karen Haltunen, *Confidence Men and Painted Women: A Study of Middle-Class Culture in America, 1830–1870* (1982); Alan Dawley, *Class and Community: The Industrial Revolution in Lynn* (1976); Bruce Laurie, *Working People of Philadelphia: The Coming of Industrial Order: Town and Factory Life in Rural Massachusetts* (1983); W. J. Rorabaugh, *The Alcoholic Republic: An American Tradition* (1979); Christine Stansell, *City of Women: Sex and Class in New York, 1789-1806* (1986); and Sam Bass Warner, Jr., *The Private City* (1968). For an innovative discussion of the effects of early industrialization on the countryside, see Christopher Clark, *The Roots of Rural Capitalism: Western Massachusetts, 1789–1860* (1990).

The concept of the business class is developed in Michael Katz et al., *The Social Organization of Early Industrial Capitalism* (1982). Surveys of reform movements closely linked to the Second Great Awakening include Alice F. Tyler, *Freedom's Ferment: Phases of Social History from the Colonial Period to the Outbreak of the Civil War* (1944); and Ronald G. Walters, *American Reformers, 1815–1860* (1978). Studies of the relationship between religious evangelism and reform are particularly abundant for communities in New York State. See Paul E. Johnson, *A Shopkeeper's Millennium: Society and Revivals in Rochester, New York, 1815–1837* (1978), and Mary Ryan, *Cradle of the Middle Class: The Family in Oneida County, New York, 1790–1865* (1981). For more general studies of the religious ferment during the early republic, see John Butler, *Awash in a Sea of Faith: Christianizing the American People* (1990); Nathan O. Hatch, *The Democratization of American Christianity* (1989); and R. Lawrence Moore, *Selling God: American Religion in the Marketplace of Culture* (1994).

President's Levee

Andrew Jackson's chaotic 1829 inauguration, represented in
this painting by Robert Cruikshank as "all Creation going to
the White House," was the first "people's inaugural."

A Democratic Revolution

1820–1844

★   ★   ★

The Industrial Revolution transformed the lives of millions of American men and women. In traditional society, where people lived and worked together in self-sufficient, close-knit communities, their institutions—the family, the village or urban neighborhood, the artisan's shop, the religious congregation, and the town meeting—had functioned well. But the new economy drew people out of those intimate settings and into larger spheres, and even into national and international affairs. The new world was less predictable, less personal, and far more complicated.

The dislocations and disorders caused by the Industrial Revolution had a profound effect on American politics. This turmoil fueled a process of political democratization, and it paved the way for the emergence of Andrew Jackson and his new Democratic party. In the early years of the republic the byword had been *republicanism*. Now the clarion cry was for *democracy*. The movement for democracy even reached beyond politics into American workplaces. Some workers accepted the Industrial Revolution and organized to improve their situations. Others organized to challenge the legitimacy of the business class. Virtually all workers agreed that westward expansion was necessary to preserve economic opportunity for average Americans.

Jackson defined himself as the protector of farmers and workers and made a commitment to advance their liberty by attacking the "special privileges" of the rich and the business class, protecting the Union, and removing native American tribes from the path of westward settlement. Jackson was a product of the democratization movement, and as president he transformed his office and the federal government into potent instruments of democracy.

Jackson's opponents—the Whigs—gradually defined themselves as the party of economic improvement and prosperity; they would create opportunity by using the federal government to promote business, transportation, and industry. The Whig challenge to Jackson's Democratic party began what historians have called the Second Party System—a system that endured until the rise of the Republican party in the 1850s. This fiercely competitive system of two parties, in which each party claimed to speak for "the people," completed a democratic revolution that in its scope and significance matched the Industrial Revolution.

Democratizing Politics, 1820–1829

The quest for political democracy that began in the 1780s accelerated because of the Industrial Revolution. With the exception of the most traditional elites in seaboard cities and the plantation South, virtually all Americans supported democratization of the republic—especially through the expansion of white male voting—as a way to fulfill the ideals of the American Revolution. But the Industrial Revolution increased the tempo of democratization and took it beyond extension of the franchise—into the development of modern political parties.

Democratic Institutions

Industrialization created a public that was much more complex in its composition, better informed, and more emotionally involved in politics. Rapid economic change created new economic interests and intensified conflict among social and economic groups, thus raising the stakes of politics. Many people saw the possibility of using government to promote their own interests or oppose the interests of others. Through government, they could either promote or resist the forces of industrialization. At the same time, the growing ease of communication made state and national issues more important at the local level. In addition, the accelerating growth of western communities, where enthusiasm for broad participation in political life had always been greatest, increased the pressures for democratization.

The Right to Vote. Expansion of the franchise was the most dramatic expression of the democratic revolution (see Chapter 9). With the removal of property requirements, even the poorest wage laborer could vote. By 1840 the electorate included more than 90 percent of the adult white male population. Most states also established the direct popular election of governors, presidential electors, and some judges. More than half a century after the American Revolution, the idea that all white men had the right to participate fully in the political life of the nation had finally triumphed.

Democracy, however, still excluded more than half the population. Native Americans remained nations to themselves, with no voice in the halls of government where their fate was determined. Every state denied women the franchise and the right to hold office. Almost every state denied the vote to free blacks. And in 1840 nearly 3 million African-Americans—about 17 percent of all Americans—lived in slavery, with no rights at all. But the essence of democracy's appeal was its universality, and when women and blacks launched drives for equal rights in the 1840s and 1850s, they drew heavily on the language of democracy first enunciated in the Declaration of Independence.

Political Parties. In response to the challenge posed by economic and social change, new parties emerged in every state during the 1820s and 1830s. These parties were more democratic than their predecessors, but they were concerned as much with organization and discipline as with increasing participation. Party organization was the crucial ingredient required to shape a wide diversity of interests into workable coalitions that could give the electorate clear choices and produce coherent legislation. In large and diverse states such as New York, party loyalty and discipline were crucial. Party members had to be persuaded to support the party's candidate even if they disagreed with some of his ideas. In return, party members got a chance to participate, influence government, and benefit from patronage. By the 1830s, although unrecognized by the Constitution, political parties had become central elements in American government.

During the 1820s the New York politician Martin Van Buren pioneered in making party discipline an effective tool for governing. Using skills that earned him the nickname the "Little Magician," Van Buren and his associates took over and transformed New York State's Republican party. They introduced collective leadership, strong party loyalty and discipline, and an elaborate apparatus of party organization. Widely circulated party newspapers such as the Albany *Argus* promoted the party line and helped maintain discipline. The focus of party activity was on shaping the actions of legislatures. Party members learned that they could advance their interests in the New York legislature by accepting the majority decisions of a meeting, or *caucus*, of party members. On one crucial occasion, after seventeen Republicans in the state legislature had threatened to vote against the party line, Van Buren pleaded that they "magnanimously sacrifice individual preferences for the general good." They agreed and were rewarded with a banquet where, as one observer wrote, "something approaching divine honors were lavished on the Seventeen."

In a nation as diverse as the United States parties had to embrace *platforms*, or programs of proposed action, that would appeal to a broad coalition of voters.

The Election of 1824 and the "Corrupt Bargain"

Whereas state political parties became more vigorous and organized during the early 1820s, the national parties were in disarray. The Federalist party had virtually disappeared, and the Republican party was badly fragmented. In the election of 1824 to succeed Monroe, no fewer than five presidential candidates, all calling themselves Republicans, crowded the field. Three were veterans of Monroe's cabinet: Secretary of State John Quincy Adams, the son of John Adams; Secretary of War John C. Calhoun; and Secretary of the Treasury William H. Crawford. The fourth was Speaker of the House Henry Clay from Kentucky, and the fifth was General Andrew Jackson, at that time a senator from Tennessee.

As a native of Nashville, where he was linked to the most influential families through marriage and his career as an attorney, cotton planter, and slave owner, Jackson spoke most clearly for the voters of the Old Southwest. But virtually all Americans revered Jackson as the hero of the Battle of New Orleans. Tall and rough-hewn—nicknamed "Old Hickory" by the press—he embodied the nationalistic pride that had swelled in the wake of the War of 1812. His rise to prominence from common origins demonstrated republican virtue and even suggested divine favor.

Nominated for the presidency by the Tennessee legislature, Jackson followed tradition and did not campaign actively. But his supporters vigorously promoted him as a man of integrity who would root out corruption and preserve American freedom. They did not dwell on specific issues except to condemn the practice, customary under the First Party System, of having a *Congressional caucus*—a meeting of each party's Congressional members—nominate presidential candidates. They had especially harsh words for the Congressional caucus of 1824, in which less than a third of the Republicans had chosen the "official" presidential candidate, William H. Crawford. Significantly for Jackson, the 1824 election was the first in which the majority of presidential electors were selected by the voters. Only six of the twenty-four states retained the practice of having the state legislature choose the electors.

The result was a complete surprise to political leaders: Jackson won 99 electoral votes, Adams 84, Crawford 41, and Clay only 37. Crawford, paralyzed by a stroke, won only Georgia, his home state, and Virginia, where he had been born. Adams had broader national support, largely because of his prominence as secretary of state, but the public identified him as the candidate of

New England. Clay's support was limited largely to the Ohio Valley. (John C. Calhoun had bowed to political realities and switched over to the vice-presidential race, which he won easily with the support of the Jackson forces.)

Since no candidate had received an absolute majority, the House of Representatives had to choose the president from among the three leading contenders. Many established politicians were horrified at the thought of Jackson in the White House. Clay had been particularly derisive during the campaign, scorning Jackson as a mere "military chieftain." Out of the race, Clay resolved to block Jackson's election in the House, where Clay still served as Speaker. By the time the House met on February 9, 1825, Clay had put together a New England–Ohio Valley coalition that threw the election to Adams. Adams showed his gratitude by appointing Clay secretary of state. This was a significant appointment, since it had served the last three presidents as the final stepping-stone to the highest office, but it was a fatal mistake for both men. Jackson's supporters immediately decried the arrangement as a "corrupt bargain" and began almost at once to prepare for the next election.

The Presidency of John Quincy Adams, 1825–1829

As president, Adams presented a bold and sweeping program to promote the nation's economic and social development. He fully embraced the basic features of Clay's American System: (1) a protective tariff to stimulate manufacturing; (2) internal improvements (roads and canals) to stimulate commerce; and (3) a national bank to provide a uniform currency and expand credit. But Adams had an even more expansive view of the federal government's responsibilities. In his first message to Congress in December 1825 he advocated legislation to promote "the cultivation of the mechanic and of the elegant arts, the advancement of literature and the progress of the sciences, ornamental and profound." And he called for the establishment of a national university in Washington, extensive scientific explorations of the Far West, the adoption of a uniform standard of weights and measures, and the building of a national observatory.

Many politicians attacked Adams for showing favoritism to his most loyal supporters, the business class of the Northeast. On his deathbed, Thomas Jefferson argued that Adams was seeking to establish "a single and splendid government of an aristocracy . . . riding and ruling over the plundered ploughman and beggared yeomanry." There were constitutional objections as well. Madison had vetoed Calhoun and Clay's Bonus Bill in 1817 because he felt it would have exceeded the govern-

John Quincy Adams
A famous photograph of John Quincy Adams (1767–1848), taken about 1843 by Philip Haas, suggests the tenacity and moral commitment that contributed to his seventeen-year career as a congressman from Massachusetts. Far more effective in Congress than he had been as president, Adams became a vigorous opponent of slavery.

ment's constitutional powers, and Adams's program was even more ambitious. Adams made matters worse by openly questioning the wisdom of democracy. He warned that America seemed to "proclaim to the world that we are palsied by the will of our constituents."

In the end, all that Adams was able to get from of a hostile Congress was a modest improvement in navigation and a start on extending the National Road from Wheeling, Virginia, into Ohio. He had no success in raising tariffs until the end of his term, and the tariff that was passed then was not of his devising.

In December 1827 the Jacksonians won control of Congress, and they decided to push through their own tariff to bolster their leader's prospects in the next election. The Tariff of 1824 had imposed a protective tax of 35 percent on imported iron, woolens, cotton, and hemp. The new tariff raised the rate on manufactured goods to about 50 percent of their value, providing significantly greater protection to New England cloth manufacturers. To appeal to voters in New York, Pennsylvania, Ohio, and Kentucky, where Jackson was weak, the act also increased tariffs on imported raw materials, including flax, hemp, iron, lead, molasses, and raw wool. Despite his reservations, Adams signed the legislation.

The tariff was bitterly attacked in the South, which relied heavily on trade with Britain. By raising the cost of imports from Britain, the tariff reduced the flow of British goods and made it difficult for the British to pay for the cotton they imported from the South. Southern politicians, especially in South Carolina, denounced it as the "Tariff of Abominations," favoring interests in the West and the North. Southern leaders vowed to overturn it in the future, one way or another.

Adams's problems in the South were aggravated by his apparent support for the rights of native Americans. In 1825 the Creek nation had signed a treaty with United States commissioners, ceding its remaining land in Georgia. Adams concluded that Georgia had obtained the treaty through fraud and ordered that another treaty be negotiated. The new treaty, negotiated and ratified in 1826, delayed the removal of the native Americans, but when Georgia's governor, a backwoodsman named George M. Troup, heard about the new terms, he angrily defied Adams and threatened to take control of the Creek lands. Adams declared that it was the president's duty to uphold federal jurisdiction "by all the force committed for that purpose to his charge." But Adams was helpless before Georgia's determined resistance and finally urged the Creek to leave quickly, which almost all of them did between 1827 and 1829.

Adams the patrician viewed the presidency as being above politics. He ignored his waning popularity and disregarded the need to build support within his party. He failed to use presidential patronage to reward his supporters. He retained even hostile politicians in appointed positions so long as they were competent. When he decided to run for reelection in 1828, he refused to pay any attention to his campaign. He reinforced this aloof, paternalistic image by telling supporters that he would not ask the American people to reelect him. "If my country wants my services," he said, "she must ask for them."

The Election of 1828: The Birth of the Democratic Party

As Adams's problems mounted, Jackson's campaign gathered momentum. Jackson did not campaign personally, but his organization was brilliant. He assembled a broad, seemingly incongruous coalition of political leaders: his close friends in the Old Southwest; the South Carolina supporters of John C. Calhoun, who was again his semiofficial running mate; the Crawford supporters and the Virginians who had inherited power from Jefferson, Madison, and Monroe; the former Pennsylvania Federalists, who lacked a political home; and the skilled, disciplined leaders of Martin Van

Buren's New York organization. The state leaders organized local groups that planned newspaper campaigns, mass meetings, torchlight parades, and barbecues to excite public interest.

The Democrats' Message. Jackson's supporters conveyed the same message as in 1824, but more thoroughly and with greater emotion. The republic, Jacksonians charged, had been corrupted by "special privilege," which Jackson would ruthlessly root out. Though they championed Jefferson as their hero, they emphasized, more than he or the Republicans ever had, the idea that forceful democratic measures, especially majority rule, were necessary to purify the republic. Their evolving party label reflected this new emphasis on democracy. Initially, the Jacksonians had called themselves "Democratic-Republicans," in contrast to other Republicans. But as the campaign wore on, they simplified their name to "Democrats."

Jackson's supporters attacked Adams as the very personification of the corrupt consequences of special privilege. Had he not stolen the presidency through a "corrupt bargain" with Clay? They even made the sensational (but untrue) charge that as minister to Russia, Adams had tried to procure an American girl for the tsar. In contrast, they exalted Jackson's virtue, stressing his frontier origins and his rise to wealth and fame without benefit of formal education or association with a political faction. Jackson was described as a "natural" aristocrat, a man who had achieved success by his own efforts in an environment of liberty. For the Jacksonians, their leader personified the potential of the republic and gave Americans an opportunity to express their nationalism by casting their votes for him.

Jacksonian hostility to special privilege—in particular Jackson's hatred of corrupt bankers—appealed especially to urban workers and artisans in the Northeast who felt threatened by industrialization. But it also appealed to farmers and small property owners who believed that Henry Clay's American System represented unconstitutional favoritism and had narrowed economic opportunity.

In the South the Jacksonians courted planters and small farmers opposed to the American System. On the crucial question of the Tariff of Abominations, as on other issues, Jackson avoided making concrete pledges that might alienate large numbers of voters. Instead, he allowed his supporters to publish a letter in which he declared his preference for an unspecified "judicious" tariff. More important, most white southerners felt that the famed Indian fighter shared their desire to remove the remaining native Americans from the Southeast.

In the West, although Jackson remained vague about how much support government should give to western expansion, his military record during the War of 1812 was crucial (see Chapter 8). It suggested that he would vigorously support the ambitions of westerners and of all Americans for whom the West symbolized opportunity.

The Democrats Triumph. The Jacksonian strategy worked. Whereas only about a fourth of the eligible electorate had voted in 1824, more than half voted in 1828, overwhelmingly for Jackson (see Figure 11.1). There were now only two states, South Carolina and Delaware, where the legislature chose the presidential electors. Jackson and Calhoun received 178 of 261 electoral votes. Jackson and his supporters had fashioned a unified national coalition that included urban workers, western settlers, and southern farmers—planters and yeomen alike. He was the first president to be elected from the West, rather than from Virginia or Massachusetts.

Jackson's only area of weakness was New England, which Adams swept. Jackson's election was unsettling to the northern business elite. After the election Daniel Webster, an old Federalist, predicted to his business friends in Boston that when Jackson came to Washington, he would "bring a breeze with him. Which way it will blow, I cannot tell. . . . My *fear* is stronger than my *hope*." On inauguration day, after watching an unruly crowd clamber over the elegant furniture in the White House to shake the new president's hand, Supreme Court Justice Joseph Story declared, "The reign of King 'Mob' seemed triumphant."

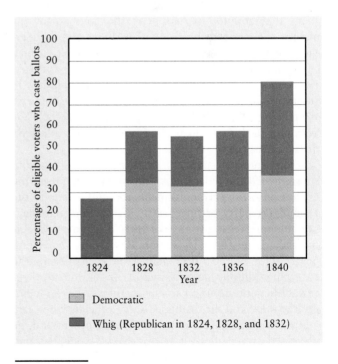

FIGURE 11.1

Changes in Voting Patterns, 1824–1840
With the return of two-party competition, voter participation soared in the critical presidential elections of 1828 and 1840.

The Jacksonian Presidency, 1829–1837

The democratizing of politics—the expansion of the franchise and the emergence of the first modern political party—had carried Andrew Jackson to the presidency. Now he turned his efforts to holding and enlarging his popular support by transforming the basic institutions of government. He expanded the powers of the presidency as an instrument of popular will. In the process, he stripped Congress of control of national politics and transferred that control to the Democratic party. Then, with powers greater than those of any president before him, he set out to smash any obstacles that impeded an independent citizenry intent on opportunity and expansion.

Party Government

To implement the people's will—the will of the majority—through party government, President Jackson reformed federal office holding. He declared that long tenure in federal jobs encouraged officeholders to view their positions as personal fiefdoms. During the election he had promised to introduce rotation in office, so that every four years officials would have to return "to making a living as other people do." He dismissed the argument that rotation would deny the government the service of experienced officials. The duties of public service, Jackson said, were "so plain and simple that men of intelligence may readily qualify themselves for their performance." Other Democrats put it more bluntly. In the words of William L. Marcy, a Jackson supporter from New York, "To the victors belong the spoils." The policy of rotation—the *spoils system*—was a distinctly democratic principle.

The spoils system, as implemented by Jackson, strengthened the federal government. Jackson used the greater power over appointments to build loyalty to the Democratic party. Stronger party loyalty in turn made it possible for Jackson to invoke party discipline in enacting and administering legislation. Rewarding loyal Democrats with public office helped build loyalty to the party. In addition, Jackson used his appointment power carefully, with attention to the quality of government. On the one hand, he dismissed some officials who were guilty of serious abuses of power. On the other hand, he protected some talented bureaucrats despite the fact that they were not Democrats.

Jackson used his highest-level political appointments to consolidate the power of his party. He selected cabinet officers purely for their ability to represent the various Democratic constituencies harmoniously. But Jackson never called cabinet meetings, relying instead

Andrew Jackson
This 1830s painting by Asher Durand captures the striking blend of romance and rugged force of character that were central to Jackson's image as a "natural aristocrat." Durand, who viewed painting as a patriotic art, was a founder of the Hudson River School of landscape art and an illustrator of James Fennimore Cooper's popular Revolutionary War novel, *The Spy.* (Collection of The New-York Historical Society)

on an informal group of advisers whose opinions he valued. Among the participants in this Kitchen Cabinet were several newspaper editors, including Francis Preston Blair of Kentucky, who edited the Washington *Globe;* Roger B. Taney of Maryland, who was to become attorney general and then chief justice of the United States; several Treasury Department officials, including Amos Kendall, also from Kentucky, who collaborated with Jackson on many of his state papers; and, most influential of all, Secretary of State Martin Van Buren.

Jackson versus the Bank

Jackson's most vigorous political offensive was his attack on the Second Bank of the United States, one of the key elements of the American System. Jackson began to dismantle the American System in May 1830, when he vetoed a bill that would extend the National Road from Maysville, Ohio, to Lexington, Kentucky. Jackson worried about the potential for corruption because the bill provided for federal purchase of stock in a Kentucky turnpike company. This issue was even more salient in Jackson's attack on the Second Bank.

The Second Bank of the United States. The Second Bank was a large commercial bank that the federal government had chartered in 1816 and partially owned (to the extent of 20 percent of the bank's stock). Its federal charter would expire in 1836. The Second Bank's most important role was to stabilize the nation's money supply. Most American money consisted of notes—in effect, paper money—that state-chartered commercial banks issued with the promise to redeem the notes with "hard" money—gold or silver coins, also known as *specie*—on demand. The Second Bank played its stabilizing role by regularly collecting these state bank notes at its various branch offices, returning them to the banks that had issued them, and demanding that the banks convert them into gold and silver coin. The intention was that, with the threat of collection hanging over them, the state banks would be conservative about extending credit. The state banks continued to issue more notes than they could redeem at any given time, thereby expanding the money supply. But under the discipline imposed by the Second Bank, they had to do so cautiously. During the prosperous 1820s, under the leadership of its president, Nicholas Biddle, the Second Bank performed especially well, maintaining steady, predictable increases in the money supply. By enhancing investors' confidence in the monetary stability of the developing West, Biddle and the bank increased the supply of capital for economic development. This was a service especially appreciated by bankers and entrepreneurs in Boston, New York, and Philadelphia.

Most Americans did not understand commercial banking, particularly the banks' capacity to enlarge the money supply through the lending of bank notes. Nor did they appreciate the role of the Second Bank in regulating credit. It was easy to believe that banking was a nonproductive, parasitic activity and that bankers earned their profits illegitimately through the exercise of special privileges. Many Americans had specific grievances against bankers. Jackson himself blamed them for financial instability in general and for the large sums he had lost in speculative investments during the 1790s. Wage earners were especially distrustful and hostile because they sometimes received payment in highly depreciated notes issued by unstable state banks. In response, they often advocated an end to all banking in the hope that there would be no money except specie (gold and silver coin). Other groups played on popular prejudices for the purpose of killing the Second Bank. Wealthy New York bankers, including supporters of Martin Van Buren, wanted to see federal monies deposited in their banks instead; some bankers in the smaller cities, including Nashville supporters of Jackson, wanted to be free of the inhibiting supervision of the Second Bank.

The Bank Veto. In 1832 Jackson's opponents in Congress, led by Henry Clay and Daniel Webster, united to embarrass him. They knew that the president opposed the Second Bank. Anticipating that many Democrats in Congress favored the Second Bank, Clay and Webster hoped to lure Jackson into the trap of a divisive and unpopular veto just before the 1832 elections. They persuaded Biddle, who would have preferred to remain neutral, to request an early recharter of the Second Bank, and they engineered the passage of a bill to accomplish that.

Jackson vetoed the bill, and that in itself was highly unusual. Before Jackson, presidents had vetoed legislation only nine times, always on constitutional grounds. But Jackson accompanied his veto with a powerful message that ranged far beyond constitutional issues to focus on the ways in which the bill was "dangerous to the liberties of the people." Using the vocabulary of the Revolution, he made the Second Bank the focus of resentment against the era's unsettling social and economic changes. He denounced the Second Bank as a nest of special privilege and monopoly power that promoted "the advancement of the few at the expense of the many." It damaged the "humbler members of society—the farmers, the mechanics, and laborers—who have neither the time nor the means of securing like favors to themselves." The president singled out the monopolists who had profited from special privileges and inside dealing. By inference, he attacked Webster, a director of the Boston branch of the Second Bank, for drawing on the Second Bank for loans and receiving fees from it for legal services. Finally, Jackson made a connection that was especially damning in the eyes of republican patriots: He emphasized the heavy investment by British aristocrats in the Second Bank.

The Election of 1832. Riding on the popular appeal of his veto message, Jackson and his new running mate, Martin Van Buren, faced Henry Clay, who headed the National Republican ticket, in the presidential election of 1832. Clay attacked Jackson for abusing patronage and the veto power, reproclaimed the American System, and called for rechartering the Second Bank. Clay was a popular campaigner, but Jackson and Van Buren carried a majority of the popular vote and overwhelmed Clay in the electoral vote, 219 to 49.

Jackson's veto and his parading of the veto in the campaign showed that he had a better sense of the public's anticorporate mood than did the champions of the Second Bank. His most fervent support came from a broad spectrum of people who resisted industrialization. But Jackson's position also won favor with some promoters of economic growth. Among them were state bankers who had originally supported the Second Bank but later concluded that its demise would open the way for more speculative investments by their banks. Also supporting Jackson were middle-class people who favored industrialization but wanted their rightful share of its benefits. Thus Jackson managed to include additional groups in his coalition, even though some held diametrically opposite positions on the value of banking and even that of industrialization.

The Bank War. Immediately after his reelection Jackson launched a new attack on the Second Bank, which became known as the "Bank war." The Second Bank still had four years left on its original charter, but Jackson decided to destroy it immediately by withdrawing the federal government's deposits. After removing two uncooperative secretaries of the treasury, he appointed Roger B. Taney, an enemy of the Second Bank who had helped Jackson with the veto message. He ordered Taney to move the government's cash to state banks—called "pet banks" by Jackson's opponents. This action probably violated the Bank's charter, but Jackson claimed that he had the authority to act because the recent election had given him a mandate to destroy the Second Bank. It was the first time a president had claimed that his electoral victory gave him the power to act independently of Congress.

Congress and the Second Bank retaliated. While the House of Representatives defended Jackson, in March 1834 the Senate passed a resolution that censured him. Henry Clay had drafted it, and he declared: "We are in the midst of a revolution, hitherto bloodless, but rapidly descending towards a total change of the pure republican character of the Government, and the concentration of all power in the hands of one man." For his part Nicholas Biddle contracted the Second Bank's loans sharply, increasing the pressure on other banks to restrict their loans and creating a brief recession in 1834. But Jackson and Taney held firm, and in 1836 the Second Bank became a state bank chartered under the laws of Pennsylvania. Jackson rewarded Taney by appointing him chief justice of the United States in 1836, after the

death of John Marshall. Until his death in 1864, Taney led the Court in giving constitutional legitimacy to Jackson's antimonopoly policies and implementing Jackson's belief that a government under control of the majority could be trusted to promote the common good.

The Tariff and the Nullification Crisis

After the 1832 election, Jackson's eagerness to defend the destiny of the republic led him to attack a state government. The occasion was the South Carolina nullification controversy, which stemmed from the chronic insecurity of that state's slaveholding elite. The only state with a slave majority—56 percent of the population in 1830—South Carolina was more like Haiti, Jamaica, or Barbados than the rest of the South. In the rice-growing districts along the coast the ratio of blacks to whites was more than ten to one. Like their West Indian counterparts, South Carolina planters lived in constant fear of slave rebellions and the power of outside authorities to abolish slavery.

During the 1820s South Carolina planters watched in apprehension as the British Parliament moved toward the abolition of slavery in the West Indies. (Parliament took this action, with compensation for slaveowners, in August 1833.) Might the United States move in the same direction? South Carolina's leaders decided to contest the limits of federal power, choosing the tariff as their target.

They had reason to focus on tariffs. The planters had lost repeatedly on tariff questions, most recently in July 1832, when Congress had passed legislation that retained the high rates of the Tariff of Abominations on manufactured cloth and iron. In effect, northern majorities in Congress had used their votes to redistribute

The Bank War
This political cartoon shows Jackson ordering the withdrawal of federal funds from the Second Bank of the United States. Crushed by the collapse of the Bank are Nicholas Biddle, whom the cartoonist represented as the devil, Biddle's cronies, and the newspapers Biddle supported in the war with Jackson. The man behind Jackson is "Major Jack Downing," the pseudonym for Seba Smith, a pro-Jackson humorist.

Charleston, South Carolina
This painting, by S. Bernard, a South Carolina artist, shows Charleston's Battery, the fashionable harborfront district. In this idealized scene, gentlemen and ladies stroll along the promenade, looking toward Britian, which they are trying to emulate. Beneath the confident exteriors of Charleston's elite residents lurked worries about their future in the only state with a slave majority.

wealth from the South to northern manufacturers, who received an artificially high price for their goods. The economic damage to southern states raised an issue endemic to American federalism: What recourse do states have when the federal government harms interests they regard as vital? (Some southern delegates to the Philadelphia convention in 1787, anticipating the threat tariffs might pose to their states, had proposed that a two-thirds majority of Congress be required to enact tariff legislation.)

Southern opposition to the tariff surged in the months after Jackson signed the bill. Antitariff forces under planter leadership won impressively in South Carolina's election that fall, and on November 24, 1832, a South Carolina state convention took a bold step. It adopted an Ordinance of Nullification, declaring the tariffs of 1828 and 1832 null and void and forbidding the collection of tariff duties in the state after February 1, 1833. Furthermore, should the federal government try to use force, South Carolina would secede.

Calhoun's *Exposition*. South Carolina's act of nullification rested on the constitutional arguments of Jackson's first vice-president, John C. Calhoun, as presented in his anonymous tract *The South Carolina Exposition and Protest* (1828). Calhoun had directly assaulted the Jack-

sonian position that majority rule should be at the heart of republican government. To protect individual liberty, the Constitution had to restrain majority rule. "Constitutional government and the government of a majority are utterly incompatible," Calhoun wrote. "An unchecked majority is a despotism," while "government is free, and will be permanent in proportion to the number, complexity, and efficiency of the checks, by which its powers are controlled."

Calhoun drew on the arguments of Jefferson and Madison in the Kentucky and Virginia resolutions of 1798. He returned to the Antifederalist argument that sovereignty lay not with the American people as a whole but with collections of people acting through their state governments. Only conventions such as those that had ratified the Constitution could determine whether acts of Congress were constitutional. If a state decided that a federal law was unconstitutional, it could "interpose" by declaring that law null and void within its borders. The challenged law would remain nullified unless three-fourths of the other states ratified an amendment assigning Congress the power in question. And if such an amendment was adopted, the dissident state then had the option of seceding from the republic. Calhoun's ideas would form the basis of *states' rights* (or *state rights*) arguments well into the twentieth century.

Calhoun did not immediately admit authorship of the *Exposition,* but he took a public position on the issue of states' rights in 1830 after a long Senate debate between Robert Y. Hayne of South Carolina and Daniel Webster of Massachusetts over the nature of the Union. The debate began in January 1830 when Senator Hayne, protesting a resolution by Samuel A. Foot of Connecticut to restrict western land sales, suggested that the West should join forces with the South to oppose the land and tariff policies of the Northeast. Webster defended his section, turning from economic issues and challenging Hayne to debate the issue of states' rights. Hayne responded with the arguments of the *Exposition,* while Calhoun looked on approvingly. Webster, often speaking directly to Calhoun, replied with a stirring defense of national power in which he concluded: "Liberty *and* Union, now and forever, one and inseparable!" What became known as Webster's "Second Reply to Hayne" circulated more widely than had any previous Congressional speech.

Jackson kept Republicans in suspense about his position until an April 1830 banquet celebrating Jefferson's birthday. Opening the formal toasts, Jackson looked squarely at Calhoun and unequivocally declared: "Our Federal Union—it must be preserved." As vice-president, it was Calhoun's turn to rise next. His glass trembling in his hand, he delivered his toast: "The Union—next to our liberty the most dear! May we all remember that it can only be preserved by respecting the rights of the states and distributing equally the benefits and burdens of the Union."

In 1831 Calhoun finally admitted his authorship of the *Exposition* and elaborated on his views. Jackson—spurred on by Secretary of State Van Buren, who wanted the vice-presidency—dropped Calhoun from the ticket in May 1832.

Jackson Defends the Constitution. Jackson's response to the Ordinance of Nullification was swift and firm. On December 10 he issued a proclamation declaring that "disunion by armed force is *treason.*" Appealing to patriotism, he declared that nullification violated the Constitution and was "unauthorized by its spirit, inconsistent with every principle on which it is founded, and destructive of the great object for which it was formed." Privately, he threatened to hang Calhoun. This was the final straw for Calhoun, who resigned as vice-president in December with three months left of his term. From then on he would defend nullification from the floor of the Senate, to which he was immediately appointed by the South Carolina legislature.

South Carolina refused to relent even when Jackson brandished federal power by reinforcing federal forts in South Carolina and sending a warship and several armed boats to the port of Charleston. Finally, in January 1833, Jackson asked Congress to pass a "force bill"

John C. Calhoun (1782–1850)
This daguerreotype, made close to the time of Calhoun's death, suggests the emotional intensity he brought to bear on the issues of states' rights and slavery.

authorizing him to use the army and navy to compel obedience.

Jackson had firmly established national supremacy, but he wanted Congress to remove a principal source of the conflict: high tariffs. Henry Clay, determined to protect America's fledgling industries for at least a few more years, worked out a compromise. He proposed a new measure that provided for a gradual, annual reduction of the tariff so that by 1842 rates would return to the modest levels set in 1816. On March 1, 1833, Congress passed both the Compromise Tariff and the force bill. Jackson was satisfied. He believed he had established that no state could nullify a law of the United States.

Having saved face on the tariff issue, South Carolina's leaders promptly repealed the nullification ordinance. No other state had joined South Carolina in its confrontation with federal power. Like Jackson, most southerners did not perceive an imminent threat to slavery. They held the Union in high regard and did not believe that restoring low tariffs warranted a challenge either to federal authority or to President Jackson, who was popular in the South. Jackson's aggressive defense of the national interest against the nullifiers won widespread support in the South as well as the North. Still, South Carolinians resented their defeat over nullification, and support for Calhoun's theories remained widespread in the South. The compromise of 1833 was only a truce, not a definitive solution to the conflict over the meaning of the Union.

Andrew Jackson's Legacy for American Government

Jackson left the federal government—in particular the presidency—far stronger than he had found it. While he defended the republican values of Jefferson, he built a far more powerful, dynamic federal government than Jefferson had favored. And the constitutional argument Jackson set forth in his proclamation against nullification would provide the basis for Abraham Lincoln's response to the secession crisis of 1861.

Jackson opposed increased powers for governments only when they fostered special privilege and corruption, as he believed they tended to do when legislatures were too powerful. "The President," Jackson declared in 1834, "is the direct representative of the American people." Acting on this belief, Jackson had freely used the veto power, fired federal officeholders and replaced them with his political supporters, defied the Supreme Court and Congress, and mobilized federal force against a disobedient state. Jackson was convinced that when the people controlled the federal government through their party and their president, the republic had nothing to fear.

Westward Expansion and Conflict

During the 1820s and 1830s Americans of virtually all regions and classes believed in the importance of new opportunities to the west of the Appalachians. They believed that average Americans had to have access to fresh land to preserve the economic and political health of the republic. In their view, democracy could prosper only if average Americans owned productive land. But the massive migration westward during the 1820s and 1830s put Americans into direct conflict with Indian tribes, which still occupied much of the land west of the Appalachians, and posed the threat of future trouble with Mexico. Contests for disputed lands and the likelihood of more such contests in the future made Americans, particularly in the West, appreciate the kind of strong central government forged by Andrew Jackson.

Removal of the Native Americans. By the 1820s most Americans had concluded that the federal government must remove Indian tribes from the path of American expansion. It was not enough to break the resistance of western Indians to white settlement. It was necessary, they believed, to remove all native Americans east of the Mississippi, even those in seaboard states who had adapted to white society and did not threaten their white neighbors. Removal was necessary because the native American tribes possessed land that white farmers coveted. Removal was Andrew Jackson's policy, as he made clear in his first inaugural address. Jackson and

most Americans justified removal with the assertion that Indians were barbaric and could never become part of American society. Some Americans, including Jackson, also rationalized the removal of Indians as a humane way to protect an inferior people from direct competition with a superior race.

The Black Hawk War. By the time Andrew Jackson was elected president, the federal government had nearly broken the back of the resistance of native Americans to removal from the Old Northwest. In 1832 Jackson finished the assault. He sent regular army troops to frontier areas of Illinois in 1832 to remove Chief Black Hawk, a leader of the Sauk and Fox tribes, from rich farmland along the Mississippi in western Illinois (see American Voices, page 338). The troops refused Black Hawk's offer to surrender and pursued him into the Wisconsin Territory. On August 3 the army ended its pursuit with the eight-hour-long Bad Axe Massacre, leaving alive only 150 of the 1,000 warriors who had followed Black Hawk. During the next five years nearly all the other tribes in the Northwest moved or were forced to move west of the Mississippi River.

Black Hawk
This portrait was painted by George Catlin (1796–1872), who visited more tribes of western Indians than did any other artist during the 1830s. He assembled nearly 600 paintings in an "Indian Gallery" and traveled with it throughout America between 1837 and 1851, appealing to intrigued but unsympathetic audiences. (Courtesy of the Gilcrease Institute)

Black Hawk

Prelude to the Black Hawk War

Black Hawk (1767–1838), or Makatai-meshekiakiak in the language of his people, was a chief of the Sauk and Fox Indians. He was born the same year as Andrew Jackson in a Sauk village where present-day Rock Island, Illinois, is located. Also like Jackson, he was a warrior, leading armies of more than 500 by the time he was in his thirties. In 1833 he dictated his life story to a government interpreter, who in turn worked with a young Illinois newspaper editor to publish the narrative. In this passage Black Hawk describes some of the events leading up to the Black Hawk War.

We had about eight hundred acres in cultivation. . . . The land around our village . . . was covered with bluegrass, which made excellent pasture for our horses. . . . The rapids of Rock river furnished us with an abundance of excellent fish, and the land, being good, never failed to produce good crops of corn, beans, pumpkins, and squashes. We always had plenty—our children never cried with hunger, nor our people were never in want. Here our village had stood for more than a hundred years. . . .

Nothing was now [1828] talked of but leaving our village. Ke-o-kuck [the principal chief] had been persuaded to consent to . . . remove to the west side

of the Mississippi. . . . I . . . raised the standard of opposition to Ke-o-kuck, with full determination not to leave my village. . . . I was of the opinion that the white people had plenty of land, and would never take our village from us. . . . During the winter [1828–1829], I received information that three families of whites had arrived at our village, and destroyed some of our lodges, and were making fences and dividing our corn-fields for their own use. . . . I went to my lodge, and saw a family occupying it. . . . The interpreter wrote me a paper, and I went back to the village, and showed it to the intruders, but could not understand their reply. I expected, however, that they would remove, as I requested them.

. . . we came up to our village, and found that the whites had not left it—but that others had come, and that the greater part of our corn-fields had been enclosed . . . the whites appeared displeased because we had come back. We repaired the lodges that had been left standing, and built others. . . .

In consequence of the improvements of the intruders on our fields, we found considerable difficulty to get ground to plant a little corn. Some of the whites permitted us to plant small patches in the fields they had fenced, keeping all the best ground for themselves. . . .

The white people brought whisky into our village, made people drunk, and cheated them out of their homes, guns, and traps!

That fall [1829] I paid a visit to the agent, before we started to our hunting grounds. . . . He said that the land on which our village stood was now ordered to be sold to individuals; and that, when sold, *our right* to remain, by treaty, would be at an end, and that if we returned next spring, we would be *forced* to remove!

I refused . . . to quit my village. It was here, that I was born—and here lie the bones of many friends and relatives. For this spot I felt a sacred reverence, and never could consent to leave it, without being forced therefrom. [1830]

I directed my village crier to proclaim, that my orders were, in the event of the war chief coming to our village to remove us, that not a gun should be fired, not any resistance offered. That if he determined to fight, for them to remain quietly in their lodges, and let them *kill them if he chose*! [Spring, 1831]

Source: David Jackson, ed., *Black Hawk, An Autobiography* (Urbana: University of Illinois Press, 1964), 88–113.

The "Five Civilized Tribes." The Cherokee and Creek in Georgia, Tennessee, and Alabama; the Chickasaw and Choctaw in Mississippi, Alabama, and Tennessee; and the Seminole in Florida—the so-called five civilized tribes—remained in the South, in control of large enclaves. The Cherokee were particularly successful because they had a centralized political system, a thriving agricultural economy, and leaders who worked to gain white sympathy by adopting the trappings of a plantation society (see Chapter 8). Tragically, the five tribes occupied high-quality cotton land that was directly in the path of white settlement.

Jackson's first move was to withdraw the federal troops protecting the tribal enclaves that had been created in the southeastern states after the War of 1812. He realized that this action would leave native Americans subject to state law, which he knew had a sharp anti-Indian edge. In 1828 Georgia declared that the Cherokee were not an Indian nation but a collection of individuals who were tenants on state-owned land. Other states followed Georgia's example. By restricting the tribal rights of native Americans, they opened the way for whites to acquire Indian lands.

Jackson then pushed through the Indian Removal

Act of 1830, which offered southern Indians land west of the Mississippi in exchange for their eastern holdings. When Jackson sent agents to negotiate with the five tribes, he instructed them to tell the Indians "as friends and brothers to listen to their father." In the West, the agents should promise the tribes, "their white brothers will not trouble them, . . . will have no claim to the land," and the Indians "can live upon it, they and all their children, as long as grass grows and water runs." Realizing that the United States was prepared to send federal troops to remove them, tribes in the North and the South negotiated almost a hundred treaties for such exchanges.

Jackson carried out his Indian policy despite two rulings by the Supreme Court that tended to uphold Indian rights. In 1827 the Cherokee had adopted a constitution and proclaimed themselves a separate nation within the United States. After Georgia's 1828 declaration denied their claim to nationhood, the Cherokee appealed to the Supreme Court, arguing that Georgia's denial of their independence as a "foreign nation" violated the U.S. Constitution. In *Cherokee Nation v. Georgia* (1831) Chief Justice John Marshall denied the Cherokee claim of independence and refused to hear their case. But speaking for a majority of the justices, he argued that the Indians were "domestic dependent nations." In another case, *Worcester v. Georgia* (1832), Marshall held that the Indian nations were "distinct political communities, having territorial boundaries, within which their authority is exclusive . . . which is not only acknowledged, but guaranteed by the United States." Jackson reputedly responded, "John Marshall has made his decision; now let him enforce it." Because of the wide popularity of Jackson's Indian policy, no significant support emerged for the Court, and Jackson took no steps to challenge Georgia.

The Trail of Tears. The Cherokee refused to budge. They repudiated a treaty, forced on them in 1835, that required them to leave by May 23, 1838. By the deadline, only 2,000 of the 17,000 Cherokee had left. During the summer Martin Van Buren, who had assumed the presidency a year earlier, sent General Winfield Scott with an army of 7,000 men to enforce the treaty. Scott rounded up 15,000 Cherokee and concentrated them in government camps, where many died. A few escaped to isolated Cherokee villages in the mountains of North Carolina. In the fall and winter the rest were forced to undertake a 1,200-mile march to the new Indian Territory in present-day Oklahoma—a route they remembered as the Trail of Tears (see Map 11.1). Only 11,000 reached Oklahoma; on the journey as many as 4,000 died of starvation and exposure, victims of racism and the ruthless hunger of whites for land. Only the Seminole remained in the Southeast. Aided by runaway slaves, many of whom had married into the tribe, the Seminole fought a guerrilla war into the 1840s against federal troops and the state militia.

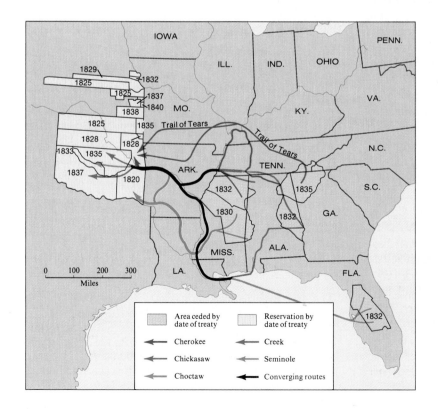

MAP 11.1

The Removal of Native Americans

This map shows the lands of the southeastern tribes before and after their removal during the 1820s and 1830s and the routes of their forced migrations. A comparison of this map with the map of land sales on page 308 shows that the tribal lands ceded in Alabama and Mississippi became those most sought after by white settlers during the 1830s. No white settlers occupied land on the new reservations before the Civil War.

Dreams of Expansion into Texas. During the 1820s, while some Americans moved onto the rich cotton lands that native Americans had once possessed, others dreamed of cultivating cotton even farther west, in Texas, on lands in Mexican territory. As they expanded the geographical reach of the American economy, they planted the seeds for a confrontation between the United States and Mexico.

Spanish, Mexican, and American Settlement. The Spanish had called the northeastern zone of their American empire Tejas or Texas, after the local native American word for "friends," and had employed Texas as a buffer against the French. With the Louisiana Purchase in 1803, Texas became Spain's buffer against the incursion of Anglo-Americans. Adventurers from the United States did arrive, encouraged by officials in the administration of James Madison. But by the time of the 1819 treaty between Spain and the United States, violent conflicts—among Spanish settlers, Spanish troops, Spanish-American republicans rebelling against Spain, and native American tribes whom the Spanish used to discourage foreign settlement—had turned Texas into an impoverished and unattractive place.

After winning independence from Spain in 1821, Mexico began to encourage immigration north of the Rio Grande. Mexican officials recognized that they could not keep illegal immigrants from the United States out of Mexico. They decided to try instead to turn them into loyal citizens and thereby perhaps block American political expansion. During the 1820s Mexico granted Stephen F. Austin and other Americans from the lower Mississippi Valley some of the best land in Texas (see Map 11.2). By 1830 about 7,000 Americans were living in Texas, outnumbering the 3,000 Mexicans there. The Americans, however, did not assimilate. They settled largely in eastern and central Texas, well removed from the largely Mexican settlements of Goliad and San Antonio to the southwest. Looking forward to planting cotton, the American Texans had imported slaves by finding loopholes in Mexico's restrictions against slavery.

The Mexican government, worried about the strength of this American community in Texas, passed laws in 1830 that restricted American immigration and prohibited the importation of slaves. (Mexico had abolished slavery the year before.) These actions and the news that American abolitionists planned to establish a refuge for free blacks in Texas led the American immigrants to begin violent protests. Meanwhile, immigration increased dramatically; by 1835, 27,000 Anglo-Americans and their 3,000 slaves lived in Texas.

One group of Americans, the "peace party," under the leadership of Stephen Austin, worked to win more self-government for Texas within Mexico. Another group, the "war party," demanded independence.

Austin won significant reforms, but before he could achieve statehood for Texas within Mexico, General Antonio López de Santa Anna became president of Mexico, appointed a military commandant for Texas, and centralized power in Mexico City. The leaders of the war party provoked a rebellion that both parties ultimately supported. On March 2, 1836, the two groups joined in proclaiming the independence of Texas and adopting a constitution that legalized slavery.

The Texas Rebellion. At first the tide of battle went against the Texans. Only four days after the declaration of independence, Santa Anna wiped out the garrison, including Davy Crockett and Jim Bowie, that was defending the Alamo in San Antonio. At Goliad he ordered the execution of 371 rebel prisoners, whom he regarded as mercenaries rather than Texans because they had arrived from the United States only recently. By the end of March, Santa Anna thought he had crushed the rebellion.

The defeat at the Alamo, however, captured the attention of New Orleans and New York newspapers,

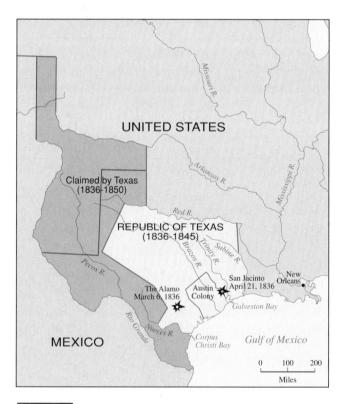

MAP 11.2

The American Settlement of Texas
In 1821 Stephen F. Austin established the first organized Anglo-American settlement in Texas, at the mouth of the Brazos. By the end of 1833, under grants from Mexican authorities, he had issued land titles to over 1,000 families. For the export of cotton, his prosperous colony had access to both Corpus Christi Bay and Galveston Bay.

Juan N. Seguín

A Tejano and the Texas Rebellion

Juan N. Seguín (1806–1890) was the most prominent of the Tejanos (Spanish-speaking inhabitants of Texas) who joined the Anglo-Americans in the 1836 rebellion against Mexico. Those, like Seguín, who fought alongside the rebels soon faced the greed and discrimination of the more recent immigrants to Texas. In 1842, three years before the annexation of Texas, Seguín left Texas for Mexico, and in 1846–1847 he led a company of soldiers in resisting the invading forces of the United States during the Mexican War.

A native of the city of San Antonio de Béxar, I embraced the cause of Texas at the sound of the first cannon which foretold her liberty, filled an honorable role within the ranks of the conquerors of San Jacinto, and was a member of the legislative body of the Republic [1837–1840]. . . .

The tokens of esteem and evidences of trust and confidence repeatedly bestowed upon me by the . . . dignitaries of the Republic, could not fail to arouse a great deal of invidious and malignant feeling against me. The jealousy evinced against me by several officers of the companies recently arrived at San Antonio from the United States soon spread among the straggling American adventurers, who were already beginning to work their dark intrigues against the native families, whose only crime was that they owned large tracts of land and desirable property.

I will also point out the origin of another enmity which, on several occasions, endangered my life. In those evil days, San Antonio swarmed with

Juan N. Seguín
After the Mexican War, Seguín returned to San Antonio where he resumed a career as a popular political leader, serving during the 1850s as a justice of the peace, an election precinct chairman, and a founder of the Democratic party in Bexar County. After his opponents charged him with treason to the Republic of Texas, he wrote his memoirs to defend his record.

adventurers from every quarter of the globe. Many a noble heart grasped the sword in the defense of the liberty of Texas, cheerfully pouring out their blood for our cause, and to them everlasting public gratitude is due. But there were also many bad men, fugitives from their country who found in this land an opportunity for their criminal designs. . . .

San Antonio claimed then, as it claims now [1858], to be the first city of Texas. It was also the receptacle of the scum of society. My political and social situation [as mayor of San Antonio, 1841–1842] brought me into continual contact with that class of people. At every hour of the day and night my countrymen ran to me for protection against the assaults or exactions of those adventurers. Sometimes, by persuasion, I prevailed on them to desist; sometimes, also, force had to be resorted to. How could I have done otherwise? Were not the victims my own countrymen, friends, and associates? Could I leave them defenseless, exposed to the assaults of foreigners who, on the pretext that they were Mexicans, treated them worse than brutes?

. . . I resolved to seek a refuge among my enemies, braving all dangers. But before taking this step, I sent in my resignation as mayor of the city to the municipality of San Antonio, stating to them that, unable any longer to suffer the persecutions of some ungrateful Americans who strove to murder me, I had determined to free my family and friends from their continual misery on my account, and go and live peaceably in Mexico. That for these reasons I resigned my office, with all my privileges and honors as a Texan.

Source: Jesús F. de la Teja, ed., *A Revolution Remembered: The Memoirs and Selected Correspondence of Juan N. Seguín* (Austin: State House Press, 1991), 73–74, 89–90.

whose correspondents romanticized the heroism of the Texans. Using some of the strongest anti-Catholic rhetoric of the day, the newspapers described the Mexicans as tyrannical butchers in the service of the pope. Thousands of adventurers, learning of Texan offers of land bounties, set sail from New York, the Gulf states, and the Mississippi Valley. Reinforced by the new arrivals and led by General Sam Houston, the Texas rebels routed the Mexicans in the Battle of San Jacinto on April 21, 1836. Although Mexico refused to recognize the new republic, it abandoned efforts to reconquer it (see American Voices, above).

The Issue of Annexation. The Texans immediately voted by plebiscite for annexation by the United States. But Jackson and Martin Van Buren, who succeeded Jackson as president in 1837, took no position on the matter. Jackson was strong-willed and decisive, but he also knew when the best policy was to do nothing. He recognized that adding Texas as a state would disrupt the even balance of free and slave states established by the Missouri Compromise. In addition, he feared that such a step would lead to war with Mexico and a division of the Democratic party into northern and southern factions. Privately, however, Jackson supported annexation and even encouraged the Texans to seize Mexican territory all the way to the Pacific Ocean.

The Early Labor Movement, 1794–1836

The movement for democratization extended beyond politics to the workshops. Some artisans believed that they had gained independence and even prosperity from the Industrial Revolution and saw little reason to challenge the inherently undemocratic nature of the new working conditions. They organized societies, associations, and unions, but only as a way to increase their share of the growing economic pie. Others organized with a more radical purpose: to resist the business class. Many artisans with traditional skills had been hurt by industrialization, and they looked with suspicion on business-class efforts to reform society. To them the political task was not to create harmony between owners and workers but to recognize the inevitable conflict of interest between people who sold their labor and people who bought it.

Artisan Self-Consciousness

The earliest labor unions drew sustenance from the craft identity and social solidarity that had existed for generations among artisans—carpenters, shoemakers, shipbuilders, and other skilled workers. The skilled shoemakers in Philadelphia were representative. They had formed the Federated Society of Journeymen Cordwainers in 1794 to press for a uniform wage for their members. (Shoemakers took the name *cordwainers* from the high-quality cordovan leather they worked.) Their repeated strikes against wage cuts had some success until 1806, when their leaders were convicted of criminal conspiracy under the common law in *Commonwealth v. Pullis.* The idea that a workers' combination was illegal—"a government unto themselves," in the words of the Philadelphia court—hampered the

union movement for many years but did not stop it.

As the Industrial Revolution gathered momentum during the 1820s and 1830s, many artisans developed a new sense of social identity. Their group consciousness did not yet include black or women workers or even the spouses who toiled alongside as "helpmates." It also did not include the growing numbers of unskilled workers, including the vast majority of factory workers. But the vision of the artisans was expanding. They began to see themselves not only as being linked with others skilled in a particular craft but as members of a larger class. During the 1820s and 1830s class-conscious artisans, many of whom had traditional skills still needed in the industrial era, led a union movement.

Workers in the Building Trades

Prominent among the leaders in unionization were workers in the building trades: carpenters, house-painters, stonecutters, masons, nailers, and cabinetmakers. These workers were able to challenge employers in a sustained way because the Industrial Revolution, far from undermining their skills, actually increased the demand for them. Workers in the building trades organized largely with the aim of increasing their remuneration—which they regarded as including leisure time as well as money—and their prospects for independence and security in the new industrial society.

Rapid urbanization during the 1820s and the building of homes, stores, and factories triggered a strong demand for construction skills. The traditional hours of work for virtually all laborers were "sun to sun," but the quickening pace of economic activity was leading many employers to demand a greater intensity of effort. In the building trades, the pressure became most intense during the spring and summer. Not only was construction then at fever pitch, but the regular working day exceeded twelve hours.

As the demand for their skills increased, so did the bargaining position of artisans in the building trades. They attempted to take advantage of this by forming labor unions and demanding a shorter workday. In 1825 about 600 carpenters in Boston struck against their contractor-employers, demanding a ten-hour day, 6 A.M. to 6 P.M., with an hour each for breakfast and dinner. Their effort failed, but this was the first great strike for the ten-hour day. Two years later a group of journeymen carpenters in Philadelphia had greater success. After a brief strike, several hundred workers won the ten-hour day and initiated coordinated action by groups of unions in the city. Their success led the building-trade workers to found the Mechanics' Union of Trade Associations. They reached out to other trades and formed the first effective citywide organization of wage earners in Philadelphia. "The real object . . . of this association," stated the constitution of the Mechanics' Union, is "to assist in establishing a just balance of power . . . between all the various classes and individuals which constitute society at large."

The building-trade workers went even further. They founded a political party, the Working Men's party, in 1828. The party's platform included equal taxation, the abolition of banks, and universal education. For a time the Working Men held enough seats to control Philadelphia's city council.

A large majority of workers considered the advancement of public education their most important goal. They were convinced that public schools would give their children skills with enduring value and allow them to advance more rapidly into the ranks of the propertied. Therefore, the Working Men's party demanded that the city and state provide all citizens with public education that would combine "one or more mechanical arts" with "literary and scientific instruction." Such training would "place the citizens of this extensive republic on an equality [and] bring the children of the poor and rich to mix together as a band of republican brethren," so that "united in youth in the acquisition of knowledge, they will grow up together, jealous of naught but the republican character of their country." The Working Men's party helped persuade Philadelphia to expand public schooling and the Pennsylvania legislature to authorize, in 1834, universal, free, tax-supported schools.

The members of the building-trade unions maintained their traditional values. They continued to take pride in their occupations and make a comfortable living, and they stressed the importance of the communal solidarity of their respective crafts. In the growing urban economy of the 1820s and 1830s their relative economic position improved, and they expanded their property holdings significantly. They saw little reason to criticize the new industrial order in a fundamental way and considerable reason to promote their own version of social harmony.

The Threatened Artisans

The position of artisans directly threatened by industrialization was less happy. These workers faced declining incomes, unemployment, and loss of status as machines took over their jobs. Hatters, printers, and weavers were among the most threatened workers, and during the 1820s and 1830s they banded together to form craft unions. Their leaders formulated a "producer's" ideology that defined their position in relation to both the business class and unskilled wage earners. They advanced a *labor theory of value*, arguing that the price of a product should reflect the labor required to make it and that most of the income from its sale should go to the person who made it. Artisans condemned the accumulation of wealth by capitalist employers and proclaimed their fear of becoming, as they put it, "slaves to a monied aristocracy."

A key group of threatened workers were the journeymen shoemakers. In the 1820s and 1830s shoe manufacturers began to change the way shoes were made. They hired more journeymen but moved them to large back-room shops where the workers cut leather into soles and "uppers." Then the masters sent out the uppers to shoe binders, usually women who worked at home binding the uppers and sewing in fabric linings. The employers then passed on the uppers and soles to journeymen who assembled entire shoes in small shops ("ten footers") commonly located in their backyards. Finally, the journeymen returned finished shoes to the central shops for inspection and packing. The new system of production made the master into a mere employer, the "shoe boss," and eroded workers' control over the pace and conditions of labor.

In 1830 the journeymen shoemakers of Lynn, Massachusetts, united to form the Mutual Benefit Society of Journeymen Cordwainers to defend their interests as employees and, insofar as possible, to establish their independence from the shoe bosses. "The division of society into the producing and nonproducing classes," they explained, "and the fact of the unequal distribution of value between the two, introduced us at once to another distinction—that of capital and labor. . . . Labor now becomes a commodity, wealth capital, and the natural order of things is entirely reversed." Therefore, "antagonism and opposition is introduced in the community; capital and labor stand opposed." In 1836 the cordwainers and journeymen printers set up national craft unions to coordinate the activities of local unions.

The new unions of cordwainers and printers, along with other artisans in similar situations, quickly turned to politics. Union members supported the Jacksonian movement, which in turn energized the workers' political efforts. Union members formed a small but vocal portion of the Democratic leadership. They became the most radical Democrats, agitating for antimonopoly legislation and antibanking regulations by the states, the adoption of universal suffrage for white men, and the abolition of imprisonment for debt. They also supported new taxes—general property taxes—that would apply to personal property such as stocks, bonds, machinery, and furniture as well as to real estate. In their political campaigns artisans appealed to the spirit of the American Revolution, which had destroyed the monopolies and special privileges created by the king, they said. Now a new revolution was needed to destroy the monopolies created by capital. Only then could individuals regain the dignity and independence befitting free citizens of a republic (see American Lives, pages 344–345).

Frances Wright: Radical Reformer

Frances Wright (1795–1852) arrived in New York City on New Year's Day, 1829, with a radical plan: to persuade the city's workers to assault business-class power. She hoped to win workers' support for a frontal attack on the religious foundations of business-class revivalism. She hoped that from New York her message would "spread far and wide, and invigorate the exertions of good and bold men throughout the land."

Born in Glasgow, Scotland, into the family of a wealthy merchant devoted to the republicanism of Thomas Paine, Wright had discovered America at age sixteen. "From that moment on," she wrote, "my attention became rivetted on this country as upon the theatre where man might first awake to the full knowledge and exercise of his powers." She was one of the many Europeans drawn to American shores by the magnet of the Declaration of Independence.

In 1818 Wright made her first Atlantic crossing. When she returned to Britain in 1821, she published an enthusiastic account of life in America, *Views of Society and Manners in America*. Translated into three languages, the book reached a large international readership.

Among the readers of the book was the French hero of the American Revolution, the Marquis de Lafayette, who became Wright's friend and patron. A few months after initiating a correspondence with Lafayette, she and her sister moved in with him, a sixty-four-year-old widower, on his country estate. Over the objections of his family, Frances stayed on in his household for almost two years. At one point she begged him either to marry her or adopt her as his daughter.

In 1824, Wright accompanied Lafayette on his triumphal return to America. During a six-week stay with Thomas Jefferson at Monticello she revealed a bold plan to set up a utopian community of whites and freed slaves, who would live together in full equality.

Encouraged by Jefferson, Wright founded the community, called Nashoba, in 1825, on 320 acres of western Tennessee wilderness. She gathered support from other young idealists, enlarged Nashoba to nearly 2,000 acres, and purchased about thirty slaves. Her scheme was to allow them to earn emancipation by working on the land. During that time Nashoba would provide their children with an education.

Wright worked alongside the slaves in the arduous clearing and ditching of the marshy land. However, the slaves saw little improvement in their lives, and the summer heat and waves of malarial fevers wore down the enthusiasm of everyone except Wright. Her dreams soared to embrace the ideals of Robert Owen, a Scottish industrialist and philanthropist who had formed his own utopian community in New Harmony, Indiana, in 1824. Following Owen's search for alternatives to private property, organized religion, and marriage, Wright declared that Nashoba would become a society "where affection shall form the only marriage, kind feelings and kind action the only religion, respect for the feelings and liberties of others the only restraint, and reunion of interest the bond of peace and security." But potential recruits were repelled by what the British author Frances Trollope described as the "savage aspect of the scene."

By 1828 Wright concluded that America had become too conservative for an "individual experiment" such as Nashoba to succeed. What was required was to reform the "collective body politic." She left Nashoba and joined forces with Owen's son, Robert Dale Owen, who had become infatuated with her, and launched a lecture campaign that took her to New York.

As a lecturer, Wright was a sensation. Rumors of free love and racial mixing at Nashoba did their part. And she challenged gender stereotypes: she was the first woman to address large mixed audiences in America. Wright would sweep onto a stage with a group of women apostles and throw off her cloak to reveal her revolutionary garb—a tunic of white muslin. Producing a copy of the Declaration of Independence, she would lecture in a resonant, musical voice. The poet Walt Whitman, who heard Wright when he was a young boy, remembered that "we all loved her; fell down before her: her very appearance seemed to enthrall us."

Frances Wright
This 1826 painting shows the thirty-two-year-old Frances Wright at Nashoba. She is wearing the simple, practical costume the New Harmony community adopted for women—a coat reaching to the knees over pantaloons.

Wright announced to her packed audiences that the "laboring class of the community" faced oppression by a "monied aristocracy" and a "professional aristocracy of priests, lawyers, and politicians." She lashed out at evangelical ministers, calling them hypocritical and unrepublican, challenging their claims of divine revelations, and describing the Benevolent Empire as the "would-be Christian Party in politics." She argued that the only path between the extremes of the enslavement of all labor and violent revolution was reform focused on education. She called on Americans to educate all children between the ages of two and sixteen in compulsory boarding schools; this would enforce social equality and insulate children from organized religion.

Among the beneficiaries would be women, who would learn to break their "mental chains" and attain equality under the law.

To nurture a radical culture among New York's workers, Wright and Owen took over an abandoned church near the Bowery, in the heart of the workers' neighborhood, and transformed it into a "Hall of Science." There they established a newspaper, *The Free Enquirer*, a printing press for other radical publications, a lecture auditorium, a day school, a deist Sunday school, a reading room, and a free medical dispensary.

Wright won a large following among artisans and journeymen, some of whom turned to politics and energized the Working Men's party. In 1829 twenty men wrote her name on their ballots for the New York assembly. Nonetheless, she failed to convert most of New York's radical workers; they believed that a maldistribution of wealth and opportunities—not religion—was at the heart of their powerlessness.

Disheartened, in 1831 Wright and Owen sold the Hall of Science to a new Methodist congregation. While Owen returned to New Harmony as a Democratic reform politician, Wright transported her freed slaves to Haiti and then sailed for Paris, where she married a French educational reformer and gave birth to a daughter.

Wright never abandoned her dreams, however. Inspired by stories of Jackson's war against the Second Bank, she returned to America in 1835. But her lectures, including speeches for Martin Van Buren, met with indifference or hostility. Newspaper editors called her the "Red Harlot of Infidelity," and pious parents used her name to frighten their children.

Wright settled in Cincinnati, where she lived out her life in oblivion, writing her memoirs, occasionally promoting her old causes, and winning a pioneering suit for divorce. In 1852 she died of complications from a broken hip. In her later years she became pessimistic about America. She felt as if she had "fallen from a strange planet among a race whose sense and perceptions are all different from my own."

During the 1830s, however, the threatened artisans shifted from politics to concentrate on the same economic issues that concerned the building trades. Following the model of the Philadelphia building trades, unions formed citywide coalitions across craft lines. In 1834 federations from Boston to Philadelphia joined to form the National Trades' Union, the first national union of different trades. By 1836 federations from as far south as Washington, D.C., and as far west as Pittsburgh and Cincinnati had joined.

In a series of strikes and boycotts during the 1830s workers across a broad spectrum of crafts successfully used their bargaining power, forcing employers to accept ten hours as the standard workday for most skilled workers in the large cities and for virtually all skilled workers in the building trades. Philadelphia was the scene of the most dramatic victories. In 1835 the Philadelphia city council set a ten-hour day for local public works, and the following year President Jackson, recognizing the importance of the Philadelphia artisans to his party, established a ten-hour day at the Philadelphia navy yard. The ten-hour day victories were significant: American skilled workers were the first in the industrializing world to wrest this concession from their employers.

Buoyed by their victories, the unions turned their energies to winning increases in wages, organizing more than fifty strikes during 1836 and 1837. In most instances the strikers won, often because the trade unions cooperated. For example, when journeymen bookbinders in Philadelphia struck for higher wages in 1836, thirty-seven trade unions from New York to Washington provided financial support that enabled them to hold out for over two months. The grateful journeymen declared that their cause had become "the sacred cause of every skilled laborer in the civilized world."

Factory Workers

The success of the artisans' organizations inspired another group of workers—factory laborers. They were a new group without a history of organization or traditional craft identity and were poorer than the artisans. Nonetheless, they marshaled the strength to resist the growing demands of their employers that they do more work for less pay.

There were about 20,000 cotton-mill operatives by the 1830s, mostly unskilled women and girls. To protest pay cuts or more stringent work rules, many of them engaged in sporadic strikes. In 1828 women mill workers in Dover, New Hampshire, had struck against two new rules. The first levied fines for lateness; the second initiated a system under which workers leaving the mill would receive certificates of regular discharge only if they had been "faithful" employees. The strikers worried that rebellious workers would be fired and then be unable to find jobs because they lacked certificates. The employers prevailed, but in 1834 more than 800 Dover women struck again to protest wage cuts.

In Lowell, Massachusetts, 2,000 women backed up a strike in 1834 by withdrawing their savings from a Lowell bank owned by their employers. The Boston *Transcript* reported that "one of the leaders mounted a pump, and made a flaming . . . speech on the rights of women and the iniquities of the 'monied aristocracy.'" But the 1834 strikes failed. The employers fired the leaders, and the rest of the workers returned to the mills. The Lowell women remained restless and militant, however. Two years later, when the mill owners raised boardinghouse charges, Lowell workers organized again. This time their rallies, marches, and slowdown of production persuaded the owners to reduce or eliminate the increases in board charges.

Victories were rare, however. Strikes of unskilled operatives almost always failed. Overpowered by the employers and viewing factory employment as temporary and peripheral to their lives, women mill workers did not react to defeat by forming strong and permanent unions.

Employers on the Counterattack

Employers had resisted workers' demands since the end of the eighteenth century, but only rarely had they acted together to combat labor. Employers' cooperation had been limited to the regulation of production or the fixing of prices. In response to the waves of strikes in 1836 and 1837, however, employers from Massachusetts to St. Louis dramatically mobilized against the unions. Among the antiunion tactics they developed was the *blacklist*. In 1836 employers in New York City agreed not to hire workers belonging to the Union Trade Society of Journeymen Tailors and circulated a list—a blacklist—of its members. The employers also used the courts. Their lawsuits targeted the *closed shop* agreement, by which employers promised to hire only union members. Most unions secured closed shop agreements when they won wage increases. During the 1830s employers sued the carpet weavers' union in Thompsonville, Connecticut; the shoemakers' unions in Geneva and Hudson, New York; the tailors' union in New York City; the plasterers' union in Philadelphia; and the union of journeymen cordwainers in Boston. Employers charged that closed shop agreements violated the common law or, in New York State, statutes that prohibited such "conspiracies."

The New York Supreme Court ruled against the Geneva shoemakers in 1835. The closed shop, the court held, had caused "an industrious man" to be "driven out of employment" and trade to be restricted. "It is important to the best interests of society," the court held, "that the price of labor be left to regulate itself." In other words, individual workers were denied the opportunity to organize. Following this precedent, a lower court found the New York tailors guilty of conspiracy.

Unions protested the decision. Twenty-seven thousand workers and their supporters demonstrated outside New York's city hall, and workers intimidated juries hearing similar cases. Later in 1836 juries acquitted the Hudson shoemakers, the Philadelphia plasterers, and the Thompsonville carpet weavers.

The rising power of organized labor was particularly threatening to the business class. Unionization—the increasingly successful effort to democratize the workplace—was only part of the threat. At least as serious was the simultaneous democratization of national politics. It appeared that workers, cooperating with other groups dissatisfied with the effects of the Industrial Revolution, might take control of government and check the power of the business class. In the mid-1830s leaders of the business class themselves attempted to use the new, more democratic political system to win support, even among American workers, for their vision of American society.

Workers Protest, 1836
This poster appealed to workers to protest the conviction of the Geneva shoemakers for conspiracy. At the meeting held in the park fronting New York's city hall, the crowd burned judges in effigy and passed resolutions calling for the creation of a new labor party.

Democrats and Whigs: The Second Party System, 1836–1844

Jackson's party and politics presented the northern business class with the first concerted challenge to its power. To check the growing power of democracy, prominent members of the business class took the lead in organizing a new national political grouping—the Whig party. The two parties that resulted, Democratic and Whig, constituted the Second Party System, which survived until the rise of the Republican party in the mid-1850s. Both political parties competed for support among farmers and urban workers, and in every electoral contest victory went to the party that appealed most successfully to Americans of modest wealth and social status.

The Emergence of the Whigs

As early as Jackson's first term, his opponents in Congress began to form an alliance. They called themselves "Whigs" and referred to Jackson as "King Andrew I." Those names conjured up associations with the pre-Revolutionary American and British parties—also called Whigs—that had opposed the power of King George III. Whigs charged that Jackson had violated the Constitution through tyrannical abuse of executive power and

that Whigs were better defenders of the republic than Democrats. In effect, the Whigs were attempting to turn Jackson's republican rhetoric against him.

Initially, the Congressional Whigs were united only by their opposition to Jackson. They included Senators Webster of Massachusetts, Clay of Kentucky, and Calhoun of South Carolina. Webster and Clay had a bond of common economic interests; Webster spoke on behalf of New England's business elite, and Clay represented the commercial interests of the Ohio and Mississippi valleys. Calhoun, having broken with Jackson over nullification, had little choice but to join the Whigs. However, as a representative of the planter class of the lower South, he had reservations about the economic ideas of his Congressional allies.

Andrew Jackson's victory over Henry Clay in the 1832 presidential election deeply troubled Jackson's Congressional opponents, who regarded his victory as a popular mandate for his position on the Second Bank. Clay and Webster feared that Jackson's election had opened the door to the destruction of all privilege and the undermining of legislative government. In Webster's home state of Massachusetts Whigs listened apprehensively as the Jacksonian George Bancroft told the workingmen of Northampton:

The feud between the capitalist and the laborer, the house of Have and the house of Want, is as old as social union. . . . It is now for the yeomanry and the mechanics to march at the head of civilization. The merchants and the lawyers, that is, the moneyed interest, broke up feudalism. The day for the multitude has now dawned.

To check such democratization, Congressional Whigs began elaborating their own plan for the nation's future. By the 1836 election they had formulated a well-defined alternative to the Democratic vision and had begun to popularize it among the northern middle class.

Whig Ideology. Whigs believed that it was "natural" for a relatively few individuals to acquire a large share of the nation's wealth, represent the people in a republican government, and use government power as they thought necessary for the welfare of all. They attempted to reconcile their elitism with republican ideals in several ways. First, they asserted that American society was really classless because it did not ascribe permanent status to groups and individuals and because its institutions fostered upward mobility. Second, they argued that in a republic it was "natural" for wealthy individuals to represent other citizens. A republican Constitution and the moral influence of religion would compel elites to govern in the best interests of all. Third, pointing to dramatic advances in banking, manufacturing, and transportation, the Whigs claimed that a strong ruling elite promoted economic growth, which strengthened the republic by creating a more prosperous citizenry and unifying labor and capital.

To the Whigs, even the most modern factories were sources of potential social harmony. In 1830 Edward Everett, a congressman from Massachusetts and a leading Whig publicist, told a Fourth of July crowd in Lowell that "the alliance which you have . . . established between labor and capital . . . may truly be called a holy alliance." He proclaimed that factories such as those at Lowell "form a mutually beneficial connection between those who have nothing but their muscular power and those who are able to bring into the partnership . . . property which was itself, originally, the work of men's hands, but has been converted, by accumulation and thrift, from labor into capital." He concluded, "Woe to the land where labor and intelligence are at war! Happy the land whose various interests are united together by the bonds of mutual benefit and kind feeling!"

The Whigs criticized Jackson and the Democrats for underestimating the possibilities for upward mobility, pitting the poor against the rich, and disrupting social harmony. They attacked Jackson's strong presidency, warning against powerful, highly individualistic executives who pandered to the growing masses of vot-

A Whig Cartoon
This political cartoon lampooned Andrew Jackson as a monarch decked out with the trappings of royalty and trampling on the Constitution. It emphasized Jackson's contempt for judges and criticized many of his political appointments. It concluded by asking, "Shall he reign over us, or shall the PEOPLE RULE?" (Collection of The New-York Historical Society)

ers. And the Whigs claimed that Democratic economic programs would turn back the clock, impoverishing and weakening the republic.

As an alternative, the Whigs offered legislative rule and a program of governmental intervention in the economy. They wanted a more vigorous national government, and wanted Congress rather than the president to lead it. And the Whigs wanted that government to enact the American System of Henry Clay and John Quincy Adams.

Calhoun's Appeal to Capitalists. The only Congressional opponents of Andrew Jackson who had reservations about the full-blown Whig ideology and program were Calhoun and his southern followers. Calhoun disliked Whig nationalism and Clay's tariff policies, but his greatest concern was the Whig objection to fixed classes. He argued that the Whig ideal of equal opportunity contradicted the realities of slavery and an industrial society. In 1837 he wrote, "There is and always has been in an advanced stage of wealth and civilization a conflict between labor and capital." He argued that southern slave owners and northern factory owners belonged to the same privileged class and faced the same threat from below. Calhoun therefore urged northern capitalists to join the planters in a defensive alliance. In his view, social harmony could be achieved only through the recognition, acceptance, and reinforcement of the existing sharp distinctions of class. Whigs, he argued, ought to unite around a common defense of privilege and social order.

The other Whig leaders refused to accept Calhoun's antidemocratic analysis. Calhoun's description of "a clear and well-defined line between capital and labor," Daniel Webster agreed, might fit the South or Europe, but in the North "this distinction grows less and less definite as commerce advances." Pointing to Massachusetts, Webster declared, "I do not believe there is on earth, in a highly civilized society, a greater equality in the condition of men than exists there." Webster maintained that Calhoun had neglected the growing importance of the northern middle class. As it turned out, it was the middle class, attracted by the promise of upward mobility, that became the backbone of the Whig, and later the Republican, party.

The Whig Coalition

Led by the Congressional Whigs, a coalition of groups emerged to run candidates at the state and local levels in opposition to the Jacksonian Democrats in the 1834 elections. These groups proved powerful enough to gain control of the House of Representatives. The coalition was strongest in New England, New York, and the new communities along the shores of the Great Lakes. The American System had a great appeal in those areas because they had the highest concentrations of prosperous farmers, small-town merchants, and machinists and other skilled industrial workers who identified with their employers. Whig politicians realized that they had interests in common with business-class enthusiasts for moral reform. Government intervention along Whig lines could be seen as part of a comprehensive program designed to restore social harmony and invigorate the Industrial Revolution. And on a practical level, Whig leaders found that workers and farmers who had been drawn to the perfectionist message of evangelical Protestantism (see Chapter 10) tended also to embrace Whig politics, with its emphasis on individual upward mobility and social improvement.

The Whig message, as publicized by Henry Clay, also won support from people of southern origin in the Ohio and Mississippi valleys. The farmers, bankers, and shopkeepers in the southern tier of the northwestern states differed from northern Whigs in their religious affiliations and culture. But they agreed that positive government action—conscious planning and collective effort—was needed for economic development. They found public investment in internal improvements particularly attractive and supported the ideal of a classless society led by "natural" elites. Consequently, they gradually formed alliances with the business class in the North.

In the South support for the Whig party was less cohesive, resting more on the appeal of specific elements in its program than on the force of the Whigs' social vision. For example, many nonslaveholding whites in the backcountry, especially in western Virginia and the deepest hill country of the other seaboard states, were Whigs because they favored a federal program of banking and internal improvement to break the grip of planter elites. A significant Whig minority also existed among wealthy planters who had invested heavily in railroads, banks, and factories and had maintained close ties to northern markets and New York capitalists. Finally, some states' rights Democrats in Virginia and South Carolina, upset with Jackson's willingness to use force to suppress nullification, joined the Whigs, at least temporarily.

The Election of 1836. In the 1836 presidential election Martin Van Buren, whom Jackson had handpicked to be his successor, was the Democratic candidate. He successfully campaigned on Jackson's record, which included not only the veto of the Second Bank but also the Bank war. The Democrats claimed that they offered Americans "liberty," in contrast with the coercion threatened by the Whigs and the social elites that the Democrats claimed that the Whigs represented. The Whigs ran three presidential candidates, hoping to maximize the opposition votes from the various sections and to force the election into the House of Representatives, which the Whigs controlled. The plan failed to accomplish this goal. The electoral votes collected by the Whigs—73 by William Henry Harrison of Ohio, 26 by Hugh L. White of Tennessee, and 14 by Daniel Webster—fell short of Van Buren's 170 votes. Van Buren's base of support in the populous states of New York, Pennsylvania, and Virginia had proved decisive. Still, the size of the Whig vote showed that the Whig message of social development—economic improvement and moral uplift—had strong appeal not only to middle-class Americans but also to farmers and workers with little or no property. Van Buren had prevailed, but his political problems were just beginning.

The Depression of 1837–1843

The prolonged and steady expansion of the economy from 1820 to 1837 had led many Americans to consider prosperity a permanent feature of life. Few realized that their prosperity still depended heavily on events in Europe. True, American production for export was declining relative to production for domestic consumption and cotton exports were important primarily to the South, but any disruption of foreign credit flowing to the South had a severe ripple effect on the entire economy. Furthermore, American industrialization and territorial expansion depended on large amounts of long-term investment from Europe, primarily from Great Britain, to finance the construction of canals and railroads. Whenever the flow of investment came to a halt, depression was likely to radiate throughout the American economy. Amplifying these problems was the fact that industrialization had made the economy more complex; its parts were more interdependent. Disruptions in any sector had more serious effects on other sectors than had been the case earlier.

The Panic of 1837. The Panic of 1837 began in Britain. In late 1836 the Bank of England, convinced that it was sending too much specie to the United States, curtailed the flow of investment. Partly as a result, British demand for cotton declined sharply, causing the bankruptcy of British and American mercantile firms whose lending was based on the use of cotton as security. These events set off a wave of bankruptcies and restrictions of credit that affected merchants and bankers throughout the United States (see Map 11.3). Without adequate credit, American trade, manufacturing, and farming slid into a depression.

Years of Depression. The depression dragged on until 1843, becoming the most severe American depression until the 1870s. The Bank of England continued to keep credit tight until the early 1840s. At the same time bumper cotton crops in the late 1830s drove down cotton prices, making matters even worse for merchants in international trade. Many states, unable to raise taxes or borrow in depressed conditions, defaulted on the bonds that they had issued to finance canal building and

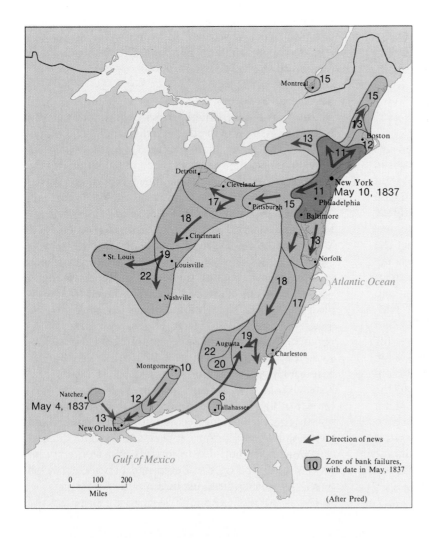

MAP 11.3

Anatomy of a Panic: Bank Suspensions in May 1837

Although the first bank failures occurred in Natchez and Tallahassee, it was the collapse of New York City banks several days later that precipitated a chain reaction of national panic. Rivers, canals, and post roads carried news of the panic from New York to St. Louis in just twelve days. The resulting pattern of bank failures provides a dramatic picture of the economic nerve system of the nation—a nerve system dominated by New York.

The Aftermath of the Panic of 1837
This cartoon pictures the Independence Day celebration in New York in 1837 as being marred by the symptoms of economic depression—unemployed workers, mothers begging and pawning their possessions, goods that cannot be sold, sheriff's sales of property, runs on banks, and alcoholism. A prison and an almshouse are in the background. (Collection of The New-York Historical Society)

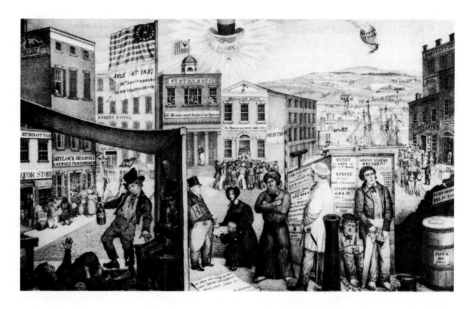

thereby undermined British confidence in American investments. To protect themselves, American banks insisted on holding larger amounts of specie. But this cautious policy reduced the amount of money available to the general public. As a result, overall spending, capital investment, and prices declined even further, deepening the depression.

By 1843, as compared with 1837, prices on average had fallen by almost half and overall investment in the American economy had declined by almost 25 percent, led by a 90 percent drop in canal construction. Investment in railroads and manufacturing also fell dramatically. Slumping investment and production forced workers out of jobs, and in 1838 unemployment rose to an unprecedented level of almost 10 percent; in seaports and industrial centers it approached 20 percent. In concert with the bankruptcies of farms and businesses, this meant that a vast spectrum of Americans were stricken. In the words of the Reverend Henry Ward Beecher:

> The world looked upon a continent of inexhaustible fertility (whose harvest had glutted the markets, and rotted in disuse), filled with lamentation, and its inhabitants wandering like bereaved citizens among the ruins of an earthquake, mourning for children, for houses crushed, and property buried forever.

Economic instability had become a significant aspect of American life. It heightened all the other disruptive forces of the Industrial Revolution, and its effects were particularly harsh on people who lacked property or skills.

Destruction of the Labor Movement. As might be expected, the depression shattered the labor movement. Union successes in the early 1830s had been based on labor shortages. But now, for the first time in fifty years,

there was a surplus of skilled workers. In 1837, 6,000 masons, carpenters, and other building-trade workers were discharged in New York City alone. The dramatic rise in unemployment among skilled workers decimated union membership.

Artisans faced additional dilemmas. Factory competition had already forced large numbers of them to abandon their crafts and consequently their union movement. During the depression increasing numbers of artisans, despairing of the possibility of organizing to oppose the forces of industrialization, dropped out of the labor movement. Consequently, most local unions and workers' assemblies and all the national labor organizations disappeared, along with their newspapers and other publications.

One of the few bright spots for the labor movement came in 1842, when Chief Justice Lemuel Shaw of Massachusetts handed down his ruling in *Commonwealth v. Hunt*. The case had begun in 1840, when the Whig district attorney for the city of Boston had brought members of the Boston Journeymen Bootmakers' Society into municipal court for trying to enforce a closed shop. Shaw overturned earlier precedent by making two critical rulings: (1) A union was a criminal organization only if its *objectives* were criminal, and (2) union members were within their rights in attempting to enforce closed shops, even by striking. This decision discouraged courts from finding that unions were inherently criminal or that the closed shop was socially harmful. But courts, which generally were dominated by unsympathetic Whig judges, usually found other grounds to restrict strikes and boycotts.

Workers, with their unions destroyed and the movement for greater democracy in the workplace faltering, increasingly turned to politics. The Democrats offered a warm welcome. President Van Buren continued Jackson's effort to court workers and in 1840 signed an executive order establishing the ten-hour day for federal employees. Ironically, this victory, the most dramatic achievement of the early labor movement, came after the unions had lost their power in the marketplace.

The Election of 1840

The election of 1840, held in the middle of the depression, created a political crisis for the Democrats in which, ironically, Andrew Jackson's success proved a liability. In turning the presidency into an agent of the people, Jackson had convinced many Americans that the president could make a difference in terms of maintaining prosperity. Most people did not understand the overwhelming influence of international forces on the business cycle and readily blamed Jackson and Van Buren for their economic troubles. In particular, they decided that Jackson had been wrong to attack the Second Bank and had been responsible for the Panic of 1837.

President Van Buren seemed helpless in the face of the political crisis. The only substantial measures successfully sponsored by his administration were the ten-hour day for federal employees and the Independent Treasury Act. That act confirmed the public's identification of the Democrats as the antibanking party by requiring the federal government to keep its cash in government vaults rather than in banks. Its chief objective was to prevent the government from playing favorites among bankers and from using federal deposits to promote banking and expand the money supply.

William Henry Harrison. The Whigs made the most of their opponents' discomfiture. The depression helped them by discrediting the Democrats, making it less important that the Whigs take clear positions on the issues. In their first national convention the Whigs renominated William Henry Harrison of Ohio, a military hero noted for his victories over native Americans at Tippecanoe and over the British in the Battle of the Thames (Ontario) in the War of 1812. Harrison lacked executive ability and was sixty-eight years old, but that mattered little to the Whig leaders, Clay and Webster. They did not want a strong president; they planned to use Harrison as a rubber stamp for Congressional enactment of the Whig program. Moreover, Harrison's military record, Virginia roots, and strong identification with western interests made him a Whig version of Andrew Jackson. Harrison believed that he matched Jackson's commitment to democracy, although he gave it a Whig twist. He believed that democracy coupled with a robust banking system provided "the only means, under

Heaven, by which a poor industrious man may become a rich man without bowing to colossal wealth."

Economic events stacked the cards against Van Buren. A more charismatic man might have been able to retain the public's favor in spite of the depression. But Van Buren was known primarily as a manipulative professional politician. And he lacked the ties with the Revolutionary generation or the military experience that might have boosted his vote-getting appeal.

The Log-Cabin Campaign. In the 1840 campaign the Whigs concentrated on organizing the electorate and demonstrating their commitment to upward social mobility rather than taking a stand on the issues. As a result, the Harrison campaign was the first in American history to be conducted as an exuberant carnival. The Whigs turned pamphleteering, songfests, parades, and well-orchestrated mass meetings into a new political style that would become the norm for American elections. Colorful Whig spectacles helped persuade participants and observers alike that they were engaged in a fundamentally democratic cause. The Whigs also made the most of the democratic message in their nomination of a popular war hero who had worked himself up from the ranks. When a Democratic newspaper unwisely de-

The Log-Cabin Campaign, 1840
Campaign banners such as this one portrayed Harrison as a simple, generous, and patriotic man of the people. (Collection of The New-York Historical Society)

scribed Harrison as a man who would be happy to retire to a log cabin if he had a pension and an ample supply of hard cider, the Whigs seized on that description to present their candidate as a simple man who loved log cabins and cider. Although Harrison was actually a man of some wealth, the 1840 election became the "log-cabin" campaign, and the candidate demonstrated his common touch by breaking with precedent and joining the campaign celebrations.

The Whigs succeeded in portraying their candidate as a man of the people and blaming the Democrats for the depression. Although their popular victory was a narrow one, the Whigs won an overwhelming electoral victory (including the votes of New York and Pennsylvania) and gained control of Congress. Popular interest in a presidential election had never been greater. Whereas less than 60 percent of the eligible voters had taken part in 1832 and 1836, more than 80 percent voted in 1840.

The Resurgence of the Democratic Party

The election of Harrison seemed to clear the way for the enactment of Henry Clay's economic program. The Whigs had the misfortune, however, of immediately losing the leader on whom they had pinned their hopes when Harrison died of pneumonia one month after his inauguration. Succeeding him was Vice-President John Tyler, a Virginian who was far from a typical southern Whig. Tyler actually opposed the urban commercial interests in his own state and had shared Jackson's hostility to the Second Bank. He had joined the Whig party because of his enthusiasm for states' rights and his disgust with Jackson's nationalism.

John Tyler. As president, Tyler betrayed the Whig party. He took it on himself to block single-handedly the Whig program of economic nationalism. He vetoed two bills sponsored by Senator Henry Clay to reestablish the national bank, and he also blocked major protective tariffs. Clay broke with Tyler in disgust. Then Tyler's cabinet, all of them Whigs, resigned, with the exception of Secretary of State Daniel Webster, who stayed on to influence the course of foreign policy.

Whig successes during the Tyler administration were few and limited: repeal of the independent Treasury in 1841 and a modest increase in tariffs in 1842. The most important legislation of Tyler's administration—the Preemption Act—passed because strong western support for it forced the Whigs to work with the Democrats. The Preemption Act of 1841 gave most American citizens and also immigrants the right to stake a claim to 160 acres of land and purchase it later at the standard price of $1.25 an acre, provided that they built

a house on the land and made other "improvements," such as clearing the land. The preemption process recognized that people commonly settled on public land before purchasing it from the government. Its intent was to give an advantage to actual settlers as opposed to land speculators; its effect was to accelerate the pace of westward expansion.

The New Democratic Coalition. Tyler's rejection of Clay's American System gave the Democrats some precious time—time they needed to consolidate their opposition to the Whigs. During the 1840s the Democratic party vigorously recruited supporters from the farming community: poor farmers in the North and planters and small farmers in the South. At the same time the party went after the votes of the urban working class, in part by strongly opposing any economic program that seemed to offer benefits to wealthy members of the business class. Immigrant workers provided a new source of support, in particular Catholic immigrants, who were repelled by the insistent Protestantism of the Whigs and appreciated the Democrats' greater acceptance of religious and economic diversity. In New York City during the 1840s about 95 percent of Irish-Catholic voters supported Democratic candidates.

A Mass-Based Political Culture. For the first time two national parties were competing vigorously for the loyalties of a mass electorate. Each party relied on a network of newspapers to convey its message; virtually every crossroads town had both a Jacksonian and a Whig newspaper. In Washington, D.C., the *Washington Globe* represented the Democrats while the *National Intelligencer* spoke for the Whigs. Each party offered a distinct vision of industrialization and of the social and political order, and they competed on terms that were reasonably equal. The Democrats held an edge in party discipline and mass loyalty. But in organizing popular appeals the Whigs had a major advantage because of their wealth and the cohesiveness of their leadership and support. That support was based on the interests of the business class, yet the Whigs also managed to make powerful inroads among workers and farmers.

The Second Party System was in place, and the new two-party competition invigorated American democracy. Both Democrats and Whigs built coalitions of diverse groups and interests. Each party tried to persuade Americans to use its ideas and rhetoric in approaching every public issue. Each party established a national identity and helped dilute and diffuse sectional disagreements. The parties were managed by professional politicians who worked to create a political "product" that would satisfy as many different kinds of voters as possible. Together, the two parties molded a new political culture.

Summary

The rise of the business class stimulated group consciousness throughout American society. All groups saw politics as the best way to advance their interests (sometimes by blocking the interests of others), and their collective pressure forced a democratization of politics—a democratic revolution—during the 1820s and 1830s. That revolution swept Andrew Jackson into the presidency, and Jackson mobilized the support of large numbers of laborers, farmers, and southern planters for the Democratic party. He was the first president to regard himself as more than just the enforcer of the nation's laws. He saw himself as an instrument of democracy—expressing the will of the majority. In the process of implementing his vision he transformed his party and the presidency into powerful instruments for majority rule. Jackson used those instruments to challenge the power of the Second Bank of the United States, defend the Union against the threat of South Carolina's Ordinance of Nullification, and remove native Americans to the west of the Mississippi. Jackson was capable of caution as well. While he sympathized with the desire of the new republic of Texas to enter the Union, he did not take up that cause lest he fracture the Democratic party into northern and southern wings and put the Union at risk.

Some workers, especially those with traditional skills, sought democracy in their places of work. They challenged the new industrial order and the power of the business class not only through politics but also through a union movement. They tried to reform working conditions by forming labor unions to demand a ten-hour day and establishing political parties to promote a more equitable society. Strikes increased during the 1830s, and the unions made some limited gains.

The democratic revolution, dramatized by Jackson's veto of the rechartering of the Second Bank of the United States, disturbed the emerging business class and stimulated the formation of the Whig party. Its initial goal was to check the power of the mass-based Democratic party. But the new political realities forced the Whigs to design a message that would have broad appeal to the common people. Led by Henry Clay and Daniel Webster, the Whigs invited middle-class Americans to join the business class and designed an ideology and a program to reconcile elitism with republican ideals. Whereas Democrats emphasized liberty, Whigs stressed material improvement and opportunity. This marked the beginning of the Second Party System. The democratic revolution was now carried forward by the intense competition between the Whig and Democratic

parties, both of which established coalitions of support that were national in scope.

The depression that followed the Panic of 1837 halted both the labor movement and Jacksonianism and contributed to the election of a Whig president, William Henry Harrison. But the betrayal of the Whigs by Harrison's successor, John Tyler, blocked the enactment of the Whig economic program.

TIMELINE

1821	Mexico encourages immigration to Texas
1825	John Quincy Adams elected president by the House of Representatives
1827	Philadelphia Working Men's party organized
1828	Tariff of Abominations Andrew Jackson elected president *The South Carolina Exposition and Protest*
1830	Jackson's Maysville Road veto Mexico restricts immigration and prohibits the importation of slaves Journeymen cordwainers organize Indian Removal Act
1831	*Cherokee Nation v. Georgia*
1832	Bad Axe Massacre Jackson vetoes renewal of the charter of Second Bank of the United States South Carolina nullifies Tariff of Abominations
1833	Force bill and Compromise Tariff
1834	Peak of the Bank war
1835	Ten-hour day for skilled workers
1836	Texans proclaim independence from Mexico Martin Van Buren elected president
1837	Depression of 1837–1843 begins with the Panic of 1837
1838	Trail of Tears
1840	William Henry Harrison elected president
1841	John Tyler succeeds to presidency Preemption Act
1842	*Commonwealth v. Hunt*

BIBLIOGRAPHY

The most useful surveys of the Jacksonian era are Edward Pessen, *Jacksonian America* (1970); Charles Sellers, *The Market Revolution: Jacksonian America, 1815–1846* (1992); Glydon Van Duesen, *The Jacksonian Era* (1959); and Harry L. Watson, *Liberty and Power: The Politics of Jacksonian America* (1990).

Democratizing Politics and the Jacksonian Presidency

Arthur M. Schlesinger, Jr., *The Age of Jackson* (1945), initiated modern reexamination of Andrew Jackson and his significance. Among the most provocative are other older studies: Lee Benson, *The Concept of Jacksonian Democracy: New York as a Test Case* (1961); Marvin Meyers, *The Jacksonian Persuasion: Politics and Belief* (1957); and John William Ward, *Andrew Jackson; Symbol for an Age* (1962). More recently scholars have studied Jacksonian democracy in the context of democratic political culture and the rise of the Second Party System. For an innovative study of Jackson as an institution builder, see Donald Cole, *The Presidency of Andrew Jackson* (1993). On the politics of the Bank war, see Robert V. Remini, *Andrew Jackson and the Bank War* (1967). On the nullification crises, see William W. Freehling, *Prelude to Civil War* (1966), and Richard E. Ellis, *The Union at Risk* (1987). On the spoils system, see Leonard D. White, *The Jacksonians: A Study in Administrative History, 1828–1861* (1954). Books treating Jackson's Indian policy and the Indians include Ralph S. Cotterill, *The Southern Indians* (1954); Grant Forman, *Indian Removal* (1953); Michael D. Green, *The Politics of Indian Removal* (1982); William G. McLoughlin, *Cherokee Renascence in the New Republic* (1986); Gary E. Moulton, *John Ross: Cherokee Chief* (1978); Francis P. Prucha, *American Indian Policy in the Formative Years* (1962) and *American Indian Treaties: The History of a Political Anomaly* (1994); and Ronald N. Satz, *American Indian Policy in the Jacksonian Era* (1975). On the settlement of Texas and the Texas rebellion, see David J. Weber, *The Spanish Frontier in North America* (1992) and *The Mexican Frontier, 1821–1846: The American Southwest under Mexico* (1982). For biographies of leading figures, see Robert V. Remini, *Andrew Jackson and the Course of American Freedom, 1822–1833* (1977), *Andrew Jackson and the Course of American Democracy, 1833–1845* (1984), and *The Life of Andrew Jackson* (1988). On John Quincy Adams, see Samuel Flagg Bemis, *John Quincy Adams and the Union* (1956), and Leonard L. Richards, *The Life and Times of Congressman John Quincy Adams* (1986). On Martin Van Buren, see John Niven, *Martin Van Buren: The Romantic Age of American Politics* (1983); Robert V. Remini, *Martin Van Buren and the Making of the Democratic Party* (1959); and James C. Curtis, *The Fox at Bay* (1970). The Great Triumverate has attracted numerous biographers. On John C. Calhoun, see Richard N. Current, *John C. Calhoun* (1963), and Charles M. Wiltse, *John C. Calhoun* (3 vols., 1944–1951); on Daniel Webster, see Irving H. Bartlett, *Daniel Webster* (1978); and on Henry Clay, see Robert V. Remini, *Henry Clay: Statesman for the Union* (1991). For the presidency of John Tyler, see Robert J. Morgan, *A Whig Embattled* (1954).

The Early Labor Movement

An earlier generation of historians of labor emphasized the organization of unions during early industrialization. See Norman Ware, *The Industrial Worker, 1840–1860* (1924), and John R. Commons, *History of Labour in the United States*, Vol. 1 (1918). More recently, historians have carefully explored the political and social context of the labor movement. See Mary H. Blewett, *Men, Women, and Work: Class, Gender, and Protest in the New England Shoe Industry, 1780–1910* (1988); Jeanne Boydston, *Home and Work: Housework, Wages, and the Ideology of Labor in the Early Republic* (1990); Alan Dawley, *Class and Community: The Industrial Revolution in Lynn Massachusetts, 1780–1860* (1981); Paul G. Faler, *Mechanics and Manufacturers in the Early Industrial Revolution: Lynn, Massachusetts* (1981); Paul A. Gilje and Howard B. Rock, eds., *Keepers of the Revolution: New Yorkers at Work in the Early Republic* (1992); Susan E. Hirsch, *Roots of the American Working Class: The Industrialization of Crafts in Newark, 1800–1860* (1978); Bruce Laurie, *Working People of Philadelphia, 1800–1860* (1980); Jonathan Prude, *The Coming of the Industrial Order: Town and Factory Life in Rural Massachusetts, 1810–1860* (1983); Ronald Schultz, *The Republic of Labor: Philadelphia Artisans and the Politics of Class* (1993); and Sean Wilentz, *Chants Democratic, New York City and the Rise of the American Working Class, 1788–1850* (1984).

Democrats and Whigs: The Second Party System

A rich literature describes the emergence of the Whigs and the larger topic—the formation of the Second Party System. Books that deal broadly with the new party structure include John Ashworth, *"Agrarians" & "Aristocrats": Party Political Ideology in the United States, 1837–1846* (1983); Richard Hofstadter, *The Idea of a Party System* (1972); Daniel W. Howe, *The Political Culture of the American Whigs* (1979); Robert Kelley, *The Cultural Pattern in American Politics: The First Century* (1979); Lawrence F. Kohl, *The Politics of Individualism: Parties and the American Character in the Jacksonian Era* (1989); Richard P. McCormick, *The Second American Party System: Party Formation in the Jacksonian Era* (1966); and Joel H. Silbey, *The Partisan Imperative: The Dynamics of American Politics before the Civil War* (1985). Studies that are more specialized include Thomas Brown, *Politics and Statesmanship: Essays on the American Whig Party*, (1985); Ronald P. Formisano, *The Birth of Mass Political Parties: Michigan, 1827–1861* (1971) and *The Transformation of Political Culture: Massachusetts Parties, 1790s–1840s* (1983); William G. Shade, *Banks or No Banks: The Money Issue in Western Politics, 1832–1865* (1972); Harry L. Watson, *Jacksonian Politics and Community Conflict: The Emergence of the Second Party System in Cumberland County, North Carolina* (1981); and Chilton Williamson, *American Suffrage from Property to Democracy, 1760–1860* (1960).

Mormon Treks across the Great Plains

After the successful establishment of Mormon communities in the valley of the Great Salt Lake, several thousand impoverished migrants, largely from Britain and Scandinavia, formed "handcart companies" and hauled their meager possessions across the Great Plains.

Freedom's Crusaders

1820–1860

★　　　　　★　　　　　★

The Industrial Revolution and territorial expansion had contradictory effects on the way Americans thought about themselves as individuals and as a society. Growing economic opportunity seemed to liberate individuals and make men and women believe that each person could become the master of his or her own fate.

But these changes also brought new restraints and obligations. The new economic order demanded social organization and an increasing degree of standardization. For one thing, men and women had to submit to common disciplines of work. And to solve a new array of social and economic problems, they had to accept a greater measure of discipline—working cooperatively, for example, within the Second Party System.

Alexis de Tocqueville observed the contest between the supremacy of the individual and the demands of social responsibility during his 1831–1832 tour of the United States. In *Democracy in America* he described the tendency of Americans to be moved in opposite ways, by self-interest but also by devotion to the interests of the community. Americans, he said, seemed at one time to be "animated by the most selfish cupidity; at another by the most lively patriotism." These opposing passions were so powerful, he thought, that Americans must have them "united and mingled in some part of their character."

It was on account of these conflicting passions that a wave of reform movements washed over America during the Industrial Revolution. The wave was so strong that it spilled out of the conservative channels first carved by business-class reformers—those who had championed regular church attendance, abstinence from alcohol, and evangelical religion—to challenge some of the basic premises of American society. The labor movement offered a sweeping criticism of industrial society but did not win wide support from middle-class Americans, and labor's power waned after the Panic of 1837. In contrast, the new reform movements won a growing middle-class following despite their radical edge. These radical movements also broke through the barriers erected by national politicians to bring order to American public life and control the debate over social issues. Radical reformers demanded action; they either sought change outside the political system or demanded that the system respond immediately to their ideals.

The effort to abolish slavery was potentially the most disruptive of the radical movements. If abolitionists could win substantial middle-class support in the North, they would pit section against section. But by the early 1840s the popular reaction to abolitionism—in the North as well as the South—was primarily outrage. It remained to be seen whether the abolitionists could mount a successful political crusade. If they did, would the dominant parties address the issue of slavery? And if that happened, could the parties still maintain their national support and the unity of the republic? The answers to all these questions would come during the late 1840s and the 1850s.

Transcendentalists and Utopians

Among the reformers who most vigorously championed individual freedom—the liberation of individuals to act freely on their personal choices—were the transcendentalists, a group of intellectuals who emerged in the New England heartland of the Industrial Revolution. At first they sought primarily to loosen the constraints imposed by the traditional Congregationalist faith, but some became so distressed about the difficulties of individual fulfillment that they rejected industrial society as well. Many of these radical transcendentalists, like other groups of Americans, withdrew into utopian experimental communities. Those communities had numerous and diverse goals, ranging from the establishment of a separate, more rewarding social order for like-minded people to the transformation of American society as a whole.

Ralph Waldo Emerson

The first transcendentalists were young men—often Unitarian ministers—and were generally members of wealthy and privileged New England families. They were American romantics who focused on ideas borrowed from the philosopher Immanuel Kant and from German romanticism, as translated by Harvard professor Edward Everett, who had studied in Germany, and the English poet Samuel Taylor Coleridge. Like the German and English romantics, they believed that behind the concrete world of the senses was another, *ideal* order of reality. This reality "transcended," or went beyond, the usual ways by which people know the world. This ideal reality could be known only by means of mysterious intuitive powers through which, at moments of inspiration, people could travel past the limits of their ordinary experience and gain mystical knowledge of ultimate and eternal things. The intellectual leader of the transcendentalists—and the most popular of all of them—was a second-generation Unitarian minister, Ralph Waldo Emerson.

Emerson resigned his Boston pulpit in 1832, at the age of twenty-nine, after a crisis of conscience that led him to choose individual moral insight over organized religion. He moved to Concord, Massachusetts, and turned to writing essays and lecturing, supported in part by a legacy from his first wife. His message centered on the idea of the radically free individual. "Our age," Emerson's great complaint began, "is retrospective." People were trapped in their inherited institutions and societies. They wore the ideas of people from earlier times—the tenets of New England Calvinism, for example—as a kind of "faded masquerade." They needed to break free of the boundaries of tradition and custom. That could be done only if each individual discovered his or her own "original relation with Nature." Emerson celebrated individuality, self-reliance, dissent, and nonconformity as the only methods by which a person could become free to discover a private harmony with what he called, in an almost mystical fashion, "currents of Universal Being." For Emerson, the ideal setting for such a discovery was nature—solitude under an open sky, among nature's rocks and trees.

Emerson's message reached hundreds of thousands of people, primarily through his lectures. Public lectures had become a spectacularly successful new way of spreading information and fostering discussion among the middle classes, across the boundaries of religious and political institutions. In 1826 an organization known as the American Lyceum was formed to "promote the general diffusion of knowledge." The Lyceum organized lecture tours by speakers of all sorts—poets, preachers, scientists, reformers—and soon took firm hold, especially in the North. In 1839, 137 local Lyceum groups in Massachusetts invited slates of lecturers to their towns during the fall and winter "season" to speak to more than 33,000 subscribers. Among the hundreds of lecturers on the Lyceum circuit, Emerson was the most popular. Between 1833 and 1860 he gave 1,500 lectures in more than 300 different towns in twenty states.

Emerson's celebration of the liberated individual tapped currents of faith that already ran deep among his middle-class audiences. The publication of the autobiography of Benjamin Franklin in 1818 had earlier given Americans a down-to-earth model of an individual determined to reach "moral perfection" through the solitary cultivation of private virtues. Charles Grandison Finney's account of his own conversion experience in 1823 also pointed in Emersonian directions. Finney, who was the foremost business-class evangelist, pictured his conversion as a mystical union of an individual, alone in the woods, with God (see Chapter 10). In addition, Emerson's notion that a solitary individual could transcend the constraining boundaries of society and discover a new self was a familiar idea to the millions of Americans who read the fiction of Washington Irving and James Fenimore Cooper.

Emerson's romantic individualism, however, was more extreme. His emphasis on nature as the route to finding God—a kind of pantheism—stood outside Christian doctrine, and after he criticized organized religion in an address to the senior class of the Harvard Divinity School in 1838, Harvard refused to invite him back for thirty years. Moreover, Emerson criticized the new industrial society. He observed the lives of New Englanders who had been forced to abandon their farms for factories and sensed "the disproportion between their faculties and the work offered them." And he worried that a preoccupation with the consumption of factory-made goods would drain the moral energy of the more affluent. "Things are in the saddle," Emerson wrote, "and ride mankind."

Emerson's genius lay in his capacity to translate radical but vague ideas into examples that made sense—and were acceptable—to ordinary middle-class Americans. He soft-pedaled some of his more radical ideas in his lectures. Thus, he described his pantheism as the idea that all of nature was saturated with the presence of God. Emerson said that if God was everywhere, then God was present in even the most routine sights of everyday life, such as a bare pasture and a railroad. In the same way Emerson took the edge off his hostility to materialism. He translated the celebration of the possibilities of human achievement into a celebration of common things that philosophers had traditionally ignored or scorned. At times he even celebrated money itself. Rather than being "the root of all evil," it "represents the prose of life. [It] is in its effects and laws, as beautiful as roses."

Emerson's Disciples

Emerson hoped to expand the influence of transcendentalism by revolutionizing literature—by creating a genuinely democratic American literature. In 1837 he had delivered an address at Harvard entitled "The American Scholar," intended as a literary declaration of independence from what he called the "courtly muse" of old Europe. He urged American writers to celebrate democracy and individual freedom and find inspiration in the "familiar, the low . . . the milk in the pan; the ballad in the street; the news of the boat; the glance of the eye; the form and gait of the body."

Henry David Thoreau. Henry David Thoreau heeded Emerson's call. Thoreau, who lived near Emerson in Concord, Massachusetts, decided to take Emerson's notion of solitude in nature literally. He built a cabin at the edge of Walden Pond, near Concord, and lived there from 1845 to 1847. In 1854 he published an account of his experiment in self-reliance, *Walden, Or Life in the Woods*. It was the story of a radical, nonconforming quest—his spiritual search for meanings that went beyond the traps and artificiality of life in a "civilized" society. On the practical side, Thoreau listed his accounts, a profit-and-loss statement that recorded his expenditures for a little sugar or a bit of string, and his income from the little surplus production he managed. He presented this accounting to lead readers to recall the pecuniary calculations of Benjamin Franklin in his *Autobiography*. Thoreau wanted to highlight his record of a "commerce" with the deeper, spiritual meaning of life. It was this kind of venture in self-discovery, rather than hermitlike subsistence farming, that he was promoting:

> I went to the woods because I wished to live deliberately, confront only the essential facts of life, and see if I could not learn what it had to teach, and not, when I came to die, discover that I had not lived.

Although Thoreau's essay had little impact outside transcendentalist circles during his lifetime, *Walden* has become an essential text of American literature and an inspiration to succeeding generations of utopian builders. And its most famous metaphor provides an enduring justification for independent thinking: "If a man does not keep pace with his companions, perhaps it is because he hears a different drummer."

Walt Whitman. Another writer who responded to Emerson's call was the poet Walt Whitman, who said that when he first encountered Emerson, he had been "simmering, simmering." Then Emerson "brought me to a boil." Whitman had been a journalist, an editor of the *Brooklyn Eagle* and other newspapers, but it was poetry that had been the "direction of his dreams." In *Leaves of Grass*, first published in 1855 and constantly revised and expanded for almost four decades afterward, he recorded his attempt to pass a number of "invisible boundaries": between solitude and community, between body and spirit, between prose and poetry, and even between the living and the dead. It was a wild, exuberant poem in both form and content. It self-consciously violated every poetic rule and every canon of respectable taste, daring readers to shut the book in revulsion or accept Whitman's idiosyncratic vision whole.

At the center of *Leaves of Grass* is the figure of the poet, "I, Walt." He begins alone: "I celebrate myself, and sing myself," loafing in nature, "observing a spear of summer grass." But because he has what Emerson calls an "original relation" with nature, the poet claims not solitude but perfect communion with others: "And what I assume you shall assume, / For every atom belonging to me as good belongs to you." Whitman was celebrating democracy as well as himself. He argued militantly that a poet in a democracy could claim a profoundly intimate, mystical relationship with a mass audience. For both Emerson and Thoreau, the individual had a divine spark. For Whitman, however, the individual had expanded to *become* divine—infusing democracy with divinity and making organized religion irrelevant.

Whitman, Thoreau, and Emerson were not naively optimistic. Whitman wrote of human suffering with as much passion as he wrote of everything else. Emerson's accounts of the exhilaration that could come in nature were tinged with anxiety. "I am glad," he said, "to the brink of fear." Thoreau's gloomy judgment of everyday life is well known: "The mass of men lead lives of quiet desperation." Still, such dark murmurings were muted in their work, woven into their triumphant and expansive assertions that nothing was impossible for an individual who could break free from tradition, law, and other social restraints.

Hawthorne and Melville. Emerson's influence also reached two great novelists, Nathaniel Hawthorne and Herman Melville. Hawthorne, who for a time was a member of Emerson's circle, and Melville had more pessimistic visions. They dwelt on the vanity, corruption, and excesses of individualism rather than on its positive potential. Both sounded powerful warnings that unfettered egoism could destroy individuals as well as their social arrangements. They embraced the ideal of individual freedom but at the same time urged the acceptance of an inner discipline.

Hawthorne's most brilliant exploration of this theme of excessive individualism appeared in his novel *The Scarlet Letter* (1850). The two main characters, Hester Prynne and Arthur Dimmesdale, challenge their seventeenth-century New England community in the most blatant way—by committing adultery, producing a child, and refusing to bend to the community's condemnation. The result of their assertion of individual freedom against communal discipline is not exaltation but tragedy. Wracked by guilt and unable to confess, Dimmesdale dies in anguish. Prynne learns from her experience that the way to a truly virtuous life can be found only by a person who is willing to do good within the social order.

Melville, strongly influenced by Hawthorne, explored the same problem in even more extreme and tragic terms and emerged as a scathing critic of tran-

Walt Whitman

Whitman (1819–1892) took dangerous steps for an artist in the nineteenth century by condemning organized religion with its "creeds and priests" and treating sex explicitly. Emerson tried to persuade him to drop those sections from *Leaves of Grass*, but Whitman explained that "if I had cut sex out," the poetry "would have been violated at its most sensitive spot."

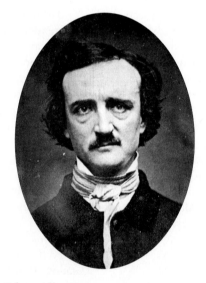

Edgar Allan Poe

Born and bred in Virginia, Poe (1809–1849) identified with the South and defended slavery. But he rose above his time and place, never using southern subjects in his work. As an editor and critic in Baltimore, Philadelphia, and New York, he advanced the ideas that art should strive for beauty, not truth, and that writers should calculate their effects on their readers with precision.

Emily Dickinson

Emily Dickinson (1830–1886), born into a well-to-do family in Amherst, was a rebellious student at South Hadley Female Seminary (now Mount Holyoke College) and might have had a brief love affair with a married Philadelphia minister. Though she was a prolific writer—in a single year, 1862, she produced 356 poems—only seven poems were published during her lifetime.

scendentalism. He made his most powerful statement in *Moby Dick* (1851). The novel begins as a whaling captain, Ahab, embarks on an obsessive hunt for a white whale, Moby Dick, that had severed his leg during an earlier expedition. Ahab is a version of Emerson's liberated individual with an intuitive grasp of hidden meanings in nature. He believes that the whale is pure, demonic evil. Ahab's form of "self-reliance" is to hunt the whale down, no matter what the cost. The trouble, as Melville tells the story, is that Ahab can hunt the whale only in a social way. Ahab's ship, the *Pequod*, is an industrial community. In fact, the novel's depiction of whaling is perhaps the most detailed literary description of an actual industry ever written in the United States or Britain. Ahab's transcendental adventure subverts the legitimate purposes of the whaling voyage. As a result, not only Ahab but the crew of workers die. Only one person, Ishmael, is left to tell the tale.

Poe and Dickinson. *Moby Dick* was a commercial failure. The middle-class audience that was the primary target of American publishers was unwilling to follow Melville into the dark, dangerous realms of individualism gone mad. It was also unenthusiastic about the visions of terror and evil that Edgar Allan Poe, a southern-born admirer of Hawthorne, created in "The Raven" (1845) and other poems and short stories. Poe won respect in New York literary circles but could not find a middle-class audience. Emily Dickinson, another poet whose work expressed doubts about individualism, did not even try to find readers. During the 1850s she kept private the poetry she had begun to write in isolation in Amherst, Massachusetts. At the same time, both *Walden* and *Leaves of Grass* also failed to find a large readership. The middle-class audience was unimpressed by Thoreau's extreme and demanding version of transcendentalism and by Whitman's boundless claims for the mystical union between the man of genius and the democratic masses. They emphatically preferred the more modest examinations of individualism offered by Emerson.

Margaret Fuller. One of the writers inspired by Emerson was Margaret Fuller (1810–1850). She edited the leading transcendentalist journal, the *Dial*, and published *Woman in the Nineteenth Century*, which appeared in the *Dial* in 1843 and as a book in 1844. Fuller proclaimed that a "new era" was coming for men and women. Although she knew the writings of Mary Wollstonecraft, her philosophy was based on a transcendental religious vision that women had an independent relationship with God that gave them an identity that had nothing to do with gender. She believed that every woman deserved psychological and social independence—the ability "to grow, as an intellect to discern, as a soul to live freely and unimpeded." She declared, "We would have every arbitrary barrier thrown down" and

Margaret Fuller
Margaret Fuller (1810–1850) learned to read the classics of six languages when she was a child, educated her four siblings, and taught in a girls' school in Providence before she became interested in women's rights and transcendentalism. In 1839 she inaugurated a transcendental "conversation," or discussion group, for elite Boston women.

"every path laid open to Woman as freely as to Man." If societies placed men and women—"the two sides of the great radical dualism" of human nature—on an equal footing, they could end all injustice. Fuller's book never attracted a large middle-class readership, but it made her ideas well known in New York literary circles and, by influencing Emerson, helped spread her message of self-help to middle-class lecture audiences. After 1845 Fuller gained visibility as the New York *Tribune*'s literary critic and as a correspondent in Italy during that country's revolution in 1848. Her friends hoped that she would become a leader in the growing women's movement, but in 1850, returning to the United States at the age of forty, she drowned in a shipwreck (see American Voices, page 362).

Brook Farm

At one time or another virtually all transcendentalists, including Emerson, felt that American society as it existed could not accommodate their aspirations for individual realization and achievement. Many of them acted on that perception by withdrawing into insular communities. Their aim was to reform society by setting an example.

The most important communal experiment of the transcendentalists was Brook Farm, founded in 1841 by a Unitarian minister named George Ripley, in West Roxbury, Massachusetts. Free from the tension and degradation of a competitive society, community mem-

AMERICAN VOICES

Margaret Fuller

Woman in the Nineteenth Century

Margaret Fuller hoped that her book *Woman in the Nineteenth Century* (1845) would win a larger audience than had the *Dial* article on which it was based. At the suggestion of her editor, Horace Greeley, she dropped the original title, "The Great Lawsuit.—Man *versus* Men; Woman *versus* Women," which she had hoped would convey how "the action of prejudices and passions which attend . . . the growth of the individual, is continually obstructing the holy work that is to make the earth a part of heaven."

. . . We would have every arbitrary barrier thrown down. We would have every path laid open to Woman as freely as to Man. . . .

What Woman needs is not as a woman to act or rule, but as a nature to grow, as an intellect to discern, as a soul to live freely and unimpeded, to unfold such powers as were given her when we left our common home . . . .

Another sign of the times is furnished by the triumphs of Female Authorship. These have been great, and are constantly increasing. Women have taken possession of so many provinces for which men had pronounced them unfit, that, though these still declare there are some inaccessible to them, it is difficult to say just where they must stop. . . .

Male and Female represent the two sides of the great radical dualism. But, in fact, they are perpetually passing into one another. . . . There is no wholly masculine man, no purely feminine woman. . . .

Nature provides exceptions to every rule. She sends women to battle, and sets Hercules spinning; she enables women to bear immense burdens, cold, and frost; she enables the man, who feels maternal love, to nourish his infant like a mother. . . .

The growth of Man is two-fold, masculine and feminine.

So far as these methods can be distinguished, they are so as

Energy and Harmony;

Power and Beauty;

Intellect and Love;

or by some such rude classification; for we have not language primitive and pure enough to express such ideas with precision. . . .

There cannot be a doubt that, if these two developments were in perfect harmony, they would correspond to and fulfill one another, like hemispheres, or the tenor and bass in music. . . .

In families that I know, some little girls like to saw wood, others to use carpenters' tools. Where these tastes are indulged, cheerfulness and good-humor are promoted. Where they are forbidden, because "such things are not proper for girls," they grow sullen and mischievous. . . .

I have no doubt, however, that a large proportion of women would give themselves to the same employments as now, because there are circum-stances that must lead them. Mothers will delight to make the nest soft and warm. Nature would take care of that; no need to clip the wings of any bird that wants to soar and sing, or finds in itself the strength . . . for a migratory flight unusual to its kind. The difference would be that *all* need not be constrained to employments for which *some* are unfit. . . .

I have urged on Woman independence of Man, not that I do not think the sexes mutually needed by one another, but because in Woman this fact has led to an excessive devotion, which has cooled love, degraded marriage, and prevented either sex from being what it should be to itself or the other.

I wish Woman to live, *first* for God's sake. Then she will not make an imperfect man her god, and thus sink to idolatry. Then she will not take what is not fit for her from a sense of weakness and poverty. Then, if she finds what she needs in Man embodied, she will know how to love, and be worthy of being loved.

By being more a soul, she will not be less Woman, for nature is perfected through spirit.

Now there is no woman, only an overgrown child.

Source: Margaret Fuller, "Woman in the Nineteenth Century," in *Woman in the Nineteenth Century and Kindred Papers Relating to the Sphere, Condition, and Duties of Woman* (New York: The Tribune Association, 1869), 13, 37–38, 63, 93, 114–116, 169–170, 174–176.

bers hoped to create a harmonious environment for the full development of the mind and soul. In the first few years the community's economy rested primarily on agriculture. The Brook Farmers sold their milk, vegetables, and hay for cash but emphasized the way in which farming allowed them to remain relatively independent from the marketplace and work close to nature. In addition, they acquired revenue by insisting that residents who did not work on the farm make cash payments—in effect, tuition for what was virtually a boarding school.

The intellectual life at Brook Farm was electric. Hawthorne lived there for a time and later used the setting for *The Blithedale Romance* (1852). All the major transcendentalists, including Emerson and Fuller, were residents or frequent visitors. A former member recalled that the transcendentalists "inspired the young with a passion for study, and the middle-aged with deference and admiration, while we all breathed the intellectual grace that pervaded the atmosphere." Music, dancing, games, plays, parties, picnics, and dramatic readings filled leisure hours. Emerson wrote that Brook Farm meant "education" to most of its residents. It was, he said, "to many the most important period of their life . . . a French Revolution in small."

Brook Farm might have represented moral progress, but it faltered in achieving economic self-sufficiency. Most of its members in the initial years were ministers, teachers, writers, and students. Relatively few families lived at Brook Farm; Ripley's message appealed mostly to young, single people from well-to-do Boston families who were Unitarians and sought alternatives to careers devoted to the acquisition of wealth. Only a few farmers and artisans joined. And for the first three years Ripley and his followers paid little attention to the need to organize their farming and crafts efficiently.

In 1844 the residents began to run Brook Farm in a more disciplined fashion, particularly in arranging housekeeping chores to free women to produce handicrafts. Under their new plan the Brook Farmers attracted some artisans and farmers. Still, the community made only marginal economic gains and did so by imposing regimented routines that depressed many of the original members. One resident wrote that "the joyous spirit of youth was sobered." Finally, after a devastating fire in 1846, the organizers disbanded and sold the farm.

The Decline of Transcendentalism

After the failure of Brook Farm the transcendentalists abandoned their attempts at comprehensive reform. Most became resigned to the structure of American industrial society; its material accomplishments seemed too great to resist. During the 1850s the transcendentalists—as poets, historians, scientists, lawyers, and ministers—became thoroughly integrated into the cultural elite of New England. Their approach to the reform of industrial communities was one of philanthropy, often focused on the education of workers. Some remained radicals on one issue, however—slavery. In the 1840s and 1850s a few aging transcendentalists and a younger generation of their disciples applied their passion for individual freedom to the liberation of slaves.

The Phalanxes

When the Brook Farmers reorganized their community in 1844, they adopted a constitution that embraced the ideas of Charles Fourier, a contemporary French utopian, as interpreted by his idealistic American disciple, Arthur Brisbane. Fourier and Brisbane envisioned

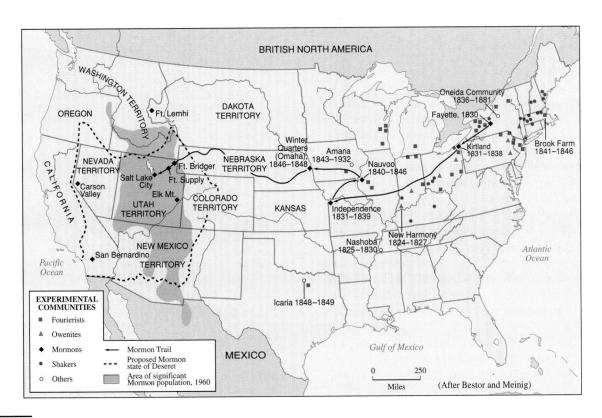

MAP 12.1

Communal Experiments before 1860
Some experimental communities sought out frontier locations, but the vast majority simply looked for secluded areas in well-settled regions. The avoidance of the South by these groups is striking. The most successful experimenters by far were the Mormons, who ultimately sought extreme isolation and built an agrarian empire in Utah.

cooperative work and living units—"phalanxes"—in which those who labored would receive the largest portion of the community's earnings. The members of a phalanx would be its shareholders; they would own all property in common, including stores and a bank as well as a school and a library. Fourier and Brisbane proposed a model for what they hoped would be a practical, more humane alternative to industrial society. "In society as it is now constituted," Brisbane wrote, "monotony, uniformity, intellectual inaction and torpor reign: distrust, isolation, separation, conflict and antagonism are almost universal: very little expansion of the generous affections and feelings obtain. . . . Society is spiritually a desert."

Brisbane skillfully promoted Fourier's ideas through his influential *The Social Destiny of Man* (1840), a regular column in Horace Greeley's New York *Tribune*, and hundreds of lectures, many of them in the towns along the Erie Canal. He inspired educated farmers and craftsmen to start close to 100 cooperative communities from Massachusetts to Michigan, mostly during the 1840s (see Map 12.1). However, almost all, like Brook Farm, were unable to support themselves and quickly died. Some contemporary observers, including the radical minister John Humphrey Noyes, believed that the Fourierists had failed because their communities lacked the strong religious ethic required for sustained altruism and cooperation.

The Shakers

When John Humphrey Noyes criticized the phalanxes, he had in mind, by way of contrast, the oldest and largest of the radical utopian experiments in America—the Shaker communities. Noyes described those communities as "the pioneers of modern Socialism."

The Shaker communities dated back to the era of the American Revolution. In 1770 Ann Lee (Mother Ann), a young cook in Manchester, England, had a vision that she was the second incarnation of Christ and thus the Second Coming. Four years later she led a band of eight followers to America, where they established a new church near Albany, New York. Because of the ecstatic dances that became part of their religious worship, they became known as "Shaking Quakers" or, more simply, "Shakers."

After Mother Ann's death the Shakers decided to withdraw from the evils of the world into strictly run communities of believers. Beginning in 1787, they founded twenty communities, mostly in New England, New York, and Ohio. During the 1820s they entered their most vigorous period of community formation, and during the 1830s they attracted more than 3,000 converts.

Shakers embraced the common ownership of property; accepted the government of the church; pledged to abstain from alcohol, tobacco, politics, and war; and made a commitment to celibacy. Men and women lived apart in gender-segregated dormitories. Applicants had to declare themselves "sick of sin" and undertake a program of systematic confession that could last for years. To the Shakers, sin was wholly the product of a society that put obstacles in the way of a chaste and self-denying life.

The Shakers' beliefs that God was "a dual person, male and female" and that Mother Ann represented God's female element provided the underpinning for their attempt to give up marriage and banish distinctions between the sexes. In practice, they maintained a traditional division of labor between men and women, but the Shakers vested the authority for governing each community—in both its religious and economic spheres—in women and men alike, the Elders and Eldresses.

New members flowed steadily into the Shaker communities, with women outnumbering men more than two to one. The communities welcomed blacks as well as whites. To Rebecca Cox Jackson, an African-American seamstress from Philadelphia, the Shakers seemed to be

The Shaker Community at Poland Hill, Maine (detail)
This Shaker community in Poland Hill, Maine, painted by Joshua H. Bussell around 1850, had typical Shaker architecture—unadorned buildings and a large central dwelling for communal living.

"loving to live forever." New members were drawn in by the highly structured nature of the community, the opportunity to escape from the stresses of American life, the chance offered to women to assume leadership roles, and the economic success of the communities. Shaker agriculture and crafts, especially furniture making, acquired a reputation for quality that enabled most of the communities to become self-sustaining and even comfortable. However, during the 1840s and 1850s the communities stopped growing, and some began to decline. Because Shakers had no children of their own, they relied on converts to replenish their numbers. During the last part of the nineteenth century most of the communities disappeared, with only a few surviving into the twentieth century.

The celibate Shaker communities could never provide a model for society as a whole; they could serve only as a refuge from industrial society. But their marriageless society highlighted the potent role of marriage and gender roles in defining social relationships in America as a whole.

The Oneida Community

In the 1830s John Humphrey Noyes established a utopian experiment after closely studying Fourierist, Shaker, and other models. He also visited many of them, including Brook Farm. Noyes intended his community to be a model for recasting all of industrial society on the basis of cooperation and Christian ethics.

Noyes and "Perfectionism." Noyes was a well-to-do Dartmouth College graduate who had left the study of law for the ministry after hearing Charles Finney preach in 1831. Noyes's divinity studies led him in radical directions, however, and the Congregationalist Church expelled him from the ministry for his unorthodox teachings. His doctrines, which Noyes promoted through the religious magazines he edited, made him the leader of "perfectionism," an evangelical cult that gathered thousands of followers during the 1830s, primarily among New Englanders who had settled in New York. Perfectionists believed that the Second Coming of Christ had already occurred. Because the Kingdom of Heaven on earth was a reality, people could aspire to perfection—to freedom from sin. To Noyes the major barrier to achieving this ideal state was marriage, which did not exist in heaven. "Exclusiveness, jealousy, quarreling have no place at the marriage supper of the Lamb," Noyes wrote. He sought to reform marriage to liberate individuals from sin, as had the Shakers. But his solution was dramatically different: Noyes and his followers embraced the doctrine of "complex marriage"— all the members of his community were married to one another.

"Complex Marriage." Like the Shakers, Noyes was attempting to gain community control over sexuality. His solution was love, usually expressed in sex without male orgasm, between successive partners, with childbearing strictly regulated by the community. Closely related objectives were to free women from being regarded as the property of their husbands and to free children, who were raised in community nurseries, from being regarded as the property of their parents. Among all the founders of communities organized along socialist lines—with common ownership of property—Noyes presented the most radical alternative to traditional marriage and family life.

In the 1830s Noyes began to collect like-minded followers in his hometown of Putney, Vermont. In 1848 the scandalousness of the doctrine of complex marriage forced Noyes to move his community to Oneida, New York. By the mid-1850s more than 200 people lived in the community, but it remained financially insecure. Its fortunes improved when the inventor of what proved to be a highly successful steel animal trap joined the community. With the profits from the production of traps, Oneida diversified into making other products, notably silverware with the brand name Community Plate. Its quality provided the basis for an economic success that continued long after 1879, when Noyes fled to Canada to avoid prosecution for adultery and the community abandoned complex marriage. In 1881 its members founded a joint-stock company, the Oneida Community, Ltd., which survived into the twentieth century.

In the case of both the Shakers and the Oneida Community, radical efforts to free individuals from sin and from the constraints of industrial society had extended to recasting the meaning of marriage and the family. Thus, in this period, when all kinds of changes seemed possible, some communitarians were willing to tinker with even the most deeply rooted institutions in American society. Neither the Shakers nor the Oneidians aroused fierce hostility to their social experiments. To most outsiders the Shakers seemed pathetic eccentrics, and the followers of Noyes were too few to be worrisome. Business-class evangelism had reinforced the institution of marriage, limiting the scope and appeal of communal experiments and restricting the ability of women to develop a full-fledged feminist ideology.

The Mormon Experience

The most successful of all the insular experiments in attracting followers was that of the Mormons, or the Church of Jesus Christ of Latter-Day Saints. The Mormons emerged from the religious ferment that swirled along the route of the Erie Canal during the 1820s and represented the greatest threat to the values of business-class evangelism.

Joseph Smith. The founder of the Mormon Church was a vigorous, powerful individual, Joseph Smith, who was born in Vermont in 1805. Smith moved at the age of ten with his rather poor farming and shopkeeping family to Palmyra in western New York. His education was rudimentary, but with his mother he heard innumerable sermons and read the Bible constantly. In a series of religious experiences that began in 1820, Smith came to believe that God had singled him out for a special, immediate, and private revelation of divine truth. Smith felt that God had called him to be a prophet with a message for redeeming a sinful society fatally flawed by excessive individualism. Ultimately he chose to stand apart from that society. In 1830 Smith published his revelations as *The Book of Mormon*, which he claimed he had translated from ancient hieroglyphics on gold plates shown to him by an angel named Moroni. The *Book of Mormon* told the story of ancient civilizations from the Middle East that had migrated to the Western Hemisphere and of the visit of Jesus Christ, soon after the Resurrection, to one of them. On a metaphorical level, the book describes the success of societies that follow the Ten Commandments and revelations.

Also in 1830, Smith organized a church in western New York. Smith's theology and leadership of the church addressed the growing tension between the claims of the individual—claims that his career as prophet typified—and the need for social order. He offered as a solution a church that would assert control over all aspects of life. Smith encouraged his followers to adopt the patterns of behavior that were central to the Industrial Revolution: hard work, saving, and risk taking. However, he also emphasized the need for a communal framework that would concentrate power in the church elders, protect the Mormon "New Jerusalem" from outside threats, and create a structure for achieving human perfection.

Nauvoo. Smith struggled to establish a sanctuary for his new community. In the face of persecution at the hands of neighboring communities, Smith and his small congregation trekked from western New York to Kirtland, Ohio, then to Independence, Missouri, and, in 1839, to Nauvoo, Illinois, a town they founded on the Mississippi River. By the early 1840s Smith, his message, and his social organization had become phenomenally successful. Nauvoo was the largest of all the utopian communities, having attracted as many as 30,000 converts, but Illinois ultimately proved to be a hostile environment. The demands of the Mormons' social order, their hostility to other sects, the secrecy with which they conducted their affairs, their block voting in Illinois elections, their great success in attracting converts, and their prosperity all fueled the resentment of their neighbors. And Smith helped turn this resentment into overt hostility when he refused to abide by any Illinois law that he did not approve personally, asked Con-

gress to turn Nauvoo into a federal territory free of state control, and declared himself a candidate for president of the United States in 1844. In addition, Smith had a new revelation that encouraged *polygamy*—taking more than one wife at the same time. This was typical of Smith's innovations: radical reforms designed to preserve a traditional institution, in this case marriage and the family. The revelation did not become public until 1852, but rumors of it, as well as disputes over economic issues, divided the Mormon community from within and encouraged assaults from without. In 1844 Smith was arrested and charged with treason for conspiring with foreign powers to create a Mormon colony in Mexico. In June an anti-Mormon mob led by members of the Illinois militia stormed the Carthage jail where Smith and his brother were being held and murdered them.

Brigham Young and Utah. Now led by Brigham Young, an early convert to the church, the Mormon elders resolved that they could ensure their religious independence only by leaving the United States and seeking a home in the wilderness. In 1846, leaving the antipolygamy minority behind, Young began a phased migration of more than 10,000 people across the Great Plains. (Under the leadership of Smith's son, Joseph Smith III, the group that remained behind formed the Reorganized Church of Jesus Christ of Latter-Day Saints, headquartered in Independence, Missouri.) Young's party reached the Great Salt Lake in what was still Mexican territory. Within a decade he and his theocracy had transformed the alkaline desert landscape by building elaborate irrigation systems. The Mormons used communal labor and developed innovative principles of communal water rights that the federal government and all the states of the semiarid West later adopted. The Mormons quickly spread planned agricultural communities along the base of the Wasatch Range in present-day Utah.

The Mormons versus the Federal Government. During the 1850s the Mormons faced challenges to their isolation, but none of those challenges disrupted their society. Many westward migrants made detours from the Oregon and California trails to purchase supplies from Mormon farmers, but that only contributed to Mormon prosperity. Potentially more serious was the effort of the federal government to assert authority over Utah, which the United States had acquired from Mexico in 1848. Congress rejected a Mormon petition to create a new state, Deseret, stretching all the way to Los Angeles and San Diego. Instead, it set up the much smaller Utah Territory in 1850, with Young as territorial governor. In 1857–1858 Democratic President James Buchanan intervened, submitting to pressure from concerned federal officials in Utah and from his Republican challengers. He removed Young from the governorship and sent a

A Mormon Man and His Wives
Mormon families, such as this one pictured in the late 1840s, achieved a degree of prosperity that was unusual for pioneer farm families, partly because of the labor of multiple wives. This homesteader's cabin, although cramped for such a large family, is well built, with a brick chimney and—a luxury for any pioneer home—a glass window.

small army to Salt Lake City. The "Mormon War," however, proved bloodless. Buchanan decided to negotiate, fearing that an attack on the "domestic institution" of polygamy might be used as a precedent to justify attacks on another "domestic institution," slavery. Ultimately he withdrew the troops and accepted his failure to establish federal control in Utah.

Republicans were more eager than were Buchanan and the Democrats to wipe out polygamy. In their 1856 platform they referred to polygamy and slavery as "relics of barbarism." But preoccupation with the Civil War prevented the administration of Abraham Lincoln from paying much attention to Utah. Consequently, the Mormons found themselves free to build their community. The Mormons did not formally abolish polygamy until 1890, six years before Utah became a state. They had succeeded where other social experiments and utopian communities had failed. They had devised the ideological, organizational, and physical means to make their community prosper and expand into the twentieth century.

The Women's Movement

Women played an instrumental role in the radical reform movements of the Industrial Revolution. They had participated in religious revivals and had joined conservative temperance, moral reform, and educational reform movements. During the 1830s some women went beyond these to movements, such as transcendentalism, that sought to remove limitations on individual freedom. Slavery was among the targets of women reformers, and it was abolitionism that radicalized many of them. Abolitionism encouraged women to develop an ideology that argued that women had social and politi-

cal rights as free individuals—rights that equaled those of men.

Origins of the Women's Movement

The Industrial Revolution shaped in complex ways the opportunities that were available to women in the home and in public life. On the surface the Industrial Revolution seemed to limit economic opportunities for women and reinforce their confinement to a "separate sphere." The Industrial Revolution sharpened the lines of demarcation between the home and the workplace while accentuating the division of labor within the home. Middle-class women were less involved in the production of goods (for example, in household workshops) and more concerned with providing personal services in the home. Partly because of the influence of revivals, mothers increasingly became the keepers of religion and morality. They were preoccupied with setting a superior moral example and providing solace and support for family members who worked outside the home.

On a psychological level, however, these changes in the role of women in the family created a basis for greater female independence and power. Middle-class women drew on the enhanced esteem attached to their family roles, reinforced each other through intensified community and kinship ties, and found sanctification for their roles in religion. With all this mutual reinforcement, middle-class women built a common identity in "womanhood." They used it to enlarge their influence over decisions in all areas of family life, including the timing of pregnancies and their husbands' choice of work. For most middle-class women greater influence over family life was enough. But some women seized on the logic implicit in the emphasis on the moral role of women to increase their involvement outside the home.

Young middle-class women in New York and New England entered the public arena through the religious revivals of the 1820s and 1830s. The evangelical revivals emphasized the power of individual free will—even for dependents such as wives and daughters—and provided a central role for women in the conversion process. The revivals also involved women more deeply in community life, enhanced their sense of self-esteem, and led them into other reform movements.

Moral reform was the first of their efforts in the public arena. Women reformers attempted to end prostitution, punish those whose sexual behavior violated the Ten Commandments, redeem fallen women, and protect single women from moral corruption. The movement began in 1834 when a group of middle-class women founded the New York Female Moral Reform Society and elected Lydia Finney, the wife of the evangelical minister Charles Finney, as its president. By 1837 the New York society had 15,000 members and 250 chapters.

The American Female Moral Reform Society. In 1840 the New York society organized a national association, the American Female Moral Reform Society, with 555 chapters throughout the North. Employing only women as its agents, bookkeepers, and staff, this society concentrated on the problems of young women who worked and lived away from their families. They focused on the need to provide moral "government" for factory girls, seamstresses, clerks, and servants who lived beyond the direct control of their families and churches. Women reformers even visited brothels, where they sang hymns, offered prayers, searched for runaway daughters, and noted the names of clients. They founded homes of refuge for prostitutes, homeless girls, and migrant women. They petitioned for state laws regulating sexual behavior—including making seduction a crime—and succeeded in arranging the passage of such laws in Massachusetts in 1846 and New York in 1848.

Women with backgrounds in evangelical reform also turned their energies to the reform of social institutions. Almshouses, asylums, hospitals, and jails became targets for improvement in a movement that involved both men and women. Women visited these places, which were growing in number during the 1830s and 1840s, with the aim of easing the condition of the residents. Dorothea Dix in particular succeeded in both reforming and expanding institutions for society's most dependent individuals: the insane and the mentally retarded (see American Lives, pages 370–371).

The energy and public accomplishments of moral reformers such as Dix inspired other women to undertake more radical reforms, including the abolition of slavery and the establishment of women's rights under the law. Dix, however, did not become active in the antislavery movement despite her personal support of it.

(She had denounced slavery and slaveholders as early as 1831.) Instead, she tried to draw other reformers to *her* cause and often succeeded. She won abolitionist support by stressing the parallels between the treatment of slaves and the treatment of the insane.

Abolitionism and Women

Under the influence of ideas and political strategy drawn from the movement to abolish slavery, a few women began to question whether they should continue to accept a restricted role in society. They faced severe opposition, but in contrast to Frances Wright, who had denounced business-class evangelism, they advanced their ideas within a religious context and thus avoided the extreme forms of public outrage Wright had encountered in championing women's rights a decade earlier (see American Lives, Chapter 11, pages 344–345).

The Grimké Sisters. The abolitionist sisters Angelina and Sarah Grimké shaped the ideas of radical women. They had left their father's South Carolina plantation, converted to Quakerism and abolitionism in Philadelphia, and become antislavery lecturers. In 1837, after some Congregationalist clergymen demanded that she cease speaking to mixed male and female audiences, Sarah Grimké responded: "The Lord Jesus defines the duties of his followers in his Sermon on the Mount. . . without any reference to sex or condition. . . . Men and women are CREATED EQUAL! They are both moral and accountable beings and whatever is right for man to do is right for woman." The next year Angelina Grimké declared that gender should not affect the manner in which people shape society:

> It is a woman's right to have a voice in all the laws and regulations by which she is governed, whether in Church or State. . . . The present arrangements of society, on these points are a *violation of human rights, a rank usurpation of power*, a violent seizure and confiscation of what is sacredly and inalienably hers.

By 1840 the Grimkés were asserting that traditional roles amounted to the "domestic slavery" of women.

Not all abolitionist women shared those views. But they all gained experience and confidence outside the home and learned much about the organizational requirements for successful reform. And as their participation in the movement grew, many women demanded equality with men within the abolitionist movement. To these women equality meant representation in antislavery societies equal to their numbers. At the same time, however, their activities, especially the vigorous antislavery lectures by the Grimkés, aroused opposition from abolitionist clergymen who believed that the women's behavior was immoral. They also drew criticism from male abolitionists who feared that such visi-

The Grimké Sisters
Sarah Moore Grimké (1792–1873) and Angelina Emily Grimké (1805–1879) joined the Philadelphia Female Anti-Slavery Society and began abolitionist lecturing in 1836. They drew crowds of thousands—and scathing criticism for having lost, as some Massachusetts clergymen put it, "that modesty and delicacy . . . which constitutes the true influence of women in society." The Grimké sisters responded with powerful statements protesting male domination of women.

ble departures from tradition would damage the political fortunes of the antislavery movement.

However, a leading abolitionist, William Lloyd Garrison, argued that "our object is *universal* emancipation, to redeem women as well as men from a servile to an equal condition." At the convention of the American Anti-Slavery Society in 1840 he insisted on the right of women to participate equally in the organization. The votes of several hundred New England women elected Abby Kelley to the organization's business committee. This event precipitated the split between the supporters of Garrison and those who left the organization to found the American and Foreign Anti-Slavery Society.

A group of women abolitionists led by Abby Kelley, Lucretia Mott, and Elizabeth Cady Stanton remained with Garrison. They recruited new women agents, including Lucy Stone, to address hostile audiences on the common interests of slaves and free women. Stanton admired Frances Wright and kept her works on her library table, but she had learned from Wright's defeats. During the 1840s women abolitionists focused on a pragmatic course of action for expanding the influence of women.

The Program of Seneca Falls

By the 1840s celebration of self—of individual identity and liberation—had become important to women in public life. Nonetheless, during the 1840s and 1850s most critics of "domestic slavery" stopped short of challenging the institution of marriage or even the con-

ventional division of labor within the family. They focused instead on using the American political system to strengthen the position of women under the law, within the existing social order. They wanted women to enter the mainstream of American life rather than separate themselves from it.

The Convention. In 1848 leaders of the nascent women's movement took a critical step by calling a convention in Seneca Falls in upstate New York. Organized by Elizabeth Cady Stanton and Lucretia Mott, who had met at the World's Anti-Slavery Convention in 1840, and joined by a few sympathetic male abolitionists, the convention outlined for the first time a coherent program for women's equality. The delegates at Seneca Falls based their program on republican ideology, adopting resolutions patterned directly on the Declaration of Independence. Among their declared principles was "that all men and women are created equal; that they are endowed by the Creator with certain inalienable rights: that among these are life, liberty and the pursuit of happiness." They asserted, however, that "the history of mankind is a history of repeated injuries and usurpations on the part of man toward woman, having in direct object the establishment of an absolute tyranny over her." To educate the public about this reality, they resolved to "use every instrumentality within our power. . . . We shall employ agents, circulate tracts, petition the State and national legislatures, and endeavor to enlist the pulpit and the press on our behalf."

Elizabeth Cady Stanton
Elizabeth Cady Stanton (1815–1902), daughter of a judge in Johnstown, New York, attended Emma Hart Willard's demanding Troy Female Seminary. In 1840 she married Henry B. Stanton, an abolitionist leader, and traveled to the World Anti-Slavery Convention in London, where she met Lucretia Mott and started down the intellectual path that led to Seneca Falls. (This photograph, with her grandson, was taken after the Civil War.)

Dorothea Dix:
Innovative Moral Reformer

Dorothea Dix (1802–1887) once wrote, "I never knew childhood." She was born in Hampden, Maine. Her grandparents, Elijah and Dorothy Dix, were prominent Bostonians, but her father, Joseph Dix, had dropped out of Harvard and married an older woman of whom his family disapproved. He had moved to Maine to manage some of his father's land developments but failed and became an itinerant (and alcoholic) Methodist minister. For Dorothea and her two brothers, family life was one of poverty, frequent moves, and emotional abuse. At age twelve she left to live with her well-to-do grandmother. But her grandmother was rigid and remote, and Dorothea proved to be precocious and willful. After two years she moved in with a great-aunt, where she remained for three years. In 1819 she returned to her grandmother's Boston mansion.

Partly because of her emotionally scarred childhood, Dorothea developed an interest in the education of children and at the age of fourteen opened her first school. In 1821, after intense private instruction and reading in the libraries of Boston, she created a school in the Dix mansion. Like other "dame" or "marm" schools, it offered private instruction to young children, either in preparation for public grammar schools, where discipline was harsh, or as a substitute for those schools. In addition, Dorothea persuaded her grandmother to allow her to open a "charity school" to "rescue some of America's miserable children from vice and guilt." She ran such schools for the next seventeen years, except during periods when illness compelled her to rest.

Dix often wrote when illness left her too weak to teach. In 1824 she published a short book of knowledge, *Conversations on Common Things*, with an emphasis on natural science and moral improvement. It went through sixty editions, the last one appearing in 1869. Between 1825 and 1832 Dix published six more books, establishing herself as a public personality. Substantial royalties, along with an inheritance from her grandmother, gave her financial independence.

Dix also used periods of recuperation to widen her social horizons. During a convalescence William Ellery Channing, the prominent Boston Unitarian minister, invited her to teach his children. She drew on her close friendship with him and incorporated Unitarian ideas

Dorothea Dix

Dorothea Dix (1802–1887) pointed to the need for institutions that would strengthen individuals in the face of the pressures of industrialization. She rhetorically asked the Pennsylvania legislature: "Is it not to the habits, the customs, the temptations of civilized life and society" that America owes the calamity of insanity? Consequently, "Should not society make the compensation which alone can be made for these disastrous fruits of its social organization?" Her call for government intervention into social relations put her on the frontier of reform.

into her work. When her health and spirits broke in 1836, she spent eighteen months on the English estate of William Rathbone, a wealthy Unitarian merchant and philanthropist. There she met British reformers who were interested in pragmatic programs to correct the maladies of industrial society, and they inspired her to look for similar possibilities in America.

Dix was ready for a career in reform when, in March 1841, she taught a Sunday School class for women incarcerated in a Cambridge, Massachusetts, jail. She was outraged to find that insane women had been put into jail along with criminals. She appeared in court to represent the women and mobilized Boston philanthropists to support her cause.

Dix felt so strongly about what she had seen in the Cambridge jail that she launched a two-year systematic investigation of the institutionalized treatment of individuals who were insane or mentally retarded. She approved of new asylum-reform programs that lavished love on mental patients. But she complained that those programs served only the families of New England's elite whereas indigent patients typically faced neglect and cruelty.

In 1843 Dix presented her findings in an extensive *Memorial to the Legislature of Massachusetts* on "the condition of the miserable, the desolate, the outcast." She mobilized powerful reformers to aid her cause. The legislature responded by enlarging the state hospital in Worcester so that it could accommodate the indigent.

Dix's success was exhilarating. She proceeded to crusade nationally to establish separate, well-funded state hospitals for the insane. Between 1843 and 1854 she traveled more than 30,000 miles and visited 18 state penitentiaries, 300 county jails and houses of correction, and more than 500 almshouses in addition to innumerable hospitals and houses of refuge. She prepared dozens of reports and memorials to state legislatures and became an exceptional student of the legislative process. Her success in arousing public opinion led many states to create or significantly expand their state hospitals.

Because Dix despaired of state governments ever being able to provide the tax revenues required to support mental hospitals, she began to propose a national responsibility. "The insane poor," she wrote, "through the Providence of God, are wards of the nation." In 1848 she asked Congress to place 5 million acres into a national trust that would fund asylums for the insane. She noted that canal and railroad developers lobbied for public lands and asked, "Why can I not too, go in with this selfish, struggling throng, and plead for God's poor . . . that they shall not be forgotten?"

Dix lobbied relentlessly from a committee room headquarters that her Congressional supporters provided. The House passed her proposal in 1850; the Senate, in 1851. In addition, she charmed Vice-President Millard Fillmore, who formed a close friendship with her. When he became president in 1850, he was ready to sign her bill. Finally, in 1854, Dix persuaded both houses of Congress to pass legislation that would have set aside 12.5 million acres for asylums. But the Democratic president, Franklin Pierce, vetoed it, claiming it was an unconstitutional encroachment on state government. In the face of the growing national crisis over slavery, Pierce and other supporters of the South feared any measure that might create precedents for the federal government to shape social relations.

Dix was depressed but soon resumed her frenetic pace. She returned to her work at the state level, founded an international movement to improve the treatment of the insane, and, when the Civil War began, accepted an appointment by Abraham Lincoln as superintendent of nurses. This job put her in charge of hospital nursing for the Union forces and made her the highest-ranking woman in the federal government. In 1866 Dix, tired and ill, returned to private life. She kept at good works but lacked the energy for new projects. In 1881 she retired to die in the New Jersey state hospital in Trenton that she had helped establish in 1845.

Dix's career illustrates the ability of women reformers to influence American society. Her moral enthusiasm was characteristic of reformers during the mid-nineteenth century, but her tactics were advanced for her time. She studied legislative behavior and, more than any other reformer before the Civil War, relied on the systematic investigation of social problems—an approach that late in the nineteenth century became a hallmark of reform and the expansion of government. It took nearly a century for the federal government to adopt the kind of social policy advocated by Dix—a redistribution of wealth that favored individuals who were unable to participate in an industrial economy.

By powerfully staking out claims for equality for women in public life, the Seneca Falls convention represented a major challenge to the idea that the assignment of separate spheres to men and women was part of the natural order of society.

The Reform Program. The ideals of Seneca Falls inspired women reformers to forge a practical program of action. Throughout the 1850s national women's rights conventions were held annually, as were numerous local and regional meetings. At those conventions women promoted a diverse reform program: establishing the right of married women to control their own property and earnings, guaranteeing mothers custody of children in the event of divorce or the father's death, ensuring women's right to sue or testify in court, revising concepts of female inferiority in established religious theology, and—above all else—winning the vote for women. The 1851 national convention of women resolved that the right of suffrage was "the corner-stone of this enterprise, since we do not seek to protect woman, but rather to place her in a position to protect herself."

Women's Property Rights. The only legislative victories of the women's movement before the Civil War came in the area of property rights. Fourteen states followed New York's pioneering law of 1848 and adopted laws protecting the property of married women after the death or incapacitation of their husbands. Joining the reformers in this effort were upper-class conservative males. Their principal motive was to protect propertied men in the event of bankruptcy (by preserving their spouses' assets intact) and to protect patriarchs with large estates who feared that dissolute or incompetent sons-in-law might lose or ruin their family holdings.

Susan B. Anthony. Despite its dearth of victories before the Civil War, the suffrage effort did advance the organization of the women's movement. Meetings and publicity widened the participation of women in women's causes, and their leaders grew in number and in their mastery of organization, as exemplified by Susan B. Anthony. Whereas many women leaders of the 1830s and 1840s had been gifted lecturers, Anthony's chief talents were organizational. Anthony was a member of a Massachusetts Quaker family that had moved to a farm near Rochester, New York. She had participated in moral reform and in a female antislavery society. She had lectured on antislavery and religion, resigned a teaching position in bitter protest over discrimination against women, and joined the temperance movement as a paid fund-raiser. In 1851, when she was thirty-one, Anthony joined the movement for women's rights and forged an enduring friendship with Elizabeth Cady Stanton. Her experience in the temperance movement had taught her "the great evil of woman's utter dependence on man for the necessary means to aid reform movements."

In promoting reforms during the 1850s Anthony created a network of political "captains," all of them women. Because each New York county had a captain, her group could collect thousands of signatures on petitions in just a few days. Anthony lobbied the state legislature relentlessly. In 1860 her efforts culminated in New York granting women the legal right to collect their own wages (which fathers or husbands previously could insist on collecting and keeping), bring suit in court, and, if widowed, acquire full control of the property they had brought to the marriage.

The organizational and legislative successes of the women's rights movement during the 1850s provided the basis for the more aggressive reform attempts that followed the Civil War (see American Voices, page 373). The political strategy of the radical women had widened their support and won the help of moderate women abolitionists. During the 1850s, however, most Americans, even most abolitionists, did not regard the issues that the women's rights movement had raised to be of great concern. Most stressed a higher immediate priority: the abolition of slavery.

Harriet Beecher Stowe and Sojourner Truth. Women who had never joined an antislavery society could join women's rights leaders in expressing evangelical outrage over slavery. The novelist Harriet Beecher Stowe, for example, did not participate in the organized movement

Susan B. Anthony
As a child, Susan B. Anthony (1820–1906) worked on the Rochester, New York, farm of her father, who had failed in textile manufacturing. She served as "headmistress" of the Female Department at Canajoharie Academy before joining the temperance movement. As she passed "from town to town," she wrote, "I was made to feel the great evil of woman's utter dependence on man for the necessary means to aid reform movements."

Lucy Stone

The Question of Women's Rights

Lucy Stone (1818–1893) graduated from Oberlin College in 1847 and came to the issue of women's rights through abolitionist lecturing. This is an excerpt from a speech she delivered extemporaneously at a national women's rights convention in Cincinnati in 1855.

The last speaker alluded to this movement as being that of a few disappointed women. From the first years to which my memory stretches, I have been a disappointed woman. When, with my brothers, I reached forth after sources of knowledge, I was reproved with "It isn't fit for you; it doesn't belong to women." Then there was but one college in the world where women were admitted, and that was in Brazil. I would have found my way there, but by the time I was prepared to go, one was opened in the young state of Ohio—the first in the United States where women and negroes could enjoy opportunities with white men. I was disappointed when I came to seek a profession worthy of an immortal being—every employment was closed to me, except that of the teacher, the seamstress, and the housekeeper. In education, in marriage, in religion, in everything, disappointment is the lot of woman. It shall be the business of my life to deepen this disappointment in every woman's heart until she bows down to it no longer. I wish that women, instead of begging of their fathers and brothers the latest and gayest new bonnet, would ask of them their rights.

The question of Women's Rights is a practical one. . . . The flour merchant, the house-builder, and the postman charge us no less on account of our sex; but when we endeavor to earn money to pay all these, then, indeed we find the difference. Man, if he have energy, may hew out for himself a path where no mortal has ever trod, held back by nothing but what is in himself; the world is all before him, where to choose; and we are glad for you, brothers, men, that it is so. But the same society that drives forth the young man, keeps woman at home—a dependent—working little cats on worsted, and little dogs on punctured paper; but if she goes heartily and bravely to give herself some worthy purpose, she is out of her sphere and she loses caste. . . . I know not what you believe of God, but I believe He gave yearnings and longings to be filled, and that He did not mean all our time should be devoted to feeding and clothing the body. The present condition of woman causes a horrible perversion of the marriage relation. It is asked of a lady, "Has she married well?" "Oh yes, her husband is rich." Woman must marry for a home, and you men are the sufferers by this; for a woman who loathes you may marry you because you have the means to get money which she cannot have. But when woman can enter the lists with you and make money for herself, she will marry you only for deep and earnest affection.

Source: Elizabeth Cady Stanton, Susan B. Anthony, and Matilda Joslyn Gage, *History of Woman Suffrage* (New York, 1881), 1, 165–166.

---

against slavery but grew angry over slavery and moved other women to share her feelings. Her novel *Uncle Tom's Cabin* delivered an abolitionist message to more homes than any antislavery campaigner ever had. Beecher charged that among the greatest moral failings of slavery was its destruction of the slave family and the degradation of slave women. This charge was substantiated by a former slave, Sojourner Truth, who was one of the many African-American women who lectured to both antislavery and women's rights conventions. Truth hammered home the point that women slaves were denied not only their basic human rights but also the protected separate "sphere" enjoyed by free women. "I have ploughed and planted and gathered into barns, and no man could head me—and ain't I a woman?" she asked in 1851. "I have borne thirteen children, and seen most of 'em sold into slavery, and when I cried out with my mother's grief, none but Jesus heard me—and ain't I a woman?"

The Antislavery Movement, to 1844

Sojourner Truth and other ex-slaves inspired what became the dominant movement to reform American society—the drive to abolish slavery. Beginning in the 1830s, white evangelists joined African-Americans in radical attacks on slavery.

By 1820 opponents of slavery, influenced by republican ideology and British antislavery advocates such as William Wilberforce, had accomplished a good deal. Congress had outlawed the importation of slaves in 1808, the earliest date permitted by the Constitution. Most northern states had already abolished slavery, and the Missouri Compromise had prohibited slavery in most of the Louisiana Purchase. But the most vocal opponents of slavery wanted to go much further. Three different approaches to ending slavery competed between 1820 and 1840: (1) gradual emancipation of the nation's slaves—1.5 million in 1820—and return of the freed slaves to Africa, with compensation paid to their former owners, (2) emancipation through slave flight or rebellion, and (3) emancipation through direct appeals to the conscience of slave owners. Then, during the 1840s and 1850s, most opponents of slavery united as they turned to political tactics and developed a fourth approach to abolition: excluding slavery from the territories.

African Colonization

The American Colonization Society. Proponents of the plan for compensated emancipation and African colonization had founded the American Colonization Society in 1817. For the most part it was led by prominent people from the Upper South who wanted to eradicate slavery in order to foster economic and social development along northern lines. Society members from New England and New York, however, were interested primarily in removing free African-Americans from the North.

Northern colonizationists regarded the North's 250,000 free blacks as "notoriously ignorant, degraded and miserable, mentally diseased, brokenspirited, acted upon by no motive to honourable exertions, scarcely reached in their debasement by the heavenly light," in the words of the American Colonization Society's 1829 report. Colonizationists often played a key role in maintaining disfranchisement and segregation. By 1860 only five northern states (Maine, Massachusetts, New Hampshire, Rhode Island, and Vermont, which together accounted for only 6 percent of the northern black population) had extended suffrage to all adult male African-Americans. New York imposed special property and residence requirements on black voters. Connecticut, New Jersey, and Pennsylvania denied African-Americans the right to vote, as did Ohio, Indiana, Illinois, and every southern state.

Southern supporters of colonization also believed that African-Americans lacked the capacity to succeed in American society. Colonization, they thought, was necessary to prevent a destructive race war, especially because slaves made up almost 40 percent of the southern population in 1820. The Kentuckian Henry Clay, for example, wanted full emancipation but declared that emancipation without colonization "would be followed by instantaneous collisions between the two races, which would break out into a civil war that would end in the extermination or subjugation of the one race or the other." By 1830 the American Colonization Society, with money raised from individuals, state governments, and churches, had succeeded in transport-

ing 1,400 African-Americans to a colony the society called Liberia, on the west coast of Africa. However, only 200 of the colonists had won freedom as a consequence of the society's efforts. In the last analysis the society was far more interested in shoring up slavery by removing free African-Americans from the South than in a program of emancipation.

Liberia. The colonists declared Liberia an independent republic in 1847 and adopted a constitution modeled after that of the United States. The country did not receive American recognition until 1862, after the Confederate states had left the Union. The African-American colonists and their descendants, who remained Protestant and continued to speak English, formed a small ruling class—little more than 10 percent of the population by the mid-twentieth century—that dominated the indigenous tribes. Liberia's economic life remained closely tied to that of the United States, and in the twentieth century American rubber companies, working with the local elite, largely controlled the economy.

A Radical Solution

Most free blacks rejected colonization. In 1817, three thousand met in Philadelphia's Bethel Church and denounced it. They informed "the humane and benevolent inhabitants of the city" that "we have no wish to separate from our present homes for any purpose whatever." They explained that they were "contented with our present situation and condition" and wanted only "the use of those opportunities . . . which the Constitution and the laws allow to all." African-Americans throughout the North seconded these sentiments at conventions and in pamphlets and newspapers. They also called for an end to slavery—through rebellion if necessary.

Walker's *Appeal*. In 1827 John Russwurm and Samuel D. Cornish began the first African-American newspaper, *Freedom's Journal*, in New York. The Boston agent for the newspaper was David Walker, a free African-American from North Carolina who made a living selling secondhand clothes. In 1829 Walker published a stirring pamphlet entitled *Appeal . . . to the Colored Citizens*. It ridiculed the religious pretensions of slaveholders, justified slave rebellion, and warned America that the slaves would revolt if justice was delayed. To white Americans Walker said, "We must and shall be free . . . in spite of you. . . . And woe, woe, will be it to you if we have to obtain our freedom by fighting." He added: "I do declare that one good black man can put to death six white men." Within a year Walker's *Appeal* had gone through three printings and had begun to reach free blacks in the South.

In 1830 Walker and other African-American abolitionists called a national convention in Philadelphia. Walker died under mysterious circumstances later that year, but the convention became an annual event. The delegates never adopted a position as radical as Walker's, but they regularly condemned slavery, colonization, and northern discriminatory legislation. They also urged free blacks to use every legal means to improve the condition of their race and asked for divine assistance in breaking "the shackles of slavery."

Nat Turner's Rebellion. In 1831 the major violence that David Walker had contemplated took concrete form when Nat Turner, a slave in Southampton County, Virginia, staged a bloody revolt. Turner had taught himself to read as a child and had hoped to be emancipated, but a new master forced him into field work and another master separated him from his wife. Turner became deeply spiritual, seeing visions and concluding that he might carry Christ's burden of suffering in a race war. Taking an eclipse of the sun as an omen, Turner plotted with a handful of relatives and close friends to meet the masters' terror with terror of their own. They killed almost sixty slave owners and members of their families, in many cases dismembering and decapitating them. Turner had hoped that an army of slaves would join his liberation force, but he had mustered only sixty men by the time a white militia formed to protect two large plantations and dispersed his poorly armed and exhausted followers. In retaliation, whites killed slaves at random all over the county. One company of cavalry killed forty in two days, putting the heads of fifteen on poles to warn "all those who should undertake a similar plot." Fifty slaves were tried formally, and twenty of them were hanged. After hiding for nearly two months, Turner was captured and hanged, still identifying his mission with that of Christ's.

Evangelical Abolitionism, to 1840

The threat of a bloody racial revolution, coupled with the inspiring example of free African-Americans who sought to eradicate slavery, had a profound effect on some young white opponents of slavery. Many were evangelical ministers and their supporters. They became evangelists against slavery, appealing to the Christian conscience of individual slave owners for immediate emancipation. Gradual change or compromise had no place in their new campaign. The issue was absolute: slave owners and their supporters were sinning by depriving slaves of their God-given status as free moral agents. If the slave owners did not repent, the evangelical abolitionists believed, they inevitably faced the prospect of revolution in this world and damnation in the next.

William Lloyd Garrison. The two most influential leaders of the antislavery movement during the 1830s were William Lloyd Garrison and Theodore Dwight Weld. Garrison was an early antislavery advocate and was less influenced by the evangelical revivals than were Weld and other white abolitionists. A Massachusetts-born printer, Garrison had collaborated in Baltimore during the 1820s with a Quaker, Benjamin Lundy, who published the *Genius of Universal Emancipation*, the leading antislavery newspaper of the decade. In 1830 Garrison went to jail, convicted of libeling a New England merchant engaged in the domestic slave trade. After seven weeks he was released because, through Lundy's intervention, Arthur Tappan, a wealthy New York merchant, paid the fine. Garrison went on to found his own antislavery weekly, *The Liberator*, in Boston in 1831. In the following year he spearheaded the formation of the New England Anti-Slavery Society.

From the outset *The Liberator* deplored gradual or compensated emancipation and demanded the immediate abolition of slavery without any reimbursement for slaveholders. Garrison condemned the American Colonization Society, charging that its real aim was to

William Lloyd Garrison
This daguerreotype captures the moral intensity Garrison displayed in 1854 when he publicly burned the Constitution and declared: "So perish all compromises with tyranny." His self-righteous defiance of proslavery laws was part of a passionate quest to destroy all institutions that prevented individuals from discovering their full potential.

strengthen slavery by removing troublesome African-Americans who were already free. He even attacked the Constitution for its recognition of slavery. It was, he pronounced, "a covenant with death, an agreement with Hell." Nothing was safe from Garrison's criticism. He denounced ministers and even the authenticity of Scripture whenever he felt slavery had been sanctioned. Increasingly, he concluded that slavery was a sign of deep corruption infesting *all* institutions and called for comprehensive reform of American society as a whole.

Garrison's radical position attracted many avid followers, and to them he became a cultural hero on the scale of Emerson or Finney. Like those men, he made thundering assertions of his own identity. In the first number of *The Liberator*, he declared: "I will be harsh as truth and as uncompromising as justice. . . . I am in earnest—I will not equivocate—I will not excuse—I will not retreat a single inch—AND I WILL BE HEARD."

Theodore Dwight Weld. In contrast to Garrison, Theodore Dwight Weld came to abolitionism from the religious revivals of the 1830s. Weld was a more restrained abolitionist. The son of a Congregationalist minister, he made a commitment to reform after hearing Charles Finney preach in Utica, New York. Weld worked within the churches of New York and the Old Northwest and shifted his focus from temperance and educational reform to abolitionism. In these churches, primarily Presbyterian and Congregational, he preached the moral responsibility of all Americans for the denial of liberty to slaves. In 1834 Weld inspired a group of students at Lane Theological Seminary in Cincinnati to form an antislavery society. When Lane's president, Lyman Beecher, tried to repress the society, the "Lane rebels" left, enrolling at Oberlin College and joining Weld in his evangelism. Weld's crusade gathered force, buttressed by the theological arguments he advanced in *The Bible against Slavery* (1837). Collaborating closely with him were two South Carolina abolitionists—Angelina Grimké, whom he married in 1838, and her sister, Sarah.

With the assistance of the Grimké sisters, Weld provided the antislavery movement with a new base of evidence in a massive book, *American Slavery as It Is: Testimony of a Thousand Witnesses* (1839). Weld addressed the reader "as a juror to try a plain case and bring in an honest verdict." The question he posed was: "What is the actual condition of the slaves in the United States?" In answering, Weld presented evidence from southerners themselves, some of it taken from the more than 20,000 editions of southern newspapers he had researched. Among the firsthand accounts he cited were those of Angelina Grimké, who recalled her childhood in Charleston. She told, for example, of a treadmill that

Charleston slave owners used for punishment and of a prominent white woman who sent slaves there regularly: "One poor girl, whom she sent there to be flogged, and who was accordingly stripped naked and whipped, showed me the deep gashes on her back—I might have laid my whole finger in them—*large pieces of flesh had actually been cut out by the torturing lash*." Weld's book sold over 100,000 copies during its first year alone.

The American Anti-Slavery Society. In 1833 Weld, Garrison, Arthur and Lewis Tappan, and sixty other delegates, black and white, met in Philadelphia to establish the American Anti-Slavery Society. They received financial support from the Tappans and with it aimed to reach the middle-class public. Led by this society, abolitionists developed two approaches: one for the general public and the other aimed at politicians. First they sought to create a moral climate so intense that slave owners would have to accept programs of abolition. They used the tactics of the religious revivalists: public meetings led by stirring speakers, small gatherings sponsored by local antislavery chapters, and home visits by agents of the movement. The abolitionists also used new techniques of mass communication. Garrison's radical individualism did not stand in the way of attempts to reach a mass market. Assisted by the new steam press, the American Anti-Slavery Society was able to distribute more than 100,000 pieces of literature in 1834 and more than 1 million in 1835. Most dramatic was the "great postal campaign" begun in 1835, which flooded the nation, including the South, with abolitionist pamphlets. In July 1835 alone abolitionists mailed more than 175,000 items through the New York City post office.

The abolitionists' second broad strategy was to mobilize public pressure on legislative bodies—in particular, Congress. In 1835 the American Anti-Slavery Society encouraged local chapters and members to bombard Congress with petitions for specific action: abolition of slavery in the District of Columbia, abolition of the domestic slave trade, removal of the "three-fifths compromise" from the Constitution, and denial of the admission of new slave states to the Union. By 1838, nearly 500,000 signed petitions had arrived in Washington.

These activities drew increasing numbers of middle-class men and women to abolitionism. During the 1830s local abolitionist societies grew swiftly, from about 200 in 1835 to more than 500 in 1836 and nearly 2,000 by 1840. Almost 200,000 people joined them. Meanwhile, the leadership of the abolitionist movement broadened beyond the original core of free blacks, Quakers, and evangelical Christians. Some transcenden-

Anti-Slavery Almanac
The heart-wrenching breakup of families by the slave trade was a common theme in abolitionist literature.

Anti-Slavery Almanac.

talists, for example, felt shattered by the stark contrast between their claims for individual potential and the reality of slavery. Thanks to their literary skills and in some instances their wealth, many became leaders of the movement in New England. Emerson was less interested in the condition of slaves than in the moral failure of a free society that tolerated slavery, but he spoke out frequently against the institution and, as the Civil War neared, condoned abolitionist violence.

Thoreau was eloquently transcendental in his condemnations of slavery and his calls for civil disobedience. In 1846 Thoreau protested the Mexican War and slavery by refusing to pay his taxes and submitting to arrest. Two years later he published anonymously an essay entitled "Civil Disobedience" that outlined how individuals, by resisting governments that sanctioned slavery and through loyalty to a higher moral law, could transcend their complicity in slavery and redeem the state from its crimes. Even if outnumbered, moral individuals could prevail if they were true to their beliefs. "A minority is powerless while it conforms to the majority," Thoreau explained. But it becomes "irresistible when it clogs by its whole weight."

The Role of Women. Women also contributed to the power of the abolitionist movement. African-American women were crucial, and one of them, Maria W. Stewart, was among the first abolitionists, speaking out in

Boston in the early 1830s. Even earlier than the Grimké sisters, she made speeches to mixed audiences of men and women. As the movement grew, thousands of white women throughout the North followed her example. They condemned the immorality of slavery, delivered lectures to audiences of men and women, supplied more than half the signatures on the petitions the American Anti-Slavery Society sent to Congress, and conducted home "visitations" to win converts among other women and their husbands.

Women abolitionists also established their own organizations, including the Philadelphia Female Anti-Slavery Society, founded by Lucretia Mott in 1833; the Boston Female Anti-Slavery Society, founded by Maria Weston Chapman and twelve other women; and the Anti-Slavery Conventions of American Women, formed by a network of local societies during the late 1830s. Among their accomplishments, the women's societies raised money for *The Liberator* and the American Anti-Slavery Society, supported agents and speakers against slavery, distributed literature, and established schools for free blacks.

By the late 1830s the abolitionist movement had mobilized and merged the reform ideas and energies of both religious revivalism and transcendentalism. What remained uncertain was the ability of its leaders to develop practical strategies that would succeed in eradicating slavery.

Hostility to Abolition

In the South the conjunction of Nat Turner's slave rebellion, the imminent abolition of slavery by the British in the West Indies, and the beginnings of Garrison's *Liberator* touched off an intense effort to defend slavery. The final effort to address the slavery problem peacefully came in 1831–1832, after Turner's rebellion, when the Virginia legislature considered a program of gradual emancipation and colonization. When the bill was rejected by a vote of 73 to 58, the possibility that southern states would legislate an end to slavery faded forever. Instead, in the 1830s the southern states toughened their slave codes, limiting the movement of slaves and prohibiting anyone from teaching them to read to prevent them from absorbing abolitionist literature. Southern legislatures banned abolitionism and passed resolutions demanding that northern states follow suit. The Georgia legislature even offered a $5,000 reward to anyone who would kidnap Garrison and bring him to the South to be tried for inciting rebellion. Public meetings routinely offered rewards for the capture of persons distributing abolitionist literature. In Nashville vigilantes whipped a northern college student for distributing abolitionist pamphlets. In 1835 a Charleston mob attacked the post office and destroyed sacks of abolitionist mail from the North. After that southern postmasters generally refused to deliver mail of suspected abolitionist origin.

The New Defense of Slavery. At the same time, southern leaders—politicians, newspaper editors, and clergymen—developed a new intellectual defense of the institution. It was new in that they moved beyond the defense of slavery as a "necessary evil" and developed a "positive good" argument linked to industrial conditions and buttressed with Christian doctrine. They argued that slavery protected slaves against the evils of the industrial system; it promoted "harmony" in relations between the races; it provided for a more efficient and orderly labor supply than was available in the North; and it had a basis in Scripture. The last argument was particularly crucial to southerners who needed a rationalization for enslaving a population that had become overwhelmingly Christian. Defenders of slavery such as Thornton Stringfellow, a Baptist minister from Virginia, claimed that St. Paul had recognized Christian churches that contained both masters and servants. Stringfellow cited Paul's injunction: "Servants, obey your masters."

According to this sharpening self-image of plantation society, only an exceptional person—the planter—deserved genuine freedom. He was seen as being surrounded by people who were incompetent and incapable of freedom. His task was to achieve a "disinterested benevolence" so that he could lead and manage. Only his exceptional willpower, reason, and self-control made society and order possible. Indeed, southern leaders such as John C. Calhoun advised the northern business elite that it could hold northern society together only by asserting the power that flowed from its "natural superiority." Calhoun exhorted northern business leaders to think and act more like southern planters.

Northern Antiabolitionists. The southern arguments won considerable support in the North. Some wealthy northerners sympathized with the South's appeal for unity among social elites and feared that the abolitionist attack on property held as slaves could turn into a general assault on property rights. Traditional elites, as well as many members of the business class, were troubled by the tactics of the abolitionists, who seemed to threaten the stability of the family by encouraging the active participation of women in their movement. The economic self-interest of northerners also prompted hostility to abolitionism. For example, some New York merchants and New England textile producers found it profitable to support the arguments of their southern customers or suppliers. And some wage earners saw abolitionism as a threat to their jobs; they feared that freed slaves, willing to work for subsistence wages, would pour into northern communities. Finally, only a small minority of any class of northerners believed in African-American equality; the rest were sympathetic to the racism of the planters and abhorred the thought of racial mixing, which the abolitionists seemed to advocate indirectly through their attacks on racism and the colonization movement. In the North the extreme tone of the abolitionists was particularly resented in the communities of the Ohio Valley, which southerners had founded and peopled and in which the fear of freed slaves was especially intense.

Northern opponents of abolition could be as violent as those in the South. Mobs, sometimes led by people whom the abolitionists described as "gentlemen of property and standing," intimidated free blacks and abolitionists. They disrupted abolitionist meetings and routinely destroyed abolitionist printing presses. Fifteen hundred New Yorkers, the first antiabolitionist mob, stormed a church in 1833 in a search for William Lloyd Garrison and Arthur Tappan. The next year prominent New Yorkers cheered a mob of casual laborers who vandalized and set fire to Lewis Tappan's house, and a white mob swept through Philadelphia's African-American neighborhoods, clubbing and stoning residents, destroying homes and churches, and forcing crowds of black women and children to flee the city. In 1835 in Utica, New York, a group of lawyers, local politicians, merchants, and bankers broke up an abolitionist convention and beat several delegates. That same year a Boston mob dragged Garrison through the streets, threatening to hang him. And two years later in Alton, Illinois, a mob shot and killed an abolitionist editor, Elijah P. Lovejoy.

The "Gag Rule." President Andrew Jackson, swayed by these demonstrations of northern hostility to abolition, privately approved of South Carolina's censorship of the United States mails. Publicly, in his annual message to Congress in 1835, Jackson called on northern states to suppress abolitionism and asked Congress to restrict the use of the mails by abolitionist groups. Congress did not respond, in part because Calhoun wanted an extreme measure—banning the delivery of abolitionist tracts in any state or territory that prohibited such material. In 1836, however, the House of Representatives did adopt the "gag rule." Under this rule, which remained in force until 1844, antislavery petitions were automatically tabled when they were received so that they could not become the subject of debate in the House. In the same year Connecticut passed a "gag law" in an attempt to suppress abolitionist speakers, but no other northern state followed suit.

The violence and suppression stunned antislavery advocates and shocked many people who had not participated in abolitionism but had joined evangelical revivals. The disorder and violence seemed to be symptoms of a deeply troubled society. Evangelical Protestants redoubled their efforts to find a means to promote social harmony. Some of the abolitionists among them worked to build the Whig party. Others focused their efforts more specifically on slavery as a political question.

The Rise of Political Abolitionism

As assaults on the antislavery movement mounted, most abolitionists dissociated themselves from Garrison's broad attack on American institutions. Many evangelical Protestants, often following the Tappans, continued to work through their churches. Some of them, working with more secular abolitionists, drew on their experience in managing the postal and petition campaigns of the 1830s and turned to practical politics. They wanted to attract moderate Americans—people who neither supported nor opposed abolition—and propose practical political solutions. They were no less radical than Garrison in terms of their commitment to abolition but were more willing to work within the existing political system. Most of these conservative abolitionists felt that American society, while seriously flawed by slavery, was at its core healthy.

Garrison and his supporters, however, became even more insistent that their American Anti-Slavery Society retain a broad platform that included equal participation for women in the society, pacifism, abolition of prisons and asylums, and in 1843 expulsion of slave states from the Union. The attacks on abolitionists had in fact made the Garrisonians even more radical. Then, in 1837, Garrison came under the influence of John Humphrey Noyes and the perfectionists. He began to emphasize his belief that institutions, rather than individuals, were the source of all sin and that virtually all American institutions were corrupt.

This growing rift in the abolitionist movement fractured Garrison's American Anti-Slavery Society in 1840. Some abolitionists left it to join the American and Foreign Anti-Slavery Society, with its leadership in New York and its major financial backing from Lewis Tappan. Others—such as Theodore Weld, who had left the organized movement along with the Grimkés in 1838—avoided both the Garrison and the Tappan camps, although Weld retained an evangelical approach to abolition. Weld tried to avoid factional disputes within the movement and in any case found both camps lacking. He disliked Garrison's dilution of abolitionism in a broad-based reform effort but found distasteful what he described as the "anti-woman" attitude of more conservative abolitionists.

The Liberty Party. In 1840 most of the abolitionist leaders who had split with Garrison began to emphasize electoral politics as a means to eliminate slavery. They established the Liberty party and nominated James G. Birney as its presidential candidate in 1840 and 1844. Birney was a former slave owner who had lived in Alabama and Kentucky; after a Princeton education and conversion by Weld to abolitionism, he had founded an antislavery newspaper in Cincinnati. In contrast with Garrison and his demands for sweeping reform of the nation's institutions, Birney was willing to work within the Constitution, and he recast abolitionism in terms of republican ideals. He and the Liberty party took the position that the Constitution did not recognize slavery, regarding it as a state institution; that the Fifth Amendment, by barring any Congressional deprivation of "life, liberty, or property," prevented the federal government from sanctioning slavery; and that slaves became automatically free when they entered areas of federal authority, such as the District of Columbia and national territories. But even this more moderate stance failed to attract a substantial following; the Liberty party won less than 3 percent of northern votes for its presidential candidate in 1844. Political abolitionism, as well as the more radical Garrisonian approach, appeared to have little future.

Summary

Industrialization challenged Americans to reconcile claims for the supremacy of the individual with society's need for cohesion. Efforts to resolve this conflict produced a widening variety of reform crusades. These crusades were considered more radical than the business-class moral campaigns.

Many of the new reformers came close to rejecting industrial society. Transcendentalists and other groups formed experimental communities that they hoped would reform society by setting an inspiring example. Religious sects such as the Shakers tried to control sin by withdrawing into insular communities. The most successful of these communities were created by the Mormons, who attempted to provide a communal structure to channel destructive individualism.

Some middle-class women who had been involved in moral reform turned to abolitionism and began to develop an ideology that challenged the traditional division of labor in the household. While they developed this challenge, they launched a movement to establish equal rights for women in public life. They did not gain suffrage but made advances in winning property rights for women.

The most dramatic outlet for reform enthusiasm was a new attack on slavery. In the 1830s a group of abolitionists emerged who shared the moral intensity of the business-class evangelists but were far more radical. In attacking slavery, the abolitionists challenged traditional property rights, and some condemned all institutions that seemed to limit human freedom.

In the late 1830s and early 1840s conservative opposition in both the North and the South nearly halted the movement to abolish slavery as well as all radical reform efforts. In response, some abolitionists tried to broaden the appeal of their message by describing slavery as being much more than the denial of freedom to individual slaves or an expression of the unbridled individualism of slaveholders.

In contrast with Garrison's demands for radical reform of all the nation's institutions, they accepted working within the Constitution. The political abolitionists moved away from directly challenging slavery and slave owners in the South. Instead, they focused on areas that were directly under federal authority, like the District of Columbia and the territories, and argued that in such places the federal government could not, under the Constitution, sanction slavery. Such abolitionists managed to form a political party and run presidential candidates in 1840 and 1844, but the political approach to abolitionism appeared to offer little more promise for winning the support of a large middle-class audience in the North than did Garrison's radical abolitionism.

TIMELINE

1817	American Colonization Society founded
1818	Publication of Benjamin Franklin's autobiography
1826	American Lyceum founded
1829	David Walker's *Appeal*
1830	Joseph Smith publishes *The Book of Mormon*
1831	William Lloyd Garrison begins publishing *The Liberator* Nat Turner's rebellion Alexis de Tocqueville begins his tour of America
1832	Ralph Waldo Emerson resigns his pulpit New England Anti-Slavery Society founded
1834	New York Female Moral Reform Society established
1836	House of Representatives adopts "gag rule"
1837	Emerson's lecture "The American Scholar" Mob kills Elijah P. Lovejoy
1839	Mormons found Nauvoo
1840	Liberty party launched with James G. Birney as its candidate
1841	Transcendentalists found Brook Farm Dorothea Dix begins her investigations
1844	Margaret Fuller's *Woman in the Nineteenth Century* Mob kills Joseph Smith James G. Birney runs again for president
1845	Thoreau withdraws to Walden Pond
1846	Mormons begin trek to Salt Lake Brook Farm disbanded
1847	Liberia declared an independent republic
1848	John Humphrey Noyes founds Oneida Community Seneca Falls convention
1850	Publication of Nathaniel Hawthorne's *The Scarlet Letter*
1851	Herman Melville's *Moby Dick* Susan B. Anthony joins movement for women's rights
1852	Harriet Beecher Stowe's *Uncle Tom's Cabin*
1854	Presidential veto of Dorothea Dix's program for national asylums
1855	First publication of Walt Whitman's *Leaves of Grass*
1858	The "Mormon War"

BIBLIOGRAPHY

General surveys of antebellum reform movements include Robert H. Abzug, *Cosmos Crumbling: American Reform and the Religious Imagination* (1994); C. S. Griffen, *The Ferment of Reform, 1830–1860* (1967); Alice F. Tyler, *Freedom's Ferment: Phases of Social History from the Colonial Period to the Outbreak of the Civil War* (1944); and Ronald G. Walters, *American Reformers, 1815–1860* (1978).

Transcendentalists and Utopians

The leading study that connects transcendentalism with reform movements is Ann C. Rose, *Transcendentalism as a Social Movement, 1830–1850* (1981). See also Catherine L. Albanese, *Corresponding Motion: Transcendental Religion and the New America* (1977). On communitarian experiments see Arthur Bestor, Jr., *Backwoods Utopias: The Sectarian and Owenite Phases of Communitarian Life in America* (1970); Lawrence Foster, *Religion and Sexuality: Three American Communal Experiments of the Nineteenth Century* (1981); Jean McMahon Humez, ed., *Gifts of Power: The Writings of Rebecca Jackson, Black Visionary, Shaker Eldress* (1981); Louis J. Kern, *An Ordered Love: Sex Roles and Sexuality in Victorian Utopias—The Shakers, the Mormons, and the Oneida Community* (1981); Spencer Klaw, *Without Sin: The Life and Death of the Oneida Community* (1995); Charles Nordhoff, *The Communistic Societies of the United States* (1875, reprinted 1960); and Stephen J. Stein, *The Shaker Experience in America* (1992). On the Mormon experience see James B. Allen and Glen M. Leonard, *The Story of the Latter-Day Saints* (1992); Leonard J. Arrington, *The Mormon Experience: A History of the Latter-Day Saints* (1992); John L. Brooke, *The Refiner's Fire: The Making of Mormon Cosmology, 1644–1844* (1994); Grant Underwood, *The Millenarian World of Early Mormonism* (1993); and Kenneth H. Winn, *Exiles in a Land of Liberty: Mormons in America, 1830–1846* (1989). Recent studies that link literary developments to reform themes and cultural history include Harold Kaplan, *Democratic Humanism and American Literature* (1972); David S. Reynolds, *Beneath the American Renaissance: The Subversive Imagination in the Age of Emerson and Melville* (1988) and *Walt Whitman's America: A Cultural Biography* (1995); R. Jackson Wilson, *Figures of Speech: American Writers and the Literary Marketplace, from Benjamin Franklin to Emily Dickinson* (1989); and Larzar Ziff, *Literary Democracy: The Declaration of Cultural Independence in America* (1981). On the linkages between religion and the utopians, see Paul E. Johnson and Sean Wilentz, *The Kingdom of Matthias: A Story of Sex and Salvation in 19th-Century America* (1995), and Timothy L. Smith, *Revivalism and Social Reform: American Protestantism on the Eve of the Civil War* (1980).

The Women's Movement

The most comprehensive history of women in the United States is Nancy Woloch, *Women and the American Experience* (1984). On the social history of women, see W. Elliot Brownlee and Mary M. Brownlee, *Women in the American Economy: A Documentary History, 1675–1929* (1976); Nancy F. Cott, *The Bonds of Womanhood: "Women's Sphere" in New England, 1780–1835* (1977); Carl N. Degler, *At Odds: Women and the Family in America from the Revolution to the Present* (1980); and Mary P. Ryan, *Cradle of the Middle Class: The Family in Oneida County, New York, 1790–1865* (1981). The most thorough description of the participation of women in benevolence and reform is Keith Melder, *Beginnings of Sisterhood: The American Women's Rights Movement, 1800–1850* (1977). For studies of more specific aspects of women's involvement in reform see Barbara J. Berg, *The Remembered Gate: Origins of American Feminism: The Woman and the City, 1800–1860* (1978); Estelle B. Freedman, *Their Sisters' Keepers: Women's Prison Reform in America, 1830–1860* (1981); Lori D. Ginzberg, *Women and the Work of Benevolence: Morality, Politics, and Class in the Nineteenth-Century United States* (1990); Nancy A. Hewitt, *Women's Activism and Social Change: Rochester, New York, 1822–1872* (1984); and Jean F. Yellin, *Women and Sisters: The Antislavery Feminists in American Culture* (1989). On Dorothea Dix, see David Gollaher, *Voice for the Mad: The Life of Dorothea Dix* (1995), and Charles M. Snyder, *The Lady and the President: The Letters of Dorothea Dix & Millard Fillmore* (1975). The leading histories of feminists and the early women's rights movement include Kathleen Barry, *Susan B. Anthony—A Biography: A Singular Feminist* (1988); Ellen Du Bois, *Feminism and Suffrage: The Emergence of an Independent Women's Movement, 1848–1869* (1978); and Eleanor Flexner, *Century of Struggle: The Woman's Rights Movement in the United States* (1959). On Margaret Fuller, see Paula Blanchard, *Margaret Fuller: From Transcendentalism to Revolution* (1978); Charles Capper, *Margaret Fuller: An American Romantic Life* (1992); and Joan von Mehren, *Minerva and the Muse: A Life of Margaret Fuller* (1994).

The Antislavery Movement

Surveys of reform that focus on antislavery include Robert H. Abzug, *Passionate Liberator: Theodore Dwight Weld and the Dilemma of Reform* (1980); David Brion Davis, *The Problems of Slavery in the Age of Revolution, 1770–1823* (1975); Louis Filler, *The Crusade against Slavery, 1830–1860* (1960); Leon F. Litwack, *North of Slavery: The Negro in the Free States, 1790–1860* (1961); Stephen B. Oates, *To Purge This Land with Blood: A Biography of John Brown* (1970); Lewis Perry, *Childhood, Marriage, and Reform: Henry Clarke Wright, 1797–1870* (1980); Benjamin Quarles, *Black Abolitionists* (1969); James B. Stewart, *Holy Warriors: The Abolitionists and American Slavery* (1976); John L. Thomas, *The Liberator: William Lloyd Garrison* (1963); and Bertram Wyatt-Brown, *Lewis Tappan and the Evangelical War against Slavery* (1959). For the role of women in the antislavery movement, consult Edmund Fuller, *Prudence Crandall: An Incident of Racism in Nineteenth-Century America* (1971); Blanche Hersh, *The Slavery of Sex: Female Abolitionists in Nineteenth-Century America* (1978); Gerda Lerner, *The Grimké Sisters from South Carolina: Pioneers for Women's Rights and Abolition* (1967); and Alma Lutz, *Crusade for Freedom: Women of the Antislavery Movement* (1968). On northern hostility to abolition, see Leonard L. Richards, *"Gentlemen of Property and Standing": Anti-Abolition Mobs in Jacksonian America* (1970).

Plantation Economy in the Old South, circa 1876

Although this detail from a painting by William Aiken Walker idealizes life on a cotton plantation—much as the defenders of slavery did—it suggests the importance of slavery and self-sufficiency to the largest plantations in the South. Small farms in the South outnumbered large plantations, but the plantations established economic and social styles that most white southerners tried to emulate.

Sections and Sectionalism
1840–1860

★   ★   ★

As the antislavery movement gathered force during the 1840s and 1850s, setting North against South, the acceleration of the Industrial Revolution accentuated the distinctiveness of the two sections. While the North grew increasingly industrial, the fortunes of the South became ever more tied to its "peculiar institution," as slavery was sometimes called. Two distinctly different economic and social systems were evolving, with two different ways of thinking about the relationship between the individual and society. And people in the two sections became acutely conscious of their differences. Indeed, they celebrated them—that is to say, *sectionalism* increased in the decades before the Civil War.

Westward expansion further intensified sectionalism. Each society, southern and northern, believed that westward expansion was necessary to preserve its way of life. In the 1840s and 1850s the acceleration of industrialization gave the North a major demographic advantage. Northerners, motivated by the push of the Industrial Revolution and the pull of fresh land, came pouring into the West in vast numbers. Southerners feared the admission of more new free states than slave states and a loss of their ability to protect slavery within the Union.

The Slave South: A Distinctive Society

On a superficial level, southern planters were similar to northern capitalists: both groups did what they considered necessary to protect their investments and maximize their profits. But the key investment for planters lay in human beings and land rather than factories and machines. That reality required a justification of slavery in which planters deemphasized or denied their economic motivations. As the profits from slave owning mounted during the 1840s and 1850s, so did the efforts at rationalization. Planters increasingly described themselves as superior beings—natural aristocrats who altruistically protected their human property.

The Slave Economy

Between 1840 and 1860 the South's economy grew rapidly and generated high incomes for both slave owners and other whites. Per capita income, even taking the meager incomes of slaves (food, clothing, and shelter) into account, increased more rapidly in the South than in the United States as a whole. In 1860 only the Northeast, Great Britain, and Australia had higher per capita incomes than the South. Southern prosperity was based on the exportation to Europe of tobacco, rice, sugar, and—above all—cotton. By the 1850s, after the Cotton Kingdom had swept across the Mississippi River into Texas, the South was producing more than two-thirds of the world's cotton. In 1860 southern cotton accounted for almost two-thirds of the total value of exports from the United States.

Southern agriculture was highly productive, generating large revenues compared with the investment of labor, capital, and land. But unlike northern farmers, southern planters did not depend on domestic consumers or improvements in farm technology. Their high profits depended on three other factors: British markets, fresh land, and slavery.

The British connection was crucial. The buoyant demand of British textile mills drove up the export price of cotton, and British mercantile houses were the major source of capital for southern planters. And because southern agriculture relied heavily on foreign markets, the region enjoyed a high degree of economic independence from the rest of the United States.

The availability of fresh land was equally significant because cotton ruined the soil more quickly than did most other crops. By 1860 nearly three-fourths of the South's cotton production came from the region's newer plantations—on lands stretching from western Georgia to eastern Texas. In the early 1850s an observer described Georgia's eastern plantation belt as "red old hills stripped of their native growth and virgin soil, and washed with deep gullies, with here and there patches of Bermuda grass, and stunted pine shrubs, struggling for a scanty subsistence on what was one of the richest soils in America." The ravaging of southern land continued into the twentieth century.

Most important, southern planters became increasingly dependent on slave labor. Slavery allowed planters to organize labor into large-scale specialized routines that resembled factory work but were far more demanding, intense, and brutal. While the northern business class relied heavily on the appeal of evangelical

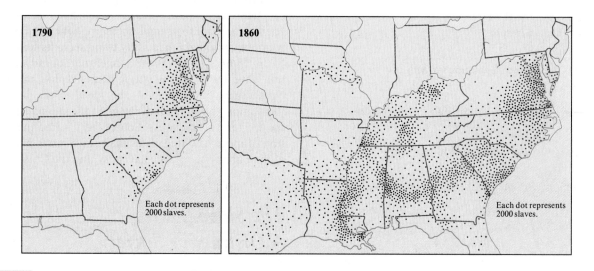

MAP 13.1

The Distribution of the Slave Population, 1790–1860
The cotton boom was largely responsible for the westward shift of the slave population. In 1790 slaves were concentrated most heavily on the tobacco plantations of the Chesapeake and the rice and indigo areas of South Carolina. By 1860 slaves were most heavily concentrated on the cotton and sugar land of the lower Mississippi Valley and along an arc of fertile cotton land—the "black belt"—sweeping from Mississippi through Georgia.

Christianity and the promise of economic rewards to discipline workers, southern planters used coercion, terror, and suppression of open communication to keep slaves in line. Planters could use those tactics as long as they insulated their society from the rest of the nation.

Immigration offered little assistance in building a southern labor force. Most migrants from the North and from Europe avoided the South, and the majority of those who did go there found jobs that did not force them to compete with cheap slave labor. Few immigrants settled there even during the 1850s, when there were growing opportunities for work in southern cities. The South actually *lost* free workers, because a significant portion of its white population, especially in the border states, migrated to the upper Ohio Valley and, during the 1850s, to Oregon and California. Few slaves arrived from Africa after 1808, when Congress banned their importation (and exportation). The high birth rate of the existing slave population provided the labor force needed for the westward expansion of the Cotton Kingdom (see Map 13.1).

The Gang Labor System. Planters who grew cotton or sugar and owned more than twenty slaves forced their slaves into intensely specialized and disciplined work. In 1860 such planters accounted for only about 10 percent of all slaveholders but owned about 50 percent of the slaves.

Those planters or their overseers assigned slaves specific tasks, which varied by season, and organized the hands into disciplined teams, or "gangs," as they were called. The gangs worked in the fields at a feverish and often brutal pace. Overseers, most of whom were white, and drivers, who were themselves slaves, used the threat of the whip to force their gangs into tight, co-ordinated units for plowing, hoeing, and picking. A traveler in Mississippi in 1854 watched an army of slaves return from the fields at the end of a summer day:

> First came, led by an old driver carrying a whip, forty of the largest and strongest women I ever saw together; they were all in a simple uniform dress of a bluish check stuff, the skirts reaching little below the knee; their legs and feet were bare; they carried themselves loftily, each having a hoe over the shoulder, and walking with a free, powerful swing.

Next marched the plow-hands with their mules, "the cavalry, thirty strong, mostly men, but a few of them women." Finally, "a lean and vigilant white overseer, on a brisk pony, brought up the rear." As large-scale cotton and sugar production grew, gang labor became more common than the somewhat less demanding "task" system that prevailed in the cultivation of other crops and had been the most common way of organizing slave labor before 1820.

Plantation owners could not have organized *free* farm workers to labor under the discipline of the gang system. On family farms and farms with only a few slaves, workers, both free and slave, insisted on a degree of independence and on work routines involving a variety of tasks. In the South as well as the North, whenever farm owners tried to organize free workers into gangs, the laborers demanded wages that made their output unprofitable. Or they simply quit, preferring to find employment as sharecroppers, casual workers, or factory hands. There was a great difference between the high wages that free laborers would have demanded from cotton planters and the cost of rearing and maintaining slaves. That saving in labor costs represented the economic gain planters reaped from slavery.

Harvesting Sugarcane
This watercolor by Franz Holzlhuber shows slaves harvesting sugarcane in the late 1850s in southern Louisiana, where American sugar production was concentrated. Sugar plantations, which had been the first to introduce gang labor, were even harder on slaves than were cotton plantations because of the continuous ditching and draining of marshlands and the laborious processing of the cane.

The Economic Impact of Slavery. The gang labor system, the availability of new land, and the enormous demand for cotton all made owning slaves extremely profitable. Planters—all except those with the poorest land—made profits from their investments in slaves that averaged about 10 percent a year in the 1840s and 1850s. Even the most successful New England textile mills rarely produced a higher rate of return.

The high profits from cotton production and slavery created two long-term economic problems. First, southern investors concentrated their resources in cotton and slaves rather than in manufacturing. Consequently, the percentage of people who lived in towns and cities and worked in manufacturing was twice as high in the North as in the South. The only major cities in the South by national standards were the old seaports of Baltimore, Charleston, and New Orleans, which remained predominantly commercial centers. A more tragic liability was slavery's discouragement of investment in human beings. Planters made little or no effort to educate or train their slaves or to provide schooling for poor whites. In fact, laws actually forbade education for slaves. Without large urban and industrial sectors and without a large force of skilled, educated workers, the South faced severe difficulties in long-term economic development.

Realities and Ideals of the Planter Class

The planters made up a tiny minority of southern whites, who by 1860 constituted a majority of the population in most southern states (see Figure 13.1). In 1860 only about 46,000 individuals—little more than 0.5 percent of the white population of the South—owned twenty or more slaves. Only about 8,000 planters owned fifty or more slaves. Small as it was, this minority increased its influence in the 1840s and 1850s and came to dominate southern society more completely than the business elite controlled the North.

The planters were able to increase their power by holding out to the majority of whites the possibility of entering their elite class. Although most planters lived in relatively unpretentious farmhouses, the enormous profits of the 1840s and 1850s enabled the wealthiest planters to build splendid plantations and indulge in displays of conspicuous consumption. In the new cotton lands of the Mississippi Valley many large cotton planters had risen from modest circumstances. Their prosperity whetted the appetites of all slave owners—more than 380,000 individuals belonging to about a fourth of white southern families—and of the small farmers who aspired to own slaves.

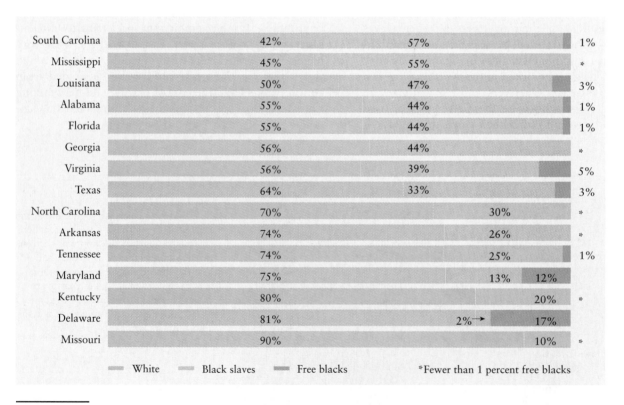

FIGURE 13.1

Proportion of Blacks and Whites in the South, 1860
Whites were in the minority in only two states of the slave South and constituted more than two-thirds of the population in eight slave states.

Mary Boykin Chesnut

A Slaveholder's Diary

Mary Boykin Chesnut (1823–1886), the wife of the South Carolina senator James Chesnut, lived most of her life on plantations near Camden, South Carolina. She made no secret of her hatred of slavery but believed that blacks were innately inferior. She revealed her views in the extensive diary she kept during the Civil War.

March 18, 1861 . . . I wonder if it be a sin to think slavery a curse to any land. [Massachusetts senator Charles] Sumner said not one word of this hated institution which is not true. Men and women are punished when their masters and mistresses are brutes and not when they do wrong—and then we live surrounded by prostitutes. An abandoned woman is sent out of any decent house elsewhere. Who thinks any worse of a negro or mulatto woman for being a thing we can't name? God forgive us, but ours is a *monstrous* system and wrong and iniquity. Perhaps the resent of the world is as bad—this *only* I see. Like the patriarchs of old our men live all in one house with their wives and their concubines, and the mulattoes one sees in every family exactly resemble the white children—and every lady tells you who is the father of all the mulatto children in everybody's household, but those in her own she seems to think drop from the clouds, or pretends so to think. Good women we have . . . the purest women God ever made. Thank God for my country-women—alas for the men! No worse than men everywhere, but the lower their mistresses, the more degraded they must be.

November 27, 1861 . . . Now what I have seen of my mother's life, my grandmother's, my mother-in-law's:

These people were educated at Northern schools mostly—read the same books as their Northern contemners, the same daily newspapers, the same Bible—have the same ideas of right and wrong—are highbred, lovely, good, pious—doing their duty as they conceive it. They live in negro villages. They do not preach and teach hate as a gospel and the sacred duty of murder and insurrection, but they strive to ameliorate of the condition of these Africans in every particular. . . . These women are more troubled by their duty to negroes, have less chance to live their own lives in peace than if they were African missionaries. They have a swarm of blacks about them as children under their care—not as Mrs. Stowe's fancy paints them, but the hard, unpleasant, unromantic, undeveloped savage Africans. And they hate slavery worse than Mrs. Stowe. . . .

We are human beings of the nineteenth century—and slavery has to go, of course. All that has been gained by it goes to the North and to negroes. The slave-owners, when they are good men and women, are the martyrs. And as far as I have seen, the people here are quite as good as anywhere else. I hate slavery. I even hate the harsh authority I see parents think it their duty to exercise *toward their children.*

Source: C. Vann Woodward, *Mary Chesnut's Civil War* (New Haven: Yale University Press, 1981), 29–30, 245–246.

The "Cavaliers" and Their Wives. The elaborate defense of slavery that began during the 1830s reinforced the message conveyed by the planters' wealth and conspicuous consumption. Planters promoted descriptions of themselves as superior, noble beings whom other whites should admire or at least treat with deference. Sermons, novels, and tracts defending slavery pictured the planter as a born leader who acted with grace and restraint. Planters were Christian patriarchs, it was said, who treated their dependents—slaves, wives, and children—with responsible generosity. They were described as hospitable, courageous, loyal, and—in the spirit of Sir Walter Scott's novels, which were popular in the South—exceptionally chivalrous. In his novel *George Balcombe* (1836) Nathaniel Beverley Tucker described planters as descendants of "the ancient cavaliers of Virginia." They were "men in whom the spirit of freedom was so blended with loyalty as to render them alike incapable of servility and selfishness."

Also idealized was the planter's wife. Defenders of southern culture believed that the planter's wife had the exceptional qualities, such as generosity, graciousness, and charm, required to match those of her spouse. Especially prized was sexual purity—contrasted with what was stereotypically described as the passionate sexuality of black women. Planters' wives became symbols of the moral superiority of whites over blacks.

The reality of plantation life was far more complex. Like northern women in their "separate sphere," most planters' wives educated their children and cared for the sick. In addition, they managed large, complicated households and often entire plantations when their husbands were absent. Southern white men did not object if white women directed the work of black men, but they firmly ruled out sexual intimacy between the two. White men brutally punished any suspected black offenders and insisted that slavery was necessary to protect southern womanhood and prevent the mixing of the races.

This belief and the strength of its appeal partly reflected the guilt of planters who routinely had sex with their female slaves and fathered children by them. As one southern woman put it, "violations of the moral law made mulattoes as common as blackberries." Planters' wives generally kept quiet about this, perhaps doing nothing more than writing in their diaries (see American Voices, page 387).

A Racist Ideology. Planters increasingly relied on a racist ideology to maintain the loyalty of non-slaveholders. Central to this ideology was the claim that blacks were an inferior race permanently unsuited for freedom and requiring rigid social control. Supporters of slavery also argued that slavery had a highly positive result. It provided what the South Carolina senator James H. Hammond described in 1858 as a "mud-sill" class—the foundation on which whites, freed from the most degrading kinds of work, had built "progress, civilization, and refinement." During the 1850s Hammond and other advocates of slavery increasingly saw slavery as guaranteeing equality, freedom, and democracy for whites and thereby protecting the highest values of the republic. As William Yancey of Alabama explained to a northern audience, "Your fathers and my fathers built this government on two ideas; the first is that the white race is the citizen and the master race, and the white man is the equal of every other white man. The second is that the Negro is the inferior race."

The planters faced no significant competition for the loyalty of non-slaveholders, who constituted a majority of the white population. Manufacturers, merchants, lawyers, doctors, editors, and ministers made up a far smaller proportion of the population in the South than they did in the North, and most were closely related to or dependent on wealthy planters. In contrast with the planters, members of the southern middle class generally supported government promotion of banking, transportation, and manufacturing, but they agreed with the planters on the prime importance of defending slavery.

Moreover, new ideas were slow to penetrate the South. Southern cities remained small, and the sparse rural population was widely scattered. The vehicles for disseminating new ideas—schools, lecturers, magazines, newspapers—that were so common in the North reached few southerners beyond the major cities. Before the Civil War no southern state had a statewide public school system, and only Kentucky and North Carolina appropriated a significant share of public revenues for education. Whereas wealthy southerners sent their children to private academies, poor whites typically taught their children at home. Whereas less than half of 1 percent of the white population in New England was illiterate in 1850, nearly 20 percent of white southerners could not read or write. This cultural isolation meant that reform movements in nineteenth-century America were limited largely to the North and that planters were able to exercise great influence over all aspects of life in the South.

Slave Life

The legal status of slaves remained unchanged in the antebellum South. The inhuman, brutal reality at the core of slavery was that slaves, in the eyes of the law, were *chattel*—personal property. They could be disciplined at will and bought and sold as if they were horses. As Thomas Ruffin, a justice of the North Carolina Supreme Court, said in 1829, "The power of the master must be absolute to render the submission of the slave perfect."

The material lives of slaves did improve, however, reflecting the prosperity of the plantation system. Most slaves were somewhat better clothed and housed than were the poorest whites in both the South and the North. The slaves' food—particularly when supplemented by greens from their own garden plots and by game and fish—was probably better than that of unskilled workers in the North. On some large plantations children, the sick, and the elderly received better care than northern society provided for those groups. But the slaves realized that planters gave them material favors primarily to protect their investment and promote a high birth rate, rarely out of benevolent concern.

The working conditions of slaves varied widely. On small farms slaves might work alongside their masters. And on every plantation some slaves were household servants, drivers who helped white overseers in the fields, or skilled workers such as blacksmiths and carpenters. However, roughly half of the slaves lived on farms or plantations that had more than twenty slaves, and they worked in the fields under the gang system.

The most oppressive conditions were found in the Old Southwest. The weather in Alabama, Mississippi, Louisiana, Arkansas, and Texas was hotter, the work routines more demanding, and the planters more harsh than was the case farther east. The slave population in those states increased from about 500,000 in 1840 to more than 1.5 million in 1860. These slaves accounted for about a fifth of the South's 2.4 million slaves in 1840 and more than a third of its 4 million slaves in 1860.

The Domestic Slave Trade. Many African-Americans came to southwestern plantations through the growing domestic slave trade, which broke up families and communities. Masters in the coastal and border states sold slaves "down the river" (the Mississippi) to increase their profits and punish those they regarded as difficult to handle. During the 1840s and 1850s profits in this trade became a major source of income for planters in the Chesapeake region and the older cotton areas of

Slaves on Auction in Richmond
The 1808 prohibition of the international slave trade forced the new cotton planters in the Deep South to import most of their slaves from the older areas of the South. Consequently, planters in those areas could reap huge profits from the slave trade. Upper South markets like this one in Richmond, Virginia, expedited that trade, and planters could use the threat of sale "down the river" to discipline their slaves.

Georgia and South Carolina, which were suffering from soil depletion. By the 1850s slave owners were shipping 25,000 slaves a year from the East to the West, and this trade helped retain the grip of slavery on the older regions of the South.

The Slave Family. In the face of intensified workloads and disrupted lives, slaves nurtured family relationships for protection and support and to foster personal identities independent of their masters. By midcentury slave families had become unusually resilient despite the lack of legal protection. Because slaves could not make contracts, marriages between them could not be legally binding. The North Carolina Supreme Court brushed aside Christian tradition in 1853 when it ruled that

> Our law requires no solemnity or form in regard to the marriage of slaves, and whether they "take up" with each other by express permission of their owners, or from a mere impulse of nature, in obedience to the command "multiply and replenish the earth" cannot, in the contemplation of the law, make any sort of difference.

A Slave Burial, circa 1860
Burials, wakes, and memorials were rituals vital to African-American culture. Slave funerals often carried on West African traditions. They were pageants that brought together friends and relatives who did not routinely see each other. By paying elaborate tribute to the dead, funerals provided a communal celebration of the living.

Frederick Douglass

Slave Songs

In this selection from his autobiography Frederick Douglass describes the singing during the days between Christmas and New Year's, which were typically allowed the slaves as holidays. He always took pains to urge his white audiences to find the hidden meanings in the words and rituals of slaves.

The fiddling, dancing, and "jubilee beating" was carried on in all directions. The latter performance was strictly southern. It supplied the place of violin, or of other musical instruments, and was played so easily that almost every farm had its "Juba" beater. The performer improvised as he beat the instrument, marking the words as he sang so as to have them fall pat with the movement of his hands. Among a mass of nonsense and wild frolic, once in a while a sharp hit was given to the meanness of slaveholders. Take the following example:

We raise de wheat,
Dey gib us de corn;
We bake de bread,
Dey gib us de crust;
We sif de meal,

Dey gib us de huss;
We peel de meat,
Dey gib us de skin;
And dat's de way
Dey take us in;
We skim de pot,
Dey gib us de liquor,
And say dat's good enough
  for nigger.
Walk over! Walk over!
Your butter and de fat;
Poor nigger you cant get over
  dat . . .

This is not a bad summary of the palpable injustice and fraud of slavery, giving, as it does, to the lazy and the idle the comforts which God designed should be given solely to the honest laborer.

. . . I did not, when a slave, understand the deep meaning of those rude and apparently incoherent sounds [of the slaves' songs]. I was myself within the circle; so that I neither saw nor heard as those without might see and hear. They told a tale of woe which was then altogether beyond my feeble comprehension; they were tones loud, long, and deep; they breathed the

prayer and complaint of souls boiling over with the bitterest anguish. Every tone was a testimony against slavery, and a prayer to God for deliverance from chains. The hearing of those wild notes always depressed my spirit, and filled me with ineffable sadness. I have frequently found myself in tears while hearing them. The mere recurrence to those songs, even now, afflicts me; and while I am writing these lines, an expression of feeling has already found its way down my cheek. To those songs I trace my first glimmering conception of the dehumanizing character of slavery, and quicken my sympathies for my brethren in bonds. . . .

I have often been utterly astonished, since I came to the north, to find persons who could speak of the singing, among slaves, as evidence of their contentment and happiness. It is impossible to conceive of a greater mistake. Slaves sing most when they are most unhappy. The songs of the slave represent the sorrows of the heart; and he is relieved by them, only as an aching heart by its tears.

Source: Frederick Douglass, *My Bondage and My Freedom* (New York, 1855), 253–54.

Nevertheless, many slaves married outside the law and lived together throughout their lives. If not broken up by sale, couples usually maintained close nuclear families within plantation communities. Parents helped their children to be as independent as possible from the discipline of the master. Mothers not only worked alongside men but also cooked, kept gardens, and raised children, often nursing babies in the field.

During this period slaves also developed elaborate kinship networks that included distant relations and even individuals who had no blood or marital ties but shared in the life of the family. Elderly slaves, for example, often played the role of community patriarch, conducting religious services and disciplining difficult children. Young slaves learned to address their elders by kin titles such as "Aunt" and "Uncle," preparing them

for the day when they might be separated from their parents. Even when parted by sale, members of both nuclear and extended families kept track of one another. Many runaway slaves returned to their home plantations and, after emancipation during the Civil War, thousands tried to reunite their families. When distances were too great to maintain marriages, many slaves started new families in their new locations. When the Union army registered African-American marriages in Mississippi at the end of the Civil War, it was found that the slave trade had separated about a fourth of the men over forty years old from their wives.

Slave Religion. In their quarters, slaves built a community life rich with mutual obligations. They shared insights regarding the world of their masters and news from the outside world. Religion was central to their culture. The Christianity of the slaves focused on the endurance of the Israelites in Egypt and the caring of Christ for the oppressed. They sometimes had to conduct their services and prayers at night or in the woods in "bush meetings" to keep them secret from their masters. Religion offered a message of hope—of eventual liberation from life's sorrows—and helped most slaves endure their bondage. Organized prayer enabled them to express love for one another and share burdens with others. Confident of their special relationship with God, the slaves prepared themselves spiritually for emancipation, which they regarded as deliverance to the Promised Land (see American Voices, page 390).

Resistance and Rebellion

Slaves resisted the growing inhumanity of bondage with the same tactics of evasion and sabotage that they had employed for generations. Slaves resisted by being deliberately careless with the master's property, losing or breaking tools, or setting fire to houses and barns. They could slow the pace of work, perhaps by feigning illness or incompetence. In the instances of greatest desperation, they could make themselves useless by cutting off their fingers or even committing suicide.

The Underground Railroad. Slave resistance sometimes took the form of flight. Tens of thousands of slaves ran away during the 1840s and 1850s, even though their chances of making it to the North or Canada were slim. In the Deep South white patrols with bloodhounds were constantly on the lookout for runaway slaves. All blacks on public roads or paths were presumed to be runaways unless they carried passes that proved otherwise. The odds for success were best for those who lived near a free state. They might receive aid from the "underground railroad," an informal network of white and, even more important, African-American abolitionists. Many escaped slaves, such as Harriet Tubman, who returned to the South nineteen times to free hundreds of slaves, risked reenslavement or death by working with the "railroad." As Tubman wrote:

> There was one of two things I had a *right* to, liberty, or death; if I could not have one, I would have the other; for no man should take me alive; I should fight for my liberty as long as my strength lasted, and when the time came for me to go, the Lord would let them take me.

Members of the small communities of free African-Americans in cities such as Baltimore, Richmond, Charleston, and New Orleans were the most important source of help. In fact, they were virtually the only free people in the South who aided escapees. In Baltimore, it was a free African-American sailor who lent his identification to Frederick Douglass, who disguised himself, used the papers to escape to New York, and then mailed the papers back to the sailor. Such acts were common despite the consequences for the benefactor if the fugitive was unable to return the papers or was captured. Despite all the obstacles, thousands of slaves escaped to freedom.

Slaves could go beyond everyday sabotage and flight to violent rebellion in which they turned on their masters and killed them. Planters used the fear of such violence to build support for slavery among non-slaveholding whites. The fear of massacre became a binding, cohesive force among whites, who recognized that their power over slaves depended on terror and that slaves might want to repay the terror. Planters could point to many slave rebellions, including the bloody revolution on the island of Santo Domingo that overthrew the French and culminated in the creation of the republic of Haiti in

Harriet Tubman
In 1849 Harriet Tubman (1823–1913, pictured far left with some of the slaves she helped to freedom) escaped from a Maryland plantation. During the next ten years she was a leader of the underground railroad and became a popular abolitionist speaker. She served as a spy for the Union army during the Civil War and then set up schools for ex-slaves in North Carolina. In 1896 she played an active role in founding the National Association of Colored Women.

1803. Within the United States revolts were local disturbances such as that of Denmark Vesey in Charleston, South Carolina, in 1822. Although such revolts were small-scale, they were numerous. As many as 200 of these small uprisings occurred during the first half of the nineteenth century, although some of the reported revolts undoubtedly took place mostly in the imaginations of slave owners. The most dramatic example of the capacity of enslaved African-Americans to fight back was Nat Turner's rebellion of 1831 (see Chapter 12).

But slaves generally recognized, especially after Turner's defeat, how heavily the odds were stacked against successful rebellion. The ratio of blacks to whites in the South was lower than that in any other slave society in the Western Hemisphere. The South was not an island that could be captured and cut off from the outside world. Southern whites were well armed, unified, and militant, and the South had no impenetrable jungles, mountains, and swamps where a guerrilla army could hide out for a long period of time.

Still, few planters were entirely certain about their security, and their anxiety rose during the 1850s. In 1856 William Proctor Gould of Green County, Alabama, warned his slaves not to become involved in an alleged conspiracy. Although they pledged their loyalty, Gould was still uneasy: "What they might have done if there had been an actual outbreak must forever remain unknown to us."

Free Blacks

While 4 million African-Americans lived as slaves in 1860, about 500,000 were free. About half of the free blacks lived in slave states, and of that number, slightly more than 85 percent lived in the Upper South. Most free African-Americans or their parents had obtained freedom before 1800. The number of slaves obtaining freedom legally, through manumission or self-purchase, then dwindled as King Cotton began to make slave owning more profitable, and as southern states restricted manumission, especially during the 1830s. Natural increase and, to a much lesser extent, escaping slaves roughly doubled the size of the free black population between 1820 and 1860, but its rate of increase was still much lower than that of the slave population.

Regardless of where they lived, free blacks were second-class citizens. They could vote only in four New England states and in New York. No state admitted to the Union after Maine in 1820 extended the suffrage to African-Americans. In New York they had to own a certain amount of property, a requirement not imposed on white voters. Every state except Massachusetts prevented them from testifying against whites in court. The federal government did not allow blacks to work for the

postal service, claim public lands, or hold a U.S. passport. Congress admitted to the Union states whose constitutions denied the vote to blacks. Virtually all public facilities were segregated throughout America, and most states, including all the southern states, denied free blacks access to public schools.

In the South free blacks faced even greater legal restrictions on their liberty, and the restrictions intensified during the 1840s and 1850s, when states tightened the system of slavery under the threat of abolitionism. Some southern states prohibited teaching slaves to read or write. They also enacted vagrancy and apprenticeship laws that were thinly disguised devices to force free blacks into slavery. Under their criminal laws, southern states subjected free blacks as well as slaves to whippings and judgments without a jury trial. By 1860 every southern state prohibited the entry of free blacks. In those states they had to carry documents establishing their free status, and in some states they needed official permission to travel across county lines. If they could not prove their status, they were subject to enslavement. Even if they had good papers, free blacks had to be careful in both the South and the North; kidnapping and sale into slavery was a constant threat.

Everywhere, free blacks endured severe discrimination when they sought work, and this discrimination intensified during the 1840s and 1850s. Most were confined by custom or law to the most menial kinds of work and to poverty. In rural areas, most were farm laborers or tenant farmers. In towns and cities, most were domestic servants or casual laborers who worked by the day. If free black women wanted to work outside of domestic service, they had almost no options except to peddle on street corners or take in laundry.

The shortage of skilled workers in southern cities, however, created opportunities. Some blacks were able to become carpenters, blacksmiths, barbers, butchers, and shopkeepers. In Charleston, Denmark Vesey, for example, won a lottery, purchased his freedom, and opened a carpentry shop. Some of these skilled workers hired other free blacks and occasionally bought slaves, usually relatives whom they wished to emancipate.

These skilled workers often formed and maintained vibrant communities of free blacks clustered in southern cities. In cities such as Baltimore, Richmond, Charleston, and New Orleans free blacks formed their own benevolent societies and churches, which became the core of their urban communities. The spirituality of the churches coupled with their practical programs of education, recreation, and social welfare provided a degree of social distance from the planter class. By 1860, as a consequence of the magnetism of urban black communities, most free blacks in the Lower South and about one-third of those in the Upper South lived in urban areas.

In some places wealthier free blacks, particularly the children of white masters and black women, felt superior to common laborers and field hands and drew apart from their communities. In New Orleans and Charleston elite free blacks formed especially close ties with the planter class and adopted its trappings of status. In New Orleans they sponsored an opera company and established literary journals. A few owned land and slaves.

Generally, however, free blacks sympathized with slaves and worked to ease their condition and even to abolish slavery. Many had been slaves, were the children of slaves, or had relatives who were slaves. They knew that so long as slavery existed even their minimal freedom was tenuous and that they had little chance to improve their status. As discrimination intensified in the 1840s and 1850s, they identified even more closely with slaves. In the North many free blacks, such as David Walker, Frederick Douglass, and Sojourner Truth, became important abolitionists. The position of free blacks in the South was much weaker, but many welcomed slaves who wanted to participate in their churches and communities. At times churches used the Sunday offering to help members who were slaves buy their freedom. Some free blacks took the risk of sheltering and protecting slaves who had escaped from their masters. A few free blacks, such as Denmark Vesey, became leaders of slave rebellions. Collectively, free blacks, despite their second-class citizenship, helped keep alive the hope of freedom from slavery.

The Northeast and the Midwest: The Industrial Revolution Accelerates

The business class of the Northeast drove industrialization forward at an increasing pace during the 1840s and 1850s and incorporated the Midwest in the expanding industrial economy. As people from the Northeast moved westward, agriculture and industry developed in close conjunction, and the economies of the Northeast and the Midwest became inextricably linked. Moreover, the economy of the Midwest became increasingly industrial in its structure. All the peoples of these two regions—even those of southern origin living in the Ohio Valley—became closely tied to the economic and social life of the North. The economic results were phenomenal. By 1860 the United States was third in the world in manufacturing, behind only Great Britain and France. Northern industrial production already was more than two-thirds that of either of those countries and was increasing even more rapidly.

Factories Triumphant

The acceleration of industrialization during the 1840s and 1850s resulted from the modernizing efforts of northern manufacturers, hundreds of whom built factories that relied on modern technology and large numbers of workers. Factory owners extended the use of power-driven machines and assembly lines from the processing of agricultural produce to the manufacture of guns, watches, sewing machines, and agricultural machinery. Manufacturers flourished not only in the first industrial towns, where falling water powered mills, but also in the older seaports and, with stunning swiftness, in the towns and cities of the Midwest. The industrialization of interior cities such as Chicago and St. Louis helped make that region a functional part of the Northeast.

The most important technological innovation adopted by manufacturers in the 1840s was the stationary steam engine, which was used to power other machines. Steam engines freed manufacturers from dependency on water power and enabled them to locate factories in the nation's largest cities: the great Atlantic seaports and the booming ports on the Great Lakes. During the 1840s manufacturers for the first time took advantage of all the benefits offered by a big-city location: easy access to the cheapest labor, highly developed markets for capital, sophisticated trading services, and urban consumers. Manufacturers in the seaports and the largest western cities, particularly Chicago, broke the near monopoly that the smaller inland cities had held on the most modern industries.

Machine Tools. The manufacturers' growing demand for machinery stimulated the machine-tool industry, which became even more critical to the advancement of industrialization. The same machines that made uniform parts for firearms were used to make parts for sewing machines. By the late 1850s five Connecticut clockmakers were using modern machine tools to make intricate works for half a million clocks a year. Some of the products of modern machine tools remained well known for generations—Colt revolvers, Remington rifles, Singer sewing machines, Waltham watches, Yale locks, and McCormick reapers.

Using the modern machine tools and new sources of power, some manufacturers introduced modern assembly lines in the 1850s. Cyrus McCormick of Chicago developed power-driven conveyor belts to assemble reapers, and Samuel Colt built an assembly-line factory in Hartford, Connecticut, to produce his invention—the "six-shooter," as it became known. By the late 1850s Colt's factory responded to the enormous demand for small arms by turning out 60,000 weapons annually.

McCORMICK'S FIRST REAPER

The McCormick Reaper, 1851
The McCormick reaper was a complex piece of machinery, but it was designed to be operated and repaired by average farmers. Company advertisements indicated that its parts were "numbered and marked with paint, showing the connection of the parts with one another so that they can readily be put together by the farmer."

In 1851, at the Crystal Palace Exhibition in London, the first world's fair in the industrial era, Cyrus McCormick and Samuel Colt displayed their machine-tooled products. The amazement of British manufacturers quickly turned to anxiety when McCormick and Colt built factories in Great Britain that used American machinery and production techniques. Two teams of technicians sent by the British government to investigate American factories reported that many different industries were organized "in large factories, with machinery applied to almost every process, the extreme subdivision of labor, and all reduced to an almost perfect system of manufacture."

The Impact of Factory Workers. The increasing scale and complexity of production, however, made it difficult for manufacturers to estimate the demand for their products. During the 1850s periods of overproduction followed by the layoff and dismissal of workers became common. One such episode coincided with the Panic of 1857—a crisis produced by overexpansion of railroad investment—and a long depression followed. Unemployment remained at about 10 percent until the outbreak of the Civil War in 1861.

Steam power and assembly lines further sharpened the class divisions that had begun to emerge in the 1820s and 1830s. To make the most of their large new investments, manufacturers increased the pace at which their workers toiled, and many workers resisted. For example, in 1845 a group of workers in Lowell, Massachusetts, under the leadership of Sarah G. Bagley, a weaver, formed the Lowell Female Labor Reform Association to protest a speedup. As working conditions became more grueling, most of the young women who had poured into factories left the paid work force to marry and raise families.

Immigration

Manufacturers turned more and more to immigrants—men and women largely from Ireland and the German states. Lacking the economic opportunities available to Americans, immigrants were willing to work for longer periods of time, at lower wages, and with greater intensity. As a result, in the 1840s immigrants began to fill the unskilled labor force.

By 1860 immigrants accounted for more than a fourth of the white adult men in the United States and more than a third of those in the North. Between 1820 and 1860 about 2 million Irish immigrants settled in the United States, along with 1.5 million Germans and 750,000 Britons (see Figure 13.2). Some of the immigrants were skilled workers, but more than two-thirds were peasants, unskilled laborers, and farmers dislocated by industrial and agricultural advances in Europe. Most of the newcomers took low-skilled jobs in factories, construction projects, docks, warehouses, and private homes. No federal legislation restricted immigration, and state immigration laws, which attempted to set minimum health standards and exclude paupers, were ineffective.

The economic situation of immigrants varied greatly by national group. The wealthiest were the British, many of whom were professionals, former landowners, and skilled workers. Many German immigrants were prosperous enough to draw on their own savings to finance travel and buy land in America. The poorest immigrants were the Irish.

The immigration of the Irish had more to do with poverty in their homeland than with economic opportunity in America. Although they arrived in increasing numbers during the 1830s, the Irish began to come in force only in 1847, after a devastating potato famine in

FIGURE 13.2

Immigration to the United States, 1820–1860

Immigration accelerated dramatically in the late 1840s. Fewer immigrants arrived in the middle and late 1850s as economic conditions improved in Ireland and the German states and the United States entered a depression.

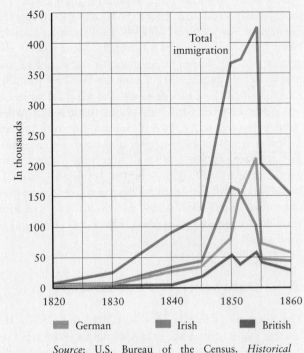

Source: U.S. Bureau of the Census. *Historical Statistics of the United States, Colonial Times to 1970*, Bicentennial Edition, Washington, DC, 1975.

Ireland. They found new homes in the Northeast, especially in the cities of New England. By 1850 the Irish accounted for more than a third of the workers in Boston. Their labor enabled Boston industrialists to compete for the first time with manufacturers in the smaller mill towns of Massachusetts and Rhode Island. By 1860 each of the largest factories producing women's clothing in Boston employed about a hundred young Irishwomen. During the late 1840s and early 1850s the Irish made only a modest contribution to the farm population. Although most had been farmers in Ireland, they were too poor to buy land in the United States.

Living conditions for many Irish immigrants, like those for other unskilled immigrants and native-born day laborers, proved to be only marginally better than the grinding poverty and rampant disease that had filled their lives in the Old World. Per capita consumption of food increased during the Industrial Revolution, and most immigrants were much better nourished than they had been in Europe. Even so, many unskilled laborers could not afford to buy the food they needed to keep up the intense pace of factory work. In addition, the stress and insecurity of work drove many unskilled workers to spend an increasing portion of their income on the entertainment and alcoholic relief found in taverns. Malnutrition increased in the largest cities, resulting in higher rates of miscarriage and death from infectious diseases.

The crowding of immigrants in the old commercial cities of the Northeast threatened public health. Sanitation systems were primitive. Poorly sealed privies drained into drinking wells, and open sewers ran through the streets. Infectious diseases ravaged the weakened, malnourished poor. Epidemics of cholera,

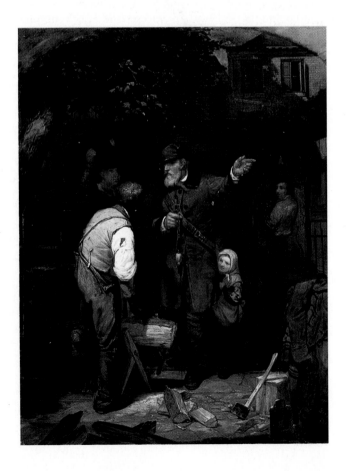

The Status of Immigrants, 1855

The painter Charles F. Blauvelt was one of the rare artists of the period who made immigrants and African-Americans his subject, and he treated both groups with realism and sympathy. In this painting he might have meant to highlight the generosity of African-Americans by portraying a black woodcutter helping lost immigrants even though the new immigrants, solely by virtue of the color of their skin, enjoyed higher status. (North Carolina Museum of Art)

yellow fever, typhoid fever, smallpox, diphtheria, and tuberculosis struck the major cities with increasing frequency. In the summer of 1849 cholera epidemics hit New York, St. Louis, and Cincinnati. More than 5,000 people, mostly immigrants, died in New York, and many entire families succumbed. Wealthy families moved out of the cities during the epidemics, while, as one observer wrote, the immigrants remained crowded "into a few wretched hovels, amidst filth and bad air, suffering from personal neglect and poisoned by eating garbage [at] which a well-bred hog on a western farm would turn up his snout." In 1860 mortality rates in New York, Philadelphia, and Boston reached a level of more than thirty-four deaths per thousand population annually, compared with about fifteen per thousand in rural areas.

Irish Identity and Anti-Catholicism

The Catholic Church. In the 1840s and 1850s the United States remained overwhelmingly Protestant in private allegiance and public culture. But many of the new immigrants—French-Canadians, many Germans, and particularly the Irish—relied on the Catholic Church not only to sustain their spiritual lives but also to reinforce their sense of class and ethnic identity. The Church's expansion closely paralleled the growth of Irish immigration, increasing from 16 dioceses and 700 churches in the 1840s to 45 dioceses and 3,000 churches by 1860. Throughout the areas settled by Irish immigrants, traveling priests were replaced by resident ones. The Irish purchased many church buildings from Protestant congregations that had moved to more spacious quarters. In towns and cities, using the church as a foundation, the Irish also built a network of charitable societies, orphanages, militia companies, parochial schools, newspapers, social clubs, and political organizations. These community institutions supported Irish immigrants in their search for housing, jobs, education, and security.

These new institutions had no equivalent in Ireland. They developed in the United States in response to the desire of Irish immigrants to maintain their native culture, to which existing American institutions were hostile or, at best, indifferent. The church network was important to immigrants in large cities, especially those who worked in factories. It provided community services and a sense of group identity, much as a labor union might have done. The institutions that the Irish created had a great impact on later groups of Catholic immigrants. Because the Irish arrived early and because many spoke English, they built the church structure and the urban political machinery through which most European Catholic immigrants established a place for themselves in American life.

The relative autonomy of Catholic communities disturbed many American Protestants, still the dominant majority in almost all of the United States. During the 1830s, when Irish immigration first started to increase, lurid anti-Catholic propaganda began to circulate. Its authors raised the specter of a sinister, highly organized menace. According to the propaganda, the pope, acting through Catholics over whom he exerted total authority, was plotting to subvert republican institutions.

Samuel F. B. Morse. A leading anti-Catholic propagandist was Samuel F. B. Morse, who would later make the first commercial adaptation of the telegraph. In 1834 Morse published *Foreign Conspiracy against the Liberties of the United States* anonymously. The book came out under his own name in 1835 and was endorsed by Protestant ministers of many denominations. Morse declared that the "past history" of Roman Catholics and "the fact that they everywhere act together, as if guided by one mind, admonish us to be jealous of their influence, and to watch with unremitted care all their movements in relation to our free institutions." He warned in particular of the political facility of Irish Catholics, who "in an especial manner clanned together, and kept alive their foreign feelings, associations, habits and manners." Morse advocated the formation of an "Anti-Popery Union" to resist the perceived Catholic threat.

Millions of young Americans read *Foreign Conspiracy* in Protestant Sunday schools and public libraries and schools. It became a textbook for anti-Catholic crusaders. In 1838 the citizens of Sutton and Millbury, Massachusetts, asked Congress to investigate "whether there are not now those amongst us, who, by their oath of allegiance to a foreign despotic Prince or Power, are solemnly bound to support his interests and accelerate his designs."

Native American Clubs. The anti-Catholic movement became exceptionally intense because of the dislocations associated with industrialization. It appealed especially to mechanics who had lost their jobs or feared that they might lose them as a consequence of the factory system. By attacking Catholics, they could blame cheap immigrant labor for their economic situation and at the same time persuade themselves that they had a superior culture and religion. Threatened workers took the lead in organizing Native American Clubs, which called for an extension of the waiting period before naturalization from five to twenty-one years, the restriction of public offices to native-born Americans, and exclusive use of the (Protestant) Authorized Version of the Bible in public schools.

Even workers who felt secure in their jobs were afraid that their children would face competition from immigrants. They strongly opposed proposals from

Riot in Philadelphia
Philadelphia's anti-Irish rioting climaxed in Southwark on June 7, 1844. Pennsylvania's governor, John Cadwalader, had called out the militia to protect Catholic churches, including one (pictured in background) in which young Irish-Americans had stored muskets for self-defense. The Protestant rioters and the militia exchanged musket fire, and the rioters even fired a cannon into the militia. Militia reinforcements ended the riots, but Philadelphia's politics became focused on ethnic and racial issues.

Catholic clergymen and Democratic legislators in many northeastern states that Catholics' taxes be reserved for parochial (religious) schools—thus weakening the public schools. Another source of anti-Catholic sentiment was the temperance movement as a number of evangelical ministers denounced the abuse of alcohol among Irish immigrants. Such appeals won recruits to the business class among native-born Protestant workers and impeded the development of a labor movement across ethnic and religious lines. Many Protestant laborers became convinced that they had more in common with their employers than with Catholic workers.

In almost every city with a large Catholic immigrant population, the anti-Catholic movement turned to violence. In 1834, in Charlestown, Massachusetts, a quarrel between Catholic laborers in an Ursuline convent and Protestant workers in a neighboring brickyard turned into a full-scale riot. The anti-Catholic mob, convinced that a young Protestant woman was being held against her will, drove out the residents of the convent and burned it to the ground. Urban rioting escalated during the 1840s as the Irish began to acquire political power in eastern cities. In Philadelphia the violence peaked in 1844 after the Catholic bishop persuaded public school officials to use both Protestant and Catholic versions of the Bible. Anti-Irish rioting, provoked by the city's Native American Clubs, lasted for two months and escalated into open warfare between the Protestants and the Pennsylvania militia, causing many casualties.

Business-Class Consumption

In the mid-1850s the annual increase in per capita income approached 2.5 percent, a remarkable rate that

the United States has never since matched. The nation achieved this rate despite the great surges of immigration during the 1840s and 1850s, which tended to reduce per capita income.

These phenomenal income gains allowed native-born Americans with property or skills to reap an extraordinary material bonanza. During the 1840s and 1850s industrialization brought a sweeping wave of consumption to middle-class life in the North. New consumer goods served as badges of economic success and membership in the business class. The availability of inexpensive mass-produced goods, many of them new during the 1840s and 1850s, made the trappings of status widely accessible to the middle class. The new material culture reinforced a prideful sense of northern uniqueness that increasingly united affluent and upwardly mobile Americans from New England through the Great Lakes states.

Middle-Class Housing: The Balloon Frame. When they could afford it, middle-class families built their homes of brick and stone. But wooden residences became much more numerous during the 1840s, and they were constructed very differently from log cabins or traditional frame buildings. In the 1830s American carpenters had devised a faster method to construct housing: the *balloon frame.*

Traditional wood construction depended on the careful fitting together of heavy timbers; experienced housewrights fashioned a strong frame with mortise-and-tenon joints, whereas western farmers fitted trimmed logs together. The balloon frame, much lighter in weight (as its name implied) but almost as strong, formed a house with a vertical grid of thin wooden studs joined by nails to cross-pieces at the top and bottom. Once the carpenter had thrown up the frame, he

Constructing a Balloon-Frame House
The fragile-looking balloon frame shown on the left provides a surprisingly strong skeleton for the substantial type of house on the right. Because people of modest means could build balloon-frame houses with the labor of family members, friends, or low-skilled carpenters, they could afford houses that had been available only to the very wealthy before the 1830s.

simply nailed wood sheathing to the studs as walls and then added a layer of clapboard siding. Even an inexperienced carpenter could erect a balloon frame. The process saved enough labor to reduce the cost of housing by 40 percent—and it was quick. The balloon frame made it possible for western cities such as Chicago, where it was first introduced, to spring up almost overnight. The four-room balloon-frame house became the standard residence, replacing the one-or two-room house of preindustrial society.

Architects published self-help manuals with detailed plans of simple houses for carpenters and families building their own homes. In the 1840s and 1850s the manuals featured larger houses with more bedrooms to enhance the privacy of each family member. The leading architectural philosopher of the era was Andrew Jackson Downing, who lauded such designs in his most famous book, *The Architecture of Country Houses* (1850). Downing argued that his new houses would promote a "refinement of manners" and strengthen the life of the family, which was "the best social form." Within the single-family home, he proclaimed, "truthfulness, beauty, and order have the largest dominion." Ample homes, even if more standardized, would provide a medium for the success of republican ideals.

Household Goods. Prosperous urban families furnished their homes with an array of new comforts, decorations, and devices. Furnaces heated both interiors and water. Europeans marveled at them and at the American desire for warmth. One visitor complained that it was impossible to escape hot air: "It meets you the moment the street-door is opened to let you in, rushes after you when you emerge again, half-stewed and parboiled into the wholesome air." In most homes, beds with springs of woven rope or iron wire replaced beds with wooden slats. Homemade featherbeds, mattresses, and down pillows spread rapidly after mass-produced ticking and sheeting became available in stores. Households acquired goods that made traditional chores more efficient. Beginning in the 1850s, some women purchased treadle-operated sewing machines. Most prosperous urban households had stoves with ovens, including broilers and movable grates, instead of open hearths. Women used a variety of pots, pans, and kettles; mechanical equipment such as grinders and presses; and washboards. And these households had iceboxes, which ice-company wagons filled daily. As early as 1825 the Underwood Company of Boston was marketing well-preserved Atlantic salmon in jars. With the introduction of the Mason jar in 1858, households vastly increased their ability to preserve other perishable foods.

The new household furnishings also included mass-produced clocks. Before 1820, townspeople and villagers relied on public clocks or bells, and country folk told time by the sun. By the 1840s, inexpensive clocks and watches manufactured in Connecticut had become the main methods of keeping time. Clocks had revolu-

Advertisement for Stoves, 1856
The broadside advertisement represented an early effort to use the mass media to sell expensive household goods. Manufacturers gave romantic names to the various stove models, such as "Medallion" and "Black Warrior," pictured here, to appeal to prosperous urban families.

tionary effects, allowing people to organize themselves to meet the more intense pace of daily life produced by the Industrial Revolution.

Middle-Class Literature

During the 1840s and 1850s American democracy came to include a "democracy of print." Middle-class Americans provided a virtually insatiable market for books, magazines, and newspapers. By 1850 nine of ten adult white Americans could read, and millions bought books. Libraries were growing in both number and size. By 1860 there were over 50,000 public libraries, containing nearly 13 million volumes. Readers and libraries were, however, concentrated in the North. The books were no doubt the most forceful component of the new material culture of the northern middle class; they fostered a powerful sense of community and reinforced the values of individualism, self-control, and republican virtue.

The Industrial Revolution swept over American publishing, dramatically widening popular access to information. The Napier steam-driven press (1825) and the Hoe rotary press (1847) made it possible to mass-produce cheap books. Publishing houses in New York, Philadelphia, and Boston competed with each other, offering discounts to booksellers, advertising in magazines and newspapers, sending sales agents into the field, and recruiting authors the way manufacturers recruited engineers and designers. Between 1820 and 1850 American book publishers such as Harper Brothers and G. P. Putnam's Sons increased their annual sales from about $2.5 million to $12.5 million. The religious press also contributed to the explosion. Dozens of Bible societies (led by the American Bible Society, founded in 1816) and tract societies published more than 1 million Bibles and 6 million books, pamphlets, and magazines each year.

Irving and Cooper. Fiction constituted a large part of the literary consumption of middle-class Americans. America's first successful writers of fiction were Washington Irving and James Fenimore Cooper. In *The Sketch Book*, Irving painted unforgettable portraits of two characters who became part of American folk culture, Ichabod Crane and Rip Van Winkle. An equally celebrated fictional character was the frontier scout Leatherstocking in the novels of Cooper. Beginning with *The Pioneers* (1823) and *The Last of the Mohicans* (1826) and ending with *The Deerslayer* (1841), Cooper built an enormously popular legend around his hero. The key personality trait of Leatherstocking—or "Hawkeye," "Natty Bumppo," or "Deerslayer," as he was also known—was his solitude in nature. His moral goodness grew directly out of his "original relation" with nature. He was a radically free individual, at odds with law and custom and comfortable only in the forest, a model of American self-reliance and nonconformity. Cooper fashioned his hero to represent the nobility, innocence, and strength of frontier Americans. Preoccupied with defending American democracy to Europeans, Cooper struck a responsive chord in his American readers. Corresponding in popularity to Irving and Cooper among American poets was Henry Wadsworth Longfellow. Poems such as *Hiawatha* (1855) and *The Courtship of Miles Standish* (1858) used the American past and American settings in imaginative ballads infused with the themes of God, nature, and moral improvement. For most nineteenth-century Americans, Longfellow defined poetry.

Currier & Ives
By the 1850s the most popular prints showed idealized images of a prosperous rural life. This verdant scene, one of several entitled *Home, Sweet Home*, dates from 1869. The apparently unscathed Union soldier returns to a perfect home, an orderly oasis in the woods.

The Beecher Family: Cultural Innovators

The evangelical reform movements of the nineteenth century were led by powerful individuals with a highly developed sense of self. Prominent among them were the members of an extraordinary family—the Beechers. No family had a greater influence on business-class reform.

Born in New Haven, Connecticut, Lyman Beecher (1775–1863) studied theology at Yale University and as the pastor of churches in New York and Boston became a central figure in the Benevolent Empire. He published a best-selling book of sermons on temperance and helped found the American Bible Society. Married three times, Lyman had thirteen children, eleven of whom survived into adulthood.

Lyman paid close attention to the spiritual development of his children. He believed in the presence of original sin, and he expected each child to undergo a deep and intense conversion experience. Eventually all his children found Lyman's spiritual code too strict. But Lyman moderated a harsh Calvinist determinism by preaching that individuals were responsible for their own salvation. This approach to personal salvation helped most of his children develop a sense of individuality and self-confidence in their spiritual progress. And, in adulthoods inspired by Lyman's evangelical appeals to individual action, some of them turned from spiritual to worldly matters, embracing the belief that they were responsible for the moral welfare of others. Seven of Lyman's nine sons joined the ministry, and three of his four daughters became influential social reformers.

Lyman's most accomplished son was Henry Ward Beecher (1813–1887). A minister at the Congregationalist Plymouth Church in Brooklyn, Henry held audiences spellbound with sermons of hope and optimism.

The Beecher Family
Taken at the studio of the photographer Mathew Brady around 1859, this Beecher family portrait includes Lyman (center, seated) and nine of his children: his sons, from the left, Thomas, William, Edward, Charles, and Henry Ward, and his daughters, from the left, Isabella, Catharine, Mary, and Harriet.

He became noted during the 1850s for his denunciations of slavery as morally evil. However, his abolitionism was moderate. Although he believed that the system of slavery was sinful, he argued that individual slaveholders were not, and he worked, along with his father, to maintain church unity across sectional lines. Both he and Lyman embraced African colonization and the free-soil movement. Henry's flamboyancy and political influence, particularly within the new Republican party, increased in the 1850s.

None of the other six Beecher sons who became ministers were as influential or prosperous as Henry. They lived out their lives in the genteel poverty that was typical of the Protestant ministry in the nineteenth century.

It was the Beecher daughters who became cultural innovators—even celebrities. While Lyman's sons found legitimate and familiar channels for fulfilling their father's expectations, his daughters had to struggle to define their social roles. They had to innovate, working out their concern for the self-improvement of individuals within the family and for the reform of society. In the process they discovered ways of influencing the public beyond the limits imposed by women's separate sphere. But the Beecher daughters never agreed on a common agenda. The differences among them reflected the difficulties and ambiguities middle-class women generally experienced in finding their special mission.

Lyman's oldest daughter, Catharine (1800–1878), never married or had a home of her own and was often at odds with the rest of her family. Nonetheless, she became the nation's leading advocate on behalf of family life and a separate sphere in which women would draw on their superior moral authority. Her passion for educational reform extended beyond schools to the family. She led in the development of a popular self-help literature designed to inspire middle-class wives and mothers. In manuals and magazines Catharine Beecher taught middle-class women how to make their homes more efficient and more moral. To improve their homes, she argued, women had to first improve themselves with better health practices, physical activity, and diet. Catharine's *Treatise on Domestic Economy* (1841) was reprinted almost every year during the 1840s and 1850s, becoming the standard text on housekeeping, child-rearing, and self-improvement for women.

Harriet Beecher Stowe (1811–1896), after the death of her mother in 1816, was placed under Catharine's care and attended one of her model schools, the Hartford Female Seminary. She found Catharine overbearing and chafed under her surrogate mothering. Harriet broke away from her sister's dominance in 1836 when she married a minister, Calvin Stowe. Despite having five children in the first seven years of marriage, she managed to publish her first article for money in 1838 and her first volume of fiction in 1843. (She had two other children later.) She gradually discovered that she could earn an income that helped relieve the chronic financial problems that stemmed in part from Calvin's ill health. Hiring others to care for their children, she wrote *Uncle Tom's Cabin* in 1852. It brought her worldwide fame and made her one of the wealthiest authors in the world. In 1853 she took over the support of her family, including the management of its money. As her income grew during the 1860s and 1870s, she contributed to the support of her father and his third wife and sustained four of her adult children through a variety of financial difficulties.

In her novels Harriet popularized the same moral ideas that Catharine promoted. Her most successful novel, *Uncle Tom's Cabin*, carried the advancement of American family life into the realm of politics and the sectional crisis. She appealed to women as mothers to recognize how slavery destroyed family life and to use their moral authority to reform the nation.

Isabella Beecher Hooker (1822–1907), the youngest Beecher daughter, was the only one to challenge traditional assumptions of womanhood. Envying Harriet's fame, she became the leading advocate for women's rights in Connecticut, securing the passage of a bill giving property rights to married women in 1877. She joined the more radical New York branch of the suffrage movement and quickly assumed a leadership role. (The more moderate New England suffragists had named her half brother Henry as its president.) But she was ostracized from her family only in 1875, when she defended the editor Victoria Woodhull, a free-love advocate who had published an article charging Henry Ward Beecher with adultery. During the sensational trial that followed, Isabella attacked the double standard that condemned Woodhull but exonerated Henry. Harriet and Catharine insisted on their brother's innocence and felt that Isabella was unfaithful to the family. Isabella was bitter that the family did not appreciate her work for suffrage and women's rights.

Mary Beecher Perkins (1805–1900) was the most traditional of the daughters, remaining aloof from the reform impulses that gripped her three sisters. She particularly disapproved of Isabella but supported all of them by offering her Hartford, Connecticut, home as a refuge. Ironically, it was Mary's granddaughter, Charlotte Perkins Gilman (1860–1935), who spun the family's reform history in a radical direction. During the 1890s Charlotte left her husband and family to lead a liberated life and developed a powerful feminist argument for the economic independence of women.

Women Novelists. A group of women writers were even more popular. They, at least as much as Irving, Cooper, and Longfellow, defined a new American literature—and new American themes. In their writing they reinforced the values promoted by business-class evangelism.

Female writers contributed to a redefinition of the role of women in middle-class life. Women formed growing majorities in most religious congregations, and middle-class women in northern communities played increasingly important roles in reform movements. They were marrying later or not at all. They were having fewer children and employing two or three times as many servants by the 1860s as they had at the end of the Revolution. And they were prodigious readers, constituting a majority of the reading public. In the 1850s, according to the estimate of *Harper's Magazine*, four out of five readers of books or magazines were women. And women were writing many of those books and editing and filling the pages of magazines with stories and poems.

Novels by the leading women writers of the day often sold hundreds of thousands of copies in the North. Catharine Maria Sedgwick won wide popularity in the 1820s, as did Caroline Howard Gilman and Caroline Lee Hentz in the next decade. But the largest audiences were reached by Harriet Beecher Stowe in the 1840s and 1850s, and by Sara Parton, Augusta Evans Wilson, and Susan Warner in the 1850s. Their sentimental melodramas, often punctuated by tearful domestic scenes, shared an assumption that had become increasingly popular in America since the 1790s: women occupied a "separate sphere" with its own morality and possibilities.

The dominant message was that women could achieve their potential only within the sphere of marriage and the family. For women, as Hentz wrote in *Ernest Linwood* (1856), "In the depth of the heart there is a lower deep, which is never sounded save by the hand that wears the *wedding-ring*." In her last novel, *Married or Single* (1857), Sedgwick concluded that "God has appointed marriage" for woman; marriage is "the great circumstance" of a woman's life.

For these writers marriage did not imply a submissive or passive role; they were claiming a superior status for women within the sphere of family life. Women, they suggested, were ultimately responsible for forming the character of their husbands and sons. In *Means and Ends* (1839), Sedgwick wrote, "By an unobtrusive and unseen process, are the characters of men formed, at home, by the mother . . . where the moral basis is fixed."

The most successful woman novelist of the period was Harriet Beecher Stowe. *Uncle Tom's Cabin* (1852), which sold 350,000 copies in its first year, was not merely an antislavery novel but an extended discussion of the role of women and the family. Time after time,

women and even little girls are shown to be morally more sensitive than and superior to the men around them. In Stowe's portrayal of slave society it is women who offer the best hope of eventual freedom for slaves and of salvation for both African-Americans and whites. Home and family held deeply religious meanings for Stowe. In *The Minister's Wooing* (1859) she wrote that home was the "appointed sphere for woman, more holy than cloister, more saintly and pure than church and altar."

The commercial success of women novelists put an ironic twist on their celebration of the private sphere of marriage and family. These writers were actually engaged in a very public—and commercial—enterprise. They often began their careers writing under assumed names—almost always female names—but eventually dropped their anonymity. Bargaining with their publishers, often making their own livings, and even supporting their families, they were among the first successful professional women in the United States. Their success seemed to support Caroline Lee Hentz's judgment that "Mind, we verily believe, is of no sex."

These writers offered a new justification for the independent woman—a justification used by the increasing numbers of women who participated in religious congregations and reform organizations in the North. If talented and energetic women could find a way to give their unusual abilities a *moral* use, the contradiction between "domestic" and "public" life could then be softened. Given such a formula, women writers and their heroines could be seen as female versions of ministers. Stowe told her readers that she would make them feel "as if you had been hearing a sermon." Hentz spoke of her writing career as a legitimate calling, or "vocation . . . for which God has endowed me." These novelists, reaching a wide audience, encouraged northern middle-class women to attempt to improve both family life and society at large.

Education

A hallmark of the northern business class was its investment in young people. Parents who aspired to higher status and income for their children tried to provide them with a healthier environment, better food, basic academic skills, and the personal and social qualities appropriate to urban life. They spent more money educating their children, kept them in school longer, and devoted more attention to their upbringing.

The improvement of schools attracted the support of women. From Maine to Wisconsin women vigorously supported the movement led by Horace Mann to expand and standardize public elementary schools. During the 1840s and 1850s thousands of young middle-class women became teachers. Part of the reason was economic. Towns wanted to hire teachers at the lowest possible wages and began, especially after the Panic of 1837 had restricted public credit, to fill teaching positions with young women rather than men. School boards recognized both the rise in the number of women with schooling and the degree to which the lack of jobs for them had depressed their wages.

Teaching drew young women into its ranks through its moral appeal as well as its economic reward. The message of Catharine Beecher was the most powerful. Along with other members of her distinguished family, she was a powerful reformer of American culture. Beecher founded academies for young women in Hartford and Cincinnati in the 1820s and 1830s and became the intellectual leader of the thousands of young women who took teaching jobs. Her message to them was that women had a special calling in education. Because "to enlighten the understanding and to gain the affections is a teacher's business," and because "the mind is to be guided chiefly by means of the affections," she asked, "is not *woman* best fitted to accomplish these important objects?" To Beecher, "moral and religious education must be the foundation of national instruction" and education must be carried out by "energetic and benevolent women" (see American Lives, pages 400–401).

Family Planning and Population Growth

Northern families found the time and money to educate their children partly by limiting the size of their families. Families in cities and towns relied on primitive but moderately effective means of birth control: abstinence, coitus interruptus, condoms fashioned from animal skins and intestines, and abortions induced by potent herbs. Business-class families led the movement to restrict family size. They, more than families that owned little property, recognized the value of urban-based skills. More important, they did not feel a pressing need for their children to bring home wages or support them in old age. Rather, they felt pressure to buy new goods and, in order to purchase more goods, to restrict the number of children they had.

Some rural parents in long-settled agricultural areas of the Northeast also limited the size of their families. Farmers wanted to provide their children with ample land, which rising prices made more difficult to buy, or to prepare them for skilled urban employment. In frontier areas fertility rates declined more slowly. There, only the most highly mobile, disrupted families restricted family size. On the frontier, where the price of land remained low, the labor of children retained greater relative value.

As a consequence of the birth control practiced by northern families, the average size of an American family declined from 5.8 to 5.3 members (including adults)

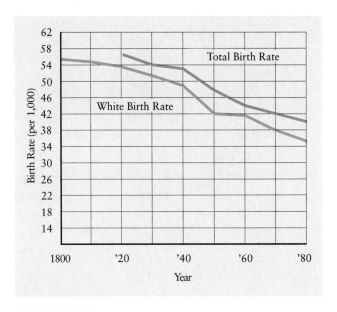

FIGURE 13.3

Birth Rate by Race, 1800–1880
Although American birth rates fell steadily from 1800 to 1880, the sharpest decline took place during the 1840s.

between 1800 and 1860. The national birth rate, however, continued to be high—from forty-five to fifty live births per thousand people per year, compared with thirty per thousand in Europe (see Figure 13.3). The vast majority of American parents, even in the Northeast, remained confident about their ability to provide for a large number of children.

The high birth rate and increasing immigration caused the American population to swell from 17 million in 1840 to over 31 million in 1860. By 1860 the American population exceeded the British in size and was about to overtake both the German and the French. The North dominated this demographic surge; between 1840 and 1860 the northeastern and Great Lakes states accounted for nearly two-thirds of the growth in the nation's population.

The Midwest

Most settlers moving to the West during the 1840s and 1850s migrated from New England and the Middle Atlantic states to the Old Northwest—Ohio, Indiana, Illinois, Michigan, and Wisconsin—and Missouri. Some pushed beyond the Mississippi into the fertile prairies of Iowa and Minnesota (see Map 13.2). This large geographical area became known as the Midwest. Migrants to the Midwest established wheat farms, settled the towns that serviced those farms, and built other, in-

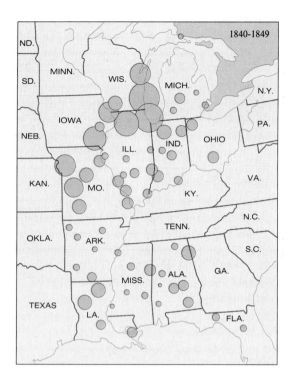

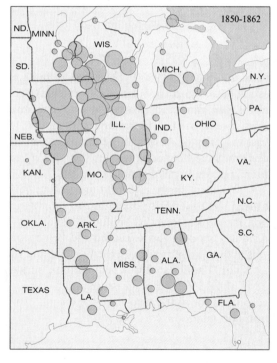

MAP 13.2

Western Land Sales, 1840–1862

Land offices continued to open up on the frontier to sell government land. Each circle centers on a land office, and the size of each circle depends on the relative amount of land sold at that office. During the 1840s and 1850s the tide of settlement shifted to the west and northwest into Indiana, Michigan, Iowa, Wisconsin, and Minnesota.

creasingly industrial towns. The demographic balance in the Midwest shifted dramatically in favor of settlers of northeastern rather than southern origin, and the growth of the Midwest dominated the growth of the West. By 1860 the westward movement had taken about half the nation's 31.4 million people west of the Appalachian Mountains (see Figure 13.4). But the great majority of westerners lived in the states of the Old Northwest (the "East Central North" states) rather than in Texas and the Old Southwest (the "East Central South" states).

Agriculture was buoyant in the Midwest, and it depended increasingly on the Northeast. Farmers relied on northeastern markets and on the products of industrial technology. The availability of low-cost labor-saving machinery quickened settlement, particularly on the fertile grain-producing prairies bordering the Great Lakes. John Deere's steel plow, superior in strength to the cast-iron plow, won widespread acceptance during the 1850s. In 1837, as a blacksmith in Grand Detour, Illinois, Deere had made his first steel plow from old saws; ten years later, in Moline, he opened a factory that used mass-production techniques. In addition, various companies—McCormick, Hussey, Atkins, and Manny—made reapers that grain farmers found invaluable. Previously, one worker with a cradle scythe had cut 2 to 3 acres a day. In the 1850s, with a self-raking reaper, a farmer could cut 12 acres daily. Largely because midwestern farmers had begun to use the products of modern factories in their fields, their productivity and incomes increased more than 20 percent during the 1850s.

The flow of cheap midwestern food stimulated the growth and productivity of northeastern communities. Midwestern wheat and flour enabled people in the Northeast to improve their diets. As a consequence, infants and nursing mothers became healthier and infant mortality declined. This helped keep the rate of population growth high in the Northeast despite the falling birth rate. Unskilled factory workers could not afford to share fully in the new agricultural bounty, but their diets also improved. Consequently, they were better able to endure the long hours of work that factories required. The "breadbasket" of the Midwest became vital to the health and productivity of the Northeast.

The Railroads. It was another product of industrial technology—the railroad—that cemented the union between the Northeast and the Midwest. As late as 1852 canals were still carrying twice as much tonnage as were railroads, but in the next five or six years track mileage increased dramatically. The new railroads included trunk lines that stretched across New York and Pennsylvania to provide through traffic from New York City and Philadelphia to Cleveland and Chicago (see Map 13.3). More convenient and faster than canals, the railroads had become the main carriers of freight by 1859.

FIGURE 13.4

Population by Region, 1820–1860 (as percentages of U.S. total)

Between 1820 and 1860 the most dramatic population growth took place west of the Appalachians. The population of the Northeast and the South Atlantic regions declined from 76 percent of the national total in 1820 to 50 percent in 1860.

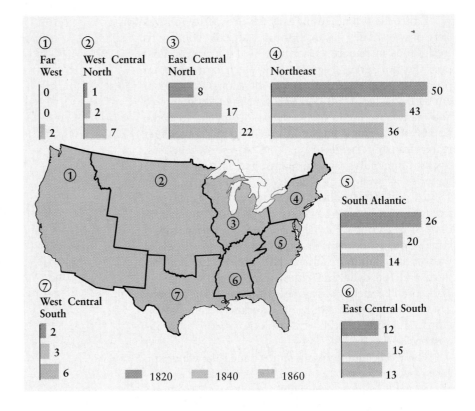

MAP 13.3

Railroads of the North and South, 1850–1860

The decade before the Civil War witnessed explosive growth in the nation's railroad network, but it was geographically uneven. The Northeast and Midwest acquired extensive, dense railroad systems that stimulated economic development. The South built a much simpler system. Numerous highly competitive companies built railroad lines, often using different track gauges that hindered the efficient flow of traffic and made the transshipment of goods slow and expensive. Such problems were frustrating to the military and proved especially severe in the South during the Civil War.

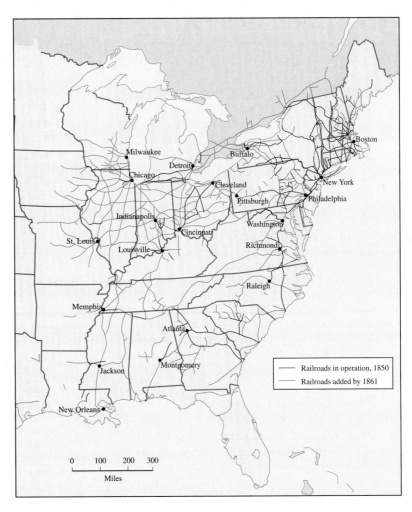

Railroads promoted midwestern prosperity in a variety of ways. They hastened the advance of people onto fresh lands in remote areas that canal and river transport did not serve. They made western farming more profitable by lowering the costs of transporting farm goods (see Map 13.4). And they promoted commerce and manufacturing in the Midwest. Springing up at the points where trunk lines converged or rail routes met water transport were grain storehouses, warehouses, docks, flour mills, packing plants, and farm machinery factories as well as mercantile and financial firms. In 1846 Cyrus McCormick moved his reaper production from western Virginia to Chicago to be closer to his customers. St. Louis and Chicago became boom towns largely because of the railroads. By 1860 they surpassed Boston and Baltimore in size and became the nation's third and fourth largest cities, respectively, after New York and Philadelphia. Taking advantage of the stationary steam engine, St. Louis and Chicago became major industrial centers with strong links to northeastern industrial centers and markets.

The trunk-line railroads undermined the economic base of western cities that had been key regional centers along water routes, especially Cincinnati, Pittsburgh, Buffalo, and Rochester. Thousands of dockworkers, teamsters, and warehouse workers in those cities lost their jobs when the railroads provided efficient through traffic. During the depression of the late 1850s many of those workers roamed the country in search of casual employment or charity.

Railroads also became a force in modernizing the iron industry, a critical component of northeastern manufacturing. This industry responded to the demand of railroads for high-quality iron. By 1860 the rail mills, which were located primarily in and around Philadelphia, were the largest and most technically advanced iron mills in the country. The engineering requirements for train engines had a similar effect on steam engine production. Moreover, to service complex locomotives, the railroads built a large network of machine shops that extended into the Midwest. The spread and expansion of these shops disseminated industrial skills and fostered the development of a skilled labor force.

Links of Culture. The migration of people and capital ensured that cultural links between the Northeast and the Midwest would follow the powerful economic ties despite the high degree of geographical mobility. In migrating westward, people who owned property or had skills faced formidable risks. They knew that in new communities, as in old ones, economic success depended heavily on the quality and strength of personal relationships. In the new communities throughout the Midwest the first residents with property and aspirations created networks among themselves. The first merchants, artisans, and professionals established loyal

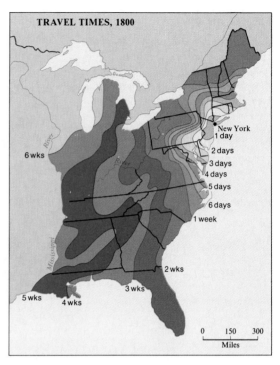

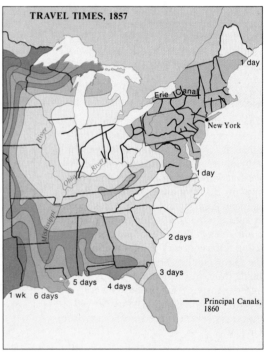

MAP 13.4

The New Mobility of Goods and People, 1800–1857

The transportation revolution dramatically decreased travel times by 1860. In 1800 a traveler from New York required an entire day to reach Philadelphia and a full week to reach Pittsburgh or western New York State. In 1860 a day on the railroad could take a New York traveler as far west as Cleveland. In a week the traveler could reach the Kansas Territory or the uppermost reaches of the Mississippi River.

clienteles, sound reputations, and good credit ratings. From this core came the leaders and prime beneficiaries of the Industrial Revolution. These people celebrated their success, becoming the greatest "boosters" of the new communities.

Later-arriving migrants sought out family members or established friends. Often wives corresponded with sisters, cousins, and old friends to identify communities where their families would find support. As a result, westward migrants usually moved to communities founded by people of similar backgrounds. New Englanders, for example, largely avoided the towns of the Ohio Valley that southerners had established and settled in newer places in northern Ohio, northern Illinois, and Wisconsin. And in their new communities migrants sought out familiar churches, fraternal lodges, crafts, and professions as places to form new friendships.

The first generations of community leaders became patrons of new migrants. They backed ambitious young men who had some education, skill, or family connections and helped them acquire skills or lent them money to start new businesses. Often they supported their daughters' decisions to marry industrious migrants. Many of the young men in turn scouted western opportunities for relatives still living in the East. Conversely, success in the new communities usually required membership in the stable core of local property owners. Through this mechanism the business class of the Midwest established powerful links with its members in the older towns and cities of the Northeast.

Conflict over the Trans-Mississippi West, 1844–1846

In the 1840s American territorial ambitions soared, reaching beyond the area of the Louisiana Purchase to encompass huge new chunks of the continent. Those ambitions meant that the United States could come into conflict with Mexico and Great Britain, the two nations whose territory or claims to territory could block American expansion to the Pacific. At the same time the South and the North came into conflict over the lands west of the Mississippi. Southern leaders recognized that the settlement of northerners in the Old Northwest had become more rapid than that of southerners in the Old Southwest and feared that if that trend extended west of the Mississippi, free states would outnumber slave states. Southern politicians launched a program of acquiring territory to protect slavery on their southern and western boundaries. This policy led the United States toward a war of conquest against Mexico. Ultimately, it put the South on a fateful collision course with the industrializing North.

Manifest Destiny

In the 1840s Americans, both southern and northern, developed a continental vision—captured by the term *Manifest Destiny*. It was coined in 1845 by John L. O'Sullivan, the editor of the *Democratic Review* and the *New York Morning News*, who wrote: "Our manifest destiny is to overspread the continent allotted by Providence for the free development of our yearly multiplying millions." O'Sullivan's vision was shared equally by southern imperialists who wanted to export slavery to new territories and by a northern business class that wanted to expand its dynamic mix of industry and agriculture.

Manifest Destiny expressed the romantic faith of Americans in their special mission to bind together nature, westward settlement, and political freedom. Virtually every aspect of mainstream American culture reinforced the imagery. Artists, for example, gave the message visual form. Thomas Cole (1801–1848) and Asher B. Durand (1796–1886), who started their careers as print engravers, established a national tradition of landscape art. They and their disciples, who were collectively known as the Hudson River School, along with the so-called Rocky Mountain painters, who began working in the 1850s, all viewed painting as a patriotic art—a visual expression of Manifest Destiny. As Philip Hone, one of Cole's patrons, remarked, "Every American is bound to prove his love of country by admiring Cole."

Although other terms had been used to describe the nation's expansionist spirit, Manifest Destiny precisely captured the mood of the 1840s and 1850s and became a permanent part of the American vocabulary. O'Sullivan left the geographical scope of Manifest Destiny vague; America's continental mission might encompass only Oregon, where Britain and the United States had conflicting claims, or it could include parts of Canada and follow the colonization of Texas as a model to reach all of Mexico and even the Caribbean islands.

O'Sullivan meant to imply that the United States had a divinely inspired mission to bring its neighbors, including Mexico, within the American democratic experiment. For behind the rhetoric of Manifest Destiny was cultural arrogance—the assumption of the cultural and even racial superiority of Americans. As "inferior" peoples were brought under American rule, they would be pushed to adopt American forms of government, convert to Protestantism, and learn from American teachers. This arrogance would long shape the nation's relationships with the rest of the world. Also behind the rhetoric of Manifest Destiny were the powerful economic motives that led Boston and New York merchants, southern planters, and small farmers throughout the nation to agree that the United States must expand to the shores of the Pacific.

The Great American Desert and Oregon Fever

By 1840 settlers had pushed westward into Texas, but few other Americans had crossed the 95th meridian. Beyond this north-south line, which lay not far beyond the western boundary of Arkansas and Missouri, stretched what most Americans called the Great American Desert. For fifty years mapmakers had put that label on the Great Plains because they believed the 1820 report of an army explorer, Major Stephen H. Long, who claimed that the entire area between the Missouri River and the Rocky Mountains was "almost wholly unfit for cultivation." This assumption led the federal government to regard the 95th meridian as a permanent frontier between white settlement and the Indian reservations that Andrew Jackson had carved out to the west.

For farmers who poured into the prairies of the Mississippi Valley from New England, New York, and Ohio in the 1840s and 1850s, the 95th meridian was not a meaningful barrier. They had plenty of room to settle in Wisconsin, Iowa, and Minnesota and did not feel overcrowded on the land until after the Civil War. However, for farmers who had filled in the best lands of Louisiana, Arkansas, Missouri, and the Ohio River Valley during the 1830s, the barrier was real. It forced those who sought new land to settle in Texas, which was still alien territory with an uncertain political future; to consider settling among the New Englanders, New Yorkers, and immigrants in the Midwest; or to cast their eyes beyond the Great Plains to the forested valleys of Oregon.

Oregon under Joint Occupation. The United States and Britain both had claims to Oregon. In 1818 a British-American convention had failed to resolve the dispute, establishing the Canadian-American boundary only as far west as the Rocky Mountains. But the convention provided that both British and Americans could settle anywhere in the Oregon Territory, which then stretched from the 42nd parallel in the south (the border with Mexico) to 54° 40' in the north (the border with Russian territory) (see Map 13.5).

Settlement had proceeded without conflict under the joint occupation agreement. The Hudson's Bay Company carried on a lucrative fur trade, while several hundred Americans, including a large group of Methodist missionaries, settled there during the 1830s. Most took up land south of the Columbia River, in the Willamette Valley, which was of little interest to the Hudson's Bay Company. Based on this settlement, the United States established a claim, unchallenged by the British, to the zone between the 42nd parallel and the Columbia River.

In 1842 American interest in Oregon increased dramatically. Navy lieutenant Charles Wilkes published widely circulated reports on his four years of Pacific explorations. He wrote glowingly of the potential harbors

he had found in the Strait of Juan de Fuca, Admiralty Inlet, and Puget Sound, which were of great interest to the New England merchants plying the China trade. Also in 1842 the first large party, over a hundred people, crossed the Oregon Trail, which fur traders and explorers had blazed through the Great Plains and the Rocky Mountains. Their reports told of a mild climate and fertile soil. This publicity and the beginnings of recovery in the rest of the nation from the depression that had followed the Panic of 1837 bred ambitious planning. "Oregon fever" suddenly raged.

The Oregon Trail. The following May a thousand men, women, and children gathered in Independence, Missouri, for the overland trek on what soon became known as the Oregon Trail (see Map 13.6). They were farming and trading families from Missouri, Ohio, Indiana, Illinois, Kentucky, and Tennessee; they had more than 5,000 oxen and cattle and over 100 wagons. With military-style organization and formations, they overcame flooding streams, dust storms, illness and death, insects and snakes, hunger and thirst, bruised feet and ruined clothes, overweight furniture and equipment, dying livestock, and encounters with Indians. (Most of those encounters, however, involved peaceful trade; over the life of the Oregon Trail fewer than 400 travelers died as a result of Indian attacks.) The trail was an ordeal for all, but women found it especially difficult. It

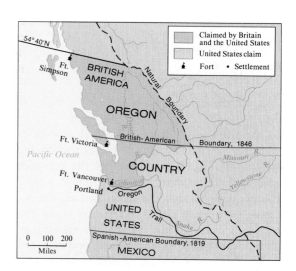

MAP 13.5

Territorial Conflict in Oregon
The American and British governments disputed whether the Oregon Territory should be divided along the Columbia River to include Ft. Vancouver or along the more northerly boundary that eventually divided the two countries. An agreement granting the citizens of each country equal access to Oregon enabled thousands of Americans to pour into the area.

MAP 13.6

Settlement of the Trans-Missouri West, 1840s
In the 1840s several trails carried settlers thousands of miles through unfamiliar and rugged terrain to the trans-Missouri West. Although greed and violence were common on the westward treks, cooperation, trade, and mutual assistance among migrants and with native Americans were more typical.

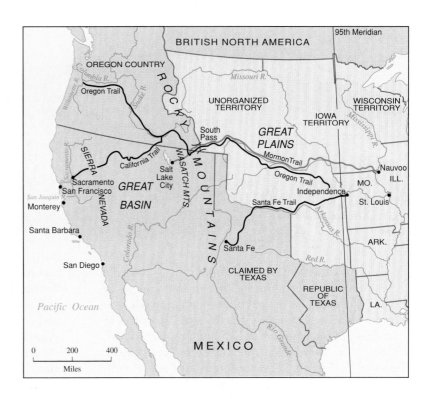

required them to submit to male discipline, add to their traditional chores the strenuous work of driving wagons and animals, and give up domesticity and female friends. After six months on the trail they reached the Willamette Valley—more than 2,000 miles across the continent. During the next two seasons another 5,000 people, still largely from the Ohio Valley, reached Oregon. By the Civil War some 350,000 people had attempted the Oregon Trail, heading for California as well as Oregon; some 34,000 died in the effort—about 17 deaths per mile. The walking migrants wore 3-foot-deep paths, and their wagons carved 5-foot-deep ruts across sandstone formations; the tracks are still visible in southern Wyoming well over a century later.

California. The land-hungry farmers streaming toward Oregon felt more secure settling in areas where the United States had staked out a claim, and they knew more about Oregon than about any other region in the Far West. However, about one in ten of the pioneers traveling the Oregon Trail turned left just past Fort Hall on the Snake River and struggled southward down the California Trail into Mexican territory. Almost all settled in the interior valley of the Sacramento River.

California had been the most remote corner of Spain's American empire, and Spain had been slow to develop its resources. In fact, Spain established a significant foothold there only in the late eighteenth century, when it built a system of missions and *presidios* stretching from San Diego to San Francisco (see Chapter 8). Almost immediately, in the 1780s, New England merchants began trading with the Spanish settlements in

California, largely for sea otter pelts that they carried to China. Their commerce increased after Mexico won its independence from Spain in 1822. At the same time, other American traders carried on a small but lucrative trade in gold, furs, and mules between Independence, Missouri, and Santa Fe, following the Santa Fe Trail.

To promote economic development, the new Mexican government welcomed Yankee traders to California. To the same end, it secularized the missions and promoted large-scale cattle ranching on former mission lands. Secularization also released the mission Indians, who numbered about 21,000 in 1821. Many left coastal communities for interior areas of California, where 200,000 Indians lived, but many others remained to become laborers, often in peonage on large *ranchos*. Some intermarried with the local *mestizos* ("mixed blood" Spanish-Indians). All of this meant prosperity to the New England merchants who brought hides and tallow from California ranchos home to the boot and shoe industry. To handle the business, beginning in the 1820s, New Englanders dispatched dozens of resident agents to the coastal towns of California. More often than not they fell in love with California, married into the families of the elite Mexicans—the *Californios*—became Catholics and Mexican citizens, and adopted the dress and manners of the *Californios*. A crucial exception was Thomas Oliver Larkin, the most successful merchant in Monterey. Larkin established a close working relationship with Mexican authorities and often lent them money but remained an American citizen and plotted for the peaceful annexation of Upper California. In 1843 he became the U.S. consul in California.

The Monterey Colonial House
Thomas O. Larkin's house, completed in 1837, represented the fusing of American and Mexican building traditions and set architectural fashions during the early 1840s for the American and Mexican elite in Monterey. The house combined eastern features, such as a symmetrical facade and a timber frame supporting an upper story, with adobe construction.

In contrast with most of the Americans who lived in the coastal towns of California, the settlers in the Sacramento Valley had no desire to assimilate into Mexican society. Their legal standing was tenuous. Most had received dubious land grants or had simply squatted without any title. They hoped to emulate the Americans in Texas by colonizing, extinguishing what they regarded as an inferior culture, and making California another example of the beneficent workings of Manifest Destiny. Their number grew swiftly, to about 700 in 1845, while the coastal population of 7,000 Mexicans, an uncounted number of Indians, and roughly 300 Americans remained stable.

Southern Imperialism

During the 1840s the South aggressively tried to protect slavery where it existed by extending it to new lands. Some planters wanted to make sure they did not run out of fertile land. Southern politicians also realized that every new free state in the West increased the threat of abolition by shifting power in Congress toward the North. Moreover, if the federal government did not protect slavery in the West, it would sanction what white southerners believed to be a denial of their rights as free Americans. They feared that if Congress failed to protect southern rights in the territories, it might not respect those rights within the states of the South.

Anxiety about the future of slavery in the West was nothing new. Southerners had pressed for the acquisition of Louisiana and Florida in order to gain new lands where slavery could expand. They had also cited the Monroe Doctrine to warn the British not to interfere with slavery anywhere in the Western Hemisphere. When Britain abolished slavery in the West Indies in 1833, southern planters feared that pressures for emancipation would release a wave of slave rebellions like Nat Turner's. The planters also were afraid that Britain would actively encourage abolition in the United States to undermine the American plantation economy and increase the international competitiveness of British plan-

tations in India and Egypt. Calhoun proposed that the British wished to abolish slavery in the United States and Brazil to "transfer the production of cotton, rice, and sugar etc. to her colonial possessions, and . . . consummate the system of commercial monopoly, which she has been so long and systematically pursuing." The annexation of Texas, which had declared independence in 1836, had offered an opportunity to avoid abolitionist containment of slavery, but both Andrew Jackson and Martin Van Buren had deflected this push in the interest of party and national unity.

During the 1840s the planters' worries intensified. They noted that in 1839 Britain, along with France, had intervened in Mexico to force it to pay its debts, and they heard rumors that Britain wanted California as payment. They saw evidence that Britain was encouraging Texas to remain independent, was expanding its involvement in Central America, and had designs on Cuba. It all seemed to add up to a grand scheme by the British to block American expansion by establishing an antislavery barrier from the West Indies through Mexican territory—a barrier sweeping from Texas all the way to California. The result, southerners feared, would be not only an end to economic opportunity but increasing pressure for emancipation in the South. A surrounding ring of free territory could provide bases for abolitionist raids on plantations and provide havens for runaway slaves.

The Election of 1844

Oregon fever opened the door for southern leaders who wanted to protect slavery through a program of territorial expansion. Suddenly, in 1843, northerners as well as southerners were calling for territorial expansion. This northern support for expansion finally made it possible for southern leaders to champion the annexation of Texas without threatening the unity of the Democratic party.

In 1843 Americans throughout the Ohio Valley and the Great Lakes states called on the federal government to renounce joint occupation and oust the British from Oregon. Democrats and Whigs jointly organized "Oregon conventions" throughout the Midwest. In July a bipartisan national convention demanded that the United States seize Oregon all the way to 54° 40' north latitude, the southern limit of Russian-controlled Alaska.

Meanwhile, President John Tyler, disowned by the Whigs, had joined the Democratic party in the hope of becoming its nominee in 1844. In 1843 Tyler settled on a program designed to please expansionists among both southern and northern Democrats: the annexation of Texas and the seizure of Oregon to the 54° 40' line.

As a first step toward annexing Texas, Tyler appointed Senator John C. Calhoun of South Carolina as secretary of state in 1844. Calhoun had rejoined the Democratic party because he feared the national economic program and abolitionist tendencies of the Whigs. Convinced that it was necessary to prevent British domination of the West, Tyler and Calhoun submitted an annexation treaty to the Senate in April. In July Calhoun brushed aside an offer from the British, now fearful of American hostility, to settle the Oregon question.

The treaty encountered opposition from two leaders with presidential ambitions in 1844: the Democrat Martin Van Buren and the Whig Henry Clay. Each feared alienating northern voters by supporting the annexation of Texas. At their urging, Whigs and northern Democrats united to defeat the treaty.

The Candidacy of James K. Polk. The economic issues that had dominated the presidential campaign of 1840 gave way to the issues of Texas and Oregon in 1844. The Democrats had great success in unifying their party on Texas. They passed over both Tyler, who had failed to win the trust of his adopted party, and Van Buren, whom southern Democrats despised for failing to support their position on Texas. Instead, they selected former Governor James K. Polk of Tennessee, a slave owner who was Andrew Jackson's personal favorite. Polk was unimpressive in appearance, but he was a man of iron will and boundless ambition for the nation. He and the Democrats called for the annexation of Texas and the taking of all of Oregon. "Fifty-four forty or fight!" became the war cry of his campaign.

The Whigs were less successful in uniting their party. They nominated Henry Clay, who once again championed his American System of internal improvements, high tariffs, and national banking. Throughout his campaign Clay was defensive about his opposition to the annexation of Texas. He finally suggested, but only hesitantly, that he might support annexation under certain circumstances. His position annoyed many southern Whigs, who were willing to bolt the party, sacrificing its economic program in return for the annexation of Texas. At the same time, Clay disappointed the thousands of northern Whigs who opposed any expansion of slavery. His waffling on Texas led them to support the Liberty party candidate, James G. Birney of Kentucky. Birney won less than 3 percent of the popular vote, but he might have taken enough votes from Clay to deprive Clay of the electoral votes of New York and Michigan, with which he would have won. That was the conclusion of Clay's supporters, who blamed his defeat on the desertion of both proslavery and abolitionist Whigs.

Polk and a Democratic majority in Congress were elected by voters who had accepted the argument of Tyler and Calhoun that the British were determined to block the expansion of the republic into Oregon and Mexico. Many Americans who might have otherwise opposed the extension of slavery had accepted Tyler and Calhoun's linkage of the Texas and Oregon issues and endorsed Polk's territorial ambitions. Thus, the strategy that Tyler and Calhoun devised and Polk implemented of uniting Democrats around expansion in Texas and Oregon had succeeded.

Congress Votes for Texas Annexation. Polk's victory led northern Democrats in Congress to reject Van Buren's leadership, close ranks with southern Democrats, and annex Texas even before Polk's inauguration. In February 1845 proannexation Democrats finessed the opposition of antislavery senators by approving annexation through a joint resolution, which required majority votes in both houses rather than the two-thirds Senate vote needed to ratify a treaty. Mexico challenged the legality of annexation—it had never recognized Texas's independence—and broke diplomatic relations with the United States. The continuing dispute with Mexico would soon give Polk the opportunity he sought to go beyond his party's 1844 platform and acquire New Mexico, Alta (Upper California), and perhaps more Mexican territory (see Chapter 14).

A Polk Political Banner, 1844
The "lone star" outside the group of twenty-six stars represents Texas. The banner was intended to leave no doubt about the importance of the annexation of Texas to Polk's presidential campaign.

Summary

During the 1840s and 1850s southern society became increasingly dependent on slavery. Planters exploited the system of slavery more aggressively as a source of profits and developed an elaborate defense of it in order to control slaves and guarantee the loyalty of non-slaveholding whites. In response to the cruel realities of slavery, which included harsh work routines and trading in human lives, slaves devised elaborate networks of family and community support. Outside the formal system of slavery in the South there was a large community of free African-Americans. They, as well as free blacks in the North, had second-class citizenship but helped keep alive the hope of freedom from slavery.

Meanwhile, industrialization tightened its hold on northeastern society by stimulating economic productivity, middle-class consumption, and business-class culture. Industrialization also promoted immigration, which accelerated during the 1840s and 1850s. Many of the new immigrants, especially those from Ireland, were poor and encountered a virulent anti-Catholic movement. Industrialization accelerated the settlement of the Old Northwest, helping to fill the land of the Great Lakes Basin and the prairies of the Mississippi Valley with people from the Northeast and stimulating the commerce and industry in new midwestern towns and cities. Settlers in the Midwest replicated the links among agriculture, community life, and industry that prevailed in the Northeast. In short, industrialization bound together the Northeast and the Midwest.

Both northerners and southerners agreed on the need for continued westward expansion and on the Manifest Destiny of continental expansion. Consequently, during the 1840s they embarked on great migrations across the Great Plains to British-American Oregon and to the vast territories of Mexican California. These migrations and the nationwide support they received created an opportunity for southern leaders such as John C. Calhoun to develop a program of expansion that promised to relieve anxiety over British and abolitionist threats to slavery. In 1844 James K. Polk won the presidency by promising to implement part of this program: annexing Texas and taking all of Oregon. Temporarily masked by national support for Polk's 1844 platform was the fact that the South's commitment to a slave-labor system had placed the region in direct competition with the North over the future of the West.

TIMELINE

1841	Catharine Beecher's *Treatise on Domestic Economy*
	James Fenimore Cooper's *The Deerslayer*
1842	Charles Wilkes reports on Pacific explorations
	Migration to Oregon begins
1843	Calhoun warns of a British conspiracy to block expansion
	Thomas Oliver Larkin becomes U.S. consul in California
	Oregon conventions organized
1844	Anti-Catholic rioting in Philadelphia
	Tyler appoints John C. Calhoun as secretary of state
	James K. Polk elected president
1845	Lowell Female Labor Reform Association formed
	Editor John L. O'Sullivan coins the term *Manifest Destiny*
	Texas admitted to the Union as a slave state
1846	Democratic Congress restores the Independent Treasury
	Walker Tariff passed
	Mexican War begins
	Cyrus McCormick opens Chicago factory
1847	Refugees from Irish potato famine arrive in large numbers
	Hoe rotary press introduced
1849	Cholera epidemics in cities
1850	A. J. Downing's *The Architecture of Country Houses*
1851	Crystal Palace Exhibition
1852	*Uncle Tom's Cabin*
1857	Economic panic begins depression
1858	Mason jar introduced
1859	Railroads carry more freight than do canals

★   ★   ★

BIBLIOGRAPHY

There are no general surveys of the social history of sections and sectionalism during the 1840s and 1850s; useful books on major aspects of the subject include Stuart M. Blumin, *The Emergence of the Middle Class: Social Experience in the American City, 1760–1900* (1989); Albert Fishlow, *American Railroads and the Transformation of the Ante-Bellum Economy* (1965); Robert W. Fogel, *Without Consent or Contract* (1989); David Alan Johnson, *Founding the Far West: California, Oregon, and Nevada, 1840–1890* (1992); James Oakes, *The Ruling Race: A History of American Slaveholders* (1982); and William R. Taylor, *Cavalier and Yankee: The Old South and American National Character* (1961).

The Slave South

The culture of the planter class and non-slaveholding whites can be explored in O. Vernon Burton, *In My Father's House Are Many Mansions: Family and Community in Edgefield, South Carolina* (1985), and Drew Gilpin Faust, *Southern Stories: Slaveholders in Peace and War* (1992). The best studies of women in southern slave society are Catherine Clinton, *The Plantation Mistress* (1983), and Elizabeth Fox-Genovese, *Within the Plantation Household: Black and White Women of the Old South* (1988). Efforts to connect southern culture with southern politics include George M. Frederickson, *White Supremacy: A Comparative Study in American and South African History* (1981), and J. Mills Thornton III, *Politics and Power in a Slave Society: Alabama, 1800–1860* (1978). On the nature of violence in southern society, see John Hope Franklin, *The Militant South 1800–1861* (1956), and Bertram Wyatt-Brown, *Southern Honor: Ethics and Behavior in the Old South* (1982).

On the role of family life and religion in helping African-Americans cope with the oppression of slavery, the pioneering studies were John W. Blassingame, *The Slave Community: Plantation Life in the Antebellum South* (1979); Eugene D. Genovese, *Roll, Jordan, Roll* (1974); Herbert G. Gutman, *The Black Family in Slavery and Freedom, 1750–1925* (1976); and Lawrence W. Levine, *Black Culture and Black Consciousness* (1977). More recent studies include Jacqueline Jones, *Labor of Love, Labor of Sorrow: Black Women, Work, and the Family from Slavery to the Present* (1986), and Deborah G. White, *Ar'n't I a Woman? Female Slaves in the Plantation South* (1985).

On slave revolts see Herbert Aptheker, *American Negro Slave Revolts* (1943); Stephen B. Oates, *The Fires of Jubilee: Nat Turner's Fierce Rebellion* (1975); Eugene D. Genovese, *From Rebellion to Revolution: Afro-American Slave Revolts in the Making of the Modern World* (1979); and Winthrop D. Jordan, *Tumult and Silence at Second Creek: An Inquiry into a Civil War Slave Conspiracy* (1993). On the ambiguous position of free blacks in slave society, see Ira Berlin, *Slaves without Masters: The Free Negro in the Antebellum South* (1974).

The Northeast and the Midwest

The economic changes in the North during the 1840s and 1850s can be studied in many of the economic history sources listed in Chapter 10.

On the sources and character of European immigration, consult Maldwyn Allen Jones, *American Immigration* (1960), and Philip Taylor, *The Distant Magnet: European Immigration to the U.S.A.* (1971). The most useful introduction to the nature of immigrant communities during the 1840s and 1850s is Oscar Handlin, *Boston's Immigrants: A Study in Acculturation* (1979). See also Kathleen Neils Conzen, *Immigrant Milwaukee, 1836–1860* (1976), and Bruce Laurie, *Working People in Philadelphia, 1800–1850* (1980).

No scholarly book surveys the development of middle-class society culture in the decades before the Civil War. Explorations of the relationship between women's roles and the development of popular literature include Ann Douglas, *The Feminization of American Culture* (1977), and Mary Kelley, *Private Woman, Public Stage: Literary Domesticity in Nineteenth-Century America* (1984). On birth control see Linda Gordon, *Woman's Body, Woman's Rights: A Social History of Birth Control in America* (1976), and James Reed, *From Private Vice to Public Virtue: The Birth Control Movement and American Society since 1830* (1978). On educational reform see Lawrence A. Cremin, *American Education: the National Experience, 1783–1876* (1980); Carl F. Kaestle, *Pillars of the Republic: Common Schools and American Society, 1780–1860* (1983); and Stanley K. Schultz, *The Culture Factory: Boston Public Schools, 1789–1860* (1973). On the Beecher family see Jeanne Boyston et al., eds., *The Limits of Sisterhood: The Beecher Sisters on Women's Rights and Woman's Sphere* (1988); Milton Rugoff, *The Beechers: An American Family in the Nineteenth Century* (1981); and Kathryn Kish Sklar, *Catharine Beecher: A Study in American Domesticity* (1973), which is a definitive biography.

Conflict over the Trans-Mississippi West

Manifest Destiny is treated in Norman Graebner, *Empire on the Pacific: A Study of American Continental Expansion* (1955); Reginald Horsman, *Race and Manifest Destiny: The Origins of American Racial Anglo-Saxonism* (1981); Frederick Merk, *Manifest Destiny and Mission in American History* (1963); and Albert K. Weinberg, *Manifest Destiny: A Study of Nationalist Expansionism in American History* (1935).

In recent years a number of books have opened up exciting new approaches to the history of western America. Leading examples of this scholarship include Patricia Nelson Limerick, *The Legacy of Conquest: The Unbroken Past of the Unbroken West* (1987); Clyde A. Milner II, *The Oxford History of the American West* (1994); Kevin Starr, *Americans and the California Dream, 1850–1915* (1973); David J. Weber, *The Mexican Frontier, 1821–1846* (1982); and Richard White, *"It's Your Misfortune and None of My Own": A History of the American West* (1991). This newer scholarship presents a more complete view of women in the West. See, for example, Susan Armitage and Elizabeth Jameson, eds., *The Women's West* (1987); John Mack Faragher, *Women and Men on the Overland Trail* (1979); Julie R. Jeffrey, *Frontier Women: The Trans-Mississippi West, 1840–1860* (1979); and Joanna L. Stratton, *Pioneer Women: Voices from the Kansas Frontier* (1981).

On the politics of expansion to the Pacific see William J. Cooper, *The South and the Politics of Slavery, 1828–1856* (1978); and Charles G. Sellers, *James K. Polk: Continentalist, 1843–1846* (1966).

John Brown (1800–1859)

Just before his hanging, John Brown wrote out a prophetic
message: "I John Brown am now quite *certain* that the crimes
of this *guilty land*: will never be purged *away*; but with Blood."

CHAPTER 14

Disrupting the Union
1846–1860

★   ★   ★

For nearly a generation after the Missouri Compromise in 1820 the two major parties succeeded in preventing the issue of slavery from polarizing the nation. They were able to do this even after the democratization of politics under the Second Party System and after a confrontation between evangelical abolitionism and the proslavery movement. The two parties devised programs that were *national* in appeal and built coalitions of groups and interests that were national in scope. Both parties struggled to avoid the slavery issue because they recognized its potential for fracturing the parties and the nation along sectional lines. In the early 1840s prospects for continuing to blunt the divisive potential of slavery seemed bright because abolitionism was stalled by the antiabolitionist movement and the split between Garrisonians and anti-Garrisonians.

The sectional arrangement of 1820 had survived into the 1840s for another reason as well: northern and southern societies had been able to expand into the West without appearing to threaten each other. But the Mexican War—and the acquisition of immense new territories in the West—changed everything.

After the Mexican War national politicians searched for a formula to resolve the status of slavery in the new lands, but their compromises became increasingly fragile as Americans took matters into their own hands. Abolitionists fought off slave catchers in northern towns, and free-soilers and defenders of slavery attacked each other in "Bleeding Kansas." When the radical abolitionist John Brown attempted to incite a slave rebellion, many southerners became convinced that only secession could protect their "peculiar institution."

The Mexican War and Its Aftermath, 1846–1850

Territorial expansion was the main goal of President James K. Polk, who had been elected on a platform that called for taking all of Oregon and annexing Texas. He and his administration were convinced that they had a national mandate for an even more ambitious and aggressive program of westward expansion. They believed that Americans wanted Polk to go beyond his party's 1844 platform and acquire additional lands—New Mexico, Alta (Upper) California, and perhaps even more of Mexico's territory. The war of conquest that followed brought huge new territories into the United States and doomed the Missouri Compromise as a means of reconciling the interests of the South and the North in the West.

The Mexican War, 1846–1848

Polk's Expansionist Program. Polk took office in March 1845 with the intention of completing the annexation of Texas and acquiring at least California and New Mexico from Mexico. Shortly after his inauguration Polk told his secretary of the navy that he regarded the acquisition of California to be as important as the "Oregon question." He would try diplomacy but was prepared to go to war if that failed. In April he sent a confidential agent to Mexico to see whether Mexico's government was willing to resume diplomatic relations and negotiate a settlement that would resolve differences over Texas and possibly even transfer California to the United States.

On July 4, 1845, Texas formally decided to join the United States but claimed that the Rio Grande was its western and southern boundary despite the fact that its boundary had never extended beyond the Nueces River under Spanish and Mexican rule and that the Mexican government had rejected the claim. Polk agreed with Texas, and to strengthen his hand in negotiations he ordered Brigadier General Zachary Taylor, an army veteran with almost forty years of service, to lead several thousand troops to occupy the disputed territory south of the Nueces. Taylor camped near the town of Corpus Christi, just south of the Nueces at its mouth (see Map 14.1). By October, Taylor had doubled his force, making it the largest concentration of American troops since the War of 1812.

In November, after learning that Mexico would receive an American minister, Polk dispatched a secret emissary to Mexico City. Polk instructed John Slidell to buy New Mexico and California and secure acceptance of the Rio Grande boundary for as much as $30 million and American assumption of the claims of American citizens against the Mexican government. But Slidell was instructed not to discuss the right of the United States to annex Texas and to make no deal that sacrificed the Rio Grande boundary. Mexico, however, rejected the legality of the American annexation of Texas and refused to see Slidell when he arrived during the first week of December. The central objective of the Mexican government was to maintain national honor and protect valuable lands from an aggressive neighbor. Mexican leaders hoped that the United States would become embroiled in a war with Britain that would divert it from its southwestern ambitions. But Mexico was prepared to fight if necessary.

The same week Slidell arrived in Mexico City, Polk unveiled a new policy toward Britain. In a bellicose State of the Union Message to Congress the president claimed that British intentions in the Pacific Northwest violated the Monroe Doctrine. Polk intended to drive the British from Oregon and discourage them from taking California, which they wanted as compensation for debts owed to them by Mexico.

Meanwhile, Polk advanced his plans to take Alta California. His strategy was to foment a revolution that would lead, as had been the case in Texas, to the creation of an independent republic and a request for annexation. In October 1845 Polk's secretary of state, James Buchanan, advised Thomas O. Larkin, the U.S. consul in the major port of Monterey, that the United States would protect Californians if they sought independence from Mexico. If the Californians "should desire to unite their destiny with ours," Larkin added, Americans would welcome them as "brethren." Larkin began a quiet campaign among leading citizens, including some powerful *Californios*, in the coastal settlements to win support for a peaceful shift of sovereignty. However, Polk also prepared for war. He sent secret orders for John Sloat, the commander of the U.S. naval squadron in the Pacific, to seize San Francisco Bay and California's coastal towns if Mexico declared war on the United States. And Polk followed the activities of a young army officer, Captain John C. Frémont, who, under War Department orders, had struck out from St. Louis and marched deep into Mexican territory in the spring of 1845 with an "exploring" party of heavily armed soldiers. Frémont later wrote that "in arranging this expedition, the eventualities of war were taken into consideration." In December 1845 he reached California's Sacramento Valley and received permission from the Mexican commander in Monterey to winter in California if he stayed away from the coastal communities. In March, however, Frémont engaged in a show of force, even building fortifications near Monterey. But when Mexican authorities threatened to fight and Larkin warned Frémont that conflict would ruin the chances for the peaceful acquisition of California, he withdrew across the Oregon border.

In January 1846, when Polk learned of the failure of Slidell's mission, he increased the military pressure on Mexico. In the disputed territory between the Rio

MAP 14.1

The Mexican War, 1846–1848

This map shows the major military expeditions that seized the northern frontier of Mexico and occupied Mexico City. In the last phase of the war, as Winfield Scott assembled an invasion army off the coast of Mexico, Santa Anna tried to take advantage of the division of American forces by attacking the army of Zachary Taylor. At Buena Vista (February 1847) Taylor's smaller forces repulsed Santa Anna, who had to return to defend Mexico City. Scott's most significant victory in his march on Mexico City came in the mountains, at Cerro Gordo.

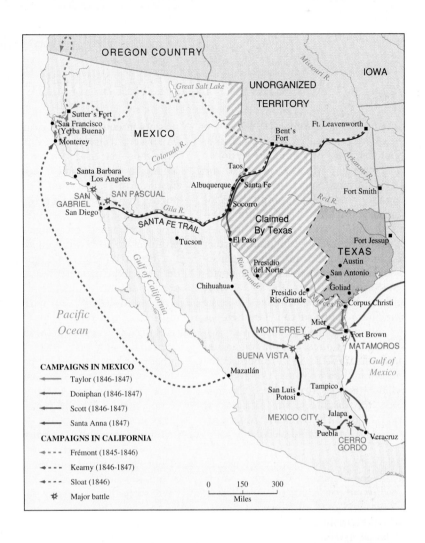

Grande and the Nueces, Polk created an incident designed to insult the Mexicans by sending General Taylor southward to establish a fort near the Rio Grande. As Ulysses S. Grant, a young officer serving with Taylor, said much later, "We were sent to provoke a fight, but it was essential that Mexico should commence it." Also, Secretary of State Buchanan sent secret orders to Frémont, which reached him in Oregon in May. Frémont destroyed the orders, along with a letter from Thomas Hart Benton, an expansionist senator from Missouri who chaired the Committee on Territories. The precise contents of the communications from Washington are unknown, but Frémont marched back to California and established a base near Sacramento. He later described his return as "the first step in the conquest of California."

News of skirmishing between Mexican and American forces near the Rio Grande reached Polk in early May. On May 9 he delivered a war message he had drafted long before, saying that Mexico "has passed the boundary of the United States, has invaded our territory, and shed American blood upon the American soil." Congress declared war four days later, and that action was followed by large, almost hysterical demonstrations of support across the nation. An editorial in the New York *Herald* declared that the war would "lay the foundation of a new age, a new destiny, affecting both this continent and the old continent of Europe."

Meanwhile, Polk worked to avoid a simultaneous war with Britain, even though that meant betraying his promise to northern Democrats. He recommended that the Senate adopt the British proposal to divide the Oregon country at the 49th parallel. The Senate agreed, ratifying the Oregon Treaty on June 15, 1846. (In 1848 Congress organized the Oregon Territory, and in 1859 it admitted the state of Oregon to the Union.)

The War in California. In June 1846 the Americans in the interior, although unaware of the formal state of war between the United States and Mexico, staged a revolt and captured the town of Sonoma with the support of Frémont's forces. Frémont did not have formal authority to take California, so he prevented the rebelling Americans from flying the Stars and Stripes. The Americans designed a crude flag displaying the strongest animal in California and proclaimed the Bear Flag Republic on July 4. Commander Sloat, knowing that hostilities with Mexico had broken out south of the Nueces, landed 250 marines and seamen in Monterey. He declared that California "henceforward will be a portion of the United States" and raised the American flag.

Captain Franklin Smith

Behind the Lines in the Mexican War

Captain Franklin Smith (1807–?) was the quartermaster for the First Mississippi Regiment of volunteers stationed in Carmargo, Mexico, in 1846 and 1847. Carmargo, just south of the Rio Grande, was a major supply base for Zachary Taylor's army. Smith organized supply trains sent from Carmargo to Monterrey and points farther south; he followed and at times participated in a bitter guerrilla war in northern Mexico between the U.S. Army and the Mexican rancheros. After the war Smith returned to a law practice in Canton, Mississippi. Little is known about his life there except for an unsuccessful effort in 1855 to publish the journal he had kept in Carmargo. He believed his descriptions of "the miseries, the disgraces, the infamies of war" might help persuade Americans to find a way to avoid a civil war.

October 3d, 1846. In the evening Col. Redd commanding [sic] the Georgia Cos. [volunteer companies] called at my tent and took supper with me. He is a young man about 23 gallant and brave as a lion. . . . He thinks now they [the Mexicans] are learning to shoot better and from late indications are united and patriotic, he thinks the fighting has just commenced. He says it is his intention not to trouble Genl. Patterson with prisoners—but hang all Mexicans who give him battle here to Monterrey or present themselves in hostile array. I told him I thought he ought not to hang but if he killed them that hanging would have a tendency to arouse the spirit of indignation and produce probably a rise en masse.

January 19th, 1847. America was designed to be the defender not the oppressor of man—An asylum for truth, justice, and liberty! And whenever she forgets the old reading and her early teachings and begins a career of conquest and dominion . . . which will end in her overthrow. . . . Our liberties may prove unsafe in our own hands (God grant they may not) but one thing is certain they would be very unsafe in the hands of the Mexicans. We should therefore whip the Mexicans first and then examine the ancient land-marks of our constitution and the principles of our Revolution and see how far we have strayed . . . from the line of Right.

January 29th, 1847. Had these people [the Mexicans] sense they would desire to have the laws of the American Union extended over them to shield them from Robbers, their own government and the Comanches to whose inroads in turn they are perpetually exposed. . . . But . . . their hatred to the Americans is deep seated. Those who have joined us will become outcasts—with the great mass hatred to Americans will become an inheritance from father to son. I believe if this war is continued beyond May rivers of blood will flow before it ceases while thousands and tens of thousands of our brave men will perish . . . one thing I am satisfied that the longer the war lasts the more national it will become and the more will disappear the prospect of the two races ever living together in harmony.

January 31st, 1847. The Col. then gave orders to burn the Ranche which consisted of one dwelling-house main ranche, one out house as a kitchen, and one other out house filled with corn shucks, fodder, and wool—This was a proper order. The Ranche was undoubtedly the head quarters of the Robbers. . . . The main building contained lances, escopettes [short muskets], swords, pistols, and all the appliances of war.

Source: Joseph E. Chance, ed., *The Mexican War Journal of Captain Frank Smith* (Jackson: University Press of Mississippi, 1991), 31–32, 157, 179, 196, 199–200.

American forces quickly moved to gain control of New Mexico and all of California. A small army under General Stephen Kearney captured Santa Fe without opposition in August and then marched on to California. By autumn Frémont and Commodore Robert F. Stockton, who had assumed command of the U.S. forces in California, seemed to have subdued the province. But in the southern part of Alta California the Mexicans mounted stiff resistance, driving the Americans from Los Angeles and winning a victory over Kearney's forces at the Battle of San Pascual outside San Diego. Only reinforcements under Stockton turned the tide, allowing Kearney and Stockton to retake Los Angeles in a decisive battle at the San Gabriel River. By mid-January 1847 the combined American forces had also captured San Francisco, Santa Barbara, and San Diego. In his diary, Polk wrote that he would accept no treaty that failed to cede New Mexico and California to the United States.

Across the Rio Grande. On May 1, even before Congress declared war, Zachary Taylor's army moved decisively toward the Rio Grande. After two bloody battles in which the outnumbered American forces displayed their great advantage in artillery, Taylor crossed the Rio Grande and occupied Matamoros. On September 25, 1846, after a fierce six-day battle, Taylor took the interior town of Monterrey (see American Voices, above). In

November a U.S. naval squadron in the Gulf of Mexico seized Tampico, Mexico's second most important port, as a base for an inland assault. In December another force, under Colonel Alfred A. Doniphan, set out on a 600-mile march south from Santa Fe toward Chihuahua, which it took in March 1847. By the end of 1846 the United States controlled a long line across northeastern Mexico.

Polk expected that the Mexicans, having lost large territories and with no chance of winning Britain as an ally, would sue for peace. But he had underrated Mexican national pride and strength. Under the leadership of General Antonio Lopez de Santa Anna, who was elected president in December 1846, Mexico refused to agree to a peace, let alone a cession of territory. Polk, supported by Winfield Scott, the commanding general of the army, decided to strike deep into the heart of Mexico. In November 1846 Polk decided to send Scott to storm the port of Veracruz and advance 260 miles inland to Mexico City. But while Scott gathered his forces, a large Mexican army under Santa Anna attacked the depleted units of Zachary Taylor at Buena Vista on February 22, 1847. The outcome was uncertain and the fighting was intense, but superiority in artillery enabled Taylor to eke out a victory and hold the American line in northeastern Mexico.

In March 1847 Scott captured Veracruz. Leading Scott's 14,000 troops were talented West Point officers who would become famous in the Civil War: Robert E. Lee, George Meade, and P. G. T. Beauregard. Scott then boldly moved his army inland. Well-read soldiers realized that they were following the route of Cortés's Spanish conquerors three centuries earlier and even looked

Mexican War Volunteers, 1846
This daguerreotype by an unknown photographer shows volunteers from Exeter, New Hampshire, preparing for war. When news of Zachary Taylor's victories reached most towns, men scrambled to volunteer before the war was over. In New York, Herman Melville wrote that "people here are all in a state of delirium. . . . Nothing is talked of but the 'Halls of the Montezumas.'"

for the locations of Cortés's battles. Scott's forces persistently outflanked the enemy during a 7,400-foot climb over rugged terrain. At Cerro Gordo his troops crushed Santa Anna's attempt to block their march, although both armies suffered heavy casualties. On August 20, at the Battle of Churubusco, near Mexico City, Santa

Street Fighting in Monterrey, 1846
The taking of Monterrey, which Spain's troops had been unable to capture during Mexico's war for independence, was a bloody affair of house-to-house fighting. Americans, however, immediately romanticized it. This is a typical lithograph of the day, picturing soldiers fighting in what seems to be a medieval setting.

Anna lost more than 4,000 of the 25,000 soldiers in his army while Scott's forces, which casualties and garrison requirements had already reduced to 10,000, sustained 1,000 casualties. Scott finally seized Mexico City on September 14, 1847, and a new Mexican government had no choice but to make peace.

National euphoria had accompanied the early phase of the war, peaking with Taylor's occupation of Matamoros. Many Americans initially viewed the war as a noble struggle to promote republican ideals in the spirit of the American Revolution. A U.S. victory, they believed, would secure American institutions in the West and free Mexico from a corrupt, weak regime that might fall under the influence of ambitious European monarchies. And at the end of the war, whatever they thought about its goals, even more Americans agreed with Polk's judgment that the war had demonstrated that a democratic republic could fight a foreign war "with the vigor" characteristic of "more arbitrary forms of government."

A few Whigs, such as Charles Francis Adams of Massachusetts and Joshua Giddings of Ohio, called "conscience Whigs" because of their antislavery views, had denounced the war from the start as part of a proslavery conspiracy. Most Whigs, however, had participated in or at least tolerated the national enthusiasm for the early phase of the war. But by the time news of Scott's victory in Mexico City reached Washington, the nation was badly divided over its war aims, and Whig opposition had become stronger and bolder.

Whig leaders in the North were ready to move toward antislavery positions partly because their championing of Henry Clay's American System no longer seemed to help them win national elections. In July 1846 Polk and the Congressional Democrats acted on their belief that they had a popular mandate not only to pursue territorial expansion but also to overturn the American System. They restored the Independent Treasury (see Chapter 11) and passed the Walker Tariff, which dramatically reduced tariffs and paid only lip service to the principle of protectionism. The Walker Tariff paralleled Britain's repeal of the Corn Laws (tariffs on imported bread grains) in the same year and seemed to herald the adoption of free trade throughout the Anglo-American world. Trade and tariff revenues were so buoyant that the Polk administration did not have to raise taxes to pay for the war. Existing taxes funded more than 60 percent of the $100 million of wartime costs, and borrowing covered the rest. After the war the continued robustness of customs duties enabled the federal government to pay off nearly all its Mexican War debts by the time of the Civil War. Demoralized by the popularity of the Polk administration's economic programs, Congressional Whigs lost their enthusiasm for campaigning on the American System.

Northern Whigs who were critical of the Mexican War drew confidence from the elections of 1846, which gave their party control of Congress, and increasing numbers of northern Whigs began to agree with the conscience Whigs. Additional slave states in the West might jeopardize the expansion of free agriculture and assure control of the federal government by the Democratic representatives of planters and immigrants. They grew more vocal as the casualties mounted, particularly during the bloody march to Mexico City. Of the 92,000 Americans who bore arms during the war, over 13,000 were killed or died of disease. After Taylor's victory at Buena Vista, the House passed a resolution thanking him—but not until the Whigs had amended it to declare that the war had been "unconstitutionally and unnecessarily begun by the President."

The Wilmot Proviso. It was a Democrat, however, who had devised the most disruptive way of opposing the war. On a warm August evening in 1846, David Wilmot, a congressman who was trying to broaden his base of support in his Pennsylvania district, proposed a simple amendment to a military appropriations bill: slavery would be prohibited in any territory acquired from Mexico. This provision, known as the Wilmot Proviso, quickly became the rallying point for northerners who feared the expansion of slavery into the West.

The Wilmot Proviso gained strong bipartisan support from northern Democrats as well as Whigs, particularly after Scott's costly invasion of Mexico. In the House a minority of Democrats, including key supporters of Martin Van Buren, joined forces with most Whigs to pass it on several occasions, but the predominantly southern, more proslavery Senate killed it each time. The legislatures of fourteen northern states passed resolutions urging their senators to vote for it.

Meanwhile, the most fervent expansionists among the Democrats became even more aggressive. They argued that the rising cost of the war meant that the nation should enlarge its war aims. The national Democratic party leaders—Polk, Secretary of State Buchanan, and senators Stephen A. Douglas of Illinois and Jefferson Davis of Mississippi—all wanted the United States to take at least part of Mexico south of the Rio Grande.

That goal put the Democratic leadership at odds with the vocal antislavery minority of northeastern Democrats and many midwestern Democrats, who were already disappointed that Polk had failed to acquire more of Oregon. Moreover, a few southern Democratic leaders worried that the Mexican people would oppose slavery; that the United States could not absorb the Mexicans, whom they regarded as an "inferior" people; and that prolonging the war dangerously risked augmenting the power of the federal government. This group included John C. Calhoun, who supported the taking of only Alta California and New Mexico, the most sparsely populated areas of Mexico.

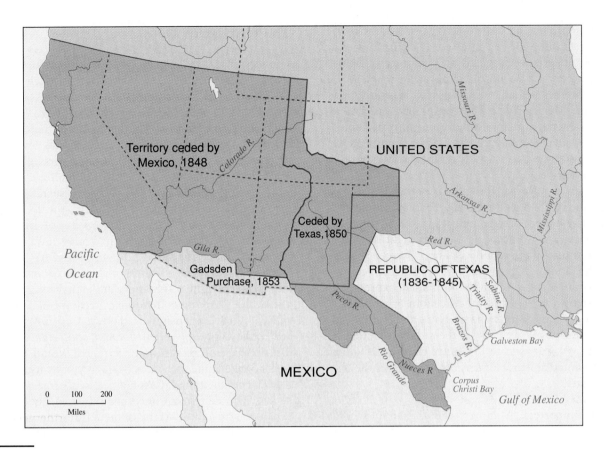

MAP 14.2

The Mexican Cession
The Mexican cession encompassed an area that includes not only California, almost all of New Mexico, and more than half of Texas but also Nevada, Utah, most of Arizona, and parts of Wyoming, Colorado, Kansas, and Oklahoma. After Mexico ratified the Treaty of Guadalupe Hidalgo, Polk told Congress that the new territories "constitute of themselves a country large enough for a great empire, and their acquisition is second in importance only to that of Louisiana in 1803."

Treaty of Guadalupe Hidalgo. Once again, as during the administrations of Jackson and Van Buren, the president put the interests of party unity foremost. He and Buchanan retreated from their early support of "All Mexico" and backed Calhoun's policy. Moreover, Polk wanted to make certain that hostilities were over and achieve a settlement with Mexico well before the elections of 1848. Consequently, Polk endorsed the Treaty of Guadalupe Hidalgo (February 2, 1848), in which the United States promised to pay Mexico $15 million in return for more than one-third of the territory of Mexico: Texas north of the Rio Grande, New Mexico, and Alta California (see Map 14.2). In addition, the United States also agreed to assume all the claims of its citizens, totaling $3.2 million, against the Mexican government. The Senate quickly ratified the treaty in March 1848.

The Polk administration had gained northern Mexico, as well as Texas and Oregon, without sacrificing party unity. But now the nation faced an even more contentious issue: What would be the future of slavery in the newly acquired territory?

The Free-Soil Movement

The Wilmot Proviso energized those abolitionists who had been seeking a political, legislative solution to the problem of slavery. After the defeat of the Liberty party in 1844, its founders had relaxed even further the intensity of their moral demands, deemphasizing the natural rights of slaves. In the Wilmot Proviso the political abolitionists further recast abolitionism, defining the problem of slavery not as an individual sin but as a threat to republican institutions. This new approach had the desired effect: the Wilmot Proviso was the first proposal that attracted broad popular support to the antislavery movement.

Between 1846 and 1848 antislavery leaders redefined their position. They stressed that there was a tyrannical "Slave Power" conspiracy composed of southern planters and those northern business people who depended on them. That conspiracy had produced, they claimed, the Mexican War. The conspiracy was said to draw its strength from an absolute control over human beings that endangered the republic. To defeat the Slave Power it would be necessary to prohibit slavery in the national territories.

The new antislavery program became known as *free soil*, and in 1848 its proponents reorganized the old Liberty party under a new name, the Free Soil party. Its platform promised to keep the West, thought to be the key to the future of the republic, pure of slavery and secure for freedom. The Free Soil party retained an enthusiasm for individual freedom but ultimately expressed a greater interest in protecting the freedom of whites occupying new lands than in championing the freedom of slaves. That shift of emphasis led the radical abolitionist William Lloyd Garrison to denounce the free-soil doctrine as "whitemanism," a racist effort to make the territories white.

Free-Soil Supporters. Although many Americans did not believe that slave owning was sinful or that African-Americans deserved equality, they could be convinced that slavery threatened liberty and economic opportunity for white people in the West. Those conservative supporters dominated the free-soil movement, but there were radical supporters as well. Despite Garrison's hostility, the new political approach won the support of many women abolitionists, who were denied the political rights that white men enjoyed. Women in the American and Foreign Anti-Slavery Society established dozens of new female societies throughout the Great Lakes states to work for free soil.

Frederick Douglass was also a major supporter of free soil. He had emerged during the 1840s as a leading antislavery strategist, the most electrifying of all abolitionist orators, and the foremost African-American abolitionist (see American Lives, pages 424–425). Douglass was unhappy with the Free Soil party's racism and watered-down platform with regard to slavery and free blacks; he urged free-soilers to pay greater attention to emancipation in the South and civil rights for African-Americans in the North. But Douglass and many other radical abolitionists, both black and white, reluctantly decided that supporting the growing free-soil movement was the only sensible political choice. They believed that the terror used to maintain slavery would ultimately require a violent confrontation between slavery and freedom, and they felt that the free-soil movement was the only viable way to provoke it. In short, free soil had radical dimensions in that it threatened both slavery and the Second Party System.

The Election of 1848

The sectional divisions among Democrats that had surfaced during the Mexican War affected the election of 1848. Free-soil and midwestern Democrats unhappy with Polk's Oregon treaty probably would have forced their party to dump Polk in the 1848 election. But before that could happen an exhausted Polk, who had worked from dawn late into the night throughout his presidency, declined to run; he would die three months after leaving office (see Table 14.1). In search of a replacement who could unify the party, the Democrats nominated the dull Senator Lewis Cass of Michigan. Cass was an expansionist who had advocated the purchase of Cuba, the annexation of Mexico's Yucatan Peninsula, and the acquisition of all of Oregon. In an effort to keep both southerners and northerners in the party, the Democrats left their platform deliberately vague on the expansion of slavery. Cass promoted a new policy concept called *popular sovereignty*. Under this policy, each territorial government would have the right to determine the status of slavery in its territory.

The nomination of Cass did not satisfy free-soil Democrats, who demanded unambiguous opposition to the expansion of slavery. Many of them threw their support to the newly formed Free Soil party. To win Democratic votes, the Free Soil party nominated Martin Van Buren for president. Though still a Democrat, he ran out of a combination of idealism and vindictiveness. He had converted to free-soil beliefs and to support of the Wilmot Proviso, but he also wanted to punish southern Democrats for denying him the nomination in 1844. The Free Soil party appealed to Whigs by nominating Charles Francis Adams, the son of John Quincy Adams, for vice-president. Adams had inherited many of the conscience Whig supporters of his father, who died in 1848 after distinguished service as an antislavery congressman from Massachusetts.

The Candidacy of Zachary Taylor. The division among Democrats created an opportunity for the Whigs, who did their best to suppress their own sectional disputes. Whig leaders avoided adopting a specific platform, even though northern Whigs generally supported the Wilmot Proviso. The Whigs nominated General Zachary Taylor. The fact that he came from Louisiana and owned a hundred slaves was less important to northern Whigs than his vagueness on the issue of slavery in the territories and his popularity throughout the nation. Known as "Old Rough and Ready," Taylor possessed a common touch that had won him the affection of his troops and made him the greatest hero of the Mexican War. Numerous biographers described him as a "natural" American leader. "Our Commander on the Rio Grande," wrote Walt Whitman, "emulates the Great Commander of our revolution"—George Washington.

TABLE 14.1

American Presidents and the Sectional Crisis, 1841–1861

	Term in Office	Party	Fate
William Henry Harrison	1841	Whig	Died in office
John Tyler	1841–1845	Whig	Broke with Whig party
James K. Polk	1845–1849	Democrat	Did not seek second term; died three months after leaving office
Zachary Taylor	1849–1850	Whig	Died in office
Millard Fillmore	1850–1853	Whig	1852 Whig nomination won by Winfield Scott
Franklin Pierce	1853–1857	Democrat	1856 Democratic nomination won by James Buchanan
James Buchanan	1857–1861	Democrat	Democratic party split, nominating Stephen Douglas and John Breckinridge

The tactic of running a military hero worked for the Whigs, just as it had when Harrison had run in 1840. Taylor won the election with 47 percent of the popular vote and 163 electoral votes against Cass's 42 percent and 127 electoral votes. Taylor carried seven free states but was stronger in the South, where he won 51 percent of the popular vote and carried eight states, or nearly two-thirds of that region's electoral votes. In the North the Free Soil party of Van Buren and Adams made a strong showing, receiving over 290,000 votes, more than 10 percent of the total. The Free Soil party drew voters away from both Taylor and Cass in the North but hurt the Democrats more than it hurt the Whigs. Van Buren received about 14 percent of the northern vote and might have taken enough votes from Cass in New York to cost Cass the state and the national election.

The swift growth of the Free Soil party and the popularity of the Wilmot Proviso left southerners—both Whigs and Democrats—stunned and fearful. Slave owners became even more aggressive in seeking the expansion of slavery, demanding more explicit commitments from the two major parties. Consequently, in the future the two national parties would have difficulty maintaining ambiguity on the status of slavery in the territories.

Alternatives to the Wilmot Proviso

The election of 1848 persuaded virtually all southern politicians that they could not win support that was national in scope for their territorial ambitions. They also realized that they would have to secure a future for slavery in territory already acquired as well as in new acquisitions from Mexico or Cuba. After the election they concentrated on meeting the challenge of the Wilmot Proviso by trying to establish slavery firmly in the territories taken from Mexico. They advocated three different approaches to achieve that objective.

Calhoun's "Common Property" Doctrine. John C. Calhoun put forward the most extreme position—explicit support for the spread of slavery into federal territories. He held that Congress had no constitutional authority to regulate slavery in the territories and thus could not exclude slavery from a territory prior to admission to statehood. According to Calhoun's common property doctrine, the citizens of any state had the same rights as the citizens of any other state to take their property into areas owned commonly by the states. His argument won support from many Democrats and Whigs in the Deep South but repelled too many northerners in both parties for it ever to win much support in Congress.

Extending the Missouri Compromise Line. Most southern leaders in both parties advocated or were willing to accept a more moderate position: an extension of the Missouri Compromise line through the Mexican cession (the territory purchased from Mexico) to the Pacific coast. This proposal would guarantee slave owners access to at least some western territory, particularly southern California; would remove the antislavery threat from the Deep South's western boundary; and would almost certainly add slave states to the Union. This approach even appealed to some northern Democrats. Buchanan and Douglas, for example, hoped the offer to prohibit slavery in northern territories would prevent free-soil Democrats from bolting the party. But free-soil Democrats and Whigs opposed *any* expansion of slavery as a matter of principle and rejected the plan.

Popular Sovereignty. The third alternative was popular sovereignty, Lewis Cass's position in the 1848 election. Because it relieved Congress of the responsibility of addressing the slavery issue by passing it on to territorial governments, popular sovereignty won support from many northern Democrats who otherwise might have converted to free soil.

Frederick Douglass: Development of an Abolitionist

Frederick Douglass was born a slave in 1818 on the eastern shore of Maryland. He took his mother's family name of Bailey—derived perhaps from the Muslim *Belali*. He never knew who his father was, although talk in the slave-quarters had pointed toward a man Douglass later described as "his master."

For most of his time in slavery Douglass's master was Thomas Auld, who acquired the young Frederick in 1827 as part of a property settlement and sent him to live with his brother Hugh in Baltimore. There were no other slaves in that home, and Frederick was treated much like the other children. He listened to Sophia Auld read the Bible, learned to read from a spelling book borrowed from the Auld children, figured out the meaning of *abolition* by reading newspapers, and heard about slaves running away to the North. At the age of twelve he purchased a copy of *The Columbian Orator*, a collection of speeches for young boys learning to declaim the virtues of the republic—including its devotion to "the rights of man." Enthralled, Douglass memorized and recited the speeches to his friends, including the free blacks he sought out at Methodist and Baptist churches.

In 1833 Thomas Auld returned Frederick to the sleepy eastern shore town of St. Michaels, perhaps to prevent him from running away or becoming mixed up in antislavery agitation. Frederick hoped that Auld would get religion and free him. When he did not, Frederick became rebellious, organizing a Sabbath school and resisting the routines of work. In 1834 Auld hired Douglass out to Edward Covey, a farmer with a reputation for "breaking" unruly slaves. After six months of disciplined labor and regular beatings Frederick had a brutal fight with Covey. Douglass recalled that the battle "was the turning point in my '*life as a slave.*' . . . I was nothing before; I WAS A MAN NOW." From that point he was determined "to be a FREEMAN."

The next year Auld hired Douglass out to a more lenient master. Douglass again organized a school and, with six other slaves, hatched a plan for an escape up the Chesapeake. Betrayed by a fellow conspirator, he found himself in jail, facing sale into the Deep South. But Auld again intervened, returning Douglass to Balti-

Frederick Douglass
The daguerreotype of Douglass was taken when he was in his twenties. Describing Douglass, an admirer wrote: "He was more than six feet in height, and his majestic form . . . straight as an arrow, muscular, yet lithe and graceful, his flashing eye, and more than all, his voice, that rivaled Webster's in its richness, and in the depth and sonorousness of its cadences, made up such an ideal of an orator as the listeners never forgot."

more with a promise that if Frederick applied himself to a trade, he would free him at the age of twenty-five.

Douglass did apply himself. He became a journeyman caulker in the shipyards and in 1838 struck a deal with Hugh Auld that allowed him to control his living and working arrangements in return for a guaranteed weekly payment. Douglass plunged into the life of Baltimore's free African-American community, almost 30,000 in number. He courted a free woman, Anna Murray, and joined a group of black caulkers—all free but him—called the East Baltimore Mental Improvement Society. But this life came to an abrupt end when he fell two days behind in his payments to Hugh Auld, who then ordered him to give up his independent earnings, employment, and housing. Unwilling to surrender the small measure of independence he had gained, Douglass decided to run away (see Chapter 13). Less than a month later, in the fall of 1838, he stepped off a ferry in New York City; a few days later he married Anna.

Frederick and Anna settled first in the seaport of New Bedford, Massachusetts, where he took a new name—Douglass—to avoid capture. He found work, made his first antislavery speech to a white audience, and heard William Lloyd Garrison lecture. At a meeting of the Massachusetts Anti-Slavery Society in 1841 he delivered a powerful address that won the admiration of Garrison and other leading abolitionists, who hired him as an agent of the American Anti-Slavery Society. His celebrated lecturing took him to hundreds of communities in the Northeast, where audiences were spellbound by his speeches. Elizabeth Cady Stanton described an 1842 address in Boston's Faneuil Hall:

> Around him sat the great antislavery orators of the day watching the effect of his eloquence on that immense audience, that laughed and wept by turns, completely carried away by the wondrous gifts of his pathos and humor. On this occasion, all the other speakers seemed tame after Frederick Douglass.

In his speeches Douglass denounced both slavery in the South and racial discrimination in the North. He was uncomfortable, however, with Garrison's Perfectionism and in particular with Garrison's insistence on expulsion of the southern states, which Douglass believed would leave the slaves completely at the mercy of their owners. Douglass did not take issue with Garrison's radicalism publicly, for he hoped it would motivate white America to take practical steps—such as abolishing slavery in the District of Columbia—toward the eradication of slavery. His differences with Garrison grew, however, and in 1847 he returned from a British tour determined to chart an independent course. (In an important way his independence was more secure because in 1846 admiring British abolitionists financed the purchase of his freedom from Auld to ensure that he would not be arrested as a fugitive.)

Douglass moved to Rochester, New York, where he founded an antislavery newspaper, the *North Star*, financed heavily by Gerrit Smith, a Liberty party leader.

The next year Douglass attended the Buffalo convention that created the Free Soil party, and the *North Star* extended a cautious endorsement to the party. In that year he also attended the Seneca Falls convention, writing in the *North Star*: "We are free to say that in respect to political rights, we hold woman to be justly entitled to all we claim for men."

In 1851 Douglass publicly defied the American Anti-Slavery Society by defending the Constitution, and in 1852 he delivered what became known as his "Fifth of July" speech, probably the most moving and influential of his career. He denied that the Constitution was proslavery. "In *that* instrument," he declared, "I hold there is no warrant, license, nor sanction of the hateful thing; but, interpreted as it *ought* to be interpreted, the Constitution is a GLORIOUS LIBERTY DOCUMENT."

Douglass's involvement in practical politics deepened during the 1850s. Although he believed that violence would be necessary to abolish slavery, he was cautious in encouraging slave insurrections, declining to join John Brown's raid on Harpers Ferry. Nonetheless, suspicion that he was a key conspirator led Douglass to flee to Canada and Britain. When he resumed speechmaking in America in the summer of 1860, the victory of the Republican party and its program of free soil seemed imminent.

Douglas remained a leader of former abolitionists and African-Americans for the rest of his life. During the Civil War he pressed Abraham Lincoln and the Republicans to embrace abolition of slavery as a war aim and was delighted when Lincoln adopted his view of the Constitution. He also helped the War Department recruit black soldiers. Throughout Reconstruction he spoke and lobbied effectively for equal treatment—including the right to vote—for African-Americans. But his service to the Republican party went virtually unrewarded. Republican presidents appointed him to the minor positions of marshal (1877) and then recorder of deeds for the District of Columbia (1881). It was not until the age of seventy that he finally received a significant appointment as minister to Haiti.

Before his death in 1895 Douglass's optimism finally waned. In 1894 his last major speech warned that the "presence of eight millions of people in any section of this country constituting an aggrieved class, smarting under terrible wrongs, denied the exercise of the commonest rights of humanity . . . is not only a disgrace and scandal to that particular section but a menace to the peace and security of the people of the whole country."

It seemed an inherently fair, democratic approach. Popular sovereignty, however, was a vague and slippery concept. It did not specify at what point the people of a territory could legalize or prohibit slavery; nor did it say how much authority territorial governments could exercise in regulating slavery. If Calhoun's doctrine was correct, the constitutional protection of slavery meant that territorial governments could decide the status of slavery only at the *end* of the territorial process, when they framed a constitution and applied for statehood. Southern Democrats preferred this interpretation, believing that it gave slavery a good chance to become established in the territories. In contrast, Northern Democrats believed that territorial legislatures had the power to exclude slavery and could do so as soon as a territory was organized.

As long as each side left this ambiguity unresolved, popular sovereignty held the greatest possibility for maintaining the unity of the Democratic party—and national unity—on the slavery issue. However, the ability of popular sovereignty to unify was tested far sooner than anyone expected in another major sectional confrontation.

The Compromise of 1850

The "Forty-Niners." In January 1848 workmen building a mill for John A. Sutter discovered flakes of gold in the Sierra Nevada foothills. Sutter was a Swiss immigrant who had arrived in California in 1839, become a Mexican citizen, and established a kind of feudal barony in the Sacramento Valley, well removed from the Mexican authorities. He tried to keep the discovery of gold a secret, but by May Americans from San Francisco were pouring into the foothills (see Map 14.3). In September the news reached the Northeast, but newspaper readers remained skeptical until December, when Polk confirmed the gold discoveries in his annual message to Congress. By January 1849 sixty-one crowded ships had departed from northeastern ports to sail around Cape Horn for San Francisco. By May 12,000 wagons had crossed the Missouri River, headed for the goldfields. In 1849 alone, more than 80,000 migrants—the "forty-niners"—arrived. The pace of growth would remain hectic. In 1852 there would be more than 200,000 Californians, and by 1860 the state's population would reach 380,000.

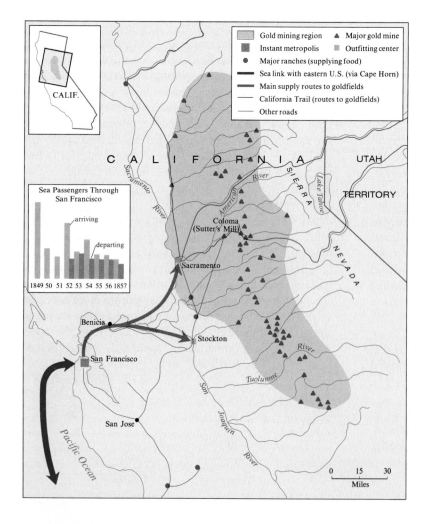

MAP 14.3

The California Gold Rush

Hundreds of thousands of fortune seekers converged on the California goldfields beginning in 1849. Miners traveling by sea landed at San Francisco, which became an instant metropolis. They outfitted for their journey inland at Sacramento and Stockton, which were commercial outposts of San Francisco. The vast population influx put pressure on existing ranches for food and stimulated new farming enterprise in the Sacramento, American, and San Joaquin River valleys.

Gold Prospectors
Working at the head of the Auburn Ravine in about 1850, these prospectors used a primitive technique—panning—to separate gold from sand and gravel. Most of the wage laborers in the early years of the gold rush were Indians or Chinese, who numbered over 25,000 in California by 1852.

Taylor and California Statehood. In California, which was not yet organized into a territory, American settlers—especially the forty-niners, who lived in crowded, chaotic towns and mining camps—demanded effective government. President Zachary Taylor advised the Californians to apply for statehood immediately. Taylor's objectives were simple: to satisfy the forty-niners' demands, to avoid wrestling with the ambiguities of popular sovereignty, and to provide dramatic evidence that the Whigs could promote westward expansion without intensifying the slavery issue. Behind his approach lay his desire to establish the Whigs as the dominant national party. On the one hand, he hoped to draw Free Soil party voters and free-soil Democrats into the Whig party; on the other hand, he hoped to persuade southern Whigs that they could protect slavery in the South without insisting on slavery in the territories.

Taylor made his proposal when he took office in March 1849. By November California voters had ratified a state constitution and applied for statehood. In the swift process of constitution making, the advocates of slavery fared poorly. Few of the many southerners who flocked to the goldfields, San Francisco, and the farms of the Sacramento Valley owned slaves or wanted to own them. Only ranchers in sparsely populated southern California had a strong interest in promoting slavery. Consequently, the California constitutional convention, copying much of the new Iowa state constitution, prohibited slavery. When Congress convened in December 1849, President Taylor urged the admission of California and New Mexico as free states.

Southern defenders of slavery were startled and alarmed by the swift victory of the antislavery forces in California. Popular sovereignty seemed to offer only empty promises of protection. Vast numbers of northerners now seemed likely to overwhelm slavery anywhere that they settled in the new territories, just as they had in California. Popular opposition to slavery in

California was usually racist, as hostile to African-Americans as it was to the institution of slavery, but that provided no comfort to southern slave owners. The farmers from Tennessee and the Irish immigrants from New York were in different wings of California's Democratic party but they shared a hatred of slavery and African-Americans. They agreed that the future of California should resemble that of the free-soil Midwest.

The imminent prospect of California's admission to the Union also disturbed southerners because it threatened the carefully maintained regional balance in the Senate. In 1845 the admission of Texas and Florida had given slavery a temporary edge of fifteen slave states against thirteen free states, but the admission of Iowa in 1846 and Wisconsin in 1848 reestablished the balance. California's admission would give the free states a political advantage in shaping states carved from the Mexican cession and the unorganized areas of the Louisiana Purchase. Moreover, southerners feared that the new state of California would create a base for abolitionists within the territory acquired from Mexico.

Southern leaders were willing to accept California's admission as a free state only if the federal government guaranteed the future of slavery. Southerners were not agreed on what they needed for an adequate guarantee, but they knew it was more than popular sovereignty in the Mexican cession. And so, in passionate debates that lasted for eight months, southern leaders forced Congress to examine all the issues surrounding the current and future status of slavery.

The most extreme southern position was taken by Calhoun, who doubted that the North and the South could arrive at a lasting compromise. In what would be his farewell address, read to Congress on his behalf shortly before he died, Calhoun said the nation could prevent the South's secession and eventual civil war only by guaranteeing slavery in all the territories and adopting a constitutional amendment to establish a per-

William H. Seward

Seward (1801–1872) was a New York State senator
(1830–1834) and a Whig governor of New York (1838–1842)
before serving two terms (1849–1861) in the U. S. Senate.
After failing to win the Republican nomination for president in
1856 and 1860, he entered Lincoln's cabinet as secretary of
state, an office he held until 1867. As early as 1835, after a trip
through Virginia, he denounced slavery as "incompatible with
all . . . the elements of the security, welfare, and greatness of
nations."

Salmon P. Chase

Trained as a lawyer, Chase (1808–1873) was drawn to the
antislavery movement by his defense of fugitive slaves. He
served as U.S. senator (1849–1855), Republican governor of
Ohio (1855–1860), secretary of the treasury (1861–1864),
and chief justice of the Supreme Court (1864–1873).

manent balance of sectional power. He was thinking of
an amendment that would turn the presidency into a
dual office, providing executives from both the South
and the North and giving each president full veto
power.

Antislavery advocates in both parties lent credence
to Calhoun's prediction of civil war. Senators Salmon P.
Chase, an Ohio free-soiler who had been elected by a
Democratic–Free Soil party coalition, and William H.
Seward, a New York Whig, urged the government to
contain slavery within its existing limits. Their goal was
its ultimate extinction. Seward declared that the government had a responsibility to "a higher law than the
Constitution, which regulates our authority over the
domain . . . the common heritage of mankind."

The issues were finally being clearly drawn, as were
the risks to the future of the nation. The clash in Congress tore both national parties along sectional lines and
stirred fears that the Union might dissolve.

Forging a Compromise. Having moved to the brink of
disaster, senior Whigs and Democrats did their best to
back away and reach a compromise. Through a long,
complex legislative process the Whig leaders Henry
Clay and Daniel Webster and the Democrat Stephen A.
Douglas organized a package that, when implemented,
consisted of six distinct laws. Those laws were known
collectively as the Compromise of 1850. The Compromise, enacted in September, attempted to mollify the
South by adopting the Fugitive Slave Act. That act replaced a weak 1793 law with a strong one that put the
federal government at the disposal of slave owners chasing runaway slaves. The intent was to remove the free
states as havens for runaway slaves and reduce the ability of abolitionists to use free-soil bases to attack slavery. The Compromise tried to satisfy the North by
establishing the principle of popular sovereignty in the
Mexican cession. The Compromise of 1850 (1) admitted California as a free state, ending the equal balance
of free and slave states, (2) organized (by two of the six
laws) the rest of the Mexican cession into the territories
of New Mexico and Utah on the implied basis of popular sovereignty, (3) resolved a boundary dispute between New Mexico and Texas in favor of New Mexico
through federal assumption of the $10 million in un-
paid debts of the Republic of Texas, (4) abolished the
slave trade, but not slavery, in the District of Columbia,
and (5) passed the Fugitive Slave Act.

The Compromise averted a secession crisis in 1850—
but only barely. In the end northern Democrats and
southern Whigs accounted for most of the votes for the
Compromise. Northern Whigs such as Seward and
southern Democrats such as Jefferson Davis opposed it.
Most southern Democrats objected to admitting California under any terms and regarded the Fugitive Slave
Act as an inadequate protector of slavery. Robbed of

their longtime leader by Calhoun's death before the vote, they would soon regroup to become an increasingly potent obstacle to sectional compromise. Northern Whigs opposed both the fugitive slave law and popular sovereignty. Those Whigs held their ground even after Vice-President Millard Fillmore of New York, a northern Whig who supported popular sovereignty, succeeded to the presidency in July 1850. (Taylor had died suddenly of a violent stomach ailment and heat prostration suffered during a Fourth of July celebration.) In other words, most northern Whigs and southern Democrats in Congress were willing to defy the leadership of their parties and risk the Union for the sake of their principles. The Compromise did not augur well for the future.

Sectional Strife and the Third Party System, 1850–1858

The Compromise of 1850 was intended to prevent the slavery issue from disrupting politics and government. Both northern Democratic and southern Whig leaders hoped that the Compromise would be as effective as its predecessor in 1820 had been and that the new compromise—particularly its fugitive slave law and popular sovereignty elements—would enable each party to maintain a national base of support. But any such hopes were quickly dashed as northern hostility to slavery swelled and southern demands for slavery's protection grew more insistent.

The Fugitive Slave Act

The most controversial element of the Compromise proved to be the Fugitive Slave Act. Under its terms, federal judges or special commissioners determined the status of blacks who denied that they were runaways. The accused African-Americans were denied jury trials and the right to testify. A commissioner would receive a $10 fee if an alleged fugitive was found guilty but only $5 if the accused was found innocent—a tremendous incentive to render a guilty verdict. Federal marshals were instructed to support slave catchers and could impose heavy penalties on anyone who helped a slave escape or obstructed the efforts of slaveholders to recover their slaves. Even slaves who had long before fled to freedom were subject to recapture. The law was effectively enforced, and many fugitives were convicted and reenslaved.

Resistance in the North. The plight of the runaways and the appearance of slave catchers in northern communities personalized the message of abolitionism, and

popular hostility to the Fugitive Slave Act grew. Abolitionists organized vigilante groups to block enforcement of the law. Frederick Douglass abandoned pacifism, declaring that "the only way to make the Fugitive Slave Law a dead letter is to make half a dozen or more dead kidnappers." In October 1850 Theodore Parker and other Boston abolitionists defied the law by helping two slaves escape to freedom and driving a Georgia slave catcher out of town. In September 1851, in the Quaker village of Christiana, Pennsylvania, more than twenty African-American men, including two escaped slaves, exchanged gunfire with a group of slave catchers from Maryland; the slave owner was killed, and his son was severely wounded. President Fillmore sent marines and federal marshals to arrest thirty-six blacks and four whites around Christiana and had them indicted for treason. But the jury acquitted one defendant, and a public uproar forced the government to drop charges against the rest. In Syracuse, New York, 2,000 rioters broke into a courthouse and freed a fugitive slave in October 1851.

Some northern legislators and judges openly resisted federal authority. Several state legislatures passed *personal liberty* laws to protect accused fugitive slaves from federal officers. Those laws attempted to exempt state officials from enforcing proslavery laws such as the Fugitive Slave Act. In 1857 the supreme court of Wisconsin, in the case of *Ableman v. Booth*, held that a state court had the power to declare an act of Congress unconstitutional. The Fugitive Slave Act, the court ruled, violated the Constitution and could not be enforced in Wisconsin. In 1859 the case reached the Supreme Court, where Chief Justice Taney ruled against Wisconsin.

Uncle Tom's Cabin. It was in reaction to the Fugitive Slave Act that Harriet Beecher Stowe composed her abolitionist novel *Uncle Tom's Cabin.* Published first in 1851–1852 as a serial in a Washington free-soil newspaper, the *National Era,* the novel tells of a compassionate but weak slaveholder in Kentucky who is forced by debts to sell two slaves, Uncle Tom and a five-year-old boy, to a slave trader. The beautiful Eliza Harris, the boy's mother, refuses to be separated from her son. With the child in her arms, she crosses the Ohio River on cakes of ice just ahead of the vicious slave trader. Eliza escapes to freedom and reaches the house of an Ohio politician who had voted for a fugitive slave law, having set aside his "private feeling." His wife persuades him to trust his heart rather than his head and to help Eliza and her child escape to Canada. Meanwhile, Tom is eventually sold to Simon Legree, a brutal overseer on a southern plantation. Legree beats Tom to death but never conquers the slave's Christian soul.

Uncle Tom's Cabin further intensified northern hostility to the Fugitive Slave Act. When the novel first appeared in book form in 1852, more than 300,000

Uncle Tom's Cabin
In these illustrations from the original 1852 edition of *Uncle Tom's Cabin*, the engraver portrayed Eliza Harris (top) and Tom (bottom panel).

Americans bought copies. Countless families saw an emotionally charged stage version produced by theater companies throughout the North. For most of those people Stowe's novel connected the abstract moral principles of abolitionism with heartrending personal situations to which they could respond with anger or grief.

The Southern Response. To the South's political leaders the Fugitive Slave Act was important because it meant that the government recognized and protected their "property" everywhere. The fierce northern defiance of the act mobilized leading southern politicians, who were already upset by the admission of California, the introduction of popular sovereignty, and the abolition of the slave trade in Washington, D.C. To protect what they called Southern Rights, they organized special conventions in South Carolina, Georgia, Mississippi, and Alabama in 1850 and 1851. The governor of South Carolina declared that there was not "the slightest doubt" that his state would secede from the Union to protect slavery. Although all the conventions considered secession, moderates in Georgia, Mississippi, and Al-

abama defused the crisis by persuading the conventions to support the Compromise of 1850. In return, the moderates agreed to support secession in the future if Congress abolished slavery anywhere, failed to recognize slavery in a new territory, or refused to admit a state into the Union because its proposed constitution permitted slavery. The victorious Georgia Unionists declared in the Georgia Platform that the protection of Southern Rights and the "preservation of our much beloved Union" depended most importantly on "a faithful execution of the Fugitive Slave Law." Moderate arguments carried less weight in South Carolina, where secession failed only because many secessionists doubted that they could go it alone, without the cooperation of other states.

The Election of 1852: A Shift in Party Balance

The northern Whigs, who dominated their party, carried their powerful hostility to the Fugitive Slave Act and popular sovereignty into the 1852 election. They passed over President Fillmore because he had vigorously enforced the act and supported popular sovereignty. Instead they nominated another general from the Mexican War, Winfield Scott, in the hope that a popular general, like Harrison in 1840 and Taylor in 1848, would attract national support. The southern Whigs were not satisfied by the Scott nomination and the offhanded endorsement of the Compromise of 1850 that the northern Whigs and Scott offered to keep southerners in the party. Many southern Whigs, particularly in the Deep South, withheld support from their party; some went so far as to vote for the Democratic ticket.

The Whigs had problems in the North too; whereas their economic program still had supporters, many northern Whigs wanted the party to address slavery and immigration issues in a straightforward, compelling fashion. Also, the deaths of Henry Clay and Daniel Webster in 1852 had robbed the party of its most articulate leaders and most effective voices for national unity.

Franklin Pierce. The Democrats displayed no more vision in 1852 than did the Whigs, but they were more successful in avoiding a division along sectional lines. Some southern Democrats wanted to nominate a candidate who supported Calhoun's radical position that the federal government should protect slavery in all the territories. Most realized, however, that that would ensure defeat for the party in the North. The Democratic convention passed over all the advocates of popular sovereignty, including Lewis Cass, Stephen Douglas, and James Buchanan, none of whom could obtain the neces-

Franklin Pierce
In this engraving (circa 1847), Pierce poses as a brigadier general of volunteers in the Mexican War.

sary two-thirds majority. On the forty-ninth ballot it chose Franklin Pierce of New Hampshire. The public knew Pierce only as a handsome and congenial New Englander with no identifiable enemies, but southern Democrats were assured that he would be sympathetic to the South's interests.

Pierce and the Democrats crushed the Whigs in the 1852 election. The Democrats not only attracted southern Whigs but also won back some of the northern Democrats who had voted for the Free Soil party in 1848. Pleased by the outcome of popular sovereignty in California, those free-soilers were satisfied that the popular sovereignty provisions of the Compromise of 1850 would effectively prevent the expansion of slavery. Even Martin Van Buren, the former candidate of the Free Soil party, supported Pierce. Votes for the Free Soil party and its candidate, John P. Hale of New Hampshire, declined to about 5 percent of the total, only about half the share the party had won four years earlier. Although General Scott attracted more popular votes than Taylor

had in 1848, Scott carried only four of the thirty-one states.

The Whigs never again waged a national campaign. The Compromise of 1850 had driven a wedge between northern and southern Whigs. The task of maintaining the political unity of the nation now fell to the Democrats.

In trying to maintain itself as a *national* party, the Democratic party had some powerful assets. Most Democratic leaders took the broadly appealing stance of supporting popular sovereignty. The Democrats also had a diverse base of voters, including the growing number of immigrant voters in northern cities and the many settlers of southern ancestry in the Ohio Valley. They also appealed to the many voters across the country who thought that preserving the Union was more important than preserving slavery or freeing the slaves.

But the Democratic party also had some important liabilities. Its program of popular sovereignty was unacceptable both to many southerners—those who insisted that slaves be treated as property throughout the Union—and to northerners who wanted the federal government to prohibit slavery in the western territories. The Democratic party was unattractive to those northern voters who resented the recruitment of immigrants, particularly Catholics, into the party and to those who wanted vigorous federal programs to promote economic development.

Pierce's Expansionist Foreign Policy

President Pierce set out to broaden his support and divert attention from sectional disputes with a familiar Democratic strategy: an expansionist foreign policy. Pierce hoped that, like Polk in the early phases of the Mexican War, he could broaden his support among Americans, both northern and southern, who were interested in spreading republican institutions and expanding trade opportunities. Pierce cast his eyes toward Latin America, particularly Mexico, the Caribbean, Central America, and across the Pacific toward Japan.

Unlocking Japan. Pierce inherited a diplomatic opportunity in Japan. American trade with China had declined in the 1840s, and in response some northeastern merchants had scouted new markets in the western Pacific. In 1846 they had persuaded the federal government to send its first mission to Japan. In 1852 President Fillmore followed up by authorizing a naval expedition under Commodore Matthew C. Perry. Pierce continued the support of Perry, and in 1854 Perry's squadron of four "black ships" led Japan to sign a treaty of friendship. President Pierce rejected Perry's desire to acquire Pacific territory, including Formosa, but was unhappy that the treaty fell far short of establishing full diplomatic and trading relations. In 1854 he sent Townsend Harris, a tough, experienced China trader, to Japan with full authority to negotiate a commercial treaty. Harris played successfully on Japanese fears of Russia and other European powers. In 1858, on an American warship in Edo (later Tokyo) Bay, Japan signed a full commercial treaty with the United States. This was the first such treaty Japan had made with any industrial power.

The Gadsden Purchase. Pierce inherited an array of Mexican-American problems, including a dispute over New Mexico's southern boundary and American acquisition of transit routes across northwestern Mexico. Pierce and his secretary of war, Jefferson Davis, hoped to pressure the Mexican government of Santa Anna, who had just returned to the presidency, to sell land to America as part of a comprehensive settlement. Pierce sent James Gadsden, a South Carolina politician and railroad promoter, to Mexico to negotiate with Santa Anna. Gadsden threatened force if Mexico did not cede a major portion of northern Mexico and Baja (Lower) California. Santa Anna refused but agreed to a settlement that included the sale of about 30,000 square miles south of the Gila River, territory Gadsden wanted for a southern railroad to the Pacific Ocean. Completed in 1854, the Gadsden Purchase, as it became known, represented the last territory acquired from Mexico, but it served to rub salt in Mexico's wounds, reminding it of the power of its northern neighbor.

Cuba. The early expansionist plans of the Polk administration had included purchasing Cuba from Spain. But those schemes had accomplished little despite the vigorous efforts of some southerners and their northern supporters, such as the New York newspaper editor John Louis O'Sullivan. Those expansionists tried to stir up a revolution in Cuba in the hope that widespread republican hostility to the Spanish monarchy would then lead to the admission of Cuba, which they hoped would turn out to be a slave state. The expansionists funded three filibustering expeditions to the island by a Cuban exile, General Narciso López.

President Pierce resumed those efforts in 1853 by covertly supporting another such expedition to Cuba—to be led by John A. Quitman, a former governor of Mississippi. While Quitman built up his forces, the Pierce administration nearly precipitated a war. In February 1854 Spanish officials in Cuba confiscated the cargo of the American ship *Black Warrior*, which had violated port regulations, creating an incident that could provide an excuse for taking Cuba by force. In March Pierce asked Congress for permission "to obtain redress for injuries received, and to vindicate the honor of our flag." Secretary of State William L. Marcy, who hoped that expansionism would win him the presiden-

tial nomination in 1856, instructed Pierce's minister in Spain, Pierre Soulé, a Louisianan who advocated taking Cuba, to demand an apology and a large indemnity for the *Black Warrior*'s losses. The Spanish government stalled, and by May Pierce had learned that northern Democrats in Congress would not support a war to add a new slave state. He accepted the Spanish terms for settling the *Black Warrior* claims and tried to signal Quitman to abandon his expedition by issuing a proclamation that the federal government would prosecute anyone who violated the neutrality laws.

Pierce meanwhile attempted to purchase Cuba. In April Marcy authorized Soulé to offer as much as $130 million for Cuba and, if he failed, to attempt "to detach that island from the Spanish dominion." After Soulé failed to start a revolution in Cuba, Marcy instructed him to meet with James Buchanan, the U.S. minister to Great Britain, and John Y. Mason, the minister to France, to devise an alternative plan. In October the three sent Pierce an inflammatory message that became known as the Ostend Manifesto. In it, they invoked the rhetoric of Manifest Destiny and declared that the United States would be justified "by every law, human and Divine" in "wresting" Cuba from Spain "if we possess the power." In November, within two weeks of the document's arrival in Washington, it had been leaked to the press, triggering a new wave of northern resentment against the South. Pierce halted his own efforts to acquire Cuba and finally persuaded Quitman to give up his filibustering plan, which he had never completely abandoned.

Nicaragua. In 1855 another American, William Walker, led an invasion of Nicaragua. Born and raised in Tennessee, Walker had acquired a taste for Latin American adventures in California, where he had won popularity for his schemes to annex Sonora and Baja California. In 1854 he had led forty-eight followers to La Paz to participate in a rebellion against Mexican rule. After the rebellion failed, he landed in Nicaragua with sixty men and made himself dictator of that country. He announced a grand scheme to create a new nation that would include Central America and Cuba. Most of his followers had the simpler mission of bringing Nicaragua into the Union as a slave state. In 1856 Walker announced the reestablishment of slavery in Nicaragua. His government was recognized by the Pierce administration and won an endorsement in the Democratic party platform, but Walker alienated his Central American neighbors and was driven out of power in 1857. He died before a Honduran firing squad in 1860. The resistance of Latin American nations, coupled with the growing force of free-soil sentiment in the North, meant that foreign policy and plots for taking Manifest Destiny to Latin America could not be the Democrats' key to national cohesion.

Kansas-Nebraska and the Republicans

The Democrats' main hope for sustaining their party as a national institution now depended on the success of popular sovereignty. The doctrine was put to its first test since California in the northern—and largest—portion of the Louisiana Purchase.

The Kansas-Nebraska Act. Because the Missouri Compromise guaranteed free soil in the Louisiana Purchase north of 36° 30', southerners had largely blocked the political organization of that area, allowing only the admission of Iowa to the Union in 1846 and the formation of the Minnesota Territory. Even though most of the unorganized area was in the "Great American Desert," the appetite of people in the Ohio River Valley and the Upper South for new land made them impatient. The same sense of confinement that had sent thousands of them to Oregon led them to demand that the government organize the vast northern region of the Louisiana Purchase into territories and open it for settlement. The Democratic senator Stephen A. Douglas of Illinois became their foremost spokesman. He championed development of the West and wanted Chicago to become the eastern terminus of a transcontinental railroad. He also yearned to be president. In 1854 he introduced a bill to extinguish native American rights and organize a large territory in what he called Nebraska.

Douglas's bill conflicted with the plans of southern senators, who wanted to guarantee slavery in the territories and hoped that New Orleans, Memphis, or St. Louis would be chosen as the eastern railroad terminus. To win southern support Douglas made two major concessions. First, he agreed with southerners that the popular sovereignty principle embraced by the Compromise of 1850 had voided the Missouri Compromise's prohibition of slavery in the northern part of the Louisiana Purchase. Second, he advocated the formation of two new territories, Nebraska and Kansas, rather than one, giving slaveholders a chance to dominate the settlement of Kansas, the more southern territory (see Map 14.4). Douglas believed that the demographic advantage of non-slaveholders in Kansas, coupled with a physical environment that he thought would be hostile to plantation agriculture, would ensure that Kansas, like California earlier, would remain free. Those concessions attracted the support of almost all southerners in Congress, and the Kansas-Nebraska Act passed in May 1854 despite the opposition of northern Whigs and half of Douglas's own northern Democrats, who were less sanguine about the future of free labor in the West.

Throughout the North abolitionists and free-soilers denounced the Kansas-Nebraska Act; Douglas had seriously misread northern opinion. The repeal of the Missouri Compromise seemed to attack freedom in an area that had been secure for more than a generation. Suddenly the idea caught fire that a Slave Power conspiracy had undertaken a dangerous program of aggression. Many free-soilers became convinced that the federal government had been captured by slaveholders and had abandoned sectional neutrality.

Formation of the Republican Party. Many northern Whigs, adrift without a national party, seized the opening Douglas had created. They began to cooperate with "Anti-Nebraska" Democrats. The two groups then joined with supporters of the Free Soil party. In 1854 they began to organize a new party, reviving the Jeffer-

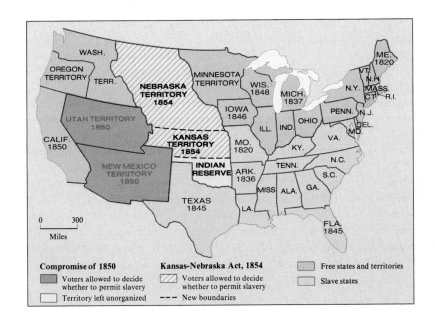

MAP 14.4

The Compromise of 1850 and the Kansas-Nebraska Act, 1854

Vast territories were at stake in the contest over the extension of slavery. The Compromise of 1850 and the Kansas-Nebraska Act provided that the future of slavery in most of the West—in the Kansas, Nebraska, Utah, and New Mexico territories—would be decided by popular sovereignty.

sonian term *Republican* for themselves. The Republicans emphasized absolute opposition to the expansion of slavery into any new territories—generalizing the principle of the Wilmot Proviso—and ran their first candidates in the Congressional elections of that year.

The Know-Nothings. Another party—the "Know-Nothings"—was already attracting support from former Whigs. The party had its origins in the anti-immigrant, anti-Catholic passions that had flared in the 1840s. In 1850 various secret anti-Catholic societies had banded together in the Order of the Star-Spangled Banner; a year later they formed a new political party, the American party. Its members sometimes answered outsiders' questions by saying "I know nothing," which gave the party its nickname. The program of the Know-Nothings, however, was not mysterious. They supported the program of the Native American Clubs and in addition advocated literacy tests for voters, which they thought would disfranchise most recent immigrants. The Know-Nothings attempted to unite northern and southern voters behind a program of nativist opposition to Catholics—both Irish and German—and the "alien menace."

Republicans and Know-Nothings Cooperate. In the 1854 elections in the North, the Republicans cooperated with the better established Know-Nothings. Whereas the Republicans stressed free soil, the Know-Nothings emphasized anti-Catholic nativism. The Republicans and Know-Nothings were wary of each other, uncertain which party had the better formula for long-term political success. But a coalition of the two new parties had much to recommend it. The conspiracy theory of the Know-Nothings—suggesting a threat to republican institutions—paralleled the free-soilers' description of the Slave Power conspiracy and created the ideological basis for the coalition. Many Republicans were uncomfortable with fervent anti-Catholicism but appreciated the fact that outside the South Know-Nothings applauded free-soil policy, regarding its potential antiblack thrust as being consistent with the Know-Nothing program of excluding everyone but white Protestants from America. There were also practical political reasons for a coalition. Neither of the national parties, the Whigs and the Democrats, had supported their programs, and most of the supporters of both the Know-Nothings and the Republicans were former Whigs. In 1854 the Know-Nothings won a number of seats in Congress and temporarily gained control of the state governments of Massachusetts and Pennsylvania. Together, the Republicans and Know-Nothings won a majority in the House of Representatives in 1854. Suddenly the Republican–Know-Nothing coalition seemed a potent alternative to the Democrats and popular sovereignty.

Republican Ideology versus the Defense of Slavery

Like most American political parties, the Republican party was a coalition, and its platform contained proposals designed to appeal to each of the groups that made up its alliance. But the party's ideas and political language were not just the sum of those proposals. Republican ideology was strongly shaped by a perception of the different kinds of human personalities and societies that developed under slavery and freedom.

In the Republican view, slavery produced only two classes of people: masters and slaves. The master class was corrupted by wielding power that knew no limits. In their dealings with slaves—and with their poorer white neighbors—slave masters would inevitably claim limitless privilege and inflict limitless injustice. This kind of excess could only produce habits of subservience, ignorance, and sloth among slaves and poor whites.

In the Republicans' description of a free society no person had unlimited power over another. The ancient division of society into permanent classes was eradicated by freedom and mobility. As Abraham Lincoln, a Whig who became a Republican after the passage of the Kansas-Nebraska Act, put it, in northern society "there is no permanent class of hired laborers among us." Every man had a chance to become an owner and an employer, and "if any continue through life in the condition of the hired laborers, it is not the fault of the system, but because of either a dependent nature which prefers it, or improvidence, folly, or singular misfortune." In the faith of Lincoln and his fellow Republicans the typical men and women of such a society would be proudly independent, creative, ambitious, and energetic. Such people would be disciplined not by authority but by their own free determination to meet their responsibilities to their families, churches, and communities. Thus, the Republicans asserted the values of individualism and republicanism in the face of increasing class divisions and tensions in the industrializing North.

Southerners saw things very differently. They had long defended slavery on racist grounds; black people, they claimed, were inferior, lacked any capacity for freedom, and were dependent on their benevolent masters. Many southerners invoked St. Paul's recognition of unequal stations in life. But in the 1850s, in response to northern attacks on slavery and celebrations of free labor, a new defense of slavery began to take shape. Proslavery novelists, for example, produced more than a dozen books between 1852 and 1854 to counter the searing images of *Uncle Tom's Cabin*. In two books, *Sociology for the South; or, the Failure of Free Society* (1854) and *Canni-*

bals All: or, Slaves without Masters (1857), a Virginia planter, lawyer, and writer, George Fitzhugh, delivered the most elaborate proslavery statement.

In a free-labor system, the new argument ran, labor is simply a commodity whose price is determined by the ruthless laws of the market. In the market, greed is the only morality, supply and demand the only law, and money the only goal. Every member of such a society, rich or poor, becomes grasping and selfish. Anyone too old, too weak, or too young to sell labor in the market is "free" only to be hungry and homeless. In such a world self-interest dominates; no one has a sense of community, civic values, or responsibility for others.

Whereas slavery requires some people to work to enrich others, the argument continued, it produces a master class that differs greatly from the ruling class of a capitalist society. Masters assume lifelong responsibility for their slaves, including the old and the sick. The slave owner, unlike the capitalist employer, is committed to community and civic responsibility. The master class in a slave society—whether in ancient Greece or Rome or in the American South—cultivates the graces and virtues that can thrive only in a frankly aristocratic culture.

Thus, in each section ideologies were taking shape that defined the differences between North and South in ways that utterly precluded political compromise. Each ideology suited the interests and world view of the dominant groups—the planters in the South and the business class in the North. Northerners and southerners argued that slavery and free labor were not simply different labor systems but expressed different social orders and produced irreconcilably different kinds of men

and women. Every passing year made it more likely that a majority of the voters in each section would decide that societies as different as the North and the South could no longer be joined in a constitutional union.

"Bleeding Kansas"

The Kansas-Nebraska Act channeled the clash of rival ideologies into the settlement of the newly organized territory. In 1854 thousands of settlers began a rush into Kansas. Many believed they had a mission to defend the fundamental principles of their society, whether northern or southern; they were putting popular sovereignty to the test. On the side of slavery, Senator David R. Atchison of Missouri organized residents of his state to cross into Kansas and intervene in crucial elections (see American Voices, page 436). Opposing him were the agents of the New England Emigrant Aid Society, organized by abolitionists in 1854 to colonize Kansas with free-soilers. The preference of the Pierce administration was clear. In March 1855 the administration recognized a Kansas territorial legislature that had been elected largely by Missourians who had crossed the border simply to cast ballots. The territorial legislature declared that questioning the legitimacy of slavery was a felony and that aiding a fugitive slave was a capital offense. Pierce assisted the legislature with federal troops and proslavery judicial appointees.

Violence peaked in the summer of 1856. A proslavery gang, 700 strong, sacked the free-soil town of Lawrence, destroying two newspaper offices, burning down buildings, and looting stores. While Lawrence

Free-State Battery, 1856
For these free-soil settlers in Topeka, Kansas, there was a very real sense that the Civil War began in 1856 rather than 1861. Their cannon had seen service in the Mexican War.

Hannah Anderson Ropes

Six Months in "Bleeding Kansas"

In September 1855 Hannah Anderson Ropes moved with her two children from Brookline, Massachusetts, to join her husband in Lawrence, Kansas. But in March 1856, terrified by the violence, she returned to Brookline two months before the sack of Lawrence. During her six months in Kansas, Anderson wrote long letters to her mother and kept a diary.

November 21, 1855. Last week . . . a man living about six miles from here upon a claim . . . was shot down by a party of Missourians, without any provocation. The border Missourians are a horseback people; always off somewhere; drink a great deal of whiskey, and are quite reckless of human life. There is no necessity for hard work to those who have long lived in this country, the earth yields so abundantly. They ride fine horses, and are strong, vigorous-looking animals themselves. To shoot a man is not much more than to shoot a buck. After killing this poor Yankee, they stood around him till they saw a man approach, and then rode deliberately away.

My dear mother, this is Saturday evening. . . . How strange it will seem to you to hear that I have loaded pistols and a bowie-knife upon my table at night, three of Sharp's rifles, loaded, standing in the room. . . . All the week every preparation has been made for our defence; and everybody is worn with want of sleep. . . .

The Missourians have taken awful oaths to destroy this Yankee town, and a price is set upon the heads of some of our most honored citizens. Already they have assembled to the number of two hundred at Franklin, a little town south of us, and many more at Douglas, a village farther up the river. They are moving with great secretiveness; but when was a Yankee "caught napping," in the faintest prospect of danger?

To-night everybody is at the hall. My orders are, if fire-arms sound like battle, to place Alice [her daughter] and myself as near the floor as possible, and be well covered with blankets. We already have one bullet in the wall, and, since that, one struck the "shakes" close by the bed's head and glanced off. Now, for the first time, I begin to take an interest in Lawrence, as a city; and, prospectively, her destiny is almost as my own. How well her men bear themselves . . . [is] now so important as a matter of national history. . . .

December 5, 1855. Mother of mine, . . . we now have an armed force of five hundred men, who are under the command of Dr. Robinson, now commander-in-chief, and Col. Lane, both of whom have had experience in actual battle, in Mexico and California. Out of my south window I can see them drilling. . . . Boys there are in the ranks; but the soberness of manhood is upon them, and the determination of "Seventy-six" in their step. The blood warms in my veins as I look. . . .

Undated, December 1855. How we, at the North, have always believed implicitly in the chivalry of the South, and the wide-hearted generosity of the West. It is not till we arrive in Kansas, away from everything dear and familiar . . . that the truth really dawns upon us. Mother, there is no indignity to be mentioned which has not been heaped upon us. By it I feel myself robbed of a large estate—my faith in human nature.

Undated, March 1856. I am not only proud, but thankful, very thankful, that New England is the land of my birth. Her laws and institutions are dearer to us than ever before; and Kansas, without a similar elevating basis of social and moral restraint, would not be worth travelling two thousand miles to secure. . . .

Source: Hannah Anderson Ropes, *Six Months in Kansas by a Lady* (Boston: John P. Jewett and Co., 1856), *passim.*

---

burned, an abolitionist from New York and Ohio named John Brown, together with his four sons and two helpers, was on his way to Lawrence with a free-state volunteer militia to defend the town. Brown, born in 1800, had started more than twenty business ventures in six states, had gone through bankruptcy, and had often had to defend himself against lawsuits. Nonetheless, he had an intelligence and a moral intensity that won the trust of influential people, including leading abolitionists, whom he sought out beginning in the early 1830s. According to a free-soil minister who sheltered him, Brown believed "that God had raised him up on purpose to break the jaws of the wicked." The day after Brown heard about the sack of Lawrence, he acted with a vengeance. He and his followers, with broadswords honed like razors, murdered and mutilated five proslavery settlers in Kansas. We must "fight fire with fire" and "strike terror in the hearts of the proslavery people," Brown declared. The "Pottawatomie massacre," as the killings became known, provoked reprisals and initiated a guerrilla war that cost about 200 lives.

The violence even reached the civilized halls of Congress. In an inflammatory speech, "The Crime against Kansas," Senator Charles Sumner of Massachusetts denounced the Pierce administration, the South, and Senator Andrew P. Butler of South Carolina, who Sumner said had taken "the harlot slavery" as his mistress. Butler's nephew and protégé, Preston Brooks, a member of the House, took personal offense at Sumner's attack and decided to punish him according to the southern code of chivalry. Brooks accosted Sumner at his desk while the Senate was not in session and beat him on the head with a walking cane. Sumner struggled to his feet, wrenched his desk loose from the screws that held it to the floor, and finally fell, unconscious and bleeding. Sumner did not return to the Senate for two and a half years; Massachusetts kept his seat open for him to honor him, and create a symbol of his martyrdom. The House censured Brooks, but South Carolina voters returned him to Congress with an almost unanimous show of support. Many of them sent him new canes to replace the one he had broken in the attack.

The Election of 1856

The violence in Kansas and the halls of Congress dominated the presidential election of 1856. The Democrats stayed with their policy of popular sovereignty, but with their party's center of gravity now resting in the South, they had to go beyond generalities and explicitly reaffirm the Kansas-Nebraska Act. To strengthen the party in the North in the face of Pierce's close association with Bleeding Kansas, the Democrats turned away from him and nominated James Buchanan of Pennsylvania. A tall, dignified, white-haired figure of sixty-four years, Buchanan had more than forty years of experience in politics but was an unimaginative, uninspiring, and timid leader. Fortunately for his candidacy, he had been minister to Great Britain during the controversy over the Kansas-Nebraska Act and had no record on that volatile issue.

The Republicans counted on a northern backlash against the Democrats over Bleeding Kansas despite the success of Pierce's third territorial governor, John W. Geary of Pennsylvania, in establishing peace in Kansas in September. The Republican platform denounced the Kansas-Nebraska Act and insisted that the federal government prohibit slavery in all the territories. The platform also called for federal subsidies to transcontinental railroads, reviving the element of the Whig economic program that was most popular among midwestern Democrats. The Republicans nominated John C. Frémont, a celebrated army explorer with a meager political record. He was a genuine free-soiler and was famous throughout the nation for his role in the conquest of California.

The Know-Nothings had appeared to be strong early in 1856, but they proved to be only a minor factor in the election. They had quickly split into warring factions—North and South—over Kansas-Nebraska. The Republicans cleverly maneuvered the northern party—called the North American party—into endorsing Frémont. Meanwhile, the southern fragment of the American party nominated Millard Fillmore. He ran strongly in many southern states, but in the North most Know-Nothings disappeared into the ranks of the Republican party. By incorporating anti-Catholic nativism but emphasizing free soil, the Republican message resonated more closely with the deepest concerns of northern voters.

FORCING SLAVERY DOWN THE THROAT OF A FREESOILER

A Free-Soil Cartoon, 1856
This Republican cartoon, published during the presidential campaign of 1856, proposes that the Democrats and their platform would compel free-soilers in Kansas to accept slavery. Using a black man to symbolize slavery and presenting him in a derogatory fashion suggest the racist aspect of the free-soil message.

For the Republicans the great issue of the election was the expansion of slavery. They grabbed the offensive—and adopted the Slave Power conspiracy theory—charging that the South, through the Democratic party, was seeking to extend slavery throughout the nation. The sense of destiny and impending doom that the election created was captured by the poet Walt Whitman, a former Democrat who campaigned for Republicans in 1856. "No man knows what will happen next," Whitman wrote, "but all know some such things are to happen as mark the greatest moral convulsions of the earth."

Many southern Democrats threatened to press for secession if Frémont won. Fearful of such a cataclysm—and still believing that popular sovereignty could solve the crisis—enough northern Democrats remained loyal to give the election to Buchanan. He drew 1.8 million votes to 1.3 million for Frémont. But the Republican party stunned the nation by running up impressive victories in the free states. Frémont attracted enough former Whigs, Know-Nothings, and free-soil Democrats to carry eleven free states. Buchanan took only five, and the race was very close in two of them—Illinois and Pennsylvania. A small shift of the popular vote to Frémont in those two states would have won him the presidency, even though he received no support in the South. In the slave states the race was simply a contest between Buchanan and Fillmore, who won only Maryland.

The Third Party System. A dramatic restructuring of parties had suddenly taken place: the Third Party System—with Democrats and Republicans replacing Democrats and Whigs—had become a reality. The implications for the sectional crisis were ominous. The Republican party was within striking distance of the presidency after only one campaign despite the fact that it was a sectional party, with no support in the South. And the Democratic party had succeeded in bridging sectional conflicts only by the slenderest of margins. Many Americans, both in the North and the South, sensed that they stood on the brink of a revolution. The future of the Union would depend on the ability of President Buchanan to persuade the North that slavery would not threaten free labor in the West and to convince the South that the federal government would protect slavery.

The Democratic Blunders of 1857–1858

The *Dred Scott* Decision. However attractive to northern voters, the free-soil program of the Republicans had never been subjected to a clear test of its constitutionality. The Supreme Court had never reviewed the free-soil doctrine or the contrary proposition of John C. Calhoun that the Constitution protected slavery in the territories and that the people of a territory could prohibit

Dred Scott

Dred Scott's odyssey began in St. Louis in 1834, when he was sold to John Emerson and taken to Illinois, then to Fort Snelling in Wisconsin Territory, and finally back to Missouri. After Emerson died, Scott sued Emerson's wife for his freedom. Two months after the Supreme Court decision, the former Mrs. Emerson, who had married an antislavery politician from Massachusetts, freed Scott.

slavery *only* at the moment of admission to statehood, not before. Many on both sides of the issue hoped the Court would resolve the question in their favor. In 1857 the Court made an effort.

In 1856 the case of Dred Scott, a slave suing for his freedom, reached the Supreme Court. Scott had lived for a time with his master, an army surgeon, in the free state of Illinois and the Wisconsin Territory, where the Northwest Ordinance (1787) and the Missouri Compromise (1820) prohibited slavery. In his suit, which began in 1846 in the courts of Missouri, Scott claimed that his residence in a free state and a free territory had made him a free man. In March 1857, only two days after Buchanan's inauguration, the Court reached a decision in *Dred Scott v. Sandford*.

There was little consensus among the justices on the issues raised by the case, but seven members of the Court agreed on one critical matter—Scott remained a slave. There was no majority opinion—every justice wrote his own—but Chief Justice Roger B. Taney's was the most influential. Taney ruled that blacks, free *or* slave, could not be citizens of the United States and that Scott therefore had no right to sue in a federal court. Taney could have stopped there. Instead, he insisted on going further and making two broad points. First, he ruled that the Fifth Amendment's prohibition of taking property without due process of law meant that Congress could not pass a law depriving persons of their slave "property" in the territories. Thus, the Missouri Compromise, voided three years earlier by the Kansas-Nebraska Act, had *always* been unconstitutional, and Scott's residence in the Wisconsin Territory had not freed him. Second, Congress could not extend to territorial governments any powers that Congress itself did not possess. Since Congress had no power to prohibit slavery in a territory, neither did the government of that territory. Thus Taney endorsed Calhoun's interpretation of the constitutional protection of slavery and definition of popular sovereignty.

Five of the seven justices, including the chief justice, who was from Maryland, were southern Democrats. They and President Buchanan—who privately twisted the arm of his fellow Pennsylvanian, Justice Robert C. Grier, to join the five—had a specific political purpose in mind when they arranged the decision. They prayed that it would be accepted by Democrats and Republicans alike out of respect for the Court and for law and order and thus ease the sectional crisis. Buchanan also wanted a decision that would strip Republicans of their free-soil platform.

But the Court's decision did just the opposite of calming the sectional waters. In a single stroke the Democratic Supreme Court had declared the Republicans' antislavery platform unconstitutional. It was a decision the Republicans could not tolerate. Led by Senator William H. Seward of New York, they accused the Supreme Court and President Buchanan of participating in the Slave Power conspiracy. Even many northern Democrats were outraged, including Stephen Douglas, who had labored so hard to protect his party's strength in the North by invoking the popular sovereignty doctrine.

The Lecompton Constitution. President Buchanan then made an even more serious blunder by deciding to support the proslavery forces in Kansas. In early 1858 he recommended the admission of Kansas as a slave state under the so-called Lecompton constitution. Most observers—including Stephen Douglas—believed that that constitution had been obtained by fraud, particularly because the antislavery majority in Kansas had previously rejected the constitution in a referendum. Douglas thought that admitting Kansas under the Lecompton constitution would be a travesty of democracy, a parody of popular sovereignty, and an embarrassment to the party in most of the North. Angered, Douglas broke

with Buchanan and the southern Democrats and mobilized western Democrats and Republicans in the House of Representatives to defeat the Lecompton constitution. (Kansas finally entered the Union as a free state in 1861, after secession was well under way and many southern representatives had left Congress.)

Buchanan's support for the Lecompton constitution meant that he had decided to worry more about the anxieties of the South than about those of the North. It was a catastrophic choice. He failed to organize Kansas on a proslavery basis, fractured the Democratic party, and provided the Republicans with more evidence that an insidious Slave Power was threatening the rights of free labor and, ultimately, the existence of the republic. Buchanan had made it virtually impossible for either the Democratic party or popular sovereignty to provide the basis for preserving national unity.

Abraham Lincoln and the Breaking of Union, 1858–1860

The disintegration of the national Democratic party that had begun over Bleeding Kansas accelerated after the elections of 1856 and the *Dred Scott* decision. Former Democrats and Whigs continued to switch to the new Republican party. During this crisis of Union Abraham Lincoln emerged as the pivotal figure in American politics. His rise to power illustrates how the issue of slavery came to dominate politics and change the way Americans thought about the future of their society.

Lincoln's Early Career

Economic development and the rise of the business class in the small towns of the Ohio River Valley shaped Lincoln's early career. His restless farming family of modest means had moved from Kentucky, where Lincoln was born in 1809, to Indiana and then to Illinois. In 1831 Lincoln set out on his own, settling in New Salem, a small town on the Sangamon River in central Illinois. He rejected the farming life and began working as a store clerk. He had already displayed signs of business entrepreneurship, having twice, in 1828 and 1831, taken flatboats laden with farm produce down the Mississippi River to New Orleans. The profits helped him become a partner in a general store in New Salem.

In New Salem Lincoln was equally at home with the rough, footloose young men of the town and its emerging business class. He excelled in the games, pranks, and fights of a gang of young men who hung out in a local saloon, and in 1831 they elected him captain of the company of New Salem men who volunteered for the Black Hawk War. He had little formal schooling, but with the help of the local schoolmaster he mastered English grammar and elementary mathematics. Another villager introduced him to Shakespeare. During Lincoln's first winter in town he became a regular participant in the New Salem Debating Society.

Illinois State Legislator. Lincoln's ambition was, as a friend later described it, "a little engine that knew no rest." That ambition ran not to business but to politics. In 1832 Lincoln ran for the state legislature on a business-class program of increased state investment in internal improvements and education. Universal education, he said in his campaign, would give people "the advantages and satisfaction to be derived from all being able to read the scriptures and other works, both of a religious and moral nature, for themselves."

Lincoln lost the 1832 election but won almost all the votes cast in New Salem and rapidly extended his influence. He was appointed postmaster and deputy county surveyor and began to study law with a prominent attorney who was also a state legislator and the foremost Whig in the county. In 1834 Lincoln ran again for the state legislature and won. Admitted to the bar in 1837, he moved to Springfield, the new state capital. There he met Mary Todd, the daughter of a successful Kentucky businessman and politician; they married in 1842. They were a picture in contrasts. Her tastes were aristocratic; his were humble. She was volatile; he was easygoing and deliberate. Bouts of depression, which plagued Lincoln throughout his life, tried her patience. Yet those episodes were integral to the remarkable growth of his personality and mind.

During Lincoln's four terms in the lower house of the Illinois legislature he had a powerful influence on the building of the Whig party. As Whig floor leader and chairman of the finance committee, Lincoln promoted state banking and extensive internal improvements—turnpikes, canals, and railroads—that the Whigs hoped would increase their appeal in the normally Democratic areas of southern and central Illinois. In 1840 he made two long campaign tours on behalf of William Henry Harrison in southern Illinois, and in 1844 he campaigned for his political hero, Henry Clay, in the southern Indiana towns of his boyhood. In 1846 Lincoln drew on his expanded network of Whig friends and supporters to win election to Congress.

Congressman. Until entering Congress in 1847, Lincoln had successfully avoided taking a stand on the contentious issue of slavery. But now the Mexican War and its implications for the future of slavery forced him to state his position.

Lincoln had concluded, perhaps as early as one of his youthful trips to New Orleans, that slavery was unjust. And in 1838 he had spoken out in general terms against the mob violence that was directed at abolitionists and had resulted in the killing of Elijah Lovejoy in nearby Alton. But Lincoln's roots in the Ohio River Valley towns settled largely by migrants from southern states and his desire to build Whig support in those towns worked against any sympathy for abolitionism, which emphasized the sinfulness of slaveholding. He knew, moreover, that abolitionism was a threat to the Whigs. This had come home to him in 1844 when he had watched the Whig abolitionists in New York throw their votes to James G. Birney, the Liberty party candidate, and seemingly deny Henry Clay the presidency. And he did not believe that the federal government had any authority to tamper with slavery where it existed.

Lincoln entered Congress in 1847 with a firm conviction that the Whigs had to abstain from abolitionism yet find a way to hold the allegiance of the growing number of people opposed to slavery. Consequently, he supported the appropriations bills necessary to sustain American forces in Mexico but, at the same time, condemned the Polk administration for its war of aggression, introduced resolutions pressing Polk on the constitutionality of the war, and, most important, voted for the Wilmot Proviso in its various forms. In addition, Lincoln introduced a resolution for the gradual abolition of slavery in the District of Columbia. His bill would have provided compensation to slave owners and required approval by a referendum of the "free white citizens" of the District. It was this kind of moderate program of opposition to slavery's expansion and encouragement of gradual emancipation, coupled with the colonization of freed slaves in Africa and elsewhere, that Lincoln argued was the only practical way to solve the problem of slavery. It was on the basis of this program that he argued in 1848, while campaigning for Zachary Taylor in Massachusetts, Chicago, and even his own district, that antislavery Whigs should remain in the party because Whigs and supporters of the Free Soil party had similar views on the spread of slavery.

Corporate Lawyer. The abolitionists denounced Lincoln's approach. In response to his gradualist proposal for emancipation in the District of Columbia, the abolitionist Wendell Phillips called Lincoln "the slave hound of Illinois." But Lincoln's position, particularly his condemnation of the Mexican War, put him too far out of step with the voters in his district, and he went into a prudent retirement from politics that lasted from 1849 until 1854. While he engaged in an increasingly lucrative legal practice, one in which some of the leading railroads and manufacturers in Illinois became his clients, Lincoln agonized over the disintegration of the Whig party and

Abraham Lincoln
Abraham Lincoln became the most photographed man of his time, yet none of the photographs suggests how striking and sparkling people found him. The photography of that day required subjects to stand absolutely still, their heads against a rack, for long periods, and this caused Lincoln to lapse into a sad and abstracted mood.

The Campaign of 1854. Lincoln's dual quest for the moral high ground on slavery and a way to preserve the Union brought him back into politics in 1854, after the passage of Stephen Douglas's Kansas-Nebraska Act. That act "aroused" him "as he had never been before." The opening of Kansas to popular sovereignty placed freedom and slavery on the same ethical level and at the same time threatened the Union. Moreover, the act created an opportunity for the Whigs to win the allegiance of Democrats who feared that Douglas was betraying them by opening the West to slavery and to blacks. Lincoln made a last, desperate effort to save the Whig party in Illinois. He plunged into the campaigns with an attack on Douglas, support for Whig candidates, and his own campaign for both the Illinois legislature and the U.S. Senate.

Lincoln stated his position in what became known as his Peoria address. He did not want to threaten slavery in areas where it existed. White southerners were, he said, "just what we would be in their situation." He believed that "some system of gradual emancipation might be adopted," but "for their tardiness in this, I will not undertake to judge our brethren of the south." But the Kansas-Nebraska Act had repealed the Missouri Compromise and threatened to expand slavery. Politicians had to face the ethical issue that slavery was founded, he said, "in the selfishness of man's nature," whereas opposition to it was based "in his love of justice." However, the risks to the Union were obvious. Those principles were in "eternal antagonism" and "when brought into collision so fiercely as slavery extension brings them, shocks, and throes, and convulsions must ceaselessly follow."

Lincoln concluded his Peoria address by appealing to supporters of the Free Soil party and abolitionists to join the Whigs in restoring the Missouri Compromise. By joining forces they could both block slavery's extension and uphold the Union. In short, Lincoln expressed what would become key tenets of the Republican party: moral opposition to slavery, assertion of the right of the national government to exclude slavery from the territories, and the conviction that the nation must eventually cut out slavery like a "cancer."

Republican Party Leader. After a handful of Anti-Nebraska Democrats in the state legislature blocked Lincoln's election to the Senate, he decided, finally, to abandon the Whig party. That way, he might win the support of Anti-Nebraska Democrats who could not bring themselves to endorse a Whig. As the violence escalated in Kansas and the Whig party splintered, he worked to unite all the Anti-Nebraska forces—conservative Whigs, members of the Free Soil party, abolitionists, Know-Nothings, and bolting Democrats—in opposition to the Democratic party and to Stephen

the apparent failure of moderate approaches to resolve the sectional crisis. In a speech eulogizing Henry Clay after his death in 1852, Lincoln condemned both the proslavery fanatics who denied the tenet of the Declaration of Independence that "all men are created equal" and the abolitionists, who would "shiver into fragments the Union of these States; tear to tatters its now venerated constitution; and even burn the last copy of the Bible, rather than slavery should continue a single hour."

Douglas and the doctrine of popular sovereignty. In May 1856, in a state convention of all the dissident groups, Lincoln emerged as the most powerful leader in the coalition that formed the Republican party in Illinois, and Illinois Republicans put him forward as their favorite-son candidate for vice-president.

The *Dred Scott* decision in 1857 gave Lincoln new ammunition in his campaign to win over Democrats. He warned that the Supreme Court, in its "next Dred Scott decision," would simply "decide that no State under the Constitution can exclude" slavery. If the followers of Buchanan had their way, "we shall *awake* to the *reality . . .* that the *Supreme* Court has made *Illinois* a *slave* State." The Court now seemed to be a partner in the Slave Power conspiracy. Although Republicans would abide by the Court's decision, they dedicated themselves to reversing it.

By 1858, Lincoln's position in the Illinois Republican party was even stronger, and he again received the party's nomination as the challenger to Stephen Douglas for U.S. senator. In accepting the nomination he delivered the most radical statement of his career. Quoting from the Bible, "A house divided against itself cannot stand," he warned that the nation could not resolve the slavery issue without a crisis. There were only two possible outcomes:

> I believe this government cannot endure permanently half *slave* and half *free*. I do not expect the Union to be dissolved—I do not expect the house to *fall*—but I do expect it will cease to be divided. It will become *all* one thing, or *all* the other.

Thus Lincoln dismissed as insignificant the differences between Douglas and Buchanan on the issue of slavery. Americans had to choose, according to Lincoln, between opposition and advocacy.

Lincoln versus Douglas

Lincoln's challenge to Douglas's bid for reelection as a senator from Illinois proved to be the highlight of the 1858 elections. The political duel attracted national interest because of Douglas's prominence and his break with the Buchanan administration. Adding to the excitement was Lincoln's reputation as a formidable attorney, politician, and stump speaker. To increase his national exposure, Lincoln challenged Douglas to a series of seven debates.

During those debates Lincoln attacked slavery as an institution that subverted equality of opportunity. He expressed doubts about the innate abilities of African-Americans and explicitly rejected formulas that would give them social and political equality, but he declared that blacks were entitled to "all the natural rights enumer-

Stephen Douglas
This photograph, taken in Mathew Brady's New York studio in 1860, suggests why Stephen Douglas (1813–1861) was known as the "Little Giant."

ated in the Declaration of Independence." This meant, Lincoln explained, that "in the right to eat the bread, without leave of anybody else, which his own hand earns," the black was "the equal of every living man."

Lincoln described the master conspiracy he saw at work. The Kansas-Nebraska Act (which Douglas had introduced), the *Dred Scott* decision, and Buchanan's cynical endorsement of the fraudulent Lecompton constitution were part of a master plan to extend slavery throughout the territories. If the South succeeded, it would eventually insist that slavery be legalized throughout the United States. Lincoln then pressed Douglas to explain how he could accept the *Dred Scott* decision and at the same time advocate popular sovereignty.

In a debate in Freeport, Illinois, Douglas responded by elaborating on a reformulation of popular sovereignty that he had been working on since mid-1857. In what became known as the Freeport doctrine, he asserted that settlers could exclude slavery from a territory in practice simply by not adopting local legislation to protect it. In other words, he claimed that even if territorial governments followed Taney and did not prohibit slavery, municipalities could still do so by failing to support the "peculiar institution." In effect, this was a legalistic formulation of his view that demography and geography made the victory of slavery in the territories almost impossible. To southerners the Freeport doctrine meant that they could be denied the victory won in the *Dred Scott* decision.

The Republicans made great gains in 1858, including control of the House. Lincoln, however, was not among the victors. Douglas was reelected to the Senate by a narrow margin in the state legislature, but Lincoln had virtually buried popular sovereignty in Illinois. Douglas's victory resulted from the overrepresentation in the legislature of the staunchly Democratic counties in southern Illinois rather than any popularity of the Freeport doctrine, which was too flimsy a basis for rebuilding the Democratic party.

The Election of 1860

The Congressional elections of 1858 made southern Democrats intensely nervous. They knew that the Republicans might win in 1860, so they increased their demands. The more moderate party members, known as Southern Rights Democrats, insisted that the Democratic party and the federal government make specific commitments to protect slavery, such as the enactment of a territorial slave code that would counter the Freeport doctrine. One of their leading spokesmen was Senator Jefferson Davis, a Mississippi planter and Mexican War hero. More radical southern Democrats, such as Robert Barnwell Rhett of South Carolina and William Lowndes Yancey of Alabama, demanded that Douglas and his followers support relegalization of the international slave trade. Called *fire-eaters*, those radicals were secessionists who hoped to drive a wedge between the North and the South. In response, Douglas made it plain that if the Democratic party platform included such proposals in 1860, he would not support it. He had no choice in drawing a hard line. If he did not, he would sacrifice his home base of support.

John Brown's Raid. In the meantime a shocking event further deepened the anxiety of southerners. One night in October 1859, John Brown, leader of the Pottawatomie massacre, led eighteen heavily armed followers, both black and white, in a raid that seized the federal arsenal at Harpers Ferry, Virginia. Brown's explicit purpose was to arm a slave rebellion and create an African-American state in the South. The local militia and U.S. Marines under the command of Colonel Robert E. Lee quickly reclaimed the arsenal; they captured Brown and killed ten of his party.

Republican leaders dismissed Brown as a criminal, but Democrats in both the North and the South called Brown's plot, in the words of Stephen Douglas, "a natural, logical, inevitable result of the doctrines and teachings of the Republican party." Fueling the Democratic charges were letters, discovered near Harpers Ferry and widely published in the press, that incriminated six leading abolitionists, known as the Secret Six, for financing Brown's raid. The group included two Unitarian ministers, Thomas Wentworth Higginson and Theodore Parker. Parker used his home as a station on the underground railroad for escaped slaves, and Higginson had run unsuccessfully as a Free Soil party candidate for Congress in 1850. During the Civil War he would command a regiment of African-American soldiers. Higginson admitted his involvement and declared that Brown's "acquittal or rescue would do half as much good as being executed; so strong is the personal sympathy with him."

Virginia gave the abolitionists the Christian martyr they wanted. The governor charged Brown with trea-

John Brown Pledging Allegiance to the Flag
This is the earliest known photograph of John Brown, probably taken in 1846. In 1847 Frederick Douglass had dinner with Brown and learned that he had a plan to establish abolitionist bases in the Appalachian Mountains and induce slaves to escape to freedom.

Harpers Ferry Armory
The town of Harpers Ferry was strategically situated at the confluence of the
Shenandoah and Potomac rivers, at the
point where the Baltimore and Ohio
Railroad crossed the Potomac. Adding
to the town's strategic importance were
the federal armory (including the machine shops at the right in the photograph), the federal arsenal (an arms
storehouse), and on a nearby island in
the Shenandoah, Hall's Rifle Works,
where sixty gunsmiths produced
firearms for the U.S. Army. At the left is
the fire-engine house where Brown and
his raiders made their last stand.

son, a state court sentenced him to death, and Brown
was hanged. At a church meeting in Concord, Massachusetts, Henry David Thoreau described Brown as "an
angel of light," "the bravest and humanest man in all
the country." Emerson proclaimed that Brown would
"make the gallows as glorious as the cross." Slaveholders were horrified, assuming that those widely publicized utterances revealed the sentiments of the entire
North and that abolitionists were organizing new slave
rebellions. More than ever slaveholders were convinced
that a Republican victory in 1860 would lead to the destruction of slavery.

The Democrats Divide. When the Democratic party
convened in Charleston, South Carolina, in April 1860,
the southern wing was determined to force the party to
embrace the program of Jefferson Davis and his followers: positive protection of slavery in the territories in
line with the *Dred Scott* decision. Northern Democrats
refused. They wanted only a vague endorsement of popular sovereignty and the suggestion that disputed issues
be left to the Supreme Court. When the convention
adopted the northern platform, the delegates from eight
southern states left the hall. Because Buchanan had lost
the confidence of northern Democrats, he was not a
contender for the nomination, and Douglas led the balloting for a presidential candidate. However, his determined foes denied him the two-thirds majority that the
party rules required for nomination. The party adjourned and then reconvened in Baltimore in June.
Most of the southerners reappeared but soon walked

out again. The Baltimore convention then nominated
Stephen Douglas. The bolting southerners convened
separately in Baltimore and nominated Buchanan's vice-
president, John C. Breckinridge of Kentucky. The Democratic party had finally broken into two sectional
pieces.

The Republicans Choose Lincoln. The Republicans
sensed victory and acted cautiously. They settled on
Abraham Lincoln, who had a more moderate position
on slavery than the best-known Republicans, Senator
William H. Seward of New York and former Governor
Salmon P. Chase of Ohio. Lincoln also conveyed a compelling egalitarian image that could appeal to small
farmers and workers. And Lincoln's home territory—
the Ohio River Valley of Illinois and Indiana—was a
crucial "swing" area in the competition between Democrats and Republicans.

The Republican platform also attempted to strike a
moderate tone. It adhered to free-soil doctrine but ruled
out direct interference with slavery in the South. It denied the right of states to secede. It also endorsed the
old Whig program of economic development, which
had gained increasing support among Democrats in the
Midwest, especially after the onset of depression conditions in 1857.

Douglas campaigned nationally against three com-
petitors, each of whom was, for all practical purposes, a
regional candidate. However, in September and October
he concentrated his efforts in the South, having concluded that Lincoln would win in the North. Douglas

underscored the seriousness of the sectional crisis by shattering tradition and campaigning personally. He warned Breckinridge supporters about secession, telling them that the North and northern Democrats would not allow them to destroy the Union and arguing that *his* Democratic party provided the only feasible instrument for compromise. Competing with Breckinridge and Douglas in the South and also offering a Unionist message was John Bell, a former Tennessee senator who became the nominee of the Constitutional Union party, a residue of southern Whiggery. The forces of moderation were ebbing in the South. Since the shock of John Brown's raid on Harpers Ferry, waves of hysteria over slave rebellion had swept through the region. Southern panic intensified during the presidential campaign. Fires of unknown origin and the deaths of whites under peculiar circumstances initiated reports of arson and poisoning.

Lincoln's Victory. Lincoln won only a plurality of the popular vote—about 40 percent of the total—but received a majority of the electoral vote (see Map 14.5). His victory in the North was overwhelming: he won every state except New Jersey. Of crucial importance to

Lincoln's election were Pennsylvania, Indiana, and his home state of Illinois, all of which had cast their electoral votes for Buchanan in 1856. In ten of the slave states Lincoln was excluded from the ballot; in the other five slave states he won no electoral votes. Breckinridge won every state in the Deep South as well as Delaware, Maryland, and North Carolina. Bell carried the Upper South states where the Whigs had been strongest: Kentucky, Tennessee, and Virginia. Douglas won electoral votes in only two states—Missouri, which he carried, and New Jersey, where he won three of the state's seven electoral votes—despite winning 21 percent of the popular vote. His broad support was wasted in a winner-take-all system.

The Republicans had united the Northeast, the Midwest, and the Far West behind free soil. They had been able to absorb abolitionism and still unify enough businessmen, workers, and farmers to achieve victory. A political party with support in only one section of the country and a clear mission had finally come to power. To many southerners, it now seemed time to think carefully about the meaning of Lincoln's 1858 words, that the Union must "become all one thing, or all the other."

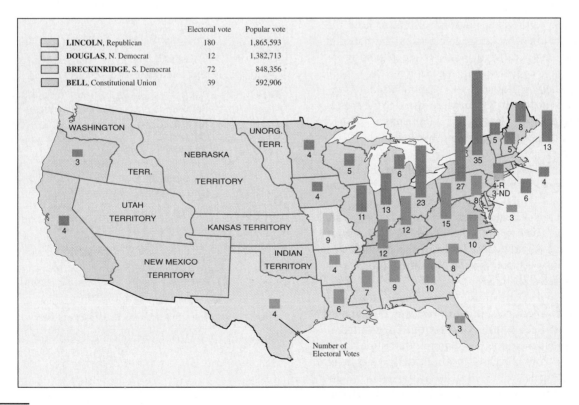

MAP 14.5

The Election of 1860

Four presidential candidates vied for election in 1860. Douglas's few electoral votes are striking in light of his strong showing in the popular vote. In most states Douglas ran second to Lincoln or Breckinridge, who took all of the electoral votes in the states that they won.

Summary

The American experience, so full of material and spiritual promise, took a tragic turn in the 1840s, when the South's ambitions led the United States into a war of conquest against Mexico. President Polk's policy of territorial expansion was successful, but the new territories and continued western expansion doomed the Missouri Compromise as a means of accommodating the interests of the South and the North in the West. The sectional threat to the unity of the two major political parties and to the Union became so great that leaders of both parties joined in framing a settlement, known as the Compromise of 1850. The Compromise temporarily preserved the Second Party System, but most southern Democrats and most northern Whigs did not support it. They stood ready to risk the Union if they could not dominate the West.

The Compromise of 1850 and the Second Party System died in the violence of the 1850s, casualties of the first armed struggles over slavery. Antislavery northerners defied the Fugitive Slave Act, battling southern slave catchers. When northern Whigs opposed the act, southerners deserted the party, killing it as a national organization.

The ability of the U.S. political system to hold the Union together then rested exclusively on the national appeal of the Democratic party and its doctrine of popular sovereignty. But that doctrine brought only more violence—"Bleeding Kansas"—as opponents and supporters of slavery fought a guerrilla war over the meaning of popular sovereignty. Bleeding Kansas pushed North and South farther apart and weakened the Democratic party.

Northern Whigs and supporters of the Free Soil party joined dissident Democrats and Know-Nothings to establish the Republican party, which supported free soil. By 1856 the Second Party System of Democrats and Whigs had given way to the Third Party System of Democrats and Republicans. In 1856 the Republicans united a majority of voters in the Northeast and Northwest around free-soilism.

The national Democratic party finally fractured over the *Dred Scott* decision and President Buchanan's support for the Lecompton constitution. Former Democrats and Whigs continued to switch to the Republican party. In 1859 John Brown, an abolitionist veteran of the Kansas struggle, captured a federal arsenal in Virginia and tried to start a war against slavery. Southerners then demanded more protection for slavery than northern Democrats would provide. Consequently, in the 1860 election the Democrats divided along sectional

lines. At the same time Abraham Lincoln succeeded in uniting northern society around the free-soil vision and won the presidency for the Republican party.

TIMELINE

1845	Polk's inauguration
	Frémont sets out from St. Louis
	Texas accepts admission to the Union
	Polk sends Zachary Taylor south of the Nueces River
	Slidell's mission
	Frémont reaches the Sacramento Valley
1846	Polk sends Taylor south of the Rio Grande
	United States declares war on Mexico
	Oregon treaty ratified
	"Bear Flag Republic" proclaimed; Sloat seizes Monterrey
	Walker Tariff passed
	Wilmot Proviso introduced in Congress
	Taylor's victory at Monterrey
1847	Taylor's victory at Buena Vista
	Scott captures Mexico City
1848	Gold discovered in California
	Treaty of Guadalupe Hidalgo
	Free Soil party organized
	Taylor elected
1849	Taylor proposes immediate admission of California
1850	Compromise of 1850
1851	Christiana riot
	American party formed
1852	*Uncle Tom's Cabin* appears in book form
	Franklin Pierce elected president
1853	Perry's expedition to Japan begins
1854	Kansas-Nebraska Act
	Republican party formed
	Ostend Manifesto
	Know-Nothing movement peaks
1856	"Pottawatomie massacre"
	James Buchanan elected president
1857	*Dred Scott v. Sandford*
	Panic of 1857
1858	Buchanan backs Lecompton constitution
	Lincoln-Douglas debates
1859	John Brown's raid on Harpers Ferry
1860	Abraham Lincoln elected president

BIBLIOGRAPHY

Histories that discuss the disruption of the Union between the Mexican War and the onset of the Civil War in a comprehensive fashion are rare. The best is David M. Potter, *The Impending Crisis, 1848–1861* (1976).

The Mexican War and Its Aftermath

Study of expansionism in the 1840s should begin with Frederick Merk, *The Monroe Doctrine and American Expansion, 1843–1849* (1972). On the coming of the Mexican War, consult Paul H. Bergeron, *The Presidency of James K. Polk* (1987); David Pletcher, *The Diplomacy of Annexation: Texas, Oregon, and the Mexican War* (1973); and Charles G. Sellers, *James K. Polk: Continentalist, 1843–1846* (1966). On the fighting of the war, see K. Jack Bauer, *The Mexican War, 1846–1848* (1974), and Otis A. Singletary, *The Mexican War* (1960). For an analysis of the relationship between the war experience and American culture, see Robert W. Johannsen, *To the Halls of the Montezumas: The Mexican War in the American Imagination* (1985), and John H. Schroeder, *Mr. Polk's War: American Opposition and Dissent* (1973). For the Mexican viewpoint see Gene M. Brack, *Mexico Views Manifest Destiny, 1821–1846: An Essay on the Origins of the Mexican War* (1975). On Congressional politics during the 1840s, see Chaplain Morrison, *Democratic Politics and Sectionalism: The Wilmot Proviso Controversy* (1967); Merrill Peterson, *The Great Triumvirate: Webster, Clay, and Calhoun* (1987); and Joel H. Silbey, *The Shrine of Party: Congressional Voting Behavior, 1841–1852* (1967). On the Compromise of 1850, see Holman Hamilton, *Prologue to Conflict: The Crisis and Compromise of 1850* (1964). For an interpretation stressing the contingency of the South's commitment to the Union, consult William W. Freehling, *The Road to Disunion: Secessionists at Bay, 1776–1854* (1991).

Sectional Strife and the Third Party System

General studies of sectional conflict in the 1850s include Avery O. Craven, *The Growth of Southern Nationalism* (1953), and Roy F. Nichols, *The Disruption of American Democracy* (1948). On the Fugitive Slave Act, consult Stanley W. Campbell, *The Slave Catchers* (1970). The best study of the politics of southern expansionism is Robert E. May, *The Southern Dream of a Caribbean Empire, 1854–1861* (1973). The leading studies of Frederick Douglass include Philip S. Foner, *Frederick Douglass: A Biography* (1964); Nathan I. Huggins, *Slave and Citizen: The Life of Frederick Douglass* (1980); William S. McFeely, *Frederick Douglass* (1991); and Benjamin Quarles, *Frederick Douglass* (1948). Essential sources on Douglass include three versions of his autobiography: *The Narrative of the Life of Frederick Douglass, An American Slave* (1845), which he wrote as an antislavery tract; *My Bondage and My Freedom* (1855), which provides an elaborate and highly personal analysis of slavery; and *Life and Times of Frederick Douglass, Written by Himself* (1881).

On the development of the Republican party, see Eric Foner, *Free Soil, Free Labor, Free Men: The Ideology of the Republican Party before the Civil War* (1970); William E. Gienapp, *The Origins of the Republican Party, 1852–1856* (1987); and Michael Holt, *The Political Crisis of the 1850s* (1978). The crisis over Kansas is discussed in James A. Rawley, *Race and Politics: Bleeding Kansas and the Coming of the Civil War* (1969), and Gerald W. Wolff, *The Kansas-Nebraska Bill: Party, Section, and the Coming of the Civil War* (1977). On the Buchanan administration, see Kenneth M. Stampp, *America in 1857: A Nation on the Brink* (1990). On *Dred Scott*, see Don E. Fehrenbacher, *The Dred Scott Case: Its Significance in American Law and Politics* (1978). For a biography of Stephen A. Douglas, see Robert W. Johannsen, *Stephen A. Douglas* (1973). The best biography of John Brown is Stephen Oates, *To Purge this Land with Blood: A Biography of John Brown* (1970).

Abraham Lincoln and the Breaking of Union

Abraham Lincoln has inspired a host of biographies. Classic studies include James G. Randall, *Mr. Lincoln* (1957, distilled by Richard N. Current from Randall's four-volume *Lincoln the President*, with vol. 4 completed by Current); Carl Sandburg, *Abraham Lincoln: The Prairie Years* (1929); and Benjamin Thomas, *Abraham Lincoln: A Biography* (1952). The most recent major biography of Lincoln is David Herbert Donald, *Lincoln* (1995). For a stimulating set of essays, see Richard N. Current, *The Lincoln Nobody Knows* (1958). The most valuable book on Lincoln's formative political years is Don E. Fehrenbacher, *Prelude to Greatness: Lincoln in the 1850s* (1962). For other interpretations, see George B. Forgie, *Patricide and the House Divided* (1979); Stephen Oates, *With Malice toward None: A Life of Abraham Lincoln* (1977); and Garry Wills, *Lincoln at Gettysburg* (1992).

**The Seventh Regiment Departing for the War,
April 19, 1861** (detail)

Stunned by the massive demonstrations of support for the
Union after Lincoln's call to arms, a New York woman
wrote, "It seems as if we never were alive till now; never had
a country till now." Thomas Nast evoked that spirit in this
painting done in 1869.

CHAPTER 15

Two Societies at War

1861–1865

★   ★   ★

For the political leaders of the South, the victory of Abraham Lincoln and the Republicans in the fateful election of 1860 presented a clear and immediate danger to the institution of slavery. They knew that Lincoln regarded slavery as morally wrong and had united northern society in opposing the "Slave Power" and the extension of slavery into the territories. Moreover, unlike any preceding president, he owed the South not a single electoral vote. Soon, southern leaders were certain, he would appoint abolitionists and free blacks to federal jobs in the South and reopen the flow of abolitionist literature. The result would be disastrous waves of bloody slave revolts. White southerners believed that no loyal American should have to fear such a cataclysm. They were convinced that the Constitution protected slavery. Moreover, in their view slavery was a bulwark of democracy: by guaranteeing equality and freedom for whites, it protected the highest values of the republic.

Many southerners swiftly concluded that they could save slavery from the Republican threat only through secession: southern states would leave the Union and establish their own nation, in accordance with John C. Calhoun's constitutional theory that sovereignty lay not with the American people as a whole but with collections of people acting through their state governments. If Lincoln would not recognize states' rights, the South would fight.

And so came the Civil War. Called the "War between the States" by Confederates and the "War of the Rebellion" by Unionists, it tested the founding principles of the republic. It resolved once and for all the great dividing issue of slavery. And it cost more lives than all the nation's subsequent wars put together.

Choosing Sides, 1861

The two societies, South and North, were poised for confrontation in 1861. Many southerners were convinced that in defending states' rights and slavery they were being more true in their Americanism and more stalwart in their support of republican ideals than were Republicans in the North. By contrast, Lincoln and his party regarded secession as despicable and treasonous. There was only the slimmest chance that during the early months of 1861 the nation's politicians could emulate the architects of the great compromises of 1820, 1833, and 1850 and once again postpone the sectional confrontation.

The Secession Crisis

The movement toward secession was most rapid in South Carolina—the home of Calhoun and the state with the greatest concentration of slaves. The fire-eaters took the lead in organizing a convention to consider se-

cession, which most of them had been calling for since 1850. On December 20, only six weeks after Lincoln's election, the convention unanimously enacted an ordinance dissolving "the union now subsisting between South Carolina and other States."

During the next six weeks fire-eaters in six other cotton states called conventions. They moved quickly, before southern Unionists could mount an effective opposition. Meanwhile, vigilante groups and military companies organized. They sometimes engaged in strong-arm intimidation of Unionists, who were often willing to secede but usually preferred to wait until Lincoln had shown his hand. In early January, in an atmosphere of public celebration, Mississippi enacted a secession ordinance. In less than a month Florida, Alabama, Georgia, Louisiana, and Texas also left the Union (see Map 15.1). The jubilant secessionists proclaimed a new nation—the Confederate States of America. In early February commissioners from those states, meeting in Montgomery, Alabama, adopted a provisional constitution and named Jefferson Davis provisional president. Secession proceeded so briskly that all this was done before James Buchanan left the White House.

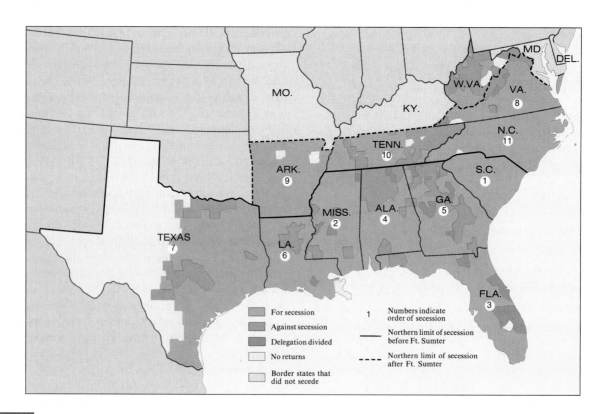

MAP 15.1

The Process of Secession
Comparing the order of secession with the distribution of slaves in Map 13.1 (page 384), it is clear that states with the highest concentrations of slaves led the movement to secede. The secession of the Upper South followed the Confederate firing on Fort Sumter. The map also shows how delegates to the secession conventions or special sessions of legislatures voted. Significant minorities in most states opposed secession.

Panic was less severe in the Upper South, where concentrations of slaves were not as large. Nevertheless, secessionist fervor had been gathering momentum there from the time of Lincoln's election, and many political leaders in the eight Upper South states (Arkansas, Delaware, Kentucky, Maryland, Missouri, North Carolina, Tennessee, and Virginia) defended the right of any state to secede. In January 1861 the Virginia and Tennessee legislatures pledged to resist any federal invasion of the seceded states. But they went no further. Upper South leaders proposed federal guarantees for slavery in the states where it existed, hoping to relieve the anxieties of the seceding states and bring them back into the Union.

While the seceding states acted, the Union government, still under control of the Democrats, floundered. President Buchanan did not support secession, but the southerners in his cabinet persuaded him that if he confronted the seceding states, he would alienate southern Unionists and accelerate the secession drive. In his last message to Congress in December 1860 he declared secession illegal but said that the federal government lacked the authority to force a state to return to the Union. South Carolina responded quickly by claiming that Buchanan's message implied recognition of its independence and by demanding the surrender of Fort Sumter, a federal garrison in Charleston harbor. But even Buchanan was reluctant to turn over federal property; he decided to test cautiously the secessionists' resolve. In January 1861 he ordered an unarmed merchant ship to reinforce Fort Sumter. When South Carolinians fired on the ship as it entered the harbor, Buchanan backed off, declining to send the navy to escort the ship into the harbor.

The Crittenden Plan. As the South Carolina crisis worsened, Buchanan urged Congress to find a compromise. The proposal that received the most support was submitted by Senator John J. Crittenden of Kentucky, an aging follower of Henry Clay. Crittenden proposed amending the Constitution with a set of provisions that could never be changed. Congress would be prohibited from abolishing slavery in the states, and the Missouri Compromise line would be extended westward across the territories as far as the California border. Whereas slavery would be barred north of the line, it would be recognized and protected south of the line, including in any territories "hereafter acquired."

After consulting with President-elect Lincoln, Congressional Republicans rejected Crittenden's plan. Lincoln feared that extending the Missouri Compromise line would encourage the South to embark on an imperialist expansion of slavery into Mexico, the Caribbean, and Latin America. If adopted, Lincoln charged, Crittenden's plan would be "a perpetual covenant of war against every people, tribe, and State owning a foot of land between here and Tierra del Fuego." Lincoln was determined not to repudiate the Republicans' chief plank: free soil in the territories.

Lincoln Takes Command. In his inaugural address on March 4, 1861, Lincoln carefully balanced the possibility of reconciliation with his firm commitment to protect the Union. He promised to welcome back the seceded states after time had allowed passions to cool and repeated his support for guaranteeing slavery in states where it existed. But he continued to stand by free soil, offering no compromise on the future of slavery in the territories. Most important, he stated that secession was illegal and that acts of violence in its support constituted insurrection. He announced equally clearly that he intended to enforce federal law throughout the Union and—of particular relevance to Fort Sumter—hold federal property in the seceded states. If force was necessary to preserve the Union, he promised to use it. The choice would be the South's—return to the Union or face war.

Lincoln had hoped to wait out the Fort Sumter crisis, but the garrison urgently needed supplies. He was reluctant to appear aggressive, but he was also unwilling to abandon the fort, fearing that his efforts to maintain the Union would lose credibility. Consequently, only a month after his inauguration, Lincoln dispatched an armed relief expedition and informed South Carolina of his intentions.

Jefferson Davis and his government received word of Lincoln's action on April 8. They welcomed Lincoln's move, believing that his show of force would set the wavering southern states against the North and win foreign support for the Confederate cause. The next day they resolved to take the fort before Union reinforcements arrived. Jefferson Davis authorized General P. G. T. Beauregard, the Confederate commander in Charleston, to take the fort—by force if necessary. When Major Robert Anderson refused to surrender, the Confederates opened fire. On April 14, after two days of bombardment that destroyed large portions of the fort but killed no one, Anderson surrendered. The next day Lincoln called 75,000 state militiamen into federal service for ninety days. As he put it, they were needed to put down an insurrection "too powerful to be suppressed by the ordinary course of judicial proceedings." War had come.

In the North, Fort Sumter became a symbol of national unity and Major Anderson became a hero. Northern states responded enthusiastically to Lincoln's call to arms. Governor William Dennison of Ohio, when asked to provide thirteen regiments of volunteers, sent twenty. "The lion in us is thoroughly roused," he explained. Many northern Democrats were equally fervent. As Stephen Douglas explained just six weeks before his death: "There are only two sides to the question. Every man must be for the United States or against it. There can be no neutrals in this war, *only patriots—or traitors.*"

The Contest for the Upper South

After the fall of Fort Sumter, Lincoln hoped to hold as many of the eight states of the Upper South as possible. If he could keep them from seceding, he might swiftly restore the Union. In the event of war, the Upper South would be of great strategic value. Those eight states accounted for two-thirds of the South's white population, more than three-fourths of its industrial production, and well over half of its food and fuel. They were home to many of the nation's best military leaders, including Colonel Robert E. Lee of Virginia, a career officer whom General-in-Chief Winfield Scott recommended to Lincoln as field commander of the new Union army. And they offered key geographical advantages. Kentucky, with its 500-mile border on the Ohio River, was essential to the movement of troops and supplies. Maryland was vital to national security because it surrounded the nation's capital on the north. It also contained the major port of Baltimore and adjoined the industrial state of Pennsylvania. Virginia was psychologically strategic as the home of Washington and Jefferson.

Virginia, North Carolina, Tennessee, and Arkansas. Lincoln never had a chance to hold Virginia. His inaugural address, with its implied threat of invasion, had silenced Unionists in eastern Virginia. His call to arms prompted them to embrace secession. After the fall of Fort Sumter, William Poague, a former Unionist lawyer who quickly enlisted in a Virginia artillery unit, explained that "the North was the aggressor. The South resisted her invaders."

On April 17 Virginia's secession convention passed an ordinance of secession by a vote of 88 to 55, an almost direct reversal of the vote taken earlier that month. The dissenting votes came mainly from the mountainous northwestern counties, where whites resented the power of the Tidewater planters and often looked to Ohio and Pennsylvania for trade and leadership. On April 18 General Scott offered Robert E. Lee field command of the Union troops. Despite his description of himself as "one of those dull creatures that cannot see the good of secession," Lee not only declined the offer but resigned from the army. "Save in defense of my native state," Lee told Scott, "I never desire again to draw my sword." At the same time Virginia's militia seized the federal armory and arsenal at Harpers Ferry and the Gosport navy yard at Newport. The Upper South states of North Carolina, Tennessee, and Arkansas promptly joined Virginia in the Confederacy and sent their militias to that state's defense.

Western Virginia, Maryland, Kentucky, and Missouri. Lincoln moved aggressively to hold the rest of the Upper South in the Union. In May he ordered General George B. McClellan, who had assembled a Union force in Ohio, to cross the Ohio River into Virginia. By June Mc-

Clellan's army had secured the route of the Baltimore and Ohio Railroad, which linked Washington with the Ohio River Valley. In July he established control of northwestern Virginia. In October the voters in fifty western Virginia counties overwhelmingly approved the creation of a new state. West Virginia was admitted to the Union in 1863.

In Maryland southern sympathizers were quite militant, but Lincoln made it clear he would use force to keep the state in the Union. Less than a week after Fort Sumter fell a pro-Confederate mob attacked Massachusetts troops marching between railroad stations in Baltimore and caused the war's first combat deaths: four soldiers and twelve civilians. A few days later Maryland secessionists destroyed railroad bridges and telegraph lines. Without delay Lincoln stationed Union troops along the state's railroad lines and imprisoned many suspected secessionists, including Baltimore's police chief and members of the state legislature. He released them only in November 1861, after the Union party had won a decisive victory in state elections.

In Kentucky secessionist and Unionist sentiments were evenly balanced, and Lincoln at first moved cautiously, trying to avoid pushing it into the Confederacy. He asserted his right to send troops into the state but took no immediate military action. In August, after Unionists had won control of the state legislature, he took steps to shut off Kentucky's thriving export trade in horses, mules, whiskey, and foodstuffs to the Lower South and to the Confederate troops on its borders. Then the Confederacy played into Lincoln's hands by moving troops into Kentucky, seizing Columbus and Bowling Green. Outraged by this aggression, the Kentucky legislature called on the federal government to protect it from invasion. In September, Union troops—Illinois volunteers under the command of the relatively unknown brigadier general Ulysses S. Grant—crossed the Ohio River to drive out the Confederates. Thus the Confederates inadvertently helped keep Kentucky in the Union. Over the course of the war about three-fifths of the white Kentuckians who took up arms did so for the Union.

In Missouri, Lincoln moved promptly to control communications and trade on the upper Mississippi and Missouri rivers. By July a small Union force stationed in St. Louis, composed largely of regiments organized by the city's German-American community, had defeated Confederate sympathizers commanded by Governor Claiborne Jackson. Confederate guerrilla bands led by William Quantrill and Jesse and Frank James—dubbed "bushwhackers" (ambushers) by Unionists—waged campaigns throughout the war. But the Union maintained control of the state, and most Missouri men who fought joined the Union armies—80,000 whites and 8,000 blacks. Of the eight states of the Upper South, Lincoln had kept four (including Delaware) and a portion of a fifth (western Virginia) in the Union.

War Aims and Resources, North and South

Setting Out War Aims. On July 4, 1861, Lincoln made his first major statement of war aims to a special session of Congress: the war was a noble crusade in which the future of democracy throughout the world would be determined. The issue of the war was "whether a constitutional republic, or a democracy—a government of the people, by the same people—can or cannot maintain its territorial integrity against its domestic foes." The war would test "whether discontented individuals, few in number, can arbitrarily break up their government and thus practically put an end to free government upon the face of the earth." Only by crushing the rebellion would the nation survive.

Lincoln did not foresee in 1861 how difficult it would be to crush the rebellion. The Union had to break the will of the southern people, not just smash the Confederate armies. To win, the Union had to fight a *total war*—a war against an entire society, not just its armies. But Lincoln's conception of the Union's war aims, which was well developed even at the war's outset, advanced the great task. His lofty statements of what was at stake helped rally the people of the Union to make a deep and sustained commitment to the war. Like Lincoln, they came to perceive the war as a democratic crusade against southern society.

Confederate leaders also called on their people to fight for democracy. At his inauguration in February 1861, Jefferson Davis identified the Confederate cause with the principles of the American Revolution. He claimed that southerners were fighting, just as their grandfathers had, against tyranny and on behalf of the "sacred right of self-government." A month later, shortly after his election as vice-president of the Confederacy, Alexander Stephens of Georgia defined more explicitly what Confederate democracy meant: the Confederacy's "cornerstone rests upon the great truth that the Negro is not equal to the white man, that slavery—subordination to the superior race—is his natural or normal condition." Slavery made democracy for whites possible, he argued, and the alternative to slavery for blacks was serfdom—dependence on economic elites—for whites.

Davis and other Confederate leaders stressed that their strategy for protecting democracy was defensive: to defend the independence of the Confederacy. As Davis put it in his inaugural, the Confederacy sought "no conquest, no aggrandizement, no concession of any kind from the states with which we were lately confederated; all we ask is to be let alone." This strategy gave Confederate leaders a major advantage. Although they might dream about a battlefield victory that would force formal recognition, they were willing to settle for the Union's abandoning the fight and implicitly accepting Confederate independence. If they could make the cost of the war high enough to induce the North to quit, their cause would be victorious. A draw on the battlefield would be good enough.

Resources, Human and Material. The Union entered the war with some obvious advantages. Lincoln's success in securing the border slave states gave the Union nearly total control over the Ohio River. With nearly two-thirds of the American people, about two-thirds of the nation's railroad mileage, and very nearly 90 percent of American industrial output, the North's economy was far superior to the South's (see Figure 15.1). The North produced all goods in larger quantities and had an especially great advantage in the manufacture of cannon and rifles because of earlier advances in mass-production technology.

But the Confederate position was not as weak as these figures might suggest. Virginia, North Carolina,

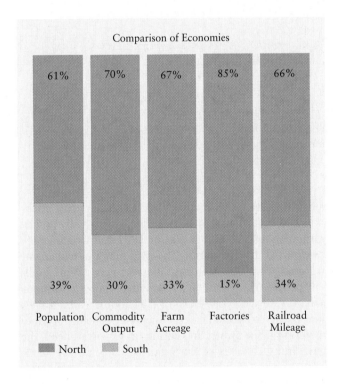

FIGURE 15.1

Economies, North and South, 1860
The economic advantages of the North were even greater than this chart suggests because the population figures included slaves, commodity output was dominated by farm goods, farm acreage included unimproved acres (greater in the South), and southern factories were, on average, much smaller than northern factories.

Source: Stanley Engerman, "The Economic Impact of the Civil War," in Robert W. Fogel and Stanley L. Engerman, *The Reinterpretation of American Economic History* (New York: Harper & Row, 1971), 371; U.S. Census data.

Industrial Richmond
Located at the falls of the James River, Richmond had flour mills, tobacco factories,
railroad and port facilities, and, most important, a profitable and substantial iron
industry. In 1861 the Tredegar Iron Works, employing nearly 1,000 workers, was the
only facility in the South that could produce large machinery and heavy weapons.

and Tennessee had substantial industrial capacity. Richmond, with its Tredegar Iron Works, was already an important industrial center, and in 1861 the Confederacy
transported to Richmond the gun-making machinery
captured at the U.S. armory at Harpers Ferry. With 9 million people, the Confederacy could mobilize enormous
armies. And while one-third of that number were slaves,
their masters expected to keep them in the fields, producing food for the armies and cotton for export. Indeed, the
agricultural capacity of the South was crucial. The Confederacy was self-sufficient in food production and dominated world production of cotton—by far America's
most lucrative export commodity. "King Cotton" could
provide revenue to purchase the clothes, boots, blankets,
and weapons that the Confederacy needed but could not
produce. Used as a weapon of diplomacy, cotton might
induce the British, who depended on imports of southern
cotton to supply their textile and clothing factories, to
recognize the independence of the Confederacy and supply it with military and economic aid.

The Confederacy thus had sufficient resources to
wage an extended and punishing war. It had other assets as well, notably a strong military tradition and a
healthy supply of trained military officers. Moreover, it
enjoyed important strategic advantages. It would be
fighting largely on familiar terrain among local supporters. And even though its railroad system was inferior to
the North's, it could move troops and supplies rapidly
by interior lines within a defensive perimeter extending
from Virginia to Texas. Its long, irregular coastline
made it difficult to blockade. Finally, with its defensive
stance the South could take full advantage of a new
weapon—the rifle-musket (see New Technology, page
455). For the first time in military history well-protected
riflemen could repulse cavalry. Britain's Enfield rifles,
together with 100,000 captured Union rifles and the
production of the Richmond armory, enabled the Confederacy to provide every infantryman with a modern
weapon by 1863.

Thus the odds did not necessarily favor the Union,
despite its superior resources. The citizens of the Union
would have to decide to fight a total war and then learn
how to fight such a war on both the battlefield and the
home front. The decision and learning were painful and
slow in coming. As late as November 1864 the outcome
could have gone either way.

The Rifle-Musket

1861 Springfield Rifle
The rifle-musket strengthened defensive forces by weakening the offensive power of artillery. Civil War artillery pieces had much shorter ranges than did the rifle-muskets, and when armies brought their artillery close enough to be effective as offensive weapons, the defending infantrymen were usually able to pick off the artillerymen.

In 1855 U.S. Secretary of War Jefferson Davis ordered an end to the production of the smooth-bore musket and began equipping American soldiers with rifle-muskets. Most Union infantrymen used the Springfield rifle, a rifle-musket first manufactured by the U.S. armory at Springfield, Massachusetts. Confederate soldiers often used the Enfield rifle, a similar weapon manufactured in Britain. These new weapons accounted for most of the casualties of the war.

Hunting rifles dating back to the eighteenth century had tapered barrels that were *rifled*—lined with spiral grooves—to give the bullet greater speed and accuracy. Unlike the smooth barrels of muskets, however, the grooved rifle barrel quickly accumulated gunpowder and required frequent cleaning, which was inconvenient and dangerous in combat.

In the early 1850s James S. Burton, an American mechanic working at the Harpers Ferry armory, developed a new bullet based on the innovations of Captain Claude E. Minie of the French army. Burton's cylindro-conoidal bullet, radically different from the round bullets of the day, was cast with a cavity at its base. When the rifle hammer exploded powder at the base of the barrel, hot gas expanded the cavity and forced the bullet to engage the grooves of the rifling as it sped through the barrel. The bullet thus cleaned the grooves with each shot.

For the first time infantrymen could be efficient, effective riflemen. Rifle-muskets built to fire the new bullets could hit targets half a mile away, whereas the maximum range of a musket was barely 250 yards. Firing two shots a minute, a veteran with a rifle-musket could kill reliably at 300 yards; his aim with a musket was assured only at 100 yards or less.

The new gun was called a rifle-musket rather than a rifle because it retained certain characteristics of the musket. It fired a single shot, was loaded through the muzzle, and had a long barrel, usually 40 inches. Like the musket, the rifle-musket was cumbersome to load. Before aiming and firing, a soldier had to take out a paper-wrapped cartridge of gunpowder, rip open the cartridge with his teeth, pour the powder down the barrel, insert the bullet into the barrel, jam the bullet and

powder down with a ramrod, half cock the hammer, insert a percussion cap, and finally cock the hammer. Some soldiers could do all this lying on their backs, but most, in order to fire two or three times a minute, had to load from a kneeling or standing position, often exposing themselves to enemy fire.

The rifle-musket was not a modern rifle; it was not breech-loading and did not fire multiple rounds. Although modern rifles were refined during the war and adopted in limited quantities, both sides preferred to stay with the familiar and proven rifle-musket.

The rifle-musket revolutionized warfare and military strategy. Its greater range and accuracy and relatively quick reloading enormously strengthened defensive forces. Defenders could fire on attackers almost continuously and, if the defenders were ensconced in well-protected positions with a broad field of vision, they could usually keep attackers from getting close enough for hand-to-hand combat. (Bayonets accounted for less than 1 percent of all wounds in the Civil War.) If attacking forces did manage to break through defensive lines, they were usually so weakened that they had to retreat or surrender in the face of counterattacks. Elaborate entrenchments strengthened defensive positions even more. Used by both sides in almost every battle by 1863, these trenches, together with the rifle-musket, enabled infantrymen to turn back assaults by forces three to four times their size. The trench warfare that developed around Petersburg, Virginia, in the last weeks of the Civil War presaged the trenches of World War I and the further strengthening of defensive positions by true rifles, automatic rifles, and machine guns.

Infantry commanders, however, were slow to change the tactics that they had inherited from the days of the musket and bayonet. Commanders still attacked in dense close-order formations with thousands of infantrymen, assaulting enemy positions in successive waves. In battle after battle charging infantrymen went down like harvested wheat. The terrible losses at Gettysburg finally forced a reformation of military tactics.

War Machines, North and South

In mobilizing their peoples for war, Abraham Lincoln and Jefferson Davis faced similar challenges: to establish their powers as commanders-in-chief, recruit troops for their armies, suppress dissent, and pay for the enormous costs of the conflict. Lincoln, aided by a strong party and a talented cabinet, quickly consolidated his power and organized a strong central government. Davis was less successful, but his task was more formidable. He had to fight a war while leading eleven states that were deeply suspicious of centralized government.

Mobilizing Armies

At first both Lincoln and Davis mobilized troops by calling for volunteers. But the initial surge of enlistments fell off in 1862 as Americans saw the realities of war—heavy losses to disease and dreadful battle carnage. Thus both presidents faced the necessity of a draft.

The Confederacy, with its relative shortage of military manpower, was the first to act. In April 1862, after the defeat at Shiloh (see page 462), the Confederate Congress imposed the first draft in American history. One law extended all enlistments for the duration of the war; another made all able-bodied men between eighteen and thirty-five subject to serve in the Confederate army for three years. In September a standoff at Antietam prompted the Congress to raise the upper age limit to forty-five. The same law exempted one white man—planter or overseer—for each twenty slaves. Drafted men could hire substitutes, and by 1863 the price for a substitute was $300 in gold—about three times the annual wage of a skilled worker in Richmond. (The substitute law was repealed in 1864.) Impoverished young farmers in the South angrily complained that it was "a rich man's war and a poor man's fight." Conscription proved unenforceable in some parts of the South, and nearly half the eligible nonvolunteers never served.

In midsummer 1862 the Union undertook a quasi-draft. The Militia Act of 1862 used the draft as a threat. When Lincoln's secretary of state, Edwin M. Stanton, announced that any state that failed to meet its quota of volunteers would be subject to the draft, enough volunteers came forward to satisfy Union needs for a year. In 1863, as the scale of hostilities increased, Congress passed the Enrollment Act, which subjected to the draft all able-bodied male citizens and aliens applying for naturalization aged twenty to forty-five. Each Congressional district was assigned a quota, based on its population, which it could meet with either conscripts or volunteers. Districts used cash bounties to compete for volunteers, sometimes bidding against one another to entice recruits. The federal government also offered

bounties for enlistment and permitted men to avoid the draft by providing a substitute or paying a $300 commutation, or exemption, fee. The 46,000 draftees and 118,000 substitutes who enlisted under the act amounted to only about 10 percent of the Union soldiers. However, the bounties stimulated the voluntary enlistment or reenlistment of almost a million men.

Meanwhile, the Lincoln administration took steps to suppress any dissent that might impede mobilization. In September 1862 Lincoln proclaimed that during the "insurrection" all persons who discouraged enlistment, resisted the draft, or were guilty of any disloyal practice were subject to martial law. He did this so that they would be tried by military courts rather than local juries. He suspended normal constitutional guarantees, such as the writ of habeas corpus (designed to protect people from arbitrary arrest and detention). By the war's end his administration had imprisoned nearly 15,000 individuals, mostly in the border states, where pro-Confederate political movements were strongest.

The Draft Riots.   Lincoln faced the most violent internal challenge of the war after the passage of the Enrollment Act of 1863. Conscription and the high commutation fee—at least half of a worker's annual income—generated resentment among men who were unenthusiastic about the war but could not afford to buy their way out. Democratic opponents of Lincoln exploited this resentment in urban working-class districts by making racist appeals to recent immigrants and wage earners. The Democrats argued that Lincoln was drafting poor whites in order to free the slaves and flood the cities with black workers. Thus the draft became a focal point for preexisting hostility to Republicans and African-Americans.

In July 1863 hostility to the draft spilled onto the streets. After draftees' names were announced in New York City, ferocious rioting broke out among immigrant Irish workers. For five days mob violence ran rampant in what was the most terrible riot in American history. Men and women rioters burned the draft office, sacked the homes of important Republicans, and assaulted the police. The rioters lynched and mutilated at least a dozen African-Americans, drove hundreds of black families from their homes, and burned down the Colored Orphan Asylum. Lincoln's reaction was swift and strong: he rushed in Union troops. The police and soldiers of the Army of the Potomac, who had faced the Confederates at Gettysburg two weeks earlier, killed more than a hundred rioters and suppressed the urban insurrection.

President Davis was never able to match this degree of force. Most Confederate leaders, such as Governors Joseph Brown of Georgia and Zebulon Vance of North Carolina, had powerful states' rights convictions and wanted to avoid creating a national government as centralized and powerful as the one they had left. Because the Confederate constitution vested sovereignty in the

Draft Riots in New York City
The riots—the worst in all of U.S. history—demonstrated that powerful issues of class and race were not far from the surface of American politics. But business-class denunciation of the riots and of Peace Democrats strengthened Lincoln's hand. (This engraving appeared in the *Illustrated London News* on August 8, 1863.)

individual states, state governors could thwart the president's will. Brown and Vance simply ignored Davis's first draft call in early 1862. In parts of the South state judges issued writs of habeas corpus ordering the Confederate government to release draftees. The Confederate Congress was reluctant to impose its authority on the state courts; it granted Davis the authority to suspend the writ of habeas corpus and thus enforce conscription for only two brief periods totaling sixteen months. Its failure to appoint a supreme court contributed to this jurisdictional dilemma.

Nevertheless, Davis's failure to organize an effective draft did not cripple the Confederacy. About four-fifths of the Confederate men eligible for the draft actually served; by contrast, only half the eligible Union men served. Moreover, the Confederate government was able to keep armies in the field by requiring volunteers to extend their enlistments. But as the scale of the fighting grew, as casualties mounted, and as the Union gained control of more Confederate territory, the manpower crisis became severe. By 1864 Confederate generals could not rotate their soldiers to rest areas for relief.

Mobilizing Money

The financial requirements of fighting a total war were enormous. In the Union war costs drove up government spending from less than 2 percent of the gross national product to an average of 15 percent, close to the 20 percent reached in the early 1990s. To finance those expenditures the Republicans had to go beyond their 1860 economic platform and build the kind of revenue system needed to establish a powerful modern state. The financial demands on the Confederacy were even greater,

but it avoided using any revenue machinery that required coercion by the central government.

Taxes, almost all of them new, financed about 20 percent of Union war costs. For the first time the government levied an income tax—a graduated tax reaching a maximum rate of 10 percent. The Union placed excise taxes on virtually all consumer goods, license taxes on a wide variety of activities (including every profession except the ministry), special taxes on corporations, stamp taxes on legal documents, and taxes on inheritances. Each wartime Congress also raised tariffs on foreign goods, doubling the average tariff rate by the end of the war.

The Union government financed about two-thirds of its war costs by running deficits and borrowing money through the sale of bonds by the U.S. Treasury. Secretary of the Treasury Salmon P. Chase had no prior financial experience, but he learned quickly from Jay Cooke, a Philadelphia banker. Chase and Cooke adopted four key policies. First, they made interest on the bonds payable in gold, making the bonds financially attractive. Second, they kept income tax rates low, thereby winning support among the wealthy for the bond program. Third, they pioneered techniques for marketing bonds. Although banks and wealthy people in America and Britain bought most of the bonds, Cooke's newspaper advertisements and his 2,500 subagents persuaded nearly a million northerners—a fourth of all ordinary families—to buy them too. Working through a private financier, the Lincoln administration was innovative in developing the propaganda techniques that would become essential to funding all the major wars of the twentieth century.

Fourth, Chase led in creating a national banking system—an important element in every modern centralized government. The National Banking acts of 1863 and 1864 established this system to induce bankers to purchase bonds. The federal government offered state-chartered banks national charters, allowing them to issue national banknotes. The national banks could acquire the notes only with U.S. bonds, which they were required to buy with at least one-third of their capital. But because the national banks were more heavily regulated, state banks did not rush into the new system. So, in 1865 the federal government placed a crippling tax on the notes of state banks. By the end of 1865 the number of national banks had tripled, and their purchases of U.S. bonds had increased nearly four times.

The Union also financed the war by issuing paper money backed by faith in the government rather than by specie. In February 1862 Congress passed the Legal Tender Act, authorizing the issue of $150 million of Treasury notes, which became known as *greenbacks*. Congress required the public to accept those notes as legal tender. Only tariff duties and interest on the national debt still had to be paid in gold or silver coins. This paper money, amounting to nearly $500 million by the end of the war, funded only 13 percent of the war's cost. If the Union government had been weaker—less able to tax its citizens or induce Americans and Europeans to lend it money—it would have had to rely more heavily on the creation of money.

In short, the Union government built the financial foundations of a modern industrial nation-state. Imposing broad-based taxes, borrowing from the middle class as well as the wealthy, and creating a functional money supply mobilized huge sums for the Union cause. In the process, the Union's program of public finance created ties of mutual dependency between the war effort and the millions of Americans who had paid taxes, lent their savings, and accepted paper money.

In sharp contrast with the Union, the Confederacy covered less than 5 percent of its expenditures through taxation. The Confederate Congress fiercely opposed taxes on cotton exports and on the property of planters. It did pass a modest property tax in 1861 but exempted property in the form of slaves and left its collection to the states. Only one state, South Carolina, imposed the tax; the others generally borrowed money or paid the Confederacy with state-issued IOUs. In 1863 the Congress passed a more comprehensive tax law, but it still exempted property in slaves. As a result, the tax burden fell primarily on middle-class citizens and non-slaveholding small farmers, who commonly refused to pay, especially when Confederate armies were far away. An 1864 revision that included a 5 percent property tax on slaves came too late to raise much revenue or restore popular faith in the fairness of the Confederate tax system.

The Confederacy was able to borrow enough money for only 35 percent of its war effort. Although wealthy planters had enough capital to fund a relatively large part of the war, most rebuffed pleas that they buy Con-

federate bonds by pledging their cotton revenues. At first they were unwilling to accept low interest rates; later they began to doubt that the Confederacy would prevail. Europeans came to share those doubts, and the only major loan to the Confederacy came from a French banking house in 1863.

And so the Confederacy was forced to finance about 60 percent of its expenses with unbacked paper money. This created a new problem—soaring inflation, which was compounded by a flood of counterfeit copies of the poorly designed and badly printed Confederate notes. The great battles and sieges created growing numbers of refugees, and this added to inflationary pressures by reducing the food supply and thereby raising food prices even higher. In the early spring of 1863 a wave of riots broke out in southern cities. In more than a dozen towns women ransacked shops and supply depots for food. In Richmond several hundred women broke into bakeries, crying, "Our children are starving while the rich roll in wealth."

The inflation worsened in 1863 as an inflationary psychology—a panic—took hold. Southerners became convinced that inflation would accelerate and rushed to spend their depreciating paper money before it became even less valuable, producing runaway inflation—the only such episode in America since the Revolutionary War. By the spring of 1865 prices had risen to ninety-two times their 1861 levels. A South Carolina judge wrote, "You take your money to the market in the market basket, and bring home what you buy in your pocketbook."

The runaway inflation severely hampered Confederate mobilization. The orderly supply of armies became impossible when farmers refused to accept Confederate money. Confederate supply officers then tried to confiscate what they needed, leaving behind worthless IOUs. Some cavalry units just took what they needed without even pretending to pay. Ironically, partly because it was so fearful of taxation, the Confederacy was forced to resort to great violations of property rights to sustain the war effort.

Economic Programs

Lincoln mobilized men by introducing conscription, used force to suppress war resistance, and taxed the people of the North at unprecedented rates. But economic reforms were also needed to increase the effectiveness of wartime organization and win the support of those who voted, paid taxes, and fought. Consequently, Lincoln and the Republican leadership enacted virtually the entire economic program that they had inherited from Henry Clay and the Whigs.

The many Republicans who had begun their political careers as Whigs had been waiting more than twenty years for this opportunity. They faced the continued opposition of northern Democrats, but the war had eliminated almost all southern Democrats from Congress while those northern Democrats who had become Republicans relaxed their resistance to national banking and protective tariffs. Most fundamentally, the Republicans won new support from workers and small farmers, arguing that the Republican economic program would help prevent a return to the depression conditions of the late 1850s. And, by celebrating economic opportunity in the North and focusing on the threat that slavery posed to opportunity, the Republicans diverted attention from the failures and limitations of American industrialization. Finally, the southern challenge to northern society helped persuade many farmers and workers to set aside their doubts about the Whig platform and support the nationalizing economic program of the Republican party and the business class in order to win the war.

Each element of the Republican economic program won a substantial following. The tariff received support from manufacturers and those laborers and farmers who feared cheap foreign labor. Capitalists large and small applauded the national banking system. Republican land policy, designed to accelerate free-soil settlement, won the enthusiastic support of almost all farmers. In 1862 Congress passed the Homestead Act, giving heads of families or individuals age twenty-one or older the right to 160 acres of public land after five years of residence and improvement. Although the act contained many loopholes, allowing speculators to put together large blocks of property, numerous small farmers also acquired land. In 1862 Lincoln followed through on the Republican promise to build transcontinental railroads. Congress chartered the Union Pacific and Central Pacific railways and subsidized them lavishly. It gave the railroads twenty sections (20 square miles) of federal land in alternate plots for every mile of track they put down. Congress provided a similar charter and subsidy to the Northern Pacific in 1864.

The Confederate government, however, undertook almost no restructuring of national economic life. True to its states' rights philosophy, the Confederacy left much governmental intervention in the economy in the hands of the state governments operating under their police powers. When the Davis administration did intervene, it did so out of desperation over the inadequacy of the economy for fighting a total war. Consequently, the Confederacy adopted extremely coercive programs. With an economy that was less developed than that of the North, the Confederacy took extraordinary measures: it built and operated its own shipyards, armories, foundries, and textile mills; commandeered food and scarce raw materials such as coal, iron, copper, and lead; requisitioned slaves; and exercised direct control over foreign trade. The unprecedented nature of these encroachments was all the more resented as the war wore

on, because the Confederate government failed to explain its wartime needs or cope with misery on the home front.

Rather than undertaking reforms designed to maintain loyalty and support through economic self-interest, the Confederate leadership relied on a defense of slavery and racial solidarity. Jefferson Davis told whites that they were fighting to be able to expand westward into new territories. Without expansion, he said, "an overgrown black population" would "crowd upon our soil . . . until there will not be room in the country for whites and blacks to subsist in." Containment would destroy slavery "and reduce the whites to the degraded position of the African race."

The Home Front: Civilian Support for the War

In both the Confederacy and the Union, civilians made enormous contributions to the war effort. No civilian effort was more important than relieving the suffering on the battlefield.

The Sanitary Commission. In the North the most important voluntary agency was the United States Sanitary Commission, which prominent New Yorkers established in April 1861 and Lincoln endorsed two months later. Its task was to provide medical services and prevent a repeat of the debacle of the Crimean War between Britain and Russia (1854–1856), in which disease accounted for over three-fourths of the British casualties. Through its network of 7,000 local auxiliaries, the Sanitary Commission gathered supplies; distributed clothing, food, and medicine to the army; improved the sanitary standards of camp life; recruited battlefield nurses; and recruited doctors for the Union Army Medical Bureau, which came to be led by an innovative surgeon general, William A. Hammond. Hammond professionalized the bureau, increasing the number of surgeons, building more hospitals, organizing a trained ambulance corps, and integrating the services of the Sanitary Commission into the war effort.

The results of all this organized medical effort were not readily visible. Diseases—primarily dysentery, typhoid, and malaria but also childhood diseases such as mumps and measles, to which many rural men had not developed an immunity—killed twice as many Union soldiers (about 250,000) as combat did. Surgeons inadvertently took more lives by spreading infection than they saved. Nurses could do little more for the wounded than dress their wounds and comfort them with reminders of home. Still, the rate of mortality from disease and wounds was substantially lower than in other major nineteenth-century wars, partly because of the attention given to sanitation and the quality of food.

The health care available to Union troops surpassed that in the Confederacy. Great numbers of southern women volunteered as nurses, but the Confederate health care and hospital system remained disorganized. Thousands of Confederate soldiers suffered from scurvy because of the lack of vitamin C in their diets, and they died from camp diseases at even higher rates than did Union soldiers.

Women in the War Effort. Most of the Sanitary Commission nurses and workers were women. Organized by Dorothea Dix, the first woman to receive a major federal appointment—as superintendent of female nurses—the nurses overcame prejudice against women treating men and opened a new occupation to women. The nurse Clara Barton, who later founded the American Red Cross, recalled, "At the war's end, woman was at least fifty years in advance of the normal position which continued peace would have assigned her." Barton might have been overly optimistic, but the war effort did open the way for middle-class women to participate not only in nursing but also in government as they either replaced male clerks who went to war or took new jobs in the expanding bureaucracies. This was true not only in the North but also in the South, where women staffed the efficient Confederate postal service.

Hospital Nursing
Most Civil War nurses served as unpaid volunteers and spent most of their time cooking and cleaning for their patients. A sense of calm prevailed in this Union hospital in Nashville, well removed from the battlefield. In contrast, conditions at field hospitals were chaotic under the pressure of heavy casualties and shifting battle sites.

While some women assumed new kinds of jobs, far more women in both the North and the South dramatically increased their responsibilities in their households, on their farms, in schools, and in textile, clothing, and shoe factories. They made mobilization possible in both the Union and the Confederacy by substituting their labor for that of men. On plantations some women took over the management of slaves and production. On small farms in both the South and the North women worked with far greater intensity and effort than they had before the war, taking on chores that men had done. Some farm women not only performed demanding chores but took jobs outside the home to make ends meet.

Military Deadlock, 1861–1863

Between 1861 and 1863 the Lincoln administration created a complex war machine and a powerful structure of command and production. Northern government, industry, and finance capital worked in an integrated manner, making the North's advantages in population and material resources available to the Union army. But the Union had not yet fully resolved to fight a total war against southern society. The Confederacy, successfully prosecuting its limited, defensive war, forced the Union into a deadlock on the battlefield.

Early Stalemate, 1861–1862

The First Battle of Bull Run. At the war's beginning Lincoln rejected the military strategy proposed by his general-in-chief, Winfield Scott, who was a Virginia Unionist. This strategy, dubbed the Anaconda (a large constricting snake) Plan by its opponents, involved blockading the South on all sides from the sea and the Mississippi River and then gradually squeezing the Confederacy into submission through psychological pressure and economic sanctions. Instead, Lincoln chose a more aggressive beginning—a swift assault on P. G. T. Beauregard's Confederate force of over 20,000 based at Manassas, a major rail junction in Virginia only 30 miles southwest of Washington. Lincoln, along with many Union commanders with Mexican War experience, believed in vigorous offensives; he recognized that northern public opinion called for a strike toward Richmond, the Confederate capital, and he hoped an early Union victory would discredit the secessionists. Consequently, in mid-July 1861, Lincoln sent Union General Irvin McDowell with an army of more than 30,000 to attack Beauregard's army.

Northern newspapers and southern spies advertised the advance of McDowell's army, so Beauregard had plenty of time to establish his army south of Bull Run, a small stream north of Manassas. He also brought reinforcements by rail from the Shenandoah Valley, thus seizing the advantage provided by having interior lines. McDowell attacked strongly on July 21, but panic swept through his troops during a Confederate counterattack. For the first time the Union troops, who had fought almost fourteen hours with little water to relieve the Virginia heat, heard the startling scream of the rebel yell. "The peculiar corkscrew sensation that it sends down your backbone under these circumstances can never be told," one Union veteran wrote. "You have to feel it."

McDowell's troops retreated to Washington, scrambling along with the many civilians who had come down from the capital with their Sunday picnic baskets and binoculars to observe the battle. The Confederate troops also dispersed. They were as confused as the beaten Union soliders, and they lacked wagons and supplies to pursue McDowell's army. While Confederate leaders rejoiced in their victory, Lincoln replaced McDowell with General George B. McClellan of Pennsylvania and Ohio. He also signed bills for the enlistment of 100,000 additional men, who would serve for three years in what would soon be named the Army of the Potomac. In November 1861, when Winfield Scott retired, Lincoln made McClellan general-in-chief. Although neither Lincoln nor Davis fully anticipated total war as yet, it was now clear that the war would not be quick or easy.

The War in the West. While eastern armies were fighting to capture the opposing capital or demoralize the enemy's army, Union and Confederate troops in the West struggled to dominate territory—the great interior river valleys. Union control of communications and transportation along those strategic rivers would divide the Confederacy into isolated pieces and reduce its ability to supply and move armies. The Confederacy had already lost the Ohio Valley when Kentucky remained in the Union. Retaining the Tennessee and Mississippi valleys was vital to the South's communications with its vast western territory.

In 1862 the Union launched a series of highly innovative land and water operations designed to seize control of the Tennessee and Mississippi rivers. In February, in a brilliant tactical maneuver, Ulysses S. Grant, still a relatively unknown Union commander, used riverboats clad with iron plates to take Fort Henry on the Tennessee River and Fort Donelson on the Cumberland. Grant then moved south along the Tennessee to take control of critical railroad lines. Meanwhile, as the southern part of a giant pincer movement, Admiral David G. Farragut struck from the sea. In April 1862 he led a Union squadron up the Mississippi from the Gulf of Mexico and took New Orleans. In one naval offensive the Union had captured the South's financial center and largest city, acquired a major base for future operations, and denied the Confederacy an important port (see Map 15.2).

Union Soldiers Camped Near Cumberland Landing, 1862
The Civil War armies required encampments that were huge and intricate. The logistic demands on the Union armies were great because they generally fought in enemy territory and maintained long supply lines. The rule of thumb was that a Union army of 100,000 men consumed 600 tons of supplies a day and required 2,500 supply wagons and at least 35,000 animals.

MAP 15.2

The Western Campaigns, 1861–1862
Control of the great valleys of the Ohio, Tennessee, and Mississippi rivers was at stake during the early part of the Civil War. By the end of 1862, Union armies had kept Missouri in the Union and driven the Confederate armies out of Kentucky and half of Tennessee. They also controlled New Orleans and almost all of the Mississippi River, and at Shiloh they had proved that they could not be driven out of the Lower South.

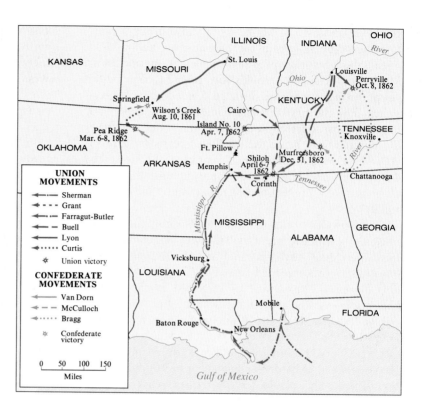

Shiloh. Confederates under Albert Sidney Johnston and P. G. T. Beauregard slowed Grant's advance by catching him by surprise a few miles from the Tennessee River near a small log church named Shiloh. In the ensuing battle on April 6–7, 1862, Grant relentlessly threw troops into the battle and forced a Confederate withdrawal. About 20,000 men were killed or wounded at Shiloh, making it the bloodiest battle to that point. Grant described a large field "so covered with dead that it would have been possible to walk over the clearing in any direction, stepping on dead bodies, without a foot touching the ground."

Grant's victory at Shiloh was a major turning point: it marked the beginning of the end of Confederate power in the Mississippi Valley. By June the Union controlled the Mississippi as far south as Memphis, Tennessee. Also, the ghastly triumph at Shiloh began to transform the Union leaders' strategic thinking. Shiloh persuaded Lincoln and the most foresighted generals that a long, protracted war would be necessary, even in the West. Grant later wrote that after Shiloh he "gave up all idea of saving the Union except by complete conquest."

The Eastern Theater, 1862. After Bull Run both the Union and the Confederacy continued to seek a victory in the East that would end the war. Confederate and Union commanders jockeyed for position around Washington and Richmond. Each tried to outflank the other, place his army between the capital and its defenders,

and, if possible, punish the opposing army. As they maneuvered, the commanders used virtually identical battlefield tactics, since almost all had been taught by the same instructors and had read the same textbooks at West Point.

After meticulously training 150,000 men during the winter of 1861–1862, McClellan moved his troops up the peninsula between the York and James rivers toward Richmond. In a maneuver that required skillful logistics, he transported about 100,000 troops by boat down the Potomac River and Chesapeake Bay and then up the peninsula. But he failed to anticipate some major problems. In May a Confederate army under Thomas J. ("Stonewall") Jackson marched rapidly north up the Shenandoah Valley, threatening the army of Nathaniel P. Banks that was protecting Washington. To head off Jackson, Lincoln diverted 30,000 troops from McClellan's army. Jackson proved himself a brilliant general by defeating three Union armies in five battles in the valley. Then, in June, as McClellan finally moved toward Richmond, Robert E. Lee, the new commander of the Army of Northern Virginia, with a force of 85,000, attacked him ferociously in the Seven Days' battles (June 25–July 1). McClellan's troops inflicted heavy casualties (20,000 to the Union's 10,000), but he was unwilling to renew the offensive unless he received 50,000 fresh troops. Lincoln believed that McClellan would only find another excuse not to attack Lee and the president withdrew the Army of the Potomac from the peninsula. Richmond remained secure.

Lee's First Invasion of the North. Lee then went on the offensive, hoping for victories that would humiliate Lincoln's government. Lee sent Jackson to destroy a Union army under John Pope in northern Virginia before McClellan returned. On August 29–30, only 20 miles from Washington, Jackson's troops, joined by the forces of Lee and General James P. Longstreet, routed Pope's army in the Second Battle of Bull Run. Lee struck north through western Maryland, and Lincoln ordered McClellan to confront Lee's army. Lee almost met with disaster when he divided his force—sending Stonewall Jackson to capture Harpers Ferry—and a copy of his orders to Jackson fell into McClellan's hands. Once again, however, McClellan hesitated, and Lee had time to occupy a strong defensive position behind Antietam Creek, near Sharpsburg, Maryland. Although outnumbered 87,000 to 50,000, Lee repelled McClellan's attacks until Jackson's troops arrived, just as Union regiments were about to overwhelm Lee's right flank (see Map 15.3).

The fighting at Antietam was some of the most savage of the war. A Wisconsin officer described his men as "loading and firing with demoniacal fury and shouting and laughing hysterically." At a critical point in the battle a sunken road, Bloody Lane, filled with Confederate bodies two and three deep, and the attacking Union troops knelt on "this ghastly flooring" to shoot at the retreating Confederates.

McClellan might have defeated Lee with another major effort, but the casualties appalled him and he feared that enemy troops might outnumber his own. He let Lee fall back to Virginia while he buried the dead and set up field hospitals for the wounded. September 17, 1862, at Antietam proved to be the bloodiest single day in U.S. military history. Lee lost somewhat fewer men than did McClellan, but Lee's losses represented one-fourth of his army. Together, the Confederate and Union dead numbered 4,800 and the wounded 18,500, of whom 3,000 soon died. (In comparison, 6,000 Americans were wounded or killed on D-Day in World War II.)

The military setbacks prior to Antietam had begun to erode popular support for the war. To rally public opinion, Lincoln declared Antietam a victory. Privately, he believed that McClellan should have fought Lee to the finish. McClellan was a masterful organizer of men and supplies but had never been willing to risk a major com-

---

MAP 15.3

The Eastern Campaigns, 1861–1862

The greatest concentration of major Civil War battlefields was in the corridor between Washington and Richmond. There, during the eastern campaigns of 1861 and 1862, the audacity and imagination of Confederate generals Robert J. "Stonewall" Jackson and Robert E. Lee almost produced decisive victories. But, as often in the Civil War, the victors were usually too exhausted to exploit their triumphs.

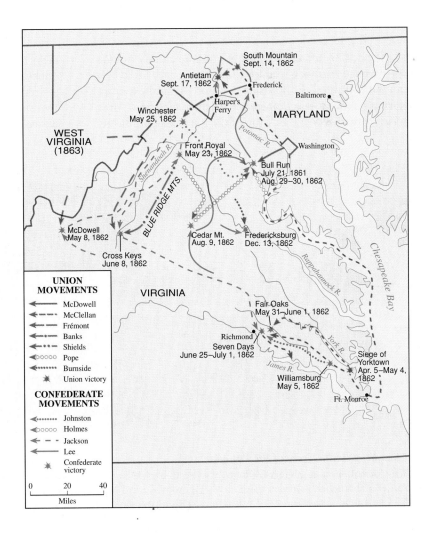

Antietam

This painting, *The Battle of Antietam: The Fight for Burnside's Bridge,* is the work of Captain
James Hope of the 2nd Vermont Volunteers, who was a survivor of Antietam. The Rohrbach
Bridge, nicknamed "Burnside's Bridge," was the scene of some of the heaviest fighting.

mitment of his forces, perhaps because he could not face
the carnage that would follow. Lincoln replaced McClellan with Ambrose E. Burnside, who proved to be a more
daring but even less competent battlefield tactician. After
losing large parts of the Army of the Potomac in futile at-

tacks against well-entrenched Confederate forces at Fredericksburg, Virginia, on December 13, Burnside offered
to resign his command. Lincoln replaced him with
Joseph ("Fighting Joe") Hooker. As 1862 ended, the war
was still a stalemate.

Lincoln with the Army of the Potomac

This formal photograph records Lincoln's visit to McClellan's headquarters near the
Antietam battlefield. On this visit Lincoln vigorously urged McClellan to advance on Richmond.
McClellan did not respond and was removed from command a month later.

Emancipation

As the war dragged on during 1861 and 1862, Lincoln, some of his generals, and some Republican leaders began to redefine it as a struggle not only against Confederate armies but also against southern society. In particular, Lincoln and his administration decided that they had to attack the very cornerstone of southern society—the institution of slavery.

At the beginning of the war a few abolitionist leaders had hoped that the South would be allowed to secede so as to rid the Union of the stain of slavery. But other abolitionists tried to persuade the Republican party to make abolition a goal of the war. They argued on grounds not just of morality but of "military necessity": it was the labor of the slaves that enabled the Confederacy to feed and supply its armies. Frederick Douglass wrote that "the very stomach of this rebellion is the Negro in the form of a slave. Arrest that hoe in the hands of the Negro, and you smite the rebellion in the very seat of its life."

"Contrabands." It was the slaves themselves who forced the issue of emancipation. From the very outset of the war, slaves exploited the disorder of wartime to seize their freedom. Over the course of the war tens of thousands escaped from plantations and ran to Union lines.

The first Union officials who dealt with the status of escaped slaves were the commanders in the field. In May 1861 General Benjamin Butler, who had taken military control of Annapolis and Baltimore, was commanding a fort on the Virginia coast. When three slaves escaped to his lines, he refused to return them to their master. He did not declare them free but labeled them "contraband of war." His term stuck, and for the rest of the war slaves found behind Union lines were known as *contrabands*. By August 1861 a thousand contrabands were camping with Butler's army.

The increasingly large number of runaway slaves behind Union lines forced the Union government to establish a policy regularizing their status. In August 1861 Lincoln signed the First Confiscation Act, authorizing the seizure of all property—defined to include slaves—used to support the rebellion. This law applied only to slaves within reach of Union armies and it did not actually emancipate them. The act was designed only to undermine the Confederate war effort, but it did begin the process that would end in abolition.

As early as the summer of 1861 almost all Republicans opposed slavery and were ready for some kind of emancipation. But they divided into three groups over the timing and method. The conservatives, the smallest of the three groups, wanted to end slavery but believed that this should occur slowly as the federal government blocked the extension of slavery into the territories; emancipation in existing states, they believed, should be left to state governments. More numerous were the radicals, who wanted the government to abolish slavery straightaway, wherever it existed. The moderates, the most numerous of all and led by Lincoln, wanted emancipation to proceed more expeditiously than did the conservatives but feared that immediate abolition would cause a dramatic loss of Union support in the border states and stimulate a racist backlash in northern cities.

But as battlefield casualties mounted in 1861 and 1862, so did popular support for punishing slave owners by taking away their slaves; so did support for emancipation as a means of mobilizing slaves against their masters; so did moral enthusiasm for freeing the slaves and thus ennobling the carnage on the battlefield; and so did the influence of the radical Republicans. Their leaders included Salmon P. Chase, Secretary of the Treasury; Charles Sumner, the chairman of the Senate Committee on Foreign Relations; and Thaddeus Stevens, the chairman of the House Ways and Means Committee. Both Sumner and Stevens held stern and uncompromising views on slavery, but Stevens was the more masterful in manipulating Congress, where he served as a representative from Pennsylvania from 1849 to 1853 and from 1859 until his death in 1868. Among all the Republicans in Congress, Stevens was probably the one most completely committed to racial equality.

In the spring of 1862 Lincoln and moderate Republicans in Congress began to move slowly toward abolition. In April 1862 Congress enacted legislation abolishing slavery in the District of Columbia while promising compensation to the former slave owners in the hope of winning their loyalty to the Union. In June Congress took its second step, abolishing slavery in the federal territories. This law affected only a few slaves but represented the fulfillment of the free-soil platform. Congress took a more radical step in July when it passed the Second Confiscation Act, which went beyond the first one by declaring "forever free" all captured and fugitive slaves of rebels. Although it affected only those slaves under the direct control of the Union army, it did for the first time embrace emancipation as an instrument of war. Also in July, Lincoln read a draft of a proclamation to his cabinet, testing out an even more radical conception of emancipation, one that would transform the Union armies into agents of liberation.

The Emancipation Proclamation. Lincoln was pondering how he could use his power to emancipate the slaves not affected by previous actions. Some lived in areas loyal to the Union, but most were in areas controlled by the Confederacy. He was certain that he had to leave the former alone because the Constitution protected slavery within the Union, but he believed he could free the latter under his wartime power to take enemy resources. He worried, however, that if he did that while the war was going badly, he would be seen as cynically trying to

Lincoln and His Cabinet
The painting portrays Lincoln reading the preliminary Emancipation Proclamation to his cabinet on September 21, four days after the Battle of Antietam. Lincoln had first presented a draft proclamation to the cabinet on July 22, but Secretary of State William H. Seward had persuaded him to "postpone its issue until you can give it to the country supported by military success."

divert attention from military defeats. And abolishing slavery while the Union was losing the war would in fact be an empty gesture; if the tide of battle did not go Lincoln's way, he could free no additional slaves. After Antietam, Lincoln decided that the time had come. He declared Antietam a victory and told his cabinet that he took it as "an indication of the Divine Will" that he should "move forward in the cause of emancipation." On September 22, 1862, he issued a preliminary Emancipation Proclamation, declaring that on January 1, 1863, slaves in all states wholly or partly in rebellion would be free. Thus Lincoln gave the rebellious states a hundred days to return to the Union and keep slavery intact. None chose to do so.

The proclamation was politically astute as well as constitutionally correct. Lincoln wanted to keep the loyalty of the border states, where racism was most severe, so he left slavery intact there. He also wanted to win the allegiance of the areas occupied by Union armies—western and middle Tennessee, western Virginia, and southern Louisiana, including New Orleans—so he left slavery untouched there. Thus, the Emancipation Proclamation had no immediate, practical effect on the life

of a single slave. Abolitionists were disappointed, but they were confident that emancipation would have to go further. Wendell Phillips believed Lincoln was "only stopping on the edge of Niagara." Jefferson Davis called the proclamation the "most execrable measure recorded in the history of guilty man." Lincoln predicted that the proclamation would change the nature of the war; it would become a war of "subjugation" in which "the old South is to be destroyed and replaced by new propositions and ideas."

Many Union officers doubted whether they wanted to fight for emancipation and worried that the proclamation would incite slave rebellions. McClellan, who had aspirations for a political career as a Democrat, privately admitted that he "could not make my mind to fight for such an accursed doctrine as that of a servile insurrection." But McClellan reminded his officers that the "remedy for political errors . . . is to be found only in the action of people at the polls."

The Elections of 1862. The Democrats, in fact, made emancipation the primary issue in the elections of 1862. Leading Democrats used emancipation to focus popular frustration over the seeming futility of the bloody war. They denounced emancipation as unconstitutional; some warned of massive bloodshed in the South and claimed that a "black flood" would sweep away the jobs of white laborers. Horatio Seymour, candidate for governor of New York, declared that if abolition was the purpose of the war, then the South could not—and should not—be conquered. Seymour won his election; other Democrats did well in New York, Pennsylvania, Ohio, and Illinois; and Democrats gained 34 seats in Congress. But this was the smallest loss since 1842 of Congressional seats in an off-year election by the party controlling the presidency. Moreover, Republicans held a 25-seat majority in the House and gained 5 seats in the Senate. They blamed their losses on the inability of soldiers at the front to vote.

Lincoln would have preferred a stronger showing in the elections but saw no reason to retreat. After the election he did not hesitate to remove McClellan, whose views on emancipation were well known, from command of the Army of the Potomac. In December the House endorsed the preliminary proclamation and passed an act requiring West Virginia to abolish slavery as a condition of statehood. In his message to Congress that month Lincoln promised that slaves freed "by the chances of war" would remain free. And on New Year's Day, 1863, Lincoln signed the Emancipation Proclamation. As a gesture to those who feared slave rebellions Lincoln hedged a bit, making it clear that he wanted slaves to "abstain from all violence." But in other ways he went beyond the September proclamation, justifying emancipation as an "act of justice" as well as a military tactic and expressing his intention to accept slaves freed by the proclamation into military service. In one stroke Lincoln had changed the meaning of the war, focusing it on abolition and revolutionizing southern society. "If my name ever goes into history," he said, "it was for this act."

The Thirteenth Amendment. During 1864 and 1865 the pace of legal emancipation accelerated. Maryland and Missouri amended their constitutions to free their slaves, and the three occupied states of Tennessee, Arkansas, and Louisiana followed suit. But what would happen elsewhere in the South after the war was over? Abolitionists worried that the Emancipation Proclamation, based on the president's wartime powers, would lose its force. There was nothing in the Constitution to prevent southern states from reestablishing slavery after the war. To solve that problem, Congress, urged on by Lincoln, began the final step toward the full legal emancipation of slaves. On January 31, 1865, it approved the Thirteenth Amendment, which prohibited slavery altogether. By the end of the year the necessary number of states had ratified the amendment.

Union Gains in 1863

The Fall of Vicksburg. During 1863 the Union made substantial progress in the western theater of the war. This progress began as Grant drove south along the Mississippi to the west of the river and hammered persistently at Confederate defenses around Vicksburg, Mississippi (see American Voices, page 468). Then, in a clever maneuver, he moved his troops across the river, swung them around the city, and attacked from the east. After a six-week siege the exhausted and starving garrison surrendered on July 4, 1863. Five days later Port Hudson, Louisiana, fell to Union forces, and a week later an unarmed merchant ship completed an uneventful trip from St. Louis to New Orleans. The Union now controlled the whole length of the Mississippi. Grant's campaign had split the Confederacy in two, cutting off Louisiana, Arkansas, and Texas from the remaining Confederate states.

Later in 1863 the Union also gained control of eastern Tennessee and the vital railroad hubs of Knoxville and Chattanooga. On September 9, Union forces under William S. Rosecrans occupied Chattanooga, Tennessee, which commanded the gateway to Georgia. Faced by large Confederate forces, Rosecrans was defeated by Braxton Bragg in the Battle of Chickamauga on September 19–20. The Union troops retreated to Chattanooga, where they faced a siege by Bragg. Grant finally charged to the rescue and, in the Battle of Chattanooga on November 24–25, drove the Confederates into Georgia.

Davis and the other civilian leaders of the Confederacy keenly felt the great Union pressure in the West and wanted to throw in reinforcements to defeat Grant in Mississippi or Rosecrans in Tennessee. But Lee, buoyed by a brilliant victory over Hooker at Chancellorsville in May, persuaded them to let him instead invade the North again. He argued that this would relieve the pressure on Vicksburg by drawing Union armies east and enable his army to resupply itself from the rich northern countryside. If he could win a large victory and then go on to capture Washington or another large city, the Union might lose its will to fight, and the setbacks in the West would be irrelevant.

Gettysburg. Lee won approval for his strategy and moved north, determined to win a great victory on northern soil. In June 1863 he maneuvered his army west to the Shenandoah Valley and then north through Maryland into Pennsylvania. The Union army also moved quickly west to stay positioned between Lee and Washington. Then, in the middle of the campaign, Hooker resigned and Lincoln replaced him with George G. Meade. Two days later the two great armies met in an accidental but momentous confrontation at Gettysburg, Pennsylvania. The battle was precipitated by Lee's

Elizabeth Mary Meade Ingraham

A Vicksburg Diary

Elizabeth Mary Meade Ingraham (1806–?) was the sister of Union General George Meade but sided with the Confederacy. In 1831 she and her husband, who had been an agent of the Bank of the United States, moved from Philadelphia to Mississippi, where they lived on Ashwood Plantation, 30 miles from Vicksburg. Her diary, which covers the six weeks between May 2 and June 13, 1863, describes how Grant's Vicksburg campaign changed the relationship between masters and slaves.

May 4. Osterhaus' Division, scum of St. Louis, camped in the big field. All the corn ruined in the field, and nearly all consumed in the granaries. . . . Nancy [a slave] sent me a little. Elsie, faithful and true, and Jack and Emma [all slaves] very attentive.

May 8. The last thing Eddens [a slave] did was to save some meat for me. He slept in the spare room Sunday night, and Monday at noon he had quit our service. . . . Parker, Sol, Mordt, Jim Crow, Isaiah, and Wadloo, have quit us, but the rest are here, and very attentive and willing. . . . I have a few mean ones [slaves] . . . , who tell what they know and implicate the faithful ones, and the servants have had a hard time. They [Union officers] have forced them to work for them. . . .

May 13. Elsy still faithful, feeds us, and does what she can; Rita Jane too; Bowlegs very attentive. Emma beginning to tire of waiting on me, did not come up at noon; Nancy not true.

May 15. Edward's [her son] sash and six pairs of gloves taken out of my wardrobe. I am afraid Emma has done this; don't feel as if I could trust any one but Elsy; she feeds and takes care of me.

May 18. [We] have reason to think the hands will all leave; only a question of time, they are not quite ready; Elsy still true; but Jack doubtful. . . .

May 27. Negro meetings are being held, and the few whites left begin to be very anxious. . . . Powers was burnt out by his own negroes. I fear the blacks more than I do the Yankees. Jack trying to persuade Elsie to leave. . . . She tells him to get her a home and a way of earning a living, and she is ready to go, but [I] told her, if he left here, to move up into the wash-house with her children. I would give her $12, a month and free her four children.

June 3. Our darkeys in great commotion, yesterday, on account of Secesh [secessionists], who, about twenty-five in number, have been going the rounds, and setting the negroes to work; they whipped one fellow . . . and hung another; and we thought last evening all ours but a few meant to go. . . . I wish the Secesh would come. . . .

June 6. Martha with her thee children and Emma, left at midnight Friday . . . and the rest are packing to-day. Hays resolved to go, and I dread lest he take his wife with him, for I can hardly get along as it is, and shall die if I have the cooking to do.

June 10. Fanny, John Smith, and the children, Buck and his family, Dave and his, Kate and hers, making in all thirteen who have gone—Dave intending to come back, but the Yankees would not let him. . . . those who have stayed are utterly demoralized; if they work for you, the job is only half done.

Source: W. Maury Darst, "The Vicksburg Diary of Mrs. Alfred Ingraham," *Journal of Mississippi History* 44 (May 1982), 148–179.

---

awareness that he was on the brink of losing his supply lines to Virginia and Meade's concern that Lee might get control of a major junction of roads at Gettysburg.

On the first day of battle, July 1, Lee was able to bring more troops into action and drove Meade's advance guard to the south of town (see Map 15.4). Meade moved cautiously, waiting for the reinforcements that would give him numerical superiority. He placed his troops in well-defended positions on the hills outside town. Reinforcements for both sides arrived all day and throughout the night. By the morning of the second day Meade outnumbered Lee 90,000 to 75,000. Although aware that he was outnumbered, Lee was bent on victory. He attacked Meade's army on both flanks. The flanking efforts failed. General Richard B. Ewell, assigned to attack the Union right, was unwilling to risk his men in an all-out assault against the forces dug in on Cemetery Hill. Longstreet, assigned the Union left, was unable to attack quickly enough to prevent Meade's forces from strengthening their hold on Little Round Top.

Despite the failures of the previous two days, Lee decided to proceed with a final frontal assault on the center of the Union lines. He had enormous confidence in his troops and mistakenly believed that they faced demoralized Union soldiers stretched out in a thin defensive line. Also, he realized that an attack was the only alternative to a retreat into the South with the loss, perhaps forever, of an opportunity to inflict a crushing psychological defeat on the North.

On the third day, after the heaviest artillery barrage of the war, Lee ordered 14,000 men under General George E. Pickett and two other officers to take Cemetery Ridge. Lee was unaware that Meade had reinforced the center of his line with artillery and his best troops. When Pickett's men charged across a mile of open terrain, they were cut down by massive, withering enemy fire. Once again, artillery and the rifle-musket demonstrated their potency against a traditional infantry assault, but Lee, along with commanders on both sides, had to use the technique because officers could not control troops beyond voice or vision. Thousands of the charging Confederates were killed, wounded, or captured, and the few who managed to charge over the Union fortifications were shot or forced to surrender. When ordered to rally his troops to repel a possible counterattack, Pickett answered, "General Lee, I *have* no division, now."

Gettysburg took more lives than did any other Civil War battle. Meade lost 23,000 killed or wounded; Lee lost 28,000, one-third of the Army of Northern Virginia. Lee could never again invade the North. But he still had a substantial force, thanks largely to Meade, who was so pleased with his victory and wary of Lee that he allowed the remaining Confederate soldiers to escape. Lincoln believed that Meade could have ended the war at Gettysburg. "As it is," Lincoln brooded, "the war will be prolonged indefinitely." Lincoln's pessimism was justified; the two sides were still deadlocked.

The victory at Gettysburg did, however, increase popular support for the war in the North. During the fall of 1863, in state and local elections in Pennsylvania, Ohio, and New York, Democrats once again tested support for the war by challenging Republicans on the issue of emancipation, accusing them of favoring social equality for blacks. For governor of Ohio, the Democrats nominated Clement L. Vallandigham after Lincoln had banished him from the Union for treasonously denouncing the war as one fought "for the freedom of the blacks and the enslavement of the whites." Republicans benefited from the patriotic pride in the victory at Gettysburg, the heroics of African-American soldiers, and white embarrassment over the New York draft riots that summer. Lincoln intervened in the election, declaring that when the war was won, "there will be some black men who can remember that, with silent tongue,

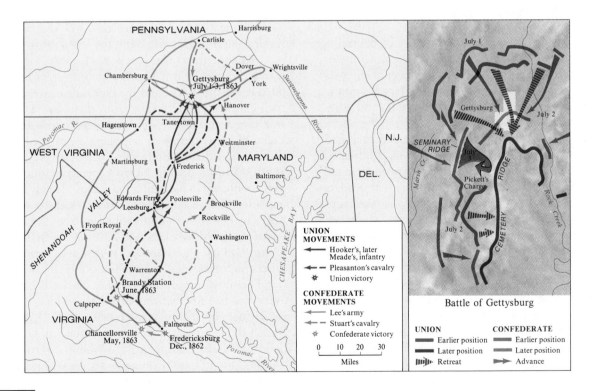

MAP 15.4

The Battle of Gettysburg
Lee's invasion of the North after Confederate victories at Fredericksburg and Chancellorsville was designed to threaten northern cities, persuade Europeans that the Confederacy would win the war, and strengthen the hand of the Peace Democrats. Lee's strategy might have ended the war if he had won at Gettysburg.

and clenched teeth, and steady eye, and well-poised bayonet, they have helped mankind on to this great consummation; while, I fear, there will be some white ones, unable to forget that, with malignant heart, and deceitful speech, they have strove to hinder it." Lincoln made stick the charge that to oppose emancipation was to oppose northern victory. Republicans swept to decisive victories across the three key states, including Ohio, where Vallandigham's opponent won a record share of the vote.

At the same time, the Confederate defeat at Gettysburg contributed to growing war weariness in the South. As a consequence of flagging morale, the Confederate elections of 1863 went sharply against the Jefferson Davis administration. Former secessionists lost ground, and former Whigs gained. As it turned out, the strongest support for Davis was in Union-occupied districts, where regular elections were impossible. Large minorities in the new Confederate Congress were outspokenly hostile to the Davis administration. Some advocated peace negotiations, but more criticized the ineffectiveness of the war effort. The Confederate vice-president, Alexander Stephens, compared Davis to "my poor old blind and deaf dog."

Wartime Diplomacy

Gettysburg also advanced the Union cause by neutralizing the European powers as factors in the outcome of the war. Great Britain in particular had been a key participant as an arms supplier to both the North and the South and as a potential source of economic and additional military aid to the Confederacy.

At the beginning of the war the Confederacy had begun diplomatic efforts to gain foreign recognition of its independence. Because Great Britain depended on the South for four-fifths of its raw cotton, southern leaders hoped that it would offer the Confederacy enough support to cause the Union to give up the fight. Moreover, France's Emperor Napoleon III might be of assistance. He dreamed of an empire in Mexico and by the summer of 1862 had sent thousands of troops to overthrow a republican regime there. In June 1863 the French army, which had grown to 35,000, succeeded, and in 1864 Napoleon installed as emperor of Mexico Archduke Ferdinand Maximilian, the brother of the emperor of Austria. France was bound by a diplomatic agreement to defer to the British in American affairs, but if Britain recognized the independence of the Confederacy, France was virtually certain to follow and might even challenge Union power west of the Mississippi.

Shortly after hostilities began, Great Britain proclaimed its neutrality. This meant that Britain recognized the Confederacy as a belligerent power and therefore regarded it as having the right, under international law, to borrow money and purchase weapons in neutral nations. A concerned Lincoln administration protested that the conflict was a domestic insurrection and not a war and that Britain's declaration of neutrality might be taken to imply recognition of the Confederacy as a sovereign state. Lincoln feared that the British might next help break the ever-tightening naval blockade of the southern coast he had established in April 1861.

The dispute with Britain came to a head over two issues. First, in November 1861, a Union sloop seized a British steamer, the *Trent*, on the high seas; two Confederate commissioners, James Mason and John Slidell, who were on their way to Britain and France, were arrested. In response, the British demanded the release of the diplomats and ordered troops to Canada. Then, in the spring of 1862, British shipbuilders agreed to supply cruisers to the Confederacy. That summer a British firm also contracted to build the "Laird rams," two well-armed ironclads designed to break the blockade. The cruisers included the *Alabama*, which sailed from Liverpool in the summer of 1862 and sank or captured more than a hundred Union merchant ships.

Lincoln, Secretary of State William H. Seward, and the minister to Great Britain, Charles Francis Adams, released Mason and Slidell in December 1861 and adroitly avoided provoking Britain into siding with the Confederacy. In the summer of 1863 they even persuaded the British to impound the Laird rams.

"King Cotton" was less powerful than Lincoln had feared. Before the war British manufacturers had stockpiled textile products, and the blockade enabled them to reap extremely high profits from their sale. During the war they were able to buy raw cotton from Egypt and India. British munitions suppliers, who sold to both sides, and British shipowners, who profited from the South's attacks on the North's merchant marine, also had no interest in hastening the end of the war by choosing sides. British consumers had no wish to raise food prices by disrupting imports of grain from the North. In addition, British workers and reformers were enthusiastic champions of abolition, which the Emancipation Proclamation seemed to establish as a Union war aim.

The most important influence on the British, however, was Lee's defeat at Gettysburg, which convinced the British of the military might of the Union. The British did not want to risk their Canadian colonies or their merchant marine by provoking a strong, well-armed United States. Consequently, they decided not to recognize the Confederacy and remain neutral. Napoleon still favored recognition but had no enthusiasm for facing Union forces alone, particularly after Lincoln, to warn France and Mexico, sent General Banks on a successful mission to capture Brownsville, Texas, just north of the Mexican border, late in 1863.

The Union Victorious, 1864–1865

Despite Gettysburg, the outcome of the war remained very much in doubt well into 1864. Even though the Confederacy could no longer mount an invasion of the North, the Union's failure to crush Lee's army at Gettysburg meant that the Confederacy had new chances to erode northern support for the Union cause. If the war went poorly for the Union, the election of 1864 might enable the Democrats to challenge Lincoln's definition of war aims and persuade northern voters that the Union should end hostilities and begin negotiations with the Confederacy. Confederate leaders believed that such an outcome would result in de facto independence of the Confederacy. Two major developments, however, strengthened the ability of the Union to prosecute a total war: the enlistment of African-American soldiers and the discovery of generals capable of fighting a modern war.

African-American Soldiers

From the beginning of the war, both free blacks and fugitive slaves had sought to enlist in the Union army to advance the cause of freedom. Abolitionists and a few Union generals had tried to help. Frederick Douglass embraced the liberating power of military service in the cause of Union: "Once let the black man get upon his person the brass letters, 'U.S.,' let him get an eagle on his buttons and a musket on his shoulder and bullets in his pockets, and there is no power on earth which can deny that he has earned the right to citizenship in the United States." But that was exactly what northern whites feared: enlistment of African-Americans could threaten traditional race relations in the North. And most Union generals doubted that they would fight. Consequently, until the Emancipation Proclamation the Lincoln administration gave little encouragement to black aspirations for military service. Nonetheless, in 1862 several regiments of free and "contraband" blacks formed in South Carolina, Louisiana, and Kansas.

The logic of tying the abolition of slavery to the war effort, combined with the carnage of battle, helped produce a change in popular attitudes and government policy. Increasingly after the Emancipation Proclamation, northern whites concluded that if blacks were to benefit from a Union victory, then they, too, should share in the fighting and dying. In early 1863 the War Department began to authorize the enlistment of free blacks in the North and slaves in the areas of the South occupied by Union armies. During the summer of 1863, when the army's demand for soldiers increased and white resistance to the draft grew as well, the Lincoln administration began to recruit as many African-Americans as it could.

The performance of the first African-American regiments also helped shift policy. One of those regiments was the First South Carolina Volunteers, under the command of Thomas Wentworth Higginson, a white abolitionist. In January 1863 he wrote a glowing news-

Black Soldiers in the Union Army

These are the proud soldiers of a guard detail of the 107th Colored Infantry at Fort Corcoran, near Washington, D.C. In January 1865 their regiment participated in the daring capture of Fort Fisher, which protected Wilmington, North Carolina, the last of the Confederate ports open to blockade runners. Their chaplain declared that in nine battles the regiment "never faltered, gave way, or retreated, unless ordered by the General commanding."

paper account of the fighting of his troops: "No officer in this regiment now doubts that the key to the successful prosecution of the war lies in the unlimited employment of black troops." In July northerners read of the heroic and tragic attack on Fort Wagner, South Carolina, by another black regiment, the 54th Massachusetts Infantry, which was led by Robert Gould Shaw, the son of a prominent abolitionist. These accounts convinced many white northerners, including Union officers, of the value of black soldiers.

By the spring of 1865 there were nearly 200,000 African-Americans, primarily former slaves, serving as soldiers and sailors, constituting about 10 percent of those who served in the Union forces. Their regiments contributed to the Union cause in a number of major battles during 1864–1865, especially in Grant's grinding siege of Petersburg. During the election of 1864 Lincoln claimed that their participation in the war effort was so great that if the Union renounced emancipation and the recruiting of black soldiers, "we would be compelled to abandon the war in three weeks."

Black soldiers knew that they were fighting for freedom and were shifting the military odds in favor of the Union. Moreover, they hoped that victory would not only end slavery but also help them achieve full equality in American society. Nonetheless, the racial attitudes of northern whites did not undergo a fundamental change during the war, and the Union army, while developing more confidence in blacks as fighting soldiers, still held them in a second-class status. The army kept them in segregated regiments, used them primarily for menial labor or for garrisoning forts and guarding supply lines in occupied southern territory, routinely denied them commissions, and paid them less than white soldiers ($7 versus $13 per month) until June 1864, when the protests of black soldiers finally led Congress to equalize pay. In addition, the Lincoln administration did not protect captured African-Americans from Confederate violations of their rights as prisoners of war. The War Department ended exchanges of prisoners of war in 1863 when the Confederacy threatened to execute or enslave black prisoners of war. On the occasions when the Confederates acted on those threats, however, Lincoln was unwilling to take sterner measures. In July 1863 he threatened retaliation—execution of rebel soldiers or their employment at hard labor on public works—but never followed through.

Despite second-class citizenship, black soldiers persisted and endured. They did so because they understood what was at stake. One soldier found himself facing his former master, who had been taken as a prisoner of war. "Hello, Massa," he said, "bottom rail on top dis time." The worst fears of the secessionists had come true; in a real sense, the great slave rebellion had materialized, though not as a slave revolt.

The New Military Strategy

Lincoln and Grant. The successful Vicksburg and Chattanooga campaigns convinced Lincoln that in Ulysses S. Grant he had finally found a military leader who produced results. He realized that Grant understood how to fight a modern war—a war relying on industrial technology and directed at an entire society.

During his cadet days at West Point, Grant had been bored with studying conventional strategies—ones that stressed, for example, the advantages of interior lines of supply. Now new strategies offered a chance to win the war. During what was the first major war fought with railroads, the telegraph, and ironclad ships, Grant emphasized taking advantage of the ability to move troops and supplies rapidly and overcoming the Confederate advantage of interior lines.

Unlike McClellan and Meade, Grant was willing to accept heavy casualties in assaults on strongly defended positions. He was convinced that only by going on the offensive, even when it meant a great loss of life, could the Union end the war swiftly. "To conserve life, in war," Grant wrote, "is to fight unceasingly." Grant's tactics earned him a reputation as a butcher—a reputation enhanced by his persistent efforts to destroy armies in retreat. Grant was certain that the only way to victory was to crush the southern people's will to resist.

Lincoln, frustrated with the stalemate on the battlefield and worried about reelection in 1864, finally implemented his own approach to modern war. In March 1864 he placed Grant in charge of all the Union armies and created a command structure appropriate to the large, complex organization that the Union army had become. From then on, the president would determine general strategy and Grant would decide how best to implement it. Aiding the process was General Henry W. Halleck, the consummate office soldier. He served as chief of staff, channeling communications and lifting administrative burdens from both Lincoln and Grant. Along with the Prussian general staff, the Union's military command structure was the most efficient in the world.

Lincoln, advised by Grant, drew up a new strategy to break the Confederacy's will to resist. Instead of launching campaigns to take specific places, cities, and territory, he planned a simultaneous crushing advance of all the Union armies, mustering the maximum manpower and resources in their support. Grant would seek victories with a will and power that, Lincoln hoped, would overcome any obstacle.

In early May 1864 Grant ordered the 115,000-man Army of the Potomac, commanded by General George Meade, to destroy Lee's remaining 75,000 troops regardless of the cost in Union lives. He ordered General William Tecumseh Sherman, who shared Grant's views

Grant Planning an Attack
On June 2, 1864, the day this photograph was taken, Grant moved his headquarters to the Bethesda church, carried the pews out under the shade of the surrounding trees, and planned the costly attack he would make at Cold Harbor the next day. While Grant leaned over the pew, gesturing at a map, other officers read reports of the war in newspapers that had just arrived from New York City.

on the nature of warfare, to move simultaneously to invade Georgia and take Atlanta. As Sherman prepared, he wrote that "all that has gone before is mere skirmish. The war now begins."

The Wilderness Campaign. In Virginia, Grant advanced toward Richmond, hoping to force Lee's 75,000 troops to fight in open fields where the Union's superior manpower and artillery could prevail. Lee, remembering Gettysburg, maintained strong defensive positions, attacking only when he held a superior position. He twice seized such opportunities, making the Union take 32,000 casualties in return for 18,000 of his men in the battles of the Wilderness on May 5–7 and Spotsylvania Court House on May 8–12. Grant drove toward the railroad junction at Cold Harbor to outflank Lee, who countered and met Grant there, 10 miles from Richmond. Disregarding his earlier losses, Grant attacked Lee on June 1–3, but broke off after losing 7,000 more men in a frontal assault that lasted less than sixty minutes.

During this monthlong Wilderness campaign Grant eroded Lee's forces, which suffered 31,000 casualties, but Grant paid with 55,000 of his own men. A Union captain, Oliver Wendell Holmes, Jr., wrote, "Many a man has gone crazy since this campaign began from the terrible pressure on mind and body." Another Union officer described his men as feeling "a great horror and dread of attacking earthworks again." During 1861–1863, battles

had been relatively brief, typically lasting one to three days with intervals between the bloodlettings. But with the Wilderness campaign the fighting took on a sustained quality. In Virginia, Grant's relentless offensive tactics and Lee's successful defensive tactics had turned the war into one of grueling attrition (see Map 15.5).

The Siege of Petersburg. On June 12, in a surprise maneuver, Grant pulled away from Lee and Richmond, now heavily fortified, and swung south toward Petersburg, a major railroad center. By occupying it, he hoped to force Lee into the final battle of the war. Lee, however, alertly entrenched his troops at Petersburg and denied Grant the advantage of position. In June 1864 Grant laid siege to Petersburg.

Protracted trench warfare, which foreshadowed that of World War I, ensued. The spade had become more important than the sword as soldiers on both sides, including many who had been engineers in civilian life, built complex networks of trenches, tunnels, artillery emplacements, barriers of debris, and clearings designed to be killing zones. The two armies extended the trenches for almost 50 miles around Richmond and Petersburg as Grant inched toward control of Richmond's railroads. An officer described the continuous artillery firing and sniping as "living night and day within the 'valley of the shadow of death.'" The stress was especially great for the Confederate troops because of the

MAP 15.5

The Closing Virginia Campaigns

In 1865 the armies of Grant and Lee were locked in a deadly dance across the Virginia countryside. By threatening Lee's lines of communication, Grant attempted to force him into open battles. Until April 1865, Lee resisted, taking strong defensive positions that forced Grant to accept protracted sieges and steady casualties, which threatened to undermine northern support for the war.

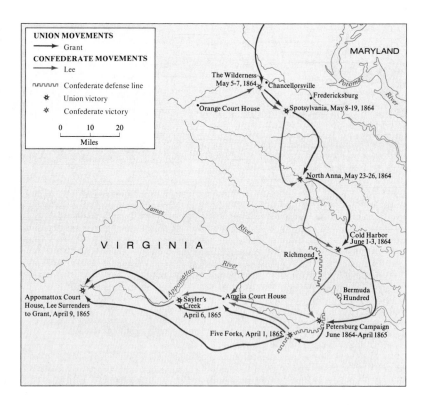

Confederacy's manpower crisis. Some of the Confederate regiments had to spend six months in the muddy, sickening trenches without rotation to the rear.

Lincoln and Grant were confident that their siege would eventually prevail, but time was not on their side. They feared that the enormous casualties and military stalemate might lead to Lincoln's defeat in the November election and, as a consequence, to the abandonment of the Union war effort (see American Voices, page 475).

The Shenandoah Campaign. The daring raids of 15,000 Confederate cavalry and other troops under Jubal Early made matters worse for the Union. Based in the Shenandoah Valley, Early's force crossed the Potomac in early July, passed Union defenses in Maryland only 5 miles north of the White House, and caused Grant to send some of his best troops from Petersburg to chase Early back to the Shenandoah. Before returning, two of Early's brigades invaded Pennsylvania and burned the town of Chambersburg when the city council refused to pay a ransom of $500,000.

The Union struck back with a vengeance. To punish and control the valley, which served as both a refuge for Confederate cavalry and a breadbasket for the Army of Northern Virginia, Grant created a new army, the Army of the Shenandoah, under his favorite cavalry officer, Philip H. Sheridan. Grant ordered Sheridan not only to destroy Early's forces but also to turn the Shenandoah Valley into "a barren waste . . . so that crows flying over it for the balance of this season will have to carry their

provender with them." During the fall Sheridan's troops conducted a scorched-earth campaign in the valley, destroying grain supplies, barns, farming implements, and gristmills, and burning the homes of people suspected of sheltering the "bushwhackers" who had murdered three of Sheridan's officers. The goal was to destroy the valley's economy and break the will of its people to resist the Union. For the first time in the Civil War a major army terrorized civilians.

Guerrillas had conducted terrorist activities against civilians in "Bleeding" Kansas during the 1850s and in the Upper South, particularly in the Shenandoah Valley and Missouri, since the outset of the war. Early's attack on Chambersburg was part of a gradual escalation of such warfare. And soldiers on both sides, frustrated and angered by the indecisiveness of the war, were increasingly tempted to commit acts of vengeance against hostile civilians. But with Sheridan's campaign, terror directed at civilians took on a far more organized form.

The new terrorism was limited for the most part to the destruction of property rather than life, but it nonetheless went beyond the military norms of the day. Conventional generals such as McClellan regarded civilians as innocents whom the military should protect and feared terrorism for the way it could disrupt military discipline. The decision of Lincoln, Grant, and the other Union generals in 1864 to carry the war to Confederate civilians in an organized fashion changed the definition of conventional warfare. The direction of organized terror against civilians was another way in which the Civil War approached the total warfare of the twentieth century.

Elisha Hunt Rhodes

The Diary of a Union Soldier

In June 1861 nineteen-year-old Elisha Hunt Rhodes left his widowed mother and enlisted in the Second Rhode Island Volunteers. Over the next four years he participated in every campaign of the Army of the Potomac. Surviving twenty major battles, he rose from private to lieutenant colonel and commander of the regiment.

April, 1861 [Pawtuxet]
Sunday night after I had retired, my mother came to my room and with a spirit worthy of a Spartan mother of old said, "My son, other mothers must make sacrifices and why should not I? If you feel that it is your duty to enlist, I will give my consent." She showed a patriotic spirit that much inspired my young heart.

July 21, 1861 [Bull Run]
On reaching a clearing . . . we were saluted with a volley of musketry, which, however, was fired so high that all the bullets went over our heads. I remember that my first sensation was one of astonishment at the peculiar whir of the bullets, and that the Regiment im-

mediately laid down without waiting for orders.

As I emerged from the woods I saw a bomb shell strike a man in the breast and literally tear him to pieces. I passed the farm house which had been appropriated for a hospital and the groans of the wounded and dying were horrible. I then descended the hill to the woods which had been occupied by the rebels. . . . The bodies of the dead and dying were actually three and four deep . . . while the trees were spattered with blood.

September 23, 1862 [Antietam]
Sunday morning we found that the enemy had recrossed the river. O, why did we not attack them and drive them into the river? I do not understand these things. But then I am only a boy.

July 3, 1863 [Gettysburg]
Soon the Rebel yell was heard, and . . . the Rebel General Pickett made a charge with his Division and was repulsed after reaching some of our batteries. Our lines of Infantry in front of us rose up and poured in a terrible fire. As we were only a few yards in rear of

our lines we saw all the fight. The firing gradually died away, and but for an occasional shot all was still. But what a scene it was. Oh the dead and dying on this bloody field.

December 22, 1864 [entrenchments near Petersburg]
We do not fear the result of an assault by the enemy on our works. . . . The forts and batteries . . . are within range of each other and are connected by curtains or rifle pits. In front of our works are deep ditches now filled with water and in front of this an abatis [barrier] made of limbs and trees driven slanting into the ground and with the points sharpened. Then we have wires stretched about in every direction about six inches or a foot above the ground. And still in front of all this the trees are slashed and are piled up in great confusion. I wish the Rebels would try to take our lines. It would be fun for us.

Source: Robert Hunt Rhodes, ed., *All for the Union: The Civil War Diary and Letters of Elisha Hunt Rhodes* (New York: Orion, 1991), passim.

Sherman, Atlanta, and the Election of 1864

As the siege at Petersburg dragged on, Lincoln and Grant knew that their hopes of proving to voters that the war could be won rested with Sherman in Georgia. At the beginning of the siege in Virginia, Sherman had penetrated to within about 30 miles of Atlanta, a great railway hub that controlled the heart of the Confederacy. Although his army outnumbered that of General Joseph E. Johnston, 90,000 to 60,000, he declined to attack Johnston directly and decided to pry him out of his defensive positions. Sherman feared that his supply line, extending by rail all the way to Louisville, was overexposed to Confederate cavalry and guerrilla attacks and recognized the advantage to its defenders provided by the rugged terrain of northern Georgia. Johnston, for his part, was unwilling to risk his smaller army and

gradually fell back southward toward Atlanta. Finally, on June 27, at Kennesaw Mountain, Sherman engaged Johnston in a set battle but took 3,000 casualties while inflicting only about 600. Sherman seemed to be stalled in his effort to destroy Johnston's army; Confederate morale soared.

In July, Jefferson Davis, tired of Johnston's defensive tactics, replaced him with General John B. Hood. Sherman, however, welcomed the change, which one of his generals remarked was "to have our enemy grasp the hot end of the poker." What followed, as one Union soldier described it, was "a common slaughter of the enemy," out in the open and unprotected by fortifications. By late July, Sherman was laying siege to Atlanta. But the next month brought little gain; both Sherman and Grant seemed to be bogged down in hopeless campaigns.

As Union and Confederate audiences focused on the fate of Atlanta, the 1864 presidential campaign began. In June the Republican party convention endorsed all of Lincoln's war measures, demanded the unconditional surrender of the Confederacy, and called for a constitutional amendment to abolish slavery. To emphasize the need for restoration of the Union and attract Democratic support, the party temporarily renamed itself the National Union party and nominated for vice-president Andrew Johnson, a Tennessee Democrat who had remained loyal and stayed in the Senate until 1862, when Lincoln named him military governor of Tennessee.

By August many Republican leaders thought Lincoln would lose the presidency to General George B. McClellan, the likely Democratic nominee. With the armies of Grant and Sherman stalled, the expanded war effort seemed almost hopeless. Some Republicans talked about calling a new convention and dropping Lincoln from the ticket. The Republican National Committee urged Lincoln to abandon emancipation as a war aim and offer Jefferson Davis peace in return only for "acknowledging the supremacy of the constitution." Lincoln was tempted, but he refused to abandon emancipation even though he had decided he would be beaten "and unless some great change takes place *badly* beaten." Meanwhile, Republicans rushed through the admission of Nevada to the Union, believing that its electoral votes might tip a close election in their favor.

The Democratic national convention met in late August, nominated McClellan, and declared that party's opposition to emancipation—and to Lincoln's harsh treatment of internal dissent. A slight majority—the War Democrats—wanted to continue the war, despite their criticisms of the Lincoln administration. But the rest—the Peace Democrats—wanted to end the fighting. By threatening to bolt the convention, they obtained nearly unanimous agreement on a platform calling for "a cessation of hostilities, with a view to an ultimate convention of the states, or other peaceable means, to the end that, at the earliest practicable moment, peace may be restored on the basis of the Federal Union." McClellan himself was a War Democrat, but he gave private assurances to the Peace Democrats that he would recommend an immediate armistice and a peace convention. Alexander Stephens, the vice-president of the Confederacy, declared that the platform offered "the first ray of real light I have seen since the war began." Stephens believed that if Confederate forces could hold on to Atlanta and Richmond through the election of 1864, Lincoln might well go down to defeat. A Democratic victory would probably mean the "cessation of hostilities," and Stephens sensed that once the fighting had stopped, Union leaders would be unable to get it going again and the Confederacy would, in effect, be independent.

The Fall of Atlanta. Stephens made his remarks before he learned the fateful news: on September 2 Atlanta fell to Sherman. In a stunning move, he had pulled his troops back from the trenches and had swept around the city to destroy its roads and rail links to the rest of the Confederacy. After failing to stop Sherman, Hood abandoned Atlanta, fearing that Sherman would be able to trap and destroy his army. Sherman wired Lincoln: "Atlanta is ours, and fairly won." In her diary Mary Chesnut recorded that she "felt as if all were dead within me, forever." For the first time she despaired of the possibility for a Confederate victory: "We are going to be wiped off the earth."

Amid the 100-gun salutes in northern cities that greeted the news of Sherman's victory, McClellan repudiated the Democratic peace platform, and Republicans abandoned all efforts to dump Lincoln. They campaigned hard, pinning the peace platform to McClellan's campaign and charging, with some accuracy, that groups of Peace Democrats—or Copperheads (poisonous snakes), as the Republican press called them—had hatched or were hatching treasonous plots in the border states and the southern part of the Old Northwest.

Lincoln's Election. Lincoln's victory in November was not a landslide, but it was clear-cut. He won 212 of 233 electoral votes, carrying every state except Delaware, Kentucky, and New Jersey. He increased his percentage of the popular vote in the free and border states from the 48 percent he had received in 1860 to 55 percent. His opposition was concentrated in border districts and the immigrant wards of large cities. Republicans also won 145 of the 185 seats in the House of Representatives and increased their Senate majority to 42 of 52 seats. The margin of victory in many places came from Union soldiers. The soldiers cast absentee ballots or returned home, briefly furloughed by commanders to cast ballots in areas where the Democrats had blocked absentee balloting. More than three-fourths of the Union troops voted for Lincoln. They wanted the war to continue until the Confederacy met every Union demand, including emancipation. As in 1863, the elections of 1864 lent democratic sanction to the Union war effort. Grant wrote a friend that "the overwhelming majority received by Mr. Lincoln and the quiet with which the election went off . . . will be worth more than a victory in the field both in its effect on the Rebels and in its influence abroad."

Sherman's "March to the Sea"

After abandoning Atlanta, Hood moved into northern Georgia to cut Sherman's supply lines but was forced to retreat to Alabama. Once Sherman set out for the sea,

Hood marched north to Tennessee, convinced that his only chance was to lure Sherman into giving chase. But Sherman declined to follow. He decided that rather than wear out his troops or spread them dangerously thin by protecting captured territory, he would simply "cut a swath through to the sea." Lincoln and Grant were dubious, but Sherman prevailed, arguing that if he marched through Georgia, "smashing things" all the way to the Atlantic coast, he would divide the Confederacy and win a major psychological victory. It would be "a demonstration to the world, foreign and domestic, that we have a power Davis cannot resist."

As he marched, Sherman carried out the concept of total war that he and Sheridan had pioneered—destruction of the enemy's economic and psychological resources. "We are not only fighting hostile armies," Sherman wrote, "but a hostile people, and must make old and young, rich and poor, feel the hard hand of war." Union armies "cannot change the hearts of those people of the South but we can make war so terrible . . . that generations would pass away before they would again appeal to it." He promised to "make Georgia howl!"

Sherman left Atlanta in flames. He destroyed Confederate railroads, property, and supplies, terrorizing the civilian population, in a 300-mile march to the sea. A Union veteran wrote that "[we] destroyed all we could not eat, stole their niggers, burned their cotton & gins, spilled their sorghum, burned & twisted their R.Roads and raised Hell generally." A Union officer described the march as "probably the most gigantic pleasure excursion ever planned." Letters from Georgia describing the havoc so demoralized Confederate soldiers at the front that many deserted and fled home to their loved ones. When Sherman reached Savannah, Georgia, in mid-December, the 10,000 Confederate troops defending the city evaporated almost at once. Sherman presented the city to President Lincoln as a Christmas gift (see Map 15.6).

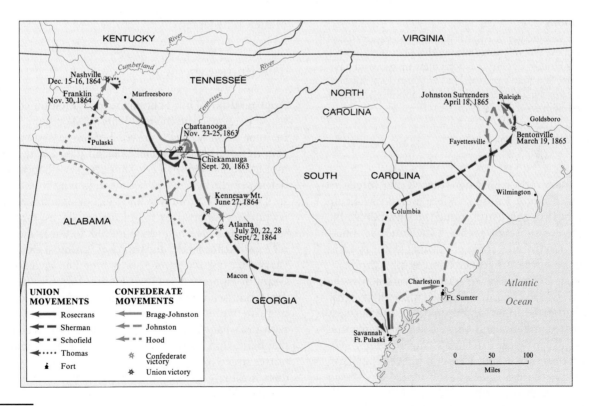

MAP 15.6

Sherman's March through the Confederacy
The Union victory at Chattanooga in November 1863 was almost as critical as those at Gettysburg and Vicksburg. Having already split the Confederacy along the Mississippi, the Union was now in position to split the Confederacy again with a line running from Kentucky through Tennessee and Georgia to the sea. Sherman captured Atlanta and then, largely ignoring John B. Hood's failed invasion of Tennessee, swept to the Atlantic.

Atlanta in Ruins
Not all of the destruction in Atlanta came at the hands of Sherman's forces. The wreckage seen in this photograph is of a factory that Hood's retreating troops blew up to avoid having it fall under Sherman's control. But Union troops finished the work, destroying a Georgia Central roundhouse and car sheds (on the right).

In February 1865 Sherman turned his forces to sweep through South Carolina. He planned to link up with Grant at Petersburg and, along the way, punish the state where secession had begun. "The truth is," Sherman wrote, "the whole army is burning with an insatiable desire to wreak vengeance upon South Carolina." His troops cut a comparatively narrow swath across the state but ravaged the countryside even more thoroughly than they had in Georgia. On February 17 the business district, most churches, and the wealthiest residential neighborhoods of South Carolina's capital, Columbia, burned to the ground. "*This* disappointment," Jefferson Davis moaned, "to me is extremely bitter." By March Sherman had reached North Carolina and was on the verge of linking up with Grant and crushing Lee's army (see American Lives, pages 480–481).

Confederate Morale. Sherman's march, together with Lincoln's victory in 1864, proved that the Union had both the armies and the willpower to prevail in a total war. Moreover, the military setbacks that culminated with Sherman's march to the sea, coupled with the early "20-Negro Exemption," exposed an internal Confederate weakness: rising class resentment on the part of poor whites. Southern men resisted conscription at rates that increased dramatically; in 1865 desertion became epidemic. In all, over 100,000 Confederates deserted. Many linked up with draft evaders to form guerrilla forces that ruled backcountry areas. To add to the South's troubles, secret societies of Unionists operated openly in the Appalachian Mountains, the hill country of Alabama, the Ozarks of Arkansas, parts of Texas, and all other areas where there were few slaves. These Unionists aided northern troops and sometimes enlisted in the Union army when it marched nearby.

By 1865 the Confederacy was experiencing a profound manpower crisis. In March its leaders decided on an extreme measure: arming its own slaves. Howell Cobb, a powerful Georgia politician, had pointed out that "if slaves will make good soldiers our whole theory of slavery is wrong." Nonetheless, urged on by Lee, the Confederate Congress voted to enlist black soldiers. Davis added an executive order granting freedom to all blacks who served in the Confederate army. The war ended too soon, however, to reveal whether any slaves would seek freedom by joining their masters in defense of the Confederacy.

The End of the War

Appomattox. While Sherman marched, Grant continued his siege of the entrenched Army of Northern Virginia. In April 1865 he finally forced Lee into a showdown by gaining control of a crucial railroad junction near Richmond and cutting off Lee's supplies. Lee abandoned the defense of the city and turned west, hoping to meet Johnston in North Carolina. While Lincoln visited the ruins of Richmond, mobbed by joyful former slaves, Grant pursued Lee and his small army of 25,000. Grant swiftly cut off Lee's escape route, and on April 9, almost exactly four years after the attack on Fort Sumter, Lee surrendered to Grant at Appomattox Court House, Virginia. In accepting, Grant set a tone of egalitarianism and generosity. He wore an unpressed jacket and muddy trousers, in contrast with Lee's handsome uniform and sword in its gold-inlay scabbard, and allowed Lee's enlisted men to take their horses home for spring planting. Afterward, Grant's soldiers willingly shared their ample rations with hungry Confederates.

Nine days later General Johnston signed an armistice with Sherman near Durham, North Carolina. He surrendered later in the month; by May 26 all the other Confederate generals had also surrendered. There was no formal conclusion to the hostilities: the Confederate army and government simply dissolved. After fleeing from Richmond, hoping that the South would continue to resist, Jefferson Davis was captured by Union cavalry in Georgia.

The armies of the Union had destroyed the Confederacy. During four years of war they had destroyed much of the South's productive capacity. Its factories, warehouses, and railroads were in ruins, as were many of its farms and cities. Almost 260,000 Confederate soldiers—nearly one in three—had paid for secession with their lives. And most significant, the Union armies had destroyed slavery (see Map 15.7).

The Union's victory had been tragically costly. From Fort Sumter to Appomattox, more than 360,000 Union soldiers had died and hundreds of thousands of others had been maimed and crippled. But the hard and bitter war had been won. Americans from the North and South, both blacks and whites, had to turn to the tasks of peace. Lincoln had spoken at Gettysburg of "finishing the work." It was time to decide exactly what that "work" was. Freed slaves faced the question of what freedom would bring. Their former masters began to try to salvage what they could from defeat. People in all parts of the North pondered the meaning of a victory so costly and so complete. They wondered whether the "terrible, swift sword" of the "Battle Hymn of the Republic" should be put away in reconciliation or loosed again in a hard and bitter peace.

Lee's Surrender
Lee surrendered to Grant in the parlor of a modest farmer, Wilmer McLean, who could not escape the war. McLean had fled to Appomattox for peace and quiet after leaving a Manassas home, which Confederate soldiers had used as a headquarters and Union forces had shelled during the first major battle of the war.

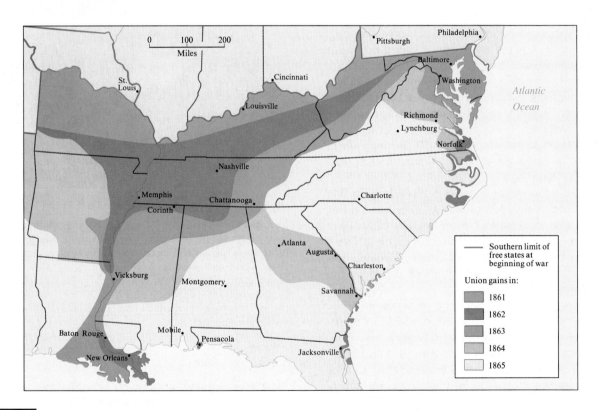

MAP 15.7

The Conquest of the South, 1861–1865
This map reveals how the Union slowly took control of Confederate territory. Nearly half of the territory of the Confederacy held fast until the last year of the war. The Union's victory depended primarily on its ability to control strategic lines of communication and destroy the armies of the Confederacy.

William Tecumseh Sherman: An Architect of Modern War

William Tecumseh Sherman's (1820–1891) obsession with social order motivated the innovations that made him one of the most important architects of modern warfare and a major force in the Union victory in the Civil War.

Sherman's ancestors had long been socially prominent in Connecticut, but after his attorney father, Charles R. Sherman, moved to Lancaster, Ohio, the family fell on hard times. After Charles's death in 1829 his wife could afford to keep only two of their eleven children. At the age of nine, the sixth child, Tecumseh (named after the Indian chief, whom Charles described as "a great warrior"), went to live with Thomas Ewing, a close family friend and a wealthy Lancaster lawyer.

On the one hand, "Cump" (as Tecumseh's own family had nicknamed him) appreciated the privileges provided by Ewing. On the other hand, Cump never got over the embarrassment of his father's financial failure and his family's inability to provide him with a home. His foster mother's insistence that a priest baptize Cump into her Catholic faith and give him a Christian name ("William Tecumseh") only heightened his sense of not belonging. In 1836 he left to enter West Point, where Ewing, who had been elected to the Senate in 1831, had found a place for him.

Sherman adopted the army as a second family. He chafed at cadet discipline but was an excellent student and found that the corps of professional officers gave him a sense of belonging. After his graduation in 1840, assignments in Florida, Alabama, South Carolina, and Georgia appealed to his curiosity about American life and geography.

The Ewings pressured Sherman to leave the army, particularly after their daughter Ellen agreed to marry him, but he refused, fearing greater dependency. Also, Sherman saw opportunity in the Mexican War. But by the time he arrived in California in early 1847 to take up his assignment there was little to do except paperwork.

In 1853 Sherman, depressed by his slow advance, resigned from the army. Unstable financial times, however, ruined his career as head of the San Francisco and

William Tecumseh Sherman
Sherman's severity in this May 1865 photograph might have partly reflected his difficulty in sitting still for Mathew Brady as much as his sense of victory. When he was seated, he crossed and uncrossed his legs incessantly, and a journalist described his fingers as always "twitching his red whiskers—his coat buttons—playing a tattoo on the table—or running through his hair." In the field Sherman smoked cigars and talked continuously.

New York branches of a St. Louis bank, and he became a reluctant business partner of two Ewing foster brothers. In 1860 he rejoined the army as superintendent of the brand-new Louisiana Military Seminary (which would eventually become Louisiana State University).

Sherman's earlier assignments in the South had already made him sympathetic to the planter class. By 1860 he was certain that slavery was necessary for southern social order. But his conviction that the Union was the primary instrument for national stability had deepened during the chaotic 1850s. Sherman's Whig ideology, army loyalties, and personal insecurities combined to give the concept of the Union great symbolic force.

When Louisiana troops seized the U.S. arsenal at Baton Rouge in January 1861 and deposited captured weapons at his academy, Sherman resigned his position. He told his southern friends that secessionists had driven him away. "There can be no *peaceable secession*," he wrote. Secession represented the "tendency to anarchy" and constituted treason. The only way to crush it was to show the secessionists that they could not get away with it. "If war comes, as I fear it surely will," he told the southerners, "I must fight your people whom I best love."

Sherman understood how costly and bloody the war would be. He believed that the Union could smash southern society, but he doubted that the administration of Abraham Lincoln had the will to do so, and Sherman had no desire to associate himself with another failed enterprise. While he hung back, Senator Ewing and one of Sherman's younger brothers, John Sherman, who had just been elected to the Senate from Ohio, persuaded him to become a colonel of a newly formed brigade.

Bull Run, Sherman's first taste of combat, drove him into a depression over the ability of a democracy to wage war. "The want of organization and subordination of our people is a more dangerous enemy than the armies of the South," he wrote. By October 1861 Sherman had risen to the rank of brigadier general and had command of all the Union forces in Kentucky, but he became darkly pessimistic amid the political and military chaos of that border state. Suddenly, in November, the Lincoln administration relieved the seemingly erratic Sherman of his command.

General Henry Halleck continued to support Sherman, however, particularly because he agreed with his warnings about southern strength. Sherman's powerful family also continued to lobby for him. In February 1862 Halleck restored a well-rested Sherman to a command under Ulysses S. Grant in Kentucky. Grant provided just the sense of direction and confidence that Sherman needed. He agreed with Sherman's stress on adequately supplying and disciplining armies and on the swift and decisive deployment of forces. Most important, he was willing to share with Sherman the credit for victories.

Under Grant's leadership, Sherman enjoyed a string of successes. He distinguished himself at Shiloh, and his friends and family in Washington made certain Lincoln immediately promoted him to major general. As military governor of Memphis he pacified a strategic sector of the Mississippi River. Then he served under Grant in the campaign that led to Vicksburg's fall. In Tennessee he began to implement his concept of a war against southern society, employing harsh tactics to deal with anti-Union guerrillas. "When one nation is at war with another, all the people of one are enemies of the other," he wrote. After guerrillas fired on a boat with Unionist passengers and goods near Randolph, Tennessee, he sent a regiment to level the town. He told a Vicksburg citizens' committee that "we are justified in treating all inhabitants as combatants . . ."

In March 1864 Sherman became commander of all military operations in the West. Now only Grant was more powerful, and he consulted closely with Sherman as they drew up a coordinated plan to destroy the Confederacy. Over the next year, Sherman's taking of Atlanta, his "march to the sea," and his sweep through the Carolinas demonstrated his tactical genius and understanding that the Civil War was a war between two societies. He preferred psychological warfare to the bloody, direct confrontations of armies.

After the Union victory Sherman received international acclaim. His former troops revered him, grateful American businessmen made him wealthy, and world leaders honored him. Sherman felt that he had at last established his own identity.

Sherman remained active in public life, but only within the military. He led a war against the Great Plains Indians and then served as commanding general of the army between 1869 and his retirement in 1883. Between 1868 and 1888 politicians, both Democrats and Republicans, regularly approached him to run for the presidency. However, Sherman's distaste for democratic politics had grown even stronger. In fact, Sherman never even voted in a presidential election, except in 1856, when he cast a ballot for Buchanan. In 1883 he ended talk of his candidacy with the often-quoted words "I will not accept if nominated and will not serve if elected." He felt that the honor of having played a central role in preserving the Union was enough. His tombstone epitaph, which he wrote, read simply "Faithful and Honorable."

Summary

The Democrats had divided along sectional lines in the 1860 elections because southerners sought more protection for slavery than northern Democrats would provide. When the Republicans won the presidency, the South concluded that it could no longer both preserve slavery and remain in the Union. The South then seceded and used force to discourage the North from trying to maintain the Union.

The conflict became a total war, one of unsurpassed cost in American lives and resources, because of the great strength of the two regions and because of their conflict over fundamental political and social values. Between 1861 and 1863 the Confederacy several times came close to a decisive victory—at Bull Run, at Antietam, and at Gettysburg. Meanwhile, the Union learned that to win it had to wage total war and smash southern society.

As the Civil War became a war between two peoples, the South and the North each had to address major issues of social unity. For the South, the key questions were: Would slaves work loyally in the fields to sustain their masters and the war effort? And would non-slaveholding whites fight and die in a war if they believed they were simply defending the interests of slave owners? For the North, the central issue of national unity was whether workers and farmers would conclude that they were fighting only to defend the interests of the northern business class and therefore refuse to fight and die.

The year 1864 turned out to be decisive. The North proved to be better organized and more unified. It had acquired the necessary military leadership, resources, and political support to wage total war. Critical to the massive mobilization was the enactment of the Republican economic program, the establishment of emancipation as a war aim, and the enlistment of vast numbers of former slaves.

During 1864 President Lincoln mounted two great offensives. The South resisted vigorously and once again came close to wearing down the will of the North to fight. But the equally stubborn determination of the Union armies, combined with their superior strength and a fortunate victory at Atlanta before the election of 1864, made both offensives successful. The war ended when Sherman's march through Georgia and South Carolina and Grant's relentless pursuit of Lee convinced ordinary southerners that they could not win the war.

TIMELINE

1861	Confederate States of America formed (February 4)
	Abraham Lincoln inaugurated (March 4)
	Confederates fire on Fort Sumter (April 12)
	Virginia convention votes to secede (April 17)
	Lincoln blockades of southern coast
	General Benjamin Butler declares runaway slaves "contraband of war"
	Lincoln states war aims (July 4)
	First Battle of Bull Run (July 21)
	Lincoln signs First Confiscation Act
	Fifty counties in western Virginia vote to form new state (October)
	George B. McClellan made general-in-chief of Union army (November)
1862	Congress passes Legal Tender Act (February)
	Congress passes Second Confiscation Act
	Battle of Shiloh (April 6–7)
	David G. Farragut takes New Orleans (April 25–29)
	Confederacy introduces first draft
	Seven Days' battles (June 25–July 1)
	Second Battle of Bull Run (August 29–30)
	Homestead Act
	Battle of Antietam (September 17)
	Preliminary Emancipation Proclamation (September 22)
	Battle of Fredericksburg (December 13)
1863	Lincoln signs the Emancipation Proclamation (January 1)
	Enrollment Act establishes draft in the North
	Battle of Chancellorsville (May 2–4)
	France sets up Mexican regime
	Battle of Gettysburg (July 1–3)
	Fall of Vicksburg (July 4)
	New York City draft riots
	Britain impounds Laird rams
	Union forces seize Brownsville, Texas
1864	Ulysses S. Grant takes command of all Union armies (March 9)
	Grant's Wilderness campaign
	Siege of Petersburg begins (June 15)
	Jubal Early's raids
	Atlanta falls to William T. Sherman (September 2)
	Shenandoah campaign of Philip H. Sheridan
	Lincoln's reelection
	Sherman's march through Georgia
1865	Congress approves Thirteenth Amendment
	Columbia, South Carolina, burns (February 17)
	Robert E. Lee surrenders
	Ratification of Thirteenth Amendment

★   ★   ★

BIBLIOGRAPHY

The best up-to-date, comprehensive one-volume surveys of the Civil War are James M. McPherson's *Battle Cry of Freedom: The Civil War Era* (1988) and *Ordeal By Fire: The Civil War and Reconstruction* (1993). An excellent brief survey is Charles P. Roland, *An American Iliad: The Story of the Civil War* (1991). Compelling older surveys include Shelby Foote, *The Civil War: A Narrative*, 3 vols. (1958–1974), and Allan Nevins, *War for the Union*, 4 vols. (1959–1971).

Choosing Sides

Classic studies of the secession crisis include Richard N. Current, *Lincoln and the First Shot* (1963); David M. Potter, *Lincoln and His Party in the Secession Crisis, 1860–61* (1950); and Kenneth M. Stampp, *And the War Came: The North and the Secession Crisis, 1860–61* (1950). Histories of the secession of the Deep South include William L. Barney, *The Secessionist Impulse: Alabama and Mississippi in 1860* (1974), and Michael P. Johnson, *Toward a Patriarchal Republic: The Secession of Georgia* (1977). On the Upper South, see Daniel W. Crofts, *Reluctant Confederates: Upper South Unionists in the Secession Crisis* (1989).

War Machines

To study northern society and politics during the war, consult Iver Bernstein, *The New York City Draft Riots* (1990); Gabor S. Boritt, ed., *Lincoln the War President: The Gettysburg Lectures* (1992); Adrian Cook, *The Armies of the Streets: The New York City Draft Riots of 1863* (1974); George M. Fredrickson, *The Inner Civil War: Northern Intellectuals and the Crisis of Union* (second edition, 1993); J. Matthew Gallman, *The North Fights the Civil War: The Home Front* (1994); Mary E. Massey, *Bonnet Brigades: American Women and the Civil War* (1966); William Q. Maxwell, *Lincoln's Fifth Wheel: The Political History of the United States Sanitary Commission* (1956); Mark E. Neely, Jr., *The Fate of Liberty: Abraham Lincoln and Civil Liberties* (1991); Phillip S. Paludan, *The Presidency of Abraham Lincoln* (1994); Susan M. Reverby, *Ordered to Care: The Dilemma of American Nursing, 1850–1945* (1987); Joel Silbey, *A Respectable Minority: The Democratic Party in the Civil War Era* (1977); Hans Trefousse, *The Radical Republicans* (1969); and Garry Wills, *Lincoln at Gettysburg* (1992). Important biographies on Union leaders include Michael Fellman, *Citizen Sherman: A Life of William Tecumseh Sherman* (1995); John F. Marszalek, *Sherman: A Soldier's Passion for Order* (1993); William McFeely, *Grant: A Biography* (1981); Stephen B. Oates, *With Malice towards None: The Life of Abraham Lincoln* (1977); Stephen W. Sears, *George B. McClellan: The Young Napoleon* (1988); and the Abraham Lincoln studied cited in Chapter 14.

Among the best histories of the Confederacy are George C. Rable, *The Confederate Republic: A Revolution against Politics* (1994), and Emory M. Thomas, *The Confederate Nation: 1861–1865* (1979). Important biographies on leading Confederates include William C. Davis, *Jefferson Davis, the Man and His Hour: A Biography* (1991), and Thomas E. Schott, *Alexander H. Stephens of Georgia: A Biography* (1988).

Studies of non-slaveholding whites in the Confederacy include Paul Escott, *After Secession: Jefferson Davis and the Failure of Southern Nationalism* (1978); Drew Gilpin Faust, *The Creation of Confederate Nationalism: Ideology and Identity in the Civil War* (1988); and Philip S. Paludan, *Victims: A True History of the Civil War* (1981).

Studies of wartime emancipation include Herman Belz, *A New Birth of Freedom: The Republican Party and Freedmen's Rights, 1861–1866* (1976); John Hope Franklin, *The Emancipation Proclamation* (1963); Louis S. Gerteis, *From Contraband to Freedom: Federal Policy toward Southern Blacks, 1861–1865* (1973); James M. McPherson, *The Struggle for Equality: Abolitionists and the Negro in the Civil War and Reconstruction* (1964); and Benjamin Quarles, *The Negro in the Civil War* (1953). The best scholarship on the lives of slaves during the war is found in Ira Berlin et al., eds., *Freedom: A Documentary History of Emancipation, 1861–1867*, Series I, Volume I: *The Destruction of Slavery* (1985) and Series I, Volume III: *The Wartime Genesis of Free Labor: The Lower South* (1990). See also Winthrop D. Jordan, *Tumult and Silence at Second Creek: An Inquiry into a Civil War Slave Conspiracy* (1993).

Fighting the Civil War

The most useful introductions to the military aspects of the war are T. Harry Williams, *The History of American Wars* (1981) and *Lincoln and His Generals* (1952). On the experiences of Civil War soldiers, see Albert Castel, *Decision in the West: The Atlanta Campaign* (1992); Gerald F. Linderman, *Embattled Courage: The Experience of Combat in the American Civil War* (1987); James M. McPherson, *What They Fought For, 1861–1865* (1994); Reid Mitchell, *Civil War Soldiers* (1988) and *The Vacant Chair: The Northern Soldier Leaves Home* (1993); and Joseph T. Glatthaar, *The March to the Sea and Beyond: Sherman's Troops in the Savannah and Carolinas Campaign* (1985). On the participation of African-Americans in the war, see Ira Berlin et al., *Freedom: A Documentary History of Emancipation, 1861–1867*, Series II, *The Black Military Experience* (1982), and Joseph T. Glatthaar, *Forged in Battle: The Civil War Alliance of Black Soldiers and White Officers* (1990). On Confederate military tactics, see Grady McWhiney and Perry D. Jamieson, *Attack and Die: Civil War Military Tactics and the Southern Heritage* (1982), and Steven E. Woodworth, *Jefferson Davis and His Generals: The Failure of Confederate Command in the West* (1990). An innovative exploration of the dynamics of violence is found in Charles Royster, *The Destructive War: William Tecumseh Sherman, Stonewall Jackson, and the Americans* (1991). The most graphic account of a single battle is Stephen W. Sears, *Landscape Turned Red: The Battle of Antietam* (1983). On the most violent guerrilla war ever fought in the United States, see Michael Fellman, *Inside War: The Guerrilla Conflict in Missouri during the American Civil War* (1989). On the Civil War in the Far West, consult Alvin M. Josephy, Jr., *The Civil War in the American West* (1991). For insightful analyses of the war's outcome see Richard E. Beringer et al., *Why the South Lost the Civil War* (1986); Joseph T. Glatthaar, *Partners in Command: The Relationships between Leaders in the Civil War* (1993); Herman Hattaway and Archer Jones, *How the North Won: A Military History of the Civil War* (1983); and Archer Jones, *Civil War Command and Strategy: The Process of Victory and Defeat* (1992).

Robert B. Elliott

Robert B. Elliott (1842–1884) was born in Boston and educated there and in Jamaica and England. After studying law and serving in the navy during the Civil War, he moved to Charleston and served in the state legislature (1868–1870), Congress (1871–1874), and as speaker of the South Carolina house (1874–1876). This 1874 lithograph, *The Shackle Broken by the Genius of Freedom,* shows him addressing state legislators on civil rights. After Reconstruction he left politics and practiced law in New Orleans.

CHAPTER 16

The Union Reconstructed

1865–1877

★   ★   ★

When the Confederacy collapsed in the spring of 1865, President Lincoln hoped that he could achieve a swift reconciliation between the triumphant North and the shattered South. In his second inaugural address Lincoln had spoken of the need to "bind up the nation's wounds." But many questions remained unanswered. Who would control the rebuilding of the Union—the president or Congress? How long should the rebuilding last? How far should it go: should it exclude former Confederates from politics and reward freedmen with land confiscated from their former masters?

At the end of the war most Republican leaders defined the task of rebuilding simply as a matter of *restoration*. These moderates wanted to establish loyal, pro-Union state governments and restore the southern states' representation in Congress. But freedmen, former abolitionists, and some Republican politicians favored a more radical plan—one requiring a degree of *reconstruction* of the South. In their view, steps should be taken to ensure a measure of political and even economic equality for the freed slaves and to prevent the return to power of unrepentant planters. For radicals, the key to reconstructing the South was to make the Republican party dominant there.

When northern Republicans adopted a policy of radical reconstruction in 1867, ex-Confederates and their Democratic sympathizers in the North maintained that their goal should be the *redemption* of the South. They claimed that the Union victory had defeated democracy in the South, depriving southerners of control over their economic, social, and political systems. The Union would be rebuilt, the redeemers claimed, only when white southerners regained power over their states and their own affairs.

The Reconstruction Era—the years from 1865 to 1877—was shaped by continuous struggles among the groups holding these differing views. It was a time of

485

unparalleled peacetime turmoil and violence. In the struggles, every kind of tactic was brought to bear: the assassination of one president and the impeachment of another; the adoption of three amendments to the Constitution and a welter of new legislation; the use of violence, including nighttime terrorism by robed whites in the South; the creation of new institutions by African-Americans; and conventional compromises and deals by politicians on all sides.

Presidential Restoration

Lincoln and his successor, Andrew Johnson, took the initiative in rebuilding the Union. Both believed that the southern states had never legally left the Union, that rebuilding the nation was simply a process of restoring state governments loyal to the Union, and that this political process could take place quickly, largely under presidential direction. This moderate approach put the presidents on a collision course with those Republicans in Congress who sought a reconstruction of southern society.

Restoration under Lincoln

The process of rebuilding had actually begun during the war as Lincoln tried to subvert the southern war effort. Lincoln thought that a policy of moderation and reconciliation in the portions of the South occupied by federal troops would induce the Confederates to abandon the rebellion. In implementing his restoration plan, Lincoln relied on his power as military commander in chief. He assumed that states could not legally secede and that reorganizing the Union was purely an administrative mat-

ter. (In 1869, in *Texas v. White*, the Supreme Court accepted Lincoln's constitutional interpretation, ruling that secession was impossible under the Constitution.)

Lincoln's Plan. In December 1863 Lincoln announced his restoration plan. He offered a general amnesty to all Confederate citizens except high-ranking civil and military officials. Citizens of states seeking to reconstitute their governments would have to take an oath pledging their *future* loyalty to the Union and accepting the Union's wartime acts and proclamations concerning slavery. When 10 percent of the number of voters in 1860 had taken the loyalty oath, those individuals could organize a new state government.

Lincoln aimed his plan at former southern Whigs, many of whom he had known well as former political allies. Under his plan they would step forward, declare allegiance to the Union, and take charge of southern state governments. That is what happened in three states under military occupation: Louisiana, Arkansas, and Tennessee. The former Whigs who organized loyal governments under Lincoln's supervision often retained their economic power. In Louisiana, for example, Whig sugar planters who declared their loyalty to the Union received help from Generals Benjamin F. Butler and Nathaniel P. Banks, who used their troops to enforce labor discipline, transforming slaves into wage laborers and enabling the former Whigs to save their plantations.

Radical and Moderate Republicans. Many members of his own party, including some of his fellow moderates, disapproved of Lincoln's plan. Their opposition was based in part on a different constitutional interpretation. They argued that the southern states *had* left the Union and were now the equivalent of conquered provinces with territorial status. As such, they were subject to Congressional rule rather than executive authority.

Radical Republicans

Lincoln's readmission plan was harshly criticized by radical Republicans. One of their leaders was Thaddeus Stevens (front row, second from left), pictured here with fellow members of Congress in a photograph by Mathew Brady. Stevens outlined a radical economic plan that called for a redistribution of land in the South. He believed that the former slaves needed more than the vote to control their fate—they needed land. He was unable to muster support for this radical plan.

The most strenuous criticism came from a group of radical Republicans, some of whom had abolitionist backgrounds. Led by Senator Charles Sumner of Massachusetts and Representative Thaddeus Stevens of Pennsylvania, the radicals wanted a harder, slower peace. In Stevens's words, the federal government should "revolutionize Southern institutions, habits, and manners." He declared that "the foundations of their institutions . . . must be broken up and relaid, or all our blood and treasure will have been spent in vain."

Stevens, Indiana Congressman George W. Julian, and African-American leaders, including Frederick Douglass, staked out the most radical definition of what reconstruction should mean. The core of their program was an economic one: confiscation and redistribution of southern plantations to the freed slaves and to white farmers who had been loyal to the Union. The program was meant to fulfill the dreams of the former slaves, whose expectations had been raised by emancipation, and of the poor white farmers of the South. To the former slaves, emancipation and freedom meant control over their lives. But to control their fate in an agricultural economy, they knew they needed to own land. But Stevens and Julian were unable to recruit other members of Congress to support a large-scale redistribution of land in the South. The majority of radical Republicans regarded such a plan as a violation of the Constitution's protection of property rights and a threat to the capitalist order.

The radical Republicans did agree on three key points: (1) The leaders of the Confederacy should not be allowed to return to power in the South, (2) steps should be taken to establish the Republican party as a major, even dominant, force in southern political life, and (3) the federal government should ensure that African-Americans participated in southern society with full *civil* equality by guaranteeing their voting rights. The last point was especially important. As Frederick Douglass declared in May 1865, "Slavery is not abolished until the black man has the ballot."

Moderate Republicans in Congress shared the radicals' view that Lincoln's program was too lenient, and they endorsed the first two points of the radical program. But as a group they hesitated to go further and support black suffrage and civil equality. Like virtually all conservative Republicans and Democrats, some moderates were profoundly racist and believed that African-Americans could never become responsible citizens. Like Lincoln, other moderates had confidence in blacks' abilities. But they wanted to avoid the violent resistance that southern whites might mount in response to drastic changes in the relationship between the races.

The Wade-Davis Bill. In 1864 the radical and moderate Republicans in Congress devised an alternative to Lincoln's program that was based on the two reconstruction principles on which they could agree. In the Wade-Davis bill, passed by Congress on July 2, 1864, they set harsher conditions for former Confederate states to rejoin the Union. A *majority* of a state's adult white men would have to swear an oath of allegiance to the Union. The state could then hold a constitutional convention, but no one could vote in the election for delegates or serve as a delegate unless he swore that he had never carried arms against the Union or aided the Confederacy in any way. Requiring this pledge, which became known as the *ironclad oath*, would exclude most southern whites, therefore leaving the task of constitution making to those white men who had overtly opposed the Confederacy. Finally, the bill required that slavery be prohibited and that Confederate civil and military leaders be permanently disfranchised.

The Wade-Davis bill proposed going further than Lincoln's plan in punishing ex-Confederates, especially those who had led the rebellion. Despite this difference, Lincoln seemed ready to compromise with the Congressional Republicans. Rather than openly challenging Congress by vetoing the Wade-Davis bill, he executed a "pocket" veto by not signing it before Congress adjourned. At the same time he initiated informal talks with members of Congress aimed at producing a compromise solution when the war ended. He even suggested that he might support the radical program of establishing federal control over race relations in the South and guaranteeing the vote to African-Americans there. In the last speech he ever delivered, on April 11, 1865, Lincoln demonstrated that he was moving pragmatically to endorse freedmen's suffrage, beginning with those who had served in the Union army and those who were educated.

The Assassination of Lincoln. Whether Lincoln and his party could have forged a unified approach to reconstruction is one of the great unanswered questions of American history. On April 14, 1865—Good Friday—Lincoln was shot in the head at Ford's Theater in Washington by an unstable actor named John Wilkes Booth. Ironically, Lincoln might have been spared if the war had dragged on longer, for Booth and his Confederate associates had originally plotted to kidnap the president to force a negotiated settlement. After Lee's surrender, Booth became desperate for revenge. In the middle of the play he entered Lincoln's box, shot him at close range, stabbed a member of the president's party, and fled. Booth was hunted down and killed by Union troops. Eight people were eventually convicted as accomplices by military courts, and four of them were hanged.

Lincoln never regained consciousness and died on April 15. The Union—and the hundreds of thousands of African-Americans for whom his name had become synonymous with freedom—went into profound mourning. Even Lincoln's critics suddenly conceded his greatness. Millions of Americans honored his memory by waiting in silence to watch the train carrying his body back to Illinois for burial.

Lincoln's death dramatically changed the prospects for a moderate reconstruction. At one stroke John Wilkes Booth had sent Lincoln to martyrdom, convinced many northerners that harsher measures against the South were necessary, and forced the presidency into the hands of Vice-President Andrew Johnson.

Restoration under Johnson

Andrew Johnson was a self-made man and former slaveholder from the hills of eastern Tennessee. A Jacksonian Democrat, he saw himself as the champion of ordinary white people. He hated what he called the "bloated, corrupt aristocracy" of the Northeast, and he blamed southern planters for the Civil War. His political career had led from the Tennessee legislature and governorship to the U.S. Senate, where he remained, loyal to the Union, after Tennessee seceded. He served as military governor of his home state after federal forces captured Nashville. In 1864 the Republicans nominated him as vice-president in an effort to promote wartime political unity and to court the support of southern Unionists.

Like Lincoln, Johnson believed that the southern states had retained their constitutional status and that reunification was exclusively an executive matter. During the summer of 1865, when Congress was not in session, Johnson unilaterally executed his own plan for restoration. He insisted only that the states revoke their ordinances of secession and ratify the Thirteenth Amendment, which abolished slavery. He offered amnesty and a return of all property except slaves to almost all southerners if they took an oath of allegiance to the Union. Southerners who were excluded from amnesty—high-ranking Confederate military officers and civil officials and persons with taxable property of more than $20,000—could petition Johnson personally. By December 1865 all the former Confederate states had functioning governments and had met Johnson's requirements for rejoining the Union.

Johnson's plan would not become complete until Congress accepted the senators and representatives from the former Confederacy. Under the Constitution, Congress is "the judge of the elections, returns and qualifications of its own members" (Article I, Section 5), and it would not convene again until December 1865. This step need not have been a problem for Johnson. Whereas most moderate Republicans in Congress hoped to make changes in Johnson's program to bring it closer to the Wade-Davis bill, they supported the basic outline of his program. Perhaps most important, they agreed with Johnson that the federal government should not protect African-American suffrage or civil equality. Even most radicals were optimistic. They liked the stern treatment of Confederate leaders, and they hoped that the new southern governments would respond positively to Johnson's conciliatory attitude and offer the vote at least to African-Americans who were literate and owned property (probably no more than 10 percent of adult black men).

During the summer and fall, however, Johnson lost the support of radical Republicans. They first became angered over a telegram that Johnson had sent in August to the provisional governor of Mississippi, who was presiding over the state's constitutional convention. Johnson urged that the vote be given to literate African-Americans on the grounds that "the radicals, who are wild upon negro franchise, will be completely foiled." The telegram also embarrassed Republican moderates, who had hoped to win the support of the radicals as well as that of Johnson for a compromise program.

In the fall of 1865 news reports of conditions in the South alarmed the moderates and further outraged the radicals. They learned that ex-Confederates were frequently attacking freedmen and white Union supporters, that the new provisional governments were making

Andrew Johnson
The president was not an easy man. This photograph of Andrew Johnson (1808–1875) conveys some of the personal qualities that contributed so centrally to his failure to reach an agreement with Republicans on a program of moderate reconstruction.

no effort to enfranchise African-Americans, and that ex-Confederates had taken control of southern governments. Southern voters elected to Congress nine men who had served in the Confederate Congress, seven former officials of Confederate state governments, four generals and four colonels from the Confederate army, and even the vice-president of the Confederacy, Alexander Stephens. It turned out that Johnson had been exceedingly liberal in pardoning ex-Confederate leaders. He seemed less interested in punishing them than in humbling them by making them submit to his personal power.

As radical Republicans increased their attacks on Johnson, he shifted away from his strongly bipartisan stance. He began to believe he could build a coalition of white southerners, northern Democrats, and conservative Republicans to support the creation of a democracy for white southerners. To avoid embarrassing potentially supportive Republicans or ex-Whigs in the South, his banner would be "National Union." Democrats in both the North and the South praised Johnson as the leader they needed to restore their party on a national basis. As the president warmed to Democratic applause, he granted more and more pardons to wealthy southerners—an average of a hundred a day in September.

The president's movement toward the Democrats further agitated radical Republicans and dismayed the moderates. By December 1865, when Congress convened, the moderates had become convinced that they had to join the radicals in order to protect the Republican party. It would be necessary, they concluded, to take action to guarantee the civil rights of former slaves and establish the Republican party in the South.

The Republican party acted quickly to reject the newly elected southern representatives and proposed that Johnson work with Congress on a new program for reconstructing the South. A House-Senate committee—the Joint Committee on Reconstruction—was formed to develop that program in cooperation with the president.

The Joint Committee conducted public hearings on conditions in the former Confederacy and publicized alarming reports from army officers, federal officials, and white and black southerners. The testimony augmented the newspaper reports by revealing an astonishing level of violence and providing disturbing details on how southern planters and legislatures were attempting to resubjugate the freed slaves. Although most moderates were still not ready to impose black suffrage on the South, almost all of them were shocked by what they regarded as a movement to circumvent the Thirteenth Amendment.

Acting on Freedom: African-Americans in the South

While congressmen discussed conditions in the South, African-Americans were already far advanced in acting on their idea of freedom. They were exultant and hopeful; their main concern was economic independence, which they assumed was necessary for true freedom. During the Civil War they had acted on this assumption throughout the South whenever Union armies drew near. But many officers actively sympathized with the planters, allowing those who expressed loyalty to the Union to retain control of their plantations and their former slaves. Other officers wished to destroy the power of the planters but preserve a class system in the South. In 1863, General Lorenzo Thomas, for example, devised a plan to lease plantations in the Mississippi Valley to loyal northern men who would hire African-American laborers under conditions set by the army.

During the final months of the war, when the Union directed its military operations against civilians, freedmen found greater opportunities to win control of land. Most visibly, General William T. Sherman reserved vast tracts of coastal lands in Georgia and South Carolina—the Sea Islands and the abandoned plantations within 30 miles of the coast—for black settlers and gave them

Schoolhouse, Port Hudson, Louisiana
This was probably the first schoolhouse built for freedmen by Union forces. In front, African-American soldiers from the Port Hudson "Corps d'Afrique" pose with their textbooks. In 1865 and 1866 most new schools in the South were established by blacks forming societies and raising money among themselves.

Eliphalet Whittlesey

Report on the Freedmen's Bureau

In October 1865, Colonel Eliphalet Whittlesey, an assistant commissioner for the Freedmen's Bureau in North Carolina, wrote the following report on the activities of the Bureau. He was later promoted to general and served as a trustee of the national Freedman's Savings Bank in Washington, D.C. He was typical of many Freedmen's Bureau officials in that he saw his role as one of mediating between two worthy groups: former slaves and former masters.

On the 22d of June I arrived at Raleigh with instructions . . . to take the control of all subjects relating to "refugees, freedmen, and the abandoned lands" within this State. I found these subjects in much confusion. Hundreds of white refugees and thousands of blacks were collected about this and other towns, occupying every hovel and shanty, living upon government rations, without employment and without comfort, many dying for want of proper food and medical supplies. A much larger number, both white and black, were crowding into the towns, and literally swarming about every depot of supplies to receive their rations. My first effort was to reduce this class of suffering and idle humanity to order, and to discover how large a proportion of these applicants were really deserving of help. . . .

It was evident at the outset that large numbers were drawing rations who might support themselves. . . . orders were issued that no able-bodied man or woman should receive sup-

plies, except such as were known to be industrious, and to be entirely destitute. . . . The homeless and helpless were gathered in camps, where shelter and food could be furnished, and the sick collected in hospitals, where they could receive proper care. . . .

Suddenly set free [the freedmen] were at first exhilarated by the air of liberty, and committed some excesses. To be sure of their freedom, many thought they must leave the old scenes of oppression and seek new homes. Others regarded the property accumulated by their labor as in part their own, and demanded a share of it. On the other hand, the former masters, suddenly stripped of their wealth, at first looked upon the freedmen with a mixture of hate and fear. In these circumstances some collisions were inevitable. . . .

. . . [M]any freedmen need the presence of some authority to enforce upon them their new duties. . . . The efforts of the bureau to protect the freedmen have done much to restrain violence and injustice. Such efforts must be continued until civil government is fully restored, just laws enacted, or great suffering and serious disturbance will be the result. Contrary to the fears and predictions of many, the great mass of colored people have remained quietly at work upon the plantations of their former masters during the entire summer. . . . In truth, a much larger amount of vagrancy exists among the whites than among the blacks. . . .

The report is confirmed by the fact that out of a colored population of nearly 350,000 in the State, only about 5,000 are now receiving support from the government. . . . Our officers . . . have visited plantations, explained the difference between slave and free labor, the nature and the solemn obligation of contracts. The chief difficulty met with has been a want of confidence between the two parties.

. . . Rev. F. A. Fiske, a Massachusetts teacher, has been appointed superintendent of education, and has devoted himself with energy to his duties. . . . the whole number of schools . . . is 63, the number of teachers 85, and the number of scholars 5,624. A few of the schools are self-supporting, and taught by colored teachers, but the majority are sustained by northern societies and northern teachers. The officers of the bureau have, as far as practicable, assigned buildings for their use, and assisted in making them suitable; but time is nearly past when such facilities can be given. The societies will be obliged hereafter to pay rent for school-rooms and for teachers homes. The teachers are engaged in a noble and self-denying work. They report a surprising thirst for knowledge among the colored people—children giving earnest attention and learning rapidly, and adults, after the day's work is done, devoting the evening to study. . . .

Source: Report of the Joint Committee on Reconstruction, 39th Cong., 1st sess. (Washington, D.C.: U.S. Government Printing Office, 1866), II: pp. 186–192.

"possessory titles" to 40-acre tracts. Sherman had little use for radicals and freedmen; he only wanted to relieve the pressure that African-American refugees were placing on his army as it marched across the Lower South. But the freedmen assumed that Sherman's order meant that the land would be theirs—a reasonable expectation after one of Sherman's generals told a large group of freedmen "that they were to be put in possession of lands, upon which they might locate their families and work out for themselves a living and respectability."

The Freedmen's Bureau. The resettlement of freedmen was organized by the Bureau of Refugees, Freedmen, and Abandoned Lands, which Congress created in March 1865. Known as the Freedmen's Bureau, it was charged with feeding and clothing war refugees of both races, renting confiscated land to "loyal refugees and freedmen," and drafting and enforcing labor contracts between freedmen and planters. The Freedmen's Bureau also worked with the large number of northern voluntary associations that sent missionaries and teachers to the South to establish schools for former slaves (see American Voices, page 490).

By the end of the war the army and the Freedmen's Bureau had resettled about 10,000 families on half a million acres of "Sherman" land in Georgia and South Carolina. Reports of such actions inspired many African-American families to stay on their old plantations in the hope that they would own some of the land after the war. When the South Carolina planter Thomas Pinckney returned home, his freed slaves told him, "We ain't going nowhere. We are going to work right here on the land where we were born and what belongs to us." One Georgia freedman offered to sell to his former master the share of the plantation he expected to receive after the federal redistribution.

Johnson's amnesty plan allowed pardoned Confederates to recover their land if Union troops had confiscated or occupied it. In October, Johnson ordered General Oliver O. Howard, head of the Freedmen's Bureau, to tell Sea Island blacks that they did not hold legal title to the land and that they would have to come to terms with the white landowners. When Howard reluctantly obeyed, the dispossessed farmers protested: "Why do you take away our lands? You take them from us who have always been true, always true to the Government! You give them to our all-time enemies! That is not right!" When some of the Sea Islanders refused to deal with the restored white owners, Union soldiers forced them to leave or work for their old masters.

The former slaves resisted efforts to remove them. Often led by African-American veterans of the Union army, they fought pitched battles with plantation owners and bands of ex-Confederate soldiers. Whenever possible, landowners attempted to disarm and intimidate the returning black soldiers. One soldier wrote from Maryland: "The returned colard Solgers are in Many cases beten, and their guns taken from them, we darcent walk out of an evening. . . . they beat us badly and Sumtime Shoot us." In this warfare federal troops often backed the local whites, who generally prevailed in recapturing their former holdings.

A New Labor System. Throughout the South high postwar prices for cotton prompted returning planters not only to reclaim land but also to establish a labor system that was as close to slavery as they could make it. On paper, emancipation had cost the slave owners about $3 billion—the value of their capital investment in former slaves—a sum that equaled nearly three-fourths of the nation's economic production in 1860. The *real* losses of planters, however, depended on whether they lost control of their former slaves. Planters attempted to reestablish that control and to substitute low wages for the food, clothing, and shelter that their slaves had previously received. They also refused to sell or rent land to blacks, hoping to force them to work for low wages.

The freedmen resisted the new wage system as well as the loss of land. During the growing seasons of 1865 and 1866 thousands of former slaves abandoned their old plantations and farms. Many freedmen sought better lives in the towns and cities of the South. Those who remained in the countryside either refused to work in the cotton fields or tried to reduce the amount of time they worked there. When they could, freedmen developed their own garden plots, guaranteeing themselves a subsistence level of rations during the postwar disruptions. Freedmen who did return to work in white-owned cotton fields refused to submit to the grueling gang system that had been the major tool of economic exploitation under slavery. Now they wanted a pace of work and independence that reflected their new status. What was freedom all about if not to have a bit more leisure time, to work less intensely than they had as slaves, and to work for themselves and their families?

Wage Labor of Ex-Slaves
This photograph, taken in South Carolina shortly after the Civil War, shows former slaves being led from the cotton fields. Although they now worked for wages, they were probably organized into a gang not far removed from the earlier slave gangs. Their plug-hatted crew leader is dressed much as his slave-driving predecessor would have been.

The Black Codes. The efforts of former slaves to control their own lives ran counter to deeply entrenched white attitudes. Emancipation had not destroyed the racist assumptions and fears that the planters had fostered in order to maintain and defend slavery. Former slave owners and many poorer whites who looked to them for leadership attempted to maintain the South's caste system. Beginning in 1865, southern legislatures enacted laws—known as Black Codes—that were designed to keep African-Americans in a condition close to slavery.

The codes varied from state to state, but virtually all required the arrest of blacks for vagrancy if they were found without employment. In most cases they could not pay the fine, and the county court would then hire them out to an employer, who could hold them in slaverylike conditions. Several state codes established specific hours of labor, spelled out the duties expected of laborers, and declared that any laborer who did not meet those standards was a vagrant. The codes usually restricted black employment opportunities outside agriculture by requiring licenses for those who wished to pursue skilled work or even "irregular job work."

The state legislatures went even further, sanctioning the efforts of local governments to circumscribe the lives of blacks. Localities set curfews, required black agricultural workers to obtain passes from their employers, insisted that blacks who wanted to live in town obtain white sponsors, and, in an effort to prevent political gatherings, sharply regulated meetings of blacks, including those held in churches. Fines and forced labor were the penalties for violators.

Congressional Initiatives

Reports of southern repression aroused moderate Republicans in Congress, who decided to provide some guarantees of the civil rights of freedmen. The moderates first drafted a bill to extend the life of the Freedmen's Bureau and enlarge its powers, including the authority to establish courts to protect the freedmen's rights.

The news from the South had not, however, convinced Republicans that they should confiscate land and give it to the freedmen. A large majority of Republicans voted down an amendment to the Freedmen's Bureau bill proposed by Thaddeus Stevens that would have made "forfeited estates of the enemy" available to freedmen. Still, Republicans were now willing to go further in creating opportunities for land ownership. Thus the Freedmen's Bureau bill countermanded Johnson's order to Howard to evict the freedmen from the confiscated lands on the Sea Islands. Also, two days after the bill's passage, the House passed another bill, sponsored by George Julian, that became the Southern Homestead

Act of 1866. It designated about 45 million acres of public land in Alabama, Arkansas, Florida, Louisiana, and Mississippi for 80-acre grants to settlers who cultivated the land for five years. Congress prohibited anyone who had supported the Confederacy from filing a claim until 1867. Although Republicans were unwilling to violate planters' property rights, they offered freedmen the same chance to acquire land that northerners had enjoyed since the passage of the Homestead Act of 1862.

Republicans approved the Freedmen's Bureau bill almost unanimously, but in February 1866 Johnson vetoed it. The bill was unconstitutional, he argued, because the Constitution did not authorize a "system for the support of indigent persons" and because the states most directly affected by its provisions were not yet represented in Congress. His veto, implying that *any* Reconstruction legislation passed without southern representation was unconstitutional, enraged moderate Republicans. They tried to override the veto but failed, just barely, to hold the votes of enough conservative Republicans to collect the necessary two-thirds majority.

Democrats applauded Johnson's firmness. To celebrate the veto and Washington's birthday, a group of Democrats went to the White House to serenade him. The president emerged to deliver an impromptu, impassioned speech that suggested to many listeners that he was drunk. Accusing the radical Republicans of being traitors, he likened Stevens and Sumner to Confederate leaders because they all were "opposed to the fundamental principles of this Government." He mentioned himself two hundred times in the speech and suggested that the radicals were plotting to assassinate him.

The First Civil Rights Bill. Johnson's veto and his Washington's birthday speech pushed the moderate Republicans close to a complete break with him. But they still expected his cooperation on their second major piece of legislation, a civil rights bill. Passed in March 1866, it defined the citizenship rights of freedmen—for example, the rights to own and rent property, make contracts, and have access to the courts. And it authorized federal authorities to bring suit against anyone who violated those rights and guaranteed that appeals in such cases could be heard in federal courts. The moderate Republicans were prepared to expand federal protection of civil rights, though they were still not ready to guarantee black suffrage.

Against the advice of his cabinet, Johnson vetoed the civil rights bill. He restated his constitutional point about absent southern representation and added a new objection, with the votes of Democratic wards in the large cities in mind. The bill, he argued, discriminated against whites by providing immediate citizenship for newly freed slaves. Under federal law, he pointed out, immigrants had to wait five years.

Johnson's veto was the last straw for almost all moderate Republicans. They now agreed with the radicals that Congress must take charge of Reconstruction. In April moderates engineered an override of Johnson's veto, and in July—after watering down the Freedmen's Bureau bill by requiring freedmen to buy the confiscated land on the Sea Islands—they won the votes of enough conservative Republicans to pass the Freedmen's Bureau bill over a second veto.

The Fourteenth Amendment. The central part of the independent plan that moderates and radicals now undertook was to provide freedmen with constitutional as well as legislative protection. In April the Joint Committee on Reconstruction drafted and submitted to Congress a proposal for a fourteenth amendment to the Constitution. It did not provide what the radicals wanted—a guarantee of black suffrage—but it went beyond the Civil Rights Act of 1866.

Section 1 declared that "all persons born or naturalized in the United States" were citizens. No state could abridge "the privileges or immunities of citizens of the United States," deprive "any person of life, liberty, or property, without due process of law," or deny anyone "the equal protection of the laws." The drafters intended these phrases to be vague but hoped that their force would increase over time, especially since Section 5 gave Congress the power to enforce the amendment. Section 2 penalized any state that denied suffrage to any adult male citizen. A state's representation in the House of Representatives would be reduced by the percentage of adult male citizens who were denied the vote.

Rising violence against African-Americans throughout the South clinched the support of moderates for the amendment. Most dramatic were three days of race rioting in Memphis in May. Forty-six blacks and two whites were left dead, and hundreds of black houses, churches, and schools were looted and burned. In June 1866 Congress forwarded the Fourteenth Amendment to the states for ratification.

President Johnson attacked the Fourteenth Amendment. Even its moderate provisions went too far in protecting African-Americans for his taste, and he wanted to create an issue for the 1866 elections. At his urging, ten ex-Confederate states, joined by Delaware and Kentucky, turned it down, denying the amendment the necessary approval of three-fourths of the states. Among the former states of the Confederacy, only Tennessee approved the amendment, and it was formally readmitted to the Union in July 1866.

The Congressional Elections of 1866. Johnson planned to attack the Fourteenth Amendment and advance his National Union movement during the Congressional elections of 1866. In July a National Union Convention met to unite his supporters from around the nation. But

Resistance in the South

The engraving, subtitled "Verdict, 'Hang the D---Yankee and Nigger,'" appeared in *Harper's Weekly* in March 1867. It may have led readers to recall the killing of the Republicans who attended the black suffrage convention in New Orleans the previous summer. There are no reliable estimates of the number of Republicans, white and black, killed by ex-Confederates during Reconstruction.

the Republican and Democratic politicians in attendance were unwilling to share power across party lines, and the convention did not attempt to create a new national party. Another problem for Johnson's movement was a major race riot in the South just two weeks before the convention assembled. A white mob in New Orleans attacked the delegates to a black suffrage convention and, aided by the local police, killed forty people, including thirty-seven blacks. Popular support in the North for radical Reconstruction seemed to grow instantly.

In August and September Johnson tried to win back support in a disastrous "swing around the circle"—a railroad tour from Washington to Chicago and St. Louis and back. It was unprecedented for a president to campaign personally, and Johnson made matters worse by engaging in shouting matches with hecklers and insulting members of the hostile crowds. His message was consistent: Congress had acted illegally by approving the Fourteenth Amendment without the participation of all the southern states, southerners were now loyal to the Union, and the real traitors were the radical Republicans who were delaying restoration of the Union.

Moderate and radical Republicans responded by escalating their attacks on Democrats. They charged that ex-Confederates wanted to resume the Civil War and, in a practice that became known as "waving the bloody shirt," charged that the Democratic party had caused the Civil War and then sided with the traitors. Indiana's Republican governor, Oliver Morton, described the Democratic party as "a common sewer and loathsome receptacle, into which is emptied every element of treason North and South, every element of inhumanity and barbarism which has dishonored the age."

The 1866 Congressional elections brought a humiliating defeat for the president, who still had two years left to serve. The Republicans won a three-to-one majority in Congress (margins of 42 to 11 in the Senate and 143 to 49 in the House) and gained control of the governorship and legislature in every northern state, as well as West Virginia, Missouri, and Tennessee. The moderate Republicans interpreted the election results as a clear call for radical Reconstruction rather than mere restoration of the South. The most important policy shift was the moderates' acceptance of the radicals' proposition that the federal government must guarantee the vote for black men, at least in the South.

Radical Reconstruction

In the months following the 1866 elections, moderates and radicals in Congress joined together to take control of Reconstruction. They agreed on a more radical program than even the one proposed in the Wade-Davis bill. Congressional Reconstruction began by treating the South as conquered territory. It proceeded to protect the civil rights of former slaves through the Fourteenth Amendment to the Constitution, protect their suffrage through the Fifteenth Amendment, and establish state governments in the South in which former slaves played important roles.

The Congressional Program

In March Congress passed the Reconstruction Act of 1867, designed to implement the radical plan. It organized the South as a conquered land, dividing it (with the exception of Tennessee) into five military districts, each under the command of a Union general. Each commander was ordered to register all adult black men in his district but was given considerable discretion in registering former Confederates. After the registration, the commander was to supervise the election of a convention to write a state constitution and make certain that the constitution included guarantees of black suffrage. Congress would readmit the state to the Union if its voters ratified the new constitution, if that document proved acceptable to Congress, if the new state legislature approved the Fourteenth Amendment, and if enough states had already ratified the Fourteenth Amendment to make it part of the Constitution. Johnson vetoed the act, but Congress overrode the veto. In 1868 six states—North Carolina, South Carolina, Florida, Alabama, Louisiana, and Arkansas—met the requirements and were readmitted to the Union. (See Table 16.1 for a summary of the Reconstruction laws and constitutional amendments.)

Such measures were radical, but a few radical Republicans argued that even more dramatic steps were needed to guarantee racial equality. They pressed for the distribution of land to former slaves, federal support for black schools, and disfranchisement of ex-Confederates. Congressman George Julian warned that "the power of the great landed aristocracy in these regions, if unrestrained by power from without, would inevitably assert itself." But even the most extreme radicals accepted the new Reconstruction policies as all they could get in 1867.

The Tenure of Office Act. Republicans also acted to check the power of President Johnson to undermine their Reconstruction plan. At the same time the Reconstruction Act of 1867 became law, Congress passed the Tenure of Office Act, which required Senate consent for the removal of any official whose appointment had required Senate confirmation. Congress chiefly wanted to protect Secretary of War Edwin M. Stanton, a Lincoln appointee and the only member of Johnson's cabinet who favored radical Reconstruction. In his position Stanton could do much to prevent Johnson from frustrating the goals of Reconstruction. Congress also required the president to issue all orders to the army through its commanding general, Ulysses S. Grant, who was also a supporter of radical Reconstruction. In effect, Congress was attempting to reconstruct the presidency as well as the South.

Johnson appeared to cooperate with Congress at first, appointing generals recommended by Stanton and Grant to command the five military districts in the South. But he was just biding his time. In August 1867, after Congress had adjourned, he "suspended" Stanton until Congress reconvened and replaced him with Grant on a temporary basis, believing that Grant would act like a good soldier and follow orders. Next Johnson replaced four Republican generals who commanded southern districts, including Philip H. Sheridan, Grant's favorite cavalry general.

TABLE 16.1

Primary Reconstruction Laws and Constitutional Amendments

Law (Date of Congressional Passage)	Key Provisions
Thirteenth Amendment (January 1865*)	Prohibited slavery
Civil Rights Act of 1866 (April 1866)	Defined citizenship rights of freedmen Authorized federal authorities to bring suit against those who violated those rights
Fourteenth Amendment (June 1866†)	Established national citizenship for persons born or naturalized in the United States Reduced state representation in House of Representatives by the percentage of adult male citizens denied the vote
Reconstruction Act of 1867 (March 1867‡)	Divided the South into five military districts, each under the command of a Union general Established requirements for readmission of ex-Confederate states to the Union
Tenure of Office Act (March 1867)	Required Senate consent for removal of any federal official whose appointment had required Senate confirmation
Fifteenth Amendment (February 1869)	Forbade states to deny citizens the right to vote on the grounds of race, color, or "previous condition of servitude"
Ku Klux Klan Act (April 1871)	Authorized president to use federal prosecutions and military force to suppress conspiracies to deprive citizens of the right to vote and enjoy the equal protection of the law

*Ratified by three-fourths of all states in December 1868.
†Ratified by three-fourths of all states in July 1868.
‡Ratified by three-fourths of all states in March 1870.

Johnson, however, had misjudged Grant, who wrote a letter protesting the president's thwarting of Congress and then deliberately leaked it to the press. When the Senate reconvened in the fall, it intensified the political drama by overruling Stanton's suspension. Grant increased the pressure on Johnson by resigning so that Stanton could resume his office. Johnson overreacted, publicly protesting Grant's resignation. Grant responded by becoming an open enemy of the president.

The Impeachment of Johnson. Johnson decided to challenge the constitutionality of the Tenure of Office Act. In February 1868 he formally dismissed Stanton. This time Stanton barricaded the door of his office and refused to admit the replacement Johnson had appointed. Three days later, on February 24, the House of Representatives lashed out at Johnson by using the power granted by the Constitution to impeach—to charge federal officials with "Treason, Bribery, or other high Crimes and Misdemeanors." The House overwhelmingly (128 to 47) brought eleven counts of criminal misconduct, nine of which dealt with violations of the Tenure of Office Act, against the president.

The trial in the Senate, which the Constitution empowers to act as a court in impeachment cases, lasted eleven weeks and was presided over by Chief Justice Salmon P. Chase. On May 16 thirty-five senators voted for conviction, one vote short of the two-thirds majority required. Seven moderate Republicans had broken ranks, voting for acquittal along with twelve Democrats. The reluctant moderates were overwhelmed by the drastic nature of impeachment and conviction; Congress had removed federal judges from office, but never before had it seriously considered removing a president. Whereas these moderates agreed that Johnson had broken the law, they felt that the real issue was a disagreement between Congress and the president over a matter of policy. They feared that a conviction based on a policy dispute would establish a dangerous precedent and undermine the presidency. The Civil War had demonstrated to them the need for a strong federal government administered by a powerful executive. These moderates doubted that the nation could preserve internal unity, advance the Republican economic program, and defend itself against foreign enemies without a strong presidency.

The radical Republicans had failed to convict Johnson, but they had defeated him politically. For the remainder of his term Johnson was forced to allow Reconstruction to proceed under Congressional direction.

The Elections of 1868. The impeachment controversy made Grant, already the North's most popular war hero, a hero of Reconstruction as well, and he easily won the Republican presidential nomination. In the fall campaign he supported radical Reconstruction and "waved the bloody shirt," but he also urged reconciliation between the sections. His Democratic opponent was Horatio Seymour, a former governor of New York and a Peace Democrat who almost declined the nomination, certain that Grant would win. In the face of rising violence in the South, Seymour and the Democrats received little support for their claim that the government should let southern state governments reorganize on their own. Grant won about the same share of the northern vote (55 percent) that Lincoln had in 1864, collected a majority of the national popular vote, and received 214 of 294 electoral votes, including those of six of the eight reconstructed states. The Republicans also retained two-thirds majorities in both houses of Congress. The Republicans were convinced they had a strong popular mandate for their program of radical Reconstruction.

The Fifteenth Amendment. The Republicans quickly produced the last major piece of Reconstruction legislation—the Fifteenth Amendment. Intended to guarantee black male suffrage, the amendment forbade states to deny their citizens the right to vote on the grounds of race, color, or "previous condition of servitude."

Some radical Republicans would have preferred more aggressive protection of black citizenship such as prohibiting state governments from using property ownership or literacy tests to disqualify blacks as voters. But Republican moderates did not want to ban tactics that northern and western states might want to employ to deny immigrants the vote. Massachusetts and Connecticut used literacy as a requirement for voting, as did California, which sought to deny the vote to Chinese immigrants. Even though it failed to prohibit such tactics, the Fifteenth Amendment was much more effective than the Fourteenth in promoting African-American suffrage. The amendment was passed in February 1869, and Congress required the unreconstructed states of Virginia, Mississippi, Texas, and Georgia to ratify it before they were readmitted to the Union.

The Issue of Suffrage for Women

Radical Reconstruction could have changed the legal status of women. Instead, by referring to adult "male citizens," the Fourteenth Amendment wrote the term "male" into the Constitution for the first time and, in effect, sanctioned the denial of suffrage for women. Under the Fourteenth Amendment, suffrage limitations based on gender—alone among all the possible restrictions on suffrage—would not reduce a state's representation in Congress.

Former abolitionists such as Elizabeth Cady Stanton and Susan B. Anthony were deeply disappointed. They had organized a massive petition drive that had collected almost 400,000 signatures in support of the Thirteenth Amendment; they believed that their male collaborators would reciprocate by supporting universal suffrage. In fact, many did, but most assumed that the public was not ready for the idea. As Wendell Phillips told women leaders, "One question at a time. This hour belongs to the Negro."

The leaders of the women's movement did not oppose ratification of the Fourteenth Amendment. They accepted defeat at the federal level and focused on the reform of state constitutions. Through a new organization, the American Equal Rights Association—which they formed in 1866 at the first women's rights convention since the Civil War—they launched a campaign to win *universal* suffrage at the state level.

The Fifteenth Amendment wounded those who sought the vote for women even more deeply; it made no reference to gender and thus permitted states to deny

A Woman Suffrage Quilt Made around 1875
Homemade quilts provided funds and a means of persuasion for the temperance and antislavery movements. But woman suffrage quilts, such as this detail from "The Suffragette Quilt" (circa 1860–1880), picturing a women's rights lecturer, were rare. The leaders of the woman suffrage movement usually regarded quilts and needlework as representing the domestic subjugation of women.

suffrage to women. In response, Stanton and Anthony concluded that feminists should develop a program independent of any political party. They broke with Republican abolitionists and refused to support the Fifteenth Amendment unless it was accompanied by a new amendment enfranchising women. Stanton argued that ratification of the Fifteenth Amendment alone would create an "aristocracy of sex." She declared, "All manhood will vote not because of intelligence, patriotism, property or white skin, but because it is male, not female." In promoting a new amendment she made a special appeal to women of the business class:

> American women of wealth, education, virtue and refinement, if you do not wish the lower orders of Chinese, Africans, Germans and Irish, with the low ideas of womanhood to make laws for you and your daughters . . . to dictate not only the civil, but moral codes by which you shall be governed, awake to the danger of your present position and demand that woman, too, shall be represented in the government!

Other advocates of woman suffrage, including Lucy Stone and Frederick Douglass, saw the politics of suffrage differently. The Fifteenth Amendment had opened up a schism in the ranks of the women's movement. In 1868 Stone and Douglass broke with the American Equal Rights Association of Stanton and Anthony and formed a new group, the New England Woman Suffrage Association. Their goal was to maintain an alliance with Republicans and support the Fifteenth Amendment. They believed that this was the best way to enlist Republican support for women's suffrage after Reconstruction issues had been settled.

The differences between the two groups increased in the postwar years. In 1869 the American Equal Rights Association renamed itself the National Woman Suffrage Association and elected Stanton as its first president. It concentrated on mobilizing local suffrage societies in communities around the country. Meanwhile, the New England Woman Suffrage Association reorganized itself as the American Woman Suffrage Association. Its members elected Henry Ward Beecher, a prominent Brooklyn minister, as its president and cultivated strong ties with Republicans and men who had been abolitionists.

For twenty-one years the two national organizations competed for the leadership of the women's movement. The "American" association tended to focus on suffrage, whereas the "National" association developed a more comprehensive reform posture. While the split weakened the movement in the short run, the formation of the "National" association meant that a major part of the women's movement had broken away from abolitionism and Republicanism and was free to develop independent political strategies.

The South during Radical Reconstruction

Between 1868 and 1871 all the southern states met the Congressional stipulations and rejoined the Union. The Reconstruction governments under Republican control remained in power for periods ranging from a few months in Virginia to nine years in South Carolina, Louisiana, and Florida. African-Americans were at the center of forming and maintaining these Republican governments. In Alabama, Florida, South Carolina, Mississippi, and Louisiana they constituted an outright majority of registered voters. They provided the votes for Republican victories there and in Georgia, Virginia, and North Carolina as well, where they accounted for nearly half the registered voters. But the Republican governments were more than African-American regimes; they also drew support from whites who had not owned slaves and from white northerners who had moved south after the war (see Map 16.1).

Democratic ex-Confederates satirized and stereotyped the Republicans who dominated the reconstructed state governments. They mocked and scorned black

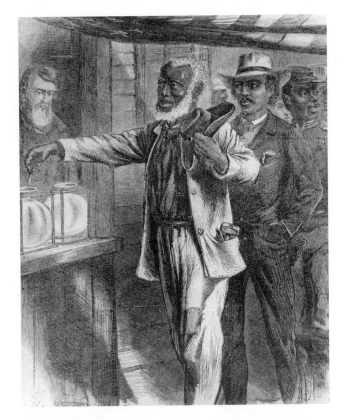

The First Vote
This lithograph appeared in *Harper's Weekly* in November 1867. The voters represent elements of African-American political leadership: an artisan with tools, a well-dressed member of the middle class, and a Union soldier.

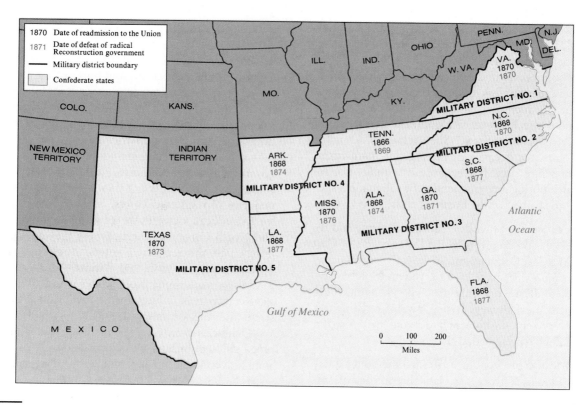

MAP 16.1

Reconstruction

The federal government organized the Confederate states into five military districts during radical Reconstruction. For each state the first date indicates when that state was readmitted to the Union; the second date shows when radical Republicans lost control of the state government. All the ex-Confederate states rejoined the Union from 1868 to 1870, but the periods of radical rule varied widely. Radicals lasted only a few months in Virginia; they held on until the end of Reconstruction in Louisiana, Florida, and South Carolina.

Republicans as ignorant field hands who could only play at politics, and they referred to whites who became Republicans as *scalawags*—an ancient Scots-Irish term for underfed, runty, worthless animals. White settlers who had come from the North were denounced as *carpetbaggers*—transient exploiters who carried all their property in cheap suitcases called carpetbags. Carpetbaggers held more than half the Republican governorships in the South and almost half of the southern seats in Congress.

Actually, few southern Republicans conformed to these stereotypes. Some carpetbaggers had come south to seek personal profit, but they also brought capital and skills to invest in the region's future. Most were former officers of the Union army who had fallen in love with the South—its climate, people, and economic opportunities. Many carpetbaggers were professionals and college graduates. The scalawags were even more diverse. Some were wealthy ex-Whigs and even former slave owners. Some of these groups saw Republicanism as the best way to attract northern capital to southern railroads, mines, and factories. Immigrant workers and

farmers were often found among the Republicans. The largest such group were the Germans in southwest Texas. They sent to Congress Edward Degener, an immigrant and a San Antonio grocer whom Confederate authorities had imprisoned and whose sons had been executed for treason. But most numerous among the scalawags were yeomen farmers from the backcountry districts who wanted to rid the South of its slaveholding aristocracy. Scalawags had generally fought against, or at least refused to support, the Confederacy; they believed that slavery had victimized whites as well as blacks. "Now is the time," a Georgia scalawag wrote, "for every man to come out and speak his principles publickly and vote for liberty as we have been in bondage long enough."

African-American Political Leadership. The Democrats' stereotypes of black political leaders were just as false. Until 1867 most African-American leaders in the South, attracted to the movement for black suffrage, came from the elite that had been free before the Civil War. When Congress began to organize Republican governments in 1867, this diverse group of ministers, artisans, shopkeepers, and former soldiers reached out to the freedmen. African-American speakers, some financed by the Republican Congressional Committee, fanned out into the old plantation districts and drew ex-slaves into political leadership. Still, few of the new leaders were field hands; most had been preachers or artisans. The literacy of one ex-slave, Thomas Allen, who was a Baptist minister and shoemaker, helped him win election to the Georgia legislature. "In my county," he recalled, "the colored people came to me for instructions, and I gave them the best instructions I could. I took the *New York Tribune* and other papers, and in that way I found out a great deal, and I told them whatever I thought was right."

Many of the African-American leaders who emerged in 1867 had been born in the North or had spent many years there. They moved south when Congressional Reconstruction began to offer the prospect of meaningful freedom. Like white migrants, many were veterans of the Union army. Some had fought in the antislavery crusade, some were employed by the Freedmen's Bureau or northern missionary societies, and a few were from free families and had gone north for an education. Others had escaped from slavery and were returning home. One of these was Blanche K. Bruce, who became one of two black U.S. senators from Mississippi. He had received tutoring on the Virginia plantation of his white father. During the war Bruce escaped to Kansas from Missouri, where his father had moved, and then returned to Missouri, establishing a school for African-Americans in Hannibal. He arrived in Mississippi in 1869 and entered politics; in 1874 he became the second African-American elected to the Senate and the first elected to a full term until 1966.

Although the number of African-Americans who held office during Reconstruction never reflected the black share of the electorate, they held positions of importance throughout most of the South, and their significance increased in every state under Republican rule. Sixteen African-Americans served in the U.S. House of Representatives in the Reconstruction Era. In 1870 Mississippi sent Hiram Revels, a minister born in North Carolina, to the Senate as its first African-American member. In 1868 African-Americans won a majority in one house of the South Carolina legislature; subsequently they won half the state's eight executive offices, elected three members of Congress, and won a seat on the state supreme court. Over the entire course of Reconstruction twenty African-Americans served as governor, lieutenant governor, secretary of state, treasurer, or superintendent of education, and more than six hundred served as state legislators. Almost all the African-Americans who became state executives had been freemen before the Civil War, whereas most of the legislators had been slaves. Because these African-Americans

represented districts that large planters had dominated before the Civil War, they embodied the potential of Reconstruction for revolutionizing class relationships in the South.

The Radical Program. Southern Republicans believed that the South needed to be fundamentally reconstructed. They wanted to end its dependence on cotton agriculture and unskilled labor and create an economy based on manufacturing, capital investment, and skilled labor. Southern Republicans fell far short of making this vision a reality, but they accomplished much more of it than their critics gave them credit for.

Southern Republicans made their societies more democratic. They repealed Black Codes and rejected new proposals for enforcing labor discipline. They modernized state constitutions, extended the right to vote, and made more offices elective. They established hospitals, penitentiaries, and asylums for orphans and the insane. South Carolina purchased medical care for poor people, while Alabama provided them with free legal counsel. Republican governments built roads in areas where roads had never existed. They supervised the rebuilding of the region's railroad network and subsidized investment in manufacturing and transportation. They undertook major public works programs. And they did all this without federal financing. To pay for their ambi-

Hiram R. Revels
In 1870 Hiram R. Revels (1822–1901) was elected to the U.S. Senate from Mississippi to fill Jefferson Davis's former seat. Revels was a free black from North Carolina who had migrated to the North and attended Knox College in Illinois. He recruited blacks for the Union army and as an ordained Methodist minister served as chaplain of a black regiment in Mississippi, where he settled after the war.

tious programs they introduced the taxes that northern states had relied on since the Jacksonian period. These were general property taxes that taxed not only real estate but the trappings of wealth—personal property such as furnishings, machinery, tools, and even cash. The goal was to force planters to pay their fair share of taxes and to force uncultivated land onto the market. In many plantation counties, especially in South Carolina, Louisiana, and Mississippi, former slaves served as tax assessors and collectors, administering the taxation of their onetime owners.

The most important accomplishments of the southern Republicans came in education. Republican state governments viewed schooling as the foundation for a democratic order in the South. Led by both black and white superintendents of education, many of whom had served in the Freedmen's Bureau, the Reconstruction governments built public schools that served more people, black and white, than had ever been reached by free education in the South. African-Americans of all ages rushed to attend the newly established schools, even when they had to pay tuition. An elderly man in Mississippi explained his desire to go to school: "Ole missus used to read the good book [the Bible] to us . . . on Sunday evenin's, but she mostly read dem places where it says, 'Servants obey your masters.' . . . Now we is free, there's heaps of tings in that old book we is just suffering to learn." By 1875 about half of all the children in Florida, Mississippi, and South Carolina were enrolled in school.

Virtually all the new schools were segregated by race; only Louisiana attempted to establish an integrated system. But most African-Americans seemed to agree that segregation was an issue for a later day; most shared Frederick Douglass's judgment that what was

most important was the fact that separate schools were "infinitely superior" to no schools at all.

Social Institutions in Freedom. The building of schools was part of a larger effort by African-Americans to fortify the institutions that had sustained their spirit during the days of slavery. Most important, they strengthened family life as the cornerstone of new communities. Families moved away from the slave quarters, usually building homes scattered around or near their old plantations and farms. Sometimes they established entirely new all-black villages. Husbands, wives, and children who had been separated by the slave trade often reunited, sometimes after journeys of hundreds of miles. Couples stepped forward to record marriages that had not been recognized under slavery. As slavery crumbled, mothers rescued their children from the control of planters and overseers. Many women refused to work in the fields. Instead, they insisted on tending gardens, managing households, and bringing education and religion to their children. Wives asserted their independence, opening individual bank accounts, refusing responsibility for their husbands' debts at country stores, and bringing complaints of abuse and lack of child support to the Freedmen's Bureau.

Christianity had played a central role in nineteenth-century slave society, and freed slaves buttressed their new communities by founding their own churches. They rejected participation in biracial congregations, which usually accorded blacks only second-class status, requiring them to worship in segregated balcony pews and denying them rights in church ownership or governance. Instead, they purchased land and built their own churches. These churches joined together to form African-American versions of the Southern Methodist

A Freedmen's School
An 1866 sketch from *Harper's Weekly* of a Vicksburg, Mississippi, school run by the Freedmen's Bureau illustrates the desire for education by ex-slaves of all ages. Because most southern blacks were farmers, schools often offered night classes that left students free for field work during the day.

and Southern Baptist denominations. The largest new denominations were the National Baptist Convention and the Colored Methodist Episcopal Church. The vigorous new churches served not only as places of worship but as schools, social centers, and political meeting halls. The ministers were community leaders and often held political office during Reconstruction. Charles H. Pearce, a Methodist minister in Florida, declared, "A man in this State cannot do his whole duty as a minister except he looks out for the political interests of his people." The religious message of black ministers, who called for a recognition of the brotherhood of man and a special destiny like that of the "Children of Israel," provided a powerful religious bulwark for the Republican politics of their congregations.

The Planters' Counterrevolution

Even if radical Reconstruction had been adopted right at the end of the Civil War, it would have sparked southern resistance to federal power. But coming after Johnson's lenient policy of restoration, which had enabled ex-Confederates to regain control of the South, the reaction was especially intense. Former slave owners were the most bitter opponents of the Republican program, especially the effort to expand political and economic opportunities for African-Americans, because it threatened their vested interest in traditional agriculture and their power and status in southern society. Led by former slave owners, the ex-Confederates staged a massive counterrevolution—one designed to "redeem" the South by regaining control of its state governments.

The former slave owners united under the Democratic banner to oppose the Republicans. In the eight southern states where whites formed a majority of the population—all except Louisiana, Mississippi, and South Carolina—planters sought to return ex-Confederates to the rolls of registered voters. They appealed to racial solidarity and southern patriotism, and they attacked black suffrage as a threat to the social status of whites. Relying primarily on conventional, albeit unsavory, means of political competition, Democrats recovered power in Tennessee in 1869 and Virginia in 1870.

But the Democrats were prepared to go far beyond conventional techniques. Throughout the Deep South and almost everywhere that Republicans and Democrats were nearly equal in number, planters and their supporters engaged in terrorism against people and property. They organized secret societies to frighten blacks and Republican whites from voting or taking other political action.

The Ku Klux Klan. The most widespread of these groups, the Ku Klux Klan, was organized in Tennessee in 1865 and quickly spread throughout the South. The

Klan's first leader was Nathan Bedford Forrest, a former Confederate general. A skilled and ferocious leader, Forrest was notorious in the North for an incident at Fort Pillow, Tennessee, in 1864, when his troops killed African-American soldiers holding the fort after they had surrendered. Forrest based the initial organization of the Klan on Confederate army units and openly threatened to kill Republicans if they tried to suppress the Klan.

By 1870 the Klan was operating almost everywhere in the South as a military force serving the Democratic party. The Klan murdered and whipped Republican politicians, burned black schools and churches, and attacked party gatherings. In October 1870 a group of Klansmen assaulted a Republican rally in Eutaw, Alabama, killing four African-Americans and wounding fifty-four. For three weeks in 1873 Klansmen laid siege to the small town of Colfax, Louisiana, which was defended by black veterans of the Union army who were holding the county seat after a contested election. On Easter Sunday, armed with a small cannon, the whites overpowered the defenders and slaughtered fifty blacks and two whites after they had surrendered under a white flag. Such terrorist tactics enabled the Democrats to seize power in Georgia and North Carolina in 1870 and make substantial gains elsewhere. An African-

Klan Portrait, 1868
Two armed Klansmen from Alabama pose proudly in their disguises. Northern audiences saw a lithograph based on this photograph in *Harper's Weekly* in December 1868.

Harriet Hernandes

The Intimidation of Black Voters

The following testimony was given in 1871 by Harriet Hernandes, a black resident of Spartanburg, South Carolina, to the Joint Congressional Select Committee investigating conditions in the South. The terrorizing of black women through rape and other forms of physical violence was among the means of oppression used by the Ku Klux Klan.

Question: How old are you?

Answer: Going on thirty-four years. . . .

Q: Are you married or single?

A: Married.

Q: Did the Ku-Klux come to your house at any time?

A: Yes, sir; twice. . . .

Q: Go on to the second time. . . .

A: They came in; I was lying in bed. Says he, "Come out here, sir; come out here, sir!" They took me out of bed; they would not let me get out, but they took me up in their arms and toted me out—me and my daughter Lucy. He struck me on the forehead with a pistol, and here is the scar above my eye now. Says he, "Damn you, fall." I fell. Says he, "Damn you, get up." I got up. Says he, "Damn you, get over this fence!" and he kicked me over when I went to get over; and then he went on to a brush pile, and they laid us right down there, both together. They laid us down twenty yards apart, I reckon. They had dragged and beat us along. They struck me right on top of my head, and I thought they had killed me; and I said, "Lord o' mercy, don't, don't kill my child!" He gave me a lick on the head, and it liked to have killed me; I saw stars. He threw my arm over my head so I could not do anything with it for three weeks, and there are great knots on my wrist now.

Q: What did they say this was for?

A: They said, "You can tell your husband that when we see him we are going to kill him. . . ."

Q: Did they say why they wanted to kill him?

A: They said, "He voted the radical ticket [slate of candidates], didn't he?" I said, "Yes," that very way. . . .

Q: When did [your husband] get back home after this whipping? He was not at home, was he?

A: He was lying out; he couldn't stay at home, bless your soul! . . .

Q: Has he been afraid for any length of time?

A: He has been afraid ever since last October. He has been lying out. He has not laid in the house ten nights since October.

Q: Is that the situation of the colored people down there to any extent?

A: That is the way they all have to do—men and women both.

Q: What are they afraid of?

A: Of being killed or whipped to death.

Q: What has made them afraid?

A: Because men that voted radical tickets they took the spite out on the women when they could get at them.

Q: How many colored people have been whipped in that neighborhood?

A: It is all of them, mighty near.

Source: Report of the Joint Select Committee to Inquire into the Condition of Affairs in the Late Insurrectionary States, House Reports, 42d Cong., 2d sess. (Washington, D.C.: U.S. Government Printing Office, 1972), Vol. 5, South Carolina, December 19, 1871.

American politician in North Carolina wrote, "Our former masters are fast taking the reins of government" (see American Voices, above).

Congress responded to the Klan-led counterrevolution by passing the Force Acts in 1870 and 1871, which included the Ku Klux Klan Act (1871). The acts authorized the president to use federal prosecutions, military force, and martial law to suppress conspiracies to deprive citizens of the right to vote, hold office, serve on juries, and enjoy equal protection of the law. For the first time, the government had made private criminal acts violations of federal law. Federal agents penetrated the Klan and gathered evidence that provided the basis for thousands of arrests, and federal grand juries indicted more than 3,000 Klansmen. In South Carolina, where the Klan was most deeply entrenched, federal troops occupied nine counties, made hundreds of arrests, and drove as many as 2,000 Klansmen from the state. The U.S. attorney general brought several dozen notorious Klansmen to trial and sent most to jail. Elsewhere, victories were only temporary. Justice Department attorneys usually faced all-white juries, and the department lacked the resources to prosecute effectively. Only about 600 Klansmen were convicted under the Force Acts, and only a small fraction of them served significant prison terms.

The Grant administration's war against the Klan raised the spirits of southern Republicans, but if they were going to prevail, they required what one carpet-bagger described as *"steady, unswerving power from without."* In particular, to defeat the well-armed paramilitary forces of the ex-Confederates, they needed sustained federal military aid. However, after seeming to defeat the Klan, northern Republicans increasingly lost enthusiasm for fighting—let alone enlarging—what amounted to a guerrilla war. Republican leaders continued to "wave the bloody shirt," but with each election it had less appeal to voters. Northerners grew weary of the financial costs of Reconstruction and the continuing bloodshed it seemed to produce. Moreover, they became preoccupied with the severe economic depression that began in 1873. Conservative and even moderate Republican leaders began to regard southern Republican governments as too radical and to conclude that they had much in common with southern economic elites. Racism played a role as well; many moderate Republicans in the North began to conclude that Republican defeats in the South reflected the incompetence of black politicians. Because of diminishing federal help, Republican governments in the South eventually found themselves overwhelmed by ex-Confederate politicians during the day and by terrorists at night. Democrats overthrew Republican governments in Texas in 1873, in Alabama and Arkansas in 1874, and in Mississippi in 1875.

The defeat in Mississippi demonstrated the crucial role of federal aid. As elections neared in 1875, paramilitary groups such as the Rifle Clubs and Red Shirts operated openly. Often local Democratic clubs paraded armed, as if they were militia companies. They identified black leaders in assassination lists called "deadbooks," broke up Republican meetings, provoked rioting that left hundreds of African-Americans dead, and threatened voters, who still lacked the protection of the secret ballot. Mississippi's Republican governor, Adelbert Ames, a Congressional Medal of Honor winner from Maine, appealed to President Grant for federal troops, but Grant refused, fearing damage to Republicans in northern elections and lacking the heart for more bloodshed. Ames then contemplated organizing a state militia but ultimately decided against it, believing that only blacks would join. Rather than escalate the fighting and turn it into a racial war, he conceded victory to the terrorists.

By 1877 Republican governments, along with token U.S. military units, remained in only three states: Louisiana, South Carolina, and Florida. Southern Republicans had done their best to reconstruct southern society, but the ex-Confederates had exhausted northern Republicans. They even won some sympathy from the northern Republicans, who finally abandoned the southern members of their party (see American Lives, pages 504–505).

The Economic Fate of the Former Slaves

The greatest failure of radical Reconstruction lay in not redistributing land, along with the resources required to cultivate it, from planters to former slaves. The only major federal program enabling freedmen to obtain land, the Southern Homestead Act, turned out to provide little assistance. Although the land was free, very few freedmen had the capital to move their families and buy the necessary seeds, tools, and draft animals to get in their first crop. Fewer than 7,000 ex-slaves claimed land, and only about 1,000 eventually qualified for ownership, most of them in sparsely populated areas of Florida. Compounding the problem, state governments rarely had the resources to help freedmen buy and settle land. Alone among the Republican state governments, South Carolina purchased land from planters and resold it to former slaves on long-term credit. Between 1872 and 1876 the South Carolina land commission enabled more than 14,000 African-American families (accounting for about one-seventh of the state's black population) to purchase homesteads.

Without guaranteed economic independence, the content of freedom depended largely on thousands of conflicts between freedmen, acting individually and collectively, and the planter class. Here too the federal government failed to assist the freedmen in a significant way. The vast majority of army officers and federal marshals held the racist assumption that had been behind the Black Codes—that former slaves were suited only for agricultural labor. If these agents of the federal government had different ideas at first, they usually came to support the economic interests of the planters. A Louisiana freedman described the process as follows: "Whenever a new Provost Marshall comes he gives us justice for a fortnight or so; then he becomes acquainted with planters, takes dinners with them, receives presents; and then we no longer have any rights, or very little." In disputes between employers and laborers, federal marshals generally sided with the planters and sustained their authority. Army commanders complied with the requests of planters for help in forcing African-Americans to work. They expelled former plantation workers from towns and cities and punished them for disobedience, theft, vagrancy, and erratic labor.

Even agents of the Freedmen's Bureau often supported the planters. Many Bureau officials interpreted their mandate to promote a transition to free labor as meaning that they should teach former slaves to be industrious, reliable agricultural workers. They preached the gospel of work to African-Americans. To discourage labor violence, they warned that it was better "to suffer wrong than to do wrong." They urged former slaves to vindicate the cause of abolition by staying at home and working even harder than they had under slavery.

Nathan Bedford Forrest: A Violent Defender of Honor

There was much violence in the life of Nathan Bedford Forrest (1821–1877). Most of the violence was focused on the protection of slavery during the Civil War and on the defeat of radical Reconstruction afterward. More than any other white southerner, Forrest was responsible for defeating Reconstruction governments and efforts to extend democracy to African-Americans.

At the age of twenty-four Forrest demonstrated his readiness to use violence when he leapt to the defense of his family's honor. Armed with only a pistol and a bowie knife, he fought off four men who had a grudge against his uncle, a merchant in the hamlet of Hernando, Mississippi. The uncle died from a bullet meant for his nephew, but young Forrest had shown that he could meet violence with violence. He became a local hero and soon used his pistol again, facing down a well-armed planter who had just killed a friend of his. The local citizens rewarded Forrest's courage by making him town constable and county coroner, and a respectable young woman from Hernando agreed to marry him.

Forrest's father had been a yeoman farmer and blacksmith who followed the frontier from North Carolina to Tennessee, where Bedford, the oldest child of eleven, was born. His family moved to northern Mississippi in 1834, but three years later, when he was only sixteen, his father died, leaving Bedford the primary breadwinner. He had no more than six months of schooling but supported the family, working on its small farm and then joining an uncle's horse-trading business. At the age of twenty-one, when his mother remarried, he left home for Hernando.

Recognized and respected in Hernando, the hard-driving young Forrest was able to scratch his way up the social ladder in the booming cotton economy. He took over his uncle's store, ran a stagecoach service between Hernando and Memphis, opened a brickyard, again traded horses and cattle, and then turned to buying and selling slaves. By 1850 he owned three of his own. In 1851 Forrest's ambition took him and his family to nearby Memphis, Tennessee. In that Mississippi River town he became one of the largest interstate slave traders and entered the ranks of the planter class. He

Nathan Bedford Forrest
In his often violent career Forrest was a farmer, slave trader, planter, politician, cavalry general, Grand Wizard of the Ku Klux Klan, and railroad entrepreneur. This portrait was done by Nicola Marshall, circa 1866. (Collection of the Tennessee State Museum)

purchased large land holdings, including a Mississippi plantation of more than 3,000 acres worked by dozens of slaves. He even entered politics, winning election to the Memphis Board of Aldermen in 1857.

The Civil War created new opportunities for Forrest. His reputation for boldness and shrewdness, as well as his riding and shooting skills, won him an appointment from the governor of Tennessee as a lieutenant colonel. He organized a cavalry regiment and, after distinguishing himself at Shiloh, was promoted to brigadier general in July 1862. In the course of the war he became the premier cavalry officer of the Confederacy, perhaps the best on either side. The Confederate government failed to make the best use of Forrest and his troops, but he almost always carried out his missions with dramatic success, protecting Confederate armies in retreat, raiding Union lines of communications, and attacking Union posts, often deep behind enemy lines.

Forrest's intimate knowledge of the countryside and the people of the Mississippi, Tennessee, and Cumberland river valleys, superb organizational skills, powerful tactical sense of when to use bluff and deception, sobriety, and ability to inspire his troops served him well. He had a ferocious temper and used it to good advantage in combat, turning a zest for fighting into enraged fury whenever his honor or the honor of his troops seemed to be at stake. He counted thirty Union soldiers that he had killed personally—one more than the number of horses shot out from under him. And he was wounded by saber cut or gunfire several times, including once by a junior Confederate officer whom Forrest quickly stabbed to death.

Forrest's code of honor, readiness for violence, racism, and commitment to slavery, all honed and hardened by war, have suggested to many that Forrest played a role in the slaughter of black troops at Fort Pillow, Tennessee, on April 12, 1864. Forrest approached the assault on the fort with a combination of anger and contempt for the garrison there—largely white pro-Union Tennesseans and former slaves. The war in western Tennessee had taken a bitter turn in 1864, involving civilians more directly in combat, and Forrest was outraged at rumors that the garrison had been harassing local whites loyal to the Confederacy. Although Forrest's direct role in the slaughter remains uncertain, it is clear that his troops believed that they were acting as he wished, that they experienced the same fury he usually displayed in battle, and that he accepted the outcome with equanimity.

The war left Forrest exhausted but determined to recreate as much of his old life as possible. That meant adapting to the new economic system and, when necessary, to the reality of Union victory. In 1866, to restore his plantation labor force, he rented his Mississippi land to seven former Union officers and worked closely with the Freedmen's Bureau, writing some of the highest-wage contracts. He drew on some of his old slave-trading skills to bring in workers from as far away as Georgia. At the same time he moved into new enterprises: provisioning the reorganized plantations, selling fire and life insurance, and contracting for paving the streets of Memphis and for laying railroad track. In building the Memphis and Little Rock Railroad, Forrest used labor supplied by the Freedmen's Bureau. Meanwhile, he sought a pardon from President Johnson, which was granted in 1868.

But Forrest was determined to oppose a radical Reconstruction. As conflicts between ex-Confederates and coalitions of former Unionists and freedmen intensified, Forrest's ambition, racism, and loyalty to his comrades—a sense of honor defined by shared wartime experiences—led him to support the effort to restore the social world of 1860. In 1867 he joined secret organizations in Memphis and Nashville that became chapters of the Ku Klux Klan. He soon became the Klan's Grand Wizard and turned the organization into a major force throughout most of the South. Under cover of his insurance business Forrest corresponded with perhaps thousands of Confederate veterans and traveled to neighboring states to confer with other ex-generals.

In 1868 the Republican governor of Tennessee, "Parson" William G. Brownlow, threatened to organize a militia of eastern Tennessee Unionists to root out the Klan. Forrest told his former troops to prepare for civil war, warning a reporter from the Cincinnati *Commercial* that he could "raise 40,000 men in five days, ready for the field." Forrest's intimidation worked, as it had so often in the past. Brownlow resigned early in 1869 to take a seat in the U.S. Senate, and his replacement sought to appease the Democrats and the Klan. Victorious in Tennessee and hoping to reduce pressure from Washington on the Klan, Forrest ordered its members to destroy their regalia and moderate their excesses, such as whippings and jailbreaks. Forrest knew full well that he had no power to implement such an order.

Forrest might have continued a secret life within the Klan, but after his political victory he appeared to devote his full attention to his businesses. He tried to combine northern capital with new sources of cheap labor. Marketing bonds in New York, he established the Selma, Marion, and Memphis Railroad. He promoted Chinese immigration to the South and made extensive use of convict labor on his railroad and plantation crews. But he achieved only modest success in the depression of the 1870s and became embroiled in complicated, massive litigation. In 1877 he died of a debilitating intestinal illness that might have been related to his wartime wounds.

One Bureau official told some freedmen that their former master "is not able to do without you, and you will . . . find him as kind, honest, and liberal as other men" and that "you can be as free and as happy in your old home, for the present, as anywhere else in the world." The agents of the Freedmen's Bureau who did side with African-Americans were stymied by northern racism, lack of funds, understaffing, poor coordination within the Bureau, and uncooperative military authorities.

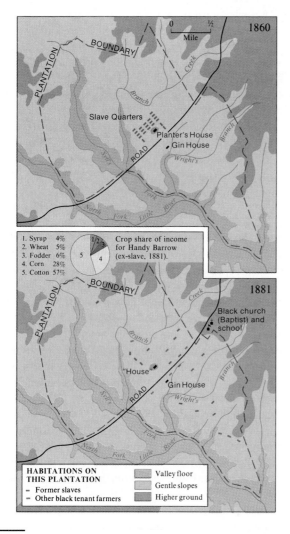

MAP 16.2

The Barrow Plantation

Comparing the 1860 map of this central Georgia plantation with the 1881 map reveals the changing patterns of black residence and farming. In 1860 the slave quarters were clustered near the planter's house, which sat on a small hilltop. The free sharecroppers of 1881 built cabins along the spurs or ridges of land between the streams, scattering their community over the plantation. A black church and school were built by this date. A typical sharecropper on the plantation earned most of his income from growing cotton.

Sharecropping. The Freedmen's Bureau did help change, however, the way planters controlled the labor of their former slaves. It encouraged, even compelled, planters and freedmen to agree on written contracts through a formal bargaining process. The labor contract system was a poor substitute for land ownership, but it assisted the freedmen in attaining something else they greatly desired: the elimination of gang labor.

As early as 1865 written contracts between freedmen and planters provided that the former slaves would work for wages. But the contracts also provided for less supervision, a slower pace of work, and more free time than had been typical under slavery as well as the elimination of drivers and overseers. By 1866 the process of bargaining between planters and freedmen had become more difficult, partly because a shrinking money supply had reduced the amount of cash available to pay wages. To resolve the growing number of conflicts over labor contracts, Freedmen's Bureau agents introduced a form of compensation that was common, though not typical, in northern agriculture: payment of agricultural workers in shares of the crop rather than in wages. This system was known as *sharecropping*. While it came to involve many poor whites in the South, it was far more important for blacks. For them, sharecropping became the dominant mode of agricultural labor (see Map 16.2).

At first freedmen were enthusiastic about sharecropping. It increased their control over working conditions and allowed them to improve their standard of living. Under typical sharecropping contracts, sharecroppers turned over half to two-thirds of their harvested crops to their landlord. The owner's share was not necessarily excessive, because the landlord commonly provided land, seed, fertilizer, tools, and assistance in marketing.

The sharecropping system joined laborers and the owners of land and capital in a common sharing of risks and returns. But it produced little upward mobility. By the end of Reconstruction only a fraction of sharecroppers, no more than one-quarter of the total, had managed to save enough to rent land with cash payments, as most landless whites did. Even though these so-called tenant farmers could take their crops directly to market, they remained impoverished.

Land Ownership. Virtually all African-American farmers struggled long and hard to buy the land they tilled, and some of the cash renters gradually succeeded. They were willing to pay exorbitant prices for land just for the sake of being independent. But the system was stacked against them. African-American renters had far less access to land ownership than did their white counterparts. Planters made agreements among themselves to drive up the price of land to blacks or even refuse to sell to them. Some planters used the Ku Klux Klan to intimi-

Sharecropping
This sharecropping family seems proud of its new cabin and crop of cotton, which it planted in every available bit of ground. But the presence of the white landlord in the background suggests the forces that led families like this one into debt peonage.

date blacks who tried to buy land. Despite the adversity, by 1910 black farmers owned nearly a third of the land they cultivated. But black farm owners usually occupied marginal land—in the coastal swamps of Georgia and South Carolina, for example—and the land usually cost far more than its productivity warranted.

Debt Peonage. The financial condition of all African-American farmers was extremely difficult. Sharecropping, cash renting of land, and land ownership enabled former slaves to raise their incomes but also increased their financial needs. They wanted more food and better clothing than they had received under slavery; they often needed more farm supplies than their landlords were willing to provide; and renters and owners had to purchase all their seed, fertilizer, and equipment. The purchase of major farm supplies almost always required borrowing, but southern banks were reluctant to lend money to black farmers, whom they saw as bad risks, and cash was generally in short supply.

The owners of country stores stepped in. Eager to lend money, they furnished everything black farmers needed and extended credit for the purchases. The country merchants took advantage of the weak bargaining power of the former slaves, especially the sharecroppers, by charging unusually high prices and interest rates. In effect, these storekeepers became rural loan sharks. Once sharecroppers accepted credit from country merchants, high interest rates made it difficult for them to settle their accounts. At best they broke even after paying their debts. Most sharecroppers fell deeper and deeper into debt.

Throughout the South, when Democrats regained control of state governments, they passed laws that gave force to this economic system by providing merchants with the right to take liens on crops. Merchants could seize crops to settle sharecroppers' debts and seek criminal prosecution of sharecroppers who could not pay the full amount of the interest they owed. Indebted African-American farmers faced imprisonment and forced labor unless they toiled on the land according to the instructions of the merchant-creditor. Increasingly, merchants and landlords cooperated to maintain this lucrative system, and many landlords became merchants. The former slaves had become trapped in the vicious circle of *debt peonage,* which tied them to the land and robbed them of their earnings.

In sum, despite the odds against them, the freedmen won some modest economic gains. But the gains came only within the restrictions of the system of debt peonage that replaced slavery. Thus, most African-Americans and many whites remained mired in an agricultural poverty created by racism and economic forces.

The North during Reconstruction

Although the Republicans in Congress failed to break the hold of the planter elite on the South, they did reconstruct the economy of the North. They enacted nearly all of their nationalizing economic program—national banking, tariff protection, and subsidies for internal improvements—despite resistance from the Democrats. The Republican program promoted unprecedented economic growth and industrial development.

A Dynamic Economy

The Civil War disrupted the nation's economic life, yet by the 1870s Americans had become more productive than ever before. Northeastern industry led the way. Production of iron more than doubled between the end of the Civil War and 1870 and doubled again by 1880. Steel production grew even more rapidly, increasing fivefold between 1865 and 1870 and then nearly twenty times by 1880. The era began an *age of capital*—a period that lasted until World War I and was marked by great increases in investment in factories and railroads. It also began the era of big business, which was characterized by the rise of giant corporations.

The Republican Economic Program. During Reconstruction, Republicans expanded the ambitious economic program they had enacted during the war. The broad support middle-class northerners gave to the program indicated that they now largely shared business-class values.

The scope of the program was vast. Republicans strengthened government regulation of the banking system, winning praise from investors who appreciated a more predictable economic environment. Republican Congresses expanded subsidies to national rail systems and chartered new railroads, expanded the national postal system, and financed major river and harbor development throughout the North. They also funded the cavalry forces that fought the nation's wars against the Indians in the Great Plains (see Chapter 17). In fact, military spending accounted for 60 percent of the federal budget by 1880. Republicans also used the Homestead Act of 1862 to subsidize the settling of the Great Plains.

Revenues raised from the Civil War tax system paid for those programs. Postwar Congresses kept the high tariffs, which had proved lucrative and appealed to average Republicans because they seemed to provide protection against foreign workers. Congress also retained the "emergency" wartime taxes on alcohol and tobacco, which were popular among many Republicans because they taxed "sin."

The tariffs and "sin" taxes not only funded programs but also provided money to pay back Americans who had bought Union bonds during the war. Because the taxes increased the cost of everyday items, average Americans were paying a far higher share of their income for debt repayment than were the wealthy. Moreover, the repayment was going largely to the wealthy, who owned a disproportionate share of Civil War bonds. Republicans were intentionally redistributing wealth from the poor to the rich, who were more likely to save and invest, as a way of increasing the supply of capital and accelerating the rate of economic growth.

The most popular Republican economic program was the Civil War pension program, which the government extended and broadened virtually every year. It provided disabled veterans and the widows and children of Union veterans with generous benefits, which were particularly welcome during the severe depressions of the 1870s and 1890s. At the same time, the pensions solidified the Republican loyalty of the families of men who had served in the Union army.

An ideological shift also contributed to the Republicans' success in enacting their economic program. The Civil War had led many Americans to relax their traditional suspicion of concentrations of power in both business and government. This was particularly true of the men and women who had served in the Union army and the Sanitary Commission. The war had given them their first direct experience of living and working within modern bureaucracies—elaborate hierarchies that imposed a high degree of job specialization and rigorous discipline. Wartime service also had taken them, usually for the first time, far from home and placed them in intimate contact with people who came from distant places but served in the same cause. And the Union had won the war. This disciplined, collective, national—and successful—experience predisposed northerners to accept American business, the Republican party, and the federal government as the central agencies of national economic development.

Republican Foreign Policy

Some Republican leaders were alert to new possibilities for expansion abroad. The most important advocate of expansion was William H. Seward, Lincoln and Johnson's secretary of state. Believing in the importance of foreign commerce to the long-term health of the republic, Seward promoted the acquisition of colonies that could be used as trading bases in the Caribbean and the Pacific. But Seward was ahead of his time. During the Reconstruction Era most Americans wanted to concentrate on developing their own territory.

Seward inherited his most pressing foreign policy issues from the Civil War. In Mexico, Napoleon III's puppet government under Archduke Maximilian was still in power; the threat this European regime posed to American interests in the Southwest was especially great since it might draw die-hard Confederate soldiers to its support. "On to Mexico," Grant only half jokingly told an aide just a day after he accepted Lee's surrender at Appomattox. It was a good guess as to where the next war might take place. Within a year President Johnson and Seward sent General Philip Sheridan with 50,000 battle-hardened Union veterans to the Mexican border, while Seward negotiated the withdrawal of French troops. The threat of force worked. The French left in 1867, abandoning Maximilian to a Mexican firing squad.

The American government was also troubled by another Civil War issue: Great Britain's allowing the *Alabama* and other Confederate cruisers to sail from British shipyards to raid Union commerce. Seward claimed that Britain had violated international laws of neutrality and owed compensation for damages. Britain, fearing that Americans might build ships for British enemies in a future war, accepted Seward's legal analysis and agreed to submit the *Alabama* claims to arbitration. However, Charles Sumner, chairman of the Senate Foreign Relations Committee, insisted that the compensation cover "indirect" damages. Including lost shipping revenue and the costs of Britain's prolonging the war, his estimates reached more than $2 billion. Sumner was angry over British aid to the Confederacy during the war and wanted to acquire Canada as part of the financial deal with Britain. In 1866 Congress restricted Canadian trade and fishing privileges in an attempt to force Canadians to support annexation. However, with the stakes so high, the British refused to agree to a settlement during Johnson's presidency.

Meanwhile, American expansionist ambitions in the Caribbean and the Pacific met with only mixed success. Supporting the U.S. Navy's demands for a base in the Caribbean, Seward negotiated a treaty with Denmark to purchase the Virgin Islands, but the Senate rejected the $7.5 million price. The Senate also turned down his proposal to annex Santo Domingo (the present-day Dominican Republic), which had won independence from Spain in 1865. Seward did persuade Congress to annex the small Midway Islands west of Hawaii after his effort to acquire the Hawaiian Islands had failed. Most important, in 1867 Seward persuaded the Senate to ratify a treaty to buy Alaska from Russia and to appropriate the $7.2 million for the purchase. Critics referred to Alaska as "Johnson's Polar Bear Garden" and "Seward's Folly," but its acquisition promised to obstruct British ambitions in North America. Also, the price was reasonable when weighed against even the low estimates that Congress made of Alaska's fish, fur, lumber, and mineral resources.

When Ulysses S. Grant became president in 1869, he took up the cause of expansion in the Caribbean. He was influenced by American investors and adventurers in Santo Domingo, including Orville E. Babcock, his former military aide, who became his personal secretary in the White House. Grant proposed a treaty to annex the country as a colony for freed slaves dissatisfied with Reconstruction. The Senate defeated Grant's imperial ambition in 1870. Leading the attack was Charles Sumner, who feared that annexation would threaten the independence of the neighboring black republic of Haiti. "These islands by climate, occupation, and destiny . . . belong to the colored people," he declared.

Grant's secretary of state was the genteel Hamilton Fish, a former Whig who had been governor of New York and a U.S. senator. Fish had less interest than Seward in acquiring new territory and concentrated on settling differences with Britain. Part of his goal was to strengthen the ties of capital and commerce between the two nations. Interest in annexing Canada still remained high, but Fish finally persuaded Grant that the British North America Act of 1867, uniting Canada in a confederation (the Dominion of Canada) and providing for greater self-government, had removed any serious Canadian interest in annexation. Fish then quickly negotiated the Treaty of Washington in 1871, which submitted for arbitration all the outstanding issues between the two countries, including the *Alabama* claims. In 1873 the British government obeyed the ruling of an international tribunal established under the treaty and presented a $15.5 million check to the U.S. government. A period of unprecedented goodwill between America and Britain followed.

The Politics of Corruption and the Grant Administration

During the Grant administration the Democratic party, seeking to reestablish its national base of power, made the Republican economic program its primary target. Since the key elements of Republican policy had wide support, the Democrats avoided attacking specific programs. Instead, they renewed their traditional assault on "special privilege."

Democrats warned that Republican programs were creating islands of privilege, enabling wealthy individuals to buy favors from the federal government and allowing the Republicans to buy support from the people that their programs served. The result, Democrats charged, was an increasing concentration of wealth and power in the hands of the wealthy and a corruption of the republic. By stressing corruption, the Democrats tried to appeal to Americans who valued honesty and still cherished the Jeffersonian ideal of a society composed of independent and virtuous farmers, artisans, and small entrepreneurs. The Democrats claimed they would restore the competitive economy that had been lost during the Industrial Revolution and the Civil War.

"Grantism"
Grant was lampooned on both sides of the Atlantic for the scandalous behavior of his administration. The British magazine *Puck* showed Grant only barely defying gravity in protecting corrupt members of his administration. Despite the scandals, the British public welcomed Grant with admiration on his triumphal foreign tour in 1877.

Dissident Republicans. Some Republicans joined the Democratic chorus condemning Grant's policies. The dissidents included radicals on Reconstruction such as Charles Sumner, but most numerous and influential were men such as Charles Francis Adams—wealthy, well-educated members of established northeastern families—who resented the critical role professional politicians had come to play in the party. They attacked Grant for turning the Republican party into a self-serving bureaucracy with too many professional politicians in executive positions, especially cabinet posts. And they faulted their party for requiring government workers to pay a portion of their salaries into the party's treasury.

The dissidents coined the term *Grantism* to describe this new system of party patronage. To counter it they endorsed a program of civil service reform, beginning

with a *merit system* to replace the spoils system established under Jackson. A civil service commission would administer competitive examinations as the basis for appointments.

The Liberal Republicans and the Election of 1872. When the dissident Republicans failed to replace Grant as the party's nominee in 1872, they called themselves the Liberal Republicans and formed a new party. The name reflected their commitment to liberty, competition, and limited government. Their platform emphasized civil service reform and—in an appeal for Democratic support—amnesty for all former Confederates and removal of troops from the South. For president they nominated Horace Greeley, the influential editor and publisher of the New York *Tribune*. In an attempt to steal the Liberals' thunder, the Democrats nominated Greeley too, but with little enthusiasm. Although Greeley supported reconciliation with ex-Confederates, he had earlier favored a radical approach to Reconstruction, and he supported high tariffs, which conflicted with the views of the Democrats.

In the election of 1872 Grant won an even larger percentage of the popular vote—56 percent—than he had in 1868. In fact, this was a higher percentage of the popular vote than any candidate had won since Andrew Jackson in 1828. Grant carried every northern state and, because of support for him among African-American voters and the distaste of ex-Confederates for Greeley, Grant also carried all the states of the former Confederacy except Tennessee, Georgia, and Texas.

Crédit Mobilier and the Whiskey Ring. During Grant's second term the issue of corruption in the Republican party erupted again. In 1873 a Congressional committee confirmed newspaper reports of a complicated deal in which high-ranking Republicans appeared to have cheated the taxpayers. The scandal centered on Crédit Mobilier, a construction company that contracted for work on the Union Pacific Railroad. It turned out that Crédit Mobilier was a dummy corporation. Union Pacific stockholders had formed it and made enormous purchases from it, sometimes for services that were never delivered, and paid for those purchases with Union Pacific stock and federal subsidies. In an attempt to prevent a Congressional investigation, the insiders had sold Crédit Mobilier stock at a discount to several members of Congress.

An even more dramatic scandal, which reached into the White House itself, involved the Whiskey Ring, a network of large whiskey distillers and Treasury agents who defrauded the Treasury of millions of dollars of excise taxes on liquor. The ring was organized by a Union general, John A. McDonald, whom Grant had appointed to the post of supervisor of internal revenue in St. Louis. Grant's private secretary, Orville Babcock, kept a protective eye on McDonald's activities and funneled some of the spoils into the campaign chests of the Republican party. The game was up in 1875 when Benjamin Bristow, an upright and ambitious secretary of the treasury, exposed the ring and brought indictments against more than 350 distillers and government officials. Babcock was later acquitted, but more than a hundred men, including McDonald, went to prison.

The Whiskey Ring scandal ruined Grant's second term and crushed whatever prospects he might have had for a third. Grant had ordered Bristow to "Let no guilty man escape," but Grant protected his good friend Babcock with extraordinary measures, possibly even perjuring himself in a deposition he gave in the presence of Chief Justice Morrison Waite.

The Depression of 1873–1877. These scandals occurred in the midst of the worst depression the nation had ever endured. By 1876 nearly 15 percent of the labor force was unemployed, and thousands of farmers had gone bankrupt. The precipitating event was the Panic of 1873, which involved the bankruptcy of the Northern Pacific Railroad and its major investor, Jay Cooke. Both Cooke's privileged role as a financier of the Civil War and the extensive Republican subsidies to railroads suggested to many suffering Americans that Republican financial manipulations had caused the depression.

To Americans who had suffered economic loss or even ruin, the Grant administration seemed unresponsive. Especially troublesome was the important issue of how much paper money should be in circulation. Rapidly falling prices hurt small farmers and all others who were heavily in debt. Forced to repay debts with dollars that were swiftly increasing in value, they called on the federal government to increase the nation's money supply, an action that they hoped would stop prices from falling. The Grant administration ignored the debtors' pleas for relief and further angered them by insisting that Civil War bondholders be fully repaid in gold, even though they had bought their bonds with greenbacks and had received only the guarantee that the interest on the bonds would be paid in gold. In 1874 the Democrats gained sufficient support from Republicans to push through Congress a bill that would have increased the number of greenbacks in circulation and eased the money pinch. But President Grant vetoed it, fueling Democratic charges that Republicans served only the special interests of capitalists. In the election of 1874 the Democrats rode their criticism of Grant's leadership to gains in both houses of Congress and a majority in the House of Representatives—for the first time since secession.

Before the new Congress met, however, the lame-duck Republicans passed the Specie Resumption Act of 1875. This law provided that the federal government would exchange gold for greenbacks, thus making federal paper money as "good as gold." It put the nation's money supply squarely on the gold standard, a step that increased the confidence of investors in the economy and helped foreign trade. But by increasing the value of greenbacks the act induced wealthy Americans to hoard them, reducing the amount of money in circulation, pushing prices up more sharply, and increasing still more the burden of carrying debts. The severe financial pain felt by many Americans worsened even further the political prospects of the Grant administration.

The Political Crisis of 1877

Republican leaders approached the 1876 presidential campaign with a sense of foreboding. If they were to thwart the Democrats, they had to shake themselves free of the atmosphere of scandal and special privilege that had come to surround President Grant. They turned to the electoral-vote-rich state of Ohio for a candidate—Governor Rutherford B. Hayes, who had won three closely contested races. His scandal-free terms had won him a reputation for honesty, he had a good Civil War record, and he was a supporter of civil service reform. He was a moderate on Reconstruction and a former Whig whose election strategy included an appeal to southern conservatives, especially former southern Whigs.

The Democrats concentrated on the Grant scandals. They nominated Governor Samuel J. Tilden of New York, a well-known fighter of corruption who had helped break the control of the infamous Tweed Ring over New York City politics. Their platform emphasized reform, especially of the civil service, promising to save the nation from "a corrupt centralism which has honeycombed the offices of the Federal government itself with incapacity, waste, and fraud."

The Election of 1876. On election night the outcome seemed clear; headlines announced that Tilden had won. The Democrats celebrated, and the Republicans were plunged into gloom. In Ohio, Hayes went to bed convinced that he had been defeated. Tilden had won a bare majority of the popular vote—51 percent. The Democrats had made deep inroads in the North, carrying New York, New Jersey, Connecticut, and Indiana, and had apparently swept the southern states (see Map 16.3).

But by dawn two or three sleepless politicians at Republican headquarters in New York City had woven a daring strategy. Republicans still controlled election procedures in three southern states: Louisiana, South

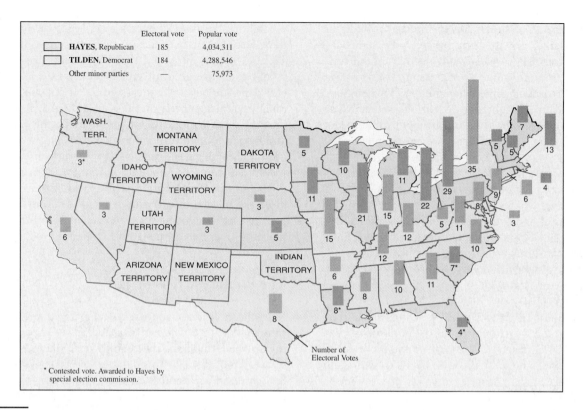

MAP 16.3

The Election of 1876

Tilden made such large inroads in northern states that Hayes could not win without the contested votes of three states in the Deep South. (Hayes also needed to defeat the efforts of the governor of Oregon to replace a Republican elector from that state with a Democrat.)

Carolina, and Florida. If they could argue that Democratic fraud and intimidation had affected the election results in those states, they could certify Republican victories and report Republican electoral votes. Of course, newly elected Democratic officials in the three states would send in electoral votes for Tilden. As a result, there would be two sets of electoral votes from those states when Congress counted them early in 1877. If Congress accepted all the Republican votes, Hayes would have a one-vote electoral majority. The audacious announcement came: Hayes had carried the three southern states and won the election.

The Compromise of 1877. The Constitution had not established a method to resolve this unprecedented dispute over the validity of electoral votes, and the long period of uncertainty between the election in November and the inauguration the following March was filled with rumors: There might be a violent coup by Democrats if the Republicans tried to steal the election; Presi-

dent Grant might use the military to prevent Tilden from taking office; there might be a new election or even a new civil war. The commander of the army, General William T. Sherman, believed that he might be the only person able to preserve the peace, and he deployed four artillery companies in Washington. While the rumors flew, various interests tried to gain advantage from the situation. Railroad promoters jockeyed for new federal subsidies, promising to deliver blocs of support in Congress to the party that made the best promises. Politicians on all sides flirted with the opposition, hoping for rewards.

In the end, political compromise and accident won out. Congress decided to appoint an electoral commission to settle the question. The commission included seven Republicans and seven Democrats. The fifteenth and deciding vote would go to Justice David Davis of the Supreme Court, a man with a reputation for being free of party loyalty. But Davis resigned from the Court at the crucial moment to accept election to the Senate

Anti-Republican Sentiment, 1876
This Democratic cartoon portrays Union soldiers, with bayonets fixed, coercing African-Americans to vote Republican. The carpetbag in the foreground identifies the politics of the civilian at the voting table. To the far left, the individual casting a watchful eye on the proceedings is probably an ex-planter, supposedly powerless in the new politics of the South.

from Illinois, and the deciding vote fell to Joseph P. Bradley, a lifelong Republican. When the commission completed its careful investigation of the election results in Florida, Louisiana, and South Carolina, the decision on each state was made by a straight party vote of eight to seven.

It remained to be seen whether Congress would accept the result. The Senate was controlled by the Republicans, and the House by the Democrats. Southern Democrats held the balance of power, and Hayes's representatives sought their support. Some of those southerners were convinced that Hayes had made various promises to the "negotiators"—to confine federal troops to their barracks throughout the South, appoint Democrats to major offices, and support the construction of a railroad across Texas to the Pacific. Whether or not such promises were actually made, enough southerners in the House accepted the commission's findings to make Hayes president.

This sequence of events is often referred to as the Compromise of 1877, but historians remain uncertain about whether any kind of deal was really struck. Dur-

ing his campaign Hayes had promised to end the military occupation of the South. He had also planned to appoint a few Democrats to his cabinet. And his faction of the Republican party did not support the Texas railroad scheme. The alleged compromise might have been a fiction created by southern Democrats to justify their votes for Hayes.

The End of Reconstruction. The only thing known for certain was that Reconstruction had ended. The outcome was mixed and unclear; no single position had emerged triumphant. In 1877 political leaders on all sides were ready to say that what Lincoln had called "the work" was complete. But for many Americans, especially the freed slaves, the work had clearly not been completed. To be sure, they had won three amendments to the Constitution, established public schools for African-American children, and gained some access to land for former slaves. But any work toward further improvement in the condition of African-Americans had been abandoned and left to the slow, frustrating, and imperfect processes of history.

Summary

In 1865, after the Civil War ended, President Abraham Lincoln's plan for quickly restoring the Union encountered opposition from radical Republicans in Congress, who believed that freedmen must have the vote, and moderate Republicans, who wished to punish the South and establish their party there. Lincoln was assassinated before he could negotiate a unified Republican position.

Possibilities for a swift sectional reconciliation continued into the administration of Andrew Johnson, but he could not satisfy both moderate Republicans and the defeated Confederacy. His difficulties in working with Congress deepened the contest for the control of Reconstruction and resulted in an erratic policy that intensified the South's resistance to federal power.

Congressional Reconstruction extended the civil rights of former slaves through the Fourteenth Amendment, protected their suffrage through the Fifteenth Amendment, and encouraged the formation of southern state governments in which freedmen played crucial roles. Republicans, however, failed to equip those governments to defeat the old planter elite, which managed to regain control through political appeals to racial solidarity and by means of terror and intimidation. Northern Republican leaders tired of the conflict and began to doubt the abilities of African-American political leaders. During the economic depression of the 1870s they increasingly concluded that they had substantial interests in common with white Southern elites.

By 1877 all the Reconstruction state governments had been ousted. The freedmen won some modest economic gains during Reconstruction, but without access to land ownership they became ensnared in a system of debt peonage and again found themselves dependent on the planters, who were now their landlords.

The Republicans proved to be more successful in consolidating the power of industrial capitalism than in reconstructing the South. Democrats attacked the Republican economic program with a Jacksonian critique of "special privilege," but most northerners came out of the Civil War more receptive to concentrations of power and to the values of the business class. Many believed that the Republican program was necessary for sustained prosperity and a strong nation. Although scandals inflamed opposition to the Grant administration, the Republicans took the election of 1876 by capitalizing on the South's hunger for an end to Reconstruction and for some influence in national politics. What is sometimes called the Compromise of 1877 kept the Republicans in control of the federal government by cementing an alliance between the northern business class and southern economic elites.

TIMELINE

1863	Lincoln announces his restoration plan
1864	Wade-Davis bill passed by Congress Lincoln gives Wade-Davis bill a "pocket" veto
1865	Freedmen's Bureau established Lincoln supports limited suffrage for freedmen Lincoln assassinated; Andrew Johnson succeeds as president Johnson implements his restoration plan Joint Committee on Reconstruction formed
1866	Republicans fail to override Johnson's veto of Freedmen's Bureau bill Civil Rights Act passes over Johnson's veto Memphis and New Orleans riots Johnson makes disastrous "swing around the circle" American Equal Rights Association founded Johnson defeated in Congressional elections
1867	Reconstruction Acts Tenure of Office Act Purchase of Alaska
1868	Impeachment crisis Fourteenth Amendment ratified Ulysses S. Grant elected president
1869	*Texas v. White*
1870	Ku Klux Klan at peak of power First Force Act passed by Congress Fifteenth Amendment ratified
1871	Ku Klux Klan Act passed by Congress Treaty of Washington
1872	Grant's reelection as president
1873	Panic of 1873 ushers in depression of 1873–1877 Crédit Mobilier scandal breaks
1874	Democrats win majority in House of Representatives
1875	Whiskey Ring scandal undermines Grant administration
1877	Compromise of 1877 Rutherford B. Hayes becomes president Reconstruction ends

BIBLIOGRAPHY

Among the best general studies are three older works: W. E. B. Du Bois, *Black Reconstruction* (1935), the first book to challenge traditional racist interpretations of Reconstruction; John Hope Franklin, *Reconstruction: After the Civil War* (1961); and Kenneth M. Stampp, *The Era of Reconstruction, 1865–1877* (1965). More modern studies are Eric Foner, *Reconstruction: America's Unfinished Revolution, 1863–1877* (1988), currently the best survey of Reconstruction, and James M. McPherson, *Ordeal by Fire: The Civil War and Reconstruction* (1993).

Presidential Restoration

For important studies of presidential efforts to rebuild the Union, see the books on Abraham Lincoln listed in Chapter 15 and the following works on Andrew Johnson: Albert Castel, *The Presidency of Andrew Johnson* (1979); Eric L. McKitrick, *Andrew Johnson and Reconstruction* (1960), which initiated scholarly criticism of Johnson; and James Sefton, *Andrew Johnson and the Uses of Constitutional Power* (1979). Books that focus on Congress include LaWanda Cox and John H. Cox, *Politics, Principle, and Prejudice, 1865–1867* (1963); David Donald, *The Politics of Reconstruction, 1863–1867* (1965); and William B. Brock, *An American Crisis: Congress and Reconstruction, 1865–1867* (1963). For insight into developments in the South, see Dan T. Carter, *When the War Was Over: The Failure of Self-Reconstruction in the South, 1865–1867* (1985). Michael Perman, *Reunion without Compromise: The South and Reconstruction, 1865–1868* (1973), analyzes how the South manipulated Johnson.

Radical Reconstruction

For studies of Congress's role in radical Reconstruction, see Michael Les Benedict, *A Compromise of Principle: Congressional Republicans and Reconstruction* (1974); William Gillette, *Retreat from Reconstruction, 1863–1879* (1979); and Hans L. Trefousse, *Impeachment of a President: Andrew Johnson, the Blacks, and Reconstruction* (1975). William S. McFeely, *Grant: A Biography* (1981), deftly explains the politics of Reconstruction. Also helpful is Brooks D. Simpson, *Let Us Have Peace: Ulysses S. Grant and the Politics of War and Reconstruction, 1861–1868* (1991). Study of the South during radical Reconstruction should begin with the wealth of literature on the experience of blacks. Among the most useful works are Ira Berlin et al., *Freedom: A Documentary History of Emancipation, 1861–1867: The Wartime Genesis of Free Labor: The Lower South* (1990); Robert Cruden, *The Negro in Reconstruction* (1969); Jacqueline Jones, *Labor of Love, Labor of Sorrow: Black Women, Work, and the Family from Slavery to the Present* (1985); and Leon F. Litwack, *Been in the Storm So Long: The Aftermath of Slavery* (1979). The economic condition of the freedmen and the postwar South is the focus of Robert Higgs, *Competition and Coercion: Blacks in the American Economy, 1865–1914* (1977); Jay Mandle, *The Roots of Black Poverty: The Southern Plantation Economy after the Civil War* (1978); Roger L. Ransom and Richard Sutch, *One Kind of Freedom: The Economic Consequences of Emancipation* (1977); Jonathan M. Wiener, *Social Origins of the New South: Alabama, 1860–1885* (1975); and Gavin Wright, *The Political Economy of the Cotton South* (1978). Specialized studies of African-Americans and race relations, often focusing on particular states, include John Blassingame, *Black New Orleans, 1860–1880* (1973); Barry A. Crouch, *The Freedmen's Bureau and Black Texans* (1992); Barbara Fields, *Slavery and Freedom on the Middle Ground: Maryland during the Nineteenth Century* (1985); Thomas Holt, *Black over White: Negro Political Leadership in South Carolina during Reconstruction* (1977); Peter Kolchin, *First Freedom: The Responses of Alabama's Blacks to Emancipation and Reconstruction* (1972); Howard N. Rabinowitz, *Race Relations in the Urban South, 1865–1890* (1977); Willie Lee Rose, *Rehearsal for Reconstruction: The Port Royal Experiment* (1964); and Joel Williamson, *After Slavery: The Negro in South Carolina during Reconstruction, 1861–1877* (1965). Other state studies of Reconstruction politics appear in Richard Lowe, *Republicans and Reconstruction in Virginia, 1856–1870* (1991), and Otto Olsen, ed., *Reconstruction and Redemption in the South* (1980). The best study of carpetbaggers is Richard N. Current, *Those Terrible Carpetbaggers: A Reinterpretation* (1988). On yeomen farmers, consult Steven Hahn, *The Roots of Southern Populism: Yeoman Farmers and the Transformation of the Georgia Upcountry, 1850–1890* (1983). The most thorough study of the Ku Klux Klan is Allen W. Trelease, *White Terror: The Ku Klux Klan Conspiracy and Southern Reconstruction* (1972). Biographies of Nathan Bedford Forrest include Brian S. Wills, *A Battle from the Start: The Life of Nathan Bedford Forrest* (1992), and John A. Wyeth, *That Devil Forrest: A Life of General Nathan Bedford Forrest* (1989). To survey Reconstruction politics in the South, consult Michael Perman, *The Road to Redemption: Southern Politics, 1869–1879* (1984).

The North during Reconstruction

On state politics in the North, see Eugene H. Berwanger, *The West and Reconstruction* (1981), and James Mohr, ed., *The Radical Republicans in the North: State Politics during Reconstruction* (1976). Studies on national politics that extend beyond Reconstruction include Paul H. Buck, *The Road to Reunion, 1865–1900* (1937), and Morton Keller, *Affairs of State: Public Life in Late Nineteenth-Century America* (1977). The best studies of classical liberalism and liberals during the Reconstruction Era are John G. Sproat, *"The Best Men": Liberal Reformers in the Gilded Age* (1968), and Robert Kelley, *The Transatlantic Persuasion: The Liberal-Democratic Mind in the Age of Gladstone* (1968). On political corruption, see Mark W. Summers, *The Era of Good Stealings* (1993). On the monetary difficulties of the 1870s, see Walter T. K. Nugent, *The Money Question during Reconstruction* (1967). On the Compromise of 1877, see K. I. Polakoff, *The Politics of Inertia: The Election of 1876 and the End of Reconstruction* (1973), and C. Vann Woodward, *Reunion and Reaction* (1956).

The Declaration of Independence

★　　　★　　　★

The Unanimous Declaration of the Thirteen United States of America

When in the Course of human events, it becomes necessary for one people to dissolve the political bands which have connected them with another, and to assume among the Powers of the earth, the separate and equal station to which the Laws of Nature and of Nature's God entitle them, a decent respect to the opinions of mankind requires that they should declare the causes which impel them to the separation.

We hold these truths to be self-evident, that all men are created equal, that they are endowed by their Creator with certain unalienable rights, that among these are Life, Liberty, and the pursuit of Happiness. That to secure these rights, Governments are instituted among Men, deriving their just powers from the consent of the governed. That whenever any Form of Government becomes destructive of these ends, it is the Right of the People to alter or to abolish it, and to institute new Government, laying its foundation on such principles and organizing its powers in such form, as to them shall seem most likely to effect their Safety and Happiness. Prudence, indeed, will dictate that Governments long established should not be changed for light and transient causes; and accordingly all experience hath shown, that mankind are more disposed to suffer, while evils are sufferable, than to right themselves by abolishing the forms to which they are accustomed. But when a long train of abuses and usurpations, pursuing invariably the same Object evinces a design to reduce them under absolute Despotism, it is their right, it is their duty, to throw off such Government, and to provide new Guards for their future security.—Such has been the patient sufferance of these Colonies; and such is now the necessity which constrains them to alter their former Systems of Government. The history of the present King of Great Britain is a history of repeated injuries and usurpations, all having in direct object the estab-lishment of an absolute Tyranny over these States. To prove this, let Facts be submitted to a candid world.

He has refused his Assent to Laws, the most wholesome and necessary for the public good.

He has forbidden his Governors to pass Laws of immediate and pressing importance, unless suspended in their operation till his Assent should be obtained; and, when so suspended, he has utterly neglected to attend to them.

He has refused to pass other Laws for the accommodation of large districts of people, unless those people would relinquish the right of Representation in the Legislature, a right inestimable to them and formidable to tyrants only.

He has called together legislative bodies at places unusual, uncomfortable, and distant from the depository of their public Records, for the sole purpose of fatiguing them into compliance with his measures.

He has dissolved Representative Houses repeatedly, for opposing with manly firmness his invasions on the rights of the people.

He has refused for a long time, after such dissolutions, to cause others to be elected; whereby the Legislative powers, incapable of Annihilation, have returned to the People at large for their exercise; the State remaining in the mean time exposed to all the dangers of invasion from without and convulsions within.

He has endeavoured to prevent the population of these States; for that purpose obstructing the Laws of Naturalization of Foreigners; refusing to pass others to encourage their migrations hither, and raising the conditions of new Appropriations of Lands.

He has obstructed the Administration of Justice, by refusing his Assent to Laws for establishing Judiciary powers.

He has made Judges dependent on his Will alone, for the tenure of their offices, and the amount and payment of their salaries.

He has erected a multitude of New Offices, and sent hither swarms of Officers to harass our People, and eat out their substance.

He has kept among us, in times of peace, Standing Armies without the Consent of our legislature.

He has combined with others to subject us to a jurisdiction foreign to our constitution, and unacknowledged by our laws; giving his Assent to their Acts of pretended Legislation:

For quartering large bodies of armed troops among us:

For protecting them, by a mock Trial, from Punishment for any Murders which they should commit on the Inhabitants of these States:

For cutting off our Trade with all parts of the world:

For imposing taxes on us without our Consent:

For depriving us of many cases, of the benefits of Trial by jury:

For transporting us beyond Seas to be tried for pretended offences:

For abolishing the free System of English Laws in a neighbouring Province, establishing therein an Arbitrary government, and enlarging its Boundaries so as to render it at once an example and fit instrument for introducing the same absolute rule into these Colonies;

For taking away our Charters, abolishing our most valuable Laws, and altering fundamentally the Forms of our Governments:

For suspending our own Legislatures, and declaring themselves invested with Power to legislate for us in all cases whatsoever.

He has abdicated Government here, by declaring us out of his Protection and waging War against us.

He has plundered our seas, ravaged our Coasts, burnt our towns, and destroyed the lives of our people.

He is at this time transporting large armies of foreign mercenaries to compleat the works of death, desolation, and tyranny, already begun with circumstances of Cruelty & perfidy scarcely paralleled in the most barbarous ages, and totally unworthy the Head of a civilized nation.

He has constrained our fellow Citizens taken Captive on the high Seas to bear Arms against their Country, to become the executioners of their friends and Brethren, or to fall themselves by their Hands.

He has excited domestic insurrections amongst us, and has endeavoured to bring on the inhabitants of our frontiers, the merciless Indian Savages, whose known rule of warfare, is an undistinguished destruction of all ages, sexes, and conditions.

In every stage of these Oppressions We have Petitioned for Redress in the most humble terms: Our repeated Petitions have been answered only by repeated injury. A Prince, whose character is thus marked by every act which may define a Tyrant, is unfit to be the ruler of a free people.

Nor have We been wanting in attention to our British brethren. We have warned them from time to time of attempts by their legislature to extend an unwarrantable jurisdiction over us. We have reminded them of the circumstances of our emigration and settlement here. We have appealed to their native justice and magnanimity, and we have conjured them by the ties of our common kindred to disavow these usurpations, which, would inevitably interrupt our connections and correspondence. They too have been deaf to the voice of justice and of consanguinity. We must, therefore, acquiesce in the necessity, which denounces our Separation, and hold them, as we hold the rest of mankind, Enemies in War, in Peace Friends.

We, therefore, the Representatives of the United States of America, in General Congress, Assembled, appealing to the Supreme Judge of the world for the rectitude of our intentions, do, in the Name, and by Authority of the good People of these Colonies, solemnly publish and declare, That these United Colonies are, and of Right ought to be FREE AND INDEPENDENT STATES; that they are Absolved from all Allegiance to the British Crown, and that all political connection between them and the State of Great Britain, is and ought to be totally dissolved; and that as Free and Independent States, they have full Power to levy War, conclude Peace, contract Alliances, establish Commerce, and to do all other Acts and Things which Independent States may of right do. And for the support of this Declaration, with a firm reliance on the Protection of Divine Providence, we mutually pledge to each other our Lives, our Fortunes, and our sacred Honor.

John Hancock

Button Gwinnett	George Wythe	James Wilson	Josiah Bartlett
Lyman Hall	Richard Henry Lee	Geo. Ross	Wm. Whipple
Geo. Walton	Th. Jefferson	Caesar Rodney	Saml. Adams
Wm. Hooper	Benja. Harrison	Geo. Read	John Adams
Joseph Hewes	Thos. Nelson, Jr.	Thos. M'Kean	Robt. Treat Paine
John Penn	Francis Lightfoot Lee	Wm. Floyd	Elbridge Gerry
Edward Rutledge	Carter Braxton	Phil. Livingston	Step. Hopkins
Thos. Heyward, Junr.	Robt. Morris	Frans. Lewis	William Ellery
Thomas Lynch, Junr.	Benjamin Rush	Lewis Morris	Roger Sherman
Arthur Middleton	Benja. Franklin	Richd. Stockton	Sam'el Hunington
Samuel Chase	John Morton	Jno. Witherspoon	Wm. Williams
Wm. Paca	Geo. Clymer	Fras. Hopkinson	Oliver Wolcott
Thos. Stone	Jas. Smith	John Hart	Matthew Thornton
Charles Carroll of Carrollton	Geo. Taylor	Abra. Clark	

The Articles of Confederation and Perpetual Union

★ ★ ★

BETWEEN THE STATES OF NEW HAMPSHIRE, MASSACHU-
SETTS BAY, RHODE ISLAND AND PROVIDENCE PLANTA-
TIONS, CONNECTICUT, NEW YORK, NEW JERSEY, PENN-
SYLVANIA, DELAWARE, MARYLAND, VIRGINIA, NORTH
CAROLINA, SOUTH CAROLINA, GEORGIA.*

Article 1.

The stile of this confederacy shall be "The United States of
America."

Article 2.

Each State retains its sovereignty, freedom and independence,
and every power, jurisdiction, and right, which is not by this
confederation expressly delegated to the United States, in
Congress assembled.

Article 3.

The said states hereby severally enter into a firm league of
friendship with each other for their common defence, the security of their liberties and their mutual and general welfare;
binding themselves to assist each other against all force offered to, or attacks made upon them, or any of them, on account of religion, sovereignty, trade, or any other pretence
whatever.

*This copy of the final draft of the Articles of Confederation is taken from
the *Journals*, 9:907–925, November 15, 1777.

Article 4.

The better to secure and perpetuate mutual friendship and intercourse among the people of the different states in this
union, the free inhabitants of each of these states, paupers,
vagabonds, and fugitives from justice excepted, shall be entitled to all privileges and immunities of free citizens in the several states; and the people of each State shall have free ingress
and regress to and from any other State, and shall enjoy
therein all the privileges of trade and commerce, subject to the
same duties, impositions, and restrictions, as the inhabitants
thereof respectively; provided, that such restrictions shall not
extend so far as to prevent the removal of property, imported
into any State, to any other State of which the owner is an inhabitant; provided also, that no imposition, duties, or restriction, shall be laid by any State on the property of the United
States, or either of them.

If any person guilty of, or charged with treason, felony, or
other high misdemeanor in any State, shall flee from justice
and be found in any of the United States, he shall, upon demand of the governor or executive power of the State from
which he fled, be delivered up and removed to the State having
jurisdiction of his offence.

Full faith and credit shall be given in each of these states
to the records, acts, and judicial proceedings of the courts and
magistrates of every other State.

Article 5.

For the more convenient management of the general interests
of the United States, delegates shall be annually appointed, in
such manner as the legislature of each State shall direct, to
meet in Congress, on the 1st Monday in November in every

year, with a power reserved to each State to recal its delegates, or any of them, at any time within the year, and to send others in their stead for the remainder of the year.

No State shall be represented in Congress by less than two, nor by more than seven members; and no person shall be capable of being a delegate for more than three years in any term of six years; nor shall any person, being a delegate, be capable of holding any office under the United States, for which he, or any other for his benefit, receives any salary, fees, or emolument of any kind.

Each State shall maintain its own delegates in a meeting of the states, and while they act as members of the committee of the states.

In determining questions in the United States, in Congress assembled, each State shall have one vote.

Freedom of speech and debate in Congress shall not be impeached or questioned in any court or place out of Congress: and the members of Congress shall be protected in their persons from arrests and imprisonments, during the time of their going to and from, and attendance on Congress, *except for treason*, felony, or breach of the peace.

Article 6.

No State, without the consent of the United States, in Congress assembled, shall send any embassy to, or receive any embassy from, or enter into any conference, agreement, alliance, or treaty with any king, prince, or state; nor shall any person, holding any office of profit or trust under the United States, or any of them, accept of any present, emolument, office or title, of any kind whatever, from any king, prince, or foreign state; nor shall the United States, in Congress assembled, or any of them, grant any title of nobility.

No two or more states shall enter into any treaty, confederation, or alliance, whatever, between them, without the consent of the United States, in Congress assembled, specifying accurately the purposes for which the same is to be entered into, and how long it shall continue.

No state shall lay any imposts or duties which may interfere with any stipulations in treaties entered into by the United States, in Congress assembled, with any king, prince, or state, in pursuance of any treaties already proposed by Congress to the courts of France and Spain.

No vessels of war shall be kept up in time of peace by any State, except such number only as shall be deemed necessary by the United States, in Congress assembled, for the defence of such State or its trade; nor shall any body of forces be kept up by any State, in time of peace, except such number only as, in the judgment of the United States, in Congress assembled, shall be deemed requisite to garrison the forts necessary for the defence of such State; but every State shall always keep up a well regulated and disciplined militia, sufficiently armed and accoutred, and shall provide, and constantly have ready for use, in public stores, a due number of field pieces and tents, and a proper quantity of arms, ammunition and camp equipage.

No State shall engage in any war without the consent of the United States, in Congress assembled, unless such State be actually invaded by enemies, or shall have received certain advice of a resolution being formed by some nation of Indians to invade such State, and the danger is so imminent as not to admit of a delay till the United States, in Congress assembled, can be consulted; nor shall any State grant commissions to any ships or vessels of war, nor letters of marque or reprisal, except it be after a declaration of war by the United States, in Congress assembled, and then only against the kingdom or state, and the subjects thereof, against which war has been so declared, and under such regulations as shall be established by the United States, in Congress assembled, unless such State be infested by pirates, in which case vessels of war may be fitted out for that occasion, and kept so long as the danger shall continue, or until the United States, in Congress assembled, shall determine otherwise.

Article 7.

When land forces are raised by any State for the common defence, all officers of or under the rank of colonel, shall be appointed by the legislature of each State respectively, by whom such forces shall be raised, or in such manner as such State shall direct; and all vacancies shall be filled up by the State which first made the appointment.

Article 8.

All charges of war and all other expences, that shall be incurred for the common defence or general welfare, and allowed by the United States, in Congress assembled, shall be defrayed out of a common treasury, which shall be supplied by the several states, in proportion to the value of all land within each State, granted to or surveyed for any person, as such land and the buildings and improvements thereon shall be estimated according to such mode as the United States, in Congress assembled, shall, from time to time, direct and appoint.

The taxes for paying that proportion shall be laid and levied by the authority and direction of the legislatures of the several states, within the time agreed upon by the United States, in Congress assembled.

Article 9.

The United States, in Congress assembled, shall have the sole and exclusive right and power of determining on peace and war, except in the cases mentioned in the 6th article; of sending and receiving ambassadors; entering into treaties and alliances, provided that no treaty of commerce shall be made, whereby the legislative power of the respective states shall be restrained from imposing such imposts and duties on foreigners as their own people are subjected to, or from prohibiting the exportation or importation of any species of goods or commodities whatsoever; of establishing rules for deciding, in all cases, what captures on land or water shall be legal, and in what manner prizes, taken by land or naval forces in the service of the United States, shall be divided or appropriated; of granting letters of marque and reprisal in times of peace; appointing courts for the trial of piracies and felonies committed on the high seas, and establishing courts for receiving and determining, finally, appeals in all cases of captures; provided, that no member of Congress shall be appointed a judge of any of the said courts.

The United States, in Congress assembled, shall also be the last resort on appeal in all disputes and differences now subsisting, or that hereafter may arise between two or more states concerning boundary, jurisdiction or any other cause whatever; which authority shall always be exercised in the manner following: whenever the legislative or executive authority, or lawful agent of any State, in controversy with another, shall present a petition to Congress, stating the matter in question, and praying for a hearing, notice thereof shall be given, by order of Congress, to the legislative or executive authority of the other State in controversy, and a day assigned for the appearance of the parties by their lawful agents, who shall then be directed to appoint, by joint consent, commissioners or judges to constitute a court for hearing and determining the matter in question; but, if they cannot agree, Congress shall name three persons out of each of the United States, and from the list of such persons each party shall alternately strike out one, the petitioners beginning, until the number shall be reduced to thirteen; and from that number not less than seven, nor more than nine names, as Congress shall direct, shall, in the presence of Congress, be drawn out by lot; and the persons whose names shall be so drawn, or any five of them, shall be commissioners or judges to hear and finally determine the controversy, so always as a major part of the judges who shall hear the cause shall agree in the determination; and if either party shall neglect to attend at the day appointed, without shewing reasons which Congress shall judge sufficient, or, being present, shall refuse to strike, the Congress shall proceed to nominate three persons out of each State, and the secretary of Congress shall strike in behalf of such party absent or refusing; and the judgment and sentence of the court to be appointed, in the manner before prescribed, shall be final and conclusive; and if any of the parties shall refuse to submit to the authority of such court, or to appear or defend their claim or cause, the court shall nevertheless proceed to pronounce sentence or judgment, which shall, in like manner, be final and decisive, the judgment or sentence and other proceedings begin, in either case, transmitted to Congress, and lodged among the acts of Congress for the security of the parties concerned: provided, that every commissioner, before he sits in judgment, shall take an oath, to be administered by one of the judges of the supreme or superior court of the State where the cause shall be tried, "well and truly to hear and determine the matter in question, according to the best of his judgment, without favour, affection, or hope of reward:" provided, also, that no State shall be deprived of territory for the benefit of the United States.

All controversies concerning the private right of soil, claimed under different grants of two or more states, whose jurisdictions, as they may respect such lands and the states which passed such grants, are adjusted, the said grants, or either of them, being at the same time claimed to have originated antecedent to such settlement of jurisdiction, shall, on the petition of either party to the Congress of the United States, be finally determined, as near as may be, in the same manner as is before prescribed for deciding disputes respecting territorial jurisdiction between different states.

The United States, in Congress assembled, shall also have the sole and exclusive right and power of regulating the alloy and value of coin struck by their own authority, or by that of the respective states; fixing the standard of weights and measures throughout the United States; regulating the trade and managing all affairs with the Indians not members of any of the states; provided that the legislative right of any State within its own limits be not infringed or violated; establishing and regulating post offices from one State to another throughout all the United States, and exacting such postage on the papers passing through the same as may be requisite to defray the expences of the said office; appointing all officers of the land forces in the service of the United States, excepting regimental officers; appointing all the officers of the naval forces, and commissioning all officers whatever in the service of the United States; making rules for the government and regulation of the said land and naval forces, and directing their operations.

The United States, in Congress assembled, shall have authority to appoint a committee to sit in the recess of Congress, to be denominated "a Committee of the States," and to consist of one delegate from each State, and to appoint such other committees and civil officers as may be necessary for managing the general affairs of the United States, under their direction; to appoint one of their number to preside; provided that no person be allowed to serve in the office of president more than one year in any term of three years; to ascertain the necessary sums of money to be raised for the service of the United States, and to appropriate and apply the same for defraying the public expences; to borrow money or emit bills on the credit of the United States, transmitting, every half year, to the respective states, an account of the sums of money so borrowed or emitted; to build and equip a navy; to agree upon the number of land forces, and to make requisitions from each State for its quota, in proportion to the number of white inhabitants in such State; which requisitions shall be binding; and thereupon, the legislature of each State shall appoint the regimental officers, raise the men, and cloathe, arm, and equip them in a soldier-like manner, at the expence of the United States; and the officers and men so cloathed, armed, and equipped, shall march to the place appointed and within the time agreed on by the United States, in Congress assembled; but if the United States, in Congress assembled, shall, on consideration of circumstances, judge proper that any State should not raise men, or should raise a smaller number than its quota, and that any other State should raise a greater number of men than the quota thereof, such extra number shall be raised, officered, cloathed, armed, and equipped in the same manner as the quota of such State, unless the legislature of such State shall judge that such extra number cannot be safely spared out of the same, in which case they shall raise, officer, cloathe, arm, and equip as many of such extra number as they judge can be safely spared. And the officers and men so cloathed, armed, and equipped, shall march to the place appointed and within the time agreed on by the United States, in Congress assembled.

The United States, in Congress assembled, shall never engage in a war, nor grant letters of marque and reprisal in time of peace, nor enter into any treaties or alliances, nor coin money, nor regulate the value thereof, nor ascertain the sums and expences necessary for the defence and welfare of the United States, or any of them: nor emit bills, nor borrow money on the credit of the United States, nor appropriate money, nor agree upon the number of vessels of war to be built or purchased, or the number of land or sea forces to be raised, nor appoint a commander in chief of the army or navy, unless nine states assent to the same; nor shall a question on any other point, except for adjourning from day to day, be determined, unless by the votes of a majority of the United States, in Congress assembled.

The Congress of the United States shall have power to adjourn to any time within the year, and to any place within the United States, so that no period of adjournment be for a longer duration than the space of six months, and shall publish the journal of their proceedings monthly, except such parts thereof, relating to treaties, alliances or military operations, as, in their judgment, require secrecy; and the yeas and nays of the delegates of each State on any question shall be entered on the journal, when it is desired by any delegate; and the delegates of a State, or any of them, at his, or their request, shall be furnished with a transcript of the said journal, except such parts as are above excepted, to lay before the legislatures of the several states.

Article 10.

The committee of the states, or any nine of them, shall be authorized to execute, in the recess of Congress, such of the powers of Congress as the United States, in Congress assembled, by the consent of nine states, shall, from time to time, think expedient to vest them with; provided, that no power be delegated to the said committee, for the exercise of which, by the articles of confederation, the voice of nine states, in the Congress of the United States assembled, is requisite.

Article 11.

Canada acceding to this confederation, and joining in the measures of the United States, shall be admitted into and entitled to all the advantages of this union; but no other colony shall be admitted into the same, unless such admission be agreed to by nine states.

Article 12.

All bills of credit emitted, monies borrowed and debts contracted by, or under the authority of Congress before the assembling of the United States, in pursuance of the present confederation, shall be deemed and considered as a charge against the United States, for payment and satisfaction whereof the said United States and the public faith are hereby solemnly pledged.

Article 13.

Every State shall abide by the determinations of the United States, in Congress assembled, on all questions which, by this confederation, are submitted to them. And the articles of this confederation shall be inviolably observed by every State, and the union shall be perpetual; nor shall any alteration at any time hereafter be made in any of them, unless such alteration be agreed to in a Congress of the United States, and be afterwards confirmed by the legislatures of every State.

These articles shall be proposed to the legislatures of all the United States, to be considered, and if approved of by them, they are advised to authorize their delegates to ratify the same in the Congress of the United States; which being done, the same shall become conclusive.

The Constitution of the United States of America

★   ★   ★

We the People of the United States, in Order to form a more perfect Union, establish Justice, insure domestic Tranquility, provide for the common defence, promote the general Welfare, and secure the Blessings of Liberty to ourselves and our Posterity, do ordain and establish this Constitution for the United States of America.

Article I

Section 1 All legislative Powers herein granted shall be vested in a Congress of the United States, which shall consist of a Senate and a House of Representatives.

Section 2 The House of Representatives shall be composed of Members chosen every second Year by the People of the several States, and the Electors in each State shall have the Qualifications requisite for Electors of the most numerous Branch of the State Legislature.

No Person shall be a Representative who shall not have attained to the Age of twenty-five Years, and been seven Years a Citizen of the United States, and who shall not, when elected, be an Inhabitant of that State in which he shall be chosen.

Representatives and direct Taxes shall be apportioned among the several States which may be included within this Union, according to their respective Numbers, *which shall be determined by adding to the whole Number of free Persons, including those bound to Service for a Term of Years, and excluding Indians not taxed, three fifths of all other Persons.** The actual Enumeration shall be made within three Years after the first Meeting of the Congress of the United States, and within every subsequent Term of ten Years, in such Manner as they shall by Law direct. The Number of Representatives shall not exceed one for every thirty Thousand, but each State shall have at Least one Representative; and *until such*

enumeration shall be made, the State of New Hampshire shall be entitled to chuse three, Massachusetts eight, Rhode Island and Providence Plantations one, Connecticut five, New-York six, New Jersey four, Pennsylvania eight, Delaware one, Maryland six, Virginia ten, North Carolina five, South Carolina five, and Georgia three.

When vacancies happen in the Representation from any State, the Executive Authority thereof shall issue Writs of Election to fill such Vacancies.

The House of Representatives shall chuse their Speaker and other Officers; and shall have the sole Power of Impeachment.

Section 3 The Senate of the United States shall be composed of two Senators from each State, *chosen by the Legislature thereof,*† for six Years; and each Senator shall have one Vote.

Immediately after they shall be assembled in Consequence of the first Election, they shall be divided as equally as may be into three Classes. The Seats of the Senators of the first Class shall be vacated at the Expiration of the second Year, of the second Class at the Expiration of the fourth Year, and of the third Class at the Expiration of the sixth Year, so that one-third may be chosen every second Year; *and if Vacancies happen by Resignation, or otherwise, during the Recess of the Legislature of any State, the Executive thereof may make temporary Appointments until the next Meeting of the Legislature, which shall then fill such Vacancies.*‡

No person shall be a Senator who shall not have attained to the Age of thirty Years, and been nine Years a Citizen of the United States, and who shall not, when elected, be an Inhabitant of that State for which he shall be chosen.

The Vice President of the United States shall be President of the Senate, but shall have no Vote, unless they be equally divided.

Note: The Constitution became effective March 4, 1789. Provisions in italics have been changed by constitutional amendment.

*Changed by Section 2 of the Fourteenth Amendment.

---

†Changed by Section 1 of the Seventeenth Amendment.

‡Changed by Clause 2 of the Seventeenth Amendment.

The Senate shall chuse their other Officers, and also a President pro tempore, in the absence of the Vice President, or when he shall exercise the Office of President of the United States.

The Senate shall have the sole Power to try all Impeachments. When sitting for that Purpose, they shall be on Oath or Affirmation. When the President of the United States is tried, the Chief Justice shall preside: And no Person shall be convicted without the Concurrence of two thirds of the Members present.

Judgment in Cases of Impeachment shall not extend further than to removal from Office, and disqualification to hold and enjoy any Office of honor, Trust or Profit under the United States: but the Party convicted shall nevertheless be liable and subject to Indictment, Trial, Judgment and Punishment, according to Law.

Section 4 The Times, Places and Manner of holding Elections for Senators and Representatives, shall be prescribed in each State by the Legislature thereof; but the Congress may at any time by Law make or alter such Regulations, except as to the Places of Chusing Senators.

The Congress shall assemble at least once in every Year, and such Meeting *shall be on the first Monday in December, unless they shall by Law appoint a different Day.**

Section 5 Each House shall be the Judge of the Elections, Returns and Qualifications of its own Members, and a Majority of each shall constitute a Quorum to do Business; but a smaller number may adjourn from day to day, and may be authorized to compel the Attendance of absent Members, in such Manner, and under such Penalties, as each House may provide.

Each House may determine the Rules of its Proceedings, punish its Members for disorderly Behavior, and, with the Concurrence of two thirds, expel a Member.

Each House shall keep a Journal of its Proceedings, and from time to time publish the same, excepting such Parts as may in their Judgment require Secrecy; and the Yeas and Nays of the Members of either House on any question shall, at the Desire of one-fifth of those Present, be entered on the Journal.

Neither House, during the Session of Congress, shall, without the Consent of the other, adjourn for more than three days, nor to any other Place than that in which the two Houses shall be sitting.

Section 6 The Senators and Representatives shall receive a Compensation for their Services, to be ascertained by Law, and paid out of the Treasury of the United States. They shall in all Cases, except Treason, Felony and Breach of the Peace, be privileged from Arrest during their Attendance at the Session of their respective Houses, and in going to and returning from the same; and for any Speech or Debate in either House, they shall not be questioned in any other Place.

No Senator or Representative shall, during the Time for which he was elected, be appointed to any civil Office under the Authority of the United States, which shall have been created, or the Emoluments whereof shall have been increased, during such time; and no Person holding any Office under the

United States, shall be a Member of either House during his Continuance in Office.

Section 7 All Bills for raising Revenue shall originate in the House of Representatives; but the Senate may propose or concur with Amendments as on other Bills.

Every Bill which shall have passed the House of Representatives and the Senate, shall, before it becomes a Law, be presented to the President of the United States; If he approve he shall sign it, but if not he shall return it, with his Objections to that House in which it shall have originated, who shall enter the Objections at large on their Journal, and proceed to reconsider it. If after such Reconsideration two thirds of that House shall agree to pass the Bill, it shall be sent, together with the Objections, to the other House, by which it shall likewise be reconsidered, and if approved by two thirds of that House, it shall become a Law. But in all such Cases the Votes of both Houses shall be determined by Yeas and Nays, and the Names of the Persons voting for and against the Bill shall be entered on the Journal of each House respectively. If any Bill shall not be returned by the President within ten Days (Sundays excepted) after it shall have been presented to him, the Same shall be a Law, in like Manner as if he had signed it, unless the Congress by their Adjournment prevent its Return, in which Case it shall not be a Law.

Every Order, Resolution, or Vote to which the Concurrence of the Senate and the House of Representatives may be necessary (except on a question of Adjournment) shall be presented to the President of the United States; and before the Same shall take Effect, shall be approved by him, or being disapproved by him, shall be repassed by two thirds of the Senate and House of Representatives, according to the Rules and Limitations prescribed in the Case of a Bill.

Section 8 The Congress shall have Power To lay and collect Taxes, Duties, Imposts and Excises, to pay the Debts and provide for the common Defence and general Welfare of the United States; but all Duties, Imposts and Excises shall be uniform throughout the United States;

To borrow money on the credit of the United States;

To regulate Commerce with foreign Nations, and among the several States, and with the Indian Tribes;

To establish an uniform Rule of Naturalization, and uniform Laws on the subject of Bankruptcies throughout the United States;

To coin Money, regulate the Value thereof, and of foreign Coin, and fix the Standard of Weights and Measures;

To provide for the Punishment of counterfeiting the Securities and current Coin of the United States;

To establish Post Offices and post Roads;

To promote the Progress of Science and useful Arts, by securing for limited Times to Authors and Inventors the exclusive Right to their respective Writings and Discoveries;

To constitute Tribunals inferior to the supreme Court;

To define and punish Piracies and Felonies committed on the high Seas, and Offenses against the Law of Nations;

To declare War, grant Letters of Marque and Reprisal, and make Rules concerning Captures on Land and Water;

To raise and support Armies, but no Appropriation of Money to that Use shall be for a longer Term than two Years;

To provide and maintain a Navy;

---

*Changed by Section 2 of the Twentieth Amendment.

To make Rules for the Government and Regulation of the land and naval Forces;

To provide for calling forth the Militia to execute the Laws of the Union, suppress Insurrections and repel Invasions;

To provide for organizing, arming, and disciplining the Militia, and for governing such Part of them as may be employed in the Service of the United States, reserving to the States respectively, the Appointment of the Officers, and the Authority of training the Militia according to the discipline prescribed by Congress;

To exercise exclusive Legislation in all Cases whatsoever, over such District (not exceeding ten Miles square) as may, by Cession of particular States, and the acceptance of Congress, become the Seat of Government of the United States, and to exercise like Authority over all Places purchased by the Consent of the Legislature of the State in which the Same shall be, for the Erection of Forts, Magazines, Arsenals, dock-Yards, and other needful Buildings;—And

To make all Laws which shall be necessary and proper for carrying into Execution the foregoing Powers, and all other Powers vested by this Constitution in the Government of the United States, or in any Department or Officer thereof.

Section 9 *The Migration or Importation of such Persons as any of the States now existing shall think proper to admit, shall not be prohibited by the Congress prior to the Year one thousand eight hundred and eight but a tax or duty may be imposed on such Importation, not exceeding ten dollars for each Person.*

The privilege of the Writ of Habeas Corpus shall not be suspended, unless when in Cases of Rebellion or Invasion the public Safety may require it.

No Bill of Attainder or ex post facto Law shall be passed.

No capitation, or other direct, Tax shall be laid, unless in Proportion to the Census or Enumeration herein before directed to be taken.*

No Tax or Duty shall be laid on Articles exported from any State.

No Preference shall be given by any Regulation of Commerce or Revenue to the Ports of one State over those of another: nor shall Vessels bound to, or from, one State, be obliged to enter, clear, or pay Duties in another.

No Money shall be drawn from the Treasury, but in Consequence of Appropriations made by law; and a regular Statement and Account of the Receipts and Expenditures of all public Money shall be published from time to time.

No Title of Nobility shall be granted by the United States: And no Person holding any Office of Profit or Trust under them, shall, without the Consent of the Congress, accept of any present, Emolument, Office, or Title, of any kind whatever, from any King, Prince, or foreign State.

Section 10 No State shall enter into any Treaty, Alliance, or Confederation; grant Letters of Marque and Reprisal; coin Money; emit Bills of Credit; make any Thing but gold and silver Coin a Tender in Payment of Debts; pass any Bill of Attainder, ex post facto Law, or Law impairing the Obligation of Contracts, or grant any Title of Nobility.

No State shall, without the Consent of the Congress, lay any Imposts or Duties on Imports or Exports, except what may be absolutely necessary for executing its inspection Laws: and the net Produce of all Duties and Imposts, laid by any State on Imports or Exports, shall be for the Use of the Treasury of the United States; and all such Laws shall be subject to the Revision and Control of the Congress.

No State shall, without the Consent of the Congress, lay any duty of Tonnage, keep Troops, or Ships of War in time of Peace, enter into any Agreement or Compact with another State, or with a foreign Power, or engage in War, unless actually invaded, or in such imminent Danger as will not admit of delay.

Article II

Section 1 The executive Power shall be vested in a President of the United States of America. He shall hold his Office during the Term of four Years, and, together with the Vice President, chosen for the same Term, be elected, as follows:

Each State shall appoint, in such Manner as the Legislature thereof may direct, a Number of Electors, equal to the whole Number of Senators and Representatives to which the State may be entitled in the Congress; but no Senator or Representative, or Person holding an Office of Trust or Profit under the United States, shall be appointed an Elector.

The Electors shall meet in their respective States, and vote by Ballot for two Persons, of whom one at least shall not be an Inhabitant of the same State with themselves. And they shall make a List of all the Persons voted for, and of the Number of Votes for each; which List they shall sign and certify, and transmit sealed to the Seat of the Government of the United States, directed to the President of the Senate. The President of the Senate shall, in the Presence of the Senate and House of Representatives, open all the Certificates, and the Votes shall then be counted. The Person having the greatest Number of Votes shall be the President, if such Number be a Majority of the whole Number of Electors appointed; and if there be more than one who have such Majority, and have an equal Number of Votes, then the House of Representatives shall immediately chuse by Ballot one of them for President; and if no Person have a Majority, then from the five highest on the List the said House shall in like Manner chuse the President. But in chusing the President, the Votes shall be taken by States, the Representation from each State having one Vote; a quorum for this Purpose shall consist of a Member or Members from two thirds of the States, and a Majority of all the States shall be necessary to a Choice. In every Case, after the Choice of the President, the Person having the greatest Number of Votes of the Electors shall be the Vice President. But if there should remain two or more who have equal Votes, the Senate shall chuse from them by Ballot the Vice President.

The Congress may determine the Time of chusing the Electors, and the Day on which they shall give their Votes; which Day shall be the same throughout the United States.

No Person except a natural born Citizen, or a Citizen of the United States, at the time of the Adoption of this Constitution, shall be eligible to the Office of President; neither shall any Person be eligible to that Office who shall not have at-

---

*Changed by the Sixteenth Amendment.

*Superseded by the Twelfth Amendment.

tained to the Age of thirty five Years, and been fourteen Years a Resident within the United States.

In Case of the Removal of the President from Office, or of his Death, Resignation, or Inability to discharge the Powers and Duties of the said Office, the same shall devolve on the Vice President, *and the Congress may by Law provide for the Case of Removal, Death, Resignation, or Inability, both of the President and Vice President, declaring what Officer shall then act as President, and such Officer shall act accordingly, until the Disability be removed, or a President shall be elected.**

The President shall, at stated Times, receive for his Services a Compensation, which shall neither be increased nor diminished during the Period for which he shall have been elected, and he shall not receive within that Period any other Emolument from the United States, or any of them.

Before he enter on the Execution of his Office, he shall take the following Oath or Affirmation:—"I do solemnly swear (or affirm) that I will faithfully execute the Office of President of the United States, and will to the best of my Ability, preserve, protect and defend the Constitution of the United States."

Section 2 The President shall be Commander in Chief of the Army and Navy of the United States, and of the Militia of the several States, when called into the actual Service of the United States; he may require the Opinion, in writing, of the principal Officer in each of the executive Departments, upon any Subject relating to the Duties of their respective Offices, and he shall have Power to Grant Reprieves and Pardons for Offences against the United States, except in Cases of Impeachment.

He shall have Power, by and with the Advice and Consent of the Senate, to make Treaties, provided two thirds of the Senators present concur; and he shall nominate, and by and with the Advice and Consent of the Senate, shall appoint Ambassadors, other public Ministers and Consuls, Judges of the supreme Court, and all other Officers of the United States, whose Appointments are not herein otherwise provided for, and which shall be established by Law: but the Congress may by Law vest the Appointment of such inferior Officers, as they think proper, in the President alone, in the Courts of Law, or in the Heads of Departments.

The President shall have Power to fill up all Vacancies that may happen during the Recess of the Senate, by granting Commissions which shall expire at the End of their next Session.

Section 3 He shall from time to time give to the Congress Information of the State of the Union, and recommend to their Consideration such Measures as he shall judge necessary and expedient; he may, on extraordinary Occasions, convene both Houses, or either of them, and in Case of Disagreement between them, with Respect to the Time of Adjournment, he may adjourn them to such Time as he shall think proper; he shall receive Ambassadors and other public Ministers; he shall take Care that the Laws be faithfully executed, and shall Commission all the Officers of the United States.

Section 4 The President, Vice President and all civil Officers of the United States, shall be removed from Office on Impeachment for, and Conviction of, Treason, Bribery, or other high Crimes and Misdemeanors.

Article III

Section 1 The judicial Power of the United States, shall be vested in one supreme Court, and in such inferior Courts as the Congress may from time to time ordain and establish. The Judges, both of the supreme and inferior Courts, shall hold their Offices during good Behaviour, and shall, at stated Times, receive for their Services a Compensation, which shall not be diminished during their Continuance in Office.

Section 2 The judicial Power shall extend to all Cases, in Law and Equity, arising under this Constitution, the Laws of the United States, and Treaties made, or which shall be made, under their Authority;—to all Cases affecting Ambassadors, other public Ministers and Consuls;—to all Cases of admiralty and maritime Jurisdiction;—to Controversies to which the United States shall be a Party;—to Controversies between two or more States;—*between a State and Citizens of another State;**—between Citizens of different States;—between Citizens of the same State claiming Lands under Grants of different States, and between a State, or the Citizens thereof, and foreign States, Citizens or Subjects.

In all Cases affecting Ambassadors, other public Ministers and Consuls, and those in which a State shall be Party, the supreme Court shall have original Jurisdiction. In all the other Cases before mentioned, the supreme Court shall have appellate Jurisdiction, both as to Law and Fact, with such Exceptions, and under such Regulations as the Congress shall make.

The trial of all Crimes, except in Cases of Impeachment, shall be by Jury; and such Trial shall be held in the State where said Crimes shall have been committed; but when not committed within any State, the Trial shall be at such Place or Places as the Congress may by Law have directed.

Section 3 Treason against the United States, shall consist only in levying War against them, or in adhering to their Enemies, giving them Aid and Comfort. No Person shall be convicted of Treason unless on the Testimony of two Witnesses to the same overt Act, or on Confession in open Court.

The Congress shall have Power to declare the Punishment of Treason, but no Attainder of Treason shall work Corruption of Blood, or Forefeiture except during the Life of the Person attainted.

Article IV

Section 1 Full Faith and Credit shall be given in each State to the public Acts, Records, and judicial Proceedings of every other State. And the Congress may by general Laws prescribe the Manner in which such Acts, Records, and Proceedings shall be proved, and the Effect thereof.

Section 2 The Citizens of each State shall be entitled to all Privileges and Immunities of Citizens in the several States.

---

*Modified by the Twenty-Fifth Amendment.

*Restricted by the Eleventh Amendment.

A Person charged in any State with Treason, Felony, or other Crime, who shall flee from Justice, and be found in another State, shall on demand of the executive Authority of the State from which he fled, be delivered up, to be removed to the State having Jurisdiction of the Crime.

No Person held to Service or Labour in one State, under the Laws thereof, escaping into another, shall, in Consequence of any Law or Regulation therein, be discharged from such Service or Labour, but shall be delivered up on Claim of the Party to whom such Service or Labour may be due.*

Section 3 New States may be admitted by the Congress into this Union; but no new State shall be formed or erected within the Jurisdiction of any other State; nor any State be formed by the Junction of two or more States, or parts of States, without the Consent of the Legislatures of the States concerned as well as of the Congress.

The Congress shall have Power to dispose of and make all needful Rules and Regulations respecting the Territory or other Property belonging to the United States; and nothing in this Constitution shall be so construed as to Prejudice any Claims of the United States, or of any particular State.

Section 4 The United States shall guarantee to every State in this Union a Republican Form of Government, and shall protect each of them against Invasion; and on Application of the Legislature, or of the Executive (when the Legislature cannot be convened) against domestic Violence.

Article V

The Congress, whenever two thirds of both Houses shall deem it necessary, shall propose Amendments to this Constitution, or, on the Application of the Legislatures of two thirds of the several States, shall call a Convention for proposing Amendments, which, in either Case, shall be valid to all Intents and Purposes, as Part of this Constitution, when ratified by the Legislatures of three fourths of the several States, or by Conventions in three fourths thereof, as the one or the other Mode of Ratification may be proposed by the Congress; Pro-

vided that no Amendment which may be made prior to the Year One thousand eight hundred and eight shall in any Manner affect the first and fourth Clauses in the Ninth Section of the first Article; and that no State, without its Consent, shall be deprived of its equal Suffrage in the Senate.

Article VI

All Debts contracted and Engagements entered into, before the Adoption of this Constitution, shall be as valid against the United States under this Constitution, as under the Confederation.

This Constitution, and the Laws of the United States which shall be made in Pursuance thereof; and all Treaties made, or which shall be made, under the Authority of the United States, shall be the supreme Law of the Land; and the Judges in every State shall be bound thereby, any Thing in the Constitution or Laws of any State to the Contrary notwithstanding.

The Senators and Representatives before mentioned, and the Members of the several State Legislatures, and all executive and judicial Officers, both of the United States and of the several States, shall be bound by Oath or Affirmation, to support this Constitution; but no religious Test shall ever be required as a Qualification to any Office or public Trust under the United States.

Article VII

The Ratification of the Conventions of nine States shall be sufficient for the Establishment of this Constitution between the States so ratifying the Same.

Done in Convention by the Unanimous Consent of the States present the Seventeenth Day of September in the Year of our Lord one thousand seven hundred and Eighty seven and of the Independence of the United States of America the Twelfth. In Witness whereof We have hereunto subscribed our Names.

---

*Superseded by the Twelfth Amendment.

Go. Washington
President and deputy from Virginia

New Hampshire	*New Jersey*	*Delaware*	*North Carolina*
John Langdon	Wil. Livingston	Geo. Read	Wm. Blount
Nicholas Gilman	David Brearley	Gunning Bedford jun	Richd. Dobbs Spaight
	Wm. Paterson	John Dickenson	Hu Williamson
Massachusetts	Jona. Dayton	Richard Bassett	
Nathaniel Gorham		Jaco. Broom	*South Carolina*
Rufus King	*Pennsylvania*		J. Rutledge
	B. Franklin	*Maryland*	Charles Cotesworth Pickney
Connecticut	Thomas Mifflin	James McHenry	Pierce Butler
Wm. Saml. Johnson	Robt. Morris	Dan. of St. Thos. Jenifer	
Roger Sherman	Geo. Clymer	Danl. Carroll	*Georgia*
	Thos. FitzSimons		William Few
New York	Jared Ingersoll	*Virginia*	Abr. Baldwin
Alexander Hamilton	James Wilson	John Blair	
	Gouv. Morris	James Madison, Jr.	

Amendments to the Constitution

★   ★   ★

Amendment I [1791]*

Congress shall make no law respecting an establishment of religion, or prohibiting the free exercise thereof; or abridging the freedom of speech, or of the press; or the right of the people peaceably to assemble, and to petition the Government for a redress of grievances.

Amendment II [1791]

A well regulated Militia, being necessary to the security of a free State, the right of the people to keep and bear Arms shall not be infringed.

Amendment III [1791]

No Soldier shall, in time of peace, be quartered in any house, without the consent of the Owner, nor in time of war, but in a manner to be prescribed by law.

Amendment IV [1791]

The right of the people to be secure in their persons, houses, papers, and effects, against unreasonable searches and seizures, shall not be violated, and no Warrants shall issue, but upon probable cause, supported by Oath or affirmation, and particularly describing the place to be searched, and the persons or things to be seized.

Amendment V [1791]

No person shall be held to answer for a capital or otherwise infamous crime, unless on a presentment or indictment of a Grand Jury, except in cases arising in the land or naval forces, or in the Militia, when in actual service in time of War or pub-

lic danger; nor shall any person be subject for the same offence to be twice put in jeopardy of life or limb; nor shall be compelled in any criminal case to be a witness against himself, nor be deprived of life, liberty, or property, without due process of law; nor shall private property be taken for public use, without just compensation.

Amendment VI [1791]

In all criminal prosecutions, the accused shall enjoy the right to a speedy and public trial, by an impartial jury of the State and district wherein the crime shall have been committed, which district shall have been previously ascertained by law, and to be informed of the nature and cause of the accusation; to be confronted with the witnesses against him; to have compulsory process for obtaining witnesses in his favor, and to have the Assistance of Counsel for his defence.

Amendment VII [1791]

In suits at common law, where the value in controversy shall exceed twenty dollars, the right of trail by jury shall be preserved, and no fact tried by a jury, shall be otherwise reexamined in any Court of the United States, than according to the Rules of the common law.

Amendment VIII [1791]

Excessive bail shall not be required, nor excessive fines imposed, nor cruel and unusual punishments inflicted.

Amendment IX [1791]

The enumeration in the Constitution, of certain rights, shall not be construed to deny or disparage others retained by the people.

---

*The dates in brackets indicate when the amendments were ratified.

Amendment X [1791]

The powers not delegated to the United States by the Constitution, nor prohibited by it to the States, are reserved to the States respectively, or to the people.

Amendment XI [1798]

The Judicial power of the United States shall not be construed to extend to any suit in law or equity, commenced or prosecuted against one of the United States by Citizens of another State, or by Citizens or subjects of any foreign state.

Amendment XII [1804]

The Electors shall meet in their respective States and vote by ballot for President and Vice-President, one of whom, at least, shall not be an inhabitant of the same State with themselves; they shall name in their ballots the person voted for as President, and in distinct ballots the person voted for as Vice-President, and they shall make distinct lists of all persons voted for as President, and of all persons voted for as Vice-President, and of the number of votes for each, which lists they shall sign and certify, and transmit sealed to the seat of the government of the United States, directed to the President of the Senate;—the President of the Senate shall, in the presence of the Senate and House of Representatives, open all the certificates and the votes shall then be counted;—The person having the greatest number of votes for President, shall be the President, if such number be a majority of the whole number of Electors appointed; and if no person have such majority, then from the persons having the highest numbers not exceeding three on the list of those voted for as President, the House of Representatives shall choose immediately, by ballot, the President. But in choosing the President, the votes shall be taken by States, the representation from each State having one vote; a quorum for this purpose shall consist of a member or members from two-thirds of the States, and a majority of all the States shall be necessary to a choice. And if the House of Representatives shall not choose a President whenever the right of choice shall devolve upon them, before *the fourth day of March* next following, then the Vice-President shall act as President, as in the case of the death or other constitutional disability of the President.*—The person having the greatest number of votes as Vice-President, shall be the Vice-President, if such number be a majority of the whole number of Electors appointed, and if no person have a majority, then from the two highest numbers on the list, the Senate shall choose the Vice-President; a quorum for the purpose shall consist of two-thirds of the whole number of Senators, and a majority of the whole number shall be necessary to a choice. But no person constitutionally ineligible to the office of President shall be eligible to that of Vice-President of the United States.

Amendment XIII [1865]

Section 1 Neither slavery nor involuntary servitude, except as a punishment for crime whereof the party shall have been duly convicted, shall exist within the United States, or any place subject to their jurisdiction.

*Superseded by Section 3 of the Twentieth Amendment.

Section 2 Congress shall have power to enforce this article by appropriate legislation.

Amendment XIV [1868]

Section 1 All persons born or naturalized in the United States, and subject to the jurisdiction thereof, are citizens of the United States and of the State wherein they reside. No State shall make or enforce any law which shall abridge the privileges or immunities of citizens of the United States; nor shall any State deprive any person of life, liberty, or property, without due process of law; nor deny to any person within its jurisdiction the equal protection of the laws.

Section 2 Representatives shall be apportioned among the several States according to their respective numbers, counting the whole number of persons in each State, excluding Indians not taxed. But when the right to vote at any election for the choice of electors for President and Vice-President of the United States, Representatives in Congress, the Executive and Judicial officers of a State, or the members of the Legislature thereof, is denied to any of the male inhabitants of such State, being twenty-one years of age, and citizens of the United States, or in any way abridged, except for participation in rebellion, or other crime, the basis of representation therein shall be reduced in the proportion which the number of such male citizens shall bear to the whole number of male citizens twenty-one years of age in such State.

Section 3 No person shall be a Senator or Representative in Congress, or elector of President and Vice-President, or hold any office, civil or military, under the United States, or under any State, who, having previously taken an oath, as a member of Congress, or as an officer of the United States, or as a member of any State legislature, or as an executive or judicial officer of any State, to support the Constitution of the United States, shall have engaged in insurrection or rebellion against the same, or given aid or comfort to the enemies thereof. Congress may by a vote of two-thirds of each house, remove such disability.

Section 4 The validity of the public debt of the United States, authorized by law, including debts incurred for payment of pensions and bounties for services in suppressing insurrection or rebellion, shall not be questioned. But neither the United States nor any State shall assume or pay any debt or obligation incurred in aid of insurrection or rebellion against the United States, or any claim for the loss or emancipation of any slave; but all such debts, obligations and claims shall be held illegal and void.

Section 5 The Congress shall have power to enforce, by appropriate legislation, the provisions of this article.

Amendment XV [1870]

Section 1 The right of citizens of the United States to vote shall not be denied or abridged by the United States or by any State on account of race, color, or previous condition of servitude—

Section 2 The Congress shall have power to enforce this article by appropriate legislation.

Amendment XVI [1913]

The Congress shall have power to lay and collect taxes on incomes, from whatever source derived, without apportionment among the several States, and without regard to any census or enumeration.

Amendment XVII [1913]

The Senate of the United States shall be composed of two Senators from each State, elected by the people thereof, for six years; and each Senator shall have one vote. The electors in each State shall have the qualifications requisite for electors of the most numerous branch of the State legislatures.

When vacancies happen in the representation of any State in the Senate, the executive authority of such State shall issue writs of election to fill such vacancies: *Provided*, That the legislature of any State may empower the executive thereof to make temporary appointments until the people fill the vacancies by election as the legislature may direct.

This amendment shall not be so construed as to affect the election or term of any Senator chosen before it becomes valid as part of the Constitution.

Amendment XVIII [1919]

Section 1 After one year from the ratification of this article the manufacture, sale, or transportation of intoxicating liquors within, the importation thereof into, or the exportation thereof from the United States and all territory subject to the jurisdiction hereof for beverage purposes hereby prohibited.

Section 2 The Congress and the several States shall have concurrent power to enforce this article by appropriate legislation.

Section 3 This article shall be inoperative unless it shall have been ratified as an amendment to the Constitution by the legislatures of the several States, as provided by the Constitution, within seven years from the date of submission hereof to the States by the Congress.*

Amendment XIX [1920]

The right of citizens of the United States to vote shall not be denied or abridged by the United States or by any State on account of sex.

Congress shall have power to enforce this article by appropriate legislation.

Amendment XX [1933]

Section 1 The terms of the President and Vice-President shall end at noon on the 20th day of January, and the terms of Senators and Representatives at noon on the 3d day of January,

*Repealed by Section 1 of the Twenty-First Amendment

of the years in which such terms would have ended if this article had not been ratified; and the terms of their successors shall then begin.

Section 2 The Congress shall assemble at least once in every year, and such meeting shall begin at noon on the 3d day of January, unless they shall by law appoint a different day.

Section 3 If, at the time fixed for the beginning of the term of the President, the President elect shall have died, the Vice-President elect shall become President. If a President shall not have been chosen before the time fixed for the beginning of his term, or if the President elect shall have failed to qualify, then the Vice-President elect shall act as President until a President shall have qualified; and the Congress may by law provide for the case wherein neither a President elect nor a Vice-President elect shall have qualified, declaring who shall then act as President, or the manner in which one who is to act shall be selected, and such person shall act accordingly until a President or Vice-President shall have qualified.

Section 4 The Congress may by law provide for the case of the death of any of the persons from whom the House of Representatives may choose a President whenever the right of choice shall have devolved upon them, and for the case of the death of any of the persons from whom the Senate may choose a Vice-President whenever the right of choice shall have devolved upon them.

Section 5 Sections 1 and 2 shall take effect on the 15th day of October following the ratification of this article.

Section 6 This article shall be inoperative unless it shall have been ratified as an amendment to the Constitution by the legislatures of three-fourths of the several States within seven years from the date of its submission.

Amendment XXI [1933]

Section 1 The eighteenth article of amendment to the Constitution of the United States is hereby repealed.

Section 2 The transportation or importation into any State, Territory, or possession of the United States for delivery or use therein of intoxicating liquors, in violation of the laws thereof, is hereby prohibited.

Section 3 This article shall be inoperative unless it shall have been ratified as an amendment to the Constitution by conventions in the several States, as provided in the Constitution, within seven years from the date of submission hereof to the States by the Congress.

Amendment XXII [1951]

Section 1 No person shall be elected to the office of President more than twice, and no person who has held the office of President, or acted as President, for more than two years of a term to which some other person was elected President shall be elected to the office of the President more than once. But this Article shall not apply to any person holding the office of

President when this Article was proposed by the Congress, and shall not prevent any person who may be holding the office of President, or acting as President, during the term within which this Article becomes operative from holding the office of the President or acting as President during the remainder of such term.

Section 2 This article shall be inoperative unless it shall have been ratified as an amendment to the Constitution by the legislatures of three-fourths of the several States within seven years from the date of its submission to the States by the Congress.

Amendment XXIII [1961]

Section 1 The District constituting the seat of Government of the United States shall appoint in such manner as the Congress may direct:

A number of electors of President and Vice-President equal to the whole number of Senators and Representatives in Congress to which the District would be entitled if it were a State, but in no event more than the least populous State; they shall be in addition to those appointed by the States, but they shall be considered, for the purposes of the election of President and Vice-President, to be electors appointed by a State; and they shall meet in the District and perform such duties as provided by the twelfth article of amendment.

Section 2 The Congress shall have power to enforce this article by appropriate legislation.

Amendment XXIV [1964]

Section 1 The right of citizens of the United States to vote in any primary or other election for President or Vice-President, for electors for President or Vice-President, or for Senator or Representative in Congress, shall not be denied or abridged by the United States or any State by reason of failure to pay any poll tax or other tax.

Section 2 The Congress shall have power to enforce this article by appropriate legislation.

Amendment XXV [1967]

Section 1 In case of the removal of the President from office or of his death or resignation, the Vice-President shall become President.

Section 2 Whenever there is a vacancy in the office of the Vice-President, the President shall nominate a Vice-President who shall take office upon confirmation by a majority vote of both houses of Congress.

Section 3 Whenever the President transmits to the President pro tempore of the Senate and the Speaker of the House of Representatives his written declaration that he is unable to discharge the powers and duties of his office, and until he transmits to them a written declaration to the contrary, such powers and duties shall be discharged by the Vice-President as Acting President.

Section 4 Whenever the Vice-President and a majority of either the principal officers of the executive departments or of such other body as Congress may by law provide, transmit to the President pro tempore of the Senate and the Speaker of the House of Representatives their written declaration that the President is unable to discharge the powers and duties of his office, the Vice-President shall immediately assume the powers and duties of the office as Acting President.

Thereafter, when the President transmits to the President pro tempore of the Senate and the Speaker of the House of Representatives his written declaration that no inability exists, he shall resume the powers and duties of his office unless the Vice-President and a majority of either the principal officers of the executive department or of such other body as Congress may by law provide, transmit within four days to the President pro tempore of the Senate and the Speaker of the House of Representatives their written declaration that the President is unable to discharge the powers and duties of his office. Thereupon Congress shall decide the issue, assembling within forty-eight hours for that purpose if not in session. If the Congress, within twenty-one days after receipt of the latter written declaration, or, if Congress is not in session, within twenty-one days after Congress is required to assemble, determines by two-thirds vote of both Houses that the President is unable to discharge the powers and duties of his office, the Vice-President shall continue to discharge the same as Acting President; otherwise, the President shall resume the powers and duties of his office.

Amendment XXVI [1971]

Section 1 The right of citizens of the United States, who are eighteen years of age or older, to vote shall not be denied or abridged by the United States or by any state on account of age.

Section 2 The Congress shall have power to enforce this article by appropriate legislation.

Amendment XXVII [1992]

No law varying the compensation for services of the Senators and Representatives, shall take effect, until an election of Representatives shall have intervened.

The American Nation

Admission of States into the Union

State	Date of Admission	State	Date of Admission	State	Date of Admission
1. Delaware	December 7, 1787	18. Louisiana	April 30, 1812	35. West Virginia	June 20, 1863
2. Pennsylvania	December 12, 1787	19. Indiana	December 11, 1816	36. Nevada	October 31, 1864
3. New Jersey	December 18, 1787	20. Mississippi	December 10, 1817	37. Nebraska	March 1, 1867
4. Georgia	January 2, 1788	21. Illinois	December 3, 1818	38. Colorado	August 1, 1876
5. Connecticut	January 9, 1788	22. Alabama	December 14, 1819	39. North Dakota	November 2, 1889
6. Massachusetts	February 6, 1788	23. Maine	March 15, 1820	40. South Dakota	November 2, 1889
7. Maryland	April 28, 1788	24. Missouri	August 10, 1821	41. Montana	November 8, 1889
8. South Carolina	May 23, 1788	25. Arkansas	June 15, 1836	42. Washington	November 11, 1889
9. New Hampshire	June 21, 1788	26. Michigan	January 26, 1837	43. Idaho	July 3, 1890
10. Virginia	June 25, 1788	27. Florida	March 3, 1845	44. Wyoming	July 10, 1890
11. New York	July 26, 1788	28. Texas	December 29, 1845	45. Utah	January 4, 1896
12. North Carolina	November 21, 1789	29. Iowa	December 28, 1846	46. Oklahoma	November 16, 1907
13. Rhode Island	May 29, 1790	30. Wisconsin	May 29, 1848	47. New Mexico	January 6, 1912
14. Vermont	March 4, 1791	31. California	September 9, 1850	48. Arizona	February 14, 1912
15. Kentucky	June 1, 1792	32. Minnesota	May 11, 1858	49. Alaska	January 3, 1959
16. Tennessee	June 1, 1796	33. Oregon	February 14, 1859	50. Hawaii	August 21, 1959
17. Ohio	March 1, 1803	34. Kansas	January 29, 1861		

Territorial Expansion

Territory	Date Acquired	Square Miles	How Acquired
Original states and territories	1783	888,685	Treaty of Paris
Louisiana Purchase	1803	827,192	Purchased from France
Florida	1819	72,003	Adams-Onís Treaty
Texas	1845	390,143	Annexation of independent country
Oregon	1846	285,580	Oregon Boundary Treaty
Mexican cession	1848	529,017	Treaty of Guadalupe Hidalgo
Gadsden Purchase	1853	29,640	Purchased from Mexico
Midway Islands	1867	2	Annexation of uninhabited islands
Alaska	1867	589,757	Purchased from Russia
Hawaii	1898	6,450	Annexation of independent country
Wake Island	1898	3	Annexation of uninhabited island
Puerto Rico	1899	3,435	Treaty of Paris
Guam	1899	212	Treaty of Paris
The Philippines	1899–1946	115,600	Treaty of Paris; granted independence
American Samoa	1900	76	Treaty with Germany and Great Britain
Panama Canal Zone	1904–1978	553	Hay–Bunau-Varilla Treaty
U.S. Virgin Islands	1917	133	Purchased from Denmark
Trust Territory of the Pacific Islands*	1947	717	United Nations Trusteeship

*A number of these islands have recently been granted independence: Federated States of Micronesia, 1990; Marshall Islands, 1991; Palau, 1994.

Presidential Elections

Year	Candidates	Parties	Percent of Popular Vote	Electoral Vote	Percent Voter Participation
1789	**George Washington**	No party designations	*	69	
	John Adams†			34	
	Other candidates			35	
1792	**George Washington**	No party designations		132	
	John Adams			77	
	George Clinton			50	
	Other candidates			5	
1796	**John Adams**	Federalist		71	
	Thomas Jefferson	Democratic-Republican		68	
	Thomas Pinckney	Federalist		59	
	Aaron Burr	Democratic-Republican		30	
	Other candidates			48	
1800	**Thomas Jefferson**	Democratic-Republican		73	
	Aaron Burr	Democratic-Republican		73	
	John Adams	Federalist		65	
	Charles C. Pinckney	Federalist		64	
	John Jay	Federalist		1	
1804	**Thomas Jefferson**	Democratic-Republican		162	
	Charles C. Pinckney	Federalist		14	
1808	**James Madison**	Democratic-Republican		122	
	Charles C. Pinckney	Federalist		47	
	George Clinton	Democratic-Republican		6	
1812	**James Madison**	Democratic-Republican		128	
	DeWitt Clinton	Federalist		89	
1816	**James Monroe**	Democratic-Republican		183	
	Rufus King	Federalist		34	
1820	**James Monroe**	Democratic-Republican		231	
	John Quincy Adams	Independent Republican		1	
1824	**John Quincy Adams**	Democratic-Republican	30.5	84	26.9
	Andrew Jackson	Democratic-Republican	43.1	99	
	Henry Clay	Democratic-Republican	13.2	37	
	William H. Crawford	Democratic-Republican	13.1	41	
1828	**Andrew Jackson**	Democratic	56.0	178	57.6
	John Quincy Adams	National Republican	44.0	83	
1832	**Andrew Jackson**	Democratic	54.5	219	55.4
	Henry Clay	National Republican	37.5	49	
	William Wirt	Anti-Masonic	8.0	7	
	John Floyd	Democratic	‡	11	
1836	**Martin Van Buren**	Democratic	50.9	170	57.8
	William H. Harrison	Whig		73	
	Hugh L. White	Whig		26	
	Daniel Webster	Whig	49.1	14	
	W. P. Mangum	Whig		11	
1840	**William H. Harrison**	Whig	53.1	234	80.2
	Martin Van Buren	Democratic	46.9	60	

*Prior to 1824, most presidential electors were chosen by state legislators rather than by popular vote.
†Before the Twelfth Amendment was passed in 1804, the electoral college voted for two presidential candidates; the runner-up became vice-president.
‡Percentages below 2.5 percent have been omitted. Hence the percentage of popular vote might not total 100 percent.

Year	Candidates	Parties	Percent of Popular Vote	Electoral Vote	Percent Voter Participation
1844	**James K. Polk**	Democratic	49.6	170	78.9
	Henry Clay	Whig	48.1	105	
	James G. Birney	Liberty	2.3		
1848	**Zachary Taylor**	Whig	47.4	163	72.7
	Lewis Cass	Democratic	42.5	127	
	Martin Van Buren	Free Soil	10.1		
1852	**Franklin Pierce**	Democratic	50.9	254	69.6
	Winfield Scott	Whig	44.1	42	
	John P. Hale	Free Soil	5.0		
1856	**James Buchanan**	Democratic	45.3	174	78.9
	John C. Frémont	Republican	33.1	114	
	Millard Fillmore	American	21.6	8	
1860	**Abraham Lincoln**	Republican	39.8	180	81.2
	Stephen A. Douglas	Democratic	29.5	12	
	John C. Breckinridge	Democratic	18.1	72	
	John Bell	Constitutional Union	12.6	39	
1864	**Abraham Lincoln**	Republican	55.0	212	73.8
	George B. McClellan	Democratic	45.0	21	
1868	**Ulysses S. Grant**	Republican	52.7	214	78.1
	Horatio Seymour	Democratic	47.3	80	
1872	**Ulysses S. Grant**	Republican	55.6	286	71.3
	Horace Greeley	Democratic	43.9		
1876	**Rutherford B. Hayes**	Republican	48.0	185	81.8
	Samuel J. Tilden	Democratic	51.0	184	
1880	**James A. Garfield**	Republican	48.5	214	79.4
	Winfield S. Hancock	Democratic	48.1	155	
	James B. Weaver	Greenback-Labor	3.4		
1884	**Grover Cleveland**	Democratic	48.5	219	77.5
	James G. Blaine	Republican	48.2	182	
1888	**Benjamin Harrison**	Republican	47.9	233	79.3
	Grover Cleveland	Democratic	48.6	168	
1892	**Grover Cleveland**	Democratic	46.1	277	74.7
	Benjamin Harrison	Republican	43.0	145	
	James B. Weaver	People's	8.5	22	
1896	**William McKinley**	Republican	51.1	271	79.3
	William J. Bryan	Democratic	47.7	176	
1900	**William McKinley**	Republican	51.7	292	73.2
	William J. Bryan	Democratic; Populist	45.5	155	
1904	**Theodore Roosevelt**	Republican	57.4	336	65.2
	Alton B. Parker	Democratic	37.6	140	
	Eugene V. Debs	Socialist	3.0		
1908	**William H. Taft**	Republican	51.6	321	65.4
	William J. Bryan	Democratic	43.1	162	
	Eugene V. Debs	Socialist	2.8		
1912	**Woodrow Wilson**	Democratic	41.9	435	58.8
	Theodore Roosevelt	Progressive	27.4	88	
	William H. Taft	Republican	23.2	8	
	Eugene V. Debs	Socialist	6.0		

Year	Candidates	Parties	Percent of Popular Vote	Electoral Vote	Percent Voter Participation
1916	Woodrow Wilson	Democratic	49.4	277	61.6
	Charles E. Hughes	Republican	46.2	254	
	A. L. Benson	Socialist	3.2		
1920	Warren G. Harding	Republican	60.4	404	49.2
	James M. Cox	Democratic	34.2	127	
	Eugene V. Debs	Socialist	3.4		
1924	Calvin Coolidge	Republican	54.0	382	48.9
	John W. Davis	Democratic	28.8	136	
	Robert M. LaFollette	Progressive	16.6	13	
1928	Herbert C. Hoover	Republican	58.2	444	56.9
	Alfred E. Smith	Democratic	40.9	87	
1932	Franklin D. Roosevelt	Democratic	57.4	472	56.9
	Herbert C. Hoover	Republican	39.7	59	
1936	Franklin D. Roosevelt	Democratic	60.8	523	61.0
	Alfred M. Landon	Republican	36.5	8	
1940	Franklin D. Roosevelt	Democratic	54.8	449	62.5
	Wendell L. Willkie	Republican	44.8	82	
1944	Franklin D. Roosevelt	Democratic	53.5	432	55.9
	Thomas E. Dewey	Republican	46.0	99	
1948	Harry S. Truman	Democratic	49.6	303	53.0
	Thomas E. Dewey	Republican	45.1	189	
1952	Dwight D. Eisenhower	Republican	55.1	442	63.3
	Adlai E. Stevenson	Democratic	44.4	89	
1956	Dwight D. Eisenhower	Republican	57.6	457	60.6
	Adlai E. Stevenson	Democratic	42.1	73	
1960	John F. Kennedy	Democratic	49.7	303	64.0
	Richard M. Nixon	Republican	49.5	219	
1964	Lyndon B. Johnson	Democratic	61.1	486	61.7
	Barry M. Goldwater	Republican	38.5	52	
1968	Richard M. Nixon	Republican	43.4	301	60.6
	Hubert H. Humphrey	Democratic	42.7	191	
	George C. Wallace	American Independent	13.5	46	
1972	Richard M. Nixon	Republican	60.7	520	55.5
	George S. McGovern	Democratic	37.5	17	
1976	Jimmy Carter	Democratic	50.1	297	54.3
	Gerald R. Ford	Republican	48.0	240	
1980	Ronald W. Reagan	Republican	50.7	489	53.0
	Jimmy Carter	Democratic	41.0	49	
	John B. Anderson	Independent	6.6	0	
1984	Ronald W. Reagan	Republican	58.4	525	52.9
	Walter F. Mondale	Democratic	41.6	13	
1988	George H. W. Bush	Republican	53.4	426	50.1
	Michael Dukakis	Democratic	45.6	111*	
1992	Bill Clinton	Democratic	43.7	370	54.0
	George H. W. Bush	Republican	38.0	168	
	H. Ross Perot	Independent	19.0	0	

*One Dukakis elector cast a vote for Lloyd Bentsen.

Supreme Court Justices

Name	Terms of Service	Appointed by	Name	Terms of Service	Appointed by
John Jay*, N.Y.	1789–1795	Washington	Joseph McKenna, Cal.	1898–1925	McKinley
James Wilson, Pa.	1789–1798	Washington	Oliver W. Holmes, Mass.	1902–1932	T. Roosevelt
John Rutledge, S.C.	1790–1791	Washington	William R. Day, Ohio	1903–1922	T. Roosevelt
William Cushing, Mass.	1790–1810	Washington	William H. Moody, Mass.	1906–1910	T. Roosevelt
John Blair, Va.	1790–1796	Washington	Horace H. Lurton, Tenn.	1910–1914	Taft
James Iredell, N.C.	1790–1799	Washington	Charles E. Hughes, N.Y.	1910–1916	Taft
Thomas Johnson, Md.	1792–1793	Washington	**Edward D. White**, La.	1910–1921	Taft
William Paterson, N.J.	1793–1806	Washington	Willis Van Devanter, Wy.	1911–1937	Taft
John Rutledge, S.C.	1795	Washington	Joseph R. Lamar, Ga.	1911–1916	Taft
Samuel Chase, Md.	1796–1811	Washington	Mahlon Pitney, N.J.	1912–1922	Taft
Oliver Ellsworth, Conn.	1796–1800	Washington	James C. McReynolds, Tenn.	1914–1941	Wilson
Bushrod Washington, Va.	1799–1829	J. Adams	Louis D. Brandeis, Mass.	1916–1939	Wilson
Alfred Moore, N.C.	1800–1804	J. Adams	John H. Clarke, Ohio	1916–1922	Wilson
John Marshall, Va.	1801–1835	J. Adams	**William H. Taft**, Conn.	1921–1930	Harding
William Johnson, S.C.	1804–1834	Jefferson	George Sutherland, Utah	1922–1938	Harding
Brockholst Livingston, N.Y.	1807–1823	Jefferson	Pierce Butler, Minn.	1923–1939	Harding
Thomas Todd, Ky.	1807–1826	Jefferson	Edward T. Sanford, Tenn.	1923–1930	Harding
Gabriel Duvall, Md.	1811–1835	Madison	Harlan F. Stone, N.Y.	1925–1941	Coolidge
Joseph Story, Mass.	1812–1845	Madison	**Charles E. Hughes**, N.Y.	1930–1941	Hoover
Smith Thompson, N.Y.	1823–1843	Monroe	Owen J. Roberts, Penn.	1930–1945	Hoover
Robert Trimble, Ky.	1826–1828	J. Q. Adams	Benjamin N. Cardozo, N.Y.	1932–1938	Hoover
John McLean, Ohio	1830–1861	Jackson	Hugo L. Black, Ala.	1937–1971	F. Roosevelt
Henry Baldwin, Pa.	1830–1844	Jackson	Stanley F. Reed, Ky.	1938–1957	F. Roosevelt
James M. Wayne, Ga.	1835–1867	Jackson	Felix Frankfurter, Mass.	1939–1962	F. Roosevelt
Roger B. Taney, Md.	1836–1864	Jackson	William O. Douglas, Conn.	1939–1975	F. Roosevelt
Philip P. Barbour, Va.	1836–1841	Jackson	Frank Murphy, Mich.	1940–1949	F. Roosevelt
John Cartron, Tenn.	1837–1865	Van Buren	**Harlan F. Stone**, N.Y.	1941–1946	F. Roosevelt
John McKinley, Ala.	1838–1852	Van Buren	James R. Byrnes, S.C.	1941–1942	F. Roosevelt
Peter V. Daniel, Va.	1842–1860	Van Buren	Robert H. Jackson, N.Y.	1941–1954	F. Roosevelt
Samuel Nelson, N.Y.	1845–1872	Tyler	Wiley B. Rutledge, Iowa	1943–1949	F. Roosevelt
Levi Woodbury, N.H.	1845–1851	Polk	Harold H. Burton, Ohio	1945–1958	Truman
Robert C. Grier, Pa.	1846–1870	Polk	**Frederick M. Vinson**, Ky.	1946–1953	Truman
Benjamin R. Curtis, Mass.	1851–1857	Fillmore	Tom C. Clark, Texas	1949–1967	Truman
John A. Campbell, Ala.	1853–1861	Pierce	Sherman Minton, Ind.	1949–1956	Truman
Nathan Clifford, Me.	1858–1881	Buchanan	**Earl Warren**, Cal.	1953–1969	Eisenhower
Noah H. Swayne, Ohio	1862–1881	Lincoln	John Marshall Harlan, N.Y.	1955–1971	Eisenhower
Samuel F. Miller, Iowa	1862–1890	Lincoln	William J. Brennan, Jr., N.J.	1956–1990	Eisenhower
David Davis, Ill.	1862–1877	Lincoln	Charles E. Whittaker, Mo.	1957–1962	Eisenhower
Stephen J. Field, Cal.	1863–1897	Lincoln	Potter Stewart, Ohio	1958–1981	Eisenhower
Salmon P. Chase, Ohio	1864–1873	Lincoln	Bryon R. White, Colo.	1962–1993	Kennedy
William Strong, Pa.	1870–1880	Grant	Arthur J. Goldberg, Ill.	1962–1965	Kennedy
Joseph P. Bradley, N.J.	1870–1892	Grant	Abe Fortas, Tenn.	1965–1969	Johnson
Ward Hunt, N.Y.	1873–1882	Grant	Thurgood Marshall, Md.	1967–1991	Johnson
Morrison R. Waite, Ohio	1874–1888	Grant	**Warren E. Burger**, Minn.	1969–1986	Nixon
John M. Harlan, Ky.	1877–1911	Hayes	Harry A. Blackmun, Minn.	1970–	Nixon
William B. Woods, Ga.	1881–1887	Hayes	Lewis F. Powell, Jr., Va.	1971–1987	Nixon
Stanley Matthews, Ohio	1881–1889	Garfield	William H. Rehnquist, Ariz.	1971–1986	Nixon
Horace Gray, Mass.	1882–1902	Arthur	John Paul Stevens, Ill.	1975–	Ford
Samuel Blatchford, N.Y.	1882–1893	Arthur	Sandra Day O'Connor, Ariz.	1981–	Reagan
Lucius Q. C. Lamar, Miss.	1888–1893	Cleveland	**William H. Rehnquist**, Ariz.	1986–	Reagan
Melville W. Fuller, Ill.	1888–1910	Cleveland	Antonin Scalia, Va.	1986–	Reagan
David J. Brewer, Kan.	1890–1910	B. Harrison	Anthony M. Kennedy, Cal.	1988–	Reagan
Henry B. Brown, Mich.	1891–1906	B. Harrison	David H. Souter, N.H.	1990	Bush
George Shiras, Jr., Pa.	1892–1903	B. Harrison	Clarence Thomas, Ga.	1991–	Bush
Howell E. Jackson, Tenn.	1893–1895	B. Harrison	Ruth Bader Ginsburg, N.Y.	1993–	Clinton
Edward D. White, La.	1894–1910	Cleveland	Stephen G. Breyer, Mass.	1994–	Clinton
Rufus W. Peckham, N.Y.	1896–1909	Cleveland			

*Chief Justices are printed in bold type.

The American People:
A Demographic Survey

★   ★   ★

A Demographic Profile of the American People

Year	Life Expectancy from Birth		Average Age at First Marriage		Number of Children Under 5 (per 1,000 Women Aged 20–44)	Percent of Women in Paid Employment	Percent of Paid Workers Who Are Female
	White	Black	Male	Female			
1820					1,295	6.2%	7.3%
1830					1,145	6.4	7.4
1840					1,085	8.4	9.6
1850					923	10.1	10.8
1860					929	9.7	10.2
1870					839	13.7	14.8
1880					822	14.7	15.2
1890			26.1	22.0	716	18.2	17.0
1900	47.6	33.0	25.9	21.9	688	21.2	18.1
1910	50.3	35.6	25.1	21.6	643	24.8	20.0
1920	54.9	45.3	24.6	21.2	604	23.9	20.4
1930	61.4	48.1	24.3	21.3	511	24.4	21.9
1940	64.2	53.1	24.3	21.5	429	25.4	24.6
1950	69.1	60.8	22.8	20.3	589	29.1	27.8
1960	70.6	63.6	22.8	20.3	737	34.8	32.3
1970	71.7	65.3	22.5	20.6	530	43.3	38.0
1980	74.4	68.1	24.7	22.0	440	51.5	42.6
1990	76.2	71.4	26.1	23.9	377	57.4	45.2

Source: *Historical Statistics of the United States, Colonial Times to 1970* (1975); *Statistical Abstract of the United States*, 1991.

American Population

Year	Population	Percent Increase	Year	Population	Percent Increase
1610	350	—	1810	7,239,881	36.4
1620	2,300	557.1	1820	9,638,453	33.1
1630	4,600	100.0	1830	12,866,020	33.5
1640	26,600	478.3	1840	17,069,453	32.7
1650	50,400	90.8	1850	23,191,876	35.9
1660	75,100	49.0	1860	31,443,321	35.6
1670	111,900	49.0	1870	39,818,449	26.6
1680	151,500	35.4	1880	50,155,783	26.0
1690	210,400	38.9	1890	62,947,714	25.5
1700	250,900	19.2	1900	75,994,575	20.7
1710	331,700	32.2	1910	91,972,266	21.0
1720	466,200	40.5	1920	105,710,620	14.9
1730	629,400	35.0	1930	122,775,046	16.1
1740	905,600	43.9	1940	131,669,275	7.2
1750	1,170,800	29.3	1950	150,697,361	14.5
1760	1,593,600	36.1	1960	179,323,175	19.0
1770	2,148,100	34.8	1970	203,235,298	13.3
1780	2,780,400	29.4	1980	226,545,805	11.5
1790	3,929,214	41.3	1990	248,709,873	9.8
1800	5,308,483	35.1	1993	259,383,000	4.3

Note: These figures largely ignore the native American population. Census takers never made any effort to count the native American population that lived outside their political jurisdictions and compiled only casual and incomplete enumerations of those living within their jurisdictions until 1890. In that year the federal government attempted a full count of the Indian population: the Census found 125,719 Indians in 1890, compared with only 12,543 in 1870 and 33,985 in 1880.

Source: Historical Statistics of the United States, Colonial Times to 1970 (1975); Statistical Abstract of the United States, 1995.

White/Nonwhite Population

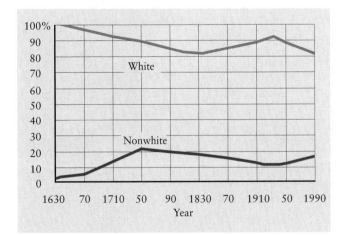

Urban/Rural Population

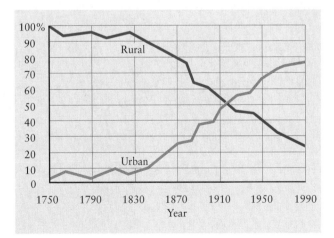

The Ten Largest Cities by Population, 1700–1990

		City	Population			City	Population
1700	1.	Boston	6,700	1910	1.	New York	4,766,883
	2.	New York	4,937*		2.	Chicago	2,185,283
	3.	Philadelphia	4,400†		3.	Philadelphia	1,549,008
					4.	St. Louis	687,029
1790	1.	Philadelphia	42,520		5.	Boston	670,585
	2.	New York	33,131		6.	Cleveland	560,663
	3.	Boston	18,038		7.	Baltimore	558,485
	4.	Charleston, S.C.	16,359		8.	Pittsburgh	533,905
	5.	Baltimore	13,503		9.	Detroit	465,766
	6.	Salem, Mass.	7,921		10.	Buffalo	423,715
	7.	Newport, R.I.	6,716				
	8.	Providence, R.I.	6,380	1930	1.	New York	6,930,446
	9.	Marblehead, Mass.	5,661		2.	Chicago	3,376,438
	10.	Portsmouth, N.H.	4,720		3.	Philadelphia	1,950,961
					4.	Detroit	1,568,662
1830	1.	New York	197,112		5.	Los Angeles	1,238,048
	2.	Philadelphia	161,410		6.	Cleveland	900,429
	3.	Baltimore	80,620		7.	St. Louis	821,960
	4.	Boston	61,392		8.	Baltimore	804,874
	5.	Charleston, S.C.	30,289		9.	Boston	781,188
	6.	New Orleans	29,737		10.	Pittsburgh	669,817
	7.	Cincinnati	24,831				
	8.	Albany, N.Y.	24,209	1950	1.	New York	7,891,957
	9.	Brooklyn, N.Y.	20,535		2.	Chicago	3,620,962
	10.	Washington, D.C.	18,826		3.	Philadelphia	2,071,605
					4.	Los Angeles	1,970,358
1850	1.	New York	515,547		5.	Detroit	1,849,568
	2.	Philadelphia	340,045		6.	Baltimore	949,708
	3.	Baltimore	169,054		7.	Cleveland	914,808
	4.	Boston	136,881		8.	St. Louis	856,796
	5.	New Orleans	116,375		9.	Washington, D.C.	802,178
	6.	Cincinnati	115,435		10.	Boston	801,444
	7.	Brooklyn, N.Y.	96,838				
	8.	St. Louis	77,860	1970	1.	New York	7,895,563
	9.	Albany, N.Y.	50,763		2.	Chicago	3,369,357
	10.	Pittsburgh	46,601		3.	Los Angeles	2,811,801
					4.	Philadelphia	1,949,996
1870	1.	New York	942,292		5.	Detroit	1,514,063
	2.	Philadelphia	674,022		6.	Houston	1,233,535
	3.	Brooklyn, N.Y.	419,921†		7.	Baltimore	905,787
	4.	St. Louis	310,864		8.	Dallas	844,401
	5.	Chicago	298,977		9.	Washington, D.C.	756,668
	6.	Baltimore	267,354		10.	Cleveland	750,879
	7.	Boston	250,526				
	8.	Cincinnati	216,239	1990	1.	New York	7,322,564
	9.	New Orleans	191,418		2.	Los Angeles	3,485,398
	10.	San Francisco	149,473		3.	Chicago	2,783,726
					4.	Houston	1,630,553
					5.	Philadelphia	1,585,577
					6.	San Diego	1,110,549
					7.	Detroit	1,027,974
					8.	Dallas	1,006,877
					9.	Phoenix	983,403
					10.	San Antonio	935,933

*Figure from a census taken in 1698.
†Philadelphia figures include suburbs.
‡Annexed to New York in 1898.
Source: U.S. Census data.

Foreign Origins of the American People

Immigration by Decade

Year	Number	Percent of Total Population	Year	Number	Percent of Total Population
1821–1830	151,824	1.6	1921–1930	4,107,209	3.9
1831–1840	599,125	4.6	1931–1940	528,431	0.4
1841–1850	1,713,251	10.0	1941–1950	1,035,039	0.7
1851–1860	2,598,214	11.2	1951–1960	2,515,479	1.6
1861–1870	2,314,824	7.4	1961–1970	3,321,677	1.8
1871–1880	2,812,191	7.1	1971–1980	4,493,000	2.2
1881–1890	5,246,613	10.5	1981–1990	7,338,000	3.0
1891–1900	3,687,546	5.8	1991–1993	3,705,000	1.4
1901–1910	8,795,386	11.6	Total	27,043,835	
1911–1920	5,735,811	6.2			
Total	33,654,785		1821–1993 Grand Total	60,698,620	

Source: U.S. Bureau of the Census, *Historical Statistics of the United States, Colonial Times to 1970* (1975), Part I, pp. 105–106; *Statistical Abstract of the United States,* 1995.

Regional Origins

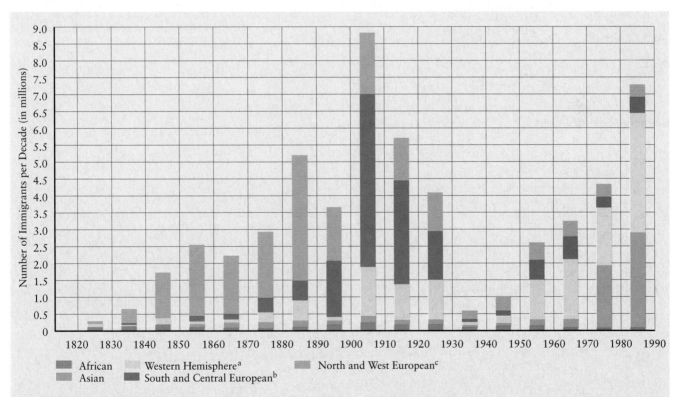

a Canada and all countries in South America and Central America.

b Italy, Spain, Portugal, Greece, Germany (Austria included, 1938–1945), Poland, Czechoslovakia (since 1920), Yugoslavia (since 1920), Hungary (since 1861), Austria (since 1861, except 1938–1945), former U.S.S.R. (excludes Asian U.S.S.R. between 1931 and 1963), Latvia, Estonia, Lithuania, Finland, Romania, Bulgaria, Turkey (in Europe), and other European countries not classified elsewhere.

c Great Britain, Ireland, Norway, Sweden, Denmark, Iceland, Netherlands, Belgium, Luxembourg, Switzerland, France.

Source: Stephan Thernstrom, ed., *Harvard Encyclopedia of American Ethnic Groups* (1980), p. 480; and U.S. Bureau of the Census, *Statistical Abstract of the United States,* 1991.

The Labor Force

(thousands of workers)							
Year	Agriculture	Mining	Manufacturing	Construction	Trade	Other	Total
1810	1,950	11	75	—	—	294	2,330
1840	3,570	32	500	290	350	918	5,660
1850	4,520	102	1,200	410	530	1,488	8,250
1860	5,880	176	1,530	520	890	2,114	11,110
1870	6,790	180	2,470	780	1,310	1,400	12,930
1880	8,920	280	3,290	900	1,930	2,070	17,390
1890	9,960	440	4,390	1,510	2,960	4,060	23,320
1900	11,680	637	5,895	1,665	3,970	5,223	29,070
1910	11,770	1,068	8,332	1,949	5,320	9,041	37,480
1920	10,790	1,180	11,190	1,233	5,845	11,372	41,610
1930	10,560	1,009	9,884	1,988	8,122	17,267	48,830
1940	9,575	925	11,309	1,876	9,328	23,277	56,290
1950	7,870	901	15,648	3,029	12,152	25,870	65,470
1960	5,970	709	17,145	3,640	14,051	32,545	74,060
1970	3,463	516	20,746	4,818	15,008	34,127	78,678
1980	3,364	979	21,942	6,215	20,191	46,612	99,303
1990	3,186	730	21,184	7,696	24,269	60,849	117,914
1994	3,409	669	20,157	7,493	25,699	65,633	123,060

Source: Historical Statistics of the United States, Colonial Times to 1970 (1975), 139; Statistical Abstract of the United States, 1995, Table 653.

Changing Labor Patterns

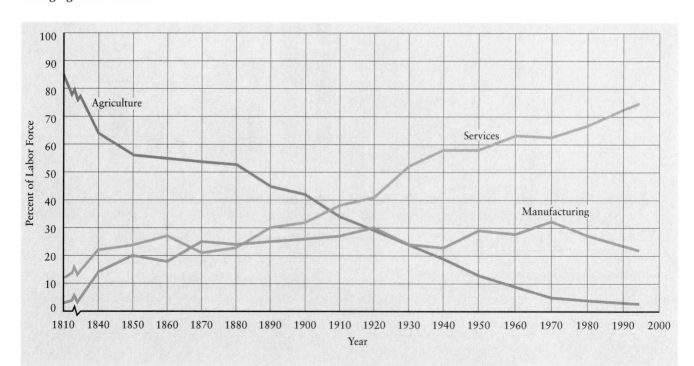

The Aging of the U.S. Population

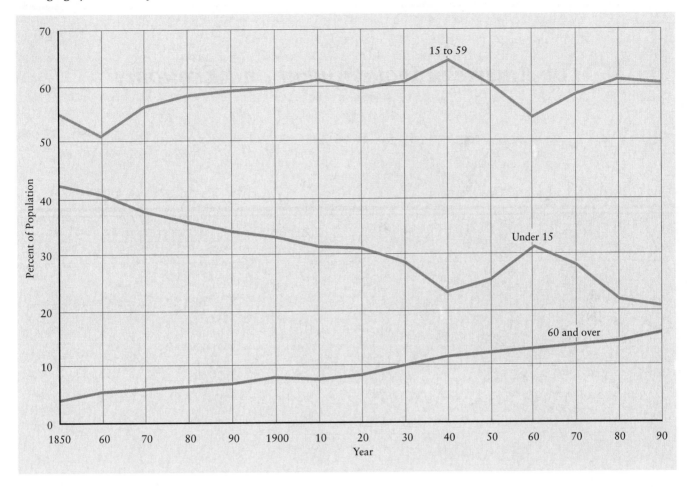

The American Government and Economy

★　　　　★　　　　★

The Growth of the Federal Government

Year	Employees (millions)		Receipts and Outlays ($ millions)	
	Civilian	Military	Receipts	Outlays
1900	0.23	0.12	567	521
1910	0.38	0.13	676	694
1920	0.65	0.34	6,649	6,358
1930	0.61	0.25	4,058	3,320
1940	1.04	0.45	6,900	9,600
1950	1.96	1.46	40,900	43,100
1960	2.38	2.47	92,500	92,200
1970	3.00	3.06	193,700	196,600
1980	2.99	2.05	517,112	590,920
1990	3.23	2.04	1,031,321	1,252,705
1993	3.04	1.70	1,153,535	1,408,675

Source: Statistical Profile of the United States, 1900–1980; Statistical Abstract of the United States, 1995.

Gross National Product, 1840–1990

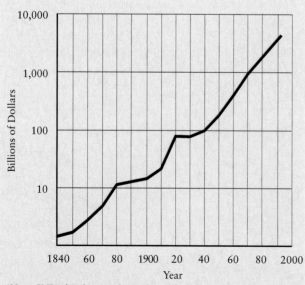

*Note: GNP values have not been adjusted for inflation or deflation. GNP is plotted here on a logarithmic scale.
Source: Statistical Abstract of the United States, 1995.

GNP per Capita, 1840–1990

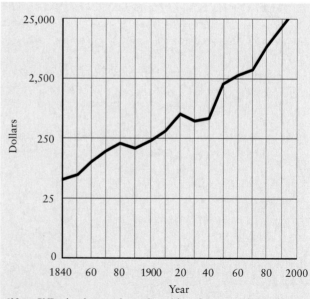

*Note: GNP values have not been adjusted for inflation or deflation. The GNP is plotted here on a logarithmic scale.

Consumer Price Index and Conversion Table

This index estimates how consumer prices changed on the average over ten-year intervals. Such estimates are highly uncertain, particularly when they are used to make comparisons over long periods of time. This is partly because it is extremely difficult to measure how the typical mix of goods (each with its own price) purchased by consumers changes over time.

To convert £ (pounds Sterling, until 1770) or $ (U.S. dollars, beginning in 1780) from any date in the past to the equivalent in 1990 dollars, multiply the historical price by the appropriate number in this column. For example, £10 Sterling in 1730 would equal about $867 in 1990. (£10 × 86.7 = $867); or $10 in 1870 would equal about $99 in 1990 ($10 × 9.9 = $99).

Year	Price Index (1860 = 100)	Conversion Multiplier
1700	130	53.3
1710	100	69.3
1720	76	91.3
1730	80	86.7
1740	66	105.1
1750	84	82.6
1760	96	72.3
1770	100	69.3
1780	165	9.5
1790	148	10.6
1800	151	10.4
1810	148	10.6
1820	141	11.1
1830	111	14.1
1840	104	15.1
1850	94	16.6
1860	100	15.6
1870	157	9.9
1880	123	12.7
1890	109	14.3
1900	101	15.5
1910	114	13.7
1920	240	6.5
1930	200	7.8
1940	168	9.3
1950	288	5.4
1960	354	4.4
1970	464	3.4
1980	985	1.6
1990	1563	1.0

Source: Adapted from John J. McCusker, "How Much Is That in Real Money? A Historical Price Index for Use as a Deflator of Money Value in the Economy of the United States," *Proceedings of the American Antiquarian Society*, Vol. 101, pt. 2, (1991), 297–390.

Illustration Credits

★   ★   ★

Chapter 1   P. 2: Oronoz. **P. 4:** Dumbarton Oaks Research Library and Collections, Washington, D.C. **P. 5:** Robert Knight/Leo de Wys. **P. 6:** Ohio Historical Society. **P. 8:** Library of Congress. **P. 9:** Amerind Foundation, Dragoon, AZ. Photo by Robin Stancliff. **P. 12:** Musée Condé/Giraudon/Art Resource. **P. 13:** J. Bourdichon. *Les quatres etats de la societé: le travail,* 15th century. Giraudon/Art Resource, NY. **P. 15:** Mathias Grünwald, *Isenheim Altar Piece* (central panel), early 16th c., Musée Unterlinden, Colmar/Giraudon/Art Resource. **P. 16:** *Pepper Harvesting in Malabar,* 14th c. French ms. illus. Bibliothèque Nationale, Paris. **P. 17** (top): Ergun Çagutay: Istanbul (From *Sahinsahname,* Vol. I, Universite Kutuphanesi, Instanbul). **P. 17** (bottom): Piero della Francesca, *The Ideal City,* 15th c. Scala/Art Resource. **P. 23:** Corbis-Bettmann. **P. 25:** *Don Luis de Velasco Murdering the Jesuits,* 1571. Courtesy of the John Carter Brown Library at Brown University. **P. 29:** Cornelius de Zeeuw. *Pierre de Moucheron and His Family,* n.d. Rijksmuseum, Amsterdam. **P. 31:** *Sir Walter Raleigh and His Son,* unknown artist, 1602. By Courtesy of the National Portrait Gallery, London. **P. 32:** *Elizabeth I* (Armada Portrait). Anonymous. Private collection. Bridgeman Art Library, London.

Chapter 2   P. 36: Ashmolean Museum, Oxford. **P. 41:** Nettie Lee Benson Latin American Collection, University of Texas at Austin, General Libraries. **P. 44:** John White, *Indians Fishing,* British Museum. **P. 46:** Collection of the Maryland Historical Society, Baltimore. **P. 49:** Colonial Williamsburg Foundation. **P. 51:** Collection of the Maryland Historical Society, Baltimore. **P. 53:** Paul Rocheleau. **P. 54:** Courtesy of the American Antiquarian Society. **P. 56** (top and center): Courtesy Essex Institute, Salem, MA. **P. 56** (bottom): Courtesy of the Pilgrim Society, Plymouth, MA. **P. 59:** Courtesy of the American Antiquarian Society. **P. 61:** Anon. *Elizabeth Freake & Baby* c. 1671–74. 17th-c. Worcester Art Museum, Worcester, MA. Gift of Mr. and Mrs. Albert W. Rice. **P. 63:** Shelburne Museum, Shelburne, VT. Photograph by Ken Burris. **P. 65:** *Pocahantas, Daughter of Powhatan Chief.* Unidentified artist, after 1616. National Portrait Gallery, Smithsonian Institution/Art Resource, NY.

Chapter 3   P. 68: *Bristol Docks and Quay* (detail), early 18th c., City of Bristol Museum and Art Gallery/Bridgeman Art Library, London. **P. 70:** Mansell Collection. **P. 74:** *James II,* by Godfrey Kneller, late 17th c. Courtesy of the National Portrait Gallery, London. **P. 75:** New York State Historical Association, Cooperstown. **P. 79:** Benin Bronze Plaque: *Mounted King and Attendants,* c. 1550–1680. The Metropolitan Museum of Art, NY. The Michael C. Rockefeller Memorial Collection. **P. 82:** The Library Company of Philadelphia. **P. 84** (left): National Maritime Museum, London. **P. 84** (right): Library of Congress. **P. 87:** Colonial Williamsburg Foundation. **P. 88:** Courtesy, Georgia Department of Archives and History, Atlanta. **P. 89:** Abby Aldrich Rockefeller Folk Art Center, Williamsburg, VA. **P. 90:** Thomas Coram, *View of Mulberry Plantation (slave quarters).* Gibbes Museum of Art/CAA Collection, Charleston. **P. 91:** Maryland Historical Society, Baltimore. **P. 97:** National Trust Photographic Library/John Hammond.

Chapter 4   P. 102: Colonial Williamsburg Foundation. **P. 104:** Anon (American), *The Cheney Family,* c. 1795, National Gallery of Art, Washington. Gift of Edgar William and Bernice Chrysler Garbisch. **P. 105:** The Connecticut Historical Society, Hartford. **P. 106:** *Lady Undressing for a Bath.* Attributed to Gerardus Duyckinck, c.1730–40. National Gallery of Art, Washington. Gift of Edgar William and Bernice Chrysler Garbisch. **P. 112:** Courtesy, Museum of Fine Arts, Boston. Bequest of Maxim Karolik. **P. 114:** Philadelphia Museum of Art, from the Clarence W. Brazer Collection. **P. 117:** John Steper and Henry Dawkins, *A Southeast Prospect of the Pennsylvania Hospital,* c. 1761. The Library Company of Philadelphia. **P. 127:** Joseph Badger, *Rev. Jonathan Edwards,* 1720. Yale University Art Gallery. Bequest of Eugene Phelps Edwards, 1938. **P. 128:** Stock Montage, Inc. **P. 129:** Private Collection. **P. 132:** *View from Bushango Tavern, 5 Miles from York Town on the Baltimore Road,* July 1788, *Columbian Magazine.* Collection of The New-York Historical Society.

Chapter 5   P. 136: Ralph Earl, *Occupation of Concord by the British,* (detail), n.d. Photograph Courtesy Concord Antiquarian Museum, Concord, MA. **P. 141:** Courtesy, American Antiquarian Society. **P. 143:** Print Collection. Miriam and Ira D. Wallach Division of Art, Prints and Photographs. The New York Public Library. Astor, Lenox and Tilden Foundations. **P. 144:** Courtesy of the John Carter Brown Library at Brown University, Providence, RI. **P. 147:** John Singleton Copley, *Samuel Adams,* c. 1772. Courtesy, Museum of Fine Arts, Boston. Deposited by the City of Boston. **P. 148:** Anon, *Patrick Henry,* n.d., Shelburne Museum, Shelburne, VT. Photograph by Ken Burris. **P. 149:** Courtesy of the Essex Institute, Salem, MA. **P. 155:** Print Collection. Miriam and Ira D. Wallach Division of Art, Prints and Photographs. The New York Public Library. Astor, Lenox and Tilden Foundations. **P. 157:** Courtesy of the John Carter Brown Library at Brown University, Providence, RI. **P. 158:** Joseph Cole, *George Hewes,* 1835. Courtesy of The Bostonian Society/Old State House. **P. 159:** Library of Congress. **P. 161:** *William Pitt* from (book) *Aubenteuil, Essais Historiques et Politiques sur la Revolution* *de l'Amerique.* The Metropolitan Museum of Art, Bequest of Charles Allen Munn, 1924 (24.90.1792) **P. 163:** Library of Congress.

Chapter 6   P. 168: Anon., *Attack on Bunker's Hill, with the Burning of Charles Town.* (detail), c. 1783. National Gallery of Art, Washington. Gift of Edgar William and Bernice Chrysler Garbisch. **P. 171:** *Family of George III,* by John Zoffany, late 18th- early 19th-c., Royal Collection, St. James's Palace. © H.M. Queen Elizabeth II. **P. 172:** Library of Congress. **P. 173:** Anne S. K. Brown Military Collection, Brown University Library, Providence. **P. 174:** Thomas Sully, *George Washington at the Battle of Trenton,* 19th- c. The Union League of Philadelphia. **P. 176** (top): Library of Congress. **P. 176** (bottom): Charles Willson Peale, *Joseph Brant,* 1797. Independence National Historical Park Collection, Philadelphia. **P. 178:** Library of Congress. **P. 182:** Virginia Historical Society, Richmond. **Pp. 183 and 184:** Anne S. K. Brown Military Collection, Brown University Library, Providence. **P. 185:** Library of Congress. **P. 186:** Benjamin West, *American Commission of the Preliminary Peace Negotiation with Great Britain,* (detail), 1783. Courtesy of The Winterthur Museum, Winterthur, DE. **P. 188:** Woodcut from *A Now Touch on the Times...By a Daughter of Liberty, Living in Marblehead,* 1779. Collection of the New-York Historical Society **P. 191:** Massachusetts Historical Society, Boston.

Chapter 7   P. 197: Frederick Kemmelmeyer, *The American Star.* Metropolitan Museum of Art, Gift of Edgar William and Bernice Chrysler Garbisch, 1962. **P. 200** (left): Mather Brown, *Portrait of John Adams,* late 18th c., Boston Atheneum. **P. 200** (right): Unknown, *Abigail Adams,* New York State Historical Association, Cooperstown. **P. 201:** John Singleton Copley, *Judith Sargent (Murray) at Age 19.* Private Collection. Photo courtesy Frick Art Reference Library. **P. 204:** *Gouverneur Morris,* attributed to James Sharples, c. 1800. City of Bristol Museum and Art Gallery, England. **P. 207:** National Portrait Gallery, Washington, DC/Art Resource. **P. 208:** Gilbert Stuart, *Portrait of James Madison,* c. 1805–07, Bowdoin College Museum of Art, Brunswick, ME. Bequest of James Bowdoin III. **P. 211:** Collection of The New-York Historical Society. **P. 218:** Print Collection, Miriam and Ira D. Wallach Division of Art, Prints & Photographs. The New York Public Library, Astor, Lenox & Tilden Foundations **P. 219:** North Wind Picture Archive. **P. 220** (left): Rembrandt Peale, *Thomas Jefferson,* c. 1800. White House Historical Collection. Photograph by the National Geographic Society **P. 220** (right): John Trumbull, *Alexander Hamilton,* n.d., Yale University Art Gallery, New Haven. **P. 221** (top): Ralph Earl, *Oliver Ellsworth and Abigail Wolcott Ellsworth,* c. 1792, Wadsworth Atheneum, Hartford, CT. Gift of the Ellsworth Heirs. **P. 221** (bottom): John Rubens Smith, *The Shop and Warehouse of Duncan Phyfe,* c. 1816–17. (detail). Watercolor, pen and brown ink on paper. The Metropolitan Museum of Art, Rogers Fund, 1922. **P. 223:** Courtesy of the Winterthur Museum. **P. 224:** By permission of the Huntington Library, San Marino, CA.

Chapter 8   P. 228: Thomas Birch, *Conestoga Wagon on the Pennsylvania Turnpike,* 1816. Shelburne Museum, Shelburne, VT. Photograph by Ken Burris. **P. 230:** Unknown, *Treaty of Greenville,* n.d., Chicago Historical Society **P. 233:** Thomas Cole Ruckle, *Fairview Inn,* c. 1889. Collection of the Maryland Historical Society, Baltimore. **P. 234:** Courtesy of the Wethersfield Historical Society, CT. **P. 235:** John Caspar Wild. *View of Cincinnati,* c. 1835. M. and M. Karolik Collection. Courtesy, Museum of Fine Arts, Boston. **P. 238:** *A View of New Orleans Taken from the Plantation of Marigny Nov. 1803,* by Boqueto de Woiserie. Chicago Historical Society. **P. 239:** Missouri Historical Society, St. Louis. **P. 241:** Library of Congress. **P. 242:** Library Company of Philadelphia. **P. 245:** Jean Hyacinthe de Laclotte, *Battle of New Orleans* n.d., New Orleans Museum of Art. Gift of Edgar William and Bernice Chrysler Garbisch. **P. 247:** *Dr. & Mrs. Brewster,* John Brewster, Jr. Old Sturbridge Village, Stur-

bridge, MA. Photo: Henry E. Peach. **P. 248:** Rare Book Department, Free Library of Philadelphia. Photo: Joan Broderick. **P. 250:** Lewis Miller, *Slave Trader, Sold to Tennessee,* n.d., Abby Aldrich Rockefeller Folk Art Center, Williamsburg, VA. Gift of Dr. and Mrs. Richard M. Kain in memory of George Hay Kain. **P. 252:** Blue Ridge Heritage Archive. Ferrum College, Ferrum, VA. **P. 255:** Mount Bethel A.M.E. Church, Philadelphia. **P. 256:** *Benjamin Hawkins and the Creek Indians.* c. 1805. Oil on canvas. 35⅞″ × 49⅞″. Greenville County Museum of Art, Greenville, SC. **P. 258:** *Se-Quo-Yah,* 19th c., Lithograph printed by Lehman & Duval after a painting by Charles Bird King, Philadelphia Museum of Art, given by Miss William Adger.

Chapter 9   P. 264: *Launching of the Ship Fame* (detail) by George Ropes, Jr. Courtesy Peabody Essex Museum, Salem, MA. **P. 265:** Ralph Earl, *Elijah Boardman,* 1782, Oil on canvas, The Metropolitan Museum of Art, NY, Bequest of Susan W. Tyler, 1979. (1979. 395) **P. 268:** Shelburne Museum, Shelburne, VT. Photograph by Ken Burris. **P. 271:** Chester Harding, *John Marshall,* c. 1830, Boston Atheneum. **P. 274:** George Lehman, *Dance in a Country Tavern,* n.d., Historical Society of Pennsylvania, Philadelphia. **P. 275:** Samuel Finley Breese Morse, *The Old House of Representatives,* 1822. Oil on canvas, 86½ × 130¾ in (219.71 × 332.11 cm). In the Collection of the Corcoran Gallery of Art, Museum Purchase, Gallery Fund. **P. 277:** Collection of The Litchfield Historical Society, Litchfield, CT. **P. 280:** Ambrose Andrews, *Schuyler Family,* c. 1824, Collection of The New-York Historical Society. **P. 282:** After William John Wilgus, *Ichabod Crane and the Headless Horseman,* c. 1855, National Gallery of Art, Washington. Gift of Edgar William and Bernice Chrysler Garbisch. **P. 284:** Collection of The New-York Historical Society. Lithograph by Kennedy and Lucas after a painting by A. Rider. **P. 286:** Unknown American, *The Sargent Family,* c. 1800, National Gallery of Art, Washington. Gift of William and Bernice Chrysler Garbisch. **P. 287:** Miniature Panorama: *Scenes from a Seminary for Young Ladies,* c. 1810–1820, Watercolor and ink on silk, St. Louis Museum of Art. Purchase and Funds Given by Decorative Arts Society. **P. 288:** John L. D. Mathies, *Jemima Wilkinson,* c. 1816, Collection of the Yates County Historical Society. Reproduced Courtesy the Village Board, Penn Yan, NY. **P. 289:** Free Library of Philadelphia. Photo by Will Brown.

Chapter 10   P. 294: Mary Keys, *Lockport on the Erie Canal,* 1832, Watercolor, 19½″ × 24½″, Munson-Williams Proctor Institute of Art, Utica, NY. **P. 296** (top): Collection of The New-York Historical Society. **P. 296** (bottom): The Cincinnati Historical Society. **P. 298:** Courtesy of the National Museum of History and Technology, Smithsonian Institution, Washington, D.C. **P. 299:** Barfoot for Darton, *Progress of Cotton: No 6, Spinning,* n.d., lithograph, Yale University Art Gallery, The Mabel Brady Garvan Collection. **P. 303:** William Giles Munson, *The Eli Whitney Gun Factory,* c. 1826–28, Yale University Art Gallery, The Mabel Brady Garvan Collection. **P. 305:** *Eli Whitney,* Samuel F. B. Morse, Yale University Art Gallery. Gift of George Hoadley, B.A. 1801. **P. 306:** Artist unknown, *The Yankee Pedlar,* c. 1830, Courtesy of the IBM Corporation, Armonk, NY. **P. 311:** John William Hill, *Erie Canal,* 1831, Collection of The New-York Historical Society. **P. 313:** Pavel Petrovich Svinin, *Deck Life on the Paragon,* watercolor on paper, The Metropolitan Museum of Art, New York, Rogers Fund, 1942. **P. 315:** Nicolino Calyo, *George Cousin, the Patent Chimney Sweep Cleaner,* 1840–44, Museum of the City of New York, Gift of Mrs. Francis P. Garvan in memory of Francis P. Garvan. **P. 316:** Nicolino Calyo, *The Hot Corn Seller,* 1840–44, Museum of the City of New York, Gift of Mrs. Francis P. Garvan in memory of Francis P. Garvan. **P. 318:** Artist unknown, *York Pennsylvania Family with Negro Servant,* c. 1828, The Saint Louis Art Museum, Bequest of Edgar William and Bernice Chrysler Garbisch. **P. 320:** Oberlin College Archives. **P. 321:** Courtesy of the Newberry Library.

Chapter 11 **P. 326:** Robert Cruikshank, *President's Levee or All Creation Going to the White House,* n.d., © by the White House Historical Association, Washington, D.C. Photograph by the National Geographic Society. **P. 330:** Philip Haas, *John Quincy Adams,* (daguerreotype), c. 1843, The Metropolitan Museum of Art, Gift of I. N. Phelps Stokes, Edward S. Hawes, Alice Mary Hawes, Marion Augusta Hawes, 1937. **P. 332:** Collection of The New-York Historical Society. **P. 334:** Library of Congress. **P. 335:** S. Bernard, *View along the East Battery, Charleston,* Oil on canvas, c. 1831 23½ × 35¼ in, Yale University Art Gallery, Mabel Brady Garvan Collection #1932.282 **P. 336:** The Gibbes Museum of Art Carolina Art Association, Charleston, SC. **P. 337:** George Catlin, *muk a tah mish o kah kaik, the Black Hawk,* mid 19th c., watercolor on paper. Courtesy of the Thomas Gilcrease Institute of American History and Art, Tulsa, OK. **P. 341:** Archives Division, Texas State Library. **P. 345:** General Research Division, The New York Public Library, Astor, Lenox and Tilden Foundations. **P. 347:** From *The Union,* 1835. Courtesy The New York Public Library. **Pp. 348, 351 and 352:** Collection of The New-York Historical Society.

Chapter 12 **P. 356:** C.C.A. Christensen, *The Handcart Pioneers,* 1900. Courtesy Museum of Church History and Art, Salt Lake City, UT. **P. 360 (left and right):** Corbis-Bettmann. **P. 360 (center):** The American Antiquarian Society, Worcester, MA. **P. 361:** Culver Pictures. **P. 364:** Joshua H. Bussell, *The Shaker Community at Poland Hill, Maine,* c. 1850, Collection of the United Society of Shakers, Sabbathday Lake, ME. **P. 367:** Culver Pictures. **P. 369 (left and center):** Library of Congress. **P. 369 (right):** Collection of Rhoda Jenkins and John Barney, Greenwich, CT. **P. 371:** Courtesy Trenton State Hospital. **P. 372:** Corbis-Bettmann. **P. 375:** Unknown, *William Lloyd Garrison,* (daguerreotype), 19th c., The Metropolitan Museum of Art, Gift of I. N. Stokes, Edward S. Hawes, Alice Mary Hawes, Marion Augusta Hawes, 1937.

Chapter 13 **P. 382:** William Aiken Walker, *Plantation Economy in the Old South,* (detail), c. 1876, The Warner Collection of Gulf States Paper Corporation, Tuscaloosa, AL. **P. 385:** Franz Holzlhuber, *Sugarcane Harvest in Louisiana & Texas,* c. 1856–60, Collection of Glenbow Museum, Calgary, Alberta, Canada. **P. 389 (top):** Eyre Crowe, *Richmond Slave Market Auction,* n.d., The Collection of Jay P. Altmayer. **P. 389 (bottom):** John Antrobus, *Plantation Burial,* c. 1860, The Historic New Orleans Collection. **P. 391:** Sophia Smith Collection, Smith College, MA. **P. 394:** Culver Pictures. **P. 395:** Charles Blauvelt, *A German Immigrant Inquiring His Way,* c. 1855. North Carolina, Museum of Art, Raleigh. Purchased with funds from the State of North Carolina. **P. 397:** Library of Congress. **P. 398 (top):** Engraving by W. W. Wilson, *Constructing a Balloon Frame House,* c. 1855, The Metropolitan Museum of Art, Harris Brisbane Dick Fund, 1934. **P. 398 (bottom):** Culver Pictures. **P. 399:** Currier and Ives, *Home Sweet Home,* c. 1869, Museum of the City of New York. The Harry T. Peters Collection. **P. 400:** Stowe-Day Foundation, Hartford, CT. **P. 406:** The Pat Hathaway Collection of California Views. **P. 411:** From the Collection of the Dallas Historical Society.

Chapter 14 **P. 414:** John Steuart Curry, *John Brown Mural,* in the Kansas State Capitol, 1941, Kansas Historical Society. Photo as published in *"The Story of America"* © National Geographic Society, 1984. **P. 419 (top):** Courtesy the Amon Carter Museum, Fort Worth, TX. **P. 419 (bottom):** Samuel Chamberlain, *Street Fighting in the Calle de Iturbide,* 1855–61, The West Point Museum, United States Military Academy. From *The Old West: The Mexican War.* Photo by Paulus Leeser © 1978 Time/Life Books, Inc. **P. 424:** The Historical Society of Pennsylvania, Philadelphia. **P. 427:** California State Library, Sacramento. Daguerreotype Collection. **P. 430 (top):** Culver Pictures. **P. 430 (bottom):** Corbis-Bettmann. **P. 432:** Chicago Historical Society. **P. 433:** Corbis-Bettmann. **P. 437:** The Kansas State Historical Society, Topeka. **P. 439:** Library of Congress. **P. 440:** Missouri Historical Society, St. Louis. **P. 443:** The Lincoln Museum, Fort Wayne, Indiana, a part of the Lincoln National Corporation. **P. 444:** National Portrait Gallery, Washington, D.C./Art Resource. **P. 445:** The Ohio Historical Society, Columbus. **P. 446:** National Park Service, Harper's Ferry.

Chapter 15 **P. 448:** The Seventh Regiment Fund, Inc., (detail), New York City **P. 454:** Virginia State Library and Archives, Richmond. **P. 455:** CBH Jackson Collection, Smithsonian Institution. From *Echoes of Glory: Arms and Equipment of the Union.* Photograph by Larry Sherer © 1991 Time-Life Books Inc. **P. 457:** Culver Pictures. **P. 460:** Massachusetts Commandery Military Order of the Loyal Legion and the US Army Military History Institute. **Pp. 461 and 464:** Library of Congress. **P. 466:** From *The Civil War: Twenty Million Yankees.* Photograph by Larry Sherer © 1985 Time/Life Books, Inc. Courtesy of the United States Senate Collection. **Pp. 471, 473 and 478:** Library of Congress. **P. 479:** L.M.D. Guillaume, *The Surrender of General Lee to General Grant, April 9, 1865,* Appomatox Court House National Historical Park. **P. 480:** National Archives (Mathew Brady Collection).

Chapter 16 **P. 484:** Chicago Historical Society. **Pp. 486 and 488:** Library of Congress. **P. 489:** Chicago Historical Society. **P. 491:** Collection of The New-York Historical Society. **P. 493:** Library of Congress. **P. 496:** Collection of Mrs. Nancy W. Livingston and Mrs. Elizabeth Livingston Jaeger. Photograph Courtesy of the Los Angeles County Museum of Art. **P. 497:** Corbis-Bettmann. **P. 499:** Library of Congress. **P. 500:** From *Harper's Weekly,* June 23, 1866, Courtesy of the Newberry Library, Chicago. **P. 501:** Rutherford B. Hayes Presidential Center, Spiegel Grove, Freemont, OH. **P. 504:** Collection Tennessee State Museum. Photo by Karina McDaniel. Courtesy Tennessee State Library & Archives, Nashville, TN. **P. 507:** Brown Brothers. **P. 510:** Historical Pictures/Stock Montage, Inc. **P. 513:** *Frank Leslie's Illustrated Newspaper,* Sept. 23, 1876. Courtesy of the Newberry Library, Chicago.

Copyright Notices

★　　　　　★　　　　　★

Index

★　　★　　★